World Literature Since 1945

World Literature Since 1945

CRITICAL SURVEYS OF THE
CONTEMPORARY LITERATURES OF
EUROPE AND THE AMERICAS

EDITED BY
Ivar Ivask
AND
Gero von Wilpert

FREDERICK UNGAR PUBLISHING CO.
New York

This is a joint publication of Alfred Kröner Verlag, Stuttgart,
and Frederick Ungar Publishing Co., New York

Copyright © 1973 by Frederick Ungar Publishing Co., Inc.

Printed in the United States of America

Library of Congress Catalog Card Number 72–79930

Designed by Irving Perkins

ISBN 0-8044-3122-1

Contents

v

Preface

World Literature since 1945 tries to offer a balanced survey of developments in the individual literatures of the western world since the end of World War II, as well as to give some idea of the supranational correlations in western literature as a whole. The focus is not on international best sellers and popular successes but rather on literary works of true merit, some of which may be inaccessible to the foreigner; indeed, some of them seem to defy translation. This is not to disparage the great value of literature in translation. But it can never entirely replace the study of the various modern western literatures in their own habitat, so to speak, as they have evolved following the laws of their own natures.

Each nation's or language's literature included in this book is examined as a distinct organic whole, with an eye toward its growth within the particular social and political setting of its homeland, its promises for the future, and, finally, its place in the totality of western literature. Nonwestern literatures have not been included because they do not share the common traditions that form the basis of meaningful comparisons.

The contributors to *World Literature since 1945* are leading literary scholars who have been selected not only because they are specialists in their individual fields but also because they have cultivated a wide interest in literary developments in other countries or languages and thus are well aware of international cross-currents. An approximate guide for the length of each article was determined by the editors, in keeping with the importance of postwar literary activity in each literature. Some literatures of narrow scope (Basque, Breton, Byelorussian, Frisian, Gaelic, Lusatian, among others) had to be passed over because their contribution to world literature in recent decades was not deemed substantial enough.

The twenty-eight articles in the book follow a common plan. The starting date of the survey falls between 1940 and 1945, depending on the decisive literary and political events in each country. The stress is on those literary currents that emerged after the war's end; writers whose principal work was published before 1945 are not emphasized. Most contributors found it appropriate to organize their articles by literary genres.

The articles are not galleries of biographical portraits, nor do they try to cover in detail a writer's individual development from one work to the next. They are rather meant to convey an understanding of the broader context, the general literary situation and the predominant trends within each literature. This approach made it necessary to omit some writers who are not necessarily less worthy than some of those included and to pass over the more peripheral aspects of a writer's work.

Several editorial aids enhance the usefulness of *World Literature since 1945* as a reference tool. Each author's dates are given at his first appearance within each article. The title of a literary work is given in its original language at the first appearance, followed by the date of publication and by a literal English translation; thereafter, the literal translation is used. Appended to each article is a listing of published English translations of works mentioned, with publication data. The appendixes to articles on literatures not widely represented by English translations also include a listing of anthologies. Finally, each article concludes with a secondary bibliography of international scope.

May this book, the result of international collaboration, contribute to bringing about a better cultural understanding among the nations of the western world.

IVAR IVASK   GERO VON WILPERT
Norman, Oklahoma, November 1972   Stuttgart, November 1972

Introduction

THE IMPACT OF WORLD WAR II on all areas of human life, not least on literary activity, was enormous. But although every country of the western world was affected by war, the specific nature of the impact varied from country to country, even among those of continental Europe.

In Germany, the focal point of the cataclysm, it will still take several more decades before one can gain a full understanding of the profound damage the country's self-destruction did to its literature, of the losses that, in addition to the casualties caused by emigration, genocide, and military events, remain invisible, because a number of writers were misguided at a crucial phase of their development and their creativity nipped in the bud. Postwar Germany has also been beset by the havoc wrought by a self-imposed spiritual isolation that has thrown Germany out of phase with the main literary currents of western Europe. This disruption is most painfully manifested in a severely debilitating generation gap, however much this was (reverently) disclaimed. The older generation was so hopelessly discredited that younger writers refused to allow it any further influence on literary life; they were less and less willing to concern themselves with the nuances of difference among the supporters of the Nazi regime, the writers of the so-called inner emigration, and those writers who went into exile. All nuances concerning their elders paled in light of the increasing sociopolitical commitment of the young, which frequently meant a categorical rejection of all older institutions.

In the countries of western Europe overrun and occupied by the German army, there was no need to wait until the war's end to recollect the nation's spiritual and cultural heritage. That memory, on the contrary, often became the inspiration for national resistance movements and thus guaranteed a high degree of continuity in those nations' literatures. But in these countries, too, the end of the war led to thorough stocktakings. The tragic losses among intellectuals, by execution or deportation, were charged against those writers whose minds had not been strong enough to avoid contamination by fascist ideology; despite their earlier literary merits, these writers were discounted in the reconstruction of a free literature. Support of the occupation regime or opposition to it also contributed, in different ways, to losses detrimental to the continuity of national literatures in the twentieth century.

World War II and its aftermath left perhaps their deepest mark on the countries of eastern Europe, where liberation was accompanied, or quickly followed, by radical changes in political and social structure. After a short period of transition, communist regimes established themselves, and under their direction literature was called upon to activate the people's class consciousness. The leading spokesmen of the new "people's republics" were often either writers who had taken refuge in the Soviet Union during the war or those who had been active in the underground. They stood for a communist literature based on the Soviet doctrine of socialist realism; and socialist realism gradually displaced middle-class or formalist trends. There was, however, a difference in the various literatures in their degree of tolerance of nonideological writing. Nonetheless, some writers committed to discredited schools of thought moved, as did their readers, to the west, where they produced a literature in exile that was splintered among various countries and whose survival is far from certain.

In some noncommunist countries of southern Europe, reactionary political and cultural tendencies came to the fore in the postwar period and brought with them literary censorship much like that of eastern Europe, as well as a lively literary activity outside the home country. Consequently, since the war's end the number of writers in exile from both southern and eastern Europe has grown rather than decreased. The widely differing reasons for emigrating prevented, however, the formation of a unified front.

In the countries that were, relatively speaking, less directly affected by World War II—Great Britain, the United States, and the Latin American nations—the year 1945 is not so firm a dividing line. But here, too, there emerged new currents paralleling those of western Europe. A young generation, deeply committed to social causes and socialist views and critical of the established order, arose in England and the Americas, making substantial contributions to the totality of western literature during the last twenty-five years. Indeed, the burgeoning growth of Latin American literature may well be the most astounding literary phenomenon of the last decades.

The past quarter-century, which has witnessed major changes in all countries, new political constellations in most of them, and almost parallel lines of development in the two political camps, may well mark the beginning of a new era, whose end cannot be foreseen and whose essential quality cannot as yet be determined.

The early phase of postwar literature, from 1945 to 1950, was dominated by writings on the recent experiences of war, persecution, underground activity, and massive destruction. This retrospection was soon followed by a more forward-looking mood, particularly in those countries that had undergone major social changes after the war. The 1950s can be called an era of social criticism and socialist commitment, of high hopes and deep disappointments. This mood has largely persisted to the present in the literatures of the communist countries.

In the western countries, however, the early 1960s was marked by an interlude of experimental artifice and esoteric frivolity, leading to a new surrealism as well as concretism of various kinds. Surprisingly, this non-committal toying with literature was strongest in countries with a rich literary tradition and a large audience. (Whether this toying was a symptom of abundance or of insufficiency I will not presume to decide here.) There was little or none of this experimentation in small nations, whose writers depend to a greater degree on local reception rather than on the applause of international connoisseurs.

Alongside this experimenting, there began to appear a new political and social concern among the young, prompted by international power politics, the civil wars in Asia, the emergence of the "third world," and the rise in large western democracies of reactionary and repressive tendencies. Despite its partisan approach, the younger generation succeeded in bringing about fresh appraisals of the foundations on which a free and open democracy must rest. And the influence of these writers has continued into the early 1970s. Many among the young writers regard social problems as their central, if not exclusive, concern. Their style and rhetoric are those of the early agitators or of the socialist realists of eastern Europe.

Because of the influence of this "new left," the postwar writers of the west have, to an extent hardly equaled by any previous era, concentrated on their own time, its conditions, its grievances, and its social and political problems. The timeless problems of the human condition—death, transcendence, personal responsibility—which had been ardently debated by the existentialists—are now dealt with in the realm of the grotesque or the absurd.

The predominantly social commitment of literature is a further illustration of the east-west political polarization with regard to concepts of a desired structure of society. On one side, western European and North and South American writers question the very nature of man, debunk heroic virtues, demolish literary form and structure down to the very elements of language. They search for new forms of expression, demythologize the world—this is a literature of uncertainty and quest. On the other side, writers in eastern Europe are often inspired by an uncritical optimism, an idealization of the positive hero, a simplistic theme of social betterment—this is a literature of (premature) solutions. But the true value of a work of literature is determined not by its immediate effect on the masses but by the depths of its artistic influence on man's social consciousness and self-awareness.

Literary currents that before World War II often ran side by side and were at times even fused in a single work have become absolute and have made claims of exclusivity since the war, thus determining the character of the period. Only a small number of works, less ideological and consequently more honest, have shown the beginnings of a rapprochement between the tendency to be monolithic and the tendency to be all-embracing. But the influence of trivial literature and of the standardizing mass media has tended to deepen the antagonism rather than to achieve any general rapprochement in contemporary literature.

GERO VON WILPERT

IHAB HASSAN

American Literature

THE IDENTITY of the American writers who established themselves after World War II was collectively, as well as individually, distinct. They dissociated themselves from the inheritance of the 1930s. For them, the threat of totalitarianism, on the left or the right, made ideology repugnant and official views of reality suspect. The war, which absorbed much of their energies, also gave them unflinching clarity, insight into existence, a prevision of things to come. Whatever illusions they did retain seemed necessary to survival; whatever techniques of literary evasion or assault they invented furthered the same end.

Survival has indeed been the secret, paramount question of contemporary man. In America particularly, change changed at a dizzying rate. Man has been rushing, ever faster, toward a destiny overcast with clouds of apocalypse. This spirit, mounting steadily through the 1960s, has invoked not only the Doomsday Bomb. Memories of holocaust from Auschwitz to Hiroshima, the poverty and political dissent at home, the explosion of the earth's population, ravages to the natural environment, heinous conflicts breaking out in every part of the world—all this sustained a momentous gloom that no writer dared ignore. Science can capture the moon or alter the genes of mankind; but none knows how the ultimate moral and political decisions can be made. A massive invasion of privacy has taken place as the media of control and communications exchanged functions.

Some think technology heroic, others viciously rampant, yet many agree

1

that the collapse of older values left the world in organized chaos, a demonic mixture of order and anarchy. For the individual, violence, nihilism, dehumanization—all the faces of anomie—offer dire alternatives to the surrealism of mass society, of the superstate. The experience, shared abroad, has deepened the affinities between American and European literature.

America, however, has always thrived on great contradictions. If the writer can not escape the deep bemusement of his country—it amounts to a crisis of confidence in the "American way of life"—neither can he deny the enormous vitality that still throbs around him. The energy of hope sustains creation, experiment, rebellion. He feels new forms, languages, values, perhaps even a novel consciousness, moving within himself. The American Dream has given way to a nightmare, and the nightmare has yielded to still other dreams in the small hours of dawn.

But it is an error to speak of the postwar period as if it possesses a simple generic character. Each decade has witnessed shifts of tone, of interest. The 1940s, for instance, gradually broke with the legacy of naturalism; with the blessings of the New Critics, writers favored mythic, elegant, or ironic forms. In the 1950s literary structures were opened up to a more jagged, roguish, or grotesque sense of reality; beside the gothic manner, the neopicaresque was rife. With the 1960s, new elements became pronounced: eroticism, fantasy, gallows humor, comic surrealism, the absurdist mode. Some authors have carried these tendencies into the 1970s, toward a "literature of silence," which mocks, subverts, or transcends its own act. Throughout, the violent American dialectic of denial and celebration, protest and acceptance, has persisted.

The trends of contemporary literature have been, of course, more numerous, and many of them have jostled in the same work. Yet if we look at what has happened since 1940, we can discern some breakthroughs of the cultural imagination, breakthroughs that have distinguished the postwar age. The literature of certain minorities or "countercultures" has attained signal importance. Thus, Jewish authors have commanded unprecedented attention. Their works have not been exclusively Jewish in character. Their brilliance, indeed their sheer number, has carried the names of these authors to a wide public.

The "beat" movement, short in span and ambiguous in achievement, introduced, nevertheless, a distinct quality of energy into the postwar period. Drawing on European existentialism, on oriental mysticism, on native traditions of rhapsodic dissent and transcendental affirmation—Thoreau, Emerson, Whitman—the beats spoke for the beleaguered self, the natural and spontaneous man, in open or improvised forms.

Black literature has also grown in diversity and intensity, through the black-power movement. More conscious of its ethnic heritage and political trial than ever before, black literature has found among countless writers new voices of anger or hope.

Finally, cutting across genres and subcultures, a fantastic vision—grim but also antic, at ease in the void, erudite in absurdity, inspired madly—has projected an image of man no art can wholly contain.

While many established writers continued to publish in the postwar period, the writers I will discuss all began to publish during or after World War II. Almost all of them were born after 1910, the year I have chosen as a plausible cut-off point. Each section—fiction, poetry, drama—begins with a brief introduction and moves from portraits of prominent authors in the genre—the order is chronological—to glimpses of prevalent types and trends. Thus, some balance between individual talent and critical abstraction is attempted.

But who are the "major figures" of the period? This, a classic question of literary history, is troublesome in contemporary context; for the stature of major figures may be itself a quality of retrospection. Still, the energy and scope of certain writers have permitted us to single them out over the last three decades. Their work seems to have given the era its color and to have grasped its roots. Thus, a special place is given to Saul Bellow (born 1915), Norman Mailer (born 1925), Robert Lowell (born 1917). In the end, however, the question of major figures may prove less premature than obsolete.

FICTION

When Ernest Hemingway (1899–1961) and William Faulkner (1897–1962) died, the new literature had already undergone several changes of heart. Many major novelists of the 1920s and 1930s continued, of course, to publish after World War II. But hints of a different social and aesthetic climate were seen in the works of a number of authors who had already established themselves by the end of the war. These authors, important as they may be, can be treated in this survey only in a transitional manner; they served as precursors of postwar fiction.

Of these, perhaps the most influential, certainly the most elusive, has been the Russian-born Vladimir Nabokov (born 1899). Though he became an American citizen only in 1945, he created in *Lolita* (1955, 1958) a monstrously true and merry statement about life in America. His novels written originally in English—*The Real Life of Sebastian Knight* (1941); *Bend Sinister* (1947); *Lolita; Pnin* (1957); *Pale Fire* (1962), perhaps the best; and *Ada* (1969), his most ambitious—revealed a self-delighting mind, a geometer of never-never-land, recovering through shifting parodic patterns of language some lost vista of memory, some artifice of eternity.

Throughout his work the theme of man's life in dream or art has played around the edge of reality until reality has burned in insubstantial fire. Still, the cerebral quality of Nabokov has prevailed even in his explorations of bizarre sensuality; his prodigious wit and learning, his characters and plots, can become too rarefied or wan.

James Gould Cozzens (born 1903) has been far more uneasy in his relation to the postwar world. His best work, *Guard of Honor* (1948), dealt with black segregation on a southern Air Force base. An innate conservative, Cozzens has stressed the limitations of men, the enduring stability of institutions. First ignored, then sporadically prized, his works, from *The Last Adam* (1933) to *By Love Possessed* (1957), were often turgid novels of manners expressing, among dissolving values, a kind of stoic nostalgia.

Conservative in a different way, Robert Penn Warren (born 1905) has written with greater skill and power. He was originally associated with the brilliant southern movement, which, in the 1930s, included the New Critics and the Fugitive Poets. Skeptical of reason, science, and industrialism, as well as of romantic individualism, Warren sought in religious myths and Christian metaphor a definition of the human community. His distinguished novel, *All the King's Men* (1946), suggested by the career of the Louisiana demagogue Huey Long, forced politics into the frame of human truth.

Warren's works reflected the transition from naturalism to symbolism, which so many postwar novelists have assumed as complete. Nelson Algren (born 1909), more sentimental about the colorful and seamy sides of cities, only modified naturalism with poetry and wild humor. His best novel, *The Man with the Golden Arm* (1949), was a taut, frightening tale of dope addiction in Chicago, moving in its great compassion. But in Algren's later work, *A Walk on the Wild Side* (1956) and *The Neon Wilderness* (1958), anger showed a soft, lurid edge. A radical eccentric, ebullient even in pessimism, Algren's perceptions had a certain extravagance that prefigured black humor in later years.

But the directions of the new fiction were far more various than Cozzens, Warren, and Algren could suggest. In broad terms, its development seems to have been a continuous movement from realism toward a new surrealism, toward a loosening of forms, toward the inspired absurdities of John Barth's (born 1930) *Lost in the Fun House* (1968). The postwar novelists have also recognized the enormous diversity of American culture. Between the appearances of that culture—clichés of mass media and technocratic bureaucracy—and its inner motives, there has been a huge discrepancy. The opposing self has pursued, beyond disaffiliation, a new concept of love or of freedom. The pursuit of love has brought men to the threshold of mystical experience, as the search for freedom has brought them to the frontiers of nihilism; thus, saintliness and crime have violently merged in quest of a new consciousness.

The hero, vicar of the self in the new fiction, has served to mediate the contradictions of culture. His dominant aspect has been that of the rebel-victim. He is an actor but also a sufferer. Almost always, he is an outsider, a demonic or sacrificial figure, anarchic, grotesque, innocent, or clownish, wavering between martyrdom and frenzied self-affirmation. Thus, the rebel-victim incarnates the eternal dialectic of the primary "yes" and the ever-lasting "no"; and his function is to create those values whose absence in culture is the cause of his predicament and ours. His morality is largely existential, defined by his actions and even more by his passions—a self-made morality, full of ironies and ambiguities. The will of the hero, how-ever, is always in some sense redemptive; he differs from the redemptive mythic scapegoat only in his allegiance to the forms of art.

As the fictional hero has attempted to mediate the contradictions of culture, and even to create a new consciousness, so has the form of the novel itself attempted the same task on a deeper level. Realism and sur-realism, comedy and tragedy, event and symbol have tended to fuse in evasive forms, equal to the perplexities of the day. Between the irrational force of human instincts and the insane power of the superstate, the novel has struck its own incongruous bargains with terror and slapstick, poetry and fantasy. The fiction of Joyce, Kafka, or Beckett displayed greater technical virtuosity. But the American postwar novelist, with his special knowledge of violence—violence in dream and fact—has become a "con-noisseur of chaos." His language has mimed its way madly, merrily, to desperate truth.

Thus, the novel has met the challenge that one of its practitioners, Philip Roth (born 1933), defined in 1961 in *Writing American Fiction:* "The American writer in the middle of the 20th century has his hands full in trying to understand, and then describe, and then make *credible* much of the American reality. It stupefies, it sickens, it infuriates, and finally it is even a kind of embarrassment at one's own meager imagination."

MAJOR NOVELISTS

Saul Bellow

Saul Bellow was among the first postwar writers to declare the promise of the new literature. Born in Canada, he grew up in Chicago during the 1930s, sweeping past the entrenched naturalism of that era. Like all writers of magnitude, he has put his stamp on reality in a style recognizably his own. He brought a strong sense of the traditional European novel—Balzac, Dickens, Dostoevski—to his free-wheeling American art.

Widely read in philosophy and history, sociology and anthropology,

Bellow, although primarily a novelist of ideas, has nevertheless chosen the turbulence of city streets as the ambience of fiction. His Jewish urban characters, conscious of their ancient heritage, have embodied the perplexities of the American Jew seeking a new definition of his fate. Similarly, Bellow's language has recovered elements of the Yiddish oral tradition for literary use. But the central quest of his work has been persistently larger: he has asked how man may survive as a creature fully possessed of his humanity, in touch with the "axial lines of existence," although the world has turned upside down. The quest has been typically comic; the seeking hero—suffering, laughing, always physically or spiritually on the move— assumes the role of the neopicaresque.

Bellow's humor, however ribald or anguished the occasion seemed, has humanized failure; even his grotesques showed dignity. His narrative, usually in the confessional mode of autobiography, journal, or letter, has made a place for conscience in the midst of flux. He has also explored the archetypal American themes—sex and success, power and death—in contexts that have demanded a new vision. But as the times changed more rapidly, Bellow began to retrench. In his most recent work he has drawn back from the extremes of contemporary experience. The inestimable gift of awareness, which he has lavished upon his best characters, has become a little scantier; and his forms have displayed less inventiveness.

Bellow's first novel, *Dangling Man* (1944), owed more to the examples of Kafka and Dostoevski than that of Theodore Dreiser (1871–1945). Its hero, Joseph, reveals the bitter ironies of existential man, caught between metaphysical absurdity and social regimentation in times of war. Turned inward upon itself, colorless in style, and thinly dramatic, the novel was important more in establishing a certain mood of postwar fiction—grim fantasy and scratchy intelligence—than in serving as a measure of Bellow's ability.

In *The Victim* (1947) Bellow carried the mummery of guilt, dread, and self-justification further. Addressing itself explicitly to anti-Semitism in America, the novel spins around two characters—one Gentile and the other Jew, really a double—creating a universal fable of human ambiguities. Dour, ironic, and compassionate, the book found a form adequate to its complexities. It stands as a landmark of serious Jewish fiction, taking bold measure of its moral and cultural perplexities.

The turning point in Bellow's career came with *The Adventures of Augie March* (1953). Moving toward a more open form, making richer use of the variousness of American culture, exploiting the culture's dreams and humor, Bellow shaped all into a language of the self seeking a "special fate." Augie's character is his fate. In some ways innocent to the end, perhaps a trifle the "schlemiel," Augie can still say: "I did have opposition in me, and great desire to offer resistance and to say 'No!' " Evading corruption, "world-wide Babylonishness," avoiding despair, Augie hears in laughter the mystery of life: "That's the *animal ridens* in me, the laughing creature forever rising up." This long book reopened the novel to the blatancy of experience and set an example to writers who had surrendered their art to Jamesian refinements or Jungian myths.

At the height of his creative powers Bellow returned to the leaner form of the novella and wrote, in *Seize the Day* (1956), a short masterpiece about the encounter with error. Moneyless and all too mortal, Tommy Wilhelm finally gains an inner perspective in which failure ceases to be a personal thing and death no longer seems the final degradation, the apotheosis of all errors.

Of all Bellow's works, it was *Henderson the Rain King* (1958) that gave the most expansive sense of life. Conceived as a romance, a quest through Africa (visited by Bellow only in the mind), the novel raised fantasy, desire, and perception to the level of wisdom. Henderson's heart cries: "I want, I want, I want." Yet he commits himself to an ideal of service or altruism, which he understands at last in the presence of a sacred lioness. His knowledge of death, his subsequent intuition of existence, achieved among high African adventures that reflect back upon western civilization, are sustained by a magic style, which leaps here and there with waggish or woeful exuberance. Thus, the endless availability of Augie gave way to the greater mystery of Henderson's responsibility.

Bellow has not to date surpassed the achievement of *Henderson the Rain King*. *Herzog* (1964), a quasi-epistolary novel, though it bristled with metaphor and idea, ended by giving a confined sense of fate. Lucid at times, biting with the double edge of self-pity, Herzog, despite all his letters, does not carry the reader to a fate larger than his own. In *Mr. Sammler's Planet* (1970) Bellow disciplined himself into a firmer moral tone. Placing man between past and future, history and science fiction— there are many references to H. G. Wells in the book—old Mr. Sammler copes with the present only in terms of his humanist loyalties. A survivor of Nazi mass murders and burials, Sammler had also known literary Bloomsbury and now makes his home in the human mazes of New York. With his durable memory, his "civil heart," his sanity, he holds at bay the vehemence and monstrosity of the world.

The energy of Bellow's imagination, once dominant on contemporary literature, seems to wait upon deeper fulfillment.

Norman Mailer

Perhaps more than any other American writer, Norman Mailer has been the chief representative of the age. This claim rests on the extraordinary vitality of his imagination, his readiness to respond to the largest problems of the times in original manner—rests, indeed, on his power to shape the moment rather than on any specific masterpiece of fiction. Like Heming-way, he has created a brawling legend of his life, and as much as any work of art, the legend has been a projection of his energy. At the center of both life and art, a great ambition took form: to wrest from the contradictions of history and nature, from the warring cosmos itself, a finer fate for man. This romantic heroism of Mailer's has been qualified, on the one hand, by intellectual wit and, on the other hand, by a mystical intuition of existence; modern ideas and primitive magic keep his spirit on the stretch.

At every turn, Mailer has resisted the technocratic or totalitarian organi-zation of the psyche, which he identifies with cancerous invasion, with death moving into contemporary society. His own intellectual development provides a critique of changing American values. Liberalism, Marxism, the new left have served as successive stages in an ideological reevaluation of the possibilities of life, a radical review of history. Mailer's technique has similarly undergone mutations. Breaking with realism early, his novels adopted symbolic and "pop" forms. The style has become increasingly more supple, colorful, humorous, distinctive.

Mailer's *The Naked and the Dead* (1948), which remains one of the best war novels, presented an overview of soldiers on an island in the Pacific. But the blundering campaign of Anopopei also mirrors vaster political issues pertaining to the postwar world. The various symbolic levels of the novel are dramatized in the conflict between three central characters: General Cummings, a visionary totalitarian; Lieutenant Hearn, a misanthropic liberal; and Sergeant Croft, a demonic individualist. Hor-ror, defeat, and death prevail; the drive toward omnipotence, as private motive or historical destiny, fails. The power of *The Naked and the Dead* derives mainly from its vision—fractured by Mailer's narrative shifts and "Time Machine" flashbacks—of dispossessed humanity, from the "raucous stricken bosom of America," waiting in vain for some emergent fate. Thus, Mailer took his first long step beyond the pieties of ordinary war fiction.

In *Barbary Shore* (1951) Mailer wrote a febrile allegory concerning the failure of revolutionary socialism, reflected in the lives of various patho-logical characters sharing a Brooklyn rooming house. Melodramatic in parts, the novel has often been dismissed by critics who failed to note that Mailer strained, with some success, for a new perception of politics and eroticism united in madness.

With *The Deer Park* (1955) Mailer became more explicitly the hiero-phant of sexual mysteries; and his political passion began to take on existential rather than Marxist hues. Set in a luxurious desert colony of Hollywood stars and film makers, the book exposed, with equivocal comedy, the nihilism, cowardice, and hypocrisy of a segment of American society. Only the narrator, who is also a writer, escapes that desert waste-land because he remains open to love and danger.

In a collection of essays and stories, *Advertisements for Myself* (1959), Mailer found his true voice, the right tone and style of an apocalyptic imagination. The crucial essay in the book, *The White Negro,* defined the mystique of the "hipster": American existentialist, obeying the "rebellious imperatives of the self," attuned to danger and the music of his instincts. In a sense, the White Negro turns the collective death of the age against itself; with murder and creation in his heart, he strives to keep man alive. The other pieces in the book confirmed the image of Mailer as prophet and outrageous clown, an inspired intelligence—sometimes mean or erratic— taking on the whole of culture in quest of a new vision. *The Presidential Papers* (1963) and *Cannibals and Christians* (1966) continued that tradition of shamanistic commentary.

Mailer also pursued his experiments with the novel in two highly successful works: *An American Dream* (1965) and *Why Are We in Vietnam?* (1967). In *An American Dream* Mailer impersonated the writer of hard-boiled, action-packed, lurid detective stories, to create an American myth deeper than parody, taller than the tall tale. The hero, Stephen Rojack— intellectual athlete, a Kennedy *manqué*—enters into a magic compact with love and death, experiences all the evils that a metropolis like New York can offer in thirty-two violent hours, and emerges on the other side of loss and terror, still affirming the ambiguous possibilities of heroism in America. Intense, obscene, droll, the novel reveals, through its amazing sensuous texture, a supernatural realm in which gods and demons still grapple for the liberty of man.

In *Why Are We in Vietnam?* Mailer impersonated the voice of a youthful Texan, D. J., who might have also been a Harlem "spade." The scabrous narrative treats the Vietnam war only obliquely; it relates a climactic hunt for a grizzly bear in the Brooks Range of Alaska, within the Arctic Circle, where all the electromagnetic forces of American reality converge. The hunt, reminiscent of Faulkner's *The Bear* (1942), initiates D. J. into the deep corruptions of his elders, the primal force of instinct, and the murderous love of comrades. In its erotic and scatological conceits, the novel brings poles together: nature and civilization, Harlem and Texas, renewal and waste. The insane quality of American violence appears as a perversion of freedom and vitality, which the brave possess in their dreams. Writing in the headlong disc-jockey language of teenagers, Mailer, ruthless comedian, drives toward a truth no ordinary satire could attain. Here language—spoof, rhyme, and pun—explodes into dirge or song.

In critical circles, it has become fashionable to say that Mailer has ended up as the genius journalist of the age. The opinion is based on his later works: *The Armies of the Night* (1968), about the protest march on the Pentagon; *Miami and the Siege of Chicago* (1968), about the Republican and Democratic presidential conventions; and *Of a Fire on the Moon*

(1971), about the first moon landing. But this opinion is tendentious. The usual categories of fiction and fact, novel and history, have often been broken down in recent literature. Furthermore, the imagination of Mailer, transcending the mock heroics of his egoism, has always compelled events to yield a complex sense of human destiny.

PROMINENT NOVELISTS

Wright Morris

One of the first novelists to emerge after World War II, Wright Morris (born 1910) provided a link between two eras of fiction. He not only harked back to Hemingway and Sherwood Anderson (1876–1941) but also foreshadowed the sophisticated humor and anxieties of a generation younger than his own. Solitary, prolific, enjoying fitful public acclaim, laboring more often in obscurity, Morris has sought to repossess the reality of America by penetrating its past, stripping its myths. Morris grew up on the plains of Nebraska; his characters—frail, inward people—return to their midwestern past to find, between the rawness and illusion of American life, some viable identity of their own.

Morris's novels have varied greatly in quality. Some seemed opaque, tedious, or frivolous; a few attained permanent distinction. From his first novel, the autobiographical *My Uncle Dudley* (1942), through more than a dozen works, Morris has tried to impose the field of his inner vision on fragments of experience. Certain characters have recurred, particularly the boy in *My Uncle Dudley,* who became the seeking consciousness of later works of fiction. The entanglements of familial relations move back and forth in time, through the peculiar aura of style.

Isolation, silence, memory, and, above all, the muteness or failure of love are the concerns of Morris's best work. Like Sherwood Anderson before him, Morris has recorded the ordeals of the passionate life in country and town, woman's incapacity to give of herself, the pathos of man's dream. Thus, in *Man and Boy* (1951), *The Works of Love* (1952), *The Deep Sleep* (1953), *The Huge Season* (1954), *The Field of Vision* (1956), and *Ceremony in Lone Tree* (1960), he pursued the American self among the debris of love and recollection.

Satire and nostalgia have been mingled in Morris's work. However, in such later works as *What a Way to Go* (1962), a kind of lightness, an amusing triviality, began to show. Morris, hoping to catch the new mood of erotic comedy, shifted his focus. But his lasting contribution lay elsewhere. Trained initially as a photographer, Morris composed in his best novels a montage of static scenes through which the lost life of Americans was glimpsed.

Bernard Malamud

While Wright Morris has recovered the American past in the lives of his midwestern characters, Bernard Malamud (born 1914) has reclaimed another region of history—the legacy of the Jew. In his work the old world struggles in the midst of the new; legend blends into the hues of social reality; and Jewish conscience, turning itself outward into the world, discovers the universal fate of suffering man. Malamud's heroes, usually ordinary and solitary people, graced with no rare beauty, wealth, or talent, testify to the possibilities of human dignity; prisoners of circumstance, they still find the means of regeneration. Thus, the morality of Malamud, hedged with necessary humor and irony, has given a new dimension to the heritage of Judaism. His lucid style, made spare with pain, rich with Yiddish inflections, tenacious in its poetry, carries its burden without buckling, carrying compassion into our midst.

His first novel, *The Natural* (1952), received belated recognition. Obscure in parts and original in conception, it enmeshed the life of a modern baseball hero into a pattern of Arthurian quest motifs and ancient vegetation rituals. In *The Assistant* (1957), however, Malamud developed the theme of spiritual conversion in flawless form. Set in a drab milieu of immigrant shopkeepers and minority groups, the novel transforms downbeat city streets into some wry version of the pastoral. The weight of ignorance and poverty, the alienation of the Jew in a land of Gentiles, the persistence of hope, inform the love story of Frank Alpine and Helen Bober. An Italian among Jews, Frank discovers himself, discovers purgation in humility, discovers rebirth through sacrifice.

The stories in *The Magic Barrel* (1958), *Idiots First* (1963), and *Pictures of Fidelman* (1969), although of mixed quality, probed the moral center of the hero as *schlemiel-schlimazel*—the aches and indignities that add up, often crazily, to a kind of nobility. In his next novel, *A New Life* (1961), Malamud returned to the theme of ironic redemption, this time in an academic setting. But in *The Fixer* (1966), Malamud created a more compelling fiction. Drawing freely on an historical incident of Jewish persecution—the trial of Mendel Beillis, accused in Kiev, in 1913, of the "ritual murder" of a Christian child—this work distilled history into a parable of terror and absurdity resisted to the end. Marred perhaps only in its abrupt ending, *The Fixer* asserted the special cogency of its theme in an epoch all too familiar with pogroms.

J. D. Salinger

The meteoric career of J. D. Salinger (born 1919) seems to have ended in silence and voluntary obscurity. There was a time, in the early postwar years, when his stories, deft and teasing, satisfied the needs of a youthful generation opposed to the spiritual vulgarity of their culture. Collected later in *Nine Stories* (1953), the best of them portrayed children or adolescents, various misfits in middle-class suburbia, who long for simplicity and truth. Their longing expresses itself, within an allusive frame, in tender or bitter quixotic gestures.

In Salinger's single novel, *The Catcher in the Rye* (1951), the early postwar era found its poignant testament of loss. The hero, Holden Caulfield, a fugitive prep-school student with red hunting cap askew, roams New York City, encountering only mendacity and phoniness. He ends in a sanatorium, from which he recounts, in the first person, his tale, tangy with the colloquial idiom of hurt adolescence. Like Huck Finn, this latter-day picaresque refuses civilization; but unlike his tough predecessor, Holden discovers no "territory ahead," only madness within. Humor, irony, and wistfulness barely conceal the sadness of city life, the equivocations of society, the reign of solitude.

With time, the religious interests of Salinger—Zen Buddhism, primitive Christianity—deepened. Sentiment and satire gave way to a sacramental view of existence. And language itself, the very pride of the artist, began to move toward silence. The evidence was in his later novellas, which reflected the extraordinary Glass family in a mirror darkly. *Franny and Zooey* (1961) and *Raise High the Roofbeam, Carpenters, and Seymour: An Introduction* (1963) astonished the critics with their prolix and convoluted shapes, their digressions and asides. In them, Salinger shattered the story form into countless fragments: speeches, letters, diaries, telephone conversations, messages scrawled everywhere. It was as if his purpose to redeem the "desecrations" of language by parody and discontinuity could be thus attained.

Kurt Vonnegut

Part satirist and part visionary, Kurt Vonnegut (born 1922) has recently enjoyed a sudden vogue, particularly among youths hoping for a better life on earth. A dark comedian even more than a satirist, Vonnegut has expressed his rage, guilt, and compassion, his sense of being a man alive in a world of death, in frightening dystopias. But as sly prophet, he has presented alternatives to the human condition in science fictions, disporting the virtues of his favorite Tralfamadorians. His urgency and rectitude carry themselves lightly in fantasy, in not-so-black humor. But his gruff sentimentality undercuts his power to cope with intolerable realities.

Player Piano (1952), both minatory and tedious, dealt with an anti-utopia ruled by engineers, a managerial society of boredom and computers. In *The Sirens of Titan* (1959), however, Vonnegut created a witty galactic fantasy, exposing the warped purpose of the planet Earth, envisioning the mystery of love in the universe. *Mother Night* (1961, 1966) has perhaps been Vonnegut's most complex work. A study of contemporary nihilism and totalitarianism, of pretense become reality, the novel explored the psyche of an American Nazi, a double agent really, through many reversals, through his search for conscience and being. In *Cat's Cradle* (1963), Vonnegut turned to an apocalyptic confrontation between science and religion, between facts and fictions of a different kind—"the heartbreaking necessity of lying about reality, and the heartbreaking impossibility of lying about it."

Slaughterhouse-Five (1969) revealed the full capabilities of Vonnegut. Centering on an awful event, the firebombing of Dresden in World War II, which the author himself survived as a prisoner of war hiding in the cold-meat locker beneath a slaughterhouse, the book unites realism and science fiction, accusation and exorcism, terror and love, in an original form.

Vonnegut has at times been too shy of his powers, or downright nostalgic or cute. There is something secretly recessive in his vision. But he has also averred human presence despite the insistencies of death, and has imposed a limit on endless cycles of waste and retribution. His irony, his peculiar humor, are only part of his moral measure. He has also devised a style, both lax and gnomic, "telegraphic schizophrenic," which carries his sense of discontinuity, beyond outrage or comedy, toward a sacramental end. In some ways a determinist, he also dreams.

James Purdy

Violence and nostalgia, those twin forces of American literature, have converged in the work of James Purdy (born 1923). He has evolved an original style, deceptively simple, which vaguely recalls Kafka as well as Purdy's fellow Ohioan, Sherwood Anderson. Purdy's humor—black, surreal—has disguised the world of violated innocence; gothic terror and Arcadian dream have sustained the tension of his imagination. Bitterly opposed to materialism and conformity in America, Purdy has created allegorical fantasies that celebrate the spiritual ache of wayward individuals: children, pariahs, and perverts.

Purdy's first collection. *The Color of Darkness* (1957), composed of eleven stories and a novella, received due recognition in England before it did in America. A later collection, *Children Is All* (1962), confirmed the skill of Purdy in expressing hypnotically what his characters, trapped in fear or guilt, can hardly permit themselves to express.

But it was *Malcolm* (1959) that first showed the scope of Purdy's extraordinary vision. Describing the encounters of a fatherless youth with various cruel or grotesque figures, the novel created a comic parable of initiation into the modern world, a world loveless and void. Malcolm is the exploited innocent who manages to preserve his innocence; but he is also a "cypher . . . a blank," around which human rapacity takes shape. *The*

Nephew (1960), unlike *Malcolm,* seems almost a realistic novel; it shares a partial fidelity to midwestern life with a later Purdy work, *Jeremy's Version* (1970).

Two other recent novels revealed Purdy in full possession of his powers. *Cabot Wright Begins* (1964) mocked the outrageous falsity of contemporary culture. Its sly treatment of various New York characters, among them a cheerful rape artist, Cabot Wright, adapted the pornographic manner to social criticism. More tragic, *Eustace Chisholm and the Works* (1967) explored Purdy's perennial theme, love disturbed, with a nearly religious intensity. Set in Chicago in the mid-1930s, the novel traces the fate of various misfits and outsiders through the Depression ending with the war. But the center of the tale is erotic torment; and the climax in an army camp unites politics and sex in terror.

Purdy's voice can be querulous, his world can be too cramped, its blackness almost willed; and women seldom bring life or grace into it. But he understands the inner chaos of men too well, the archetypal night of their souls. Like some absurd lapidary or icy expressionist, he has found the manner to cut the lineaments of dread and innocence into the gross matter of existence.

Truman Capote

The gothic vision was also manifest in the early works of Truman Capote (born 1924). Born and raised in the deep south, Capote's earliest work was in the manner of that region, albeit more exotic than anything written by Faulkner or Eudora Welty (born 1909). His earliest fiction had the quality of nightmare or nocturnal romance. *Other Voices, Other Rooms* (1948), a tour de force in its style and mythic sensibility, enfolds the reader in an inscape of fright and poetic perversion. The initiation of the boy, Joel Knox, to the mysteries of the spectral Cloud Hotel is part of his quest for the other—god, father, or lover; it ends in his discovery of a new self. The same dark surrealism pervades most of *A Tree of Night, and Other Stories* (1949). But in *The Grass Harp* (1951), a humorous daylight romance, the tone changed to one of reverie and nostalgia.

Humor has mediated between the public world and the private motive in Capote's work. His film script, *Beat the Devil* (1953), the essays of precise observation in *Local Color* (1950), the reportage of *The Muses Are Heard* (1956) crackled with outlandish laughter. So did his next work, the novella *Breakfast at Tiffany's* (1958), which marked the end of the southern phase of Capote's fiction. Set mainly in New York, the book celebrated wild Holly Golightly, a sort of bitter-sweet, erotic picaresque.

At his worst, Capote has seemed almost camp; at his best, he has tempered whimsy with shrewd insight. *In Cold Blood* (1966) went beyond all his former work. It heralded a new genre—the "non-fiction novel," the author called it—which recognizes the convergence of fiction and fact, especially in times of outrage. Based on an account of a grisly murder in Kansas (Capote spent years in research, notes, tapes, interviews), the book ultimately raised vast questions about American society and the anger of men. Its impact thus exceeded the force of actuality; and its covert art of selection and juxtaposition, its nets of imagery, its sympathy for stunted life managed to keep its violence controlled.

John Hawkes

The gothic strain, filtering through the work of so many writers of the period, became almost the principle of design in the fiction of John Hawkes (born 1925). Faulkner, Djuna Barnes (born 1892), and Nathanael West (1903–1940) helped shape the bizarre poetic sensibility of Hawkes. His satirical impulse led him to burlesque the "mystery of human feeling at its origin"; the malice of familiar objects, the terror of love gone coldly mad, the fascinations of unstated evil, the ancestral magic of death, of disease, has held his world in surreal fixity.

Hawkes's first book, *The Cannibal* (1949), was a war novel that departed completely from the naturalistic conventions of that form. It was an allegory of cyclical crime and retribution, set in occupied Germany, compressing the military events of 1870, 1914, and 1945 into grim archetypes: murder, madness, and cannibalism. In Hawkes's stories and novellas —*Charivari* (1950), *The Goose on the Grave* (1954), *The Owl* (1954)—the climate of menace, of macabre humor, persisted while social and dramatic content tended to fade.

Hawkes found new subjects for his subsequent novels, although his angle of vision has remained the same. *The Lime Twig* (1961), set in England, evoked a mythical world of power and evil in the racing underworld. *Second Skin* (1964) brought more light into Hawkes's world. The New England coast—rocks, cloudy sun, and sea—reflects cruelty, desire, reflects the endurance of Skipper, the narrator, who refuses to partake in the doom of his entire clan. The complex action moves back and forth in time, from the Pacific to New York to Maine; it comprises lovers and enemies; it ends with Skipper's evasion of death. The sentences are linked; the novel, more than a collection of images and rhythms, is a coherent unity. Hawkes surmounted his innate weakness—a language, although original, too retrogressive and discrete, defying the broader synthesis of experience. Very probably, he has carried the poetic novel as far as it can go.

William Styron

A Virginian by birth, William Styron (born 1925) began his literary career in the southern manner; but he soon showed an independent sensibility. Brilliant in parts, shifting from rhetoric to sudden poetry, dramatically rich, his work has sought, between violence and ambiguity, some definition of personal integrity.

The influence of Faulkner was apparent in Styron's first novel, *Lie Down in Darkness* (1951). But the book, intense and darkly lyrical, also harked back to the baroque tradition of John Donne and Sir Thomas Browne. Nonetheless, it has remained Styron's most vivid, most personal expression. The novel presented a southern family locked in a domestic tragedy; love wears the face of guilt, and the search for childhood innocence leads only to self-destruction. Through the various characters, Styron made a symbolic statement on the decay of the south and on the larger trials of the modern world.

Styron's later novels expanded his range; seldom shoddy or trite, they did not burn, however, so incandescently as *Lie Down in Darkness*. *The Long March* (1952) depicted a Marine camp realistically. And *Set This House on Fire* (1960), a work less esteemed in America than in Europe, where the action takes place, presented the existential themes of alienation and murderous freedom.

The most controversial, perhaps the most ambitious, of Styron's novels, *The Confessions of Nat Turner* (1967), purported to be a "meditation on the history" of a nineteenth-century slave rebellion in Virginia. Styron found in the event a mirror of the contemporary black movement in America. Written in a sequence of dreams, reflections, and actions, mostly from the point of view of the black rebel Nat Turner, the book raised complex issues of literary and historical authenticity. Bold in conception, tense and magnificent in some scenes, the novel nevertheless failed to probe the deepest insights of its subject.

John Barth

One of the most ingenious avant-gardists of the contemporary period, John Barth has tested the very limits of the novel. A virtuoso of language, he has mimed old genres mischievously, mixed fantasy and philosophy in parodic forms, and turned history into farce. A radical skeptic by temperament, he has understood the comedy of nihilism in our time and the existential clownery of art. The phenomenal world seems to him gratuitous, reality merely a "nice place to visit." Only in the region of "ultimacy," entered through the portals of the imagination, is man funny, free, and lucid. Yet an excess of consciousness, "cosmopsis," has also poisoned the will of man to be or act or love.

Although Barth's first two novels departed only mildly from standard structures, their playing with reality was peculiarly mordant. In *The Floating Opera* (1956, 1967) Barth declared his theme: the uninvolved life, lived from heartbeat to heartbreak, in total absence of intrinsic values. In *The End of the Road* (1958, 1967) Barth used the sexual triangle to expose crippled will and identity. The central character, Jake Adams, carries "all non-mystical value-thinking to the end of the road."

But it was in *The Sot-Weed Factor* (1960, 1967), set in colonial Maryland, that Barth revealed the full measure of his inventiveness. One of the longest and most riotous books of the postwar period, the novel parodied, with philosophical vengeance, eighteenth-century gothic and picaresque tales; it was the imitation of a novel by an author who was impersonating the role of Author. The result of this technical *tour de force* seemed close to a metaphysical joke. The mystery of human personality, the madness of history, the surrealism of nature—all came within its dark and delightful purview.

Pushing farrago still farther, Barth constructed in *Giles Goat-Boy* (1966) a mosaic allegory of all the destructive wisdom of the twentieth century. The epic hero, a goat-man, part Christ and part Pan, struggles toward the salvation of the human race. He nearly attains it in the embrace of his beloved Anastasia, within the bowels of a monstrous computer, WESCAC. The immense panorama of travesty in the novel, however taut and complex beneath, tended to pall; in places, imagination gave way to preciosity.

The parodic rage of Barth found a different expression in the short stories in *Lost in the Fun House*. Living voice, printed word, and magnetic tape constitute a kind of aural montage, a generic conceit. The narrative swallows itself by the tail, as in *Anonymiad;* or vanishes entirely in a Chinese box, as in *Menelaiad;* or ends in the silence of the tale, the teller, and the told, as in *Title*. Like Samuel Beckett, Jorge Luis Borges, and William Burroughs (born 1914), Barth seems to hear a brilliant stillness within contemporary literature.

John Updike

John Updike (born 1932) shares the ironic temper of Barth. His satiric focus, however, is narrower, his inventions less exuberant. He has written in a crisp, probing idiom, precise yet astonishing in imagery, sterile in an oddly poetic way. He has chosen subtle middle-class characters who seldom suffer the extreme passions of their day. Updike, therefore, has often seemed a novelist of manners, a clever writer, deft up to a certain depth. Yet he has also tried to sound some major themes: love, death, freedom, the burden of redemption in the contemporary world.

The short stories in *The Same Door* (1959) and in *Pigeon Feathers* (1962) demonstrated formal brilliance. In *Rabbit, Run* (1960), however, Updike created a work of greater power. "Rabbit" Angstrom represents the contradictory urges of the new hero to discover, beyond responsibility, beyond love even, a special fate for himself. Running from one failure to another, disengaging himself from the embroilments of sex and society, he evades all corruptions but his own. Yet Rabbit remains alive to his spiritual quest: in the secular wasteland of the novel, he alone dramatizes the existential condition of man deprived of grace.

The Centaur (1963) was denser and more problematic than *Rabbit, Run.* The novel reflects, in the myth of Chiron, the travails of a modern schoolteacher, Caldwell. The various levels of the story, mythic and realistic, allegorical and literal, collide in shifting perspectives, refracting degeneration, revealing death. Profoundly moving in parts, merely clever or obscure in others, *The Centaur* seemed a testimony of vast artistic ambitions partially fulfilled.

In *On the Farm* (1965), which takes place in his native Pennsylvania, Updike returned to straightforward narrative; he continued in this vein in *Couples* (1968), set in a small eastern American town, affluent and sexually frenetic. Increasingly, Updike has turned toward love as the mirror of human maladies. Yet his skill, evident in *On the Farm,* failed in *Couples* to convey, beyond the intricacies of shuddering flesh, a carnal meaning.

Updike can be too detached, cerebral. And his witty language, cramped with minutiae, can intrude upon the reader. At his worst, he has lacked the courage of any large feeling. But his satire, in *Bech* (1970) for example, has been adroit and wickedly amusing. Updike sees more than the pretensions of society; he sees its spiritual vacuity. He is, therefore, less a satirist than a religious writer.

FICTION: TYPES AND TRENDS

The Short Story

The short story goes back to the nineteenth-century masters: Hawthorne and Poe, Crane and James. In the earlier part of the twentieth century, Anderson, Hemingway and Faulkner helped to mold its character. In the postwar period, the short story, sharply defined by its scope and form, proved more resistant to various trends than the novel. It has remained, nevertheless, popular. The mass market for newspapers, for magazines ranging from pulp to academic to avant-garde, has made story writing both lucrative and reputable.

Many contemporary virtuosos of the short story are known as well for their longer fiction: J. D. Salinger, John Cheever (born 1912), Flannery O'Connor (1925–1964), Bernard Malamud, Truman Capote, John Updike, James Purdy. But there are also writers whose achievement has seemed more intensely representative, their angle of vision more acute, in the shorter form. *The Prince of Darkness, and Other Stories* (1947) by J. F. Powers (born 1917), and *Children Are Bored on Sunday* (1953) by Jean Stafford (born 1915) provided examples of poignant achievement in short fiction. Quiet as it may still seem, the short story has evolved to a degree that lyric ceremony has often yielded to sexual violence or absurdist humor, as in Alfred Chester's (born 1928) *Behold Goliath* (1964) or Donald Barthelme's (born 1931) *Come Back, Dr. Caligari* (1964).

The War Novel

It was natural that World War II itself should provide young writers who have just climbed out of their uniforms with an experience large and troubling enough to compel the fictional imagination. Novelists of Hemingway's and John Dos Passos's (1896–1970) generation had found in World War I a symbol of general collapse as well as personal disillusionment. But the next generation entered World War II with few illusions; and what they saw in its unspeakable ravages seemed to them not only the collapse of an old order but also a dread prophecy of the future.

The war yielded great variety in theme, manner, and artistic quality. The conflict between officers and enlisted men; the contrast between American and European or oriental women; the character of the American soldier in war and peace; the meaning of courage, love, or death—these were among the themes that came out of the war. John Hersey's (born 1914) *A Bell for Adano* (1944), John Horne Burns's (1916–1953) *The Gallery* (1947), Irwin Shaw's (born 1913) *The Young Lions* (1948), Norman Mailer's *The Naked and the Dead,* Herman Wouk's (born 1915) *The Caine Mutiny* (1951), and James Jones's (born 1921) *From Here to Eternity* (1951)—of these, the works of Burns, Mailer, and Jones stood out—suggested that realism tended to prevail in the earliest war fiction. In *The Naked and the Dead,* however, there were already hints of another, surrealistic form, reminiscent of Dos Passos. In John Hawkes's *The Cannibal,* Thomas Berger's (born 1924) *Crazy in Berlin* (1958), Joseph Heller's (born 1923) *Catch-22* (1961), and Kurt Vonnegut's *Slaughterhouse-Five,* the form was broken wider open to reckon with the deepening absurdities of the age.

The most representative author of war fiction was perhaps James Jones. His first novel, *From Here to Eternity,* set in the Schofield barracks of Hawaii just before the attack on Pearl Harbor, movingly depicted the struggle of one soldier to maintain his identity, his dignity as a man. The novel displayed raw power and compassion, characters stubborn in their vivid life, and a sense of outrage sustained in dramatic action and social fact. Its hero says, "Men are killed by being always alike, always unremembered."

The same feeling informed *The Pistol* (1958), which examined the nature of authority in its inevitable clash with personal "salvation." But it was in *The Thin Red Line* (1962) that Jones gave his fullest, most technical account of the war. The "system" was no longer solely responsible for all human violations; men conspired, through their lack of "realism," to defeat themselves. In the vast, murderous spectacle of jungle combat, which Jones described minutely, evil disguises itself as softness or illusion, as romantic heroism, as social cant that can not stand the test of natural survival.

Jones has been accused of uncouth writing, sensationalism, and sentimentality. But although he sometimes has given evidence of these faults, he possesses gifts greater than subtlety: a capacity to respond to life in narrative terms, an enduring honesty in statement, a covert uncanny sensitivity. Nor has his achievement been limited entirely to war fiction, as *Some Came Running* (1957) and *The Merry Month of May* (1971) showed.

The Southern Novel

The tradition of southern fiction is perhaps the oldest in the United States. It goes back to the gothic works of Charles Brockden Brown (1771–1810) and Edgar Allan Poe. Then, in the twentieth century, William Faulkner reinvented the south in his myth of Yoknapatawpha County, in which history and poetry violently met. The heroic legacy of Faulkner was fully available to such later writers as Robert Penn Warren, as well as to women novelists who chose to explore more delicate nuances of feelings.

The best of the women writers—and a figure of transition like Warren himself—Eudora Welty has captured the concrete quality of life, love, humor, and grotesqueness in her native Mississippi. Her fine stories were collected in *A Curtain of Green* (1941) and *The Wide Net* (1943). Her novels have included *Delta Wedding* (1946), *The Golden Apples* (1949), *The Ponder Heart* (1954), and *Losing Battles* (1970).

Welty represents a vanishing way of southern life. Rural and largely conservative, tragic in its sense of the past, acquainted with bloody defeat and its lingering symbols, struggling still with the guilt of slavery, the south has presented a strong regional identity. That identity stands in opposition to the popular assumptions about American culture: progress, egalitarianism, rationalized existence. The southern mind has been preeminently aware of custom and ceremony, responsive to the mythic or elemental; a mind eager to preserve the sense of person, family, and community, the folklore of the land; a mind dwelling on the cadences of oral discourse, gossip, rhetoric, and living story. This has been, in brief, the image of "Dixie." But the novelists who began writing during or after the war— Carson McCullers (1917–1967) and Flannery O'Connor, for instance— gave it darker colorations.

The characters of Carson McCullers were almost all grotesques, inhabitants of provincial Georgia, left behind on islands of time and their own hermetic souls. For them, the alchemy of love distilled only pain. "There are the lover and the beloved," McCullers wrote, "but these two come from

" In McCullers's first and longest work, *The Heart Is a* ...40), a sexless deaf-mute, Singer, serves as mock con- ...ose citizens he can neither hear nor redeem. And in her ...*llad of the Sad Cafe* (1951), the three central charac- ...ters—the Amazon-like Miss Amelia, a hunchback, and a criminal—play out the ballad of privacy and maimed desire, while a chain gang sings, suffers, endures.

More precise in embodying mystery through manners, her great rigor equal to her wit and compassion, Flannery O'Connor was hailed as one of the most impressive postwar writers before her untimely death in 1964, and her reputation continues to grow. In her native Georgia, she saw Protestant fundamentalism run wild, and worship, heresy, and nihilism burst within the Bible Belt. A devout Catholic herself, she once defined her subject as the "action of grace in territory held largely by the devil."

This religious idea shaped O'Connor's first novel, *Wise Blood* (1952), a taut and terrifying tale of a young revivalist preacher, converted to the Church Without Christ. In her second novel, *The Violent Bear It Away* (1960), O'Connor developed in the ritual of baptism a metaphor of the human struggle *against* salvation. Thus, the boy Tarwater holds out fanatically against his fate, until he experiences evil firsthand.

O'Connor also wrote extraordinary short stories, collected in *A Good Man Is Hard to Find* (1955) and *Everything That Rises Must Converge* (1965). As complex in comic shadings as in dramatic detail, the stories dwelt rather too insistently on horrors that make the human condition intolerable without grace. O'Connor's ascetic control of nuance in the face of baleful passion, her realism in dark places of the soul, empowered her to state the disorders of the contemporary spirit in ineluctable forms, southern only in texture, as universal as death.

Flannery O'Connor was also the author of thoughtful essays, posthumously published in the collection *Mystery and Manners* (1969).

The Jewish Novel

The Jewish novel has shown no evidence of decline, as has southern fiction. Not all Jewish writers, of course, have concerned themselves exclusively with the "Jewish experience." Some, like Mailer, Bellow, and Salinger, have accepted no restriction on their material; others, like Malamud, writing mainly about Jews, have moved always into a far broader nexus of life.

In its tradition—northern, urban, liberal or radical in politics—the postwar Jewish novel could claim writers as different as Henry Roth (born 1906), Daniel Fuchs (born 1909), and Nathanael West (1906–1940) as precursors. Orthodox Judaism, which rests on a particular faith and history, a sense of community, a special language, has submitted to subtle

mutations in postwar America. Memories of the Nazi holocaust and ne.
of Israel's victories have possessed the Jewish American novelist, who participated in the crucial events of his people only vicariously; even the anti-
Semitism he might recall from his own childhood has waned. Anxious and
ambivalent, he has often expressed the tensions of skepticism and belief, of
assimilation and identity, of new, mixed marriages and old family manners,
in complex, ironic forms.

The premature death of Edward Lewis Wallant (1926–1962) deprived
American literature of a novelist of unusual talent and integrity. Although
he often wrote about Jews, his constant theme—the regeneration of feeling
in love or grief, in response to the sacramental nature of existence—applied to all. His best work, *The Pawnbroker* (1961), grimly follows Sol
Nazerman, former victim of Nazi torture, to his rebirth in "agonizing sensitivity" in New York decades later.

Daniel Stern (born 1928) wrote about concentration camps in *Who
Shall Live, Who Shall Die* (1963) and about the improvised life—urgent,
dislocated, but hopeful—in postwar New York in *After the War* (1967).
Stern is best known for *The Suicide Academy* (1968), in which he created
a compelling metaphor of the contemporary world, balanced intricately in
the dance of love and death or in the dialogue of black and Jew. The
atmosphere of "para-reality," funny and darkly scintillant, leaves the
reader with a brilliant sense of himself.

For Bruce Jay Friedman (born 1930), black humor—he even edited an
anthology by that name—has been the form for skepticism and fear and
the horrors of love. Beneath the breakneck gaiety of his novels *Stern*
(1962) and *A Mother's Kisses* (1964) is an exacerbated sensitivity to anti-
Semitism and to the farce of sex.

But of the younger Jewish novelists, Philip Roth has been the most
popular. He first made an impression with a collection of stories, *Goodbye,
Columbus* (1959), which exposed the new Jewish sensibility in a setting of
social and moral ambiguity. With *Portnoy's Complaint* (1969) Roth
created a scandal. Focusing on a Jewish family, and particularly on the
relationship between possessive mother and prodigal son, Roth wrote a
ribald fantasy of guilt and onanism, altruism and prurience. The humor of
the novel caught the latest erotic mood of fiction and deflected violence
toward insight. The sexual conflict between Gentile and Jew in Roth's
earlier stories here moved to a deeper level—involving self-knowledge and
self-fantasy. Still, despite his great skill and hilarity, Roth has not always
guarded himself against a certain triviality.

The Black Novel

The character of black fiction changed rapidly as both Africans and
Negro Americans developed a new cultural and political sense of them-

selves. Nevertheless, certain common features of the black novel have emerged since Richard Wright (1908–1960) began to give it shape with *Uncle Tom's Children* (1938), *Native Son* (1940), and *Black Boy* (1945). Memories of slavery, protest, and fury; the sometimes-impossible search for dignity, for identity, in a world dominated by white values; the conflict between the artistic and political natures of the writer; his sexual complexities; the existential quality of his life; his need for an ethnic definition of himself—all these appeared, sometimes in hints, sometimes in full shape, in Wright's work.

These were also the challenges that Ralph Ellison (born 1914) met in his outstanding novel *Invisible Man* (1952). Born in Oklahoma, Ellison did not feel all the restraints that the former slave states imposed on blacks. His sense of the human condition, therefore, tended to be more complex, more expansive than that of some other black writers. A natural artist—he has also studied sculpture and music—Ellison has shown a sophisticated sense of fictional form, the "mixture of the marvelous and the terrible," as well as a sense of jazzlike improvisation. He has learned from his own experience and from the blues how anger, incongruity, and agony can sustain a provisional vision of things.

The task of the ironic, picaresque, nameless hero of *Invisible Man* is exactly this: to move from invisibility to vision. Through the dangers, corruptions, and temptations awaiting him, he recapitulates the history of his own race. Exploited by all—white communists and African nationalists, southern bigots and northern liberals, women and men alike—he proceeds, less in the manner of an arrow than a boomerang, from innocence to disillusionment to the edge of a new wisdom. *Invisible Man* was a profound and brilliant work, perhaps too prolix in parts, yet original in its syncopation of reality, musical in its organization of themes. More than an example of black fiction, this novel was an early landmark in all of postwar American literature.

James Baldwin (born 1924) has made an impact in more diverse ways: in fiction, in drama, above all in essays that are at once lucid and impassioned, burning with self-knowledge. His statements in *Notes of a Native Son* (1955), *Nobody Knows My Name* (1961), and *The Fire Next Time* (1963) sounded a crescendo of anger that echoed mutely his own growing perplexity in relation to even more militant blacks.

Baldwin's first novel, the autobiographical *Go Tell It on the Mountain* (1953), depicted the family of a Harlem preacher, a proud, lust-driven man, haunted by the power of a terrible God. Religion howls in poetry; prophecy, sin, and madness shake the soul of young Johnny, bastard stepson of the family, who makes his way through torment to manhood. In two subsequent novels, *Another Country* (1962) and *Tell Me How Long the Train's Been Gone* (1968), Baldwin attempted to place racial and political tensions within the framework of love. His intricate and sinuous style, graceful or apocalyptic as the occasion required, was unmistakable; but the nature of his material defied dramatic control.

The difficulties of any writer in a revolutionary movement can be immense; it has therefore been all the more remarkable that black authors, who have not always agreed on a common stance, have done so well. Some, writing in the shadow of Wright, Ellison, and Baldwin, came to be known only in the 1960s. John A. Williams (born 1925), active in many political and literary endeavors, moved deeply by black anger, still committed to art, produced fine, laconic novels in *Sissie* (1963) and *The Man Who Cried I Am* (1967). Paule Marshall (born 1929), born in Brooklyn of Barbadian parents, drew on her knowledge of South, Central, and North America in *Brown Girl, Brownstone* (1959) and *Soul Clap Hands and Sing* (1961). William Melvin Kelley (born 1937), a recipient of numerous literary awards, proved his great talent in *A Different Drummer* (1962) and *Dem* (1967).

Alienation and Anarchy

By far the largest part of contemporary literature has come under the rubric of alienation—alienation certainly from the dominant culture, alienation sometimes from self and nature. The fictional hero has been an outsider because the very conditions of life, and his own consciousness, have required estrangement. The forms of estrangement, however, have evolved curiously in the postwar years.

Paul Bowles (born 1910) was one of the earliest writers to turn his back on American, indeed, on western culture. The characters of his novels *The Sheltering Sky* (1949) and *Let It Come Down* (1953) are expatriates in a stark and pitiless land, North Africa; and their existential quest, which recalls Albert Camus's *L'étranger,* ends in annihilation. In a sense, Bowles presaged, in a style of classic restraint, the wandering "beats" and, more precisely, the violent "hipster."

The beat movement, of course, had a sacramental aspect lacking in Bowles's world. Emerging from the coffee houses of San Francisco, Venice West (near Los Angeles), and Greenwich Village, these new bohemians spread across the land, challenging the forms and values of American culture, devising a shaggy life style of their own that featured sex, drugs, jazz. Love and anarchy jostled in the movement, as Jack Kerouac (1922–1969) perhaps best exemplified. His novel *On the Road* (1957) attempted to recover the spontaneity of jazz, the perception of haiku, the wildness and openness and joy of the American continent. Kerouac's next novel, *The Subterraneans* (1958), was a love idyll of the underground, sung in sweet, "spontaneous prose," loose in syntax, flowing with the natural line of feeling. But his best work may have been *The Dharma Bums* (1958), which celebrated the "rucksack revolution," the splendors of eastern religion and of the American west, the cities with their gritty loves in the background, the very wonder of creation.

The hipster, more hardened and dangerous, went farther in metaphysical rebellion than the beat, and none went farther in his fictional exploration of that state than William Burroughs. Indeed, Burroughs defined a limit beyond which neither language nor form could go in the American novel. The violence of his work has been cold and total. Yet his style, mechanical and desiccated, could still break into outrageous humor and poetic hallucination. In Burroughs's best work, *Naked Lunch* (1959), he offered a lunatic scenario, a grisly montage of satire and horror—reminiscent in parts of Hieronymus Bosch—showing humanity in the demonic control of abstract powers, working through sex, through drugs, through language itself, to reduce life to death and excrement. An experimentalist in the American vein of anti-literature, Burroughs found words abysmally corrupt—"To speak is to lie," he wrote—and thus has turned, in the technological nightmares of his more recent "science fiction" (which I will discuss with that genre), to the "Cut-Up Method," which demands composition by random collages of clippings.

Other novels have expressed alienation in terms of violence and perversion so shocking as to approach Burroughs's: John Rechy's (born 1934) *City of Night* (1963), Burt Blechman's (born 1927) *Stations* (1964), Hubert Selby's (born 1926) *Last Exit to Brooklyn* (1964). But none of these has exceeded the satanic wit and distrust of language in Burroughs's work.

Alienation and anarchy has also resorted to the new antics of an archaic figure—the amorous rogue, master of chicaneries. J. P. Donleavy (born 1926) burst on the scene in 1955 with Sebastian Dangerfield, hero of *The Ginger Man* (which he revised in 1958 and 1965), scruffy, zany sensualist, lurching through Dublin, improvising his life from day to day with all the gusto and desperation he can muster. But the comic vitality of the novel, which ridiculed mediocrity and convention, also had a nasty edge; it carried knowledge of the void, doom. Written in an original, elliptic style, interspersed with acrid twaddling songs, *The Ginger Man* offered a vision of human singularity.

The novel of alienation reached the limits of outrage in *Naked Lunch;* and it prompted the bitter tomfooleries of *The Ginger Man*. But it has also generated, in such works as *The Dharma Bums,* a redemptive impulse beyond alienation. The theme of redemption has been clear in the work of Ken Kesey (born 1935). His fine first novel, *One Flew over the Cuckoo's Nest* (1962), set in a mental institution, showed how the unbroken spirit of one man, an outsider to the deadly "combine" of contemporary social existence, could free his fellow inmates, free them even from their own fear before life.

The redemptive impulse, the movement out of alienation, seems more cruel in the work of Jerzy Kosinski (born 1933). Born in Poland, Kosinski could draw on European as well as American conditions of demonic solitude. His shattering first novel, *The Painted Bird* (1966), depicted with preternatural clarity the tortures and savageries a boy, taken for a gypsy or Jew, tries to escape in Nazi-occupied Poland. *Steps* (1968) pursued, through lacunae of the unspeakable, the adventures of a young man in America. The hero, forced by memory and circumstance to act as predator, is also a symbol of the contemporary self, pure in its extreme alienation, struggling to reenter the world with the lucidity of hatred. Spare in style, learned in the dark nuances of the human, consummately parabolic, Kosinski has transcended all the platitudes of alienation and has thus moved to redefine, if not redeem, the estrangement of man from society.

From Satire to the Novel of the Absurd

One of the most recent and more salient trends of American fiction has been a variant of fantasy, satirical only in part, inward with absurdity. Both celebration and despondency have mingled in its motive, although its humor has tended to be Stygian. The authors drawn to the genre have displayed great inventiveness, verbal magic, and virtuosity, versatility even in despair. Yet the line from Nathanael West and Vladimir Nabokov to John Barth, Joseph Heller, Thomas Berger, Donald Barthelme, Thomas Pynchon (born 1937), Terry Southern (born 1928), and Jerome Charyn (born 1937) was not as straight, perhaps, as critics might conveniently wish.

In a special sense, the satirical work of Mary McCarthy (born 1912), conventional as it has been, may be apposite to the new spirit of comedy. Her acidulous observations of leftist intellectuals in *The Oasis* (1949), of collegiate intriguers in *The Groves of Academe* (1952), of women and wives, lesbians and big-city careerists in *The Group* (1963) conveyed a cold intuition of American life and manners.

A satirist of more benign disposition, John Cheever has approached American experience with a sacramental wink at life. He sees people and events with a kind of eccentric clarity. Love and celebration, whimsy and irony, made his history of a New England family—*The Wapshot Chronicle* (1957) and *The Wapshot Scandal* (1964)—a testimony not only American in its generosities but also human in its dalliance with fate. Despite eroticism and exuberance, however, Cheever has also known the "nightmare of our existence," and wrote, "Life in the United States in 1960 is Hell."

The contemporary hell has seemed to the absurdist an organized chaos—a kind of institutionalized madness. This was how the world appeared in Joseph Heller's *Catch-22* (1961), a masterpiece of black comedy. Ostensibly a "war novel," dealing with the attempts of Air Force Captain Yossarian to stay alive through bombing missions without end, the book created a surreal universe of drollery and death. Serious, satirical, and unspeakably funny, the novel bursts in fragments of dialogue, narrative, caricature, joke, reflection, flashback that only Heller's imagination could contain, only his discontinuous form could render with integrity.

Conscience has modified the sense of incongruity in another novelist too sophisticated for piety, too vigorous for despair—Thomas Berger. His style—extravagant, buffoonish—has recovered for man a kind of quixotic innocence or simplicity, a knowing craziness. Like the hero of his Reinhart novels—*Crazy in Berlin* (1958), *Reinhart in Love* (1962), *Vital Parts* (1970)—Berger has impersonated the Fool or Scapegoat of tradition, carrier away of death, and has made his home in the fictive and real worlds with equal poise.

In the fiction of Terry Southern, satire and black humor, parody and pornography, have carried the special aura of camp. But in his best works —*Flash and Filigree* (1958) and *The Magic Christian* (1960)—he was also pitiless in his contempt for human deceit and folly.

A more serious humorist, a creative fantast, Donald Barthelme, has experimented with nonlinear narratives and absurdist techniques—his works have contained pictures, questionnaires, captions of various sizes— while maintaining his commitment to a world wildly out of joint. His novel *Snow White* (1967) and the stories in *City Life* (1970) showed fierce wit and verbal agility as well as a genuine, if totally oblique, moral perception of human lunacy.

But none has pushed the absurd novel farther toward autodestruction and nihilistic play than Thomas Pynchon. Arcane humor; bizarre characters; cryptic plots and counterplots; a style almost too brilliant in puns, allusions, innuendos—all served his purpose of obliterating meaning. His first novel, *V* (1963), designed a labyrinthine story of mock quests leading nowhere. In *The Crying of Lot 49* (1966) Pynchon continued his inspired reduction of the world's absurdity with mock-apocalyptic fervor. As in his previous work, sex, violence, madness, and technology composed an entropic hallucination of the void, an epistemological conundrum.

Science Fiction

Fantasy has also taken the special form of science fiction, which has increasingly captured the attention of "serious" authors. Through this genre, both the creative and destructive potential of the contemporary world has been projected; the imagination has found a mode of confronting stunning changes, in politics or technology, in culture or consciousness. Science fiction has tended, therefore, to be prophetic and visionary in projections of utopia or, more frequently, satirical and minatory in projections of dystopia.

Dystopias have attracted some authors who were known equally for fiction of another kind. William Burroughs, for instance, has turned in his more recent work—*The Soft Machine* (1961, 1965), *The Ticket That Exploded* (1962), and *Nova Express* (1964)—to an intergalactic adventure and morality drama, involving the conflict between forces of good and evil, freedom and repression, couched in technological vocabulary, simulating a space-age nightmare. Kurt Vonnegut also found science fiction most congenial. One of his characters, Eliot Rosewater, says: "You're [science fiction writers] all I read any more. You're the only ones who'll talk about the really terrific changes going on, the only ones crazy enough to know that life is a space voyage. . . ." Such Vonnegut novels as *The Sirens of Titan* and *Cat's Cradle* have employed the techniques of science fantasy in both a satirical and a visionary vein.

The genre, however, has developed in many more ingenious ways in the hands of professional science fiction writers, the best of whom include Ray Bradbury (born 1920), Alfred Bester (born 1913), Robert Heinlein (born 1907), and Isaac Asimov (born 1920).

POETRY

Postwar American verse has been both abundant and contrary. Styles have broken out, changing rapidly; cliques have formed and disappeared; poets have proliferated. Poets of quality have been no fewer than novelists; they have published, taught, read more widely than ever before; fellowships have come their way, and small magazines have honored their work; translators have rendered them into foreign tongues. Yet poets have also paid a heavy psychic toll to Mammon, in suicide, madness, mute despair; and in the end, the impact they have made on the age seems less than they have deserved.

Literary historians have consistently argued that the first breakthrough of the twentieth century came when Ezra Pound (1885–1972) and T. S. Eliot (1888–1965), writing in London, turned to French symbolism, English metaphysical verse, or ancient Provençal lyrics to fashion in modernism a language that brought Victorian or Georgian modes to an end. This new language was formal, erudite, compressed in thought, elusive in rhythms, quick to the uses of irony and wit, rich in conceits or catachresis, inclined to mythical allusions. The New Critics, who included such notable poets as John Crowe Ransom (born 1888) and Allen Tate (born 1899), soon lent their intellectual authority to this movement. Editors and professors, through critical quarterlies, through college courses, supported its orthodoxies.

When the reaction to orthodoxy finally came, it took a multitude of forms; and some postwar poets who began in one manner shifted dramatically to another. Different models, as indigenous as Walt Whitman, Carl Sandburg (1878–1967), or Robert Frost (1874–1963) were rediscovered. Instead of the decorous and polyglot cadence of the modernist tradition, the raucous sounds of American speech crept into verse. Curiously enough, an aspect of the later Pound—idiomatic, immediate, discontinuous, as in the *Cantos*—was recovered together with the poetry of William Carlos Williams (1883–1963), who provided an informal paradigm, the accents and diction of urban life, a poetry of experience. The rebellious romanticism of E. E. Cummings (1894–1962) and the mystic tone of H. D. (1886–1961, pseudonym of Hilda Doolittle) seemed also apposite. The earlier tradition of Eliot, which had become academic, yielded to new styles of confession or protest, surrealism or bardic rage, claiming the ancestry of Whitman.

Discriminations between the two main trends of postwar poetry have been at best tentative, at worst misleading. Yet certain terms have come into use, sharpening both contrast and controversy. Robert Lowell casually distinguished between "cooked" and "raw" verse; and Lawrence Ferlinghetti (born 1919) between poetry of the "ivory tower" and poetry of the "streets." Others pitted "academic" against "beat." In some sense, these labels referred to the old strains in American literature, which Philip Rahv (born 1908) called "pale face" (Poe, James) and "red skin" (Melville, Twain). Indeed, they revived Nietzsche's fundamental distinction between Apollonian and Dionysian temperaments. Perhaps we can simply refer to the older, modernist style as "closed," the newer style as "open," keeping in mind that boundaries have never been so clear as to warrant a last judgment, that most poets in their individual careers have progressed from closed to open styles.

The progress of postwar poets may have followed certain patterns, but their appearance in the public domain, the making and fading of their reputations, has seemed more erratic. These mutations of taste have been reflected in leading anthologies of the period, in their receptivity to closed or open styles. The opposition of these styles was acknowledged in a work edited by Paris Leary and Robert Kelly called *A Controversy of Poets* (1965).

The path to the proverbial wood of contemporary verse, which sometimes can hardly be discerned from its trees, was cleared by four poets who began to publish before World War II but who remained very much part of contemporary poetry. These authors of transition have also exemplified, each in his manner, some tendency of the period.

Richard Eberhart (born 1904) brought to his earliest verse, *A Bravery of Earth* (1930) and *Reading the Spirit* (1937), a breathless romantic intensity, a lyric presence often awkward or naïve. Yet in their most vital rush, and their intuition of death, these volumes were immemorially wise. Three decades later, Eberhart expressed in his *Collected Poems* (1960) other moods: visionary, reflective, didactic, erotic.

Less prolific, Stanley Kunitz (born 1905), a superb craftsman, won little acclaim for *Intellectual Things* (1930) and *Passport to the War* (1944). It was only with *Selected Poems: 1928–1958* (1958), hailed by Lowell among others, that Kunitz was recognized for his precise language—dense yet natural, metaphysical yet unassuming.

Accomplished in poetry as he was in fiction and criticism, Robert Penn Warren was part of the southern movement called the Fugitives, led by John Crowe Ransom and Allen Tate. This movement was conservative in cultural outlook, formalist in literature. Power and intelligence informed Warren's verse, and a ballad naïveté toughened its texture. From *Thirty-six Poems* (1935) to the long narrative work *Brother to Dragons* (1953) Warren moved between rhetoric and love. Through a textbook he edited with Cleanth Brooks (born 1906), *Understanding Poetry* (1938), he influenced the first decade of postwar writing with the precepts of New Criticism.

Quite the opposite from Warren, Kenneth Rexroth (born 1905) espoused the cause of various antiformalists, the San Francisco poets, the beats. His verse—from *In What Hour* (1940) through *The Collected Shorter Poems* (1968)—has displayed a curious mixture of oriental imagism and anarchic fervor in forms stark and free.

The romantic primitivism of Eberhart, the close modulations of language of Kunitz, the complex of irony and earthiness of Warren, and the rebellious prosody of nature of Rexroth all found their way into contemporary poetry. It remained for younger poets to reconcile the richness of their legacy to the great violence within their lives and without.

A MAJOR POET: ROBERT LOWELL

The stature of Robert Lowell has grown continuously over the years. His name has exerted, perhaps prematurely, the authority of a major figure. From the start, Lowell struggled with his daimon; the inhibition of his own violence, the sad or sudden paralysis of self, has given his poetry its peculiar power. Against inner torment—in some deep, distasteful sympathy with Milton's Satan, Lowell also cried, "I myself am hell"—he pitted the disintegration of the outside world. And he found in madness a state that could subsume all hells. A central voice, apocalyptic and anecdotal, revolting against its own origins, putting contemporary existence on trial, has been heard in unmistakable cadences throughout his poetry.

A descendant of Puritans, racked by rebellious guilt, bent under history and bending it back upon itself, Lowell found in Catholicism the lines of his own spiritual force. The best poems in his first volume, *Land of Unlikeness* (1944), reappeared in a stronger second volume, *Lord Weary's Castle* (1946). In both, Lowell revealed his dark apprehension of Christ, who contains hope of redemption for all things dead or dying, "lust and dust." The very structures of the poems imitated the movements of grace. Their characteristic language was thick, alliterative, gnarled by kinesthetic metaphors, dialectic conceits, elliptic syntax, nearly obsessive rhythms—in short, a triumph of the closed style, Hopkinsian, at times grotesque. Some of Lowell's best poems—certainly his most savage—came from these early books, Charon-rowed across some private Styx.

In *The Mills of the Kavanaughs* (1951) Lowell offered seven dramatic monologues. The title poem, unusually long and even, developed reveries, memories, thoughts of a young woman whose husband, a naval officer, has committed suicide. Mythic allusions, particularly to Pluto and Persephone, guide the obscure narrative toward a recognition of Death, "who takes the world on trust." Some shorter poems in the collection, notably *Mother Marie Therese,* seem better realized. But the interest of the volume was prefigurative; it suggested a shift toward a more restful dramatic manner.

Life Studies (1960) brought the shift to light. Almost prosaic in parts, strong and yet endlessly subtle in sounds, philosophic without vehemence, elegiac and confessional without laxity, the poems probed past and present, self and civilization, family and friends. Lowell spoke through these poems more clearly in his own voice, his Catholic insistencies muted, the great lunacy of existence still there, calm. Autobiography—explicit in the prose sketch *91 Revere Street*—served as the form of anguish or vulnerability by which the poet could engage the world. Mischief and satire, a kind of new-found slyness, appeared; ironic, Lowell wanted to undercut nostalgia as well as pain. He could write masterfully, in *Waking in the Blue,* even from the "house of the 'mentally ill.' "

Lowell had come into a versatile mood. He produced another volume, *Imitations* (1961), in which he rendered poems by Sappho, Villon, Baudelaire, Rimbaud, Rilke, and Eugenio Montale among others, "one voice running through many personalities." He also completed a translation of Racine's *Phaedra* (1961), and wrote verse plays, *The Old Glory* (1965).

Lowell had begun to strike his major note. In *For the Union Dead* (1964) he confronted with casual grandeur all the burning themes of the times: faith, history, love, modern death in all its savage and servile forms. Informally, he took the measure of the world in the breath of a line, the turn of a metaphor. He reduced the world in the scale of irony and thus loomed larger, impersonal confessor. Each poem, supremely *made,* judged time.

Lowell next published *Near the Ocean* (1967), illustrated by Sidney Nolan; and *Notebook: 1967–68* (1969), which Lowell described as "one poem, jagged in pattern, but not a conglomeration or sequence. . . . My plot rolls with the seasons. The separate poems are opportunist and inspired by impulse. Accident threw up subjects, and the plot swallowed them—famished for human chances." Addressed to the events of the day—the Vietnam war, the Newark riots, Che Guevara's death, the murders of Martin Luther King and Robert Kennedy, the French student uprisings—and dedicated to renowned figures, the best poems stubbornly dealt, in a language of new-made complexity, with the senseless contingency of all our lives. Some of the poems, however, were oblique and merely knowing, grotesque in levity.

In some peculiar sense, the work of Robert Lowell seems a miraculous anachronism—the heroic effort of Poesy to aver its excellence although it can not vouch for the survival of man. Nature he has scarcely understood, and in America he feels ill at ease. Yet Lowell will be remembered as one of its poets. Indubitably, the changeful genius of his language has given his audience a larger dominion over reality, perhaps over death itself.

PROMINENT POETS

Theodore Roethke

Although Theodore Roethke (1908–1963) was born a few years earlier than most of the chief postwar poets, his first book of verse, *Open House* (1941), did not appear until the war had begun; his subsequent achievement proved him very much part of the contemporary world. His was an extraordinary achievement, recognized gradually, attaining full recognition posthumously with *The Collected Poems* (1966).

Roethke felt close to the romantics—Blake, John Clare, Wordsworth, Whitman, Yeats. He distrusted reason, "that dreary shed"; he chose to proclaim "the condition of joy" in the universe. He was, perhaps above all else, a poet of nature, which he knew meticulously and in all its secret and sensuous forms; he was an Orphic poet really, who became what he saw in sacramental celebration of the unity of all things: "And everything comes to One." Roethke grew up in the shade of a greenhouse, which his parents tended in Saginaw, Michigan; it later became his "symbol of the whole of life."

Yet nature did not by itself define Roethke's sensibility, both tortured and naïve, so human and animal. He was also a poet of the unconscious, of childhood, leaning to beginnings, clutching for roots. He returned always, farther back than where life began, to start again. And, like many romantics, he reached for death. He was a dream poet, wishing his way everywhere; a love poet, sensual and pure; an author of nonsense verse and childhood lyrics. A bare self ("I'm naked to the bone")—undergoing journeys to the interior, moving outward toward a woman, an animal, a flower—spoke in rhythms of its own.

Roethke's earliest work was spare, minimal; the poems, tight and brief. He disliked the "obscure" intellectual idiom of modernism; he wanted the poet to "scorn being 'mysterious' or loosely oracular, but be willing to face up to genuine mystery." Roethke's last poems, those in the volume *The Far Field* (1964), gathered his purpose in wider reflective forms. "A man learning to sing," he also asked questions about final things, seeking light, seeking acceptance of being. Writing in a longer line, a meter between verse and prose, his eye close on the object, he recalled both Whitman and D. H. Lawrence. "We need," he said, "the catalogue in our time."

There were moments when Roethke came too close to the great authors who influenced his work, or when his poetry gave itself to clichés of doxology. These moments were infrequent. More often, he was a poet of the indicative; being, not doing, was his joy. He was the recipient of some aboriginal magic, nature-blessed. He was master of some uneasiness no world could allay.

John Berryman

The poetry of John Berryman (1914–1972) underwent several transformations in three decades, and in its last phase, *The Dream Songs* (1969), it took a bewildering and original turn. By his own admission, the earliest models of his poetry were Yeats and, somewhat later, Auden; both "saved me," he wrote, "from the then crushing influences of Ezra Pound and T. S. Eliot." His first books—*Poems* (1942) and *The Dispossessed* (1948)—had a deep, brooding tone, wrenched syntax and rhythms, a slashing cerebral quality.

Berryman's Sonnets, written in the 1940s but not published until 1967, sang of a disastrous love affair. Painfully personal, these poems still locked the poet within their tortuous structures. But a dramatic concept was beginning to take hold in Berryman's imagination. Character, narrative, and most important, the sense of a shifting, complex point of view, determined his approach; cunningly, he "administered" the pronouns of his verse. The result was a long poem, narrative and meditative, *Homage to Mistress Bradstreet* (1956), sustained by an eight-line stanza and the dominant persona of Anne Bradstreet, who may have been the first Puritan poet of America.

Despite the great strain of the long poem, Berryman returned to another form of it in *77 Dream Songs* (1964), to which he added *His Toy, His Dream, His Rest* in 1968. He conceived the dream units in these books—eighteen lines, six-line stanzas, mostly rhymed—as part of a whole poem concerning the "turbulence of the modern world, and memory, and wants." The central imaginary character, named Henry, was, according to Berryman, a "white American in early middle age sometimes in blackface, who has suffered an irreversible loss and talks about himself sometimes in the first person, sometimes in the third, sometimes even in the second; he has a friend, never named, who addresses him as Mr. Bones and variants thereof." Berryman's explanation hardly began to touch the difficulties, rewards, and subterfuges of the poem, a metaphysical minstrel show, full of low comedy and terror and grief, full of "hell-spinning puns" and coarse jokes. The poem was allusive, jagged, close to the truth or insanity of dreams.

As a poet, Berryman was extreme; some called him too obscure, idiosyncratic, deliberately offensive. Yet he created a unique language that can "suffer living like a stain," and he made of his poet's "strangeness" a gift to men.

Allen Ginsberg

Perhaps more than any other contemporary American poet, Allen Ginsberg (born 1926) has created a legend of himself, a series of public figures of odium or adoration. He has been the "beat bard," the mad, flailing genius, the Dionysiac opening sexuality wide, the radical anarchist, the drugged prophet of a new consciousness, the obscene clown, the far traveler (India to Japan to Peru), the bearded guru of oriental wisdom, the Jewish apocalyptic crying doom. This means that Ginsberg's poetry has been an agent, certainly a part, of a profound cultural transformation in America—among the young, perhaps, a change of heart.

The experiences that went into his poetry were personal, harrowing. Coming from a family of Jewish immigrants, he also grew up with Marx and Lenin. Poverty, idealism, hysteria, ruled the household. His parents were estranged, his mother—the Naomi of *Kaddish* (1961)—monstrously mad. Ginsberg learned about drugs, insanity, homosexuality, the sheer violence of life; about anger, sweetness, and lamentation. He also has inner strength, vast book knowledge. At Columbia University, he studied with Lionel Trilling and became acquainted with writers—William Burroughs, Jack Kerouac, Gregory Corso (born 1930), among others—who gave the beat movement its shape. Thereafter, he gave himself to various causes, worldly or vatic, with shrewdness, generosity, boundless energy.

Ginsberg found his poetic models in Whitman, but the blatant and outrageous psalmist rather than the "good grey poet"; in William Carlos

Williams, who wrote an introduction to Ginsberg's first work, *Howl, and Other Poems* (1956); in the "spontaneous bop prosody" of Kerouac and the "breath" measure of Charles Olson (1910–1970); in "extreme rhapsodic wails" heard in madhouses; in rippling sounds of sacred mantras, sutras, biblical texts. But his true source was, at his frequent insistence, inspiration, divine possession, the music of the spheres. "Who denies the music of the spheres denies poetry," he wrote, "denies man, & spits on Blake, Shelley, Christ & Buddha. Meanwhile have a ball. The universe is a new flower. America will be discovered. Who wants a war against roses will have it."

Still, against the need for ecstasy stood other ragged needs. When Ginsberg began to publish in the 1950s, memories of Hitler and Stalin were alive, and McCarthyism was rampant through the early Eisenhower years. There was, and still remains, a cause for outrage. Consent and fury—with time, more consent than fury—therefore went into the making of *Howl*, which begins with the now-famous line: "I saw the best minds of my generation destroyed by madness, starving hysterical naked."

In a sense, the work of Ginsberg has denied the poem as made object, as artifact; it is a spiritual process, illumination, "complete statement of Person," "self-prophetic" command, or simply Poesy. Critical criteria have tended, therefore, to fail his critics. Still, his poems have varied greatly in appeal, power, or inspiration. *Kaddish* contained some of his best work. *Reality Sandwiches* (1963, 1966) seemed less satisfying. *T. V. Baby Poems* (1968) and *Planet News* (1968) had syntactic subtlety, music, and hallucination. People, places, politics, psychedelics, ecology, love, nature, and war were among the concerns of Ginsberg in these books, which were journals of a turned-on psyche, mediated little by conscious form, yet shaped by breath and vision, oracular, mantic, surreal, naked.

Some of Ginsberg's poems could be complacent, otiose, boring; they appealed to only a part of the mind, and left the rest dozing. Others were written, as he said, in heaven. On the whole, his work has increased the possible, attesting to the immensity of "is," and his language has given poets new daring and new awe in verbal freedom.

POETRY: TYPES AND TRENDS

Variations of Formalism

The earliest trend in contemporary poetry showed variations of closed style. Gradually, the variations evolved the closed style toward more open or experimental forms; yet the original derivation from the tradition of Ezra Pound and T. S. Eliot endowed these works with a tone, perhaps academic, that they never lost. Excellent poets, representing many variations of formalism, had otherwise little in common. Their work, nonetheless, conditioned the taste of audiences during the first decade after the war.

One of the most accomplished of these poets, Elizabeth Bishop (born 1911), displayed from the start, in *North and South* (1946), freshness of imagery, high precision of the mind. The rich colors of her verse have been ultimately intellectual, exact hues of a world full of concrete things (like Marianne Moore's [1887–1972]) and flat cadences. Bishop's own objectivity in discerning the aspect and relation of things was visual, and so clear as to be dreamlike, fantasmic, like some imaginary iceberg, "jewelry from a grave" sparring with the sun. An impeccable craftsman, Bishop proved herself in her second volume, *Poems* (1955), to be a poet's poet, not prolific but inevitable in her finest work, witty and graceful in the rest, a quiet moralist withal.

Delmore Schwartz (1911–1966) was of a more passionate temper than Elizabeth Bishop. As a young man Schwartz made a place for himself— with short stories, poems, plays, criticism—in the leading quarterlies and became an editor of *Partisan Review*. His early efforts were quickly recognized for their energy, their resourcefulness. In *In Dreams Begin Responsibilities* (1938)—which derived its title from a poem by Yeats, and included a story, a play, and some verse—Schwartz tried to supplant older styles of the 1920s and 1930s without entirely succeeding. His concerns— time, love, the noumenal and phenomenal worlds—were expressed with precocious ease, the music sensuous, the mind playful and philosophic. Schwartz continued to experiment with mixed forms in subsequent volumes: *Shenandoah* (1941), a play in prose and verse; *Genesis* (1943), a long narrative; *Summer Knowledge* (1959).

The impact of Randall Jarrell (1914–1965) owed something to the very great breadth of his knowledge, his genius in teaching and criticism as well as in poetry. His essays in *Poetry and the Age* (1953) were crucial in interpreting old and new poets to students of literature; his insights into contemporary culture, in *A Sad Heart at the Supermarket* (1962), were both astringent and funny. Jarrell's early volumes of verse—*Blood for a Stranger* (1942), *Little Friend, Little Friend* (1945), *Losses* (1948)— reflected his war experiences: he was in the Air Force and wrote about bombing missions, soldiers writing home, extermination camps. Jarrell could write about these experiences with poignancy, coming close to sentimentality at times, but always saved by a very keen intelligence, which turned a discrete event into a symbolic human and historical statement. Jarrell turned in his later work—*The Woman at the Washington Zoo* (1960), *The Lost World* (1965)—to broad dramatic representation of individuals caught in the pathos and horror of a world no saner in peace than in war.

Richard Wilbur (born 1921), more than any other poet, has been considered the epitome of formalist grace. Ceremonial, detached, allusive, a craftsman of beauty and scope, he mastered various complicated verse forms, from riddles and alliterative verse to sonnets and *ballades*. Eliot himself recognized the distinctive note of Wilbur in *The Beautiful Changes* (1947). *Ceremony, and Other Poems* (1950) and *Things of This World* (1956), which contained some of his best poems, followed. Celebration, everyday things, the illusionism of art, the whimsical epiphanies of men—these were some of his concerns. His classic, comic sense found an outlet in superb translations or adaptations from the French: *The Misanthrope* (1955), *Candide: A Comic Opera* (1957) with Lillian Hellman (born 1905) and Leonard Bernstein, and *Tartuffe* (1963). With *Advice to a Prophet* (1961), Wilbur began to change his manner: the poems, still urbane, exhibited a rougher texture, a new strength, also a new faltering. *Walking to Sleep* (1969), which contained many translations, gave no clear sense of his destination as a poet. It seemed as if his temperament was finally too guarded or fastidious to engage the fullest life of the age.

The variations of formalism were very considerable, and lacked nothing in quality. Other poets, such as J. V. Cunningham (born 1911), Reed Whittemore (born 1919), Isabella Gardner (born 1915), Howard Nemerov (born 1920), Daniel Hoffman (born 1923), Anthony Hecht (born 1923), William Jay Smith (born 1918), Louis Simpson (born 1923), Donald Justice (born 1925), William Meredith (born 1919), and Edgar Bowers (born 1924) have further amplified the range of closed styles. But it was true, as James Dickey (born 1923) said, that among the lesser academic poets, "painfully contrived arguments in rhyme substituted for genuine insight."

The Black Mountain Poets

During the early 1950s an extraordinary confluence of talent appeared at Black Mountain College in North Carolina. Many became known later as leaders of the artistic avant-garde in numerous fields: John Cage (music), Josef Albers (painting), Buckminster Fuller (architecture), Robert Rauschenberg (painting), Merce Cunningham (dance), David Tudor (music), M. C. Richards (pottery). The group also included poets: Charles Olson, Robert Creeley (born 1926), Robert Duncan (born 1919), who were on the staff of the experimental college; and Edward Dorn (born 1929), Joel Oppenheimer (born 1930), and Jonathan Williams (born 1929), who studied there. Two magazines, *Black Mountain Review* and *Origin,* served as outlets for these poets and attracted others, like Denise Levertov (born 1923), Paul Blackburn (born 1926), and Paul Carroll (born 1927)—later the editor of *Big Table*—who were not formally associated with the college. The influence of the group was slow in spreading; its members published mainly in pamphlets put out by private presses or ephemeral magazines. Their poetry was therefore ignored by the establishment of letters for many years.

Without a doubt, the central figure of the groups was Charles Olson, who served as rector of Black Mountain College from 1951 to 1956. His affinities were with the poetic tradition of Whitman and Williams, the Pound of ideograms and *Pisan Cantos* (1948), Louis Zukovsky (born 1904) and his open forms. But Olson, like Robert Duncan and Edward Dorn, was also prodigiously learned in wayward things; he made original use of geology and geography, myth and history. His poems, written for his own speaking voice, spoken, in fact, to students and friends, had a special style—unfinished, telegraphic, scattered like letters or lecture notes. These poems were not meant for Empsonian scrutiny.

Olson's manifesto, *Projective Verse,* first appeared in *Poetry New York* (1950). But it was only when Donald Allen reprinted it in his anthology *The New American Poetry* (1960) that it caught the public eye. Olson insisted that "form is never more than an extension of content," and urged "composition by field," as "opposed to inherited line, stanza, over-all form." He conceived the poem as a high-energy construct seeking discharge, and demanded that each perception lead immediately to a fuller perception. "MOVE, INSTANTER, ON ANOTHER!" he cried.

Above all, Olson contributed a number of technical observations on "breath," the measure of syllable and line and composition. "Breath" served to give a natural life to each part of the poem, to emphasize the kinetic participation of form in the objects of reality, to recover the "full relevance of human voice." Projective verse lent itself to vast individual variations: the "Hebraic-Melvillian bardic breath" of Allen Ginsberg, the gnostic and visionary verse of Robert Duncan, the wry reticences of Robert Creeley, the elemental simplicity of Gary Snyder (born 1930).

In Olson's own poetry, complex typographic variations, rhythmic breaks of the line from within or without, collages of quotations, were submitted to the lyric control of "breath," to the underlying mystic chant. His major themes in *The Distances* (1960) were change, ancient cultures moving or dying, the collapse of human configurations of meaning, modes of the spirit in their physical setting. Ponderous, humorous, self-deprecating, Olson led his readers on a heroic journey. In *The Maximus Poems* (1960) and *Maximus Poems IV, V, VI* (1969) he made his native Gloucester, Massachusetts, the focus of time and place. As a fishing village, it stood for the origin of culture, which Olson associated with fishing more than hunting, and stood also as a coordinate in the migration of symbols to the west. Despite the undeniable value of these works, Olson has proved a seminal rather than a major poet.

Denise Levertov was born in England into a family with a mystic and

Hasidic tradition. Her development, under the influence of William Carlos Williams and H. D. as well as the Black Mountain group, could be seen in the contrast between *The Double Image* (1946), published while she was still living in England, and *Here and Now* (1957), which appeared in America. The form of the American poems seemed broken—bits and pieces, yet still wholly harmonious within. Her more recent work—*The Jacob's Ladder* (1961), *O Taste and See* (1964)—proved her mastery of certain spiritual ventures, uttered simply as in prosaic dreams. Writing about marital love or sensuous objects, her imagination has meshed into the ambiguous order of reality on some deep level of art.

Robert Creeley has been enigmatic in a different way. His poems have usually been of the "minimal" kind, brief, short-lined, laconic, open to the indeterminacy of the blank page. But their wry humor and reveries have concealed intense feelings about living "as we can, each day another," wasting nothing. Subtle concentration, sly broken music, and diction chosen to slide on the syntax distinguished the personal lyrics of *For Love* (1962), a collection of two earlier books. *Words* (1967) revealed Creeley in a more extreme mood. He created partial patterns, resisted completeness; recurrence, remembrance, rhyme, all the elements of relation or conclusiveness, were alien to him. "Only disconnect": this has been his motto, the very stutter in his reading voice.

No literary school can, or should, attain complete unity. Thus, the open styles of the Black Mountain poets remained plural. Writers younger than Olson, such as Edward Dorn, Paul Blackburn, Paul Carroll, Jonathan Williams, and Joel Oppenheimer, all have struck distinct notes.

The San Francisco Poets

Poetic activity in San Francisco during the middle and late 1950s was even more diversified. In the cafés, bookshops, and "pads" of the north shore, literature was written or argued, poetry was sold or sung. Kenneth Rexroth served both as dean of the writers who came flocking to the new bohemia and as their chief polemicist. The new poets—some natives of the city, others late comers to it—had no single program or persuasion other than their distaste for academic formalism. The beats, the Black Mountain teachers, and poets from the east and northwest converged for a time to participate in the San Francisco renascence.

Brother Antoninus (born 1912), a lay Dominican born William Everson, came from Sacramento, California. His raging poetry, enhanced by a Dionysian style of reading, first became known in San Francisco. Writing in the great tradition of Spanish baroque ecstasy, of possession and confession, guilt and sensuality, he cried from the depths, "I am burned black." Sometimes his early work seemed a cross of Whitman and Hopkins, a nature poem tortured in sound and spirit; and the influence of Robinson Jeffers (1887–1962) could also be discerned in the long, loose lines of *The Residual Years* (1948). In his later work—*The Crooked Lines of God* (1959), *The Hazards of Holiness* (1962), *The Rose of Solitude* (1967) —the religious and biblical accents became primary.

The central, yet contrasting, figures of the San Francisco renascence were Robert Duncan and Lawrence Ferlinghetti. Robert Duncan could also be placed among the Black Mountain poets. But it was in the Bay area—he was born in Oakland—that his impact finally became felt. Brilliant, curious, and learned, he found his inspiration in older poets, inevitably Pound, Williams, and H. D., but also in such contemporaries as Jack Spicer (1925–1965) and Helen Adam (born 1909), balladeer of the marvelous; in musicians, such as Satie, Stravinsky, and Schönberg; in painters, both old masters and the San Francisco postexpressionists. Yet his imagination ran wilder among ancient creation myths, mystical Jewish texts like *The Zohar*, fairy tales, treatises of magic, astrology, alchemy.

Despite Duncan's admiration for Olson's projective verse, his own seemed restrained, hermetic except in melody. His early works—often illustrated by Jess Collins, who prompted Duncan to experiment with collage techniques, discontinuity in composition—were privately printed. *Selected Poems* (1959) indicated the range of his poetic complexity and of his mannerisms. More impressive, *The Opening of the Field* (1960) and *Roots and Branches* (1964) developed his central themes: immanence, mythopoesis, homosexual love, despondency. "Our consciousness," he said, "and the poem as a supreme effort of consciousness, comes in a dancing organization between personal and cosmic identity." The method of the poems was far more musical than dramatic, since music, the author came to believe, moved at the heart of nature. Aesthetic, erotic, mystical, the poetry of Robert Duncan seems to have been created from the intellectual order not of one mind but of existence.

The poetry of Lawrence Ferlinghetti has been far more exoteric. Born in New York, he settled in San Francisco in 1951; and through his City Lights Bookshop and Press he contributed vigorously to the emergent literary movement, publishing, among many works by new writers, Ginsberg's *Howl*. The oral quality of Ferlinghetti's verse, whether colloquial or declamatory, its topical and satiric touch, made it suitable to café readings, often to the accompaniment of jazz. In his books—*Pictures of the Gone World* (1955), *A Coney Island of the Mind* (1958), *Starting from San Francisco* (1961)—Ferlinghetti was irreverent, humorous, mundane. Yet, putting aside the clownish guise, he was able to burst into sudden anger at sham or injustice, burst with the authentic power of poetry.

Other poets of the original San Francisco renascence included James

Broughton (born 1913), Philip Lamantia (born 1925), Jack Spicer, Madeline Gleason (born 1913), Robin Blaser (born 1925). But as new poets came on the scene, the movement became increasingly heterogeneous and spread to various parts of the country.

Beats, Nature Mystics, and Others

The paths of the beats and San Francisco writers crossed in time, in place, and in poetic mind; their personal friendships, their life styles, their vehement rejection of formalism and middle-class values served as common ground. Yet the beats also had a separate identity. The initial associations of Jack Kerouac, Allen Ginsberg, Gregory Corso, William Burroughs were in New York. The beat poets drifted in and out of San Francisco, joining Gary Snyder, Philip Whalen (born 1923), Michael McClure (born 1932) in readings there; they also published in the *Black Mountain Review*. Their spirit was antic, reckless, at times violent. Blasphemy and obscenity were expressions of their revolt, and of their search for beatitude.

More immediately, the beats admired, as did other antiformalists, Kenneth Patchen (born 1911), who had worked in steel mills and coal mines in his youth and had written in a special vernacular, mixing prose and poetry, surrealism and revolution, humor and horror. His numerous works—which included *First Will & Testament* (1939), *The Dark Kingdom* (1942), *Cloth of the Tempest* (1943), the inspired diary *Memoirs of a Shy Pornographer* (1945), and *Red Wine and Yellow Hair* (1949)—revealed a phantasmagoric world, violent, ugly, obscene.

Among older poets, besides Kenneth Rexroth the beats also found a surprising champion in Karl Shapiro (born 1913). His transformation from a disciple of Eliot and Auden, writing in the closed style of *Person, Place and Thing* (1942) and *V-Letter* (1944), into the later poet was striking. There was evidence even in the early work of jagged perception, a brusque personal idiom, whether he spoke of war or injustice. The change clearly began to show in the polemic essays of *Beyond Criticism* (1953) and *In Defense of Ignorance* (1960), in which Shapiro attacked excessive intellectualism, the literary and cultural dogmas of the age; thus, he shifted his allegiances from Eliot to Lawrence, from Auden to Henry Miller (born 1891). But it was in the rugged, sometimes cranky verse of *Poems of a Jew* (1958) and, more particularly, of *The Bourgeois Poet* (1964), that Shapiro showed his development most clearly. Abandoning rhyme, abandoning even meter, he ended by frankly adopting the prose poem—autobiographical, grotesque, bitterly satiric, awry with energy.

Neither Patchen nor Shapiro could be considered remotely as beat poets. Ginsberg, of course, was paragonal, though he grew into a role that set him apart; and Kerouac, who wrote some poems, was better known for his spontaneous prose. It was Gregory Corso who perhaps best exemplified the beat poet. Born in New York, abandoned by his mother, raised in orphanages and by foster parents, acquainted with reformatories and prisons (including the infamous Tombs of Manhattan), he was first published by the Harvard *Advocate*. He counted Ginsberg among his close friends, and later Ferlinghetti, who printed his *Gasoline* (1958). *The Happy Birthday of Death* (1960) mingled impish prophecy with the eroticism of death. Yet Corso was essentially an innocent beneath the hoodlum's or wild man's skin, a child of sorrows who never surrendered his faith in man. *Long Live Man* (1962), a kind of hymn to human choice and life's variousness, full of paranoia too, projected him, swinging and shrieking self, into the pure energy of the universe. His response to vatic and historical realities, in *Elegiac Feelings American* (1970), was denser, more resonant, than in any previous book.

Gary Snyder knew many of the beats, and even suggested the hero in Kerouac's *The Dharma Bums*. But his own inclinations took him closer to nature mysticism than any of the others. A native of San Francisco, he worked as logger, forest ranger, seaman; and he studied mythology, linguistics, oriental cultures, spending years in Japan, acquiring the discipline of Zen. His poems were influenced by the rhythms of his physical work, by the geology of his environment in the Sierras, Oman, and Kyoto, by Indian folk tales, classical Chinese poetry, and haiku.

Snyder's own poetry has been wholly integral, its body, speech, and mind uniting in free forms. *Riprap* (1959) gave a tranquil, concrete vision of the northwest landscape: mountains, rivers, trees. *Myths & Texts* (1960) was more ambitious. Standing for the two sources of knowledge, symbol and sensation, the title also referred to a spiritual-ecological-historical system that the various poems explored with wondrous particularity. In some poems, too, Snyder began a quiet synthesis of Marx and Zen, a politics of nature that appealed to the postrevolutionary sensibilities of some youths, and found its fullest expression in *Revolution within the Revolution within the Revolution* (1970). Naming the names, arranging the sounds with effortless wisdom, relying on nouns and participles affirming being, and sometimes on a dramatic structure akin to Japanese No plays, the poems of *A Range of Poems* (1967) and *The Back Country* (1968) spread slowly through the consciousness of readers in witness of being. An extraordinary collection of Snyder's essays, *Earth House Hold* (1969), presented his views discursively.

A number of other poets declared their affinities with the beat and San Francisco writers without belonging completely to either circle. The most remarkable of these were Philip Whalen, Michael McClure, Richard Brautigan (born 1935), John Wieners (born 1934), and David Meltzer (born 1937).

The New York Poets

A very different group of poets, intensely cosmopolitan in spirit, formed naturally in New York. Their affinities were with the European avant-garde, going back to Stéphane Mallarmé and Tristan Corbière, Alfred Jarry and Guillaume Apollinaire, Vladimir Mayakovski, Tristan Tzara, and André Breton. They were also close to the various circles of Action Painting, the Museum of Modern Art, *Art News,* The Living Theatre, and the Artists' Theatre in New York. Their concept of poetry has demanded a humorous or hallucinatory refusal of sense, structure, coherence; it has relied on a spatial disposition of poetic clues that invoke a new quality of attention. Their language, so it seems, is all primary colors and play.

Kenneth Koch (born 1925) has written in a state of perpetual excitement, trying to populate some gorgeous region of language in which pleasure and illogic and invention are all one. His first major work, *Ko, or a Season on Earth* (1959), was a monstrous mock-epic, a statement on chaos or mutability, on natural glee, on the subversion of poesy by itself. *Thank You, and Other Poems* (1962) and *The Pleasures of Peace* (1968) revealed Koch's maniacal will to gaiety, creation, and outrage. Parodying all genres and conventions, Koch seems to have spun free both of form and absurdity, celebrating the terror of possibility.

Frank O'Hara (1926–1966) cultivated a more prosaic manner, sometimes fairly distasteful, refusing to refine the indiscriminateness of urban life by art. Yet the manner was ultimately sophisticated; and it expressed the desire of a complex personality to find itself, beyond wit or learning, gossip or chic, beyond its own "catastrophe." *Meditations in an Emergency* (1957) and *Lunch Poems* (1965), eschewing rhythm, assonance, and often rhyme, offered an inclusive landscape of modernity, brittle and hard, bright-surfaced here, deathly there. Between self-hatred and fidelity to fact, the poems of O'Hara took their free shape.

John Ashbery's (born 1927) poetry has perhaps been the most mysterious of the New York group. Word-by-word and line-by-line clear, elegant, and sometimes waggish, his poems have been so discontinuous, his sense so recalcitrant, as to defy the closure of a "complete" reading—much like a parable by Kafka, a dadaist joke, a dream. In comparison with his later work, the early *Turandot, and Other Poems* (1953) and *Some Trees* (1956) seemed obedient to conventions of the masters. The change was subtle. *The Tennis Court Oath* (1962), *Rivers and Mountains* (1966), and *The Double Dream of Spring* (1970) had an arcane mythology, limpid too, controlled yet utterly wild. They were experiences in pure poetry, disquieting and marvelously weird. Their author, a cool fantasist lost in reality, still managed to evoke feelings of innocence, courtesy, or love. Yet the strange seemliness of Ashbery has concealed a kind of savagery.

The New York poets, who count Barbara Guest (born 1920), James Schuyler (born 1923), Ted Berrigan (born 1934), Edward Field (born 1924), and David Shapiro (born 1947) among their other members, have been antiformalist in a sense, inventors of new open styles. Yet their openness has been as cryptic as dada or surrealism; and their aversion to statement, theme, content, and directness betrays a formal concern with the origins of language, the wordless music of consciousness.

The Postromantics

No adequate rubric can describe the number of poets who have eluded the previous categories of verse. Yet they have shared a certain slant of sensibility, certain attitudes toward the traditions of poetry. Their tradition has been largely romantic, but they have also caught the wryness and derangement of the contemporary world. They themselves were postromantic, eclectic in their inspiration, finding it in Yeats or Williams, Stevens or Pound, Lowell, Roethke, or Olson; and their own verse evolved in independent modes, vital, fluid, or visionary, yet still secretly measured. Very often, they chose the confessional mode, or else they chose to speak through some subjective agent, an internal mask, a hidden persona of the poet. In a sense, then, the postromantics have held the large middle ground of poetry, assimilating influences, moving through various individual talents toward some still unknown future of poetry.

The direction of these writers was vaguely suggested by James Dickey, who said, "Of late my interest has been mainly in the conclusionless poem, the open or generalizing poem, the un-well-made-poem." His own poetry, vitalist in origin, has incarnated his "best moments," which have in them elements of danger, of joy, and of repose. An enthusiastic outdoorsman, a decorated pilot in both World War II and the Korean war, he knew nature, the strange reciprocities of men and beasts, the pervasiveness of death, the will to transcendence.

Interested initially in poems with a basic narrative structure, Dickey wrote *Into the Stone* (1960) and *Drowning with Others* (1962); dream and fact united in a single state of conscience as of consciousness, sometimes hallucinatory in power. *Buckdancer's Choice* (1965) has perhaps been his most impressive volume. Finding no expiation in art for human violence, Dickey turned the past on the present, the self toward the other, nature against man, questioning the cosmic, the moral, and the aesthetic order of things. Again, but more insistently than ever, the voice that spoke in *The Eye-Beaters* (1970) was the personal voice seeking spiritual legitimacy in a brutish and energetic world.

Robert Bly (born 1926) attracted attention both for his poetry and for the combative magazine called by each decade, called now *The Seventies,* which he has edited with the help of James Wright (born 1927). Much of

Bly's work has seemed quiet, even flat, nature poetry—he hailed from Minnesota—with sudden bursts of surrealist imagery. His books—*Silence in the Snowy Fields* (1962) and *The Light around the Body* (1967)—revealed what Bly could do when his associative powers and straggling music hit original heights. Behind many of the seemingly simple, declarative poems has lurked the presence of the German sixteenth-century mystic Jakob Böhme, the urge to absolve man of his false identity, released in death. Yet Bly has also written precisely about politics, the degradations of his country, the wars that man has made as if he were annointing himself. His true spiritual quality is fluid, slow, regenerative, running deep beneath the great plains of the midwest, pushing suddenly through bole and flower.

A close associate of Bly's, James Wright, visionary of the human, wrote mainly a free verse given structure only by its parallelisms of syntax and feeling. His first book, *The Green Wall* (1957), influenced by Robert Frost and Edward Arlington Robinson (1869–1935), departed from the well-wrought preciocities fashionable among neophytes of the period. In that volume as in his next, *Saint Judas* (1959), Wright chose a poetry of experience about ordinary events or solitary people, a poetry transformed from within by an intensity that, in his public readings, became almost frightening. *The Branch Will Not Break* (1963) established him as an original voice speaking of elemental occurrences, conversing with death, in a style more direct and colloquial yet still inward. With Bly and Wright foremost in mind, the poet Donald Hall (born 1928) said: "This new imagination reveals through images a subjective life which is *general,* and which corresponds to an old objective life of shared experience and knowledge." This sacramental subjectivity gave the poetry of Wright strange subliminal force in *Shall We Gather at the River* (1968).

More than Wright, Bly, or Dickey, W. D. Snodgrass (born 1926) wrote in the confessional mode—witty, candid, and self-ironic. His world was essentially the human world, apprehended through autobiography and all its peculiar embarrassments. His first book, *Heart's Needle* (1959), was also one of the first to adopt the stance of self-exposure among poets trained in verbal politeness. Though Snodgrass has favored regular verse forms, his language has been direct, homey in the nuances of American speech, and striking in its sudden personal twists. Speaking of his love, his divorce, or his own daughter, Snodgrass has managed also to make echoes of the Korean war part of his voice. Impish in humor, complex in his sincerity, still somehow cool, he sought in his first book to know, above all else, his "name." Disguise, confession, and self-division—these have been the curse and cure of Snodgrass, the burden he sought to depose in *After Experience* (1968), reaching for some form of reconciliation.

In the poetry of W. S. Merwin (born 1927) the confessional element, although present, has been muted by larger concerns, which he has shared, from a certain distance, with Wright and Bly. Merwin has steadily moved toward his own version of an open form. His first book of verse, *A Mask for Janus* (1952), made an impression of enchantment and intimate ease. Intricacy and decorum and mythic sheen were qualities of *The Dancing Bears* (1954), too, and its vision was one of recurrence in mutability. But in *Green with Beasts* (1956) and *The Drunk in the Furnace* (1960), Merwin adopted a more disjunctive, discursive manner, challenging his Orphic themes, restating them on deeper levels, "living forward" through the menaces of nature. His best poems to date can be found in *The Moving Target* (1963) and *The Lice* (1967). Gnomic, abrupt, mysterious, drawing on imagination refined by some invisible element of the earth, Merwin exposed his lines of verse—with little punctuation, with no cleverness or willfulness—to silence, to some immense freedom akin to prophecy.

The most exacerbated poet of this postromantic company was undoubtedly Sylvia Plath (1932–1963), who spent the latter part of her life in England, married to the British poet Ted Hughes. Ailing, inspired, at times mad, she died by her own hand. And she wrote verse of grotesque power and originality, macabre in its badinage, bloody in laying the soul bare. *The Colossus* (1960, 1962) revealed her austere sense of herself in bitter dramas of love and dying, in pastorals of decomposition. Taking risks with her great intelligence, she ended, almost always, by enlarging the apprehension of her subject. It was these larger intensities that she brought to *Ariel* (1965, 1966), a superior volume. Its poems ranged widely; they were about family, love, disease, politics, Christian myth, the poisoning of nature, the contortions of consciousness. Inventive, bizarre, slangy, terrifyingly plain, they moved beyond their own center of fear toward some reconciliation in love that Sylvia Plath was never permitted to reach. Yet she bequeathed brilliance, daring of language in the extreme, a desperate motion of the mind.

Many other postromantic poets have enlarged this indefinite region of postwar sensibility. Thus, John Logan (born 1923), Galway Kinnell (born 1927), Anne Sexton (born 1928), X. J. Kennedy (born 1929), May Swenson (born 1919), and A. R. Ammons (born 1926) can be counted among poets of the new subjectivity.

The Black Poets

The tradition of black poetry goes back to Paul Laurence Dunbar (1872–1903) in the nineteenth century. And it was developed further by James Weldon Johnson (1871–1938) and Claude McKay (1890–1949). But its real origins were older, deeper in black culture, deriving from folk tales, myths, dances; from work songs, the blues, spirituals; from jazz; from words of confidential wisdom passed from father to son and mother to daughter; from the vernacular of jokes. The soul of black poetry was sound, not print or image. With the Harlem renascence of the 1920s, the sounds of black speech entered into more complex literary forms; and the black intellectual, although he still stood some distance from his people, began to realize his inheritance.

Foremost among the poets of that period, and an uneasy influence on postwar poets as Richard Wright was on postwar novelists, Langston Hughes (1902–1967) voiced his ethnic passion in numberless plays, poems, stories, and essays. More than anyone else, he articulated the concept of American negritude, helping new writers, carrying their cause both at home and abroad, editing such pioneering anthologies as *The Poetry of the Negro, 1746–1949* (1949), *Poems from Black Africa* (1963), and *New Negro Poets: U.S.A.* (1964). His own innovations were manifest in *Selected Poems of Langston Hughes* (1959). Other poets of Hughes's generation also prepared the way for postwar black verse. These included Melvin B. Tolson (1900–1966), Arna Bontemps (born 1902), and Countee Cullen (1903–1946).

With the emergence of the black-power movement in the 1950s and 1960s, however, a new type of poetry came into being. It was, of course, more militant and proud. But it was also more communal, gravid with the sense of a black destiny; its themes were urgent and large. The new poetry sprang from the ugly ghettos of America and took loudly to the streets. It was elemental as well as revolutionary, more aware of its origins than ever before, more dedicated to the mission of overcoming the double consciousness of blacks in white America; it was therefore blatant sometimes in its desire to build morale, in its sheer lust for rhetoric. But the music saved it, through such geniuses as John Coltrane, Aretha Franklin, Sun Ra, Ray Charles, who gave their cadences to language.

The ideal of the black poet as "juju" revolutionary is one that various writers have approached differently. Robert E. Hayden (born 1913), a professor at Fisk University, seemed controlled in his passion, sometimes allusive and analytical, sometimes fully responsive to the folklore of his people, in *A Ballad of Remembrance* (1962) and *Selected Poems* (1966). Dudley Randall (born 1914), owner of the Broadside Press in Detroit, published many unknown poets in attractive pamphlets. Brooding, quiet, and craftsmanlike, his own work—in *Poem Counterpoem* (1966) and *Cities Burning* (1968)—has generally adhered to strict forms. Writing and teaching in Chicago for many years, Gwendolyn Brooks (born 1917) has exerted considerable influence on students of poetry. Her books—*A Street in Bronzeville* (1945), *Annie Allen* (1949), *Selected Poems* (1963)—have given a strong impression of order and concentration, of a deep, sad, and vivid life.

But the ideal of the "juju" poet was more fully exemplified by writers still younger in age, closer to the center of the black movement. LeRoi

Jones (born 1934) came to be one of these. As an editor of *Yugen* magazine in New York, his initial associations were with the beats; and he admired the projective verse of Olson. Jones, however, moved rapidly away from white culture. After Zen and the Yoruba craze, he became a black nationalist and uses the name of Amiri Imamu Baraka. As a founder of the Jihad Press and Spirit House in Newark, he worked with black radical artists: the poets Edward Spriggs (born 19??), and Yusef Iman (born 19??); the musicians Pharaoh Saunders and Sun Ra. Jones's early poetry, *Preface to a Twenty Volume Suicide Note* (1961)—energetic, existential, open—blasted the sodden or vicious quality of life in middle-class America. In *The Dead Lecturer* (1964) and *Black Art* (1966), however, his anger was sharply focused on racial matters; the lines darted sometimes into strange intensities, sometimes beat the slow rhythm of declarative statements.

The black-power movement has triggered the creative temper in various parts of the land. From Indianapolis, the voice of Marie Evans (born 1923) was heard; from New York, Audre Lorde (born 1934) and Sonia Sanchez (born 1935) compelled attention to their verse. In San Francisco, a group of young poets gathered around the *Journal of Black Poetry;* and another group formed around *Umbra* in New York. It became evident that in still younger authors, like Ishmael Reed (born 1938) or Clarence Major (born 1936), and in such "cosmic" musicians as Sun Ra, the experiments of black poetry are far from ended.

DRAMA

Of all the literary genres in America, drama has the shortest and the most spare tradition. Neither the Puritan inheritance nor the harsh quality of frontier life contributed to the development of a native theater. It was not until the early part of the twentieth century that an original American drama came into being. The dominant figure of that movement was Eugene O'Neill (1888–1953), who combined elements of naturalism, expressionism, and Greek tragedy in a distinctive dramatic language of great power. Throughout the 1920s and 1930s, other notable playwrights— Maxwell Anderson (1888–1959), Robert E. Sherwood (1896–1955), Elmer Rice (1892–1967), Thornton Wilder (born 1897), Clifford Odets (1906–1963), Lillian Hellman—gave diversity and magnitude to the achievement of the American theater.

While some of the older playwrights struck new paths after World War II, it was Tennessee Williams (born 1914) and Arthur Miller (born 1915) who most clearly determined the earliest directions of postwar drama and who dominated its stage for well over a decade. Between Williams's *The Glass Menagerie* in 1945 and the newer-wave plays like Jack Gelber's (born 1932) *The Connection* and Edward Albee's (born 1928) *The Zoo Story,* both produced in 1959, few dramatists challenged the authority of Williams and Miller. The New York theater was mainly given to commercial plays and musicals, productions of considerable sparkle and sophistication, but seldom of enduring value. The atmosphere was not conducive to serious experiments.

Thus American drama began to lag, once again, behind other genres in the first decades of the postwar era. With few exceptions, it seemed enervated or derivative. The new breakthrough came through the influence of a European movement designated as the theater of cruelty (Antonin Artaud) or the theater of the absurd (Samuel Beckett).

By the late 1950s Williams and Miller had nearly exhausted themselves in repetition. The psychology of Williams and the sociology of Miller seemed no longer adequate to the cruelties or evasions of the day. Meanwhile, in Europe the seminal ideas of Jacques Copeau and particularly of Artaud were rediscovered. Beckett, Brecht, Genet, and Ionesco, each unique in dramatic style, laid the foundation of a new theater, at once dazzling and simple, and created dramatic languages of enormous possibility. A renewed interest in mime and gesture, in the space of silence, in simplicity, contributed to a fresh approach to reality.

It was a reality that postwar American writers could understand, although they chose to respond to it in ways of their own. Their dark sense of life, their intuition of the void, may not have been as deep as their European compeers. Nevertheless, the new American dramatists have recognized the random, contradictory, and mysterious quality of existence represented by the theater of the absurd. They have sensed that art and history, that politics and metaphysics, that language itself have been called into doubt as the chatter of harassed minds.

The opportunity for developing a new American drama came in the 1950s, when authors, actors, and directors began to move away from the high-rent districts of Broadway into lofts, cellars, and abandoned warehouses located in various parts of New York, mostly Greenwich Village. The economic and psychological conditions of the Off-Broadway theater were conducive to experiment; some of the best plays of the younger dramatists—Edward Albee, Jack Gelber, Kenneth H. Brown (born 1936) —first saw the footlights in outlying districts. But a reaction to the Off-Broadway theater soon took place as its iconoclasm hardened into convention. By the middle of the 1960s an even more informal and experimental theater, employing "happenings" and mixed media, discovering still younger dramatists and painters and musicians, assumed the name of

"OOB"—Off-Off-Broadway. Small restaurants, bars, churches, and coffee houses became the scenes of rehearsed or spontaneous spectacles. At times, the theatrical scene was the street.

New York, however, did not have a monopoly on the theater. Guerrilla theater—performed by student or amateur groups, hippies, yippies, or political dissenters—moved into the parks, the streets, even the courtrooms of America. At the same time, fine repertory companies—in Washington, Houston, Cleveland, Detroit, Milwaukee, Minneapolis, and San Francisco—encouraged often by grants from the Ford Foundation, produced the work of known and unknown contemporary dramatists across the country. By 1970 the prospects of American drama appeared considerably more exciting than in 1950.

PROMINENT DRAMATISTS

Tennessee Williams

Thomas Lanier Williams, better known by his pen name, Tennessee Williams, was the most prolific of early postwar dramatists and perhaps the most lurid. A romantic, a solitary fantasist of desire, he could combine poetic delicacy with primal violence, capture the frailty of man's spirit and his voracity. Enacting the explosive drama of the subconscious, Williams also exposed a civilization in which deviants or outsiders, the "fugitive kind," always perish. These, however, were as often victims of their own guilt or illusion as they were prey to the world's brutality. Williams's vision owed something to the southern gothic tradition, from Poe to Faulkner, and owed even more to the erotic mysteries of D. H. Lawrence, whom Williams admired. His dramatic sensationalism—his ready use of nymphomania, homosexuality, rape, castration, murder, cannibalism—which has accounted for his popular success, can also be seen as a projection of an imagination haunted by death.

But drama, in Williams's view, brings time to a stop and thus assuages the tragedy of man. In an essay called *The Timeless World of a Play,* he wrote: "About their lives people ought to remember that when they are finished, everything in them will be contained in a marvelous state of repose which is the same as that which they unconsciously admired in drama. The rush is temporary. The great and only possible dignity of man lies in his power deliberately to choose certain moral values by which to live as steadfastly as if he, too, like a character in a play were immured against the corrupting rush of time." The arrest of time presumes a suspension of realism, and a movement into a world of poetry, dream, or terror, a world of grotesque distortions. That world the characters of Williams inhabit, although they bring to it familiar grievances, memories, names.

Williams's first play, *Battle of Angels,* failed when it was produced in Boston in 1940, although Margaret Webster directed it and Miriam Hopkins took the lead. Success came five years later with *The Glass Menagerie,* a vaguely autobiographical family drama, which created in Amanda Wingfield the eternal southern lady, steeped in genteel illusions, who contributes to the breakdown of her ailing, inward daughter, entombed in a room full of glass statuettes. Symbol and theme, character and setting, act in poetic synergy to make this drama among the finest of its period.

The impact of Williams's next work, *A Streetcar Named Desire* (1947), was greater. The element of southern nostalgia found even more complex expression in Blanche DuBois, dreamy and dissolute, corrupt and spiritual. Set in a dingy, yet still exotic, quarter of New Orleans, the play offered a parable of the conflicts and values of American society at midcentury, sustaining its themes with surges of dramatic vitality. More important, perhaps, the play mediated the awesome polarity of nature and civilization so central to Williams, a polarity that collapsed in his later melodramatic work.

Cat on a Hot Tin Roof (1955), however, could never be dismissed as melodrama. Set on a southern plantation dominated by the patriarchic figure of Big Daddy, the play showed how money and sex, greed and mendacity, tear at the invisible fabric not only of a particular family or culture but also of life itself.

Sometimes, Williams rewrites his earlier plays; he has also sometimes expanded a one-acter into a full drama. Solitude, sexual hunger and deviation, the dread of death have always entered into his most startling plays: *Summer and Smoke* (1948), *Suddenly Last Summer* (1957), *Sweet Bird of Youth* (1959), *The Milk Train Doesn't Stop Here Any More* (1963). Occasionally, redemptive elements of lusty comedy (*The Rose Tattoo* [1951]) or surreal comedy (*Camino Real* [1953]) or plain sex comedy (*Period of Adjustment* [1960]) have relieved the aura of modernized Grand Guignol in his work. But there is no doubt that the essential Williams believes in the "horror at the heart of the meaninglessness of existence."

Williams took the full measure of American reality, and without drabness or determinism has offered major insights into its social and historic qualities. True, he has repeated himself, has employed the clichés of melodrama, has surrendered at times to pathology, and has exuded self-hate in places. But the dialogue of Williams has echoed the morbid poetry of the age; and his characters, supercharged with their own emotions, compel audiences to share their fates. Above all, he has expanded the sensibility of postwar drama with Orphic knowledge, however mixed.

Arthur Miller

Unlike Williams, Arthur Miller has had no interest in sexual wayward-ness or romantic agony. A moralist foremost, endowed with broad social awareness, Miller has placed an idea of commitment and responsibility at the heart of his drama. He believes that, as life is accountable rather than absurd, so are human beings responsible to one another and to themselves. If the individual is seldom defined by his milieu, neither can he escape entirely the impersonal forces that affect his image of himself, his *name*.

At its best, Miller's dramatic vision has had power, integrity. But it also has retained, perhaps from the theater of the 1930s, a certain awkward simplicity. His first play, *The Man Who Had All the Luck* (1944), ran for four performances only, although it called the attention of critics and producers to a new talent. *All My Sons* (1947) made a much wider impression. Miller implicated the domestic tragedy of Joe Keller, a war profiteer who manufactures faulty airplane engines, into larger issues of pragmatism and idealism, crime and atonement, justice and love. Techni-cally artificial in places, and morally elusive in its final perceptions of guilt, the play indicated serious promise rather than achievement.

The achievement came with *Death of a Salesman* (1949). This work created the unforgettable figure of the aging Willy Loman. Moreover, it penetrated the mythology of America; illusions lead to Willy's ruin as salesman, husband, father, his ultimate ruin as a man. Through memory and introspection, a "mobile concurrency of past and present" retrieves his life, the bitterness and "ecstasy of spirit" that he chases to the end. The play put not only the Lomans but a whole society on trial; above all, it questioned the human condition that corrupts the need of love and reduces a bright dream to suicide.

In the early 1950s Miller withstood the inquisition of the House Un-American Activities Committee, a manifestation of the wave of anticom-munist hysteria that was sweeping the country. From the experience came *The Crucible* (1953). Set in Salem during the notorious witchhunts of the seventeenth century, the play explored the inevitable clash of private and public motives, the mysterious capacity of terror to create a reality inde-pendent of fact or history, the administration of conscience. Increasingly, Miller was drawn, in wonderment or even in horror, toward the inner sources of tragedy, the origins of human force. Thus, *A View from the Bridge* (1955, 1957)—this play, before it was expanded into two acts, was staged with another short play, *A Memory of Two Mondays* (1955)— probed the soul of a betrayer.

For nine years Miller was silent, disappointed in what he conceived to be public misunderstanding of his plays, engrossed in his own life—divorce from his first wife, marriage to and divorce from Marilyn Monroe, a third marriage. When he returned to the theater with *After the Fall* (1964), he offered his most introspective and autobiographical play. A kaleidoscopic succession of scenes takes the protagonist, Quentin, in search of his past, in search of himself, beyond cruelty, egotism, and failure, to a lucid life in the shadow of despair. Rejecting his faith in absolutes—socialism, innocence, even love—Miller traced the roots of the world's violence to the self, and went on to accept man's terrible complicity in the real. *Incident at Vichy* (1965), a long one-acter, focused this theme by narrowing the action to a Nazi hunt for Jews. With his same moral concern, Miller returned to the family situation in *The Price* (1968). The play showed nothing new, except a tough recognition of the near impossibility of altruism in human relations.

Miller has confronted the issues of his day with a tortured determination to shirk no truth or responsibility. He has engaged the world with conscience and ideas with naïve passion; he has sustained the theater with his morose art. Yet the cumulative reaction to his work remains mixed, and this too is understandable. For Miller has seldom displayed the verve, poetry, or spiritual complexity that the greatest dramatists usually have commanded.

Edward Albee

The most impressive of the younger dramatists who succeeded Williams and Miller was Edward Albee. His theater has been close to the style of the European absurdists; echoes of Beckett, Genet, Ionesco, and Dürrenmatt can be heard in his plays. Still, Albee's language has been entirely his own, taut or sinuously coiled, striking suddenly with venom. He has understood the human drive toward self-annihilation, has exposed the pretensions of familial, conjugal, and romantic love. Always, he has tried to lay existence before his audiences, open and bare, white to the marrowbone.

But Albee's drama has also pushed misanthropy and misogyny beyond themselves in search of new sources of vitality. Cruelty, hatred, or spite has shattered human complacencies; savage invective, absurd cliché, or gallows humor has jarred audiences into feeling the outrages of quotidian life. His compassion has gone particularly to men and women who suffer intensely without knowing how to grasp their suffering. Indeed, the development of Albee's work in a decade suggested a genuine movement toward acceptance of reality, a complex interdebtedness akin to love.

Albee's *The Zoo Story,* rejected at first by New York producers, opened in Berlin in 1959. A year later it was presented with Beckett's *Krapp's Last Tape* at the Off-Broadway Provincetown Playhouse, registering a macabre success. The play portrayed in one wrenching scene, which takes place at a simple bench in Central Park, two men, Jerry and Peter—the truculent outsider and the complacent insider; instinct against society; two sides of human nature locked in a struggle of mutual recognition, of love really, culminating in death. *The Death of Bessie Smith* (1959, 1960), which also had its premiere in Berlin, seemed more conventional in its cinematic realism, its direct approach to racism in America.

Two plays related to each other—*The Sandbox* (1959) and *The American Dream* (1960, 1961)—followed. *The Sandbox* borrowed characters from the later and longer play, then incomplete, to create a vicious and surreal pastiche of the family. Albee described *The American Dream* as an "attack on the substitution of artificial for real values in our society, a condemnation of complacency, cruelty, emasculation and vacuity; it is a stand against the fiction that everything in this slipping land of ours is peachy-keen."

The first full-length play of Albee, and still his best known, was *Who's Afraid of Virginia Woolf?* (1962). Four people—George and Martha, the central characters, and Nick and Honey—confront each other in every combination possible, clawing egos, stripping bodies, heaving their fears loose into the night. The drama, set in an ordinary living room of a professor's house, moves with enormous dynamism from dangerous conviviality to demonic abuse to an exorcism that leaves the audience wholly spent in horror and recognition. Its ritual structure circles narrowly around the center; there, at the hollow center, a myth sustained by human dread of reality threatens to swallow up all the characters. Exposure of the myth—it could be God as well as the imaginary son of George and Martha—opens the way for harrowing reconciliation.

The realm of the invisible seemed also to be the central theme of Albee's most ambiguous drama, *Tiny Alice* (1965). A philosophical teaser, wavering between fact and fantasy, the work presented the struggle of Brother Julian to justify his Christian faith in terms of his concrete existence, his suffering. At around the same time, Albee turned to adapting novels or plays of other writers: *The Ballad of the Sad Cafe* (1963), *Malcolm* (1966), *Everything in the Garden* (1968). His next original work, *A Delicate Balance* (1966), clearly showed a desire to transcend absurdity and hatred. More than any other work of Albee, *A Delicate Balance* sought a working concept of human responsibility, a minimal love.

Like Williams and Miller before him, Albee has not been an innovator in the forms of drama. Yet there is no doubt that he has pushed postwar drama into new regions of sensibility. He has expressed the destructive conjunctions of human passions in ritual or musical patterns. His vision of man's failure is so uncompromising as to possess a unique dignity. And more than his predecessors, he has denounced, in essays and interviews, the material conditions that have corrupted the art of drama in America.

DRAMA: TYPES AND TRENDS

Originals and Adaptations

The original ventures of American novelists and poets in playwriting, as well as the adaptations of various authors from genres other than drama, have filled a distinct vacuum in the postwar American theater.

In *The Last Analysis* (1965) Saul Bellow wrote a satire on psychoanalysis, or rather, on what he called the "peculiarly literal and solemn manner in which Americans dedicate themselves to programs, fancies, or brainstorms." Though livened with wild comedy, the play failed to sustain the interest of audiences. Similarly, Joseph Heller, despite his outrageous humor, fell short of dramatic success in his play *We Bombed in New Haven* (1968). J. P. Donleavy's *Fairy Tales of New York* (1961) and John Hawkes's *The Innocent Party* (1967) hardly succeeded more. Perhaps only James Purdy's short play, *Cracks* (1961), a work Beckettian in overtones, came close to fulfilling the conditions of drama.

Poets of the New York school have also turned to drama in an attempt to create—out of verse, parody, and politics—a new experimental form, funny and free. John Ashbery's *The Heroes* (1960), Frank O'Hara's *Try! Try!* (1960), and Kenneth Koch's *The Election* (1960) were instances of their quizzical attitude toward society. The work of a different kind of poet, Lawrence Ferlinghetti's *Unfair Arguments with Existence* (1963), proved hard to produce. The outstanding poetic contribution to the theater came from Robert Lowell. In *The Old Glory* Lowell transformed stories of Hawthorne and Melville into a dramatic trilogy that was a troubling statement on man and history in times of revolutions.

Curiously enough, adaptations very often met the challenge of the theater better than works intended originally for dramatic performance. Thus, for instance, Carson McCullers adapted her own novella into a fine stage production, *The Member of the Wedding* (1950); so did Truman Capote with *The Grass Harp* (1952). Albee, a highly skilled original dramatist, did only fairly with McCullers's *The Ballad of the Sad Cafe,* Purdy's *Malcolm,* and Giles Cooper's play *Everything in the Garden.*

"Middle Drama"

By far, the greatest number of plays in the postwar period have fitted a strictly commercial concept of theater. Musical comedies—lavish, raucous, and bright—have dominated Broadway. But a certain type of melodrama has also infiltrated the neon realm. Though wide in appeal, this type has exhibited more serious pretensions. Its masters have been William Inge (born 1913), Arthur Laurents (born 1918), and Robert Anderson (born

1917), who have shared the dubious distinction of placing the human condition in a soft focus.

William Inge is known for a number of plays that are still better known as Hollywood films: *Come Back, Little Sheba* (1950), *Picnic* (1953), *Bus Stop* (1955), and *The Dark at the Top of the Stairs* (1958). A midwesterner by birth, Inge has a certain intuitive grasp of grass-roots America. But his view of love has tended toward superficiality, and his skillful forms have relied on easy pathos. Arthur Laurents has shown similar limitations in his treatment of social problems. His best play, *Home of the Brave* (1945), dealt in unglamorous fashion with war in the south Pacific and anti-Semitism in America. *The Time of the Cuckoo* (1953) and especially *A Clearing in the Woods* (1957) appealed to the popular interest in psychoanalysis as a means of apprehending character and motive on the stage. Robert Anderson won some attention with his play *Tea and Sympathy* (1953), about a prep-school boy accused of homosexuality. He also wrote *All Summer Long* (1955) and *Silent Night, Lonely Night* (1960).

All these playwrights have shown a certain theatrical flair; they propagated the old ideal of the well-made play. They also attempted to engage significant issues of their day. But their statements were finally too soft, simple, or equivocal.

Off-Broadway

The Off-Broadway theater, especially during the 1950s, helped, with new honesty and resourcefulness, to remake American drama. Authors, actors, and directors of that theater took risks; they showed greater awareness of avant-garde movements in Europe; above all, they saw the changing character of American society and challenged its values and assumptions. In their hands, absurdity took on the hues of ideology, utopia, or gallows humor. The most talented companies of the early years of Off-Broadway, struggling perpetually to avoid financial ruin, were The Living Theatre (1951–63) of Julian Beck and Judith Malina, two brave and inspired artists in their own right, and the Artists' Theatre (1953–56) of Herbert Machiz. The Circle in the Square, the Phoenix Theatre, the Theater de Lys, the Cherry Lane—all located in or around Greenwich Village—were particularly hospitable to serious and experimental drama.

The turning point of the new theater came when *The Connection* (published in 1960) was produced by The Living Theatre in July, 1959. The author, Jack Gelber, conceived that work as an improvisational drama with live jazz, on the theme of drug addiction, revealing a "petty and miserable microcosm" of the human condition, a universe of self-annihilation, but avoiding pessimism when its most lucid junkie, Solly, says: "The man is you. . . . You are the man. You are your own connection. It starts and stops here." *The Connection* proved highly controversial because its shape, its subject, its obscene language, jarred the deadened sensibilities of the day. Unfortunately, Gelber's next work, *The Apple* (1960), failed to enhance his achievement. Nor did *Square in the Eye* (1966) surpass his first play.

Subsequent directions of the Off-Broadway theater have been various, and its authors eclectic. Murray Schisgal (born 1926) found English producers more receptive to his earliest efforts, two one-act plays called *The Typists and The Tiger* (1963), staged in London in 1960, three years later in America. Gifted in dialogue, both satiric and compassionate, Schisgal perceived the waste and rage of treadmill lives in humorous terms. Subsequently, Schisgal has failed to create the authentic new statement that his first work intimated.

A more subtle and probing writer, Jack Richardson (born 1935) has not achieved the wide reputation he fully deserves. His first play, *The Prodigal* (1960), retold the myth of Orestes, pitting his original conceptions of Agamemnon and Aegisthus against one another, raising fundamental questions about history, morality, and dream. Despite the limpidity of its style and the classicism of its patterns of dramatic confrontations, *The Prodigal* was also able to strike at the center of contemporary chaos. *Gallows Humor* (1961) claimed "tragicomedy" as its mode. The drama developed two moments in the lives of a condemned man and of his executioner, two moments of freedom struggling against the institutional death, which men call social order.

Kenneth H. Brown made a lasting impression with his play *The Brig* (1964). Set in a Marine stockade, with barbed wire and cagelike cells as part of its decor, the drama relied on harsh noise and gesture, ritual and explosive action, to enhance an atmosphere of terror, monotony, and utter degradation. Without characters—the prisoners were mere numbers—or traditional plot, *The Brig* offered itself as an almost unbearable experience of absolute and arbitrary authority, of human madness as will to power. Its kinship to Artaud's concepts of a sensuous and cruel theater was clear; yet in the original production of The Living Theatre, it was even clearer that Brown had gone farther, creating a dramatic symbol, outside of verbal discourse, beyond naturalism or surrealism, based on the ancient, the unacknowledged dread of his audience.

In a lighter, whackier mood, Arthur Kopit (born 1937) has written plays full of frippery, parody, and acrid black humor. *Oh Dad, Poor Dad, Mamma's Hung You in the Closet and I'm Feelin' So Sad* (1960), directed with bravura by Jerome Robbins, suggested in its very title the macabre sex and absurdism of its genre; a growing Venus flytrap, a talking piranha, sliding chairs, and banging doors are part of its set. But Kopit's comic gift—elements of the Marx Brothers and of pseudo-Harlequin are in it—seem finally too facile, a witty evasion—camp. Still young as a dramatist, his future development is hard to foretell.

There have been, of course, other dramatists of the Off-Broadway theater worth mentioning: William Hanley (born 1931), Arnold Weinstein (born 1927), William Snyder (born 1928), among others. Clearly, no single direction, no uniformity of theme or method, has prevailed. Off-Broadway has produced such signal works as Gelber's *The Connection,* Albee's *The Zoo Story,* and Brown's *The Brig;* it has welcomed the admirable, and rather classic, plays of Richardson; and it has presented the extravaganzas of Schisgal and Kopit.

Off-Off-Broadway

Inevitably, as some dramatists of the Off-Broadway theater achieved renown they began to turn to the financial rewards of larger media. Inevitably, too, the Off-Broadway theater gradually surrendered to commercialization as its audiences and advertisements spread wider. A time came for a more reckless or untrammeled drama. Thus, the Off-Off-Broadway theater came into being.

The arbitrary beginning may have been a performance of Alfred Jarry's *Ubu Roi* at a Greenwich Village coffee house called Take 3, in September, 1960. Soon, the practice spread to other locations (particularly active on Monday nights when Off-Broadway was dark), although civic rulings and licensing problems nearly crippled these efforts. The most notable sponsors of the new theater were Joseph Cino's The Caffe Cino; the Judson Poets' Theatre, organized by Al Carmines, assistant minister of the Judson Memorial Church, where many of the performances took place; Ellen Stewart's resourceful La Mama Experimental Theatre Club; Theatre Genesis, run by Ralph Cook, lay minister of the Church of Saint Mark's In The Bowery; and Joseph Chaikin's The Open Theatre, which included some of the most active participants in Off-Off-Broadway.

In style, Off-Off-Broadway has favored short and striking plays, several of which could be grouped in an evening. Rarely naturalistic, they have been comic in devious and disturbing ways, and consummately American in violence or extravagance. Although Off-Off-Broadway's artistic and political tempers are mainly radical, it has avoided direct statement, preaching, ideology. Above all, it has employed the resources of a "total theater": mixed media, physical shock and improvisation, a language even less restricted to words than European dramas of the absurd.

Although a great many playwrights have contributed to Off-Off-Broadway, several are particularly known for their flair and stamina. Jean-Claude Van Itallie (born 1935) has had plays produced both in America and abroad. He is perhaps best known for *America Hurrah* (1966), which used horrendous dolls, larger than life-size, to deride the vulgarity and violence, the bloated quality, of culture in the United States. Noise, glare, caricature, and grotesquerie—obscene drawings, too!—carried the coarse point to the audience. His other plays have included *War* (1967) and *Serpent* (1969).

Paul Foster (born 1931) also has a small international following. *Hurrah for the Bridge* (1964) and *Tom Paine* (1968), performed at La Mama, displayed unusual dexterity in mixing media and techniques. In *Balls* (1964) Foster held the stage with two Ping-Pong balls swinging in the void while a tape carries sounds from the sea and hypnotic voices weave pleasure, pain, determination, protest, fear, through time and eternity.

Young and prolific, Sam Shepard (born 1943) has written plays for Off-Off-Broadway characterized by a special subjective vitality and a highly visual sense of drama. In *Chicago* (1965), no narrative or logical thread related the action. In a longer work, *La Turista* (1968), he moved from one parodic mode to another, in absurd tableaux full of unstated violence, composing, in the end, an ineluctable statement on the psychic disease of man.

There were, of course, many other authors—Lanford Wilson (born 1938), the poet Joel Oppenheimer, Megan Terry (born 19??), Ronald Tavel (born 1940), Maria Irene Fornes (born 1930), Rosalyn Drexler (born 19??)—who have contributed to the diversity of Off-Off-Broadway. There are also painters, dancers, sculptors, and musicians who have helped to broaden the conception of theatrical events. These events were called happenings ever since Allan Kaprow, a pop painter, staged *18 Happenings in 6 Parts,* at the Reuben Gallery, October 4, 1959. It is probable that the work of Marcel Duchamp and of John Cage—Cage directed an ur-happening at Black Mountain College in 1952—has influenced the form.

Black Drama

Black drama has thrived on and off Broadway; it gained its identity from its particular concerns. Committed to a racial cause, it has seldom permitted itself the luxury of absurdist philosophy or sheer entertainment. Its themes have been, often violently, cultural; its forms have varied from ritual to propaganda, from magic to fantasies of revenge. What it lacks in universality, it attempts to gain in black consciousness, "negritude." Holding some uneasy region between art and politics, it has challenged the canons of western aesthetics but has not always succeeded in formulating a theory of its own. Within its expanding domain, it has evinced different styles, attitudes.

James Baldwin, better known as a novelist and essayist, has also written plays. Like many black writers, increasingly he found "the war between his social and artistic responsibilities all but irreconcilable." *The Amen Corner* (1968), written almost fifteen years before its publication, reflected his early interest in religious and domestic conflicts. A later work, *Blues for Mr. Charlie* (1964), showed how much black anger had developed in less than a decade. Dedicated to Medgar Evers, a civil-rights worker murdered in 1963 in Mississippi, the play presented a vaguely similar incident in which the white killers remained defiantly free. Set in "Plaguetown, U.S.A.," the play echoed some themes from Camus's *La peste* (The Plague). Awkward or sentimental in parts, *Blues for Mr. Charlie* still managed to create an effect more complex than stark political protest.

Lorraine Hansberry's (1930–1965) smooth plays had wider success. She died before the black movement hit its shrillest note; her dramas recognized the universality of suffering even when fury and frustration threatened to overwhelm their characters. *A Raisin in the Sun* (1959), set in Chicago's south side, elicited the matriarchic resentments and the self-hatred of which a minority was capable, even in its quest for dignity. *The Sign in Sidney Brustein's Window* (1965) exposed those failures of white liberalism—piety, self-deception, ease of commitment—that militant blacks have contemned with special fury.

Hansberry's best play, *Les Blancs* (1970), was produced posthumously. Set in a medical mission in the heart of Africa—very much like Albert Schweitzer's at Lambaréné—it explored the large issues of colonialism, Christianity, and revolution with firm insight, and with theatricality equal to its compassion. An enemy of nihilism and despair, Hansberry also opposed absurdism in literature. But her meliorism did not always evade the pieties of which she accused liberals; nor did her dramatic vision always transcend the soft rhetoric of her characters.

At the other pole of black drama, LeRoi Jones has used the theater, as he has used his poetry, mainly as a political weapon, an extension of black power. To him, the theater is not a medium of "protest," which blacks see as a concession to the white world; it is rather an expression of black culture, a mode of self-consciousness as well as of assault. In 1964, Jones organized the Black Arts Repertory Theatre School in Harlem; and later he founded Spirit House, a community theater, in Newark. He wrote: "Our theater will show victims so that their brothers in the audience will be better able to understand that they are the brothers of victims, and that they themselves are blood brothers. . . . We will scream and cry, murder, run through the streets in agony, if it means some soul will be moved, moved to actual life understanding of what the world is, and what it could be."

To his own dramatic works, Jones has brought intense poetry and rage. His first one-act play, *The Toilet* (1963), a homosexual fantasy of politics and violence set in a public urinal, served only to presage his obsessions. *Dutchman* (1964), however, was a dramatic masterpiece. The action between a white woman, Lula (or Eve), and a black man, Clay (or Adam), takes place in a subway car—the symbolic "flying underbelly of the city," perhaps of existence. The action moves with truth, ferocity, and surprise toward a climax that contains the racial history of America. *The Slave* (1962), set against an apocalyptic background of racial strife, lacked tension because its dramatic situation seemed starkly murderous, one-sided. But in *Slaveship* (1967) Jones resorted to a series of tableaux, a historical pageant of the Negro, a kind of "total theater" that, although partial in its ideology, deployed in dramatic "metalanguage" an experience larger than any of its verbal parts.

Black drama continues to find new paths of expression in authors still relatively unknown: Adrienne Kennedy (born 1931), Ron Milner (born 1938), Ed Bullins (born 1935), Ben Caldwell (born 19??), Jimmy Garrett (born 19??), among others. And black community theaters have spread from New York—westward across the United States and eastward to Africa.

No conclusion is really possible to a literature still as current and vital as contemporary American literature. Even the putative death of art—death of the novel or death of the theater—becomes a new motive for the imagination to discover new media. Still, we may well wonder what forms of literary innovation the 1970s will witness. The answer, at very best, can only be tentative.

The experimental urge in fiction reveals itself in fantasy and humor, in surreal language and discontinuity, and sometimes in typographic play. This urge has been strong in such novelists as Heller, Barth, Pynchon, and Barthelme. It continues in gifted younger novelists: Richard Brautigan, Ronald Sukenick (born 1932), Jerome Charyn, Charles Newman (born 1938), Ishmael Reed, Rudolph Wurlitzer (born 19??), and Robert Coover (born 1932). In all these novelists, different as they are from one another, the effort to reconceive the very nature of narrative fiction is brilliantly manifest.

In poetry, the influence of pop lyrics, sung to the sophisticated sounds of the new rock music, may also extend to verse. The work of Bob Dylan (born 1941) in particular, consummate in its artistry and complex in its vision, is of central importance. In contrast with pop lyrics, another experimental genre, concrete poetry, offers itself mainly to visual rather than auditory appreciation. The assumption of the genre is that the printed form of the poem, the arrangement of lines, letters, and spaces, also creates the poem's meaning. Practitioners of concrete poetry include Mary Ellen Solt (born 1920), Emmett Williams (born 1925), and Aram Saroyan (born 1943). Still other directions of poetry in the 1970s may be discovered in anthologies such as Paul Carroll's *The Young American Poets* (1968).

Black drama promises to continue its lively explorations of the ritual and communal resources of the theater; and new white dramatists, such as David Rabe (born 19??) and Michael Weller (born 1942), show that serious talent is still drawn to the stage. Furthermore, new theatrical organizations dedicate themselves to the discovery and performance of experimental works that neither Broadway nor Off-Broadway theaters may find economical to produce. These organizations, which enjoy some of the most gifted directors in New York, include the Public Theater of Joseph Papp, the Performance Group of Richard Schechner, the American Place Theatre of Wynn Handman, the Chelsea Theater Center of Robert Kalfin, and the New Theatre Workshop of Stephen Aaron.

These are only a few names and trends that may assert themselves in the 1970s. Yet other names or other trends may finally prove more central. In the end we can only be certain of this: that contemporary American literature attempts to take the full measure of life in the contemporary world. The American imagination has been neither paltry nor laggard in making that world human and habitable.

SECONDARY WORKS

BIBLIOGRAPHIES AND GUIDES

Blanck, Jacob Nathaniel. *Bibliography of American Literature,* 5 vols. to date. New Haven, 1955–69

Burke, W. J. and W. D. Howe. *American Authors and Books,* 2nd ed. New York, 1962

Ghodes, Clarence. *Bibliographical Guide to the Study of the Literature of the U.S.A.,* 2nd ed. Durham, N.C., 1963

Hart, James D. *The Oxford Companion to American Literature,* 4th ed. New York, 1965

Herzberg, Max John, ed. *The Reader's Encyclopedia of American Literature.* New York, 1962

Leary, Lewis. *Articles on American Literature, 1900–1950.* Durham, 1954; supplemented by *Index to Articles on American Literature, 1951–1959, Prepared in the Reference Department of the University of Pennsylvania Library.* Boston, 1960

Leary, Lewis, ed. *Contemporary Literary Scholarship: A Critical Review.* New York, 1958

Spiller, Robert E. et al., eds. *Literary History of the United States: Bibliography and Supplements I and II,* 2 vols. New York, 1963, 1972

GENERAL WORKS

Cunliffe, Marcus. *The Literature of the United States.* Baltimore, 1954

Lüdeke, Henry. *Geschichte der amerikanischen Literatur,* 2nd ed. Bern, 1963

Quinn, Arthur Hobson et al. *The Literature of the American People: An Historical and Critical Survey.* New York, 1951

Schöne, Annemarie. *Abriß der amerikani-*

schen Literaturgeschichte in Tabellen. Bad Homburg, 1967

Schulze, Martin. *Wege der amerikanischen Literatur.* Berlin, 1968

Spiller, Robert E. *The Cycle of American Literature,* 3rd ed. New York, 1967

Spiller, Robert E. et al., eds. *Literary History of the United States,* 2 vols., 3rd ed. New York, 1963

Straumann, Heinrich. *American Literature in the Twentieth Century.* London, 1951

Taylor, Walter Fuller. *The Story of American Letters,* rev. ed. Chicago, 1956

Thorp, Willard. *American Writing in the Twentieth Century.* Cambridge, Mass., 1960

WORKS ON CONTEMPORARY LITERATURE

Aldridge, John W. *After the Lost Generation.* New York, 1951

———. *Time to Murder and to Create: The Contemporary Novel in Crisis.* New York, 1966

Alvarez, A. *Beyond All This Fiddle.* London, 1968

Balakian, Nona and Charles Simmons, eds. *The Creative Present: Notes on Contemporary American Fiction.* New York, 1963

Baumbach, Jonathan. *The Landscape of Nightmare: Studies in the Contemporary American Novel.* New York, 1965

Bigsby, C. W. E. *Confrontation and Commitment: A Study of Contemporary American Drama, 1959–1966.* Kansas City, Mo., 1968

Blau, Herbert. *The Impossible Theater.* New York, 1964

Broussard, Louis. *American Drama: Contemporary Allegory from Eugene O'Neill to Tennessee Williams.* Norman, Okla., 1962

Brustein, Robert. *The Third Theatre.* New York, 1969

Bryant, Jerry H. *The Open Decision: The Contemporary American Novel and Its Intellectual Background.* New York, 1970

Cambon, Glauco. *Recent American Poetry.* Minneapolis, Minn., 1963

Carroll, Paul. *The Poem in Its Skin.* Chicago, 1968

Dickey, James, ed. *From Babel to Byzantium.* New York, 1968

Dodsworth, Martin, ed. *The Survival of Poetry.* London, 1970

Downer, Alan S. *Recent American Drama.* Minneapolis, 1961

Eisinger, Chester E. *Fiction of the Forties.* Chicago, 1963

Fiedler, Leslie. *No! In Thunder.* Boston, 1960

———. *Waiting for the End.* New York, 1964

Galloway, David. *The Absurd Hero in American Fiction.* Austin, Tex., 1966, 1971

Gardner, R. H. *The Splintered Stage: The Decline of the American Theatre.* New York, 1965

Geismar, Maxwell. *American Moderns: A Mid-Century View of Contemporary Fiction.* New York, 1958

Gilman, Richard. *Common and Uncommon Masks: Writings on Theatre, 1961–1970.* New York, 1971

Gossett, Louise Y. *Violence in Recent Southern Fiction.* Durham, N.C., 1965

Gottfried, Martin. *A Theater Divided: The Postwar American Stage.* Boston, 1968

Gould, Jean. *Modern American Playwrights.* New York, 1966

Hamilton, Ian, ed. *The Modern Poet.* London, 1969

Harper, Howard M., Jr. *Desperate Faith: A Study of Bellow, Salinger, Mailer, Baldwin, and Updike.* Chapel Hill, N.C., 1967

Hassan, Ihab. *Radical Innocence: The Contemporary American Novel.* Princeton, N.J., 1961

Hausermann, Jans-Walter. *Moderne amerikanische Literatur.* Bern, 1965

Hicks, Granville. *The Living Novel: A Symposium.* New York, 1957

Hill, Herbert, ed. *Anger and Beyond: The Negro Writer in the United States.* New York, 1966

Hoffman, Frederick J. *The Art of Southern Fiction: A Study of Some Modern Novelists.* Carbondale, Ill., 1967

Howard, Richard. *Alone with America.* New York, 1969

Hungerford, Edward B., ed. *Poets in Progress: Critical Prefaces to Ten Contemporary Americans.* Evanston, Ill., 1962

Jarrell, Randall. *Poetry and the Age.* New York, 1955

Kazin, Alfred. *Contemporaries.* Boston, 1962

Klein, Marcus. *After Alienation: American Novels in Mid-Century.* Cleveland, 1964

Klein, Marcus, ed. *The American Novel since World War II.* Greenwich, Conn., 1969

Kostelanetz, Richard, ed. *On Contemporary Literature.* New York, 1964

Lewis, Allan. *American Plays and Playwrights of the Contemporary Theatre,* rev. ed. New York, 1970

Ludwig, Jack. *Recent American Novelists.* Minneapolis, 1962

McCarthy, Mary. *Sights and Spectacles: Theatre Chronicles, 1937–1956.* New York, 1956

Malin, Irving. *Jews and Americans.* Carbondale, Ill., 1965

——. *New American Gothic.* Carbondale, Ill., 1962

Mills, Ralf J., Jr. *Contemporary American Poetry.* New York, 1965

Nathan, George Jean. *The Theatre in the Fifties.* New York, 1953

Nemerov, Howard, ed. *Poets on Poetry.* New York, 1966

Ossman, David. *The Sullen Art.* New York, 1963

Ostroff, Anthony, ed. *The Contemporary Poet as Artist and Critic.* Boston, 1964

Parkinson, Thomas, ed. *A Casebook on the Beat.* New York, 1961

Podhoretz, Norman. *Doings and Undoings: The Fifties and After in American Writing.* New York, 1964

Ransom, John Crowe et al. *American Poetry at Mid-Century.* Washington, D.C., 1958

Rosenthal, M. L. *The New Poets.* New York, 1967

Rubin, Louis D., Jr. *The Faraway Country: Writers of the Modern South.* Seattle, 1963

Schechner, Richard. *Public Domain.* New York, 1969

Schultz, Max F. *Radical Sophistication.* Athens, Ohio, 1969

Scott, Nathan A., Jr., ed. *Adversity and Grace: Studies in Recent American Literature.* Chicago, 1968

Stepanchev, Stephen. *American Poetry since 1945.* New York, 1965

Tanner, Tony. *City of Words.* New York, 1971

Waldmeir, Joseph J., ed. *Recent American Fiction: Some Critical Views.* Boston, 1963

Weales, Gerald. *American Drama since World War II.* New York, 1961

HORST W. DRESCHER

British Literature

THE POLITICAL AND SOCIAL RECONSTRUCTION after World War II affected the literature of the British Isles as much as it did that of the continent. A new world had emerged, bringing with it new themes, calling for fresh orientations. The extent of the changes to come could still only be guessed at. In the British Isles, however, traditions did prevail longer than on the continent. Contemporary British writers, with few exceptions, have not experimented with form but have been chiefly interested in the concrete problems of current society, in its cultural and social aspects—in other words, in literature as document of the times. Some discussion of the sociopolitical background is therefore a necessary requisite for a study of contemporary literature.

For many, especially among the young, 1945 stood for the electoral victory of the Labour Party in Britain, signaling the beginning of a new social order built according to the ideas of modern socialism. The Labour Party promised full employment through the nationalization of key industries. Indeed, both parties were in favor of a welfare state and had developed plans to implement it during the war years. But the desire for decisive reforms in the social structure of the country, for equal educational opportunities, and for the reduction of inequalities between rich and poor was felt by the electorate to be more easily attainable under a Labour government than under the Conservative Party of Winston Churchill.

The great hopes aroused by the Labour victory were soon shown to be

65

utopian dreams that could not stand up to pragmatic considerations. The new government showed itself ready, indeed compelled, to compromise. The creation of the welfare state and the political and social consequences resulting from it were, it is true, a first, decisive, and initially highly promising step toward the realization of socialist ideals. But disappointment in what it was not achieving grew stronger. The welfare state did indeed bring with it financial amelioration, and removed discriminations under which large groups of the population had been suffering. But there was little talk of immediate implementation of more sweeping values and ideals. And the general indifference of the working class was largely unchanged. Nevertheless, British society managed in those years to break successfully with its past—to accept the dissolution of its empire and to move toward closer ties with continental Europe.

When the Conservative Party regained power in 1951, it took over the various features of the welfare state. And in the years that followed, both parties came increasingly close to each other in their views. Many people saw this as a confirmation of their fears that independent political decision was no longer possible and that it actually made little difference which party one voted for. Thus, general disillusionment grew stronger, particularly among the young people, who felt themselves frustrated in their hopes for a new society. They increasingly stood on the sidelines, refused on principle to cooperate, and strongly criticized state, church, and society. They became resigned to the status quo and no longer tried to make constructive criticisms.

In international politics, too, a great deal happened to strengthen the general skepticism and the sense of personal helplessness. Protests and doctrines lost their meaning when countries took violent action. In 1956 the Hungarian uprising was suppressed by the Soviet Union according to the best tactics of imperialistic power politics, in full view of a helpless world. In the same year, England and France attempted to seize the Suez Canal after Egypt announced its intention of nationalizing it.

In Britain itself, protests against the atomic arms race resulted in the first Aldermaston March. The marchers acted as individuals and not as members of a party or political group. They believed—at least at the beginning—that in passive resistance they had found a suitable practical expression of men's anger at finding themselves the pawns of international interests. These and other events helped to create the climate of opinion that influenced young writers in their work. And it also clearly produced favorable conditions for these writers' initial successes.

These sociopolitical developments were ignored as far as possible by a hostile establishment—the aristocracy and the upper middle class—with its stress on tradition, proper upbringing, and conservativism in politics. They closed their eyes to the bitter realities of the postwar years and thus hoped to preserve for themselves an oasis of peace and comfort. The reaction of the younger generation was quite different: in their disappointment and disillusionment, they attacked these problems with special ferocity.

During the 1950s young writers who were fiercely critical of the establishment were called "angry young men." Their protests often arose out of their own discontent and despair, and were not unmixed with a certain degree of self-pity. They rejected conventional morality because they believed that these values prevented people from recognizing their own potential and stood in the way of self-development. Moreover, they felt that there was scarcely any room left for individual initiative in a world hemmed in by values of the marketplace and pressures to conform. The heroes of this literature are completely antipolitical, for in their eyes party and politics are part of the hated establishment. These novels and plays, although they presented a totally disillusioned view of contemporary problems, have had continued success because of their strong emotional appeal.

This "angry" attitude toward state and society found its first literary expression in the novel. John Wain (born 1925) and Kingsley Amis (born 1922), in their respective first novels, introduced characters who thought of themselves as outsiders. Their protests were directed against the hated class structure and against the welfare state, from which they ultimately derived no benefit. Indeed, their protests were directed indiscriminately against everything that pertained to the establishment, unlike the focused criticism of more recent fiction, which is intended to promote positive action.

For the most part, the protests of Amis, Wain, and their followers were accompanied by the resigned admission that they were ultimately unable to alter anything. They realized that at the end of all their angry outbreaks, and despite all their opposition, they were nonetheless attracted by the advantages they could reap from society. Thus, Charles Lumley in Wain's *Hurry On Down* (1953), after an undistinguished educational career, embarks on an erratic course through various odd jobs, unrelated to his education, as a protest against middle-class life. But he finally puts down his anchor in the haven of bourgeois morality. Jimmy Porter's hate-filled tirades in John Osborne's (born 1929) play *Look Back in Anger* (1956) are the elixir of his life, concocted with relish. He gets drunk with his own rhetoric, trembles with satisfaction (according to the stage directions) when he is successful in his verbal attacks and hurts his adversary.

The angry-young-man attitude led to a literary fashion that embraced all literary forms, although not always successfully. One manifestation was the playwriting competition initiated by the Sunday paper *The Observer,* in the autumn of 1956. Only a small proportion of the approximately 3,000 manuscripts submitted were poetic plays. The chief subjects were the Hungarian revolution, the problems of the nonwhite populations of the

United States and Great Britain, the nuclear arms race, and generalized political and social protest in the manner of *Look Back in Anger.* It became clear that writers chiefly wanted to present specific current problems, using all the resources of the naturalistic theater, including everyday language.

Attempts to divide contemporary British literature into genres are fraught with problems, because there has been so much cross-fertilization among the genres. Yet categorizing contemporary literature by themes also has its dangers: on one hand, the various genres do still have their own special demands; on the other hand, labels such as "angry young men" tend to undercut all individuality of expression and to lead to unintelligent generalizations. Thus, I have chosen a roughly chronological approach, sometimes emphasizing genre, sometimes emphasizing theme, depending upon the dominant concerns of the individual writers.

One final preliminary point: The title of this article is "British Literature," and my central focus is the literature of Britain. But I have also included the major English-language writers of contemporary Ireland, both insofar as they can be compared to their British counterparts and—in some cases—insofar as specifically Irish conditions have made their work quite different from the literature of Britain.

THE POSTWAR WORK OF PREWAR WRITERS

After the war, a number of major prewar authors continued their careers or returned to literature after a hiatus. They had in common a strongly personal view of life, which accounts as much as anything for their astonishing durability.

The first novels of Graham Greene (born 1904), who will certainly occupy a central position in future evaluations of twentieth-century British literature, were early proof of his unusual talent. In *Brighton Rock* (1938) he took up for the first time a theme that would recur in all his novels—the conflict between the powers of good and evil in a world that has forgotten God. Greene has been a master at combining different kinds of narrative to produce the greatest possible effect on the reader; *Brighton Rock* is an entertainment, a psychological casebook, a thriller, and a work of sociology all in one. The foreground, that is, the narrative, has served Greene as an excuse for the specific message of his novels. But this cannot hide the fact that Greene the writer is in continuous conflict with Greene the convinced Catholic—as in *The Power and the Glory* (1940).

In his more recent novels Greene has returned to his favorite setting, the world of exotic places: Haiti, Africa, Saigon. The theme remains the exploration of good and evil, of the poverty and the pain that make up human existence. Greene's talent as a storyteller, his sure feeling for what is exciting and spell-binding, has hidden certain weaknesses that arise from his compulsive thinking and theorizing. But when he does not feel this compulsion—in his "entertainments," as he calls them—the strength of the narrative comes into its full force. Written in the best tradition of English adventure stories, these entertainments are outstanding examples of their genre—technically brilliant, certainly more than mere pastime reading.

J. B. Priestley (born 1894) became known for *The Good Companions* (1929), a picaresque novel in the tradition of Charles Dickens (1811–1870) and Henry Fielding (1707–1754). Priestley tried to capture the atmosphere of the late 1920s, particularly stressing the changes that took place in society. His subsequent novels showed shifts in subject matter and technique. In *Lost Empires* (1965), about the great days of the English music hall, Priestley repeated his earlier triumphs. Bleakness marked the atmosphere of his *It's an Old Country* (1967), in which an Australian travels through England in search of his father.

Before World War II Priestley was even more popular as a dramatist than as a novelist. After the war Priestley had success on the stage with *The Linden Tree* (1947) and a stage adaptation of Iris Murdoch's *A Severed Head* (1964).

The writings of the Anglo-Irish Joyce Cary (1888–1957) gave the impression of direct experience, told mostly from the point of view of a first-person narrator. In novels set in the Africa of his own experience, Cary was chiefly concerned with the direct conflict between alien ways of life and thought. Since *The Horse's Mouth* (1944), which was without a doubt Cary's most distinguished book, the theme of nonconformism became central—nonconformism in religion, in society, and in politics. Cary thought of his novels chiefly in groups of three, linked thematically. The summit of his work, the trilogy ending with *The Horse's Mouth,* was followed by a less successful postwar trilogy: *Prisoner of Grace* (1952), *Except the Lord* (1953), and *Not Honour More* (1955). Cary no longer was able to reach the intensity of his previous works. With his creative imagination waning, he made an almost desperate attempt to keep the action vivid in these last novels.

Among other novelists who published their main body of work before 1945 but also produced noteworthy works after the war were Elizabeth Bowen (born 1899), Rosamond Lehmann (born 1903), Rebecca West (born 1892), and Ivy Compton-Burnett (1892–1969). Elizabeth Bowen, who broke a silence of close to ten years with the publication of *The Little Girls* (1964); Rosamond Lehmann, who had a postwar success in *The Echoing Grove* (1953); Rebecca West, who published *The Fountain Overflows* in 1957 as the first volume of a series—all belong to that generation of female writers which has never considered the contemporary world to be of primary interest; instead, they have written from a private, self-enclosed world. The result has been finely drawn psychological portraits in meticulously described settings.

Ivy Compton-Burnett in a certain sense created her own tradition. Her novels remind one of the Victorian predilection for melodramatic action. Spare in description, they consist almost exclusively of dialogue. With studied quiet and calm, she bared the motives behind selfishness and cruelty. In her fiction the unscrupulous and self-assertive oppress those weaker than themselves. The strong use their apparent superiority whenever opportunity occurs. In Compton-Burnett's work, evil and sinfulness grow so wildly over everything that they eventually strangle all life. Behind the façade of moral self-judgment, destruction is at work. There are only masters and servants in her work. This deliberate narrowing of patterns of action and characterization has in it the inevitable danger of repetition. And the portrait of human relationships in her numerous novels is consistently dark and hopeless, yet intelligently presented with her special virtuosity.

Charles Morgan (1894–1958), Aldous Huxley (1894–1963), George Orwell (1903–1950), and Compton Mackenzie (born 1883) should also be mentioned with the older generation. But their work—with the exception of Orwell's *Animal Farm* (1945) and *1984* (1949)—belongs even more clearly to the prewar period. Charles Morgan's philosophical novels found more response in France and Germany than in his own country. The people in his novels are embodiments of problems or ideals rather than rounded characters living in the real world. The philosophical and speculative element in Morgan's fiction was also present in his problem plays, but these were not the equal of his novels.

The theater immediately after the war seldom concerned itself with the happenings of the most recent past or with the present. Old themes and techniques dominated until the landmark appearance of Osborne's *Look Back in Anger*. The well-made play dominated the West End stage. Noël Coward (born 1899) perpetuated the traditions of the comedy of manners; his plays have been distinguished by witty but often frivolous dialogue.

In addition to the various kinds of realistic drama practiced by such writers as Priestley and Coward—who continued to follow the theater of George Bernard Shaw (1856–1950), W. Somerset Maugham (1874–1965), and John Galsworthy (1867–1933)—there were the plays of the self-taught Sean O'Casey (1884–1964), chief representative of the Irish Renaissance. O'Casey, certainly the most important Irish dramatist of the twentieth century thus far, wrote several plays after 1945, among them the tragicomedies *Oak Leaves and Lavender* (1946) and *Cock-a-Doodle Dandy* (1949), and the comedies *The Bishop's Bonfire* (1955) and *The Drums of Father Ned* (1958). In O'Casey's early work one cannot fail to hear the voice of accusation in his primarily realistic descriptions of the world of socially underprivileged Dublin. After he moved to London, however, he turned more toward expressionistic theater. Vivid dialogue, rich fantasy, unexpected humor, and a great skill in characterization made almost all of O'Casey's plays unusually effective on the stage.

In the late 1920s a number of young poets met together at Oxford. Their leftist political leanings were later expressed in a passionate partisanship for the republican side in the Spanish civil war. The most impressive among the group—which considered William Butler Yeats (1865–1939) and Gerard Manley Hopkins (1844–1889) its precursors—was W. H. Auden (born 1907). Other prominent members of the group were Stephen Spender (born 1909), Louis MacNeice (1907–1963) from Northern Ireland, and the Anglo-Irish C. Day Lewis (born 1904).

Auden has produced a large body of work, which can be divided into three phases. Three poems from the first phase described particularly clearly his position during the 1930s: *1929* (1930), *Spain 1937* (1937), and *September 1, 1939* (1939). During the war Auden's attitude changed; indeed, the second phase of his literary development was already manifested in *September 1, 1939,* which was written after the final defeat of the republicans in the Spanish civil war. Auden turned in disappointment away from communism as World War II was beginning. His overriding theme became one of search—of departure into an unknown and unexplored future. His *For the Time Being* (1944) showed a strong affinity to T. S. Eliot's (1888–1965) *Four Quartets* (1944).

This second stage in Auden's career ended with *The Age of Anxiety* (1947). In this baroque pastoral poem, he enlarged the theme of search to include the whole of mankind. The restlessly searching wanderer, a symbolic figure, finds release in a salvation grounded in a faith in God. *The Age of Anxiety* can be seen as a thematic variant on *For the Time Being.*

Auden's more recent poems, which he collected in the volume *City without Walls* (1969), reflected the changing age and spoke for the present even more than *For the Time Being* had. In contemporary New York Auden experienced the dark vision of a disastrous future. Technology and created needs have led to the spiritual regression of man. Auden's vision, it is true, resulted from his own personal pessimism. But this does not minimize the validity of his frightening question of whether present progress does not contain within itself the seeds of destruction.

The intellectual poetry of Louis MacNeice and C. Day Lewis became more meditative as they grew older. Lewis was strongly influenced by Auden and at first wrote like him, also inspired by the Spanish civil war; but he found his own voice in his nature poetry. MacNeice's poetry was concerned with the present time, as were his plays both for the theater and for radio. Stephen Spender, a critic and translator as well as a poet, has often chosen the world of technology as the subject of his thoughtful poems. He has examined man's place in modern civilization. For him, there is no point in discussing gains made through technological advances—only the dilemma and desperation of the individual in his oppressive surroundings.

TRANSITIONAL FIGURES

This preceding group of novelists, playwrights, and poets belongs in the main to the prewar era, even though some of their later works took into account the changed world. A slightly younger group of writers, although they began their careers before World War II, are more figures of transition, since they significantly enriched their work after 1945.

The Welsh poet Dylan Thomas (1914–1953), who died so young, brought out his most important poetic work, *Death and Entrances,* in 1946. Like the Scottish Hugh MacDiarmid (born 1892, pseudonym of Christopher Murray Grieve), whose poetic gifts were proof that the Scottish idiom is still very much alive as a vehicle for serious poetry, Thomas was an outstanding regionalist poet of contemporary Britain. His verse plays—*The Doctor and the Devils* (1953) and *Under Milk Wood* (1954)—his film scripts, essays, short stories, and a fragment of a novel, showed his many-sided talent.

Thomas's poetry, written out of his own experiences, contained peculiarly striking images and other creative uses of language. He himself spoke of his poetry as thoughts about man's struggle for understanding and for truth. The combining of several different levels of speech, the use of onomatopoeia, of similar sounding words or series of words, of words of his own invention, of mysterious symbols often to the point of self-parody, of abbreviations and economies in punctuation—all these elements of ambiguity were part of Thomas's work. *Death and Entrances* established him as principally a religious poet; religion was the central theme of such poems in the volume as *Vision and Prayer, Ceremony after a Fire Raid, Fern Hill,* and *A Refusal to Mourn.*

Under Milk Wood has been a great success on the stage since 1956. It tells the story of an ordinary day in a small Welsh fishing village. It is not, however, really a stage play at all but, as the author called it, a "play for voices," coming out of darkness, out of his own home. *Under Milk Wood* depicts a grotesque dream world in which normal values are irrelevant. But the work is not simply a parody on civilization; rather, it is a poetic expression of man's innocence, and it focuses on the theme of love. Thomas wrote very freely in *Under Milk Wood,* mingling religious and sexual themes. Life, death, and corruption are intensely experienced, profoundly understood. The expression of natural goodness and joy was also present in his last poems, published in *Collected Poems* (1952).

Dylan Thomas was as celebrated as a public figure as he was as an artist. He enjoyed reciting his poems in front of large audiences, remained a constant enigma to admirers and critics, and became a legend during his lifetime. Some called him a genius; others, a charlatan. Indeed, some of Thomas's work was mediocre, but his better achievements belong to the best of the period.

After the end of World War II there was constant talk of a crisis in poetry. This was not because of a lack of good younger poets or of distinguished older poets. It was simply that poetry sold badly and there was little demand for it. The need to explain poetry to a vanishing audience gave rise to an important group of poet-critics: William Empson (born 1906), Edwin Muir (1887–1959), and D. J. Enright (born 1920). Their critical work, like their poetry, has reflected the effort to find fresh openings and interpretations.

Poetic theater came to new life with Christopher Fry (born 1907), whose first verse play, *A Phoenix Too Frequent* (1946), was based on the widow of Ephesus episode in Petronius's *Satyricon*. With *The Lady's Not for Burning* (1949), Fry began a cycle of four verse plays portraying, to the accompaniment of the changing seasons, the course of human life. The first play, a cheerful work but with serious undertones, symbolized spring. It was followed by *Venus Observed* (1950), representing autumn, and *The Dark Is Light Enough* (1954), representing winter, in nature as in human life. Finally, after a long interval, came *A Yard of Sun* (1970), the summer play.

Fry's plays of the four seasons brought new life to the stagnating West End theater. The monotony of the well-made play seemed at last to have been dispersed by the dramatic power of Fry's language and his soaring imagination. Behind the ambiguity of the word play and the images, the real and imaginary worlds lie side by side—which is not the case in the realistic theater of illusion. Fry has been criticized for putting too great a stress on language to the detriment of action and dramatic density. But others have felt that in his works language at last came into its own again on the stage. He is, in a sense, a successor to the Elizabethan dramatists.

Fry's plays, like Dylan Thomas's, have been based on individual experience and cannot be interpreted as direct statements about contemporary life. What Fry offers is diversion from the chaos of destruction, a reminder of the healing powers of nature, and, in his religious plays, a certainty about the consoling power of religion. He has not been primarily interested in experimenting with dramatic forms; he prefers to present a world view. For Fry, art is a catalyst through which the claims of daily reality can be transcended.

Fry brought new life to the theater. But he was an exception in the early 1950s. The West End stage was still dominated at that time by light entertainment; and even today the general tendency is toward social comedy and easy problem plays. The best-known exponent of the problem play is Terence Rattigan (born 1911). *The Winslow Boy* (1946), a play with slightly sentimental overtones, was his first considerable success after the war. *The Deep Blue Sea* (1952) was successful the world over, as was *Ross: A Dramatic Portrait* (1960), based on the life of T. E. Lawrence. Rattigan's most recent play, *A Bequest to the Nation* (1970), also concerns an historical character—Lord Nelson—and the circumstances surrounding him, his wife, and Lady Hamilton shortly before the Battle of Trafalgar. Rattigan glossed over facts and dates. The psychology of the characters is simple; the civilized manner in which they confront and forgive each other is both honest and uncomplicated. *A Bequest to the Nation* offered no very exact depiction of historical events, but it did charm and entertain.

British fiction gained increased strength right after 1945—in the social and psychological novels of Evelyn Waugh (1903–1966), Anthony Powell (born 1905), C. P. Snow (born 1905), L. P. Hartley (born 1895), and Henry Green (born 1905). These five writers all began their careers well before World War II; but all published major works after 1945.

Evelyn Waugh created a fictional world whose value many now question because of its insistence on social status and class distinctions. It is the world of the English upper-middle and upper classes, from which Waugh himself came. His work can be divided into two phases: The first includes the works from *Decline and Fall* (1928) to *Put Out More Flags* (1942). The second period began with *Brideshead Revisited* (1945), included *The Ordeal of Gilbert Pinfold* (1957), a short novel with autobiographical overtones, and ended with his last great work, *Unconditional Surrender* (1961).

Waugh's first group of novels were very like each other in subject matter, technique, and style. Irony and satire both played an important part. The setting was the urbane world of West End clubs, Mayfair, and St. James's. Waugh mocked this world, yet not without admiration for the spirited and carefree behavior of young people in the early 1930s. His characters are charming scoundrels, convinced they have discovered the only acceptable way of life; they are not unsympathetic, despite their negative qualities.

A different quality emerged in Waugh's second group of novels. These resembled the first only in their satirical descriptions of society; satire remained a continuing literary strength for Waugh. In *Brideshead Revisited* he treated for the first time a theme that became central for him—Catholicism in England. His nostalgic reminiscences lead him back into a calm and ordered world. The subtitle of *Brideshead Revisited* is "The Sacred and Profane Memories of Captain Charles Ryder." Ryder, the first-person narrator of the novel, describes past experiences. The action is told in flashbacks in which Waugh at times goes even further back and relates events that lie in a deeper past than the past actions of the story. The distance of the narrator from the events experienced is thus not always static but varies from instant to instant.

Although Waugh's personal belief in the Catholic religion became evident toward the end of the first phase of his career, in *Brideshead Revisited* he offered an unambiguous and penetrating account of his own position. His medium of expression was Ryder, whose purpose is to relay Waugh's own observations and opinions about the other characters in the novel and the sense and purpose of their actions—in other words, the specific goals he has set himself in his novel. As Waugh stressed in his preface, he wanted to show the workings of divine grace within a small group of people. The change that occurs at the end of the novel, Ryder's inner approach to real faith—for Waugh the Catholic faith—has led to much criticism and many reservations about the motives of the sudden conversion of the agnostic Ryder. All the same, *Brideshead Revisited* remains a valid attempt to bring to life, in the manner of Proust, a period of the past through the recollections of a first-person narrator.

Waugh's talent was not of the experimental kind but was derived from his sure possession of the skills of social comedy and satire. The *Sword of Honour* trilogy—*Men at Arms* (1952), *Officers and Gentlemen* (1955), and *Unconditional Surrender* (1961)—was, taken as a whole, Waugh's most considerable literary achievement. It is true that the overall plan of the work, its series of character portrayals, offered nothing substantially new. But in these three novels Waugh gave a very detailed account of the armed forces and of modern war. Coming from a writer known for his right-wing politics, the trilogy was a surprisingly ruthless satire on all tendencies toward militarism and its associated values. The protagonist, Guy Crouchback, sees the illusions he had nurtured at the beginning of the war fade into sober disappointment, a disappointment engendered by the anonymous powers of the war machine.

With the new, down-to-earth attitude of the gentleman-officer Crouchback, Waugh's myth of the aristocrat and gentleman seems to have changed also. It looks as if he had at last, although reluctantly, found a new, modified attitude toward the present, an attitude more suited to the real world. The temper of the time is opposed to the gentleman. The romantically idealized picture of an aristocratic society belongs to the past. Crouchback, unlike Ryder in *Brideshead Revisited,* accepts this necessary development and no longer seems to escape its consequences. In a certain sense, he is a precursor of the anti-hero so prevalent in the novels of writers of the next generation.

The Ordeal of Gilbert Pinfold confirmed Waugh's bias, evident in all his works, toward the fabular and the grotesque. It tells the story of a successful author whose creative powers are failing. Waugh's novels all had an autobiographical basis, and this description of a fifty-year-old successful writer was quite clearly derived from his own experiences.

Society occupied a key position in Waugh's works, although it was presented in a form different from that of the great novels of the nineteenth century. Real conflicts seldom occur, and descriptions of social position and differences in status are used almost exclusively for comic effect. We find similar uses of comedy in the works of Anthony Powell; but C. P. Snow, whose series *Strangers and Brothers* had characteristics of the *Bildungsroman,* pushed the comic element into the background.

The early work of Anthony Powell can be compared to Waugh's social satires. But when Powell, after a long interval, took up his literary activity again in 1951, it was clear from the first volume of his projected twelve-volume cycle, *A Dance to the Music of Time,* that he was offering a different and more complex narrative perspective. The first nine novels of *A Dance to the Music of Time* formed three trilogies: (1) *A Question of Upbringing* (1951), *A Buyer's Market* (1952), *The Acceptance World* (1955); (2) *At Lady Molly's* (1957), *Casanova's Chinese Restaurant* (1960), *The Kindly Ones* (1962); (3) *The Valley of Bones* (1964), *The Soldier's Art* (1966), *The Military Philosophers* (1968). The tenth volume, *Books Do Furnish a Room,* the first part of the last trilogy, was published in 1970.

The individual novels are sometimes hard to follow, taken on their own, because of the complexity of the action and the interrelationships of the characters. Again and again characters appear whom the reader is expected to know from previous books. New ones are introduced. In the center is Nicholas Jenkins, both narrator and commentator, a figure who resembles his author in many ways. Jenkins is the link between one novel and the next, one period and the next. He guides the reader through all the volumes, observes and at the same time represents society in its dance through time.

At the risk of oversimplification, one could say that each of the three trilogies is devoted to one period in the life of its narrator. In the first trilogy Jenkins appears as pupil in a public school in the early 1920s, as student at Oxford, and then as a young adult in the London of the late 1920s. The second trilogy continues the narrator's life during the 1930s and ends with the threat of a new war. The action of the third trilogy takes place during World War II and ends at the point of Jenkins's return to private life. Powell used a good deal of autobiographical material, as did Evelyn Waugh in his *Sword of Honour* trilogy.

In Waugh's *Brideshead Revisited* the Proustian method of linking the present to the past is only barely perceptible; in Powell's *The Music of Time,* however, the past is totally recalled in the Proustian sense and woven into the fabric of the present. It is true, however, that Powell has not insisted on the exclusively *personal* elements of his recollections. Despite the stylistic imitation of Proust, which has shown itself most strongly in the accuracy of the details and in the significance of seemingly trivial objects and events, this important difference must not be overlooked.

Powell's metaphorical title for the twelve-volume cycle, *A Dance to the Music of Time,* which was taken from the short description of Poussin's painting in the Wallace Collection in London, explains the structure of the entire cycle. Jenkins observes the movements and behavior of his fellow participants in the dance. While their gazes are directed toward the outside, he is looking inward. He wants to discover the reasons for the moves they make. He is the conductor of this dance to the music of time. He selects the situations in which the characters, including himself, are made known to us. He programs their reactions. But only when the narrator is able to play the notes of this music *freely* according to his own ideas does his concert become viable. A mechanistic, strictly chronological, reconstruction of the past would be contrary to Powell's intention. Only the possibility of time freed from the strict measure of time (Proust's *temps délivré*) can enable us to recall all the nuances of a remembered event. Only thus will be born the melody of awareness, which is the accompaniment to which this dance moves.

Characters appear, leave the stage, and return once more in new groupings. Past time is continuously present in the present of the telling. Characters reappear, alter the situation, bring new impetus to the story, disappear again, are present backstage, as it were, until the author places them once more in the center of the action. In the third trilogy, because of the historical facts of the war, unambiguously time-bound events force their way into what was initially the self-enclosed world of the novel. And thereby the closed form of the dance is opened, if not actually disrupted. The choreography no longer follows its own independent laws.

Environment and character are the decisive elements in Powell's epic story of society. They complement each other and constantly produce fresh variations on the theme. *A Dance to the Music of Time* is a social comedy in which the characters are given representational value; at times they unfortunately slide into the clichés of type casting. Yet Powell is mainly interested in depicting their personal development and the human relationships that bind them together. Only after this is he concerned with external problems: historical events, religion, cultural and spiritual questions.

Jenkins, as the center of the narrative, is less involved than Charles Ryder in Waugh's *Brideshead Revisited.* His view of the past lacks the strong feeling of nostalgia that pervades Waugh's novel. Jenkins's attitude is neither that of moralist nor that of a mythologizing observer. Even if it becomes clear that the "keeping to themselves" of the upper-middle and upper classes will lead to their disappearance in the not-too-distant future, there is in Powell nothing resembling Waugh's fears about the disappearance of the ideals of these classes. For Powell, such a social development is not a total disruption, but an inevitable shift, something that cannot be undone but must be borne by the losers with dignity.

Critics seem to have difficulty in evaluating C. P. Snow objectively. Many dislike the uniformity of his themes, the pseudoscientific background, and the homespun psychology of his novels. His attempt to find a link between scientific and cultural ideas has also met with rejection. Other critics have praised him immoderately for his goals, while ignoring his shortcomings.

After some unimportant early works, Snow published *Strangers and Brothers* in 1940, the first volume of the series called by that name, which he brought to an end in 1970, with *Last Things*. Snow's series does not have the unity of Powell's, each volume of which tells a section of the story but only assumes its rightful place in the context of the work as a whole. Like Powell, however, Snow did make use of a first-person narrator. Lewis Eliot, like Nicholas Jenkins, is both observer and commentator, but he takes a more active role as a participant. His function thus changes from that of pure storyteller to intermediary between people and between interest groups. He is a friendly adviser before whom one lays one's problems and whose opinion is valued as that of a thoroughly integrated man. The role of worldly father confessor that Snow gave his narrator is not always effective. At times it deprives the characters and the action of credibility.

Each of the *Strangers and Brothers* novels has its own distinct place in the sequence of the story. But the novels are written so that each can be read independently. The story of Lewis Eliot's life forms the framework, more or less. But one can distinguish between novels in which he is chiefly commentator and observer, that is, where the story of his friends and acquaintances is primary, and the four novels in which his own life story forms the central subject of the book.

A more meaningful division might be a chronological arrangement of the books according to the time period each covers. Yet although the action takes place according to a time scheme that Snow planned from the outset, the novels were not published in order of the chronology of the events. Thus, one has to keep in mind both the order of the action and the order in which the individual novels were published.

Snow used character analyses to link characters and action as closely together as possible. This aim was realized through the medium of the narrator, Lewis Eliot, who not only reports on events and persons but gives his own thoughts and ideas as well. Snow was interested, moreover, in the private attitudes of his characters, especially in relation to their external behavior; individual actions and the general concerns of public life are interwoven in mutual dependence. A purely private sphere of life, unrelated to society, does not exist for Snow. He is always concerned with the juxtaposition and interrelations of public interest and personal ambition, of the state of society and individual character.

As the title of the series, *Strangers and Brothers,* indicates, Snow sees human beings simultaneously as individuals facing each other as strangers and as fellow men whose lives are connected by multiple social relationships. Only when strangers become brothers will life side by side become life together; only then will mutual understanding work to the advantage of the individual and of society. But Snow showed precisely how difficult such understanding is to achieve, through the central concerns of his characters: the strivings for success, esteem, possessions, and power are seen as decisive factors in human thought and action.

Snow's novels have provided insights into the intellectual and social life of England. His characters are scientists, lawyers, politicians, administrators: this is a world Snow knew well from his own experiences. Although he used the methods of traditional realism, he did identify rather too closely with his first-person narrator. Everything is seen and described through the eyes of Eliot. And this means that those characters in the novel whose opinions and modes of behavior are different from Eliot's are seldom presented favorably. They are either regarded as incomprehensible and unintelligent or are simply let to appear in their less sympathetic traits. But the subjectivity of such a view is in itself excusable in novels written in the first person, especially since Snow was so successful in breathing life into the narrator.

Snow has not been the least concerned in finding new literary forms or techniques. In this traditionalism his work has resembled that of most of his contemporaries, including the younger generation. And Snow has expressed great enthusiasm in his criticism for the trend away from a preoccupation with aesthetics. Experimental literature—he includes mainly James Joyce (1882–1941), Virginia Woolf (1882–1941), Ezra Pound, T. S. Eliot, Franz Kafka, and Samuel Beckett—opened an abyss between author and reader, which he felt had to be bridged.

Henry Green has stood on the periphery of the contemporary novel. He has shown a certain affinity to E. M. Forster (1879–1970), Joyce, Woolf, Thomas Mann, and other great novelists of the beginning of the century. But Green's work is different from theirs in that he creates no past for his characters. Their life stories are seldom told, and then only in parts. Green's interest lies in external behavior.

Green's novels are hard to classify. A connection might be made with Anthony Powell, whose *The Acceptance World* pointed to a similar accommodation to existing conditions. Green has tried to show that loneliness can only be assuaged through mutual understanding and love. But against this stands man's inability to communicate with others. The poetic density, the immediacy, and the tight construction of Green's novels are indicated by their participial titles: *Living* (1929), *Party Going* (1939), *Caught* (1943), *Loving* (1945), *Concluding* (1948), *Doting* (1952). The titles *Back* (1946) and *Nothing* (1950), while not participles, are equally terse.

Living, rooted in Green's own experiences, portrayed the life of a factory worker in the metal industry of the midlands. He told the story naturalistically, without artifice. But he symbolically associated the workers with the pigeons they keep in roof coops—free but tied to their familiar surroundings. *Living* and *Party Going* were proletarian novels, primarily naturalistic; but in *Party Going* the symbolism was much more elaborate and detailed.

In *Caught* and *Loving* Green juxtaposed the different social classes in England during World War II. In *Back,* the story of the return home of a war veteran, Green created a poetic novel; for once there was nothing about social confrontation. *Concluding, Nothing,* and *Doting* described the effects of the welfare state on man and society, and thus were completely contemporary, but without the poetic content of *Back.* The easy conversational tone of these novels was that of a rather routine craftsman.

L. P. Hartley has combined symbolism with psychological awareness. In his *Eustace and Hilda* trilogy (1944–47) he described the tyrannical influence of an older sister on a younger brother. The central symbolism is introduced in the first book, *The Shrimp and the Anemone* (1944). Eustace observes how an anemone sucks a small shrimp dry. He cannot make up his mind on whose side he ought to be. When finally he and his sister try to free the shrimp, they kill the anemone in the process. In the relationship of the brother and sister, Eustace takes on the role of the shrimp, and Hilda the anemone. They are inseparable, first as children, then as young man and woman tied to each other in mutual destruction. Hartley developed a similar theme with even more insistent symbolism in *The Go-Between* (1953).

With *Facial Justice* (1960) Hartley came close to the philosophy of Huxley's *Brave New World* (1932) and Orwell's *1984.* The action of *Facial Justice* takes place in England after the end of an atomic world war. People gradually begin to forget the life in caves that they had been compelled to lead. Uniformity of behavior and even of physical appearance has become necessary for life together. The heroine is singled out because of the beauty of her face; she must be made to approximate more nearly the average. Hartley's future world clearly has points of resemblance to the present. In *The Brickfield* (1964) and *The Betrayal* (1966) Hartley returned to the psychological novel and once again revealed his powers of suggestion.

FRESH VOICES IN THE POSTWAR NOVEL

The years between 1950 and 1960 were a particularly fruitful period for contemporary British literature. Although the new movement in the theater, which began with Osborne's *Look Back in Anger,* was of great importance, the novel served even more to create the literary climate of the 1950s. Authors who first came to prominence after 1950 strove to describe and analyze contemporary problems. Only rarely did they look back to World War II and before.

A new readership emerged, corresponding to the changed preoccupations of the writers. Readers, guided by the best-seller lists and skilled book salesmanship, turned more and more into mere consumers of literature. They simply followed current literary fashion, while lacking the educational standards that older writers had expected of their audience.

The chief characteristic of the large group of new writers was their reluctance to create new literary forms. The experiments were with fresh themes and subjects, so as to relate the changes in traditional ideas; novelty of content seems to have been the only common criterion. Considerations of form were pushed into the background; writers used what was available, modified just a little to strengthen the relevance of their material. One cannot claim that such an attitude necessarily entailed a falling off in quality. But this lack of formal experimentation, which still characterizes British fiction, should it continue for too long, might eventually bring about the frequently heralded death of the novel. For the moment, however, the British novel continues to show astonishing faculties of life and regeneration.

Contemporary society, the structures it has developed, its people and institutions have become subjects of intense discussion. In the novel, in the drama, and in poetry, there have been constant attempts to define a person's own position in a system of social relationships that are, for the most part, felt to be imposed from above. The typically English interests in class distinctions, in upbringing and behavior, in manners and conventions, in social change and acquired rights, have been reflected in literature, especially in the novel. And there are few writers who feel they can manage without the inexhaustible variety of themes that spring from the many and changing relationships between the individual and society.

Angus Wilson (born 1913), whose literary criticism, especially on Dickens, has illuminated his work as a novelist, began his literary career relatively late, with two collections of short stories—*The Wrong Set*

(1949) and *Such Darling Dodos* (1950)—in which he described the world of the English middle class. There followed the novels *Hemlock and After* (1952) and *Anglo-Saxon Attitudes* (1956). Both were in the style of his short stories and contained extremely vivid characterizations. But as novels they lacked unity. *Hemlock and After* has about thirty characters. Some are of the middle class, and others belong to a parasitical lower class whose arrogance and depravity renders them victorious over the middle class.

Anglo-Saxon Attitudes, a broad survey of a society peopled by a multitude of characters, some very eccentric, was more unified than *Hemlock and After*—reminiscent of early Dickens in its breadth of action and its many different scenes. In *Anglo-Saxon Attitudes* Wilson took up a major theme of his short stories—the criticism of an incorrectly understood and socially fatal liberal intellectualism. He also described the combination of private and professional conflicts that can only be resolved through the painful path of self-discovery, by means of total and unsparing self-examination. An older man sees himself compelled, through inner motivation and outer circumstances or both, to revise the role in society that he has occupied so far or to exchange it for an entirely new one. The reversal of customary habits and the acquisition of new ideas, with all the personal and professional consequences they entail, can only occur with much difficulty and suffering, and necessitates giving up part of one's private life.

The title of Wilson's *The Middle Age of Mrs. Eliot* (1958) pinpoints the heroine's age. She sees herself confronted, through the sudden accidental death of her husband, with totally new situations. Depending only on herself, she must now try to find a way out of the chaos of her present. After a series of false starts she finally sees her way to making the necessary new beginning. The structure of *The Middle Age of Mrs. Eliot,* unlike *Anglo-Saxon Attitudes,* is uniform. The different scenes do not veer away from each other, but combine into a whole. While in *Anglo-Saxon Attitudes* the great number of characters has a tendency to threaten to splinter the action, in *The Middle Age of Mrs. Eliot* none of the secondary characters ever overshadow the focus on Meg Eliot.

In his fourth novel, *The Old Men at the Zoo* (1961), Wilson tried his hand at a novel of the future (as it was then), whose action takes place in 1970. The negative utopia of a fascist occupation of Britain lacked immediate political relevance. But as a parable the story had considerable meaning. A form of civilization that has not grown up organically and is not founded on true ideals will turn to cruelty and brutality when the test comes. This is not only true of the state; this is true of the individual also. *The Old Men at the Zoo* tells a very impressive story of the consequences that will follow if, in pursuit of a goal, all human emotions and all feelings are put aside. The portrait of the brutal person is depicted with great intensity. The setting has symbolic significance, unusual for Wilson. As England becomes the stage for various interests, the zoo becomes a place of intrigue, battle, and personal conflict. The changes in the zoo administration reflect the political and social situation.

Late Call (1964), Wilson's greatest achievement thus far, is a dense and compact novel, set in the present. The action takes place in one of the "new towns" of Great Britain and depicts life in such a "drawing-board environment." Sylvia Calvert has to come to terms with surroundings strange to her. Her alternatives are either submitting to an unaccustomed way of life—and this would be a self-imposed task for the ego—or going her own way and, when no longer young, creating a new life for herself. The search for an identity is the central theme of the novel. *Late Call* also touches on the barrier of communication between parents and their grown-up children.

In *No Laughing Matter* (1967), a thinly disguised family chronicle, Wilson aimed at a total vision of society over the past fifty years by chronicling the story of a London middle-class family. In this survey of time and society, he abandoned the traditional novel form and combined fiction with drama. The story contains short dramatic interludes, which parody the different types of contemporary drama. The frequent use of interior monologue also contributed to the dramatic quality of the novel.

Wilson's play, *The Mulberry Bush* (1956), was in the tradition of the drama of ideas (Ibsen and Shaw). As in his fiction, the relationship of the author to the events and the characters was marked by ironic distance.

Until *No Laughing Matter,* Wilson eschewed experimentation. One reason may have been his extraordinary gift for characterization. Certain types—old ladies, egotistical mothers, men broken by family and profession, artists and writers—occur again and again, but always in different constellations. Wilson has been criticized for overloading his novels with characters. But the central themes—the changes that take place in human beings as a consequence of the breaking up of traditional values, and the demand for a continuous review of oneself to identify self-deception and false pretensions—are never obscured by the multiplicity of characters. The tragedy of mankind, shown in the discrepancy between what is and what ought to be, has given the humanist Wilson constant material for reflection and for appropriate character portrayals.

Doris Lessing's (born 1919) first work, the novel *The Grass Is Singing,* was published in 1950. Since then her oeuvre has comprised poems, plays, short stories, and essays. But her novels have been her most important work.

Under the influence of her own experiences, Lessing, who grew up in Rhodesia, used her *Children of Violence* pentalogy (1952–69) to investigate racial conflict and the relationship between rulers and ruled. The tone of these novels was determined by violence, including the violence of war. In the fifth volume Lessing concentrated on a wider theme, which had only been touched on marginally in the pentalogy until then but which has stood in the very forefront of her short stories—the place of woman in a society in which the male is dominant. Lessing is convinced that prejudice against women, like the oppression of the black people of the world, can only be removed by left-wing political action. Martha Quest in *Children of Violence* equates both her restless political activity and her restless sexual activity with complete feminine independence.

With *The Golden Notebook* (1962) Lessing joined those contemporary novelists who have continued the tradition of the long psychological novel, even though with different objectives (others are J. B. Priestley and Angus Wilson). *The Golden Notebook* consists of four parts, four notebooks, in which a writer who is trying to overcome a temporary uncreative period jots down events in her life. She has made her name with a best seller, believes herself independent in every respect, yet cannot get rid of an ultimate sense of dependence in her subconscious. The conflict between her desire to lead her life according to her own rules independent of external influences and her love for a young American writer almost destroys her.

Only a small part of *The Golden Notebook* is told through traditional narrative. The greater part is taken up by the notebooks. In the first notebook the heroine tells about her life in Rhodesia, which had been the subject of her first successful novel; the second notebook deals with her experiences as a member of the Communist Party; the third describes her work on a novel; the fourth is a diarylike notebook, with chronological entries about her private life. A short section called "The Golden Notebook" can be interpreted as an attempt at synthesizing the scattered and unconnected fragments of the story. *The Golden Notebook* raises questions of form and content with great insistence. Is this a work of autobiography or a sociological study? Is it to be evaluated as a political tract or as a case history? Doris Lessing has, at any rate, transcended the purely personal. For her, writing is seeking after new possibilities of communication.

In a superficial way, P. H. Newby (born 1918) can be compared to Doris Lessing in that both have written "colonial novels." But Newby's novels *The Picnic at Sakkara* (1955) and *A Guest and His Going* (1959) could not compete with the comic and satirical colonial novels of Cary and Waugh. And Powell has certainly shown greater depth and immediacy as a comic writer with his satirical descriptions of society in large cities. Newby's Anglo-Egyptian novels did indeed bring him a solid readership, but the critics have been less than uniformly enthusiastic. Newby's more serious side, which he revealed in his first novel, *A Journey to the Interior*

(1946), showed that there is more to be looked for in his novels than entertainment alone. The theme of search, the compulsion of Newby's characters to examine themselves, and the changes that take place in the individual as a result of his new awareness—all this has linked Newby's work to the general concerns of the contemporary novel. Thus, the role of outsider, which critics have often given to Newby, would hardly seem accurate, since it it true mainly of his subject matter but not his themes.

ANGRY YOUNG NOVELISTS

The group of writers referred to since the 1950s as "angry young men" had its beginning with John Wain and Kingsley Amis. Although most contemporary British writers are difficult to classify, the angry young men have shown a strong bond of unity, a unity that includes playwrights as well as novelists. The much-publicized angry young men—necessary, durable, and refreshingly uncomplicated as their works have been—offered no advance for literature. The unity of their work, and thus its power of expression, existed at the cost of creative individuality. In limiting their focus to British society and institutions, they led the novel away from the context of universal human experience into a narrow provincialism. The apparently endless interest of the British in class distinctions and the manipulation of social systems has yielded a literature that is set almost exclusively in contemporary Britain. This literature is a criticism of society, but a society confined to the experiences of an expected readership.

One can argue about the suitability of the phrase "angry young men." But there can be no dispute about the wide influence exerted by this disillusioning view of our time and its people. Without claiming to give a value judgment, I use the phrase merely as a collective description of those authors whose central characters have represented the type of angry young man. This character type, very variously delineated, is the picaresque anti-hero of the modern novel. He is in no sense a malicious rebel. His protest is loud and strong, but is too easily dissipated in wildly uncontrolled comic situations (this is especially true of Amis). These angry young men did not succeed in making any theoretical diagnosis of the illnesses of contemporary society.

Joe Lunn in *Scenes from Provincial Life* (1950) by William Cooper (born 1910) was perhaps the first embodiment of this state of rebellion against conformity and the pressure of traditional bourgeois conventions. John Wain's *Hurry On Down* prepared the ground on which the novels of Amis, John Braine (born 1922), Keith Waterhouse (born 1929), Alan Sillitoe (born 1928), and David Storey (born 1932), and the plays of John

Osborne, Ann Jellicoe (born 1928), Shelagh Delaney (born 1939), and Peter Shaffer (born 1926) could flourish. One of the essential requirements was the unadorned use of everyday language.

Wain's anti-hero Charles Lumley considers himself a social outsider. He is politically indifferent, mistrusts all ideologies, feels himself cheated, sees in the established social order a natural enemy, and has no scruples about profiting, should opportunity occur, from the system he has rejected. Rejecting the apparent order of normal life, he does not take up the profession for which his university education has prepared him but follows various other pursuits, among others, window cleaner, chauffeur, and smuggler. His protest ironically represents both the absolute rejection of material possessions and the bourgeois pursuit of them. He tries to evade the difficult demands of an achievement-oriented society, and hopes thereby to establish new criteria. But Lumley, like all the angry young men, lacks the power and persistence to play this role convincingly to himself and others to the end; he is thus also unable to do without the comforts of economic security.

Jim Dixon in Kingsley Amis's *Lucky Jim* (1954) strives for the same ideal. But this ideal vision shatters against reality. These young men are by no means as revolutionary as they would like to be. Wain's Charles Lumley is confronted by an all-too-human dilemma when he falls in love with a girl who is neither accustomed nor prepared to renounce a certain standard of life. Through the intervention of friends Lumley obtains a high-paying job and is once again part of the society he struggled against and wanted to escape from. Thus, his original state of rebellion is changed into one of resignation.

The end of *Hurry On Down* seems as forced as that of *Lucky Jim.* Charles Lumley has not found what he hoped for in his search: liberation from the chains of convention and a solution to his own old problems of dissatisfaction and alienation. The isolation of the individual is emphasized by frequent metaphors of imprisonment. Man lives as prisoner of his social class. Ironically, Lumley, richer through his experiences, has at the end acquired a more sober evaluation of his position but has gained no genuine freedom. In him Wain created not only a new type of anti-hero but a totally new protagonist in the novel, a protagonist characterized by his difficulty in coming to terms with a world into which he obtained automatic entrance through his upbringing and education.

Living in the Present (1955), Wain's second novel, picaresque in structure like *Hurry On Down,* was an unsuccessful attempt to unmask nihilism and indifference as the fashionable diseases of our day. The action turns into melodrama; humorous situations turn into empty, often vulgar farce; the intended criticism dissipates itself in bewildering changes of scene and can be discerned only in faint allusions. Wain's third novel, *The Con-*

tenders (1958), was closer to *Hurry On Down*. Young people are brought up solely in terms of the unsparing competitive struggle they will be engaged in later in life. Their upbringing is not so much a real education as it is training in highly specialized skills that will enable them to be first in the race. Love played a secondary role in Wain's first three novels, but in *A Travelling Woman* (1959) he was almost exclusively concerned with sexual relationships.

From the point of view of literary technique, *Strike the Father Dead* (1962) has been Wain's most interesting novel to date. He described a father-son conflict, which is only resolved when the father frees himself from false ideas of honor. The subject matter was reminiscent of Samuel Butler's (1835–1902) *The Way of All Flesh* (1903). And indeed the literary generation of the 1950s, which rejected experiment, produced novels traditional enough to be compared to those of the eighteenth and nineteenth centuries. The turning away from London as the scene of the action and the preference for a provincial background, in writers like Braine, Sillitoe, Amis, and Wain, reminds one of the writers of the end of the nineteenth century and—with Amis and Wain—also of the eighteenth-century picaresque tradition. The story of *Strike the Father Dead* is told from a multiple first-person point of view. Each narrator has his own assumptions and acts according to his own limitations. In Wain's *The Smaller Sky* (1967) the feeling of oppression and the threats to the individual stand in the center of the grotesque comedy.

Wain's protagonists try to break away from a world which they believe does not understand them and which uniformly strangles every attempt at individuality. These attempted breakaways often end in compromise despite the semblance of freedom. Wain has described a world that is against man. He has rejected every kind of view that tries to make the life of the individual conform to a uniform pattern. Inner and outer freedom are necessary prerequisites for the search after truth. Wain has also rejected all theories about group behavior, as exemplified, for instance, in the collective description "angry young men." He turned his back on this label, which he saw as a gross simplification.

Jim Dixon in Kingsley Amis's *Lucky Jim* represented a further development of the picaresque anti-hero, with the stress on the humorous and satirical elements. But Jim Dixon is more than merely a comic character who runs into difficulties chiefly through his own fault and who finally, by rare good fortune, finds happiness in love and work. Dixon is not at all industrious: he engages himself only in his own concerns, and then only reluctantly. His attitude is always that of passive waiting. The world around Dixon is unreal, dishonest, built on false premises, destined in advance to be a disappointment. And Dixon, who finds himself confronting this world, suffers from the same symptoms. He is himself a cheat and an opportunist, who makes unjustified claims and tries to impress others with qualities of his own invention. He shows up society's need of approval by endeavouring to use it for his own purposes. But he is well aware that he himself is not so very different. He is as indignant about the arrogance of the upper class as he is about his own deficiencies. In private life, too, he has to admit that his position rests solely on false pretenses.

Jim Dixon's self-analysis is as sharp as his judgment on his fellow players in this many-sided comedy: his attitude is critical, ironic, unsentimental, and with a sure instinct for identifying phoniness. Amis wanted to depict the brittleness of the cultural and social façade in the English welfare state and the meaninglessness of the contemporary culture industry. He turned his back on the fatal longing for a "Merry Old England," which belongs inexorably to the past.

Amis's *That Uncertain Feeling* (1955) and *I Like It Here* (1958) fell below the standard of *Lucky Jim* and lacked its unity. Nevertheless they also revealed his talent for comic characterization. They did suffer, however, from a repetition of certain basic scenes to keep the comedy going. In the end the characters turn into caricatures, and the whole thing culminates in clowning and tomfoolery.

Amis's *Take a Girl Like You* (1960) lacked the pronounced comic element of its predecessors. The struggle of the heroine for her virtue bears a resemblance to Restoration comedies, but only superficially. There are no illusions in *Take a Girl Like You*. Sex is a household appliance. Therefore, the characters' responses to things are rather simple: the constant problem is how best to amuse oneself without making firm commitments. For Amis, Jenny and Patrick are typical representatives of a society that bears all the marks of uniformity of the welfare state, a society that levels differences and forces people to conform. In *I Want It Now* (1968) Amis was once again in conflict with contemporary society. There was his usual emphasis on witty and satirical, often even grotesque elements. *I Want It Now* was a successful combination of intelligent entertainment and sharp satire.

As critic, Amis prefers the pose of an antiintellectual. Such was his pose when he declared his preference for science fiction and the James Bond books of Ian Fleming (1908–1964). Amis has rejected the usual high-brow attitude of superiority toward popular culture.

The figure of angry anti-hero has also appeared in the work of Thomas Hinde (born 1926). In the picaresque adventures in *Happy as Larry* (1957), the title character has experiences similar to those of his forerunners in the novels of Amis and Wain.

John Braine can also be grouped with the angry young men in that he has taken the present for his subject matter and has pursued an analysis of social and cultural problems of the welfare state. But Braine's novels have been less episodic and much less humorous than have Amis's. Braine places his characters in the very midst of the bustle of contemporary life. The principal theme of his first novel, *Room at the Top* (1957), was the social rise of Joe Lampton, a young man of the working class, and the changes in his personality that accompany the rise. In *Life at the Top* (1962) Braine continued the story of *Room at the Top*.

Unremovable class distinctions are responsible for Joe Lampton's situation. The motive of his actions is not so much anger as envy, with a liberal sprinkling of opportunism. Braine introduced an age-old theme, but he dressed it in modern clothes: a young man from the provinces seeks his fortune in the town and undergoes changes that are detrimental to the growth of his personality. The story is told entirely from the hero's point of view and thus gives us his view of the world and his prejudices. Lampton's concept of "zombie" plays an important part. Zombies are people with a one-sided view of life, out of touch with their surroundings and lacking humanity—virtual corpses. Joe Lampton's struggle against zombie-ism ends tragically. Once he has obtained entry into society at the top, he himself turns into just such a figure of convention, lacking all individuality. Success has turned him into a zombie.

Some critics have included *Room at the Top* among works of leftist social criticism. But Braine was primarily concerned with personal problems. The interaction between characters and events is very complex. Joe Lampton is the embodiment of a man with practically no scruples, striving for recognition and success. The anti-hero of Braine's *The Vodi* (1959), on the other hand, has already given up and made the best of things. Only with the break of a close human tie does a new strength of will awaken in him.

In *The Jealous God* (1964) Braine's central theme was the intellectual limitations and narrowness of small-town conventions. But once again he was primarily interested in the development of his chief character's personality. In *The Crying Game* (1968) there was clearly a social and political context. But here, too, Braine did not analyze contemporary problems so much as he searched for human individuality. Thus, Braine's work must be seen as somewhat separate from the social criticism of the angry young men.

The term "angry young men" when applied to contemporary British novels often refers only to purely external manifestations, to the behavior of some of their characters. What has stood in the way of a sober, unemotional, and balanced interpretation of the works of these novelists is the tendency to equate the authors with their characters in all particulars. Unquestionably, a great deal of autobiographical material has found its way into the work of these novelists. But it would be wise not to make this the sole basis for one's judgment.

ANGRY YOUNG DRAMATISTS

The attitude of the angry young man led to a dangerous narrowing, if not isolation, of the English novel. In the theater the situation was different. The developments initiated by John Osborne, with goals similar to those of the novelists, turned into a movement whose intention was at last to break through the long-criticized monotony of the British drama. The English theater was, until the mid-1950s, dominated by the West End, which offered mainly light entertainments. Only occasionally did one find attempts at introducing new approaches and ideas. The Theatre Workshop, founded by Joan Littlewood in 1945, was one such endeavor.

The real starting point for the new English drama was the founding of the English Stage Company at the Royal Court Theatre, on Sloane Square, not far from the taste-shaping West End. In 1956 George Devine, together with Ronald Duncan and Lord Harewood, took over the management of the theater. Devine was convinced that the English drama was stagnating for lack of suitable encouragement to young authors. He felt this was due to a complete absence of experimental theaters willing to include controversial plays in their repertory. He intended the Royal Court in part to give established novelists and poets the opportunity to try their hand at writing for the stage. But he was primarily interested in encouraging the rising generation. Devine's hopes were that many authors would welcome this opportunity. But he was disappointed by the initially small response he received.

Among the few manuscripts sent in during the first season was *Look Back in Anger* by John Osborne. Until then Osborne had received rejections for his play because it was believed to be totally contrary to the taste of the public. But the time was ripe for a play like *Look Back in Anger*. The internal politics of Great Britain in 1956, in addition to the international situation, had created a climate of protest, especially among the young.

Because of *Look Back in Anger* and the plays on related themes that followed, the public and the critics alike recognized that a new school of playwrights had appeared, concerned with a common thesis. But all these writers had in common was an attitude of protest against traditional ties, class distinctions, national interests, the established church, trade unions, family, marriage, and private property. The great variety of opinions expressed by these writers was completely overlooked. People associated *Look Back in Anger* with the novels of Amis and Wain and felt that the term "angry young man" described Osborne as well. But this label was applied far too freely and uncritically, as it had been to the novel.

Look Back in Anger gave expression to the accumulated discontent of a whole generation and to the frustrations of an overlooked minority at outmoded social structures and political events. But the inner cohesion of *Look Back in Anger* distinguished it from most other plays of its period. This cohesion was achieved mainly through the principal character, Jimmy Porter, who was very different from what in the early 1950s was thought of as a hero of a play.

The unexpected originality of *Look Back in Anger* lay in both its subject matter and its language. The play departed from the usual drawing-room comedy, from the escapist world of a theater detached from everyday problems. The setting of *Look Back in Anger* in itself was sufficient indication of the freshness of the play: a one-room attic flat in a town in the midlands, poorly furnished, with gas burner, skylight, slanted walls, and an old chest. In the middle of all this is Jimmy Porter reading the Sunday paper; his wife, Alison, is at an ironing board with one of Jimmy's old shirts. For many, it was a familiar sight. For some, the setting elicited uneasy feelings.

In form, *Look Back in Anger* was a thoroughly conventional three-act play, employing the traditional methods of dramatic realism. It is essentially a monologue of the protagonist, interrupted only briefly by the other characters. These others barely have existences of their own; they exist only in their different relations to Jimmy Porter. Concepts like gentleman, Public School, and Oxford and Cambridge are irrelevant to Jimmy Porter, whose declared intention is to shock. And he seizes on everything that gives him an occasion to do so. Only when he succeeds in hitting out against his wife Alison, the hated image of bourgeois life, does he feel better.

Osborne has shown in a variety of ways that he is interested in a theater of feeling. The accusation of sentimentality has disturbed him little. But if the appeal to the feelings is put too much in the forefront, then the thinking and the ordering of thoughts and arguments can become defective, and the social criticism can lose its force. What remains is simply unordered emotions. And this is what we occasionally see in *Look Back in Anger*. Jimmy Porter's attitude to the problems raised, personal as well as public, gave rise to the many misunderstandings of the nature of this new anti-hero in British drama. It is important to see that the frustrations of Jimmy Porter arise ultimately from his inability to meet the demands made by life.

Look Back in Anger is not a propaganda play, and Jimmy is more than simply a mouthpiece of protest. To regard the play so narrowly would be to underestimate it. For many in the audience, Jimmy seems to be a rebel. But Osborne has created a character who cannot adapt to the current situation but who has the heightened sensibility to recognize its false values. He is, however, unable to find anyone with whom to share his sense of solitariness and helplessness. Jimmy's is the dilemma of the intelligent man who does not see himself as passive, yet for whose abilities the world has no use. Jimmy Porter represents his generation insofar as he gives loud and strong expression to his helpless anger at a hostile world. Less representative are his self-pity, his personalization of problems, and his inability to work out alternatives. Jimmy voices not really a political creed but the anxiety of modern man. In this the play transcended the specific coloration of the 1950s; *Look Back in Anger* provides questions but no answers.

Osborne's second play, *The Entertainer* (1957), was also produced by the Royal Court and also was centered around one character. Like Jimmy Porter, Archie Rice realizes he is a failure, even though he does not complain so sharply or bitterly. In *The Entertainer,* however, Osborne turned away from the strictly realistic and naturalistic tradition and tried his hand at experimenting. The story of the out-of-work music-hall entertainer Archie Rice is told as if it were itself a series of stage turns, with songs and music-hall interludes. *The Entertainer* is a mixture of music-hall entertainment and naturalistic drawing-room drama. At one moment Archie is a performer who entertains an imaginary public with tired jokes and coarse allusions. The next moment he is at home in his small house with his family, in the midst of the daily quarrels that never cease. Along side his despairing efforts to make his comeback on the stage are the unpleasant scenes in the circle of his family. Archie belongs to a lost generation. He tries to grapple with an age that has made the music hall, and therefore also his own way of life, obsolete.

Some critics have asserted that *The Entertainer* bore certain resemblances to the style of Brecht, because of the play's structure and the insertion of songs. But one should not overlook the inspiration of the specifically British institution of the music hall. The music hall works both as a technical device and as a symbol of the present, which struggles desperately against the changing times and tries to revive traditions that have long lost their validity. The songs are an important contribution; some of them have clear undertones of social criticism. The function of literature as document of the times and as a criticism of culture and society was illustrated anew in this play; there were allusions to the Suez crisis, to England's threadbare empire, and to the bitterness of the younger generation.

The World of Paul Slickey (1959), "A Comedy of Manners with Music," has been Osborne's farthest-reaching attempt to date to free himself from the realism of *Look Back in Anger*. It was primarily a social satire. In the "historical" play *Luther* (1961) Osborne did not attempt to re-create an historical character faithfully; instead, he concentrated on the psychology of a reformer. In twelve separate scenes he showed Luther's development from his beginnings as a novice undergoing a crisis of existence and identity, filled with doubt and despair as to the best and most direct way to God, to his development into a man of strength and confidence, sure enough of himself to battle with the authorities of the Catholic church—during which battle he acquires still more strength and confidence.

Luther was a more powerful historical drama than Osborne's earlier *A Subject of Scandal and Concern* (1960) and more like Brecht's *Leben des Galilei*. But once again, one must think carefully before making comparisons with Brecht. Osborne made very little attempt to remain true to historical fact. And he showed no interest in social history either. The reason for the revolt of Luther and of Holyoake in *A Subject of Scandal and Concern* is purely personal. The main source of the conflict is the struggle of the individual—modern man—against his own anxieties and fears.

The isolation of the individual has been the subject of other British historical plays. In Robert Bolt's (born 1924) *A Man for All Seasons* (1961) as well, the protagonist, Sir Thomas More, a man of high integrity, loses touch with a corrupt society and finds he no longer has anything in common with it. These historical protagonists resemble Jimmy Porter in a number of ways; thus the popularity of these plays with a public that identified with Jimmy. Osborne did not give up his critical attitude toward society, even when he made use of historical subjects. The symbolic content always refers to the present. Unlike the social drama of the 1930s, the development of the hero does not depend primarily on historical facts or environmental influences. Psychological and physiological determinants are the sources of his actions and omissions. The hero's preferred means of communication—which reinforces our sense of his isolation—is monologue rather than dialogue.

A Patriot for Me (1966) was a play on two levels. In the specific case of the young Austrian officer Redl, Osborne portrayed the ineradicable fear of being recognized as a homosexual in a society which is prepared to accept such deviation silently but which relentlessly pursues any individual whose homosexuality becomes public. The play simultaneously depicted the disintegration of a supposedly firm state system and the increasing breakdown of a social structure built solely on the privileges of the upper class.

Osborne's most powerful statement so far on the subject of isolation was in *Inadmissible Evidence* (1965). The stage directions place the play in a world half way between fantasy and reality. Osborne wanted to leave the audience uncertain as to whether the happenings on the stage are about real or dream figures and events. As a result, the play constantly moves between two levels, which, however, merge into each other. With *Inadmissible Evidence* Osborne brought the technique of the "one-man play" to perfection. The protagonist's monologues are more impressive than anything Osborne has written since. For the first time, too, he succeeded in depicting the isolation of the individual through constant crises. As before, the protagonist is given no convincing opposite number; the audience sees everything from the point of view of one character. But in this play it is no disadvantage that his views carry all the weight. Since he is the sole representative of the play, even on the physical plane, his perspective is the only decisive one. He has no need of opposite numbers, since the conflict arises purely out of his own personality.

Osborne's most recent play, *West of Suez* (1971), suffered from an overabundance of the same social criticism that had been treated in detail in his previous plays. It did not add a new point of view, nor did it round out any of the previous statements.

Osborne's lively, taut language, his openness, and his ability to give full effect to scenic detail have shown his mastery of his art. His plays have shocked, it is true; but they have also renewed the long-lost contact between the stage and the public.

Osborne's colleagues in the theater of the "angry generation" have included Shelagh Delaney, Ann Jellicoe, and Peter Shaffer. Delaney, who said of herself that she, unlike the brigade of angry young men, knows exactly where her anger is directed, wrote her very considerable first play at the age of eighteen. *A Taste of Honey* (1958) tackled three basic problems: love between people of different races, homosexuality, and prostitution. The mother-daughter conflict that leads to the onset of revolt in *A Taste of Honey* was also the starting point of Delaney's *The Lion in Love* (1960). This play did not, however, repeat the success of *A Taste of Honey*.

Ann Jellicoe's *The Sport of My Mad Mother* (1957) gave every impression of being a stage improvisation, which was exactly what the author intended. There is no concrete situation; emotions take the place of real relationships. A group of neglected youngsters comes under the influence of a teacher who takes over the function of mother. Ecstatic relationships give way to confrontations that culminate in a suicide. *The Knack* (1961) was about the art of seducing girls. Of the three male characters, one possesses this knack to perfection, the second wants to acquire it, and the third feels it is unimportant. Both of these plays showed a masterly use of language and gave proof of Jellicoe's keen ear and feeling for the world of the adolescent. In *Shelley* (1965), a documentary play, Jellicoe turned to a form much less suited to her talents.

Peter Shaffer, who has combined richness of invention with technical skill, criticized the hypocrisy of society and the alienation it causes in *Five Finger Exercise* (1958). *The Royal Hunt of the Sun* (1964) was an historical drama about the conquest of Peru by the Spaniards. When the two civilizations confront each other, the higher and older succumbs. The spectacular visual aspects of the production overshadowed the intellectual content of the play. *The Private Ear and the Public Eye* (1962), two one-act plays, and *Black Comedy* (1965), a play about mistaken identity, gave further evidence of Shaffer's talent.

THE DRAMA: REFORMERS AND ABSURDISTS

It would be a mistake to credit the renewal of the theater in the 1950s solely to Osborne and the angry generation. Similar claims can be made for Arnold Wesker (born 1932) and Harold Pinter (born 1930).

Arnold Wesker is a far more committed writer than Osborne. And in Wesker the autobiographical element is even stronger. Wesker wants to stir up the working class, to rouse it from its cultural lethargy, and to awaken in it an active interest. He looks on art and literature as ways of coming to awareness, of speaking truthfully about the human situation to those who live in the dark. For Wesker, the intellectual's task is to uncover man's psychic situation, and the task of the artist is to reveal man's human predicament.

Wesker has used his plays to present his socialist convictions again and again to the public. For Wesker, the arts and the work of artists are the only means of freeing the working class from its indifference and hostility to culture, and of leading it to a socialism that looks beyond wages and welfare states. But Wesker has tempered his socialism with "humanity," a term that includes reason, understanding, self-confidence, and firmness. He does not want to see the theater in the service of the class struggle; he does not want a Marxist theater. The principal message of his work so far has been that man must always try to play a positive role in life and must take care not to lead an unthinking, animallike existence.

The indolence and indifference of the masses and the negative effects of the welfare state have been the central subjects of Wesker's plays. Wesker has recognized the human predicament and has tried to give voice to existing problems and to seek solutions. What in Osborne is wild accusation is in Wesker grounded in facts, even though the characters may discuss topics with all the passion they can command.

Although Wesker's literary work and life are closely linked, this does not mean that his plays have been merely autobiographical reports in dramatic form. In his Chicken Soup trilogy—which consists of *Chicken Soup with Barley* (1959), *Roots* (1959), and *I'm Talking about Jerusalem* (1960) —despite its autobiographical basis, he considered universal questions: We break up human relationships; what possibilities are there of preventing this? And, more generally, what constitutes a human relationship?

Chicken Soup with Barley covers twenty years in the life of the Jewish family Kahn and their communist friends. The action begins as Mosley's Black Shirts try to march through London's East End and the workers who live there come to bar their path. Everything that happens—on the personal, the social, and even the international level—is shown in relation to this one family and their friends. Two themes—the gradual disintegration of the family, shown symbolically by the failing health of the father; and the parallels in the social and political sphere, the political disillusionment—are closely connected. But the personal events are always primary. Wesker's strong commitment is somewhat neutralized by the symbolic framework of the last scene. Concern for one's neighbor is not best expressed in large spheres of action but in the small acts, trivial in themselves, of practical neighborly love. Wesker's message was one of a practical socialism, not of slogans and manifestos.

Roots covers a considerably shorter time span than *Chicken Soup with Barley*—about three weeks in the life of Beatie Bryant, a girl from Norfolk working as a waitress in London, whom Ronnie Kahn wants to marry. Her parents are farm laborers. Ronnie tries to rouse Beatie out of the inertia engendered by her surroundings. He struggles against her indifference and tries, in the spirit of his mother, to introduce her to socialist ideals. He wants to convince her of the superficiality and cheapness of the contemporary entertainment industry and to train her eye for real art and introduce her to classical music and good books. He wants to show her how to discover her own ideas so that she can break away from the indifference of her class.

Roots was the most impressive realization so far of Wesker's central theme. Only social relations—in the widest sense—can lead to salvation. We must build bridges by talking to each other, by discussing our problems, by speaking the same language. Ronnie is Wesker's mouthpiece, and Beatie, as pupil-listener, represents the audience.

In *I'm Talking about Jerusalem* Wesker returned to events related in *Chicken Soup with Barley*. (In *Roots* the Kahn family as a whole does not appear.) *I'm Talking about Jerusalem* is directly connected to a scene in the second act of *Chicken Soup with Barley,* in which Ada and Dave decide to leave the city and industrial society behind and to establish an ideal way of life on the land—a life of nature and manual skills, the opposite of industrial mass production. For thirteen years Dave tries to establish himself in the new environment, but he fails because of his surroundings and because of personal problems. The allegorical element, strongest in this final play, made it less theatrically effective than the other two.

The central subject of the trilogy is Ronnie's growing doubts about his political ideals and about himself. As a child he experienced militant communism. At the end of *Chicken Soup with Barley* he remains without illusions and without a clear objective. *I'm Talking about Jerusalem* shows the effect of Dave's failed experiment on Ronnie.

Wesker's Chicken Soup trilogy by and large belonged to the naturalistic theater, even though he became increasingly unrealistic from one play to the next. His naturalism was shown in the language and in the setting as a whole. The dialogue is for the most part colloquial, reflecting Wesker's very accurate ear for social and regional dialects. Language stands for class, reflects education or the lack of it, and distinguishes one character from another more profoundly than any gesture or action. A further aspect of the trilogy's naturalism is the inclusion of historical events. The personal life of the Kahns is lived against the authentic background of current events, and thus the fictional elements merge with the factual. Yet naturalism does give way to allegory at the end of *Roots*. And *I'm Talking about Jerusalem* is altogether allegorical. Furthermore, Wesker consciously violated the unities of time and place both within the three plays and in progressing from one play to the next.

The Kitchen (1960) exists on two levels: the real and the allegorical. Wesker's cooks and kitchen aides are of various nationalities. The routine in the kitchen confronts them with the necessity of working together. This is clearly meant to reflect the wider context of the world outside. Wesker makes the hotel kitchen symbolize modern life, and even has one character make the explicit comparison.

Chips with Everything (1962) is set in a Royal Air Force training camp. As in *The Kitchen,* the events and the people are intended to be a microcosm of the contemporary social and political system in Great Britain. On one side are the men; on the other, the officers. Within both sections there is a further hierarchical structure built on rank and service. The play openly criticized the ruling class, be it in the army or in all of Britain. *Chips with Everything* also was at a remove from naturalism. The reduction of scenery corresponded to a reduction in dialogue. And the play was somewhat reminiscent of Osborne's *The Entertainer* in its use of short scenes and of songs. One general weakness of *Chips with Everything* was its characters, who are never more than types. And the attempt to break away from naturalism, together with the stereotyped characters, resulted in an overstylization.

In *Their Very Own and Golden City* (1966) Wesker took up important points raised in *Chips with Everything,* but from a different angle: the relationship of the outsider to established society, and the attempts of society to bring him back again into its fold. An architect has a dream wish to build towns that will be administered by all the inhabitants on a communal level—a symbol of many similar desires in Britain after the war. The plans are favorably received, the idealism that brought them into being is acknowledged, but everything remains as before. The town-planning experiment in cooperative socialism is a failure. The architect is faced with the need to compromise. To preserve at least some remnants of his ideals, he accepts the help offered by the Conservative minister of housing, in order to be able to build the town of his dreams.

The action of *Their Very Own and Golden City* served Wesker as excuse to criticize the trade unions. They fail just at the moment when they could have helped to cooperate in a large project intended to further their own cause. In their shortsightedness they fail to recognize the meaning of true socialism. But Wesker did not discuss these questions with the same persistence as in his earlier plays; the didactic element was less pronounced.

In its structure, *Their Very Own and Golden City* is Wesker's most interesting play to date, because of its use of flashforwards (in contrast to the more familiar flashback). The continuity of scenes at the end of the second act reminds one of the technique of running film together. Various episodes follow one another in quick succession, and this gives the impression of continuous time, of time passing before the eyes of the spectator without break or interruption. Unity of time and place is unimportant here. The action spans about sixty-five years and takes place in various locales. The division of time into regular intervals corresponding to the different scenes follows no regular pattern. The action taking place in the present occupies only a few hours of one day; the future events transpire over days, weeks, months, years.

In *The Four Seasons* (1965) Wesker broke radically with his past subject matter and also continued his movement away from naturalism. In his earlier plays his chief interest lay in the portrayal of character against an accurately defined social background. In *The Four Seasons* all this is changed. What remains is the description of a purely personal relationship. *The Four Seasons* is completely apolitical, and without a real plot. It is a very simply constructed story about the personal relationship of two people, told to the rhythm of the four seasons. The setting is itself a sign of the writer's poetic expressionism. The house changes in front of the eyes of the spectators as the seasons change. Wesker is well aware of the problems inherent in his attempts to move away from naturalistic language and to free his characters from the world that produced them. His development as playwright has led him away from naturalism to a form closer to a narrative-theater technique.

Uncertainty, meaninglessness, the lack of any objective in life—these have been the distinguishing marks of the theater of the absurd and of Harold Pinter. Any clear and unambiguous statement is immediately followed by a corresponding opposite statement; things and the appearances of things are never what they seem. This technique leads to lack of clarity, to mysteriousness, and finally to pessimism.

Pinter's first play, *The Room* (1957), was performed at the University of Bristol. His first play to receive a professional production was *The Birthday Party* (1958). These two plays, together with *The Dumb Waiter*

(1957) and *A Slight Ache* (1959), constitute Pinter's early phase. The action of *The Birthday Party* takes place in a setting whose seclusion offers the characters refuge and protection, even though perhaps only for a short time. Elements of the uncertain and the incalculable are brought from the outside into this place of seeming security. Two mysterious men turn up in a shabby little boarding house. Stanley lives there, the only guest, and it looks as if the men have come to fetch him away. Perhaps they are hired murderers. In the second act they overwhelm Stanley with contradictory accusations in a sort of cross-examination. The meaning of their accusations remains completely unclear, both to Stanley and to the audience. On the occasion of Stanley's birthday there is a small celebration. He and the others play a game of blindman's buff. The third act gives us what seems to be the first clear information: Stanley has suffered a nervous breakdown; the two mysterious strangers promise to look after him. But once more the meaning of the words is ambiguous. Stanley finally comes down to breakfast. Without a word the two men lead him out to the waiting car.

The Birthday Party was by no means Pinter's finest play, but it established clearly some of his recurrent techniques and attitudes. His characters are in a state of bewilderment and insecurity. They are in no position to give an account of what is happening. The dialogue seems confused, aimless, spoken in a vacuum. There is no communication between the speakers; their speech and actions are unmotivated, lacking order and sense. Pinter's characters are on the fringe of existence. The lack of cohesion in his plays is a reflection of a world that has lost faith, a world in which fright and fear are dominant, a world in which the search for truth, which alone could give support to the individual, leads nowhere. Pinter has often pointed to the congruence of fright, fear, and absurdity. Feelings of fear are dissolved by threats from outside, by anonymous powers. The outside world, which is cold and hostile, does not belong to the protected private sphere symbolized by the enclosed room.

The Caretaker (1960), like Pinter's later one-act play *Silence* (1969), was reminiscent of Samuel Beckett. But whereas the tramps in Beckett's *En attendant Godot* are types, Pinter's characters have more individual traits. *The Caretaker* combines the comic and tragic, but it is not the farce it is often said to be. The life of Aston, who picks up the tramp Davies from the street and takes him "home," is as aimless as the tramp's own life. Aston's "home" is a room filled with old lumber, standing and lying about in wild disorder. Thus, it is no symbol of apparent security (as in Pinter's earlier plays) but part of the disorder that lies over everything, including Aston's own aimless life.

Pinter has turned more and more to the short play—including some written for radio and television. Among these plays are *A Night Out* (1960), *The Dwarfs* (1960), *The Collection* (1961), *The Lover* (1963),

The Tea Party (1965), *The Basement* (1967), and *Landscape* (1969). He has also written a number of screenplays, among them that of the film version of L. P. Hartley's novel *The Go-Between*.

The full-length *The Homecoming* (1965) again raised the question of human identity, a theme Pinter had dealt with in *The Caretaker*. This theme has been treated in contemporary literature in many variations. The characters in *The Homecoming* live between reality and fantasy but do not distinguish between the two. Wish fulfillment and reality merge. The audience learns little about the background of their behavior. Max, a former butcher, surly and fault-finding, lives with his two sons, Lenny and Joey, and his brother Sam in an old house in north London. Teddy, the eldest son, who has been a professor of philosophy in an American university for several years, comes on a visit with his wife Ruth, whose existence the family is ignorant of. They arrive late at night, and only Lenny observes their arrival. Max is indignant that Ruth has slept there without his knowledge, and accuses Teddy of having brought a whore into his house. Without further explanation, there follows a reconciliation, and Ruth goes to bed with Joey, the youngest brother. In the meantime Teddy packs his bags to return to America. At the end everyone agrees that Ruth should be established as a prostitute in Soho, under Lenny's protection.

The Homecoming lends itself to many interpretations. Perhaps Ruth is not Teddy's wife at all; perhaps he is glad to be able to free himself of a nymphomaniac. On the other hand, the entire action may just be a play improvised by the members of the family. The basic absurdity of what transpires is intended to show the impossibility of recognizing motives: absolute truth does not exist.

The surface atmosphere of Pinter's *Old Times* (1971), a three-character play, is that of a cozy conversation, in which the characters exchange partly melancholy, partly joyful memories. But what actually takes place on stage is a contest of two of the characters over the third. This situation is reminiscent of the power struggle waged with acerbity within the family in *The Homecoming*. In both plays characters are concerned with upholding or regaining positions they feel are of vital importance. In *Old Times,* however, the struggle between the rivals does not take place in the open, but is hidden behind words and double meanings.

In *Old Times* Pinter continued the themes and techniques of his preceding plays. Particularly close to it were the one-act plays *Landscape* and *Silence*. In these plays, too, the focus is on a question about the past, which proves to be as uncertain as the memories that try to keep it alive. The problem of identity cannot be solved, since man is not a closed unit, but a combination of various traits that render a clearcut characterization impossible. The ambiguity is shown exclusively through language, which takes the place of overt action. The mastery with which Pinter handles language has endowed his plays again and again with a special fascination.

The situations described by Pinter, however absurd, are rooted in ordinary, everyday life. The language used by his characters is appropriate to their background. Pinter's subtle command of regional and social dialects makes it possible for him to use nuance of speech as a part of his characterization. Thus, vulgarity of expression is as significant as any illogical or incorrect use of words. Pinter, who has acknowledged his indebtedness to Beckett and Kafka, is an uncompromising naturalist in language, however unnaturalistic other aspects of his plays may be.

The plays of N. F. Simpson (born 1919) have shown numerous parallels to the theater of the absurd. *A Resounding Tinkle* (1956) and *One Way Pendulum* (1959) depicted an upside-down world: the ordinary becomes something special, the exceptional becomes normal. For Simpson, as for Pinter, the use of language is basic to his dramatic technique. James Saunders (born 1925) started his career with short plays in the style of Ionesco. But he has since tried to find new openings for the theater of the absurd, by combining it with the drama of ideas.

John Arden (born 1930), who also belongs to this group of new dramatists, began writing one-act plays in the late 1950s. His plays for the stage and for television cannot be easily categorized. His characters often represent group interests; confrontations are determined by their standing in the social hierarchy. In *Live Like Pigs* (1958) a group of gypsies confronts respectable citizens and the officials of their bureaucracy. The four soldiers in *Serjeant Musgrave's Dance* (1959) argue against war. They form themselves into a group and oppose the representatives of authority: mayor, police, church. In *The Workhouse Donkey* (1963) there are characters representing different interest groups. But the individuality of these characters does come through when they begin to act as spokesmen for their group.

Arden is considered the most important of the new historical dramatists —better than Robert Bolt and John Osborne. Neither Bolt nor Osborne has the power of historical imagination Arden has shown in his historical plays, although Bolt comes nearer. Arden's feeling for his chosen period is strong, even when there are anachronisms in the setting. And Arden is a regionalist. He set *Live Like Pigs* and *The Workhouse Donkey* in middle-sized industrial towns in the north of England. *Serjeant Musgrave's Dance* was also set in the north of England, around eighty years ago. The historical plays *Left-Handed Liberty* (1965) and *Armstrong's Last Goodnight* (1965) dealt respectively with the period of King John and with the early sixteenth century.

The Happy Haven (1960) differed in technique from Arden's other plays. Masks, open stage, and a chorus were all used in this cynical picture of life in a home for the aged. In its attempts to present a thesis, the play lacked effectiveness. But it was an interesting experiment. Arden is not one of those contemporary writers who address themselves to the world at large. And his plays do not force one to take a position—although this is something that is expected today.

Brendan Behan (1923–1964) left behind at his early death three considerable achievements: two plays, *The Quare Fellow* (1956) and *The Hostage* (1958); and the autobiography *Borstal Boy* (1958). The two plays were halfway between the Irish theatrical tradition and the new British drama. The connection between the writer and his writings was an especially close one for Behan, and the legends about his personal life have not always helped toward an objective judgment of his literary achievements. Behan's special achievement lay in his language. It is the colloquial speech of Dubliners: unpolished, rough, strong. The language of *Borstal Boy* was even stronger—full of obscenities and underworld slang.

The plays of Bernard Kops (born 1926) and Henry Livings (born 1929) have been like Wesker's plays. Kops's *The Hamlet of Stepney Green* (1956) is set in the working-class environment of a Jewish family. Kops's strength has been his ability to depict the lives of simple people. Livings's *Nil Carborundum* (1962) was directed against the meaninglessness of the old-fashioned military drill; but the play lacked the wider implications of Wesker's *Chips with Everything*.

The actor Peter Ustinov (born 1921) has written a number of commercially successful plays. His comedies have been intelligent and amusing. Ustinov's main interest is characterization; the plays develop through the characters. Ustinov writes for the present moment, and his success with the public can be attributed to his topicality. But it has made the critics regard him, if not exactly as a hack, then at any rate as a writer for his own day only.

In *The Love of Four Colonels* (1951), Ustinov's first international success, an Englishman, an American, a Frenchman, and a Russian, representing the allied military occupation, try their luck at love. *Romanoff and Juliet* (1957) was a comedy that, in paraphrase of Shakespeare, presented the love of the Russian naval officer Romanoff and the American college girl Juliet; this subject gave Ustinov the opportunity to poke gentle fun at the cold war. In *Photo Finish* (1962) an eighty-year-old man looks back at the various stages of his life and sees himself face to face with his younger selves. *The Life in My Hands* (1963) was a didactic contribution to the struggle for the abolition of the death penalty. And *Halfway Up the Tree* (1968) was a popular comedy. Ustinov's characters are eccentric, obstinate, and convinced of their own importance. They are for the most part aging or elderly, and this gives rise both to the inevitable conflict between generations and to a reassessment of the past.

John Whiting (1915–1963) received recognition only after his death.

But to call him the precursor of the new English dramatists, as some have, is to overestimate his role. His chief works were *A Penny for a Song* (1951), *Marching Song* (1954), and *The Gates of Summer* (1956). Whiting wrote his last play, *The Devils* (1961), at the request of the Royal Shakespeare Company, after a long interval during which he had retired from writing for the theater. *The Devils* was an adaptation of Aldous Huxley's novel *The Devils of Loudun* (1952). In his depiction of the good and evil in man, of the powers of darkness and self-destruction, Whiting reached a degree of intensity that he tried for in vain in his completely original efforts.

WORKING-CLASS NOVELISTS

The late 1950s and the 1960s saw the rise of novels of working-class background, and the chief practitioner has been Alan Sillitoe. With the exception of the heavily allegorical novel *The General* (1960), his fiction consists of realistic descriptions of workers' lives in present-day Britain. Sillitoe has neither sentimentalized nor idealized this milieu. His characters accept their origins, are proud of them, and in no way deny their proletarian ways of thought. The behavior of Joe Lampton in Braine's *Room at the Top* is alien to them. In Sillitoe's best works—the novel *Saturday Night and Sunday Morning* (1958); the title story of the collection *The Loneliness of the Long-Distance Runner* (1959)—he succeeded in making his implied social criticism part of the fiction itself without being overly propagandistic. He applied the same methods less successfully in *Key to the Door* (1961) and *The Death of William Posters* (1965). In these works there are interventions whose sole purpose is to emphasize the author's partisanship, his commitment to the interests of the working class.

Central to *Saturday Night and Sunday Morning* is the working-class character Arthur Seaton, who rebels against every kind of authority, which he sees as forcibly perpetuated by a morally corrupt society. In his rebelliousness Arthur may resemble the angry young·men, but his rebellion has a different motivation. The conflict grows out of the place of the working class in the socioeconomic structure of contemporary Britain. For Arthur, the world is divided into the little man and worker on the one hand, and the boss, the government official, the teacher, the policeman, and the rich on the other. The establishment is fighting for its very existence, and therefore overlooks nothing that will strengthen the status quo.

Arthur's views determine the course of the novel's action. The narrowness of the point of view prevents *Saturday Night and Sunday Morning* from breaking up into a number of small episodes. And the novel is infused with the jargon and slang of its protagonist. Sillitoe offered no ideology, no political solutions, pronounced though his commitment as socialist writer is. Thus, *Saturday Night and Sunday Morning* should not be read exclusively as the struggle of a man against a society that is hostile to him, a politically inspired struggle; the struggle should be equally seen as carried on within himself. While the external struggle remains without a satisfactory solution, Arthur comes to recognize himself as an individual. He learns that the struggle against society, important and necessary though it seems to him to be, must never be carried on at the cost of one's selfhood.

Key to the Door, the story of three generations of the working-class family Seaton, lacked the compactness of *Saturday Night and Sunday Morning.* In *The Death of William Posters,* whose protagonist is somewhat reminiscent of Arthur Seaton, Sillitoe did not succeed in repeating the masterly characterization of *Saturday Night and Sunday Morning,* let alone of his short stories. His short stories, perhaps even more convincingly than his novels, have shown Sillitoe to be a nonconformist who seldom has a good word for the society around him.

In his poetry Sillitoe has criticized the cleanliness, law-abidingness, narrowmindedness, love of order, and prudence of his contemporaries. In his collection *The Rats, and Other Poems* (1960), the rats are synonymous with the rulers, the government officials, the establishment—in short, all who submit to the compulsions of the system and adapt to it for the sake of their own advancement.

Margot Heinemann's (born 1913) novel *The Adventurers* (1960) described people of the working class who are torn between revolutionary fervor and opportunistic career goals. The central characters are the communist intellectual Adams and the ambitious miner's son Danny. After receiving a college education, Danny turns his back on the working class. Like Braine's Joe Lampton, he is looking for room at the top, where money and influence are important. Adams, on the other hand, moves from London to a small Welsh mining village to share the cares and deprivations of the workers. Neither the discovery of Stalin's mistakes at the Twentieth Congress of the Communist Party nor the brutally crushed counterrevolution in Hungary shakes his faith in communism. Heinemann so clearly insisted on the moral superiority of Adams over Danny that she left no questions about her own position.

Jack Lindsay's (born 1900) four novels that form *Novels of the British Way* (1953–57) described the class conflict on the social and political levels. His characters have hardly any individual traits but reflect the usual characteristics of the working class. Clichés take the place of insights. Only in his later novels—*All on the Never-Never* (1961) and *The Way the Ball Bounces* (1962)—did he make any attempt at individual characterization, even if his view was still conditioned by "socialist realism." Such a tendentious approach to the class struggle, which has also marked Heinemann, has not characterized Sillitoe's work or two other novels of the working class: *All in a Lifetime* (1959) by the well-known literary critic Walter Allen (born 1911), and *Border Country* (1960) by the cultural historian Raymond Williams (born 1921).

David Storey is also, because of his background, a writer of the working class. Just as Sillitoe's characters look on a world regulated and administered from above as an impenetrable jungle, so Storey's characters see this world as hostile and mechanistic. In Storey's first novel, *This Sporting Life* (1960), he placed the class struggle into the microcosm of a rugby team, in a mining town in Yorkshire. Storey used the world of rugby symbolically to stress the class differences that still exist in British society, as seen in the spectrum from the players to the men who give the money to the team.

This Sporting Life was the first contemporary working-class novel to take as its subject matter the sport-for-profit theme. The professional player is merchandise that is bought and sold, as is the worker at his factory bench. The sole difference is that the player has the possibility of becoming, for a short time, an idol of a fanatic crowd, put on display as society's darling. Storey's descriptions of the game have a brutal directness. Human beings seem to be reduced to machines, but they fight with tigerish fury. The animal metaphors running through the whole novel illustrate the Darwinian theory applied to the rules of social play.

In Storey's second novel, *Flight into Camden* (1960), a Yorkshire miner leaves his natural surroundings and moves to Camden, London. Although in the earlier story of the animallike rugby player Arthur Machin external events predominate and are realistically related, in *Flight into Camden* the inner world of the hero receives symbolic value. Although *Radcliffe* (1963) is set in contemporary industrial society, its symbolism derives from the description of the decline of an old and respected family.

Since *Radcliffe* Storey has turned more toward the stage. In *The Restoration of Arnold Middleton* (1967) the history teacher Middleton builds an inner world that serves as a refuge from his profession and family. He retires more and more deeply into this world. In the plays *In Celebration* (1969) and *The Contractor* (1969) Storey returned to his earlier naturalistic style. In *In Celebration,* to celebrate their parents' wedding anniversary, three sons return home. Despite success in their professional lives, they cannot shake off the burden of their social origin: their father was a miner. The principal event in *The Contractor* is the building of a festive tent. This activity forms the framework for the ideas of the characters. Their thoughts, hopes, and desires are expressed in seemingly irrelevant talk, as they hand each other the objects used in the building trade. On the surface, the play is about a tent and the people who are concerned in its erection; but the imagery suggests the many layers of meaning.

The four main characters in Storey's play *Home* (1970) are presented statically, through very stylized conversations. The play's effectiveness did not arise from the content of their speeches but from the typical theater situation of people on the stage, moving and speaking, and people in the audience, observing, listening, and understanding more through instinct than through their intellect. Storey has developed his voice as a playwright, his own dramatic style.

Keith Waterhouse, who practices the writer's craft, as he has said, more as a business than as an art, is, like Storey, both a novelist and a playwright. With the exception of *There Is a Happy Land* (1957), his novels have been set in the present and are closely related to the work of the angry generation. Waterhouse's novels have been about the fate of individuals, the lives of outsiders.

Waterhouse's first tragicomic protagonist, the title character in *Billy Liar* (1959), like Jim Dixon in Amis's *Lucky Jim,* puts himself into uncomfortable situations. His narrow small-town existence gives him no opportunity for self-development. Instead, he lives in a fantasy world. But in Waterhouse's novels, it is not just environment that molds characters: the protagonists are also driven by their own inner compulsions. They are not only the prisoners of their backgrounds; their assumption of the role of outsider is an integral part of their personality. Billy feels unsure of himself, sees difficulties everywhere that seem unconquerable, and escapes into his dream world.

The thirty-six-year-old Leonard Jubb in Waterhouse's *Jubb* (1963) is an exhibitionist and a voyeur, living a fringe existence in society, lacking individuality. He associates sexuality with thoughts of impotence, older women, perversion, and arson. While Billy's fantasies and the fears of the protagonist of *The Bucket Shop* (1968) are harmless and give rise to comic characterization, Jubb moves along the path of self-destruction.

Waterhouse writes like a journalist, and his novels are documents of the times. But from the linguistic point of view, *Billy Liar* deserves special interest. Waterhouse attempted, by mixing of standard English, clichés, idioms, technical jargon, and language taken from the Sunday press, to give immediacy to his material. In *Jubb* he achieved immediacy by abandoning a chronology of events. Only recollections relevant to the narrator are set down in a strictly personal sequence. This was one of the few attempts at innovation on contemporary British fiction.

Stan Barstow's (born 1928) first novel, *A Kind of Loving* (1960), continued the traditions of the writers of the 1950s. Two motifs have dominated Barstow's novels: the link with his origin as a miner's son and the transferring of the main action away from London to the provinces.

While Stanley Middleton (born 1919) and J. D. Scott (born 1917) have also preferred a provincial setting for their fiction, the misunderstood and rejected rebels in the novels of Colin MacInnes (born 1914) live in London. MacInnes's characters represent the lowest level of existence, and he has described them with psychological insight and compassion, yet without sentimentality. They and their surroundings are faithfully portrayed, but in language that lacks subtlety.

INNOVATIVE NOVELISTS

In the 1950s almost all British novels were realistic, following the tradition of the novels of the eighteenth and nineteenth centuries. They were stimulating mainly because of their content. There have been only a few authors of note who tried to go their own way and to experiment with new forms. Among them are William Golding (born 1911), Iris Murdoch (born 1919), Muriel Spark (born 1918), and Lawrence Durrell (born 1912).

The characters in the novels of William Golding seem to be at the mercy of the powers of darkness. Evil in allegorical form runs through Golding's entire oeuvre. His first novel, *Lord of the Flies* (1954), was early evidence of his experimental daring. It tells the story of a group of schoolboys, brought up in the Christian tradition, who, after a plane crash, land on an island in the south seas and live a life there of hate and mutual distrust. As soon as the reins of enforced self-control are loosened, primeval instincts rise to the surface. The small number of those who try to fight this tendency are sacrificed to the evil masses. The children's original attempt at a constructive democratic form of communal life ends up in its very opposite. The result is life organized to the tiniest detail at all levels, dominated by fear, superstition, power, and sheer strength. The parallels with the adult world cannot be overlooked. For example, as the boys get ready to set their island on fire, an atomic war rages far off.

The Inheritors (1955), Golding's next novel, which the author considers his best work, sought to give an explanation of the destructive drive in man he so vividly presented in *Lord of the Flies*. The action takes place in the time of the Neanderthal man and is told from the perspective of a prehistoric man. *Homo sapiens,* the new species, gains the upper hand and destroys his predecessors. The form of *The Inheritors* can be compared to *Lord of the Flies* and *Pincher Martin* (1956). All three end with a sudden change in perspective, which makes the reader see the previous happenings with different eyes.

The Spire (1964) had a religious subject. Jocelin, dean of a cathedral in the Middle Ages, has what he thinks is a holy vision, a high spire rising up over the nave of the church. He receives permission to build this spire. But his confidence diminishes as the spire advances; too much sacrilege and evil are involved in its construction. The actual process of building the spire seems to have nothing in common with the original sacred intention. The symbol in the title can be variously explained. This spire can stand for purity, divine grace, prayer, and security for the body of the church. But it is equally a sign of sin and guilt, a monument to human presumptuousness. The central symbol of the pyramid in *The Pyramid* (1967) is much less carefully worked out. The narrator visits the place in which he was born, a small town, and remembers people and encounters from the past. He begins to realize that he has failed in situations in which love and understanding were expected from him.

Golding has discussed central questions of human existence. In so doing, he has attempted to pull off the mask of the pretense of civilization.

Iris Murdoch, born in Dublin and now teaching philosophy at Oxford, insists that she has tried to keep philosophical questions out of her novels. Nevertheless her philosophy, her ethics, and her theory of the novel cannot be separated. Her characters find themselves in a state of moral contradiction from which they can escape only by discovering the right ideology. Murdoch's own position grew out of her interest in the philosophy of Sartre, but as her ideas developed she began to reject Sartre's form of existentialism. For Murdoch, only by controlling subjectivity and recognizing the objective existence of one's fellow men will love and understanding grow. She rejects the idea of continuous moral self-examination, because this brings with it a total concentration on the self and drives away love. Threadbare moralities, neurosis, conventionality, and the drive for power result from such self-centeredness. Love and freedom must be brought in as counterweights.

Murdoch's first novel, *Under the Net* (1954), combined the psychological and the picaresque. The principal character and the richly picaresque episodes remind one of Wain's *Hurry on Down* and Amis's *Lucky Jim*. But Murdoch did not continue in this vein. In her succeeding novels the characters have distinct, developed personalities as well as a symbolic function. Magic, double meaning, and symbolism all play a part in *The Flight from the Enchanter* (1956) and *The Sandcastle* (1957). Murdoch did away with comic descriptions in *The Bell* (1958), in which she told of the disintegration of a lay religious community. The symbolism, especially of the title, is all-important. The dissolution of the lay community is brought about by the failures of its members. These failures on the personal and communal level result from a lack of love and a failure in love—both produced by neurosis and conventionality. The failures of the lay community are projected by analogy onto the whole of the human race and its religions.

Murdoch's more recent novels—including the allegorical *A Severed Head* (1961) and *The Unicorn* (1963)—have lacked the poetic intensity and tight construction of *The Bell*. *The Italian Girl* (1964) was disappointing, in part because of the intrusiveness of the imposed symbolism. In *The Red and the Green* (1965) Murdoch described the fate of an Anglo-Irish family during the Easter Rebellion of 1916.

Despite her individuality in subject and technique, Murdoch, like Muriel Spark, who resembles her in some ways, does belong to the large context of contemporary literature. Her characters feel compelled to search for self-awareness and identity.

The very versatile Muriel Spark made her reputation chiefly through her fiction. She wrote her poetry before joining the Catholic church; it is important only as introduction to her subsequent creative work. In *The Ballad of the Fanfarlo* (1952), her longest poetic work, she explored for the first time the question of human identity, which became a central concern of her novels. Spark is concerned with religious questions but does not use the novel to spread religious doctrines; and her work goes beyond specifically religious and ecclesiastical matters.

Spark's first novel, *The Comforters* (1957), told a story of people suffering from compulsive neuroses. Each of the main characters is obsessed by intruding visions and voices. Among the results of these obsessions is an inability to communicate—the outcome of living in a private world of illusion, which makes one less than ready to put oneself into the place of others. An isolated existence of this sort leads to the distortion of the real world and the creation of an imaginary world corresponding to the person's private situation. Art provides the aesthetic dimensions of such imagined reality. *The Comforters* reflects, in the person of a writer converted to Catholicism, Spark's own understanding of the relationship between truth and fiction in narrative art. Caroline Rose is at work on a book that confronts problems of form of the modern novel. She feels herself surrounded by voices that tell her the plot of a novel in which she herself is a character. The imagination enlarges the confines of everyday reality and opens up new possibilities of direct relationships.

The events in Spark's *Memento Mori* (1959), an unmercifully comic novel, are likewise marked by the supernatural. Mysterious telephone calls remind the old and ailing characters in the novel that death awaits them. The caller is never identified. The only thing of importance is the reaction of those on the other end of the line to the truth that they must die.

Spark has chosen to set her novels in small, self-enclosed worlds, but each one is a distinctly different world. There is the world of old people in *Memento Mori;* of unmarried men in *The Bachelors* (1960)—a novel that further enriched her gallery of eccentric characters; and the domestic world of *The Girls of Slender Means* (1963). Her novels are similarly limited in narrative perspective. Spark puts herself in the place of her characters, lives their lives, and tries to tell their story solely from their point of view. *The Ballad of Peckham Rye* (1960) was similar in content and structure to Spark's other novels. A diabolical Scotsman, Dougal Douglas, frightens the inhabitants out of their small-town isolation and calm. In its satirical description of different types of society, this novel, which consists mostly of dialogue, resembles Spark's play *Doctors of Philosophy* (1963).

In *The Prime of Miss Jean Brodie* (1961) and Spark's succeeding novels, social satire, the surrealistic situations, the interest in eccentrics became less pronounced. The tone became more serious, with inner events taking precedence over outer. And the personality of her characters, rather than the atmosphere of their surroundings, became primary. Her real subject matter has become the unfolding of individual human qualities.

Spark's *The Mandelbaum Gate* (1965) and *The Public Image* (1968) were excellent examples of the theme of search for an identity. In *The Mandelbaum Gate* a British woman travels to divided Jerusalem to visit the holy places there. The characters encountered on her long journey are shown to be divided personalities whose lives constantly move between emotion and reason. The city divided by the Mandelbaum Gate is both symbol and geographical reality. The conflict in *The Public Image* arises from the confrontations between the self-imposed responsibility of a person seeking to discover his own personality and the demands made by the world at large to live according to its guiding lights.

Muriel Spark has been labeled Catholic writer, moralist, satirist, and surrealist. But these labels, while they indicate specific characteristics, fail to indicate the complexity of her work.

Lawrence Durrell has been the greatest innovator among contemporary British writers. His tetralogy, *The Alexandria Quartet,* explored many new narrative techniques. Durrell's quartet of novels has no continuous time sequence in the traditional sense. The first three novels—*Justine* (1957) and *Balthazar* (1958), both written in the first person, and *Mountolive* (1958), which is in the third person—are roughly simultaneous: they cover many of the same events. Durrell spoke of them as "siblings"; he rejected the term "sequel," because the novels subsequent to *Justine* do not continue the story but stand in a spatial relationship to each other. Only the fourth novel, *Clea* (1960), again in the first person, can be thought of as a continuation in time—to all three previous novels at once. The first three develop the story in three-dimensional space: in depth, breadth, and length; the fourth novel brings the dimension of time, continuing the action chronologically. The main events occur during the mid-1930s; the epilogue, *Clea,* brings the action to 1942, the year of the bombardment of Alexandria during World War II. The spell-binding city of Alexandria is the link between memory and present time—between Darley's island and the world outside—a continuous background against which the events take place. Again and again the city and its surrounding countryside are invoked, depicted, almost personified. The city has many meanings; it is unreal, yet concrete. It shapes the thoughts and feelings of its inhabitants.

Equally important for the unity of the novels are the characters, especially Darley, the narrator of the three first-person novels. In each of the novels, several main figures step into the foreground; with the exception of Mountolive, they have key roles in all four novels, although none of the main characters has the same function in all of them. The significance of the unifying setting of Alexandria and of the chief characters as links in the story becomes clear in the third novel, *Mountolive.* Although the story moves in an unexpected direction in *Mountolive,* it can be easily fitted into the existing framework, and the fitting together makes clear how the first two novels are related to each other. The various love affairs described in the first volume are taken up again in the succeeding novels and reexamined in constantly new and different perspectives.

It is clear from the overall structure of *The Alexandria Quartet,* with its three novels of spatial dimensions and one novel of time dimension, that Durrell's intention was not to tell a chronological story. Past events exist only in the memory of the characters. Brief moments that are of extreme importance to the person concerned take up a great deal of story time; on the other hand, years containing few significant events are glossed over. This subjective or psychological understanding of time is totally independent of the objective interval of time actually taking place; but psychological time seems to become real time during the course of the story. Durrell's stress on the subjective experiencing of time places him in a tradition which goes all the way back to Laurence Sterne (1713–1768) but which was not taken up again until the twentieth century—by Proust, Joyce, Woolf. Durrell's originality stems from the fact that he refrained from imitating Proust and his successors, whose novels exemplified Henri Bergson's "continuous time." In Bergson's theory, present and past merge together so that the happenings of the past thrust their way into present awareness and produce a situation of continuous relationships. The concept of continuous time does not correspond to Durrell's space-time continuum.

In the construction of *The Alexandria Quartet* Durrell attempted to transfer a scientific theory onto the literary field. He believed he could find in a theory of physics, in Einstein's concept of space and time, the unity he had looked for in vain in modern literature. Thus, he said in the foreword to *Balthazar* that he was trying to write a novel on four levels whose structure was determined by the theory of relativity—three dimensions in space, one in time. Some critics have questioned Durrell's claim of relativity: Is it indeed possible to construct and work out a novel on the basis of the idea of a four-dimensional continuum? Durrell himself gave an answer to this. In no sense did he regard his tetralogy as a continuum in the strictly scientific sense. In any case, *The Alexandria Quartet* was a major experiment—one of the few attempts to break through the conservatism of the contemporary British novel.

Durrell regarded *Tunc* (1968) and its continuation *Nunquam* (1970) as one novel on two levels. The modern world and man's place in it are subject to the control of anonymous powers, who administer everything according to antihumanitarian principles. The symbol of these powers is the international firm Merlin. A young inventor who asks for help from this firm soon finds himself restricted in his further development. The firm supports his inventive genius but sets limits on his creative freedom. *Nunquam,* as complementary novel, continues the story of the main characters; but their relationships to one another are changed. The interconnection of actions, characters, and situations reminds one of *The Alexandria Quartet.* In the signed letter at the end of the book, Durrell stated that he tried to play with ideas and images that are connected to concepts of culture.

Durrell's extensive oeuvre has been marked by a variety of genres and by a considerable variation in quality. His poetry has shown little originality. His three poetic dramas—*Sappho* (1950), *An Irish Faustus* (1963), and *Acte* (1965)—were outmoded in form at their conception. Durrell's international reputation rests on his fiction.

POETRY: THE "MOVEMENT" AND THE "GROUP"

The 1950s were a productive period for poetry in Britain as well as for fiction and drama. At times there was overlapping: the same names kept recurring. Two anthologies helped to make known a group of young poets, the majority of whom were or had been active in the universities. They were referred to as the "movement." The critic D. J. Enright included in the anthology *Poets of the 1950s* (1955) Kingsley Amis, Robert Conquest (born 1926), Donald Davie (born 1922), John Holloway (born 1920), Elizabeth Jennings (born 1926), Philip Larkin (born 1922), John Wain, and himself. The anthology *New Lines* (1956), edited by Robert Conquest, contained the same poets with one addition—Thom Gunn (born 1929).

Both editors held similar views about the task and work of the poet. In his introduction Conquest stressed the necessity of putting the intellectual element once again into the foreground and of choosing simple verse forms, in order to avoid the emotionally charged statements and the rich imagery of the romantics. The same reaction against the kind of over-luxuriousness of feelings found in war literature, with its almost total concentration on personal experience, was even more pronounced in the novel than in poetry. One thinks of Amis, Wain, and Philip Larkin, whose novels *Jill* (1946) and *A Girl in Winter* (1947) were decidedly anti-romantic. Larkin's development as poet, starting with *The North Ship* (1945), showed his constant preoccupation with rationality and irrationality in his search for truth. Larkin believes that the poet is impelled to try to feel something because he believes in it or to believe in something because he feels it. His poems are good examples of the effective use of simple words.

Donald Davie looked at the world in his early poems from the distance of an independent observer. Neoclassical influences can be seen in his work. Davie seems peculiarly traditional among contemporary British poets, even though in *Events & Wisdoms* (1964) he experimented with words. Robert Conquest introduced aesthetic and philosophical questions into his poetry, but only rarely arrives at an answer. His interest in science fiction, which he shares with Kingsley Amis, led him to write the rather mediocre novel *A World of Difference* (1955) and to edit, with Amis, several collections of science fiction.

The simplicity of Elizabeth Jennings's poetry has resulted from her deliberate rejection of rhetoric and symbolism. She has often chosen themes that could just as well be dealt with in theoretical essays. John Holloway's ideas have been particularly typical of the aims of the "movement." One of the most pressing tasks of the poet, he believes, is to develop a characteristic style and manner of expression out of the inexhaustible store of commonly owned language.

Next to Larkin, Thom Gunn possesses the most powerful and the most self-willed talent among the "movement" poets. But his four volumes of poems—*Fighting Terms* (1954), *The Sense of Movement* (1957), *My Sad Captains* (1961), and *Touch* (1967)—were only partly related to "movement" poetry. Gunn has not rejected romanticism or the mythologizing of his subject. But he has subjected his central theme—the search of modern man for his identity—to the strict discipline of the intellect. His descriptions remain factual, and in the "unpoetic" poems of the world of "Teddy Boys" and "Rockers" take on the character of news items. Gunn's almost exclusive use of everyday words and expressions underlines this quality and cuts short an emotionally loaded description almost before it has begun. His rejection of rhyme in favor of a syllable-counting principle in *My Sad Captains* and *Touch,* together with his diction, gave the impression of a curiously divided, fragmentary prose. Gunn has united contemplation with the life of action in his poems.

A second group of poets, mainly associated with Cambridge, became known as the "group." The "group," which counted the most powerful figure in contemporary poetry, Ted Hughes (born 1930), among its numbers, has produced fewer well-known poets but is more progressive than the formalist, politically conservative "movement."

The phrase "neometaphysical" poetry, often associated with the "group," can be applied especially to Roy Fuller (born 1912) and Norman MacCaig (born 1910) but also to some extent to the poetry of Gunn and Hughes. Roy Fuller's first volume of poetry, *Poems* (1939), showed the influence of Auden: one even finds lines in memory of a friend killed in the Spanish civil war. In *The Middle of War* (1942) Fuller revealed the beginnings of a style of his own, which took firm root in *Epitaphs and Occasions* (1949), *Counterparts* (1954), and *Brutus's Orchard* (1957). The loose poetic form of his earlier poems yielded to terseness, a defensively ironic attitude, the skillful manipulation of paradoxes and antitheses, and elegant verse construction. The atmosphere of the majority of the poems is dark and melancholy, although less so in *Brutus's Orchard,* which ends with *Mythological Sonnets.* Here Fuller went from the metaphysical sphere to the mythological.

The Scotsman Norman MacCaig has only rarely touched on contemporary life in his poetry. Instead, he has offered metaphysical speculations on timeless themes: the nature of the resemblances between two things or persons, the relation between observation and what is observed, the power of the mind to give meaning or being to an object or a piece of scenery, the relation of the self to the outside world. MacCaig's love poetry has dissected the power of love to change man and leave him either in chaos or in peace. He showed himself as a neometaphysical poet in *Riding Lights* (1955), *The Sinai Sort* (1957), *A Common Grace* (1960), and *A Round of Applause* (1962). John Donne (1572–1631) has undoubtedly been a great influence on him. In MacCaig's descriptions of nature—the mountains and lochs of Scotland, the moors, the animal world—accuracy of observation has gone hand in hand with awareness of the complexities that lie hidden behind external appearances and reveal themselves to man's mind.

In Ted Hughes's first book of poetry, *The Hawk in the Rain* (1957), many thought they recognized the influence of Donne. But the metaphysical element was far less marked than in Fuller, MacCaig, or even Gunn. As Hughes himself said, his poetry has been chiefly concerned with the struggle between the life force and death. In his early poems and the radio play *The Wound* (1962) he pursued this theme with great intensity. The image of the life force firmly resisting death has constantly recurred in his animal and nature poems. The most striking characteristic of Hughes's poetry is the passion and power of the language, which, together with the content, caused it to be called a poetry of violence. The stress on violence in *The Hawk in the Rain* elicited the shortsighted view that Hughes cultivated brutality to disguise his own insecurity.

Hughes's second volume of poems, *Lupercal* (1960), showed that he acquired a more personal style. The earlier echoes of Hopkins and Dylan

Thomas were assimilated. He no longer concentrated with the same intensity on the details of violence but made the contemplation of violence central.

His recent poems have shown his progress toward a "philosophical" explanation of his basic theme—the conflict between life and death. Descriptions have become secondary, and his message has acquired depth through mythological symbolism. What Hughes has aimed for in his poetry is unity of tone. To his dynamic language he sacrificed a regularity of syntax and a logical cohesion; his recent poems are without rhyme or verse divisions. Hughes has long stopped playing the role of outsider earlier attributed to him. He has shown himself to be the leading poet of his generation.

Charles Tomlinson (born 1927) accused the *New Lines* poets (*New Lines II* appeared in 1963) of being unable to include in their observations the mysterious world lying outside their limited experience. In his opinion, British poetry, with a few exceptions, had become provincial; he felt it had to rejoin the literary development of Europe and to expand the achievements of Yeats and Eliot. Tomlinson's closeness to the French symbolists was shown in a poem like *Antecedents* in the collection *Seeing Is Believing* (1958). He indirectly accused his contemporaries—above all Amis and Larkin—of having let the great developments in poetry pass them by.

Tomlinson's poetry is visual. He contemplates a piece of scenery or an object and tries to imitate or to describe impressionistically its reception by the senses. The collections *A Peopled Landscape* (1963) and *American Scenes* (1966) reflected his American experiences and his interest in modern American poetry.

The Irishmen Patrick Kavanagh (born 1905) and Denis Devlin (born 1908) have continued the traditions of the Irish Renaissance. Thomas Kinsella's (born 1928) poetry is equally far removed from the British poetic tradition.

Seamus Heaney (born 1939) published his first collection of poems, *Death of a Naturalist,* in 1966. The subject of his poems has been the landscape of his homeland, Northern Ireland. Heaney has rendered his impressions in powerful language; he has shown his rage against Ireland's past with great force. The collection *Door in the Dark* (1969) contained tough poetry. But many of the characters, whom he has given heroic mantles, are clichés.

NEW DIRECTIONS?

If one takes a look at the most recent trends in contemporary British literature, one soon realizes that the generation that rose to prominence during the 1950s is still dominant—in fiction and drama as well as in poetry. Of course, new names have emerged.

One of the most prolific recent novelists has been Anthony Burgess (born 1917). His first work was the *Malayan Trilogy* (1956–59), which described life in the then British protectorate during a period of transition. In these novels Burgess tried to depict the effects of Britain's indifference to her disintegrating empire. The decay of traditional values in a welfare state forms the subject matter of *The Right to an Answer* (1960), in which a man returns to provincial England after a long period overseas. Burgess has worked over autobiographical material without too much thought or pretense at originality. Loyalty, the relations between countries and races, and a coming to terms with future developments have been the central themes of his work.

A Clockwork Orange (1962), however, gave proof of Burgess's willingness to experiment—rare in the contemporary British novel—by using, for example, numerous neologisms taken from rock language and from Russian words. *Honey for the Bears* (1963), politically and sexually explosive, showed Burgess as a master of satire and black humor. There was a strong element of the grotesque in such novels as *The Doctor Is Sick* (1960), *Inside Mr. Enderby* (1963), and *Enderby Outside* (1968).

Dan Jacobson's (born 1929) carefully constructed novels have dealt mainly with South African problems: *A Dance in the Sun* (1956), *The Evidence of Love* (1960), and *The Beginners* (1966). In *The Tape of Tamar* (1970), an adaptation of biblical material, he used a modern colloquial language.

Brigid Brophy's (born 1929) fame rests on her outspoken attitudes toward marriage as well as on her novel *The Snow Ball* (1964). In *The Snow Ball* she cleverly dissected the façade of morality and attacked the male domination of society. The Irish Edna O'Brien (born 1932) has centered her writings on the problems of woman as sexual object and has displayed similar feelings of resentment toward everything masculine. In three related novels—*The Country Girls* (1960), *The Lonely Girl* (1962), and *Girls in Their Married Bliss* (1964)—she told of the love affairs of two young girls who have moved from Ireland to London. *August Is a Wicked Month* (1965), the story of an emancipated woman, described the gains of acquired freedom—isolation and loneliness.

Discussion of the intellectual and sexual emancipation of women seems to be an inexhaustible theme of the 1960s and the 1970s. Margaret Drabble's (born 1939) *The Garrick Year* (1964), *The Millstone* (1965), and *Jerusalem the Golden* (1967) were further manifestations of the women's liberation movement.

Michael Frayn's (born 1933) *The Russian Interpreter* (1966), which recalled Kingsley Amis, described with humor and understanding the picaresque adventures of an Englishman abroad. The tradition of social criticism in the novel has been carried on by Simon Raven (born 1927). His still incomplete series, *Alms for Oblivion*—the first volume, *The Rich Pay Late,* appeared in 1964—has dealt with the changed world of the upper middle class in postwar England.

Aidan Higgins's (born 1927) fine collection of short stories *Felo de se* (1960) offered precise depictions of great charm of the Irish landscape. His central theme was the drive of an individual toward self-destruction. This theme recurred in his novel *Langrische, Go Down* (1966), originally conceived as a short story, which traced the decay of the Irish Protestant aristocracy during the 1930s. Another Irishman, John McGahern (born 1934), has written gloomy, acerbic novels. *The Barracks* (1963) and *The Dark* (1965) gave proof of his sharp eye for the strange paradoxes of the Irish mind.

What has been true of recent fiction has also been true of poetry. One looks almost in vain for new talent. The leading poets of the 1955–60 era, even more so than the leading novelists, are still those most dominant today.

In the theater the situation is also similar. The new dramatists of the 1950s have continued to develop, trying to avoid the dangers of repetition. If one can note a common characteristic of the youngest generation of playwrights, it is simply that they have made increasing use of the medium of television.

Edward Bond's (born 1934) controversial play *Saved* (1965) showed him to be an exponent of the "theater of cruelty." Bond tried to analyze the group behavior of young people whose immaturity expresses itself in cruelty and brutality. Their frenzy of destruction and their pleasure in cruelty reflect their insecurity. Their repressed aggression hits out not at predetermined goals but, in order to escape from boredom, at anything at all, as in a game. Even a baby can be tortured to death. In the bestial act against the defenseless child, the complete intellectual vacuum and spiritual solitariness of the characters are laid bare. Their actions are meant to signify the atavistic return of contemporary man to his primitive bestiality.

Bond has wanted to change society through his plays, for he is convinced that society today is in no way capable of driving out the animal in man; rather, it cultivates it. He welcomes every effect, however shocking, that will make man come to his senses. In *Early Morning* (1968) the regression to primitive life is even more marked. The monster man takes the greatest pleasure in feeding on his own kind. His limbs continue to grow without stopping so that murder and death can go on for all eternity—a horrifying picture. *Narrow Road to the Deep North* (1968), called a comedy by Bond, takes place in an imaginary Japan of the past. As in his previous plays, the main character is caught in a trap; he does not struggle to escape and instead commits suicide. Bond has used almost exclusively the lowest possible form of language in his dialogue. The directness and obscenity of this idiom is part of the shock effect that is his goal.

Bond further pursued his "shock therapy," consistently and graphically, in *Lear* (1971), about the dark evil of power. Lear's suffering, according to Bond's interpretation, is primarily a political tragedy.

Bond considers existing society primitive, dangerous, and corrupt. He calls himself an anarchist, because government is anticreative and only oriented toward law and order, and he, as artist, is searching for personal justice. The time has come to stop telling people that the few shall lead the many. Bond considers man's gravest danger the fact that he lives in a social order for which he is not biologically equipped. The human organism, for instance, is not suited for work in factories. This has led to the development of an aggressive society, in which things like hydrogen bombs exist. This situation is aggravated by the educational system. Bond equates schools with prisons: both serve, according to Bond, to create slaves, or at least people who have so adapted themselves to the prevailing forms of society that they will conform to it. He does not object to knowledge itself, only to the force-feeding of knowledge. By nature man is not violent; on the contrary, love is the natural condition in which man is born—the ability to love and be loved. Bond feels that this ability is being beaten out of man so that he can conform more willingly.

David Mercer's (born 1928) first published work was the trilogy *The Generations* (1961–63), which cast light on contemporary political and social problems. He sees his ideological development as having moved from liberal socialism through Marxism to a nondoctrinaire communism. One central theme has run through all of Mercer's recent plays—the interrelationship between individuals and institutions, seen from a psychological viewpoint. *A Suitable Case for Treatment* (1962), *For Tea on Sunday* (1963), and *In Two Minds* (1967) used psychological disturbances in man as an expression of social alienation.

In his short playwrighting career Joe Orton (1933–1967) wrote two of the most commercially successful plays of the 1960s: *Entertaining Mr. Sloane* (1964) and *Loot* (1965). The vitality of his plays springs from the discrepancy between what takes place on the stage, that is, the behavior of the characters, and their way of expressing themselves. The respectability, propriety, and euphemistic circumspection of their words stand in crude contrast to their scandalous thought and actions.

Rosencrantz and Guildenstern Are Dead (1967) made Tom Stoppard (born 1937) famous overnight. The play takes the two characters out of their limited role in *Hamlet* and creates a private life for them. It is clear from the first appearance of Rosencrantz and Guildenstern that nothing can ever change for them, that they are forever compelled to remain outsiders who never quite understand what is happening. If they force themselves to act independently, then they deny their own natures, and fatal consequences will result. Stoppard wanted to undermine and parody the critical assumption that dramatic characters have no existence outside the limits imposed on them by their author.

In Peter Barnes (born 1931) the element of burlesque has been basic, particularly in *The Ruling Class* (1968), which satirized the British aristocracy. *Leonardo's Last Supper* (1969) and *Noonday Demons* (1969) revealed Barnes's powers of irony.

If one looks at the newest currents in contemporary British literature, one is still struck by the discrepancy between intellectual content and artistic achievement. If one compares the conservatism of the British novel with such developments as the *nouveau roman* in France, one can observe the absence of a new form to reflect the new content and new attitudes. The contemporary British novel still continues the traditions of the novelists of the eighteenth and nineteenth centuries. But the subject matter, with a few exceptions, is contemporary.

The problems of contemporary British fiction are that it is primarily nationally oriented, that it turns inward, that it ignores the manifold experiments with form undertaken by writers in other countries. Drama and poetry have been less tradition-bound. The search for new themes has coincided in these genres with a greater willingness to try out new forms. But the novel—in the past the glory of British literature—may pass out of international notice unless the narrow choice of themes can be overcome and writers can step away from depicting only matters of contemporary concern.

SECONDARY WORKS

BIBLIOGRAPHIES AND GUIDES

Bateson, F. W., ed. *The Cambridge Bibliography of English Literature,* 5 vols., Cambridge, 1940–66

Eagle, Dorothy, ed. *The Concise Oxford Dictionary of English Literature,* 2nd ed., New York, 1970

Harvey, Sir Paul and Dorothy Eagle, eds. *The Oxford Companion to English Literature,* 4th ed. Oxford, 1967

Temple, Ruth and Martin Tucker, eds. *Twentieth Century British Literature: A Reference Guide and Bibliography.* New York, 1968

GENERAL WORKS

Allen, Walter. *The Modern Novel in Britain and the United States.* New York, 1964

Brown, John Russell, ed. *Modern British Dramatists.* Englewood Cliffs, N.J., 1968

Daiches, David. *A Critical History of*

English Literature, 2 vols. London, 1961

Erzgräber, Willi, ed. *Englische Literatur von Wilde bis Beckett: Interpretationen.* Frankfurt, 1970

Ford, Boris, ed. *The Pelican Guide to English Literature,* 7 vols. Baltimore, 1954–61

Gascoigne, Bamber. *Twentieth-Century Drama.* New York, 1966

Lumley, Frederick. *New Trends in 20th Century Drama,* 3rd ed. London, 1967

Mehl, Dieter, ed. *Das englische Drama,* 2 vols. Düsseldorf, 1970

Sampson, George. *The Concise Cambridge History of English Literature,* 3rd ed. Cambridge, 1970

Standop, Ewald and Edgar Mertner. *Englische Literaturgeschichte,* 2nd ed. Heidelberg, 1971

Temple, Ruth and Martin Tucker, eds. *Modern British Literature,* 3 vols. New York, 1966

Wilson, F. P. and Bonamy Dobrée, eds. *The Oxford History of English Literature,* 12 vols. London, 1961–69

WORKS ON CONTEMPORARY LITERATURE

Allen, Walter. *The Novel Today.* London, 1959

Allsop, Kenneth. *The Angry Decade: A Survey of the Cultural Revolt of the Nineteen-Fifties.* London, 1958

Armstrong, William, ed. *Experimental Drama.* London, 1963

Bergonzi, Bernard. *The Situation of the Novel.* London, 1970

Borinski, Ludwig. *Meister des modernen englischen Romans.* Heidelberg, 1963

Burgess, Anthony. *The Novel Now.* New York, 1967

Drescher, Horst W., ed. *Englische Literatur der Gegenwart in Einzeldarstellungen.* Stuttgart, 1970

Fraser, G. S. *The Modern Writer and His World.* Baltimore, 1964

Fricker, Robert. *Das moderne englische Drama.* Göttingen, 1964

———. *Der moderne englische Roman.* Göttingen, 1966

Gindin, James. *Postwar British Fiction.* Berkeley, Cal., 1962

Jennings, Elisabeth. *Poetry Today (1957–1960).* London, 1961

Kahrmann, Bernd. *Die idyllische Szene im zeitgenössischen englischen Roman.* Bad Homburg, 1969

Karl, Frederick R. *A Reader's Guide to the Contemporary English Novel.* New York, 1970

Kazin, Alfred. *Contemporaries.* Boston, 1962

Kermode, Frank. *Continuities.* New York, 1969

———. *Puzzles and Epiphanies: Essays and Reviews 1958–1961.* New York, 1962

Kitchin, Laurence. *Drama in the Sixties.* New York, 1966

———. *Mid-Century Drama,* 2nd rev. ed. New York, 1962

Marowitz, Charles et al., eds. *The Encore Reader: A Chronicle of the New Drama.* New York, 1965

Marowitz, Charles and Simon Trussler, eds. *Theatre at Work: Playwrights and Productions in the Modern British Theatre.* New York, 1968

McCormick, John. *Catastrophe and Imagination: An Interpretation of the Recent English and American Novel.* New York, 1957

Newby, P. H. *The Novel 1945–1950.* London, 1951

O'Connor, William Van. *The New University Wits and the End of Modernism.* Carbondale, Ill., 1963

Oppel, Horst, ed. *Das moderne englische Drama: Interpretationen.* Berlin, 1963

———. *Die moderne englische Lyrik: Interpretationen.* Berlin, 1967

———. *Der moderne englische Roman: Interpretationen.* Berlin, 1965

Press, John. *Rule and Energy: Trends in British Poetry since the Second World War.* New York, 1963

Raban, Jonathan. *The Technique of Modern Fiction.* Notre Dame, Ind., 1969

Rabinovitz, Rubin. *The Reaction against Experiment in the English Novel 1950–1960.* New York, 1967

Ratcliffe, Michael. *The Novel Today.* London, 1968

Rippier, Joseph. *Some Postwar British Novelists.* Frankfurt, 1965

Rosenthal, M. L. *The New Poets: American and British Poetry since World War II.* London, 1967

Salem, Daniel. *La révolution théâtrale actuelle en Angleterre.* Paris, 1969

Schleussner, Bruno. *Der neopikareske Roman: Pikareske Elemente in der Struktur moderner englischer Romane, 1950–1960.* Bonn, 1969

Schlüter, Kurt. *Kuriose Welt im modernen englischen Roman.* Berlin, 1969

Scholes, Robert. *The Fabulators.* New York, 1963

Shapiro, Charles, ed. *Contemporary British Novelists.* Carbondale, Ill., 1965

Spender, Stephen. *The Struggle of the Modern.* Berkeley, Cal., 1963

Taylor, John Russell. *Anger and After: A Guide to the New British Drama.* London, 1962

Tynan, Kenneth. *Curtains.* New York, 1961

Wagner, Walter, ed. *The Playwrights Speak.* New York, 1968

Weise, Wolf-Dieter. *Die "neuen englischen Dramatiker" in ihrem Verhältnis zu Brecht.* Bad Homburg, 1969

DETLEF KULMAN

Bulgarian Literature

BULGARIAN LITERATURE, the oldest of the Slavic literatures, has a history of eleven hundred years. Despite the influence of neighboring Byzantine literature, it acquired a distinctive national character during the Middle Ages. But the Turkish invasions of the fourteenth century and the subsequent Turkish domination of Bulgaria relegated creative writing to the field of folk literature for centuries—until the south Slavic renascence in the second half of the eighteenth century. This renascence (*vuzrazhdane*), during which the Bulgarians fought against Turkish rule, reminded the Bulgarians of their heroic past and thus laid the foundation for a new literature.

Having been neglected because of an unfavorable political and cultural climate for hundreds of years, literature in the independent Bulgaria of 1878 could only be described as primitive and provincial compared with that of most other European countries. Not until the adoption of symbolism in the first two decades of the twentieth century did Bulgaria finally enter the literary mainstream, thanks partly to the growing influence of western Europe. Between the two world wars, critical realism dominated literature, and the first proletarian and socialist writers came to the fore.

With the communist coup of September, 1944, political, social, and cultural life underwent fundamental changes. Breaking drastically with the past, Bulgaria became closely allied with the Soviet Union, which had helped to liberate the country from fascism, and adopted the Marxist-

Leninist ideology as its new creed. The sometimes violent process of reorganization and reorientation, amounting to a cultural revolution, had a particularly strong impact upon literature. A new era began, typified by a program of socialist realism borrowed from the Soviet Union.

In May, 1945, Premier Georgi Dimitrov formulated the new goals of literature in a letter to the Bulgarian Writers' Union. Through the methods of socialist realism and its insistence on *partinost* (party-mindedness), literature was to serve the people and support the aims of the Communist Party.

The result of this new program for literature was a thematic monotony and a structural and stylistic standardization, at least in the beginning. The recognition a writer achieved depended upon his choice of subjects, which were prescribed and were supposed to contribute to the building of the new society. The subjects were drawn mainly from three fields: the antifascist movement and the partisan struggle, including the September revolutions in 1923 and 1944; the building of socialist Bulgaria and the glorification of the communist labor heroes; gratitude and love for the Soviet Union and appreciation for Soviet-Bulgarian friendship.

This period of generally drab and monotonously standardized literature lasted until the Twentieth Congress of the Communist Party of the Soviet Union in 1956, which condemned the "cult of personality" (actually, the tyranny of Stalin) and denounced dogmatism. After the party resolutions came the plenary April session of the Central Committee of the Bulgarian Communist Party, which opened the way for a period of liberalization.

The year 1956 marked a definite turning point in postwar Bulgarian literature. The first period of communism was over; a new literature— much of it written by younger men and women—sought fresher, less rigid forms; devoted itself more intently to everyday problems; and widened its scope by tackling moral and ethical issues. Bulgarian literature is now in a state of flux: some writers of the period 1945–56 have already been forgotten by Bulgarian readers, while it is still too soon to assess definitively many of the younger literary figures.

POETRY

The quantity of poetry published between 1945 and 1956 was not matched by its quality. Anthologies, cycles of poems, and verse narratives were offered to the reader as utilitarian poetry. In these works stereotyped images and standardized actions recurred over and over. A paucity of invention in language went hand in hand with political slogans. War and patriotism—specifically the partisan groups, the triumph of Soviet communism, and, a little later, such contemporary political problems as spreading socialism throughout the country—provided the subjects for pseudoliterary, not to say propagandistic, works. *Partizanski pesni* (1947, Partisan Songs) by Veselin Andreev (born 1918); *Poema za vintovkata* (1947, Poem on the Rifle) by Mladen Isaev (born 1907); *Stikhove v palaskite* (1954, Poems from a Cartridge Belt) by Veselin Khanchev (1919–1966)—the titles alone of such cycles offer sufficient indication of their content.

Behind these personal experiences of war lay a faith that out of the destruction would arise a new world and a new race of men. The individual poems of these cycles, usually unpretentious in form, were inspired by socialist fervor. In their sharp confrontation of love and hate, life and death, heroism and brutality, they were far from lacking in dramatic tension.

Among the older poets was Lamar (born 1898, pseudonym of Lalyo Marinov), who wrote several narrative poems on topical themes and, later, sonnets. Khristo Radevski (born 1903), an early communist, turned increasingly, with considerable success, to the field of fable and satire. Elisaveta Bagryana (born 1893), Bulgaria's leading woman poet, recaptured the strong expressiveness of her early work in the cycle entitled *Ot bryag na bryag* (1963, From Shore to Shore), after the less successful *Pet zvezdi* (1953, Five Stars). Outstanding among the poets who extolled the building of the new socialist society was Pen'o Penev (1930–1959), who continued in the poetic tradition of Nikola Vaptsarov (1909–1942). Unfortunately, Penev succumbed to psychological depression and committed suicide before he was thirty.

In the late 1950s the horizons of poetry began to broaden. As poets began to write about nature, love, and personal experience, poetry became increasingly apolitical, more intellectual, less closely linked with daily events, and hence more international. Purely external description and stereotyped characterization yielded to a less idealized, more critical stance, which was closer to reality. Many of these works, however, were no more than isolated experiments in technique, without a concomitant poetic theory. This has been true of the poems in free verse of Vladimir Bashev (1933–1969) and Lyubomir Levchev (born 1935), who were the most significant poets of the 1960s.

DRAMA

With the establishment of the socialist republic, the theater assumed a new and important role in Bulgarian literature—as a medium of education. Drama was supposed to reflect the evolution of the new man and his new morality. But the requirement that the hero be a positive figure prevented the development of the conflict necessary to drama. *Borbata produlzhava*

(1945, The Fight Continues) by Krum Kyulyakov (1893–1955) was Bulgaria's first play about its communist revolution. Lozan Strelkov (born 1912) also took the partisan movement as the subject for his heroic drama *Razuznavane* (1949, Reconnaissance). The lyric poet, short-story writer, and dramatist Orlin Vasilev (born 1904) treated communism more convincingly, especially in *Zaroveno sluntse* (1959, The Buried Sun), which dealt with the cult of personality. The plays of Todor Genov (born 1903) and Emil Manov (born 1918) are never mentioned today because their heroes failed to meet the requirements of the party position.

Recent years, however, have brought a change. In *Prokurorut* (1965, The Public Prosecutor) Georgi Dzhagarov (born 1925), freeing himself from conventions of form, developed the moral conflict of a Marxist intellectual in a taut, rigorously handled plot. Valeri Petrov (born 1920) wrote the very successful *Kogato rozite tantsuvat* (1965, When the Roses Dance), a grotesque play that exploited the style of Shakespearean comedy. In historical drama Kamen Zidarov (born 1902) won recognition for his traditional verse play *Ivan Shishman* (1959, Ivan Shishman), as did Magda Petkanova (born 1900) for her *Samuil* (1965, Samuil).

FICTION

The major achievements in contemporary Bulgarian literature have been in fiction. Here again the works of the immediate postwar period reflected events of the war and the establishment of socialism. Stoyan T. Daskalov (born 1909), whose extensive but mediocre oeuvre will probably not be read years from now, was, for a time, the most celebrated writer on socialism and the war. Georgi Karaslavov (born 1904) described Bulgarian peasant life in his panoramic *Obiknoveni khora* (1952–66, Simple People), but this work lacked the force of his prewar novels.

The novels of Dimitur Dimov (1909–1966) transcended the previous limits of Bulgarian fiction and earned an international recognition for Bulgarian literature. In his most famous novel, *Tyutyun* (1951–54, Tobacco), an analysis of the period from 1933 to 1944 in Bulgaria, Dimov reduced the obligatory party-mindedness to a tolerable level of personal engagement with communism. This novel, controversial when it first appeared, presented nonidealized communists with all their human weaknesses and faults.

Dimitur Talev (1898–1966) was as successful as Dimov. But unlike Dimov, Talev, more than any other writer, consciously perpetuated the traditions of Bulgarian fiction. In his tetralogy consisting of *Zhelezniyat svetilnik* (1952, The Iron Candlestick), *Ilinden* (1953, The Elias Day), *Prespanskite kambani* (1954, The Bells of Prespo), and *Glasovete vi chuvam* (1966, I Hear Your Voices), he described the history of Macedonia from the mid-nineteenth century to 1905. Talev's grandiose panoramic design was modeled on the novels of Tolstoi and Sholokhov. Their techniques were reflected in the shifting back and forth between descriptions of intimate family life and historical events.

In addition to many animal stories, Emiliyan Stanev (born 1907) wrote a highly praised novel, *Ivan Kondarev* (1958–64, Ivan Kondarev), which dealt with the preparation for and the outbreak and suppression of the September revolution of 1923.

Recently, Bulgarian writers of fiction have tried different forms and have tackled previously neglected subjects and themes. The sketches of Nikolay Khaytov (born 1919) and Yordan Radichkov (born 1929) have described events in the daily life of the common man in lively, colorful language. The humorous or satirical story, a genre with a long tradition, has provided opportunities for veiled social criticism.

There is scarcely an event in Bulgarian history that has not become the subject for contemporary fiction. Moreover, some writers have begun a serious investigation of moral and philosophical problems. These writers have carried Bulgarian literature far beyond the boundaries envisioned for it by the dogmatists of the early years of the people's republic.

BULGARIAN WORKS IN ENGLISH TRANSLATION

ANTHOLOGIES

Kirilov, N. and F. Kirk, eds. *Introduction to Modern Bulgarian Literature.* New York, 1969

Stanev, Emiliyan, ed. *The Peach Thief, and Other Bulgarian Stories.* London, 1968

INDIVIDUAL WORKS MENTIONED IN ARTICLE

Dzhagarov, Georgi. *Prokurorut* as *The Public Prosecutor.* London, 1969

Talev, Dimitur. *Zhelezniyat svetilnik* as *The Iron Candlestick.* New York, 1964

SECONDARY WORKS

Bogdanov, Ivan. *Bulgarskata literatura v dati i kharakteristiki: 817–1965.* Sofia, 1966

Istoriya na bulgarskata literatura v 4 toma, 3 vols. to date. Sofia, 1962ff.

Kolevski, Vasil. *Literaturata na svobodata: Problemi na socialisticheskiya*

realizum v bulgarskata literatura sled deveti septemvri. Sofia, 1969

Konstantinov, G. et al. *Bulgarski pisateli: Biografii, bibliografiya.* Sofia, 1961

Likova, Rozaliya. *Suvremenni avtori i problemi.* Sofia, 1968

Manning, Clarence A. and Roman Smal-

Stocki. *The History of Modern Bulgarian Literature.* New York, 1960

Markov, D. *Bolgarskaya literatura nashikh dnei.* Moscow, 1969

Minkov, Tsvetan. *Ocherki po bulgarska literatura.* Sofia, 1948

Ocherki istorii bolgarskoi literatury XIX–XX vekov. Moscow, 1959

Penev, Pencho. *Suvremenna bulgarska drama.* Sofia, 1967

Problemi na suvremennata bulgarska literatura: Sbornik statii. Sofia, 1964

Schmaus, Alois. *Die bulgarische Literatur.* In Wolfgang von Einsiedel, ed., *Die Literaturen der Welt.* Zürich, 1964

IHAB HASSAN

Canadian Literature

As a nation, Canada is relatively young. The British North America Act established the confederation only in 1867. For a long time Canadian culture looked to England or to France, and later to the dynamic country south of its borders. The sparse towns and vast spaces of Canada were open to the cultural colonialism of older and more populous societies. Canadian artists, sensing the provincialism of their native land, often emigrated to the more exciting cities of Europe or the United States, thereby delaying the emergence of a native culture. Those who remained confronted a spiritual solitude more fearsome than physical hardship.

The contemporary Canadian writer, nevertheless, inherited the national myth. The natural frontier, hostile or beneficent, was always palpable; so was "the deep moral silence . . . the riddle of unconsciousness" (in the words of Northrop Frye [born 1912]) that nature presented. Immense in open space, Canada also seemed to hold a great future, which its people often regarded in messianic terms; technology was therefore more esteemed than art. Moreover, in communities faced with so many rigors, the cohesive instinct excluded individual expression; against the ethos of the pioneer or the *coureur de bois,* the Presbyterian and Catholic churches enforced orthodoxy. Intellectual and rhetorical more than poetic, Canadian writing tended toward didactic forms, confirming a collective human identity against all threats.

A serious creative literature appeared, however, after World War I.

128

Popular regional novels, historical romances, and homiletics continued to be published. But other authors began to create a literary climate that could help release the imaginations of younger writers. By the end of World War II Toronto and Montreal had become considerably vigorous and varied literary centers, for English- and French-speaking writers respectively; Vancouver hardly lagged behind. The munificent Canada Council took an active part in promoting new talent; the Canadian Broadcasting Corporation offered a public voice. University faculties turned their attention to their national literature; and academic critics of exceptional talents—Northrop Frye, George Woodcock (born 1912) A. J. M. Smith (born 1902)—established the frame of its reference. Such periodicals as *Canadian Literature, Tamarack Review, Delta,* and *Prism* provided a responsible forum of literary discussion. Young Canadian writers could easily take their place in world culture. The era of the "global village," as the Canadian genius Marshall McLuhan (born 1911) put it, had arrived.

FICTION

IN ENGLISH

The modern Canadian novel began to take shape when realism replaced history, romance, and nostalgia, when human, moral, and psychological complexities asserted themselves on the natural world. This trend, transforming the experience of Canadian reality into a fictional art, could be discerned in Mazo de La Roche's (1885–1961) *Jalna* (1927), which was still touched by idyllic light; the trend was continued in Frederick Philip Grove's (1872–1948) *Fruits of the Earth* (1933), and culminated in the works of Morley Callaghan (born 1903) and Hugh MacLennan (born 1907), the two most celebrated novelists of Canada, both of whom began their careers in the 1920s.

Morley Callaghan, perhaps the most prominent of Canadian novelists, developed from the melodramatic naturalism of *Strange Fugitive* (1928) to the moral and symbolic intricacies of later books, from *Such Is My Beloved* (1934) through *The Loved and the Lost* (1951) and *The Many-Colored Coat* (1960). Hugh MacLennan made his central concern in numerous essays and realistic novels the definition of a national identity. His work tackled the largest social issues of his age: the conflict of cultures and languages in *Two Solitudes* (1945), puritanism in *Each Man's Son* (1951), and the malaise of contemporary civilization in his best work, *The Watch that Ends the Night* (1959).

Of the writers who began to publish after the second world war, Ethel Wilson (born 1890) was among the first to become known abroad. Her works, usually set in British Columbia, have sustained contradictory moods, and her wisdom has always probed the meaning of love within the cycles of nature. From her first novel, *Hetty Dorval* (1947), to her best works, *The Equations of Love* (1952) and *Swamp Angel* (1954), she rendered sibylline insights into forms that seem both decorous and wholly independent, even eccentric.

It remained, however, for younger novelists to express best the contemporary sensibility and thus to project the Canadian presence into the world of metaphor.

Mordecai Richler (born 1931) has exposed the hypocrisies of urban culture and contemporary politics with anger, with gusto, always driving toward the radical truth, driving his characters to act upon that truth. The settings and subjects of his novels have changed—from Spain in *The Acrobats* (1954), to the Jewish community of Montreal in *Son of a Smaller Hero* (1955), to the leftist bohemias of London in *A Choice of Enemies* (1957), to the Laurentian "virgin land" in *The Apprenticeship of Duddy Kravitz* (1959), his most exuberant novel. Versatile—he also writes essays, film and television scripts, stories—tough-minded, and quarrelsome, Richler is one of the two most exciting novelists of today's Canada.

The other is Leonard Cohen (born 1934), who seems close to the mystique of American hippies—Cohen spends a good deal of time in the United States—just as Richler seems close to the ethos of the English "angry young men." Erotic and visionary, anarchic and surrealistic, Cohen developed a very personal style, at once quiet and explosive—hallucinogenic in a word—which he has put to unnerving use in his poems and songs. His first novel, *The Favorite Game* (1963), vaguely autobiographical, concerned a young Jewish poet. But not until *The Beautiful Losers* (1966) did Cohen reveal his astonishing gifts. Canadian history, religion, and myth; Indian nature and white culture; the mysteries of time, love, and identity—all converge on the actions or dreams of three characters caught in a haunting triangle.

Other notable Canadian novelists writing in English include Sinclair Ross (born 1908), Margaret Laurence (born 1926), John Buell (born 1930), Norman Levine (born 1924), and Mavis Gallant (born 1922).

IN FRENCH

Although French culture is older than English in Canada, literature in French began to flourish late, perhaps only in the mid-1930s, and it gathered momentum only after World War II. The growing nationalism of the province of Quebec, the violent separatism of some of its groups, served as profound challenges to the literary imagination.

The immediate predecessors of the contemporary French Canadian novelists often chose rural backgrounds or historical themes. The best of them—such as Ringuet (1895–1960), author of *30 arpents* (1938, Thirty Acres)—brought certain modern analytical perceptions and colloquial idioms to traditional material. After the war, however, the shift to urban settings became pronounced. This was evident in the fiction of Gabrielle Roy (born 1909) who, although born in Manitoba, wrote about the awakenings and ordeals of Montreal slum-dwellers in *Bonheur d'occasion* (1945, Happiness of Occasion). Lucid, tender, penetrating, Roy has brought a special intuition to humble or caged humanity, even to prosaic bank clerks, in *Alexandre Chenevert, caissier* (1954, Alexandre Chenevert, Cashier).

More satiric, Roger Lemelin (born 1919) evoked the color and misery of Quebec in *Au pied de la pente douce* (1944, At the Foot of the Gentle Slope), *Les Plouffe* (1948, The Plouffe Family), and *Pierre le magnifique* (1952, Pierre the Magnificent). The most austere and classic of these urban novelists may well be André Langevin (born 1927), who enlarged his descriptions of lower- or middle-class life in *Poussière sur la ville* (1953, Dust over the City) and *Le temps des hommes* (1956, The Time of Men) into tragic parables of the human condition.

More prolific, varied, and contradictory than any of these novelists, Yves Thériault (born 1915) began by portraying the liberation of sensuality and violence in *Contes pour un homme seul* (1944, Stories for a Solitary Man) and *La fille laide* (1950, The Ugly Girl). His best work, *Agakuk* (1958, Agakuk), about an Eskimo family, explored both symbolic and immediate experience, presented both the sexual and the social complications of Canadian life. Thériault's opposition to instinctual as well as cultural repression became, as the critic Edmund Wilson noted, the concern of another group, which focused on the decadence of the somber *maisons seigneuriales,* carriers of Jansenist traditions and the stifling values of provincial Canada throughout its history. This group has included the poet Hector de Saint-Denys Garneau (1912–1943), the essayist Jean Le Moyne (born 1913), and the novelist and poet Anne Hébert (born 1916), who wrote in *Les chambres de bois* (1958, The Wooden Rooms) a dreamlike study of an ingrown and neurotic family, hardly belonging to the twentieth century, from which escape is necessary to attain a new life.

The academic temper of Canadian criticism discouraged experimentalism for many decades; the *nouveau roman* has hardly flourished among French writers on this side of the Atlantic. Some of the younger authors, nevertheless, have voices or manners of their own. The most striking of these is Marie-Claire Blais (born 1939). She presented a spare, terrifying world—loveless, ultimately mysterious—in such novels as *Tête blanche* (1960, White Head) and *Le jour est noir* (1962, The Day Is Black). Her narrative, shifting from soliloquy to action or dream, has remained severe, original, and concise even in its ultimate strangeness.

Other French Canadian novelists of the contemporary period include André Giroux (born 1915), Félix-Antoine Savard (born 1896), Robert Charbonneau (born 1911), Jean Simard (born 1916), and Gérard Bessette (born 1920).

POETRY

IN ENGLISH

Before World War II such poets as E. J. Pratt (1883–1964), F. R. Scott (born 1899), A. J. M. Smith, and Dorothy Livesay (born 1909) established a tradition of modernist verse, deriving largely from the mythical and metaphysical style of T. S. Eliot and Ezra Pound, yet stressing narrative and dramatic rather than lyrical modes. During the 1940s and 1950s, certain magazines—*Contemporary Verse* in Vancouver; *Northern Review,* which consolidated *Preview* and *First Statement,* in Montreal; *Alphabet* in Toronto—played a crucial role in developing contemporary Canadian verse.

Among the older postwar poets, Earle Birney (born 1904) has raised most insistently the question of Canadian identity. A versatile craftsman, a prolific writer and editor, he has pushed the implications of his national concerns into a larger didactic view of the world in an age of technology, as *Ice Cod Bell or Stone* (1962) showed. A. M. Klein (born 1909), a poet of great learning and power, has explored social and religious themes in forms wrought with originality. His novel, *The Second Scroll* (1951), has been called a "twentieth-century Pentateuch." Some of his best work, such as the collection *The Rocking Chair, and Other Poems* (1948), flashed with a dark visionary wit, which transcended what in some of Klein's poetry remained more precise Jewish experience. Equally independent, Margaret Avison (born 1918) has been a self-critical artist, given to bold metaphysical perceptions as well as to personal themes. Her playful intelligence was evident in *Winter Sun* (1960).

Montreal and Toronto continue to serve as centers of poetic activity; the mood of Montreal tends toward social and religious radicalism; of Toronto, toward mythic and reflective forms. Thus, in Montreal Irving Layton (born 1917), Louis Dudek (born 1918), Raymond Souster (born 1921), and P. K. Page (born 1916) have created a literary climate that encourages some of the best Canadian verse. Among the younger writers of Montreal, Leonard Cohen, as original a poet as he is a novelist, has developed, through several volumes of verse, an idiom concrete, conversational, and insidiously mystical. In Toronto Eli Mandel (born 1922), James Reaney (born 1926), and Jay Macpherson (born 1931) have favored a subtle and witty style. Macpherson's *The Boatman* (1957) presented fine lyrics, usually formally strict, cunningly interlaced.

Still younger poets, notably Margaret Atwood (born 1939) and Daryl Hine (born 1936), are already moving beyond promise toward genuine achievement.

IN FRENCH

The modern tradition of French Canadian poetry goes back to Émile Nelligan (1879–1941), brilliant, somber, and intense. His work, created out of deep spiritual solitude, foreshadowed the mood of certain poets, caught in the melancholy isolation of their Canadian experience. The most haunted of these, Hector de Saint-Denys Garneau, displayed original perceptions of sin and death in largely conventional metric forms. His works, *Regards et jeux dans l'espace* (Glances and Games in Space) and *Solitudes* (Solitudes), were collected posthumously in *Les poésies complètes* (1949, The Complete Poetry).

Anne Hébert, whose fiction I already mentioned, has conveyed her sense of life, in tombs or shuttered rooms, with reticence and power. With Rina Lasnier (born 1915), the themes of death and isolation have become part of a larger perspective; images of love and joy flit through her poems. Her force, essentially religious, revealed itself in *Madones canadiennes* (1944, Canadian Madonnas), and *Présence de l'absence* (1956, The Presence of Absence). A virtuoso in many genres, including the prose poem, Lasnier remains one of the most compelling poets of her generation.

Increasingly, however, the new poets of Montreal have turned to French models—Henri Michaux, Pierre Jouve, René Char, Jacques Prévert— while at the same time they have continued to define their own concerns, be they magic or myth, social commitment or revolt against the values of Canadian life. This new movement did not exclude, however, the appearance of an author such as Paul-Marie Lapointe (born 1929), a contemporary nature poet whose volume *Arbres* (1960, Trees) was experimental and at the same time immediate in communicating pure sensations. More conscious of his specific role as a Canadian poet, Jean-Guy Pilon (born 1930) has approached the human condition affirmatively, but without rhetoric or sentimentality. His *Recours au pays* (1961, Recourse to the Land) and *Pour saluer une ville* (1963, To Salute a City) suggested even in their titles the tendencies of his imagination.

Other talented poets of today's French Canada include Alain Grandbois (born 1909), Gilles Hénault (born 1920), Roland Giguère (born 1929), Fernand Ouellette (born 1930), Pierre Trottier (born 1925), and Gatien Lapointe (born 1931).

DRAMA

No major dramatic talent or trend has yet emerged in Canada, although some fine writing has been commissioned for radio or television by the Canadian Broadcasting Corporation, and such authors as Robertson Davies (born 1913) and Paul Toupin (born 1917) have written interestingly for the theater.

FRENCH CANADIAN WORKS IN ENGLISH TRANSLATION

ANTHOLOGIES

Roy, George Ross, ed. *Twelve Modern French Canadian Poets*. Toronto, 1958
Silvestre, Guy and H. Gordon Green, eds. *Un siècle de littérature canadienne/ A Century of Canadian Literature*. Montreal, 1967

INDIVIDUAL WORKS MENTIONED IN ARTICLE

Blais, Marie-Claire. *Tête blanche* as *Tête Blanche*. Boston, 1961
Langevin, André. *Poussière sur la ville* as *Dust over the City*. New York, 1955

Lemelin, Roger. *Au pied de la pente douce* as *The Town Below*. New York, 1948
———. *Pierre le magnifique* as *In Quest of Splendour*. Toronto, 1955
———. *Les Plouffe* as *The Plouffe Family*. Toronto, 1948
Ringuet. *30 arpents* as *Thirty Acres*. Toronto, 1961
Roy, Gabrielle. *Alexandre Chenevert, caissier* as *The Cashier*. New York, 1955
———. *Bonheur d'occasion* as *The Tin Flute*. Toronto, 1958
Thériault, Yves. *Agakuk* as *Agakuk*. Toronto, 1963

SECONDARY WORKS

Berthelot-Brunet, H. *Histoire de la littérature canadienne-française*. Paris, 1948
Klinck, Carl F. et al. *Literary History of Canada: Canadian Literature in English*. Toronto, 1965
Lamontagne, Leopold, ed. *Visage de la civilisation au Canada français*. Quebec, 1970
Logan, J. D. and D. G. French. *Highways of Canadian Literature,* 3rd ed. Toronto, 1967

Marcotte, Gilles. *Une littérature qui se fait*. Montreal, 1962
Rièse, Laure. *L'âme de la poésie canadienne française*. London, 1955
Robidoux, R. and A. Renaud. *Le roman canadien-français du XXe siècle*. Quebec, 1968
Roy, Camille. *Histoire de la littérature canadienne,* 14th ed. Quebec, 1950
Smith, A. J. M., ed. *Masks of Fiction*. Toronto, 1961

————. *Masks of Poetry*. Toronto, 1962

Story, Norah. *The Oxford Companion to Canadian History and Literature*. Oxford, 1967

Sylvestre, Guy. *Écrivains canadiens— Canadian writers*. Montreal, 1964

Tougas, Gérard. *Histoire de la littérature canadienne-française,* 2nd ed. Paris, 1964

Viatte, Auguste. *Histoire littéraire de l'Amérique française*. Quebec, 1954

Watters, Reginald Eyre and Ingliss Freeman Bell. *On Canadian literature 1806–1960: A Check List*. Toronto, 1966

Wilson, Edmund. *O Canada*. New York, 1965

ANTONÍN MĚŠŤAN

Czech and Slovak Literature

CZECH LITERATURE

SINCE THE BEGINNING of the romantic period Czech literature has been strongly influenced by nonliterary considerations. At first, literature was used consciously as a weapon in the struggle to maintain Czech as the language of cultivated readers, rather than having it supplanted by German, the language of the Austrian empire, of which Bohemia and Moravia were part. Then, in the second half of the nineteenth century, Czech literature was used as an instrument for upholding the political rights of the Czech people. Only toward the end of the nineteenth century did Czech writers allow aesthetic considerations to supersede its paraaesthetic uses.

After the creation of an independent Czechoslovakia in 1918, other institutions of society naturally took over the social and political functions of literature. It soon became evident, however, that the polarization of political forces—above all in the creative intelligentsia, which by and large showed a marked trend toward the left—as well as, somewhat later, the growing menace of Hitler's Germany, brought a renewed sense of commitment to Czech literature. But this time Czech writers struggled not for ethnic rights but for the defense of democracy and for social welfare. This led to a left-wing radicalization of part of Czech literature during the 1930s.

136

During the German occupation from 1939 to 1945, especially in its last years, the publication of new literary works became very difficult, finally impossible. The works that did manage to appear during the occupation endeavored to strengthen belief in the indestructibility of the Czech people as a nation. Thus, these works were actually a reversion to the age of romanticism.

At the conclusion of World War II, as in other European countries, there was a marked swing toward the left. The wave of political writing largely devoted to socialist ideals mounted high. The joy attending the end of the war, which had threatened the very existence of the Czech people, was directed into an effort to rebuild a democratic society through a radical socialist reorganization. But this period ended in disenchantment in 1948, after the communist takeover. Shortly afterward, it was decreed that literature be patterned after the Soviet model. Writing was thereby degraded into serving as a mere instrument of propaganda. In the place of the earlier spontaneous political involvement, writers were now compelled to submit to the interests of the Communist Party, a coercion that became increasingly rigorously supervised by party functionaries.

During the "thaw" following Stalin's death, there was a certain loosening of restraints in Czechoslovakia, both in political life and in literature. The Second Congress of the Czechoslovak Writers' Association in April, 1956, pointed to directions similar to those gradually emerging in the political and cultural life of neighboring Poland and Hungary. But after the abortive revolution in the autumn of 1956 in Hungary, this development in Czechoslovakia was severely crippled, and the thaw came to an end.

Czech writers had great difficulty in departing from "official literature," since strong conservative (Stalinist) factions of the Communist Party successfully prevented such a development. Not until the late 1960s was literature able, gradually, to liberate itself from the isolation that had kept it cut off artificially from developments in the west since 1948. When the Fourth Congress of the Writers' Association, in June, 1967, gave the signal to combat the ruling forces, Antonín Novotný, first secretary of the Czechoslovak Communist Party, and his cohorts tried to prevent the writers from being heard, because they saw them, with reason, as political adversaries.

The downfall of Novotný, which resulted in the so-called Prague spring (the period from January to August, 1968), did not in any way signify a turning of Czech writers to pure art. On the contrary, many writers turned into agitators and speechmakers, just as writers had done in Poland and Hungary in 1956. The "literary press," which reached mass audiences, became one of the most important weapons of those who demanded extreme changes in the conduct of public affairs.

All this liberalization halted after the Russian invasion of August, 1968.

In the spring of 1969, after the final demotion of Alexander Dubček from the leadership of the Czechoslovak Communist Party, the pressure on all Czech writers increased. Step by step, Czech literary periodicals were suspended. Since the summer of 1970 no literary journal has appeared, and censorship has been intensified.

Political developments have made exiles of Czech writers four times in this century. After both world wars most of them returned home, but those who emigrated after the events of February, 1948, and of August, 1968, have for the most part remained in exile. The emigration of 1968 included Josef Škvorecký (born 1924), Věra Linhartová (born 1938), Antonín Brousek (born 1941), and Arnošt Lustig (born 1926). The most important organs of the new emigration are the magazines *Text* in Munich and *Listy* in Rome. All of the émigrés face the eternal problem of writers in exile: Should they continue to write in Czech, for a small circle of Czech émigrés? Or should they publish in languages of their adopted countries?

POETRY

Immediately after World War II, Czech poetry, which had usually avoided political themes before the war, expressed thanks to the Soviet army, which was then welcomed as liberators. Vítězslav Nezval (1900–1958), one of the greatest Czech poets of the first half of the twentieth century, was renowned before World War II as a surrealist, an admirer of French poetry, and a friend of many internationally famous writers. He started his postwar poetic activity with the collection *Rudé armádě* (1945, To the Red Army). Although his creative originality began to wear thin, Nezval's inexhaustible inventiveness, his mastery of language, and his astonishing use of metaphor continued to characterize some of the works he wrote after 1948. His volumes of verse *Z domoviny* (1951, From the Homeland) and *Chrpy a města* (1955, Cornflowers and Towns) testified to his still-considerable creative power. The influence of his works, especially those of the prewar years, is still perceptible in the writing of a number of poets.

Nezval's friend Jaroslav Seifert (born 1901), who also came to prominence during the 1920s, was, like Nezval, a prewar communist. He hailed the end of the war with the volume *Přílba hlíny* (1945, Helmet of Earth), marked by a patriotic and socialistic tone, but he soon turned his back on political writing. In collections such as *Mozart v Praze* (1946, Mozart in Prague), *Šel malíř chudě do světa* (1949, A Painter Went Penniless Out into the World), and *Maminka* (1954, Mama), his virtuosity shone forth. Because he was an outspoken advocate of liberalization at the Second Congress of the Czechoslovak Writers' Association in 1956, he was compelled to keep silent for a number of years. Undaunted, he picked up the threads of his previous work in *Koncert na ostrově* (1965, A Concert on the Island). He became politically involved again during the "Prague spring." Surprisingly, he was elected chairman of the Czech Writers' Association in June, 1969.

In 1945 František Halas (1901–1949), a prewar communist, published the collection of political verse *Barikády* (Barricades). His wish to express his political views in poetry was only a passing phase, and he returned to his sense of the tragedy of life—surprising in a communist—in *Já se tam vrátím* (1947, I Shall Return There). Some of Halas's readers construed his poems as the expression of secret religious reflections. The high officials of the Communist Party reacted harshly against such possible interpretations, and for a long time after his death his work was in disfavor.

Vladimír Holan (born 1905), one of the most important of all Czech poets, called his first volume of postwar verse *Dík Sovětskému svazu* (1945, Thanks to the Soviet Union). In 1947 he published the collection of poems *Rudoarmejci* (Soldiers of the Red Army). After 1948, when he was harassed and for a time forbidden to publish, he returned to writing pure poetry and to translating. Not until 1963 was he able to publish again his reflective works, such as *Noc s Hamletem* (1964, A Night with Hamlet) and *Bolest* (1965, Pain).

The prolific poet František Hrubín (1910–1971) greeted the year 1945 with his patriotic collections of verse *Chléb s ocelí* (1945, Bread with Steel) and *Jobova noc* (1945, Job's Night). Later he restricted himself almost exclusively to poems for children. At the Second Congress of the Czechoslovak Writers' Association in 1956, he, like Seifert, was a staunch supporter of liberalization. But when the political climate became again repressive, he turned his attention to describing life in a Bohemian village, as in *Srpnová neděle* (1958, A Sunday in August). In his last years, he returned to pure lyric poetry, as in the volume *Černá denice* (1968, The Black Morning Star).

The Catholic poet Jan Zahradníček (1905–1960), who had previously been a symbolist, did not conceal his disillusion with the events after the liberation of Czechoslovakia in May, 1945. He stressed the religious aspects of Czech history in his touching volumes *Svatý Václav* (1946, Saint Wenceslaus) and *Stará země* (1946, The Ancient Land). His irritation with doctrinaire communism was clearly expressed in his poem *La Salletta* (1947, La Salletta). Zahradníček was imprisoned in the 1950s, and when he returned to his work, he was physically broken. Not until 1969 did the authorities allow publication of the poems he wrote from 1956 to 1960—*Čtyři léta* (Four Years).

The painter and poet Jiří Kolář (born 1914) received international recognition, especially for his collages. He was also an admirer and translator of American poetry: Walt Whitman, Edgar Lee Masters, Carl

Sandburg. In spite of the war, he remained true to his surrealistic bent, as can be seen in his collection *Limb, a jiné básně* (1945, Limbo, and Other Poems). During the time that Stalinism dominated Czechoslovak communism, Kolář wrote verses for children. In 1966 he went back to experimenting with verse forms in the collection *Vršovický Ezop* (The Aesop of Vršovice). His *Nový Epiktet* (1968, The New Epictetus) and *Návod k upotřebení* (1969, Directions for Use) departed completely from traditional poetic composition and were a bridge to concrete poetry.

All these poets began writing before 1945. Younger writers, who did not begin publishing until after 1948, found that their books published in the late 1940s and early 1950s were not successful. These poets are known only as translators. The group around the magazine *Květen* (1955–59) was the first to take again a firm hand in the development of Czech poetry. Celebrating daily life, these poems rapidly attracted interest and recognition, especially of young readers.

Jiří Šotola (born 1924) began to publish in 1946, but it was not until after 1956, with the publication of *Svět náš vezdejší* (1957, Our Everyday World), that he became the herald of a new movement through his clear renunciation of sentimentality. Perhaps the most individualistic member of this group is Miroslav Holub (born 1923). His highly intellectual verse has made use of his experiences as a physician and biologist. Among his best collections have been *Denní služba* (1958, Day Service) and *Kam teče krev* (1963, Where the Blood Flows). In *Ačkoli* (1969, Although) he expressed a new synthesis of science, philosophy, and lyricism. The poetry of Miroslav Florian (born 1931) has been characterized by a lyrical admiration of nature and subtle psychological insights. These talents were evident in *Stopy* (1960, Traces) and *Svatá pravda* (1969, The Sacred Truth).

A still younger generation of poets, which came forward in the 1960s, was too young to be fully aware of the oppression of the Stalinist years. The protest of these writers against the social conventions and their naïve romanticism showed strong similarities to the ideas of their contemporaries in the western world.

Among the best-known poets of the young generation is Jana Štroblová (born 1936). Adhering to the forms of rather traditional poetry, she focused on the feelings of young people in *Protěž* (1958, Edelweiss) and *Hostinec u dvou srdcí* (1966, The Inn of the Two Hearts). Her collection *Torza* (1970, Torsos) contained some striking nature poems.

Antonín Brousek revealed himself to be an unconventional intellectual poet in *Spodní vody* (1963, Underground Waters). Ivan Wernisch (born 1942), on the other hand, has written in a decidedly popular tone, since his first work, *Kam letí nebe* (1961, Where the Sky Flies), approaching the naïveté of folk art.

The most radical deviation from the principles of socialist realism (glorification of the communist way of life through everyday instances) has been the movement of concrete poetry. Among its best-known representatives is Josef Hiršal (born 1920). His collection *Job-Boj* (the title is a pun; literally, Job Fight) appeared in 1968. In the search for wider possibilities, Hiršal produced in 1969 a cycle of "auditive poetry" on Czech radio. In this project he was aided by other Czech poets, such as Jiří Kolář, as well as the Austrian poet Gerhard Rühm. These broadcasts were sound collages composed with the aid of tape recordings.

FICTION

The development of Czech fiction, which has always been more politically committed and therefore more vulnerable to attack than poetry, has been full of large gaps as a consequence of the harsh official policies since 1948.

The stories of Jan Drda (1915–1970) in *Němá barikáda* (1946, The Mute Barricade) can be best seen as an effort to create a national myth by depicting and idealizing the uprising against the Nazi occupation in May, 1945. After 1948 Drda was a high official in the party for a long term, as well as chairman of the Writers' Association, which was at that time completely obedient to the party line. In his official capacity, as well as in most of his works of this period, he made every effort to conform to the Soviet pattern as closely as possible. Only in 1968 and 1969 did he redeem himself in the eyes of the progressives by his journalistic activities.

Jiří Mucha (born 1915), who served during the war as an officer in the British RAF, regarded the war from an entirely different point of view. After his return to Prague, he published the volume of stories *Problémy nadporučíka Knapa* (1946, The Problems of First Lieutenant Knap), in which he was primarily concerned with the psychological problems of men in war. He continued to focus on psychological questions in his subsequent works, such as *Studené slunce* (1968, Cold Sun), which was based on his own experiences as a political prisoner in the 1950s.

There were numerous novels and stories about World War II that treated specifically Jewish themes. Among the most noteworthy were the story *Romeo, Julie a tma* (1958, Romeo, Juliet, and Darkness) by Jan Otčenášek (born 1924); the novel *Pan Theodor Mundstock* (1963, Mr. Theodor Mundstock) by Ladislav Fuks (born 1923); and the collection of short stories *Démanty noci* (1958, Diamonds of the Night) by Arnošt Lustig.

But the most important Czech novel about World War II has probably been Josef Škvorecký's *Zbabělci* (1958, The Cowards). Škvorecký, a disciple of Ernest Hemingway in style, vigorously attacked the then-official line about World War II. This line was that of Jan Drda's *The Mute Barricade,* which declared that the uprising of May, 1945, was but the final consummation of a continuous Czech resistance against the Nazis. *The Cowards* was confiscated by order of the highest party authorities immediately after its appearance, therefore becoming a sensational hit both in Czechoslovakia and abroad. The few copies that were salvaged passed from hand to hand until a new printing was permitted in 1964. After some uncontroversial works, Škvorecký again attracted attention with the novel *Lvíče* (1969, The Young Lion). In it he frankly described conditions in a Prague publishing house in which he had worked as editor for a long time.

Many writers endeavored, after 1948, to conform to the requirements of socialist realism, so as to win popularity among readers. The results were the same as in other eastern-bloc countries: practically nobody read these works but the official critics and the censors. Some writers preferred voluntarily to remain silent, others were not allowed to publish, and still others were jailed. Some went to live in exile in the west. For the exiles it was obviously difficult to publish in Czech, and some began writing in the language of their adopted country.

Among the few who have remained active since 1948 is Vladimír Neff (born 1909), who wrote about two families of Prague entrepreneurs in a cycle of five novels—*Sňatky z rozumu* (1957–63, Sensible Marriages)—which was not unlike the works of John Galsworthy and Thomas Mann. In this cycle Neff followed the tradition of the Czech realistic historical novel and so escaped the need to conform to socialist realism.

A place apart in postwar Czech fiction has been occupied by Josef Nesvadba (born 1926), a psychiatrist who has written science fiction. In *Einsteinův mozek* (1960, Einstein's Brain), a collection of short stories, as well as in his other works, he warned against the loss of feeling in a technological civilization.

The general lack of variety in Czech fiction did not change until 1963, when interesting new works about the present were permitted to appear. These rapidly won the interest of Czech readers and somewhat later were received with respect abroad as well.

Bohumil Hrabal (born 1914) made his debut with *Perlička na dně* (1963, A Little Pearl on the Bottom), a collection of tragicomic stories, and quickly became one of the best loved of writers. Rapidly, one after the other, came *Taneční hodiny pro starší a pokročilé* (1964, Dancing Lessons for Adults and Advanced Pupils), *Pábitelé* (1964, Babblers), and other works. His surprising partiality for eccentric characters and human peculiarities has persisted in his work, as can be seen in *Morytáty a legendy* (1968, Ballads of Bloody Deeds and Legends).

The works of Vladimír Páral (born 1932)—such as *Veletrh splněných přání* (1965, The Fair of the Fulfilled Wishes), *Soukromá vichřice*

(1966, Private Stormwind), and *Katapult* (1967, Catapult)—have described with honesty the lives of modest socialist citizens, who accept the system as it exists and adapt themselves to it. Through repetition of words, phrases, and paragraphs, as well as isolated situations, Páral has succeeded—in such works as *Milenci a vrazi* (1969, Lovers and Murderers) —in presenting the lives of his protagonists as being of monotonous sameness, interrupted only by the same amatory adventures.

The long-discouraged theme of romantic love received tragicomic coloring in Milan Kundera's (born 1929) collection of stories *Směšné lásky* (1963, Ridiculous Loves). Kundera intertwined the important theme of police despotism in the period since 1948 with a love theme in the novel *Žert* (1966, The Joke). In his fiction as well as in the play *Majitelé klíčů* (1962, The Owners of the Keys) Kundera has placed characters in difficult situations they themselves must master. Moral principles do not suffice; the intellect must be brought to bear on the circumstances.

Quite unlike these writers of youthful intellectual fiction is Věra Linhartová. Her first work, *Prostor k rozlišení* (1964, Tales without Sequence), provoked puzzlement. Other works, such as *Meziprůzkum nejblíž uplynulého* (1964, A Plea to Share the Most Recent Past) and *Rozprava o zdviži* (1965, Discourse about the Elevator), showed that she is not a mere intellectual trifler but a serious writer who challenges her reader to cooperate. In *Dům daleko* (1968, House in the Distance), composed like a sonata in three movements, Linhartová moved further away from the traditional narrative than anyone else in Czech fiction.

DRAMA

Contemporary Czech acting, direction, stage design, and various technical innovations grew out of the old Czech theater tradition and can be considered among the greatest theatrical achievements in the world. Nevertheless, the number of significant plays since World War II has not been great. This is in part accounted for by the fact that since around 1958 the interest of the younger audiences and the younger writers in Czechoslovakia has been concentrated on the intimate theater, which developed a style of presentation that departed from fixed dramatic rules.

Before the war the major figure in Czech theater was Jan Werich (born 1905), an outstanding actor and coauthor of many plays. He operated, in collaboration with Jiří Voskovec (born 1905), Osvobozené Divadlo (The Liberated Theater). In their productions elements from dadaism, surrealism, and political cabaret were combined. Works produced at the Osvobozené Divadlo later became models for the intimate theater. After 1945, Werich produced nothing and Voskovec emigrated to the United

States, changed his first name to George, and became a prominent film and stage actor.

Between the end of World War II and the flowering of the exceedingly popular intimate theater in the late 1950s, Czech theater suffered a rather lengthy period of stagnation. Its repertory was made up of a small selection of Czech and foreign classics as well as mechanical socialist-realist dramas from the Soviet Union and other eastern-bloc countries. These were supplemented by equally dogmatic new Czech plays. Vašek Káňa (born 1905) was typical of those playwrights who wrote downright indigestible didactic plays. His *Parta brusiče Karhana* (1949, The Brigade of Karhan the Knife Grinder) was a montage of never-ending communist tirades declaimed overemotionally while real machines were operating on stage. This work was produced very frequently in eastern-bloc countries; the Poles even made a film of it.

Miroslav Stehlík (born 1916), a writer of greater skill than Káňa, tried to work within older conceptions of realistic drama. In one trilogy he portrayed the transformation in the social structure of a village in Bohemia extending from prewar times through the Nazi occupation to the forced collectivization after Czechoslovakia became a communist state in 1948. Stehlík's dramas, especially *Selská láska* (1956, Peasant Love), teem with class enemies, but occasional realistic details are evidence of his gift for observation.

Pavel Kohout (born 1928), party official, army officer, diplomat, journalist, and long-time advocate of the hard party line, after writing several poetic exercises devoted to the greater glory of the party, of Stalin, and of the Soviet Union, endeavored to achieve popularity with three plays. Aiming at psychological depth, Kohout wrote *Zářijové noci* (1955, September Nights), which, although intended as a criticism of conditions in the army, proved to be quite tame; *Sbohem, smutku* (1957, Goodbye, Sadness), an attempt to take an optimistic position contrary to Françoise Sagan's *Bonjour tristesse;* and *Taková láska* (1957, Such a Love).

In recent years Kohout's loyalty has increasingly deviated from the official party line. At the Fourth Congress of the Czechoslovak Writers' Association in June, 1967, he was one of the most outspoken participants. In 1968 he was actively involved in ousting the conservative wing of the party hierarchy, which he himself had previously been a member of. His *Tagebuch eines Konter-Revolutionärs* (1969, The Diary of a Counter Revolutionary), which first appeared in German in Switzerland, could not be published in Czechoslovakia.

In 1956, under the shadow of official theater, several young people began to meet together in order to create something entirely novel in the way of entertainment. Some of them later became active as promoters of the most important little theaters in Prague. At the start, their program, which consisted of songs, jazz, and the recitation of stories, contained little of what is traditionally thought of as theater.

As early as 1958 the Divadlo na Zábradlí (Theater on the Balustrades) began to operate. Its name took hold rapidly not only in Czechoslovakia but abroad. The world-famous mime Ladislav Fialka performs here. The first playwright of the Divadlo na Zábradlí, who was also the first director of the theater, until 1962, was Ivan Vyskočil (born 1929). His dramatic montages, at first written in collaboration with Jiří Suchý (born 1931), later with Václav Havel (born 1936), concealed behind a façade of black humor disturbing questions that young audiences felt were vitally important. Characteristic of Vyskočil's work were two plays he wrote with Jiří Suchý: *Kdyby tisíc klarinetů* (1958, If a Thousand Clarinets) and *Faust, Markéta, služka a já* (1959, Faust, Marguerite, the Serving Maid, and I). Vyskočil later turned to writing stories. The collection *Kosti* (1966, Bones) pictures a world full of absurdities that, on closer inspection, turn out not to be absurd at all because our environment is full of them and we have learned to come to terms with them.

An even more important playwright of the Divadlo na Zábradlí was Václav Havel. He made his debut with *Zahradní slavnost* (1963, The Garden Party), influenced by techniques of the theater of the absurd. It is a penetrating satire on a system that converts even the clearest concepts into empty phrases. Also strongly influenced by techniques of theater of the absurd was *Vyrozumění* (1965, The Memorandum), in which Havel openly assailed the machinery of bureaucracy, which oppresses the people and furthers its own selfish aims. *Ztížená možnost soustředění* (1969, The Increased Difficulty of Concentration) posed the question of how man can achieve happiness. Havel's work has evoked much criticism as well as admiration in Czechoslovakia; its importance in contemporary European theater, however, is incontestable.

Another playwright of the Divadlo na Zábradlí, Miloš Macourek (born 1926), has written some of his plays in collaboration with other dramatists: one of his collaborators on *Smutné vánoce* (1960, Sorrowful Christmas), was Ivan Vyskočil. Macourek has also written short stories.

Other writers who contributed to the revival of Czech drama were Ivan Klíma (born 1931), in such plays as *Zámek* (1965, A Castle), and Josef Topol (born 1935), whose *Konec masopustu* (1963, The End of Shrovetide) used the stylized Czech ritual of Mardi Gras.

In 1959 the Divadlo Semafor (Semaphore Theater) was opened. Both its directors, Jiří Suchý and Jiří Šlitr (1924–1969), learned their craft from Jan Werich and Jiří Voskovec. But the Divadlo Semafor developed into its own highly original form as a musical theater. In its first ten years it put on forty-six productions and always has played to full houses. Šlitr was especially important as a composer, singer, and actor; Suchý wrote most of the dialogue and the lyrics. The individual songs and skits were combined quite freely with humorous text. The humor and the definitely antisentimental tone of Suchý's dialogue was frequently imitated. Suchý has also published many short stories, not all of which are very good. In *Med ve vlasech* (1970, Honey in Her Hair) he collected almost all his short fiction.

In a short time, other small theaters were established in Prague and in other Czech cities, after the pattern of these intimate theaters. They have continued to make further innovations. The great interest of the public, especially of youth, in these theatrical experiments has not diminished.

SLOVAK LITERATURE

Nineteenth-century Slovak literature performed many of the same extra-literary functions as did Czech literature. But conditions in Hungary, of which Slovakia was then a region, were much less favorable than in Austrian-controlled Bohemia and Moravia, and this oppression impeded the development of Slovak literature. After Bohemia, Moravia, and Slovakia were united into the new nation of Czechoslovakia in 1918, Slovak literature rapidly began to catch up with the Czech lead.

Toward the end of the nineteenth century, Slovak writers, like Czech writers, became more interested in literature as an art form; the establishment of the state of Czechoslovakia in 1918 held out the promise to Slovak writers, as it did to Czech writers, that they could now leave literature's paraaesthetic functions to other institutions of the state. But Slovak writers realized quite soon after World War I that circumstances demanded that they write politically committed works. A special incentive in Slovakia for committed literature was a resentment of Czech domination in national politics and a need to assert their own—Slovak—identity.

When Hitler annexed Bohemia and Moravia in 1939, he created a nominally independent state of Slovakia; and the Nazis did not directly influence Slovak cultural life until 1944. Thus, during the war Slovak literature enjoyed better conditions for development than did Czech literature. The activity of the surrealists had special significance, because it was interpreted by the Slovak people as democratic opposition to the German-sponsored fascist regime. Between 1945 and 1948, Slovak writers shared with their Czech counterparts the same enthusiasm and the same illusions, and surrealism still dominated Slovak literature. The communist takeover in 1948 brought quick disenchantment in Slovakia. The situation was aggravated by the return of centralizing pressure from Prague. Dissatisfaction with the state of affairs in public life and with the enforced socialist realism in art imposed from above became even more intense in Slovakia than it did in Bohemia and Moravia, but the dissatisfaction could not express itself to any extent in literature.

After a brief period of relaxation after Stalin's death, Slovaks were disillusioned by the renewed repressions following the Hungarian revolution and by the anti-Slovak policy of Novotný and his cohorts, despite the fact that some Slovaks exerted considerable influence in the national government. The tension over the anti-Slovak attitudes began to be aired about 1963, especially in Slovak literary journals. From 1963 to 1967 Slovak writers spearheaded the resistance to Novotný, making headway against dogma much sooner than the Czechs. Yet what they preached most of all was the legitimacy of Slovakia's ethnic interests. Only secondarily did they stress the need for a general democratization in public life.

Slovak nationalism was also apparent during the "Prague spring" of 1968. Until today, it has not become clear why the Slovak writers failed to take an active part in the historic Fourth Congress of the Czechoslovak Writers' Association in June, 1967, in which decisive struggle against Novotný was embarked upon.

Today the west is the home for émigré Slovak writers, both those who left during the 1940s and those who left after 1968. Slovak literature in exile, however, is not particularly rich. Some of the émigré writers, such as Ladislav Mňačko (born 1919) now publish almost exclusively in languages other than Slovak.

POETRY

Unlike Czech poets, the most important Slovak lyric poets did not become politically committed during the period 1945–48. The surrealists, the most outstanding Slovak poets, continued to go their own way. Consequently, when Slovak surrealists after 1948 joined in panegyrics to Stalin, industrial production, and the collectivization of agriculture, the rupture with the past was much more striking than in Czech literature. It was not until 1960, and even more conspicuously after 1963, that Slovak poetry returned to its pre-1948 voice.

Štefan Žáry (born 1918), one of the most talented Slovak surrealists, was, like so many of his colleagues, influenced by the great Czech poet Vítězslav Nezval. Also fluent in French and Spanish poetry, loyal to his own poetic origins, and maintaining his surrealistic idiom, Žáry wrote in an antimilitaristic, humanist vein in his first postwar collections—*Pavúk pútnik* (1946, The Wandering Spider) and *Zasľúbená zem* (1947, The Promised Land). But in 1948 he glorified the Slovak heroes of the nineteenth and twentieth centuries in his *Meč a vavrín* (Sword and

Laurels), using the verse forms of Slovak folk poetry and the Slovak romantics.

Žáry's collection *Cesta* (1952, The Road) linked him with those writers who endeavored to comply with the demands of socialist realism without suppressing their own creativity. But in 1960 he returned much more thoroughly to his earlier poetic goals. *Zázračný triezvy koráb* (The Magic Sober Ship) and *Ikar večne živý* (The Immortal Icarus) contained poems in which he soared freely over the philosophical and human problems of space flights.

Another surrealist, Pavel Bunčák (born 1915), published in 1946 the collection *S tebou a sám* (With You and Alone), one of the major works of postwar Slovak surrealism. Since *Zomierať zakázané* (1948, Dying Is Forbidden) he has been writing dull, dutifully optimistic works. His interest in Polish poetry and his translations from Polish were the sole evidence for many years that Bunčák was not dead as a poet. But *Prostá reč* (1963, Simple Speech) signified a turning point in that it gave evidence of his renewed creative power.

Ján Rak's (1915–1969) postwar poetry followed a path similar to that of so many Slovak surrealists. In his first postwar works—*Nezanechajte nádeje* (1946, Don't Give Up Hope) and *V údolí slnka* (1946, In the Valley of the Sun)—he was still writing surrealistic poems. But the title of his next work, *Pieseň mierových rúk* (1949, Song of the Hands of Peace), indicated that after 1948 he switched to political poetry. Not until the poems in *Plenér* (1962, In the Open), which could be called impressionistic, was there an indication that Rak had veered in a new direction. The poems collected in *Poslední gladiátori* (1970, The Last Gladiators), which appeared only after his death, showed very clearly that he, too, wished to return to his poetic beginnings.

Vladimír Reisel (born 1919), a prominent theorist and champion of surrealism, was still developing his own definition of surrealism in 1946, in the poems in *Zrkadlo a za zrkadlom* (The Mirror and Behind It). After 1948 he, like so many others, abandoned his predilections, and his collection *Svet bez pánov* (1951, The World without Masters) contained pallid poems. He lost his readership without gaining favor with the official critics. Only gradually did his poetry regain resonance and color. Since his collection *More bez odlivu* (1960, The Tideless Sea) he has taken his place once more among major Slovak poets. Love has been the central theme of Reisel's more recent works: *Láska na posledný pohľad* (1964, Love at Last Sight) and *Smutné rozkoše* (1966, Melancholy Rapture). In them his poetic talent was again evident.

Laco Novomeský (born 1904), before the war an avant-garde poet, a communist journalist and politician, for a long time published nothing after the war except the collection *Pašovanou ceruzkou* (1948, With a Smuggled Pencil), which he had written during the war. His prewar work was influenced by Nezval, Mayakovski, and Yesenin. His experience as an important cultural organizer and a politician seemed to assure him great authority and influence after the war. He was indeed active in various party and state offices after 1945, but during the period in which the party line hardened, he was condemned as a nationalist and imprisoned. For a time after his release, he was forbidden from partaking in political activity. Not until 1963 could he publish his long poem *Vila Tereza* (Villa Tereza), in which he described his ties with the Soviet Union. In *Stamodtial, a iné* (1964, From Yonder, and Other Poems) he wrote about his experiences after 1945. In recent years Novomeský has again become politically active in Slovakia.

Ján Kostra's (born 1910) first postwar collection, *Presila smútku* (1946, The Overwhelming Sorrow), reminiscent of Czech proletarian poetry of the 1920s, was followed by the poem *Na Stalina* (1949, On Stalin). But by 1953, in *Javorový list* (Maple Leaf), Kostra was once again writing pure poetry. He showed considerable virtuosity by his translations of Nezval, Hrubín, and Baudelaire, as well as by his later original works: *Šípky a slnečnice* (1958, Hedge Roses and Sunflowers) and *Báseň, dielo tvoje* (1960, The Poem, Your Work). In recent years he has devoted himself to eternal themes of poetry—love and friendship—as can be seen in *Len raz* (1968, Only Once).

Andrej Plávka (born 1907), a conservative in art, has linked himself consciously to the Slovak poets of the nineteenth century. His first book of poetry, *Ohne na horách* (1947, Fire on the Peaks), took as its subject the Slovak uprising of 1944. For a while he wrote party propaganda, an example of which is *Sláva života* (1955, The Glory of Life). His later works, such as *Korene* (1965, Roots), are far more appealing, but he still continued to use poetic techniques of the past.

A number of poets after 1948 considered the artist's mission that of political agitation. Pavol Horov (born 1914) attempted to write propagandistic poetry in *Slnce nad nami* (1954, The Sun above Us). Then there was a striking change in his work. His volumes of poetry *Vysoké letné nebo* (1960, The High Sky of Summer) and *Koráby z Janova* (1966, The Ships from Genoa) revealed a reflective poetry with a touch of sentimentality akin to his mature writing during World War II.

Those Slovak poets who entered literary life shortly after 1945 shared the dilemma of their Czech contemporaries. Between 1945 and 1948 the young writers, fascinated by Slovak surrealism, were only just beginning to find their poetic voices. But after 1948 they had to conform for a number of years to the prescriptions of socialist realism if they wished to see their works in print. Some of the younger writers themselves believed in the value of socialist realism. Among them was Milan Lajčiak (born 1926), a party official and diplomat, who pleased the officials of the party more than he did his readers with his first book, *Súdružka moja zem* (1949, My Comrade, My Country). He published similar poetic products in rapid succession. His collection *Kniha istoty* (1960, Book of Certainty) made it clear that the political and cultural thaws in Czechoslovakia since Stalin's death had affected him little.

The poems of Vojtech Mihálik's (born 1926) first book, *Anjeli* (1947, The Angels), were in the spirit of Christian humanism. But *Plebejská ko-šeľa* (1950, Plebeian's Shirt) showed a radical change. He wrote many poems devoted to the "building of socialism." Later, however, Mihálik turned to other themes and showed himself to be a very competent crafts-man, especially in *Útek za Orfeom* (1965, Flight after Orpheus). At the end of August, 1968, he attacked the Soviet Union vigorously in the poem *Rekviem* (Requiem), but in 1969, in *Čierna jeseň* (Black Autumn), he took a stand against the ideas of democratization that were gaining such force in 1968. Mihálik has been very active politically since 1969; at present he is chairman of a chamber of the Czechoslovak Parliament.

The writers who have come to the fore since around 1960 have had it much easier because of the retreat during the 1950s from the extremes of dogmatism. Miroslav Válek (born 1929) elicited astonishment with his surprisingly mature collection *Dotyky* (1959, Touches), which was rapidly followed by other equally accomplished works. His poetry was quickly appreciated by the young and found many imitators. Válek has avoided false pathos, but traces of sorrow and fear of the unknown, instead of the false optimism required by the official line, can be found in his poems. He later became an official in the Slovak Writers' Association. Today he is the Slovak minister of culture.

FICTION

Slovak writers of fiction, like their Czech counterparts and those of other eastern-bloc nations, were more disturbed by the developments after 1948 than the poets were. There was an additional hindrance in Slovakia: Hun-garian tyranny during the nineteenth century prevented the complete un-folding of critical realism in fiction. Because it came so late to Slovakia, critical realism dominated fiction well into the twentieth century, even after 1945. After 1948 novelists shifted to the "higher plane" of socialist realism. Many long-winded works were written during the early years of communist rule, among which were a number of trilogies (most of which were never completed) in the leisurely tradition of the nineteenth century. Few of these works succeeded in achieving more than superficial descriptions. The representative writers of the early postwar years were Peter Jilemnický (1901–1949) and Fraňo Kráľ' (1903–1955).

Peter Jilemnický, an early communist, began his writing career in his native Czech, but, after becoming a teacher in Slovakia he published only in Slovak. Even before the war he had been an uncompromising champion of socialist realism, to which his stay of two years in the Soviet Union contributed. His novel *Kronika* (1947, Chronicles) described the anti-German uprising in Slovakia in August, 1944, in which, however, Jilemnický had not taken part because he was in a concentration camp. He pictured the communists as the chief organizers of the uprisings, and his glorification of the communists became adopted as canon in other works about the uprising.

Fraňo Kráľ' became a high party official after 1945. In his novel *Za krajší život* (1949, Toward a Better Life) he offered an autobiographical account of the life of a party official. In his last novel, *Bude ako nebolo* (1950, It Will Be As It Has Not Been), he wrote the typical tedious story of the "building of socialism." For a number of years this work was prescribed to young Slovak writers as the model they had to copy in dealing with contemporary problems. Slowly, however, both Jilemnický and Kráľ' lost their binding power on Slovak novelists.

The first novel of František Hečko (1905–1960), *Červené víno* (1948, Red Wine), about life in a tiny wine-growing village in western Slovakia, was written completely in the objective spirit of critical realism. But in his second novel, *Drevená dedina* (1951, The Wooden Village), whose theme was the collectivization of agriculture in northern Slovakia, Hečko attempted to meet all requirements of socialist realism. Only his storytelling talent saved this work from oblivion. Hečko planned a trilogy of novels about life in Slovakia during World War II, but he died soon after finishing the first part, *Svätá tma* (1958, Sacred Darkness), in which he criticized sharply, from the communist viewpoint, the Nazi-supported Tiso regime that ruled "independent" Slovakia during the war.

The writing career of Rudolf Jašík (1919–1960) lasted only five years. In his first novel, *Na brehu priezračnej rieky* (1956, On the Bank of a Clear Stream), he described life in one of the most impoverished regions of Slovakia before 1939. The novel *Námestie svätej Alžbety* (1958, St. Elizabeth's Square), about the love of a Slovak man for a Jewish girl during the war, was one of the most widely read books of its day. *Mŕtvi nespievajú* (1961, The Dead Don't Sing), about the fate of Slovak soldiers fighting against the Soviet Union, was unfinished when Jašík died.

Dominik Tatarka (born 1913) has been one of the most individual

Slovak writers. His novel *Farská republika* (1948, The Republic of Priests), about the church-dominated fascist state in Slovakia, was a deeply penetrating psychological analysis of his people during World War II. Tatarka's works after 1950 were no longer marked by psychological analysis, an omission that did not exactly increase their worth. Yet, he was one of the first in Slovakia to criticize Stalinism, in the political satire *Démon súhlasu* (1956, The Demon of Consent). At first, the work was permitted to appear only in a magazine; it was not published as a book until 1963. Since then Tatarka has published well-balanced works of psychological depth, such as *Prútené kreslá* (1963, The Wicker Armchair), which described the atmosphere in Paris just before World War II.

Ladislav Mňačko was for a long time extolled by the communists as a writer to be emulated. After some completely unsuccessful poetic efforts and some too-obviously-plotted plays, he published a novel, *Smrť sa volá Engelchen* (1959, Death Is Called Engelchen [Little Angel]), about the battles of the Czech and Slovak partisans on the border of Moravia and Slovakia during the closing phases of World War II. During the less restrictive atmosphere of the early 1960s, Mňačko wrote *Oneskorené reportáže* (1963, Belated Reportage), in which he condemned the methods of Stalinism. This work led to a rift with the Novotný group. After being deprived of his citizenship and living for a while in the west, Mňačko returned to Czechoslovakia and published the novel *Ako chutí moc* (1968, How Power Tastes), which had previously appeared in translation in the west. After the disastrous events of August, 1968, he went abroad again and wrote in German an attack against the Russian invasion in the novel *Die siebente Nacht* (1968, The Seventh Night). This work and another novel, *Vorgang* (1970, An Occurrence), could not be published in Slovakia. Mňačko's lively journalistic style, combined with a decided knack for sensationalism and publicity, has made him one of today's most widely known contemporary Czechoslovak writers.

Alfonz Bednár (born 1914), an accomplished translator from the English, surprised the public by publishing his own novel, *Sklený vrch* (1954, The Glass Mountain). At its appearance it caused a sensation; it was regarded as an attack on the tedious novels extolling production records. In succeeding works Bednár began to make cautious analyses of postwar developments. But it was not until 1968, in the short novel *Balkón bol privysoko* (The Balcony Was Too High), that he more openly criticized the postwar period, especially the manipulation of the whole society. More recently, he has turned in part to surrealism.

The writer who won perhaps the greatest popularity during the relaxation of the political atmosphere after 1963 was Ladislav Ťažký (born 1921). After some works that attracted little attention he published the novel *Amenmária* (1964, Mother of God!), which can be described as a story of the fate of the Slovaks during World War II, especially of Slovak soldiers in the Soviet Union. In his later works Ťažký has continued to focus on World War II, as in the novel *Pivnica plná vlkov* (1969, Cellar Full of Wolves), which described the life of Slovak peasants during the war and after 1945. Ťažký has tried to open up the techniques of realistic narration and has also experimented with language itself.

DRAMA

Slovak poetry, and to some extent also Slovak fiction, underwent exciting growth after the founding of the state of Czechoslovakia in 1918. But this was not true of the drama. Before 1918 there was practically no professional theater in Slovakia. The consequences of this have not yet been overcome. After World War II the older Slovak playwrights wrote practically nothing. After 1948 the Slovak stage presented, in addition to works of non-Slovak playwrights, a few new plays by its own writers; only the titles of these works are remembered today.

The only Slovak playwright who has won wider than local recognition is Peter Karvaš (born 1920). His sharp criticism of the Slovak petty bourgeoisie and its conduct during the war, as revealed in *Polnočná omša* (1959, Midnight Mass), brought his work to the attention of readers abroad. Karvaš showed himself to be a perceptive psychologist in *Antigona a tí druhí* (1962, Antigone and the Others), a play he wrote in a concentration camp during the war. His play *Jizva* (1963, The Scar) caused an international sensation; it was the first play in Slovakia to picture the persecution of innocent people after the communist takeover. Karvaš is also a fine writer of fiction, as he demonstrated in the stories in *Nedokončená pre detský hlas* (1968, The Unfinished for a Child's Voice).

In recent years little theaters have sprung up in Slovakia, especially in Bratislava, on the pattern of those in Prague. Suffering from the lack of original Slovak works, the repertory of such theaters as the Divadlo na Korze (Theater on the Boulevard) in Bratislava consists predominantly of foreign plays. The interesting cabaret theater called Tatra-Revue in Bratislava was closed down in February, 1970, for political reasons—just one more example of the dominance of politics over literature in Czechoslovakia since 1948.

CZECH AND SLOVAK WORKS IN
ENGLISH TRANSLATION

ANTHOLOGIES

French, A., ed. *A Book of Czech Verse.*
London, 1958
Harkins, William E., ed. *Anthology of
Czech Literature.* New York, 1953
Hughes, Ted and Daniel Weisbort, eds.
*Modern Poetry in Translation, no. 5:
The Czech Poets.* New York, 1965
Osers, Ewald and J. K. Montgomery, eds.
Modern Czech Poetry. London, 1945
Otruba, Mojmír and Zdeněk Pešat, eds.
*The Linden Tree: An Anthology of
Czech and Slovak Literature, 1890–
1960.* Prague, 1962
Theiner, George, ed. *New Writing in
Czechoslovakia.* Baltimore, 1969
Weiskopf, Franz Carl, ed. *Hundred
Towers: A Czechoslovak Anthology of
Creative Writing.* New York, 1945

INDIVIDUAL WORKS MENTIONED
IN ARTICLE

Fuks, Ladislav. *Pan Theodor Mundstock*
as *Mr. Theodore Mundstock.* New
York, 1968
Havel, Václav. *Vyrozumění* as *The
Memorandum.* New York, 1967
———. *Zahradní slavnost* as *The Garden
Party.* London, 1969
Holub, Miroslav. *Ačkoli* as *Although.*
New York, 1971
Jašík, Rudolf. *Námestie svätej Alžbety*
as *St. Elizabeth's Square.* New York,
1965
Kohout, Pavel. *Tagebuch eines Konter-
Revolutionärs* as *The Diary of a Coun-
ter Revolutionary.* New York, 1972
Škvorecký, Josef. *Zbabělci* as *The Cow-
ards.* New York, 1969

SECONDARY WORKS

Buriánek, František. *Česká literatura 20.
století.* Prague, 1968
———. *Současná česká literatura.* Prague,
1960
Česká literární bibliografie 1945–1963,
3 vols. Prague, 1963–64
Harkins, W. E. and K. Šimončič. *Czech
and Slovak Literature.* New York, 1951
Havel, Rudolf and Jiří Opelík, eds.
Slovník českých spisovatelů. Prague,
1964
Meriggi, Bruno. *Storia delle letterature
ceca e slovacca.* Milan, 1958
Mišianik, Ján et al. *Dejiny slovenskej
literatúry,* 2nd ed. Bratislava, 1962
Mráz, Andrej. *Dejiny slovenskej literatúry.* Bratislava, 1948
Mukařovský, J., ed. *Dějiny české literaturgeschichte.* Munich, 1970

Mukařovský, J., ed. *Dějiny české litera-
tury,* 3 vols. Prague, 1959–61
Novák, Arne et al. *Stručné dějiny litera-
tury české.* Olomouc, 1946
Pražák, Albert. *Dějiny slovenské litera-
tury.* Prague, 1950ff.
Ripellino, Angelo M. *Storia della poesia
ceca contemporanea.* Rome, 1950
Součková, Milada. *A Literary Satellite:
Czechoslovak-Russian Literary Rela-
tions.* Chicago, 1970
Števček, Pavol. *Nová slovenská literatura.*
Prague, 1964
Václavek, Bedřich. *Česká literatura XX.
století.* Prague, 1947
Vlček, Jaroslav. *Dějiny české literatury,*
3 vols., 5th ed. Prague, 1960
———. *Dejiny literatúry slovenskej,* 4th
ed. Bratislava, 1953

WILHELM FRIESE

Danish Literature

THE SCANDINAVIAN LITERATURES in the late nineteenth century exhibited striking similarities in subject matter, themes, and style. Around the turn of the century, however, these correspondences gave way increasingly to national and regional currents. In Denmark Johannes V. Jensen (1873–1950) and Martin Andersen Nexø (1869–1954) introduced Jutland and Bornholm into literature; in addition, Jensen's belief in technical progress and Andersen Nexø's confidence in the power of proletarian solidarity burst through provincial narrowness and turned Jutland and Bornholm into microcosms. In form, however, their works remained within the tradition of realism; indeed, in the first half of the twentieth century, realism was the mode of the greater part of Danish literature.

During the early twentieth century the influence of Danish writing on European literature, especially German, became slighter and slighter, and the interrelationships among the various Scandinavian literatures decreased considerably. Nevertheless, Martin Andersen Nexø's propagandizing for socialism and communism and Johannes Jørgensen's (1866–1956) proclamations of the value of Catholicism had worldwide readership.

Of course, Danish writers *were* strongly influenced by the main political events and the intellectual and literary trends of the major European cultures. Nietzsche's ideas and language and the stylistic features of expressionism found their way into Danish literature, although, according to the influential contemporary literary critic Torben Brostrøm (born 1927),

155

expressionism in Denmark, unlike Germany, produced only "good-natured and easygoing" results.

Danish writers also adopted surrealism and the stream-of-consciousness technique, both of which opened up new possibilities for psychological realism. But in the 1920s, ideological problems were discussed more intensively than aesthetic issues. The 1930s, with the growing political danger from the south, united former ideological opponents in a "cultural front" against fascism, and the oppressive years of the German occupation (1940–45) brought forth political concerns that pushed literary experiments into the background.

POETRY

In the years before and during World War II there was little in Danish poetry that could be called "modern." A socially involved and political literature—particularly the poetry of resistance, which was printed illegally in considerable quantity during the war—demanded a readily comprehensible language. Thus, the public largely ignored the work of the more experimental poets: the violent language and explosive imagery of Tom Kristensen (born 1893); Emil Bønnelycke's (1893–1953) ecstatic prose poetry; Jens August Schade's (born 1903) cosmic whimsies reminiscent of Marc Chagall; and Gustaf Munch-Petersen's (1912–1938) surrealistic images.

The war and the bleakness of the subsequent years caused the authors of the 1940s to return to the moods of the 1920s. Ethical and existential questions replaced the sociological and psychological problems of the prewar period, and causes for historical developments were sought less in the social realm than in the domain of the demonic. The circle around the journal *Heretica* (1948–53) rebelled against the overvaluing of rationalism. The postwar generation's deep-seated feeling of anxiety (Kierkegaard's *Begrebet angst* [1844, The Concept of Dread] acquired an immediate significance) was best articulated by the influential cultural critic Vilhelm Grønbech (1873–1948). At the same time he pointed out the significance of myths for modern man. For him, the poem was no longer a weapon. It had become a form of knowledge; and since general truths no longer said anything, verse had to contain a personal truth.

In *Heretica* Paul La Cour (1902–1956) published a poetic work written in the form of a diary—*Fragmenter af en dagbog* (1948, Fragments of a Diary). Although La Cour had demanded in the 1930s that art reform itself by focusing on social problems, he later asserted the value of imagery for poetry; only the image could express the unity of the world and communicate truth. The collections *Mellem bark og ved* (1950, Between

Bark and Wood) and the posthumously published *Efterladte digte* (1957, Posthumous Poems) made an honest effort to solve this postulate. Yet La Cour's demands that art be its own concern were repeatedly counterbalanced by his ever-present consciousness of the community of man.

The symbolic world of the *Heretica* circle also characterized Jørgen Gustava Brandt's (born 1928) first collection of poems, *Korn i Pelegs mark* (1949, Grain in Peleg's Field). He tried to find beauty both by contemplating objects and by attempting to achieve a mystical experience. Brandt gradually departed from the ideological and aesthetic ideas of his early poetry. Yet the central themes of sacrifice and love and his frequently recurring religious concepts—all of which appeared more than a decade later in *Fragmenter of imorgen* (1960, Fragments of Tomorrow)— showed his continuing ties to his intellectual and literary origins. Although *Fragments of Tomorrow,* an "Offertory in Eight Songs," ends in a mystical-religious experience of love, the individual remains bound to this world. He cannot achieve a unity between inner and external reality, but seems divided. Indeed, Brandt used a classic image of dividedness for the title of one of his volumes—*Janushoved* (1962, Janus Head). However, from *Etablissementet* (1965, The Establishment) through *I den høje evighed lød et bilhorn* (1970, In Lofty Eternity an Auto Horn Honked) the environment became more accessible and comprehensible to the speaker of Brandt's poems.

By means of abrupt leaps, random images, and extremely concentrated language, Ole Sarvig (born 1921) in his early collections of verse—from *Grønne digte* (1943, Green Poems) through *Menneske* (1948, Man)— depicted the situation of man in the mid-twentieth century. In our chaotic, gloomy times, with the barren materialism of modern urban culture, the lonely and isolated individual finds his salvation in an affirmation of Christ, even if this affirmation is uttered hesitantly. The "I" is redeemed through his meeting with a "Thou," through love and the secret of divine grace.

In *Min kærlighed* (1952, My Love) Sarvig finally experienced the redeemer. Sarvig's works suggest that perhaps a new Christianity, without traditions, is developing in our age—a Christianity of the individual (here the legacy of Kierkegaard is evident). The themes of the poems occurred again in several of Sarvig's novels. In *Stenrosen* (1955, Stone Roses), *De sovende* (1958, The Sleepers), and *Havet under mit vindue* (1960, The Ocean beneath My Window) he described in lyric, symbolic-realistic prose the difficulties of the individual striving for self-awareness and seeking the redeeming, compassionate "Thou."

Ole Wivel (born 1921) was not able to find God in the church or in other institutions of official Christianity. In *I fiskens tegn* (1948, Under the Sign of the Fish)—a title that evokes the early Christian symbol for Christ—and even more so in *Jænvdøgnselegier* (1949, Elegies like Day and Night) Wivel invoked, through almost apocalyptic images, the isolation of modern man and the deep despair and yearning of the individual for the hidden God. Man lives in a state of uncertainty and emptiness, in which language has been corrupted. T. S. Eliot's *The Waste Land* was clearly the model for this work.

In *Den skjulte Gud* (1952, The Hidden God) Wivel hoped to meet the God of his search in the old and still-unified folk culture. This discovery could then lead Wivel in *Månen* (1952, The Moon) to use his hope to perceive the closeness of God to the world in a manner similar to the way the light of the sun is perceived by means of the moon. The poems in *Templet for Kybele* (1961, The Temple for Cybele) revolved about the identity of the individual. It has not been easy for Wivel, who has sought values in a world that no longer knows any values, both to maintain an ethical stance and to satisfy art's demands. In both *Nike* (1958, Nike) and *Gravskrifter* (1970, Epitaphs) he turned his attention to critical observation of his age.

Like Sarvig and Wivel, the early poetry of Erik Knudsen (born 1922)— *Til en ukendt Gud* (1947, To an Unknown God)—tried to find the "unknown God." Yet as early as *Blomsten og sværdet* (1949, The Flower and the Sword) he began to believe that the dangerous situation in our world is caused by social conditions. Even though he has had doubts about the efficacy of the poet's word, he has nevertheless made an effort to unmask the idols of contemporary culture and the brutality of capitalism in simple and clear poems—from the collection *Brændpunkt* (1953, Focal Point) to the political texts in *Babylon marcherer* (1970, Babylon Marches). He effectively satirized the Danish welfare society in *Frihed— det bedste guld* (1961, Freedom—the Best Gold). *Det er ikke til at bære* (1963, It Is Unbearable), in which he took up the same theme by using motifs from Büchner's *Leonce and Lena,* was less successful.

The problem of living in the contemporary world has also been a central theme in Thorkild Bjørnvig's (born 1918) poems, but he has sought solutions more in art than in society. In *Stjærnen bag gavlen* (1947, The Star behind the Gable) Eros, resembling a distant star, leads man out of the narrowness of life; and only art can grasp Eros. The poems in *Anubis* (1955, Anubis) treated the ambivalent relationship between art and basic human experiences. The individual must accept the inexorable law of dying; only in this manner can he overcome the horror of death and gain the strength to withstand life. Both in these themes and in the sonnet form he used here Bjørnvig showed the influence of Friedrich Hölderlin and of Rilke.

Rilke occupied Bjørnvig's attention for years; this intense involvement resulted in a scholarly treatise and translations of several volumes. Bjørnvig also adopted from Rilke the idea that life can be mastered only through art. Only art can transform chaos into order and harmony, as a number of poems in *Figur og ild* (1959, Figure and Fire) proclaimed. Both *Figure and Fire* and Bjørnvig's later *Vibrationer* (1966, Vibrations) and *Ravnen* (1968, The Raven) used compressed language to present a wealth of reflections on contemporary man.

Unlike any of these poets is Klaus Rifbjerg (born 1931), who has expressed himself more violently than any other contemporary Danish writer. In one of his first poems Rifbjerg introduced himself self-assuredly, albeit ironically, as a "poseur from the beginning." There is scarcely a genre in which this unusually prolific author has not tried his hand. From 1959 to 1963 Rifbjerg and Villy Sørensen (born 1929) edited the journal *Vindrosen,* the mouthpiece of the new generation of authors emerging after World War II. Year after year Rifbjerg has published poems, novels, stories, film scripts, and essays.

In Rifbjerg's first collections of poems—*Under vejr med sig selv* (1956, Having Come to Myself), *Efterkrig* (1957, After the War), and *Konfrontation* (1960, Confrontation)—the speaker stood exposed, facing the world irreverently and coolly; he recorded, without illusions, the phenomena of existence. With unusual syntax and an inexhaustible supply of fresh, modern words, Rifbjerg defined the position of a generation that believes that it is accepting life as it is. He thus departed from the symbolic, existential literature of the immediate postwar years.

As early as *Camouflage* (1961, Camouflage), however, with its imploring and ecstatic verses and surrealistic associations, Rifbjerg tried to comprehend the meaning of existence and to know the present by examining personal memories and past events. In simple diction borrowed from everyday language, he depicted childhood memories in the *Amagerdigte* (1965, Amager Poems). In *Fædrelandssange* (1967, Songs of the Homeland) he celebrated his Danish island homeland in a radiant mood, full of optimism. At the same time he has not forgotten the confusions of the world, as can be seen in the critical and demythologizing poems in *Mytologi* (1970, Mythology).

Rifbjerg's renunciation of the metaphysical view of life of the poetry of the first postwar years was repeated by many of his contemporaries. Before long, however, many of them recognized that neither a skepticism toward ideologies nor a method of observation that proceeded calmly and without presuppositions was enough for survival in this world.

In Ivan Malinovski's (born 1926) collection of poems, *Galgenfrist* (1958, Respite from the Gallows) the speaker not only stood under the imminent threat of the atomic bomb but was aware of living constantly in the shadow of death. The certainty of death and the feeling of the futility of existence are existential experiences. This nihilistic position, however, later led Malinovski not to defeatism but to the defiant activist behavior in *Åbne digte* (1963, Open Poems) and *Poetomatic* (1965, Poetomatic). The title of one of Malinovski's collections provides a cautiously optimistic motto for our times: *Leve som var der en fremtid og et håb* (1969, Live as if There Were a Future and a Hope).

Cecil Bødker (born 1927) does not entertain much hope for either the future or the present. In her view, man lives in a state of constant restlessness, but wherever he walks, everything turns to ashes under his feet. The concrete details and abstract images in the poems from *Luseblomster* (1955, Dandelions) to *Anadyomene* (1959, Anadyomene) have also marked Bødker's prose works. The volume of stories *Øjet* (1961, The Eye) described the inner chaos of modern man, which is leading him to catastrophe. In *Tilstanden Harley* (1965, The Condition of Harley) the oppressive impact drives the individual to flee from himself and others, away from all human contacts. Bødker's vision in the satirical novel *Pap* (1967, Cardboard) was even gloomier. The world of the future described here has already largely become a reality in our world of systematic conformity.

The confrontation with the confusing chaotic condition of the world has led Jess Ørnsbo (born 1932) to seek a unity in the confusion. However, since an "emptiness between things" remained, he set out in *Digte* (1960, Poems) and *Myter* (1964, Myths) to examine ancient and modern myths. In *A som Alfred eller det rullende alfabet* (1969, A as in Alfred, or the Rolling Alphabet) he tried to describe the grotesqueness of human existence.

Similar themes characterized Inger Christensen's (born 1935) collections *Lys* (1962, Light) and *Græs* (1964, Grass), but she concentrated primarily on the words themselves, which are, in the last analysis, the primary creators of poetic reality. *Det* (1969, It) was a comprehensive cycle of poems concerning the process of poetic and human development. The condensed language of Christensen's verse has also characterized her prose works, which have dealt with such basic human experiences as loneliness, love, and death.

There are a number of other contemporary poets worth mentioning. Halfdan Rasmussen (born 1915), since the volume *Digte under besættelsen* (1945, Poems During the Occupation), has used strict rhythms and simple stanzaic forms. Robert Corydon's (born 1924) pictorial language has been inspired by modern painting. Per Højholt (born 1928) has experimented with language to test the possibilities of the modern lyric. Uffe Harder (born 1930) and Jørgen Sonne (born 1925) brought the major currents of contemporary world poetry to Denmark.

Especially important is the very popular Benny Andersen (born 1929), who in realistic, humorous works—from *Den musikalske ål* (1960, The Musical Eel) through *Det sidste øh* (1969, The Last Oh)—captured the everyday life of people and revealed the lighter side of existence. Piet Hein (born 1905), using the pseudonym Kumbell, has commented on contemporary and general problems of life in ironic, barbed short verses. Frank Jæger (born 1926), on the other hand, has focused in his poems and stories on life's quiet pleasures, loneliness, and the peacefulness of the Danish landscape.

Vagn Steen's (born 1928) *Digte?* (1964, Poems?) provide examples of concrete poetry, the wording of which was intended to provoke and activate the reader. Hans-Jørgen Nielsen's (born 1941) works *vedr. visse foreteelser: en hvidbog* (1967, concerning specific phenomena: a whitebook) and *fra luften i munden: fantasistykker* (1969, from the air into the mouth: fantasies) were more radical experiments than Steen's. Both authors have reduced customary language to a skeleton and have sought reality in the juxtaposition of nonsense. But they never lose sight of the humor in their toying with the raw material of language.

FICTION

The reconsideration of ethical values and metaphysical thought after World War II made realistic and naturalistic fiction, which had been unchallenged up to this time, look very superficial and threadbare. The last works of H. C. Branner (1903–1966) and Martin A. Hansen (1909–1955) departed from the psychological and sociological realism of their early novels. New dimensions for the Danish novel were opened up by the rediscovery of the symbol and the myth—which in the tales of the modern Scheherazade Karin Blixen (1885–1962; the most famous of her numerous pseudonyms was Isak Dinesen) seemed somewhat exotic in Danish literature. Yet neither the novels of these authors nor the bizarre tales of Albert Dam (1880–1972) had a significant influence on contemporary fiction.

One of the most important works of fiction in the early postwar period was Villy Sørensen's *Sære historier* (1953, Strange Stories), which in the form of parables described the workings of unconscious forces in man, the equivocal relationship between art and life, and the confusions of contemporary man. The omnipresent narrator introduced archetypal figures, and in tangibly real pictures presents basic human experiences. Traumas, repressions, basic drives, and instincts were described through constantly changing symbols.

Several stories in Sørensen's *Ufarlige historier* (1955, Harmless Stories) dealt with the possibility of rescuing the ego from its divided state. Sørensen did not interpret the human condition in terms of eternal truths and values; he analyzed existence with existentialist terminology and with the categories of depth psychology.

In his *Formynderfortællinger* (1964, Tales of a Guardian) Sørensen questioned the maturity of the individual; not only the ward but also the guardian is not free. For Sørensen, literature is a form of knowledge, and, like the Austrian Hermann Broch, his aim has been to combine scientific insight and poetic form. In Thomas Mann's work Sørensen found the model for writing legends and for maintaining an ironic distance from mythical subject matter. The stories of Franz Kafka served him as models for writing parables. In Sørensen's work, however, Kafka has been mixed with a strong dose of Hans Christian Andersen.

Sørensen's importance as a short-story writer has been equalled by his significant contributions as critic and philosopher to the cultural debates of his nation. In the latter capacity he prefers the *Hverken-eller* (1961, Neither-Nor), as he entitled a collection of essays, to the simplifying "either-or." For Sørensen, all of his works, but particularly his stories, represent segments of "an expedition in search of truth."

Peter Seeberg's (born 1925) first novels and stories, on the other hand, tell of the search for *reality*. For the characters in *Bipersonerne* (1956, Insignificant People), existence consists of senseless incidents, and the individual creates reality only through his own actions. Since the main character in *Fugls føde* (1957, Birdseed) does not dare to act, he does not succeed in holding on to reality. In the volume of short stories entitled *Eftersøgningen* (1962, Research), however, Seeberg dropped his search for reality. In *Research,* he was concerned with the meaning of life and the identity of the individual. A man's action or inaction can turn into guilt, but the individual finds his way to his true self only through the acceptance of responsibility, as the main characters in the realistically written novel *Hyrder* (1970, Shepherds) discover.

Leif Panduro (born 1923) has used absurd farce to unmask the irrationalities of our civilization, which are still represented as normal by many. After *De uanstændige* (1960, The Indecent Ones) and *Øgledage* (1961, Days of the Lizards), two novels about the difficulties of growing up, the author's uncontrollable pleasure in spinning yarns increased even more. Psychoanalysis has served as the godfather of all his novels. The title character in *Fern fra Danmark* (1963, Fern from Denmark) is confused and frightened as he faces his own past. In *Fejltagelsen* (1964, The Error), the main character flees into an imaginary illness in order to escape responsibility. And in *Den gale mand* (1965, The Crazy Man) the repressions and the schizophrenia of a man end in catastrophe. The ironic and satirical novel *Vejen til Jylland* (1966, The Road to Jutland) concludes in a more conciliatory manner. But the title figure in *Daniels anden verden* (1970, Daniel's Other World) demonstrates once again the schizophrenic condition that exists in the relationship of the individual to his environment.

In Peter Ronild's (born 1928) *Kroppene* (1964, The Bodies), written on the model of the *nouveau roman,* the first-person narrator registers concrete situations dispassionately, without any moral judgment. The theme of man governed by his instincts emerged again in Ronild's collection of stories *Fodring af slanger i vissent græs* (1966, Feeding Snakes in Dry Grass). However, in the portrayal of a modern idler in *Tal sagte, månen sover* (1968, Speak Softly, the Moon is Sleeping), the author showed another, and far more cheerful, side of himself.

The title story in Sven Holm's (born 1940) volume *Den store fjende* (1961, The Great Enemy) attempted to offer a sociopsychological description of man: the instinct for aggression, which derives from an inner fear, causes his self-destruction. In *Fra den nederste himmel* (1965, From the Lowest Level of Heaven), Holm adapted Sørensen's theme of the guardian. The three parts of this work treated in allegorical form the maturing of an individual. Holm was less concerned with strained effects in *Termush, Atlanterhavskysten* (1967, Termush, Atlantic Coast), in which the survivors of a future atomic war are brought to the realization that the "great enemy" of man is man himself. The farcical plot of the novel *Min elskede: En skabelonroman* (1968, My Beloved: A Novel of Stereotypes) should not distract the reader from seeing that Holm bitterly satirized human social behavior in our time. Yet his concluding word to the reader made it clear that he has not yet given up all hope for a better future.

In Ulla Ryum's (born 1937) *Spejl* (1962, Mirror)—whose second part, in the form of an absurd, surrealistic verse drama, serves as a mirror image of the first part, which is written in realistic prose—the characters try in vain to escape the narrowness of their individuality. Also self-obsessed is the protagonist in Ryum's *Latterfuglen* (1965, The Mockingbird). The unusual and unexpected conclusion of *The Mockingbird* is well suited to the incomprehensible events related in the novel. The incomprehensibility of man became the subject of *Jakkelnatten* (1967, Punch and Judy Night): although the public personality of an artist can be ascertained, his real self remains impenetrable.

Sven Åge Madsen's (born 1939) novel *Besøget* (1963, The Visit), which was reminiscent of Kafka, still had a recognizable plot. In his next works, however, he made a decisive break with traditional novelistic technique: he himself designated *Lystbilleder* (1964, Portraits of Joy) a "non-novel." The five characters who are authors in *Tilføjelser* (1967, Supplements) demonstrate the uncertainty and insecurity of the literary profession. This experimenting with language was continued in *Liget og lysten* (1968, The Corpse and the Desire). From the world of trivial literature and its stylistic devices Madsen created synthetic figures as a means of parodying the banal truths of life. In *Maskeballet* (1970, The Masked Ball), a work presented in the form of a cycle of stories, Madsen reverted to a realistic manner of writing.

The traditional novel of psychological realism has still continued to flourish in Denmark, although contemporary authors have adopted elements of the style and the themes of the most recent literary trends. The prolific poet Klaus Rifbjerg is known outside Denmark mainly as a novelist. His novel *Den kroniske uskyld* (1958, Chronic Innocence) seems to have been written under the influence of the numerous portrayals of isolated, dreamy, and aggressive young people—the kind of novel initiated by Salinger's *The Catcher in the Rye* (1951). *Chronic Innocence* presented a group of adolescents who have to lose their youthful innocence when they collide with the world of adults.

Rifbjerg's *Operaelskeren* (1966, The Opera Fan) was similarly realistic. In this novel love and passion turn the life of a rational scientist into a drama more unreal than the one on stage. *Arkivet* (1967, The Archive) and *Lonni og Karl* (1968, Lonni and Karl), which was inspired by the youthful revolutionary movement of the 1960s, recounted banal, everyday occurrences.

The title figure of Rifbjerg's *Anna (jeg) Anna* (1969, Anna [I] Anna) attempts a rebellion against her bourgeois environment, but an aura of romanticism and resignation hovers over her attempt to escape. Rifbjerg seems to believe that it is impossible for contemporary man to cast off the role assigned him by society; this notion was clearly brought out in *Marts 1970* (1970, March 1970), a novel that successfully combined humor and fantasy.

Other novelists who have favored psychological realism include Ole Juul (born 1918), Hans Lyngby Jepsen (born 1920), Hans Jorgen Lembourn (born 1923), and Tage Skou-Hansen (born 1925). Skou-Hansen's novels have treated individual moral problems. Although his early novels, such as *De nøgne træer* (1957, The Naked Trees) and *Dagstjernen* (1962, The Star of the Day), were set in Denmark during Nazi occupation, in *Hjemkomst* (1969, Homecoming) the setting became more global.

Poul Ørum (born 1919) selected his materials from everyday life and effectively shaped the destinies and conflicts of his characters in *Lyksalighedens ø* (1958, Island of Happiness), *Natten i ventesalen* (1962, The Night in the Waiting Room), and *Et andet ansigt* (1970, Another Face). Willy-August Linnemann (born 1914) frequently placed the action of his novels in the Danish-German border area. In a series of novels published between 1958 and 1966 Linnemann made the reader sense the hidden face of God behind the lives depicted. In his five Schleswig novels, which were published between 1968 and 1972, he traced the history of a family through the years following World War II.

Because of the limited audience of the Faeroe Islands (the islands, which are a part of the Kingdom of Denmark, have only about 35,000 inhabitants, who speak a language of their own) William Heinesen (born

1900) chose to write in Danish in order to address a broader readership than the Djurhuus brothers (Hans Andrias, 1883–1951; Jens Hendrik Oliver, 1881–1949), the two most important authors of Faroese literature during the first half of the twentieth century. In the 1930s and 1940s Heinesen wrote novels critical of society, but since 1950—from *De fortabte spillemænd* (1950, The Lost Musicians) through *Det gode håb* (1964, The Good Hope) and the narrative volume *Don Juan fra Tranhuset* (1970, Don Juan of Tranhuset)—he has played the role of the humorous narrator who enjoys telling stories. Even though Heinesen has given up the language of his homeland, in his works, including his collections of verse, the bare rocks and steep cliffs of the Faeroe Islands in the Atlantic and the capital city, Thorshaven, are still central to his work.

DRAMA

In the first half of the twentieth century Kaj Munk (1898–1944), Carl Erik Soya (born 1896), and especially Kjeld Abell (1901–1961) provided the Danish theater with several successful works. The novelist H. C. Branner wrote several topical ideological dramas in the 1950s. In the last fifteen years, however, there has been no outstanding Danish playwright.

A few authors have been making honest efforts to imitate the themes and forms of the theater of the absurd: Henning Nielsen (born 1924), Knud Holst (born 1936), and the novelists Sven Holm and Leif Panduro. But none of these writers' one-act plays has been very successful. Certain elements of this theater—the clownlike, ironic, and satiric qualities—enrich the comic revue, that typically Danish stage entertainment, which purports to be not only an amusement but also an instrument of social criticism. These authors have attacked the complacent citizens of the welfare state either good-naturedly or viciously.

The plays of Klaus Rifbjerg, like his novels, have been set in a bourgeois milieu. *Hvad en man har brug for* (1966, What a Man Needs) dealt with the inner emptiness of a man standing at the peak of a successful career. *Voks* (1968, Wax) presented the instability and crass egotism of contemporary people; on the other hand, *År* (1970, Years), depicted, through somewhat ironic images, the simple, unheroic everyday life of a Danish family during the Nazi occupation.

If Klaus Rifbjerg's dramas have projected general European problems onto the Danish milieu, Ernst Bruun Olsen (born 1923), very aware of the stage tradition of his country, has focused on more specifically Danish issues. In the musical *Teenagerlove* (1962, Teen-Age Love), one of the most successful works of the contemporary Danish theater, the criticism of this activist author was aimed at the dehumanizing practices of the pleasure industry in capitalist society. Yet, ironically, the sentimental, melodramatic plot of this play turned it into a product of the very industry it wanted to expose. In several "folk comedies with songs" Bruun Olsen ridiculed the adoption by the Danish Social Democratic Party of bourgeois values and recalled with some yearning and melancholy the beginnings of the party. In the historical drama *De fredsommelige* (1969, The Peacemakers) he raised his index finger in the manner of Bertolt Brecht—but a little too obtrusively.

The most striking characteristic of Danish literature after World War II has been the end of the dominance of a literature that was realistic or naturalistic in form and radical and socially activist in theme. During the past twenty-five years Danish writers have been very receptive to the most recent developments in world literature. It is true that contemporary Danish literature is no longer in the position it held at the turn of the twentieth century, when writers like Jens Peter Jacobsen (1847–1885), Herman Bang (1857–1912), and Martin Andersen Nexø had international reputations. However, because of the best poetry of Sarvig, Wivel, Bjørnvig, Brandt, and Christensen, and also because of such outstanding works of fiction as the stories of Sørensen and the novels of Rifbjerg, contemporary Danish literature need not fear comparison with the literary production of other European countries.

DANISH WORKS IN ENGLISH TRANSLATION

ANTHOLOGIES

Bredsdorff, Elias, ed. *Contemporary Danish Plays*. Freeport, N.Y., 1970
———. *Contemporary Danish Prose.* Copenhagen, 1958
Holm, Sven, ed. *The Devil's Instrument, and Other Danish Stories.* Chester Springs, Pa., 1971
Jansen, F. J. Billeskov, ed. *Anthology of Danish Literature.* Carbondale, Ill., 1972
Keigwin, Richard Prescott, ed. *In Denmark I Was Born: A Little Book of Danish Verse.* Copenhagen, 1950
Mogensen, Knud K., ed. *Modern Danish Poems,* 2nd ed. Copenhagen, 1951

INDIVIDUAL WORKS MENTIONED IN ARTICLE

Holm, Sven. *Termush, Atlanterhavskysten* as *Termush.* London, 1969
Kierkegaard, Søren. *Begrebet angst* as *The Concept of Dread.* Princeton, N.J., 1957
Panduro, Leif. *Vejen til Jylland* as *One of Our Millionaires Is Missing.* New York, 1967
Sørensen, Villy. *Sære historier* as *Tiger in the Kitchen, and Other Strange Stories.* Freeport, N.Y., 1969

SECONDARY WORKS

BIBLIOGRAPHIES AND GUIDES

Engelstoft, P. and S. Dahl, eds. *Dansk skønlitterært forfatterleksikon 1900–1950,* 3 vols. Copenhagen, 1954–64

Mitchell, P. M. *A Bibliographical Guide to Danish Literature.* Copenhagen, 1952

Vor tids Hvem-skrev-hvad, efter 1914, 2 vols. Copenhagen, 1968

GENERAL WORKS

Albeck, G. et al. *Dansk litteraturhistorie,* 4 vols. Copenhagen, 1964–66

Billeskov Jansen, F. F. *Danmarks digtekunst,* 3 vols., 2nd ed. Copenhagen, 1964ff.

Brix, Hans. *Danmarks digtere,* 3rd ed. Copenhagen, 1951

Danske digtere i det 20. århundrede, 3 vols., 2nd ed. Copenhagen, 1965–66

Durand, Frédéric. *Histoire de la littérature danoise.* Paris, 1967

Friese, Wilhelm. *Nordische Literaturen im 20. Jahrhundert.* Stuttgart, 1971

Kristensen, Sven Møller. *Dansk litteratur, 1918–1952* (with a supplement 1952–64), 7th ed. Copenhagen, 1965

Mitchell, P. M. *A History of Danish Literature,* 2nd ed. New York, 1972

Svendsen, Werner and Hanne Marie. *Geschichte der dänischen Literatur.* Neumünster, 1964

Woel, Cai M. *Dansk litteraturhistorie 1900–1950,* 2 vols. Copenhagen, 1956

WORKS ON CONTEMPORARY LITERATURE

Brandt, Jørgen Gustava. *Præsentation: 40 danske digtere efter krigen.* Copenhagen, 1964

Bredsdorff, Thomas. *Sære fortællere: Hovedtræk af den ny danske prosakunst i tiåret omkring 1960,* 2nd ed. Copenhagen, 1968

Brostrøm, Torben. *Poetisk kermesse.* Copenhagen, 1962

———. *Ti års lyrik: Kritik og kronik, 1956–65.* Copenhagen, 1966

———. *Versets løvemanke,* 2nd rev. ed. Copenhagen, 1964

Claudi, Jørgen. *Contemporary Danish Authors.* Copenhagen, 1952

Enberg, Harald. *Dansk teater i halvtredserne.* Copenhagen, 1958

———. *Teatret 1945–52.* Copenhagen, 1952

Frederiksen, Emil. *Ung dansk litteratur 1930–50.* Copenhagen, 1951

Kruuse, Jens. *Gentagelser.* Copenhagen, 1954

Nielsen, Frederik. *Dansk digtning idag,* 2nd ed. Copenhagen, 1963

Svendsen, Hanne Marie. *Romanes veje: Værkstedssamtaler med danske forfattere.* Copenhagen, 1966

Vosmar, J., ed. *Modernismen i dansk litteratur.* Copenhagen, 1967

Wivel, Ole. *Poesi og eksistens.* Copenhagen, 1953

IVAR IVASK

Estonian Literature

THE ESTONIAN NATION can look back on an old rich tradition of folk songs and folklore, and the first book written in Estonian was printed as early as the sixteenth century. But written Estonian literature came of age only in the second half of the nineteenth century. Friedrich Reinhold Kreutzwald (1803–1882) is generally regarded as its founder. Following the example of the Finnish writer Elias Lönnrot's *Kalevala* (1835–49), Kreutzwald synthesized in the national epic *Kalevipoeg* (1857–61, The Son of Kalev) both authentic folk material and his own creative imagination. *The Son of Kalev* had a profound influence on the awakening national consciousness of a peasant people that had been serfs to German landowners for centuries.

Estonian literature reached a level of excellence comparable to general European standards at the end of the nineteenth century: with the impressionistic nature poetry and symbolist lyrics of Juhan Liiv (1864–1913); with the naturalistic and historical novels of Eduard Vilde (1865–1933); and with the plays of August Kitzberg (1855–1927), who at times drew his inspiration from Estonian folklore. Further refinements in style, new themes, and greater awareness of international literary currents were introduced by Noor Eesti (Young Estonia), a group that favored a stronger orientation toward the sister nation Finland and toward France as a counterbalance to the predominant cultural influence of Germany and Russia. Outstanding members of the Noor Eesti movement were the short-story writer and essayist Friedebert Tuglas (1886–1971, pseudonym of Friedebert Mihkelson); the formally perfect symbolist poet Gustav Suits (1883–1956); and the reformer of the Estonian language, Johannes Aavik (born 1880).

The program of Noor Eesti—"Let us be Estonians, but let us also become Europeans"—was fully realized during the period of national independence (1918–40), during which all literary genres (with the exception of drama) were greatly enriched. Suits became the first professor of Estonian and world literature at Tartu University. Criticism flourished through the writings of such outstanding critics as Johannes Semper (1892–1970), Ants Oras (born 1900), and Aleksander Aspel (born 1908). The most lasting achievements of the interwar years were the poetry of Marie Under (born 1883) and the novels of A. H. Tammsaare (1878–1940, pseudonym of Anton Hansen). A title such as *Ja liha sai sõnaks* (1936, And the Flesh Became Word) indicates the vitality and metaphysical intensity that has characterized all of Under's poetry. Tammsaare's fame rests on the monumental five-volume novel *Tõde ja õigus* (1926–33, Truth and Justice), which recreated the Estonian experience during the half-century from 1875 to 1925. The Soviet occupation in 1940 interrupted these literary developments, and the German occupation that followed (1941–44) did nothing to revive them.

Since the Soviet reoccupation in 1944 and the incorporation of Estonia into the Soviet Union, Estonian literature has been divided into two branches. One of these is the literature of the approximately 75,000 refugees in the west, concentrated in Sweden, the United States, and Canada. The other branch—the literature written inside the Estonian Soviet Socialist Republic—is under Communist Party control. During the early postwar years, 1945 to 1960, the writing in Soviet Estonia could not compare, in quantity (of first editions) or quality, with the work of Estonians in exile. Not until several years after Stalin's death could personal styles, experiments with form, and psychologically convincing characterizations make their appearance.

In Estonian émigré poetry, surrealism emerged in 1946—in Ilmar Laaban's (born 1921) collection *Ankruketi lõpp on laulu algus* (The Anchor Chain's End Is the Beginning of Song). By 1953 a Kafkaesque atmosphere was effectively evoked in the émigré novel—in *Hingede öö* (All Souls' Night) by Karl Ristikivi (born 1912). Soviet Estonian literature did not approach such modernity until the 1960s. Exile literature, on the other hand, can offer no parallel to the surprising development of the theater of the absurd in Soviet Estonia.

POETRY

Because of the rich heritage of the folk song, lyric poetry has been the strongest and most original genre in Estonian literature. The modern classics Gustav Suits, Marie Under, and Henrik Visnapuu (1890–1951) concluded their life's work in exile. Under—in *Sädemed tuhas* (1954, Sparks under Ashes)—and Suits—in *Tuli ja tuul* (1950, Flames and Wind)—wrote very moving poetry about the tragedy of exile and the solitude of old age. The spirit of these writers was never broken.

Bernard Kangro (born 1910) has been in many ways a key figure in Estonian exile literature. In addition to his great productivity as a poet (thirteen volumes from 1935 to 1969, collected in *Minu nägu* [1970, My Face]), as a novelist (twelve titles from 1949 to 1971), as a playwright (collected edition: *Merre vajunud saar* [1968, Island Lost in the Sea]), and as a critic, Kangro has edited the important literary quarterly *Tulimuld* since 1950 and has directed the leading émigré publishing house, the Estonian Writers' Cooperative, in Lund, Sweden.

Kangro's earlier poetry was famous for its botanically exact evocation of nature and its often incantatory, yet folkloristically thorough, descriptions of the pagan beliefs of his peasant ancestors. His poetry written in exile has been characterized by symbolism of his native soil, patriotic feelings, and a metaphysical alienation from an absurd history. Kangro's novels culminated in the six-volume cycle on the university town of Tartu in the 1930s. In these novels, past and present, dream and reality, were kaleidoscopically refracted from various narrative perspectives (reminding one of Lawrence Durrell). A lyrical tone has permeated Kangro's novels and plays.

The poems of Arno Vihalemm (born 1911), frequently epigrammatic and ironic, have offered a refreshing blend of parody, colloquialisms, and puns. They clearly reveal that their author is also a painter. His major collections include *Kaja kivi südames* (1954, Echo in the Stone's Heart), *Consolationes* (1961, Consolations), and *Tsoo-loogia ehk ingel lindudega* (1966, Zoology or Angel with Birds). Unlike Vihalemm's humorous and sensitive verse, the intellectualized poetry of art critic Aleksis Rannit (born 1914), frequently inspired by works of art or artists, has tended to be hermetic and preoccupied with questions of technique at the expense of poetic experience. His fourth collection, *Kuiv hiilgus* (1963, Dry Brilliance), probably came closest to realizing his formal ideal.

Among younger émigré poets, Kalju Lepik (born 1920) prefers rustic pithiness, yet he has considerable scope. His strongest poems, such as those in *Kivimurd* (1958, The Stone Quarry), combined effectively an almost surrealistic association of images with elements of the folk song. This prolific, experimental poet has had the most obvious influence on the young poets inside Soviet Estonia.

Raimond Kolk's (born 1924) early collections, written in south-Estonian dialect, were lyrical in tone and tinged with gentle sadness. In his later poems, written in standard Estonian, he has shown an interest in irony and satire; outstanding was *Müüdud sõrmus* (1959, The Sold Ring). In such novels as *Et mitte kunagi võita* (1969, In Order Never to Win) Kolk illuminated some of the complexes of the emigrant mind.

Unlike Kolk and Lepik, but like the surrealist Ilmar Laaban, Ivar Grünthal (born 1924) is an entirely urban poet. A virtuoso of form, he is particularly fond of the sonnet and has managed to pack it with a hyper-tense content culled from contemporary experience. Grünthal's interests range from physiologically detailed eroticism (he is a professional physician) to metaphysical speculations and political invective. Among his six volumes of poems, the love lyrics of *Must pühapäev* (1954, Black Sunday) reached the widest audience. His novel in verse, *Peetri kiriku kellad* (1962, The Bells of Saint Peter's), attempted to synthesize the metrical sophistication of a Pushkin and a realism of almost Joycean complexity. In 1957 Grünthal founded in Sweden the liberal literary journal *Mana*, which he edited for several years.

In Soviet Estonia it was not until the 1960s that poetry was able to return to the best national traditions and to open itself to postwar developments in western literature.

The poets of the prominent Arbujad (Magicians of the Word) group of the 1930s either had been forced into emigration (like Kangro), had died in Siberia (like Heiti Talvik [1904–1947]), or had entered a period of silence as poets, during which they devoted themselves to translating. August Sang (1914–1969), who has translated Goethe, Pushkin, Baudelaire, and Brecht, was the first Arbujad poet to publish an important collection of verse in Soviet Estonia. His *Võileib suudlusega* (1963, Sandwich with a Kiss) expressed in simply worded quatrains—yet at times with the biting wit of Heine—some of the experiences witnessed during the worst years of Stalinist terror. Sang emerged as a man of gentle wisdom and inner resilience.

Betti Alver (born 1906, pseudonym of Elisabet Lepik) also occupied herself with translation during a period of almost twenty years; her version of Pushkin's *Yevgeni Onegin* (1964) is among the best done in any language. A selection of both older and more recent verse, *Tähetund* (1966, Stellar Hour), and her latest collection, *Eluhelbed* (1971, Flakes of Life), confirmed her position as the greatest living poet in Estonia today. Her best poems have managed to be personal and impersonal at the same time; rooted in a definite historical period, yet timeless; classically transparent in form, yet rich in symbolic levels of meaning.

In 1965 the theologian and linguist Uku Masing (born 1909), another poet of the Arbujad school, courageously had his visionary-mystical collection of poems, *Džunglilaulud* (Jungle Songs), published in Sweden. Critics have compared him with Hölderlin, Blake, and Rilke.

But the pioneer of greater freedom of expression in Soviet Estonian poetry was the younger poet Jaan Kross (born 1920). His first collection, *Söerikastaja* (1958, The Coal Sorter), was distinguished both by courage in expressing his convictions and by joy in formal experimentation. (The poem *Irax* [Irax], written as early as 1952, is the wittiest known satire on Stalin in Soviet Estonian literature.) Kross's three subsequent volumes of poetry were dominated by water symbolism and metaphors of flying. In 1971 a collected edition was published—*Voog ja kolmpii* (The Wave and the Trident).

A polemicist and a wide-ranging translator (Lewis Carroll, Brecht, Paul Éluard, Peter Weiss) as well as a poet, Kross also opened new doors for Soviet Estonian fiction in 1970 by imaginatively employing the interior monologue in his historical novellas (collected edition: *Klio silma all* [1972, Under Clio's Eye]). He showed himself to be a psychologically penetrating novelist in the first part of his novel *Kolme katku vahel* (1970, Between Three Pestilences), which dealt with the life of the Estonian-born chronicler Balthasar Russow, during the eventful sixteenth century. Through gripping episodes, he made Estonian history come alive and gave it new depth. Kross has also written libretti for operas by the Estonian composer Eduard Tubin, and one day he may well try his hand at drama; there has already been a strong dramatic streak in his poems and stories.

Artur Alliksaar (1923–1966) was as much of an inspiration to young Estonian poets as was Kross. His poetic play *Nimetu saar* (1966, The Nameless Island) marked the founding of the Estonian theater of the absurd. *Olematus võiks ju ka olemata olla* (1968, Nonbeing Might Just as Well Not Have Been) gave a preliminary overview of his rich, largely unpublished poetry, and frequently brought to mind the *greguerías* of the Spaniard Ramón Gómez de la Serna and the surrealist aphorisms of Ilmar Laaban. But this resemblance may well have been coincidental.

Paul-Eerik Rummo's (born 1942) collection *Ankruhiivaja* (1962, The Anchor Heaver) signaled the emergence of a talented new generation of poets in Estonia. Rummo's subsequent collections—*Tule ikka mu rõõmude juurde* (1964, Come Always to My Joys) and *Lumevalgus— lumepimedus* (1966, Snowbrightness—Snowblindness)—earned him a deservedly high reputation with both critics and readers. He has been able to fuse modernity with the simplicity of folk song, reminding one of García Lorca. His play *Tuhkatriinumäng* (1969, The Cinderella Game), which had an American production in 1971, has been the most stimulating and most discussed work of the Estonian theater of the absurd. On his search for Cinderella, the prince discovers that the land is full of castles with princesses as well as Cinderellas. "Who is the genuine Cinderella?" thus becomes the question for the very meaning of life in a world that has turned into a confusing labyrinth.

More philosophical and learned than Rummo is Jaan Kaplinski (born 1941), whose second volume of poems *Tolmust ja värvidest* (1967, Out of Dust and Colors) ranged in theme from an ecological concern for nature to oriental mysticism. Kaplinski has passionately and movingly defended the rights of small nations and minor languages, be they American Indian or Estonian. His prophetic fervor reminds one at times of the visionary poet Uku Masing.

FICTION

The senior writer of fiction in exile, Karl Rumor (1886–1971, pseudonym of Karl Ast), known for his short stories and travel books, published his only novel, *Krutsifiks* (The Crucifix), in 1960. It was one of the most fascinating stylistic achievements in postwar Estonian prose (both at home and in exile). It described with baroque exuberance the activities of a religious fanatic in tropical South America. The complex metaphysical symbolism of the novel made it worthy of several rereadings.

Albert Kivikas (born 1898), August Gailit (1891–1960), and August Mälk (born 1900) were among the most productive and popular novelists before World War II; Gailit and Mälk were also widely translated. In exile they continued to write on their accustomed level of excellence, yet without significant new breakthroughs in either form or content.

Karl Ristikivi has also shunned experimentation, yet he probably is the most representative Estonian novelist in exile. He had already been known in Estonia as the heir of A. H. Tammsaare because of his first three realistic novels sensitively dealing with the working class and the middle class of Estonia's capital, Tallinn. Two additional novels published in exile continued to explore the same milieu. Then in 1953 Ristikivi made a surprising break in *All Souls' Night,* whose landmark importance I already mentioned. This allegory of exile seemed to herald a new direction in his work.

Ristikivi, however, did not continue in the vein of *All Souls' Night* but turned instead to the historical novel, producing with astonishing ease nine novels from 1961 to 1971. He has been called a "skeptical humanistic optimist." This paradox illuminates quite well the engaging mind behind these novels, which took their subject matter from the Middle Ages and the Renaissance, as well as the life of Catalan refugees in Paris during the 1940s. Parallels to the tragic history of Estonia abound, yet Ristikivi obviously wanted to place his ideas in a more universal context. Among the best of Ristikivi's historical novels have been *Rõõmulaul* (1966, Song of Joy) and *Lohe hambad* (1971, The Dragon's Teeth).

The poet Bernard Kangro remained the most innovative novelist of the middle generation. Valev Uibopuu (born 1913), on the other hand, seems at first reading rather traditional. Nevertheless, the subdued expressiveness of his few novels and novellas have subtly enriched the resources of Estonian fiction. In the novel *Janu* (1957, Thirst) the last summer of a mortally ill girl becomes the symbolic analysis of a whole life and at the same time the evocation of the last summer of independent Estonia. Uibopuu's way of seeing the world was suggested by such titles as *Mosaiik* (1962, The Mosaic) and *Lademed* (1970, Layers).

Arved Viirlaid (born 1922), also known for his poetry, focused in several of the eight novels he published between 1949 and 1965 on the dramatic events that engulfed Estonia during World War II (in which he was a soldier), on the subsequent Soviet annexation, and on the reign of Stalinist terror. In *Ristideta hauad* (1952, Graves without Crosses) he depicted with stark realism the desperate fight of Estonian partisans in the forests. *Sadu jõkke* (1965, Rain for the River), based on first-hand sources, retold the harrowing experiences of an Estonian officer in a Siberian forced-labor camp and his escape from the Soviet Union. Viirlaid has not been averse to presenting real heroes, although they possess understandable bitterness and pessimism as they see the lack of hope for the nationalist cause both at home and in the isolation of exile. Viirlaid is the most widely translated Estonian émigré novelist.

Among a talented younger generation of writers in exile, Ilmar Jaks (born 1923) is perhaps the most interesting. He fought as a volunteer in Finland, returned to Estonia at the end of World War II, and then fled to Sweden via Leningrad. Jaks views life from a considerably more absurd and grotesque angle than the older writers. His novel *Eikellegi maal* (1963, In No-Man's Land) summed up, in Kafkaesque fashion, his experiences as soldier and refugee. His volumes of stories—*Aruanne* (1958, Account Rendered), *Mapp* (1970, Portfolio), and *Keldrist pööningule* (1971, From Basement to Attic)—have dealt ironically and often humorously with the life among Estonian émigrés.

The novelists writing in Soviet Estonia have not yet equaled the many-faceted achievements of Estonian émigré novelists. The most interesting authors of the socialist-realist school have been Rudolf Sirge (1904–1970) and Aadu Hint (born 1910). Sirge's *Maa ja rahvas* (1956, Land and People) described the turbulent events in a rural community during the communist takeover of 1940–41. Sirge did not shrink from dealing with the deportations and the difficulties of forced collectivization. Aadu Hint, in his somewhat uneven tetralogy *Tuuline rand* (1951–66, Windy Shore), traced the social situation of Estonia's island and seashore population from the 1905 revolution against the tsar and the German landowners to 1940, when the Soviets seized power. The contributions of Jaan Kross to the novel have already been discussed together with his poetry.

Perhaps the most unexpected development in Soviet Estonian fiction has been the sudden emergence of a new epic cycle. The inspiration was Kreutzwald's *The Son of Kalev*. But while Kreutzwald fashioned a male protagonist out of ancient legends, the folklorist August Annist (1899–1972) decided to weave authentic folk songs into a trilogy in which women were the protagonists. He prepared himself for this task by translating masterfully not only the *Kalevala* but also the Iliad and the Odyssey. The first two parts of Annist's trilogy have been published: *Lauluema Mari* (1966, Mari, The Mother of Song) and *Karske Pireta, maheda Mareta ja mehetapja Maie lood* (1970, The Stories of Sober Pireta, Gentle Mareta, and the Husband-Killer Maie).

Three younger Soviet Estonian writers of fiction have made interesting contributions and have gained some international notice. Arvo Valton's (born 1935) collections of novellas—such as *Rataste vahel* (1966, Between the Wheels) and *Kaheksa jaapanlannat* (1968, Eight Japanese Girls)—showed a certain indebtedness to Kafka, as well as an intellectual kinship with the Polish absurdist Sławomir Mrożek. His stories have been primarily preoccupied with the plight of average people caught in the machinery of bureaucracy and oppressive daily routine. In his sense of the grotesque Valton is comparable to the émigré writer Ilmar Jaks.

Enn Vetemaa (born 1936) is a poet, playwright, and novelist. His best-known short novels have been *Monument* (1965, The Monument) and *Pillimees* (1967, The Musician), both dealing with the conflict of political guilt and human and artistic integrity in contemporary Soviet Estonia. Yet by choosing as his setting the mazelike streets of old Tallinn and referring to Gothic gargoyles, by quoting from the Bible and Dante, Vetemaa made the present action assume a more universal dimension of metaphysical conflict. His latest novel, *Kalevipoja mälestused* (1971, The Memoirs of the Son of Kalev), set straight the record of the national hero's exploits—from the son of Kalev's own point of view this time. The tale was told with humorous gusto and numerous devices of comic alienation, which will no doubt alienate the less sophisticated reader and honest patriot.

Mati Unt (born 1943) has distinguished himself both as a writer of fiction and as a playwright. He distrusts all mass slogans and calls for uncompromising honesty toward oneself and others. His early works—*Hüvasti, kollane kass* (1963, Goodbye, Yellow Cat), *Võlg* (1964, The Debt), and *Elu võimalikkusest kosmoses* (1967, On the Possibility of Life in Space)—described the life of young people in the university town of Tartu with an immediacy recalling Salinger. While Vetemaa has been preoccupied with the image of medieval-street labyrinths, Unt is obsessed with closed windows. His most recent stories and parables were collected in *Kuu nagu kustuv päike* (1971, The Moon as a Dying Sun). This volume also contained his play *Phaethon, päikese poeg* (Phaëthon, Son of the Sun), which pitted a young idealist against the interests of the state. The mythological context was no more than a pretext.

DRAMA

Although the Estonian stage has always been lively, Estonia has failed so far to produce a great playwright. Both the dispersal of exile and the most restrictive period inside Estonia, from 1944 to 1963, discouraged experimental drama. Only after 1965 did the conditions relax sufficiently in Soviet Estonia to permit a certain renaissance of the theater. I have already mentioned the pioneering work of the poet Artur Alliksaar in absurdist drama and the masterful application of the techniques of the theater of the absurd of another poet, Paul-Eerik Rummo. To this same movement also belong the plays by Enn Vetemaa and Mati Unt.

The poet and versatile translator Ain Kaalep (born 1926), in *Iidamast ja Aadmast* (1967, About Idam and Adam), used Brechtian dramatic techniques to produce a highly original variation on the story of Adam and Eve, which takes place in a futuristic totalitarian state of cybernetic apes. Less experimental and more popular are the plays by Juhan Smuul (1922–1970). Well known as the author of travel books, ballads, and humorous tales based on the lives of the Estonian islanders, he may well have done his best work in such plays as the Molièresque monologue *Polkovniku lesk* (1965, The Colonel's Widow) and the allegorical parody *Pingviinide elu* (1968, The Life of the Penguins), which described with astonishing frankness the ideological rifts between Stalinists and liberals, between nationalists and russophiles, between the old and the young.

A quarter century has passed since the fateful bifurcation of Estonian literature. In fiction the émigré writers still hold an edge, while the Soviet Estonian dramatists have lately produced a theater not only of national relevance but even of international interest. The young poets of Soviet Estonia are moving gradually ahead of the émigrés, partly because of their greater youth: the youngest poet to publish his first collection in the west was born in 1940, while his counterpart in Estonia was born in 1950. Inevitably, younger émigrés and their offspring will adopt the language of their new countries. And unless the process of russification in Soviet Estonia can be halted, Estonian literature—both east and west—may go into a decline.

ESTONIAN WORKS IN ENGLISH TRANSLATION

ANTHOLOGIES

Matthews, W. K., ed. *Modern Estonian Poetry.* Gainesville, Fla., 1953

Oras, Ants, ed. *Estonian Literary Reader.* Bloomington, Ind., 1963

Pranspill, Andres, ed. *Estonian Anthology.* Milford, Conn., 1956

INDIVIDUAL WORKS MENTIONED IN ARTICLE

Kreutzwald, Reinhold. *Kalevipoeg* as *The Hero of Estonia.* London, 1895

Viirlaid, Arved. *Ristideta hauad* as *Graves without Crosses.* Toronto, 1972

————. *Sadu jõkke* as *Rain for the River.* Cape Town, 1964

SECONDARY WORKS

Harris, Edward Howard. *Estonian Literature in Exile.* London, 1949

————. *Literature in Estonia,* 2nd ed. London, 1947

Ivask, Ivar. *Baltic Literatures in Exile: Balance of a Quarter Century.* In *Journal of Baltic Studies,* III, 1, 1972

————. *The Main Tradition of Estonian Poetry.* In Viktor Kõressaar and Aleksis Rannit, eds., *Estonian Poetry and Language.* Stockholm, 1965

Jänes, Henno. *Geschichte der estnischen Literatur.* Stockholm, 1965

Kääri, Kalju and Harald Peep. *A Glimpse into Soviet Estonian Literature.* Tallinn, 1965

Mägi, Arvo. *Estonian Literature.* Stockholm, 1968

Mägi, Arvo, Karl Ristikivi, and Bernard Kangro. *Eesti kirjandus paguluses.* Lund, 1972

Nirk, Endel. *Estonian Literature.* Tallinn, 1970

Oras, Ants. *Acht estnische Dichter.* Stockholm, 1964

————. *Storia della letteratura estone.* In Giacomo Devoto, ed., *Storia delle letterature baltiche.* Milan, 1957

Oras, Ants and Bernard Kangro. *Estonian Literature in Exile.* Lund, 1967

Sõgel, Endel, ed. *Eesti kirjanduse ajalugu,* 3 vols. Tallinn, 1965–69

Suits, Gustav. *Eesti kirjanduslugu I.* Lund, 1953

Valgemäe, Mardi. *Recent Developments in Soviet Estonian Drama.* In *Bulletin/ Institute for the Study of the USSR* (Munich), XVI, 9, 1969

K A I   L A I T I N E N

Finnish Literature

THE BEGINNING of Finnish literature goes back to the fifteenth century—with the translation of the New Testament. But its real development did not come until the nineteenth century—signaled by the appearance of two works: *Kalevala* (1835–49, Poems of the Kaleva District), an epic put together from reworked folklore materials by Elias Lönnrot (1802–1884); and the first significant novel, *Seitsemän veljestä* (1870, Seven Brothers) by Aleksis Kivi (1834–1872), which firmly established the tradition of portraying the common people in the mode of humorous realism.

By the end of the nineteenth century, the liberal ideas and social criticism developing in the other Scandinavian countries, especially in Norway, began to affect Finnish literature. Finnish neoromanticism at the turn of the century, which spread to all the arts, had an international cast insofar as it showed connections with *art nouveau* and symbolism, but it also was marked by a distinctly national interest in nature and folk poetry.

The period between the two world wars was distinguished by the mature writings of those authors who had first made their appearance at the beginning of the century: Joel Lehtonen (1881–1934), Volter Kilpi (1874–1939), and Frans Eemil Sillanpää (1888–1964). In the 1920s a group of writers called the Fire Bearers was formed; they demanded an orientation to recent developments in European literature and wrote in free verse. The 1930s, however, brought a return to classical meter and a tendency toward symbolism in lyric poetry. Ethical and psychological problems became dominant during this period.

After 1945 rapid changes took place in literary life, brought about by the defeat in war, the end of the alliance with Germany, and the development of a better relationship with the Soviet Union. Finland's cultural orientation shifted from Germany to France and the English-speaking world. National self-criticism became stronger, and an international outlook was reflected in the number and variety of translations. New, often only short-lived literary magazines and publishing ventures were founded, which served as a forum and inspiration for young authors; these included *40-luku, Ajan kirja,* and *Näköala.* The latter two combined in 1951 to form *Parnasso,* which is still published.

By 1970, Finland had seven large or medium-sized publishing houses that put out original Finnish works and translations into Finnish, as well as two Swedish publishing houses. Single titles have had printings as large as those in England or Germany. A system of grants was created in 1948 and extended in 1969 to make living conditions easier for authors by giving them monthly stipends of about $320 for one, three, and five years. In addition, there are subsidies for projects and old-age pensions for writers, as well as yearly national literary prizes. Numerous private foundations also award grants to writers. A professional organization, the Finnish Association of Authors, was founded in 1897 and had about 420 members in 1970. An association of authors writing in Swedish was established in 1919 and has a present membership of about 175.

THE OLDER GENERATION

Lyric poets were the first writers to react to the postwar situation. Two authors, who had been recognized in the 1920s but then forgotten again, stepped into the foreground: Aaro Hellaakoski (1893–1952) and P. Mustapää (born 1899, pseudonym of Martti Haavio). The need to adjust to the radically changed postwar world, a concern for the fate of their country, and a sense of the importance of finding adequate new forms all gave impetus to their renewed creative efforts. Their work pointed the way, both intellectually and stylistically, for the younger poets of the 1950s.

Hellaakoski showed from the beginning a strong ethical commitment, which took on an almost religious character in his late work. In *Sarjoja* (1952, Suites), the last volume published during his lifetime, he used long, meditative verse lines not unlike Rilke's in *Duineser Elegien* and Eliot's in *Four Quartets.* Mustapää worked with mythological material and archaic stylistic elements, sometimes in self-parody. He paid particular attention to imagery and rhythm. In *Jäähyväiset Arkadialle* (1945, Farewell Arcadia),

Koiruoho, ruusunkukka (1947, Wormwood, Rose Blossom), and *Linnustaja* (1952, The Bird Catcher) he used images of past memories to make statements about the relativity of life. To comment on current events, Mustapää used motifs from old ballads and idylls as well as concentrated images.

Viljo Kajava's (born 1909) poetry has been marked by a Whitmanesque praise of life. In *Siivitetyt kädet* (1949, Winged Hands) and *Hyvä on meri* (1950, The Sea Is Good) he opened up fresh possibilities for Finnish poetry by bringing to it new ideas from Sweden. Arvo Turtiainen (born 1904) established himself at the same time as Kajava and achieved recognition for the volumes *Minä rakastan* (1955, I Love) and *Syyskevät* (1959, Autumn Spring). Turtiainen's work has been characterized by a vital concept of man, a vibrantly lyrical portrait of nature, and striking descriptions of Helsinki.

Both Turtiainen and Jarno Pennanen (1906–1969) began as members of the leftist group Kiila (The Wedge). Among Pennanen's intellectual and experimental works were the volume of surrealistic prose poems *Lähettämättömiä kirjeitä* (1947, Unmailed Letters) and the posthumously published memoirs *Tervetultua—tervemenoa* (1970, Welcome and Parting). Aale Tynni (born 1913), whose range extends from lyrical songs to sharply drawn pictures of people and current events, also belongs to the group of poets who established themselves soon after World War II. Tynni has also done numerous translations.

Finnish novelists and essayists responded to the war both directly and indirectly. The earliest and best-known expression of the indirect response was Mika Waltari's (born 1908) *Sinuhe, egyptiläinen* (1945, Sinuhe the Egyptian), which became an international bestseller. Despite its historical subject, the novel was ultimately concerned with the problems of postwar resignation, the loss of civil liberties, and the fate of small nations put under pressure by the powerful. Waltari also dealt with similar themes in his later historical novels, in which he often, as in *Sinuhe the Egyptian,* opposed a realist and an idealist.

Elvi Sinervo (born 1912), a member of the Kiila group, reacted optimistically to the postwar world. Her novel *Viljami Vaihdokas* (1946, Viljami Changeling) depicted the maturing of a dreamy, imaginative boy, who finds in communism the route to his humanity.

The prominent critic of the arts and travel writer Olavi Paavolainen (1903–1964) expressed his reaction to the war directly. He wrote about his experiences in Soviet Karelia and at the Finnish headquarters in *Synkkä yksinpuhelu* (1946, Dark Monologue), in which he criticized Finland's prewar German orientation. An important follower of Paavolainen was the outstanding stylist Matti Kurjensaari (born 1907), an essayist and novelist.

The work of Pentti Haanpää (1905–1955) and Toivo Pekkanen (1902–1957) showed similarities to prewar literature. Both Haanpää and Pekkanen were concerned with social justice. Haanpää continued the tradition of portraying common people in an ironic manner. He described the average people of northern Finland in numerous novels and stories, giving special attention to social conflicts. Two other novels of Haanpää had a somewhat different focus: *Yhdeksän miehen saappaat* (1945, The Boots of the Nine Men), a critical examination of war; and *Jauhot* (1949, Flour), an account of Finland's years of famine in the nineteenth century.

Pekkanen, a writer with a strong intellectual bent, became known in his younger years for his portrayals of the working class. Later he published a trilogy about the growth of an industrial city, some stylistically refined fantasies, and the moving memoirs *Lapsuuteni* (1953, My Childhood).

THE 1950s

As in the period 1945–50, during the 1950s new voices made themselves heard in lyric poetry. Within a few years Finnish poetry experienced a thorough renewal. Free verse, strong, concrete images, suggestive language, and themes close to everyday life replaced older conventions in Finnish poetry. The influences on these younger writers were varied: international modernism, Rilke and Eliot, Swedish writers of the 1940s, Hellaakoski and Mustapää, and even early Finnish folk poetry.

Aila Meriluoto (born 1924) was one of the first writers of this younger generation to establish a reputation. In *Lasimaalaus* (1946, Stained Glass) she introduced the technique of Rilke's object-poems to Finnish poetry. In its protest against traditional world views, this volume was a forerunner of more recent philosophies of life. The intellectual, fragmentary poems of Lasse Heikkilä (1921–1961) reflected Swedish influences. Lassi Nummi (born 1928), who at the beginning of his career wrote an experimental prose work, *Maisema* (1949, Landscape), using a "subjective camera technique," later brought to his poetry new idyllic tones and the inspiration of music. *Keskipäivä, delta* (1967, Noon, Delta) synthesized his work. Lauri Viita (1916–1965) renewed the language of poetry in the powerful volume *Betonimylläri* (1947, The Miller of Concrete), based upon personal rhythm and colloquial speech. In addition to further volumes of poetry, Viita wrote a novel about the destinies of a working class family, *Moreeni* (1950, The Moraine), which was also marked by an individual, imaginative style.

Despite common stylistic elements, there were great differences in philosophy of life among the new poets. The only uniting factor was a kind of relativism: a distrust of set programs—be they national, religious, or ideological; a dislike of worn phrases; and a political detachment.

This relativism appeared in an especially marked and personal manner in the work of Paavo Haavikko (born 1931), who may in many ways be considered the key figure in his generation. His best volumes of poetry— *Synnyinmaa* (1955, Fatherland), *Talvipalatsi* (1959, Winter Palace), *Puut, kaikki heidän vihreytensä* (1966, Trees, All Their Verdure), and *Neljätoista hallitsijaa* (1970, Fourteen Rulers)—showed him as a virtuoso in language and a master of irony. He works as surely and inimitably with lush complicated images as with grotesque colloquial turns of phrase. He has often used historical material but has connected it to the present through paradoxical twists, achieving remarkable double perspectives by mirroring the present in the past and the past in the present.

Haavikko has always regarded man as living in a changing world in which nothing is certain, and "one must know almost everything oneself." This world, however, has appeared in his poetry not as illusion but as a very final reality. In his most recent poems he has been concerned with the uses of power, as well as with the position of the intellectual and the possible ways he can be effective under the pressure of political maneuverings. Haavikko has also written fiction and some unusual plays: *Münchhausen* (1958, Münchhausen) and *Agricola ja kettu* (1968, Agricola and the Fox).

Helvi Juvonen (1919–1959), who has been the only Finnish modernist to exhibit religious traits, was more traditional than Haavikko. Her very clear and concentrated message found expression best in the volumes *Pohjajäätä* (1952, Permafrost), *Kalliopohja* (1955, Rock Bottom), and *Sanantuoja* (1959, The Messenger). The titles themselves were indicative of her demand for strength and clarity, which were for her artistic and intellectual imperatives. Many of her poems have been studies of the cruelty of life and the suffering of mankind. But they have also shown suffering overcome through honest self-knowledge or through melting into nature.

Nature has been central in the work of another great modernist woman poet, Eeva-Liisa Manner (born 1921), whose work has been both powerful and refined. Besides nature, Manner's other recurring themes have been music, childhood, and—later on—Chinese philosophy. The pitilessness of man, which she has pursued in topical poems, caused her to turn inward and create her own harmonious poetic world with a dreamlike richness of imagery. Manner's volumes of poetry have included *Tämä matka* (1956, This Journey), *Orfiset laulut* (1960, Orphic Songs), *Niin vaihtuvat vuoden ajat* (1964, Thus the Seasons Change), *Kirjoitettu kivi* (1966, The Inscribed Stone), and *Fahrenheit 121* (1968, Fahrenheit 121). She has also written a number of plays.

Eila Kivikkaho (born 1921) began writing traditional lyrics, but then adopted a more modern imagistic language in the volume *Niityltä pois* (1951, Away from the Meadow). Her striving for concentrated expression has often led to aphorism and occasionally to the use of the classic Japanese poetic form, *tanka*. Anja Vammelvuo (born 1921), important also for her fiction, has published social and political as well as love poetry.

Tuomas Anhava (born 1927) has a style and point of view close to that of Paavo Haavikko. The intellectual poems of his early career contained echoes of English and American verse, especially of Pound. Later he became involved with Japanese and Chinese poetry. Anhava is an alert observer, and his range of expression has noticeably increased. He has also earned credit as a translator and critic. Indeed, he was one of the first representatives of new criticism in Finland.

Fiction during the 1950s showed various tendencies, both opposed to and parallel to developments in poetry. Some authors continued in traditional narrative forms, which they led in new directions or used as a means of national self-criticism. Others struck out on new paths and gave up the form of the conventional novel as well as the traditional image of man. Most authors, however, settled somewhere between these two extremes and have developed a modified realism, characterized by an objective, uncomplicated narrative style with few flourishes and a general avoidance of psychological commentary.

The traditional fictional portrayal of the common people was continued most clearly by Veikko Huovinen (born 1927), whose comic novel *Havukka-ahon ajattelija* (1952, The Philosopher of Havukka-aho) presented the "philosophy" of an eccentric forestry worker. Huovinen's later work has shown his talent for satire and also his pessimism; both traits can be seen in a grotesque novel about Hitler, *Veitikka* (1971, Rogue).

In the work of Matti Hälli (born 1913), who has published problem novels as well as stylistically refined stories, humor is a basic element. Aapeli (1915–1967, pseudonym of Simo Puupponen), achieved recognition with masterful sketches and books for young people.

Väinö Linna (born 1920) has been the most noteworthy contemporary practitioner of the traditional novel. He has written long novels critical of his country. His war novel, *Tuntematon sotilas* (1954, The Unknown Soldier) was an instantaneous success, becoming for a time the dominant topic of literary conversation. It sold about 400,000 copies, an all-time record for a Finnish novel. Using the traditional elements of realism and humor, Linna gave a naturalistically unvarnished picture of the experiences of a small unit in the war. He was sharply critical of the attitudes of the officers, that is, of the middle and upper classes.

Linna continued to observe his own people with a critical eye in the trilogy *Täällä Pohjantähden alla* (1959–62, Here under the North Star) in which, starting with the fate of a poor cottager's family, he portrayed the social problems of the Finnish rural population from the turn of the twentieth century through the mid-1950s. The most impressive thing in the trilogy is the description of the civil war of 1918 and its aftermath. Linna is a master of the broad Tolstoian epic, with its crowd scenes, dramatic situations, and effective dialogue. His particular merit is his ability to combine criticism of his own country, vivid descriptions of characters, and skillful handling of plot.

Paavo Rintala (born 1930) has also striven to deflate national myths in his trilogy *Mummoni ja Mannerheim* (1960–62, Grandma and Mannerheim) and in *Leningradin kohtalonsinfonia* (1968, Leningrad Fate Symphony).

The first Finnish novelist to free himself from the older narrative manner was Jorma Korpela (1910–1964). His novels presented humanity in a new light. *Tohtori Finckelman* (1952, Doctor Finckelman) investigated the destructive forces hidden in the human psyche and the drive to misuse power. The novels and stories of Juha Mannerkorpi (born 1915) have been built upon penetrating psychological analyses and have achieved an existentialistic awareness of the human condition. Pentti Holappa (born 1927), for a long time a well-known columnist for a large daily newspaper, has used the technique of the *nouveau roman* in such novels as *Tinaa* (1961, Tin). Instead of linear narrative action, Holappa presented incongruent parallel versions of the lives of his characters. Iris Kähäri (born 1914) and Marko Tapio (born 1924) have also come up with experimental solutions to narrative problems; these solutions have been original in both style and structure. In 1967 Tapio began a broadly conceived series of novels under the title *Arktinen hysteria* (Arctic Hysteria), in which he intends to give a cross section of Finnish society.

One Finnish writer well known beyond the borders of his country is Veijo Meri (born 1928). His work has been characterized by an objective, almost documentary, narrative style, reporting the actions and reactions of men without commentary and leaving it to the reader to draw conclusions about motives and causal connections. Meri has often described setting from the point of view of his characters, so that its composition and shading vary according to their moods. Frequent changes of perspective are common, because the characters are often in motion, usually on fruitless journeys. Meri's work has been shot through with a grotesque humor reminiscent of Gogol' or Hašek; the dialogue and behavior of his characters is disconnected and unpredictable. One of Meri's peculiarities is to interrupt the action frequently with excursuses and anecdotes, which enlarge time and space in his novels.

Among Meri's best-known novels are *Manillaköysi* (1957, The Manila Rope), an account of a nightmarish returning home on leave (this novel has been translated into fourteen languages); *Sujut* (1961, Even), the story of a deserter; *Irralliset* (1959, Foundlings), a novel describing the destinies of small-town people; and *Peiliin piirretty nainen* (1963, The Woman Drawn on the Mirror), which depicted the last day in the life of an artist and the effect of his death on the people around him. Meri has also published plays and stories.

Two women, Eila Pennanen (born 1916) and Eeva Joenpelto (born 1921) have written objective descriptive fiction. Pennanen began by writing psychological and historical novels and later switched to describing critically contemporary phenomena, attacking ossified prejudices and false roles. In her novels and in the stories in *Kaksin* (1961, Together) she brought into focus the contrasts between generations. Eeva Joenpelto has also described the conflict of generations in such novels as *Neito kulkee vetten päällä* (1955, Virgin Walking on the Water) and *Kipinöivät vuodet* (1961, The Sparking Years), in which industrialization and the urbanization of peasant communities formed the social background.

Man's situation in a time of social change has been the concern of the novelist Leo Kalervo (born 1924). Marja-Liisa Vartio (1924–1966) posed similar questions in her early works. But in her later novels, especially in the posthumously published *Hänen olivat linnut* (1967, The Birds Belonged to Her), she turned away from these problems and let her imagination roam, guided by her stylistic mastery, to create sharp caricatures of two elderly ruminating women.

Antti Hyry (born 1931) has explicitly aimed at the ideal of objective realistic depiction. He has described the outer world minutely, but the feelings of his characters are only suggested. Again and again he has returned to the north-Finnish milieu, of which he shows a penetrating knowledge. He has been called a representative of the *nouveau roman,* but he is much less a theoretician than is usual for the exponents of the so-called new novel. In the collection *Junamatkan kuvaus* (1962, Account of a Train Ride) Hyry showed himself to be an outstanding storyteller.

THE 1960s

Again as before, lyric poetry led the innovations in Finnish literature. Pentti Saarikoski (born 1937) pointed the way with *Mitä tapahtuu todella?* (1962, What Really Happened?). This work was marked by strong, colloquial diction, the incorporation into the text of various quotations, a clear leftist commitment, and an open, fragmentary structure. As the title indicates, Saarikoski tried to see behind isolated phenomena in an attempt to solve the great problems of society. Several other books of the 1960s set themselves this task, and they displayed similar attitudes: criticism of the capitalistic system, and alignment with the new left. To be sure, there are other things in the work of Saarikoski: tender love lyrics, resigned self-analysis, and lovingly drawn descriptions of experiences in Prague and Dublin. He is also an important translator, his range extending from classical antiquity to Joyce and Salinger; his Finnish version of *Ulysses* has received great praise.

Many other poets have also taken explicit positions in response to current events and international crises. Matti Rossi (born 1934) wrote fierce poems about the Vietnam war as early as 1965, and in the volume *Tilaisuus* (1967, Opportunity) he expressed himself strongly on international conflicts.

Arvo Salo (born 1933) had a great theatrical success with the play *Lapualaisooppera* (1966, Lapua Opera), which depicted, in a pacifist spirit and Brechtian style, the fascist machinations and putsch attempts in Finland during the 1930s. Salo, together with Marja-Leena Mikkola (born 1939), introduced the political cabaret to Finland. Many poems of the 1960s were set to music, and some authors performed their protest songs themselves and successfully issued them on records; one such poet has been Aulikki Oksanen (born 1944), who first achieved recognition with two densely textured novels. Attacks on consumer ideology, war, and capitalist exploitation have been the main subjects; still, a few beautiful and simple love poems may also be found among the texts of the political cabarets.

Despite the growing number of political poems, poetry in the 1960s remained, for the most part, politically unaffiliated, although socially conscious. New experiments in style and form may be observed in this period. Väinö Kirstinä (born 1936) has written some dadaist and concrete poetry. Anselm Hollo (born 1934) adopted elements from modern English and American verse; indeed, he could be classified as an English poet in that for years he wrote in and translated into English. The verse of Jyrki Pellinen (born 1940) has used language in an intentionally unclear way in an attempt to explore its limits and possibilities.

The work of some poets is a direct continuation of the poetry of the 1950s. Pertti Nieminen (born 1929) began as a translator of Chinese lyrics. At first he published refined imagistic poems, but later turned to writing imaginative fables, in which he set current phenomena in a bizarre light. Maila Pylkkönen (born 1931) has written extensive poetic monologues. Tyyne Saastamoinen's (born 1924) concentrated poetry—subjective and fanciful—has exhibited some characteristics of surrealism. The clear, aphoristic, philosophical lyrics of Mirkka Rekola (born 1931) have shown a talent for compression of details and an unusual philosophy of life.

In fiction many of the trends of the 1950s have continued, but more attention was given in the 1960s to social problems, and writers became readier to take positions on current questions. A new feature was subjective spontaneity in narration, which can perhaps be traced to the influence of Henry Miller. There has lately been a great deal of variety in geographical setting and range of expression. In the stories of Timo K. Mukka (born 1944), set in northern Finland, the landscape takes on a balladesque character charged with religious and sexual significance. Pekka Kejonen (born 1940) has described young drunkards and lovers in his novels. Pekka Parkkinen (born 1940), who is also a poet, has written intensely about Paris and Portugal. Jarkko Laine (born 1947) has described the younger generation's pleasure in vagabondage and its passion for pop culture.

There was an increase in intellectual content and experimental features during the 1960s, as in the fantasy tales of Pekka Suhonen (born 1938), which have shown a knowledge of cultural history. The novels of Aapo Junkola (born 1935) have tried to analyze the sway of prejudice over thought and action. Many elements of the poems, novels, and plays of Juhani Peltonen (born 1941) are fanciful, yet his dreamlike or mythologically stylized world shows decidedly topical features. The style of the novels of Anu Kaipainen (born 1933) could almost be called expressionistic. Her *Arkkienkeli Oulussa* (1967, An Archangel in Oulu) described events in a northern town, while in *Magdaleena ja maailman lapset* (1969, Magdalene and the Children of This World) she combined the thematic material of an old ballad with the present.

Numerous novels have depicted the conflicts of generations, regions, or social classes. Kerttu-Kaarina Suosalmi (born 1921) described the relations among members of the educated middle class in the novel *Hyvin toimeentulevat ihmiset* (1969, Well-off People). Similar material has appeared in stories by Eeva Kilpi (born 1928) and—from the point of view of the younger generation—in the novels of Hannu Mäkelä (born 1943).

Lassi Sinkkonen (born 1937) and Alpo Ruuth (born 1943) brought new perspectives on the life of the working class. Sinkkonen's novel *Sumuruisku* (1968, The Spray Gun) showed the problems of alienation and adjustment of a worker in a communist-run automobile repair shop. Ruuth's *Kämppä* (1969, The Log Cabin) dealt with the conflicts arising in a circle of friends that lead to its ultimate dissolution. Both novels were written in the strong colloquial language of Helsinki. This increased use of colloquial speech was a characteristic of fiction during the 1960s.

Hannu Salama (born 1936) became the center of a literary scandal in the 1960s, which catapulted him into unintended success. He was prosecuted for blasphemy because of a few passages in the novel *Juhannustanssit* (1964, Midsummer Night's Dance), which presented a gripping naturalistic account of a midsummer festival and its fateful ending. Salama's conviction was nullified by a constitutional act of pardon by President Kekkonen. Salama wrote about a milieu similar to that of *Midsummer Night's Dance* in short stories and in the novel *Minä, Olli ja Orvokki* (1967, I, Olli, and the Girl Orvokki), a pitiless description of intrigues and moral duplicity within a small circle of friends. His most important work to date, *Siinä näkijä, missä tekijä* (1972, No Deed Remains Unseen), was a strong novel about the communist resistance in Finland during the war.

Toward the end of the 1960s, Finnish dramatic literature came back to life after a long repose. In addition to those poets and novelists already mentioned who also wrote plays, other interesting plays have been written by Lauri Leskinen (born 1918), Reino Lahtinen (born 1918), Lauri Kokkonen (born 1918), and Pekka Lounela (born 1932).

The prospects for Finnish literature during the 1970s are very good. It has shed the provincialism that earlier characterized it and, like Finland itself, has become immersed in the problems of the contemporary world. Finnish literature today is also characterized by a considerable variety both in subject matter and in technique.

While poetry has been the most innovative genre, writers of fiction—and, more recently, of drama—have added to the interest of Finnish literature. In the last ten years a new Finnish genre—social and political reports that are documentary in content but frequently close to literature in style—has assumed an important role in Finnish literary activity.

FINNISH WORKS IN ENGLISH TRANSLATION

INDIVIDUAL WORKS MENTIONED IN ARTICLE

Kivi, Aleksis. *Seitsemän veljestä* as *Seven Brothers.* New York, 1962
Linna, Väinö. *Tuntematon sotilas* as *The Unknown Soldier.* New York, 1957
Lönnrot, Elias. *Kalevala* as *The Old Kalevala, and Certain Antecedents.* Cambridge, Mass., 1969
Meri, Veijo. *Manillaköysi* as *The Manila Rope.* New York, 1967
Pekkanen, Toivo. *Lapsuuteni* as *My Childhood.* Madison, Wisc., 1966
Waltari, Mika. *Sinuhe, egyptiläinen* as *The Egyptian.* New York, 1954

SECONDARY WORKS

Hein, Manfred Peter. *Moderne finnische Lyrik.* Göttingen, 1962
Koskimies, R. *Elävä kansalliskirjallisuus,* 3 vols. Helsinki, 1944–49
Laitinen, Kai. *Suomen kirjallisuus 1917–1967,* 2nd ed. Helsinki, 1970
Suomen kirjallisuus, 8 vols. Helsinki, 1963–70
Tarkiainen, V. *Finsk litteraturhistoria.* Helsinki, 1950
Tarkka, Pekka, ed. *Suomalaisia nykykirjailijoita,* 2nd ed. Helsinki, 1968

French Literature

FRENCH LITERATURE since 1945 has offered a great many serious works, and some masterpieces. Its failure to measure up to the period between the two world wars should be seen as part of a more general trend, not as something peculiar to France. At any rate, French literature since World War II has overcome one of its less attractive traits—a sense of superiority that isolated it to some extent from other literatures. Now, no longer ignoring the existence of other literature, French writers have become receptive to influences of all kinds, especially the American novel (Faulkner, Hemingway, Dos Passos), German philosophy (Heidegger), German and Spanish drama (Brecht and García Lorca), and early twentieth-century fiction (Kafka, Joyce, James) that had been admired but not emulated. Although some have claimed that French literature is in a state of decline, it still maintains its high reputation: it is the most translated and most written about of all European literatures, and it holds the record number of Nobel Prizes (six since 1945).

Social conditions have been favorable for French literature since World War II. A wider public has appeared through increased access to education, through the reform of university programs, through radio and television, and through the reduction or even removal of the obstacles and prohibitions barring access to certain areas of literature. Today, the whole of literature—without any restrictions on moral, aesthetic, or historical grounds—has become, potentially or in fact, the object of immediate consumption and general acceptance. And yet, whether to defend itself against this advance of the public, against this promiscuity, or whether to guard its privileges against other media, such as television and films, French literature is becoming more and more intellectual, striving after refinements that ultimately are intended only for the eyes of other writers, and engaging in a self-analysis suitable only for literary theorists. Hence, the literature of recent years, more subtle than twentieth-century literature before World War II, has been, nonetheless, less fertile and less alive.

THE HERITAGE

The literature of the immediate present is so far removed from prewar literature that we sometimes have to make an effort to remember that prewar writers continued to publish in the years following the liberation. Yet, 1945 did not mark a sudden break. Each year there were tenuous, imperceptible breaks, one slight shift after another, although their overall effect now strikes us as amounting to an almost radical contrast.

Three authors who can be described as the last great classicists concluded their careers between 1940 and 1955. Paul Valéry (1871–1945) published a year before his death *Propos me concernant* (1944, Remarks about Myself), an outline of an intellectual biography embodying the features of his character-persona Monsieur Teste, and the last volume of *Variété* (1924–44, Variety). And his unfinished play *"Mon Faust"* (1946, "My Faust"), which might have been one of his masterpieces, was published soon after his death. In the last years of his life, Paul Claudel (1868–1955) published *Présence et prophétie* (1942, Presence and Prophecy), *L'histoire de Tobie et de Sara* (1942, The Story of Tobias and Sara), and various fragments of a biblical commentary, which, taken together, constitute one of his major works. And André Gide (1869–1951) published, apart from the last part of his often monotonous *Journal* (1950, Journal), a very fine novella, *Thésée* (1946, Theseus), which ends with a serene farewell and testament: "I have no regrets as my solitary death draws near. I have enjoyed the benefits of the earth. It is pleasant for me to think that, after me, and thanks to me, men will find themselves happier, better, and freer. For the good of future humanity, I have lived."

These three writers can be called the last great classicists not only because none of their successors has attained the same stature but also because the concept of literature has radically changed; and it may well be that there is a relationship between their "classic" concept of literature and the possibility of personal greatness.

Gide felt that the tradition he had maintained was dying, but by whose hand he was not sure. The taste of the public for shock and surprise, which

Gide detected after the war and which was denounced by Valéry in his poetics and by Claudel in his continual indictment of modernity, was not the fundamental cause of the break. Even more, the rupture had to do with a loss of faith in literature. The last classicists (whether Gide, Valéry, Claudel, or Thomas Mann) believed in literature. Although their art represented a considerable innovation at the beginning of the twentieth century, they never challenged the concept of literature itself: its function was accepted, and its tradition was venerated.

The period after World War II has seen the development of two very different literary movements. The first, the existentialist, is a literature of *content,* which, by using simplified, sometimes slipshod means and a style of writing that is sometimes "colorless," expresses a vision of man and the universe. The second, the formalist or structuralist, seems to be interested only in structure, without worrying too much about what it expresses and even at times going so far as to say that there is nothing to express—that there is no meaning. Despite their differences, both existentialism and formalism have undermined the traditional definition of literature as a relationship between form and content, a relationship to which the last great classicist works owed their strength.

In fiction before World War II, Jules Romains (1885–1972), Roger Martin du Gard (1881–1958), and François Mauriac (1885–1970) were masters of a narrative tradition divided between the sociological epic (in the form of vast novel cycles) and the psychological tragedy condensed into a short novel of about two hundred pages. This tradition persisted after the war and still persists today, but it has not found the same masters.

Either because they were growing old or because their confidence was to some extent shaken by the new atmosphere, these three masters added nothing decisive to their work. At his death in 1958, Roger Martin du Gard left thousands of pages of a huge novel that was much more personal than his earlier works—*Souvenirs du Colonel de Maumort* (Reminiscences of Colonel de Maumort)—which has not yet been published. The manuscript contains some very fine moments—in particular an admirable episode entitled *La baignade* (The Bathing Place); but perhaps it was not just by chance that the author was unable to put it into its final form. Aware that traditional techniques were worn out, Martin du Gard attempted in this work a first-person narrative very different from the objectivity of *Les Thibault* (1922–40, The Thibault Family), but he did not succeed in mastering it.

After a long period during which he wrote no novels, François Mauriac temporarily abandoned his political journalism to write *Un adolescent d'autrefois* (1969, A Former Adolescent). But this novel was not up to the standard of such earlier novels as *Le nœud de vipères* (1932, The Nest of Vipers), and he wrote it only because the student riots of May, 1968, prompted the old writer to look back on his own youth. Mauriac, too, was unable to accept the way in which the novel had begun to evolve since before the war, and was greatly inhibited by the changes.

Apart from the traditional novel—which followed the lines laid down by the great masters of the nineteenth century, from Honoré de Balzac (1799–1850) to Guy de Maupassant (1850–1893)—there developed after World War I a literature that was markedly original in spirit and in form. A poetic and imaginative fiction, receptive to the play of language, shifted the boundaries separating the genres, reflecting the euphoric easing of tensions after World War I and celebrating the modern world greeted so magnificently by Guillaume Apollinaire (1880–1918) on the threshold of the century. This prose included the "novels" of such writers as Jean Giraudoux (1882–1944), Jean Cocteau (1889–1943), Valéry Larbaud (1881–1957), and Paul Morand (born 1888), storytellers who were often also writers of verse. Their works belong to a world that has disappeared, a world of luxury and ease that the anguish of today rejects. Yet Paul Morand, with *Venises* (1971, Venices), a nostalgic evocation of a city he has known and loved for half a century, has just reminded us of his exquisite mastery as a writer. And the posthumous publication of an unfinished novel by Giraudoux, *La menteuse* (1969, Lying Woman), compels us not to dismiss too easily a writer who, as the novelist and critic Maurice Blanchot (born 1907) rightly saw, was one of the first to free the novel from its subjugation to realism.

The heritage of the period between the two wars includes one movement—surrealism—that warrants special treatment, because it continues to exercise its sway. Most contemporary poets and readers of poetry have learned from surrealism that poetry must ultimately "lead somewhere," that it is something other than a harmless confection of images and words, that it is intimately involved with and acts upon life. Surrealism expressed an ambition that has characterized almost all contemporary literature—to be more than literature. Its indictment of categories of society and of thought still determines our way of looking at things.

But the gap between surrealism and the most recent metamorphoses of literature continues to widen all the same. In the first place, surrealism, although a movement of rebellion, was imbued with enthusiasm, enthusiasm for language itself and enthusiasm for the imagination. The literature of the last twenty-five years, including poetry, however, has been conscious of the inadequate, precarious, and provisional nature of language and very much aware of the great distance separating language and life. It is an expression of rebellion, anguish, or criticism, without any compensating factor. Whether it takes the form of a cry of despair or a theoretical analysis, the literature of the present and the future would seem incapable of finding its consolation or its solution in the beauty of language.

The wane of surrealism had two major manifestations. First, some writers won a hold on the public after 1940 only by moving away from their surrealist beginnings. Paul Éluard (1895–1952) and Louis Aragon (born 1897), for example, owed their popularity to their political commitment, to their poems inspired by the resistance. Aragon has succeeded in remaining in the forefront because he has moved close to the most recent trends, such as that represented by the review *Tel Quel*.

A second manifestation of change is that the surrealists who occupy the highest place in the godless, demythologized pantheon of the literary consciousness of today are not André Breton (1896–1966) and not even Éluard or Aragon, but the dissident or banished surrealists, such as Antonin Artaud (1896–1948) and Georges Bataille (1897–1962). Breton never ceased to reproach them for inhabiting a world of hiatuses and anguish that he found unbearable; but his fundamental objection was that they had rejected lyricism. Despite what he added to his work before his death in 1966, Breton was an isolated figure after the war, an historical monument, inasmuch as he continued to represent the original spirit of surrealism, seeking the "gold of the time" and believing he could capture it without assuming the commitments and suffering the poisoned anguish of historical time.

THE OLDER GENERATION OF NOVELISTS

After 1945 there were many writers active who had begun their careers between 1925 and 1930. Their work still cannot be spoken of merely as historical fact, even though they no longer dominate contemporary literature. This group included Georges Bernanos (1888–1948), André Malraux (born 1901), Louis Aragon as a novelist, Henry de Montherlant (1896–1972), Marcel Jouhandeau (born 1888), Pierre Drieu la Rochelle (1893–1945), Antoine de Saint-Exupéry (1900–1944), Louis-Ferdinand Céline (1894–1961, pseudonym of Louis-Ferdinand Destouches), and even Jean Giono (1895–1970), Julien Green (born 1900), and Charles-Ferdinand Ramuz (1878–1947).

The essential contribution of these writers was through the novel—but novels that were early provokers of the public reaction, "This is no novel!" The end increasingly outweighed the means; invention, description, and the creation of characters were decidedly of secondary importance. Although these means were used, they were strained and shamelessly subordinated to the basic purpose, which was to establish the author's relationship to the world, to capture, or rather to form, a way of looking at things and a style of living. The novel became for them a way of posing questions and answering them.

Hence the neglect of narrative, sometimes elliptical and condensed, sometimes discursive; hence the digressions and the irregularity of the flow, the stresses being placed according to internal resonance and not according to the logic of the events related; hence the unity—and often the monotony —of perspective and coloring. The world described was the world that fascinated the writer and formed his thought, not the outward diversity of the real world.

The differences among these writers was great, but for all of them the novel was first and foremost an essay on the self, a transmuted confession, an attempt to give concrete expression to a particular idea. It is not coincidental that in addition to their novels, all these authors wrote essays. And the regularity with which they alternated between fiction and expository prose can be found in no preceding generation of novelists.

When we think of their work, what springs to mind is not stories or characters, or even a narrative style, but a voice telling us of the values for which each lived. If anything grouped these writers together and defined them, it was undoubtedly their common ethical concern. They contrasted what was and what they were with what they wanted to be and do. In this connection Malraux once rightly spoke of a "Corneillian tradition." For Malraux, the value was heroism; for Saint-Exupéry, courage and duty; for Montherlant and Drieu la Rochelle, the quest for virility (but through the adoption of a political stand for Drieu la Rochelle); for Aragon, social justice; for Ramuz and Giono, the naturalness of a certain way of life; for Bernanos, honor—Christian and French—and saintliness; and for Jouhandeau, the quest for salvation, sometimes in demoniac guise. They all tried to offer a key to life. Thus, their masters were not Valéry or Claudel or Gide or Marcel Proust (1871–1922), that is, not the writers who laid the foundations for a new narrative structure; instead, they seemed the descendants of François-René de Chateaubriand (1768–1848), of Maurice Barrès (1862–1923), of Charles Péguy (1873–1914), or in the case of Bernanos, of Léon Bloy (1846–1917).

The very fact that they used the novel more than they served it, that they had no ambition to find a new basis for it, made them all the more inclined to abandon it if what they wished to convey could be put over by more effective means. In part, the invention and "dishonesty" of fiction alienated them from the genre that, by gift and training, they had initially chosen. This alienation also arose from a purely artistic crisis—a feeling that the novel had been surpassed in the creation of illusion by films, and even by television—and from their refusal or inability to join younger novelists in seeking new paths for fiction.

Unlike Malraux or Montherlant, Georges Bernanos possessed the traditional gifts of the novelist: an art of imagining events, an ability to compress time and still give a sense of its flow, and an ability to sympathize with characters very unlike himself. Bernanos's *Sous le soleil de Satan* (1926, Under the Sun of Satan) marked the debut of a true novelist; and *Journal d'un curé de campagne* (1936, The Diary of a Country Priest) showed his artistic maturity. But in the last ten years of his life he devoted himself almost entirely to political writings—to the articles collected in *Lettre aux Anglais* (1942, Letter to the English), *Écrits de combat* (1944, Combat Writings), *La France contre les robots* (1947, France against the Robots), *Le chemin de la Croix-des-âmes* (1948, The Croix-des-Âmes Road), and the posthumously published *Les enfants humiliés* (1949, The Humiliated Children).

Bernanos did not switch to the essay because he had run out of material for creative fiction. In 1934 he had written, "I had to wait until I was thirty-eight before I could start drawing on an inner experience that, as is sufficiently proved by my first book (if I may be forgiven for saying so myself), suffers from an excess of richness rather than a poverty." His last novel, *Monsieur Ouine* (1943, Mr. Ouine), perhaps his masterpiece, was, if anything, overly rich; the unfinished novel *Un mauvais rêve* (1951, A Bad Dream) gives the same feeling; and his play *Dialogues des Carmélites* (1949, Dialogues of the Carmelites), which was also published posthumously, undoubtedly demonstrated that his inventive genius remained intact to the end. But the pressing demands of the times in which he lived, and his attempt to combat—without any illusions—the trend toward decadence and disaster led him to turn away from his visionary world, which continued nonetheless to nourish his last imaginative works.

The development of André Malraux was different, although his abandonment of fiction was even more determined. Until 1940, he was primarily a novelist; *La tentation de l'occident* (1926, The Temptation of the West) and a few shorter essays were much less important than the five novels that appeared over regular intervals: *Les conquérants* (1928, The Conquerors), *La voie royale* (1930, The Royal Way), *La condition humaine* (1933, The Human Condition), *Le temps du mépris* (1935, The Time of Contempt), and *L'espoir* (1937, Hope). Malraux originally intended *Les noyers de l'Altenburg* (1943, The Walnut Trees of Altenburg) as the first novel of a multiple-volume work, *La lutte avec l'ange* (The Struggle with the Angel), which he never completed.

After *The Walnut Trees of Altenburg* Malraux devoted himself to writings on the philosophy of art, of which the most important were *Saturne* (1950, Saturn), an essay on Goya; *Les voix du silence* (1951, The Voices of Silence); *Le musée imaginaire de la sculpture mondiale* (1953–55, The Imaginary Museum of World Sculpture); and *La métamorphose des dieux* (1958, The Metamorphosis of the Gods). In 1967 Malraux published the first volume of his *Antimémoires* (Anti-Memoirs), which did contain a few fragments of narrative fiction. These fragments, however, were all related to his old works—to *The Walnut Trees of Altenburg* and to *The Royal Way*. *Anti-Memoirs* was primarily a journal of his meetings with Nehru, with Mao, of his conversations with Charles de Gaulle. Although Malraux announced a sequel to *Anti-Memoirs,* he does seem to have given up the novel as an art form.

For Malraux, the novel was always based on a participation in history in the making. His characters only take shape when they can live outside themselves and become part of a movement that transcends them. To seek refuge from the self in action is not to act for oneself but to participate in an impersonal action. For the agnostic, this transcendental energy has only one name—history. Thus, in Malraux's novels the theme of revolution and virile brotherhood (*The Human Condition*) alternates with the theme of the solitary adventure (*The Royal Way*).

In a flash, however—in 1940, to be precise—Malraux saw the vast flow of what until then he had believed to be the goal of history crumble before his eyes. At that point, he encountered national solidarity, which inspired the *Camp de Chartres* (Chartres Prisoner-of-War Camp) parts of *The Walnut Trees of Altenburg*; later he would say, "I espoused the cause of France." Why then did he not write the epic of the French resistance? It is as if the national myth were powerless to replace the revolutionary myth in his work. And, indeed, they were not comparable: the resistance was not, and could not be, a movement of history, as revolution is for a Marxist or para-Marxist writer. In *The Walnut Trees of Altenburg* Malraux attempted to make up for this loss by leaving history and seeking permanent human values, this being the theme of the intellectuals conversing beneath the arches of the monastery of Altenburg.

Malraux exalted permanent human values again in *The Voices of Silence,* in which the history of art played the role political events had played in his novels. There was the same dispossession of the self for the sake of a transcendental energy. But unlike his novels, in *The Voices of Silence* the history has already been made, without Malraux's personal involvement in it. He could not find creative inspiration in this sort of history. And no doubt there would not have been an *Anti-Memoirs,* but instead a continuation of the unfinished *The Metamorphosis of the Gods,* if Malraux had not entered the lists again by acting as de Gaulle's minister of culture for more than ten years.

Yet Malraux's experience in government in turn was powerless to give fresh impetus to his novel writing. As minister of culture, he participated in an administrative rather than an historic action. But even if he had been minister for foreign affairs or minister for Algerian affairs, the France of de Gaulle was in any event no longer the kind of country that could direct history. What remained for Malraux was an evocation of the great men he encountered. But Nehru and Mao represented historical goals that were not his; and de Gaulle, although an illustrious figure, belonged more to the past than to history in the making. In his most recent work, *Les chênes qu'on abat* (1971, Felled Oaks), he gave an account of his last meeting with de Gaulle.

Two writers who did not survive the war bore witness both to the ethical inspiration of their generation and to the crisis of the novel, whose validity was already being questioned. Antoine de Saint-Exupéry, who disappeared while on a reconnaissance mission over occupied France in 1944, divided his literary work between reportage in the form of novellas—*Vol de nuit* (1931, Night Flight) and *Pilote de guerre* (1942, Combat Pilot)—and reportage in the form of essays—*Terre des hommes* (1939, World of Men). He was unwilling, and no doubt unable, to embark on a novel proper. His posthumously published *Citadelle* (1948, Citadel), a long allegorical tale, seemed to some to be closer to a novel; but in fact it was rather a philosophical tract. Saint-Exupéry's literary reputation, which has been very high in recent years and has spread beyond the borders of France, was enhanced by the heroism of his life and death. He was certainly not the great writer he has been thought to be, and people are beginning to realize this; nevertheless, he was representative of his generation.

Pierre Drieu la Rochelle was also a victim of the war, but on the other side, so to speak, since he committed suicide in 1945 after the collapse of the Nazis, whose cause he had espoused out of a misguided Europeanism. Drieu la Rochelle wrote intellectual problem novels and essays closely akin to confessions, but almost none of his books was able fully to contain his intriguing yet irritating mind—obsessed by the "immediacy of the twentieth century," grappling unhesitatingly with its demands, haunted by the problem of how to reconcile mind and body, seeking a life that would be an all-out risk and that would find its personal justification through its involvement in the collective destiny. His most successful work was his last, the posthumously published *Récit secret* (1958, Secret Account), in which Drieu la Rochelle revealed his deep-seated suicidal tendencies and made it understandable how such intelligence and such high demands could be transformed into impotent anguish.

Henry de Montherlant—whom many, particularly Bernanos, regarded as the major writer of his generation—used both the essay and the novel to express his concept of "wisdom," an art of living that consisted in following the contradictory impulses of his nature through a principle of alternation, since he was unable to reconcile them: the Christian versus the profane, the pagan, the stoic; the taste for commitment, sacrifice, and austerity versus the taste for sensuality, indulgence, and hedonism.

Montherlant's early novels, from *Le songe* (1922, The Dream) to the tetralogy *Les jeunes filles* (1936–39, The Girls), all showed a remarkable and persuasive lightness of touch. From 1942 onward, from *La reine morte* (1942, Queen after Death) through *Le cardinal d'Espagne* (1960, The Cardinal of Spain) and *La guerre civile* (1965, Civil War), drama became his favorite means of expression. While his plays served the same ethic and taught the same lessons as his novels, Montherlant the dramatist remained as respectful of the traditional rules of the genre as Montherlant the novelist was free with those of the novel. This is why his plays, despite their success, did not have the same importance as his novels. He added nothing new to the drama; instead, he took a content that remained the same—and about which one could have many reservations—and arrayed it in fine, but outmoded costumes. One exception was *La ville dont le prince est un enfant* (1951, The City Whose Prince Is a Child), a play deeply rooted in Montherlant's own knowledge of religious schools and of adolescent passions, which had the seriousness of tragedy without its formal trappings.

Although Montherlant may have been overestimated at one time, his present fall from favor is equally unjust. In his later essays, such as those in *Va jouer avec cette poussière* (1966, Go Play with This Dust), which showed an astringent yet serene aloofness from the contemporary world, admirable touches often redeemed what could otherwise have been trite and repetitious. Of Montherlant's other postwar works, *La rose de sable* (1954, The Sand Rose), a late publication of a novel written before the war, is clearly dated. But one of his most recent novels, *Le chaos et la nuit* (1963, Chaos and Night), may well be his masterpiece, even though it was almost unnoticed when it was published. It told the story of the last days of a Spanish refugee, a survivor of the civil war, who had gradually become alienated from all his beliefs and acquaintances, and who decides to return to Spain although he knows that there he is a wanted man. He dies by an unknown hand in his hotel room, after attending a bullfight, which symbolically anticipates his murder. *Chaos and Night* is a complex, ambiguous, and very free work, in which we listen to the reflections of the author, become involved in the realistic illusion of the narrative, and at the same time meditate on the lesson of the enigmatic fable it relates.

The French-Swiss Charles-Ferdinand Ramuz was yet another writer caught between the novel and the essay. For him, truth meant harmony with nature, which surrounds and explains man.

Jean Giono has sometimes been compared by critics with Ramuz, although their styles were completely different; and nature in Giono's work was more the cosmos of a pagan epic. Before the war Giono used the novel as a means of preaching. From 1947, when he returned to his literary career with *Un roi sans divertissement* (A King without Amusement) and *Noé* (Noah), he abandoned preaching for a kind of fiction that seemed to seek for nothing beyond itself. And although in his problem novels he had been fairly free with the laws of the genre and used such forms as the folk tale and the epic, in his later fiction he reverted to more traditional forms, recapturing in *Le hussard sur le toit* (1951, The Horseman on the Roof), *Le bonheur fou* (1957, Mad Joy), and *Angelo* (1958, Angelo) the tone of Stendhal's (1783–1842, pseudonym of Marie-Henri Beyle) Italian chronicles.

These chronicles, in which Giono delighted in recapturing the distant past—for example, the Italy of the *carbonari,* duels, inns—did have a significance, but in a way quite unlike his earlier work. Giono's shift from commitment to escapism meant that he—a pacifist disoriented by the war—no longer believed in the possibility of living an authentic life, even as an exception to the general rule, in the modern world. Gone was the embodiment of values in one's own existence, which obsessed his generation and which had obsessed him before the war. Giono no longer attempted to teach us how to live happily and freely; he wanted his writing to give the *feeling* of happiness and freedom. Happiness was not the happiness of Angelo on the roads of Italy but the happiness of Giono dreaming and writing about Angelo, and the happiness of his reader.

For Giono, life became a void that could be filled only by playing with life, through words that play with life, through literature. One might think that this concern with language, which separated Giono from writers who, both in his generation and in the next, regarded it as a mere tool, would have found him disciples among those of the most recent literary trends. Yet, those of today who have defined literature as language above all have scarcely any interest in him. This is because for Giono language was a game that accepted and took delight in itself and was willing to conform to certain traditions (for example, the scope and tone of the chronicle); in more recent years, on the other hand, language has become the means for a joyless destruction.

The work of Louis Aragon has provided one of the most complex and original examples of the multiple possibilities of the novel and its place in literature. Aragon, at the outset, was in no way a novelist, even though his surrealistic imagery and arabesques of language found better expression in the partially narrative prose of *Le paysan de Paris* (1926, The Peasant of Paris) than in the poems of *Le mouvement perpétuel* (1925, Perpetual Motion). His definitive turn to the novel coincided with his becoming politically active. Adherence to communism dominated his "realistic" novels of the 1930s: *Les cloches de Bâle* (1933, The Bells of Basel) and *Les beaux quartiers* (1936, The Good Neighborhoods). Since Aragon's goals were to contribute to the emancipation of man and to work for the advent of true social justice—and in so doing not only recount the revolutionary legend but also (unlike Malraux) depict bourgeois society in all its machinations and selfishness—he felt he had to use the most popular literary form and to make it perfectly readable.

According to the dogma of socialist realism—and Aragon's six-volume *Les communistes* (1949–50, The Communists) bordered on propaganda —the revolutionary novel had to follow the traditional novel form. Aragon's contribution to literature, however, cannot be dismissed as that of a militant. At the same time as these novels about the "real world," he was writing his "scenes of private life." Works such as *Les voyageurs de l'impériale* (1943, The Outside Passengers) and *Aurélien* (1944, Aurélien) and, even more explicitly, *La mise à mort* (1965, The Death Blow) and *Blanche et l'oubli* (1967, Blanche and Forgetfulness) were full of revelations about himself, revelations about Aragon the lover that provide us with glimpses of the myth he created around his wife, Elsa.

Other gifted writers belonged to the generation that began writing in the period between the two world wars. But their work showed no real development after World War II and is now rather remote from us.

Julien Green, whose last important novel, *Moïra* (Moïra), was published in 1950, has been devoting himself more and more to writing his memoirs. Unlike other major novelists of his generation, Green was never concerned with ethical humanism. His masterpieces—*Le voyageur sur la terre* (1927, The Pilgrim on Earth), *L'autre sommeil* (1931, The Other Sleep)—expressed an anguish that links them more to the later existentialist novel and the novel of the absurd; Green's fictional world, created out of full-bodied, believable characters who usually live in the provinces, unfolded itself in traditional narrative forms. Probably partially the changes in the genre of the novel but even more so Green's religious conversion has paralyzed his creative impulse; hence his turning to the diary form.

Marcel Jouhandeau has continued to publish very regularly since World War II, but has added nothing essential to an enormous oeuvre, whose strangeness and beauty are better appreciated in a collection of extracts. On the surface, Jouhandeau's universe is that of the nineteenth-century novel: stories of marriage, adultery, petty theft, and even crime take place in the imaginary village of Chaminadour, in the French provinces (it has been said that the provinces have provided the most fertile raw material for the novel). Moreover, his style is classical, and he in no way puts language under attack. However, one feature of Jouhandeau's work links him with the contemporary novel: he has not put his fictional universe into a vast narrative cycle, as a nineteenth-century novelist would have done. Instead, he uses aphorisms, portraits, and meditations; or he merely collects the various banal incidents that could be the starting point for a sweeping epic. As a result, his novels are fragmented, and we have—like points of a graph that are not joined together—only the main indications of an experience, and reflections that he could have called, as he did one of his expository works, *Essai sur moi-même* (1947, Essay about Myself).

Of all the writers of this generation, the one who has become most immediately relevant today is Louis-Ferdinand Céline, despite his temporary obscurity because of his anti-Semitic and anti-French attitudes, which made him an object of contempt during and after World War II. *Voyage au bout de la nuit* (1932, Journey to the End of the Night) was hailed as an event when it first appeared, but no one could then surmise the full depths of its influence. Going against the mainstream of the humanist, ethical literature of the day, it revealed a world without values, seen in all its nakedness. Céline was one of the first to live what was to become the subject matter of literature—the absurdity of human existence. Moreover, the essential relationship between the absurd and the obscene—the obscene considered as a test of sincerity—would be found again in Georges Bataille, in Antonin Artaud, and in Jean-Paul Sartre (born 1905). Indeed, Sartre's *La nausée* (1938, Nausea) has a quotation from Céline on its title page.

Céline's influence was to make itself felt on style even more than on sensibility. It has been rightly claimed that Céline's revolution was to substitute the spoken word for the written word. Yet Céline did not write simply the way people speak. His language—very highly wrought to achieve a sort of spontaneity or perpetual invention—took from the spoken language what went beyond the commonplace and the stereotype.

In Céline's alchemy of language slang is combined with metaphor and, particularly in *Journey to the End of the Night,* with cadences and breaks worthy of the symbolists. Sentences are often left unfinished; and trite, hackneyed phrases are replaced by exclamation marks or points of ellipsis. Was he attempting to destroy language so that nothing remained, in order to demonstrate its impotence, to say that there is nothing to be said, since everything is fake and nothingness? This is the interpretation of some of Céline's present-day admirers. Or was he attempting to destroy language in order to break its usual sequence to set it on another course and make it capable of lending enchantment to pain and giving life to dreams?

A certain magic did mark *Journey to the End of the Night,* as well as *Mort à credit* (1936, Death on the Installment Plan), which, although less spontaneous and less lyrical, pushed even further the construction of a scatological fairyland. In his last works, *D'un château l'autre* (1957, Castle to Castle) and *Nord* (1960, North), and in his posthumously published works, *Le Pont de Londres* (1964, London Bridge) and *Rigodon* (1969, Rigadoon), the language (now the rhetoric of a counterrhetoric) was transformed into a kind of death rattle and was destroyed to no purpose. Language thus testified to the self-destruction of the author himself.

In his drive to self-destruction Céline was constantly close to a literature that, like Artaud's work, suffered from its distance from life. However painful they might be, books like *Bagatelles pour un massacre* (1938, Bagatelles for a Massacre) and *L'école des cadavres* (1938, The School of

Corpses) do not arouse disgust or disapproval so much as a harrowing sympathy for a man who was prey to obsessions of persecution and hatred and to prophecies of the end of the world. In some works, however, Céline did succeed in combining enchantment, scorn, and delirium in a totally original way. In *London Bridge* this magical Céline was present again, but not in *Castle to Castle,* an account of the tragicomedy of his collaboration with the Nazis, enmeshed in an historical truth that it cannot transmute.

FROM EXISTENTIALISM TO THE NEW NOVEL

During the first decade following World War II, literature was dominated by the works of two very different writers, but two who are associated with each other under the label of *existentialism*. This label is an oversimplification, but it does point to similarities that cannot be ignored. These two writers—Jean-Paul Sartre and Albert Camus (1913–1960)—together gave the novel a metaphysical rather than an ethical content, and a new structure.

The most immediate and natural effect of the end of the war, however, was not the existential novel but a literature inspired by the times and by specific events rather than by a general vision of man, one that sought to give spontaneous expression to the contemporary situation rather than to transform techniques. The underground literature of the war—the outstanding examples of which were the poems of Aragon and Éluard and the novellas and accounts of Vercors (born 1902, pseudonym of Jean Bruller) (*Le silence de la mer* [1942, The Silence of the Sea] and *La marche à l'étoile* [1943, The March toward the Star])—was followed, quite naturally, by a retrospective look at the resistance. The best of these retrospective accounts were perhaps Roger Vailland's (1907–1965) *Drôle de jeu* (1945, A Strange Game) and Romain Gary's (born 1914) *Éducation européenne* (1945, A European Education).

The battles of the war provided the inspiration for *La vallée heureuse* (1946, The Happy Valley) by Jules Roy (born 1907) and *Week-end à Zuydcoote* (1949, Weekend at Dunkirk) by Robert Merle (born 1909). But the most important literature about the war was concerned with the world of the concentration camps. David Rousset's (born 1912) *L'univers concentrationnaire* (1946, The Concentration Camp Universe) was not a novel, since it was an attempt to give a structural description of the world of the camps; but it drew widely and powerfully on the narrative and descriptive techniques of the novel. In Robert Antelme's (born 1915) *L'espèce humaine* (1947, The Human Species), a deportee suffers his martyrdom without being able to reflect on its meaning, and a second character is able to do so by vicariously experiencing it through the other.

These years of captivity provided Jean Cayrol (born 1911) with the material for his trilogy *Je vivrai l'amour des autres* (1946–47, I Will Live the Love of Others). In this fictionalized account, the concentration camp, far from being an historical accident, becomes a symbol for man's earthly condition. Cayrol described this miserable, "Lazarus-like" condition in so uncompromising a way that he approached the world of Céline's outcasts and Samuel Beckett's (born 1906) tramps; but Cayrol interpreted this world exclusively in terms of religious redemption.

The most lasting literature of the immediate postwar years was not, however, these eye-witness accounts. It was a literature of thinkers, of philosophers—the writings of Sartre and Camus.

The first difference between Sartre and Camus and the group of "ethical novelists" who had come to the fore between the wars was naturally one of literary chronology. Although Sartre is almost the same age as Malraux, he published his first novel ten years later—*Nausea* in 1938. His status as a writer was confirmed during the war years with the play *Les mouches* (1943, The Flies) and the treatise *L'être et le néant* (1943, Being and Nothingness), and right after the liberation with the first two novels of his trilogy *Les chemins de la liberté* (The Roads to Freedom): *L'âge de raison* (1945, The Age of Reason) and *Le sursis* (1945, The Reprieve). Camus began his career as a novelist in 1942 with *L'étranger* (The Stranger) and confirmed his importance during the late 1940s and early 1950s.

But this chronological gap between Sartre and Camus and the generation of Malraux and Bernanos was not the only difference. There were subtle but important differences in their thinking. Sartre and Camus, like the earlier writers, sought an ethic, under the names of freedom, commitment, and revolt; and both Malraux and Montherlant had already combined the ethical statement with a metaphysical conception of man, presenting the human condition either tragically or with resignation. And it is not even altogether accurate to say that the interwar writers went from the ethical to the metaphysical while Sartre and Camus went from the metaphysical to the ethical; more precisely, the former merged what the latter were to separate.

The interwar writers, even if they were also essayists, reacted totally and vitally through the work of art; each book sprang forth from an *experience,* a moment, or a mood. The postwar writers were philosophers (Sartre) or thinkers (Camus), and the dialectic of their *thought* dictated the order of their works, each one being a proposition or an experiment leading toward a conclusion. *Nausea* treated in isolation, or rather in abstraction, a pointless existence, just as *The Stranger* treated an absurd existence. *The Roads to Freedom* was primarily concerned with a provisional solution to the problem of freedom; Camus's *La peste* (1947, The Plague) dealt in the same way with the problem of evil and revolt, and *La chute* (1956, The

Fall) with the problem of guilt. Each of these works of fiction was constructed like a theoretical essay, its aim being to analyze fully a proposition.

Hence an important stylistic change. There was no longer any question of being carried away by an impulse, of arousing the emotions, or seeking to transmute experience. The aim was to be complete, clear, accessible, simple. All earlier major novelists were to some extent poets. Sartre and Camus, although their prose styles were very different—Sartre discursive and familiar, Camus elliptic and aristocratic; Sartre closer to Émile Zola (1840–1902), Camus to Benjamin Constant (1767–1830)—were both prose writers who refused the allurement of poetry (the only exception was a few lyrical essays Camus wrote as a young man during the late 1930s). Their writing was as antiromantic as their vision, tending sometimes toward what the critic Roland Barthes (born 1915) later called *"le degré zéro"*—a style almost devoid of color, approaching the technique of naturalistic reporting (I myself once ventured to describe the literature they dominated as "metaphysical naturalism" rather than existentialism). Sartre was perfectly at home in the political polemics of the periodical *Les temps modernes,* as was Camus in the editorials he wrote for the newspaper *Combat.*

It was no accident that both Sartre and Camus regarded the theater as a more satisfactory means of expression than the novel, Sartre because he sought political effectiveness, and Camus no doubt because he was interested in the structure of tragedy and even in the staging of plays. But both of them probably favored the drama primarily because it uses a simple language, which rejects poetic overtones, and—inasmuch as only one character speaks at a time—it avoids confusion and the superimposition of voices and visions.

For, insofar as he is the only one to think, the philosopher-novelist has to find some way of stilling his voice or effacing it. The omniscient narrator who, in the nineteenth-century novel, constantly intruded his point of view on that of his characters and commented on and announced events, this narrator who was not involved in the events of the story, had no place in an objective narrative that must adopt, and never go beyond, the field of vision of the character, a narrative that is committed and told from the point of view of the one who is involved, who is living the story, a narrative that is determined by an actor, not a narrator. This objective writing, which practices what is known in cinematic terms as reduction of the visual field, had been used by Stendhal (unlike Balzac), by the naturalistic novelists (Gustave Flaubert [1821–1881], Maupassant), by some American novelists (Dos Passos, Hemingway), and by Kafka. In stripping the narrative of amalgams, additions, and subjective vibrations, these men gave it maximum realism.

This concern for objectivity was undoubtedly all the greater in the postwar philosopher-novelists because they were so aware of their intellectuality. That is why they put so much stress on the process, already initiated, by which the latent content of the novel, traditionally intermingled with its surface content, could rise to the surface and occupy it entirely. The characters, the plot, and the setting became more and more clearly only *media;* they faded before a truth that could be (and this was what determined whether the work was successful) a vision or merely an idea.

In any event, there was an attempt (mainly by Sartre, it is true, but Camus also wrote on the novel while the earlier novelists never did) to formulate a dogmatic aesthetic designed to provide the novel with a new and durable basis. At the same time that *Nausea* appeared, Sartre published in the *Nouvelle revue française*—together with an article on phenomenology, which was the manifesto of a philosophical realism, paying tribute to the philosopher Edmund Husserl for having given us *things, things in themselves,* free from all idealistic secretions—an article entitled *M. François Mauriac et la liberté* (1939, François Mauriac and Freedom). This article was the first of a series of studies in which Sartre contrasted true and false practitioners of the novelist's art. The false ones included Mauriac, Giraudoux, Giono, and Malraux; the true novelists were Faulkner and Dos Passos.

Sartre's basic idea here was that the novelist cannot be both inside and outside at the same time. Either his field of vision is God's, who sees simultaneously the end and the beginning and pierces through appearances (in which case he is explaining a destiny, not portraying a life), or his field of vision coincides with the instant actually lived by someone, and his art is alive, encouraging a free response from the reader to the very freedom of the character. This theorizing, which would be found (with different conclusions) in what ten years later was to be the *nouveau roman* (new novel), was one of the main differences between Sartre and his predecessors.

Literary reasons alone cannot account for the enormous success of Sartre between 1945 and 1955. He was not of the first rank as a novelist, a dramatist, a prose stylist, or even a philosopher, but he was nonetheless an outstanding writer because the range of his work was so broad and, more importantly, because he gave his contemporaries precisely what they needed. The disillusionment and despair arising from the horror of wartime events created a need for resolute thinking, for an orthodoxy that would face the world as it was, that would be alive to the world's problems, and that would not delude itself. People were attracted by the authority and systematic vigor in the contemporaneity and frankness of Sartre's thinking.

Nausea was a completely ahistorical metaphysical novel, whose success lay more in showing than in proving. Admittedly, Roquentin's interior monologues sometimes take the form of a meditation with a definable pattern and conclusions. The famous passage of the existential revelation, in the public park of Bouville, tells us explicitly that man is superfluous, that his existence is purposeless, that the world and himself are totally contingent. But we *feel* the nauseous disgust and the soft, heavy atmosphere much more than we follow the stages of a demonstration. The images, evoking the gratuitousness and obscenity of forms, and the writing itself, with its stricken, paralyzed quality, are more persuasive than any philosophy. But philosophy enters into the moral question that the book poses. On the last pages, the music of a record provides a gleam of the hope of salvation. The melody does not exist softly and insipidly like man; it has a rigorous necessity. Perhaps man can participate in the same way and *be* rather than merely exist, by creating or living "perfect moments."

Shortly after *Nausea,* Sartre published a treatise significantly called *L'imaginaire* (1940, Imagination). But he promptly rejected this aesthetic temptation, through a break between a visionary universe, which inspires a genuine artistic creation, and a philosophy seeking after values, which threatens the vitality of the novel and is likely to break away from it sooner or later. From *Nausea* to *The Roads to Freedom,* via *The Flies,* Sartre went from the entrapment of existence in the world to its liberation, its return to itself. Consciousness was shown to have no basis, no value. But if the nausea provoked by this recognition is overcome by admitting it lucidly, this was enough to discover the "roads of freedom." Having no basis, man is his own basis; the fact that he is abandoned means that he is free. Freedom, finally, is the exalting, life-giving word (although proclaimed without the fervor attached to it by surrealism) that makes it possible to face up to the world. Life begins "on the other side of despair."

In a key scene in *The Flies* between Jupiter and Orestes, the freedom of man is contrasted with the order of the world; and the circumstances in which the play was written and performed—in Paris during the Nazi occupation—gave a clearly political connotation to a general philosophical concept. Echoing Orestes, Mathieu Delarue, the hero of *The Roads to Freedom,* decides to "accept responsibility for existence." All the characters in the trilogy thus live the experience of their freedom and are shown in their progress toward an unforeseeable future. Nothing weighs on them or forces them to be this rather than that—not God's commandments or moral imperatives or their past or their passions or their concept of themselves or their social position. They are, of course, in a particular situation. But the situation determines nothing; it is the setting for a choice or a decision. Does Mathieu love Marcelle? Will Marcelle keep the child? Does Daniel believe in God? Will Mathieu become a communist? Will he kill himself? Will Daniel kill the cats? One cannot know, because the questions can only be settled by the act that they will freely choose. And this act allows of no hierarchy; to commit oneself or not to commit oneself is to be equally free. Freedom is not an exceptional form of action; it is the common fabric of existence, to which we are all condemned. This condemnation is the only value there is and it is called *responsibility*. Thus, "existentialism is a humanism," the only humanism that is consistent and free from illusion.

But this humanism of freedom raised a primary difficulty that threatened imaginative literature itself, insofar as the experiential, obsessional world could be forced out by the movement of the thought that sets it free. A play like *Huis clos* (1945, Closed Door), an admirable evocation of the hell that for each of us is "other people," and also stories like *Intimité* (1939, Intimacy) and the best of *The Roads to Freedom*—for example, the scene in *The Reprieve* between the two sick people lying on their stretchers and exchanging tender words as they satisfy their natural needs—conveyed the anguish and solitude, the impossibility of communication, and an eroticism deeper and stronger than any thought. The obsession with the original defilement and the horror of the viscous humors in which life has its origin block the movement leading to freedom and life. That is why Sartre, who drew his strength as a novelist from such obsessions, was to abandon the novel, since he wanted above all not to be carried away.

Sartre was never to write the projected fourth volume of *The Roads to Freedom*. Instead, after the third part, *La mort dans l'âme* (1949, Sick at Heart), he abandoned the novel in favor of the theater, which is more suited to showing action than to evoking the climate of life and is a better vehicle for words of command. His skillfully written and very popular plays—*Les mains sales* (1948, Dirty Hands), *Le Diable et le bon Dieu* (1951, The Devil & the Good Lord), *Nekrassov* (1955, Nekrassov), *Les séquestrés d'Altona* (1960, The Condemned of Altona)—had to confront another difficulty—the difficulty of the meaning that should be given to freedom itself.

At the very moment that Sartre the novelist was affirming the absolute value and equivalence of *all* freedom, Sartre the political thinker, in the manifesto launching *Les temps modernes* (October, 1945), was accusing bourgeois literature of having chosen the freedom of noncommitment: "The writer is *situated* in his age; every word has repercussions. Every silence too. I hold Flaubert and Goncourt responsible for the repression that followed the Commune because they did not write a line to prevent it. . . ." Taking the place of existentialism in Sartre's work, Marxism brought with it a hierarchy of freedom and destroyed the mystique of humanism. What Sartre had taken for the metaphysical absurd became the social absurd. Hell was no longer the hostility of individual consciousnesses, but class inequality. Freedom was not a value, but a potential value that could be realized only once social alienation had been removed. Freedom for its own sake became freedom for a particular end; man the "useless passion" became effective passion.

In *Dirty Hands,* in which we see Hugo kill Hoederer on the orders of the party, thus giving his freedom a practical content in line with the movement of history, Sartre left the conclusion ambiguous, since perhaps Hugo also killed out of jealousy, and the party, changing its line, would later disown him. Sartre's subsequent plays left no room for subjective interpretations; they reflected the conviction that one must work for social emancipation and that this emancipation is achieved through collective action. In *The Devil & the Good Lord,* Goetz, a German mercenary soldier fighting in the civil wars of the Reformation, arbitrarily chooses now good, now evil; and since he always fails, he proves the absurdity of all subjective morality. And in *The Condemned of Altona,* Frantz, the Nazi who isolates himself in his guilt, assuming responsibility for the history of his party and its action, ends in madness, since no one person can be solely responsible. But this is more a condemnation of subjectivity than a definition of objectivity. And the question remains as to what community one can put one's trust in.

For a time a hard-line communist, later the founder of a short-lived movement of the noncommunist left, then a communist once more, and today attracted by Maoism and the new left, director of the newspaper *La cause du peuple,* breaking and then renewing his ties with his friends at *Les temps modernes*—Sartre, although he is uncertain of his position, has in any event given up writing novels and plays, which he has condemned as ineffective, subjective, and in danger of being taken over immediately by the bourgeoisie (in this spirit he refused the Nobel Prize).

Nevertheless, Sartre still writes—and writes well—almost as if to say that his farewell is prolonged by a weakness that delays the substitution of action for words. *La critique de la raison dialectique* (1960, Critique of Dialectical Reason) opened the paths of historical pragmatism to philosophy. *Les mots* (1964, The Words) analyzed, without self-indulgence, his literary vocation. In it Sartre accused himself of only being interested in words, his own and those of others; but he made these accusations in a style new to him: sharp, lively, brilliant, almost the style of Voltaire (1694–1778, pseudonym of François-Marie Arouet). *L'idiot de la famille* (1971, The Idiot of the Family) was a monumental study of Flaubert (the 2000 pages of the first two volumes is only a beginning). In "settling accounts" with the man who for a long time has been in his eyes the very model of the writer, he is also settling accounts with literature itself and putting an end to a long fascination. Sartre said that he will continue the book only because he has begun it and that he will write no more afterward. Nevertheless, *The Idiot of the Family* represents, objectively, a beginning, although it may be a subjective farewell. It is a model of how to integrate Marxist criticism and psychoanalytical criticism, an attempt at totalization as opposed to the open grillwork of structuralist criticism. Sartre clearly still has much more to offer. But the exigencies and the scruples of a moral conscience, which has made Sartre unwilling to share what cannot be grasped by all, has made him suppress—at least in part—the richness of his artistic and philosophical mind.

Sartre's influence on fiction in the ten years after the war was substantial. There was an "existentialist," even a specifically Sartrian flavor in many novels, above all in those of Simone de Beauvoir (born 1908). Her first novel, *L'invitée* (1943, The Invited Woman), remains her masterpiece. Her subsequent novels, *Le sang des autres* (1944, The Blood of Others), *Tous les hommes sont mortels* (1947, All Men Are Mortal), and *Les Mandarins* (1954, The Mandarins), in all of which one can see the influence of both Sartre and Camus, were weakened by a too-obvious didacticism, and Beauvoir abandoned fiction fairly soon to write essays (*Le deuxième sexe,* [1949, The Second Sex]) and memoirs (*Mémoires d'une jeune fille rangée* [1958, Memoirs of a Dutiful Daughter], *La force de l'âge* [1960, The Prime of Life], *La vieillesse* [1970, Old Age]), in all of which she never resisted an opportunity to denounce the bourgeoisie.

The novels of Raymond Guérin (1905–1954)—*Quand vient la fin* (1941, When the End Comes), *L'apprenti* (1946, The Apprentice), *Les poulpes* (1953, The Octopi)—pitiless and bitter indictments of the absurdity of existence, can be compared to *Nausea*. But they completely lacked any spirit of positive humanism. Violette Leduc (born 1907) can also be grouped with the existentialists. Her first essay, *L'asphyxie* (1946, Asphyxiation), was published by Camus. Her novel *La bâtarde* (1964, The Bastard), prefaced by Simone de Beauvoir, more a "scandalous" autobiography than a novel, was both deliberately frank and revolutionary in its social implications.

In the work of Henri Calet (1903–1955) one can find, together with a restrained pathos, the same refusal to compromise, the same iconoclasm, and the same determination to conceal nothing. Both Calet's *La belle lurette* (1935, Ages Ago) and René Etiemble's (born 1909) *L'enfant de choeur* (1937, The Choir Boy) were significant precursors of postwar fiction.

The works of Boris Vian (1920–1959)—such as *L'écume des jours* (1947, The Scum of Days), which showed the influence of Sartre—belonged to the folklore atmosphere of the liberation and the existentialism of the cellars of Saint-Germain-des-Prés. Vian's refusal to make any commitment, his poetic handling of language, and the melancholy of an adolescent inspiration won him a special place in contemporary literature, despite his premature death.

The strength of the work of Marguerite Duras (born 1914), who began by publishing in Sartre's *Les temps modernes,* has been strictly objective writing, showing life as it is—in the silences, in the unspoken that underlies the spoken. Her short novels—among them *Les petits chevaux de Tar-*

quinia (1953, The Little Horses of Tarquinia), *Le square* (1955, The Square), *Moderato cantabile* (1957, Moderato Cantabile), and *Détruire, dit-elle* (1969, Destroy, She Said)—have been sustained by the images, obsessions and moods of an extremely rich and personal inspiration. Her work, like that of other members of her generation, has been moving increasingly (although within the art of the implicit) toward revolutionary indictment. Marguerite Duras's work, however, has also provided a link between the existentialist novel and the "new novel."

Among other existentialist novelists, one could also mention Marcel Mouloudji (born 1922) and Colette Audry (born 1906). But apart from Sartre, existentialism produced only one writer of the first rank—Albert Camus.

The progression of Camus's career was very close to Sartre's. Taking a metaphysical realization as his starting point, he sought an ethic and a commitment. *The Stranger* corresponds to *Nausea;* Camus's concept of the absurd was not far from Sartre's notion of contingency. The "sensibility of the absurd that can be found scattered through the century" (as Camus stated in *Le mythe de Sisyphe* [1942, The Myth of Sisyphus], which set out to analyze the absurd philosophically) was embodied in *The Stranger*.

Meursault, the protagonist of *The Stranger,* to whose field of vision the narrative is restricted, is, like each and every one of us, absurd man; although he wants to find a justification for existence, he cannot. The feeling of the absurd derives from the conflict between a subjective desire for a valid life in a rational universe and objective reality, which thwarts this desire. So we become indifferent, we become strangers to ourselves. Meursault, however, does not destroy himself but allows himself to live; but in so doing, he allows himself to be condemned to death. How have we the courage to live in this absurd world? In *The Myth of Sisyphus* Camus replied that life and an ethic are possible, provided that the truth of the absurd is accepted and provided that all illusions—suicide, religious faith, and hope—are rejected. The one irreducible value that makes life possible is lucidity.

Thus, at worst life is still bearable; the absurd is not all-pervading. "The absurd is contradictory in existence. It excludes value judgments, and value judgments exist. They exist because they are linked with the very fact of existence," Camus wrote in an essay, *Remarque sur la révolte* (1945, A Note on Revolt), a few years after *The Myth of Sisyphus*. By living and acting, man reveals a meaning, which is illuminated by one experience in particular—rebellion. Rebellion proves that we are not prepared to accept the unacceptable, that we cannot let everything go unchecked, and that there are things worth defending. And what is worth defending is not the individual alone, but man: "The individual is not, in himself, an embodiment of the values he wishes to defend. All humanity comprises them. When he rebels, a man identifies himself with other men."

The Plague embodied the transcending of the absurd. And it is significant that this book, at the same time it was an allegory of the eternal human condition, was a chronicle of the recent past. One can recognize in the city of Oran—fallen prey to the plague, shut in by its own tragedy, but calling for devotion and sacrifice—France during the Nazi occupation. And indeed, it was in the resistance that Camus himself demonstrated, and lived to the full, values that cannot be reduced to the absurd. In *The Plague* the values that come to the fore are caring for others, understanding, and limiting the spread of evil. There is a kind of prudence here that limits the meaning of commitment and contrasts it with the Sartrian choice.

In *L'homme révolté* (1951, The Rebel) Camus described these themes clearly in theoretical terms. The ethic born of the rebellion against evil rediscovers the obsession with evil by asking what its consequences will be. How can we ensure that a new evil will not arise from our actions? Under the influence of events (the disillusionment after the liberation of France, the degradation of the revolutionary spirit by the dictatorships in the Soviet Union and in the "people's democratic republics"), the threat of the evil that can arise from action in the service of good never ceased to haunt Camus. He denounced the concrete forms taken by modern rebellion and condemned the Marxist and Hegelian religion of history, at the risk of cornering himself into a passive ethic of nonintervention, understanding, and charity.

The path Camus followed in his plays paralleled that of his novels and essays. Just as the lyrical monologue of *Caligula* (1938, Caligula) corresponded to his first essays, *Le malentendu* (1944, The Misunderstanding)—a somewhat melodramatic play in which a man is murdered by his mother and sister, who do not recognize him—was an extension of *The Stranger*. *L'état de siège* (1948, State of Siege) took up again the theme of *The Plague*. And *Les justes* (1949, The Just), which portrayed Russian terrorists as "scrupulous murderers," tormented by the contradiction between the end and the means, was linked to *The Rebel*. After *The Just* Camus abandoned the theater, disillusioned by a failure that contrasted with the success of his novels, although his plays were no more unconventional in technique than Sartre's.

In *The Fall,* a novel that is a long monologue by a single character, Camus attempted to go beyond his previous work. The hero, an outwardly decent man, one day perceives the hypocrisy of his virtues, accuses himself, and becomes both judge and penitent. Thus, good conscience, subjective morality, and minimum intervention, with which Camus had appeared to be satisfied, are deprived of their mystique. But how can the will to act for the common good be reconciled with the need to accept final responsibility for such action oneself and prevent it from being deflected and despoiled by history? Cut off prematurely, the work of Camus did not reach any conclusion. But might it have done so? He would doubtless have tried to seek a conclusion without returning to the complacency of the inner conscience, but without ever accepting Sartre's delegation of responsibility—in other words, by relying on a dialectic of the wrong versus the right. In this unstable equilibrium, in the "agonized serenity" (to quote an expression of a poet he loved, René Char [born 1907]) of those moments in which contradictions seem about to meet, the genius of Camus would have found the subject matter of other narratives. Putting together and restoring the unique, contrary throb of life: this is the rhythm of his last works, such as *L'exil et le royaume* (1957, Exile and the Kingdom). And it is a rhythm of poetry.

Unlike Sartre, Camus was first and foremost an artist, a man who believed in art. He did not go along with the tendency to despise or question the validity of language. Close in this to the great writers of the early twentieth century, and to Gide in particular, he strove to combine a new sensibility with a traditional language handled with mastery and brilliance. He obscured the force of the language in *The Stranger* through the objectivity of the writing, but he gave language free expression not only in the lyricism of his early essays but also in the tense and insistent rhythm of *The Fall*.

Camus did not have the vigor and originality of Sartre the philosopher, and certain passages of *The Rebel* come perilously near the scholarly dissertation. He was also not capable of creating the obsessional universe that gave the work of Sartre its creative power. The poverty of Camus's fictional imagination was evident. A few banal events, which reappeared from one book to the next (the subject of *The Misunderstanding* was announced in *The Stranger;* and there is a reference in *The Plague* to the subject of *The Stranger*), served merely as a pretext. And the characters have no real life: Meursault and Caligula are myths, and both Rieux and Tarrou in *The Plague* are simply mouthpieces of the author. *The Stranger* is more a long story than a novel; *The Plague* is an allegorical chronicle, halfway between Anatole France (1844–1924, pseudonym of Anatole-François Thibault) and Kafka; *The Fall* is a mythic monologue. If Camus was not a great novelist, he was a great writer, a true writer, who used art to express the perplexities of his time.

Although existentialism dominated fiction from 1945 to 1955, the novel wore other colors as well during this period, beyond the specifically war fiction I have already mentioned.

Among writers who did not challenge the traditions of the novel, one of the best was Louis Guilloux (born 1899), whose *Le sang noir* (1935,

Black Blood) was one of the finest books of the interwar period, some-where between Malraux's *The Human Condition* and Céline's *Journey to the End of the Night*. *Le jeu de patience* (1949, The Game of Patience), the story of a little Breton town during the occupation, reaffirmed Guil-loux's exceptional gifts as a storyteller. Marcel Arland (born 1899), whose *L'ordre* (1929, Order) had been awarded the Prix Goncourt, continued after the war to add to his substantial oeuvre. Arland has combined his interest in philosophy (which he taught) with a stylistic grace and a skill at handling dialogue and narration. His postwar works have included *Il faut de tout pour faire un monde* (1947, You Need a Little of Everything to Make a World), *L'eau et le feu* (1956, Water and Fire), and *Le grand pardon* (1965, The Great Pardon).

Other worthy traditional novelists of the immediate postwar period—all of whom began writing before the liberation—were Henri Bosco (born 1888) (*Le mas Théotime* [1946, The Théotime Farm], *Malicroix* [1948, Malicroix]); André Dhôtel (born 1900) (*Les rues dans l'aurore* [1945, The Streets at Dawn]); Marguerite Yourcenar (born 1903, pseudonym of Marguerite de Crayencour) (*Mémoires d'Hadrien* [1951, Memoirs of Hadrian], *L'œuvre au noir* [1969, A Study in Black]); and Paul Gadenne (1918–1956) (*Siloé* [1941, Siloam], *L'invitation chez les Stirl* [1955, The Invitation to the Stirl Home]). Among those who started writing after 1945, particularly noteworthy was Pierre Gascar (born 1916), whose novels—such as *Les meubles* (1949, Furniture) and *Le temps des morts* (1953, The Season of the Dead)—with their heavy obsessional atmo-sphere, showed some characteristics of existentialism.

Affected by contemporary events, but reacting against the existentialist novel, against its criticism of society and of language, against its pessimism and its philosophical seriousness, was a group of young writers around 1950 whose masters were Paul Morand, Jacques Chardonne (1884–1968) and Marcel Aymé (1902–1967). These novelists were for the most part politically to the right, ill at ease in the atmosphere of France after the liberation, skeptical about any progressivist ideology, and eager to please, to write well, and also to shock.

Jacques Laurent (born 1919), who wrote the enormously popular novel *Caroline chérie* (1947, Caroline Darling), ridiculed Sartre in polemical essays, attacking his problem novels and the ponderousness of his Ger-manic philosophy. Antoine Blondin (born 1922) showed brilliant verve in *L'Europe buissonnière* (1949, Truant Europe). And Roger Nimier (1925–1962) wrote charming yet irritating, individualistic novels: *Les épées* (1949, The Swords), *Le hussard bleu* (1950, The Blue Horseman). These three writers have been the most significant representatives of a neoclassi-cal group, which still exists in a way but which failed to form a genuine school as an alternative to existentialism and the *nouveau roman*.

More spontaneous, and without any theoretical or political afterthought, have been the novels of Françoise Sagan (born 1935), including *Bonjour tristesse* (1954, Hello Sadness) and *Un certain sourire* (1956, A Certain Smile). Sagan has been allied to the neoclassical school by her style and above all by her desire to speak for a young generation which became conscious of itself only after the war and which reacted against its elders by displaying a kind of lucidity that was both frivolous and despairing.

Unaffected by any events, currents, or countercurrents of the day, the tradition of poetic fiction was continued into the postwar period; these novels often embodied the values of the surrealists. The underrated writer Georges Limbour (1901–1970), who took part in the surrealist movement, began his career before the war by writing poetry (*Soleils bas* [1924, Low Suns]), short fiction (*L'illustre cheval blanc* [1930, The Illustrious White Horse]), and the novel *Les vanilliers* (1938, The Vanilla Plants), which was undoubtedly his masterpiece. After the war he wrote *Le bridge de Madame Lyane* (1948, Mrs. Lyane's Bridge) and *La chasse au mérou* (1953, The Quest for Rockfish). He animated these symbolic tales with an admirable poetic use of language, and combined adult nostalgia with the beautiful dreams of childhood.

André Pieyre de Mandiargues (born 1909), who began by writing surrealistic and romantic tales—*Le musée noir* (1946, Black Museum) and *Soleil des loups* (1951, The Wolves' Sun)—came closer to the dimensions and even the laws of the novel with *La motocyclette* (1963, The Motorcycle) and *La marge* (1967, The Margin), both of which considerably enlarged his public. His is a world of erotic fantasy, the unusual, and the fabular, marked by a somewhat decadent aestheticism but always embodied in persuasive imagery and served by a subtle and controlled art.

Marcel Schneider (born 1913) found inspiration in German romanticism for *Le granit et l'absence* (1947, Granite and Absence) and *Le chasseur vert* (1950, The Green Huntsman). Noël Devaulx (born 1905), whose first stories, *L'auberge Parpillon* (1945, The Parpillon Inn), were discovered and introduced to the public by Jean Paulhan (1884–1968), has not found the audience he deserves. Serious, rigorous, at times fairy-tale-like, but never superfluous, Devaulx's work is an obsessive questioning, a fantasia of death.

But the most important contemporary practitioner of the poetic novel has undoubtedly been Julien Gracq (born 1910). Gracq, who declared his debt to André Breton by publishing an essay on him in 1948, started writing in 1938, the year Sartre's *Nausea* was published, with the novel *Au château d'Argol* (The Castle of Argol). Bordering on the gothic novel, it attested to the continuing effectiveness of the imaginary and the irrational. The novels that followed, *Un beau ténébreux* (1945, A Dark Stranger) and *Le rivage des Syrtes* (1951, The Banks of the Syrtes) showed a fidelity to mythology and imagery comparable to that of the romantic and surrealist poets. But the descriptions, the analyses, and the dialogue were handled with the skill of a genuine novelist and also with a flair for the dramatic. (Gracq, incidentally, tried his hand at the theater with *Le roi pêcheur* [1948, The Fisher King].)

A Dark Stranger and *The Banks of the Syrtes* are dramatic novels because their subject is the intrusion of drama in lives of people who believed themselves to be safe from it. Allan, the dark stranger, appears, and the daily routine is transformed into destiny, with everyone overwhelmed by "this rising tempest"; Aldo, a patrician youth, arrives on the banks of the Syrtes, and the war between the realms of Orsenna and Farghestan, which had lain dormant for three centuries, bursts forth anew. Allan will die; Orsenna will be destroyed. Yet the drama is kept at a distance, like an image always sought after but never really attained. Or rather, behind the apparent story, told in a very precise descriptive style, is an implicit story, a myth. Each character, each place, and each scene is presented not so much for its own sake as to represent magic forces or realities which we sense around us but which the analytical voice of reason cannot name. And the enchantment of these novels is both sustained and reinforced by a highly wrought and brilliant style. The sentence structure, eloquent and serene, is also powerfully dramatic, yet has a surface calm.

Gracq's most recent novel, *Un balcon en forêt* (1958, Balcony in the Forest), set in the war year of 1940, brought fable closer to contemporary reality. The same is true of two of the three stories collected under the title *La presqu'île* (1970, The Peninsula)—one set at the end of World War I, the other simply a story of a man waiting for a woman, the analysis of his wait, and the detailed description of places that are easily identifiable, although the names were changed. Has Gracq rejected his surrealist past? Does he now think that the real is richer than the imaginary? We must not forget, however, that the surrealist mind was also of this world. And Gracq's descriptions, however precise, still are suffused with imagination and are a far cry from the realistic reporting of today.

Several writers of this same generation, who were related (at first, closely related) to the existentialist movement, drew away from it to pursue a much freer form of fiction, with a greater importance given to the play of language itself.

Raymond Queneau (born 1903) was connected with the surrealist movement from 1924 to 1929. For a time he was a contributor to Sartre's *Les temps modernes,* and his poems and songs—those in *Si tu t'imagines* (1951, If You Imagine) were tinged with the existentialist folklore of Saint-Germain-des-Prés. *Le chiendent* (1933, The Bark-Tree) presented a desert-like vision of the world, not far from contingency and the absurd. But this vision was presented indirectly, from the angle of ironic fantasy. And one can find in Saturnin's slangy monologue a prophetic caricature of existentialism. The most striking thing about *The Bark-Tree* was the verve, the freedom, and the comicality of the language; it was a vast play on words, and Queneau's master was clearly James Joyce. He mingled the resources of slang with the standard language; he wrote as people spoke. And linguists will find in him an invaluable source of information on the varieties of language, even of spelling.

In *Pierrot mon ami* (1942, Pierrot, My Friend), although the dialogue was based on the spoken language, the brawl at the beginning is recounted in the manner of the Iliad. In *Les temps mêlés* (1941, Mixed Time) Queneau told a story in three different forms (poetry, fiction, and drama). And in *Exercices de style* (1947, Exercises in Style) he presented the same absolutely insignificant incident (a quarrel in a Parisian bus) in ninety-nine versions, each one differing in syntactic structure, verb tense, figures of speech, and so on.

Yet Queneau is as much a dreamer as a talker. His world is nourished by a reality that is out of step and somewhat clandestine. The world of his fiction—*Loin de Rueil* (1945, Far from Rueil), *Le dimanche de la vie* (1952, The Sunday of Life), *Zazie dans le métro* (1959, Zazie in the Subway), *Les fleurs bleues* (1965, The Blue Flowers)—is a world of outcasts, of ghostlike harum-scarums, of Pierrots and Harlequins without masks, of the marionettes of the amusement parks, of roustabouts haunting fairgrounds, the outskirts of towns, and movie houses.

In Queneau's world, social outcasts become the representatives of humanity, swarming in a no-man's-land, in all places that are out of bounds. The obsession with death, the void, night, and absence casts a black shadow over this itinerant spectacle. But Queneau does not subject this world to the cold lucidity of factual reporting. His purposes are served by humor—grating and sneering but also compassionate, humane, and liberating.

Before Queneau, the novel had never been treated so freely, never been so "mixed up," so dislocated, to allow scope for all the rhythms and nuances of language; his work is a repertory of linguistic structures constantly brought up to date. Under attack, diverted and forced out of its habitual mold, language serves Queneau as magic without illusion, camouflaging the void without filling it. It continues, however, to be a source of entertainment for the writer, who, without being taken in, never tires of his inventiveness.

Jean Genet (born 1910), like Queneau, also was an early contributor to *Les temps modernes* and became friendly with Sartre; and Sartre wrote an important study of Genet, *Saint Genet, comédien et martyr* (1952, Saint Genet, Actor and Martyr). Also like Queneau, Genet rejected society and the traditional forms of expression. And he, too, at the outset, accepted this marginal situation and found his pleasure in the play of language. However, Genet's marginality expressed itself in the direct confessions of *Journal du voleur* (1949, The Thief's Journal) and in fiction that was never very far from his actual experience: *Notre-Dame des Fleurs* (1948, Our Lady of the Flowers), *Miracle de la rose* (1944, Miracle of the Rose); and his language was not the spoken language but the language of poetic transfiguration.

In *The Thief's Journal* Genet was concerned with the singularity of a particular kind of person—the homosexual thief. But in his more recent work, particularly in his plays, he has modified and broadened his scope considerably. What has happened to Genet is what happens to most of those who start from a negation: as they continue writing and living they convert it sooner or later into an affirmation; they remake an ethic, even if they do not wish to do so, by inverting their scale of values. That extreme limit, that purity of evil which he strove to attain like an ascetic, contained a challenge within itself: "Saintliness is my goal. . . . I want to act so that everything I do may lead me to what is unknown to me." Why not, indeed, give the name of saintliness to the culmination of an effort infinitely more difficult than that associated with conventional morality, because this effort isolates the person and does not tell him where it is leading?

Although Genet had felt himself a part of a subculture, he realized that the criminal world had universal significance only up to a point. In his recent plays, unlike his confessional narrative works, Genet has portrayed different kinds of minorities, for whom society bears the responsibility and who may appear as the spearhead of future society: the blacks, the third-world peoples. It is as if Genet had ended up by interpreting his own image as it had already been interpreted by his friends of *Les temps modernes,* as the symbol of social alienation. Going from himself (or his own kind) to others, he has thus moved toward universality. And he bridged the gap between the private world and the other world by taking as the subject of his plays people playing at being others or people playing at being themselves without succeeding—servants taking the role of their mistress in *Les bonnes* (1947, 1954, The Maids); blacks disguising themselves as whites in *Les nègres* (1958, The Blacks)—or people acting in private as they would like to behave in public, as in *Le balcon* (1956, The Balcony).

The master has within him the slave, the slave the master, and rebellion leads to a communication and reveals an identity. Can the theater help to transform the world he indicts, or is his solution to stop writing and, like Sartre—but for motives much closer to Artaud's—ally himself with the Black Panthers or with Arab guerrillas? After having accepted language and used it with a delight that contained a certain self-indulgence and affectation, Genet became tempted to reject it to the extent that it had no effect on his life. He once said that, despite the beauty of the words, the best western theater is nothing but "crap," since it fails to immerse us in the sacred, which is implicit in the ritual theater of Japan but which in western civilization is still most effectively evoked by the mass. Since it cannot be life, sacred life, literature is haunted by the specter of its own bankruptcy.

Michel Leiris (born 1901) has been associated with all the decisive currents since World War I: the poetic fervor of surrealism; the broad-scale inquiries of the school of sociological critics before World War II; the existentialist humanism of *Les temps modernes*; and the radical indictment that tends toward the renunciation of all literature for the sake of revolutionary action. Leiris's work has had great variety. Apart from the books he wrote as a professional ethnologist (*L'Afrique fantôme* [1934, Phantom Africa]), he also wrote poetry (*Haut mal* [1934, Sacred Illness]).

But Leiris's most remarkable work, after the personal reminiscences of *L'âge d'homme* (1939, Manhood), is the autobiographical sequence of *La règle du jeu* (The Rules of the Game): *Biffures* (1948, Crossings Out), *Fourbis* (1955, Gadgets), *Fibrilles* (1966, Fibrils). This sequence, which at first attracted few readers, has recently won a large audience. It is a self-portrait illuminated and warmed by the sunshine of childhood; a psycho-analysis that has plasticity, sinuousness, precision, and seductiveness. Leiris sometimes reminds one of Proust, but he expects from self-awareness a freeing and a transformation of the self, the "rules of the game." These works, he said, "merely recount observations or experiences from which I hope to infer laws that will in the end reveal . . . the golden rule I ought to choose (or ought to have chosen) to preside over my game."

But is this revelation not too late? Is there still time to retrace all these forks in the road and patiently decipher all these erasures and torn scraps, in order to discover a direction that could be followed with less uncertainty in the future? If it is too late to make a new life for oneself, what can one do, except write? But writing has no meaning unless it leads somewhere, unless it is, at the same time, living. The paradox of art lies in this exalta-tion which it inspires in us and which indicates that it is a symbol of what transcends it.

In his preface to *Manhood* Leiris made some important remarks on "literature compared to the art of bullfighting." Literature must be a commitment, must risk life or death. The confession is in itself a kind of risk, and we sense what the author has had to overcome in order to draw an uncompromising self-portrait, laying bare his fundamental masochism and his own cowardice. But his life has been more than that; it has been governed throughout by a demand for poetry, by a desire for the exaltation of what "makes us cry out in wonder," the "going beyond the self," the "high vision" whose literary expression is justified only if it recaptures the authentic cry, the ineffable moment of illumination.

In Leiris, language is the guiding thread, the culmination, but also the inadequacy. It is the guiding thread because through certain linguistic memories Leiris rediscovers his experience of life. In the child who said *"la fière"* (the proud) instead of *"la fièvre"* (the fever), the adult rediscovers the secrets of a world of poetry. But, in learning the real words, he realized that there was someone else, the interlocutor, for whom and with whom he had to speak. To go from *la fière* to *la fièvre* is to enter the objective world, and this progression reflects Leiris's social and political concerns, marked by his visits first to Cuba, then to China. How can the language of daily life be reconciled with the language of poetry? How can the dream be recaptured in deeds, in revolutionary action? The pathos and significance of Leiris's work lie in this dilemma, and we sense that the author would be ready to subscribe to the renunciation of literature were it not that he still believes—and here we see the last traces of the old surrealist fervor—in the possibility of a magic language capable of transforming the life of all.

Difficult and enigmatic, but now gaining increasing recognition, Maurice Blanchot began to write before the war, with the critical studies collected under the title *Faux-pas* (1943, False Step). These studies contained a rigorous criticism of the realistic novel, which he accused of lagging behind poetry. "The characteristic of the novel," wrote Blanchot, "is to have its substance in its form," namely, the movement of the words.

Blanchot's first novel, *Thomas l'obscur* (1941, Thomas the Obscure), was written somewhat in the style of Giraudoux, whom Blanchot the critic praised. But in *Aminadab* (1942, Aminadab) the influence of Giraudoux gave way to that of Kafka. Blanchot clearly did not regard language as an aesthetic exercise. And in his subsequent novels—*Le Très-Haut* (1948, The Almighty), *L'arrêt de mort* (1948, Death Sentence), *Le dernier homme* (1957, The Last Man), *L'attente, l'oubli* (1962, Waiting, Forgetting) —which had an extraordinary tone of cold vehemence, an eloquence without eloquence, and a dispassionate shudder, Blanchot's style was neutral and impersonal. Rather than an individual or a writer, an anonymous witness speaks, conveying a truth, the only truth. It is the one truth which language strives to express but which in fact it cannot express: the truth of the void, absence, nothingness, and death; a truth that is perpetually waiting to be told and remains unsaid.

Everything in these works of Blanchot is situated in a strange, elusive intermediate zone between life and death, in which life moves toward death but in which death cannot take place. This is a world between language and silence, in a mute downward slide, a motionless movement, forever going over the same ground. What Blanchot has demonstrated in his fiction, and has commented on in his critical essays (which, from *L'espace littéraire* [1955, Literary Space] to *L'entretien infini* [1970, Infinite Conversation], have become more and more closely linked to his fiction) is the straining of language toward the "dangerous horizon where it seeks in vain to disappear," the desire for an inaccessible nonlanguage.

The myth of Orpheus teaches us that we cannot look night in the face, that profundity is revealed only if it is concealed in the work. But what good is this dissimulation, this constant fruitless harking back to what eludes us? The logic of the metaphysical experience (or mystical experience, but in a negative sense) leads the writer's work toward renunciation. Strangely enough—although it should be noted that, even if Blanchot has changed his political attitudes, he has always been mindful of the movement of history—this tendency has been confirmed by a recent kind of revolutionary extremism, as if the unsaid were not only the forbidden area of being and of death but also the area forbidden to all of mankind by bourgeois civilization, so that no one, for the moment, can speak for all men.

In the fiction of Blanchot nothing of the traditional novel remains. They are stylistic, autobiographical exercises, disembodied narratives in which the character is merely the spokesman for the anonymous and the story is merely the path described by the words. Blanchot made no attempt to define new laws for the novel but rather to find any means of expressing something essential, the quest for which led him to an awareness of the inexpressible.

This bursting of the bounds of the novel, and even of literature itself, perhaps found its most decisive expression in the work of Georges Bataille. That we have seen the collected works of Bataille and of Artaud published before those of André Breton is a remarkable sign of the times.

An unlimited curiosity and a vast erudition enabled Bataille to cover the most varied fields in his essays—from sociology and even political science and economics in *La part maudite* (1949, The Cursed Part) to aesthetics in *Manet* (1955, Manet) and *Lascaux, ou la naissance de l'art* (1955, Lascaux, or the Birth of Art). And in the connections Bataille established between such disparate domains, one can see the first signs of structuralism. Whatever he had to say was subordinated to the same fundamental quest and had the same intensity. This intense quest was amplified in his philosophical investigations in *L'expérience intérieure* (1943, Inner Experience) and *Le coupable* (1944, The Guilty) and in his "fiction" from *L'anus solaire* (1931, The Solar Anus) to *Le bleu du ciel* (1957, The Blue of the Sky).

Bataille's fiction took the form sometimes of narrative, sometimes of myth, sometimes even of an apparently realistic account. Sometimes it burst into a series of isolated aphorisms of existential philosophy, as in *Histoire de rats* (1947, Story of Rats). Bataille used a violent, taut, abrupt approach to express the tension of a life always seeking the extreme states in which man's truth, man's movement toward the absolute, bursts forth in both pleasure and pain, in eroticism and death. His central goal was to approach the sacred domain in which man escapes from the ordinary, in which he can find revealed the dizzy ecstasy that summons man to confront it in a panicky delirium.

With Bataille, fiction turned its back completely on the world of ordinary, sometimes insignificant occurrences, the empty moments of life that Breton had condemned in those novels that used them as their raw material. Bataille knew only moments of crisis, of excess. "Only the stifling, the intolerable experience allows the author to reach the distant vision expected by a reader weary of the narrow limits imposed by the conventions. How can we waste time on books that the author has clearly not been compelled to write?" Thus wrote Bataille in the preface to *The Blue of the Sky,* the novel of his that, however, conformed most to traditional narrative form. Eroticism, a profane and profanatory mystique, and a longing after the sacred elements of primitive civilizations were all attempts of Bataille's to break into a domain in which the rational and partial sense is lost, in which life and language come up against the impossibility of ordering themselves and continuing.

It remains to be seen how this "sovereign operation" can be reconciled with other activities, those directed by the revolutionary political impulse, which Bataille shared and which inspired him to write numerous essays on the structure of fascism and of communism. But Bataille was separated from the writers who tended toward an acquiescent slide into silence; the brilliance of the cry and the imagery could still be heard in his shattered voice. Bataille, who wrote *La haine de la poésie* (1947, Hatred of Poetry), was a poet.

At first sight, the writings of the essayist Jean Paulhan seem diametrically opposed to the works of Bataille: by the style, which had a completely classical elegance (Paulhan dedicated *Les fleurs de Tarbes* [1941, the Flowers of Tarbes] to André Gide); by the tone, which was ironically allusive; and by the content, since his analysis of terrorism (reflecting the tendency of modern literature to want to be more than just literature) would seem to lead to a rehabilitation of rhetoric. Paulhan thus invited us to accept rather than question the power of language, and politically he tended toward conservative nationalism.

Yet Paulhan accepted language to analyze it as a medium of mirages, optical illusions, and misunderstandings. In *The Flowers of Tarbes,* for example, he showed that when we read we see the negative of the writer's photograph, that what is an object for the reader is a word for the writer. Paulhan attempted to decipher the secrets and contradictions of language, and he recognized the horizon of the mysterious, the uncertain, and the unsaid. Coming between surrealism and existentialism, he exercised considerable influence in his role as editor of the *Nouvelle revue française.* But his work, which has just recently been collected, has much more than historical importance today. It was a necessary parallel to the attack on language that has burst the bounds of literature, first and foremost in the novel.

Although in recent years writers have continued to question every assumption of the novel, an important group of them has defined new rules for it instead of abandoning it. It is almost as if a reconstruction has followed the revolutionary violence. But before discussing the reconstruction—the *nouveau roman*—I would like to consider the altogether individualistic contribution of Samuel Beckett (born 1906). Born in Dublin like James Joyce, who had a very great influence on him, Beckett began writing in English before he wrote in French; he remains a bilingual writer in that he himself translates most of his French works into English and in that he still occasionally writes a major work in English (such as *Happy Days* [1961], which he translated into French as *Oh les beaux jours* [1963]). Beckett's work has shared in the pessimistic vision of existentialism and in the seemingly despairing use of language of the writers I have just discussed.

Beckett's work, too, has rested between the absurd and silence. And such novels as *Molloy* (1950, Molloy), *Malone meurt* (1951, Malone Dies), *L'innommable* (1953, The Unnamable), *Comment c'est* (1961, How It Is) were as far removed from the traditional novel as such plays as *En attendant Godot* (1953, Waiting for Godot), *Fin de partie* (1957, Endgame), *Happy Days* were from any theatrical tradition. But Beckett was not interested in the theoretical redefinition of the novel that younger writers were pursuing. His singularity and his greatness rest in his ability to sustain genuine creation in an almost total void, giving spontaneity and richness to what is left of the basic elements of the novel and the drama.

It is true that nothing happens in Beckett's novels; we do not know where they take place, and an anonymous voice talks endlessly of what it is unable to name. A consciousness condemned to talk in vain, because it cannot find the final word that would enable it to return to silence, harps endlessly on the same theme. This final word is not a truth that would put an end to speech by giving it its object but rather the disappearance of all objects—nothingness. This endless murmuring belongs to a being that is forced to talk to itself as long as it lives a life that looks to death as the only release and suffers at being separated from it. This voice is the murmuring of existence itself, at its most secret and also at its most common. Nothing remains in the world except this perpetual voice, incapable of seeing, of identifying, or of explaining. There is no here, no now, no yesterday (the impossibility of reconstituting a memory is one of the constant themes of Beckett's novels), no I, no you, no he. Beckett captures moments when everything seems about to come to an end, in a faded twilight, in the half light of the blind.

In Beckett's plays, too, nothing happens. The characters wait for someone, like Godot, who does not come; or the infirm look at one another, resigned to an intolerable situation that has no end. "The end is in the beginning, and yet we go on," says one character in *Endgame*. In *Happy Days* a woman whose body is gradually sinking into the ground until only her head remains recalls insignificant memories and strings together phrases so banal that they lose all sense.

However, the essential monologue in the novels is given concrete form: Molloy and Malone are monstrous invalids in whom life is revealed in its worst physiological tyranny, and who are witnesses of the impotent horror of being a body. In Beckett's plays the voice becomes divided; and its several forms engage in dialogue and confront situations: the sadomasochistic relationship, the relationship of master and slave, links the characters in *Waiting for Godot* and those in *Endgame*. Although nothing happens, there is a mounting tension and sometimes even a kind of hope: if Godot were to arrive, if death were to retreat, if happy days were to return, everything would be transformed. It does not happen, of course, but the tension sustains the action on stage; Beckett succeeds in keeping us in suspense right to the very end.

In recent French literature Beckett is the only one who has shown us that, while the novel or play can divest itself of all its outward appearances and conventions, to remain a true creation it must preserve a movement, a tension, that compels us to go on reading, page after page.

The practitioners of the *nouveau roman,* despite their diversity, have been distinctive as a group in their desire to give the novel, which they regard as the major genre—if not the only genre—a clear definition. Their realization that the possibilities of the traditional novel had been exhausted did not lead them to burst open its bounds and overlap all genres; rather, it led them to create a new aesthetic for the novel, thus resuming an attempt begun and abandoned by Sartre.

Nathalie Sarraute (born 1900) in *L'ère du soupçon* (1956, The Age of Suspicion) and Alain Robbe-Grillet (born 1922) in *Une voie pour le roman futur* (1956, A Way for the Novel of the Future) both recorded the disappearance of the traditional novel. Sarraute insisted that there can no longer be any possibility of keeping the reader in suspense by some exciting plot, of establishing lifelike characters, of describing a natural or social setting, or even of giving a new analysis of human emotions. The traditional novel could only yield bloodless imitations of Balzac or Constant.

But psychological reality remained the supreme goal for Saurraute, although the means she has used is no longer the analysis which establishes character once and for all and which converts the living into something dead and treats states of mind divorced from actions. Nor has her means been the interior monologue. For her, psychological reality is inseparable from behavior, and only dialogue—or the capturing of those inner sensations through which we are in a state of dialogue with ourselves, which she terms "tropisms"—can give the reader the "illusion of reenacting the events himself with a more lucid awareness, with more order, clarity, and force than he can in real life, without their losing that element of indetermination, opacity, and mystery that they have for the one who experiences them."

Robbe-Grillet replied to Sarraute that her approach was still anthropomorphic, that it still postulated its own reality, which makes us lose the only reality with which we should be concerned—the reality of appearances, the reality of the object: "The operation that she [Sarraute] attempts to impose on the world threatens to dissolve and annihilate it completely. In neglecting the surface of things for an ever more distant, ever more inaccessible depth, are we not impelled to reach only shadows, reflections, patches of mist?"

For Robbe-Grillet, the novel had to cease being *visceral, metaphorical,* or *incantatory,* had to become *visual* and *descriptive.* Whether realistic or romantic, the traditional novel endeavored to discover reality beneath appearances; and that reality was always presented as meaningful. Robbe-Grillet felt that recent novels of the absurd were making a similar mistake in having non-meaning as their content. We have discovered, he said, that the "world is neither significant nor absurd; it simply *is.*" The *nouveau roman* set out to describe this state of being, this *"is."*

The difference between Sarraute and Robbe-Grillet was in the definition of the goal, not in the literary expression. Whether concerned with psychological tropisms, with the sensations underlying conversations, or with a visual inventory that goes so far as to measure the distance from a table to a window, the *nouveau roman* has tried to make the "world speak"; the traditional novel, Robbe-Grillet claimed, had merely "spoken of the world." The object must emerge and manifest itself directly, without any intervention, without the analytical, explanatory voice of the narrator. The words must act as objects; they are objects. And the order of the words must follow the sequence of their appearance, not in a sequence dominated from beginning to end by a conscious mind. But insofar as there is succession and continuity, is not such a conscious mind postulated?

The first novels of Robbe-Grillet—*Le voyeur* (1955, The Voyeur) and *La jalousie* (1957, Jealousy)—still seemed to follow a story: the murder of a girl by a traveling salesman, the jealous vigil of the husband watching the movements of the wife and the lover, as through the slats of a blind.

Yet, in fact, the aim of the narrative is to blot out the story that we suspect. The action that would set a traditional novel in motion (the murder, the triangle) breaks through only imperceptibly. The action is simply the void between objects that prevents the descriptions or accounts of insignificant facts (such as the movements of the shadows of the objects in *Jealousy*) from running together completely.

In his latest novel, *Projet pour une révolution à New York* (1970, Project for a Revolution in New York), Robbe-Grillet went much further. The story is completely destroyed in that the same beginnings of a plot constantly reappear in different contexts. They are situations, or a series of images whose beginning or outcome are nowhere to be found, and the novel is a structural reordering of the same combinations, the same collages.

Claude Simon's (born 1913) early novels—*Le vent* (1957, The Wind), *L'herbe* (1958, The Grass), and *La route des Flandres* (1960, The Flanders Road)—were in the Faulknerian tradition, with particular interest in the element of time in the novel. But his recent novels—the monumental *Histoire* (1967, Story) and *Les corps conducteurs* (1971, Conductive Bodies)—showed many tendencies of the *nouveau roman*.

At first sight the novels of Nathalie Sarraute seem very different, since they have characters and action. In *Le planétarium* (1959, The Planetarium), she depicted a foolish young man who wants to be an artist, a maniacal aunt, a divided family, and a famous woman writer seen both in her moments of glory and in her moments of absurdity. *Les fruits d'or* (1963, The Golden Fruits) was a satire on snobbery and its unfounded judgments, and *Entre la vie et la mort* (1968, Between Life and Death) was the story of the creation of a book, that very book. But just as Robbe-Grillet has suppressed the story by superimposing images and structural links, in other words, by burying it, Sarraute has dissolved it by exposing it to the open air, by leaving it to fade away. Seemingly linked to the frame of a character, the psychological elements that Sarraute describes in her first book, *Tropismes* (1938, Tropisms), free themselves from it and perform an anonymous dance at the far boundaries of visibility and existence.

Is this not to rediscover, by taking it to its extreme, the aesthetic aim of the "reduction of the visual field" professed by Sartre? But Sartre, although he effaced the narrator, wanted to make what the narrator had to say all the more clear. And one feature common to all the writers of the *nouveau roman* is that for them there is no other meaning than that of the writing itself. The world has no other meaning than what is conveyed through what is said. One might be tempted to see in this assertion the existentialists' concerns: a metaphysics of absence, the impossibility of communication, contingency, and the absurd. But the writers of the *nouveau roman* do not want to be metaphysical; they claim that no vision of things precedes the moment in which they appear in the written word and that even then their only meaning is their written expression.

There are, of course, individual inspirations that have brought diversity to this theoretical unity. The ductility, subtlety, and art of intellectual dramatization of Sarraute are quite distinct from the elliptical acuity of Robbe-Grillet and from the controlled lyrical power of Simon. She reminds us of Virginia Woolf, the others of Guy de Maupassant or William Faulkner or Henry Miller.

Three other writers of the *nouveau roman* have contributed important work. Robert Pinget's (born 1920) *L'inquisitoire* (1962, The Inquisitory) was strongly influenced by Robbe-Grillet's brand of "reportage." Michel Butor (born 1926), whose earlier *L'emploi du temps* (1956, Passing Time) and *La modification* (1957, The Change) were novels in the traditional sense, superimposed images and assembled and dismantled structures in *Mobile* (1962, Mobile), *Réseau aérien* (1962, Aerial Network), and *Description de San Marco* (1963, Description of San Marco). J. M. G. Le Clézio's (born 1940) *Le procès-verbal* (1963, The Interrogation), *La fièvre* (1965, Fever), and *La guerre* (1970, War) showed that he has taken from the literary climate of the *nouveau roman* only what suits his abundant inspiration. He probably has the most natural and spontaneous novelistic gift of any of the serious newcomers to French fiction.

Considering the way the *nouveau roman* as a whole has been tending, we may well wonder what has become of the desire of these novelists to redefine with precision the genre itself. Collages of images, symmetrical arrangements, and structural permutations have nothing to do with that narrative movement, of which Beckett still has retained the essential. We may admire a page chosen at random, but we do not feel at all compelled to read the next one immediately. The novel is in danger of becoming a prolix and basically inferior form of poetry. The writers of the review *Tel Quel* have replied that it is becoming a "text." Ultimately, the boundaries among all the genres are disappearing; literature is becoming the unified domain of all writers.

Even if one does not share the point of view of *Tel Quel,* and even though the theory is more interesting than the practice, one must admit that the young writers of *Tel Quel*—founded in 1960 by Philippe Sollers (born 1936), who has been by far the most gifted representative of the group— have brought about the most recent metamorphosis of literature.

Sollers, who began by writing a fairly traditional novel, *Une curieuse solitude* (1958, A Strange Solitude), and who, with *Le parc* (1961, The Park), followed in the footsteps of Robbe-Grillet, has recently, with *Drame* (1965, Drama) and *Nombres* (1968, Numbers) illustrated a very ambitious theoretical program through which he is attempting to bring his literary creation into line with the challenges of psychoanalysis and Marxism, as well as with the tools of linguistics. According to Sollers, the writer does not have to give expression to a world that has already found expression, a world that has made him what he is. Nor can he create by himself alone a work of art in his own image. He must be the artisan of a writing that is both anonymous and "plural," writing that can open a new field—signs freed from their alienating meanings. In other words, until there is a new culture, born of revolution, writing cannot contain any meaning; it can only be the incitement to future meaning by being the energy of the sign.

How this liberation of writing is linked with social liberation, which the writers of *Tel Quel* conceive in the most orthodox form of communism, is not for me to discuss here. In any case, what retains our interest in the works that derive from this theory is mainly their theoretical program. If literature is to become an undifferentiated text, tending no longer either toward fiction or poetry, we are likely to conclude from these texts (the "fiction" of Jean-Louis Baudry [born 1935], Jean Thibaudeau [born 1935], and Jean Ricardou [born 1932], or the "poems" of Marcelin Pleynet [born 1933], and Denis Roche [born 1937]) that this is at the expense of the vitality and effectiveness of the sources, however distorted, of the novel and of poetry, and that the greatest single strength of these texts lies in their declaration of intent.

CONTEMPORARY POETRY: OLD MASTERS

A number of poets whose literary careers began well before 1940 reached full maturity or completed their work during the war years or shortly after—and in some cases adopted fresh approaches and reached a wider audience.

Between the two wars, surrealism was the most important movement. But André Breton, in his *Manifeste du surréalisme* (1924, Surrealist Manifesto), saluted as a master one poet who never belonged to the movement—Pierre Reverdy (1889–1960). He was some ten years older than his disciples, and his genius flowered extremely early; his first publications date from 1915. But Reverdy continued to write right up to his death. In addition to two journallike works that contained valuable revelations about his attitudes toward his art—*Le livre de mon bord* (1948, My Log Book) and *En vrac* (1956, Pell-Mell)—Reverdy continued to create very fine poems: those in his last major collection, *Main d'œuvre* (1949, Handiwork), which included poems from 1913 to 1949; and those in *Les libertés des mers* (1959, Freedoms of the Seas).

We are only now beginning to set a high enough value on Reverdy's poetry, which is in fact among the finest of any writer of this century.

Overshadowed by the brilliance of the surrealist movement, Reverdy was taken between the wars as a mere precursor of surrealism and was too quickly seen from a purely historical point of view, as an example of the so-called literary cubism of the 1910s. Rereading him today, however, we can see that he had little connection with the theories of poetry of the early twentieth century. In Reverdy's poetry one can find a balanced objectivity recalling the experiments of Guillaume Apollinaire and Max Jacob (1876–1944), an explosive force resulting from the liberation of the image, and the shock value of unusual metaphorical sequences (as in the surrealists). But these characteristics were all subsumed into a dramatic force that was entirely Reverdy's own.

Far from being receptive to the world's diversity, Reverdy preferred to express a fundamental relationship between the world and himself; and one can say that he simply rewrote the same poem time and time again. This poem contained hardly any adjectives, metaphors, or images; nouns were its most important elements, and verbs expressed actions rather than states of being. The protagonists in this drama are the objects the poem evokes, in muted yet insistent tones. For, however briefly, a drama is enacted. Something *happens* at the juncture between life as it is lived, as it flows by and onward, and the world evading life's advances. The pulse of night and day, the sky adrift, the fleeting images of the wind, the clock ticking, the lamp that measures time, the roads, crossroads of night where the traveler's footfall echoes, faces turning away, the backs of people departing, doors and windows half opened and then slammed again—these key images are always images of flight, of transience, of time passing; and they are drawn in the language of the most simple experience.

Reverdy's poetry suggested neither the absolute dominance of the imagination over the mind nor the total subordination of man to objects; instead, it depicted man's movement among real objects and his painful confrontation with them. Reverdy's was a poetry of pathos, of the inner self, a dense crystallization of brief moments of experience.

Although Jules Supervielle (1884–1960) wrote nothing after the outbreak of the war as important as *Gravitations* (1925, Gravitations) or *Le forçat innocent* (1930, The Innocent Convict), his *Poèmes de la France malheureuse* (1941, Poems for Unhappy France) showed that he shared the wartime vogue for politically committed poetry. He later published the collections *Oublieuse mémoire* (1949, Forgetful Memory) and *L'escalier* (1956, The Staircase), as well as various plays, among which *Le voleur d'enfants* (1949, The Child Stealer) was outstanding. From *Les poèmes de l'humour triste* (1919, Poems of an Unhappy Mood), up to his last collection, *Le corps tragique* (1959, The Tragic Body), the tone of Supervielle's poetry was altered by the varying literary landscapes it passed through: a modernism akin to Blaise Cendrars (1887–1961) and Valéry Larbaud in

Débarcadère (1922, Landing Stage); and surrealism after that. But despite his having dedicated a poem to Lautréamont (1846–1870, pseudonym of Isidore Ducasse), Supervielle had no fundamental connection with the surrealists, who in turn ignored him.

Some of Supervielle's poetry was not unlike the early work of Henri Michaux (born 1899)—fabular travels of exploration through the inner recesses of mind and body, a sort of coenesthetic dream voyage. And this vein was part of Supervielle from the beginning to the end of his career. But at the same time his poetry contained elements of mythology and a feeling profoundly in tune with the cosmos and with eternity. Whatever the source of the inspiration—whether it be the body seen as a cage in which the mind is imprisoned, the pampas, a bird, or a tree—Supervielle's poetry possessed the lyricism of a continuous flow of song. In his odes, fables, elegies, epics, or simple songs, the melodic line was always there to make the poem immediately graspable.

Supervielle managed to give the most modern poetry the transparency and simplicity of a familiar tale. The reason for this was the continual presence of a discursive, anecdotal thread: for Supervielle was a teller of tales, as was shown by his stories and plays, which so resembled his poetry. Images, myths, and emotions appeared in well-regulated order. And whether he was telling a tale, enlarging on it, recounting the creation of the world, or inventing the words of God to man or of man to the unknown, the poet's meaning shone clearly through his limpid language.

Pierre Jean Jouve (born 1887) struck out in many more new directions in his poetry after the war than did Supervielle. From the beginning, Jouve's poetry was dominated by forebodings of disaster; he wistfully longed for "paradise lost," and, still more strikingly, he prophesied doom. Jouve has always seen history as the embodiment of an eternal drama, as in the collection *La Vierge de Paris* (1946, Our Lady of Paris). The poem *La chute du ciel* (The Sky Is Falling) was a striking combination of details of present disaster (the ruins of bombed towns, the passerby "measuring out his cross upon the sidewalk") and the guessed-at struggle of supernatural forces. But Jouve's poetry, while kindled by the fire of contemporary experience, has also pursued its own path in spirit and form. And his later collections—*Ode* (1951, Ode), *Langue* (1952, Language), *Lyrique* (1956, Lyric), and *Moires* (1962, Watered Silks)—which have used a more rigorous, more harmonious form often very close to traditional versification, have evoked a more tranquil atmosphere, even when, as in his most recent collection, *Ténèbre* (1965, Darkness), his subject was the approach of death through illness.

Jouve has also added to his considerable achievements in narrative myths since the war, with the fine tale *Aventure de Catherine Crachat* (1947, Adventure of Catherine Crachat), and in expository prose with essays like *Le Don Juan de Mozart* (1948, Mozart's Don Juan), *Wozzeck, ou le nouvel opéra* (1953, Wozzeck, or the New Opera), *Le tombeau de Baudelaire* (1958, The Tomb of Baudelaire), and the autobiographical reflections in *En miroir* (1954, In a Mirror). Though of impressive breadth and variety, Jouve's work has been too hermetic, too difficult, and too frequently intractable to appeal to the ordinary public. Nonetheless, he has greatly influenced such younger poets as Pierre Emmanuel (born 1916) and Yves Bonnefoy (born 1923).

Saint-John Perse (born 1887, pseudonym of Alexis Léger) developed even more than his contemporary Jouve after the war. Between *Anabase* (1924, Anabasis) and *Exil* (1942, Exile), Saint-John Perse, during most of that time secretary general of the French Foreign Office, occupied himself exclusively with his official activities and not with poetry. He was admired by some important writers, including Proust and Breton, but his silence almost led to his being consigned to oblivion, especially since the general public had not heard of him at all.

In 1940, however, Saint-John Perse came to the United States as a refugee and began writing poetry again. *Exile* was a major émigré poem. And *Vents* (1946, Winds) evoked the great currents that destroy, set in ferment, and rebuild the world of men; it bore witness to the great world-wide disaster during which it was written. *Amers* (1957, Seamarks) also told of the loneliness of the poet on the coast of a foreign continent, dreaming of the beacons lighting up the shores of his own country, which he refused to return to. Despite its context, however, this poetry was time-lessly outside all particular literary and historical periods.

Saint-John Perse's early poems belonged to the climate of postsym-bolism. The privileged, the rare, the precious, and the exotic characterized his earlier work. But his poetry, like that of Claudel, who used the same meter, that is, the *verset* (a biblical verse form), was cosmic poetry. It evoked and celebrated the world in its elemental manifestations: snow, rain, wind, sea, and sunlight. What the poet perceived was eulogized; the liturgical unfolding of his *versets* was a ceremony in honor of the cosmos. Saint-John Perse took the entire universe in his grasp, and thereby went beyond symbolist subjectivity and, like all the poetry of his time, moved toward the concrete.

The subject of Saint-John Perse's poetry has not been sensory data alone. He has proclaimed the ancient alliance between man and the world, the time-honored meaning of history and culture. His wondering gratitude has been directed above all toward man's imprint upon the world and toward the saga of human civilization. His is not only a poetry of the cosmos but also an epic enumeration of the works of man, a poetry of memory as well as sensation. Indeed, the cosmic imagery is perhaps no more than a stage setting of changelessness and evanescence in which the human adventure—

the epic poem's true subject—is carried on. Monuments lost in the sand, corroded bronzes at the bottom of the seas, traces of vanished roads, abandoned temples, dead languages, undeciphered hieroglyphs, outworn trades, obsolete words, forgotten sciences—all are so many landmarks held upright by the blaze of poetry, with the eternal profile of the pillar standing among the ruins, as a sign of victory for man, and defeat for death.

Saint-John Perse's series of cosmological poems—*Pluies* (1944, Rains), *Neiges* (1944, Snows), *Winds, Seamarks*—and even *Oiseaux* (1963, Birds) suggested that he made a distinction between various moments in time and that the last collection constituted a final rejection of history. But one cannot attribute such a fixed progression of thought to Saint-John Perse. In *Chronique* (1960, Chronicle) he took up history again, and the very early *Éloges* (1911, Praises) was clearly cosmological.

In fact, although one must acknowledge his varying emphases, Saint-John Perse's poetry has been at once a poetry of human civilization and of nature; and if he has simplified his language, his methods have remained the same. With all its verve and provocative force, his poetry is able to control as much as it unleashes, to subdue these elements to rhythm, to rhetorical cadence, to the strict architecture of a language suited as much to the prose writer or chronicler as to the poet. His images communicate surprise, abruptness, shock; Saint-John Perse has combined symbolist glitter with the surprise elements of more recent poetic developments. But he has firmly subordinated imagery to the structure of the poem; the imagery illuminates rather than dazzles, and it is as precise as it is recondite. Saint-John Perse's poetry is a meeting point of opposite impulses and traditions and, like classical verse, it can support a detailed explication; for each word, each image, is exactly justified, however much the *verset's* stately progress carries us forward and enchants us.

Neither Reverdy, Supervielle, Jouve, nor Saint-John Perse belonged to the surrealist movement. They were of a previous generation; their origins lay elsewhere; their purposes were different. And, since World War II, there no longer is a surrealist movement, apart from certain tiny groups of no importance. But there has remained a state of mind created by surrealism, to which Louis Aragon, the poet who moved furthest from it, paid homage in *Le roman inachevé* (1956, The Unfinished Novel).

Éluard and Aragon became the two great popular poets of the resistance by adopting communism (of a very national kind). But the passage from surrealism to communism was not so strange, for surrealism had sought an anonymous style. And is not political poetry anonymous poetry established on a firm basis? When Éluard quoted Lautréamont's statement, "Poetry shall be created by everyone," he invited people to forget, during the time of fervor, that poetry was a highly specialized profession.

Paul Éluard was not the most important figure in the surrealist movement, but he was certainly the greatest poet—and the only one who was exclusively a poet. He was also the one who wrote the most moving and lasting poems of the resistance. His militant collections—*Au rendez-vous allemand* (1944, At the German Rendezvous), *Poèmes politiques* (1948, Political Poems), and *Une leçon de morale* (1949, A Lesson on Morality)—contained a few poems that broke down the barrier between poetry and public and were on everyone's lips: *Liberté* (Liberty) above all; but also *Hommage à Gabriel Péri* (Homage to Gabriel Péri), *Critique de la poésie* (A Critique of Poetry), and *Couvre feu* (Curfew).

But committed poetry for Éluard was never simply poetry of circumstance, a flash in the pan. If we read *Choix de poèmes* (Selected Poems), a selection chosen by Éluard himself in 1946, we can find the very early *Poèmes pour la paix* (Poems for Peace), which date from 1918; they tell of the joy of women reunited with their husbands home from the front. At the end of *La vie immédiate* (1932, Life at Close Quarters), there is a *Critique of Poetry* that prefigured the one in *At the German Rendezvous* and says the same thing: the happiness of men is more important than the words of poets. Even in Éluard's early poetry there was, mingled with the more personal vein, a humanistic, social note, a theme present long before World War II and his conversion to communism. Along side *Médieuses* (Médieuses) and *Les yeux fertiles* (The Fertile Eyes), poems of pure love written during the 1930s, in *Chanson complète* (1939, Total Song) he announced the tragedy and bore witness to its first victims. Poems like *La victoire de Guernica* (The Victory of Guernica) and *Les vainqueurs d'hier périront* (Yesterday's Victors Shall Perish) were the first of the kind of poem Éluard was to bring to fruition in *Liberty*.

This is not to say that Éluard's poetry did not develop. His early collections, such as *Mourir de ne pas mourir* (1924, Dying of Not Dying) and *Capitale de la douleur* (1926, Capital of Grief), revealed a private voice, enclosed in its inner space, face to face with its dreams, in a sort of half light in which nothing can be heard but the heart beating. In his collections of poetry after 1940 the overall tone changed considerably, especially in the movement away from solitude and toward communion.

But in Éluard's development there were no ruptures. His loneliness was always a longing for communion; his night, a hope for day. Éluard was France's last great lyric poet, for his poetry saw in love the privileged path to understanding the world, and his mode of expression remained from first to last not merely images or metaphors but—better yet—pure song. His songs are friends to memory; these poems were among the last that we can easily learn "by heart."

It is now twenty years since Éluard died, and, although he reached a sizeable audience toward the end of his life, he is viewed as somewhat remote. This is easily explicable, for he was in many ways closer to the tradition of Charles Baudelaire (1821–1867) and even of Paul Verlaine (1844–1896) than to more recent tendencies. More "modern" writers (Henri Michaux, Francis Ponge [born 1899], Jacques Prévert [born 1900]) have denied the primacy of lyric poetry and have been unconcerned with the poem as *form*. Éluard was censured by Breton because he asserted the superiority of poetry over dream and of the "arrangement in poem form" over the word-for-word transcription of the dream. And the most recent poets, even though they no longer find their chief source of inspiration in dream, do not organize their poems so much as they disorganize them! Yet, even if Éluard has lost present favor, his place in literary history is assured.

As a surrealist, Louis Aragon was more a prose poet than a writer of verse. And as a communist in the 1930s he was much more important as the novelist of *The Good Neighborhoods* (1936) than as the poet of *Hourra l'Oural* (1934, Hurrah for the Urals). It was World War II, with its combination of patriotic fervor and revolutionary zeal, that brought Aragon the poet both his eminence and his audience. However, the patriotic, neoclassical, and popular poetry that Aragon wrote then resulted rather from willed choice and a sort of program than from inner personal necessity. He wrote the kind of poetry that he would have hoped to have seen written by others.

Aragon's wartime poetry was simple poetry reflecting everyone's preoccupations, a lyricism poured into metrical molds that made it easy to memorize. This explains his use of the alexandrine; this also explains his rather curious defense of rhyme: "I say it is not true there can be no new rhymes in the world, when the world is new" (*La rime en 1940* [1941, Rhyme in 1940]). And in his use of it there was perhaps more dexterity than inspiration.

Constantly mingled with Aragon's political subject matter was an almost Petrarchan love motif: Elsa in *Les yeux d'Elsa* (1942, The Eyes of Elsa), like Bérénice in his novel *Aurélien,* established the myth of a beloved woman's face, which is at the same time the face of a whole people. And Aragon's finest poems explored the theme of love. He did have difficulty in achieving candor and passion (or desire for passion), which his own nature and the very profusion of his talents almost disqualified him from feeling. Equally antagonistic to passion was the virtuosity that enabled him to try out any and every device of versification, from classicism and romanticism to the most up-to-date styles. But the emotional sincerity that Aragon sought at first (and so often in vain) from the future, he later found in the past, in *The Unfinished Novel* and *Les chambres* (1969, The Rooms), which were created out of the emotions of memory.

Aragon's and Éluard's departure from surrealism enabled them eventually to attract a large audience. André Breton, on the other hand, always identified himself with surrealism. Leader of the movement from its very beginnings, he was also the only one who remained faithful to its spirit. Such fidelity naturally meant less development. But despite the fact that Breton's inspiration was the same at all periods of his career, he nevertheless wrote important works after 1940. His great poems of the 1940s—*Fata Morgana* (1940, Fata Morgana), *Pleine marge* (1943, The Further Edge), *Ode à Charles Fourier* (1947, Ode to Charles Fourier), *Les états généraux* (1947, The Estates General)—had the same eloquence, the same luminosity, the same great metaphorical vitality as the poems of *Clair de terre* (1923, By Earthlight). *Arcane 17* (1944, Arcanum 17) revealed the same style of poetic prose that made his *Nadja* (1928, Nadja) so extraordinary. And in his essays, restatements of the true surrealism, *La lampe dans l'horloge* (1948, The Lamp in the Clock) or *Flagrant délit* (1949, Caught in the Act), there was the same authoritarian zeal as before.

But although Breton's techniques and ideas did not change, his relationship to reality did—because the world had changed. The altered world caused adjustments in Breton's thinking and led to the appearance of a new tone, compounded of bitterness and nostalgia. Breton was forced to admit his failure: surrealism, which had scorned literature and wanted to alter life, in the end altered literature without affecting the world. But Breton was determined not to recant. What could he do but take a fresh and melancholy grip on the past? His last publications were songs of disappointed hopes and missed chances. Breton began to look toward Charles Fourier and the social utopias of the nineteenth century, toward the Germans Heinrich von Kleist and Johann Hölderlin, toward Gérard de Nerval (1808–1855), toward the poetic dreams of the romantic period. Breton did not react to circumstances as Aragon and Éluard had, accepting the time and trying to keep in step with it. *Arcanum 17* is a work of "discommitment," if there is such a thing, in which the poet found in "personal ways of feeling" an antidote to the tragedies of history.

But Breton was physically detached from the resistance by having emigrated to the United States. Although he certainly espoused and defended the Allied cause, particularly in his many radio broadcasts, he never gave the events of the war the status and dignity of a source of poetic inspiration. There was no room, in his view, for nationalist and political enthusiasm: at the very most, one might take up a defensive position, so to speak, or fight to keep the damage to a minimum, but not to establish an absolute value. Breton shared none of the hopes characteristic of the immediate postwar period. He and his friends had called for a revolutionary transformation of society, but although his colleagues seemed to be content with the directives of "strange comrade Stalin," Breton utterly rejected orthodox communism, and his friendship with Trotski was essentially similar to his admiration for Fourier, a sort of nostalgia.

Once, like his friends, he had hoped for destruction—the destruction of a society, of a culture, of a Europe whose "defeatists" they claimed to be. But he began to perceive not only that no improvement had come about in the world but that what changes had occurred were such that tended to discourage men from wanting further change. We had desired the end of the world—he said in *The Lamp in the Clock,* written just after the first atomic explosion—and here the end of the world is, staring us in the face, but "we want nothing more to do with it." For it was the world of history that man should have destroyed, but now history may destroy the world of man. It is easy to understand why Sartre wrote that Breton was an "exile in our midst" at a time when literature was committing itself to political optimism. Breton not only disdained any political stance that did not incarnate an absolute but also was a lucid enough observer to see clearly how treacherous were the paths to which others had blindly committed themselves.

From a literary point of view, Breton is closer to more recent tendencies, and Philippe Sollers has often cited him. But although the group around the review *Tel Quel* has borrowed from Breton the notion of literature as a unified field of activity and the idea that writing must not be the mode of expression of a finite and limited man but rather an activity directed toward totality, it is a long way from Breton's intuition and poetic necessity to *Tel Quel*'s theoretical concerns. For they have attempted to integrate the chief contemporary theoretical disciplines with each other; and they have suspected poetry of being invented by, and in league with, the bourgeoisie. Whatever he wrote, Breton was a poet, by virtue of the imagery, the sense of discovery, the thrill of life that accompanied his every word. Whether his mood was nostalgia or excitement, whether he was rejecting or asserting, his work was still a sublime instance of poetry as an attitude to life.

Breton was surrounded to the end by the remnants of the surrealist group, and even after his death the group kept going, along with its successive reviews: *Bief, Le surréalisme même, La brèche,* and others. But no important new work resulted; the journals had to struggle to survive; the demonstrations that the group organized had a prehistoric flavor. Breton himself, toward the end of his life, was tempted to wind up the movement; the few interesting writers who were associated with its last gasps (such as Julien Gracq) were not activists but rather nostalgic admirers of a past whose splendors they themselves had not known. What mainly remains today of surrealism is its history.

To this history, which is also the history of dadaism, also belong Tristan Tzara (1896–1963), Philippe Soupault (born 1897), and Benjamin Péret (1899–1959). But what they produced after the war was considerably less important than their earlier work. At most, they played a part in the literary conflicts of the time: Péret, faithful to André Breton to the end, attacked in *Le déshonneur des poètes* (1945, The Poets' Shame) the patriotic, "propagandist" litanies of Aragon, Éluard, and Pierre Emmanuel. Tristan Tzara replied to Péret in *Le surrealisme et l'après guerre* (1947, Surrealism and the Postwar World), diagnosing the death of that movement: because surrealism had wanted to be outside the world, it could no longer find a place in the "circuit of ideas."

But this was mere pamphleteering. Robert Desnos (1900–1945), on the other hand, was about to find a new vein, if one is to judge by the poems he wrote during the war, such as *Fortunes* (1942, Fortunes), which had a simple, tightly strung lyricism. But he died in 1945, a few days after he was freed from a concentration camp.

One group of the 1930s related to surrealism was the writers around the review *Le grand jeu*. They developed surrealism's "occultist" side; but in opposition to surrealist dogmatism they proclaimed that spiritual experiences could not be precisely formulated. Among them, Roger Vailland was to take up political positions after the war similar to those of Tristan Tzara and become a "committed" writer. René Daumal (1908–1944) was by far the most important poet in this occultist movement. He has won an increasing following through posthumous publications, above all *Mont-Analogue* (1952, Mount Analogue), which has a preface by André Rolland de Renéville (born 1903). *Mount Analogue* strikingly recounts the myth of a voyage in search of an invisible world—a voyage that ends in death. Also important in this group was Roger-Gilbert Lecomte (born 1909), whose manifesto in the first issue of *Le grand jeu* ("We do not wish to write; we let ourselves be written") seems to have anticipated more recent theories, although Lecomte was speaking of lived experience and inspiration rather than analytical intelligence.

But no writer has received more posthumous attention over the last few years than has Antonin Artaud. He left hardly more than the shreds and tatters of literary creation—or rather of his *refusal* to create. Yet these fragments tower above the carefully constructed and widely glorified works of many other writers. Artaud appeared suddenly out of limbo, and he seems to have been the precursor and discoverer of all that now most concerns and disturbs us.

After the war Artaud produced very important works, such as *Au pays des Tarahumaras* (1945, In the Land of the Tarahumaras) and *Lettres de Rodez* (1946, Letters from Rodez), as well as *Artaud de Mômo* (1947, Artaud the Boogieman) and *Van Gogh, le suicidé de la société* (1947, Van Gogh: The Man Suicided by Society). But his immediacy is not to be explained by the fact that his last works were deeper and richer; the current enthusiasm for Artaud includes not only these later works but a rediscovery of his prewar writings, such as *L'ombilic des limbes* (1925, Umbilical Limbo); his meditations on the theater, *Le théâtre et son double* (1938, The Theater and Its Double); his experiments in tragedy, *Les*

Cenci (1935, The Cenci), *Héliogabale* (1935, Heliogabalus)—in short, Artaud's entire oeuvre.

Artaud's popularity may seem strange, for he was, as well as a genius, also a pathological case: a powerful enemy within himself separated him from himself, deprived him of speech, imprisoned him. Sometimes, reading him, we sense the wind of madness, with its accompanying deprivation of free will. But Artaud was able to make his sick obsessions the means to a revelation that involves us; and he even makes us question our customary policy of locking away the insane, by castigating the policy as social hypocrisy designed to protect us from our fear of recognizing ourselves in them.

By forcing us outside our usual reassuring boundaries, Artaud proves to us that we also inhabit those dangerous regions beyond all frontiers. In his ravaged body, his stammering, inconsequential phrases, we suddenly recognize the truth, the one truth. Artaud is the hero, or rather anti-hero, of a literature that has nothing whatever to do with escapism: what justifies literature is truth itself, not the creation of an opus or an escape to the "beautiful object."

In 1922 Jacques Rivière (1886–1925), editor of the *Nouvelle revue française,* rejected the poems Artaud had just submitted, complaining that they were shapeless. Artaud in reply expressed his disgust for the "Vermeer of Delft side of poetry." In the 1920s people agreed with Rivière, but today they think Artaud is right. And compared to Artaud, surrealism itself looks like an outburst of lyrical euphoria that suffers from a certain "Vermeer of Delft" side. The truth revealed and proclaimed by Artaud is life seen as evil and inadequate, seen also as an intensity of rebellion, ecstasy, and paroxysm.

Artaud consistently rejected the idea of literature as a fictitious and distanced version of life. He sought desperately for a word gesture—a word cry in his poems, a word action in a theater that would no longer be a spectacle played by actors for an audience but a ceremony or a happening lived and shared. From Artaud, from his thought and his theatrical experiments, comes today's anti-theater and the audience participation that has succeeded Brecht's theater of alienation—all the tendencies, in fact, that seek to raise art to the level of life, even at the risk of destroying art.

CONTEMPORARY POETRY: NEW MASTERS AND NEW PROSPECTS

The climate for poetry after the end of World War II was favorable: there were many poetry magazines, such as Pierre Seghers's (born 1906) *Poésie, Confluences,* and *Fontaine,* and there was rich variety among them. Some writers spoke in a more-or-less traditional lyrical voice, others created poetic myths, and yet others used rhetorical or realistic approaches.

The lyricism of Jean Tardieu (born 1903) as in *Le témoin invisible* (1943, The Unseen Witness) and *Une voix sans personne* (1954, A Voice without an Owner) has been extremely pure, sometimes close to classical versification. And he has used a symbolism reminiscent of the German romantics. His poetry has also displayed irony and parody, as in *Monsieur Monsieur* (1951, Mister Mister); but these tendencies found their true outlet in Tardieu's plays.

Henri Thomas (born 1912), a novelist and translator, also has written poetry: *Travaux d'aveugle* (1941, Work in the Dark) and *Le monde absent* (1947, The Absent World). He has displayed a frail, ingratiating charm, rather like that of Verlaine.

Philippe Jaccottet (born 1925), who is also a translator, has been at his best perhaps in poetic prose rather than in his verse. His work leads to silence, to something unsayable that seems also to be indestructible. His poems contain distinct, dense, long-pent-up voices, which mingle cadence and image in nostalgic autumn colors, as in *L'effraie* (1954, The Barn Owl) and *Airs* (1967, Airs).

Lebanon-born Georges Schehadé (born 1910), who has written a number of plays including the delightful *Monsieur Bob'le* (1951, Monsieur Bob'le), clearly belongs to the lyric tradition. His poetry has been outstanding for its innocence and purity. His words shine with a dewlike freshness, but his simple, even naïve at times, graceful, and amusing poetry can also turn iron-hard and give glimpses of true profundity.

By contrast, the poetry of André Frénaud (born 1907)—such as *Poèmes de dessous le plancher* (1949, Poems from under the Floorboards) and *Il n'y a pas de paradis* (1962, There Is No Paradise)—has been characterized by sheer abundance and epic vigor. His method of combining the disorder and the discontinuity of modernism with classical rhythms, his method of mixing together anecdotes, notes, experiences, and lyrical solemnity, reminds one sometimes of Apollinaire. But his best poems have a tragic discordancy, a nakedness shot with sudden flashes through which one glimpses his most private voice.

Aimé Césaire (born 1913), both a dramatist and a poet, has also revealed an epic strength and abundance, in *Les armes miraculeuses* (1946, The Miraculous Weapons) and *Cahier d'un retour au pays natal* (1947, Diary of a Return to the Native Land). Césaire, from Martinique, is the first great black poet to write in French, and in return for what French culture (particularly surrealism) has given him he has enriched French literature with the picture of a new sensibility and of a new humanity.

But René Char, more than anyone else, today most brilliantly and masterfully embodies the lyrical impulse in poetry. Char's poetry best illustrates the essence of the poem, as Maurice Blanchot said, echoing Heidegger's evaluation of Hölderlin. Although he was associated with the second wave of surrealists, and his first works were published before the war—*Ralentir travaux* (1930, Slowing Down the Work), *Le marteau sans maître* (1934, The Hammer without an Owner)—he found his true voice only after 1945. *Feuillets d'Hypnos* (1946, Leaves of Hypnos) was a verse diary of Char's combat action as a leader of the Maquis in Provence. *Leaves of Hypnos* overshadowed all other committed poetry because of its direct narration of scenes actually experienced. For instance, the poet witnesses the execution of one of his comrades and is powerless to intervene because the village in which this happens would have been massacred by the Germans in reprisal. There is no propaganda in *Leaves of Hypnos,* no political blandishment, but rather a morality, an affirmation of courage and comradeship, with no illusions and no program for the future.

The reserved, dense, often aphoristic lyricism of Char was quite unlike the melodious effusiveness of Éluard and Aragon. But although his poetry has always contained a thread of reference to the world of history, the collections *Le poème pulvérisé* (1947, The Pulverized Poem), *Fureur et mystère* (1948, Frenzy and Mystery), *Recherches de la base et du sommet* (1955, Researches Fundamental and Supreme), *La parole en archipel* (1962, Words in Archipelago), not to mention his plays, among which *Le soleil des eaux* (1949, The Water Sun) was especially notable, have made it clear that Char's poetry is very far from the literature of political commitment. He has been concerned with what is sacred in the universe, with a mysterious relationship between human order and cosmic sensations, always going beyond any possible definition of its meaning.

Char has confined his poetry to experience, and has entrusted this experience to the fullness and perfection of form. and he accepts language itself. Whereas surrealism tended toward liberation, toward a dislocation of the linguistic mechanism, Char has condensed the richest experience into the hardest and most explosive language. He has often ended up with maxims like those of Heraclitus, subsuming contradictions in the unity of a single tension. Imagery and metaphor (which have not always avoided preciosity; a meadow, for instance, is "day's tool case") have been important elements in his poetry. But he uses them to create a passing glow, a flash of light rather than an object intended to be looked at. Like Char's aphorisms, his imagery and metaphors constitute a kind of gesture, a form of energy.

By condensing language, reducing it to the fundamental nuclei of its energy, Char isolates upon a page a number of atoms, so to speak, whose explosion will set off a chain reaction. His poetry sparks off and instigates much more than it actually relates; its unity is not that of a unifying consciousness but of a gesture that initiates. The tension maintaining the elements of language in violent equilibrium is that of a force coursing through life and opening up the future. The world's images glitter and glimmer like flint kindling the tinder of space. But this is a fire lit, rather than contained, by the poem. It gives one the taste and strength for life. The taste for life subsumes both the return toward primal innocence and a virile acceptance of life as it is. All times, like all contradictions, are fused: "Speech, storm, ice, and fire shall end by forming a common frost." Is this a prophecy or the reminiscence of a golden age? Neither. For past and future vanish in poetry's eternal present, in the golden moment of the poet's gaze riveted upon the world.

The postwar period saw some experiments that were in radical opposition to the surrealist and modernist modes of discontinuity. These writers required the poem to have unity; they asked it to follow an inner unifying logic, to become the narrative of a myth. Jouve was a major influence; but it is easy to understand why the postwar climate in general was favorable. The war had produced a world of absurdity that demanded description and interpretation at the highest level. Through the epic tradition, these writers hoped to find a meaning and a consistent form, to give answers to man's bewilderment, and to aid readers lost amidst so much obscure and disjointed poetry. Thus, these writers had nostalgia for the great eras of myth and religion. Among them, Pierre Emmanuel, in *Tombeau d'Orphée* (1941, Orpheus's Tomb), *Combats avec tes défenseurs* (1942, Combats with Your Defenders), *Babel* (1952, Babel), and *Jacob* (1970, Jacob), and Patrice de La Tour du Pin (born 1911) in *Une somme de poésie* (1946, A Sum of Poetry), were outstanding representatives of this neoepical movement. But the ambition to create organic poems presupposed a unity that our civilization does not possess. Thus, despite their strength, such works seem out of place among us, like monuments of another age.

Other poets' works, which were simply language, plays on words, and rhetoric, were certainly more modern. The best example of this kind of poetry was the work of Jacques Audiberti (1899–1965). *L'empire et la trappe* (1930, The Empire and the Monastery), *Race des hommes* (1937, Human Race), and *Des tonnes de semence* (1941, Tons of Seed) were full of verbal fireworks. This rhetorical flair characterized his novels, too, but in his plays it was more restrained, and they were probably his finest creations, especially *Le mal court* (1947, Evil Is in the Air), which was also a considerable popular success. Audiberti used a variety of traditional forms and styles: song, epic, baroque rhetoric, and even classical austerity. In his 1942 manifesto, *La nouvelle origine* (The New Beginning), he had reaffirmed François de Malherbe's (1555–1628) old ideal of the poet as verbal technician; and he mingled this with the romantic ideal of the poet as divine creator.

A newer current in poetry is one that can roughly be called "realistic." It has been characterized by a critical attitude, or an irreverence, toward poetry itself. In this anti-poetry the writer has sought, through either subject matter or language, to use jarring forms and materials. Is this to make the domain of poetry limitless? Or is it to show that nothing is poetic? A reply to these questions must depend upon one's own temperament.

Jean Follain (1903–1970), in *Exister* (1947, Existing) and *Territoires* (1953, Territories), cunningly but unaggressively made poetry out of the simplest things: a peasant's lace bonnet, the village draper's shop, the inventory of a hardware shop, a still life. He took possession of a familiar domain in which he felt perfectly at ease. But this was not to debunk but rather to evoke the same feelings as those that traditional lyric poetry produces on another level. For every one of Follain's poems was like a bright, crudely colored tarot card that we turn over to reveal fate's disquieting and touching face.

Though his methods have been different, Eugène Guillevic's (born 1907) efforts have been much of the same order as Follain's. In collections like *Terraqué* (1942, Terraqueous), *Carnac* (1961, Carnac), *Paroi* (1970, Partition), he offered an abrupt, rugged, brutal poetry, whose decor was as simple as a peasant household (wooden bench, bowl, wardrobe, and outside, tree and rock). From this poetry also emanated a disturbing, dramatic magic. But unlike Follain, Guillevic has shunned all melodic attractiveness: his poems are ungraceful successions of short, gritty, guttural words. His style clearly constituted a step beyond Follain in this "criticism" of poetry.

Jacques Prévert has also belonged to this school of realistic reappraisal, with its deflation of language and its simple inspiration. But Prévert's career has been very special, not least on account of his great popular success: *Paroles* (1946, Words), which included both old and new poems by Prévert, is the only collection of poems whose sales have equaled or exceeded that of a best-selling novel. Counting paperback editions, *Words* sold a million copies in its first twenty years. This success was partly because Prévert already had a vast audience through his screenplays for such films as *Le jour se lève* and *Les enfants du paradis*. Nonetheless, he is the one poet who will have a place in the history of literature who also belongs to popular culture.

What was so different about *Words* and the collections that followed it: *Spectacle* (1951, Show), *La pluie et le beau temps* (1955, Rain and Fine Weather), *Fatras* (1956, Hodge-Podge)? A diction rather than a style—the shorthand of a nonchalant improvisation. And the subject matter? The air and the images of the street; stories about anyone, principally love stories, but a love emptied of drama and often equated with pleasure. Although this sounds more like the song than the poem, one can soon see that literature, in the best sense of the word, has its share here as well.

However spontaneous Prévert's verve may be, it still develops, is organized, becomes an extraordinary instrument for catching words and knocking them off course. However innocent this poetry may be, it is nonetheless animated by a criticism, a reappraisal of poetry; and no doubt Prévert's irreverence, his hostility to social, religious, and national myths, his denunciation of idols and privileges all express an old anarchistic tradition. But Prévert offers more than iconoclasm; although he rejects the language of conventional propriety, he delights in a fresh, new, rejuvenated language, exercising all its potentialities.

What a distance there is from the vivacious simplicity of Prévert to the very different simplicity of Francis Ponge, whose poetry starts with the object itself and ends in abstraction, sometimes even in hermeticism. But there is reason for mentioning Prévert and Ponge together: they are two totally opposite instances of the modern tendency to create poetry by turning it inside out.

Ponge's first important publication, *Le parti-pris des choses* (1942, Siding with Things), was probably the first application to poetry of a tendency toward "objectivity" that the novel was to adopt some years later, whose intellectual basis was phenomenology. These poems seemed at first sight very modest, limited exercises. They were like still lifes: an orange, an oyster, fire, a snail, a shell, a pebble are described in such a way that the reader should exclaim, even before he has seen the title, "Why, it's about a snail, a pebble!" Clearly, Ponge's enterprise was ambitious, and he pursued this course with great determination.

Ponge was also careful, at least implicitly at the beginning, to give his poetry a theoretical basis. He took enormous care with these short poems, giving them the quality of models to be imitated, so as to teach traditional poetry a lesson. This was a challenge to the validity of poetry's claim to be an authentic, genuine contact with the world; the suspicion began to grow that poetry's territory was no more virgin than any other, that it was determined by human expectations, that its purity was sullied by human presuppositions.

Is it then nature devoid of man's presence that Ponge is seeking to evoke? Alain Robbe-Grillet recently complained that he did not admire Ponge when Ponge retained traces of anthropomorphism in his poetry. But Ponge replied that in his view any attempt to eliminate every such trace is doomed to failure. Although Ponge has desired to speak not of man but of things, it is on behalf of man that he has spoken, to man, and with man's words. On behalf of man: for the poems of *Siding with Things* and of his next collection, *L'œillet, la guêpe, le mimosa* (1946, Carnation, Wasp, Mimosa), were not only exercises but, in the fullest sense, lessons drawn from things. If we have to exercise so much care in the description of a pebble, this is because the pebble is a model: it indicates to us the direction of our lives. The world of objects suppresses useless feelings and vain disquiet. Not only lyric subjectivity but also philosophical and historical problems vanish alike before the solidity and serenity of the object. Francis Ponge's humanism is an acceptance of the world located and defined by the object.

Humanism? Yes. For if the tree or the stone has a lesson to teach us, it is that they live by their own definitions, that they are their own definitions. It is equally our duty to live by what constitutes man, that is, by "speech and morality"—or, rather, *the morality of speech.* It is our duty to live wisely, in conformity to what is ours, following step by step, word by word, those things that alone are real—objects.

And this human labor of language became both the form and the content of Ponge's work. His early work took up the "challenge of things to language" and sought to present a poetry that weighed the object exactly, was an equivalent for it, and had its completeness. In *Carnet du bois de pins* (1947, Pine Wood Notebook) Ponge presented for the first time a succession of rough drafts, a text in its successive states. This technique recurred in *La crevette dans tous ses états* (1948, The Shrimp in All Its States). *La rage de l'expression* (1952, The Frenzy to Express) indicated by its title Ponge's new intention, which superseded that of "siding with things." He wanted to find in each moment of language what he was looking for: the poet's work, his gesture toward the object.

Taken to its extreme, this approach can yield no final poem, which has to result from erasures, emendations, and recomposition: for Ponge the poem became every word that is written down, from first to last, a verbal trajectory reproduced in its entirety, for none of its individual moments can be preferred to the progressive creation of the whole. In *La fabrique du Pré* (1971, The Field Factory), Ponge gave a succession of drafts ending with the text of "The Field" itself. *Le savon* (1966, Soap), however, did not even contain a text at all, but the progress *toward* a text, consisting of variations, passages reworked, and various stylistic exercises interspersed with reflections on the text as it is written. In this work the impulses of the mind and the progressive emergence of the object were fused into a single effort until the moment is reached when the object melts in the hands (appropriately enough, since the subject matter is soap) as the effort to describe it ends.

Is this poetry? Ponge himself has made a distinction between what he has written and poetry, for he entitled one of his collections *Proêmes* (1949, Proems). This added "r" is the letter found in *"premier"* ("first") and *"création"* ("creation") and lacking in *"poème."* His is an anti-poetry that refuses to believe in "higher" or "complete" forms and feelings. But when the dexterity, precision, and the mobilization of all its resources enabled Ponge's poetry to capture its object, he gave language its full poetic dignity.

Henri Michaux has written against the poetic tradition, declaring that he does not care if he is a poet or not. He has used a great variety of styles, and if he has often been elliptical and incantatory, he can also be the opposite: he can write a dry, ironic, agile prose, almost like Voltaire's. All this, however, sprung from a single source, which by its nature was infinitely nearer poetry than were Ponge's objects; for Michaux, it was an inner, if also coenesthetic, experience, full of impulses and phantasms intimately linked with the body. But this "inner space," the space of poetic subjectivity, was depoeticized by Michaux's mode of expression. Thus, Michaux's approach was directly opposite to Ponge's; for as Ponge wrote, he turned what had previously been unpoetic into poetry.

Michaux's work has been unusual, and impossible to classify. He began his career long before World War II. *Mes propriétés* (My Properties) was published in 1929, and *La nuit remue* (The Night in Motion) in 1935. But only since the war has the true, and considerable, worth of Michaux's poetry been recognized. His early works included diaries of actual travels (*Un barbare en Asie* [1933, A Barbarian in Asia]); logbooks of imaginary voyages in strange lands, such as *Voyage en Grande Garabagne* (1936, Voyage to Great Garabagne), in which the flora and fauna and especially the customs are described in minute detail; and *Un certain Plume* (1930, A Certain Plume), the chronicle of the life and acts of a character called Plume (Pen), who is constantly the victim of an aggressive environment. But these fables, these fictions, these utopias were used mainly to reveal and unfold the same inner world with which *My Properties* was concerned. It is a world of uneasiness and anguish, in which strong external pressures assail the protagonist, who feels out of place but who reacts, struggles, intervenes, destroying what annoys him, trying to make up for what he lacks by the force of imagination, by sheer writing. These works were feverish but simultaneously detached and full of humor.

Michaux continued to write in this vein after World War II. *Ici, Poddéma* (1946, Here Is Poddéma) was another imaginary voyage. Poddéma is a land in which lips are put up for sale, words kill, in which children are manufactured to order.

During the war, Michaux wrote poems in a new spirit and a new tone: anathemas, imprecations torn from him by the horror of events. In some of these he achieved a simplicity and a solemn grandeur that reminds one of the Bible (*Épreuves, Exorcismes* [1940–45, Ordeals and Exorcisms]). Michaux's obsession with death and universal emptiness joined forces with the drama of history. And thus, Michaux's work, so deliberately odd at times that it seemed delirious and even pathological, revealed a universality nonetheless.

Michaux's Plume is ultimately only a more comic version of Sartre's Roquentin and Camus's Meursault: the hero of every poem is continually wounded and disappointed, always lacks something decisive that he cannot even give a name to; he is a "holed" man who feels only emptiness and absence inside him. Nature's infinite multiplicity weighs him down because he yearns for order and unity; but it reassures him, too, because it constitutes the mask before an emptiness that is still more terrifying. He is "between center and absence," haunted at once by obsessive absence and by excessive presence.

Michaux's work, then, is revelation and witness. But it is something else, too—witchcraft. His purpose is "to hold at arm's length the hostile forces of the world around us." He writes for reasons of "hygiene" (as he says) and "to find a way out." Abandoning the passive Plume, Michaux increasingly has turned to this force of intervention as the motif and directing force of his works. Some of his titles bear this out: *Liberté d'action* (1945, Freedom of Action), *Poésie pour pouvoir* (1949, Poetry to Enable), *Mouvements* (1951, Movements), *Passages* (1950, 1963, Passages). The haunted creature demonstrates such prodigious agility and mobility that it is impossible to take hold of him. For Michaux, this gesture, projecting ever further, beyond the reach of all snares, defines existence and life. It is also the definition of the poem.

But in the last few years, an important development has occurred in Michaux. He has begun to identify the liberating gesture with his painting rather than with his poetry. For him, "action painting" reproduces this mobility most closely; it is mobility in action, whereas literature can never do more than describe it at a distance, after the event.

A number of collections published after 1956 reflected Michaux's recent experiences with the drug mescaline: *Misérable miracle* (1956, Miserable Miracle), *L'infini turbulent* (1957, The Stormy Infinite), *Connaissance par les gouffres* (1961, Knowledge from the Abyss). Michaux's domain of imagination had been artificially, but decisively, enlarged; thanks to hallucinogenic drugs, Michaux began to see things he had never seen before. He used his drawings to capture his visions instantly, and the written text tended to be an analysis and commentary on events which preceded it and which it could never entirely reproduce. In *Les grandes épreuves de l'esprit* (1966, The Great Ordeals of the Mind) he rendered still more clearly the process from re-creation to exposition, relating the unforeseen consequences of the disorientation brought about by mescaline: the experience of mental abnormality enabled Michaux to rediscover wonder in ordinary experience.

In his latest book, *Façons d'endormi, façons d'éveillé* (1970, Ways of a Sleeping Man, Ways of a Waking Man), Michaux contrasted the passivity and meagreness of the night's dreams to the rich inventiveness of the "waking reverie." Thus, Michaux still sees salvation, his always-wished-for consummation, in the same direction. But although this latest book still contained the nervous, unexpected, familiar yet dramatic diction that is inseparably Michaux's, it also showed a further development toward analysis and explanation. One can regret that Michaux has reserved the action of poetry mainly to his visual art, important though it may be.

Even if those poets just discussed reached their true stature only after the war, all had begun writing before it. What of those writing today who were not writing in 1950? What of those who were not even writing in 1960? What new have they brought to poetry? And have they common features?

The contact between poetry and the outside world, so evident in the 1940s, has continued. But those who had been only children during the resistance recall the Nazi occupation as something not so much frightening as absurd; and they hold their elders responsible for it. Even the values that had given meaning to the struggle and to the hopes of the previous generation have now been dimmed: it is as if nothing had been worth defending or rescuing. A revolutionary atmosphere does pervade the new poetry, but the Marxist orthodoxy scarcely suits it, since Marxism is a humanism, a hope, and a heritage.

When the revolt has taken a precise political form, it has emphasized an alienation that Marxism (a doctrine of affluent countries) has tended to minimize. Édouard Glissant's (born 1928) epic poem *Les Indes* (1956, The Indies), for instance, spoke for the oppressed races and discovered behind capitalist exploitation a still more basic oppression. But the revolt of these poets has always been deeper than any political revolt could be. In the name of those young poets who felt that the world gave them nothing worthy of acceptance, Henri Pichette (born 1924), their elder by a few years, declared in his *Apoèmes* (1947, Unpoems), "I shall remake my life." And remaking one's life in this case meant remaking poetry as well.

Although Pichette, for one, later adopted a precise political position, most of these writers have found the sources of their poetry outside history. And whatever relationship they do have to history is very personal. The poet's inner anguish familiarizes him with the anguish of his epoch. And the process that brings society from alienation to unity mirrors an inner process: the moments and movements of history serve merely as landmarks and signs of private events and impulses.

This new poetry often relates to an experience realized in successive moments, but moments of *inner* time—an experience whose starting point is emptiness and absence, conjoined with or reflected in an absence of language and an inability to speak. Is expression possible? Is language possible? Being philosophers for the most part, having read Hegel, Sartre, and Blanchot, these younger poets know that the word is the thing's absence, that language brings death into the world. The poet takes his vows to the world through the intermediary of language but sees language's impotence to touch reality. Speech is empty, the world is separate: such is the starting point. But whereas their elders would be content to assert this experience, leaving themselves free to deny it at the same time, and leaving readers and critics the task of harmonizing these two opposite assertions, most of the newcomers do not so much juxtapose the data of the immediately lived experience as describe a trajectory, a thought-out itinerary. Poetry must pass from dead language to living speech, in tune with the world; and it is poetry's job, not the world's, to bring about this achievement. This passage from one language to another, or from language to speech, has often been linked with another sort of passage—that from an alienated to a liberated society.

Among poets who have come to prominence since 1950, the leading figure has been Yves Bonnefoy. His *Du mouvement et de l'immobilité de Douve* (1953, On the Motion and Immobility of Douve) precisely embodied the inner dialectic I have just been describing. Douve is the speech of poetry. Dying, dead, reborn, identified with nature, grass, flint, and then with consciousness and language, motionless and immobile, maenad, salamander, woman's body, or half-effaced fresco on the walls of a chapel, Douve incarnates the speech of poetry in all its ambiguity and its metamorphoses. Of this collection of poetry, one could say that poetry alone is the subject.

But poetry so understood is everything, both language and world. To begin with, poetry and life seem impossible. They are dead, dead with a death which everything negative in human experience demonstrates and which can only be evoked by the assemblage of all the shapes of nothingness: physical dissolution, silence, absence, desert, night. To speak the "true name," the poet must appeal to all these fragmentary names, sketch all the many profiles of a single absence. And the poem, in part, celebrates an entombment; but it also (and ultimately) celebrates a resurrection. From absence to presence, from silence to speech, a motion occurs. Better still: the word must be founded on the initial silence, life must be founded upon death.

This dialectic, by which the experience of nothingness becomes the guarantee of any assertion of authentic life, gives Bonnefoy's work its sense and its life. *Vrai corps* (True Body), a poem in *On the Motion and Immobility of Douve,* evokes the corpse made everlasting by the word denoting it. Night is "other than night"; night is a "buried day" that can be delivered from the tomb; one needs only to assert it and pass through it.

The collection's epigraph is a statement by Hegel which Georges Bataille also loved to quote and which illuminates the broadest landscape of contemporary thought and feeling: "The life of the mind is not afraid of death and does not try to steer clear of it. It is a life that copes with death and sustains itself within it."

Bonnefoy's subsequent collections of poetry, *Hier régnant désert* (1958, Yesterday Reigning Desert) and *Pierre écrite* (1963, Written Stone)—as well as *L'improbable* (1959, The Improbable) and *Un rêve fait à Mantoue* (1967, A Mantuan Dream), essays largely about painting, in which we find again the "erudite music" of the poet—showed Bonnefoy pursuing the same ideas, but in a less abstract and more polished way. *Yesterday Reigning Desert* and *Written Stone* were not assemblages of poems, but single books, works that have their own rules of sequence and are conceived of as wholes. Hand in hand with this mastery of form went a certain metrical traditionalism that sometimes included rhyme and the alexandrine line.

Bonnefoy's recent collections have blended the impulses of life and of literary creation more closely together. His writing still shows occasional moments of the harmony noticeable in his early collections. But he now refuses to accept such relief, such a refuge: the confident lyrical excitement of Bonnefoy's powerful verse is punctuated by short, terse, dismembered texts—"written stones," like so many epitaphs inscribed on tombstones. On the other hand, though the spiritual horizon is by no means lost sight of, the actual details of his progress concern the poet more deeply: in a poem like *La chambre* (The Room) the awareness of unity occurs in the here and now, is embodied in a simple human love.

Jacques Dupin (born 1927) in *Gravir* (1963, To Climb) and André du Bouchet (born 1924) in *Où le soleil* (1968, Where the Sun) wrote poetry close to Bonnefoy's in its reference to lived experience. But unlike Bonnefoy, their styles are dense, sometimes aphoristic. And the blank spaces on the page play a considerable part, especially with Bouchet.

Other young poets (those associated for instance with the review *Tel Quel*) are principally interested in the permutations of a language that, they postulate, has nothing to say. The poem speaks of nothing, of nobody. It is anonymous and incessant language, and has no other meaning than its literal text, its "textuality." Marcelin Pleynet and Denis Roche have written poems that would be reminiscent of the "automatic writing" of surrealism if it were not for surrealism's special intensity that compels us to call it poetry. The texts of *Tel Quel,* on the other hand, could be perfectly easily interchanged with prose. Lines often end with a hyphen cutting the word in two, just as in prose. More importantly, the "electricity" of poetry is totally absent. However, these writers still use such differentiating descriptive titles as "poems" or "stories." And in their "poetry" they have utilized blank spaces and divisions into lines, as in formal poetry. Even when meanings and genres are destroyed, something still remains to prevent literature from becoming nothing more than the unified field of a meaningless "textuality."

Jacques Roubaud (born 1932), whose texts, too, may seem to be in some limbo between prose and poetry, has had different concerns, of a structuralist kind, as in the most recent texts of Robbe-Grillet and Michel Butor. Roubaud in ϵ (1969, ϵ [epsilon]) neither surrendered to automatic writing nor sought to compose the absolute book, but organized the work in such a way that it can support various interpretations and various arrangements. Four different readings are suggested for ϵ: one according to the way the texts are arranged, a second according to a system of mathematical signs, a third following the progress of a game of Japanese *go,* and a fourth by reading each text separately. But these permutations are ultimately less interesting than what each reader can do with the work; and one has to admit that Roubaud is highly inventive and that he even possesses the electricity that disappeared after the demise of surrealism.

THE THEATER: BETWEEN LITERATURE AND SPECTACLE

Some of the most important dramatists of the contemporary period have also been novelists—and, more generally, simply *writers.* These include Henry de Montherlant, Jean-Paul Sartre, Albert Camus, Jean Genet, and Samuel Beckett, all of whose total literary activity I have already discussed. Perhaps—particularly abroad—they are better known as writers for the stage. But I felt it wiser to discuss their literary work as a whole together with related writers who are primarily or exclusively novelists.

Whether their plays have been produced or not, whether they have been successful or not on the stage, almost all of them can be read independent of production considerations. Whether or not they retain a place in the repertories of theaters, they will always merit attention on the shelves of libraries.

Significantly, none of these five writers began his career with the drama: each of them was temperamentally a novelist, and the theater, far from being an exclusive and spontaneous vocation, was merely one form that their literary calling took for a time. The hero who underwent successive incarnations in Montherlant's plays originated in the 1935 essay *Service inutile* (Useless Service), which defined this character and his dilemma of being caught between a desire for commitment and a nihilistic clarity of mind. Sartre used the drama to simplify his metaphysics and his ethics, to give them a wider audience and a greater influence. Camus, it is true, was always interested in the theater for its own sake, but his fiction was certainly more artistically successful.

Genet's plays, on the other hand, are both the best known and the most convincing part of his work; but much of their strength derives from his poetic and narrative gifts. And although the audience for Beckett's plays is certainly larger than the readership of his novels, he was first and above all a novelist. I shall therefore focus in this section on those authors who have written exclusively for the theater—or those at least for whom the drama is their prime mode of expression—and on those sociological considerations peculiar to the theater. But the development of the contemporary drama has followed a pattern similar to that of the novel; therefore, a number of general points have already been established.

Through the years, there have been some novelists, like Jules Romains, whose dramatic work has crowned their careers. Others, like Balzac and Stendhal, Gide and Martin du Gard, met with great failure in the theater. A number of contemporary novelists have written some first-rate plays. But they remain marginal to their fiction. After the success of *Asmodée* (1937, Asmodée), François Mauriac wrote *Les mal aimés* (1945, The Ill-Beloved) and *Le feu sur la terre* (1951, Fire on the Earth); but he will be remembered chiefly for his novels. The same can be said of Julien Green, although *Sud* (1953, South), the drama of an impossible and guilty homosexual love affair set during the American civil war, and *L'ennemi* (1954, The Enemy), which treated similar themes transposed to prerevolutionary France, were both fine plays. Since his first play, *The Fisher King,* in 1948, Julien Gracq has written nothing for the stage. And Georges Bernanos's admirable play *Dialogues of the Carmelites,* published posthumously in 1949, and not produced until 1952, owed its existence to an accident resulting from a commission: Bernanos had been asked to write a screen adaptation of Gertrude von Le Fort's novella *Die Letzte am Schafott.*

A number of masterpieces of the novel have been successfully adopted for the stage, most notably Faulkner's *Requiem for a Nun* by Camus as *Requiem pour une nonne* (1957) and Kafka's *Der Prozeß* by Gide with Jean-Louis Barrault as *Le procès* (1947, The Trial). Indeed, their version of *The Trial* foreshadowed some of the later features of the *"nouveau théâtre."*

For there is a new theater just as there is a new novel. Paris greeted Giraudoux's *La folle de Chaillot* (1945, The Madwoman of Chaillot) right after the war with an acclaim that suggested that everything was going to continue as it had before the war. Here was Giraudoux working again with Louis Jouvet—a collaboration that had dominated the prewar theater. Continuity of tradition was not to be, however. Ironically, Jouvet, who produced Giraudoux's last great success, in 1951 was to produce Genet's *The Maids,* one of the earliest masterpieces of the new theater.

The gulf between old and new was as marked in the theater as in other genres. And even before the appearance of completely new departures in the theater, a change in theatrical style seemed to be in the air. Although Paul Claudel's plays were all written prior to 1940, few were produced until 1943, the date of Jean-Louis Barrault's production of *Le soulier de satin* (1929, The Satin Slipper). After the war Claudel's work found an increasingly important place in the repertory. This was not only true in Paris, where Barrault produced *Partage de midi* (1906, Break of Noon), *L'échange* (1901, The Exchange), *Le livre de Christophe Colomb* (1930, The Book of Christopher Columbus), and, in 1960, for the opening of the new Théâtre de France, *Tête d'or* (1891, Golden Head), and where the T.N.P. (Théâtre National Populaire) produced *La ville* (1893, The City) in 1955, and where Jean-Marie Serreau produced *L'otage* (1911, The Hostage). Claudel was also produced in the provinces, where a whole flock of young companies established themselves. Besides Claudel, Brecht and García Lorca became the most important playwrights of the repertories of the new theaters. As a consequence, the stage was invaded by a lyricism and by the search for a modern epic mode, prompting a new awareness of our period by replacing cliché-ridden naturalism with a new distance between stage and spectator.

The theatergoing public has greatly increased, although there still exists the potential audience that young producers have not yet reached, an audience they feel has been confined to ghettos by capitalist society. Nonetheless, plays can be produced today even for small audiences and brief runs. The theater's variety and daring can thus rival that of the printed book (for a play production's financial outlay is now not much larger than a book's). Little experimental theaters have sprung up everywhere (Théâtre des Noctambules, Théâtre de Poche, Théâtre de la Huchette, Théâtre du Quartier Latin, Théâtre de Babylone, Théâtre de Lutèce); they manage to survive on tiny budgets provided by private donations. In the provinces dramatic centers subsidized by the French government have been created; they have some freedom from commercial pressures, yet without any political strings. There is also official support for the young companies. Festivals, supported mainly by local councils, have proliferated. All these new conditions explain fresh departures in both stage production and repertory, and also explain the increased freedom with the audience and with theatrical convention.

Nonetheless, there is still a traditional theater, just as there is still a traditional novel, and the former is perhaps even more alive than the latter, for audiences keep to their old habits even more fondly than do readers. The easy theater, the *théâtre du boulevard,* gives the public exactly what it expects: its function is to amuse; and its habit is to produce suspense in the audience, as Thierry Maulnier (born 1909, pseudonym of Jacques Talagrand) said in his preface to *Le profanateur* (1952, The Desecrator), "over some gentleman's chances of sleeping with some lady in the last act,

or over some lady's chances of rearousing the passions of some gentleman." The "masterpieces" of this sort of theater sometimes run for years,
but they are then replaced by other successes that assume exactly the
same function and so consign the earlier "masterpieces" to oblivion. Since
they do not survive by virtue of their texts, they do not belong to literature—whose nature it is to leave a history behind it.

But there is an intermediary ground between such rapidly forgotten
successes and works that play a lasting part in literary history. Some certainly very "easy" plays—such as André Roussin's (born 1911) *Am Stram
Gram* (1944, Am Stram Gram) and *La petite hutte* (1947, The Little
Hut), Roger Ferdinand's (born 1898) *Les croulants se portent bien* (1959,
Rip Van Winkle's Doing Well), the enormous output of Pierre Barillet
(born 1923) and Jean-Pierre Grédy (born 1920), or the amusing spectacles of Robert Dhéry (born 1921)—are not without quality. Such is the
domain of the *théâtre de boulevard*.

There is also a theater whose traditional nature guarantees it an audi-
ence but which certainly also belongs to literature; one thinks of Sacha
Guitry (1885–1957), Jean Sarment (born 1897), Stève Passeur (born
1899), Paul Raynal (born 1885), and Édouard Bourdet (1887–1945).
But the works of these men belong mainly to the prewar period, as does
Marcel Pagnol's (born 1895) famous trilogy: *Marius* (1929, Marius),
Fanny (1931, Fanny), and *César* (1937, César).

After the war, the spirit of the traditional theater underwent a radical
change. For it wished to embody an awareness of the altered world situation; even if it was not concerned in changing its form, it felt obliged to
change its content. "Our epoch is an historical and metaphysical one,"
wrote Maulnier in the preface from which I have already quoted; "A
sheltered bourgeoisie used to live at ease with its dreams, between four
comfortable walls. These walls have collapsed in the storm and have let in
the cold and the darkness, the problems of crime and human unhappiness,
the dumb questionings of creation in its death throes."

The majority of plays dating from during or just after the war were
concerned with the problems of the contemporary world. But a poetic
mythology—as in Jean Cocteau's *Renaud et Armide* (1943, Renaud and
Armide) and Maurice Clavel's (born 1920) *Les incendiaires* (1946, The
Incendiaries)—or an historical framework often achieved the effect of
distance. Ancient mythology and history had been drawn upon by Giraudoux, and were used again by Jean Anouilh (born 1910) in *Antigone*
(1943, Antigone), by Sartre in *The Flies,* by Georges Neveux (born
1900) in *Le voyage de Thésée* (1943, The Voyage of Theseus), by
Emmanuel Roblès (born 1914) in *Montserrat* (1948, Montserrat), by
Thierry Maulnier in *The Desecrator,* and by Gabriel Marcel (born 1889)
in *Rome n'est plus dans Rome* (1951, Rome Is No Longer in Rome).

Whether they used an historical framework or not, there were many works that can be defined as "problem plays," whose themes were taken from contemporary events—among them Georges Neveux's *La voleuse de Londres* (1960, The Lady Thief from London), Emmanuel Roblès's *La vérité est morte* (1952, Truth Is Dead), Claude-André Puget's (born 1905) *La peine capitale* (1948, Capital Punishment), and André Obey's (born 1892) *Maria* (1946, Maria) and *Les trois coups de minuit* (1958, The Curtain Rises at Midnight).

These "problem plays" had the inherent dangers of didacticism and artifice. A comic treatment of similar themes had better chances of avoiding these dangers. There has been much verve and inventiveness in Felicien Marceau's (born 1913) plays; the technical originality of *L'œuf* (1956, The Egg) and *La bonne soupe* (1958, The Good Soup) consisted in their being almost entirely monologues. Marceau's *Babour* (1959, Babour) amusingly probed the problems of sex in contemporary society. Equally lively has been Marcel Aymé's drama: *Lucienne et le boucher* (1947, Lucienne and the Butcher); *Clérambard* (1950, Clérambard); *Les oiseaux de lune* (1955, The Moon Birds), in which a strange individual has the power to turn his acquaintances into birds; *La convention Belzébir* (1966, The Belzébir Convention), which takes place in a society that permits murder upon the payment of a fee. The price both Marceau and Aymé paid for their ability to entertain was a certain vulgarity. But neither was as vulgar as Marcel Achard (born 1899), who added a few further commercial successes to his copious prewar output: *Auprès de ma blonde* (1946, Beside My Blonde), *Savez-vous planter les choux* (1951, Can You Plant Cabbages?), and especially *Patate* (1957, Spud).

In a very different category are Armand Salacrou (born 1899) and Jean Anouilh, who have both written exclusively for the stage. They are the two playwrights who can be compared most closely to the novelists of the same period. Their work has contained an equivalent for what I have already described in the existentialist novel. They combined a new content—in the sense that evident contemporaneity is mingled with a pessimistic and accusatory vision—with an evolution in form, which, however, never threatened to push content into the background.

Salacrou in *L'inconnue d'Arras* (1935, The Stranger from Arras) was toying with a metaphysical theater. This was a play that, "like our lives, emerges from nothingness only to return to it." But his plays between 1946 and 1961 were primarily dramas of social criticism: *Les nuits de la colère* (1946, Nights of Rage), whose subject was the resistance; *L'archipel Lenoir* (1947, Lenoir Archipelago); *Une femme trop honnête* (1955, Too Virtuous a Woman), which satirized the bourgeois family; and *Boulevard Durand* (1960, Boulevard Durand), in which justice is miscarried because of political allegiances.

A mainspring of Jean Anouilh's work has been a savage indictment of society, despite his belonging to the political right (although there is, to be sure, the phenomenon of right-wing anarchism). His work has had an abundance and diversity that puts it in the first rank. Anouilh was famous before the war for *L'hermine* (1931, The Ermine), *Le voyageur sans bagage* (1936, Traveler without Luggage), and *La sauvage* (1934, The Savage). The Anouilh hero, obsessed by youthful idealism and rejecting the compromises of ordinary life, had already appeared in various guises. *Antigone* gave the Anouilh hero (or heroine, in this case) the prestige of an ancient myth. Creon, who accepts the demands society makes on the individual, is not an entirely contemptible figure. But the play is naturally dominated by Antigone herself, whose unreasonable behavior is seen as reasonable.

This conflict (close to the one we find in Montherlant) between personal purity and the demands of society tended, after the war, to disappear in Anouilh's work in favor of a savage pessimism that rejected any alternative. His early division of his plays into the *pièces noires* and the *pièces roses* gave way to a uniform atmosphere of sourness and asperity. *Ardèle, ou la marguerite* (1948, Ardèle, or the Daisy) was a pitiless debunking of all respectability and all enthusiasm. A sexuality of resentment, not unlike that found in Sartre's novels, was expressed in the harrowing scene in which two children parody their parents' dissolute behavior. In *La valse des toréadors* (1952, The Waltz of the Toreadors) and *Le boulanger, la boulangère et le petit mitron* (1968, The Baker, the Baker's Wife, and the Little Baker's Boy) Anouilh continued this picture of incurable degradation and disgust. This exaggerated pessimism seems to have been caused largely by the events of the liberation of France, which Anouilh felt had involved excess and injustice, proving that evil inevitably results from the illusion of good.

Anouilh's attitude toward current events perhaps explains the temporal distancing he sought through his historical plays. (Did the break with the present drive Anouilh, like Giono, back toward the past? Or did the past serve Anouilh merely as a prudent disguise?) *Becket, ou l'honneur de Dieu* (1959, Becket, or the Honor of God) reasserted the absurdity of the noblest conflicts, and *La foire d'empoigne* (1960, Catch as Catch Can) put Louis XVIII in a better light than Napoleon. In *L'alouette* (1953, The Lark) the trial of Joan of Arc offered many analogies to the contemporary world. And in *Pauvre Bitos* (1958, Poor Bitos) a magistrate who has terrorized his town just after the liberation is persuaded to adopt the role of Robespierre at a fancy dress party.

In his most recent plays—*Cher Antoine* (1969, Dear Antoine) and *Les poissons rouges* (1970, The Goldfish)—Anouilh adopted a more confidential, autobiographical form; but he obsessively continued to attack social hypocrisy, above all the vacillations of progress and progressivist optimism. Anouilh has experimented ingeniously, sometimes daringly, in almost all of his plays: plays within plays, liberties taken with time, and so forth. But he has remained traditional in that he links a quite explicit content, based usually upon a central problem, to a form that primarily seeks to effect a convincing illusion of reality. Anouilh is neither a Beckett nor a Eugène Ionesco (born 1909), but he was one of the first to pay tribute to Beckett's *Waiting for Godot* and to Ionesco's *Les chaises* (1952, The Chairs).

Nonetheless, it was the kind of drama practiced by Anouilh that Ionesco denounced in 1953: "Our contemporary theater . . . does not fit the cultural style of our epoch; it is out of tune with the spirit of our times." This is because only its content had changed: it had shown us men of a different society and a different psychology. But we should go further, and ask if man exists at all as a being who can be expressed immediately and straightforwardly. We should go as far as putting everything in parentheses, using language and the stage setting like rockets and explosives—lighting up one knows not what. Neither Sartre nor Camus brought any real transformation about in the theater, any more than they did in the novel. And, of course, the trouble was that they were novelists. Is it not *poetry* that brings about the most radical changes?

Giraudoux's drama, today so unjustly neglected, had been a prewar expression of the tendency to transform the theater. But the true precursors of the new theater are to be found in surrealism and its forerunners. This tradition runs from Alfred Jarry's (1873–1907) *Ubu roi* (1897, King Ubu) to Apollinaire's *Les mamelles de Tirésias* (1918, The Breasts of Tiresias), from Tristan Tzara's *La première aventure céleste de M. Antipyrine* (1916, The First Celestial Adventure of Mr. Antipyrine) to Antonin Artaud's *The Cenci* to Roger Vitrac's (1899–1952) *Victor, ou les enfants au pouvoir* (Victor, or Children in Power), which dates from 1928, but only achieved a really appreciative audience when it was revived in 1962. Slowly, these plays established a countertradition leading the theater to reject realism and the portrayal of society, and laying it open to fantasy, dream, and word play.

Most of Michel de Ghelderode's (1898–1962) plays were written before 1940. Only after 1945, however, did new conditions in the theater allow him to achieve decisive successes on the stage with *Hop, Signor!* (1942, Hop, Signor!) and *Fastes d'enfer* (1938, Chronicles of Hell). These masterpieces linked burlesque, diablerie, and—despite Ghelderode's refusal to consider himself a philosopher—a metaphysical vision of the world to a lively verbal talent.

Boris Vian, too, may be classified with the precursors of the new theater. *Les bâtisseurs d'empire* (The Empire Builders), it is true, was written in

1959, and seemed to look like the work of a disciple, for Ionesco's influence was so visible in it. But *L'équarissage pour tous* (1947, Knackering for All) anticipated many future developments in the drama.

To a still-traditional form of poetic theater belonged the plays of Jules Supervielle, whose *The Child Stealer* was produced in 1948, and whose *Shéhérazade* (1949, Scheherazade) was put on that same year at the Festival of Avignon by Jean Vilar. The poetry that flows through Georges Schehadé's plays is more unusual and, one might say, more modern. In *Monsieur Bob'le, La soirée des proverbes* (1954, Evening of Proverbs), *L'histoire de Vasco* (1956, The Tale of Vasco), and *L'émigré de Brisbane* (1965, The Brisbane Émigré), he embodied a fresh and charming lyricism in a group of familiar and preposterous characters who meet as memory or quest dictate.

Aimé Césaire's *La tragédie du roi Christophe* (1964, The Tragedy of King Christophe) was a poet's play but also a political play calculated to serve "black power." It depicted a native kinglet of Haiti at the beginning of the nineteenth century, who embodies the independence of his people but is abandoned by them. *Une saison au Congo* (1966, A Season in the Congo) recounted the events that led to the death of Patrice Lumumba. Césaire's theater has occupied a place halfway between Claudel's and Brecht's.

The springs of a violent lyricism based on Arthur Rimbaud (1854–1891) and on surrealism meet, in Henri Pichette's plays, with the tones of accusation and commitment. But *Les épiphanies* (1947, The Epiphanies) and *Nucléa* (1952, Nucléa), a play against war and atomic destruction, were more like oratorios than plays, poems entrusted to an actor's voice. Their success was largely due to the presence of Gérard Philippe on the stage.

Jacques Audiberti, on the other hand, although a novelist and poet was a true man of the theater in his plays. *Quoat quoat* (1946, Quoat Quoat), *Evil Is in the Air, L'effet Glapion* (1959, The Glapion Effect) were firmly based on the structures of the drama. Their verve, fantasy, and baroque effervescence are cleverly linked to a symbolic action, whose development carries us vigorously along. *Evil Is in the Air* was Audiberti's masterpiece, and no doubt one of the best plays produced since World War II. Its freedom and its clowning did not hide its profundity. Although Audiberti had no explicit philosophy, he told us himself that he "never deviated from this single subject, the conflict between good and evil, between soul and flesh: the problem of incarnation."

The most recent theater has been characterized by two tendencies: a word play that revolutionized theatrical form and led to a questioning of language itself; and an exploration of psychology and of society. Some plays have clearly been on one side or other of this division; some have deliberately been on the border. Jean Tardieu has mastered the minor theatrical form of "stylistic exercises"—not full-length plays but playlets, monologues, and humorous sketches for small-scale theaters or cabarets. The contemporaneity of Tardieu's plays comes from their giving the problem of language its due; he is far indeed from any sociological interest.

René de Obaldia (born 1918) has written novels, notably *Tamerlan des cœurs* (1955, Tamburlaine of Hearts), as well as a number of richly parodic plays, in which one finds that rare combination of amusement and intelligence. His "chamber western," *Du vent dans les branches de sassafras* (1965, Wind in the Branches of the Sassafras), has been his best play to date. There was also burlesque and the inventiveness of the highest comedy in Roland Dubillard's (born 1923) *Naïves hirondelles* (1961, Naïve Swallows), *La maison d'os* (1962, The House of Bone), and *Le jardin de betteraves* (1969, The Sugar-Beet Garden)—but also much anguish and disquiet. The "house of bone" is the body about to give up its consciousness, during a long death agony.

The theater of Jean Vauthier (born 1910) has been a theater of language. He, too, has been concerned with the condition of man rather than of society. *Capitaine Bada* (1952, Captain Bada), his best work to date, was an extraordinary monologue that exteriorized the dreams and fantasies of the hero, a would-be author who is prevented from writing by words.

The political theater is, however, at least in quantitative terms, even more important than the poetic theater, and Brecht has had an enormous influence over the past several decades. Wishing to attract to the theater those who had never shown interest in it, and addressing themselves no longer to the traditional middle-class public but to the working class, these playwrights and directors have sought to make contact through their new public's preoccupations, which are societal and full of revolutionary feeling. The majority of the regional dramatic centers and young companies have a distinctly political outlook. A good example is the Théâtre National Populaire, directed by Jean Vilar from 1951, the year of its foundation, until 1963. His successor, Georges Wilson, who has recently left, somewhat reduced these political tendencies.

The development of Arthur Adamov's (1908–1970) career was representative of the movement from the inner to the outer, from the poetic to the political. Although his first plays, including *Le professeur Taranne* (1953, Professor Taranne), attacked, in the tradition of Strindberg and Ionesco, the human image itself, in *Le ping-pong* (1955, Ping Pong) the slot machine, which is the play's central character, is primarily a symbol of the regimented society Adamov was rebelling against. In *Paolo Paoli* (1957, Paolo Paoli), *La politique des restes* (1967, The Politics of the Remainder) and *Off Limits* (1969, the title is in English) he deepened this political commitment and simultaneously showed the tendency to return to realism: Adamov's schizophrenic lyricism reached its limit and found its antidote, as the author himself put it, in the awareness that the object (the slot machine for instance) was the "product of a particular society" and has a "particular purpose: to earn money and prestige."

Georges Michel's (born 1926) plays—*La promenade du dimanche* (1967, The Sunday Walk), *L'agression* (1967, Aggression)—belong to the theater of social criticism, as do Armand Gatti's (born 1924) *La vie imaginaire de l'éboueur Auguste Geai* (1962, The Imaginary Life of Auguste Geai the Road Sweeper), *Chant public devant deux chaises électriques* (1964, Public Song before Two Electric Chairs), and *V comme Vietnam* (1967, V for Vietnam). Gatti has shown the tendency to get lost among a maze of divergent experiments with technique. The plays of François Billetdoux (born 1927)—*Tchin-tchin* (1959, Tchin-Tchin), *Va donc chez Törpe* (1961, Well, Go Along to Törpe's Place), *Comment va le monde, môssieu? Il tourne, môssieu!* (1964, How Is the World, Mister? It's Turning, Mister!)—have been clever, even perhaps too clever. Billetdoux has followed the same path of accusation as has Gatti, but Billetdoux knows how to achieve distance and the trappings of myth.

More complex, and finding a unity among the various movements through the personality of the writer himself (either a novelist or a poet), have been the plays of Robert Pinget (*Lettre morte* [1959, Dead Letter]); Marguerite Duras (*Le square* [1957, The Square], *L'amante anglaise* [1968, The English Mistress]); Nathalie Sarraute (*Le silence* [1964, Silence], *Le mensonge* [1966, The Lie]); and Romain Weingarten (born 1926) (*Akara* [1948, Akara], *L'été* [1966, Summer]). But it is clearly in the plays of Samuel Beckett and Jean Genet that the theater expressing the personality of the writer has achieved its highest expression.

Eugène Ionesco, who came to France from Rumania in 1945, is the only writer of recent years who has earned an important place in literary history through his plays alone. His other writings, such as *Journal en miettes* (1967, Fragments of a Journal), have not been creations of a different kind, but commentaries on his one mode of creation. Rather like Samuel Beckett, Ionesco also had to face the possibility of capitulating before his philosophical dilemmas and his struggle with language. Instead, they have both created work that is classic in a sense, ample, and constantly developing, nourished by spontaneous inspiration, and sustained by the supreme mastery of the structures of expression.

Like Adamov and others, Ionesco has passed from an anti-theater limited to quirks of language and reflections of the inner self to a discussion of the problems of contemporary society. But Ionesco has been almost the only one to link a revolution in literary form to a *rejection* of political revolution, for his pessimism about history is the inevitable outgrowth of the pessimism of his philosophy.

Ionesco's first plays, all one-acters, which so questioned language and the theater itself, found an audience in the tiny experimental theaters, such as the Théâtre des Noctambules and the Théâtre de la Huchette. If we are to take Ionesco's word for it, his first effort at playwriting was an unexpected consequence of his starting to learn English by the *Assimil* method. Nothing could have been further from his mind than an interest in the theater; but he suddenly saw that the elements of cliché, the unexpected, the discontinuity, and the pointlessness of the examples of conversations contained infinitely more comic power than all the plays in the repertory.

His first intention was thus to drive to paroxysm those elements of rupture, absurdity, and artifice inherent in language and drama, and to obtain from this exaggeration new forms of comedy and tragedy, something that at any rate would be extreme and intolerable. In *La leçon* (1950, The Lesson), and *La cantatrice chauve* (1948, The Bald Soprano) the characters were little more than the mouthpieces for disjointed speech: their marionette- or robot-like gestures indicated how language can turn us into machines. At the same time, the gestures parodied the traditional theater. Here, as Ionesco said in *Jacques, ou la soumission* (1950, Jack, or the Submission), "the drawing-room comedy decomposes and goes mad!" In *The Chairs* Ionesco took his investigation further. Two old people get a deaf-mute orator to transmit an incomprehensible message, after their suicides, to an audience of empty chairs. This message no longer represents the emptiness only of language but of life and of the universe.

As Ionesco's drama has developed, it has expanded. *Amédée, ou comment s'en débarrasser* (1954, Amédée, or How to Get Rid of It) was his first three-act play. One single room no longer limits the action. There is also a street, a town and its inhabitants, the sky and its stars. There is an action, which passes through a series of comic modes (and through the parody of tragedy) to an incredible conclusion. The language has an appropriateness to what is talked about, even if that something is nothing; it is dry, terse, restrained.

But it was not really until Ionesco's next several plays, in which the character of Béranger appears—*Tueur sans gages* (1957, Killer without Wages), *Le rhinocéros* (1959, Rhinoceros), *Le piéton de l'air* (1962, A Stroll in the Air), *Le roi se meurt* (1962, The King Is Dying)—that he began to relate his questions (which remained, of course, primarily metaphysical) to the contemporary period and its problems. "It is not a particular society that I feel to be absurd; it is man himself," he has said clearly. One can see, however, how society piles absurdity upon this absurdity: in *Rhinoceros* all the people turn into insensitive pachyderms in front of the "hero," who remains isolated in his humanity; and this is how a country becomes Nazified or bolshevized.

In *A Stroll in the Air* Ionesco looked at an unreal world, which he called an anti-world: the hero rises at first into the air, as if thanks to a mystical experience, and gazes about him as if he were seeing for the first time, but then falls back onto an earth covered with mire and blood. There is no way out. In *The King Is Dying* Ionesco presented a striking image of human life as a progress toward death: Béranger I, a derisory king, accompanied by a servant, a guard, his two wives, and a doctor-executioner, performs the stages of a ceremony that ends in nothingness. In *La soif et la faim* (1964, Thirst and Hunger) Ionesco took up similar themes less convincingly.

Ionesco has offered no solutions, unless it be in the catharsis of the theater, its laughter or its derision (despite Ionesco's declaration that he only resorts to humor out of habit). Amid disquiet and risibility, amid shock elements that are sometimes comic and sometimes disturbing, we are presented with the paradox of creation following its course, although the course leads nowhere.

The new theater of Ionesco, Genet, Beckett, and Adamov is beginning to look traditional. For they have not really altered the relationship between play and spectator. Brecht had attempted to alter that relationship through distancing alienation—an approach that insisted that the theater is not life. The newest trend in altering the function of the theater has been a reversal of Brecht's approach. Continuing Artaud's protest and demands, under the immediate influence of the American troupe The Living Theater and of the Polish director Jerzy Grotowski, whose *The Constant Prince* was a great success in Paris in 1968, the youngest playwrights and directors (frequently one man occupies both functions) have sought a mixture of theater and life that will abolish the footlights, the separation between stage and spectators. They have also sought to eliminate the text as a previously written and complete creation, in favor of a collective improvization, a "happening."

In this participatory theater, there is a nostalgia for a primitive state of affairs when the theater was a collective celebration, a longing for total liberation, or rather the annihilation of the individual in favor of a communal ecstasy. It is a Dionysian theater, in which bodily expression matters more than the text.

Fernando Arrabal (born 1932), who has written, among other plays, *Le cimetière des voitures* (1958, The Automobile Graveyard), defined the theater in terms that were clearly reminiscent of Artaud: "At present, a number of different personalities in different parts of the world are trying to create a form of theater pushed to its ultimate consequences. Despite the enormous differences between our efforts, we are turning theater into a festival, a ceremony built on a rigorous pattern. Tragedy and puppet show, poetry and vulgarity, comedy and melodrama, love and eroticism, happening and set theory, bad taste and aesthetic refinement, sacrilege and the sacred, condemnation to death and exaltation of life, the sordid and the sublime, are natural parts of this festival, this ceremony of Pan."

Whatever the future of such experiments may be, they cannot by definition form part of literature. Drama has in the past been simultaneously text and spectacle; this is why it has never completely belonged to the history of literature. But if it becomes no more than a spectacle, a demonstration, a moment in the life of the collectivity, it will cease to have anything at all to do with literature.

FROM CREATION TO CRITICISM

Thought, in the form it takes in the essay, has always formed part of literary creation: Michel Montaigne (1553–1592), Blaise Pascal (1623–1662), and Charles-Louis de Montesquieu (1689–1755) were among the greatest figures in French literature. The role of the essay as part of literature certainly was major in the years following World War II. Sartre and Camus were important essayists as well as novelists and playwrights. Georges Bataille's literary contribution is difficult to classify; but if a genre must be applied, it most closely resembles the essay.

Jean Paulhan's subtle and highly individual work was devoted to the problem of language, from *The Flowers of Tarbes* and *Clef de la poésie* (1944, The Key to Poetry) to *La preuve par l'étymologie* (1953, Proof by Etymology). Language has also been the major concern of Roger Caillois (born 1913), in *Le mythe et l'homme* (1938, Myth and Man), *Babel* (1948, Babel), and *Les jeux et les hommes* (1958, Games and Men), and of Brice Parain (1897–1971). Maurice Blanchot's meditations, beginning with his analyses in *False Step*, have taken the form of a mystique of negation. All of these men have been essayists in the traditional sense— writers who manipulate general concepts or certain scientific data so as to give their personal answers to vital questions.

The leading thinkers of the most recent period appear to be *scientists*, or, more precisely, explorers of human sciences that are in process of creation. They have based their authority on the theoretical apparatus of linguistics, ethnology, semiology, and psychoanalysis—an apparatus that is anonymous and objective in theory. In the name of consciousness, by a personal decision, their forerunners denounced the illusions of consciousness, and this allowed them to speak as writers. The decisive break came with the rejection of the Cartesian *cogito*, to which Sartre's, Camus's, and Maurice Merleau-Ponty's (1908–1961) thought was still related.

This break was applied to ethnology by Claude Lévi-Strauss (born 1908), who has relied on structuralism to eradicate all ethnocentrism. In psychoanalysis, Jacques Lacan (born 1901) formulated an *anti-cogito* that exorcised psychology ("I think where I am not; therefore, I am where I do not think"). And Roland Barthes, Louis Althusser (born 1918), and Jacques Derrida (born 1932) have proposed *readings* of phenomena, of the economy, or of writing itself, by going from the superficial surface of the discourse (which corresponds to reality no better than our picture of it corresponds to physical reality) back to the underlying discourse.

One may be tempted to omit these writers from the study of literature, on the grounds that their work is scientific; but their influence on literature itself should be enough to make us take note. On the one hand, structuralism stands for an attitude, a choice that presents itself both in literature and in art: by the chilly anonymity of science these writers have expressed their deep-seated antihumanism, their rejection of any form of personal experience. On the other hand, the human sciences are still far from attaining the objective status of the natural sciences; and they have in them much that is prescientific and consequently leaves considerable room for creativity and imagination.

Thus, whether they like it or not, the anti-Cartesian essayists are part of literature and can be compared stylistically to other writers. Jacques Lacan in his *Écrits* (1966, Writings) has shown a preciosity reminiscent of Stéphane Mallarmé (1842–1898) and even of the Spaniard Luis de Góngora. Roland Barthes revealed a felicitous style and imagination in *Mythologies* (1965, Mythologies), *Système de la mode* (1967, The System of Fashion), and *L'empire des signes* (1969, The Empire of Signs). Louis Althusser, in *Lire le Capital* (1965, Reading "Capital") and *Pour Marx* (1965, For Marx), and Jacques Derrida, in *L'écriture et la différence* (1967, Writing and Difference), both used inspired, muted tones, whispering on the brink of mystery, allowing words to guide their footsteps. Michel Foucault (born 1926), an historical philosopher, certainly showed himself to be a gifted writer in *Les mots et les choses* (1966, Words and Things). And Claude Lévi-Strauss, a meticulous scientist, showed himself a writer of great talent in *Tristes tropiques* (1955, Sad Tropics) and in the finale of his impressive *Mythologiques* (1964–72, Mythologics).

Literary criticism has always belonged to literature itself, and this has never been truer than today: the argument over the "new criticism" (or criticisms) is inseparable from that over the "new novel" and the "new theater." The view of "existential" criticism is that the origin and very essence of the work can be found in the writer's experience. This experience occurs at a deep level, however, without the author's being fully aware of it; thus, the criticism has nothing to do with biographical anecdotes. Outstanding among the existential critics have been Gaston Bachelard (1884–1962) (from *La psychanalyse du feu* [1937, The Psychoanalysis of Fire] to *La poétique de l'espace* [1957, The Poetics of Space]); Georges Poulet (born 1914) (*Études sur le temps humain* [1950, Studies in

Human Time], *La distance intérieure* [1952, The Interior Distance]); and Jean-Pierre Richard (born 1922). Sartre's study of Flaubert, *The Idiot of the Family,* was also representative of this type of criticism.

But the last ten years have been even more dominated by a formalist criticism, in which the work is interpreted not by the ideology or the hidden life of its author but by the latent system of language. Seeking patterns in language, narrative, and poetics, Roland Barthes, Gérard Genette (born 1930), Tzvetan Todorov (born 1935), and Jean Cohen (born 1936) have been working toward a formalization of the theory of literature—no longer an analysis of the work but a theory of literariness, tending toward a history of texts divorced from authors and dates.

But there has also been a sociological criticism, usually Marxist. It has been developed by such critics as Lucien Goldmann (1913–1970), in such works as *Le dieu caché* (1955, The Hidden God). But Georges Blin (born 1917), in his works on Stendhal, and especially Jean Starobinski (born 1920), in *L'œil vivant* (1961–70, The Living Eye), for example, have drawn on all these approaches, without overlooking historical accuracy or the work's own reality as an individual phenomenon that can also be enjoyed. This, of course, has rubbed against the grain of current intellectual fashion, which sees in "enjoyment" a gastronomic habit connected with the much-challenged consumer society.

It is undoubtedly a sign of the times that theoretical and critical thinking has increasingly been considered as a major literary event. And it is a sign that we may well find disturbing. This movement away from "nonscientific," imaginative works and toward scientific ideas signals a victory for the intellect but a setback for the creative instinct.

FRENCH WORKS IN ENGLISH TRANSLATION

INDIVIDUAL WORKS MENTIONED
IN ARTICLE

Achard, Marcel. *Auprès de ma blonde* as *I Know My Love.* New York, 1952
———. *Patate* as *Rollo.* London, 1960
Adamov, Arthur. *Paolo Paoli* as *Paolo Paoli.* London, 1960
———. *Le ping-pong* as *Ping Pong.* New York, 1959
———. *Le professeur Taranne* as *Professor Taranne.* In *Four Modern French Comedies.* New York, 1960

Althusser, Louis. *Pour Marx* as *For Marx.* New York, 1969
Althusser, Louis and Étienne Balibar. *Lire le Capital* as *Reading "Capital."* New York, 1971
Anouilh, Jean. *L'alouette* as *The Lark.* In *Five Plays,* vol. 2. New York, 1959
———. *Antigone* as *Antigone.* In *Five Plays,* vol. 1. New York, 1958
———. *Ardèle, ou la marguerite* as *Ardele.* In *Five Plays,* vol. 2. New York, 1959
———. *Becket, ou l'honneur de Dieu* as

Becket, or the Honor of God. New York, 1960

———. *Cher Antoine* as *Dear Antoine.* New York, 1971

———. *La foire d'empoigne* as *Catch as Catch Can.* In *Seven Plays,* vol. 3. New York, 1967

———. *L'hermine* as *The Ermine.* In *Five Plays,* vol. 1. New York, 1958

———. *Pauvre Bitos* as *Poor Bitos.* New York, 1964

———. *La sauvage* as *Restless Heart.* In *Five Plays,* vol. 2. New York, 1959

———. *La valse des toréadors* as *The Waltz of the Toreadors.* New York, 1957

———. *Le voyageur sans bagage* as *Traveler without Luggage.* In *Seven Plays,* vol. 3. New York, 1967

Apollinaire, Guillaume. *Les mamelles de Tirésias* as *The Breasts of Tiresias.* In Michael Benedikt and George Wellwarth, eds., *Modern French Theatre.* New York, 1966

Aragon, Louis. *Aurélien* as *Aurélien.* New York, 1947

———. *Les beaux quartiers* as *Residential Quarter.* New York, 1938

———. *Les cloches de Bâle* as *The Bells of Basel.* New York, 1936

———. *Le paysan de Paris* as *Nightwalker.* Englewood Cliffs, N.J., 1970

———. *Les voyageurs de l'impériale* as *Passengers of Destiny.* London, 1949

Arrabal, Fernando. *Le cimetière des voitures* as *The Automobile Graveyard.* In *The Automobile Graveyard, and The Two Executioners.* New York, 1960

Artaud, Antonin. *Au pays des Tarahumaras* as *Concerning a Journey to the Land of the Tarahumaras.* In *Antonin Artaud Anthology.* San Francisco, 1965

———. *Les Cenci* as *The Cenci.* New York, 1970

———. *L'ombilic des limbes* as *Umbilical Limbo.* In *Collected Works,* vol 1. London, 1968

———. *Le théâtre et son double* as *The Theater and Its Double.* New York, 1958

———. *Van Gogh, le suicidé de la société* as *Van Gogh: The Man Suicided by Society.* In *Antonin Artaud Anthology.* San Francisco, 1965

Aymé, Marcel. *Clérambard* as *Clérambard.* In *Four Modern French Comedies.* New York, 1960

Bachelard, Gaston. *La poétique de l'espace* as *The Poetics of Space.* New York, 1964

———. *La psychanalyse du feu* as *The Psychoanalysis of Fire.* Boston, 1964

Barthes, Roland. *Mythologies* as *Mythologies.* New York, 1972.

Bataille, Georges. *Lascaux, ou la naissance de l'art* as *Lascaux, or the Birth of Art.* Lausanne, 1955

———. *Manet* as *Manet.* New York, 1955

Beauvoir, Simone de. *Le deuxième sexe* as *The Second Sex.* New York, 1953

———. *La force de l'âge* as *The Prime of Life.* Cleveland, 1962

———. *L'invitée* as *She Came to Stay.* Cleveland, 1954

———. *Les Mandarins* as *The Mandarins.* New York, 1960

———. *Mémoires d'une jeune fille rangée* as *Memories of a Dutiful Daughter.* Cleveland, 1959

———. *Le sang des autres* as *The Blood of Others.* New York, 1948

———. *Tous les hommes sont mortels* as *All Men Are Mortal.* Cleveland, 1955

———. *La vieillesse* as *The Coming of Age.* New York, 1972

Beckett, Samuel. *Comment c'est* as *How It Is.* New York, 1964

———. *En attendant Godot* as *Waiting for Godot.* New York, 1954

———. *Fin de partie* as *Endgame.* In *Endgame/Act without Words.* New York, 1958

———. *Happy Days.* New York, 1961

———. *L'innommable* as *The Unnamable.* In *Three Novels.* New York, 1965

———. *Malone meurt* as *Malone Dies.* In *Three Novels.* New York, 1965

———. *Molloy* as *Molloy.* In *Three Novels.* New York, 1965

Bernanos, Georges. *Dialogues des Carmélites* as *The Fearless Heart.* London, 1952

———. *La France contre les robots* as *Tradition of Freedom.* London, 1950

———. *Journal d'un curé de campagne* as *The Diary of a Country Priest.* New York, 1962

———. *Lettre aux Anglais* as *Plea for Liberty: Letters to the English, the*

Americans, the Europeans. New York, 1944

———. *Un mauvais rêve* as *Night Is Darkest.* London, 1953

———. *Monsieur Ouine* as *The Open Mind.* London, 1945

———. *Sous le soleil de Satan* as *Under the Sun of Satan.* New York, 1949

Billetdoux, François. *Tchin-tchin* as *Tchin-Tchin.* In *Two Plays.* New York, 1964

———. *Va donc chez Törpe* as *Chez Torpe.* In *Two Plays.* New York, 1964

Bonnefoy, Yves. *Du mouvement et de l'immobilité de Douve* as *On the Motion and Immobility of Douve.* Athens, Ohio, 1968

Bosco, Henri. *Le mas Théotime* as *Farm in Provence.* Garden City, N.Y., 1947

Breton, André. *Ode à Charles Fourier* as *Ode to Charles Fourier.* London, 1969

Butor, Michel. *L'emploi du temps* as *Passing Time.* In *Passing Time, and A Change of Heart: Two Novels.* New York, 1969

———. *Mobile* as *Mobile.* New York, 1963

———. *La modification* as *A Change of Heart.* In *Passing Time, and A Change of Heart: Two Novels.* New York, 1969

Caillois, Roger. *Les jeux et les hommes* as *Man, Play, and Games.* New York, 1961

Camus, Albert. *Caligula* as *Caligula.* In *Caligula, and Three Other Plays.* New York, 1958

———. *La chute* as *The Fall.* New York, 1957

———. *L'état de siège* as *State of Siege.* In *Caligula, and Three Other Plays.* New York, 1958

———. *L'étranger* as *The Stranger.* New York, 1946

———. *L'exil et le royaume* as *Exile and the Kingdom.* New York, 1958

———. *L'homme révolté* as *The Rebel: An Essay on Man in Revolt.* New York, 1954

———. *Les justes* as *The Just Assassins.* In *Caligula, and Three Other Plays.* New York, 1958

———. *Le malentendu* as *The Misunderstanding.* In *Caligula, and Three Other Plays.* New York, 1958

———. *Le mythe de Sisyphe* as *The Myth of Sisyphus.* New York, 1955

———. *La peste* as *The Plague.* New York, 1948

Céline, Louis-Ferdinand. *D'un château l'autre* as *Castle to Castle.* New York, 1968

———. *Mort à credit* as *Death on the Installment Plan.* New York, 1966

———. *Nord* as *North.* New York, 1972

———. *Voyage au bout de la nuit* as *Journey to the End of the Night.* New York, 1947

Césaire, Aimé. *Cahier d'un retour au pays natal* as *Return to My Native Land.* Baltimore, 1969

———. *Une saison au Congo* as *A Season in the Congo.* New York, 1969

Char, René. *Feuillets d'Hypnos* as *Hypnos Waking.* New York, 1956

Claudel, Paul. *L'histoire de Tobie et de Sara* as *Tobias and Sara.* In Richard Francis Hayes, ed., *Port-Royal, and Other Plays.* New York, 1962

———. *Le livre de Christophe Colomb* as *The Book of Christopher Columbus.* New Haven, Conn., 1930

———. *L'otage* as *The Hostage.* In *Three Plays.* Boston, 1945

———. *Partage de midi* as *Break of Noon.* In *Two Dramas.* Chicago, 1960

———. *Le soulier de satin* as *The Satin Slipper.* New Haven, Conn., 1931

———. *Tête d'or* as *Tête d'Or.* New Haven, Conn., 1919

———. *La ville* as *The City.* New Haven, Conn., 1920

Daumal, René. *Mont-Analogue* as *Mount Analogue.* San Francisco, 1968

Dubillard, Roland. *Naïves hirondelles* as *Naïves Hirondelles.* New York, 1968

Duras, Marguerite. *L'amante anglaise* as *L'Amante Anglaise.* New York, 1968

———. *Détruire, dit-elle* as *Destroy, She Said.* New York, 1970

———. *Moderato cantabile* as *Moderato Cantabile.* In *Four Novels.* New York, 1965

———. *Les petits chevaux de Tarquinia* as *The Little Horses of Tarquinia.* London, 1960

———. *Le square* (novel) as *The Square.* In *Four Novels.* New York, 1965

———. *Le square* (play) as *The Square.* In *Three Plays.* London, 1967

Gary, Romain. *Éducation européenne* as *A European Education.* New York, 1960

Gascar, Pierre. *Le temps des morts* as *The Season of the Dead.* In *Beasts and Men.* Boston, 1956

Genet, Jean. *Le balcon* as *The Balcony.* New York, 1960

———. *Les bonnes* as *The Maids.* In *The Maids and Deathwatch: Two Plays.* New York, 1954

———. *Journal du voleur* as *The Thief's Journal.* New York, 1964

———. *Miracle de la rose* as *Miracle of the Rose.* New York, 1966

———. *Les nègres* as *The Blacks.* New York, 1960

———. *Notre-Dame des Fleurs* as *Our Lady of the Flowers.* New York, 1963

Ghelderode, Michel de. *Fastes d'enfer* as *Chronicles of Hell.* In *Seven Plays,* vol. 1. New York, 1960

———. *Hop, signor!* as *Hop, Signor!* In *Seven Plays,* vol. 2. New York, 1964

Gide, André. *Journal 1942–1949* as *The Journals of André Gide,* vol. 4: 1939–49. New York, 1951

———. *Thésée* as *Theseus.* In *Two Legends: Oedipus and Theseus.* New York, 1950

Gide, André and Jean-Louis Barrault. *Le procès* as *The Trial.* New York, 1964

Giono, Jean. *Angelo* as *Angelo.* London, 1960

———. *Le bonheur fou* as *The Straw Man.* New York, 1959

———. *Le hussard sur le toit* as *The Horseman on the Roof.* New York, 1966

Giraudoux, Jean. *La folle de Chaillot* as *The Madwoman of Chaillot.* New York, 1949

———. *La menteuse* as *Lying Woman.* New York, 1972

Goldmann, Lucien. *Le dieu caché* as *The Hidden God.* New York, 1964

Gracq, Julien. *Au château d'Argol* as *The Castle of Argol.* Norfolk, Conn., 1951

———. *Un balcon en forêt* as *Balcony in the Forest.* New York, 1959

———. *Un beau ténébreux* as *A Dark Stranger.* Norfolk, Conn., 1950

Green, Julien. *Moïra* as *Moira.* New York, 1951

———. *Sud* as *South.* In J. C. Trewin, ed., *Plays of the Year,* vol. 12. London, 1955

———. *Le voyageur sur la terre* as *The Pilgrim on Earth.* New York, 1929

Guilloux, Louis. *Le sang noir* as *Bitter Victory.* New York, 1938

Ionesco, Eugène. *Amédée, ou comment s'en débarrasser* as *Amédée, or How to Get Rid of It.* In *Three Plays.* New York, 1958

———. *La cantatrice chauve* as *The Bald Soprano.* In *Four Plays.* New York, 1958

———. *Les chaises* as *The Chairs.* In *Four Plays.* New York, 1958

———. *Jacques, ou la soumission* as *Jack, or The Submission.* In *Four Plays.* New York, 1958

———. *Journal en miettes* as *Fragments of a Journal.* New York, 1968

———. *La leçon* as *The Lesson.* In *Four Plays.* New York, 1958

———. *Le piéton de l'air* as *A Stroll in the Air.* In *A Stroll in the Air & Frenzy for Two or More: Two Plays.* New York, 1968

———. *Le rhinocéros* as *Rhinoceros.* In *Rhinoceros, and Other Plays.* New York, 1960

———. *Le roi se meurt* as *Exit the King.* New York, 1968

———. *Tueur sans gages* as *The Killer.* In *The Killer, and Other Plays.* New York, 1960

Jarry, Alfred. *Ubu roi* as *King Ubu.* In Michael Benedikt and George Wellwarth, eds., *Modern French Theatre.* New York, 1966

Jouve, Pierre Jean. *Le Don Juan de Mozart* as *Mozart's Don Juan.* London, 1957

———. *Ténèbre* as *An Idiom of Night.* Chicago, 1969

La Tour du Pin, Patrice de. *Une somme de poésie* as *The Dedicated Life in Poetry and The Correspondence of Laurent de Cayeux.* London, 1948

Laurent, Jacques. *Caroline chérie* as *Caroline Chérie.* New York, 1952

Le Clézio, J. M. G. *La fièvre* as *Fever.* New York, 1966

———. *Le procès-verbal* as *The Interrogation.* New York, 1964

Leduc, Violette. *La bâtarde* as *La Bâtarde.* New York, 1965

Leiris, Michel. *L'âge d'homme* as *Manhood.* In *Manhood, Preceded by The Autobiographer as Torero.* London, 1968

Lévi-Strauss, Claude. *Tristes tropiques* as *Tristes Tropiques*. New York, 1964

Malraux, André. *Antimémoires* as *Anti-Memoirs*. New York, 1968

———. *Les chênes qu'on abat* as *Felled Oaks*. New York, 1972

———. *La condition humaine* as *Man's Fate*. New York, 1936

———. *Les conquérants* as *The Conquerors*. New York, 1929

———. *L'espoir* as *Man's Hope*. New York, 1938.

———. *La métamorphose des dieux* as *The Metamorphosis of the Gods,* vol. 1. Garden City, N.Y., 1960

———. *Les noyers de l'Altenburg* as *The Walnut Trees of Altenburg*. London, 1952

———. *Saturne* as *Saturn, an Essay on Goya*. New York, 1957

———. *Le temps du mépris* as *Days of Wrath*. New York, 1964

———. *La tentation de l'occident* as *The Temptation of the West*. New York, 1961

———. *La voie royale* as *The Royal Way*. New York, 1935

———. *Les voix du silence* as *The Voices of Silence*. New York, 1953

Marceau, Félicien. *L'œuf* as *The Egg*. London, 1958

Martin du Gard, Roger. *Les Thibault* (parts 1–6) as *The Thibaults*. New York, 1939; *Les Thibaults* (parts 7–8) as *Summer 1914*. New York, 1941

Mauriac, François. *Un adolescent d'autrefois* as *Maltaverne*. New York, 1970

———. *Asmodée* as *Asmodée*. In Richard Francis Hayes, ed., *Port-Royal, and Other Plays*. New York, 1962

———. *Le feu sur la terre* as *The River of Fire*. London, 1954

———. *Le nœud de vipères* as *Vipers' Tangle*. New York, 1947

Merle, Robert. *Week-end à Zuydcoote* as *Weekend at Dunkirk*. New York, 1951

Michaux, Henri. *Un barbare en Asie* as *A Barbarian in Asia*. Norfolk, Conn., 1949

———. *Misérable miracle* as *Miserable Miracle: Mescaline*. San Francisco, 1967

Michel, Georges. *La promenade du dimanche* as *The Sunday Walk*. London, 1968

Montherlant, Henry de. *Le cardinal d'Espagne* as *The Cardinal of Spain*. In J. C. Trewin, ed., *Plays of the Year,* vol. 37. London, 1969

———. *Le chaos et la nuit* as *Chaos and Night*. New York, 1964

———. *La guerre civile* as *Civil War*. In Robert Baldick, ed., *Theatre of War*. Harmondsworth, England, 1967

———. *Les jeunes filles* as *The Girls: A Tetralogy of Novels*. New York, 1968

———. *La reine morte* as *Queen after Death*. In *The Master of Santiago, and Four Other Plays*. New York, 1951

———. *La rose de sable* as *Desert Love*. New York, 1957

———. *Le songe* as *The Dream*. New York, 1963

Obaldia, René de. *Du vent dans les branches de sassafras* as *Wind in the Branches of the Sassafras*. In *Modern International Drama,* vol. 1, no. 2, March, 1968

Pieyre de Mandiargues, André. *La marge* as *The Margin*. New York, 1969

———. *La motocyclette* as *The Motorcycle*. New York, 1965

Pinget, Robert. *L'inquisitoire* as *The Inquisitory*. New York, 1967

———. *Lettre morte* as *Dead Letter*. In *Plays,* vol. 1. New York, 1966

Ponge, Francis. *Le savon* as *Soap*. London, 1969

Poulet, Georges. *La distance intérieure* as *The Interior Distance*. Baltimore, 1959

———. *Études sur le temps humain* as *Studies in Human Time*. Baltimore, 1956

Prévert, Jacques. *Paroles* as *Selections from Paroles*. San Francisco, 1958

Queneau, Raymond. *Le chiendent* as *The Bark-Tree*. London, 1968

———. *Exercices de style* as *Exercises in Style*. New York, 1958

———. *Les fleurs bleues* as *The Blue Flowers*. New York, 1967

———. *Loin de Rueil* as *The Skin of Dreams*. Norfolk, Conn., 1948

———. *Pierrot mon ami* as *Pierrot: A Novel*. London, 1950

———. *Zazie dans le métro* as *Zazie*. New York, 1960

Robbe-Grillet, Alain. *La jalousie* as *Jealousy*. New York, 1959

———. *Projet pour une révolution à*

New York as *Project for a Revolution in New York*. New York, 1972

———. *Le voyeur* as *The Voyeur*. New York, 1967

Roblès, Emmanuel. *Montserrat* as *Montserrat*. New York, 1950

Rouset, David. *L'univers concentrationnaire* as *The Other Kingdom*. New York, 1947

Roussin, André. *La petite hutte* as *The Little Hut*. New York, 1952

Roy, Jules. *La vallée heureuse* as *The Happy Valley*. London, 1952

Sagan, Françoise. *Bonjour tristesse* as *Bonjour Tristesse*. New York, 1955

———. *Un certain sourire* as *A Certain Smile*. New York, 1956

Saint-Exupéry, Antoine de. *Citadelle* as *The Wisdom of the Sands*. New York, 1950

———. *Pilote de guerre* as *Flight to Arras*. New York, 1942

———. *Terre des hommes* as *Wind, Sand, and Stars*. New York, 1949

———. *Vol de nuit* as *Night Flight*. New York, 1932

Saint-John Perse. *Amers* as *Seamarks*. New York, 1958

———. *Anabase* as *Anabasis,* new ed. London, 1959

———. *Chronique* as *Chronique*. New York, 1961

———. *Éloges* as *Éloges*. In *Éloges, and Other Poems*. New York, 1956

———. *Exil* as *Exile*. In *Exile, and Other Poems*. New York, 1949

———. *Neiges* as *Snows*. In *Exile, and Other Poems*. New York, 1949

———. *Oiseaux* as *Birds*. New York, 1966

———. *Pluies* as *Rains*. In *Exile, and Other Poems*. New York, 1949

———. *Vents* as *Winds,* 2nd ed. New York, 1961

Sarraute, Nathalie. *Entre la vie et la mort* as *Between Life and Death*. New York, 1969

———. *L'ère du soupçon* as *The Age of Suspicion*. New York, 1963

———. *Les fruits d'or* as *The Golden Fruits*. New York, 1964

———. *Le mensonge* as *The Lie*. In *Silence, and The Lie*. London, 1969

———. *Le planétarium* as *The Planetarium*. New York, 1960

———. *Le silence* as *Silence*. In *Silence, and The Lie*. London, 1969

———. *Tropismes* as *Tropisms*. New York, 1967

Sartre, Jean-Paul. *L'âge de raison* as *The Age of Reason*. New York, 1947

———. *Critique de la raison dialectique* as *Search for a Method*. New York, 1963

———. *Le Diable et le bon Dieu* as *The Devil & the Good Lord*. In *The Devil & the Good Lord, and Two Other Plays*. New York, 1960

———. *L'être et le néant* as *Being and Nothingness*. New York, 1956

———. *Huis clos* as *No Exit*. In *No Exit & The Flies*. New York, 1947

———. *L' imaginaire* as *The Psychology of Imagination*. New York, 1961

———. *Intimité* as *Intimacy*. In *Intimacy, and Other Stories*. New York, 1963

———. *M. François Mauriac et la liberté* as *François Mauriac and Freedom*. In *Literary and Philosophical Essays*. New York, 1955

———. *Les mains sales* as *Dirty Hands*. In *Three Plays*. New York, 1949

———. *La mort dans l'âme* as *Troubled Sleep*. New York, 1951

———. *Les mots* as *The Words*. New York, 1964

———. *Les mouches* as *The Flies*. In *No Exit & The Flies*. New York, 1947

———. *La nausée* as *Nausea*. Norfolk, Conn., 1949

———. *Nekrassov* as *Nekrassov*. In *The Devil & the Good Lord, and Two Other Plays*. New York, 1960

———. *Saint Genet, comédien et martyr* as *Saint Genet, Actor and Martyr*. New York, 1963

———. *Les séquestrés d'Altona* as *The Condemned of Altona*. New York, 1961

———. *Le sursis* as *The Reprieve*. New York, 1947

Schehadé, Georges. *L'histoire de Vasco* as *Vasco*. In Robert Corrigan, ed., *New Theatre of Europe,* vol 2. New York, 1964

Simon, Claude. *L'herbe* as *The Grass*. New York, 1960

———. *Histoire* as *Histoire*. London, 1969

———. *La route des Flandres* as *The Flanders Road*. New York, 1961

———. *Le vent* as *The Wind*. New York, 1959

Sollers, Philippe. *Une curieuse solitude* as *A Strange Solitude*. New York, 1959
———. *Le parc* as *The Park*. London, 1968
Vailland, Roger. *Drôle de jeu* as *Playing with Fire*. London, 1948
Valéry, Paul. *"Mon Faust"* as *"My Faust."* In *Plays*, vol. 3 of *Collected Works*. New York, 1960
———. *Variété* as *Variety*. New York, 1927; *Variety: Second Series*. New York, 1938
Vercors. *La marche à l'étoile* as *Guiding Star*. In *Three Short Novels by Vercors*. Boston, 1947

———. *Le silence de la mer* as *The Silence of the Sea*. New York, 1944
Vian, Boris. *Les bâtisseurs d'empire* as *The Empire Builders*. New York, 1967
———. *L'écume des jours* as *Mood Indigo*. New York, 1968
———. *L'équarissage pour tous* as *The Knacker's ABC: A Paramilitary Vaudeville in One Long Act*. New York, 1968
Yourcenar, Marguerite. *Mémoires d'Hadrien* as *Memoirs of Hadrian*. New York, 1954

SECONDARY WORKS

BIBLIOGRAPHIES AND GUIDES

Boisdeffre, Pierre de, ed. *Dictionnaire de la littérature contemporaine*, 3rd ed. Paris, 1967
Bourin, André and Jean Rousselot. *Dictionnaire de la littérature française contemporaine*, 2nd ed. Paris, 1968
Braun, Sidney D. *Dictionary of French Literature*. New York, 1964
Cabeen, David C., ed. *A Critical Bibliography of French Literature*, 7 vols. Syracuse, N.Y., 1947ff.
Dictionnaire des auteurs français. Paris, 1961
Drevet, M. L. *Bibliographie de la littérature française, 1940–1949*. Geneva, 1955
Grente, G. and A. Pauphilet, eds. *Dictionnaire des lettres françaises*, 6 vols. Paris, 1951ff.
Harvey, Paul and J. E. Heseltine. *The Oxford Companion to French Literature*. Oxford, 1959
Klapp, Otto, ed. *Bibliographie der französischen Literaturwissenschaft*, 7 vols. Frankfurt, 1960ff.
Rousselot, Jean. *Dictionnaire de la poésie française contemporaine*. Paris, 1968

GENERAL WORKS

Albérès, René-Marill. *L'aventure intellectuelle du XXe siècle*. Paris, 1959

———. *Bilan littéraire du XXe siècle*. Paris, 1956
Bédier, Joseph and Paul Hazard. *Histoire de la littérature française illustrée*, 2 vols., 3rd. ed. Paris, 1952
Boisdeffre, Pierre de. *Métamorphose de la littérature*, 2nd. ed. Paris, 1963
Bouvier, Émile. *Les lettres françaises au XXe siècle*. Paris, 1962
Brée, Germaine and Margaret Guiton. *The French Novel from Gide to Camus*. New York, 1962
Brereton, Geoffrey. *A Short History of French Literature*. Baltimore, 1954
Brodin, Pierre. *Présences contemporaines: Littérature*, 3 vols. Paris, 1954–57
Cazamian, Louis. *A History of French Literature*. Oxford, 1955
Clouard, Henri. *Histoire de la littérature française du symbolisme à nos jours*. 2 vols., 2nd ed. Paris, 1960
———. *Petite histoire de la littérature française*. Paris, 1965
Curtius, Ernst Robert. *Französischer Geist im 20. Jahrhundert*, 2nd ed. Bern, 1960
Engler, Winfried. *Französische Literatur im 20. Jahrhundert*. Bern, 1968
———. *The French Novel from Eighteen Hundred to the Present*. New York, 1968
Grossvogel, David I. *20th Century French Drama*, 2nd ed. New York, 1961

Haedens, Kléber. *Une histoire de la littérature française,* 3rd ed. Paris, 1970

Hatzfeld, Helmut. *Trends and Styles in 20th Century French Literature.* Washington, D.C., 1966

Jan, Eduard von. *Französische Literaturgeschichte in Grundzügen,* 6th ed. Heidelberg, 1967

Krause, Gerd. *Tendenzen im französischen Romanschaffen des 20. Jahrhunderts.* Frankfurt, 1962

Lalou, René. *Le roman français depuis 1900,* 2nd. ed. Paris, 1955

———. *Le théâtre en France depuis 1900,* 2nd. ed. Paris, 1958

Lanson, Gustave and P. Truffau. *Manuel illustré d'histoire de la littérature française,* 3rd ed. Paris, 1957

Magny, Claude-Edmonde. *Histoire du roman français depuis 1918,* 2nd ed. Paris, 1956

Moore, Harry T. *Twentieth Century French Literature,* 2 vols. Carbondale, Ill., 1966

Pollmann, Leo. *Der französische Roman im 20. Jahrhundert.* Stuttgart, 1970

Rousseaux, A. *Littérature du XXe siècle,* 7 vols. Paris, 1952–61

Simon, Pierre-Henri. *Histoire de la littérature française au XXe siècle,* 2 vols., 8th ed. Paris, 1965

Theisen, Josef. *Geschichte der französischen Literatur.* Stuttgart, 1964

Turnell, Martin. *The Art of French Fiction.* New York, 1968

WORKS ON CONTEMPORARY LITERATURE

Albérès, René-Marill. *Histoire du roman moderne.* Paris, 1962

Beigbeder, Marc. *Le théâtre en France depuis la Libération.* Paris, 1959

Bernier, Michel Antoine. *Choice of Action: The French Existentialists in the Political Front Lines.* New York, 1968

Bersani, Jacques et al. *La littérature en France depuis 1945.* Paris, 1970

Blanchot, Maurice. *Le livre à venir.* Paris, 1959

Boisdeffre, Pierre de. *Les ecrivains français d'aujourd'hui.* Paris, 1963

———. *Une histoire vivante de la littérature d'aujourd'hui,* 7th ed. Paris, 1968

Butor, Michel. *Essais sur les modernes.* Paris, 1964

Chiari, Joseph. *Contemporary French Poetry.* Manchester, 1952

———. *The Contemporary French Theatre.* New York, 1959

Cruickshank, John, ed. *The Novelist as Philosopher: Studies in French Fiction 1935–1960.* London, 1962

Fletcher, John, ed. *Forces in Modern French Drama: Studies in Variations on the Permitted Lie.* New York, 1972

Fowlie, Wallace. *Climate of Violence.* New York, 1967

———. *Dionysus in Paris: A Guide to Contemporary French Theater.* New York, 1960

———. *A Guide to Contemporary French Literature.* New York, 1957

———. *Mid-century French Poets.* New York, 1955

Girard, Marcel. *Guide illustré de la littérature française moderne,* 3rd ed. Paris, 1962

Gmelin, Hermann. *Der französische Zyklenroman der Gegenwart.* Heidelberg, 1950

Grossvogel, David I. *The Self-conscious Stage in Modern French Drama.* New York, 1958

Guicharnaud, Jacques. *Modern French Theatre: From Giraudoux to Genet,* 2 vols., rev. ed. New Haven, Conn., 1967

Hobson, Harold. *The French Theatre of Today: An English View.* New York, 1965

Janvier, Ludovic. *Une parole exigeante: Le nouveau roman.* Paris, 1964

Lalou, René. *Histoire de la littérature française contemporaine,* 2 vols., 3rd ed. Paris, 1953

Lange, Wolf-Dieter, ed. *Französische Literatur der Gegenwart.* Stuttgart, 1971

Larnac, J. *La littérature française d'aujourd'hui.* Paris, 1948

Lesage, Laurent. *The French New Novel.* University Park, Pa., 1962

Mauriac, Claude. *The New Literature.* New York, 1959

Nadeau, Maurice. *The French Novel since the War.* New York, 1969

———. *Littérature presente.* Paris, 1952

Nathan, Jacques. *Histoire de la littérature française contemporaine, 1919–60.* Paris, 1964

Pabst, Walter, ed. *Das moderne französische Drama.* Berlin, 1971

————. *Der moderne französische Roman.* Berlin, 1968

Peyre, Henri. *French Novelists of Today,* 2nd ed. New York, 1967

Picon, Gaëtan. *Panorama de la nouvelle littérature française,* 3rd ed. Paris, 1968

Pingaud, Bernard, ed. *Écrivains d'aujourd'hui, 1940–1960: Dictionnaire anthologique et critique.* Paris, 1960

Pollmann, Leo. *Der Neue Roman in Frankreich und Lateinamerika.* Stuttgart, 1968

Pronko, Leonard Cabell. *Avant-Garde: The Experimental Theatre in France.* Berkeley, Cal., 1964

Raible, Wolfgang. *Die moderne Lyrik in Frankreich.* Stuttgart, 1972

Ricardou, Jean. *Problèmes du nouveau roman.* Paris, 1967

Richard, Jean-Pierre. *Onze études sur la poésie moderne.* Paris, 1964

Robbe-Grillet, Alain. *For a New Novel.* New York, 1966

Rousselot, Jean. *Panorama critique des nouveaux poètes français.* Paris, 1952

Sarraute, Nathalie. *The Age of Suspicion: Essays on the Novel.* New York, 1963

Serreau, Geneviève. *Historie du nouveau théâtre.* Paris, 1966

Schöll, Konrad. *Das französische Drama seit dem zweiten Weltkrieg,* 2 vols. Göttingen, 1970

Zeltner-Neukomm, Gerda. *Das Wagnis des französischen Gegenwartsromans.* Hamburg, 1960

MANFRED DURZAK

German Literature

ANY SURVEY of the literary developments in German-speaking countries since 1945 must take into account two special circumstances. The first is the sheer quantity of material. So much has been published that, unless one merely gives an encyclopedic list of facts, one must make judgments and discriminations, which the passing of time may prove to have been immature.

The second special circumstance has to do with subject matter: unlike in most other European countries, in Germany the year 1945 signified more than just the beginning of the postwar phase. When viewed against the immediately preceding literary life in Germany, the year 1945 represented a turning point of the greatest importance. This date marked the beginning of an attempt to overcome the literary vacuum caused by the break with tradition that began when Hitler rose to power.

A continuous line of literary development, represented by late expressionism and by the new matter-of-factness (*neue Sachlichkeit*), was interrupted by force in the early 1930s and remained dormant during the years of Nazi domination. Many authors were forced to emigrate because of race or politics. The result was a cultural and literary diaspora, with a concomitant severing of connections with the land of the mother tongue. Inside Germany, the regimentation of publishing houses and the requirement of political conformity placed on all publications contributed significantly to the deterioration and monotony of the literature that could still be published in Germany. The only German writing that could be taken seriously at that time originated either in exile or in Switzerland, the one German-speaking area not included in the expansionistic ambitions of the Third Reich.

The subordination of culture to a political dictatorship made literary life provincial. The literature produced in Germany during the 1930s could develop in one of two directions. Some writers took seriously the ideological programs of the Nazi cultural policies and bowed to the postulate of "folk literature." The so-called "blood and soil" literature that resulted, closely related to the Nazi ideology of race, was characterized by an irrational mythos glorifying race and nation. Authors of such literature glorified the robust, healthful peasant life and idolized the heroic Nordic type.

This ideology can be clearly seen in a successful novel of that period like Hans Grimm's (1875–1959) *Volk ohne Raum* (A People without Space), which, although published in 1926, offered in its title a slogan readily adopted by the Nazis. Also successful during the Hitler era were *Der Femhof* (1934, The Vehmic Court) and *Frau Magdlene* (1935, Mrs. Magdlene) by Josefa Berens-Totenohl (born 1891). Erwin Guido Kolbenheyer (1878–1962), Hans Friedrich Blunck (1888–1961), and Hanns Johst (born 1890) belonged to the same category.

Parallel to this more-or-less official line in German literature of the 1930s there was an unofficial one, which considered itself a continuation of the true German literature but which, because of political pressures, was largely restricted in its scope. If writers resisted the political orientation imposed from above, they had to focus their attention totally on the private sphere. The result was an intensely personal literature. After 1945 there were attempts to exonerate this personal literature by claiming, as did Frank Thiess (born 1890), that this work was to be understood as literature of "inner emigration."

If official literature was determined by ideology, the literature of "inner emigration" was characterized by a turning toward an idyllicized nature. That this idyllicizing had a political origin, namely, that it amounted to an acquiescent acceptance of the conditions created by the Nazis, was made abundantly clear by Ernst Wiechert's (1887–1950) novel *Das einfache Leben* (1939, The Simple Life). This work, which was praised as the apotheosis of a wholesome, natural life, juxtaposed ostensibly pure humanity and oppressive civilization. Ironically, this successful novel appeared in 1939, the year of Hitler's blitzkrieg victories. In general, the men who returned from the war in 1945 found themselves confronted in Germany with a literary heritage from the Nazi era that offered scarcely anything to build on.

WEST GERMANY

Writers who had gone into exile returned only hesitantly to the western zones of postwar Germany; and—as the actions of Alfred Döblin (1878–1957) and Fritz von Unruh (1885–1970) showed—disappointment soon induced them to leave Germany again. It became fully evident just how destructive the break with tradition caused by Nazism had really been: those who returned could find no point of contact with Germany any more.

The personality and the writings of Wolfgang Borchert (1921–1947) can be taken as a point of departure for the problematic new West German literature. The dilemma of the postwar situation was mirrored both in Borchert's life and in his work. After an apprenticeship as a book dealer and a temporary job as an actor in Lüneburg, he served on the eastern front in 1941, was wounded, became politically suspect, was arrested and brought to Nürnberg. After three months of solitary confinement he was released. Because of remarks against Nazism in his letters, he was re-arrested and sentenced to a prison term of four months. In 1942–43 he served in a so-called death squad, seeing action as an unarmed messenger again on the eastern front. He fell severely ill, was discharged in 1943, and then, because of his political satires, was arrested again and imprisoned for nine months in a Berlin jail. His attempts to establish himself as an actor and cabaret performer after the war were unsuccessful because of the effects of the illnesses with which he had been afflicted during his periods of imprisonment. He died in 1947 at the age of twenty-six.

Borchert began by writing expressionistic poems at the age of seventeen and then fell under the influence of Rainer Maria Rilke (1875–1926). His radio play *Draußen vor der Tür* (1947, Outside the Door) made him famous overnight and later became a great success in the theater. This drama was a key to the postwar period, giving literary expression to the experiences of an entire generation, which recognized itself in the fate of the returning veteran, Beckmann, who cannot forget the horrible memories of the war and who tries in vain to find his place in a society in which the guilty ones, such as the general, have already reestablished themselves.

Despite the contemporary experiences to which Borchert gave literary expression, and despite the moral call for truthfulness and honor, *Outside the Door,* with its theme of the returning soldier, was clearly in the expressionist tradition. Its moral intensity and its generic closeness as a *Stationendrama* (play constructed of self-contained scenes) can be compared to Ernst Toller's (1893–1939) drama of the returning soldier, *Die Wandlung* (1919, Transfiguration). Borchert's writings typified the eclecticism of contemporary German literature; they showed the influences of such contrasting models as Toller and Rilke.

The word *"Kahlschlag"* (clearing the woods) as a formula for the first phase of German literature after 1945 largely concealed its connections to traditional literature. *"Kahlschlag"* appeared for the first time in 1949, when Wolfgang Weyrauch (born 1907) coined it in the preface to a collection of his short stories, *Tausend Gramm* (A Thousand Grams). *Kahlschlag* was an attempt to herald a radical new beginning, which certainly did not characterize form or language. The only real exception to traditionalism was the genre to which Borchert made his most important contributions—the short story. Because of its simplicity and its absence of the formal requirements of the novella and the novel, this short form of fiction, which had just been introduced into Germany in imitation of Anglo-American models, particularly of Hemingway, proved to be an adequate literary vehicle for the realism and the demand for truth of the young authors. Some stories by Borchert, such as *Die Hundeblume* (1947, The Dandelion) and *Die Krähen fliegen abends* (1947, Crows Fly in the Evening), are acknowledged today as more than just works of literature. The following passage from Borchert's *Generation ohne Abschied* (1947, Generation without Farewell) is representative of the attitude of his entire generation: "We are a generation without attachment and depth. Our depth is an abyss. We are the generation without happiness, without a home, without a word of farewell. Our sun is narrow, our love is cruel, and our youth is without youth."

Borchert was representative of postwar reactions in West Germany because he embodied two central characteristics of the young authors: their sense of hopelessness and their demand for truth. At the same time he exemplified the continuation of a diffuse literary tradition, from which he evidently could not free himself although he postulated the need for a radical new beginning. The response that Borchert's work found in the first postwar years was proof of how representative he was. Nevertheless, he did not offer a specific literary direction to West German postwar literature. On the contrary, he remained a solitary figure among young German authors because his work originated in isolation and was not supported or continued by any group.

The dominant literary figures of the first postwar years were members of the older generation—the former "inner emigrants." The reasons for this strange phenomenon lay primarily in the sins of omission of the West German cultural policies of the early postwar years. While in East Germany specific action was taken to attract prominent authors who had emigrated, and to encourage them to participate as individual representatives of a liberal democratic tradition, in West Germany little effort was made along these lines. Moreover, most émigrés maintained a wait-and-see attitude and returned home only gradually, without having been officially invited to do so. The exiled writers who returned immediately after 1945 aroused no response and soon saw themselves again isolated in their devastated homeland, which was busily preoccupied with reconstruction. Since the exiled authors had been invited neither to return nor to serve as representatives of a newly developing literary life, those other authors, who had remained in Germany and who—through flight into inwardness and to the form of the idyll—had proved themselves harmless to the Third Reich, now received widespread attention as the real literary conscience of the Nazi years and rushed to fill the cultural vacuum.

When these writers of so-called inner emigration wrote after the war, their motivation was not analysis of the political mistakes of the preceding fifteen years but rather lament. *Klage um den Bruder* (1947, Lament for a Brother), the title of a collection of sonnets by the poet and critic Hans Egon Holthusen (born 1913), can be taken as a keynote for this group. Other works that projected a similar mood included *Dies irae* (1945, Dies Irae) by Werner Bergengruen (1892–1964), the cycle of sonnets *Venezianisches Credo* (1945, Venetian Creed) by Rudolf Hagelstange (born 1912), and Georg Albrecht Haushofer's (1903–1945) posthumously published *Moabiter Sonette* (1946, Moabite Sonnets). These poems were characterized not only by an elegiac pathos lamenting the loss of feeling but also by a tendency toward strict form, with the sonnet particularly popular. The conservativeness of these lyrical questions of conscience was underscored by the very predilection for conventional literary forms. Such authors as Ernst Wiechert, Hans Carossa (1878–1956), Werner Bergengruen, Hermann Hesse (1877–1962), Ernst Jünger (born 1895), Rudolf Alexander Schröder (1878–1962), Reinhold Schneider (1903–1958), and Stefan Andres (1906–1970) became prominent in the literary life of the immediate postwar period as spokesmen for human qualities that had survived the war.

Ernst Wiechert found a broad readership for his "back-to-nature" novels —*Die Jerominkinder* (1940–46, The Jeromin Children), *Missa sine nomine* (1950, Missa sine Nomine)—which pleaded for a new morality to assuage the troubled German conscience. The postwar second printing of Wiechert's earlier *The Simple Life* became a great success. In the very popular novels of Hans Carossa—*Der Arzt Gion* (1931, Gion the Physician), *Geheimnisse des reifen Lebens* (1936, Secrets of a Mature Life), and *Das Jahr der schönen Täuschungen* (1941, The Year of Beautiful Illusions)—the function of spiritual healing was expressed even more clearly, by presenting the physician's sense of dedicated service to humanity.

Werner Bergengruen's collection of skillfully written novellas, *Der spanische Rosenstock* (1940, The Spanish Rosebush), and his historical novels with settings in his Baltic homeland—*Der Starost* (1938, The Count) and *Der letzte Rittmeister* (1952, The Last Captain of the Cavalry)—became just as popular after World War II as his earlier novel *Der Großtyrann und das Gericht* (1935, The Archtyrant and the Court). Although *The Archtyrant and the Court* had received the approval of Nazi critics as a "novel about a strong national leader set in the Renaissance," after 1945 it was interpreted as a symbolic confrontation with Nazism. Without doubt, the novel had no intended political meaning, and Bergengruen himself denied any analogy between his tyrant and Hitler. But the glorifying of the totalitarian ruler, the "archtyrant" of the autonomous city-state Cassano—who demands the solving of a crime that he himself has committed and thus dissolves all traditional human relationships—fit the concepts of Nazi literary criticism. Similarly, the spirit of self-sacrifice of the dyer Sperone—who is ready to give his life for the sake of the community and who finally arouses the conscience of the tyrant through this gesture of Christian martyrdom—could easily be accommodated to the postwar concept of "moral rearmament" in West Germany.

Hermann Hesse's overly aesthetic late fiction, such as *Narziß und Goldmund* (1930, Narcissus and Goldmund) and especially *Das Glasperlenspiel* (1943, The Glass Bead Game), which depicted a utopia in the province of Castellia devoted to the maximum development of the individual, was highly esteemed in the early postwar years, even though in some ways they seemed like second-rate psychological novels.

Ernst Jünger was also rediscovered in the postwar years, despite his latent inclination toward Nazi ideology. His novel *Auf den Marmorklippen* (1939, On the Marble Cliffs) was interpreted as an important but metaphorically indirect analysis of Nazism. In the novels *Heliopolis* (1949, Heliopolis) and *Gläserne Bienen* (1957, The Glass Bees) Jünger presented a philosophical stance through such antitheses as leaders and followers, individuals and masses. This outlook undeniably had a fascist aura.

The traditional literary outlooks of Rudolf Alexander Schröder and Reinhold Schneider were tinged with Christianity, Protestantism in Schröder's case and Catholicism in Schneider's. Schröder considered himself a late follower of the kind of symbolism developed by Stefan George (1868–1933), Hugo von Hofmannsthal (1874–1929), and Rilke at the beginning of the century. In fact, Schröder had been a personal friend of Hofmannsthal and Rilke. A traditional classicist, Schröder was prominent in almost all lyric forms. He tried to revive both the Protestant church song and the religious poem; he also wrote poems in classical strophic forms and excelled as a translator of the literature of classical antiquity.

Reinhold Schneider's strong affinity for Catholicism was revealed in his preference for historical subjects, which were used in his plays and novels to illustrate an exemplary humanitarianism based on Christian principles. The story *Las Casas vor Karl V.* (1938, Las Casas before Charles V) was typical of his interests.

The novels of Stefan Andres also had Catholic roots. The allegorical trilogy *Die Sintflut* (1949–59, The Flood) translated contemporary history into a metaphor that occasionally lapsed into artificiality. Like his other writings, *The Flood* concludes with an appeal to morality. A better work was his novella set during the Spanish civil war, *Wir sind Utopia* (1943, We Are Utopia), which illustrated through the characters of a renegade monk and a communist officer the possibility of overcoming ideological differences.

In addition to the effort to revive traditional literature in West Germany, a second phenomenon—the adoption of various literary fashions from foreign countries—was encouraged to some degree by the study of literature at the new or reopened universities. Individual German authors from the early part of the century were canonized, and a kind of eternal validity was bestowed upon the literary accomplishments of Rilke, Gottfried Benn (1886–1956), Franz Kafka (1883–1924), Thomas Mann (1875–1955), and Bertolt Brecht (1898–1956). Kafka and Mann, however, have had only limited influence. One example of Kafka's influence was Hermann Kasack's (1896–1966) novel *Die Stadt hinter dem Strom* (1947, The City toward the River), a vision of a perfect bureaucracy and soulless dictatorship, which is destructive to man. The influence of Kafka was also felt in Walter Jens's (born 1923) first novel *Nein: Die Welt der Angeklagten* (1950, No: The World of the Accused), a parable about the last man in a dictatorship, whose bureaucratic procedures are known only to a judge of the highest court.

It was in poetry more than fiction that the influence of early-twentieth-century masters was felt. Rilke, Benn, and Brecht have served as specific models for postwar poets. (And Brecht's influence on the drama has been great indeed.) The fashionableness of Rilke, Benn, and Brecht in poetry has shifted from time to time. Still, Rilke's influence was undeniable in the poetry of Wolfgang Borchert and Hans Egon Holthusen. The poetry of Peter Rühmkorf (born 1929), Alexander Xaver Gwerder (1923–1950), and Albert Arnold Scholl (born 1926) all have shown the influence of Benn. Brecht's poetry continues to influence younger writers, from Erich Fried (born 1921) to Wolf Biermann (born 1936).

A group of young authors who chose to write their works in isolation, without regard for a public, formed a loose organization of writers that, contrary to their own intentions, gradually grew after 1945 into a literary forum of West German literature. The starting point of what later became Group 47 was the journal *Der Ruf,* edited by Hans Werner Richter (born

1908) and Alfred Andersch (born 1914). When the journal appeared in 1946–47, it was intended less as a literary publication than as a medium for developing political awareness. Without denigrating the liberating role of the Allies, the young writers took a critical look at the schematic democratization which was taking place in West Germany, pleaded for a rational democratic reeducation of the German people, and pointed to the necessity of attracting the wartime emigrants back into the newly awakening cultural life, together with a reinstatement of émigré professors in the universities. But this plea had little success among the exiles.

Because some of the political opinions outlined by *Der Ruf* aroused the displeasure of the Allied cultural authorities, the journal's license was withdrawn, and the editors were denied a license for a new journal. This situation led to a kind of emergency solution in April, 1947, when Richter invited the contributors to *Der Ruf* to meet at Bannwaldsee near Füssen. The indirect result of the meeting, at which they read their works to each other and criticized the unpublishable manuscripts they had brought along, was the founding of Group 47. A programmatic formula for a literature of *Kahlschlag,* of *Nullpunktsituation* (zero-point-situation), of *Trümmer-literatur* (literature built from ruins) was now stated for the first time. At the same time that the public was accepting authors who were reviving traditionalism, the face of a new German literature was beginning to take shape at Bannwaldsee in temporary isolation.

It is best not to judge the declared intentions of the first authors of Group 47 by the literature they produced. Their imaginative works lagged far behind their theoretical program and exhibited, as the contributions in *Der Ruf* testify, the very stylistic and semantic features of literature and language from which they wanted to make a radical break. Nevertheless, through Group 47 the mainstream of West German literature developed more and more clearly from year to year. Although much attacked as an institution, Group 47 has become today synonymous with contemporary West German literature.

Whether or not Group 47 can be defined as a community of writers with a common literary program is highly debatable. The lack of uniformity becomes clear if one considers objectives that originally brought Richter into the group. These goals were: (1) to promote the formation of a democratic elite in the realm of literature and journalism, (2) to demonstrate continually practical methods of applying democracy within a circle of individualists with the hope of effecting a general adoption of the principle, and (3) to achieve both goals without a specific program and without the formal structure of a club or collective organization.

The didactic intention of using literature to promote a feeling for democracy was lost very soon. The group, which had come into existence as an institution reflecting the ideas of Richter, soon included authors of the most disparate political feelings, from lyric poets who consciously strove to be apolitical—such as Paul Celan (1920–1970) and Ingeborg Bachmann (born 1926)—to such avowed leftist authors as Erich Fried and Hans Magnus Enzensberger (born 1929).

The literary styles of these writers were also diffuse. From an author like Siegfried Lenz (born 1926), who is a conservative in form and style, through such playful formalists as Peter Härtling (born 1933) and Walter Jens, the spectrum extends to Heinrich Böll (born 1917), Günter Grass (born 1927), and Uwe Johnson (born 1934), who in very different ways analyzed the political heritage of Germany and the current situation in West Germany.

The literary position of Group 47 became supreme during the late 1950s and early 1960s, when the meetings of the Group assumed the function of a portable literary capital. When it expanded to include literary critics and publishers, Group 47 set the pattern for literary life—even if for the most part unintentionally—and, by awarding a Group 47 prize, identified literary landmarks. The role of Group 47 as the chief arbiter of literary activity did not, however, remain unchallenged. A series of attacks was launched by such former émigrés as Robert Neumann (born 1897) and such literary individualists as Hans Erich Nossack (born 1901).

This negative reaction meant that Group 47 had the unquestionable indirect influence of leading to the formation of new literary schools, which attempted to organize similarly as groups. This is true of the so-called Cologne School of new realism, which was founded by Dieter Wellershoff (born 1925) at the beginning of the 1960s and which recognized its indebtedness to the *nouveau roman*. Products of the Cologne School have included Jürgen Becker's (born 1932) short prose montages and Rolf Dieter Brinkmann's (born 1940) collections of stories, *Die Umarmung* (1965, The Embrace) and *Raupenbahn* (1966, Funicular Railway), and his novel *Keiner weiß mehr* (1968, Nobody Knows Any More), all of which revealed the influence of the American pop movement.

Group 61 of Dortmund, which stated as its objective the literary treatment of the worker's world and tried to stimulate the literary potential of the workers, also opened new literary paths. The novels *Männer in zweifacher Nacht* (1962, Men in Double Night) and *Irrlicht und Feuer* (1963, Will-o'-the-wisp and Fire) by Max von der Grün (born 1926); Günter Wallraff's (born 1942) *13 unerwünschte Reportagen* (1969, 13 Unwanted Reports), as well as his firsthand accounts of industry, *Wir brauchen dich* (1966, We Need You); and Erika Runge's (born 1939) documentary accounts of workingmen's lives, *Bottroper Protokolle* (1968, Bottrop Papers)—all expressed the ideas of the Dortmund group.

It can be said that the origins of the Cologne School and Group 61 were analogous to those of Group 47. Such a group structure has not characterized concrete poetry. These poets had to publish their works in private editions for a long time, and their experimental and highly abstract constellations of words only gradually reached the public in the second half of the 1960s. By the late 1960s Helmut Heissenbüttel's (born 1921) six *Textbücher* (1960–67, Textbooks) were distributed in a popularly priced edition. His grandiose work *D'Alemberts Ende* (1970, D'Alembert's End) revived the discussion of an experimental novel form based solely on language. By the late 1960s the works of two other concrete poets, Eugen Gomringer (born 1924) and Franz Mon (born 1926), also received more attention. Even the concrete poets, however, were not an isolated group. There is some overlapping: Heissenbüttel, for example, also belongs to Group 47.

By the late 1960s there was also an increase in West German interest in writers of the so-called Vienna group. These writers included Gerhard Rühm (born 1930), Hans Carl Artmann (born 1921), and Oswald Wiener (born 1935), as well as Graz-circle writers like Peter Handke (born 1942) and Wolfgang Bauer (born 1941), who in fact had their literary breakthroughs in West Germany.

A countermovement to the widespread interest in literary form developed in the circle around the journal *Kursbuch,* which has been appearing since 1965 under the editorship of Hans Magnus Enzensberger and has been dedicated primarily to political enlightenment and revolutionary social change. Yaak Karsunke (born 1934) and Peter Schneider (born 1940) have been closely connected with *Kursbuch.*

Despite Enzensberger's membership in Group 47, his work in *Kursbuch* can be viewed as an indirect criticism of the political ineffectuality of Group 47. Indeed, Group 47 is gradually but clearly losing its importance as the major organization of West German writers, partly because of many literary feuds within the group, partly because of the defections of its members.

EAST GERMANY

One of the most significant events of the year 1945 was the political division of Germany and the establishment of a second German literature embracing the political principles of the new official social order in the German Democratic Republic (East Germany). The separate literary development of East Germany was directed according to a program: Germany's literary past was purged ideologically, and everything was rejected that did not possess liberal-democratic, antifascist, or socialist tendencies, and thus could not be interpreted as a preparatory step toward the new literature. To be sure, the new prescriptions for literary life in East Germany proceeded gradually, and they were not always carried out with narrow dogmatism. Occasionally, pragmatic considerations played a role in determining the course to be followed.

The early phase of East German literature was relatively liberal. While in West Germany there was a general indifference to exile literature, in East Germany steps were taken from the beginning to revive interest in the works of writers of the Weimar republic who had emigrated, and to let these works serve as the basis of a new antifascist, democratic literature. This program was carried out in several ways. Since almost all of the famous pre-World War II German publishing houses were located in East Germany, particularly in Leipzig, they could be reactivated relatively quickly after the firms were reorganized as state-owned operations. After 1945 the newly founded Aufbau Verlag, today still the most influential and most important publishing house in East Germany, took over the programs of important firms in exile, such as Querido Verlag (Amsterdam), Malik Verlag (London), and Aurora Verlag (New York).

At the same time an effort was made to invite exiled writers to return home. A number of prominent authors accepted this invitation: Arnold Zweig (1887–1968), Bertolt Brecht, and Anna Seghers (born 1900) returned; Heinrich Mann (1871–1950) and Lion Feuchtwanger (1884–1958) indicated their support of the new government from abroad. Indeed, Heinrich Mann announced that he was prepared to accept the chairmanship of the newly established Berlin Academy; however, he died shortly before he was to return to East Germany.

An effort was also made to encourage the return of Alfred Döblin and Hermann Broch (1886–1951), but both hesitated to make the move. Writers who did return to settle in East Germany included the dramatist Friedrich Wolf (1888–1953), the novelists Ludwig Renn (born 1889) and Bernhard Kellermann (1879–1951), the poet (later high official in the ministry of culture) Johannes R. Becher (1891–1958), and the poets Stephan Hermlin (born 1915) and Erich Arendt (born 1903).

The contrasts between East and West German literature during the period of reconstruction were indeed striking. While in West Germany idyllic literature came into prominence and celebrated the invulnerability of humanity in an appeal to the basically decent nature of man, in East Germany a political literature was established, which could be traced back to the Weimar republic and which became intensified through experiences gained in exile. No specific literary doctrine prevailed in East Germany during this phase of reconstruction. Instead, an effort was made to form a broad antifascist and democratic united front from the various forces willing to participate in the reconstruction. The regimentation of cultural and political affairs manifested itself only in general tendencies and not through direct controls.

The guarantee of full artistic freedom was made clear at the first central cultural meeting of the German Communist Party, which was held in February, 1946. The representatives favored the idea of publishing on a broad scale the works of earlier writers; there was no suggestion that the selection of authors should be subject to political controls. Entirely positive goals also distinguished the Cultural Union for the Democratic Renewal of Germany, whose honorary chairman was Gerhart Hauptmann (1862–1946). In the early postwar years this group was a major impetus to artistic life. As a consequence, the expressionist dramatists of the 1920s were rediscovered and staged, and works of the American dramatists William Saroyan, Thornton Wilder, Tennessee Williams, and Eugene O'Neill were widely performed. Soviet cultural policies had by no means come to predominate.

This cultural situation, initially so liberal, changed at the end of the 1940s when the two German states were officially formed and the Socialist Unity Party was established in East Germany. The concept of culture was now defined in terms of Marxism and Leninism. A two-year plan for the implementation of cultural projects was rejected in favor of a new insistence upon the need to develop a "realistic" art. This so-called realism had to be distinguishable by its polemic slant from the artistic developments in West Germany, namely, from "neofascist," "decadent," or "formalist" art.

Only now did the phase of doctrinaire cultural and literary policies begin. A careful sifting of literary tradition and the creation of an index of proscribed works for the guidance of publishing firms were the first indications of the change. Such authors as Joyce, Proust, Kafka, Beckett, and Benn were now repudiated as formalists. Literature was drawn into the contemporary class struggle and was expected to become a vehicle of socialist progress. The power of the cultural functionaries was strengthened, and cultural journals and organizations of artists were brought in line with politics. The establishment of cultural foundations, the control over publishing firms, and the granting of national prizes provided a means of applying economic pressure, which in turn made it possible to regiment literary development.

This campaign enjoyed its first victory at the initial meeting of the Central Committee of the Socialist Unity Party in March, 1951, when the attack on formalism in art and literature was officially launched. In the wake of this shift in official policy, further attacks were made against even such formerly immune authors as Arnold Zweig and Bertolt Brecht. In the summer of 1952 the State Commission for Artistic Affairs, an agency for controlling cultural policies, announced the doctrine of socialist realism, which had become a rigid artistic credo in Russia after 1946.

Henceforth, socialist realism was to serve as the criterion for literature in East Germany. The critical realism of the major Weimar authors, from Heinrich Mann to Lion Feuchtwanger, was no longer satisfactory. The new doctrine required a literature which did not represent life and society as an objective process from an unbiased point of view but which showed society in its revolutionary development toward a socialist goal. The representation of concrete social problems, fidelity to truth and adherence to reality (as seen through socialist eyes), and loyalty to party doctrine were the requirements associated with this goal. Literature assumed a didactic function: its aim was to educate people to socialism indirectly, by showing how the so-called positive hero represented the proper perspective, namely, the direction that would lead to the goal of emancipation in the future. Thus, the call was for a tendentious literature in which the content was more important than the form.

This intention of indoctrinating the public with socialism led in June, 1953, to internal acts of political resistance. Writers tried to defend themselves against the massive bureaucratic influence and demanded to be judged not by functionaries of the Socialist Unity Party but by the public. Although at first glance the dissolution of the Art Commission and the establishment of the Ministry of Culture under Johannes R. Becher seemed to be an act of liberalization, in actuality only the tactics were changed. The gap between party functionary and writer was ironically eliminated by expediently turning authors into functionaries.

With the hardening of Soviet policy toward East Germany in June, 1955, even this timid attempt at liberalization was stifled. At the thirtieth meeting of the Central Committee in January, 1957, the "struggle against ideological coexistence" was announced. The internal political fronts stiffened their positions so much that so-called counterrevolutionary groups were arrested. At the same time a new bureaucratic agency, the Cultural Commission, was established under the direction of the militant old-line communist Alfred Kurella, who transformed the Academy of Arts into a communist academy and carried out ideological purges of various cultural institutions.

A reorientation of the literary policies in East Germany first became evident at two conferences that took place at the electrochemical plant at Bitterfeld. The first Bitterfeld conference, which took place on April 24, 1959, presented a program for politicized literature under the often parodied motto, "Reach for your pen, pal; socialist German national culture needs you!" This program was intended both to overcome the separation of art and life, which was allegedly a heritage of capitalism, and to create a national literature from new beginnings. The results of this "nonprofessional" literary movement remained far behind expectations.

At the second Bitterfeld conference, in April, 1964, the original goals were revised downward to practical levels. The phase of socialist reconstruction in East Germany was now declared at an end. The incompatible contradictions between bourgeois relics and socialist renewal were now considered to have actually been overcome in the reconstruction of East Germany. While literature up to this time had been asked to limit itself to presenting confrontations between hostile social classes in a simplified, black-and-white technique, now a new artistic outlook on social problems was demanded within the framework of socialist realism. Subjective elements, which had barely been considered previously, once again received greater attention.

As skeptically as one may view the results of the Bitterfeld conferences, the aftereffects can nevertheless be clearly recognized in the literature of East Germany. For example, one of the central programmatic points of the Bitterfeld resolutions—to induce writers to use industry and agriculture as settings for their novels so as to reflect the world of socialist labor directly —was put into practice in a number of novels. Franz Fühmann (born 1922), who worked for some time at the Warnow Shipyard in Rostock, described his experiences in the firsthand account *Kabelkran und Blauer Peter* (1961, Cable Crane and Blue Peter). Herbert Nachbar (born 1930) recounted his work in a fishing commune at Rügen in the novel *Die Hochzeit von Länneken* (1960, Länneken's Wedding). Other novels of this type were Erik Neutsch's (born 1931) *Spur der Steine* (1964, Trace of Stones) and Christa Wolf's (born 1929) *Der geteilte Himmel* (1963, Divided Heaven). In a certain sense Erwin Strittmatter's (born 1912) *Ole Bienkopp* (1963, Ole Bienkopp) also belonged to the group of novels of socialist labor.

This demand for a new literary orientation was accompanied by punitive actions by the authorities. At a meeting of the Socialist Unity Party in January, 1963, several authors were dropped from the rolls for ideological reasons, and Stephan Hermlin, who had served up to this time as secretary of the department of literature and language in the Berlin Academy, lost his position to Alfred Kurella. The manager of the Deutsches Theater, Wolfgang Langhoff, who had staged Peter Hacks's (born 1928) controversial play *Die Sorgen und die Macht* (1958, Worries and Power) was likewise removed from office. In 1962 Peter Huchel (born 1903) was replaced as editor of the prestigious literary journal *Sinn und Form*.

There was, however, a temporary relaxation of controls in East Germany in response to the wave of liberalization in Czechoslovakia in the 1960s. The works of Kafka were published, and several East German authors received permission to participate in meetings of Group 47. Indeed, Johannes Bobrowski (1917–1965) received the prize of Group 47 a year before his death. But the squelching of the Czechoslovak efforts at liberalization also affected the internal policies of East Germany. A renewed control was imposed upon literary life, as evidenced, for example, in the denunciation of the poet Wolf Biermann, who was prohibited from publishing his writings in East Germany.

Austria

While literature in West and East Germany has been characterized by a break with tradition, Austrian literature since 1945 has consciously acknowledged and continued its uninterrupted literary heritage. A number of émigrés, such as Hans Weigel (born 1908) and Friedrich Torberg (born 1908), returned soon after the war's end and assumed important roles in the newly developing literary life, even though other prominent émigrés, like Hermann Broch, Elias Canetti (born 1905), and Johannes Urzidil (1896–1970), continued to live in exile.

Ilse Aichinger's (born 1921) *Aufruf zum Mißtrauen* (Call to Suspicion), which was published in 1946 in the newly founded journal *Plan,* is usually considered the beginning of Austrian postwar literature. *Call to Suspicion* to a certain extent reflected the postwar interest in criticizing social conditions; but it was predominantly concerned with the specifically Austrian heritage. Another important feature of the work was its relationship to French surrealism, which has been especially important for recent Austrian poetry, as the poems of Paul Celan, Ingeborg Bachmann, and Friederike Mayröcker (born 1924) have attested. Other authors, such as Albert Paris Gütersloh (born 1887), George Saiko (1892–1962), Franz Theodor Csokor (1895–1969), and above all Heimito von Doderer (1896–1966), brought to contemporary Austrian literature the specific traditions established by the generation of Hermann Broch, Hugo von Hofmannsthal, Robert Musil (1880–1942), and Karl Kraus (1874–1936).

This continuity was strengthened even more in the 1950s, when the Austrian State Treaty was concluded, and, unlike Germany, Austria as a neutral state was relieved of any further burden of its political past. The renewed national consciousness that was developing during the 1950s also had an effect on literature, which began to be viewed as having a specifically Austrian idea of culture, distinct from that of Germany. While West German writers of the 1950s focused on eternally human issues, Austrian writers concentrated on eternally *Austrian* qualities and values. Behind both phenomena stood the hope of a world restored to unity and health; but this hope could be realized sooner in Austria through tradition than in Germany, where it ran against tradition.

Together with such younger authors as Herbert Eisenreich (born 1925) and Gerhart Fritsch (1924–1969), Heimito von Doderer was the principal representative of this phase of Austrian literature. He made his reputation as a novelist during the 1920s. But his real importance was not recognized until the 1950s, with the publication of the novels *Die erleuchteten Fenster* (1950, The Illuminated Windows), *Die Strudlhofstiege* (1951, The Strudlhof Stairway), and *Die Dämonen* (1956, The Demons). These three long novels offered comprehensive historical portraits that brought into focus the continuity not only of the geographical area encompassed by Austrian history but also of the problems connected with this territory. Ingeborg Bachmann's poetry of the 1950s had a similar representative significance.

Not until the early 1960s did a new orientation appear in Austrian literature. The publication of Hans Carl Artmann's surprisingly successful volume of poetry *med ana schwoazzn dintn* (1958, with black ink) signaled less the emergence of dialect folk poetry into literature than the appearance of a literary underground, which overshadowed established literature through forcefulness of language and vitality of form. In retrospect, a group of Viennese authors during the 1950s and early 1960s can now be discussed to a certain extent as representing a development paralleling Group 47 in West Germany. There is, to be sure, one difference: these Viennese authors, even at the height of their influence in Austria, did not actually regard themselves as an organization of writers.

In addition to Artmann, other writers prominently connected with the so-called Vienna group were Friedrich Achleitner (born 1930), Oswald Wiener, Gerhard Rühm, and Konrad Bayer (1932–1964). (Bayer, Rühm, Wiener, and Achleitner founded a "literary cabaret" in Vienna.) Friederike Mayröcker, Andreas Okopenko (born 1930), and Ernst Jandl (born 1925) were also associated with the Viennese group.

There was a certain relationship between the Vienna group and the circle of younger writers centered around Graz. The Graz journal *manuskripte* and major authors of the Graz circle—Peter Handke, Gert F. Jonke (born 1946), Wolfgang Bauer, Barbara Frischmuth (born 1941), and Michael Scharang (born 1941)—adopted many of the ideas of the Vienna group and have continued to develop them. The Viennese authors utilized and enriched forms and traditions that originated outside the realm of standard literature. Ludwig Wittgenstein's (1889–1951) philosophy of language inspired an intensive study of word patterns and an attempt to achieve an alteration of reality by destroying normalized forms of language. For these authors, the notion of a healthy traditional Austrian literary heritage is an ideological signpost from which they are determined to remain aloof.

Gerhart Fritsch's novel *Moos auf den Steinen* (1956, Moss on the Stones) had major importance as a critique of the idea of an unbroken

Austrian tradition; Fritsch severely censured the belief that tradition itself could bring about a restoration after World War II. He also unmasked the myth of the healthy, wholesome Austrian provinces. The intention to destroy myths also inspired the novels of Gert Friedrich Jonke and Oswald Wiener, as well as the plays of Wolfgang Bauer, which produced irritating shock effects by combining elements of folk theater with the "happening."

An iconoclastic motive can also be seen in the works of Thomas Bernhard (born 1931). Bernhard's novels have been documentations of reality unmistakably rooted in specific Austrian locations. In these novels the prominent presence of illness, decay, agony, and death attacked the idea that the world is healthy; indeed, Austrian reality was specifically equated with a decaying culture. Thus, Austrian literature today, undeniably more varied than in the 1950s, no longer presents the harmonious picture it did in the years following the end of World War II.

SWITZERLAND

None of the political determinants that have influenced the literature of West and East Germany, and to a lesser degree of Austria, have applied to Switzerland. Switzerland, which has been castigated as the "garden dwarf of Europe," survived the catastrophes of the war by remaining uninvolved, and thus preserved a political complacency, which was not, however, reflected in its literature. One reason for the lack of harmony in Swiss literature may be a specifically Swiss feature that has been described as "Helvetian malaise," an attitude characterized by a strange mixture of optimism and self-doubt. Another reason is the multilingual character of Switzerland, which has prevented the development of an integrated national literature that could claim to be culturally representative of the entire country. Moreover, German-Swiss authors have to use not only a literary language that is spoken by only a part of the population but one that is also considerably different from the local dialects.

Therefore, despite the unique political position of Switzerland during the 1930s and 1940s, there did not exist a continuous tradition for German-speaking Swiss writers to accept without reservation. To be sure, during the bleak years for Germany Switzerland was important as a refuge for exiles and as an asylum for German literature. Robert Musil and Georg Kaiser (1878–1945) were only two of a considerable number of writers who emigrated to Switzerland. Moreover, the Zurich Schauspielhaus became one of the few German-language stages that continued the traditions of the Weimar period in Germany, as well as giving voice, through performances of Brecht and Carl Zuckmayer (born 1896) to the new drama that developed in exile.

Along with Brecht, the Swiss dramatists Max Frisch (born 1911) and Friedrich Dürrenmatt (born 1921) were key figures in bringing German drama back to international recognition after 1945. Characteristically, both Frisch and Dürrenmatt have distanced themselves from their Swiss environment. And both writers have mercilessly attacked the myth of Switzerland: Dürrenmatt, through the small town Güllen in *Der Besuch der alten Dame* (1956, The Visit of the Old Lady); Frisch, through the small state of Andorra in *Andorra* (1962, Andorra).

These attacks have linked both Frisch and Dürrenmatt to a group of younger Swiss writers with a similar critical attitude, who have not as yet become as well known in Germany. Walter Matthias Diggelmann (born 1927), for example, in his novel *Die Hinterlassenschaft* (1965, The Estate) showed the misery of an émigré in Switzerland, a country that gives the outward appearance of being humane. Otto F. Walter's (born 1928) novels of social criticism—*Der Stumme* (1959, The Silent Man) and *Herr Tourell* (1962, Mr. Tourell)—portrayed the collapse of the individual's relationship to society and to his fellow men.

Political activism, dominated by criticism of Swiss society, has also been a central concern of a number of younger poets who came to prominence mainly in the 1960s: Urs Oberlin (born 1919), Urs Martin Strub (born 1910), and Jörg Steiner (born 1930).

Among Swiss poets the priest Kurt Marti (born 1921) holds a special place because of his powerful language and the variety of his lyrical forms. Similar to the way Hans Carl Artmann has used Austrian dialect as a new and by no means folkloric poetic language, Marti has elevated colloquial Swiss speech to a literary language. As a result, particularly with the poems in the volume *Rosa Loui* (1967, Rosa Loui), he enriched the stylized High German literary language from below. Its political themes gave immediate relevance to *Rosa Loui*. Walter Vogt (born 1927) and Ernst Eggimann (born 1936) followed Marti along the path of liberating Swiss poetry.

Marti's importance among poets is paralleled by the position of Peter Bichsel (born 1935) among the younger writers of fiction. Bichsel's combination of artistically simple language with subject matter chosen from everyday life worked more successfully in the volumes of stories *Eigentlich möchte Frau Blum den Milchmann kennenlernen* (1964, And Really Frau Blum Would Very Much Like to Meet the Milkman) and *Kindergeschichten* (1969, Children's Stories) than in the novel *Die Jahreszeiten* (1967, The Seasons).

Antithetical to Bichsel's works was the imitative virtuosity of Adolf Muschg's (born 1934) two novels: *Im Sommer des Hasen* (1965, In the Summer of the Hare) and *Gegenzauber* (1967, Countercharm). A similar talent for assimilating different models was demonstrated by Jürg Federspiel (born 1931) in the powerful novels *Massaker im Mond* (1963, Massacre on the Moon) and *Der Mann, der Glück brachte* (1966, The Man Who Brought Good Luck).

There is a rather large gap between the fame of Frisch and Dürrenmatt and the relative obscurity outside of Switzerland of the younger authors. One of the reasons for their obscurity is that Germany (now only West Germany) is still the literary center of the German-speaking world, and Swiss writers, unlike Austrian writers, are not closely connected to West German literary life. Membership in Group 47 certainly helped Frisch and Bichsel to become quickly known beyond the borders of Switzerland.

POETRY

THE QUEST FOR A WHOLESOME WORLD

The poetry published and favorably received in the years immediately following World War II hardly provided an overall view of the historical changes that took place during the period of reconstruction. Instead, these poems, usually by authors of the older generation, were retrospective flights into unscathed worlds. The wholesomeness they presented was evident from the very titles of their collections of poems. These included Friedrich Georg Jünger's (born 1898) *Die Silberdistelklause* (1947, Silver Thistle Hermitage) and *Das Weinberghaus* (1947, The House in the Vineyard), Hans Carossa's *Abendländische Elegie* (1947, Western Elegy), Rudolf Alexander Schröder's *Weihnachtslieder* (1946, Christmas Carols) and *Alten Mannes Sommer* (1947, Old Man's Summer), Hermann Hesse's *Der Blütenzweig* (1945, The Twig with Blossoms), and Elisabeth Langgässer's (1899–1950) *Der Laubmann und die Rose* (1947, The Leaf Man and the Rose). In the aftermath of a corrupt way of life, whose political failure was now obvious, these poets concentrated on the permanent and beneficent forces of nature, which was elevated through wishful thinking into an illusionary mythical counterimage of the reality of the time.

In addition to an emphasis on nature, there was also a Christian aura in the poetry of consolation written by Rudolf Schröder; by Oda Schaefer (born 1900), in the collection *Irdisches Geleit* (1946, Earthly Escort); by Hans Egon Holthusen, in *Hier in der Zeit* (1949, Here in This Time); and by Rudolf Hagelstange, in *Strom der Zeit* (1948, Current of Time). These poets combined an invocation of a pure mythological nature and of indestructible human values with Christian resignation. The result was a didactic and edifying poetry, which elicited enthusiastic response during the first postwar years. As the writings of Holthusen and some of the others demonstrated, this type of poetry did not by any means lack thought. Instead, it combined, with virtuoso skill, the symbolism of George, Hofmannsthal, and Rilke and the expressionism of Georg Trakl (1887–1914) and Georg Heym (1887–1912) with the awareness of living in a postrevolutionary period; these poets realized that they could only imitate attitudes that had been recognized earlier.

NATURE POETRY

Behind these restorative tendencies of the first years after World War II, one can recognize an artistically important trend that characterized a considerable segment of German poetry well into the 1950s—nature poetry. The central figure was Wilhelm Lehmann (1882–1968), who acquired important poetic ideas from his friend Oscar Loerke (1884–1941) and helped bring Loerke to greater importance posthumously than he had enjoyed during his lifetime. Loerke's poetry—especially that in *Atem der Erde* (1930, Breath of the Earth) and *Der Silberdistelwald* (1934, The Forest of Silver Thistles)—had a sensuous transparency that revealed the orderliness of nature while at the same time spiritualizing it.

Lehmann followed Loerke in such collections as *Entzückter Staub* (1946, Charmed Dust), *Noch nicht genug* (1950, Not Enough Yet), and *Überlebender Tag* (1951–54, Surviving Day). These poems combined motifs of nature with mythology and history, both of which areas Lehmann examined minutely with an artistic, if occasionally mannerist, refinement of language. Lehmann, one of the most successful of the nature poets, inspired many others.

Karl Krolow's (born 1915) early collections—*Hochgelobtes, gutes Leben* (1943, Highly Praised, Good Life), *Gedichte* (1948, Poems), *Heimsuchung* (1948, Visitation) and *Auf Erden* (1949, On Earth)—showed a level of artistry comparable to Lehmann's. Krolow's works written in the late 1950s, such as the volume of poems *Fremde Körper* (1959, Foreign Bodies), opened the scope of his style and subject matter to other spheres of influence besides German nature poetry: French surrealism and French symbolism.

Heinz Piontek's (born 1925) indebtedness to Lehmann was evident in his volumes of poetry *Die Rauchfahne* (1953, The Trail of Smoke), *Wassermarken* (1957, Watermarks), and *Mit einer Kranichfeder* (1962, With a Crane's Feather). A similar indebtedness to Lehmann can be seen in the Viennese poet Christine Busta's (born 1915) volumes *Der Regenbaum* (1951, The Rain Tree), *Lampe und Delphin* (1955, Lamp and Dolphin), and *Die Scheune der Vögel* (1958, The Birds' Barn). The poetry of the East Germans Peter Huchel and Johannes Bobrowski has also contained themes resembling those of the nature poets. But they followed a different path of development, of its own artistic importance aside from the similarities to the nature poetry.

THE INFLUENCE OF GOTTFRIED BENN

In 1948, after thirteen years of silence, Gottfried Benn published a volume of poetry in Switzerland, *Statische Gedichte* (Static Poems), the title of which can be interpreted as a label for his approach to poetry during his later years. Benn's reappearance as a poet proved to be a significant event, for he was a direct link between the legendary expressionist generation and the postwar writers. Benn's work also formed a bridge between contemporary poetry and symbolism, since he made the doctrine of the absolute poem, which Baudelaire and Mallarmé had promoted, the basis of his artistic credo—the poem as an autonomous, self-contained reality, which stands aloof from the changeable, inconsistent historical world.

For Benn, "world of expression" (*Ausdruckswelt*), "artistry" (*Artistik*), and "statics" (*Statik*) became the formulas for a world of poems determined by internal organization. Benn gave concrete representation to this poetic world in his late poems and also established its theoretical basis in his now-famous lecture, *Probleme der Lyrik* (1951, Problems of Poetry), which became the credo of a whole generation of young poets. Both Benn's techniques and his themes dominated German poetry of the 1950s. His characteristic techniques—assimilation of foreign words, unusual rhymes, incorporation of colloquial speech, cryptical and mythical allusions—were freely adopted by other poets, as was his thesis that nihilism produces a feeling of happiness. The result for Benn and his followers was a modish, romantic irrationalism characterized by a blindness to reality.

This imitation of Benn cut across generations. Older authors, such as Alexander Lernet-Holenia (born 1897) and Horst Lange (1904–1971) fell under the spell of Benn's influence; so did poets of the younger generation, such as Alexander Xaver Gwerder, Peter Rühmkorf, and Albert Arnold Scholl.

THE INFLUENCE OF FRENCH SURREALISM

While Benn's influence was limited strictly to West Germany, the influence of French surrealism crossed the political borders and can be seen in retrospect to have been of perhaps greater consequence than Benn. French surrealism was certainly an important influence on such poets of the Vienna group as Hans Carl Artmann and Ingeborg Bachmann. The poems of Apollinaire, Éluard, and Saint-John Perse, with their richness of word associations and their ability to assimilate the most contradictory elements and combine them into bold linguistic structures with a conscious disregard for logical connections, had a particular attraction for such poets as Paul Celan, Karl Krolow, Stephan Hermlin, and Erich Arendt.

In 1947 Paul Celan fled from his native Rumania to Vienna. In 1948 he settled in Paris and became the friend of the expressionist poet Iwan Goll (1891–1950), who was living there as an émigré. Goll directed Celan's attention to Apollinaire. The translations into German done by Celan and others brought about close ties between French and German poetry. Celan, for example, translated Rimbaud, Valéry, and René Char. In 1957 Karl Krolow published his translations of French surrealistic works in the volume *Die Barke Phantasie* (The Barge Fantasy).

French surrealism was brought to German poetry indirectly by Erich Arendt. Arendt spent many years in exile in Colombia and was influenced by ideas of the Chilean poet Pablo Neruda, who had significantly altered the techniques of the French surrealists by combining his own version of surrealism with a Marxist approach to life. Neruda's politics appealed to Arendt, a confirmed Marxist, and Arendt translated Neruda with sensitivity. Indeed, the quality of Arendt's Neruda translations established him as one of the most important contemporary German poets.

Stephan Hermlin also translated Neruda, but he stands closer to the French surrealists; he has become known particularly for his translations of Éluard. In Hermlin's own poems, which have exhibited great power of expression, he has combined the bold metaphorical techniques of Éluard with the precision of form of the French symbolists to create verbal constructions that radiate provocative ideas.

As East German poets, Arendt and Hermlin stand apart from others because of their highly receptive attitudes to other poetry. Their work is quite different both from that of the hermetic, idyllic poets, such as Peter Huchel and Johannes Bobrowski, and from the work of such younger poets as Wolf Biermann and Reiner Kunze (born 1933), who have been followers of Brecht.

FIVE REPRESENTATIVE POETS

It became common in the early postwar years to regret the paucity of new fiction and to cry in vain for plays and novels dealing with the immediate present. In poetry, however, there was a surge of activity right after the war, although most of these works have already been forgotten.

The major poetry anthologies since World War II all have shown a general uniformity within themselves, despite the generally high level of their individual selections. Only a few poets have overcome the impression of conformity through the force of their language and their special artistic visions. Five very gifted poets seem to illustrate best the similar directions followed in German poetry in spite of political borders.

Günter Eich (born 1907)—in the collections *Abgelegene Gehöfte* (1948, Isolated Farms), *Untergrundbahn* (1949, Subway), and *Botschaften des Regens* (1955, Messages of Rain)—was one of the few poets who confronted seriously the changed conditions after 1945. The poem *Inventur* (Inventory), included in his first volume, has rightly become famous as an example of a lyrical statement that concentrated language into laconic messages while it consciously rejected traditional form. Eich's achievement has been the result of a simplicity of form and language, which can be seen in his astonishing talent for compression. He has isolated simple things from their environment and has made them transparent in order to reveal their intellectual essences within the perceivable realm of the poem.

Eich's short poems have been influenced by Japanese haiku and occasionally also by the American imagism of Ezra Pound and William Carlos Williams. In his more recent collections—*Zu den Akten* (1964, File It Away) and *Anlässe und Steingärten* (1966, Causes and Rock Gardens)—the withdrawal from reality, which he had established as an absolute for his poetry, contained clearly polemical protests against the rationalism of his time. An example of this new note can be found in *Fußnote zu Rom* (1964, Footnote on Rome): "Too much of the west, / suspicious, / too much of the world left out. / No possibility / of rock gardens."

The process of artistic reduction in Eich's poetry seemed to be leading to an excessive aestheticism. In 1968 and 1970 he attempted to reverse the direction of his work by including in his collections *Maulwürfe* (Moles) short prose pieces of fifteen to twenty lines. Using puns, paradoxes, cynical remarks, word plays, and illogical combinations, he attacked in these prose works the very kind of poetry he represented and thus indirectly revised his own aesthetic stance.

Eich's development exemplifies in a certain way the dangers that have beset contemporary German poetry. Equally typical is the reorientation Eich has recently undergone. He has virtually repudiated his aesthetic phase and has returned to his starting point of 1948—taking inventory of reality and deciphering it.

Ingeborg Bachmann, an Austrian who earned her doctorate in Vienna with a dissertation about the existentialist philosopher Martin Heidegger, showed her rich poetic talent in the collections *Die gestundete Zeit* (1953, On Borrowed Time) and *Anrufung des großen Bären* (1956, Invocation of Ursa Major). With a sensitivity to language reminiscent of both Georg Trakl and Hofmannsthal and occasionally of Hölderlin, as well as of contemporary French poetry, Bachmann has transformed the awareness of the "borrowed time" of the untrustworthy present and future into poetry characterized both by eruptive animated pictures and by a precise rhythm that occasionally uses rhyme.

Bachmann has used metaphors from the world of myths and fairy tales to objectify her historical experiences. Occasionally, she has succumbed to an overly mannered system of metaphors and a rhetorical pompousness. But in such poems as *Das Spiel ist aus* (The Game Is Over), *Die große Fracht* (The Great Cargo), and *Lieder von der Insel* (Island Songs) she achieved great expressive power. Like Eich, Bachmann has also undergone a crisis as an artist: in the last decade she has been almost totally silent as a poet. Instead, she has attempted to proceed along new paths, with the lyrical prose of the monologues in *Das dreißigste Jahr* (1961, The Thirtieth Year) and with the novel *Malina* (1971, Malina).

Peter Huchel became known as early as 1925, when his first poems were published in the journals *Die literarische Welt* and *Das Kunstblatt*. But he quickly withdrew from literary life, and from 1927 he lived for extended periods of time in France, in the Balkans, and in Turkey. After the war, which he spent on the Russian front, he held various managerial positions with the East Berlin radio and then served until 1962 as editor of the journal *Sinn und Form,* which he developed into an elevated, nondoctrinaire artistic forum.

Huchel's early works showed his connection to the nature poets. His language was enriched by the peasant idiom of his native Brandenburg, and the subjects and themes of his landscape poems derived from his personal experiences in that environment. But there were also descriptions of Mediterranean lands (Italy, Provence, and the near east). The range of themes in his first volume of poetry, *Der Knabenteich* (1933, The Boys' Pool), was significantly expanded in his postwar collections—*Gedichte* (1948, Poems) and *Chausseen, Chausseen* (1963, Avenues, Avenues)—in which classical antiquity was a more apparent source. Moreover, his more recent poems have reflected the destruction and decay caused by the war and postwar events.

Huchel has conceived his poetry not as a creation outside the realms of time and space but as a richly imaged representation of a documentable reality, although his poetry has never deteriorated into versified reportage. Nevertheless, Huchel is well aware that his poems may possibly be undecipherable, because language as a means of communication is threatened today and a dialogue between author and reader is only conditionally possible.

Huchel for the most part has used free verse, but he occasionally has employed songlike rhymed verse. Even when he describes immediate reality, he does so in such compact images that there is no danger of didacticism. His avoidance of tendentiousness has put him in conflict with official East German literary doctrine and has probably been the real reason for his unpopularity with the arbiters of literature in his country. After he was removed as editor of *Sinn und Form* in 1962, he found himself forced into the role of an outsider. Finally, in 1971, he was granted permission to emigrate to Italy, where he now lives.

Johannes Bobrowski, an East German comparable to Huchel in artistic rank, was another outsider who avoided politics in his poetry. His verse closely resembled nature poetry, while at the same time it showed the influences of Friedrich Klopstock (1724–1803) and Hölderlin. Bobrowski also wrote prose works, including the novel *Litauische Claviere* (1966, Lithuanian Pianos), but he is known primarily for his poems.

Bobrowski's first lyrical efforts, published in 1943 in the journal *Das innere Reich,* evoked scarcely any response. Then in 1961 and 1962 there appeared the collections *Sarmatische Zeit* (Sarmatian Time) and *Schatten-land Ströme* (Shadowland Rivers), published in both East and West Germany. These poems and his readings at meetings of Group 47 in 1960 and 1962 made him famous. One more volume of poems, *Im Windgesträuch* (In Windswept Shrubbery), was posthumously published in 1970.

Bobrowski stated the theme of his poetry as follows: "The Germans and eastern Europe . . . a long history of misfortune and guilt . . . since the days of the Teutonic Order." Thus, in such poems in *Sarmatian Time* as *Lettische Lieder* (Latvian Songs), *Die Düna* (The Duina River), *Die Heimat des Malers Chagall* (The Homeland of Chagall the Painter), and *Der Ilmensee* (Lake Il'men) the old Baltic lands were glorified.

Shadowland Rivers, containing such poems as *Der Don* (The Don), *Kathedrale 1941* (Cathedral 1941), and *Kloster bei Nowgorod* (Monastery at Novgorod), also included descriptions of the Russian landscape, which Bobrowski came to know as a soldier and as a prisoner of war. His portrayal of the landscape is partly visual and realistic and partly, as in *The Don,* vaguely visionary and difficult to understand. Even the sense of time changes in the poems. Bobrowski contrasts direct experience, as in the poem *Heimweg* (The Way Home), with an imaginary historical perspective that evokes visions, as in the poem *Cathedral 1941.* Typical of the landscapes of his poems is their breadth and openness. But in those poems in which the landscapes consist of few features, like *Unter dem Nachtrand* (Beneath the Edge of Night), they are seemingly fluid: sky, plains, fore-ground, and horizon merge into one another. Bobrowski was especially fond of two forms: the narrative poem and the hymn. Although he clearly broke away from the strictures of rhyme and stanzaic form, he used this freedom to give rhythmic balance to his poetry.

Paul Celan combined an extremely wide variety of sources—Hasidic tradition, Russian and French symbolism, French surrealism—to create a poetry of self-contained metaphors and strict rhythms. Although his shaping of contemporary experiences—such poems as *Todesfuge* (Fugue of Death), about the horror of the concentration camps—made him famous, more characteristic of Celan was the hermetic independence of images that refer only to themselves. In his early collections—*Der Sand aus den Urnen* (1948, The Sand from the Urns) and *Mohn und Gedächtnis* (1952, Poppy and Memory)—Celan unfolded an antiworld, which revealed itself to be a descendant of French surrealism, with its occasionally mannerist genitive metaphors. The metaphors served him as a bulwark against reality.

But for Celan, poetry resided not only at the "edge of silence," as has often been stated in a standard formula associated with him. It was also a magic game of words that goes back to the Jewish cabala and revolves around the idea of representing the relationship to God through language. Celan's development could be seen in the volume *Von Schwelle zu Schwelle* (1955, From Threshold to Threshold) and reached a first climax in his fourth volume, *Sprachgitter* (1959, Talking Grilles). In *Talking Grilles* the fundamental metaphor, of which the title is a variant, can also be construed as a symbolic formula expressing Celan's view of the relationship between language and reality: In medieval cloisters the tiny windows through which the nuns could speak with the outside world were called talking grilles. In these poems language apparently had an analogous double function for Celan: to make possible and to prevent communication with reality; to preserve the hermetic zone and to send signals into the outside world.

Because of this increasing concentration on language, Celan's poetry since the mid-1950s became increasingly more compressed. The long lines, with their surrealistic metaphors, gave way to syntactically concise verses, which had the effect of expanding the words to maximum meaning in the most limited space. He began to form new nouns through contraction, and to reactivate obsolete words. A corollary to this approach was his dismemberment of words, which were sometimes broken up into parts that were separated by several lines from one another. Cryptic quotations added to the hermetic quality of his language.

Celan's focus on language and the increasing foreignness of the vocabulary were also characteristic of his later collections: *Die Niemandsrose* (1963, No-Man's Rose), *Atemwende* (1967, Reversal of Breath), and *Fadensonnen* (1968, Suns of Threads). In his last poems Celan combined elements from three different languages: Middle High German, New High German, and Hebrew. After his visit to Israel in 1969 Celan apparently tried, through his affirmation of the "fulfilled word" of Hebrew tradition, to make overt the latent affinity of his language for the language of Hasidic mysticism. It is more than mere chance that the hermetism of his poetry became poetically viable when it was blended with Judaic motifs.

POLITICAL POETRY

A trend of special importance in contemporary German poetry has been the political poem, which has had two main sources. The first was the didactic parlando poetry of Brecht, who realized with artful simplicity the lyrical value inherent in colloquial language and contemporary political themes. Brecht's political poetry was emulated both in West Germany and in East Germany. In addition to his great influence on contemporary German drama, Brecht had an importance to poetry comparable to that of Gottfried Benn in the early 1950s. The second source for political poetry was the general politicizing of life in West Germany. The late-symbolist or hermetic poem of the 1950s now became suspect as elitist aestheticism. In its place writers demanded a poetry that could deal with immediate reality and reflect social processes.

Hans Magnus Enzensberger, whose works have been dominated by social criticism, was one of the first to follow the Brechtian line of prosaic poetry directly concerned with reality. His aggressive first collection of verse, *verteidigung der wölfe* (1957, wolves' defense), combined various levels of language—slang and colloquial speech as well as professional jargon—into a lyric montage that questioned the traditional conventions of bourgeois society. Enzensberger announced his program in a line in the poem *ins lesebuch für die Oberstufe* (into the reader for the Upper Level): "read no odes, my son, read the train schedules." His essay *Scherenschleifer und Poeten* (1955, Scissor-Grinders and Poets) consciously developed a system of poetics counter to Gottfried Benn's: to replace the notion of the poem as an absolute, Enzensberger enunciated the thesis that the poem is a useful object that must provide insights in order to assume its role in the social process.

The poems of Enzensberger's next two collections—*landessprache* (1960, language of the land) and *blindenschrift* (1964, braille)—were filled with attacks on the political indifference that prevailed in the society about him. Naturally, these tendentious poems used the forms of language developed by Brecht (simplicity of sentence structure, parody, mixture of levels of language, and simplicity of vocabulary). At the same time, Enzensberger skillfully applied the international language of modern poetry —from Apollinaire to Auden. He also used elements from the romantic tradition, from folk poetry, from children's poetry. After 1965 Enzensberger's views became so radical (he now presented them in his journal *Kursbuch,* primarily to polemicize and agitate) that he stopped writing poetry and instead turned to polemical prose.

The Austrian Erich Fried, who has been living in England since 1938, likewise adopted Brecht's political poetry and made a reputation mainly with the volumes of poems he published in the 1960s: *Reich der Steine* (1963, Realm of Stones), *Warngedichte* (1964, Poems of Warning), *Überlegungen* (1964, Reflections), and *Anfechtungen* (1967, Attacks). As in Enzensberger, in Fried, too, the simple language and the parlando tone of Brechtian poetry has dominated, as have themes taken from contemporary political life. At the same time, there are elements in Fried's poetry from the world of magic, from the past, and from fairy tales. Similarly, Fried's language reaches back to old aphoristic forms, counting rhymes, and children's songs. Fried's propensity for word play and for experimental repetitions of words has inherent in it the danger of a playful formalism. However, in his most recent volume of poetry, *und Vietnam und* (1968, and Vietnam and), he returned to the aphoristic form of didactic poems. The themes of *and Vietnam and* also indicated a radicalization of Fried's politics.

The works of a number of younger authors can be classified with those of Enzensberger and Fried: Yaak Karsunke's *Kilroy und andere* (1967, Kilroy and Others) and *reden und ausreden* (1969, speeches and excuses); Friedrich Christian Delius's (born 1943) *Kerbholz* (1965, Tallies) and *Wenn wir, bei Rot* (1969, When We, on Red); and Nicolas Born's (born 1937) *Marktlage* (1967, State of the Market) and *Wo mir der Kopf steht* (1970, Where I Should Begin).

Brecht's political poetry has been even more influential in East Germany, although here the work of some of his followers has been marked by a didactic superficiality approaching agitprop literature. Nonetheless, some writers have created artistically valid poetry. Günter Kunert (born 1929), whose career was promoted by Johannes R. Becher, kept his first volume of poetry, *Wegschilder und Mauerinschriften* (1950, Road Signs and Inscriptions on Walls), consistent with the official line: in laconic, aphoristic verses modeled on Brecht he came to grips with the Nazi past. In the collections *Tagewerke* (1960, Day Labors), *Das kreuzbrave Liederbuch* (1961, The Honest Songbook), and *Erinnerung an einen Planeten* (1963, Recollection of a Planet) Kunert attempted to balance the occasional criticism and irony he aimed at his society with a basically positive attitude.

Kunert's volume *Der ungebetene Gast* (1965, The Uninvited Guest), however, took up controversial themes: his questions about society and the meaning of his own life could no longer find satisfaction in the ideologically prescribed solutions. Implied criticism of the state was evident, for example, in the ironic five-line poem *Unterschiede* (Distinctions), which described the difficult situation of an author in East Germany. These shifts in values contributed greatly to Kunert's recent isolation in East Germany.

A similar fate has fallen to Wolf Biermann, the most dynamic younger poet in East Germany and the one with the richest ideas about form. Instead of composing poems that followed paths already laid out, this guitar-playing cafe singer and balladeer went his own way. The models for his poems were François Villon, Heinrich Heine (1797–1856), and Joachim Ringelnatz (1883–1934). Other influences were Brecht's ballads and revolutionary workers' songs. Biermann's uncompromising poems in *Die Drahtharfe* (1968, The Wire Harp) and *Mit Marx- und Engelszungen* (1968, With the Tongues of Marx and Engels) led to his house arrest and to a ban on the publication of his works in East Germany.

The simple, songlike forms of Biermann's early poems (ballads, children's rhymes, love songs, folk songs) have given way in his most recent works to contemplative rhetoric and concise diction. He formulates doubts and questions as he attacks ideological dogmatism, petrified traditions, bureaucracy, and the concealment of political and economic mistakes. His criticisms of negative social forces, however, have not in any sense been an attack on communism itself but rather on its abuses.

Biermann's attitudes thus exemplify the changes that have taken place in the literature of East Germany during the last few years. The confrontation between socialism and remnants of the bourgeoisie is no longer a subject for literature; instead, the tensions that have developed within the socialist society have now become the main topic. For Biermann, the writer's primary interest is to formulate a means of coming to grips with problems that can inhibit the development of the individual in a socialist society. Typical of this kind of restriction are the threat to the individual represented by the party apparatus and the resulting stifling of sensitivity and creativity. Biermann's poetry is thus a document of a period of objective development in East Germany, even though the nation itself refuses to acknowledge his poetry officially.

Two other poets, Franz Fühmann and Reiner Kunze, both more willing to accept the official doctrine of East Germany and less original than Biermann and Kunert, can nonetheless be grouped with them.

Franz Fühmann published his first postwar poems in the journal *Aufbau*. Writing in total conformity with the official line about the fascist past, he strongly criticized capitalism and Hitler's dictatorship in the volume *Die Nelke Nikos* (1953, Nikos's Carnation), while at the same time praising Marxism, the working class, and the Soviet Union. Despite all the rhetorical power that surrounds the theme of building a new Germany, the agitprop verses of Fühmann were surprisingly conventional in wording and even occasionally descended to the level of cliché.

During the phase of national self-evaluation in East Germany, Fühmann's emphatic eulogies of socialism differed sharply from the work of the more critical authors, such as Wolf Biermann, Peter Hacks, Heiner Müller (born 1929), and Hermann Kant (born 1926). More successful were Fühmann's poems in *Die Richtung der Märchen* (1962, The Direction of Fairy Tales). Here Fühmann revived themes from fairy tales and sagas, while he tried to enrich the form of his poetry by using such devices as the *Nibelungenlied* stanza. He also achieved an intensity of expression through the use of compact metaphors.

Reiner Kunze began his literary career with the love poems and songs of *Vögel über dem Tau* (1959, Birds above the Dew). In these simple verses, resembling folk songs, he used an idyllic environment in trying to define the role of the individual. In the volume *Aber die Nachtigall jubelt* (1962, But the Nightingale Rejoices) Kunze addressed himself more firmly to present-day politics, and he was unsparing in his ironic criticism of specific practices connected with art as a business. The children's poems in this collection continued the noncontroversial line of his first volume of poetry and showed an increasing tendency toward idyllic themes.

To date, the poems in Kunze's *Widmungen* (1963, Dedications) have elicited the greatest response. Here Kunze revealed himself as an artistic eclectic who has absorbed a wide variety of formal and thematic influences, particularly from Czech poetry (which he has translated). On the whole, Kunze has not so much continued the tradition of Brecht's didactic poetry as he has developed a modern version of Anacreontic poetry, which occasionally is marked by flight from reality.

CONCRETE POETRY

Concrete poetry has also become increasingly important in the last ten years, although it dates back to the early 1950s. While it was esteemed only by an in-group at first, it is now much more widely accepted. The beginning of concrete poetry can be dated almost exactly—1954, the year of publication of Helmut Heissenbüttel's *Kombinationen* (Combinations).

Concrete poetry, which can be defined as a poetic statement about language in which the method largely becomes the content, borrowed some ideas of dadaism from Kurt Schwitters (1887–1948) and Hans Arp (1887–1966). However, at the same time it has declared itself a contemporary international movement, the aims of which can be perceived just as well in Swedish manifestos as in Brazilian blueprints.

In the German-speaking world Helmut Heissenbüttel has been the most consistent in attempting to put these theoretical aims into practice. His main experimental works have been the six *Textbooks,* which appeared between 1960 and 1967. In Heissenbüttel's work, language has become more and more reduced to its elements. The musicality and imagery of his first volume, *Combinations,* yielded in his very next volume, *Topographien* (1956, Topographies), to a skeletonizing of language that occasionally lapsed into playing games and performing tricks with the letters of the alphabet. Heissenbüttel has made a valuable contribution to German poetry by demanding that readers surrender their conventional expectations of language, that language be liberated from its worn-out formulas. But he has run the danger of lapsing into mannerism. Nonetheless, he has emerged as in ingenious theoretician of concrete poetry.

Eugen Gomringer has also reduced metaphors to single words in *die konstellationen* (1964, constellations) and *das stundenbuch* (1965, the book of hours). His symmetrical patterns of words have special significance when he does succeed in making apparent how such abstract combinations can apply to personal experiences.

Franz Mon's *artikulationen* (1959, articulations), and *sehgänge* (1962, lines of sight) went to even greater extremes in destroying the conventional patterns of language by dissolving the texts into images that consist of constellations of isolated letters. The result is to negate completely the communicative function of language. Certainly, the radicality of Mon's approach has the risk of sterile esotericism. In the serial texts of *herzzero* (1968, heart-zero) this danger was partly avoided by Mon's method of using montages and plays on words to allow the development of fields of words connected by associations. The fields of words can be viewed as "word stories," which again produce certain connections.

Other concrete poets are the Austrians Ernst Jandl and Gerhard Rühm. It is also possible to find similarities between the Viennese group of poets and the concrete poets of West Germany, although no direct connections exist.

DRAMA

THE OLDER GENERATION

During the first decades of this century the German drama achieved a high point in its development, with the expressionist plays of Carl Sternheim (1878–1942), Georg Kaiser, Ernst Barlach (1870–1938), Ernst Toller, and Fritz von Unruh. This lively activity was abruptly interrupted by the Nazi policies during the 1930s. Only a few dramatists succeeded in preserving the continuity of their productivity in emigration. They considered themselves disadvantaged in two ways. First, not only had they been displaced from the society that provided the subject matter for their dramas, but had lost the theaters that could have produced their plays. Moreover, they had no audience that could respond to their plays. The dramatists did not find emergency solutions comparable to the publishing houses and journals that existed in exile for other kinds of writers. The employment a number of them found as screenplay writers in Hollywood represented no real continuation of their work but rather a frequent degeneration to the level of writing farces.

Thus, only a few dramatists continued to develop along the paths they had been pursuing in pre-Hitler Germany. Most either stopped writing plays based on reality—like Kaiser and Sternheim, who both continued to write only plays concerning private involvements—or, like Carl Zuckmayer, Fritz Hochwälder (born 1911), and Brecht, they wrote without hope of seeing their work performed. Although some émigrés discovered with pleasure that the Zürich Schauspielhaus after 1945 would perform their plays (concern over the aggressive neighbor to the north made Swiss theaters unwilling to perform émigré plays during the period 1935–45), the new German postwar theaters showed hardly any interest in the works of exiled dramatists.

Thus, only three prewar playwrights fully succeeded in reestablishing themselves after 1945: Zuckmayer, Hochwälder, and especially Brecht. Brecht's plays, his theater practices, and his theory of the epic theater influenced the German theater tremendously after 1945. But the popularity of Zuckmayer and Hochwälder lasted only through the mid-1950s. By now both writers are virtually forgotten.

Carl Zuckmayer, who began as an expressionist, established his reputation in the late 1920s with the folkloric naturalism of such lively plays as *Der fröhliche Weinberg* (1925, The Happy Vineyard), *Schinderhannes* (1927, Schinderhannes), and *Katharina Knie* (1929, Katharina Knie). Zuckmayer made a triumphant comeback with *Des Teufels General* (1946, The Devil's General), a play written in exile. This play, which analyzed the conflict of conscience in General Harras, who comes to terms with Nazism because of his passion for flying, used the techniques of the traditional psychological theater and was regarded as a suitable representation of a typical German dilemma. When the general discovers aircraft sabotage and is unable to choose between loyalty to the system and loyalty to the saboteur, who is a friend, he voluntarily goes to his own death. The flat dramatic technique and the moralizing of *The Devil's General* are no longer convincing because of their glaring tendentiousness.

The deficiencies of Zuckmayer's subsequent plays, which attracted scarcely any notice, were evident from the start. In *Das kalte Licht* (1955, The Cold Light), a free adaptation of the life of Klaus Fuchs, who for idealistic reasons had engaged in atomic espionage, Zuckmayer attempted to present a contemporary statement, in which the outcome of top-level international intrigue is determined by the course of a love affair. Zuckmayer's most recent play, *Die Uhr schlägt eins* (1961, The Clock Strikes One), tried to depict social and personal problems; through journalistic accounts, Zuckmayer showed conflicts between generations and confrontations between opportunism and idealism. The accumulation of external theatrical effects sometimes caused the play to lapse into sensationalism.

The Austrian Fritz Hochwälder, now living in Zürich, enjoyed international success with the play *Das heilige Experiment* (1943, The Holy

Experiment), which was written in Switzerland. His dramatic technique, like Zuckmayer's, has also been conventional. In *The Holy Experiment,* using the historical metaphor of the Jesuit state in Paraguay, Hochwälder attempted to answer such fundamental moral questions as the relationship between social justice and God's realm on earth.

Hochwälder's later historical plays failed to repeat the earlier success of *The Holy Experiment.* They included *Donadieu* (1953, Gift to God), which was inspired by a ballad by Conrad Ferdinand Meyer (1825–1898); the modern mystery play *Donnerstag* (1959, Thursday); and *Der öffentliche Ankläger* (1947, The Public Prosecutor), which was based on events of the French revolution. Hochwälder's plays of the late 1950s and early 1960s—such as *1003* (1963, 1003) and *Der Himbeerpflücker* (1964, The Raspberry Picker)—which presented contemporary subjects in the manner of Georg Kaiser and occasionally of Pirandello, were less important for their pointed didacticism and moralizing than for their continuing certain traditions of the popular theater, principally those of the Vienna Volkstheater. As with Zuckmayer, Hochwälder's popularity has diminished considerably in recent years.

Bertolt Brecht can be ranked as a traditional dramatist only in that he was a link between the prewar and postwar German drama. While Zuckmayer and Hochwälder continued to use conventional techniques, Brecht's dramatic work broke with psychological or Aristotelian theater and created the "theater of alienation," or, as it is better known, epic theater.

Brecht's work, which has now become famous throughout the world, crossing all political boundaries, influenced to a greater or lesser degree every German dramatist of the 1950s and 1960s—from Friedrich Dürrenmatt to Peter Weiss (born 1916). Perhaps nowhere is his reputation greater than in East Germany, where he is revered as a canonized figure by the young dramatists.

Almost all of Brecht's plays have been influential: the realistic didactic theater of *Furcht und Elend des dritten Reiches* (1937–38, Fear and Misery in the Third Reich) and *Die Tage der Commune* (1948–49, The Days of the Commune); such purposefully grotesque reworkings of musical theater as *Die Dreigroschenoper* (1928, The Threepenny Opera), and *Aufstieg und Fall der Stadt Mahagonny* (1927–29, Rise and Fall of the City of Mahagonny); oratorical parables, such as *Der Jasager und der Neinsager* (1930, He Who Says Yes and He Who Says No), *Die Maßnahme* (1930, The Measures Taken), and *Die Ausnahme und die Regel* (1930–37, The Exception and the Rule); such didactic studies of life and character as *Die Mutter* (1932, The Mother), *Mutter Courage und ihre Kinder* (1939, Mother Courage and Her Children), and *Leben des Galilei* (1938–39, Life of Galileo); and parables of alienation that resemble fairy tales, such as *Der gute Mensch von Sezuan* (1938–42, The Good Woman of Setzuan), *Der kaukasische Kreidekreis* (1949, The Caucasian Chalk Circle), and *Turandot, oder der Kongreß der Weißwäscher* (Turandot, or the Congress of Whitewashers), which was found among Brecht's unpublished papers after his death. The rich legacy left by Brecht is in abundant evidence in the German drama of the last two decades.

A NEW BEGINNING

New playwrights gradually began to emerge after 1945. For a number of reasons, the reestablishment of the drama during the first postwar years was a slow process. On the one hand, there was no single outstanding young author. Wolfgang Borchert's *Outside the Door* remained a somewhat isolated event because of Borchert's early death in 1947.

Additional reasons for the slow recovery of the theater can be found in the structure of the German theater. Considered a traditional educational institution, the German theater was not expected primarily to foster new writing. As in the past, classic writers continued to dominate the repertory.

A special problem for the post-1945 German drama was its preceding isolation. For a decade and a half the German theater had been cut off from international developments and now found itself in urgent need to catch up with the rest of the world. Thus, the repertory of the first postwar years was dominated by many foreign authors: the plays of Tennessee Williams, Thornton Wilder, Eugene O'Neill, Christopher Fry, J. B. Priestley, Jean Giraudoux, Jean-Paul Sartre, and Albert Camus were frequently performed. In competition with these writers, only a few of the younger German authors succeeded in attracting attention. For the most part, these were dramatists whose plays followed the direction already delineated by Borchert's *Outside the Door,* that is, works that discussed the most recent period of German history and the effects of the war.

Claus Hubalek (born 1926) was one of the first to take up the ideas of Brecht. In *Der Hauptmann und sein Held* (1954, The Captain and His Hero) he presented an epic sequence of scenes forming a satiric representation of hypocritical military logic. The blundering fool Kellermann escapes sadistic treatment when he is accidentally recommended for an Iron Cross. His captain accepts him as a protégé and treats him as the hero of the company at first but later wants to have him executed when the swindle is finally uncovered. *The Captain and His Hero,* with its pointed didacticism, was more successful than Hubalek's *Keine Fallen für die Füchse* (1957, No Traps for Foxes), in which he attempted to dramatize the division of Berlin through a comedy about narrow-minded people.

To present the war in *Triumph in tausend Jahren* (1955, Triumph in a

Thousand Years), Peter Hirche (born 1923) used techniques of parables. Here, too, the purpose was to accentuate the moral bankruptcy caused by the war. The case history of a universally admired hero is examined to show how this man saves himself in a crisis by abandoning his company to its fate after it has been surrounded by the Russians.

Leopold Ahlsen (born 1927) had his most lasting success with *Philemon und Baukis* (1955, Philemon and Baucis), a play that stood directly in the tradition of the naturalistic theater and contained well-drawn characters. Old Nikolaos illustrates the conflict between conscience and obedience: out of a spirit of hospitality he protects a wounded German soldier and consequently brings down upon himself the vengeance of the Greek partisans, with whom he does sympathize.

Ahlsen's later plays continued to use the techniques of conventional drama, as for example the sketches of the French king Louis XI in *Sie werden sterben, Sire* (1963, You Shall Die, Sire) and Ahlsen's play about Luther, *Der arme Mann Luther* (1964, Poor Man Luther). In *Raskolnikoff* (1961, Raskolnikoff) Ahlsen reached back to the literary past, to Dostoevski. Ahlsen's conventional dramatic technique has also been influenced by television, the medium he has chosen to work in most in recent years.

ALLEGORIES AND POETIC PARABLES

Alongside realistic plays, the postwar German drama has also produced allegories and parables, which have reflected the influence of the poetic theater in France (Anouilh and Giraudoux) and in England (Fry), as well as of the philosophical theater (Sartre and Camus).

Richard Hey (born 1926) tried to portray the threat of totalitarian systems through fairy-tale allegory in the play *Thymian und Drachentod* (1955, Thymian and the Dragon's Death), which takes place in an imaginary kingdom. Although this play exhibited a remarkable precision, indeed elegance, of language, the distancing caused by the use of allegory proved ultimately to be an artistic dead end for Hey, as *Lysiane* (1956, Lysiane) and *Der Fisch mit dem goldenen Dolch* (1960, The Fish with the Gold Dagger) demonstrated.

Characteristics of the parable can also be found in Hermann Moers's (born 1930) play *Zur Zeit der Distelblüte* (1958, In Thistle Season), which described the situation of five prisoners sentenced for life. A thistle growing between the cracks in the wall brings the deadening order of prison life into symbolic focus. In Moers's *Der kleine Herr Nagel* (1964, Little Mr. Nail), the stylization as a parable extended even to the characters, who are skeletonized into mere functions, and who unmask the unscrupulousness of society through their mechanical behavior.

Karl Wittlinger (born 1922) also has a penchant for parable in his plays, which have been among the greatest theatrical successes in the German postwar theater, although their literary quality has been a subject of debate. *Kennen Sie die Milchstrasse?* (1956, Do You Know the Milky Way?) was a tragicomedy of alienation, which described, through a psychiatric patient, a loss of identity as a flight into illusion. The psychiatrist finally comes to share the fantasy of his patient and sets out with him to search for his imaginary homeland, a star in the Milky Way.

Wittlinger's play *Seelenwanderung* (1962, Metempsychosis) concerned the relationship between two formerly unemployed men, Bum and Axel, one of whom exchanges his soul for a successful career. *Metempsychosis* was an allegorical criticism of contemporary social conditions, although the criticism remained schematic. The comedy *Zum Frühstück zwei Männer* (1962, Two Men for Breakfast) was in the tradition of the commercial theater. Both the dialogue and the plot of this work demonstrated Wittlinger's technical virtuosity.

The influence of the poetic theater of Giraudoux, Anouilh, and Fry was particularly evident in the plays of Dieter Waldmann (1926–1971). His works also showed the love of playfulness found in the commedia dell'arte and in German romantic comedy. Waldmann displayed his virtuosity with form in his early dramas, *Der blaue Elefant* (1958, The Blue Elephant) and *Atlantis* (1963, Atlantis), in both of which he transmuted reality by using fairy-tale elements. His social criticism, which he tried to introduce simultaneously, remained in the background.

In Waldmann's most successful play, *Von Bergamo bis morgen früh* (1960, From Bergamo to Tomorrow Morning), characters from the commedia dell'arte are brought to new life, and the aesthetic transformation that Harlequin and Pierrot undergo in their impromptu play suggests a victory over reality. Despite all his virtuosity, Waldmann's dramatic efforts remained isolated achievements, without influence on other writers.

Tankred Dorst (born 1925) has participated in almost all of the movements of German drama since 1945. His first play, *Gesellschaft im Herbst* (1958, Company in the Autumn), fit perfectly into the mode of the poetic theater, since it proclaimed the aesthetic autonomy of the absolute play and exhibited an obvious dependence on Giraudoux. The farce *Freiheit für Clemens* (1962, Freedom for Clemens), on the other hand, was a philosophical parable that pointed in the direction of Sartre and Camus. *Große Schmährede an der Stadtmauer* (1961, Great Diatribe at the City Wall), which revealed its relationship to Brecht by its very subtitle *"Stück,"* was similar to *The Good Woman of Setzuan* in its dramatic construction and range of themes. *Die Mohrin* (1964, The Moorish Woman), based on a Provençal love story, was effective both in the skillful combination of various theatrical forms (marionette theater, pantomime, and ballet) and in its treatment of the theme of love in ever-changing constellations of characters and scenes.

Dorst's recent play *Toller* (1968, Toller) critically examined the role of Ernst Toller in the Bavarian soviet-style Workers Councils. In *Toller* Dorst made a contribution to documentary theater: by analyzing Toller as a model of revolutionary behavior using the techniques of epic theater, he did for the politicization of contemporary German drama what Toller had done for an earlier period.

The plays of Herbert Asmodi (born 1923)—*Pardon wird nicht gegeben* (1958, No Pardon Is Granted), *Nachsaison* (1959, Postseason), *Die Menschenfresser* (1961, The Cannibals), and *Mohrenwäsche* (1963, Whitewashing)—can also be grouped with the poetic theater. But Asmodi is less related to the allegory of fairy tales than he is to the tradition of social comedy. He has succeeded occasionally, as in *Whitewashing,* in writing sharply satirical portrayals which continued the tradition of Frank Wedekind (1864–1918) and Carl Sternheim and which were well-founded criticisms of contemporary conditions in West Germany.

While the plays of Waldmann, Dorst, and Asmodi have been most successful in their playfulness and their skillful manipulation of form, the plays of Siegfried Lenz constitute a dehydrated philosophical didactic theater that professes to be profound. His dramas not only illustrate all the disadvantages of didactic drama; they also fail to achieve the level of conceptual sharpness found in his models, Sartre and Camus. Lenz's first and most successful play to date, *Die Zeit der Schuldlosen* (1961, The Time of Innocents), showed Lenz to be an attentive reader of Werner Bergengruen's novel *The Archtyrant and the Court* and of Walter Jens's novel *No: The World of the Accused,* as well as of Sartre's *Morts sans sépulture* and Camus's *Les justes.* If, at any rate, Lenz deserved credit for the moral force of these dramatic reflections on totalitarian systems and the corruptibility of the people exposed to them, the philosophical profundity of his next plays, *Das Gesicht* (1964, The Face) and *Augenbinde* (1970, Blindfold), was reduced to the declamations of masklike figures who failed to come to life on the stage.

THE THEATER OF THE ABSURD

Just as the poetic theater and the theater of philosophical parables represented an adoption of literary trends already well established in other literatures, particularly French, so too the German theater of the absurd has been dominated by foreign models, principally Samuel Beckett and

Eugène Ionesco. In the German drama since World War II—as far as one can see at the present time—the theater of the absurd seems to be only a temporary episode and one that has been pursued by only two authors: by Wolfgang Hildesheimer (born 1916) and by Günter Grass in the early period of his career.

Hildesheimer presented his theoretical commitment to absurdist drama in *Erlanger Rede über das absurde Theater* (1966, Erlangen Lecture on the Theater of the Absurd). His first play, *Der Drachenthron* (1955, The Dragon Throne), which he published in a revised version in 1959 under the title *Die Eroberung der Prinzessin Turandot* (The Conquest of Princess Turandot), was a clever adaptation of a familiar subject. Despite Hildesheimer's stylizing of the plot and his playful reworking of the dialogue, the dramatic action remained comprehensible. But in *Landschaft mit Figuren* (1958, Landscape with Figures) and *Pastorale, oder die Zeit für Kakao* (1958, Pastoral, or Time for Cocoa) the action was dominated by visual paradoxes, independent gags involving gestures, and linguistic jokes, the absurdity of which when enacted on stage negated every tradition of realism.

The cryptic quality of Hildesheimer's scenes and combinations of scenes, which have had a cabaret quality, has increased in his most recent plays: *Die Verspätung* (1961, Lateness) and *Nachtstück* (1963, Nightpiece). His playful spirit has retreated behind a profoundly puzzling darkness. In *Lateness* he showed, in the manner of Ionesco, the senselessness of a world dissolving into codes and fragments. In *Nightpiece* this pessimism increased even more: the unbridgeable loneliness of the individual became intensified to the point of madness.

In the early plays of Günter Grass one can see illogical combinations of gags and long, drawn-out situations: *Noch zehn Minuten bis Buffalo* (1954, Only Ten Minutes to Buffalo), *Die bösen Köche* (1956, The Wicked Cooks), *Hochwasser* (1957, Flood), and *Onkel, Onkel* (1957, Uncle, Uncle). But neither the playful spirit of Hildesheimer's early plays nor the monomaniacal pessimism of his more recent plays was present in Grass's plays. The absurdity of Grass's plays approaches aesthetic nonsense, which he sometimes seems to take too seriously.

In *Die Plebejer proben den Aufstand* (1966, The Plebeians Rehearse the Uprising) Grass broke from the mode of his early plays. By following the path of Brecht both formally and thematically (the play attempted to depict in stylized fashion Brecht's behavior during the June, 1952, uprising in East Berlin) Grass made a contribution to documentary theater. But in *Davor* (1969, In Front) he returned totally to conventional dramaturgy. What was intended as a contemporary play of social criticism and as an effort to depict the restlessness and the politicization of youth in the late 1960s turned out to be a somewhat boring dramatic paraphrase of Grass's novel *Örtlich betäubt* (1970, Local Anaesthetic), which was much less conventional in form.

CRITICAL REALISM

The form that Grass was striving for in *In Front* was characteristic of another trend in contemporary German drama—a critical realism that developed both the conventional techniques of psychological theater and the ideas of Brecht's epic theater. Critical realism, with its orientation toward social realities, gained popularity during the early 1960s as a kind of countermovement to the theater of the absurd and the poetic theater. Toward the end of the 1960s it turned radical and adopted the forms of documentary theater.

In Martin Walser's (born 1927) first play, *Der Abstecher* (1961, The Detour), there were grotesque effects reminiscent of the theater of the absurd and a didacticism reminiscent of Brecht. But Walser combined these qualities into a biting satire of marriage among the lower bourgeoisie. "A German Chronicle," the subtitle of Walser's second play, *Eiche und Angora* (1962, Oak and Angora), could also be applied to two later plays, *Überlebensgroß Herr Krott* (1963, Mr. Krott Bigger than Life) and *Der schwarze Schwan* (1964, The Black Swan). In these three plays Walser was concerned with exposing the slackening of national conscience in West Germany and with criticizing present modes of behavior.

In *Oak and Angora* the thesis of Brecht's *Schweyk im zweiten Weltkrieg* (1941–44, Schweyk in the Second World War), namely, that a simple man can prevail over the "roundheads" merely by adapting in his stupid way to existing circumstances, was to a certain extent reversed into its antithesis. The naïve petty-bourgeois Alois Grübel is willing to adapt to changing social conditions, but he is always hobbling along behind new developments without ever catching up. As a result, he sometimes comes into conflict with the prevailing circumstances.

Mr. Krott Bigger than Life was a penetrating parable of the omnipotence of money, which Krott, a kind of politicized Baal, personifies allegorically. There is a definite reason to doubt the sociological truth of this parable of social criticism, for it tries to attack the capitalist system as personified by an anti-hero from the period of early capitalism. Since this type is rarely encountered any longer in contemporary business practice, Walser has only succeeded in re-creating a past era.

In *The Black Swan* Walser used various characters to show how people try to escape from their past involvements in concentration camp crimes: by hiding, like Liberé, the former concentration camp physician, in self-imposed asceticism in a sanatorium for neurotics; by adapting to the present and forgetting the past, like Professor Goothein, the former gas-chamber specialist and "black swan"; or by seeking moral retribution, like Goothein's son Rudi, who finally shoots himself. Walser used surrealistic techniques in *The Black Swan* to expose the crimes of the Nazis, employing such devices as fragments of consciousness, memories of childhood games, monologues, and debates.

Hans Günter Michelsen (born 1920), who made his name in the theater during the early 1960s, has also examined social problems critically. His one-act play *Stienz* (1955, Stienz), which was first performed in 1963, emphasized the insurmountable power of the past in the person of a retired major, whose foolish reliving of the past estranges him from the present. Michelsen was able to expand the destiny of an individual into a typical existential situation. In *Lappschiess* (1963, Lappschiess) Michelsen converted an inner monologue into a visual representation on the stage. Through an impressive interweaving of different time levels, *Lappschiess* shows the attempt of an old man and a girl to grasp the present by re-creating the past. The special interest of Michelsen's play lay in the fact that the abstract theme was not given the treatment of a parable but was presented in a concretely drawn milieu. The language was free of vacuous profundity and consisted predominantly of colloquial speech.

Michelsen's *Helm* (1965, Helm) and *Drei Akte* (1965, Three Acts) also had realistic plots. In *Three Acts* Michelsen showed clearly the systematic collapse of bourgeois life. In *Helm* the innkeeper Helm's attempt to overcome the past by inviting his former military superiors to a drunken revel of reminiscing develops into an impressive demonstration of the potential catastrophes that threaten an individual.

A mood of contemporary catastrophe and a vision of horror were also captured in the early plays of Konrad Wünsche (born 1928): *Vor der Klagemauer* (1962, At the Wailing Wall) and especially *Der Unbelehrbare* (1964, The Unteachable Man), a farce about bourgeois hypocrisy and pretense. Features of critical realism were less apparent in his historical plays, such as *Les Adieux, oder die Schlacht bei Stötteritz* (1964, Les Adieux, or the Battle of Stötteritz), about the Battle of Leipzig of 1813, and his drama of the crusades, *Jerusalem, Jerusalem* (1966, Jerusalem, Jerusalem), inspired by Torquato Tasso's *Gerusalemme liberata*.

Another exponent of critical realism in the theater is Martin Sperr (born 1944). In *Jagdszenen aus Niederbayern* (1966, Hunting Scenes from Lower Bavaria) he attacked the hypocritical morality of a Bavarian village, which joins together unanimously to hunt down a homosexual. Sperr's *Landshuter Erzählungen* (1966, Landshut Tales) demonstrated pointedly, in alternating scenes, how the competition between two contractors gradually deforms their behavior.

EAST GERMAN DRAMA

East German drama offers certain analogies to plays of critical realism, but only in a general way. East German drama has been ideologically based on the doctrines of socialist realism, and its dramaturgy has been, for the most part, strongly influenced by Brecht.

Although there have been many writers of socialist-utilitarian drama, who offer a glaringly propagandistic theater, there are only a few authors who deserve to be singled out for special mention. Helmut Baierl (born 1926) first wrote a didactic political play, *Die Feststellung* (1958, The Findings), which interpreted in complete conformity to the prescribed party line a case of escape from the German Democratic Republic. More complex was Baierl's comedy *Frau Flinz* (1962, Mrs. Flinz), which can be taken as an antithesis of Brecht's *Mother Courage and Her Children*. *Mrs. Flinz* was impressive both for its full development of the central character and its basic theatrical idea. Just as Mother Courage loses one child after another to the war because of her economic shortsightedness, Frau Flinz also loses her children, but to the new state. Her confrontation with the party culminates in a happy ending: having finally gained insight into the workings of the party, she joins it, becomes the manager of an agricultural commune, and emerges finally as a "positive heroine." Baierl succeeded in combining his didactic intent with a comic execution of the plot.

Heiner Müller also began by writing political plays: *Die Korrektur* (1959, The Correction) and *Der Lohndrücker* (1959, The Scab). But these two plays were distinctly superior to the bombast of ordinary agit-prop drama because of their brittleness of language and compression of scenes. Müller's third play, *Die Umsiedlerin, oder das Leben auf dem Lande* (1961, The Relocated Woman, or Life in the Country), showed that he was on a collision course with the party, which at its fifth meeting had expressly designated the mastery of "great form" as a goal for dramatists. As a result, Müller turned to adapting classical material, rather effectively but not without the danger of epigonism. *Herakles 5* (1966, Hercules 5) demonstrated the power of dialectical materialism through the example of Hercules, the autonomous man of action living in a demythologized world. For *Philoktet* (1966, Philoctetus) Müller used Sophocles as his model, but he offered a disillusioning interpretation of the classical myth, out of which deception and betrayal emerged as human motives. His *Ödipus Tyrann* (1967, Oedipus the Tyrant) also demythologized the Sophoclean version.

Hartmut Lange (born 1936), who now lives in West Berlin, also began his career with didactic plays and then proceeded to adaptations of literary works, such as *Die Gräfin von Rathenow* (1970, The Countess of Rathenow), an adaptation of Heinrich von Kleist's (1777–1811) *Die Marquise von O.* (1810, The Marquise of O—). Lange's most interesting work to date has been the comedy *Marski* (1965, Marski), which clearly showed its indebtedness to Brecht's *Herr Puntila und sein Knecht Matti* (1948, Mr. Puntila and His Hired Man, Matti). Marski, an estate owner, is able to bind the less affluent farmers to him through friendship and economic dependency only until there is an alternative in the form of a producers' cooperative. Finally, Marski, who becomes isolated and eventually driven to the verge of committing suicide, is converted to communism through culinary seduction.

The most talented of the East German dramatists is probably Peter Hacks, who not only put Brechtian influence to good use but also was able to draw on his vast learning. In *Eröffnung des indischen Zeitalters* (1954, Onset of the Indian Age), *Der Müller von Sanssouci* (1958, The Miller of Sanssouci), and *Die Schlacht bei Lobositz* (1956, The Battle of Lobositz), Hacks used historical subjects. *Onset of the Indian Age,* a didactic play about Columbus, demonstrated the questionable value of progress and knowledge; *The Miller of Sanssouci* repudiated a patriotic legend; and *The Battle of Lobositz,* an adaptation of Ulrich Bräker's (1735–1798) *Lebensgeschichte* (1789, Autobiography), portrayed an anti-hero during the Seven Years' War, elevating him to a paragon of a socialist citizen. All of these plays by Hacks convincingly advanced Brecht's epic theater and employed a great variety of techniques to avoid the absence of drama that has characterized so many didactic demonstrations.

Hacks came into conflict with official literary doctrine because of his 1958 play, *Worries and Power.* Since he had avoided introducing stereotyped, two-dimensional "positive heroes" as socialist models and instead showed that socialist progress was the result of dialectical developments, the chief ideologist of the Socialist Unity Party, Kurt Hager, accused him in 1962 of not portraying the new man in a manner positive enough so that people could identify with his actions. *Worries and Power* was indeed far from being a superficial, harmonious portrayal of socialist society. Instead, Hacks demonstrated that even in a socialist society unofficial privileges, disguised prosperity, and manipulated private interests exist. All of this is shown through a briquette factory that sacrifices quality for quantity to increase its output. Ironically, this factory is praised by the state, although its procedures seriously hamper the operations of another factory.

In the play *Moritz Tassow* (1965, Moritz Tassow) Hacks also chose a subject from the immediate present in East Germany—the land reform carried out at the end of the war under the direction of the Russian occupation forces. The swineherd Moritz Tassow, who has worked for twelve years for an estate owner, recognizes after the war that the hour of the proletarian revolution has come. He divides the property of the former owner's estate but finally comes into conflict with the bureaucracy of the party and the selfishness of the others.

In the comedy *Amphitryon* (1967, Amphitryon) Hacks presented one of the oldest literary subjects in an admirable inventive variation. Jupiter in particular undergoes a remarkably positive reinterpretation as a "synopsis and embodiment of all human capabilities." The play was noteworthy not only for its successful reworking of the well-known story in terms of social progress but also for its elegant, yet nonderivative, manipulation of blank verse. In the contemporary drama of East Germany Peter Hacks merits a similar status to that of Peter Weiss in West Germany.

THREE MAJOR DRAMATISTS

Because of their international reception and artistic worth, three dramatists in particular have determined the reputation of German drama since 1945: Friedrich Dürrenmatt, Max Frisch, and Peter Weiss. If spectacular success were a criterion, Rolf Hochhuth (born 1931) could also be included. However, the explosive force of his timely themes has not compensated either for his dry, highly inflated language or for his obsolete dramatic techniques, which have been largely borrowed from the philosophical tragedies of the nineteenth century.

Of the three authors, the one with the greatest individuality and theatrical vitality is without doubt the Swiss Friedrich Dürrenmatt. While there are Brechtian influences in his dramas, he has developed his own form of theater. He defined comedy in theoretical terms as a story taking the worst possible turn. In his comedies he has created a dramatic form that not only is based on historical and philosophical principles but is also, in his opinion, the only form appropriate to the chaotic condition of modern times.

Dürrenmatt's first play, *Es steht geschrieben* (1946, It Is Written), about the uprising of the Anabaptists in seventeenth-century Westphalia, was in many respects a descendant of the expressionist *Stationendrama,* particularly in its language and its dramatic techniques. The pessimistic view of history, which is, however, modulated toward the end through the theme of salvation, also pointed backward to expressionism. In 1967 Dürrenmatt published a revision of *It Is Written*; in the new version he sharpened the comedy and dropped the religious coloration of the conclusion of the earlier version.

Dürrenmatt's *Romulus der Große* (1948, Romulus the Great) was also an historical drama, but unlike *It Is Written,* in *Romulus the Great* Dürrenmatt used an almost strict neoclassic dramaturgy, including the observance of the three unities. In developing a highly causal plot, Dürrenmatt reduced world history to chance events carried out by foolish representatives. Even characters with true insight, such as Romulus and the Germanic prince Odoaker, who both want to sabotage history, are finally duped by its mechanisms: the Roman empire that Romulus wants to destroy will soon arise anew in the Gothic empire of the new ruler Theodoric. Although in his second play, *Der Blinde* (1948, The Blind Man), Dürrenmatt had approached allegorical profundity with ponderous language, in *Romulus the Great* he unveiled for the first time the unerring conciseness of his comic dialogue.

In *Romulus the Great* Dürrenmatt attacked the tendency to view history in terms of heroes; in *Die Ehe des Herrn Mississippi* (1952, The Marriage of Mr. Mississippi) he launched a sweeping attack on ideologies, which are presented in terms of allegorical personifications. This play, which borrowed some details of action from Wedekind's *Schloß Wetterstein* (1910, Wetterstein Castle) unfolds a confusing, complicated plot told in the form of a parable. The characters involved include the state prosecutor Florestan Mississippi, a representative of absolute justice; the revolutionary communist Saint-Claude; the unscrupulous, sensual Anastasia, an embodiment of amoral reality; the unprincipled career politician Diego; and the Christian dreamer Count Übelohe. The intrigue of the play arises from the personal relationships of the four men with Anastasia, who personifies the world. All four men want to influence Anastasia and are finally destroyed by her. Dürrenmatt used a bewildering variety of theatrical techniques, such as devices from motion pictures and radio plays, scenarios from the marionette theater, film projections, compressions of time, flashbacks, popular gags, and remarks addressed directly to the audience. By constantly offering new versions of the play, Dürrenmatt has indirectly indicated that he himself is not satisfied with the confusing presentation of the plot.

Ein Engel kommt nach Babylon (1953, An Angel Comes to Babylon) and *Frank der Fünfte* (1959, Frank the Fifth) both showed clearly Dürrenmatt's debt to Brecht. *An Angel Comes to Babylon,* a fairy-tale play about the beggar Akki, who is the only representative of freedom in a rigid and regulated world, has obvious parallels to *The Good Woman of Setzuan. Frank the Fifth,* a grotesque opera about the demoralizing power of money, was a not-altogether-successful variation of *The Threepenny Opera.*

Dürrenmatt's most famous play, *The Visit of the Old Lady,* is comparable to the best plays of Brecht in its sharp critical unmasking of the individual; but its dramatic construction was an independent achievement. Dürrenmatt used the provincial town of Güllen, which is described with the utmost realism, to illustrate moral corruption; the antagonism between the millionairess Claire Zachanassian and her former lover Ill, who rejected her and whose life she now demands from her former hometown for an immense sum of money, is mirrored in the relationship between the external picture of the town and the inner character of its people. At the beginning of the play the town of Güllen is in a state of total ruin, in direct contrast to the unimpaired and undiminished morality of the people. Under the influence of the reward promised by Mrs. Zachanassian, the town begins to change gradually. It shows increasing signs of prosperity, while at the same time the state of the townspeople's conscience deteriorates inexorably until they all join together to murder Ill. The economically healthy, streamlined Güllen that emerges at the conclusion of the play is revealed to be a morally corrupt, purchasable hell, which has been generalized into a symbol of modern society. Dürrenmatt, who has often run the risk of losing himself in either an overly contrived or an overly banal melodramatic plot, succeeded in *The Visit of the Old Lady* in achieving a rare balance between a well-rounded form and a complex subject.

Die Physiker (1961, The Physicists) was another Dürrenmatt play reminiscent of Brecht, although its connections to Brecht's *Life of Galileo* were chiefly thematic; the linear construction of the plot showed the influence of the techniques of psychological theater. Galileo's alternatives, before which he falters—namely, either to stand up for the truth of his discovery or to deny the truth for reasons of self-preservation—can be applied in a certain way to Dürrenmatt's hero Möbius, a genial physicist and inventor of a formula that could endanger the existence of the world. Möbius places moral responsibility above everything else and thus does not publish his discovery but hides behind feigned insanity and retreats into an insane asylum. Dürrenmatt treats Möbius ironically not only by unmasking his fellow patients as physicists and agents of enemy powers but also by having the woman doctor in charge of the establishment, who is really mad, secretly acquire Möbius's formula and dream of world domination.

The Physicists demonstrated anew the senselessness of history, as did Dürrenmatt's most recent important play, *Der Meteor* (1966, The Meteor), which described the fate of the Nobel Prize winner Schwitter. Although he tries in vain to die, Schwitter is resurrected again and again. He is thus shown to be a destructive catalyst in his environment. Since Schwitter is a writer, Dürrenmatt was able to dissect the nimbus of literary fame. *The Meteor* seems to have been an indirect expression of a crisis in the dramatist Dürrenmatt, who has not offered any important plays since 1966.

In 1967 Dürrenmatt published an adaptation of his first play, *It Is Written*; in 1968, an adaptation of Shakespeare, *König Johann nach Shakespeare* (King John in the Manner of Shakespeare); in 1969, an adaptation of Strindberg's *Dödsdansen* under the title *Play Strindberg* (Play Strindberg); and in 1970 an adaptation of Goethe's *Faust* entitled *Play Goethe* (1970, Play Goethe). His most recent play, *Portrait eines Planeten* (1972, Portrait of a Planet), was a further variation on the theme of ideological bankruptcy, here encompassing all of history and politics.

Max Frisch is not the equal of his fellow countryman Dürrenmatt either in theatrical innovation or in the sheer exuberance in writing for the stage. Frisch, who has proved himself an important novelist with such works as *Stiller* (1954, Stiller), *Homo Faber* (1957, Homo Faber), and *Mein Name sei Gantenbein* (1964, Let My Name Be Gantenbein), has presented in his dramas some of the central themes of his novels: the individual's search for his own identity, the facing up to a wasted life, the problems of communication.

Frisch's first play, *Santa Cruz* (1944, Santa Cruz), anticipated features of the contemporary poetic theater, with its echoes of Paul Claudel's *Le soulier de satin* and Hofmannsthal's *Der Abenteurer und die Sängerin* (1899, The Adventurer and the Singer). But thematically *Santa Cruz* was like later Frisch plays in that its allegorical characters illustrated the imaginary life of the individual.

Frisch must have sensed the danger of aesthetic emptiness in the techniques of *Santa Cruz,* for in his next play, *Nun singen sie wieder* (1945, Now They Sing Again), he returned to contemporary subjects and attempted to portray the moral decay caused by the war. Unlike the young dramatists in Germany who wrote about World War II, Frisch's assumptions about war were not based on any personal experience. Although it begins realistically, *Now They Sing Again* becomes excessively stylized by the end.

Die chinesische Mauer (1946, The Chinese Wall) was Frisch's first important play. This historical masquerade play, in which the figure of The Contemporary is used for unity, revealed the senselessness of history by presenting inner reflections delivered as monologues. The apocalyptic signal that triggers these reflections is the dropping of the first atomic bomb on Hiroshima. Frisch's multifaceted collective view of diverse ages would not be conceivable without Brecht's pioneering work in the open dramatic form. Despite the play's excellences, the identification of The Contemporary with the suffering Wang toward the end of the play seems an overly contrived solution.

The complexity of form of *The Chinese Wall* gave way in Frisch's next drama, *Graf Öderland* (1951, Count Öderland), to a comprehensible series of epic pictures making up two parallel levels of action. One level involves the bank cashier Schweiger, who commits a murder without a motive; the other level concerns the state prosecutor, who is uprooted from his organized life by Schweiger's deed. With an ax in his hand, the state's attorney becomes the personification of the legendary Count Öderland, whose revolution finally ended when his country entrusted him with the formation of a new government. Frisch's not-consistently-convincing demonstration of the triumph of reality over man's fantasies was reminiscent of Dürrenmatt's *The Marriage of Mr. Mississippi.* In both cases the form was strongly influenced by Brecht.

Frisch's comedy *Don Juan, oder die Liebe zur Geometrie* (1953, Don Juan, or the Love of Geometry) was more than a playful parodic reworking of a literary myth. Frisch made central a concept he had explored in *Santa Cruz* and *The Chinese Wall:* the moral constancy that is made visible in the personal love relationship. Don Juan, who is more interested in geometrical abstractions than in romance, grows into the role of the seducer against his will. But he gradually overcomes his self-centeredness and accepts his relationship with Miranda as a marriage. *Don Juan* is one of Frisch's most nearly perfect plays; he found in the myth a viable dramatic correlative for his ideas.

Frisch's parable of social criticism, *Biedermann und die Brandstifter* (1958, Biedermann and the Arsonists), his most popular play besides *Andorra,* was much less interesting than *Don Juan. Biedermann and the Arsonists* was an all-too-obvious imitation of Brecht at his most tendentious. It demonstrated with blunt didacticism how a narrow-minded man's fear and uncertainty cause him to dig his own grave.

Despite its great fame, *Andorra* must also be included among Frisch's not-entirely-successful plays. The attempt to interpret the cruelty of the persecution of the Jews in a parable centered on Andri, the outsider turned into a Jew by the people around him, failed in two ways to do justice to its subject: by the irrelevance of the plot and by the old-fashioned dramatic techniques of psychological theater, which necessitated the construction of far-fetched conflicts to convert monstrous mass cruelty into individual cases.

Evidently, Frisch himself recognized the dramatic weakness of *Andorra.* For six years he did not produce any more plays because he saw the necessity of replacing a "dramatic technique of articulation," which formed the basis of *Andorra,* with a new technique, a "dramatic technique of chance." In *Biografie: Ein Spiel* (1967, Biography: A Game), which also contained the theme of the search for identity, Frisch attempted to realize this "dramatic technique of chance," which, as an open-ended construction, presents a reality released from all causality. The depiction of how the behavioral scientist Kürmann attempts to revise his private life retroactively, primarily by nullifying his marriage to Antoinette, indicated a growing pessimism in Frisch. His earlier concept of love as a counterbalance to the senseless course of history lost its validity in *Biography.* Kürmann, who is ill and abandoned, sees no hope at all for a new life, only death before him. Although the play was not a particularly convincing demonstration of a new dramatic technique, it did show an important thematic development in Frisch's theater.

Peter Weiss has followed Brecht more closely than Dürrenmatt or

Frisch, who borrowed formal elements of Brecht's theater but little of his philosophical premises about the ability to change history and the necessity of its transformation by Marxist revolution. In *Marat/Sade* (1964, Marat/ Sade), which made Weiss internationally famous, he acknowledged a third standpoint between east and west, and since then he has unequivocally embraced socialism. His recent play *Trotzki in Exil* (1968, Trotski in Exile) fell decisively between ideological camps, and the communist critics, who at first had celebrated him enthusiastically, took umbrage at his attempt to justify Trotski historically.

Weiss's first play, *Der Turm* (1948, The Tower) was a philosophical parable reminiscent of Calderón's *La vida es sueño* and Hofmannsthal's *Der Turm* (1925, The Tower). It also sounded like Camus in its existential overtones. Weiss's second play, *Die Versicherung* (1952, The Insurance), reflected completely different trends in contemporary German drama. Constructed of shocking details and slapstick gags illogically combined, the play demonstrated the senseless cruelty of self-destructiveness and approached the theater of the absurd.

Not until *Marat/Sade* (full title: *Die Verfolgung und Ermordung Jean Paul Marats dargestellt durch die Schauspielgruppe des Hospizes zu Charenton unter Anleitung des Herrn de Sade* [The Persecution and Assassination of Jean Paul Marat Presented by the Actors' Group of the Hospice at Charenton under the Direction of Mr. de Sade]) did Weiss present his full, independent profile as a dramatist. *Marat/Sade* showed the fruitful results of his study of Brecht. Using all the different techniques of theatrical alienation, Weiss reflected upon the meaning of history through his two protagonists, Marat and Sade; Sade is also the arranger of a play within the play. Marat believes in a revolutionary transformation, while Sade recognizes that senseless cruelty is the only meaning of history. Weiss's multileveled reflections on history in dramatic form serve to reinforce a situation which acts as a leitmotif throughout the entire play and which, though constantly prevented, is finally accomplished toward the end—the murder of Marat by Charlotte Corday.

The artistic success of *Marat/Sade* resulted primarily from Weiss's having employed techniques created by Brecht; indeed, Weiss carried them further with great mastery. But he also achieved impact with his dramatic inventiveness, which was at great remove from the didactic monotony of philosophical theater.

Weiss's drama *Die Ermittlung* (1965, The Investigation), based on the Auschwitz trials held in Frankfurt, is usually mentioned as an important example of documentary theater, since it was Weiss's reworking of the actual Frankfurt trial transcripts. However, the play's construction shows striking conformity with artistic rules, a situation that Weiss himself indicated by citing Dante. And indeed, *The Investigation* shows parallels to the portrayal of hell in the *Divine Comedy*. The strict division of *The Investigation* into cantos is a correlation in form of the rationally organized system of genocide. The counterpart in Dante's time was the hierarchical closed structure of the medieval scholastic view of the world.

This artistic relevance of *The Investigation,* not only in its political ideas but also in its form, has scarcely characterized Weiss's plays that followed it. With *Der Gesang vom lusitanischen Popanz* (1967, Song of the Lusitanian Bogey), a drama attacking Portuguese colonial policies in Angola, Weiss embarked on a path toward a theater of political agitation, which in this instance was not devoid of theatricality. *Diskurs über die Vorgeschichte und den Verlauf des langandauernden Befreiungskrieges in Viet Nam* (1967, Discourse on the Progress of the Prolonged War of Liberation in Vietnam) tried to present the background of the Vietnam war through a broad panorama of the history of Vietnam up through the intervention of the Americans. The play lost all vitality through its rhetorical didacticism; it was little more than an arrangement of slogans, one following the next.

In *Trotski in Exile* Weiss once more focused on individuals and returned to more conventional dramatic techniques. One can see in this play, as in *Marat/Sade,* elements of philosophical theater—a dialectical openness— although, of course, such features seem inconsistent with Weiss's political intentions. His latest play, *Hölderlin* (1971, Hölderlin), was related linguistically, dramatically, and thematically to *Marat/Sade.* Hölderlin combines in himself the polarity of the political visionary Marat and the sober pragmatist Sade.

DOCUMENTARY THEATER

The form of Weiss's recent plays has been characteristic of a trend of the last five years—documentary theater. Such plays as Günter Grass's *The Plebeians Rehearse the Uprising,* Tankred Dorst's *Toller,* the dramas of Heinar Kipphardt (born 1922) and Rolf Hochhuth, and the first play of the poet Hans Magnus Enzensberger are other examples of the genre.

Heinar Kipphardt, who started his career with satiric comedies written while he was still living in East Germany—for example, *Shakespeare dringend gesucht* (1953, Shakespeare Urgently Sought) and *Die Stühle des Herrn Szmil* (1958, Mr. Szmil's Chairs)—first came to prominence through plays that brought documentary reality to the stage. *Joel Brand* (1965, Joel Brand), which resembled a *Stationendrama* in construction, treated Eichmann's plan to exchange deported Jews for ten thousand new trucks to be paid for by the Jewish community. The play generalized this situation into a conflict between economic bargaining and humanitarianism.

In the "staged trial transcript" *In der Sache J. R. Oppenheimer* (1964, In the Matter of J. R. Oppenheimer), Kipphardt worked again with documentary material. He presented a theme that had been treated earlier in Brecht's *Life of Galileo* and Dürrenmatt's *The Physicists*—the natural scientist's responsibility to society. Kipphardt's raw material was the behavior of the American physicist Oppenheimer, who participated in the building of the first atomic bomb, before the House Un-American Activities Committee, which accused him of having delayed the construction of the hydrogen bomb. The conflict of conscience, which Oppenheimer tried to escape by fleeing into pure research, was examined critically. As a specimen of documentary theater, however, it remains difficult to prove to what extent Kipphardt may have distorted "reality" through omissions, selectivity, and the manner of presenting documents.

In the Matter of J. R. Oppenheimer released a flood of documentary historical plays—many written for television—which have offered up just about everything from the Windisch-Graetz affair in Hungary in 1925 to the anti-Hitler conspiracy of July 20, 1944. This popularization of timely subjects—frequently with no interest in structure—has made the documentary theater just as suspect as Rolf Hochhuth's attempts to treat politically explosive contemporary themes with the techniques of confrontation of classical philosophical tragedy. Despite their obviously makeshift dramatic construction, Hochhuth's dramas, which elevate the theater once again to a moral institution, have created some sensational effects. To be sure, the effectiveness of his plays has been the result primarily of his choice of themes.

Hochhuth's "Christian tragedy," *Der Stellvertreter* (1963, The Deputy), which treated the passivity of Pope Pius XII during the period of Nazi persecution of the Jews, produced a worldwide wave of Catholic protest. Similarly, his second play, *Die Soldaten* (1967, The Soldiers), which scorned the senselessness of air attacks on enemy cities and also accused Churchill of complicity in the death of the Polish prime minister Sikorski, led to patriotic protests in England. Hochhuth slipped here into the unthinking manner of political sensationalism despite the extensive supplement of documents that he appended to the editions of his plays, which were supposed to endow his various theses with the strength of scholarly proof.

Hochhuth's *Guerillas* (1970, Guerrillas) also tended toward outright political tendentiousness. This time he took to task the "dollar imperialism" and the "plutocratic oligarchy" of the United States, and vehemently condemned the Vietnam war. His revolutionary prescription for effecting changes in the United States through a coup d'état clearly showed his extremely naïve, conspiratorial view of history, which he reduced to intrigues, espionages, and the strength of a few powerful men. His downgrading of the United States was invalidated by the mindless, overly emotional biases of the play.

Hans Magnus Enzensberger has followed a very different approach to form in drama. In his play *Das Verhör von Habana* (1970, The Havana Interrogation) he expressly rejected any claim to artistic quality and wished to have his sequence of scenes construed as a didactic reconstruction of a typical event (the Bay of Pigs invasion by exiled Cubans in April, 1961, undertaken with the support of the American CIA), which he designated as a "self-portrait of counterrevolution." Thus, to a certain degree Enzensberger assumed a position diametrically opposed to Weiss's. While Weiss has emphasized the artistic value of his documentary theater, and while Hochhuth and Kipphardt have left unclear the extent to which they feel their plays were historical reproductions or subjective interpretations, Enzensberger has primarily been concerned that his dramas receive a political interpretation.

THE SHATTERING OF THEATRICAL FORM

A position opposed to the pointedly political aims of documentary theater is immediately apparent in the plays of several other young German authors. Nonetheless, it is possible to speak of a certain political or social intent in the very shattering of theatrical form. The authors of such works have no intention of engaging in a critical examination of reality. Instead, their aim is to take a critical look at what people think of as reality, which means to look at language itself.

Bazon Brock (born 1936) tried to eliminate the boundary between art and life in his *Theater der Position* (1966–67, Theater of Position) and *Die Besucherschule* (1968, The School for Visitors). By making the audience the subject of the work of art, as in a "happening," he tried to fuse art and life.

Wolfgang Bauer has demonstrated in his plays the monotonous ritual of groups that lack all possibility of communication because they practice social restraint to avoid the extremes of either resignation or outbursts of brutality. In *Party for Six* (1967, the title is in English) Bauer completely violated all expectations of the pretense of "reality" by moving the action offstage. In *Magic Afternoon* (1968, again, the title is in English) he also eliminated the self-contained plot and offered instead trivial linguistic structures of merely esoteric value. Bauer offered another protest against social regimentation in *Change* (1969, another English title), which unveils the emptiness of social life indirectly through an excessively melodramatic plot.

Peter Handke has elevated this criticism of social behavior to a literary method. Handke began by dissecting phrases, especially those that exert real force as prescriptive rules of society. Initially, in actionless *"Sprechstücke"* (speaking plays) like *Selbstbezichtigung* (1966, Self-Accusation), *Weissagung* (1966, Prophecy), and *Hilferufe* (1967, Calling for Help), he toyed with specific verbal patterns, such as confessions, prophecies, and invocations. In *Publikumsbeschimpfung* (1966, Offending the Audience), the work that first established his reputation, he broke with the illusion that the theater is a representation of reality. Instead, the theatrical situation became the reality, and the spectators were declared to be participants in the play, "characters without an author." The ability of language to control behavior was demonstrated most convincingly in the play *Kaspar* (1968, Kaspar). Kaspar, who seems to be a mute at the beginning, is still a person, but he loses his humanity and becomes a marionette after he accepts the language drilled into him by the prompters.

Handke's pantomime *Das Mündel will Vormund sein* (1969, The Ward Wants To Be the Guardian) and his *Quodlibet* (1969; the title is in Latin: As You Like It)—with their collages of fragmented action and clichés—did not equal the effectiveness of *Kaspar*. His most recent play, *Der Ritt über den Bodensee* (1970, The Ride across Lake Constance) was another departure from theatrical illusion. Yet, the idea of being in a theater still threatened to assert itself through clichés of language and the play's intrinsic meaning as a parable, even though the actors perform their roles using their real names and act in unexpected ways. *The Ride across Lake Constance* can be appreciated from the standpoint of Handke's intention of breaking with all conventions, but it sinks into the monotony of routine exercises.

Handke has also tried to express the same criticism of the regimentation of language in the volume of poems *Die Innenwelt der Außenwelt der Innenwelt* (1969, The Inner World of the Outer World of the Inner World) and in several novels. However, with the exception of the short novel *Die Angst des Tormanns beim Elfmeter* (1970, The Goalie's Anxiety at Eleven Meters), which employed certain rudiments of a plot, he reached the point of experimental sterility, the anemia of which is not compensated for by his pretentious theoretical reflections on art.

THE NOVEL

TRADITIONALISM

The German novel immediately after the war was characterized by the desire to heal the rupture through a return to traditionalism. The leading older novelists were Hans Carossa, Hermann Hesse, Ernst Wiechert, and Werner Bergengruen. Other older traditionalists were Otto Brües (1897–

1967), whose realistic novels *Der Silberkelch* (1948, The Silver Chalice), *Simon im Glück* (1948, Simon in Happiness), and *Das vergessene Lied* (1948, The Forgotten Song) described with a great deal of humor the author's relationship to his homeland in the lower Rhine. Edzard Schaper (born 1908) gave Baltic settings to his *Der letzte Advent* (1949, The Last Advent), *Der Mantel der Barmherzigkeit* (1953, The Cloak of Mercy), and *Der Gouverneur, oder der glückselige Schuldner* (1954, The Governor, or the Blissful Debtor).

Among numerous other traditional novelists, Stefan Andres was typical and also one of the best. He wrote many realistic novels, in which he expressed faith in the curative powers of man and presented contemporary history from a Christian perspective.

Andres's most ambitious work was the trilogy *The Flood*. Conceived as a satirical analysis of Nazism, *The Flood* is set in an imaginary realm that has obvious parallels to Hitler's Germany. The first novel, *Das Tier aus der Tiefe* (1949, The Animal from the Deep), portrayed the early phase of fascism. The setting is a mythical southern Italian city, Città morta, in which a sect headed by the "confessor" Leo Olch, a disciple of Nietzsche, demands the depersonalization of man. In accordance with Olch's ideological concept of the herd, the personally insignificant Moosthaler, a professor of theology, assumes the role of leader of the regimented people and begins to rise to a position of real power.

In the second novel, *Die Arche* (1951, The Ark), the fascist situation is presented from the perspective of those who are threatened by the doctrine of normalcy. The different possible forms of resistance in a totalitarian system are presented, but the realism of the parable is changed at the end into a religious hope for salvation: the biblical myth of Noah's ark is retold.

The third novel, *Der graue Regenbogen* (1959, The Gray Rainbow), treats the postwar period. The Normalizer is dead and the war that he unleashed is ended, but the rudiments of his ideology are still present. This is made clear allegorically in the gray rainbow, which symbolizes the constant latent threat to man even after the flood. Andres's use of parable in these novels did not hide their closeness to Ernst Jünger's *On the Marble Cliffs* and Werner Bergengruen's *The Archtyrant and the Court*. None of these works convincingly portrayed the Nazi period. This had to wait for younger authors, especially Günter Grass.

Several Austrian authors may be included among the traditional novelists. However, the designation "traditionalism" when applied to Austrian writers refers solely to their conventional form and to a hope for salvation. In other respects, it was quite unlike German traditionalism: traditionalism in Austrian fiction meant the productive continuation of the narrative tradition of Hermann Broch, Robert Musil, Elias Canetti, and Joseph Roth

(1894–1939). Such novels as Albert Paris Gütersloh's *Eine sagenhafte Figur* (1946, A Legendary Figure) and *Sonne und Mond* (1962, Sun and Moon) and George Saiko's *Auf dem Floß* (1948, On the Raft) and *Der Mann im Schilf* (1955, The Man in the Reeds) continued to give adequate representation to chaotic reality on the model of Musil's negative utopia Kakanien.

Austrian traditionalism reached the artistic heights of Broch and Musil in the novels of Heimito von Doderer. With *The Strudlhof Stairway,* published in 1951, and *The Demons,* which was begun in 1937 but not finished until 1956, Doderer described a particular epoch, which at the same time can be recognized as a general portrait of Vienna. In the masterful interweaving of multiple narrative threads and levels of characters arranged around the central idea of the "humanizing" of the retired officer Melzer, Doderer's *The Strudlhof Stairway* gives a multifaceted representation of Austrian history during the first two decades of this century. The politics of the age were analyzed more thoroughly in *The Demons,* which begins with the burning of the Palace of Justice in Vienna on July 15, 1927, and traces the consequences of this event. The novel showed, through an abundance of persuasive examples, how ideology can assume a demonic factuality.

In Doderer's other novels—*Die Merowinger, oder die totale Familie* (1962, The Merovingians, or the Whole Family) and his mature work *Roman No 7* (Novel No. 7), planned in four parts, of which only two parts, *Die Wasserfälle von Slunj* (1963, The Waterfalls of Slunj) and *Der Grenzwald* (1967, The Woods at the Border), appeared during his lifetime —he continued expertly the tradition of the refined naturalistic novel. In some respects, Doderer's works can be compared with those of Thomas Mann.

NOVELISTS OF GROUP 47

World War II and its immediate aftermath was mirrored particularly in the novels of two authors who were closely associated with the beginnings of Group 47 and its later development: Walter Kolbenhoff (born 1908) and Hans Werner Richter. Kolbenhoff's first novel, *Untermenschen* (1933, Subhumans), appeared while he was in exile in Denmark. It described uprootedness, social misery, and the problem of being an outsider—all of which Kolbenhoff knew intimately from his own experiences. His second novel, *Heimkehr in die Fremde* (1948, Returning Home to Exile), was important, too, primarily as a document critical of the times, since it reflects the misery of the first postwar years. Heinrich Böll's and Gerd Gaiser's (born 1908) first novels also described the immediate postwar period.

In *Die Kopfjäger* (1960, The Headhunters) Kolbenhoff took as his subject the German economic miracle and its concomitant corruption, attributed to American power. In form this work resembles a detective story, and its intended social criticisms are submerged under the popularizing elements of the plot. Although during the late 1940s Kolbenhoff was regarded as one of the most important novelists, by now he has lost this significance.

The artistic value of the novels of Hans Werner Richter is also questionable. At present he is mentioned mainly as the leader of Group 47 and as a moderator of television discussions. In *Die Geschlagenen* (1949, The Defeated) Richter used a prosaic, journalistic style to describe, from the perspective of a simple soldier, the retreat from Italy, the battle of Monte Cassino, and the American occupation. The novel *Sie fielen aus Gottes Hand* (1951, They Fell from God's Hand), in which Richter incorporated authentic interviews into the text, described the misery of fugitives in postwar Germany and strove to present a moral inventory of conditions at that time. *Spuren im Sand* (1953, Tracks in the Sand) was a humorous novel that offered a retrospective look at his proletarian childhood in Pomerania. In *Du sollst nicht töten* (1955, Thou Shalt Not Kill) Richter once again took up the theme of the war. This account of World War II may possibly be Richter's most convincing literary accomplishment. But *Linus Fleck, oder der Verlust der Würde* (1959, Linus Fleck, or the Loss of Dignity), a persiflage on artistic activity of the postwar period, lost all opportunity at effectiveness because of its overly contrived satirical effects.

Despite his rather prolific oeuvre Richter has been scarcely able to sustain his literary reputation. In the long run, Wolfdietrich Schnurre's (born 1920) sad, witty, and laconic tales—collected in *Die Aufzeichnungen des Pudels Ali* (1953–62, The Notes of Ali the Poodle) and *Das Los unserer Stadt* (1959, The Fate of Our City)—may stand as far greater artistic accomplishments of the first postwar years than the novels of other Group 47 writers, such as Kolbenhoff or Richter.

INDIVIDUALISTS

A number of individualist novelists also appeared soon after the war. They did not promote a specific platform for West German literary life, as did Kolbenhoff, Richter, and Schnurre. Except for Alfred Andersch, these writers were not members of Group 47. And Andersch has been in more ways like the individualists than like the Group 47 novelists.

Among the individualists the most difficult writer to assess is Gerd Gaiser. In the early 1960s his work was still accorded the highest rank, but since then his impact has retreated far into the background. Gaiser's first novel, *Eine Stimme hebt an* (1950, A Voice Begins to Speak), was about a homecoming soldier—the favorite subject of the immediate postwar period. Despite its great effectiveness in depicting the social and spiritual confusions of the first postwar years, *A Voice Begins to Speak* leaned toward the biases of provincial writers in its simplified black-and-white contrasts and its antagonism toward civilization. *Die sterbende Jagd* (1953, The Dying Hunt), a melancholy swan song to a flying squadron that was gradually destroyed in World War II, was also distressing, because of its emphasis on heroic friendship, bravery, and "masculine" virtues.

Gaiser's most famous novel, *Schlußball* (1958, The Final Ball) was a superbly constructed narrative mosaic, consisting of thirty short reminiscing monologues. But Gaiser's vehement criticism of the West German economic miracle as represented by the town of Neu-Spuhl was weakened by his conservative belief in a wholesome world rooted in the soil. Indeed, it is Gaiser's ideology rather than his artistry that has been the major cause of the highly negative recent criticism of his novels.

Hans Erich Nossack has been less interested in social criticism than have Gaiser, Andersch, or Wolfgang Koeppen (born 1906). Nossack literally made a new beginning after the war, because all of his manuscripts had been destroyed during an air raid on Hamburg. Instead of directly discussing contemporary West German society, Nossack has philosophically examined, in ever new constellations, the fundamental questions of human existence and the possibility of finding fulfillment. He has used reflective monologues in his fiction to set forth his ideas.

In *Spätestens im November* (1955, In November at the Latest) Nossack showed the incompatibility of artistic creativity and human communication through the relationship between the author Möncken and the wife of an industrialist, Marianne Helldegen, as articulated in a monologue of the dead Marianne. At the same time, the novel presented a version of the traditional Paolo-Francesca love theme.

Unmögliche Beweisaufnahme (1959, The Impossible Proof), which first appeared as a section of the novel *Spirale: Roman einer schlaflosen Nacht* (1956, Spiral: Novel of a Sleepless Night), was widely regarded as Nossack's most significant achievement. Here he showed the impossibility of explaining in legal terms the reasons for the failure of a marriage that had appeared outwardly perfect. Nossack used the plight of the accused as a parable of existential involvement in guilt before an authority that summons the individual to self-judgment.

In *Der jüngere Bruder* (1958, The Younger Brother) Nossack took the homecoming theme out of the context of recent history and interpreted it philosophically. In this instance it became the search for one's own individuality, which the engineer Stefan Schneider thinks he recognizes in the mirror image of the young man Carlos Heller. In *Nach dem letzten*

Aufstand (1961, After the Last Uprising), which was closely related to the philosophical novels of Sartre and Camus, Nossack's use of a character's posthumously published notes clearly showed his inclination toward the monologue form. Nossack used a parable to present the search for individuality and for a mythical total reality in the midst of a demythologized and bureaucratized world.

In his most recent novel, *Dem unbekannten Sieger* (1970, To the Unknown Victor), Nossack approached contemporary history more directly. He demonstrated the incongruity of history and reality through a father-son relationship in which the firsthand experience of the father is contrasted with the son's writing of history through research.

If Nossack stands close to Sartre and Camus, and if within German literature he can best be compared with Hermann Broch, Wolfgang Koeppen has shown the influence not only of Alfred Döblin but also of James Joyce, John Dos Passos, and William Faulkner. In his use of multiple perspectives and in the unusually rich range and variety of his language, Koeppen has shown himself to be one of the most powerful novelists in contemporary German literature. Moreover, in his long novels one finds him coming to grips with conditions of the 1950s in West Germany with an intensity not achieved by any other novelist.

Koeppen found his own voice early, in such novels as *Eine unglückliche Liebe* (1934, An Unhappy Love) and *Die Mauer schwankt* (1935, The Wall Is Teetering), both of which were totally ignored during the Nazi period. Then in the early 1950s he published in quick succession three novels, which in many respects constitute the most important fictional depiction of the economic miracle in West Germany.

In *Tauben im Gras* (1951, Doves in the Grass) Koeppen employed the technique of multiple perspective to describe in detail a single day of the year 1950 in Munich. He showed the pandemonium of a wildly chaotic period, which Koeppen pitilessly bared to express his total distrust of ideology. The title of *Das Treibhaus* (1953, The Greenhouse) refers to Bonn, the capital of West Germany, which, for Koeppen, had a greenhouse atmosphere in 1952. In this novel Koeppen used inner monologues and the experiences of Keetenheuve, a member of parliament, to form an excellent portrait of the times. Koeppen's aggressive morality was transformed into convincing satire, despite occasional lapses into overstatement.

In *Der Tod in Rom* (1954, Death in Rome) Koeppen once again lamented the abuses of the economic miracle and the reactionary tendencies in West Germany. The novel, set in Rome, achieved a suspenseful, ghostly effect through its portrayal of revitalized fascism in Germany. Koeppen's picture of the epoch, portrayed through the same techniques of free association and inner monologue found in his other works, gave the most gloomy diagnosis of the postwar period that has been written to date.

Despite its achievement, *Death in Rome* did suffer from occasional attempts to pander to popular taste and from the overly schematized juxtaposition of the protagonists Judejahn and Pfaffrath on the one side and Siegfried and Adolf on the other.

Alfred Andersch played an important role in founding Group 47 but has since gone his own artistic way. His novels are comparable to those of Koeppen in their critical and moralistic stance, even though the scope of Andersch's themes has been broader. In virtuosity of form, however, he has not attained the level of Koeppen. Following *Die Kirschen der Freiheit* (1952, The Cherries of Freedom), an autobiographical description of his desertion, Andersch published the novel *Sansibar, oder der letzte Grund* (1957, Zanzibar, or The Final Cause), an artfully woven narrative that made extensive use of inner monologues. Here he presented a series of typical attitudes toward the Third Reich through important figures, each of whom has his own reasons for wanting to leave Germany. In *Die Rote* (1960, The Redhead), a novel that used a variety of narrative techniques, Andersch viewed critically the prosperous society of West Germany through the flight of the protagonist, Franziska Lukas. A melodramatic heightening of suspense characterized *The Redhead,* and this feature brought negative reactions from critics. In *Efraim* (1967, Efraim), Andersch retold experiences both in Hitler's Germany and in East and West Germany during the 1960s from the perspective of a Jewish protagonist, who is an English journalist born in Berlin. *Efraim* has been both highly praised and sharply rejected by critics.

An individualist par excellence is Arno Schmidt (born 1914), who, together with essays and philological works, has published a series of complex novels that are rated highly by a small group of admirers, although they are disparaged by others as esoteric playthings. Because of his peculiar spelling (his partly phonetic method of writing), punctuation, and syntax, Schmidt has made an understanding of his novels difficult. Yet, he must be credited with having anticipated linguistic collages and montages, which such authors as Helmut Heissenbüttel and Peter O. Chotjewitz (born 1934) have recently popularized.

Schmidt's novel *Das steinerne Herz* (1956, The Heart of Stone) was a confusing montage of fragmented narrative, recherché interpolations, and expository intrusions. It purports to be a multileveled reflection on contemporary life with a range of themes extending from the partition of Germany through the international arms race. The utopian novel *Die Gelehrtenrepublik* (1956, The Republic of Scholars), which takes place in the year 2009, also featured Schmidt's characteristic mixture of essay and fiction. He transplanted the political situation of the present into the future; his satire occasionally veers to the grotesque.

Schmidt's most recent work, *Zettel's Traum* (1970, Bottoms Dream), was unusual because of its physical appearance and its manner of presentation (it was printed as a manuscript facsimile with handwritten corrections by the author). Its structure, which consists of separate plot lines running parallel, pushed mannerist exclusivity so far that the book immediately became a commercial success. This voluminous work is less a novel than a compendium of cultural and literary history. Its unity is achieved only through the person of the author, who has created a monument into which he packed everything that has any relevance for him, including his philological work on Poe, his literary insights, his tremendous wealth of lexicographical knowledge. The title of *Bottoms Dream,* which evokes Shakespeare's *A Midsummer Night's Dream,* at the same time points to the title of Joyce's *Finnegans Wake* in its unconventional rendering of the possessive. One thing about *Bottoms Dream* was incontrovertible: it had very little connection to the traditional novel.

THE EAST GERMAN NOVEL

As I have already pointed out, literary life in East Germany has proceeded according to very different rules from those of West Germany, Austria, or Switzerland. The literary reputation of an East German author has depended on the fulfillment of a prescribed literary doctrine and the criteria established by authorities determining the public acceptability of a literary product. Editors, critics, and book dealers are all part of the system. In examining the East German novel, one therefore has to take into account both works that merit attention because of their success in East Germany and works whose artistic quality makes them significant from a nonideological point of view.

The writer considered the most important East German novelist of the present day is Anna Seghers, who became known in 1928 for her artistically mature performance in *Der Aufstand der Fischer von St. Barbara* (1928, The Uprising of the Santa Barbara Fishermen). Her novels written in exile, particularly *Das siebte Kreuz* (1942, The Seventh Cross), showed her to be a writer clearly bound by party ideology but at the same time well versed in the most modern narrative techniques (those of Joyce and Dos Passos).

In her novels written in East Germany after 1945 Anna Seghers has rarely attained the artistic heights of her previous works, since her artistic sensibility and the programmed doctrine prescribed from above have frequently been in conflict with one another. As a result, novels like *Die Entscheidung* (1959, The Decision) exhibited all the characteristics of compromise and were unsatisfactory because of their doctrinaire format.

Segher's novel *Die Toten bleiben jung* (1949, The Dead Stay Young) was, however, something of an exception. The death of a young Spartacist, who is shot before the gates of Berlin on a November day in 1918, serves as a catalyst for tracing the lives of the murderers and the other participants; in so doing, Seghers showed her insight into the rise of fascism in Germany. The action extends through 1954, when the son of a Spartacist is likewise murdered because of his political orientation. As in *The Seventh Cross*, in *The Dead Stay Young* a cross section of German society is presented in mosaic fashion, but the social spectrum has been widened. The narration is written in expressive language, and the individual strands of the plot are joined together with technical mastery.

Anna Seghers is typical of a number of important exiled authors who returned to East Germany after 1945 but who lost some of their artistic quality after their return. Another example is the novelist Arnold Zweig, who fell completely silent in East Germany. Willi Bredel (1901–1964), an exiled author who had long been an active communist agitator, also settled in East Germany after 1945. Twice honored with the national prize of East Germany, Bredel also rose to high cultural offices. He was vice-president of the German Academy of Arts and a member of the Central Committee of the Socialist Unity Party.

Bredel's novels have been frequently called models of communist fiction, since narrative technique, which has distinguished the best work of Anna Seghers, was, for Bredel, secondary to pointed didacticism. His best known work, the trilogy *Verwandte und Bekannte* (Relatives and Acquaintances), was published as separate volumes: *Die Väter* (1941, Fathers), *Die Söhne* (1949, Sons), and *Die Enkel* (1953, Grandchildren). In this trilogy Bredel described three generations of the Hardekopf and Brenten families of workers over a period extending from the turn of the century through 1948. Bredel used the individual lives of his characters to present important historical events, including the battles, defeats, and victories of revolutionary workers.

Bredel's *Relatives and Acquaintances* encompasses a huge number of characters and a broad spectrum of events in recent German history, and many of the situations are succinctly portrayed. Nevertheless, the naïve, straightforward narrative manner, the numerous heavy-handed descriptions, and the overly sentimentalized characterizations lessened the value of this grandiose work. Bredel's novel *Ein neues Kapitel* (1959, A New Chapter) suffered from his characteristic shortcomings.

Even Bredel, despite his dutiful fulfillment of ideological norms in his late works, occasionally fell into conflict with the official literary policy. Erwin Strittmatter, on the other hand, has had an unblemished success with the literary bureaucracy, and his influence on literary criticism in East Germany remains strong. He has received high honors, and his works have been included in the official East German anthologies.

Persistently encouraged by Brecht, Strittmatter began his career with a number of works that showed a considerable narrative talent: *Eine Mauer fällt* (1953, A Wall Collapses), *Ochsenkutscher* (1949–51, Oxdriver), *Tinko* (1954–57, Tinko), and *Der Wundertäter* (1957, The Miracle Worker). The novel *Ole Bienkopp,* his most impressive accomplishment to date, became very successful because of its linear plot, its consciously simple, direct language, and the naïve outlook of its narrator-hero, who is shown both as a child and as a young man. The central theme of *Ole Bienkopp*—the changes in the agrarian economy of East Germany after World War II—met the demands of the official literary doctrine. The difficulties and mistakes of Ole Hansen, nicknamed Bienkopp, who founds the peasant cooperative Blühendes Feld (Blooming Field), make him a symbol of the resistance to, and the erratic planning for, the building of socialism in East Germany. Yet his positive efforts and the progressive changes in the fictitious village of Blumenau nevertheless represented the successes of socialism.

Among the other authors of the older generation, Bruno Apitz's (born 1900) limited literary ouevre is significant mainly because of one novel that became a success not only in East Germany but also in the outside world—*Nackt unter Wölfen* (1958, Naked among Wolves). Based on the author's own experiences, the novel treated the last weeks of the war in the concentration camp of Buchenwald; the underground activities of the prisoners is played off against the radio announcements of the advancing Allies. An orphaned Jewish child rescued by the prisoners serves as the unifying central focus of the highly divergent narrative strands. Although Apitz eschewed the incorporation of actual documents into his text, and although he tended to oversimplify his characters, *Night among Wolves* was convincing because of its moral force.

A much younger author, Dieter Noll (born 1927), had the same broad success as Apitz with the two-volume novel *Die Abenteuer des Werner Holt* (1960–63, The Adventures of Werner Holt). The first volume presented the typical development of a young man during the Nazi period, and the second part portrayed him during the early postwar years. Both volumes have a structure and language resembling the fiction in the more sophisticated popular magazines. Because of the straightforward, chronological handling of time and the limited scope of the action revolving around a central character, Noll achieved a simplicity of construction, which could explain the success of his conventionally written novel.

Hermann Kant's novel *Die Aula* (1965, The Auditorium) was more complex. Kant, too, was concerned with describing a socially relevant problem, namely, the effects of the cultural revolution in East Germany on proletarian children, as shown by the example of a kindergarten. The result was a narrative with a mosaic structure that unites remembered past and narrated present. The linear story is dissolved into a complex narrative spectrum that presents a cross section of East German history through free association and inner monologues. The story is crystallized in the thoughts of the narrator, who is charged with delivering the final speech at the ceremony marking the closing by government order of a worker-and-peasant school. The narrator provides the central unity of the novel and brings the different time periods and strands of action into relationship with one another. Parallel to the shifts in time is the quick change in setting between East and West Germany. The subject of *The Auditorium* enabled Kant to parody the mistakes made in the course of the cultural revolution.

The choice to use complex narrative techniques was also made by Christa Wolf, the outstanding writer of fiction among the younger East German authors. In her novel *Divided Heaven* she created a complex parable of the development of socialist awareness. The message is proclaimed through the protagonist Rita Seidel, who remains loyal to East Germany despite its social problems and despite the defection of the young chemist Herrfurth to West Germany. After reaching the point of attempting suicide, Rita recovers her health and comes to understand her role as a member of the state.

Wolf's second novel, *Nachdenken über Christa T.* (1968, Thoughts about Christa T.) was a masterfully constructed narrative work in which she combined authentic documents, personal recollections, thoughts of the narrator, and fragments of narrated action. The novel also had a surprising theme: the thoughts about the life of the narrator's dead friend, Christa T., do not insist that life is only fulfilled within the framework of society; instead, they show the meaningfulness of a life on the periphery of society. Thus, in *Thoughts about Christa T.* self-realization has an individual rather than a communal meaning.

Christa Wolf has not by any means intended to contradict official literary doctrine, but she does recognize that social development in East Germany has progressed beyond the struggle for the establishment of communism and should begin to tackle more personal problems within communist society. The artistic heights achieved by *Thoughts about Christa T.* are comparable to the finest examples of the West German novel.

FOUR MAJOR WEST GERMAN NOVELISTS

Four novelists have given a particular character to contemporary West German literature, because of their influence and their artistic achievements.

The oldest of these writers is Heinrich Böll, whose early short stories and novels chronicled the years following the war with laconic seriousness and moral aggressiveness. These works were sharply critical of the forces of restoration, particularly of the Catholic church. *Wo warst du, Adam?* (1951, Where Were You, Adam?), a fragmented melancholy portrait of the senselessness of war, is told through several narrative episodes held together by the figure of the soldier Feinhals. *Und sagte kein einziges Wort* (1953, And Said Not a Single Word), narrated alternately from the different perspectives of the married couple, Fred and Käte Bogner, contained strong elements of social criticism, triggered by the housing shortage in postwar Germany. *Haus ohne Hüter* (1954, House without Guardians) described the postwar misery of neglected children and lonely war widows.

The multiple-level narrative of *House without Guardians* prepared for Böll's most complex and most ambitious work from the standpoint of form, *Billard um halbzehn* (1959, Billiards at Half-Past Nine). In *Billiards at Half-Past Nine* Böll attempted to portray the first half of the twentieth century in a novel that is conceived primarily as a coming to grips with the breakdown of morality during the Third Reich. The catalyst for the action is the birthday celebration of a highly regarded architect, the privy councillor Fähmel, who is famous for designing an abbey which his son destroyed during the war as punishment for the ideological blindness of people and which his grandson is now supposed to rebuild. The novel has a complicated structure consisting of various inner monologues, each of which simultaneously reflects the past and the present while focusing on the date of the planned anniversary celebration as the fixed center. Although this contemporary historical panorama had a strong moral message, it had clear deficiencies in its use of language, particularly in its artificial metaphors, which tend to obscure the political subject matter instead of highlighting it.

In *Ansichten eines Clowns* (1963, Opinions of a Clown) Böll used again the ambitious narrative technique of *Billiards at Half-Past Nine* and looked back at memories that are constantly interrupted by the present. *Opinions of a Clown* mirrors the consciousness of Böll's protagonist, Hans Schnier, whose inability to find employment as a clown is a by-product of industrial society. Böll's political orientation emerged here more clearly, and his criticism of the Catholic church became sharper. Schnier's lack of hope at the end indicates that Böll was beginning to distrust utopian implications associated in his earlier books with the earliest ideas of Christianity.

Böll pursued his pessimism further in the novella *Entfernung von der Truppe* (1964, Absence without Leave), the title of which immediately expresses Böll's characteristically escapist attitude: for him desertion has a fundamental significance broader than its military sense. A similar theme dominated his novel *Ende einer Dienstfahrt* (1966, End of a Mission), in which the senselessness of military drill is unmasked through a desertion from the West German army and the ritual burning of a jeep. The chronicle style of narration, reminiscent of Kleist, created an ironic distance, which made Böll's criticism all the more trenchant.

The novella *Das Brot der frühen Jahre* (1955, The Bread of Our Early Years), which uses what could have been a trite love story as a pretext for exploring the mind of the protagonist and the postwar world, has been one of Böll's most impressive accomplishments. It also helped in a general way to make the novel of social criticism an important genre once more. Böll's most recent work, *Gruppenbild mit Dame* (1971, Group Portrait with Lady), was a distinguished continuation of his fictional oeuvre.

Böll can be considered the most representative West German novelist of the 1950s. He is still regarded, particularly in eastern European countries, as the contemporary German novelist par excellence. In the 1960s Günter Grass towered above all others as the writer who helped to reestablish the reputation of the German novel in English-speaking countries.

Grass's most important work still remains his first novel, *Die Blechtrommel* (1959, The Tin Drum), which helped to revitalize the picaresque novel in Germany. This enormous book overflows with episodes and ideas. As in Döblin's works, the literary language of the book is enriched by colloquial speech, dialect, and technical jargon. It is unified by the dwarf Oskar, who possesses magical powers (an electrifying drum and a singing voice that shatters glass). From Oskar's perspective, the city of Danzig, a microcosm of the vicious world of the 1930s, is a pitifully deformed reality devoid of any conventional sense of values. *The Tin Drum,* which was recognized as an important work because of its picaresque structure and its vitality of language, inspired numerous imitations: Paul Pörtner's (born 1925) *Tobias Immergrün* (1962, Tobias Immergrün), Manfred Bieler's (born 1934) *Bonifaz, oder der Matrose in der Flasche* (1963, Bonifaz, or the Sailor in the Bottle), Heinz Küppers's (born 1930) *Simplicius 45* (1963, Simplicius 45), Gerhard Ludwig's (born 1924) *Tausendjahrfeier* (1965, Millennial Celebration), Gerhard Zwerenz's (born 1925) *Casanova, oder der kleine Herr in Krieg und Frieden* (1966, Casanova, or the Little Man in War and Peace), Günter Kunert's *Im Namen der Hüte* (1967, In the Name of Hats), and Paul Schallück's (born 1922) *Don Quichotte in Köln* (1967, Don Quixote in Cologne).

Grass's short novel *Katz und Maus* (1961, Cat and Mouse) was related to *The Tin Drum* as a portrait of the Third Reich with a setting in Danzig, but it had a surprisingly disciplined narrative structure, which well served the author's purpose of satirically unmasking the military image of the hero. In *Hundejahre* (1963, Dog Years) Grass pursued the themes of his first two books; it was filled with the same superabundant narrative fantasy and playful linguistic inventiveness as *The Tin Drum*. But *Dog Years* lacked a unifying perspective, which *The Tin Drum* derived from Oskar's point of view; the division into three different narrative perspectives in *Dog*

Years proved to be an artificial solution. The unconvincing satirical portrait of West Germany in the latter part of *The Tin Drum* degenerated even further in *Dog Years* to the level of vaudeville gags, which are not even integrated into the plot.

In his most recent novel, *Local Anaesthetic* (1970), Grass tried to capture such relevant contemporary themes as student unrest and political involvement. However, by choosing a dentist and an assistant principal of a school as his protagonists, he departed from the petty-bourgeois milieu of his earlier novels. The multileveled structure—composed of memories, reflections, advertising slogans, and segments of plot—is an "objective correlative" to the complex consciousness of Starusch, the assistant principal, even though the montage technique is not always used convincingly. A good deal of the political tendentiousness of the novel, directed against the former West German chancellor Kurt Kiesinger, has by now become obsolete. This novel, which received a mixed response in Germany, became an unexpectedly great success in English-speaking countries.

Uwe Johnson, born in Pomerania and educated in East Germany, has made the division of Germany the central theme of his novels. Johnson's choice of forms, which includes multiple perspectives, as well as his choice of themes, has made him one of the most important novelists of the present day.

In *Mutmaßungen über Jakob* (1959, Speculations about Jakob) Johnson presented a mosaic of reflections of the railroad engineer Jakob Abs and of the intellectual Jonas Blach in order to pose the question of what constitutes a meaningful life in a socialist society. This web of reflections is triggered by the puzzling death of Jakob. Questions about the causes of Jakob's death are expanded into questions about the meaning of his life and about the society of East Germany. Johnson presented an extremely pessimistic view of contemporary history: both the crushing of the Hungarian rebellion by the Russians and Suez intervention by the western powers are seen as equally disillusioning, a "choice between two insanities."

Johnson's second novel, *Das dritte Buch über Achim* (1961, The Third Book about Achim), also had a difficult structure totally justified by its theme. The montage form of this book is a necessary outgrowth of the working methods of the scholarly journalist Karsch, who is collecting material for a biography of Achim T., an East German sports idol. Again, Johnson showed the discrepancy between the life of the individual and the social role prescribed by the state through the central character: from behind his image there emerges a contradictory picture of Achim as a person who, despite his new allegiance, still represents the state as it was when he participated in the rebellion of June 17, 1953.

In *Zwei Ansichten* (1965, Two Views) Johnson took up for the third time the theme of the division of Germany, but in this novel he used a conventional narrative with more focus on characterization. In the relationship that develops by chance between a young West German journalist and an East German nurse whom he helps to escape, Johnson tried to describe the differences between the two German societies. But *Two Views* lacked artistic conviction. Both the simplicity of the plot and the schematic quality of the characters are inappropriate to the complexity and scope of the theme.

In the first part of his trilogy in progress, *Jahrestage: Aus dem Leben von Gesine Cresspahl* (1970, Days of a Year: From the Life of Gesine Cresspahl), Johnson expanded the theme of coexistence between the West German and East German states into the theme of the German-American symbiosis. He combined in diary form contemporary American life, with all its signs of crisis, and the world that Gesine's parents experienced in the England of the late 1920s and subsequently in Mecklenburg after 1933. The complex structure of *Days of a Year,* which was reminiscent of both Döblin's *Berlin Alexanderplatz* (1929, Alexanderplatz, Berlin) and Dos Passos's *Manhattan Transfer,* can be justified as an attempt to mirror in form the manifold complexities of communication in the metropolis of New York. Johnson's obsession with detail, however, occasionally led to a distortion of the narrative function of individual parts. At present Johnson, who now lives in West Berlin, is regarded along with Böll and Grass as one of the most important contemporary German novelists.

A similar position of importance can also be given to the novels of Martin Walser, whose work as a playwright I have already discussed. The structural design of his novels, however, has been frequently unsatisfactory. But Walser has perhaps the sharpest eye for social conditions in contemporary West Germany and is a virtuoso of language.

In his first novel, *Ehen in Philippsburg* (1957, Marriage in Philippsburg), Walser presented a cross section of the West German middle class. However, each of the four loosely related sections of the novel focuses upon the experiences of a character. *Marriage in Philippsburg* repudiated the concept of an ominiscient central consciousness but in so doing lacked a larger perspective on life.

Walser's novel *Halbzeit* (1960, Halftime) offered a more imposing compendium of West German society. The advertising agent Anselm Kristlein does not function as a first-person narrator in the traditional way. Rather, he is a narrating medium who provides a minutely detailed picture of bourgeois circles in West Germany. The traditional individuality and stability of the narrator are thus avoided. Instead of a narrator with a consistent personality, there emerges an aggregate of distinct sociological roles: husband, friend, businessman, and so forth. A master of mimicry, Anselm symbolizes a prosperity attuned to adaptation. The narrating medium Anselm, who is introduced into different social realms, uses an extremely complex mixture of language, which assimilates colloquial language, the jargon of political propaganda, and the language of advertising. The novel is interspersed throughout with journalistic accounts, chronicles, poems, and dialogues.

In *Das Einhorn* (1966, The Unicorn) Walser presented a variation on the role-player Anselm Kristlein. He appears here as a writer for whom a projected book about love becomes the occasion for Walser to produce another broad satire on West German society. Unlike *Halftime,* in which the overflowing richness of language tends to overwhelm the structure, *The Unicorn* has a more clearly defined form. However, the individual parts, especially the concluding section, do not form an overall unity. In his most recent work, *Fiction* (1969, the title is in English), Walser tried to develop a new, more concise form to replace that of his earlier social novels.

THE NEW REALISM

In contemporary fiction the realistic social novel has managed to maintain itself despite all modifications. Within the last five years, although the "death" of the bourgeois novel was announced by many, the "new realists" have attempted to revitalize the conventional novel. Even Böll, Grass, Johnson, and Walser, despite their experiments, are still largely within the tradition of the realistic novel.

Well known among the new realists is Siegfried Lenz, who has experimented with different variations on realism. His novel *Der Mann im Strom* (1957, The Man in the Stream) took a critical look at the social order of West Germany through the life of an aging diver. *Brot und Spiele* (1959, Bread and Games) belongs to the genre of the journalistic sports novel, and in the tale *Das Feuerschiff* (1960, The Lightship) he tried to elevate a realistically described situation to a model for political action.

Lenz's only lasting success has been *Die Deutschstunde* (1968, The German Lesson), a conventional novel-within-a-novel story in which the protagonist, Siggi Jepsen, provides a retrospective moral reexamination of the history of the Third Reich. As in Lenz's dramas, in which the form is inferior to the moral attitude of the author, the critical position toward West Germany he takes in his novels has not been transmuted into a form that has intrinsic artistic significance.

The novels of Reinhard Baumgart (born 1929) and Herbert Heckmann (born 1930) also provide nothing more than beginnings. Baumgart's *Der Löwengarten* (1964, The Lion Yard) undeniably displayed a stylistic elegance, which occasionally rises to mannerism. Because of the particular realistic milieu chosen (the film industry), the work did fall victim to the dangers of esoterica. In *Hausmusik: Ein deutsches Familienalbum* (1962, Home Music: A German Family Album) Baumgart turned to more concrete themes and described the German past, but he used a highly artificial structure to carry out these goals. Herbert Heckmann's straightforwardly narrated autobiographical novel *Benjamin und seine Väter* (1961, Benjamin and His Fathers) was enhanced by its humorous tone and the unpretentious simplicity of the story.

Alexander Kluge (born 1932) attracted notice with *Lebensläufe* (1962, Life Histories), a montage of documentary material, and with *Schlachtbeschreibung* (1964, Description of a Battle), another montage. These books initiated a new vogue for documentary literature. Among the progeny have been *Industriereportagen* (1970, Industrial Records) by Günter Wallraff and Erika Runge's *Bottrop Papers*. It should be remembered that this kind of documentary literature really harks back to Theodor Plivier's (1892–1955) *Stalingrad* (1945, Stalingrad). It is not by chance that Kluge's *Description of a Battle,* which dealt with the German attack on Stalingrad, had a close kinship to Plivier's book.

Dieter Wellershoff tried to inaugurate a new type of realistic novel in his two books *Ein schöner Tag* (1966, A Beautiful Day) and *Die Schattengrenze* (1969, The Edge of the Shadows), in which he intended to eliminate all psychology from his descriptions, as in the *nouveau roman.* While Wellershoff's work has been very derivative, the works of two more individualistic writers have more artistic interest. Hubert Fichte's (born 1935) *Das Waisenhaus* (1965, The Orphanage), *Die Palette* (1968, The Palette), and *Detlefs Imitationen "Grünspan"* (1971, Detlef's Imitations "Verdigris") presented microscopically accurate milieu studies that are impressive for their complex intensity of expression. Thomas Bernhard's *Frost* (1963, Frost), *Verstörung* (1967, Bewilderment), and *Das Kalkwerk* (1970, The Lime Works) captured a reality which had unmistakably local Austrian features but which also gave a clearly delineated panorama of a society that is already in the process of decaying.

FALSE STARTS AND DEAD-END STREETS

The novels I have grouped together under the category "false starts and dead-end streets" show a virtuosity of form, but they lack the kind of internal consistency that would make the novels into total entities. Thus, the individual books have been groping starts, which adopted various forms and themes of contemporary literature. However, the experiments failed to integrate these trends into new types of literature. The literary quality of such novels remains questionable.

A typical example of this kind of novelist is Walter Jens, who as classical philologist, professor of rhetoric, literary and television critic, and influential member of Group 47 has helped in many ways to determine the character of literary life in West Germany. His first novel, a pessimistic depiction of the future. *No: The World of the Accused,* was akin to George Orwell's *1984* and even more closely related to Kafka, whose aptness of language served Jens as a stylistic model. *Vergessene Gesichter* (1952, Forgotten Faces), a novel about actors, unquestionably achieved an intensity of mood in parts, but nonetheless smacked of being only a higher-grade popular novel.

Jens's most mature accomplishment to date, *Der Mann, der nicht alt werden wollte* (1955, The Man Who Did Not Want to Get Old), was a mosaic of reflections masterfully constructed from fictitious poetic texts, philological research, and monologues. For this novel Jens was inspired by the style of Thomas Mann as well as his themes, although in form it anticipated Uwe Johnson and Christa Wolf's *Thoughts about Christa T.* Completely unsuccessful, on the other hand, was Jens's *Herr Meister: Dialog über einen Roman* (1963, Mr. Meister: Dialogue about a Novel), a somewhat diffuse epistolary novel that begins with a formulation of the political mistakes of the recent past and ends in a mood of abstract melancholy. This work also purported to be a treatise on the impossibility of writing a novel today.

Peter Härtling, in his lyrical sequences of memories, has played off the imagination against the factuality of history, attributing the function of truth only to lyrical evocations. This was true particularly of his latest novel, *Das Familienfest, oder das Ende der Geschichte* (1969, The Family Celebration, or the End of History). His epigonal novel about a returning war veteran, *Im Schein des Kometen* (1959, In the Light of the Comet), and *Janek: Porträt einer Erinnerung* (1966, Janek: Portrait of a Recollection) also dissected the reality he wants to shape into art by rearranging historical facts with lyrical subjectivity. Only in *Niembsch, oder der Stillstand* (1964, Niembsch, or the Standstill), clearly Härtling's best book to date, did he treat an historical fact objectively. Here he used the return of the poet Nikolaus Lenau from America as an historical foil, thus providing a character who complements the lyrical moods of the novel.

An evaluation of Heinz von Cramer (born 1924) is also hard to make. His first novel, *San Silverio* (1955, San Silverio), which was strengthened by strong elements of social criticism, was greeted as a work of promise. His second work, *Die Kunstfigur* (1958, The Artistic Figure), proved to be an important political novel, which portrayed with critical conciseness the typical development of a German intellectual in recent decades. The polemicism of *The Artistic Figure* took on more subjective hues in his third novel, *Die Konzessionen des Himmels* (1961, The Concessions of Heaven), which consisted of three episodes containing anticlerical barbs. But the moral position of the author was superimposed on the characters rather than growing out of them. In Cramer's most recent work, the "syn-

thetic novel" *Der Paralleldenker* (1968, The Parallel Thinker), he assimilated techniques of pop art.

Wolfgang Hildesheimer's much-discussed novel *Tynset* (1965, Tynset)
related a finely spun net of reflections, memories, and loosely bound episodes to a fixed geographical point, Tynset. It is unclear, however, whether
Tynset was an important first step for Hildesheimer as novelist or only a
digression from his career as a dramatist.

OPEN FORM

The increasing dissatisfaction with the novel as a genre has recently
elicited many efforts to abolish once and for all the closed form of the
traditional novel in favor of an open form. Advocates of open form have
claimed that, in spite of the techniques of montage and the complex combination of the most disparate elements, most avant-garde novelists are still
trying to preserve formal integration. The objective of open form was
accomplished in one case by renouncing all pretensions to composition in
the novel and in another by reducing it to the bare forms of language.

Peter Handke's first novels—*Die Hornissen* (1966, The Hornets), *Der
Hausierer* (1967, The Peddler), and the already mentioned *The Goalie's
Anxiety at Eleven Meters*—laid the foundation for the development of
narrative modes that revolutionized the optics of the traditional narrator.
The Hornets was told from the perspective of a blind man, *The Peddler*
skeletonized the conventional design of the detective story, and *The
Goalie's Anxiety at Eleven Meters* presented reality from the perspective of
a former goalkeeper who behaves somewhat like a schizophrenic and relates all things to himself. Handke was convincing only in the third work,
in which he returned to rudiments of a story; his first two attempts failed to
engender any major new narrative form.

Also incapable of attracting disciples was Helmut Heissenbüttel's boring
satire of contemporary cultural activity, *D'Alembert's End,* which is one
long and tiringly monotonous quotation. Peter O. Chotjewitz, in *Die Insel*
(1968, The Island), *Roman: Ein Anpassungsmuster* (1968, Novel: A
Model for Emulation), and *Vom Leben und Lernen* (1969, On Life and
Learning) renounced all efforts at form and tried to provide nothing but
secondary material, which the reader as half-author is supposed to arrange
according to his own ideas. Such texts accomplish the demise of the
conventional form of the novel without giving any indication of a future
with possibilities.

Jürgen Becker has been more consequential, in that in his books—
Felder (1964, Fields), *Ränder* (1968, Edges), and *Umgebungen* (1970,
Environments)—he consciously limited himself to narrative miniatures

that, with their rigorous intensity of description, virtually represent tests of transforming reality into language. Gert F. Jonke's *Geometrischer Heimatroman* (1969, Geometrical Homeland Novel), like Handke's works, begins with a specific narrative focus. A slice of reality that is comprehensible at first glance gradually disintegrates and dissolves into its linguistic components. A different approach to open form was offered by Andreas Okopenko, who tried in his "dictionary novel," *Lexikon einer sentimentalen Reise zum Exporteurtreffen in Druden* (1970, Dictionary of a Sentimental Journey to the Meeting of Exporters in Druden), to make an entirely new beginning by arranging the words as in a dictionary. This method resulted in a "novel of possibilities," which allowed the reader to fashion his own novel and, as it were, to choose his own reading route.

Through these experiments with open form, it is possible to recognize a polarity that vacillates between a reduction of literature to patterns of words and a renunciation of large narrative form on the one hand, and the beginnings of a new kind of social novel on the other. But only in Oswald Wiener's novel *Die Verbesserung von Mitteleuropa* (1969, The Improvement of Central Europe), which tried to revolutionize society by dissolving the norms of language, did these tendencies reach a provocative intellectual intensity. Wiener revived in a surprising way the aim of the *Bildungsroman* of mirroring the development of society in the inner development of a protagonist. While the verbal privacy of the novel seemed to reject all norms of society, Wiener nonetheless opened up the thinly covered fragmentation of reality by showing the disintegration of the individual. Thus, he suggested the beginnings of a renewal, of an "improvement of Central Europe."

GERMAN WORKS IN ENGLISH TRANSLATION

INDIVIDUAL WORKS MENTIONED
IN ARTICLE

Andersch, Alfred. *Efraim* as *Efraim's Book*. Garden City, N.Y., 1970
———. *Die Rote* as *The Redhead*. New York, 1962
———. *Sansibar, oder der letzte Grund* as *Flight to Afar*. New York, 1958
Bergengruen, Werner. *Der Großtyrann und das Gericht* as *A Matter of Conscience*. New York, 1952
Bernhard, Thomas. *Verstörung* as *Gargoyles*. New York, 1970

Bichsel, Peter. *Eigentlich möchte Frau Blum den Milchmann kennenlernen* as *And Really Frau Blum Would Very Much Like to Meet the Milkman*. New York, 1969
———. *Kindergeschichten* as *There Is No Such Place as America*. New York, 1970
Biermann, Wolf. *Die Drahtharfe* as *The Wire Harp*. New York, 1968
Böll, Heinrich. *Ansichten eines Clowns* as *The Clown*. New York, 1965
———. *Billard um halbzehn* as *Billiards at Half-Past Nine*. New York, 1962

————. *Das Brot der frühen Jahre* as *The Bread of Our Early Years*. London, 1957

————. *Ende einer Dienstfahrt* as *End of a Mission*. New York, 1968

————. *Entfernung von der Truppe* as *Absent without Leave: Two Novellas*. New York, 1965

————. *Gruppenbild mit Dame* as *Group Portrait with Lady*. New York, 1973

————. *Haus ohne Hüter* as *Tomorrow and Yesterday*. New York, 1957

————. *Und sagte kein einziges Wort* as *Acquainted with the Night*. New York, 1954

————. *Wo warst du, Adam?* as *Adam*. In *Adam and The Train: Two Novels*. New York, 1970

Borchert, Wolfgang. *Draußen vor der Tür* as *The Man Outside*. In *The Man Outside*. New York, 1971

————. *Generation ohne Abschied* as *Generation without Farewell*. In *The Man Outside*. New York, 1971

————. *Die Hundeblume* as *The Dandelion*. In *The Man Outside*. New York, 1971

————. *Die Krähen fliegen abends* as *The Crows Fly Home at Night*. In *The Man Outside*. New York, 1971

Brecht, Bertolt. *Aufstieg und Fall der Stadt Mahagonny* as *Rise and Fall of the City of Mahogonny*. In booklet accompanying recorded version, Columbia K3L–243

————. *Die Ausnahme und die Regel* as *The Exception and the Rule*. In *The Jewish Wife, and Other Short Plays*. New York, 1965

————. *Die Dreigroschenoper* as *The Threepenny Opera*. New York, 1964

————. *Der gute Mensch von Sezuan* as *The Good Woman of Setzuan*. New York, 1966

————. *Der Jasager und der Neinsager* as *He Who Says Yes and He Who Says No*. In *Accent*, Autumn, 1946

————. *Der kaukasische Kreidekreis* as *The Caucasian Chalk Circle*. New York, 1966

————. *Leben des Galilei* as *Life of Galileo*. In *Collected Plays*, vol. 5. New York, 1972

————. *Die Maßnahme* as *The Measures Taken*. In *The Jewish Wife, and Other Short Plays*. New York, 1965

————. *Die Mutter* as *The Mother*. New York, 1965

————. *Mutter Courage und ihre Kinder* as *Mother Courage and Her Children*. In *Collected Plays*, vol. 5. New York, 1972

Döblin, Alfred. *Berlin Alexanderplatz* as *Alexanderplatz, Berlin*. New York, 1958

Doderer, Heimito von. *Die Dämonen* as *The Demons*. New York, 1961

————. *Die Wasserfälle von Slunj* as *The Waterfalls of Slunj*. New York, 1966

Dorst, Tankred. *Freiheit für Clemens* as *Freedom for Clemens*. In Michael Benedikt and George Wellwarth, eds., *Postwar German Theatre*. New York, 1968

Dürrenmatt, Friedrich. *Der Besuch der alten Dame* as *The Visit*. New York, 1962

————. *Die Ehe des Herrn Mississippi* as *The Marriage of Mr. Mississippi*. In *Four Plays*. New York, 1965

————. *Ein Engel kommt nach Babylon* as *An Angel Comes to Babylon*. In *Four Plays*. New York, 1965

————. *Die Physiker* as *The Physicists*. In *Four Plays*. New York, 1965

————. *Romulus der Große* as *Romulus the Great*. In *Four Plays*. New York, 1965

Frisch, Max. *Andorra* as *Andorra*. New York, 1964

————. *Biedermann und die Brandstifter* as *The Firebugs*. New York, 1963

————. *Biografie: Ein Spiel* as *Biography: A Game*. New York, 1969

————. *Die chinesische Mauer* as *The Chinese Wall*. New York, 1961

————. *Don Juan, oder die Liebe zur Geometrie* as *Don Juan*. In *Three Plays*. New York, 1967

————. *Graf Öderland* as *Count Oederland*. In *Three Plays*. London, 1962

————. *Homo Faber* as *Homo Faber: A Report*. New York, 1959

————. *Mein Name sei Gantenbein* as *A Wilderness of Mirrors*. New York, 1966

————. *Nun singen sie wieder* as *Now They Sing Again*. In Michael Roloff, ed., *The Contemporary German Theater*. New York, 1972

————. *Stiller* as *I'm Not Stiller*. New York, 1962

Gaiser, Gerd. *Schlußball* as *The Final Ball*. New York, 1960
──────. *Die sterbende Jagd* as *The Last Squadron*. New York, 1956
Gomringer, Eugen. *die konstellationen* as *Constellations*. In *The Book of Hours/Constellations*. New York, 1968
──────. *das stundenbuch* as *The Book of Hours*. In *The Book of Hours/Constellations*. New York, 1968
Grass, Günter. *Die Blechtrommel* as *The Tin Drum*. New York, 1963
──────. *Die bösen Köche* as *The Wicked Cooks*. In *Four Plays*. New York, 1967
──────. *Hochwasser* as *Flood*. In *Four Plays*. New York, 1967
──────. *Hundejahre* as *Dog Years*. New York, 1965
──────. *Katz und Maus* as *Cat and Mouse*. New York, 1963
──────. *Noch zehn Minuten bis Buffalo* as *Only Ten Minutes to Buffalo*. In *Four Plays*. New York, 1967
──────. *Onkel, Onkel* as *Mister, Mister*. In *Four Plays*. New York, 1967
──────. *Örtlich betäubt* as *Local Anaesthetic*. New York. 1970
──────. *Die Plebejer proben den Aufstand* as *The Plebeians Rehearse the Uprising: A German Tragedy*. New York, 1966
Handke, Peter. *Die Angst des Tormanns beim Elfmeter* as *The Goalie's Anxiety at the Penalty Kick*. New York, 1972
──────. *Hilferufe* as *Calling for Help*. In *TDR: The Drama Review*, Fall, 1970
──────. *Kaspar* as *Kaspar*. In *Kaspar, and Other Plays*. New York, 1969
──────. *Publikumsbeschimpfung* as *Offending the Audience*. In *Kaspar, and Other Plays*. New York, 1969
──────. *Der Ritt über den Bodensee* as *The Ride across Lake Constance*. In Michael Roloff, ed., *The Contemporary German Theater*. New York, 1972
──────. *Selbstbezichtigung* as *Self-Accusation*. In *Kaspar, and Other Plays*. New York, 1969
Hesse, Hermann. *Das Glasperlenspiel* as *The Glass Bead Game*. New York, 1969
──────. *Narziß und Goldmund* as *Narcissus and Goldmund*. New York, 1968
Hildesheimer, Wolfgang. *Nachtstück* as *Nightpiece*. In Michael Benedikt and George Wellwarth, eds., *Postwar German Theatre*. New York, 1968
Hochhuth, Rolf. *Die Soldaten* as *Soldiers: An Obituary for Geneva*. New York, 1968
──────. *Der Stellvertreter* as *The Deputy*. New York, 1964
Hochwälder, Fritz. *Das heilige Experiment* as *The Strong Are Lonely*. New York, 1954
──────. *Der Himbeerpflücker* as *The Raspberry Picker*. In Martin Esslin, ed., *The New Theatre of Europe*, vol. 4. New York, 1970
──────. *Der öffentliche Ankläger* as *The Public Prosecutor*. London, 1958
Hofmannsthal, Hugo von. *Der Turm* as *The Tower*. In *Three Plays*. Detroit, 1966
Johnson, Uwe. *Das dritte Buch über Achim* as *The Third Book about Achim*. New York, 1967
──────. *Mutmaßungen über Jakob* as *Speculations about Jakob*. London, 1963
──────. *Zwei Ansichten* as *Two Views*. New York, 1966
Jünger, Ernst. *Auf den Marmorklippen* as *On the Marble Cliffs*. New York, 1948
──────. *Gläserne Bienen* as *The Glass Bees*. New York, 1961
Kasack, Hermann. *Die Stadt hinter dem Strom* as *The City toward the River*. London, 1953
Kipphardt, Heinar. *In der Sache J. R. Oppenheimer* as *In the Matter of J. Robert Oppenheimer*. New York, 1968
Kleist, Heinrich von. *Die Marquise von O.* as *The Marquise of O──*. In *The Marquise of O──, and Other Stories*. New York, 1960
Krolow, Karl. *Fremde Körper* as *Foreign Bodies*. Athens, Ohio, 1969
Lenz, Siegfried. *Die Deutschstunde* as *The German Lesson*. New York, 1972
──────. *Das Feuerschiff* as *The Lightship*. New York, 1967
Nossack, Hans Erich. *Unmögliche Beweisaufnahme* as *The Impossible Proof*. New York, 1968
Plivier, Theodor. *Stalingrad* as *Stalingrad*. New York, 1948
Richter, Hans Werner. *Die Geschlagenen* as *The Odds Against Us*. London, 1950

————. *Sie fielen aus Gottes Hand* as *They Fell from God's Hand*. New York, 1956

Seghers, Anna. *Der Aufstand der Fischer von St. Barbara* as *The Revolt of the Fishermen*. New York, 1930

————. *Das siebte Kreuz* as *The Seventh Cross*. Boston, 1942

Sperr, Martin. *Jagdszenen aus Niederbayern* as *Hunting Scenes from Lower Bavaria*. In Michael Roloff, ed., *The Contemporary German Theater*. New York, 1972

Toller, Ernst. *Die Wandlung* as *Transfiguration*. In Harlan Hatcher, ed., *Modern Continental Dramas*. New York, 1941

Walser, Martin. *Der Abstecher* as *The Detour*. In *Plays*, vol. 1. London, 1963

————. *Ehen in Philippsburg* as *Marriage in Philippsburg*. Norfolk, Conn., 1961

Weiss, Peter. *Diskurs über die Vorgeschichte und den Verlauf des langandauernden Befreiungskrieges in Viet Nam* as *Discourse on the Progress of the Prolonged War of Liberation in Vietnam*. In *Two Plays*. New York, 1970

————. *Die Ermittlung* as *The Investigation*. New York, 1967

————. *Der Gesang vom lusitanischen Popanz* as *Song of the Lusitanian Bogey*. In *Two Plays*. New York, 1970

————. *Trotzki in Exil* as *Trotsky in Exile*. New York, 1971

————. *Der Turm* as *The Tower*. In Michael Benedikt and George Wellwarth, eds., *Postwar German Theatre*. New York, 1968

————. *Die Verfolgung und Ermordung Jean Paul Marats dargestellt durch die Schauspielgruppe des Hospizes zu Charenton unter Anleitung des Herrn de Sade* as *The Persecution and Assassination of Jean-Paul Marat as Performed by the Inmates of the Asylum of Charenton under the Direction of the Marquis de Sade*. New York, 1966

Wiechert, Ernst. *Das einfache Leben* as *The Simple Life*. London, 1954

————. *Die Jerominkinder* as *The Earth Is Our Heritage*. London, 1951

————. *Missa sine Nomine* as *Missa sine Nomine*. New York, 1953

Wolf, Christa. *Nachdenken über Christa T.* as *The Quest for Christa T.* New York, 1970

Zuckmayer, Carl. *Des Teufels General* as *The Devil's General*. In Haskell M. Block and Robert G. Shedd, eds., *Masters of the Modern Drama*. New York, 1962

Zwerenz, Gerhard. *Casanova, oder der kleine Herr in Krieg und Frieden* as *Little Peter in War and Peace*. New York, 1970

SECONDARY WORKS

BIBLIOGRAPHIES AND GUIDES

Albrecht, Günter, ed. *Lexikon deutschsprachiger Schriftsteller*, 2 vols., 6th ed. Leipzig, 1967

Arnold, Robert Franz. *Allgemeine Bücherkunde zur neueren deutschen Literaturgeschichte*, 4th ed. Berlin, 1966

Eppelsheimer, Hanns W. and Clemens Köttelwesch, eds. *Bibliographie der deutschen Literaturwissenschaft,* 9 vols. Frankfurt, 1957ff.

Goedeke, Karl. *Grundriß zur Geschichte der deutschen Dichtung,* 15 vols., rev. ed. Berlin, 1955ff.

Hansel, Johannes. *Bücherkunde für Germanisten,* 5th ed. Berlin, 1968

————. *Personalbibliographie zur deutschen Literaturgeschichte*. Berlin, 1967

Internationale Bibliographie zur Geschichte der deutschen Literatur. Berlin, 1969ff.

Kohlschmidt, Werner and Wolfgang Mohr. *Reallexikon der deutschen Literaturgeschichte*, 3 vols. Berlin, 1955ff.

Körner, Josef. *Bibliographisches Hand-*

buch des deutschen Schrifttums, 4th ed. Bern, 1966

Kosch, Wilhelm. Deutsches Literaturlexikon, 8 vols., 3rd ed. Bern, 1966ff.

Kunisch, Hermann, ed. Handbuch der deutschen Gegenwartsliteratur, 3 vols., 2nd ed. Munich, 1969–70

Lennartz, Franz. Deutsche Dichter und Schriftsteller unserer Zeit, 10th ed. Stuttgart, 1969

Nonnemann, Klaus, ed. Schriftsteller der Gegenwart: Deutsche Literatur. Olten, 1963

Wilpert, Gero von. Deutsches Dichterlexikon. Stuttgart, 1963

GENERAL WORKS

Bithell, Jethro. Modern German Literature, 3rd ed. London, 1959

Boesch, Bruno, ed. Deutsche Literaturgeschichte in Grundzügen, 3rd ed. Bern, 1967

Boor, Helmut de and Richard Newald, eds. Geschichte der deutschen Literatur, 8 vols. Munich, 1949ff.

Burger, Heinz Otto, ed. Annalen der deutschen Literatur, 2nd ed. Stuttgart, 1961–71

Calgari, Guido. The Four Literatures of Switzerland. London, 1963

Closs, August. Reality and Creative Vision in German Lyrical Poetry. London, 1963

David, Claude. Von Richard Wagner zu Bertolt Brecht. Frankfurt, 1964

Domandi, Agnes Körner, ed. Modern German Literature, two vols. New York, 1972

Duwe, Wilhelm. Ausdrucksformen deutscher Dichtung vom Naturalismus zur Gegenwart. Berlin, 1965

———. Deutsche Dichtung des 20. Jahrhunderts, 2 vols. Zürich, 1962

Friedmann, Hermann and Otto Mann, eds. Deutsche Literatur im 20. Jahrhundert, 2 vols., 5th ed. Bern, 1967

Fricke, Gerhard and Volker Klotz. Geschichte der deutschen Dichtung, 11th ed. Hamburg, 1965

Geerdts, Hans Jürgen, ed. Deutsche Literaturgeschichte. Berlin, 1965

Horst, Karl August. Kritischer Führer durch die deutsche Literatur der Gegenwart. Munich, 1962

———. The Quest of 20th Century German Literature. New York, 1971

Mann, Otto. Deutsche Literaturgeschichte. Gütersloh, 1964

Martini, Fritz. Deutsche Literaturgeschichte, 15th ed. Stuttgart, 1968

Natan, Alex, ed. German Men of Letters, 3 vols. London, 1963

Robertson, J. G. History of German Literature, 5th ed. London, 1962

Schmidt, Adalbert. Dichtung und Dichter Österreichs im 19. und 20. Jahrhundert, 2 vols. Salzburg, 1964

Schneider, Hermann. Geschichte der deutschen Dichtung, 2 vols. Bonn, 1949ff.

Welzig, Werner. Der deutsche Roman im 20. Jahrhundert, 2nd ed. Stuttgart, 1970

WORKS ON CONTEMPORARY LITERATURE

Arntzen, Helmut. Der moderne deutsche Roman. Heidelberg, 1962

Baumgart, Reinhard. Aussichten des Romans, oder Hat Literatur Zukunft? Neuwied, 1968

Berger, Manfred et al. Theater in der Zeitenwende: Zur Geschichte des Dramas und des Schauspieltheaters in der Deutschen Demokratischen Republik, 2 vols. Berlin, 1972

Demetz, Peter. Postwar German Literature: A Critical Introduction. New York, 1970

Domin, Hilde. Doppelinterpretationen: Das zeitgenössische deutsche Gedicht zwischen Autor und Leser. Frankfurt, 1966

Durzak, Manfred. Der deutsche Roman der Gegenwart. Stuttgart, 1971

Durzak, Manfred, ed. Die deutsche Literatur der Gegenwart: Aspekte und Tendenzen. Stuttgart, 1971

Flores, John. Poetry in East Germany. New York, 1971

Franke, Konrad. Die Literatur der Deutschen Demokratischen Republik. Munich, 1971

Garten, J. F. Modern German Drama, 2nd ed. London, 1964

Grenzmann, Wilhelm. Deutsche Dichtung der Gegenwart, 2nd ed. Frankfurt, 1955

Hamburger, Michael. Reason and Energy. New York, 1967

Heitner, Robert R., ed. *The Contemporary Novel in German: A Symposium.* Austin, Tex., 1967

Hensel, Georg. *Theater der Zeitgenossen: Stücke und Autoren.* Frankfurt, 1972

Heselhaus, Clemens. *Deutsche Lyrik der Moderne.* Düsseldorf, 1961

Holthusen, Hans Egon. *Das Schöne und das Wahre.* Munich, 1958

———. *Der unbehauste Mensch.* Munich, 1951

Huebener, Theodore. *The Literature of East Germany.* New York, 1970

Jens, Walter. *Deutsche Literatur der Gegenwart,* 4th ed. Munich, 1962

Kayser, Wolfgang, ed. *Deutsche Literatur in unserer Zeit,* 4th ed. Göttingen, 1964

Keith-Smith, Brian. *Essays on Contemporary German Literature.* London, 1966

Kesting, Marianne. *Panorama des zeitgenössischen Theaters.* Munich, 1969

Knörrich, Otto. *Die deutsche Lyrik der Gegenwart.* Stuttgart, 1971

Koebner, Thomas, ed. *Tendenzen der deutschen Literatur seit 1945.* Stuttgart, 1971

Krolow, Karl. *Aspekte zeitgenössischer deutscher Lyrik.* Gütersloh, 1961

Lettau, Reinhard. *Die Gruppe 47: Bericht, Kritik, Polemik.* Neuwied, 1967

Magris, Claudio. *Il mito absburgico nella letteratura austriaca moderna.* Turin, 1963

Matthaei, Renate, ed. *Grenzverschiebung: Neue Tendenzen in der deutschen Literatur der sechziger Jahre.* Cologne, 1970

Mayer, Hans. *Brecht und die Tradition.* Pfullingen, 1961

———. *Das Geschehen und das Schweigen.* Frankfurt, 1969

———. *Zur deutschen Literatur der Zeit.* Reinbek bei Hamburg, 1967

Raddatz, Fritz. *Traditionen und Tendenzen: Materialien zur Literatur der DDR.* Frankfurt, 1972

Reich-Ranicki, Marcel. *Deutsche Literatur in Ost und West.* Munich, 1966

———. *Literarisches Leben in Deutschland.* Munich, 1965

———. *Literatur der kleinen Schritte.* Munich, 1967

Rischbieter, Henning and Ernst Wendt. *Deutsche Dramatik in West und Ost.* Velber, 1965

Rühle, Jürgen. *Literature and Revolution: A Critical Study of the Writer and Communism in the Twentieth Century.* New York, 1969

Schmidt, Adalbert. *Literaturgeschichte unserer Zeit,* 3rd. ed. Salzburg, 1968

Schnetz, Diemut. *Der moderne Einakter.* Bern, 1967

Soergel, Albert and Curt Hohoff. *Dichtung und Dichter der Zeit.,* 2 vols. Düsseldorf, 1961

Taeni, Rainer. *Drama nach Brecht.* Basel, 1968

Thomas, R. Hinton and Wilfried van der Will. *The German Novel and the Affluent Society.* Toronto, 1968

Vormweg, Heinrich. *Die Wörter und die Welt: Über neue Literatur,* Neuwied, 1968

Waidson, H. M. *The Modern German Novel.* London, 1960

Weber, Dietrich, ed. *Deutsche Literatur seit 1945,* 2nd ed. Stuttgart, 1970

Wellwarth, George E. *The Theater of Protest and Paradox.* New York, 1964

Widmer, Urs. *1945 oder die "Neue Sprache."* Düsseldorf, 1966

Wiese, Benno von. *Deutsche Dichter der Moderne,* 2nd ed. Berlin, 1969

ISIDORA ROSENTHAL-KAMARINEA

Greek Literature

GREEK LITERATURE underwent fundamental changes in the 1930s as a result of the country's experiences of World War I and the subsequent defeat, in 1922, of Greek troops in Asia Minor. Some outspoken novelists dared for the first time to break with the traditional cult of the war hero in Greek literature and to write instead a courageous antiwar literature with strong social comment. The focus of stories and novels shifted from the portrayal of external behavior to the uncovering and investigating of problems resulting from social and psychological conflicts.

Poetry during the 1930s also underwent a transformation. Modernism supplanted a traditional poetry marked by lavish symbols and stylistic devices. And although fiction after 1935 did not continue along its new lines but instead returned to earlier modes (certainly influenced by political events both at home and abroad between 1935 and 1940), poetry continued to be dominated by modernism.

The horrors and sufferings caused by World War II and the severe upheavals caused by the ensuing civil war (1945–50) became the central themes of Greek literature of the 1940s. With a unity of purpose, Greek writers attacked the oppressive German enemy and his war crimes. Afterward, however, writers separated into two conflicting political camps and related their experiences from their different perspectives.

348

POETRY

Gheorghos Seferis (1900–1971), who was awarded the Nobel Prize in 1963, can be called the founder of modern poetry in Greece. His pioneering first volume of poems, *Strofi* (1931, Turning Point), departed from the accepted traditions of Greek poetry and offered a version of the symbolism practiced in France by such poets as Paul Valéry. Seferis's work was characterized by a simplicity, an economy of expression, and an awareness of the twentieth-century world.

Modernism also characterized the first books of poetry of Seferis's colleagues, Andhreas Embirikos (born 1901), Odhysseas Elytis (born 1911), and Nikos Engonopoulos (born 1910), all three of whom adopted French surrealism; of the religious Takis Papatsonis (born 1895), whose poetry also has had surrealistic traits; of the visionary Melissanthi (born 1910); of the politically committed Yannis Ritsos (born 1909) and Nikiforos Vrettakos (born 1912).

Angelos Sikelianos (1884–1951), who continued to follow an independent path, cannot be linked with the modernists. Much closer to traditional Greek poetry, Sikelianos used mythology, religion, and history to affirm his belief in an underlying harmony and unity of mankind.

Another older poet who did not embrace modernism was Kostas Varnalis (born 1884), who has also written important criticism. Varnalis has been the Nestor of the literature of the political left. Although he did write his revolutionary works in a new language, he still used forms and meters handed down by the generation of Kostis Palamas (1859–1943). Varnalis's particular strength is biting satire. Other leftist poets who continued to use traditional forms and meters were Markos Avghiris (born 1883), also known as a critic; the realistic poet Manolis Kanellis (born 1900); the Cypriots Tefkros Anthias (1904–1968) and Theodhossis Pieridhis (1908–1968).

During World War II and the civil war that followed, Greek poetry, like fiction, reflected political events. The chief concern of poets, including the modernists, during the occupation was to keep alive the idea of freedom. A great many poems were passed from hand to hand in mimeographed form. Some works that were not printed at all until after World War II became known through oral transmission.

Nikos Engonopoulos, who together with Andhreas Embirikos had established surrealism in Greek poetry, wrote the lengthy poem *Bolivar* (Bolívar) in 1942, which was circulated from person to person. Embirikos celebrated Bolívar, the symbol of freedom, as an image of Greece timelessly associated with liberty. In *Asma iroiko kai penthimo ghia to hameno anthypolohagho tis Alvanias* (1945, Heroic and Mournful Song on the Second Lieutenant Killed in Albania), Odhysseas Elytis, who had celebrated the Greek landscape through surrealism, became the poet of the Greek nation fighting for freedom. This shift enabled Elytis to subdue the natural lyricism of his luminous poetry and to open himself up to new possibilities for his poetry, which reached fruition in his complex masterpiece *Axion esti* (1961; the title is the first two words of a hymn: It Is Worthy).

Two poets who made their debuts during the 1930s, Yannis Ritsos and Nikiforos Vrettakos, did not develop into major writers until the postwar period. Ritsos and Vrettakos have had much in common: their early backgrounds, their struggles for survival, their love for humanity, their social involvement. Ritsos's sensitive, delicate poems of his early career yielded, in turn, to engrossing protest songs rich in imagery, to battle songs, to social-protest poems, to restrained complaints, and finally to simple, almost naked presentations of the sufferings of the persecuted. Vrettakos's activist tone of the war years was replaced by the warning voice of a wise, experienced man concerned about the elusiveness of peace and the state of the world, and filled with love for mankind.

In postwar Greece, all the forms of modern world poetry have been evident. There has also been a close connection between the content of poetry and the philosophical tendencies of the age. Existential anxiety, self-examination, metaphysical searching, an optimistic or Dionysian closeness to nature, a visionary religiosity, and a concern for the future of humanity have all found expression in the verse of such contemporary poets as Gheorghos Themelis (born 1909), Kostas Thrakiotis (born 1909), G. T. Vafopoulos (born 1904), Aris Dhiktaos (born 1917), Takis Sinopoulos (born 1917), Takis Varvitsiotis (born 1916), Kriton Athanassoulis (born 1916), Sarandos Pavleas (born 1917), Miltos Sahtouris (born 1919), Stelios Yeranis (born 1920), Gheorghos Kotsiras (born 1921), Klitos Kyrou (born 1921), Nikos Karousos (born 1926), and the Cypriot poets Kostas Mondis (born 1914), Kypros Hrysanthis (born 1915), and Andhreas Hristofidhis (born 1937).

A number of poets have dedicated themselves specifically to social and political problems. These include Nikos Papas (born 1906), Gheorghos Sarandis (born 1919), Tassos Livadhitis (born 1921), Manolis Anaghnostakis (born 1925), Titos Patrikios (born 1928), and Vagelis Tsakiridhis (born 1936).

The special characteristics of postwar Greek poetry have been a spare language and a new expressiveness taken over from surrealism, by which the adjective does not serve the aesthetically selective function of decorative qualifier, as in the melodic language of nuances, but rather contributes to the development of piercing images that stand in irrational relationships to each other and conjure up a new, dynamic reality. Through these adjectives, the barrenness of abstraction acquires the luminosity of images of the unconscious, of the dream, or of the almost unreal, light-drenched Greek landscape.

FICTION

Several novelists who may be considered transitional figures made major contributions to postwar Greek literature. The outstanding novelist, epic poet, playwright, and essayist Nikos Kazantzakis (1883–1957), whose reputation is international, defies classification. Although he began to write while still in his early twenties and although his monumental epic poem *I Odhysseia* (1938, The Odyssey) was published before the war, Kazantzakis's major novels were published after 1945: *Alexis Zorbas* (1946, Alexis Zorbas), *O Kapetan Mihalis* (1953, Captain Mihalis), *O Hristos xanastavronetai* (1954, Christ Recrucified), *O televtaios peirasmos* (1955, The Last Temptation), *O ftohoulis tou Theou* (1956, God's Pauper), *Anafora sto Greco* (1961, Report to Greco). Kazantzakis made many contributions to the contemporary Greek novel, including the linguistic one of preferring demotic Greek, the spoken language, to the customary literary language. Kazantzakis's major theme was the quest for freedom, even if the search can never be successful.

Another major writer of the interwar period who continued to contribute to Greek literature after 1945 was Ilias Venezis (born 1904). His major achievements remain his short stories. The collection *Ora polemou* (1946, Hour of War) captured the oppressive immediacy of events (not always a virtue). In most of Venezis's stories, including those in his later collection *I nikimeni* (1954, The Defeated), characters have to confront a complex world beyond their understanding.

Gheorghos Theotokas's (1905–1966) *Iera odhos* (1950, Sacred Road) was about the German occupation of Greece. Theotokas later used similar material for his two-volume novel *Astheneis kai odhoiporoi* (1964, Patients and Wanderers). Theotokas's novels, fine examples of realism, are distinguished by their sharp observations, sensitive psychology, and clarity of style. Stratis Myrivilis (1892–1969), who had written early in his career the well-known antiwar novel *I zoi en tafo* (1924, 1932; Life in the Grave), continued to attack war in *Kokkino vivlio* (1952, Red Book).

Other works dealing with the horrors of war were Petros Harus's (born 1902) stories in the volume *Fota sto pelaghos* (1958, Lights in the Sea);

Ioannis M. Panayotopoulos's (born 1901) novel *Aihmalotoi* (1951, Prisoners) and his volume of stories *Anthropini dhipsa* (1959, Man's Thirst); and Angelos Tersakis's (born 1907) chronicle *Aprilis* (1946, April), in which he described the Greek-Italian war in Albania.

The war in Albania was also treated by Stelios Xefludhas (born 1902) in modern prose style in *Anthropoi tou mythou* (1946, People of Myth), by Yannis Veratis (born 1904) in *To platy potami* (1946, The Broad River), and by Loukis Akritas (1908–1965) in *Armatomenoi* (1947, Armed Men). Both Veratis and Akritas continued the old tradition of war-hero worship and the affirmation of war.

In general, fiction about World War II showed a different spirit from that of the antiwar literature of the 1930s. Whether they stood politically to the right or left, the writers all emphasized the bravery of Greeks resisting the enemy and fighting for freedom. The struggle against the Germans during the period of occupation was described in Themos Kornaros's (1907–1970) *Stratopedho tou Haidhariou* (1945, Haidhari Concentration Camp), in Dhimitris Hadzis's (born 1913) *Fotia* (1946, Fire), and in Andhreas Frangias's (born 1921) *Kangeloporta* (1962, Iron-Bar Door).

Younger writers of fiction also described the horrible events of the war years, mostly in works published during the 1950s. Outstanding among these works were Rodhis Roufos's (born 1924) trilogy *I riza tou mythou* (1954, The Root of Myth), *I poreia sto skotadhi* (1955, March into Darkness), and *I alli ohthi* (1958, The Other Bank); Nikos Kasdhaghlis's (born 1928) *Ta dhondia tis mylopetras* (1955, The Teeth of the Mill-wheel); and Theophilos Frangopoulos's (born 1923) *Teihomahia* (1954, War at the Wall). Kazantzakis's *Adhelfofadhes* (1954, The Fratricides), Themos Kornaros's *Stahtes kai foinikes* (1957, Ashes and Phoenix), and Renos Apostolidhis's (born 1924) *Pyramidha 67* (1950, Pyramid 67) impressively portrayed the civil war. Although these war novels, taken collectively, varied considerably in political viewpoints, literary techniques, and expressive power, they were united by their common subject.

After the first postwar years, during which the subject of the war and its aftermath dominated, writers of fiction, like poets, began to seek new themes and new forms of expression. Political and social commitment remained strong. But one could sense an existential anxiety arising from the events narrated in a number of novels; the anxiety took the specific form of a feeling of the lack of a way out for hectically pursued man, of the senselessness of life and its absurdity. A modern mode in fiction, suggested earlier in the works of Alkiviadhis Yannopoulos (born 1896) and Yannis Sfakianakis (born 1908), now began to prevail.

The activist leftist Stratis Tsirkas (born 1911) presented events of the war years, principally centered on the circles of Greek exiles in Cairo and

Alexandria, in a majestically planned trilogy: *I leshi* (1960, The Club), *I Ariaghni* (1962, Ariagni), and *I nyhteridha* (1965, The Bat). Menelaos Lundhemis (born 1912), who had described war experiences in *Avtoi pou ferane tin katahnia* (1946, Those Who Brought the Fog), has written novels and stories about the world of the socially disadvantaged. Mihail Piranthis (born 1917) has specialized in historical and biographical novels. Yannis Manglis (born 1909) has written about the misery of sailors' and workers' lives in the prose manner of Nikos Kazantzakis. Tassos Athanassiadhis (born 1913) has written *romans fleuves,* while Alkis Angeloglou (born 1915) and Asteris Kovadzis (born 1916) are representatives of the school of lyrical prose.

Novelists who came to the fore during the 1950s were confronted by an abundance of old and new problems. Dhimitris Hadzis, a leftist activist novelist, who has lived abroad since the end of the civil war, is among the leading representatives of a realism infused with the spirit of humanity and able to express the most subtle nuances, as in *To telos tis mikris mas polis* (1963, The End of Our Little City). Spyros Plaskovitis's (born 1917) characters are torn between feelings of justice and their weakness and loneliness. Plaskovitis paid for his righteous, fearless stance toward the military regime with a five-year prison sentence.

Kostas Steryopoulos (born 1926), who is also a poet, has written esoteric fiction with little in the way of plot. Galatia Sarandi (born 1920), in stories filled with psychological nuances, has laid special stress on the psychology of woman as she responded to conditions during and after the war. Sotiris Patadzis (born 1915), focusing on the area between dream and reality, has described the inner dramas of lonely people and the sad, gloomy life in the provinces. The leftist Tatiana Milliex (born 1920) has given a modern stamp both to her own experiences and to her social criticism through an original prose style, in such works as *Kai idhou ippos hloros* (1963, And Behold a Green Horse). Eva Vlami (born 1920), with forceful narrative technique, has brought to life maritime villages as they were in a prosperous era of the past. The novels of Nikos Athanassiadhis (born 1905), such as *To ghymno koritsi* (1964, The Naked Girl), have shown his strong ties to nature. Alexandhros Kotsias (born 1926), who contributed to war fiction with *Poliorkia* (1953, Siege), has perceptively presented the discussions of young people's political groups. Nestoras Matsas (born 1931) has stressed the problems of the persecuted Jews during the war.

Among the prominent writers of the 1960s were Yerassimos Ghrighoris (born 1907), who has written stories of social criticism, and Kostas Kotsias (born 1920), another leftist writer of fiction with a very accomplished style, who had described the struggle against the German occupation in

O kapnismenos ouranos (1957, The Smoked Sky). Kostoula Mitropoulou (born 1937) has written several books that are modern in conception and form. Petros Ambadzoglou's (born 1931) *Thanatos misthotou* (1970, Death of an Employee) in a highly original way gave a critical presentation of life in a military dictatorship.

Two writers of contemporary Greek fiction have made special contributions: Andonis Samarakis (born 1919) and Vassilis Vassilikos (born 1934). Samarakis has employed a choppy style consistently denuded of all external beauty to depict—in several penetrating stories in *Ziteitai elpis* (1959, Search for Hope) and in the novel *To lathos* (1965, The Flaw)—the world of man helplessly delivered up to the compulsions and severities of society. Vassilikos, with new means of expression, has endeavored to present the conflict of the individual and society and to uncover the political crimes in a corrupt nation, in such works as *To fyllo, to pighadhi, to angeliasma* (1961, The Leaf, the Well, the Process of Becoming Angelic) and *Zita* (1966, Z).

Alexander Skinas (born 1924) has chosen the path of experimental fiction, which is new for Greece, in *Anafora periptoseon* (1966, Report of Cases).

DRAMA

Many contemporary poets and novelists have also written plays. The major writers Angelos Sikelianos and Nikos Kazantzakis are just two of a number of writers who have written modern tragedies set in antiquity or during the Byzantine period; not all of the literary tragedies are effective on the stage. Other prominent writers, such as Kostis Palamas, Gheorghos Theotokas, and Pandelis Prevelakis (born 1909), have used their plays to show the characteristics of the Greek way of life.

Until the end of the war, Greek theater did not keep up with modern international developments. A national provincialism, largely attributable to the peculiarity of social customs and the still-dependent position of women, was very hard to overcome despite repeated efforts. In the last two decades, however, younger authors have written plays concerned with the problems taken up in the contemporary drama of Europe and America.

In recent years, the ranks of established playwrights—Spyros Melas (1882–1966); Theodhoros Synodhinos (1880–1959); Dhimitris Voghris (1890–1964); Angelos Tersakis, also an important novelist—have been swelled by young writers who have written plays that are modern in form and treat contemporary problems. Iakovos Kambanellis (born 1919) attracted considerable attention right after the war. Vangelis Kadzanis (born

1935) created a sensation with his antimonarchist tragedy about the house of Atreus. Fofi Tresou (born 1929), whose plays have been put on by several theaters in Athens, has also written a tragedy of the house of Atreus with modern implications. Vassilis Zioghas (born 1935), who is also a poet, has written successful plays, several of which have been performed abroad. Marietta Rialdhi (born 1943) has written avant-garde plays directed against power. Kostas Mourselas (born 1930), Dhimitris Kehaidis (born 1933), and Petros Markaris (born 1937) have written epic dramas in the manner of Brecht. Other worthy contemporary playwrights include Margharita Lymberaki (born 1918), Stratis Karras (born 1935), and Hristos Samouilidhis (born 1927).

GREEK WORKS IN ENGLISH TRANSLATION

ANTHOLOGIES

Barnstone, Willis, ed. *Eighteen Texts: Writings by Contemporary Greek Authors.* Cambridge, Mass., 1972

Dalven, Rae, ed. *Modern Greek Poetry,* 2nd ed. New York, 1971

Decavalles, Andonis, ed. *The Voice of Cyprus: An Anthology of Cypriot Literature.* New York, 1966

Gianos, Mary P., ed. *Introduction to Modern Greek Literature: An Anthology of Fiction, Drama, and Poetry.* New York, 1969

Keeley, Edmund and Philip Sherrard, eds. *Six Poets of Modern Greece.* London, 1960

Modern Poetry in Translation, no. 4: *The Greek Poets.* New York, 1968

Richmond, John and Brian McCarthy, eds. *The Singing Cells: Modern Greek Poems.* Montreal, 1971

INDIVIDUAL WORKS MENTIONED
IN ARTICLE

Athanassiadhis, Nikos. *To ghymno koritsi* as *A Naked Girl.* New York, 1968

Kazantzakis, Nikos. *Adhelfofadhes* as *The Fratricides.* New York, 1964

——. *Alexis Zorbas* as *Zorba the Greek.* New York, 1953

——. *Anafora sto Greco* as *Report to Greco.* New York, 1965

——. *O ftohoulis tou Theou* as *Saint Francis.* New York, 1962

——. *O Hristos xanastavronetai* as *The Greek Passion.* New York, 1954

——. *O Kapetan Mihalis* as *Freedom or Death.* New York, 1956

——. *I Odhysseia* as *The Odyssey: A Modern Sequel.* New York, 1958

——. *O televtaios peirasmos* as *The Last Temptation of Christ.* New York, 1960

Samarakis, Andonis. *To lathos* as *The Flaw.* New York, 1966

Seferis, Gheorghos. *Strofi* as *Turning Point.* In *Collected Poems, 1924–1955.* Princeton, N.J., 1967

Vassilikos, Vassilis. *To fyllo, to pighadhi, to angeliasma* as *The Plant. The Well. The Angel.* New York, 1964

——. *Zita* as *Z.* New York, 1968

SECONDARY WORKS

Baud-Bovy, S. *Poésie de la Grèce moderne*. Lausanne, 1946

Dhiktaeos, Aris. *Theoria poiisios*. Athens, 1962

Dhimaris, K. T. *Istoria tis neoellinikis loghotehnias*, 4th ed. Athens, 1968

Kambanis, Aristos. *Istoria tis neas ellinikis loghotehnias,* 5th ed. Athens, 1948.

Kanellopulos, P. *Hyperion und der neugriechische Geist,* 2nd ed. Marburg, 1959

Karandonis, Andhreas. *Eisaghoghi sti neotera poiisi*. Athens, 1958

Keeley, Edmund and Peter Bien, eds. *Modern Greek Writers*. Princeton, N.J., 1972

Knös, Börje. *L'histoire de la littérature néo-grecque*. Uppsala, 1962

Kordhatos, Yannis. *Istoria tis neoellinikis loghotehnias,* 2 vols. Athens, 1962–63

Lavagnini, Bruno. *Storia della letteratura neoellenica,* 3rd ed. Florence, 1969

Mirambel, A. *La littérature grecque moderne*. Paris, 1953

Politis, Linos. *Istoria tis neas ellinikis loghotehnias*. Athens, 1968

Sahinis, Apostolos. *Neoi pezoghrafoi*. Athens, 1965

———. *I synhroni pezoghrafia mas*. Athens, 1951

Sideris, Jean. *Le théâtre néo-grec*. Athens, 1957

Spyridaki, Georges. *La Grèce et la poésie moderne*. Paris, 1954

Steryopoulos, Kostas. *Apo to symvolismo sti nea poiisi*. Athens, 1967

Valetas, Gheorghios. *Epitomi istoria tis neoellinikis loghotehnias*. Athens, 1966

Vitti, M. *Orientamento della Grecia nel suo risorgimento letterario*. Rome, 1955

GEORGE GÖMÖRI

Hungarian Literature

THE HUNGARIANS speak a non-Indo-European language—related to Finnish but completely different from the languages spoken by neighboring Slavic and Germanic peoples. All the same, the development of Hungarian literature, since the first written documents in the eleventh century, has been similar to that of other central and eastern European literatures. Although Latin was the standard literary language until the sixteenth century, the literature of the vernacular, powerfully stimulated by the Reformation, began to take dominion. By the end of the eighteenth century Magyar—the self-designation of the Hungarian language—had become the almost exclusive idiom of Hungarian writers.

Yet only in the nineteenth century, after the successful language reform of Ferenc Kazinczy (1759–1831), did Hungarian literature come of age and produce its first poets of international stature. These classical Hungarian writers—Mihály Vörösmarty (1800–1855), János Arany (1817–1882), Sándor Petőfi (1823–1849)—were more influenced by Greek and Latin authors and Shakespeare than by their German or French contemporaries. After stagnation in the second half of the nineteenth century, Hungary saw the triumphant rise of the "modern" movement, centered around the literary review *Nyugat,* which drew to it, like a magnet, the best writers of the age, including Endre Ady (1877–1919).

Hungarian writers in our century can be divided into two groups: those believing in social commitment, who have promoted reform or revolution;

and those refusing to accept such a task, in the name of art's complete autonomy. The best Hungarian writers, however, managed to solve this conflict by responding to the "challenge of the age" without lowering their artistic standards. Attila József (1905–1937), the socialist poet, is a case in point. Until recently, writers in Hungary have been working under an unwritten social and national obligation to be at the service of the community at all times. Postwar developments, however, if not quite eliminating this expectation, at least restricted and, after 1956, seriously impaired its validity.

In most literary histories the discussion of contemporary Hungarian literature begins with the year 1945. This date certainly can be taken as a starting point in at least one respect—politics. The conclusion of the war, with the liberation of Hungary by the Soviet army (and I do not use this term ironically, for whatever their later role in Hungarian politics, the Russians *did* liberate Hungary from German occupation), was the beginning of an era of radical reform long overdue in a country in which huge estates were owned by a few aristocrats and by the Catholic church, in which the landless peasantry lived in total poverty, and in which democracy was at best a tactical slogan of the ruling coalition of landowners, rich industrialists, and the military bureaucracy.

Yet although 1945 was an important milestone in the life of the nation, in literature it was not a watershed like 1849 or 1919. The liberation did bring about significant changes, such as the abolition of wartime censorship and the return to print of authors previously suppressed either for their left-wing views or for their racial origins. Many new cultural periodicals were launched, and the existence of democratic political parties ensured the possibility of free and largely unfettered debate on literary problems. Nonetheless, the first three years following the conclusion of World War II appear to have been more a *continuation* of rather than a break with the literature of preceding years. Both writers and readers needed time to get over the shock of a war that brought so much suffering and destruction to Hungary; they also needed time to digest the social revolution represented by the radical land reform.

The list of the writers who were victims of the war and of the fascist terror that gripped Hungary in October, 1944, is sadly long. Miklós Radnóti (1909–1944), a poet of classical serenity and harmony who wrote some of his best poems in the last months of his life, was shot by the Germans in 1944. Other victims of the Nazis included the sensitive poet György Sárközi (1899–1945) and his friends, the brilliant literary historians Antal Szerb (1901–1945) and Gábor Halász (1901–1945). György Bálint (1906–1943), the well-known left-wing critic, disappeared in the Ukraine; the young Transylvanian worker-poet Ernő Salamon (1912–1943) also perished in the Ukraine, shot by an Italian soldier.

These losses to Hungarian literature could not be offset by the return to Hungary of some writers and critics who had emigrated to the Soviet Union before World War II. This group included György Lukács (1885–1971), the world-famous aesthetician and literary critic; József Révai (1898–1959), an energetic Marxist critic of populist sympathies; the playwright Gyula Háy (born 1900); the film theoretician Béla Balázs (1884–1949); and the novelist Béla Illés (born 1895). With the exception of Balázs, who died soon afterward, all of them played an important part in the cultural and political debates of following years: Lukács in the first ("coalition") period, Révai in the second, in the years of direct communist rule. The return of communist writers led to the publication of books written earlier, of which Béla Illés's verbose but colorful *Kárpáti rapszódia* (1946, Carpathian Rhapsody) and Sándor Gergely's (born 1896) historical trilogy *Dózsa* (1945–48, Dózsa) were the most popular at the time. The theaters staged plays by Gyula Háy written in emigration.

At the other end of the literary spectrum during the years immediately after World War II was the so-called bourgeois prose of such authors as Sándor Márai (born 1900) and Lajos Zilahy (born 1891). Between the wars Márai had built up a considerable reputation both as a master of style and as an outstanding spokesman of upper-middle-class values. From 1945 to 1948 he published the travel diary *Európa elrablása* (1947, The Abduction of Europe) and *Sértődöttek* (1947–48, The Offended Ones), a novel dealing with the life of a middle-class family during the rise of Nazism.

Zilahy wrote apolitical best sellers before the war. In *Ararát* (1947, Ararat), later included in the Dukay trilogy (first published in English as *The Dukays* [1949], and later in Hungarian as *A Dukay család* [1969]), Zilahy told the saga of a Hungarian aristocratic family from the times of the Austro-Hungarian empire through World War II. This novel enjoyed some success in left-wing circles because of its sarcastic and critical treatment of the life of the "ten thousand families" who had owned most of Hungary.

By 1948 both Zilahy and Márai had emigrated. Márai has since written several novels, such as *Béke Ithakában* (1952, Peace in Ithaca) and *San Gennaro vére* (1965, The Blood of San Gennaro). His postwar diaries, published in two separate volumes, showed that he has not lost the passion for observing and commenting on life and art. One of the most erudite Hungarian writers, Márai is often more impressive in his diaries than in his novels, which tend to become excessively lyrical or essayistic in his hands.

A writer caught between his bourgeois background and communist sympathies, Tibor Déry (born 1894) attracted attention after 1945. His involvement in the socialist movement had forced him into emigration after 1919. Between the wars Déry lived in half a dozen different European countries: he started *A befejezetlen mondat* (1947, The Unfinished Sentence) in Vienna, worked on it in Dubrovnik, and finished the manuscript in Budapest. It soon became an "underground classic." Although it was read in manuscript and praised in print in Hungary by the prominent poet Gyula Illyés (born 1902) in 1938, the novel itself could be published only after the war. *The Unfinished Sentence* was an ambitious attempt to give a total picture of Hungarian society. Its hero, Lőrinc Parcen-Nagy, is an "alienated" man who has detached himself from his class but has not yet found a home among his proletarian comrades. Déry's novel was criticized by Lukács and others for "overemphasizing" the political sectarianism in the Hungarian workers' movement and for using a somewhat surrealistic technique.

Another book of Déry's published soon after the war was *Alvilági játékok* (1946, Games of the Underworld), a cycle of stories depicting the twilight life of a Budapest besieged by Russian troops and terrorized by local fascists. This cycle and the long and beautifully told story *Az óriás* (1948, The Giant) showed Déry's willingness to accept the Lukácsian formula of "realism" and to break with surrealist experimentation.

Apart from Déry, the most accomplished prose writer of this period was probably László Németh (born 1901). Németh had been active as a writer since the 1920s, and by the end of the war he was regarded as the most influential essayist of the populist movement, which, among other things, advocated a radical land reform in Hungary. In his essays Németh explored the possibility of a "third road" for Hungary and put forward the program of a "socialism of quality."

Németh made his name as a writer of fiction well before World War II. But his best novel, *Iszony* (1947, Revulsion), was written during the war years. Here Németh achieved an unusually high level of cohesion through both social and psychological realism. The point of departure for the story is the monologue of Nelli Kárász, a proud and cold but hardworking girl of gentry stock. Circumstances force her into a tragic marriage with the easy-going and sociable but indolent and unsophisticated son of a rich peasant. The alienation that is the central theme of the novel is only in part psychological; it also has social relevance.

Németh is an acute observer of provincial society. He is at his best when describing the life and mentality of the Hungarian middle class of the small towns—its rigid rules, elaborate pretensions, and modest ambitions. This was also the milieu of his later novel *Égető Eszter* (1956, Eszter Égető). The heroine here, however, lives a much more harmonious and satisfying life than the tragically isolated Nelli Kárász of *Revulsion*. Eszter's main aim is to create a "nest of happiness" in a sea of conflicting emotions and interests.

The lyric poets of the period 1945–48, or, rather the best of them, continued trends that had begun well before the war. The two great figures of Hungarian modernism—Milán Füst (1888–1967) and Lajos Kassák (1887–1967)—survived the war; but Füst did not publish any new poems and Kassák had little influence on the development of postwar verse. Other outstanding poets, such as Gyula Illyés, Lőrinc Szabó (1900–1957), and István Vas (born 1910), were prewar contributors to *Nyugat;* Illyés even coedited the review at one time.

Of the three, Gyula Illyés was the most enthusiastic about the political changes in the country. Because of the "lyrical realism" of his poems hailing peace, reconstruction, and the democratic land reform, he was the equivalent of a "Popular Front" poet, acceptable to populists and Marxists alike. In the 1950s, however, he wrote *Egy mondat a zsarnokságról* (One Sentence on Tyranny), a fiery poetic condemnation of totalitarianism (not published until 1956). This and the poems collected in the volume *Kézfogások* (1956, Handshakes) showed his growth into a truly popular poet who could express not only general human emotions but also particular national hopes and aspirations in an intellectual, yet direct and easily comprehensible, idiom.

Lőrinc Szabó, an anarchist rebel in the 1920s, became to some extent a member of the prewar establishment in following years. His rightist nationalism—especially his pro-German attitudes during the war—resulted in a temporary ostracism of Szabó from literary life in the years immediately after 1945. During this period he completed his autobiographical cycle of poems *Tücsökzene* (1947, Cricket's Music). This work, consisting of sonnets of the Shakespearean form, was the quintessence of Szabó's very sensuous and richly textured poetry. The most interesting qualities of these sonnets were their supple diction (which followed the rhythm of everyday speech) and their dynamic structure (the tension increased to the very last line). Szabó's subsequent poetry was of equally high quality, but not until a decade later did he produce a major work comparable to *Cricket's Music—A huszonhatodik év* (1959, The Twenty-sixth Year), a cycle of sonnets addressed to the poet's dead beloved. In this cycle the poet of sensual joy despaired over the limitations of the senses and finds the consolations offered by faith and philosophy equally unsatisfactory.

István Vas, whose *Római pillanat* (1947, A Moment in Rome) was one of the significant poetic works of the period, has been a traditionalist of the *Nyugat* school and an admirer of Horace and Hölderlin. But he used his classically coherent and disciplined form to explore modern problems. Vas, whose sympathy for socialism was coupled with a deep skepticism about the compatibility of "history," and "morality," brought back to Hungary a cycle of poems written during a trip to Italy, which, in the guise of cultural and historiographic meditation, asked some questions central to the predicament of his generation.

During the ensuing period of Stalinist controls (1948–53) Vas, like his colleague Szabó, published very little and eked out a living by translating foreign classics. In 1956, he again published a major work, the collection *A teremtett világ* (1956, The Created World), in which he clearly reestablished himself as one of contemporary Hungary's leading intellectual poets and as a staunch defender of European cultural traditions. His autobiographical novel *Nehéz szerelem* (1964–67, Troubled Love) is one of the least pretentious and most readable examples of this difficult genre.

In discussing the first postwar years, one must mention the great impact (unacknowledged until recently by Hungarian critics) that the poets of the literary review *Ujhold*—especially János Pilinszky (born 1921) and Ágnes Nemes Nagy (born 1922)—had on the evolution of modern Hungarian verse. The poets of *Ujhold,* although they regarded Mihály Babits (1883–1941) as their mentor, also developed the apolitical, "alienated" side of Attila József, who, as mentioned earlier, also revealed a committed, socialist side.

János Pilinszky is a laconic poet whose entire output can be collected in a thin volume. His philosophy is pessimistic and close to some kind of Christian existentialism; his formally disciplined and metrically traditional but dramatically soaring poems on hunger, despair, and humiliation—inspired by the inhuman sufferings of people in concentration camps and other dehumanizing situations—expressed the human condition with great authenticity. Though he became widely known only with his collection *Harmadnapon* (1959, On the Third Day), one could argue that Pilinszky's best creative period was 1948–49, the period preceding his censorship-enforced silence.

Ágnes Nemes Nagy shares the guilt complex of her generation arising from the war and from the collapse of traditional European values. While she did not accept Adorno's dictum, "No poetry after Auschwitz," her experiences did define the context within which she moves. Nemes Nagy fights the madness of the world with the weapon of her diamond-hard intellect. Her severely Protestant philosophy is one of a rationalist who believes that the poet's vocation is to name and to control the subconscious drives of the mind. She searches for the "objective correlative" in a supple but perfectly controlled verse, which, together with that of Pilinszky, has exerted considerable influence on the work of the younger poets.

The poet whose biography reflects political change most dramatically and whose creative development symbolizes the search of a whole generation is László Benjámin (born 1915). A poet of romantic, revolutionary ideals, Benjámin's love of revolution and longing for a fraternal community brought him into the Communist Party after the war. For some years he was the leading bard of socialist transformation (which included a lopsided and irrational industrialization program). His innate romanticism debased itself in the service of a regime built on fear and intimidation. By 1953, however, when the first deep cracks appeared on the "fortress of peace" of Mátyás Rákosi (then secretary-general of the Hungarian Communist Party), Benjámin's exultant optimism turned into a more introspective, self-searching mood; his book of poetry *Egyetlen élet* (1956, A Single Life) was hailed as a major literary event of the thaw. Here the poet's disillusionment took the form of a bitter and ironic attack on the inhuman practices of a political regime he had himself supported earlier. After 1956 Benjámin withdrew into complete silence, and it was only during the new liberalism of the early 1960s that he could publish his new poems and be acknowledged by critics as a leading socialist poet. Though direct and sincere in its torment, Benjámin's "confessional," autobiographical poetry is considered somewhat old-fashioned and unappealing by the younger generation.

The period 1948–53, when the Soviet demands of socialist realism and its basic ingredient, "party-mindedness" (*partinost*), were imposed upon Hungarian literature by such spokesmen of doctrinal purity as József Révai, is now regarded as the lean years of the postwar era. Having disciplined Lukács in the so-called Lukács debate (in which the Marxist critic was castigated for his preference of critical to socialist realism), Révai staged a demonstration of doubtful unity at the First Congress of Hungarian Writers (1951). Literature as a whole was now subordinated to the day-to-day demands of party politics. Among the few genuine literary accomplishments of this period are the novels of village life by Péter Veres (1897–1970) and Pál Szabó (1894–1971), the plays of Gyula Illyés, and the struggles for poetic autonomy of such younger poets as Ferenc Juhász (born 1928), László Nagy (born 1925), and István Simon (born 1926), whose talents could unfold only later in the freer atmosphere of the post-1953 thaw.

The success of Gyula Illyés in weathering the political pressures of the times were mainly due to his strategy of retreating behind the ramparts of Hungarian history in selecting material for his plays. Both his *Ozorai példa* (1952, The Example of Ozora) and *Fáklyaláng* (1953, Torch Flame) looked back to episodes from the 1848–49 struggle for independence. In *Torch Flame,* through the confrontation of Kossuth and Görgey, Illyés achieved a degree of dramatic tension unusual for the Hungarian stage of these years. His later plays on outstanding historical personalities—such as *Dózsa György* (1956, György Dózsa) and *Különc,* (1963, The Eccentric)—remained within the same tradition of "national realism." Two exceptions were *A kegyenc* (1963, The Minion), a parable on the demoralizing effect of loyalty to arbitrary power, and *A tiszták* (1970, The Pure Ones), a drama about the Cathar heretics of southern France, whose intransigence led to the total extermination of their culture.

Perhaps the most hotly debated novel of the 1948–53 period was Tibor Déry's *Felelet* (1950–52, The Answer), the second part of which invited Révai's sharp rebuke for its alleged "political deficiencies." Déry, however, withstood the pressure to rewrite his novel in the image of authority. Indeed, the Déry debate in 1952 could be regarded as the starting point of a widening rift between the Communist Party and its writer members. This process ultimately led to the "writers' revolt," the intellectual prelude to the revolutionary uprising of 1956.

While the political events of 1953 (Stalin's death, Imre Nagy's new reform program) undoubtedly stimulated the regeneration of Hungarian literature from the doldrums of previous years, the "explosion of talents" in 1954 and 1955 was due to other factors as well, including the independent initiative of younger writers and poets seeking a way out of the blind alley of party-minded stereotypes. In this move toward greater independence, poetry fared the best. Two poets—Ferenc Juhász and László Nagy, both of Marxist-populist orientation—made the first breakthrough: Juhász, with his effusive, visionary epic poem *A tékozló ország* (1954, The Prodigal Country); Nagy, with his lyric and short-epic poems later collected in the book *Deres majális* (1956, Frosty May Fair).

These works heralded a revolution in style, based on achievements by Ady, Füst, Babits, József, and Sándor Weöres (born 1913). Aiming at "Bartók's synthesis," Juhász and Nagy combined folkloric elements with expressionism and surrealism. Later, however, the ways of the two poets diverged. Juhász—whose language absorbed much of the specialized vocabulary of the natural sciences, especially that of botany and zoology—lapsed into an orgiastic verbalism. His post-1956 volumes—*Harc a fehér báránnyal* (1965, Struggle with the White Lamb) and *A Szent Tűzözön regéi* (1969, The Tales of the Sacred Fireflood)—although they contain some first-rate poems, suffer from a monstrous plethora of clustered images.

Nagy, on the other hand, underwent a crisis of conscience. This led him to a discovery of the tragic essence of existence. Although he continued to believe that man's aim should be the creation of harmony and happiness, he came to realize the terrible price that is extorted from mankind in the name of these ideas. *Himnusz minden időben* (1965, Hymn for Anytime) showed Nagy's new mastery of poetic technique and the redefinition of the world in the light of his post-1956 experiences.

Another important event of this very fluid and exciting period was the return of many poets and writers into print. Sándor Weöres, who had gained attention in the first postwar years when his ingenious and provocative *A fogak tornáca* (1947, The Portico of Teeth) was published, now brought out *A hallgatás tornya* (1956, The Tower of Silence), which established him as a leading Hungarian poet. Weöres's talent ranges from children's ditties to complex philosophical poems; he is more interested in myths and life's eternal rites than in reforms or political salvations.

The right to ignore politics in the name of art has been inherent in Weöres's poetry. By permitting Weöres to publish his book of poems *Tűz-kút* (1964, Well of Fire), the authorities implicitly agreed to respect this right. And Weöres has continued ever since in his daring pursuit of new forms and subject matter, exploring new facets of the soul and new possibilities for the ever-changing language. Though some of his poems are hard to grasp, even for the initiated, the richness of his talent and his unprejudiced attitude toward experimentation assure him no mean rank in the international fraternity of poets.

Noteworthy among the prose writers brought back from semioblivion by the thaw of 1953–54 were Lajos Nagy (1883–1954)—a writer of caustic, penetrating short stories—and Áron Tamási (1897–1966). Both published reminiscences at the time. Of the two, Tamási was the more accomplished writer. The beautiful plasticity of his language and his grasp of the "eternal reality" of nature and of man close to nature guarantee his literary survival.

Only in 1955 could Zsigmond Remenyik (1900–1962) publish his *Por és hamu* (1955, Dust and Ashes), written some four years earlier. *Dust and Ashes* was a grim and gripping novel, convincingly critical of the "good old days" of the Austro-Hungarian empire. The work of Remenyik, a man of weird exploits and adventures, who lived for some years in South America and in the United States, is insufficiently known in Hungary, though in recent years most volumes of his *Apocalypsis humana* have been published. His bitterness about injustice, his deep pessimism, and his nightmare visions, though common enough in modern fiction, made his novels and stories strikingly different from the mainstream of Hungarian tradition.

László Németh wrote many historical dramas, most of them after the war. His plays were about both Hungarian and foreign subjects (John Hus, Pope Gregory VII, Gandhi). *Galilei* (Galilei), staged in 1956, was among the best of this genre. Although the play discussed the responsibility of the scholar (and writer) to his age and to his conscience, the technique of *Galilei* was historical realism. Indeed, Hungarian drama until very recently has been unable to move beyond the limitations of the nineteenth-century theater. Brecht found few followers, even after his "discovery" in 1956; and until 1963 there were hardly any attempts to write in the style of the theater of the absurd.

Among the playwrights of the 1960s Imre Sarkadi (1921–1961) is regarded as a precursor of later trends. He presented existentialist dilemmas in *Oszlopos Simeon* (1960, Simon Stylite) and *Elveszett paradicsom*

(1961, Paradise Lost). Miklós Hubay (born 1918), Endre Illés (born 1902), Ferenc Karinthy (born 1921), and Gábor Thurzó (born 1912) have written social dramas and comedies in a more or less traditional vein, while Miklós Mészöly (born 1921), István Örkény (born 1912), and, among the younger writers, István Eörsi (born 1931), István Csurka (born 1934), and Gábor Görgey (born 1923) have recently written grotesque and absurdist plays.

The failure of the 1956 revolution threw Hungarian literature into a partial eclipse. In 1957 Tibor Déry, Gyula Háy, and other writers were imprisoned by the Kádár regime; until their release three years later, other well-known writers, such as Illyés, abstained from publication. Yet even this partial eclipse, which interrupted rather than reversed the creative upsurge of the mid-1950s, was not entirely barren: the new regime favored some writers, either previously silent or badly neglected, who did not take part in the political events of 1956 and were, on the whole, apolitical.

One newly rediscovered writer was János Kodolányi (1899–1969), whose postwar novels explored the prehistoric and biblical past: *Az égő csipkebokor* (1957, The Burning Bush), *Jehuda Bar Simon* (1957, Jehuda Bar Simon), and *Uj ég, uj föld* (1958, New Sky, New Earth). Though lacking the sophistication and epic breadth of Thomas Mann's *Joseph and His Brothers,* Kodolányi's novels were nevertheless exciting and imaginative efforts to recreate the world of ancient people living in and through myths. László Passuth (born 1900), the popular author of colorful historical novels, who wrote for the "drawer" until 1956, could now be published once again.

The most successful newcomer of these years was another apolitical writer, Magda Szabó (born 1917). Her early novels—especially *Freskó* (1958, Fresco) and *Disznótor* (1960, Pig Killing)—were preoccupied with the disintegration and crisis of the same provincial middle-class society portrayed in the novels of László Németh. Magda Szabó's psychological realism has tragic undertones: her women protagonists follow their destinies with the blind determination of the heroines of a Greek tragedy. In recent years her attention has turned toward the conflict of generations in present-day Hungary (*Mózes, egy, huszonkettő* [1967, Moses One, Twenty-two]). But her popularity is due more to her well-observed characters and realistic plots than to her subject matter.

The early 1960s was a favorable time for such nonrealistic writers of fiction as Géza Ottlik (born 1919) and Iván Mándy (born 1918), whose books explore the domain of dreams, memories, and fantasies with great evocative force. The fiction of Sándor Török (born 1904) gained new dimensions. His novels *A hazug katona* (1957, The Mendacious Soldier) and *A legkisebb isten* (1966, The Smallest God), were significant attempts to reveal the hidden possibilities of the human mind, including nonrational cognition.

In the 1960s the whole concept of socialist realism was reinterpreted and liberally broadened to include such diverse literary works as the conformist pseudodramas of József Darvas (born 1912) and Imre Dobozy (born 1917) and the slick "socialist" best sellers of András Berkesi (born 1919). It also included the laconic social reportage of Endre Fejes (born 1923) in *Rozsdatemető* (1962, Iron Scrap Cemetery) and the chilling "documentary" tales of József Lengyel (born 1896). Lengyel lived in the Soviet Union between the two wars as a communist émigré, and in 1938 he was arrested. He went through the hell of Stalin's camps and returned to Hungary only in the 1950s. His real comeback into Hungarian literature, however, took place only with the publication of his Siberian stories in the 1960s and with *Elejétől végig* (1963, From Beginning to End), a work in the style of Solzhenitsyn but written more passionately. The publication and warm critical reception of Lengyel's "true stories" indicated a real change in the atmosphere of literary life.

The liberal wave culminated around 1964 with the publication of Déry's short stories (*Szerelem* [Love]) and of Gyula Háy's *Királydrámák* (Royal Dramas); *Royal Dramas* included *Mohács* (Mohács), possibly Háy's best postwar play. Also in 1964 Tibor Cseres (born 1915) published his much-discussed novel of a Hungarian war crime, *Hideg napok* (Cold Days), and Ferenc Sánta (born 1927) published his important *Húsz óra* (Twenty Hours).

Sánta, since the publication of his first short stories in the mid-1950s, has grown into one of Hungary's most interesting writers. His novels raise disturbing moral issues and question the possible uses and abuses of power. This theme was first apparent in *Az ötödik pecsét* (1963, The Fifth Seal), and was further developed in *Twenty Hours* and in *Az áruló* (1965, The Traitor). Sánta's politically most relevant and in many respects best novel has been *Twenty Hours,* which gave—through a many-sided, semidocumentary description of a visit in a Hungarian village—the first artistically valid explanation of the events of 1956.

If Sánta's novels are representative of one main current in contemporary Hungarian fiction, there are plenty of interesting experimenters, who attract intellectual readership. Gyula Hernádi (born 1926), after the promising short novel *A péntek lépcsőin* (1959, On the Steps of Friday), became the film director Jancsó's script writer. The disjointed time-space relations and geometric imagery of his stories indicate an alienation almost too deep for words. A more comprehensible writer is Miklós Mészöly, whose impassive stance and uncompromising artistic precision relate him to certain schools of modern western fiction. His best-known novels are *Az atléta halála* (1966, The Death of an Athlete) and *Saulus* (1968, Saul).

István Örkény is another nonrealist recently becoming popular, thanks largely to his excellent grotesque miniatures—*Nászutasok a légypapíron* (1967, Newlyweds Stuck on Flypaper). He has written short stories and a short novel (collected in *Jeruzsálem hercegnője* [1966, The Princess of Jerusalem]), which confirm his gifts as a storyteller. Though a number of novelists of the younger generation could be mentioned, György Konrád (born 1933) seems the most interesting. His *A látogató* (1969, The Visitor), apart from being a brilliant stylistic performance, opened up a hitherto neglected theme in Hungarian literature—the situation of the socially and mentally deprived or underprivileged.

The leading writer of fiction of the 1960s, along with László Németh (who since *Eszter Égető* published only one new novel—*Irgalom* [1965, Mercy]) was undoubtedly the septuagenarian Tibor Déry. Since 1956 he has published two novels: one, *G. A. úr X.-ben* (1964, Mr. A. G. in X.), a negative utopia; the other *A kiközösítő* (1966, The Excommunicator), an ironic pseudohistorical novel on Saint Ambrose. He also published a very subjective but fascinating autobiography, *Nincs itélet* (1969, No Verdict). In his memoirs Déry used a spotlight technique to give substance to the shadows of his deceased mistresses, friends, and colleagues, as well as to certain episodes of his own life. The wealth of Déry's subject matter and his complete mastery over form made *No Verdict* a very accomplished book, almost a masterpiece.

Poetry has not changed dramatically since 1956. During the years of the partial eclipse a group of politically active young poets (the *Tűztánc* [Fire Dance] group, called thus after the title of a verse anthology) tried to fill the vacuum. The most important members of this group—Mihály Váci (1924–1970) and Gábor Garai (born 1929)—made a conscious effort to rekindle the socialist enthusiasm of the late 1940s—Váci more in the populist tradition, Garai in the urban Marxist (post-*Nyugat*) tradition. More pervasive, however, has been the influence of Weöres and Pilinszky, Juhász and László Nagy, and—more recently and on a more popular level—the sensual surrealism of Sándor Csoóri (born 1930) and the anarchistic dissent of Mihály Ladányi (born 1934). Among the more interesting younger poets is Dezső Tandori (born 1938). His axiomatic intellectualism and austere poetic technique are a natural enough reaction to the uncontrolled effusiveness of Ferenc Juhász and his younger followers.

Hungarian literature flourishes outside Hungary as well. Three of Hungary's neighbors have large Hungarian-speaking minorities: Rumania, Yugoslavia, and Czechoslovakia. Moreover, there is a literature of Hungarian émigrés. In this survey I can give only a brief summary of this literary activity.

Transylvania—ethnically largely Hungarian but politically Rumanian since World War I—has a long literary history, which has had both a local identity and a relationship to Hungarian culture as a whole. Although many fine Hungarian writers (including Tamási) were born in Transylvania, since World War II no outstanding prose writer has appeared in this region, and only two are worth mentioning: Gyula Szabó (born 1930) and András Sütő (born 1927). Both are critical realists. Sándor Kányádi (born 1929), János Székely (born 1929), and especially Géza Páskándi (born 1933) are gifted poets who draw their strength from the powerful emotional and intellectual reserves of the Transylvanian tradition.

In Yugoslavia since the early 1950s there has been much experimentation in all literary genres among Hungarian-language writers. The most impressive figure, however, was a traditionalist, Ervin Sinkó (1898–1967), the author of two fascinating autobiographical novels: *Optimisták* (1955, Optimists), and *Egy regény regénye* (1961, The Novel of a Novel). In Czechoslovakia another nonconformist Marxist writer and essayist, Zoltán Fábry (1897–1970), was chiefly responsible for the slow resurrection of Hungarian literature in Czechoslovakia after World War II; he stopped what seemed to be the extinction of Hungarian literature in Czechoslovakia through the chauvinistic policies of the Czech authorities during the period immediately after the war.

In western Europe and North America poetry continues to be the leading genre of Hungarian-language writers. The postromantic poet György Faludy (born 1913) and the Rabelais-like modernist Győző Határ (born 1914) were among the refugees who reached the west in 1956. Some of their younger colleagues recently made a collective appearance in the verse anthology *Uj égtájak* (1969, New Climes). In addition to the erudite and prolific essayist László C. Szabó (born 1905), Gyula Háy should be mentioned as the only outstanding playwright living in emigration. His recent plays—*A főinkvizitor* (1968, The Chief Inquisitor) and *Apassionata* (1969, Apassionata), dealt with the human predicament in totalitarian countries. While the influence of émigré writing on literature in Hungary has been rather slight, some expatriates play an important role as conveyors of Hungarian cultural values to the west.

In conclusion, Hungarian literature during the last twenty-five years has been marked by numerous achievements, despite various setbacks caused by politics. Poetry, traditionally the leading genre, has flourished throughout the period (except during the years 1948–53), and there have been great advances both in the range of subject matter and in poetic technique. The boldest innovations in poetry were made by poets with "anthropological" tendencies (Weöres, Pilinszky, Nemes Nagy, Juhász, László Nagy), who at one point or another broke with the lyrical realism and social impressionism inherent in Hungarian poetic tradition and organized their poetry around some kind of a universal myth.

After a promising start in the late 1940s, the growth of fiction was retarded by the repressive doctrines of socialist realism. But a new wave of talented novelists appeared in the early 1960s, preferring to write experimental short novels. Their work is socially and morally more probing and questioning than the critical realism of Németh or Déry. Significantly, there have been changes in Déry's work as well, the lyrical-grotesque mood often prevailing over descriptive realism.

Drama has been the slowest genre to reflect contemporary trends, with historical plays keeping their supremacy over social dramas. In the mid-1960s the theater of the absurd began to tempt the imagination of playwrights, and more recently there have appeared plays of more than local interest, such as those of Örkény.

While Hungarian literature is certainly more socialist now than it was in 1945, its basic structure has not changed radically, nor did the literary hegemony of Budapest, with its disproportionate concentration of writers, disappear. Since the war the reading public has grown considerably, and the popularity of literature (especially of poetry) is still far greater than in many western countries.

HUNGARIAN WORKS IN ENGLISH TRANSLATION

ANTHOLOGIES

Duczynska, Ilona and Karl Polanyi, eds. *The Plough and the Pen: Writings from Hungary 1930–1956.* London, 1963

Hungarian Anthology: A Collection of Poems. Toronto, 1966

Hungarian Short Stories, 19th and 20th Centuries. Budapest, 1962

Juhasz, William and Abraham Rothberg, eds. *Flashes in the Night: Stories from Contemporary Hungary.* New York, 1958

Konnyu, Leslie, ed. *Modern Magyar Literature: A Literary Survey and Anthology of the XXth Century Hungarian Authors.* New York, 1964

Kunz, Egon F., ed. *Hungarian Poetry.* Sydney, 1955

Ray, David, ed. *From the Hungarian*

Revolution: A Collection of Poems. Ithaca, N.Y., 1966

Szabolcsi, Miklós. *Landmark: Hungarian Writers on Thirty Years of History.* Budapest, 1965

INDIVIDUAL WORKS MENTIONED IN ARTICLE

Déry, Tibor. *Az óriás* as *The Giant.* In *The Giant/Behind the Brick Wall/ Love.* London, 1964
———. *Szerelem* as *Love.* In *The Giant/ Behind the Brick Wall/Love.* London, 1964

Fejes, Endre. *Rozsdatemető* as *Generation of Rust.* New York, 1970

Illés, Béla. *Kárpáti rapszódia* as *Carpathian Rhapsody.* Budapest, 1963

Lengyel, József. *Elejétől végig* as *From*

Beginning to End. In *From Beginning to End/The Spell.* Englewood Cliffs, N.J., 1968

Németh, László. *Iszony* as *Revulsion.* London, 1965

Szabó, Magda. *Disznótor* as *Night of the Pig-Killing.* New York, 1966

Zilahy, Lajos. *A Dukay család* as *The Dukays.* New York, 1949.

SECONDARY WORKS

BIBLIOGRAPHIES AND GUIDES

Benedek, Marcell, ed. *Magyar irodalmi lexikon,* 3 vols. Budapest, 1963–65

Czigány, Magda. *Hungarian Literature in English Translation Published in Great Britain, 1830–1968.* London, 1969

Tezla, Albert. *An Introductory Bibliography to the Study of Hungarian Literature.* Cambridge, Mass., 1964

GENERAL WORKS

Bóka, László and Pál Pándi. *A magyar irodalom története.* Budapest, 1957

Jones, Mervyn D. *Five Hungarian Writers.* Oxford, 1966

Klaniczay, Tibor et al. *History of Hungarian Literature.* Budapest, 1964

Reményi, Joseph. *Hungarian Writers and Literature.* New Brunswick, N.J., 1964

Szerb, Antal. *Magyar irodalomtörténet,* 3rd ed. Budapest, 1958

WORKS ON CONTEMPORARY LITERATURE

Gömöri, George. *Polish and Hungarian Poetry 1945 to 1956.* Oxford, 1966

Sivirsky, Antal. *Die ungarische Literatur der Gegenwart.* Bern, 1962

Somlyó, György. *A Short Introduction to Contemporary Hungarian Poetry.* In *New Hungarian Quarterly,* 7, 23, 1966

Sükösd, Mihály. *Hungarian Prose Literature Today.* In *Mosaic,* 1, 3, 1968

Tóth, Dezső, ed. *Élő irodalom.* Budapest, 1969

Vogel, Ferenc. *Theater in Ungarn.* Cologne, 1966

ERLENDUR JÓNSSON

Icelandic Literature

ICELANDIC LITERATURE has a continuous history going back to the period
of settlement of the country (874–930). The great medieval Icelandic
works—the eddas and the sagas—still influence literature in Iceland. Since
the language has changed relatively little, the sagas can still be read by
everybody without any major explanations. Moreover, contemporary Icelandic writers on occasion look for inspiration to their literature of the
Middle Ages, in a way similar to the way that French writers relate to the
literature of ancient Greece and Rome. More specifically, some Icelandic
poets still make heavy use of alliteration, once a common trait of all
Germanic poetry, but long since fallen into disuse outside Iceland.

POETRY

Not until the first decades of this century did Icelandic poets begin to shed
the yoke of the old metaphors, which referred to an older way of life. They
also looked for new subject matter; the wonders of city life now were
praised in lyrical poetry. When, during the 1930s, poets began to write
about current urban problems, social literature came into being. The poets
Steinn Steinarr (1908–1958) and Jón úr Vör (born 1917) both satirized
the budding bourgeois society.

After World War II both Steinarr and Vör paved the way for new poetic

372

forms. Vör rejected rhyme, alliteration, and regular rhythmic patterns. He wrote a poetic cycle, *Þorpið* (1946, The Village), about the everyday life of common people, in their own language. Steinarr kept more of the external trappings of verse, but his original perceptions were turned inward. The poetic cycle *Tíminn og vatnið* (1949, Time and Water) did not relate to common experience or logical thought, as all older poetry had done. It was a series of unconnected images that the reader perceived without emotion or even understanding. Although the name *Time and Water* recalled major themes of T. S. Eliot, Steinarr cannot be considered a disciple.

The same year that *Time and Water* was published, the first book of Hannes Sigfússon (born 1922), *Dymbilvaka* (1949, The Eve of Muted Bells), came out, obviously under the strong influence of Eliot; there are even whole sentences that are almost straight Icelandic translations of lines from *The Waste Land*. In spite of its derivativeness, *The Eve of Muted Bells* was deeply personal and powerful poetry, created from profound feelings and insight, expressed through allegories. In his more recent books Sigfússon has become political, and his art has lost much of its enchantment.

Jón Óskar (born 1921) began publishing poems in the 1940s, at about the same time as Sigfússon. He, too, likes to espouse causes and sometimes has gone on at considerable length. His best poems, however, are short, yet built around repetition. His straightforward and personal outlook has given a sense of tranquillity to his works. A contemporary of Óskar and Sigfússon, Einar Bragi (born 1921) has written more conventional poems than the other two; he is interested in lyrical form and celebrates Icelandic nature in the manner of the nineteenth-century idyllists.

The poets who experimented with new forms after World War II were generally called "atom poets"—a disparaging term. In the late 1950s there appeared a new generation of poets who were related to the atom poets but who carved out individual paths for themselves.

The foremost member of this generation has been Hannes Pétursson (born 1931), whose first book, *Kvæðabók* (1955, A Book of Poems), immediately placed him among the best poets in Iceland. Pétursson has written in traditional form, mostly about national subjects—Icelandic history and nature. His poetry is notable for meticulous workmanship. Pétursson has published four books of poetry thus far, all somewhat similar in nature, although he has been turning inward more and more. In his most recent book, *Innlönd* (1968, Inland), he stands at the border of the highland wilderness, with an exalted view of the land, pondering the eternal questions of life and death. In *Inland* the shelter of the farmlands in the valley represents life and the wilderness is associated with the unknown realm of death.

The most prolific of the younger generation of writers is Matthías

Johannessen (born 1930), a newspaper editor and the author of many books, including five books of poetry. The most recent one, *Fagur er dalur* (1966, Beautiful Valley), has been the most interesting. It begins with the poetic cycle *Sálmar á atómöld* (Hymns in the Atomic Age), which is modern religious poetry simple in form and content but filled with unexpected similes.

Some of Þorsteinn frá Hamri's (born 1938) poems used Icelandic folklore to protest present conditions indirectly by referring to ancient virtues. Quite different from Hamri is Jóhann Hjálmarsson (born 1939), neither nationalistic nor political. He has lived in southern Europe, where he got to know surrealism, which influenced him greatly. He has also been influenced by geometric painting. His poems have been somewhat cold, but they are carefully constructed and written in clear and beautiful language.

DRAMA

Playwriting has neither a long nor a distinguished history in Iceland. For centuries, settlements were so scattered that theatrical performances were impossible. Only when small towns began to spring up in the late nineteenth century were any plays written. An amateur theater was established in Reykjavík before the turn of the century. The National Theater was established in 1950, and now theatrical life in Reykjavík is quite lively for a city its size.

In recent years several authors have written passable plays, but few if any have been outstanding. Agnar Þórðarson (born 1917) has written a number of plays, including some for radio. They have been realistic, in contemporary urban settings. Jökull Jakobsson (born 1933) has written plays for the theater, radio, and television. He is less realistic than Þórðarson and tends to the sentimental. His best works have been one-act plays for radio and television. Jónas Árnason (born 1923) has written a few comedies and musicals that are not very significant but have become popular for their humor and pleasant music.

Oddur Björnsson (born 1932) is the most experimental Icelandic playwright. His most original work has been *Amalía* (1963, Amalía). This play, typical of his work, described the shattered dreams and anguish of one who must face cruel reality without the refuge of dreams.

THE NOVEL

Like the drama, the novel is a recent development in Icelandic literature. Nevertheless, the genre has achieved considerable distinction since the first

Icelandic novel was published in the middle of the nineteenth century. Indeed, since the beginning of the twentieth century, when the novel came into its own, it has been the dominant literary genre in Iceland.

The best-known novelist is Halldór Laxness (born 1902), who received the Nobel Prize in 1955. He has described most aspects of the old rural society and has perpetuated the traditional saga style of writing. Another novelist of the older generation, Guðmundur G. Hagalín (born 1898), has concentrated on the beginning of the vast changes in Icelandic society, when the people started building villages on the coast and making a living from fishing rather than from farming.

World War II was a great economic stimulus to Iceland. The standard of living soared to equal the best of the industrial nations of western Europe, and it has remained at that level. The towns, especially the capital, grew rapidly. On the other hand, urban culture did not immediately follow urbanization; the new city dwellers were literally farmers come to town. Novelists, like everyone else, were slow to adapt to urban conditions, and their orientation remained rural. This partly explains the paucity of good fiction during the 1950s. The first novelist to make his reputation after World War II was Elías Mar (born 1924), who wrote about life in the capital. But his style was entirely conventional—under the influence of Laxness. Perhaps because of Mar's inability to find his own voice, he gave up writing novels.

It is hardly coincidence that Thor Vilhjálmsson (born 1925), the first postwar novelist to do something new and original, lived abroad from the end of the war, first in Britain, where he became inspired by Eliot's idea of time, and later in France, where he was influenced by existentialism. The name of his first book was indicative—*Maðurinn er alltaf einn* (1950, Man Is Always Alone). The title alone announced that Vilhjálmsson did not intend to follow in the footsteps of his predecessors by spewing out conventional mass-market fiction. Vilhjálmsson has since written about ten books, including travel books filled with unexpected metaphors. These travel books were among the best prose written in this period. His most complex work, however, has been the novel *Fljótt fljótt sagði fuglinn* (1968, Quick, Quick, Said the Bird). This novel is like an X ray of life in the large cities of the western countries as reflected in the overburdened perceptions of a modern man.

Although a year younger than Vilhjálmsson, Indriði G. Þorsteinsson (born 1926) has been closer in many ways to the older novelists. He was born and raised in the country and became a newspaperman in Reykjavík. He has very strong ties with his home in the country and is faithful to the traditional forms of storytelling. A mixture of country boy and the urban man, Þorsteinsson has been very perceptive in dealing with the profound social changes that have occurred in his time. His heroes are frequently young men leaving the farm to go to town. His third novel, *Þjófur í paradís* (1967, A Thief in Paradise), was a tale of the pleasures and woes of life in the isolated countryside. In Þorsteinsson's most recent novel, *Norðan við stríð* (1971, North of War), he re-created and examined the atmosphere in Iceland during the British occupation of World War II.

Guðbergur Bergsson (born 1932), another very active novelist, wrote a debut novel that was realistic in both form and content. His most important work to date, *Tómas Jónsson metsölubók* (1966, Tómas Jónsson—Bestseller), was a devastating and unsavory account of the sterile and purposeless life of modern man cooped up within cold concrete walls in timelessness and passivity. No recent Icelandic book has aroused so much interest and controversy.

Steinar Sigurjónsson (born 1928) writes like Bergsson, but on a smaller scale in every way. Jóhannes Helgi (born 1926) and Ingimar Erlendur Sigurðsson (born 1933) have tried to breathe new life into the novel of social protest along the lines of the prewar writers, but they have both of them failed to rise above mediocrity. Jakobína Sigurðardóttir (born 1918) has experimented in a similar way, but without much success. She has written, however, a fairly good novel about everyday life in Reykjavík—*Dægurvísa* (1965, A Pop Song). Svava Jakobsdóttir (born 1930) has written several short stories in which woman's position in the modern world was delicately touched on.

A glance at Icelandic literature during the last few decades reveals that it is moving away from tradition without severing all ties with the past. The years between the two world wars were a fruitful era in Icelandic literature, followed by stagnation in the 1940s. Particularly in the novel the impact of Laxness and other respected authors was so overwhelming that little new or different was attempted. Since 1950 younger writers have gone their own way, whether that way was avant-garde or more conventional. Foreign literature has always influenced Icelandic literature, and the influence has been more noticeable the closer we get to the present. On the whole, an increasing diversity is the outstanding feature of Icelandic literature of the last twenty-five years.

ICELANDIC WORKS IN ENGLISH TRANSLATION

ANTHOLOGIES

Boucher, Alan, ed. *Poems of Today: From Twenty-five Modern Icelandic*

Poets. Reykjavík, 1971

Haugen, Einar, ed. *Fire and Ice: Three Icelandic Plays.* Madison, Wisc., 1967

SECONDARY WORKS

Andrésson, Kristinn E. *Íslenzkar núti-mabókmenntir 1918–1948.* Reykjavík, 1949

Einarsson, Stefán. *A History of Icelandic Literature.* New York, 1957

Gíslason, Bjarni. *Íslands litteratur efter sagatiden ca. 1400–1948.* Copenhagen, 1949

Hjálmarsson, Jóhann. *Íslenzk nútímaljóðlist.* Reykjavík, 1971

Jónsson, Erlendur. *Íslenzk bókmenntasaga 1550–1950.* Reykjavík, 1966

———. *Íslenzk skáldsagnaritun 1940–1970.* Reykjavík, 1971

Magnússon, Sigurður A. *Modern Icelandic Poetry.* In *Iceland Review,* 4, 2, 1966

———. *Nyju fötin keisarans.* Reykjavík, 1959

———. *Sað í vindinn.* Reykjavík, 1968

Schneider, Hermann. *Geschichte der norwegischen und isländischen Literatur.* Bonn, 1948

JOHANNES HÖSLE

Italian Literature

AFTER THE NAPOLEONIC WARS the nationalism that swept Europe found broad acceptance among the Italian people. And the revolutionary ideas of the romantic movement became the driving force behind the Italian risorgimento. Efforts to establish a genuinely democratic nation failed, however, because of the backwardness of the illiterate rural population, the patriarchal protectionism of the liberal circles, and the machinations of the Curia, which remained strong but gave the outward appearance of having lost its power with the founding of the Italian nation.

Although political conditions compelled the poet Ugo Foscolo (1778–1827) and the literary historian Francesco de Sanctis (1817–1882) to emigrate, they were both inspirations to Italy's role in nineteenth-century Europe, as was the cosmopolitan Alessandro Manzoni (1785–1873). The fact remains, however, that Italian literature had almost entirely disappeared from the European consciousness since the seventeenth century except for sporadic attention, such as Goethe's interest in the work of Manzoni. Economically underdeveloped Italy played no part in the growth of the novel of middle-class life, which had been developing in France and England since the eighteenth century.

The history of Italy in the twentieth century has been marked by the collapse of the revolutionary ideas of the risorgimento. The constant fear of a revolution and of social reforms led the Italian bourgeoisie to fascism, and the Curia to its unconscionable concordat with Mussolini. Until the

378

end of World War II literary life, like other aspects of nineteenth- and early twentieth-century Italy, remained elitist: authors came either from nobility (Manzoni, Giacomo Leopardi [1798–1837]), from prosperous land-owners and entrepreneurs (Giovanni Verga [1840–1922], Gabriele d'Annunzio [1863–1938]), or from the educated middle class (Giosuè Carducci [1835–1907]). And literary works reached only a small minority of the people.

Since 1945 the situation has changed. In addition to schools and universities, the media have provided a means of existence for writers. Many of them, to be sure, have thus submitted to the economic pressures they have attacked so vehemently in their writings. Elio Vittorini (1908–1966), Franco Fortini (born 1917), and Vittorio Sereni (born 1913) have coped with this situation in exemplary fashion, for through their work in the mass media they have been able continually to measure and compare their ideological positions with their actual practice.

Between 1950 and 1970 book production in the world tripled, and Italy had its share in this boom. New publishing houses learned how to make books into commercially attractive and desirable consumer articles. For the first time mass media brought Italy's literary heritage to the attention of disadvantaged classes. Paperback editions, which are sold almost exclusively at newsstands in Italy, reached a large audience whose cultural background would have kept them away from the bookstores. When Riccardo Bacchelli's (born 1891) trilogy *Il mulino del Po* (1938–40, The Mill on the Po) was serialized on Italian television, the work suddenly became a best seller, although it had sold poorly until then.

FICTION

Any survey of Italian literature since 1945 must begin with fiction. The hiatus caused by the war was more obvious in fiction than in poetry, which remained under the influence of hermeticism into the 1950s.

NEOREALISM

After World War II Italian fiction was dominated by neorealism and by the leftist politics that supported it. However, it became clear after the Hungarian uprising of 1956, at the latest, that the ideology of the Stalinist dogmatists no longer offered a valid interpretation of the new Italy. Many Italian intellectuals who up to this time had belonged to the Moscow-oriented Italian Communist Party now turned away from it in disillusionment, because the capitalistic consumer society as it developed during the

1950s in Italy needed to be assessed by new criteria. Many Italian intellectuals regarded this assessing as their most important social obligation.

Italian neorealism was originally conceived as an instrument of moral and political renewal, as a means of overcoming the period of grandiose fascist tendencies in literature, painting, and films during the twenty-year dictatorship of Mussolini. Neorealism was so much a response to Italy's participation in the war, its capitulation, the resistance movement, and a situation approaching a civil war in the areas occupied by German troops, that it would not be erroneous to restrict the concept of neorealism to the decade from 1940 to 1950.

This phenomenon was paralleled during the same decade in Italian films. The central focus of Roberto Rossellini's first films, *Roma, città aperta* (1945) and *Paisà* (1947), was the struggle carried on by Italian partisans in the cities and in the countryside. The authentic feeling of these works was never matched later, either by Rossellini or by others. Indeed, during the 1950s the Italian western displaced the increasingly superficial depictions of the war.

Mussolini's anachronistic attempt to make the Italy of the 1920s into a reincarnation of the Roman empire was unmasked as a mere folly by the alliance with Hitler, which eventually culminated in the occupation of Italy by the Germans. The misery of the war years brought Italians face to face with some important facts about their country, particularly the social differences that existed between north and south, between city and country, and between bourgeoisie and proletariat. The political, economic, and social problems of the nation—which was racked by numerous internal tensions despite the attempt of the fascist government to divert attention from the precariousness of the domestic situation by pursuing adventurous foreign policies—were discussed passionately during the postwar years.

Neorealism opened the eyes of the Italians and led to the discovery of remote provinces and of voices that had formerly been ignored in the official literature of the land. There would have been no neorealism without the diversity of the different Italies that knew nothing of each other, or without the different dialects and levels of language that writers wanted to incorporate into the literary language.

Some characteristics of neorealism were foreshadowed during the 1930s by Ignazio Silone (born 1900, pseudonym of Secondo Tranquilli). The career of Silone, who participated in the Socialist Congress of Livorno in 1921, at which the Italian Communist Party was founded, recalls in many respects the somewhat later career of Elio Vittorini. After a quarrel with the Communist Party, Silone went to Zürich, where his novel *Fontamara* (Fontamara) first appeared in 1933, in a German translation. *Fontamara* described the poverty of the *cafoni,* the exploited laborers of southern Italy, and their overtly sadistic treatment by the bureaucracy and the fascist flying squads. Silone's *Pane e vino* (1937, Bread and Wine) and *Il seme sotto la neve* (1941, The Seed beneath the Snow) were first published in Switzerland in both German and Italian editions. These works, which combined political and religious themes, although highly praised outside Italy, were received in Italy without much enthusiasm, as were Silone's later novels. Silone's pouring a new philosophical wine into the old wineskins of outmoded nineteenth-century narrative forms was disturbing to the Italian reader, who had become familiar with the forms of modern fiction.

The peasant of southern Italy (specifically, the province of Abruzzi) was also the focal point of the novels of Francesco Jovine (1902–1950). In *Le terre del Sacramento* (1950, The Sacramental Lands) the lands in the title are those areas that fell to new owners after the dissolution of the ecclesiastical state. The Pope's excommunication of the new owners places the curse of unjustly acquired property upon the "sacramental lands." When Luca, a young law student, begins to enlighten the rural population, which has been vegetating in ignorance, superstition, and misery, the fascist militia strikes down the innovative actions of the social reformer and of the peasants behind him. Jovine, like Silone, was not concerned with renewing the form of the novel; he found the narrative forms of the nineteenth century perfectly suitable and appropriate to spreading his hopes of political salvation.

An older and more important precursor of neorealism was the giant of *verismo,* Giovanni Verga. Luchino Visconti created one of the first classics of the neorealistic cinema by using Verga's *I Malavoglia* (1881, The Malavoglia Family) as the basis for his film *La terra trema* (1948). The principal foreign model for neorealism was American literature of the interwar years. Italians became acquainted with American literature through the criticism of Emilio Cecchi (1884–1966) and especially through translations by Elio Vittorini and Cesare Pavese (1908–1950), both of whose original works formed the basis of neorealism.

Elio Vittorini began his literary career in the early 1930s, with the stories in the collection *Piccola borghesia* (1931, Petty Bourgeoisie), which he wrote under the influence of John Steinbeck, William Saroyan, and Erskine Caldwell. These stories first appeared in the journal *Solaria,* which published serially Vittorini's first novel, *Il garofano rosso* (The Red Carnation), during 1933–34. Vittorini's confrontation with fascism in *The Red Carnation* and his realistic presentation of a love affair with a prostitute—realistic by comparison with the salon literature of the *"ventennio nero,"* the "black twenty years"—aroused the suspicion of the official fascist censor, who was able to prevent publication of the complete novel; it was finally published in 1948.

Vittorini provided a guide for the direction of postwar literature in

Conversazione in Sicilia (Conversation in Sicily), which was published serially during 1938–39 in the Florence journal *Letteratura* and then in a book edition disguised by the title *Nome e lacrime* (1941, Name and Tears). In *Conversation in Sicily* Silvestro, the protagonist, tells about his return to Sicily (Vittorini was born in Siracusa). The people of the island belong to a world mistreated by the fascist dictatorship, and Silvestro's mother is glorified as a mythical matriarch, whose three husbands—the revolutionary lover Gran Lombardo, the father of Silvestro, and his step-father—transform the young man's search for his childhood into a multi-faceted encounter with his native land. The vast theme of Vittorini's *Conversation in Sicily* is *il mondo offeso*—the injured world. Thus, Vittorini found himself at the exact opposite pole from Gabriele d'Annunzio, whose facile and witty affectation of superiority had enchanted the ladies of the fascist era.

Vittorini's critical work of the 1930s was marked by an antifascist activism and a fascination with American literature. The anthology *Americana* (1942, Americana), which he edited, was a challenge to the fascist regime. Through this volume, the neorealists discovered a new image of reality.

In *Uomini e no* (1945, The Human and the Inhuman), a novel about the resistance with a Milanese setting, Vittorini used a bold technique of montage. Since it became increasingly evident to him that the new subject matter had to be presented through new forms, Vittorini, although a committed communist, could not avoid coming into conflict with those left-wing writers who advocated that Italian writers follow the Soviet model of socialist realism. His own literary productivity virtually came to an end; his novel *Le donne di Messina* (1949, The Women of Messina), which he revised in 1964, marked for all practical purposes the end of his narrative creativity.

But the tireless energy of Vittorini in other literary forms was of inestimable importance to Italian intellectual life, whether by editing of the Communist Party journal) *Il politecnico* (1945–47), an activity that soon resulted in a break with Communist Party leader Palmiro Togliatti, or by publishing *Diario in pubblico* (1957, Open Diary), which, unlike Cesare Pavese's memoirs, merely contained excerpts from articles published over several decades along with retrospective critical observations on them. The opportunities Vittorini gave young writers in his editorial capacity at Einaudi, a Turin publisher, and his writings in the journal *Il menabò di letteratura* (1959–67), published in collaboration with the much younger novelist Italo Calvino (born 1923), indicated that Vittorini, an indefatigable promoter of young revolutionary forces, was throughout his life perhaps the most valuable leaven for Italian postwar literature.

In Cesare Pavese, neorealism found its most fascinating author; his suicide in 1950 made him temporarily a literary and existentialist myth. Pavese, who had studied American literature extensively in school, reported on its developments in the Turin journal *La cultura* from 1930 on.

Pavese began as a poet during the 1930s, and his early poetry will be considered with that of the hermetic poets. In his first published novel, *Paesi tuoi* (1941, Your Country), Pavese tried to transfer themes of the American west into his native Piedmont. This novel immediately attracted the attention of some prominent critics but also aroused anger in ecclesiastical circles. The action takes place in a landscape dominated by sexual symbols, between two hills resembling women's breasts. Tensions are heightened and released with the inexorability of a gathering thunderstorm.

During the war years Pavese became involved with the study of mythology and ethnology, particularly with the writings of the Hungarian Károly Kerényi and the Englishman Sir James George Frazer, which led him to basic reflections about the art of fiction. The essays and stories in the volume *Feria d'agosto* (1946, August Vacation) revealed the myths of his childhood. Behind this retreat into his own past stood the fear of taking risks, the fear of responsibility, with which he reproached himself for the rest of his life, although he had participated in the Turin resistance movement of the 1930s and had been exiled to Calabria by the fascist authorities. The short novels *Il carcere* (Prison) and *La casa in collina* (The House on the Hill), which Pavese published under a title alluding to Peter's betrayal of Christ, *Prima che il gallo canti* (1949, Before the Cock Crows), dealt with his relationship to politics.

Pavese's belief in the mythical recurrence of events provided an important structural element for his last narrative works. In both *Il diavolo sulle colline* (1949, The Devil in the Hills) and in *Tra donne sole* (1949, Among Women Only) the situation at the beginning of the first chapter is repeated at the end of the novel. The circular construction of these novels has the effect of an expanded metaphor for Pavese's belief in fate. In his final novel, *La luna e i falò* (1950, The Moon and the Bonfire), Pavese summarized masterfully his fictional world through the perspective of the artist. As in Vittorini's *Conversation in Sicily,* a man returning home gradually reveals his past. Thus, five years after the war ended, Pavese succeeded in representing the events of the Italian resistance movement as a ballad of times past.

His fiction and poetry, his posthumously published diary *Il mestiere di vivere* (1952, The Business of Living), and his collected letters published in 1966—all showed Pavese to be an undisputed twentieth-century master. With his death, Italian neorealism lost its most productive and gifted author. Because his suicide occurred during the years of the cold war, the younger generation considered him to be a victim of that conflict.

Beppe Fenoglio (1922–1963), succeeded in creating that broad, epic description of fascism, the German occupation, and the partisan war, which remained an unfulfilled intention of so many of his contemporaries. In the collection of stories *I ventitre giorni della città di Alba* (1952, The Twenty-three Days of the City of Alba) and in the novel *Primavera di bellezza* (1959, Spring of Beauty), which reflects the fascist hymn in its title, Fenoglio provided a broad saga of the Italian resistance. Fenoglio was an inexhaustible narrator who was able to bring Pavese's synthesis of Piedmont and the American west to fruition on the basis of a concrete historical situation: Fenoglio, the resistance fighter, takes the role of the hounded and driven outcast of American western movies. The fascination with American literature, above all with Hemingway, even led Fenoglio to the curious linguistic experiments of the posthumously published novel *Il partigiano Johnny* (1968, Johnny the Partisan), in which he combined colloquial Italian with American slang, not only in the dialogue but also in the descriptive passages.

Southern Regionalism

Regionalism has always been and continues to be an important characteristic of Italian literature, as it is in other aspects of Italian life. One of the most characteristic phenomena of contemporary Italian literature has been the rediscovery of the south. A central preoccupation with the south has distinguished such writers as Corrado Alvaro (1895–1956) and Carlo Levi (born 1902) from others, like Vittorini who, while writing in part about the south, have been pan-Italian in their major literary concerns.

After the war the literature of southern Italy was decisive in creating the image foreign nations had of the whole country. A sense of fate has often played an important role in the works of authors native to southern Italy. Historical facts are presented as immutable, and the inhabitants of southern Italy are shown to be victims of an historical stagnation decreed by fate. An awareness of being protectors of a world accessible only to the initiated has given a jealous exclusivity to the works of many southern Italian writers.

The chronicle of the family of Prince Fabrizio Salina in Giuseppe Tomasi di Lampedusa's (1896–1957) novel *Il gattopardo* (1959, The Leopard) was an elegy to a class condemned to extinction. As in the historical novel of the nineteenth century, the personality under whose spell all others stand is an extraordinary individual, but one who finds a dimension commensurate with his own importance only in his nocturnal study of the firmament. It is significant that it was in southern Italy that the historical novel sprouted this late offshoot. *The Leopard* was a direct descendant of Federico de Roberto's (1861–1927) analysis of social conditions in Sicily in the novel *I vicerè* (1894, The Viceroys).

It was Corrado Alvaro who was most responsible for the revival of interest in southern Italy, in *Gente in Aspromonte* (1930, People in Aspromonte). Alvaro tried, in a trilogy about the character Rinaldo Diacono, to paint a broad portrait of postwar Italy. Of the three novels, only the first—*L'età breve* (1946, The Brief Age), about Rinaldo's adolescence—appeared during Alvaro's lifetime; it was a passionate examination of the educational methods of Catholic boarding schools.

The other two novels of the trilogy, *Mastrangelina* (1960, Mastrangelina) and *Tutto è accaduto* (1961, Everything Has Happened), appeared posthumously. Some of Alvaro's incomplete work, largely fragments, were to have described everyday life under fascism in southern Italy. In Alvaro's later works essayistic and polemical elements became stronger and stronger. Indeed, in *Mastrangelina* and *Everything Has Happened* Alvaro incorporated, sometimes unchanged, pages from his own diary, which he published as *Quasi una vita: Giornale di uno scrittore* (1950, Almost a Life: Diary of a Writer).

Alvaro staged a debate with his age in the futuristic novel *Belmoro* (1957, Belmoro), in the manner of Huxley and Orwell. This attempt to revitalize the subject matter of fiction was a sign of the dissatisfaction with neorealism, a dissatisfaction that continued to spread during the 1950s. Alvaro's own voice in fiction perhaps received its best expression in his short stories, which were collected in *75 racconti* (1955, 75 Stories) and *La moglie, e i quaranta racconti* (1964, The Wife, and Forty Stories).

Carlo Levi's *Cristo si è fermato a Eboli* (1945, Christ Stopped at Eboli), which was a worldwide success, provided *the* decisive impetus for the literary rediscovery of southern Italy. After Levi, a native of Turin, had been banished to Basilicata (Lucania) by the fascist authorities, he discovered there—as a physician, painter, and ethnologist—an Italy that had remained unknown land to the intellectuals of the industrialized north. In *Christ Stopped at Eboli* the political exile Levi styled himself to some degree as a long-awaited redeemer of the regions of southern Italy, which were almost completely isolated from the rest of the world.

Five years later Levi recorded his disappointment over the nonparticipation of Italian intellectuals in government in a comprehensive documentary account, *L'orologio* (1950, The Watch). But only in *Le parole sono pietre* (1955, Words Are Stones) did Levi once again strike the tone of *Christ Stopped at Eboli*. The reports of his trips to the Soviet Union and Germany—*Il future ha un cuore antico* (1956, The Future Has an Ancient Heart) and *La doppia notte dei tigli* (1959, The Double Night of the Linden Trees)—did not go beyond the level of superficial reportage based on fleeting impressions and were too preoccupied with Levi's own personality.

Inchiesta a Palermo (1956, Inquiry in Palermo), by the Trieste-born author Danilo Dolci (born 1924), would not have captured the interest of the international public with its revelation of corruption and of the Mafia if Levi's exploration of southern Italy had not already prepared the way for it. From the perspective of a magistrate, Dante Troisi (born 1920) took aim at the socially backward Italian south in his *Diario di un giudice* (1962, Diary of a Judge) and in *La gente di Sidaien* (1957, The People of Sidaien). Primarily through the court testimonies of Italian women (who are often quoted verbatim), Troisi rendered faithfully differences in the language as it is spoken, in contrast to the artistic stylization of language in the Sicilians Giovanni Verga and Luigi Pirandello (1867–1936).

A belief in the inexorability of fate has characterized Felice del Vecchio's (born 1929) recollections of childhood, *La chiesa di Canneto* (1957, The Church of Canneto); Rocco Scotellaro's (1923–1953) *Uva puttanella* (1955, Puttanella Grapes); and Fortunato Seminara's (born 1903) *Il vento nell'oliveto* (1951, The Wind in the Olive Grove).

The specifically Sicilian misery, with its cult of bureaucracy and its idolatry of sexual potency to the point of pathologically exaggerated expectations, was the main subject of the novels of Vitaliano Brancati (1907–1954). While World War II was still being fought, he published *Gli anni perduti* (1941, The Lost Years) and *Don Giovanni in Sicilia* (1941, Don Giovanni in Sicily), which described a journey to the mainland of Italy, a stay in Rome, and the return to the deadening stagnation of Sicily. Brancati's novel *Il bell'Antonio* (1949, Handsome Antonio) presented a parable of the impotence of the fascist regime, shown through its imbalance between intention and capability. The protagonist impressively demonstrates the grotesque contrast between the showy cult of fascism and its military inadequacy. The handsome, impotent Antonio is the victim of an environment that views sex as its only purpose in life.

Unlike the neorealists, for whom the years following the collapse of the fascist regime were filled with political hope and many expectations for the future, Brancati had no illusions about a transformation of his world. The title character in *Paolo il caldo* (1955, Paolo the Hot-blooded) falls victim, in his postwar world, to the same obsessions as those of the protagonists of Brancati's novels set during the fascist years. And in the essays in *Ritorno alla censura* (1952, Return to Censorship) Brancati attacked police procedures in the new Italy.

Leonardo Sciascia (born 1921) has analyzed the history of Sicily in the narrative essays in *Le parocchie di Regalpetra* (1956, The Parishes of Regalpetra), as well as in stories and novels set both in past centuries and in the present. He has illuminated facts hidden in old papers. In *Morte dell'inquisitore* (1964, The Death of the Inquisitor) he documented the violent death of an ecclesiastical tyrant, and in *Il consiglio d'Egitto* (1963,

The Council of Egypt) he described an uprising in eighteenth-century Palermo. Sciascia's accounts of Mafia activity in *Il giorno della civetta* (1961, The Day of the Owl) and *A ciascuno il suo* (1966, To Each His Own), as well as in the play *L'onorevole* (1965, The Deputy), were consistent applications of the criteria he derived from coming to terms with the history of his own region. In Sciascia there is no arrogant assertion of the Sicilians as a "chosen people," and likewise nothing of that folklore that has turned much of the literature of southern Italy into mere sketches and amusing anecdotes.

Local color concealed the social problems of Naples in the writings of Giuseppe Marotta (1902–1963), who depicted the "eternal Neapolitan," with his propensity for the picaresque, his bombast and melancholy, in well narrated but unoriginal, anecdotal short stories, most of which were collected in the volumes *L'oro di Napoli* (1947, The Gold of Naples), *San Gennaro non dice mai no* (1948, San Gennaro Never Says No), *A Milano no fa freddo* (1949, In Milan It Is Not Cold), and *Le madri* (1952, The Mothers). Beautiful, exuberant Naples, with its brilliance and misery—the Naples of Vittorio de Sica's films starring Sophia Loren—is the real protagonist of Marotta's numerous stories.

Carlo Bernari (born 1909) and Anna Maria Ortese (born 1914) have tried to show the dark side of sun-drenched Naples, Bernari in such novels as *Tre operai* (1934, Three Workmen), and Ortese in *Il mare non bagna Napoli* (1953, The Sea Doesn't Wash Naples). But they have lapsed again and again into an artistically questionable sentimentality.

Hunger has played a central role in the stories of the Neapolitan Domenico Rea (born 1921). In an appendix to his novel *Quel che vide Cummeo* (1955, What Cummeo Saw) Rea made a penetrating analysis of the two Naples. He maintained that the other face of the city, its brutality, had been ignored by authors from Salvatore di Giacomo (1860–1934), who had an almost physical revulsion against reality, to Eduardo de Filippo (born 1900), in whose Neapolitan streets one would very much like to live in spite of its miseries.

One of the most enduring monuments of southern Italian literature has been Elsa Morante's (born 1918) novel *Menzogna e sortilegio* (1949, Deception and Enchantment). This work, utilizing all of the refinements of narrative technique, is a chronicle of a southern Italian family, depicting its concepts of honor, its taboos, its attempts to form an alliance with the aristocracy, and the resulting social lies and fantasies. This impressive novel of more than seven hundred pages has an epic breadth, and the narrative is grandly sustained in a manner that was rarely achieved by the neorealistic writers. The center of interest in Morante's *L'isola di Arturo* (1957, Arturo's Island) is the dreams and illusions of a boy growing up virtually alone on the island of Procida. Arturo glorifies his father, who is almost always away, into a mythical, heroic figure. Gradually, however, the father is revealed to his son as a cowardly and corrupt weakling.

To a certain extent, the vivid eye-witness account of the war in *La pelle* (1948 in French, 1949 in Italian; The Skin) by Curzio Malaparte (1898–1957, pseudonym of Kurt Suckert) also belongs to the literature of southern Italy. In this work the scandal-hungry reporter gathered all the shocking scenes that he could discover in his war-ravaged country. (Jacopetti followed his example in the film *Mondo cane* about a decade later.) In Malaparte's view, Naples is a disgusting and simultaneously fascinating ulcer on the European continent, a city of antiquity comparable to Nineveh and Babylon, a city in which obscenity and cruelty are often practiced for their own sake. In both *The Skin* and *Kaputt* (1944, Kaputt) Malaparte bared the wounds and weaknesses of his time with exhibitionistic sado-masochism and illuminated them with glaring searchlights.

TRADITIONALISM IN THE NORTH

The break with the past after the war was not as noticeable in a number of Tuscan novelists as it was in other writers. Just as hermetic poetry has been able to survive in Florence to the present day, traditional forms of fiction have also persisted to a large extent.

Mario Tobino (born 1910) is one of those Tuscan novelists who have followed the tradition of Federigo Tozzi (1883–1920). Most of Tobino's stories and novels have been largely autobiographical. In the novel *La brace dei Biassoli* (1956, The Ashes of the Biassoli) he told the history of his family, which came from Liguria and Tuscany. In *Le libere donne di Magliano* (1955, The Liberated Women of Magliano) a neurologist reports on the sanatorium he supervises. *Una giornata con Dufenne* (1968, A Day with Dufenne) described a class reunion.

Carlo Cassola (born 1917), who in the years after the war became one of the most popular writers of fiction in Italy, was a Roman by birth but of a Tuscan family. His novels and tales have usually been set in western Tuscany. Cassola, who was influenced by Stevenson's *Treasure Island*, Alain-Fournier's *Le grand Meaulnes*, and Thornton Wilder's *The Bridge of San Luis Rey*, has avoided stylistic and structural innovations and has chosen simple people as the protagonists in his novels. He has attempted to reproduce which he calls the "impossible film" of his characters, to show them to us as they would look in faded photographs.

The autobiographical novel *Fausto e Anna* (1952, Fausto and Anna) showed Cassola's commitment to an introspective approach. His best-selling novel *La ragazza di Bube* (1958, Bube's Girl) showed his characteristic regard for the common people caught up in the resistance movement. Influenced by Pasternak's *Doktor Zhivago*, Cassola presented the victory of poetry over ideology; the counterpoint between poetry and ideology is embodied in the lovers Mara and Bube. With *Un cuore arido* (1961, An Arid Heart) Cassola turned his attention to a larcenous religiosity: after Anna Cavorzio renounces the world to dedicate herself to the idea of strict self-control, her life becomes completely isolated, devoid of feeling.

The identification of morality and literature led temporarily to the great respect enjoyed by Vasco Pratolini (born 1913), who began his literary career with a prose style derived from the hermetic poetry of Florence. In *Via de' Magazzini* (1942, Via de' Magazzini) he found an idyllic quality in his own childhood, despite its hunger and misery. If vernacular voices had not been so overestimated in Italy right after the war, critics would have seen earlier that Pratolini's moralizing, which was based on simple black-and-white contrasts, resulted at its best in regional writing for certain Florentine districts. *Il quartiere* (1945, The District), *Cronache di poveri amanti* (1947, A Tale of Poor Lovers), and *Le ragazze di San Frediano* (1952, The Girls of San Frediano) amounted to imitations of nineteenth-century sentimentality, although they do contain a few successful pages.

Not surprisingly, the result of Pratolini's ambitious attempt to write a trilogy was far below the exaggerated expectations of the Italian critics. *Metello* (1955, Metello), *Lo scialo* (1961, Waste), and *La costanza della ragione* (1963, The Permanence of Reason), which attempted to retell a hundred years of Italian history, showed even more clearly than his earlier works that Pratolini veered toward pseudorealism.

Traditional narrative techniques have also characterized the Emilian Giorgio Bassani (born 1915). But with his *Cinque storie ferraresi* (1955, Five Stories of Ferrara) Bassani introduced a new subject into Italian postwar literature: the life of a Jewish community in an average Italian city both under facism, with its oppressive racial laws, and after the liberation. The geographically and socially restricted milieu enabled Bassani to analyze interpersonal relationships in detail. He polished his style and language, so that he was able to produce one of the few international successes of postwar Italian literature—the gripping novel *Il giardino dei Finzi-Contini* (1962, The Garden of the Finzi-Continis), a nostalgic retrospective look at prewar Ferrara. The garden of the Finzi-Continis becomes an illusory sanctuary in the midst of the impending catastrophe, which involved the deportation of almost two hundred members of the Jewish community and the shooting of eleven hostages.

Another traditionalist, Giovanni Arpino (born 1927), a native of Piedmont, probed two of Pavese's favorite landscapes: the Piedmont hinterland and the milieu of Turin workers. But, like Carlo Cassola, Arpino has described contemporary events with a very conservative prose style; he considers content more important than avant-garde experiments. In *Gli anni del giudizio* (1958, The Years of Judgment) the center of attention is the election campaign of 1953, which was conducted with uncompromising rigidity by both the Communist Party and the Christian Democrats. Arpino took up a "forbidden" theme in *La suora giovane* (1959, The Novice), the love story of a young novice and a Turin workingman. *Un delitto d'onore* (1961, A Crime of Honor) was set in southern Italy at the time when the fascists were beginning to rise to power; a schematization in the satirical portrayal of southern Italian sexual morality detracts from the realism of the work.

TWO INDIVIDUALISTS

Two writers a generation apart—Alberto Moravia (born 1907, pseudonym of Alberto Pincherle) and Italo Calvino (born 1923)—although they both have had some ties with specific literary movements and circles, have each brought an important and highly individual contribution to postwar Italian fiction.

Alberto Moravia came from a Roman Jewish family that had immigrated from Moravia. Beginning with his first novel, *Gli indifferenti* (1929, The Indifferent Ones), which attracted the attention of G. A. Borgese (1882–1952), the major critic of the time, and which influenced Sartre's *La nausée,* Moravia has enjoyed extraordinary fame as a writer of fiction well beyond the borders of Italy, a situation attributable in no small measure to his frequent use of sexual material. The structure of *The Indifferent Ones* is not unlike that of a classical drama, with due regard for the three unities. The rational clarity and the factual and precise language of Moravia's novels and stories enabled him to reach readers who were put off by the structural and linguistic experiments of other authors.

Without aligning himself to any political party, Moravia became a stimulating literary authority during the postwar years. He commented repeatedly on contemporary films in *Nuovi argomenti,* which he coedited, and in the leftist-liberal Roman weekly *L'espresso.* Acerbic polemics against fascism and the clergy, and cerebral dissections of the relationships between psychology and society, have characterized Moravia's extensive oeuvre. Not mood but total and seemingly all-encompassing clinical description of interpersonal relationships in the vein of existential nausea is a major feature of his fiction.

It is therefore all too often overlooked that Moravia's "heroes," who move in a world ruled by indifference, boredom, and disgust, carry inside them a longing for an unknown paradise. Moravia's characters, insofar as they are not already integrated into a world dominated by money, are alienated from bourgeois society; an example is the young title character of the novel *Agostino* (1944, Agostino), which portrayed a crisis of puberty. The story of a Roman prostitute during the fascist era was the focal point of *La Romana* (1947, The Woman of Rome). Here the theme of capitalist exploitation was demonstrated in a particularly graphic example: the prostitute Adriana, who is at most guilty of passivity, is innocent to Moravia because she belongs to the "people."

The lower class of Rome was the subject of Moravia's *Racconti romani* (1954, Roman Tales). Here the author juxtaposed the healthy instinct of self-preservation of the lower class with the hopeless depravity of the bourgeoisie. For Moravia, the only positive figure in the middle class is the intellectual, whom he presented in *La Ciociara* (1957, The Woman of Ciociaria), his novel about the resistance, as a man of uncompromising fervor. With his characteristic lucidity, Moravia has also depicted the abyss between the intellectual and lower-class peasants and workers. Pavese, quite unlike Moravia in many respects, tried, in *Il compagno* (1947, The Comrade) to resolve the contrast between the worker and the intellectual through a frankly mystical affirmation of the dogma of the infallibility of the proletariat, which is allegedly always unerring and instinctively correct.

Moravia's *La noia* (1960, Boredom) showed the alienation of the individual in the postwar capitalist society, using the example of a well-to-do man who fully enjoys his material advantages. Moravia's characters live under the illusion that actual contact with reality can be obtained through possessions. The result is *la noia:* boredom and disgust. In *Boredom* he showed in exemplary fashion what energies have to be released to fill this void.

Moravia's firsthand accounts of his trips to many non-European countries (he was in India with Pier Paolo Pasolini [born 1922]) have been written with the conviction that the future of the world will be decided in Asia and Latin America, not in the highly industrialized nations.

Italo Calvino began his career under the influence of neorealism, with *Il sentiero dei nidi di ragno* (1947, The Path to the Nest of Spiders), a novel about the resistance movement; indeed, novels about the resistance seemed obligatory during the early postwar years. But in this first work Calvino showed that structure was just as important to him as content. *The Path to the Nest of Spiders,* which described the war from the perspective of a boy from Genoa who joins the partisans in the hills, was consciously written as a picaresque novel.

In *The Path to the Nest of Spiders* it was evident already that Calvino was searching for his own voice, independent of neorealism. His feeling for the adventure of everyday events, his utilization of the European literary tradition of fantasy, and his interest in the folk song and fable showed that Calvino (as well as Pasolini) was compensating for the omissions of nineteenth-century Italian romanticism. Folk literature in general and the folk song and fable in particular, which were only collected by archivists in nineteenth-century Italy, were finally established as literary forms by Pasolini and Calvino. The "folk," which previously had been examined only superficially and perfunctorily and which had often been spoken of in sentimental terms, now was given the opportunity to express itself directly. This was Calvino's great achievement as editor of a comprehensive volume of fables—*Fiabe italiane* (1956, Italian Fables).

Calvino's novels with fabular subjects—*Il visconte dimezzato* (1952, The Cloven Viscount), *Il barone rampante* (1957, The Baron in the Trees), *Il cavaliere inesistente* (1959, The Nonexistent Knight)—marked the break in his own work with the neorealistic subject matter of his first novel. These works are set in the seventeenth and eighteenth centuries and in the time of Charlemagne. The first of these "ancestors" (in 1960 Calvino published the three novels together under the collective title *I nostri antenati* [Our Ancestors]) was a viscount divided into good and bad halves. The freely invented fable, the first part of which takes place in a grotesquely sinister area of eastern Europe, has a symmetrical structure, as does *The Nonexistent Knight*. Calvino manipulated narrative techniques most masterfully in *The Baron in the Trees*. This work, with its eighteenth-century background, showed that Calvino was at home in the age of Voltaire and Rousseau.

Calvino did return in short stories to the resistance, but he did not force the experiences of the World War II into simplified nationalistic or partisan statements. Instead, he used these experiences to deal with problems facing the second half of the twentieth century. The theme of his collected stories (*I racconti* [1958, Stories]) is withstanding the pressure of objects and avoiding being passive in the face of events. Calvino's people react and stand firm; an example is the crafty character Marcovaldo, who does not understand the technological nature of the city that boxes him in.

As early as the mid-1950s Calvino recognized clearly, in the story *La speculazione edilizia* (1957, Building Speculation), how rapidly Italian life had changed since World War II, how fundamentally the economic rebirth of western Europe and Italian prosperity had destroyed the myths of the resistance movement. It was no longer possible to render this changed way of life with conventional narrative techniques. The writer had to become a technician, had to analyze new phenomena. The alternatives of a humanly controlled nature, a state that could be realized by the baron in the trees with his enlightened enthusiasm, or a life as a noble savage with the naïveté of a Marcovaldo were no longer possible. Calvino's discomfort over this realization led him to extremely detailed and thoughtful critical analyses of society, such as *La giornata d'uno scrutatore* (1963, An Election Official's Day), as well as to the use of space science in *Le cosmicomiche* (1965, Cosmicomics) and its sequel *Ti con zero* (1967, T Zero). In these novels the protagonist is no longer the spontaneous, postromantic hero in search of adventure but a creature circumscribed by an abstract symbol, "Qfwfq." With *Cosmicomics* and *T Zero* Calvino arrived at the antipode of neorealistic themes. He apparently sees his shift as the writer's only possibility of coping with a radically changed world.

THE AVANT-GARDE

Carlo Emilio Gadda (born 1893) was catapulted into international literary fame after the success of his magnificent novel *Quer pasticciaccio brutto de via Merulana* (1957, That Awful Mess on Via Merulana), as well as of *La cognizione del dolore* (1958, Aquainted with Grief), which won him the International Publishers' Prize. Gadda's earlier works, such as *L'Adalgisa* (1944, The Adalgisa), the tales of *Novelle dal ducato in fiamma* (1953, Novellas of the Burning Dukedom), and the even earlier *Il castello di Udine* (1934, The Castle of Udine) started to be read with new attention by both critics and general readers.

Gadda's peculiar style, influenced by the German writer Jean Paul and the Italian writer Carlo Dossi (1849–1910), his encyclopedic knowledge, and his technical precision (he studied engineering in Milan) contributed to his strong individuality. Gadda has gone so far as to call reality and nature baroque. He approaches the grotesque phenomena of language, of nature, and of society as proof that something secret is hidden beneath the surface of things. A typical example is the murder case in *That Awful Mess on Via Merulana*. It enables the author to introduce bureaucracy and the linguistic distinctions among different classes and professions. Death, decay, and decomposition lurk behind the façades that the fascist regime and the Roman society construct to disguise their intentions. At the same time, the linguistic stratification opens up gaping abysses and makes sudden transitions possible.

Gadda's *Acquainted with Grief,* although set in South America, satirized both Italian fascism and the city of Milan, which Gadda hated with an enduring obsession. Placing the action in the remote Maradagál also gave Gadda the aesthetic distance to reveal his own jealously guarded traumatic experiences. The mother-son relationship certainly sounds like a specific pathological case; but, to Gadda's credit, he was able to present the situation as a typical example of late bourgeois decadence. The grotesque and expressionist effects of dialect and language parallel the unmasking of a seemingly correct way of life: the linguistic confusion corresponds to the chaos of the world and is the means of representing it.

After these two novels by Gadda, it became almost impossible for Italian writers to use dialect naïvely or carelessly any longer. The gradual recognition of Gadda's significance marked a distinct break in Italy with the literature of the first ten years after the war. Toward the end of the 1950s documentary and confessional literature that disregarded form was not considered creditable in many critical circles.

Although born in the nineteenth century, Antonio Pizzuto (born 1893) did not publish his first work, *Signorina Rosina* (1956, Miss Rosina), until he was in his sixties. At short intervals there followed *Si riparano bambole* (1960, Dolls Are Repaired), *Ravenna* (1962, Ravenna), *Paginette* (1964, Brief Pages), and *Sinfonia* (1966, Symphony). Pizzuto was unmistakably influenced by James Joyce and by Gadda's linguistic experiments. Pizzuto has attempted to make drastic changes in the treatment of language: the present and perfect tenses have been suppressed in favor of the imperfect; and his novels have the formal structure of musical compositions.

The neorealist Elio Vittorini introduced Lucio Mastronardi (born 1930) by publishing in his journal *Il menabò di letteratura* Mastonardi's first novel, *Il calzolaio di Vigevano* (1959, The Shoemaker of Vigevano). Mastronardi has written two further works with the same locale: *Il maestro di Vigevano* (1962, The Teacher of Vigevano) and *Il meridionale di Vigevano* (1965, The Southerner of Vigevano). All his novels are sagas of rising and falling careers of middle-class men. The expectations and the struggles for success during the period of the Italian economic miracle, as well as the abandoning of lower-middle-class ideals, have played a decisive role in Mastronardi's novels. Mastronardi could never have written as he has without Gadda and Pasolini, who served as models for his approach to language. Despite his linguistic ingenuity, his mordantly satirical representation of a provincial environment often has led him to mechanical style and psychological commonplaces.

Luciano Bianciardi (1922–1971) was influenced by both Pietro Aretino (1492–1556) and Henry Miller but also made use of nineteenth-century memoir literature. He began his career by publishing, in collaboration with Carlo Cassola, essays on the condition of miners in Tuscany—*I minatori della Maremma* (1955, The Miners of the Maremma). Then in *Il lavoro culturale* (1957, The Labor of Culture) Bianciardi wrote a pamphlet in narrative form about the collapse of political and cultural activity in a stagnating province. As a novelist, he had success with *La vita agra* (1962, The Hard Life), in which the narrator is an angry young man working in the mass media of Milan. Bianciardi here put himself into the role of the literary outcast, the great loner. Bianciardi opened up syntax and juxtaposed the empty, mechanical Milanese language derived from the economic miracle with the vitality of the Tuscan language. For the novels *La battaglia soda* (1964, The Hard Battle) and *Aprire il fuoco* (1969, Open Fire), Bianciardi drew upon Italian history after the risorgimento.

By comparing present-day Italy to its nineteenth century goals, he tried to show the failure of the modern age to carry out a historical obligation.

Luigi Malerba's (born 1927) Roman love story—if it can be called a story—*Il serpente* (1966, The Serpent) contained bitter satire, which might be overlooked because of the playful frivolity of many parts of the novel. Carlo Villa's (born 1930) *Deposito celeste* (1967, Heavenly Settlement), which lacked a linear plot, was in some ways like Malerba's *The Serpent*. The book takes place in a shop that sells devotional objects.

Giorgio Manganelli (born 1922), in *Hilarotragoedia* (1964, Hilarotragedy), with its linguistic furor, renounced any semblance of a story. Language is without "meaning" for Manganelli, but is merely an abstract form of organization. He demonstrated this idea again in *Nuovo commento* (1969, New Commentary). Manganelli and other writers who formed the avant-garde Group 63 during a meeting in Palermo in October, 1963, constitute a new breed of Italian writer. The writers of the 1940s and early 1950s generally wanted simple and folksy forms but discovered that in their overly complex world reality could no longer be presented without some kind of scientific and technical background. Gadda, an engineer, seems to have created a new labyrinth, which acts as a challenge to a whole generation of young, intellectual writers and readers.

Ottiero Ottieri's (born 1924) short novel *Tempi stretti* (1957, Hard Times) was probably the first attempt in Italy to introduce modern industrial techniques into a work of fiction. Here the highly intensified political expectations of the postwar years replaced the struggle for employment and wages. In *Donnarumma all'assalto* (1959, Donnarumma on the Attack), which dealt with the industrialization of the south, Ottieri's essayistic tendency was more apparent, and this tendency increased in the didactic novel *L'irrealtà quotidiana* (1966, Daily Unreality).

Paolo Volponi's (born 1924) first novel, *Memoriale* (1962, Memorial), dealt with the factory as a place of both self-alienation and self-confirmation. The paranoid Albino Saluggio, having returned home from war and imprisonment, is convinced that the physicians of the social welfare agency have diagnosed him as sick only to remove him from his work. Monomaniacal self-assertion in the face of the system leads Saluggio to his pathetic battle against the bureaucracy of socialism. Volponi's second novel, *La macchina mondiale* (1965, The Worldwide Machine), was ingenious but unconvincing. With the aid of a technological invention, the protagonist, Anteo Crocioni, wants to rectify a world that has turned into an insane asylum.

The relationship between industry and literature, which was discussed at length by Vittorini, Calvino, Ottieri, and others in the journal *Il menabò di letteratura* in the early 1960s, has been a dominant concern in the fiction of

Giovanni Testori (born 1923). After his debut with *Il dio di Roserio* (1954, Roserio's Idol), in which a Milanese racing hero is portrayed through the use of inner monologues, Testori soon expanded the Milanese theme to a cycle of novels, *I segreti di Milano* (1958ff., The Secrets of Milan). The linguistic verve of *Roserio's Idol* yielded completely in *The Secrets of Milan* to the naturalistic technique John Dos Passos used in novels that tried to represent the simultaneity of events. Testori's characters are often expertly drawn. His fictional world of the proletariat, with its prostitution, jealousy, exploitation, and raw sexuality, reached an international audience through the screenplay he wrote for Luchino Visconti's film *Rocco e i suoi fratelli* (1960).

Elio Pagliarani's (born 1927) major theme has been the clash of indestructible human nature with the world of industrial capitalism. In the story *La ragazza Carla* (1957, The Girl Carla), he used the avant-garde techniques of quotations and montage. The Milanese dialect of *The Girl Carla* never becomes an end in itself nor mere local color; it serves rather as a distinguishing and alienating feature in the regimented consumer society.

Goffredo Parise (born 1929) did not begin as an avant-gardist. The novel *Il prete bello* (1954, The Handsome Priest), which won him fame, described, from the perspective of an urchin, a small-town clergyman's vain and complacent existence under fascism. But by *Il fidanzamento* (1955, The Engagement), a portrait of provincial misery, Parise began to address himself to the problems of alienation in modern society. His most successful novel, *Il padrone* (1965, The Boss), dealt with the subtle forms of exploitation of postwar capitalism. In *Il crematorio di Vienna* (1970, The Crematory of Vienna) Parise described the reduction of interpersonal relationships: people no longer have names but have become mere numbers, as in Calvino's recent works.

ART AND LIFE

Gianna Manzini (born 1896), in her *Lettera all'editore* (1945, Letter to the Publisher), was the first to introduce to Italy a narrative technique reminiscent of Virginia Woolf and André Gide. With a stylistic and technical mastery that had no equal in Italy at that time, she created the novel of a novel. Subsequently, however, in *La sparviera* (1956, The Sparrow Hawk), her refined style of narration often amounted to virtuosity for its own sake.

Anna Banti (born 1895, pseudonym of Lucia Lo Presti), who for years edited the literature section of the journal *Paragone,* mutated the autobiographical element of fiction by filtering it through history and art history. She retold the destiny of the early seventeenth-century painter Artemisia Gentileschi in *Artemisia* (1947, Artemisia), for which Virginia Woolf's

Orlando and Walter Pater's essays on art were important models. Another accomplished work, *Lavinia fuggita* (Lavinia the Runaway), in the volume *Le donne muoiono* (1951, The Women Are Dying), is set in the Venice of Antonio Vivaldi.

Life and art also provided the counterpoint in two fine novels by Alessandro Bonsanti (born 1904): *La buca di San Colombano* (1964, The Hole of San Colombano) and *La nuova stazione de Firenze* (1965, The New Station of Florence). Through the journal *Solaria,* which he helped decisively to shape, and through *Letteratura,* which he founded, Bonsanti tried to keep Italian literature within an international context even under fascism.

THE LURE OF POPULARITY

Guido Piovene (born 1907) gained fame for his *Lettere di una novizia* (1942, Letters of a Novice). The self-analysis and self-deceit of ambivalent, egocentric characters was the essence of Piovene's novels and essays through *Le stelle fredde* (1970, The Cold Stars). In the volume of essays *La coda di paglia* (1962, The Wisp of Straw), in which Piovene discussed his attitudes during the period of the fascist racial laws, he tried, unconvincingly, to come to terms with his past through a literary exorcism. Piovene's dabbling in Marxism has also been unconvincing, but his travelogues *De America* (1953, About America) and *Viaggio in Italia* (1957, A Trip in Italy) were first-rate journalistic analyses of the two countries.

Mario Soldati (born 1906) has repeatedly used Catholic themes in his numerous works of fiction. In *Le lettere di Capri* (1954, The Capri Letters) he contrasted Anglo-Saxon puritanism and southern sensuality. In *La confessione* (1955, The Confession) he dealt with homosexuality in Catholic boarding schools. And in *Le due città* (1964, The Two Cities) he explored the differences between Turin and Rome. As a rule, Soldati is content with journalistic anecdotes, which he then packages as a story. This mass producer of light, entertaining literature failed to create any genuinely significant work.

Although Dino Buzzati's (born 1906) excellent novel *Il deserto dei Tartari* (1940, The Tartar Steppe) was the first successful attempt in Italy to adopt Kafka's tone and atmosphere, Buzzati ended his serious literary career all too soon with a drift into works that adapted surrealism to popular taste. In the novel *Un amore* (1963, A Love Affair), he swung over completely into the field of light literature.

Tommaso Landolfi (born 1908) has borrowed more heavily than any other contemporary Italian author from the gothic literature of romanticism, including E. T. A. Hoffmann and Edgar Allan Poe. Landolfi takes pleasure in playing the outmoded role of the dandy.

THE CATHOLIC REVIVAL

Although the French *renouveau catholique* had a broad influence on Italian literary life during the first half of the century, Italy has produced no major Catholic writer since Alessandro Manzoni. The oppressive machinery of the Curia, which skillfully insinuated itself into the life of the state after its concordat with fascism, generally stifled any intellectual initiatives inspired by the spirit of the gospel. Even after the war there was little change, despite the efforts of Pope John XXIII; and the Italian clergy remained, for the most part, represented throughout the world by Giovanni Guareschi's (born 1908) novels about Don Camillo. While it is true that these works did make it possible to laugh at the ominous tensions of international politics even during the cold war, they also showed that for the author no distinction existed between Emilian peasant cunning and Emilian religion.

Except for Ignazio Silone, who was too much an individualist to be considered part of a Catholic movement, the most important Catholic author of postwar Italy has been Luigi Santucci (born 1918), whose stories and novels have been characterized by a sense of humor more reminiscent of the Scottish novelist Bruce Marshall than of Manzoni. The stories in *Misteri gaudiosi* (1946, Joyful Secrets) and *Lo zio prete* (1951, Uncle Priest) are marked by elegance of style. It has become increasingly evident that Santucci is a spokesman for the Catholic middle class entrapped in its complexes. This was clear in his novel *Il velocifero* (1963, The Carriage), which was a particularly notable success in his adaptation of it as a play in Milanese dialect under the title *L'arca di Noè* (1964, Noah's Ark). In the novel *Orfeo in Paradiso* (1967, Orfeo in Paradise) Santucci regressed to the romantic clichés of the nineteenth century.

Two other interesting writers in the Catholic revival have been Mario Pomilio (born 1921) and Silvio d'Arzo (1920–1952, pseudonym of Ezio Comparoni). Pomilio's first novel, *L'uccello nella cupola* (1954, The Bird in the Dome), was clearly influenced by Georges Bernanos. Arzo's story *Casa d'altri* (1948, House of Others) is set in an isolated parish.

POETRY

HERMETICISM

Hermeticism (the term was first coined by the critic Francesco Flora [1891–1962]) was the most important movement in Italian poetry between the two world wars. Hermetic poetry, which remained aloof from politics until World War II, originated in part as a reaction to Giosuè Carducci's and Gabriele d'Annunzio's rhetorical cult of words, which they used to serve the political messages of the risorgimento and imperialism. Instead, the hermetics used language to explore private worlds of associations. In Gianfranco Contini (born 1912), Carlo Bo (born 1911), and Oreste Marcrí (born 1913) hermeticism found sympathetic critics and interpreters. A great deal of Italian poetry after 1945 continued the traditions of hermeticism.

The central figure in hermetic poetry was Giuseppe Ungaretti (1888–1970). In the volume of poems *Il porto sepolto* (1916, The Buried Harbor), which appeared during World War I, he rejected Gabriele d'Annunzio's rhetorical glorification of the war and the futurists' demand for a destruction of all traditional values. Ungaretti's first poems consisted of isolated fragments of words; they were, in the poet's words, a "brief tearing of silence." Only with *Sentimento del tempo* (1936, Feeling of the Times) did the word unit develop into a sentence unit. The eventual result was Ungaretti's return to the eleven-syllable line, a feature of traditional Italian poetry that came to be regarded as indispensable by Ungaretti.

In his later poetry, dating from the years immediately preceding, during, and after World War II (including the poetry written when he lived in Brazil [1936–43]) Ungaretti was drawn more and more to the literary tradition extending from Vergil to Góngora and from Shakespeare to Blake. Unlike his early poetry, in the collections *Il dolore* (1947, Pain), *La terra promessa* (1950, The Promised Land), and *Il taccuino del vecchio* (1960, The Old Man's Notebook) Ungaretti strove for grand form, the reintroduction of such difficult traditional meters of Italian poetry as ballads and sestinas, and further development of the rhetoric of Spanish Gongorism. He presented himself as a poetic seer tested by sorrow and as an oracle of misfortune. He began to regard his entire lyrical oeuvre as an autobiography, which he gathered together under the title *Vita d'un uomo* (1943, Life of a Man).

The other major hermetic poet of the interwar years was Eugenio Montale (born 1896), who was considerably influenced by T. S. Eliot. Montale's collections *Ossi di seppia* (1925, Bones of the Cuttlefish) and *Le occasioni* (1939, Opportunities) were seminal works. His stoic solipsism, his rejection of fascism, and his poetics of the unpoetic served as an example for a whole generation. A central characteristic of Montale was the rejection of lyrical melody. His encoded antifascist activism was typical of the "inner emigration" possible under the banner of hermeticism, which was able to spread in the shadow of a censorship that was mild by comparison with Nazi practices.

The volume *La bufera, e altro* (1957, The Storm, and Others) was a collection of the poems Montale wrote during the war and postwar years. In these works, in his numerous articles for the newspaper *Corriere della sera,* in the stories and sketches of *Farfalla di Dinard* (1956, The Butterfly of Dinard), and in his political autobiography in verse, *Botta e risposta* (1960, Blow for Blow), Montale revealed himself as a trenchant moralist and satirist who has come to drop his aristocratic reserve. His deceased wife occupies the center of the volume *Xenia* (1964–66, Xenia); in these poems, which show the woman in the domestic sphere of the household, Montale moved closer than ever before to the language of everyday life.

Salvatore Quasimodo (1901–1968), who gained international fame when he received the Nobel Prize in 1959, also began as a hermetic poet in the early 1930s. His earliest poems were evocations of the lost paradise of childhood. He turned his Sicilian origin into a declaration of Pan-Hellenism. Unlike Ungaretti and Montale, Quasimodo cultivated a musical effect. For example, the antepenultimate stress in Sicilian given names derived from the Greek, such as Tindari and Anepo, gave his poetry a distinctly lilting meter. One of Quasimodo's most significant accomplishments remains his translations: from classical Greek lyric poetry (1940), from the Georgics (1942) and the Odyssey (1945), and of the Gospel according to Saint John, through all of which he consciously emphasized his Pan-Hellenic background. (In a similar way, Ugo Foscolo, during the age of romanticism, developed his origins on the Greek island of Zante into an autobiographical myth.)

The programmatic title of Quasimodo's volume *La vita non è sogno* (1949, Life Is Not a Dream), as well as of the small volume *Con il piede straniero sopra il cuore* (1946, With a Stranger's Foot in One's Heart), underscored his later political activism, which occasionally got sidetracked into clichés of the risorgimento. Quasimodo was the first hermetic to reach a broad public, because the sensual melody of his lines was more easily accessible to the hearer or reader of his verse than were Montale's harsh constructions.

THE "MIDDLE GENERATION": THE MOVEMENT AWAY FROM HERMETICISM

The major poets of the next generation all came strongly under the influence of hermeticism, as their early work clearly demonstrated. Most, however, moved away from hermeticism to find their independent voices.

Alfonso Gatto (born 1909), whose career in a number of ways resembled Quasimodo's, emphasized his alienation from his environment in the very title of his first volume of poems, *Isola* (1932, Island). At first, death, the central theme of his works, was only a subjective experience for him. It took the collective catastrophe of the war to tear him loose from his isolation, as with Quasimodo. Gatto's active participation in the resistance, his membership in the Communist Party, and his subsequent dispute with the party bureaucracy expanded his poetic horizon (he even was interested in the literary cabaret, an unpopular place in Italy). In the preface to his poems on the resistance, *Il capo sulla neve* (1949, The Head on the Snow), Gatto explained the new activist program of his poetry. The title of his *Osteria flegrea* (1962, Phlegraean Inn) suggests four central motifs of his work: death, antiquity, the south of Italy, and the present time. As with so many poems by Ungaretti and Quasimodo, Gatto's *Phlegraean Inn* showed how relevant Vergil, Dante's guide on his trip to the world beyond, still is for Italian poetry of recent decades, both as a personality and as a poet.

The great neorealist novelist Cesare Pavese began his career in the 1930s under the influence of hermeticism. He wanted to escape from the impressionism of contemporary free verse because its "word music" repelled him. He was not concerned with sonorousness but with rhythmic units, which he joined together according to the logic of the thoughts. Things were named and enumerated so as to liberate their explosive intellectual charge.

Pavese's first volume of poems, the originally underestimated *Lavorare stanca* (1936, Working Causes Tiredness), in which he used anapestic cadences in many lines but in general had no dependence on traditional meter, was something completely new in hermetic poetry. While Montale's poetic ideal was a highly stylized artistic language, which became more puzzling from year to year, Pavese strove to produce a lyrical slang in the manner of the American writer Sherwood Anderson's prose style. The central figures in Pavese's narrative poems are prostitutes, peasants, workers, drunkards, and musicians, people who do not play any role in the works of other hermetic poets.

Influenced by Benedetto Croce's (1866–1952) aesthetics, Pavese at first considered large poetic compositions or cycles of poems aesthetically impossible. Later, he discovered that individual poems in a *canzoniere* (song book) could unite to form a larger structure. The construction of Elizabethan dramas and of the novels and stories of Melville also served him as models. Yet Pavese's individual poems became terser, shorter, more hermetic. Since he began to regard his poems, which he at first saw as isolated "creations," as forming an interconnected whole or a cycle, allusions could take the place of detailed images.

Mario Luzi (born 1914), another hermetic—as least as a young poet—has freed himself more and more in the postwar years from his ornate early lyrics written under the spell of Mallarmé and surrealism. His development recalls the intellectual journey of Clemente Rebora (1885–1957). Luzi's demand for truthfulness above all can be seen in the title *Onore del vero* (1957, Respect for the Truth). He has distanced himself from the lyrical experiments with big-city jargon of other poets, and he has also refrained from introducing the language of the modern technical age into his verse.

His poetic world has remained untouched by the major economic and social upheavals and consequently has shown the degree to which his native Florence and Tuscany likewise have remained unaffected by these occurrences.

Alessandro Parronchi (born 1914) has also not been concerned with the historical period of the war and its aftermath but rather with the seasons in their eternally regular recurrence. Like Luzi, Parronchi has been an advocate of the eternally "true." But Parronchi lacks the existential involvement that enabled Luzi to break through the formal rigidity of hermetic art.

A contemporary of Luzi and Parronchi, Piero Bigongiari (born 1914) continued to develop hermetic poetry consistently in imitation of Montale. Bigongiari has practiced a refined and "precious" word art. Even in the volume *Le mura di Pistoia* (1958, The Walls of Pistoia), which appeared long after the heyday of hermeticism, the objective or historical reality was still only a point of departure for the creation of hermetic symbols.

The title of Vittorio Sereni's first volume of poetry, *La frontiera* (1941, The Border), refers to his homeland on Lake Maggiore, close to the Swiss border. If not for his war experiences in Greece and his internment in Africa, Sereni would probably have remained a regionalist follower of Montale and Quasimodo. But the poems in *Diario d'Algeria* (1947, Diary from Algeria) viewed the myths of childhood from the perspective of the Italian defeat. The economic boom in Milan, which Sereni witnessed firsthand as chief editor for Mondadori, Italy's largest publishing house, caused him to revise his concept of man, as in *Gli strumenti umani* (1965, The Human Instruments). Sereni's misty Lombard landscapes have recalled again and again the moods of the lower world found in the Aeneid. In the midst of the self-alienating world of the Italian economic miracle, Sereni established for himself a narrow realm of literary autonomy, as he demonstrated in his satirical representation of the Frankfurt book fair in the story *L'opzione* (1964, The Option).

REGIONALISM AND INTERNATIONALISM

A regionalist trend, not unlike that in fiction, exists in contemporary Italian poetry. As in fiction, regionalism has been particularly strong in the south. But alongside regionalism and the home-grown phenomenon of hermeticism, contemporary Italian poetry has also shown some strong influences from abroad, especially from France.

Leonardo Sinisgalli (born 1908) became known after the publication of his *18 poesie* (1936, 18 Poems). An engineer from Basilicata, Sinisgalli has combined his *Furor mathematicus* (the Latin title [A Passion for Mathematics] of a collection of essays of 1944) with a belief in the changelessness of his southern Italian world. Sinisgalli's poems often take as their starting point the decomposed forms of former living things, which are conjured up with scientific objectivity. The objects are isolated, as in modern paintings, and because they are extracted from their environmental associations, they have the effect of an obsessive presence. The poetry of Libero de Libero (born 1906), like that of Sinisgalli—and, indeed, of Quasimodo as well—has been grounded in his homeland, which has its roots in antiquity. But his occasional surrealistic effects and his satirical vein have set him apart from his two contemporaries.

Completely outside any organized literary movement is Luciano Erba (born 1922). His ironic poetry has remained on the periphery of the postwar Italian ideological debates. In *Il male minore* (1960, The Lesser Evil) Erba took up the themes and forms of the French symbolists and developed them further.

The neorealists of the 1940s, who rejected hermeticism, found a precursor in Umberto Saba (1883–1957). The poetry of Saba, who was exiled from his native Trieste by the fascist race laws, was republished in 1945 under the title *Canzoniere* (Song Book). (Saba's first *Song Book* had appeared in 1921.) The title refers less to Petrarch than to Heinrich Heine's *Buch der Lieder*. Saba's idyllic and intimate, yet commonplace lyrical world, like the seemingly effortless parlando of his lines, stood in conscious contrast to the aristocratic isolation of the hermetics and to their metaphysical or orphic conception of poetic language.

In the 1930s Saba departed from the traditional metric forms of his earlier works. Although he did follow the traditional Italian eleven-syllable line, he gave this meter a distinctive accent by eliminating fixed caesuras and by creating new rhythmic groupings. His later poems became more compact, but also more capricious and more synthetic. Following in the footsteps of Nietzsche and Freud (whom Italo Svevo [1861–1928] had discovered for Italian literature), Saba developed in *Scorciatoie e raccontini* (1946, Side Roads and Short Tales) a very personal theory about the creative value of subconscious failures. *Storia e cronistoria del Canzoniere* (1948, History and Chronicle of the Song Book), with its strange self-irony, was a very unusual poet's autobiography.

AVANT-GARDISTS AND MARXISTS

Luciano Anceschi (born 1911), who gathered the Italian avant-garde of the 1950s around his journal *Il verri,* edited the anthology *Linea lombarda* (1952, Lombard Line), which vigorously postulated a poetry that is part of the real world. A polemical stand against Florentine hermeticism coincided with this return to the Lombard traditions. Although Rilke and Hofmannsthal remained the important foreign stimuli for the hermetics, Mayakovski and Brecht, and soon debates about structuralism as well, occupied those of the younger generation living in industrialized northern Italy.

Further stimulus came from the Bologna journal *Officina,* whose contributors included Francesco Leonetti (born 1924), Franco Fortini, and Pier Paolo Pasolini. (Pasolini edited *Officina* from 1955 to 1959.) *Officina* and *Linea lombarda* advocated a literature that would face the realities of modern capitalism instead of dwelling in an ahistorical no-man's-land.

Francesco Leonetti dwelt repeatedly on the historical and social background of Bologna and its traditional anticlericalism in his volume of poetry *La cantica* (1959, The Canticle). These poems, which originated in the cultural climate of *Officina,* stressed repeatedly Leonetti's ideological concerns; the poems were unpalatable because of their idiosyncratic and willful syntax and structure. In the novelistic pamphlet *Conoscenza per errore* (1961, Knowledge from Error) Leonetti disputed with the Christian Democratic Party of the 1950s.

Franco Fortini has had more influence on the cultural debates of the last twenty-five years than most other Italian Marxists. Nobody in postwar Italy has formulated more penetratingly the helplessness of politically committed intellectuals who also profited from the system because of their employment in the mass media. The satirical verses of Fortini's volume *L'ospite ingrato* (1966, The Ungrateful Guest) presented a razor-sharp dialectic.

Elio Pagliarani, better known for his fiction, has dealt in his poems—from the collection *Cronache, ed altre poesie* (1954, Chronicles, and Other Poems) on—with the integration of people from the provinces into industrial Milan.

In the late 1950s the need to take stock and find new directions became more and more pressing. It was at this time that the novelists Vittorini and Calvino joined to edit the new journal *Il menabò di letteratura.* Until Vittorini's death in 1966 there were in Italy few literary and cultural debates for which *Il menabò di letteratura* did not serve as a relay station. In 1961 a new tone for poetry was set by Alfredo Giuliani's (born 1924) anthology *I Novissimi: Poesie per gli anni '60* (The Latest: Poems for the 1960s), which included poems by Pagliarani, Edoardo Sanguineti (born 1930), Nanni Balestrini (born 1936), Antonio Porta (born 1935), and Giuliani himself.

How thoroughly these new avant-gardists broke with the neorealism of the early postwar period has been especially shown by Edoardo Sanguineti, whose cerebral poems—*Laborintus* (1956, Laborintus), *Erotopaegnia* (1958, Erotopaegnia)—brought Jungian archetypes to life literarily and utilized Ezra Pound's technique of building montages out of quotations from different languages. Sanguineti is a learned and subtle poet, a master of parody, whose sequences of associations have not always escaped the danger of arbitrariness. His inexhaustible literary and intellectual reservoir was also evident in his novel *Capriccio italiano* (1963, Italian Caprice), which attempted to begin at the zero degree of writing.

Antonio Porta struck the principal themes of his poetry in his first volume, *La palpebra rovesciata* (1960, The Upside-Down Eyelid): blood, aggression, and sadomasochistic horror. For Porta, a Catholic poet, reality is the state of sin, of defilement. He has used free verse to present scenes of sexual violence in rapid succession.

The impact of *The Latest* was felt soon. In October, 1963, thirty-four writers met in Palermo and joined with the authors of Giuliani's anthology to form Group 63, with Luciano Anceschi, high priest of the avant-garde of the 1950s, again serving as godfather of the undertaking.

A SINGULAR POET: PIER PAOLO PASOLINI

Pier Paolo Pasolini has had an unmistakable tendency toward exhibitionism; thus, he represents the opposite pole from Italo Calvino, who typifies Gallic understatement. Pasolini began his career with a collection of poems in Friuli dialect, *Poesie a Casarsa* (1942, Poems in Casarsa). In Casarsa Pasolini joined a movement to modernize the province of Friuli along the lines of his experiences in the resistance movement, in which he had participated with a religious fervor. His model was Marx's *Der Traum von der Sache* (*Il sogno di una cosa* [The Dream of a Thing] is the title of a novel Pasolini wrote soon after the war but did not publish until 1962). His verses in Friuli dialect were collected later in *La meglio gioventù* (1954, The Best of Our Youth). Two anthologies Pasolini edited—*Poesia dialettale del Novecento* (1952, Twentieth-Century Poetry in Dialect) and *Canzoniere italiano* (1955, Italian Song Book)—showed that the postwar literary use of dialect was not a random occurrence but that it signified a systematic inclusion of the most linguistically diverse strata in Italy.

With the novels *Ragazzi di vita* (1955, Rebellious Youths) and *Una vita violenta* (1959, A Violent Life) Pasolini called attention for the first time to the lumpenproletariat of the suburbs of Rome. The jargon of his teenagers is characterized by a monotonous basic vocabulary, unlike Carlo Emilio Gadda's masterfully controlled linguistic pluralism. Pasolini placed the reckless vitality of his consumptive and cold-nosed idlers and pickpockets in direct contrast to the Roman *dolce vita*.

Pasolini has descended repeatedly and solemnly to the dregs of the Roman underworld in all his works with the attitude of a missionary intent on achieving martyrdom. Despite his conversion to Marxism, a Catholic substratum can be perceived in poems he wrote in standard Italian; these poems were written between 1943 and 1949, but Pasolini, a skillful manager of his own fame and literary image, did not publish them until a decade later, under the title *L'usignolo della chiesa cattolica* (1958, The Nightingale of the Catholic Church). In these poems Pasolini made use of the meters of church hymns and of the satanic element in romanticism.

Pasolini's social criticism became especially clear in the volume of poetry *Le ceneri di Gramsci* (1958, Gramsci's Ashes). Here he evoked a martyr of the Italian resistance, the leading theoretician among Italian communists, who died in 1936 after years of confinement in fascist prisons. These poems, in terza rima, were modeled on numerous nineteenth-century poems, from Ugo Foscolo's to Victor Hugo's and Giosuè Carducci's. Pasolini, who seems to have been born to found a religion, is concerned with a new doctrine of salvation; thus, he appropriately entitled his next volume of poems *La religione del mio tempo* (1961, The Religion of My Time).

Pasolini has experimented masterfully with lyric forms. Long narrative poems stand next to ecstatic shouts in the tradition of hymnal poetry; and exaggerated forms of terza rima are found next to satirical epigrams. His sympathy for the lowly, the oppressed, and the outcasts of society led Pasolini to India (*Odore dell'India* [1962, Odor of India]) and to the hippies in America, whom he has described in the journal *Nuovi argomenti,* which he and Alberto Moravia have edited since 1966.

The desire for a larger public than can be reached through literature, together with the lack of demand for poetry, which Pasolini confirmed in an appendix to his most recent volume, *Poesia in forma di rosa* (1964, Poetry in the Form of a Rose), finally brought Pasolini into films. In *Accatone* (1961) he depicted a victim of bourgeois society. For *Mamma Roma* (1962) he found in Anna Magnani the ideal interpreter of the Mediterranean version of the cult of motherhood (Pasolini's use of Friuli dialect was in itself a tribute to the mothers, an existentialist return to the sources). In his filming of *Il vangelo secondo Matteo* (1964), with its polemics against the Pharisees and its message of love for sinners, Pasolini insisted above all on the social impact of the text. *Passione e ideologia* (1960, Passion and Ideology), the title of a collection of Pasolini's essays, can be taken as a signpost of Pasolini's career.

Italian-Swiss and Dialect Poetry

Giorgio Orelli (born 1921), whose first volume of poems was published by Giuseppe Ungaretti, released the poetry of Ticino (an Italian canton of Switzerland) from its provincial narrowness. A sensitive follower of the hermetics, Orelli has referred constantly to the Swiss landscape and has introduced technical words for stylistic shock. Grytzko Mascioni (born 1936), who comes from the Swiss canton of Grisons, introduced Marxism and student activism into Italian-Swiss poetry through his volume *I passeri di Horkheimer* (1968, Horkheimer's Sparrows).

Pasolini made an enormous contribution to furthering the cause of dialect poetry in contemporary Italy. And today there is worthy dialect poetry, whether it is concerned with capturing regions whose language strongly differs from Tuscan Italian, such as Trieste (whose most significant poet remains Virgilio Giotto [1887–1957]) or capturing the language of a particular social class, like Antonio Guerra (born 1920). Nonetheless, dialect poetry has diminishing possibilities because of the spread of one standard Italian language.

The career of the Venetian Giacomo Noventa (1898–1960, pseudonym of Giacomo Ca' Zorzi) followed an unusual course. He received his major formative impressions from Croce's aesthetics and from the political writer Piero Gobetti's (1901–1926) program for a "liberal revolution." Under fascism he was denied the right to live in university cities because of his great influence on intellectuals of the younger generation. His *Versi e poesie* (1956, Verses and Poems), in Venetian dialect, could not be published until long after the end of the war. Noventa created for himself a forceful means of expression through the use of Venetian dialect. The work of this ideological eccentric, who was rooted in the patriarchal structures of his homeland (in the postwar years Noventa championed a liberal Catholicism), showed the influence of the many-faceted Italian literary tradition, the urbanity and simplicity of Venetian folksongs, and the epigrammatic compression of baroque conceits.

DRAMA

DRAMA AND THEATER

Italian drama has had isolated peaks, like the plays of Carlo Goldoni (1707–1793) and Luigi Pirandello, but it has lacked continuity. And Italy has not produced a great dramatist since Pirandello. No Italian play has gained more than temporary recognition abroad, although there has been no shortage of plays, since the state-subsidized Italian theaters are required to present unfamiliar works of new authors. But contemporary Italian plays cannot compare to Italian films in social and artistic significance. This does not mean that Italy has no theatrical life. There have been many talented directors and actors. But the repertory of Italian stages consists primarily of classics—from Renaissance drama through Goldoni to Pirandello—and contemporary foreign plays.

Drama and theater have frequently followed parallel courses since the end of the Renaissance, but without cross-pollination. Vittorio Alfieri (1749–1803) and Alessandro Manzoni both wrote important plays, but hardly influenced the activity of the Italian theater. Great Italian actors like Eleonora Duse or, more recently, Vittorio Gassmann, have been objects of personal cults but have done little to stimulate serious playwriting. An academy for new actors and directors, founded in Rome by Silvio d'Amico during the fascist era, signified a new beginning. Critics like Vito Pandolfi and actors like Vittorio Gassmann acquired their training here.

Since Giorgio Strehler's presentation of Brecht at the Piccolo Teatro di Milano, the German dramatist has become the most talked-about playwright in Italy. Strehler gave the decisive thrust to Italian theatrical life of the 1950s. Jean Vilar's Théâtre National Populaire was the most influential model for Strehler and for Paolo Grassi, general manager of the Piccolo Teatro di Milano. Artistic, political, and social responsibilities were indivisible for Strehler. One aspect of his political outlook was that he and Grassi excluded the French avant-garde, from Adamov to Beckett and Ionesco, from the repertory of his theater. Strehler was always primarily concerned with presenting a coherent Marxist interpretation of the works he selected, whether it were Brecht, Chekhov, Goldoni, or Shakespeare. Thus, his inability to have freedom to pursue his clear-cut goals led to his resignation from his position as managing director.

Most Italian directors approached the international avant-garde with hesitation. Samuel Beckett was staged by Carlo Quartucci in the 1960s, and the Italian writer-director Carmelo Bene (born 1933), through his self-proclaimed "massacre of the classics" and other theatrical experiments, brought about ties between Italy and Grotowski, The Living Theatre, and Anglo-American "happenings." Critics like Alberto Arbasino and Giuseppe Bartolucci were instrumental in stressing the need to catch up to foreign developments in the theater.

PHILOSOPHICAL AND SOCIAL DRAMA

The only Italian dramatist of the fascist era to receive international attention after the war was Ugo Betti (1892–1953), who had been employed under Mussolini as judge and librarian in the ministry of justice. With an existential unwillingness to compromise, Betti presented interpersonal relationships in such works as *Corruzione al Palazzo di Giustizia* (1944, Corruption in the Palace of Justice), *Marito e moglie* (1947, Man and Wife), *Delitto all'isola delle capre* (1950, Crime on Goat Island), and *La fuggitiva* (1953, The Fugitive). A masochistic proclivity toward self-blame and an exhibitionistic desire to confess characterized Betti's works. The central theme of his theatrically effective plays was generally the unmasking of corruption.

No other Italian dramatist since Pirandello has mastered with similar theatrical skill the raveling and unraveling of plot as did Betti. However, he remained the prisoner of a narrow ideology. His characters are ambitious people in the middle and lower-middle classes, who at the moment of their unmasking seek an escape into a not very credible transcendence. Religion offers Betti's figures not the basis for a new way of life but the possibility for self-laceration, which they occasionally experience with real pleasure. The influence of Strindberg and Ibsen was unmistakably obvious in the theme of the "lie of life."

The problem of religion lies at the center of the plays of Diego Fabbri (born 1911), who found a wide audience abroad as well as in Italy during the 1950s. His protagonists are lonely people who can be redeemed only by providence. In *Inquisizione* (1950, Inquisition) the central issue is the intellectual and religious crises of a priest and of a former aspirant to the priesthood. In *Processo di famiglia* (1953, Trial in the Family) three married couples fight over an adopted child; only when the child falls into an open elevator shaft through the negligence of all do they recognize and acknowledge their guilt. In *Processo a Gesù* (1955, Trial against Jesus) Fabbri questioned the legality of Jesus's sentence. How brilliant Fabbri can also be as a writer of social comedy was clearly shown by *La bugiarda* (1956, The Deceitful Woman), one of the rare instances in contemporary Italian drama of a comedy not written in dialect.

Giuseppe Patroni-Griffi (born 1921) has used the cocktail jargon of the chic set in the mass media to create social dramas—such as *D'amore si muore* (1958, One Dies of Love) and *Metti una sera a cena* (1966, Let's Imagine an Evening at Dinnertime)—that have been only partially successful.

REGIONALISM AND DIALECT DRAMA

The most popular playwright during the years immediately following World War II was the Neapolitan Eduardo de Filippo. He began as an actor of the commedia dell'arte, but the influence of Pirandello, whom Filippo knew personally, encouraged him to write his own plays. Like Pirandello, Filippo has "translated" his dialect plays into standard Italian. Both *Napoli milionaria* (1949, Millionairess Naples) and *Filumena Marturano* (1947, Filumena Marturano) were popular plays that became worldwide successes as movies. The lower middle-class environment of his domestic plays and melodramas, the superabundance of emotions enjoyed to the full by his Neapolitans, their will to live and their skepticism—all these traits have contributed to the success of Filippo's plays. In *Questi fantasmi* (1946, Oh, These Ghosts) a "southern tragedy" of jealousy is averted because the husband, a "poor fool," takes the nocturnally appearing lover of his wife for a spirit. The world and society are as a rule hostile forces, against which the family and the clan stand in opposition. The preservation and security of the family are sought through all means, even self-deception.

A great deal of the life of the Italian theater depends even today on plays in dialect. Dialect drama continues to flourish not only in Naples, but in Venice and Genoa as well.

POLITICAL DRAMA

The admiration for Brecht and for Marxism has attracted authors, but no talented playwrights, to the theater. Carlo Terron (born 1913), Ugo Pirro (born 1920), and the novelist Giovanni Testori have not advanced beyond a few angry experiments.

Polemics in the form of cabaret texts was offered by the Parenti-Fo-Durano troop, which disbanded, however, after the financial failure of the satirical presentation *Sani de legare* (1956, So Healthy That They Had to Be Tied Down), which was mutilated by censorship. Nevertheless, one of the troop, Dario Fo (born 1926) has continued to pursue contemporary social criticism on the stage. His extraordinary talent as author, director, and actor was verified in the gangster play *Aveva due pistole con gli occhi bianchi e neri* (1960, He Had Two Pistols with White and Black Eyes). The gangster appears both as a cynical bandit and as a peace-loving priest. As unoriginal as is the subject, one borrowed from E. T. A. Hoffmann's *Fräulein von Scudéry* and Stevenson's *Dr. Jekyll and Mr. Hyde,* it nevertheless provided an ideal theme for Fo's brilliant pantomimic jokes and satirical barbs. With *Grande pantomima con bandieri e pupazzi piccoli e medi* (1968, Big Pantomime with Flags and Small and Medium-Sized Puppets), Fo departed conclusively from the theater in the traditional sense. For him, the performance has become a political agitation that Fo can stage in any public building and in any square. The play presents the political, economic, and social development of Italy and the world since 1945 in the form of a revue, and the characters speak in everyday language (including jargon) to eliminate any distance between actors and audience.

THE AVANT-GARDE

Carmelo Bene has taken the raw material for his savagely parodic plays from myths (Pinocchio, Faust, Hamlet, Christ). His objective is not artistic experimentation but rather iconoclastic aggression, in the service of which Bene applies his extraordinary sense of theatrics.

Luigi Squarzina (born 1922), who began as a traditional dramatist, established the Teatro d'Arte Italiano in Rome with Vittorio Gassmann; Squarzina has been a very knowledgeable man of the theater. But despite the interest of major theaters and actors in his plays—*L'esposizione uni-*

versale (1955, The International Exposition) and *Tre quatri di luna* (1952, Three Quarters of the Moon)—they failed to attract audiences. In *La Romagnola* (1959, The Woman from Romagna) Squarzina tried to dramatize a typical episode from the resistance movement, partly through melodrama; the result was not convincing. With *Emmeti* (1966, Emtee) Squarzina embarked on a new path. Here he made an effort to utilize the subject matter of the 1960s: a woman is pushed by the inexorable pressures of modern capitalist society.

Members of the avant-garde Group 63 have attempted to revolutionize the form of the theater by working with such experimental directors as Carmelo Bene and Carlo Quartucci. The poet Alfredo Giuliani created collages of dialogue in *Povera Juliet* (1965, Poor Juliet) and *Urotropia* (1965, Urotropia). And the novelist Giorgio Manganelli, in *Monodialogo* (1970, Monodialogue), reduced the two partners of the script to a completely depersonalized contrast of A and B: two voices seek each other and are constantly shattered against one another.

The director Luca Ronconi stands at the opposite pole from Brecht and from Brecht's most congenial contemporary Italian interpreter, Giorgio Strehler. For Ronconi, the theater is not an instrument of propaganda. With his production of the poet Edoardo Sanguineti's stage adaptation of Ariosto's *Orlando furioso* (1969, Orlando Raging) Ronconi involved the spectator in a new form. By being presented with simultaneous scenes, the crowd of visitors before the Church of San Zeno in Verona or at the 1970 festival season in Berlin was required to keep making decisions about which scene they wanted to watch. *Orlando Raging* gave the experimentalists of Group 63 their first resounding success.

Sanguineti's work for the theater had begun earlier, with *K* (1959, K), a dialogue between Kafka and Gustav Janouch. His *Traumdeutung* (1964; the title is in German: The Interpretation of Dreams) was a quartet for one female voice and three male voices. It is a composition in dialogue for voices in parallel, which pause and then begin at different moments. Sanguineti was consciously seeking a link with modern theories of musical harmony. In his adaptation of *Orlando Raging* the simultaneity of the voices was developed further and logically into a simultaneity of action.

One of the most radical experiments of the contemporary Italian theater has been Giuliano Scabia's (born 1935) *Zip, Lap, Vip, Vap, Mam, Crep, Scap, Plip, Trip, Scrap e la Grande Mam alle prese con la civiltà contemporanea* (1967, Zip, Lap, Vip, Vap, Mam, Crep, Scap, Plip, Trip, Scrap, and the Great Mam in Her Confrontation with Contemporary Civilization). In this play the substance of language was dissected into its components with the aid of modern linguistics. One characteristic of the most recent developments in the avant-garde theater has been the departure farther and farther away from literature; the value of scripts is measured only by their effectiveness on the stage. Ironically, for all its experimentalism, this avant-garde theater has led Italy back to the commedia dell'arte.

ITALIAN WORKS IN
ENGLISH TRANSLATION

INDIVIDUAL WORKS MENTIONED
IN ARTICLE

Alvaro, Corrado. *Gente in Aspromonte* as *Revolt in Aspromonte.* New York, 1962

Arpino, Giovanni. *Un delitto d'onore* as *A Crime of Honor.* New York, 1963

———. *La suora giovane* as *The Novice.* New York, 1962

Bacchelli, Riccardo. *Il mulino del Po* as *The Mill on the Po.* New York, 1950

Bassani, Giorgio. *Cinque storie ferraresi* as *Five Stories of Ferrara.* New York, 1971

———. *Il giardino dei Finzi-Contini* as *The Garden of the Finzi-Continis.* New York, 1965

Betti, Ugo. *Corruzione al Palazzo di Giustizia* as *Corruption in the Palace of Justice.* In Alvin B. Kernan, ed., *Classics of the Modern Theater.* New York, 1965

———. *Delitto all'isola delle capre* as *Crime on Goat Island.* In Robert Corrigan, ed., *Masterpieces of the Modern Italian Theatre.* New York, 1967

———. *La fuggitiva* as *The Fugitive.* In *Three Plays on Justice.* San Francisco, 1964

Bianciardi, Luciano. *La vita agra* as *La Vita Agra: It's a Hard Life.* New York, 1965

Brancati, Vitaliano. *Il bell'Antonio* as *Antonio, the Great Lover.* New York, 1952

Buzzati, Dino. *Un amore* as *A Love Affair.* New York, 1964

———. *Il deserto dei Tartari* as *The Tartar Steppe.* New York, 1965

Calvino, Italo. *Il barone rampante* as

The Baron in the Trees. New York, 1959

———. *Il cavaliere inesistente* as *The Non-existent Knight.* In *The Non-existent Knight/The Cloven Viscount.* New York, 1962

———. *Le cosmicomiche* as *Cosmicomics.* New York, 1968

———. *Il sentiero dei nidi di ragno* as *The Path to the Nest of Spiders.* Boston, 1957

———. *Ti con zero* as *T Zero.* New York, 1969

———. *Il visconte dimezzato* as *The Cloven Viscount.* In *The Non-existent Knight/The Cloven Viscount.* New York, 1962

Cassola, Carlo. *Un cuore arido* as *An Arid Heart.* New York, 1964

———. *Fausto e Anna* as *Fausto and Anna.* New York, 1960

———. *La ragazza di Bube* as *Bebo's Girl.* New York, 1962

Filippo, Eduardo de. *Filumena Marturano* as *Filumena Marturano.* In Robert Corrigan, ed., *Masterpieces of the Modern Italian Theatre.* New York, 1967

———. *Questi fantasmi* as *Oh, These Ghosts.* In *Tulane Drama Review,* 8, 1964, pp. 118–62

Gadda, Carlo Emilio. *La cognizione del dolore* as *Acquainted with Grief.* New York, 1969

———. *Quer pasticciaccio brutto di Via Merulana* as *That Awful Mess on Via Merulana.* New York, 1965

Jovine, Francesco. *Le terre del Sacramento* as *The Estate in the Abruzzi.* London, 1952

Lampedusa, Giuseppe Tomasi di. *Il gat-*

topardo as *The Leopard*. New York, 1960

Levi, Carlo. *Cristo si è fermato a Eboli* as *Christ Stopped at Eboli*. New York, 1947

——. *La doppia notte dei tigli* as *The Linden Trees*. New York, 1962

——. *L'orologio* as *The Watch*. New York, 1951

——. *Le parole sono pietre* as *Words Are Stones: Impressions of Sicily*. New York, 1958

Malaparte, Curzio. *Kaputt* as *Kaputt*. New York, 1946

——. *La pelle* as *The Skin*. New York, 1954

Malerba, Luigi. *Il serpente* as *The Serpent*. New York, 1968

Marotta, Giuseppe. *L'oro di Napoli* as *The Treasure of Naples*. New York, 1949

——. *San Gennaro non dice mai no* as *San Gennaro Never Says No*. New York, 1950

Montale, Eugenio. *Farfalla di Dinard* as *The Butterfly of Dinard*. London, 1970

——. *Le occasioni* as *Opportunities*. In *Selected Poems*. New York, 1966

——. *Ossi di seppia* as *Ossi di Seppia*. In *Selected Poems*. New York, 1966

Morante, Elsa. *L'isola di Arturo* as *Arturo's Island*. New York, 1959

——. *Menzogna e sortilegio* as *House of Liars*. New York, 1951

Moravia, Alberto. *Agostino* as *Agostino*. In *Five Novels*. New York, 1955

——. *La Ciocara* as *Two Women*. New York, 1958

——. *Gli indifferenti* as *The Time of Indifference*. London, 1953

——. *La noia* as *The Empty Canvas*. New York, 1961

——. *Racconti romani* as *Roman Tales*. New York, 1957

Ortese, Anna Maria. *Il mare non bagna Napoli* as *The Bay Is Not Naples*. London, 1955

Ottieri, Ottiero. *Donnarumma all'assalto* as *The Men at the Gate*. Boston, 1962

Parise, Goffredo. *Il padrone* as *The Boss*. New York, 1966

——. *Il prete bello* as *Don Gastone and the Ladies*. New York, 1955

Pasolini, Pier Paolo. *Ragazzi di vita* as *The Ragazzi*. New York, 1968

——. *Una vita violenta* as *A Violent Life*. London, 1968

Pavese, Cesare. *Il carcere* as *The Political Prisoner*. In *The Political Prisoner/The Beautiful Summer*. London, 1955

——. *La casa in collina* as *The House on the Hill*. New York, 1961

——. *Il compagno* as *The Comrade*. London, 1959

——. *Il diavolo sulle colline* as *The Devil in the Hills*. In *Selected Works*. New York, 1968

——. *La luna e i falò* as *The Moon and the Bonfire*. New York, 1953

——. *Il mestiere di vivere* as *The Burning Brand: Diaries 1935–1950*. New York, 1961

——. *Paesi tuoi* as *The Harvesters*. London, 1962

——. *Tra donne sole* as *Among Women Only*. In *Selected Works*. New York, 1968

Piovene, Guido. *Lettere di una novizia* as *Confessions of a Novice*. London, 1950

Pratolini, Vasco. *La costanza della ragione* as *Bruno Santini*. Boston, 1964

——. *Cronache di poveri amanti* as *A Tale of Poor Lovers*. New York, 1949

——. *Metello* as *Metello*. Boston, 1968

——. *Il quartiere* as *The Naked Streets*. New York, 1952

Roberto, Federico de. *I vicerè* as *The Viceroys*. New York, 1962

Santucci, Luigi. *Orfeo in Paradiso* as *Orfeo in Paradise*. New York, 1968

Sciascia, Leonardo. *A ciascuno il suo* as *A Man's Blessing*. New York, 1968

——. *Il consiglio d'Egitto* as *The Council of Egypt*. New York, 1966

——. *Il giorno della civetta* as *Mafia Vendetta*. New York, 1964

——. *Morte dell'inquisitore* as *The Death of the Inquisitor*. In *Salt in the Wound/The Death of the Inquisitor*. New York, 1969

——. *Le parocchie di Regalpetra* as *Salt in the Wound*. In *Salt in the Wound/The Death of the Inquisitor*. New York, 1969

Silone, Ignazio. *Fontamara* as *Fontamara*. New York, 1960

——. *Pane e vino* as *Bread and Wine*. New York, 1962

——. *Il seme sotto la neve* as *The Seed beneath the Snow*. New York, 1942

Soldati, Mario. *La confessione* as *The Confession*. New York, 1958
——. *Le Lettere di Capri* as *Affair in Capri: The Capri Letters*. New York, 1957
Ungaretti, Giuseppe. *Vita d'un uomo* as *Life of a Man*. London, 1958
Verga, Giovanni. *I Malavoglia* as *The House by the Medlar Tree*. New York, 1964

Vittorini, Elio. *Converazione in Sicilia* as *Conversation in Sicily*. Baltimore, 1962
——. *Il garofano rosso* as *The Red Carnation*. New York, 1952
Volponi, Paolo. *La macchina mondiale* as *The Worldwide Machine*. New York, 1967
——. *Memoriale* as *My Troubles Began*. New York, 1964

SECONDARY WORKS

BIBLIOGRAPHIES AND GUIDES

Bosco, Umberto. *Repertorio bibliografico della letteratura italiana*. Florence, 1953–69
Dizionario enciclopedico della letteratura italiana. Bari, 1966
Frattarolo, Renzo. *Bibliografia speciale della letteratura italiana*. Milan, 1959
Mazzotti, Artal, ed. *Repertorio bibliografico aggiunto ai "Contemporanei."* Milan, 1964
Renda, Umberto and Piero Operti. *Dizionario storico della letteratura italiana*, 4th ed. Turin, 1959

GENERAL WORKS

Amici, Gualtiero. *Il realismo nella letteratura da Verga a Mastronardi*. Bologna, 1963
Antonielli, Sergio. *Aspetti e figure del '900*. Parma, 1955
Bo, Carlo. *L'eredità di Giacomo Leopardi e altri saggi*. Florence, 1964
Burgio, Alfonso. *Storia della letteratura italiana*. Milan, 1968
Carsaniga, Giovanni. *Geschichte der italienischen Literatur*. Stuttgart, 1970
Cecchi, Emilio and Natalino Sapegno. *Storia della letteratura italiana*, 8 vols. Milan, 1965ff.
Falqui, Enrico. *Novecento letterario*, 9 vols. Florence, 1954–69
Flora, Francesco. *Storia della letteratura italiana*, 5 vols., 16th ed. Milan, 1969
Friedrich, Hugo. *Epochen der italienischen Lyrik*. Frankfurt, 1964

Luti, Giorgio. *Narrativa italiana dell'Ottocento e Novecento*. Florence, 1964
Mariani, Gaetano. *Poesia e tecnica nella lirica del '900*. Padua, 1958
Pompeati, Arturo. *Storia della letteratura italiana*, 4 vols., 4th ed. Turin, 1965
Pozzi, Gianni. *La poesia italiana del Novecento*. Turin, 1965
Russo, Luigi. *Compendio storico della letteratura italiana*. Messina, 1961
——. *I narratori, 1850–1950*. Milan, 1951
Sapegno, Natalino. *Compendio di storia della letteratura italiana*, 3 vols., 20th ed. Florence, 1965
Storia letteraria d'Italia, 13 vols., 8th ed. Milan, 1967
Vittorini, Domenico. *High Points in the History of Italian Literature*. New York, 1958
Whitfield, John H. *A Short History of Italian Literature*. New York, 1962
Wilkins, Ernest Hatch. *A History of Italian Literature*. Cambridge, Mass., 1954

WORKS ON CONTEMPORARY LITERATURE

Apollonio, Mario. *I contemporanei*. Brescia, 1956
Asor Rosa, Alberto. *Scrittori e popolo*. Rome, 1965
Avanguardia e neoavanguardia. Milan, 1966
Barberi Squarotti, Giorgio. *Poesia e narrativa del secondo Novecento*. Milan, 1967

Bartolucci, Giuseppe. *La scrittura scenica*. Rome, 1968

Bertracchini, Renato. *Figure e problemi di narrativa contemporanea*. Bologna, 1961

Bo, Carlo. *Inchiesta sul neorealismo*. Turin, 1951

Fernandez, Dominique. *Le roman italien et la crise de la conscience moderne*. Paris, 1958

Ferretti, Gian Carlo. *Letteratura e ideologia*. Rome, 1964

Flora, Francesco. *Scrittori italiani contemporanei*. Pisa, 1952

Giuliani, Alfredo. *Immagini e maniere*. Milan, 1965

Guazzotti, Giorgio. *Rapporto sul teatro italiano*. Milan, 1966

Guglielmi, Giorgio and Elio Pagliarani. *Manuale di poesia sperimentale*. Milan, 1966

Hinterhäuser, Hans. *Italien zwischen Schwarz und Rot*. Stuttgart, 1956

―――. *Moderne italienische Lyrik*. Göttingen, 1964

Kanduth, Erika. *Wesenszüge der modernen italienischen Erzählliteratur*. Heidelberg, 1968

Letteratura italiana: I contemporanei, 2 vols. Milan, 1963

Macrí, Oreste. *Caratteri e figure della poesia italiana contemporanea*. Florence, 1956

Manacorda, Giuliano. *Storia della letteratura italiana contemporanea*. Rome, 1967

Mariani, Gaetano. *La giovane narrativa italiana tra documento e poesia*. Florence, 1962

Michelis, Eurialo de. *Narratori antinarratori*. Florence, 1952

Muscetta, Carlo, *Realismo e controrealismo*. Milan, 1958

Pacifici, Sergio. *A Guide to Contemporary Italian Literature*. Cleveland, 1961

Pancrazi, Pietro. *Scrittori d'oggi*, 6 vols. Bari, 1946–53

Pescanti Botti, R. *Narratori e poeti d'oggi*. Milan, 1960

Petrucciani, Mario. *La poetica dell'ermetismo italiano*. Turin, 1955

Piccioni, Leone. *La narrativa italiana tra romanzo e racconti*. Milan, 1959

Pullini, Giorgio. *Il romanzo italiano del dopoguerra*. Padua, 1965

Quaderni del circolo filologico-linguistico padovano: Ricerche sulla lingua poetica contemporanea. Padua, 1966

Ramat, Silvio. *L'ermetismo*. Florence, 1969

Romano, Angelo. *Discorso degli anni cinquanta*. Milan, 1965

Russi, A. *Gli anni del antialienazione, 1943–1949*. Milan, 1966

Salinari, Carlo. *Preludio a fine del realismo in Italia*. Naples, 1967

Sanguineti, Edoardo. *Ideologia e linguaggio*. Milan, 1965

Tommaso, Piero de. *Narratori italiani contemporanei*. Rome, 1965

Trombatore, Gaetano. *Scrittori del nostro tempo*. Palermo, 1959

Vallone, Aldo. *Aspetti della poesia italiana contemporanea*. Pisa, 1960

Varese, Claudio. *Occasioni e valori della letteratura contemporanea*. Bologna, 1967

EMIR RODRÍGUEZ-MONEGAL

Latin American Literature

ONE OF THE MOST REMARKABLE literary phenomena of our time has been
the emergence of Latin American literature. This emergence has even been
reduced to a facile slogan ("the boom of the Latin American novel") and
has been hallowed by mass-circulation magazines. This new prominence of
Latin American literature is the result of the publication in recent years of
a great number of outstanding works, and is manifested in almost the
whole of Latin America, although there are probably centers of greater
concentration and quality (such as Mexico, Cuba, Brazil, and Argentina
for the novel; Chile and Venezuela for poetry; Uruguay for literary criticism). Behind the glare of publicity (which has shocked some scholars)
lies a real achievement. Today Latin America can offer a corpus of writing—from three or four generations—that is more than a collection of
isolated individual works: it constitutes a *literature*.

What is most striking is precisely the existence of a single literature, in
spite of the continent's division into countries and spheres of influence, into
differing ideologies and incompatible regimes, into divergent national
characteristics and cultural traditions originating from such contrasting
sources as native America, Renaissance Europe, and Europe of the nineteenth and twentieth centuries. An America that is, culturally speaking,
half caste; an America divided by every kind of antagonism and oppression;
an America whose exact position between the developed and underdevel-

oped worlds is still uncertain—this is the same America that has been able to produce a new, powerful literature.

With his usual lucidity, Octavio Paz (Mexico, born 1914) has observed that for a literature to exist, there must also exist certain channels of communication and dialogue that only good criticism can open. In Latin America these channels of communication are precarious because they are exposed to the ravages of cultural earthquakes. Every day, however, it becomes clearer that at certain privileged periods the region has had the critical tradition it needs. The following are some of the most important periods of critical communication: the outburst of cultural emancipation from Europe under Andrés Bello (Venezuela, 1781–1865); the dispute about romanticism and socialism centering on Domingo Faustino Sarmiento (Argentina, 1811–1888); the great wave of Spanish American modernism that followed the restless pioneering of Rubén Darío (Nicaragua, 1867–1916) and reverberated from one end of Latin America to the other, even reaching backward Spain.

Criticism in Latin America today does more than merely hand out accolades and condemnations. It helps situate the whole cultural movement and trace its underlying aims; it indicates new currents with clarity and imagination; it selects and scrutinizes new criticism from Europe and the United States. In Mexico and Montevideo, in Rio and Lima, this criticism is revealing the paths that the new creative writers are opening up, exploring, and developing.

The boldness of many of the new Latin American writers, the stubbornly experimental nature of some of their works, and the obvious youth of the most recent exponents should not make us forget that this new literature has its roots in the immediate past of Latin American culture. Far from being the outcome of chance, Latin American literature is the outcome of a general cultural development that has already been carefully studied by sociologists, economists, historians of ideas, and literary critics. Thus, since World War II we can speak of a tangible tradition of Latin American literature.

To define this tradition we must go back slightly in time and see what was happening in Latin America around 1940. I have not selected this date at random. The Spanish civil war had just ended in the triumph of General Franco and World War II had broken out, with the early victories of Hitler. The civil war forced some of the Iberian peninsula's most noted intellectuals to emigrate to Latin America (especially to Mexico and Argentina), thus stimulating Latin American culture. World War II was to have a similar effect, but for different reasons. The war either interrupted or hampered the flow of European magazines and books, which in Latin American countries had always fed the longings for a more refined level of civilization, and thus forced intellectuals to fill the void. The combination of immigration from Spain and the lack of European contacts led to founding publishing houses, magazines, cultural institutes, libraries, and museums in Latin America, and to revitalizing completely those already in existence. Most significantly, the new immigrants from Spain contributed to the "professionalization" of Latin American writers.

The year 1940 marked the beginning of what was to be a radical transformation of culture in every Latin American country during the following twenty years. Little by little, a reading public emerged, which, though at first only an elite (we well know of the millions of illiterates that Latin American culture carries on its back like a corpse, as Pablo Neruda [Chile, born 1904] has said), gradually developed into a larger group of readers. Between 1940 and today, therefore, it is possible to talk of a second and a third generation of readers. Those of the first generation were still more interested in foreign than in native writers and kept up their old loyalties not only to Spanish literature but even more to French. These were the years when a new Prix Goncourt novel was more widely read than a book by Jorge Luis Borges (Argentina, born 1899); when a novel by Graham Greene or Alberto Moravia attracted more readers than one by Miguel Ángel Asturias (Guatemala, born 1899) or Alejo Carpentier (Cuba, born 1904); when the poetry of Eliot or Valéry meant more to Brazilian readers than that of their own Manuel Bandeira (1886–1968).

But a second generation of readers was already beginning to explore native literature, as it rejected this Europhilia. This was the era of the great essayists, who chose to define *"mexicanidad"* or *"argentinidad"*; who tried to find out where lay Latin American identity; who *suffered* for the whole continent, as Unamuno *suffered* for his Spain. The third generation of readers—the present one—has little time, interest, or even curiosity for anything that is not Latin American. Only a minority today reads Saul Bellow or the latest Goncourt.

Although the Spanish émigrés stimulated Latin American culture, and although the blocking of European sources forced Latin Americans to be more producers than consumers of culture, neither change would have been possible without the demographic migrations that in twenty years swelled the population of all the major cities. The influx to urban centers from rural areas also increased, if only relatively, the number of people going on to secondary education. The second- and third-generation readers, products of this demographic shift, have reflected it in being much more conscious of Latin America. They form a group which is almost without European traditions, which speaks and writes mainly in the national languages (Spanish or Portuguese), and which is primarily interested in things that concern its world. For this new wave of readers, the native author holds the key to the problems that beset them. Therefore, they regard him as a collaborator and demand total commitment from him.

THE ESSAY

Curiously, it was not in the novel (as one might suppose) that this close communion between Latin American authors and readers was prepared. It is true that the novel contributed a good deal to the popularization of certain problems and themes of great interest either to a particular country or to all of Latin America. But the important preparatory work was carried out mainly in two other genres—the essay and the lyric poem—which reached a smaller public but had widespread impact. A heightening of Latin American consciousness (very evident in Mexico after its revolution and in Cuba since Castro) found its first major literary outpouring in the work of essayists, who threw themselves into a dual exploration of separate national characters and of the Latin American image as a whole.

Bello, Sarmiento, José Martí (Cuba, 1853–1895), and Euclides da Cunha (Brazil, 1866–1909) were all precursors of the contemporary Latin American essayists. But the most influential figure was José Enrique Rodó (Uruguay, 1871–1917), who initiated in his *Ariel* (1900, Ariel) the essay of elevated style and supranational (that is, Latin American) vision. Published immediately after the Spanish-American War, *Ariel* was widely read as a vindication of Latin American spirit and tradition against the materialism of Anglo-Saxon power. Very few readers realized then that *Ariel* was also a blueprint for the New Man, a subject Rodó later developed in all its ethical and aesthetic implications in his *Motivos de Proteo* (1909, The Motives of Proteus).

The exploration of Latin American consciousness Rodó began so successfully slowly emerged from a purgatory of good international intentions to become—in the work of some of his disciples and critics—a small but fascinating corpus of lively, polemical, and outspoken essays. Writers like Pedro Henríquez Ureña (Dominican Republic, 1884–1946) and Alfonso Reyes (Mexico, 1889–1959) took Rodó's message several steps further and produced some very valuable interpretations of Latin American culture. In works like Henríquez Ureña's *Seis ensayos en busca de nuestra expresión* (1926, Six Essays in Search of Our Expression) and *Las corrientes literarias en la América hispánica* (1949, Literary Currents in Hispanic America), and Reyes's *Visión de Anáhuac* (1917, Vision of Anahuac) and *La experiencia literaria* (1942, The Literary Experience), one can recognize not only Rodó's basic preoccupations but a more complete awareness of all the threads that compose the Latin American cultural fabric.

Essayists like José Carlos Mariátegui (Peru, 1891–1930) and Ezequiel Martínez Estrada (Argentina, 1895–1964) used techniques and points of view that went far beyond Rodó. In Mariátegui's *Siete ensayos de interpretación de la realidad peruana* (1928, Seven Essays on the Interpretation of Peruvian Reality) a pervasive Marxist point of view introduced a complete new set of references to Latin America. Martínez Estrada's important books included *Radiografía de la Pampa* (1933, X-Ray of the Pampa) and *La cabeza de Goliat* (1940, Goliath's Head), a symbolic, almost psychoanalytical, approach to Argentina's realities. These works explored the hidden and dark sides of Argentine life.

An exploration similar to Martínez Estrada's was carried out for Mexico by Octavio Paz, in a less apocalyptical style and with a surer poetic diction. In Paz's successful *El laberinto de la soledad* (1950, The Labyrinth of Solitude) the gods and demons of a country tortured by the clash of several cultures were exposed in lucid prose. In Brazil Gilberto Freyre (born 1900) explored the roots of the sugar-cane culture in a trilogy of socio-poetical works: *Casa grande e senzala* (1933, The Mansions and the Shanties), *Sobrados e mucambos* (1936, The Masters and the Slaves), and *Nordeste* (1937, Northeast). Freyre's more recent works, in which he tried to vindicate the Portuguese heritage, were less relevant.

These are some of the masters who began to explore traditions and made searching analyses of all aspects of their worlds, including the least visible. Their work of construction and destruction was aimed not only at their countries of origin but also at the contradictions and hopes of all of Latin America. These essayists were the true founders of the new Latin American literature.

The work of these writers and of many of their colleagues, who have carried on or refuted their theories, helped the second-generation readers to discover a supranational identity that the colonial powers denied them— and still continue to deny them. To be accepted in Europe or the United States as a true Latin American writer, one had to write folklore. Even today, worthy institutions survive (the Swedish Academy among others) that think Asturias more Latin American than Borges. It is as if Katherine Mansfield could only be accepted if she wrote about the Maoris; or Ezra Pound, about the Cherokees. That Borges is multilingual and cosmopolitan only reflects the way of life of the city in which he was born and in which he has written his most authentic work—Buenos Aires, a city almost as multilingual and cosmopolitan as New York. It is precisely *through* the contradictions of Borges's situation that the literature of the Río de la Plata region (not only Buenos Aires) learned to discover and accept its mixed identity.

For the present generation of readers, the search for identity is no longer a problem but a form of self-recognition. One cannot ask them now what was asked of so many Latin Americans for ages: But what is a Latin American? (It is easy to find in this question an echo of the famous one in Montesquieu's *Lettres persanes: "Mais comment peut-on être persan?"*) Latin Americans have discovered that the solution to the problem of national or Latin American identity cannot be established from the outside but must come from within and take the form of a search. In the work of the essayists the search has already been fruitful.

POETRY

Poets have also made a notable contribution to the search and discovery of a Latin American identity. Some of the best of those who started to publish in the early 1920s had to fight against the work left by the brilliant generation of the turn of the century—a generation called *modernista* in Spanish America and *parnasiana* in Brazil. Reacting against the verbal excesses of this generation, the poets of the 1920s turned their verse to less externally brilliant, more personal and more anguished statements. At the same time, they reacted against much of the decadent and cosmopolitan themes of the turn-of-the-century poets, and looked to the actualities of life, to an aggressively "modern" vision of the world, to a purely experimental use of diction and rhythms. They were in touch (directly or through books and magazines) with the European avant-garde movements: futurism, dada, surrealism, to name a few. Some even traveled to France and Spain to participate in the revolution in poetry.

Both Vicente Huidobro (Chile, 1893–1948) and Jorge Luis Borges were involved in the activities of the advanced European groups. Huidobro contributed poems and manifestoes to magazines edited by Apollinaire and the surrealists. He wrote some *"calligrammes"* in French. Returning to his native Chile via Spain, he helped to propagate the new poetry there. Borges met Huidobro in Spain and almost immediately became one of the most active members of the futurist movement, called "ultraism" in Spain and Spanish America. To the group he contributed his firsthand knowledge of the German expressionist poets (he was in Geneva during World War I) and a talent for organizing and defining aesthetic matters.

Back in their native countries, both Huidobro and Borges gathered around them a group of young poets and started to preach the new credo. Huidobro's action helped to develop surrealism in Chile and paved the way for several groups of outstanding poets in the years to come. In Argentina Borges started, almost singlehandedly, a new version of ultraism, less concerned with actuality, or futurity, more interested in basic themes and feelings, simple diction, colloquial tone. The influence of Macedonio Fernández (Argentina, 1874–1952), an old friend of Borges's father and a very unusual writer, channeled Borges's poetry to a search for identity, for the "real" Buenos Aires beneath the layers of foreign modes and manners, for a usable past, for a more private speech.

Although Borges soon turned against the ultraists and became a completely individual poet, more classical than romantic in his diction, and although later on he devoted his main efforts to the short story and the critical essay, his experience among the avant-garde groups left a mark on his work. The same can be said of Huidobro. He found his own voice in a verse several times removed from the rather frivolous *calligrammes* of his Parisian phase. In *Altazor* (1931, Altazor), for instance, the playing with words, even with phonemes, is not only a mere playing; it is also an undisguised way of expressing the anguish of the central character, and of the poet, both hanging from an invisible parachute over the void of reality. Huidobro's experiments with language had an enormous influence not only on the younger poets but on many later essayists and novelists.

Two other poets, who contributed notably to the avant-garde movements but were not associated directly with them, had a lasting influence on younger poets. Both Gabriela Mistral (Chile, 1889–1957) and César Vallejo (Peru, 1892–1938) were highly experimental. Mistral's *Desolación* (1922, Desolation) and *Tala* (1938, The Cutting of Trees) broke completely from modernist diction and ornamental verse. Instead, she favored a hard and sometimes harsh, spare, almost abrupt style, which seemed to link her poetry to the Spanish classics and the early Spanish version of the Bible. Deliberately out of fashion, completely personal, Mistral's poetry nevertheless became extremely popular; even before the Nobel Prize was awarded to her in 1945, her audience in Latin America was enormous. During her lifetime she was the object of a personal cult that has had no parallel in modern Latin American poetry.

Vallejo's contribution was similar. Although some of his earlier books can be linked to the avant-garde movement, and *Trilce* (1922, the title is an invented word, probably coined from *tris*te [sad] and du*lce* [sweet]) was one of the best examples of Latin American experimentalism, Vallejo's later poetry was more than a stylistic tour de force. In *Poemas humanos* (1939, Human Poems) and *España, aparta de mí este cáliz* (1939, Spain, Take Away this Cup from Me) Vallejo's relentless fight with his human condition, with his hunger, and with God, injustice, fascism, and brutality was so poignantly stated that the "message" tended to make invisible the consummate artistry. Since his death, Vallejo's popularity in Latin America has continued to grow.

In Brazil the reaction against Parnassianism was called *modernismo*. But this movement has nothing to do with Spanish American modernism; it is instead the equivalent of Argentine ultraism or Chilean surrealism. Brazilian modernism sought to free the literature of the country from the obsolete turn-of-the-century rhetoric. Although the movement started officially in São Paulo in 1922, with a Semana de Arte Moderna, and was sponsored almost immediately by all the young poets and novelists, it was more than a coordinated effort to bring Brazilian letters up to date: it was, more profoundly, a movement that set deliberately to discover the essence of being Brazilian. That is why the theoretical work of some of its members (like Mário de Andrade [1893–1945]) was even more important than the poetry. In books like *Paulicéia desvairada* (1922, A Hallucinated Song to São Paulo), or in his only novel, *Macunaíma* (1928, Macunaíma), Andrade wrote what he had preached, giving a concrete example of what the new literature ought to be.

Less gifted as theoreticians, but more creative, were two of the most outstanding Brazilian modernist poets, Manuel Bandeira and Carlos Drummond de Andrade (born 1902). Bandeira began as a post-Parnassian poet but soon was influenced by the Brazilian modernist movement. As early as in the second edition of his *Poesias completas* (1924, Complete Poetry), the poet took leave of his former self. With *Libertinagem* (1930, Libertinism), he entered into the modernist movement. The third edition of his *Complete Poetry* (1944) revealed him as one of the most important poets of his time.

His only rival, Drummond de Andrade, had already been established as a modernist poet by the publication of his first volume, *Alguma poesia* (1930, Some Poetry), but not until he published *Sentimento do mundo* (1940, A Feeling for the World) and subsequent collections of poems did Drummond de Andrade discover a way out of modernism, toward a simpler, almost colloquial poetry, a poetry deeply aware of the political and social context of man's predicament. His work has had a persistent influence on the work of younger poets.

The Brazilian modernists, as well as the Argentine ultraists and the Chilean surrealists, were simultaneously exploring new forms of poetry and discovering the reality of their own countries. But none of these poets carried out that exploration and discovery with more vitality and passion, and to a greater extent, than did Pablo Neruda, one of the world's greatest living poets. Very precocious, he started writing at the time the turn-of-the-century poets were still widely read in Chile. But he was soon to shift from the sentimental postmodernism of *Veinte poemas de amor y una canción desesperada* (1924, Twenty Love Poems and a Song of Despair) —a brilliant but dated sequence—to the Huidobrian *Tentativa del hombre infinito* (1925, Tentative of the Infinite Man) and to the highly personal and wildly experimental surrealism of *Residencia en la tierra* (1935, Residence on Earth).

Comprehending the poetry of *Residence on Earth* necessitates imagining an incredible conglomeration of the visions of Blake and the Eliot of *The Waste Land,* of Rimbaud and Walt Whitman. Written mainly when the poet was living in the far east, this book recounts Neruda's "season in hell" (to borrow a phrase from Rimbaud). Its publication in Spain, on the eve of the civil war, established Latin American leadership in Spanish poetry as unmistakably as when, more than three decades before, Rubén Darío arrived in Spain.

The Spanish civil war brutally awoke Neruda's political consciousness. He became an activist poet: words were his weapons. He wrote *España en el corazón* (1937, Spain of the Heart) and started to address the reader, the common people, directly. Of all the work he produced in this vein, the best was undoubtedly *Canto general* (1950, General Song), an epicolyrical poem in which he attempted to describe Latin America, to tell its history, to denounce the local and international villains who kept Latin America in chains. At the same time, he portrayed himself, told of his life and loves, made an inventory of the world he loved.

General Song was in the vein of much poetry already written by the romantics and modernists (Bello, Heredia, Chocano, and Darío can be mentioned as forerunners). It showed Neruda at his best—in the sequence called *Alturas de Macchu Picchu* (Heights of Macchu Picchu) or in *Mollusca gongorina,* in which he described his wonderful collection of shells. It showed him at his most ferocious—in his eloquent diatribe against United States imperialism in the Caribbean. It also showed him at his worst—in some very naïve retellings of Latin American history or in his purely political attacks on personalities of the day. But *General Song* was greater than the sum of its strengths and weaknesses, and it has been enormously influential in creating a Latin American consciousness. Indeed, the only book of poetry Che Guevara carried with him to Bolivia was *General Song.*

Since *General Song,* Neruda has tried to recover the private voice without entirely renouncing the public one. In some of his *Odas elementales* (1954–59, four volumes; Elementary Odes) but mainly in *Estravagario* (1958, Strange Vagaries) and in *Memorial de Isla Negra* (1964, Isla Negra's Memoirs) he achieved a balance between both voices and also managed to develop a comic, and even ironic, diction that was suggested in some of his earlier books but was almost submerged under the anguished utterances or the earnest preaching. Today Neruda goes on writing. His work is undoubtedly the most important in Latin American letters of this century, as has been recognized (rather belatedly) even by the Swedish Academy in awarding him the 1971 Nobel Prize.

In many respects, all the poets who came after Neruda had to establish themselves against his powerful personality. Some became pale facsimiles of the master; some reacted strongly against him but could not create a poetry of their own. The best found their own paths and are still exploring them to their limits. Perhaps the two most individual poets of the post-Nerudian era are Nicanor Parra and Octavio Paz, both born in 1914, ten years after Neruda. Being a Chilean, it was harder for Parra than for Paz to cast off the master's influence. Somehow his poetic inspiration survived, and around 1950 he found his own voice.

A collection of *Poemas y antipoemas* (1954, Poems and Antipoems) quickly established Parra as one of the most original poets of Latin America. Witty and brutal (with the superficial cynicism of a very sentimental person), but also compassionate and lucid, Parra can be best understood if one remembers his two years' stay in Oxford (1949–51) and his apprenticeship in the Auden-MacNeice school of poetry. What Parra discovered in British (and later American) poetry was his own self: a voice that cuts to the bone, a search that stops at nothing, not even love or death or political fallacies. Parra's humor is related to the blackest of Neruda's in *Residence on Earth* but he has developed it, slowly and consistently, to a point that only Quevedo reached in Spanish letters. His subsequent collections—*Versos de salon* (1960, Parlor Verses), *Canciones rusas* (1966, Russian Songs), *Artefactos* (1967, Artifacts)—confirmed and even expanded this tragic and ironic vein.

Octavio Paz's poetry evolved slowly from the overwhelming influence of older poets (in Spain, Latin America, and France) to reach in *Libertad bajo palabra* (1949, Freedom under Parole) a first maturity. But only in *Piedra de sol* (1958, Sun Stone) and *La estación violenta* (1958, Violent Season) did he become completely aware of the liberating forces inside his own poetry. His philosophic mind has been explicit in his prose works: essays like *The Labyrinth of Solitude,* the investigations of the essence of poetry in *El arco y la lira* (1956, The Bow and the Lyre) and *Los signos en rotación* (1965, The Signs in Rotation,) the literary and aesthetic criticism in *Cuadrivio* (1965, Crossroads) and *Conjunciones y disyunciones* (1969, Conjunctions and Disjunctions). Paz's philosophic bent has limited the sensuous scope of his poetry, but it has allowed him to explore regions of the mind that Neruda has left untouched.

In Paz's most recent poetry, from *Salamandra* (1962, Salamander) to *Discos visuales* (1968, Visual Disks) and *Ladera este* (1969, East Slope), his long sojourn in India and the discovery of eastern philosophies have been harmoniously blended with the visual and spatial experimentations of concrete poetry to establish a new concept of poetical space (that is, the space occupied by the poetical signs). The result is a poetry that is not only more concrete and passionate but also more deeply philosophical. Today Paz is the acknowledged master of younger poets and critics. The lucidity of his thought in both prose and poetry, the incantatory quality of his expression, the independence of his political attitudes—all have contributed to making him a deeply influential figure.

Younger poets have had to establish themselves against Neruda, on the one hand, and Parra and Paz, on the other. Some have followed the Nerudian path, adding new insights to the ones discovered by the master. The most successful has perhaps been Ernesto Cardenal (Nicaragua, born 1925), a poet and a priest who has managed to sing, almost simultaneously, in praise of Marilyn Monroe and against genocide and the atomic bomb, without losing contact with the realities (past and present) of Latin America.

In a more colloquial vein, which has coincided with Parra's (although it was developed independently), César Fernández Moreno (Argentina, born 1919) found his original voice rather late in his career. In *Argentino hasta la muerte* (1963, Argentine until Death) and *Los aeropuertos* (1967, The Airports), he rediscovered a lyrical path to a narrative poetry: he has been both extremely autobiographical and at the same time evocative of the whole Argentine reality.

In a different vein, more reminiscent of Vallejo's anguished poems, Idea Vilarino (Uruguay, born 1920) has sung of the ravages of love and illness, the nearness of death, the horror of being alive. Her sequence of slim volumes has contained some of the best poetry written in Latin America: *La suplicante* (1945, The Supplicant), *Cielo cielo* (1947, Heaven Heaven), *Paraíso perdido* (1949, Paradise Lost), *Nocturnos* (1955, Nocturnes), and *Poemas de amor* (1958, Love Poems).

Brazilian poetry evolved from the modernist movement to a more direct and colloquial, yet still poetical, speech in the work of João Cabral de Melo Neto (born 1920), the most original Brazilian poet of his generation. Irony, pity, a tragic sense of life, and a decidedly antipoetical poetry have made Melo Neto the Brazilian counterpart of Nicanor Parra. But he is also deeply rooted in his native folklore, and one of his most striking works, a dramatic poem called *Morte e vida Severina* (1956, The Death and Life of Severino) showed a commingling of Brecht's epic theater with the popular songs of the northeast of Brazil. In this very short work Melo Neto achieved a synthesis of the major themes and motifs of the Brazilian epics and novels of that ravaged part of land. Melo Neto is, of course, much more than a modern version of the folklorist poets of the nineteenth century. The range of his work can best be seen in his *Poesias completas* (1968, Complete Poetry).

In recent years, the poetic output of Latin America has been enormous. Some of the most significant poets are: José Lezama Lima (Cuba, born 1910), Sara de Ibáñez (Uruguay, 1909–1971), Jorge Gaitán Duran (Colombia, 1924–1962), Enrique Lihn (Chile, born 1929), Alvaro Mutis (Colombia, born 1923), Carlos Germán Belli (Peru, born 1927), Guillermo Sucre (Venezuela, born 1933), Jorge Teillier (Chile, born 1935), José Emilio Pacheco (Mexico, born 1939), Homero Aridjis (Mexico, born 1930). Instead of presenting a catalogue of the major works of these poets, I would rather discuss two movements that have had impact on today's poetry, inside and outside Latin America.

The concrete poetry movement started almost simultaneously all around the world but has been particularly important in Brazil, where Décio Pignatari (born 1927), Haroldo de Campos (born 1929), and Augusto de Campos (born 1931) formed the Noigandres group under the inspiration of Pound, Cummings, and Apollinaire. The group's purpose was to develop a visual and spatial poetry that could find a witty balance between the poster and the traditional printed page—a poetry that is both graphic and aural, a sign on the page and a sound in the air. Although the Noigandres group did not discover Huidobro's experiments until quite recently, a link between these Brazilian poets and new directions in Spanish American poetry was established through an acquaintance with Octavio Paz's experiments with space in *Blanco* (1967, White) and *Visual Disks*.

The other important contemporary movement is in the revolutionary and guerrilla poetry of the 1960s. Gaining strength from the Cuban revolution, and initially based there, revolutionary poetry in Latin America could claim Neruda's and Vallejo's poems about the Spanish civil war as its most decisive models. The present political situation of Latin America and the inspiration of figures like Che Guevara (Argentina, 1928–1967), who also left some narrative prose and several love poems in the style of Neruda, helped consolidate a movement of didactic and political poetry that has already produced some very interesting works.

The conflicts and hopes of being a revolutionary poet have perhaps been better presented in Cuba than anywhere else, as in the work of Pablo Armando Fernández (born 1930) and Heberto Padilla (born 1932). Padilla expressed in his *Fuera del juego* (1967, Out of the Game) the conflict of a poet who wants to help the revolution but cannot avoid being critical about it. (This predicament was also faced by the Russian poets of the 1930s.) The most original writer of this kind of committed poetry was Javier Héraud (1942–1963), a young Peruvian killed in guerrilla fighting, who anticipated in the poems of *El río* (1963, The River) his tragic destiny. With these poets the mission the older poets set for themselves—to sing of Latin America—has also become a challenge to action. Words are no longer enough.

THE DRAMA

Very little need be said in a brief survey such as this about Latin American drama. Sporadically present in the great cities, with sudden spurts of life, drama in Latin America is still to reach the level of the other genres. Many factors contribute to its underdevelopment. Although at the turn of the century the bourgeoisie supported the theater, the literary quality of the plays was very low, with some rare exceptions, like the plays of Florencio Sánchez (Uruguay, 1875–1910). The best theater either was armchair theater or had such an experimental quality that it appealed only to a minority.

More recently, the revolutionary movements in all Latin American countries have labored earnestly to create a political theater. They have thus far only produced plays that are either dramatically uninteresting or purely derivative from the Brechtian or the Jan Kott-Grotowski-Peter Brook formula. These plays have political importance for contemporary Latin America, but they have little literary value. Besides, they are clearly inferior to the work produced for the cinema by the same group of agitprop talents. Dramatic literature in Latin America has not yet reached a genuinely creative stage. The liberating forces of the region have found expression mainly in poetry, in the essay, and especially in the novel.

THE NOVEL

The sociopolitical life of Latin America since World War II, which undoubtedly encouraged the essay and lyric poetry, was, above all, grist to the mill of the new novel. Changes in Latin American life provided the three requisites for the novel to flourish: large urban concentrations, a permanent group of readers, and a wide distribution of books. The rise of the novel in Europe and the United States was associated with the rise of the bourgeoisie. In Latin America novels or semifictional narratives were written during the colonial period, and a number of outstanding novelists emerged during the second half of the nineteenth century: Alberto Blest Gana (Chile, 1830–1920), Joaquim Machado de Assis (Brazil, 1839–1908), and Eduardo Acevedo Díaz (Uruguay, 1851–1921). But one cannot really speak of a complete genre, with authors writing on many levels and creating a sustained oeuvre, until this century. And in the most professional sense of the word, the novel has only existed from 1940, a year that has been chosen as a symbolic date and should not be taken too literally.

When the novelist of the 1940s began to write, he could draw not only on the recent tradition of the rural novel in Latin America and on a few isolated examples of the urban novel but also on something more important. Through translation, and through re-creations by writers of the stature of Alfonso Reyes and Jorge Luis Borges, he could draw on the principal European and American novels of this century. And though it is important to avoid thinking that the new novelists had no Latin American predecessors, one should not fall into the trap of forgetting that the new Latin American novel owes much to Joyce, Kafka, Faulkner, and Sartre, to name a few. All that these foreign novelists of the first forty years of the century had achieved was exploited by those Latin American novelists who began to write and publish after 1940. European and American novels, a rich and universally available source for the Latin American novel, were read and reread, translated, commented on, and even plagiarized—from one end of Latin America to the other. They became a permanent source of literary inspiration.

But the creators of the new novel not only read Kafka and Faulkner. With effort, often with enormous difficulty, they absorbed the writings of their fellow Latin Americans, and slowly, from Argentina to Mexico, they got to know one another. This process, at first very slow, has been accelerated to the point where one can speak of an international language in the Latin American novel. There are strong links binding all the best-known writers today, not only those who belong to the clannish political and intellectual coteries. Thus, the process that began in 1940 has culminated in full literary contact. This new unity has been encouraged equally by foreign influence (both positive and negative) and by an awareness of the reality, the consciousness, and the mission of Latin America. The outcome has been the new Latin American novel, with a language that now burns a path from one end to the other of the Iberian-speaking world. The importance of contemporary Latin American literature can best be understood through the flowering of the novel.

In the works of novelists who established themselves before 1940, Latin American nature and Latin American landscape so dominated man, so crushed or molded him, that the human being almost disappeared or was reduced to an archetype, a symbol, not a complex character. The character Demetrio Macías in *Los de abajo* (1916, The Underdogs), by Mariano Azuela (Mexico, 1873–1952), was only a piece in a landscape ravaged by the Mexican revolution. The title character of Ricardo Güiraldes's (Argentina, 1886–1927) *Don Segundo Sombra* (1926, Don Segundo Sombra) was less an individual gaucho than the prototype of all gauchos, that is, a shadow—as his name in Spanish points out. Both Arturo Cova in *La vorágine* (1924, The Vortex) by José Eustasio Rivera (Colombia, 1888–1928), and Santos Luzardo in *Doña Bárbara* (1929, Doña Bárbara) by Rómulo Gallegos (Venezuela, 1884–1969), have to face the jungle or the *sabana* and fight for their very lives. In Gallegos's novel, nature is personified in the symbolic figure of a woman who gives the book its title. In Rivera's *The Vortex* the Amazonian jungle is lyrically addressed by the protagonist several times. Even in the work of a more sophisticated novelist like Graciliano Ramos (Brazil, 1892–1953), nature overwhelms the characters almost completely, as in his *Vidas sêcas* (1938, Barren

Lives). The same power of nature can be seen in *O quinze* (1930, The Year 1915), by Rachel de Queiróz (Brazil, born 1910), which concerned one of Brazil's worst draughts.

In these and similar novels the rendering of human conflicts was generalized; man was anonymous. Abstract economic and social forces—particularly the political power and aspirations of the ruling classes—were pitted against the disinherited and oppressed of the Andes, the Amazonian forest, the Argentine pampas, the arid northeast of Brazil. The individual was reduced to a cipher in an inhospitable universe. Geography was everything, man nothing.

For Latin American novelists writing since 1940, the center of gravity has shifted radically—from a rural landscape created by God to an urban landscape created by man and inhabited by men. The pampas and the cordillera have yielded to the great city. For earlier novelists, the city was no more than a remote presence, arbitrary and mysterious; for the new writers the city has been the axis, the place to which the protagonist of the new novel is drawn, inevitably. Suddenly, powerful fictional beings are emerging from the anonymous masses of the great cities.

This dramatic change (corresponding sociologically to the growth of large metropolitan areas, but also reflecting the spreading influence of psychoanalysis, Marxism, and existentialism) has also influenced novelists who have stuck largely to rural themes. Even if superficially these writers still record the traditional struggle of man against nature, the characters they now present are no longer abstractions to justify some political and sociological theory. They are complex and ambiguous characters who resemble real people.

We have apparently seen the end of epics about campesinos and gauchos—with their two-dimensional characterization, their all-too-mechanical "documentary" structure. Because the cities now monopolize the attention of the younger novelists, when they turn their attention to the landscape, they do so mainly to reveal the mythical side of Latin America. A new concept of man is emerging from the chaos and revolutions, the coups d'état and the forced underdevelopment. And the Latin American novelists are, willingly or not, the prophets of this new man.

They are also the creators of a new language of the novel. When I talk about the language in this context, I do not mean exclusively the use of peculiar or experimental language. In literature language is not synonymous with the general system of speech; rather, it is the tongue a certain genre or a certain writer uses. The language of the new Latin American novel is derived from the skills and techniques with which the new novelists have tried to achieve a deep vision of their environments, a vision that owes a great deal to the skills and techniques developed by poets and essayists. Perhaps because of this common fund—that is, the work of all the great Latin American writers—the new novel is not only the most complete poetic vehicle for the exploration of reality; it is also the richest literary form with which to transmit to the reader that other parallel reality —the reality of words, that is, of language.

In the history of the new Latin American novel, what first attracts the attention is the coexistence, within the same literary space, of at least four generations of writers. These four generations could easily be compartmentalized, but, in the process of literary creation, they share the same world, dispute over fragments of the same reality, explore unknown avenues of language, or share and exchange experiences, techniques, secrets of the craft.

The method of organizing writers into generations has had distinguished exponents in Germany and Spain and has been applied to Latin American literature more than once. But I would like to stress the pragmatic reasons for such a classification rather than its merely mechanical convenience, which may look artificial. The several generations, often confronted in separate sections of a textbook as different extremes, frequently share the same space and the same time, influence each other more than is at first apparent, and seem to contradict the orderly flux of time.

Besides, to belong to the same generation is no guarantee of a shared vision and language. It is impossible not to realize that the Peruvian novelist Ciro Alegría (1908–1967) and the Uruguayan novelist Juan Carlos Onetti (born 1909) were born within months of each other. Yet, on one hand, Alegría was the last of the great rural novelists of Latin America, and his masterpiece, *El mundo es ancho y ajeno* (1941, Broad and Alien Is the World), exemplified the virtues and defects of the narratives of the 1920s and 1930s. Onetti, on the other hand, was a forerunner of the experimental novelists who have focused their vision mainly on the alienation of the city dweller. The great differences between Alegría and Onetti are obvious. Yet in 1941 both competed for the same international prize, and Alegría won.

Because of such lacks of correlation between when a writer lived and how he wrote, it is probably better to refer to groups than to generations. If I do use the word "generation," it is not to force writers into pigeonholes. Indeed, all of the more original new novelists of Latin America have escaped, rather than have belonged to, their own generation.

Some writers have been decisive in the creation of the new novel. Among the many innovators, the work of four has had a lasting influence: Miguel Ángel Asturias, Jorge Luis Borges, Leopoldo Marechal (Argentina, 1900–1970), and Alejo Carpentier. Although Borges has written no novels (except a detective novel in collaboration with Adolfo Bioy Casares [Argentina, born 1914], published under a pseudonym), it seems to me impossible to attempt any serious analysis of the genre in Latin America without studying his remarkably innovative short stories. Collected under several titles—*Historia universal de la infamia* (1935, The Universal History of Infamy), *Ficciones* (1944, Fictions), *El Aleph* (1949, The Aleph), and, more recently, *El informe de Brodie* (1970, Brodie's Report)— Borges's short fiction has influenced not only the practitioners of that form but the general style and vision of the novelists as well.

Explicitly or implicitly, the works of Asturias, Borges, Marechal, and Carpentier carried a critique of earlier novelists. Surveying the impassioned testimony of reality found in the best work of Gallegos, Rivera, Güiraldes, and others, the new novelists pointed out the obsolete rhetoric that masked the essential truth of the older novels. But they did more than criticize earlier novels or deny their validity; more importantly, they searched for other ways out. It is no coincidence that their work was so strongly influenced by the avant-garde writers who in Europe were able to go beyond the heritage of naturalism. In Geneva, as a youth, Borges became familiar with German expressionism and the works of Joyce and Kafka. Some years later, Carpentier, Asturias, and Marechal avidly read the brilliant work of the French surrealists.

From the hands of these founders, Latin American fiction emerged deeply transformed, not only in appearance but also in essence. More than anything, these writers brought new visions of Latin America and new concepts of language. This is not generally acknowledged of Borges's work, which still suffers from the accusation of "cosmopolitanism," although he is very Argentine. Changes in vision and language are evident enough, however, in the work of the other three writers of fiction. Asturias's novels have generally combined the language and the imagery of the Mayan people of Guatemala with the narrative approach of the protest novel of the 1920s and 1930s. A good example of Asturias's work is a trilogy in which he denounced the exploitation of his native land by the big international interests: *Viento fuerte* (1950, Strong Wind), *El Papa verde* (1954, The Green Pope), and *Los ojos de los enterrados* (1960, The Eyes of the Buried). The best parts of these novels are the re-creations of the myths of his own people. Asturias's masterpiece, *Hombres de maíz* (1949, Men of Maize), retold in a contemporary context some of the stories from ancient sources, like the Popol Vuh, the sacred book of the Mayans.

The intention to discover what it means to be Argentine is obvious in the title of Marechal's first novel, called *Adán Buenosayres* (1948, Adam Buenosayres). In this novel he explored his native city and reproduced it in an allegory that owed its inspiration to writers as disparate as Dante, Quevedo, and Joyce. The real value of this book lies not in its too obvious intentions but in the use of colloquial speech (*"lunfardo"*) to transmit his vision of man.

In Carpentier's novels the entire Caribbean world, not only his own

Cuba, has been transformed by a poetic vision of the past (*El reino de este mundo* [1949, The Kingdom of This World], *El acoso* [1955, The Chase], *El siglo de las luces* [1962, The Century of Lights]); the present (*Los pasos perdidos* [1953, The Lost Steps]); and even a time without a time (*Guerra del tiempo* [1958, War of Time]).

In Brazil, almost singlehandedly, Mário de Andrade created in *Macunaíma* the prototype of the mythopoetic narrative, which was to be so popular two decades later. Using most of the major motifs of Brazilian folklore, and experimenting with language on a Joycean scale, Andrade drastically changed the order of importance of the elements in narrative. At a time when the best Brazilian novelists were still writing principally naturalistic novels and novels of protest, Andrade presented an alternative.

Whether intentionally or not, these writers effected in their first books such a complete and deep break with the traditional language and vision of Gallegos, Rivera, and Ramos that the older writers lost their progeny. Although when these pioneering new books were published, only a few realized their importance, those few have become the important reading public of today.

The change brought about by this first group of new novelists took place almost simultaneously with the emergence of the next generation, which included João Guimarães Rosa (Brazil, 1908–1967), Juan Carlos Onetti, José Lezama Lima, Ernesto Sábato (Argentina, born 1911), José María Arguedas (Peru, 1913–1969), Julio Cortázar (Argentina, born 1914), and Juan Rulfo (Mexico, born 1918). Although these writers have much in common, the work of each one has been deeply personal and unmistakably his own. Nevertheless, it is interesting to begin by pointing out ways in which they are alike.

In the first place, they showed traces of the previous generation. For example, how could Cortázar's *Rayuela* (1963, Hopscotch)—that supremely Argentine novel hidden under thick layers of French patina—have existed without Borges's short stories and parodies, Roberto Arlt's (Argentina, 1900–1942) novels and grotesques, Marechal's *Adam Buenosayres,* and Onetti's explorations of the dark side of sex? Cortázar, in fact, has not hesitated to acknowledge his debt to these and other writers and sometimes has done it in the novel itself—in the notes of his fictional alter ego, the ubiquitous Morelli; or in a few discrete homages in the form of episodes originally used by Marechal and Onetti.

Another thing these writers of the second generation have in common is the influence of foreign writers and movements, such as Faulkner, Proust, Joyce, the surrealist poets, the French existentialists. There are some odd anecdotes about this influence. Guimarães Rosa, for instance, has always denied that Faulkner interested him. He once told a critic that the very few Faulkner works he had read displeased him, that Faulkner's sexual attitude seemed morbid to him, that Faulkner was a sadist. Yet in the magnificent *Grande Sertão: Veredas* (1956, Big Desert: Small Paths), his only novel, Faulkner's presence—in the way of writing an intense interior monologue, in the passionate, mythical vision of a rural universe—was unmistakable. It is easy to explain, however, the seeming contradiction between his own novel and his statements about Faulkner. One does not necessarily even have to have read Faulkner to be influenced by him. Faulkner may have affected Rosa almost accidentally, by way of writers like Sartre, who certainly did learn from the great American novelist and whose influence Rosa has acknowledged.

But it is not these influences, which most writers have acknowledged, that best define this group. It is rather a common conception of the novel, no matter what the differences in writing are. If their immediate forerunners did little to innovate the external structure of the novel and were generally satisfied to follow traditional form (perhaps only *Men of Maize* and *Adam Buenosayres* tried to use time and place more complexly), the work of this second group—with very few exceptions—has attacked the very form of the novel. Indeed, this attack has been its greatest preoccupation.

Guimarães Rosa found in the interminable lyric and narrative monologues of the traditional oral poets of Brazil's backlands the shape for his sweeping novel. Onetti, on the other hand, created a Río de la Plata universe, dreamlike yet real, in a sequence of novels that was very personal despite the original debt to Faulkner's Yoknapatawpha County. These novels could be gathered under the general title, "The Saga of Santa María." The best have been *La vida breve* (1950, The Short Life), *Los adioses* (1954, The Farewells), *Para una tumba sin nombre* (1959, For a Nameless Tomb), *El astillero* (1961, The Shipyard), and *Juntacadáveres* (1964, The Body Snatcher). In some of these novels, especially in the last two, Onetti carried the construction of his narrative to the most subtle extremes of sophistication, creating a frighteningly ironic literary reproduction of the Río de la Plata area.

A kinship of interests can be seen between Onetti's world and that of Ernesto Sábato, especially in Sábato's masterpiece, *Sobre héroes y tumbas* (1961, On Heroes and Tombs). This novel, Sábato's only long one (a previous one, *El tunél* [1948, The Tunnel], was really a novella), tried to encompass in a very complex and seemingly disorganized structure three stories that coexist in time and space only because they are in the same novel. By switching back and forth from the revolutionary past of the main character's ancestors to present-day Argentina, or to Paris in the 1930s, Sábato created a poetic structure that in many ways linked Borges's experiments to Cortazar's *Hopscotch*.

Juan Rulfo's *Pedro Páramo* (1955, Pedro Páramo), the only novel he has published so far, was a paradigm of the new Latin American novel: a fiction that uses the great local (in this case Mexican) tradition of the rural and revolutionary novel but transforms it, destroys it, and recreates it through a very deep assimilation of Faulkner's techniques. *Pedro Páramo* was as dreamlike as the works of Onetti and Sábato, and strove for that precarious balance between realism and the anguish of a nightmare (it is basically a dialogue among the dead).

Less of an innovator, at least on the surface, was José María Arguedas, whose best novels were *Los ríos profundos* (1959, Deep Rivers), *El sexto* (1961, The Sixth), and *Todas las sangres* (1964, All the Bloods). His vision of the Andean Indians, seen through a knowledge of the Quechua tongue itself (in which his novels are conceived if not written), brushed aside all the good indigenist intentions of the Peruvian intellectuals who, because they did not speak the native languages, ended up writing what reads like romantic folklore. A comparison between *All the Bloods* and Alegría's *Broad and Alien Is the World* helps one to realize the importance of Arguedas's contributions to the new novel. Like Asturias in *Men of Maize,* Arguedas presented a convincing picture of the Indians' visions and dreams in a language that is Spanish and Indian at the same time.

Even more revolutionary, because they attacked not only narrative structure or characterization but language itself, were Cortázar's *Hopscotch* and Lezama Lima's *Paradiso* (1966, Paradise), the most important novels produced by this group of writers. These two masterpieces marked a culmination of a process begun by Asturias and Borges a generation before; at the same time, they opened up completely new paths for younger writers.

In *Paradise* Lezama Lima achieved, by what seems poetic magic, what Leopoldo Marechal had set about to do with almost painful deliberateness. *Paradise* is a totality, a book whose form is dictated by the nature of the poetic vision that inspires it. It is a novel that has the appearance of a novel of manners but is at the same time a treatise on the paradise of childhood and the hell of sexual deviations. It is a chronicle of the education of a young man from Havana during the 1920s. But he becomes, through the metaphorical play of language, the mirror of both the visible and the invisible world. Lezama Lima's success in so complex a feat is extraordinary.

Superficially, *Hopscotch* seems more accessible, since Cortázar was blessed not only with the rich tradition of the literature of the Río de la Plata area but also with a permanent contact with French culture (he has lived in Paris since 1952). But if Cortázar seems to have written *Hopscotch* from the center of the western intellectual world while Lezama began writing *Paradise* on the periphery of even the Latin American world, Cortázar, in fact, used culture to deny culture. In *Hopscotch* he tried to achieve a *subtraction,* not a totality; an anti-novel, not a novel. Yet, though he attacked the novel as a form, he retained in the book something that is essentially a novel.

The narrative form is questioned at the start of the book itself, by the author's telling the reader how to read it. (One is immediately reminded of Charles Kinbote's efforts, in Nabokov's *Pale Fire,* to indicate a privileged reading of "his" book.) Cortázar goes a step further and proposes a classification of readers: the female reader, or hedonistic one, who reads only for pleasure; and the accomplice reader, the one willing to help in the actual creation of the novel. To this reader, Cortázar offers a bonus, the possibility of following a sequence of chapters that will entrap him in an infinite circular reading: Chapter 58 refers to Chapter 131, which refers to Chapter 58, and so on and so forth, until kingdom come. The reader thus becomes another character in the book.

In *Hopscotch* the *form* of the novel—a labyrinth without a center, a trap that is always shutting the reader within it, a serpent biting its tail—is no more than another device to emphasize the deep, secret subject of the book: the exploration of a bridge between two existences (Oliveira, Traveler), a bridge between two muses (La Maga, Lalita), a bridge between two worlds (Paris, Buenos Aires). The novel unfolds itself to question itself the better; indeed, the title itself indicates its symbolic form (a hopscotch is a labyrinth and a *mandala,* in the Jungian sense). Yet it is also a novel about the complexities of being an Argentine (a man between two worlds) and about the *double* who menaces us in other dimensions of our lives. The *form* of the book has become what used to be called its *content.*

The most important things this group of novelists transmitted to the generation immediately following it were a consciousness of the structure of the novel and an acute sensibility to language as the basic material of narrative. It must be acknowledged that there is considerable overlapping between the second and third generations. Indeed, the masterpieces of Rosa, Cortázar, and Lezama Lima (which came out between 1956 and 1966) were published later than some of the most important novels of the following generation. The influence, then, came from coexistence: it was more properly a crossbreeding than an inheritance.

The third generation includes such writers as Clarice Lispector (Brazil, born 1924), José Donoso (Chile, born 1924), Carlos Fuentes (Mexico, born 1928), Gabriel García Márquez (Colombia, born 1928), Salvador Garmendia (Venezuela, born 1928), Guillermo Cabrera Infante (Cuba, born 1929), and Mario Vargas Llosa (Peru, born 1936). These novelists have given attention both to the external structure of the novel and to the creative and even revolutionary role of language.

Although some of them have pushed experimentation to the extreme, some are not visibly experimental. Donoso, for instance, has used the traditional narrative until quite recently. In *Coronación* (1957, Coronation), *Este domingo* (1966, This Sunday), and *El lugar sin límites* (1966, The Place with No Limits) he concentrated his inventiveness in the exploration of a subterranean reality—what lies beneath the many layers of stucco of the Chilean novel of manners. In his latest novel, *El obsceno pájaro de la noche* (1970, The Obscene Bird of Night), Donoso presented the same world of nightmares, grotesqueries, and monsters. But in telling his story, Donoso has become an experimentalist, creating a complex structure of stories within stories, legends, and even hallucinations. *The Obscene Bird of Night* is firmly linked to the novels of the preceding generation and to the works of the most experimental writers of Donoso's own generation.

For Salvador Garmendia, realism is grotesque enough. In a series of novels—*Los pequeños seres* (1959, The Little Men), *Los habitantes* (1960, The Inhabitants), *Día de ceniza* (1964, Ash Wednesday), *La mala vida* (1968, The Bad Life)—he transcended the optical details of the *costumbrista* novel and achieved a ferocious satire of mediocrity that bordered on caricature. The tenseness of his prose and the concreteness of his presentation of the external world have combined to give a surrealistic texture to his fiction. Less well known than some of his contemporaries, Garmendia deserves a major audience.

The same wide recognition is due Clarice Lispector. In several books of short stories and in two novels, Lispector has already created a world of her own. Stimulated by some of the writers of the *nouveau roman,* she produced in *A maça no escuro* (1956, The Apple in the Dark) and in *A Paixão segundo G. H.* (1964, The Passion according to G. H.) two powerful allegories of alienation. In the first, a man feels guilty of a crime he has not committed. In the second, a woman fights against an overpowering feeling of nausea. In both, Lispector described an arid, nightmarish world in a language that is both spare and lucid.

Unlike Donoso, Garmendia, and Lispector, the greater part of the novelists of this group created efficient narrative works. Carlos Fuentes has used all of the experimentation of the contemporary novel to create hard, complex books in which he denounces a reality that is excruciatingly painful to him. In *La región más transparente* (1958, Where the Air Is Clear), *La muerte de Artemio Cruz* (1962, The Death of Artemio Cruz), and *Cambio de piel* (1967, Change of Skin), and in shorter novels like *Aura* (1962, Aura) and *Zona sagrada* (1966, Sacred Zone), Fuentes wrote expressionistic allegories of his own country, his gods and monsters, his politicos and celebrities, his bourgeoisie and Indians. His world is composed of mythopoetic masks, which at different levels conceal something very different from the surface of the Mexico of today.

Mario Vargas Llosa can be grouped with these writers partly because of his precocity, but mainly because of his vision and techniques, which closely have followed those of the best novelists of the group. He has learned, simultaneously and harmoniously, from Faulkner and Fuentes, from Flaubert and the novel of chivalry, from Arguedas and Musil. He uses new techniques (discontinuity of time, interior monologue, plurality of points of view and narrators) to compose masterly visions of his native Peru that are both very contemporary and very traditional. In *La ciudad y los perros* (1963, The City and the Dogs), *La casa verde* (1965, The Green House), *Los cachorros* (1968, The Puppies), and *Conversación en "La Catedral"* (1969, Conversation in "La Catedral"), Vargas Llosa has shown himself to be a narrator with a great epic talent to whom character and plot are still of the utmost importance. His main contribution has been a revitalization of realism—a realism that does away with the manichaeism of the novel of protest. He is aware that time has more than one dimension but never lifts his feet from his solid, tormented earth. In a sense, a novel like *The Green House* can be considered a new version (with deeper probing and more stylistic control) of such older Latin American epics as Rivera's *The Vortex* and Gallegos's *Doña Bárbara*.

More clearly products of the innovations of the two preceding generations are García Márquez and Cabrera Infante. They established themselves somewhat later than Vargas Llosa, but they have already produced work of the utmost importance. In both García Márquez's *Cien años de soledad* (1967, One Hundred Years of Solitude) and Cabrera Infante's *Tres tristes tigres* (1967, Three Sad Tigers), one can clearly recognize the bonds with the world of Borges and Carpentier, Asturias and Onetti; with the fantastic visions of Rulfo and Cortázar; with the international idiom of Fuentes and Vargas Llosa. But the resemblances are only superficial and do not in themselves make *One Hundred Years of Solitude* and *Three Sad Tigers* such important novels.

At the core of both these novels stands a clear conviction of the "fictional" quality of all narration. They are, first and foremost, formidable verbal constructions, and they proclaim this either subtly and implicitly (in *One Hundred Years of Solitude*) or more militantly, almost pedantically (in *Three Sad Tigers*). In García Márquez's novel the traditional realism of the rural narratives is altered by fable and myth. People ("real" people of the novel) fly to the skies or come back from the tomb. Time is circular, and all space is contained in a book, a magic manuscript that tells the same story as *One Hundred Years of Solitude,* but in Sanskrit verse and in code. The fable is served up brilliantly, shot through with humor and imagination.

If García Márquez seems to have adapted Faulknerian techiques and those of Virginia Woolf's *Orlando* to the creation of the country of

Macondo, where Colonel Aureliano Buendía lives and dies, the reader would be well advised not to be led astray by the surface similarities. García Márquez does more than merely tell a fable of infinite charm and unquenchable humor, which envelops the reader in its fantasy. Using persuasive, even insidious practices, he erases the distinction between reality and fantasy in the body of the novel itself in order to present—in the same sentence and on the same metaphorical level—the narrative "truth" of what his fictional characters live and dream. Rooted in myth and in history, using episodes that echo the famous ones in the Bible or the *Arabian Nights* or the long-forgotten *El carnero* (The Sheep), a seventeenth-century Colombian *Decameron* by Juan Rodríguez Freile, *One Hundred Years of Solitude* achieves complete coherence only in the deep reality of its dazzling language. Most of García Márquez's readers have not noticed this, because they are carried away by a style of unparalleled fantasy, wit, and precision.

What Cabrera Infante has done is even more daring because *Three Sad Tigers* has meaning only if one examines it as a language structure. Different from *One Hundred Years of Solitude,* which is told by a ubiquitous omniscient narrator, Cabrera Infante's novel is told by the characters themselves, or, more accurately, by its "talkers," since the whole novel is a collage of voices. Evidently a disciple of Joyce, Cabrera Infante was also clearly indebted to Lewis Carroll, another manipulator of language, and to Mark Twain, who discovered before so many others the exactly appropriate tone for the dialogues or monologues of his characters. The language structure, which includes the title itself (*Tres tristes tigres*), a Spanish tongue twister, is made up of all possible meanings of a given word, and sometimes of a phoneme, of the rhythms of a sentence, of the most complicated puns. Disciple of his acknowledged masters, yes, but, above all, a disciple of his own ear, Cabrera Infante has incorporated into his novel things that are not strictly of literary origin but come from popular music and from the cinema.

When I maintain that with García Márquez and Cabrera Infante the conception of the novel as a language structure predominates, I am not denying that in both *One Hundred Years of Solitude* and *Three Sad Tigers* the "content" is of lasting importance. It would be foolish to ignore García Márquez's picture of the demented process of Colombian violence, on the surface and in its vertiginous depths. It is impossible not to recognize in Cabrera Infante's book the Havana of the end of the Batista regime in which these sad tigers are trapped, a society in agony, a candle about to be blown out—or perhaps already blown out. These things are obvious, and they also explain the success of both novels. But what makes *Three Sad Tigers* and *One Hundred Years of Solitude* the extraordinary creations they are is not their documentary value, which the reader would be able to find in other books of minor literary value; what makes them so unique is their devotion to the novel as complete fiction.

With García Márquez and Cabrera Infante the Latin American novel has entered the newest—the fourth—generation of writers. It is not easy to make generalizations about many of these writers, since most of them have published only one or two novels. But I would like to take advantage of the word "novel" in its etymological sense of "novelty," and mention a few novelists whose work seems fresh and original.

The Brazilian Nélida Piñon (born 1930) has already published four novels. *Fundador* (1969, The Founder) has undoubtedly been the best. It condenses the most striking allegorical qualities of her two earlier books, but it incorporates them into a more complex narrative structure and a surer diction. Although she began writing under the influence of Clarice Lispector, Piñon has now escaped from the rather confining and claustrophobic limits imposed upon narrative by Lispector. In *The Founder* she moves with ease from the origins of western culture and myths to the present day of revolutionary Latin America. The novel perhaps encompasses too much, in terms of space and time, and sometimes even falls into the most obvious pitfalls of allegory. But it has a hypnotic quality, a dreamlike recurrence of events and motives, which makes it a very distinguished work of fiction.

In some countries of Spanish America—Mexico, Cuba, Argentina— there is now a whole generation of novelists who are committed to total freedom of form, without respect for any law save experimentation. It is impossible to speak of all of them, and trying to point out the best will look suspiciously like cataloguing. Nevertheless, a few names should be singled out: in Mexico, Fernando del Paso (born 1932), Salvador Elizondo (born 1932), Gustavo Sáinz (born 1940), José Agustín (born 1943), and the poets José Emilio Pacheco and Homero Aridjis; in Cuba—both on the island and abroad, but anyway in a Cuba that is united by its literature— Edmundo Desnoes (born 1936), Severo Sarduy (born 1937), and Reinaldo Arenas (born 1943); in Argentina, Daniel Moyano (born 1930), Manuel Puig (born 1932), and Néstor Sánchez (born 1935).

Among these writers some seem more significant than others. Those whose work has attracted considerable attention, and have at least produced one and even two distinguished novels, are Puig, Sánchez, Sáinz, Sarduy, and Arenas. These five share the belief that the nature of fiction lies neither in theme (as the romantic creators of the rural novel believed), nor in plot, nor even in its myths and symbols. For them, the crux of the novel is language. The novel uses words not to say something in particular about the world outside literature but to transform the linguistic reality of the narration itself. What the novel "says" is this transformation through language, not what is generally discussed when talking about a novel: plot, characterization, point of view, theme, structure. For these writers, the novel is *the* reality, not a creation parallel to reality itself.

This does not mean that these novelists do not allude to extraliterary realities. They do, and that is why the novel has continued to remain so popular. But the true message of their novels is not on the level of documentation of reality, a substitution for the speech of a president or a dictator or the ministrations of the local parish priest. The message is the language.

In a book like *La traición de Rita Hayworth* (1968, Betrayed by Rita Hayworth), by Manuel Puig, the important thing is not the life of a boy who lives in a provincial town in Argentina and who goes to the movies with his mother every other afternoon; nor is it the structure, which uses Joycean interior monologues and dialogues without an explicit subject in the style of Nathalie Sarraute. What is really important in Puig's fascinating book is the *continuum* of spoken language, which is at the same time the vehicle of narrative and narrative itself. The alienation of the characters through the movies they see, which the title also indicates and which is clear in each detail of their conduct, is told by Puig with a sweeping humor and irony and an extremely fine sense of parody. It is also projected into the personal experience of the reader by the alienation of the language the characters use, a language that is almost a facsimile of radio and television soap operas and cheap magazines. The alienated language makes the alienation of the characters explicit: alienated language is alienation itself. The medium is the message.

Puig's second novel, *Boquitas pintadas* (1969, Little Painted Lips), went one step further in the exploration of this type of alienation. The whole novel follows the format of the literary serials that were so popular at the turn of the century. Again, a commonplace story of a provincial Don Juan is the pretext for a brilliant re-creation of the language spoken in Argentina in the 1930s, 1940s, and 1950s. Through letters and diaries, interior monologues, and lyrics from tangos and boleros, Puig evokes a buried world and, at the same time, rescues from the hell of despised genres a form (the serial) that still has some life in it.

Néstor Sánchez has written three novels to date: *Nosotros dos* (1966, The Two of Us), *Siberia Blues* (1967, the title is in English), and *El amhor, los orsinis y la muerte* (1969, Lohve, the orsinis, and Death). They fulfill—atlhough in a manner more like Cortázar's and that of recent French novelists—Cabrera Infante's intention of creating a structure that is, above all, a structure of sound, a verbal object. Sánchez has also been influenced by popular music (the tango in this case) and by the avant-garde European cinema. But his narrative texture, his medium, is even more complex and confusing than Cabrera Infante's—in whose works an almost Anglo-Saxon lucidity finally governs all delirium.

Unfortunately, in Sánchez, tension and ambition end up in excess. When he is at his best, he can create a narrative in which all presents and all pasts of his stories, every one of his characters are mixed. Thus, he can stress the fact that the unique central reality in his world of fiction, the only reality that is accepted and assumed with all its risks, is the reality of language—a glass that at times is beautifully clear but can turn invisible, and at times is so opaque that it lets no vision through.

In the novels of Sánchez, Cortázar's *Hopscotch* is always present (his admiration for Cortázar is so complete that it borders on mimicry). One is also aware of the presence of the rhythmic and visual world—uniform and serial at the same time—of the Alain Resnais–Alain Robbe-Grillet film *L'année dernière à Marienbad*. A comparison between Sánchez's three novels and Cortázar's most recent one, *62: Modelo para armar* (1968, 62: Model for Building), in which the master also used the serial approach, reveals how far Sánchez has gone in his explorations of a reality in which the only dimension is language.

Gustavo Sáinz has arrived at the same point, at the same vision, through an object as trivial in the world of today as the windmills were in the world of Cervantes—the tape recorder. His novel *Gazapo* (1965, the word has multiple meanings: young rabbit, shrewd fellow, great lie, blunder) is supposed to have been dictated into a dictaphone. Sáinz pretends to use the tape recorder (he actually wrote the novel with an old-fashioned typewriter) so that everything is kept within the realm of the spoken word. His characters seem to be taping what is going on in an effort to escape the tediousness of everyday life (it is well known that reality is a recurrent happening). But this taping of the characters' lives is in turn used to start fresh tapings, or to contradict them, or to form the basis for a narrative that one of the characters, perhaps the author's alter ego, is writing at the same time.

The taping of the novel's reality within the book, like the book itself, forces spoken and written word back on one another. After all, in a novel everything is words. Just as in the second part of *Don Quixote* the characters discussed the adventures attributed to them in the first part, and even the apocryphal ones that Fernández de Avellaneda invented for them in his parody, the characters in Sáinz's novel go over and over their own recorded lives. They are prisoners in the cobwebs of their own voices. If all the levels that are more or less "real" in the narrative of this novel are valid, they are so because the only reality the characters have is the reality of the book, that is, the reality of the word. Everything else is questionable—and is questioned by Sáinz.

In Reinaldo Arenas's two novels to date, the first-person narrative allows the reader to come into close contact with the characters. *Celestino antes del alba* (1967, Celestino before Dawn) is almost totally Faulknerian in its device of an idiot conveying the essence of its tale. In his second novel, *El mundo alucinante* (1969, The Hallucinating World), Arenas's precocious mastery of the medium is more evident. The novel was based on the real memoirs of Friar Servando Teresa de Mier, an eighteenth-century Mexican priest condemned to prison by the Spanish church, who managed to escape several times under the most incredible circumstances. Arenas used Friar Servando's text to compose an antitext that distorts and explodes the fabric of the original, letting the most nightmarish visions and the hidden passions of the memoirs come to life. Blasphemous and perverse, dazzlingly brilliant and chaotic, the novel is a linguistic tour de force. Written in the baroque tradition that has Lezama Lima as an acknowledged master, this novel manages to re-create the world of Friar Servando and his unvanquished freedom of spirit at the same time it creates a whole structure of verbal narrative. It is quite an achievement for such a young novelist.

I have deliberately left for the end the novelist who has gone the longest way into the exploration of language. He is Severo Sarduy, who has had three novels published—*Gestos* (1963, Gestures), *De donde son los cantantes* (1967, Where Are the Singers From?), and *Cobra* (1972, Cobra). *Where Are the Singers From?* seems to me one of the decisive works in the collective enterprise of creating a language for the Latin American novel. What this work does is to present three episodes from areas of Cuban life not yet transformed by the revolution. One of the episodes is situated in the Chinatown section of Havana and presents a limited world of transvestism and tinsel, theatrical effects and real sexual passion. The second episode shows us a half-breed and black Cuba, the colorful surface of the tropics; the narrative is a parody, a satire, and a cantata all at the same time. The third part takes place mainly in the Spanish and Catholic Cuba, the most important Cuba.

But what the book actually tells is secondary to Sarduy's purpose. What matters is how he tells it. By unifying the three diverse parts, Sarduy creates a medium that turns out to be the end, a vehicle that is itself a voyage. Here, the Havana slang of the author (not of the characters, as in Cabrera Infante) is the protagonist. His is a baroque language, not as in Carpentier but as in Lezama Lima. It is language that critically turns on itself, as happens with the group of French writers around the magazine *Tel Quel,* a group with which Sarduy has been so involved. It is a language that evolves as the novel proceeds, a language that lives and suffers, that is corrupted and dies to resuscitate itself from its own corrupted matter, like the image of Christ that is taken in procession to Havana in the third part of the novel.

With this novel by Sarduy, along with Puig's *Betrayed by Rita Hayworth,* the works of Néstor Sánchez and Reinaldo Arenas, and Sáinz's

Gazapo, the Latin American novel—which had been put on trial by Borges and Asturias; which had been brilliantly developed from different points of departure by Lezama Lima, Onetti, and Cortázar; which is being enriched, metamorphosed, and fabulized by Fuentes, García Márquez, and Cabrera Infante; and which has achieved a summit in Guimarães Rosa's novel—has now reached a veritable delirium of invention. The subterranean theme of the newest Latin American novel is language as the place (space and time) in which the novel exists. Language is the ultimate "reality" of the novel.

All these voices of the Latin American novel reinforce the general impression of continuous vitality in a genre to which, only a few decades ago, Latin America had little to contribute. Thanks to these men and women, and to their elders, the Latin American novel is beginning to take root beyond its present linguistic limits. It is being discovered, translated, and discussed, in Europe and the United States. Literary prizes and popular editions are beginning to multiply. Some impact is being made in quarters that were rather skeptical until quite recently about Latin American literature. Perhaps not since the introduction of the Russian novelists to nineteenth-century France and England, or of the modern Americans to postwar Europe, has a similar potential impact existed both for the literature itself and for its readers abroad. Today's European and American novelists—dominated by the arid writers of the *nouveau roman* or the *nouveau nouveau roman* or by the secluded, almost private fiction of the best American, British, or Italian novelists—might well consider the all-embracing and overexperimental attitude of the new Latin American novelists.

An enterprise of such vastness and courage—the summing up of a whole new society and the representation of a contradictory, as yet unclassified man through the invention of a new narrative language—has seldom been attempted with such vigor. I believe the Latin American novelists have a vision to communicate and to share—the common vision of a part of the world torn by revolution and inflation but also emboldened by anger and mounting expectations, by its awareness that it is the spokesman of an emerging world. At the same time, the novelists have a literary vision, a vision that, instead of denying the fictional quality of what it creates, emphasizes this quality to the utmost limit because it has discovered that only through total fiction can the hidden meaning of Latin America be discovered. Reality is never on the surface.

Through the expanded audience for the novel, Latin American literature now travels around the world. Translations increase; critics are beginning to take into account books that only ten years before were never considered. An area well publicized for its revolutions, earthquakes, and picturesque landscapes is now also known for its literature. The nonprofessional reader (that *common* reader, for whom Samuel Johnson wrote and whom Virginia Woolf believed herself to be) is no longer so astonished to find that Latin America, too, has a literature worthy of some consideration. In the universities of the western world it is no longer considered shocking that the literature of former colonies should be studied on an equal footing with that of Spain and Portugal.

All this change, which has been going on for decades in the Latin American consciousness, is new to the outside world. But not quite so new. Borges has been quoted by Nabokov and John Barth, by Michel Foucault and Gérard Genette; he has inspired Thomas Pynchon and Donald Barthelme; he has shared a prize, the Formentor 1961, with Samuel Beckett. Paz and Parra have stirred young audiences in London and New York. Mistral, Asturias, and Neruda have won the Nobel Prize. Latin American literature, then, is finally being recognized outside the Iberian world. It is about time.

LATIN AMERICAN WORKS IN ENGLISH TRANSLATION

INDIVIDUAL WORKS MENTIONED
IN ARTICLE

Alegría, Ciro. *El mundo es ancho y ajeno* as *Broad and Alien Is the World*. Philadelphia, 1962

Andrade, Mario de. *Paulicéia desvairada* as *Hallucinated City*. Nashville, 1968

Arenas, Reinaldo. *El mundo alucinante* as *Hallucinations; Being an Account of the Life and Adventures of Friar Servando Teresa de Mier*. London, 1971

Asturias, Miguel Ángel. *El Papa verde* as *The Green Pope*. New York, 1971

———. *Viento fuerte* as *Strong Wind*. New York, 1969

Azuela, Mariano. *Los de abajo* as *The Underdogs: A Novel of the Mexican Revolution*. New York, 1963

Borges, Jorge Luis. *El Aleph* as *The Aleph, and Other Stories*. New York, 1970

———. *Ficciones* as *Ficciones*. New York, 1962

———. *Historia universal de la infamia* as *The Universal History of Infamy*. New York, 1972

———. *El informe de Brodie* as *Doctor Brodie's Report*. New York, 1972

Cabrera Infante, Guillermo. *Tres tristes tigres* as *Three Trapped Tigers*. New York, 1971

Carpentier, Alejo. *Guerra del tiempo* as *War of Time*. New York, 1970

———. *Los pasos perdidos* as *The Lost Steps*. New York, 1967

———. *El reino de este mundo* as *The Kingdom of This World*. New York, 1971

———. *El siglo de las luces* as *Explosion in a Cathedral*. London, 1963

Cortázar, Julio. *Rayuela* as *Hopscotch*. New York, 1966

———. *62: Modelo para armar* as *62: A Model Kit*. New York, 1972

Donoso, José. *Coronación* as *Coronation*. New York, 1965

———. *Este domingo* as *This Sunday*. New York, 1967

———. *El lugar sin límites* as *Hell Has No Limits*. In *Triple Cross*. New York, 1972

Freyre, Gilberto. *Casa grande e senzala* as *The Mansions and the Shanties*. New York, 1963

————. *Sobrados e mucambos* as *The Masters and the Slaves*. New York, 1964

Fuentes, Carlos. *Aura* as *Aura*. New York, 1966

————. *Cambio de piel* as *Change of Skin*. New York, 1968

————. *La muerte de Artemio Cruz* as *The Death of Artemio Cruz*. New York, 1964

————. *La región más transparente* as *Where the Air Is Clear*. New York, 1971

————. *Zona sagrada* as *Holy Place*. In *Triple Cross*. New York, 1972

Gallegos, Rómulo. *Doña Bárbara* as *Doña Barbara*. New York, 1931

García Márquez, Gabriel. *Cien años de soledad* as *One Hundred Years of Solitude*. New York, 1970

Güiraldes, Ricardo. *Don Segundo Sombra* as *Don Segundo Sombra: Shadows on the Pampas*. New York, 1966

Henríquez Ureña, Pedro. *Las corrientes literarias en la América hispánica* as *Literary Currents in Hispanic America*. Cambridge, Mass., 1945

Lezama Lima, José. *Paradiso* as *Paradise*. New York, 1972

Lispector, Clarice. *A maça no escuro* as *The Apple in the Dark*. New York, 1967

Mariátegui, José Carlos. *Siete ensayos de interpretación de la realidad peruana* as *Seven Interpretative Essays on Peruvian Reality*. Austin, Tex., 1971

Martínez Estrada, Ezequiel. *Radiografía de la Pampa* as *X-Ray of the Pampa*. Austin, Tex., 1971

Neruda, Pablo. *Alturas de Macchu Picchu* as *The Heights of Macchu Picchu*. New York, 1967

————. *Canto general* as *General Song*. In *Twenty Poems*. Madison, Minn., 1967

————. *Odas elementales* as *Elementary Odes*. New York, 1961

————. *Residencia en la tierra* as *Residence on Earth*. In *Twenty Poems*. Madison, Minn., 1967

————. *Veinte poemas de amor y una canción desesperada* as *Twenty Love Poems and a Song of Despair*. London, 1969

Onetti, Juan Carlos. *El astillero* as *The Shipyard*. New York, 1968

Parra, Nicanor. *Poemas y antipoemas* as *Poems and Antipoems*. New York, 1967

Paz, Octavio. *Blanco* as *Blanco*. In *Configurations*. New York, 1971

————. *El laberinto de la soledad* as *Labyrinth of Solitude: Life and Thought in Mexico*. New York, 1962

————. *Piedra de sol* as *Sun Stone*. New York, 1963

Puig, Manuel. *La traición de Rita Hayworth* as *Betrayed by Rita Hayworth*. New York, 1971

Ramos, Graciliano. *Vidas sêcas* as *Barren Lives*. Austin, Tex., 1965

Rivera, José Eustasio. *La vorágine* as *The Vortex*. New York, 1935

Rodó, José Enrique. *Ariel* as *Ariel*. Boston, 1922

————. *Motivos de Proteo* as *The Motives of Proteus*. New York, 1928

Rosa, João Guimarães. *Grande sertão: Veredas* as *The Devil to Pay in the Backlands*. New York, 1962

Rulfo, Juan. *Pedro Páramo* as *Pedro Páramo*. New York, 1970

Sábato, Ernesto. *El tunél* as *The Outsider*. New York, 1950

Sáinz, Gustavo. *Gazapo* as *Gazapo*. New York, 1968

Sarduy, Severo. *De donde son los cantantes* as *From Cuba with a Song*. In *Triple Cross*. New York, 1972

Vallejo, César. *Poemas humanos* as *Poemas humanos*. New York, 1968

Vargas Llosa, Mario. *La casa verde* as *The Green House*. New York, 1968

————. *La ciudad y los perros* as *The Time of the Hero*. New York, 1966

SECONDARY WORKS

BIBLIOGRAPHIES AND GUIDES

Diccionario de la literatura latinoamericana. Washington, D.C., 1958–61

Leguizamón, Julio A. *Bibliografía general de la literatura hispanoamericana.* Buenos Aires, 1954

Levine, Suzanne Jill. *Latin America: Fiction and Poetry in Translation.* New York, 1970

Sánchez, Luis Alberto. *Repertorio bibliográfico de la literatura latinoamericana,* 3 vols. Santiago, 1955–62

Zum Felde, Alberto. *Indice crítico de la literatura hispanoamericana.* Mexico City, 1954–59

GENERAL WORKS

Alegría, Fernando. *Breve historia de la novela hispanoamericana,* 3rd. ed. Mexico City, 1966

Anderson Imbert, Enrique. *Spanish-American Literature: A History,* 2 vols., 2nd ed. Detroit, 1969

Arrom, José Juan. *Esquema generacional de las letras hispanoamericanas.* Bogotá, 1963

Aubrun, C. V. *Histoire des lettres hispano-américaines.* Paris, 1954

Bazin, R. *Histoire de la littérature américaine de langue espagnole.* Paris, 1953

Cándido, Antonio. *Formação de literatura brasileira: Momentos decisivos.* São Paulo, 1959

Coutinho, Afrânio, ed. *A literatura no Brasil.* Rio de Janeiro, 1955–59

Gallo, Ugo. *Storia della letteratura ispano-americana.* Milan, 1954

Grossmann, Rudolf. *Geschichte und Probleme der lateinamerikanischen Literatur.* Munich, 1969

Hamilton, Carlos. *Historia de la literatura hispanoamericana,* 2 vols. New York, 1960ff.

Henríquez Ureña, Pedro. *Literary Currents in Hispanic America,* 2nd ed. New York, 1963

Jones, W. K. *Breve historia del teatro latinoamericano.* Mexico City, 1956

Lazo, R. *Historia de la literatura hispanoamericana.* Mexico City, 1965

Leal, Luis. *Historia del cuento hispanoamericano.* Mexico City, 1966

Lorenz, Günter W. *Literatur in Lateinamerika.* St. Gallen, 1967

Loveluck, Juan, ed. *La novela hispanoamericana,* 3rd ed. Santiago, 1970

Sánchez, Luis Alberto. *Proceso y contenido de la novela hispanoamericana.* Madrid, 1953

Solórzano, Carlos. *El teatro latino americano en el siglo XX,* 2nd ed. Mexico City, 1964

Torres Rioseco, Arturo. *Aspects of Spanish-American Literature.* Washington, D.C., 1963

———. *Historia de la literatura iberoamericana.* New York, 1965

———. *La novela iberoamericana.* Albuquerque, N.M., 1952

———. *Nueva historia de la gran literatura hispanoamericana.* Buenos Aires, 1960

Uslar Pietri, Arturo. *Breve historia de la novela hispanoamericana.* Caracas, 1957

Valbuena Briones, Angel. *Literatura hispanoamericana,* 5th ed. Barcelona, 1965

WORKS ON CONTEMPORARY LITERATURE

Franco, Jean. *The Modern Culture of Latin America,* 2nd ed. London, 1970

Fuentes, Carlos. *La nueva novela hispanoamericana.* Mexico City, 1969

Harss, Luis and Barbara Dohmann. *Into the Mainstream: Interviews with Latin American Writers,* 2nd ed. New York, 1970

Lorenz, Günter W. *Dialog mit Lateinamerika: Panorama einer Literatur der Zukunft.* Tübingen, 1970

———. *Die zeitgenössische Literatur in Lateinamerika.* Tübingen, 1971

La novela iberoamericana: Actas del

XIII Congreso de Literatura Ibero-americana. Caracas, 1968

Ortega, Julio. *La contemplación y la fiesta,* 2nd ed. Caracas, 1969

Pollman, Leo. *Der Neue Roman in Frankreich und Lateinamerika.* Stuttgart, 1968

Rodríguez-Monegal, Emir. *El arte de narrar: Diálogos con narradores latinoamericanos.* Caracas, 1968

———. *Narradores de esta América,* 2 vols., 2nd ed. Montevideo, 1969–71

———. *Notas sobre (hacia) el Boom.* Caracas, 1972

JĀNIS ANDRUPS

Latvian Literature

ALTHOUGH LATVIAN oral folk poetry has a rich and varied history, when written Latvian literature began in the sixteenth century, it displayed from the start an hostility toward folklore. Only with the period of national awakening (1850–80) were efforts made to reestablish the broken link with the oral tradition.

Jānis Rainis (1865–1929, pseudonym of Jānis Pliekšāns) lifted Latvian poetry and drama to such a level of excellence that Latvian literature commanded an interest beyond its borders. The philosophical depth of Rainis's writings has seldom been surpassed by those of subsequent generations. As early as the first realistic novel, *Mērnieku laiki* (1879, The Times of the Land Surveyors) by the brothers Kaudzītes (Reinis, 1839–1920; and Matīss, 1848–1926), one of the main themes of Latvian literature emerged: the search for ethical values, which are seen as "goodness of heart" (*"labestība"*).

The failure of the revolution of 1905 against the local German landowners and the tsar thwarted political hopes and thus contributed to turning poetry inward. Under the influence of French symbolism, a group of Latvian decadent poets came into being. After Latvian independence in 1918, and especially toward the end of the 1920s, a new poetic world view was attempted through greater stylistic control and rejuvenation of language. Like writers of the twentieth century everywhere, the Latvian writer

449

was no longer able to perceive the world as a unity and to focus equally on internal and external events.

A separation took place in Latvian literature: writers either focused on the outer world or on man's inner life. Typical of the outer vision was Anš-lavs Eglītis (born 1906), who has remained very active as novelist and dramatist in exile. Writers who sought an inner vision of the world pre-ferred the psychological novella or short story. Mirdza Bendrupe (born 1910) was strongly influenced by Freud, while Ēriks Ādamsons (1907–1946) exaggerated psychological detail to morbid proportions. Ādamsons's decadent refinement was part of his charm and originality, especially in the context of a relatively young and optimistic literature. He expressed his remarkable talent in poetry and drama as well as fiction.

Free verse developed under the influence of German expressionism and attracted mostly politically oriented writers. Aleksandrs Čaks (1902–1950, pseudonym of Aleksandrs Čadarainis), the outstanding Latvian poet of the 1930s, successfully combined techniques of Russian imagism, especially the poetry of Yesenin, and his own fresh application of free verse to metaphorically daring descriptions of city life. His principal work, *Mūžības skartie* (1937–39, Touched by Eternity), was a lyrical-epic depiction of the bravery of Látvian soldiers during World War I.

SOVIET LATVIAN LITERATURE

Many leftist writers of the 1930s who moved to the Soviet Union perished there during the Stalinist purges, among them the outstanding poet Linards Laicēns (1883–1938). And with the Soviet annexation of Latvia in 1944, a majority of the writers still living in the country fled to the west. Thus, what had been a period of intensive experimentation came to an end.

Moscow's authority over Latvia found a mouthpiece in Andrejs Upīts (1877–1970), whose rambling novel cycles abandoned humanistic moral-izing in favor of a Marxist-colored naturalism. His works included the historical novel *Pirmā nakts* (1938, The First Night) and the war novel *Zaļā zeme* (1945, Green Earth). For the most part, Soviet Latvian litera-ture remained voiceless until the death of Stalin and the Twentieth Con-gress of the Communist Party of the Soviet Union in 1956.

Three poets, all born during the 1930s, were successful in bringing poetry back to life in the Latvian Soviet Socialist Republic. Ojārs Vācietis (born 1933) was indebted to the style of Yesenin and Mayakovski and, like them, he has walked a tightrope between acceptance and condemna-tion. Despite the influence of Yesenin and Mayakovski, Vācietis's lan-guage has always been refreshingly his own, and in his best collections—

Dzegužlaiks (1966, The Time of the Cuckoo) and *Aiz simtās slāpes* (1969, Behind the Hundredth Thirst)—he achieved a personal tone of great poignancy. With Vācietis's verses, Soviet Latvian poetry began to breathe again.

Vizma Belševica (born 1931) developed her sense of style by doing many translations. She expresses herself through the emotionally surfeited word, whether in free verse or in classical verse. She has widened the poetic metaphor to an encompassing image, often of breathtaking intensity.

Imants Ziedonis (born 1933), another in the line of Latvians who have sought the "goodness of heart," was indebted to expressionism, which he has molded to suit his personality. He enjoys being carried by the stream of language and thus has risked the danger of becoming wordy. Among his collections of poems, two are of special interest: *Motocikls* (1965, The Motorcycle) and *Es ieeju sevī* (1968, I Go into Myself). *The Motorcycle* was imbued by a boyish joy in discovery, while *I Go into Myself* revealed Ziedonis's growing meditative introspection. In his travel book *Kurzemīte* (1970, Courland) and his collection of short lyrical prose pieces, *Epifānijas* (1971, Epiphanies), Ziedonis revitalized the prose miniature as an art form. In these two books, because of their multileveled associations and compressed imagery, he achieved a more contemporary voice than in his poems.

A leading younger poet, Māris Čaklais (born 1940), is also an important essayist. His third collection of verse, *Lapas balss* (1969, Voice of the Leaf), showed an intellectual maturity and a wide thematic range.

In world literature lyric poetry has always had an easier time than other genres in diverging from political or moral controls, partly because of its more limited readership. Soviet Latvian fiction did not free itself from the demands of the Communist Party until the end of the 1960s. Ilze Indrāne (born 1927, pseudonym of Undīna Jātniece) progressed from realistic depictions of youth and country life to a freely associating impressionism in her collection of miniatures *Basām kājām* (1970, Barefoot).

Among writers of fiction of the younger generation, Alberts Bels (born 1938) has achieved a personal style and outlook: he sees reality as distinct yet interrelated planes of action. This does not facilitate the search for truth; there is, finally, no objective historic truth—a conclusion reached by the protagonist of Bels's novel *Izmeklētājs* (1967, The Prosecutor). Written in the form of a monologue, *The Prosecutor* presented a personal and human rather than an official, party-dictated perspective on recent history.

Lack of dogmatism has also marked the work of Andris Jakubāns (born 1940). He views the world through the eyes of ordinary people, whose heroism often consists of the things they do *not* do. His anti-heroes are the descendants of the third, youngest, and dumbest brother of the Latvian folk tales, who valued "goodness of heart" more than fame and fortune.

LATVIAN ÉMIGRÉ LITERATURE

Following World War II, about 75 percent of the active Latvian writers fled to the west, shifting the center of Latvian literature during the 1940s and 1950s outside their native country. The first decade of exile was filled with echoes of the catastrophic events of World War II.

Veronika Strēlerte (born 1912, pseudonym of Rudīte Strēlerte-Johansone) found symbols for the mood of the times, which she expressed in classical verse forms in such collections as *Žēlastības gadi* (1961, Years of Grace). Andrejs Eglītis (born 1912), in his numerous collections of verse, played the role of tribune of the people. His finest achievement, however, lay in the area of intimate personal expression.

A valid inner vision of a nation's tragic fate was achieved by Zinaīda Lazda (1902–1957, pseudonym of Zinaīda Šreibere). She chose a path similar to that of the anonymous women who created Latvian folksongs and thus approached a solution to a major problem of Latvian literature— how to use the spirit and style of the folksong to enrich contemporary Latvian writing. Velta Sniķere (born 1920) arrived at a somewhat similar result by pursuing another aspect of folklore—riddles and magic incanta- tions. Her personal poetic language was also influenced by Paul Valéry's *Charmes* and the late poems of Rainer Maria Rilke. Sniķere's work has closely approximated surrealism; indeed, she remains the only Latvian poet to have adopted surrealism.

A new period of intensive stylistic innovation began in the 1950s. Its originators were poets living in New York, commonly called the "Hell's Kitchen Group" (after a section of Manhattan). The first important pub- lication of the group was Gunars Saliņš's (born 1924) collection *Miglas krogs* (1957, Tavern of Mists). Endowed with a gift for poetic storytelling that is only a short step removed from the exuberant imagination of folk tales, Saliņš has woven fables around the present-day megalopolis of New York, lifting its reality to a new plane of poetic perception. In his second collection, *Melnā saule* (1967, Black Sun), he expanded his vision to include the past and the black sun of the netherworld.

The other major poet of the Hell's Kitchen Group, Linards Tauns (1922–1963, pseudonym of Alfrēds Bērzs) was more lyrical, and his poems have the transparency of old frescoes that vibrate with the light of times long past. Tauns was a visionary who transformed both New York and his native Latvian countryside into hanging gardens of his imagination. His first collection was significantly called *Mūžīgais mākonis* (1958, The

Eternal Cloud). His second, published posthumously, was *Laulības ar pilsētu* (1964, Wedding with the City). Both Tauns and Saliņš were undeniably influenced by Aleksandrs Čaks.

During the 1960s three women poets effected further stylistic changes, each in her own way. Of the three, Aina Kraujiete (born 1925?) is closest to Čaks, although her verse has shown abrupt rhythmic contrasts and has mirrored the world in fragmented images. Astrīde Ivaska (born 1926) has made an elliptic, unadorned poetic line the vehicle for a restrained, multi-leveled emotionality that demands full collaboration of the reader. She has created personal symbols and individual images, as the titles of her collections have indicated: *Ezera kristības* (1966, The Lake's Baptism) and *Ziemas tiesa* (1968, Judgment of Winter). Behind these images often lies a far-reaching historical perspective.

The poetry of Baiba Bičole (born 1931) has been buoyed by a vital sensuousness that strains to become one again with the stream of life. Her poetry has rebelled against the repressions of technology and the apocalyptic threat of our age. In the poetry of Bičole and Ivaska, the century-old attempt to bridge the gap between contemporary and folk poetry has finally been realized.

Poetry has always been at the center of Latvian literature. It is no surprise then that dramatic writing should not be among its strong points, especially in exile, with the lack of a large enough audience for a sustained theatrical life. The outstanding contemporary dramatist, Mārtiņš Zīverts (born 1903) found the one-act play particularly congenial, and he has made the scene containing a "great monologue" the focal point of his plays.

The older generation of writers of fiction in exile remained true to the earthy style and colorful use of regional dialect of the 1930s. Jānis Jaunsudrabiņš (1877–1962) published *Zaļā grāmata* (1950, The Green Book), and Zenta Mauriņa (born 1897) won a wide circle of readers in German-speaking countries with her essays and autobiographical novels, some of which were written in German. Knuts Lesiņš (born 1909), a writer who by temperament was concerned with man's inner life, tried to show man as part of the whole creation.

New modes of expression in fiction were attempted during the 1960s, with existentialism as the starting point. The novels of Guntis Zariņš (1926–1965) clearly reflected existentialist philosophy. A more thoroughly existentialist writer was Andrejs Irbe (born 1924), who in his two collections of short fiction—*Mums nav svētvakaru* (1962, No Holidays to Look Forward To) and *Marisandra kaza* (1966, Marisander's Goat)—showed contemporary man in all his loneliness. His hero is the absolute outsider, wandering around—without any link with the past; without a country, a nation, and society—trying to forget his solitude.

Benita Veisberga (born 1928), who reminds one of the Norwegian Knut Hamsun, has presented closeness to nature as an alternative for man who is both homeless and expelled from the paradise of love. In her remarkable first novel, *Es, tavs maigais jērs* (1968, I, Your Gentle Lamb), the style and atmosphere virtually became the contents of the book.

Margarita Kovaḷevska (born 1911) has depicted country and small-town life during the early twentieth century in her novels *Posta puķe* (1962, Flower of Disaster) and *Gauru gaiḷi* (1963, The Roosters of the Gauri Farmstead). Yet her protagonists are so obsessed by a hunger for life and at the same time isolated by a general mood of impending disaster that they are true children of the existential atmosphere of the postwar years. Kovaḷevska's extraordinarily colorful and powerful style lifts every-day destinies to a near-biblical plane.

Ilze Šķipsna (born 1928) opened entirely new perspectives in both style and theme in her three distinctive works of fiction. In the collection of short stories *Vēja stabules* (1961, Pipes of the Wind) she announced her movement away from outer reality with a half-wistful, half-ironic smile. The novel *Aiz septītā tilta* (1965, Behind the Seventh Bridge) was an existentialist narrative of a journey inward in search of a unity of person-ality. *Neapsolītās zemes* (1970, The Unpromised Lands) showed the overcoming of existentialism and the search for a meaningful world view. Šķipsna, too, built a bridge between today's world and folklore's realm—through the symbol of the tree of the sun, or the tree of life, whose presence can be traced back in the mythologies of the whole world, as far back as Sumeria. But folklore, for Šķipsna, is not an end in itself; she uses it to illuminate the situation of modern man.

Both the fiction and poetry of Latvia in exile continue into the 1970s with unabated creative vigor. In Soviet Latvia, it is primarily poetry that has been able to establish a precarious foothold on behalf of more indi-vidual expression. One would like to be able to claim in 1972 that the most vital activity in Latvian literature is no longer with the exile community, but in the country itself. This statement is untenable, however, since official Soviet statistics openly admit that Latvians no longer constitute more than 56 percent of the country's population, and a reversal in russification is not yet in sight. With an inevitably dwindling exile group and a diminishing population at home, Latvian literature will face a struggle for survival during the last quarter of this century.

LATVIAN WORKS IN
ENGLISH TRANSLATION

ANTHOLOGIES

The Literary Review (Baltic issue), Spring, 1965

Matthews, W. K., ed. *A Century of Latvian Poetry*. London, 1957

Rubulis, Aleksis and M. J. Lahood, eds. *Latvian Literature*. Toronto, 1964

Speirs, Ruth, ed. *Translations from the Latvian: Selected Poems by Linards Tauns and Gunars Saliņš*. Exeter, 1968

SECONDARY WORKS

Andrups, Jānis and Vitauts Kalve. *Latvian Literature*. Stockholm, 1954

Blese, Ernests. *Storia della letteratura lettone*. In Giacomo Devoto, ed., *Storia delle letterature baltiche*. Milan, 1957

Blyumfeld, L. G. et al. *Ocherk istorii latyshskoi sovietskoi literatury*. Riga, 1957

Eckardt-Skalberg, Elfriede. *Lettische Lyrik*. Hannover, 1960

Jēgers, Benjamiņš. *Bibliography of Latvian Publications Published outside*

Latvia 1940–1960. Stockholm, 1968

Johansons, Andrejs. *Latvian Literature in Exile*. In *Slavonic and East European Review*, 30, 75, 1952

————. *Latviešu literātūra*, 4 vols. Stockholm, 1953

Silenieks, Juris. *The Humanization of the Recent Soviet-Latvian Short Story*. In *Lituanus*, 16, 2, 1970

Sokols, E., ed. *Latviešu literātūras vēsture*, 6 vols. Riga, 1959–62

R I M V Y D A S   Š I L B A J O R I S

Lithuanian Literature

WRITTEN LITHUANIAN LITERATURE began with the poem *Metai* (1818, The Seasons) by Kristijonas Donelaitis (1714–1780). It was a rural epic written in a pious Protestant vein, with no clearly identifiable predecessors in foreign or oral-native literature. *The Seasons* did not directly influence subsequent developments, but it is in many ways a characteristic Lithuanian work: Lithuanian literature has remained, to the present, in close contact with the palpable realities of nature and the countryside.

Strong elements of romantic nationalism were added to this rural tradition in the nineteenth century. And Lithuanian writers did respond to the various European literary movements at the beginning of the twentieth century and throughout the period of national independence (1918–40). But in adopting international literary movements, Lithuanians retained their concern with concrete sensory experience—with the beauty of nature and its organic processes. Thus, Jurgis Baltrušaitis (1873–1944), who wrote in both Russian and Lithuanian, used the techniques of Russian and French symbolism to explore the meaning of existence. But he directed this symbolism toward man's relationship with the surrounding landscape.

In a similar manner, Jonas Aistis (born 1904) combined French modernism and expressionism with Lithuanian pastoral imagery and with the verbal texture and poetic devices inherited from the rich and ancient traditions of folklore. Bernardas Brazdžionis (born 1907), an intensely patriotic poet oriented toward Christian mysticism, expressed his faith in

456

fine rhetorical cadences replete with nature imagery. The most outstanding prose writer, Vincas Krėvė-Mickevičius (1882–1954), in his numerous short stories, plays, and novels, always centered his attention on man as a natural force, emerging from a close intimacy with nature—and as great and inexplicable as the organic laws of nature. Such an interest in nature was well suited to the writers of a small agrarian nation, one as yet not significantly affected by the industrial processes of modern civilization.

The situation changed considerably during World War II, particularly with the second Soviet occupation in 1944, which was soon followed by the incorporation of Lithuania into the Soviet Union. Lithuanian literature was split into two separately functioning entities. On one hand, the Soviet-controlled literature of Lithuania was now forced to adjust the old values and traditions to the demands of socialist realism. On the other hand, a separate Lithuanian literature was developed in the west by émigrés, who were confronted with two powerful forces: the profound homesickness of people torn suddenly from their roots; and the wide range of cultural and literary developments in the western world. Moreover, both literatures now had to meet somehow the challenge of complex urban civilizations: the huge Soviet state in the east and the modern industrial west.

LITHUANIAN ÉMIGRÉ LITERATURE

The émigré writers responded to their new situation in various ways, depending on age and on relationship to the mainstream of the Lithuanian literary tradition. Many of the established older writers in exile continued to write in the old manner, producing realistic, nature-oriented prose and poetry tinged with patriotic romanticism. The only new element in their work was the theme of exile itself. Its manifestations were a great outrage against the injustice done to their nation and a deep nostalgia for their homeland, now a receding memory.

One such writer was Antanas Vaičiulaitis (born 1906), who had established his reputation in Lithuania with his novel *Valentina* (1936, Valentina), a delicate love story written in a style that contained many elements of French and Scandinavian impressionism. In exile, Vaičiulaitis turned his attention to the short story and to the fairy tale, creating carefully balanced narratives dealing with the inner lives of little people lost among the huge shadows of an alien world.

Marius Katiliškis (born 1915), who started writing only in exile, also developed his art in terms of the old tradition. In his main novel, *Miškais ateina ruduo* (1957, Autumn Comes through the Forests), he traced the life and loves of a young lumberjack in Lithuania; natural forces manifested themselves with equal power in the soul of man and in the surrounding landscape.

The poet Kazys Bradūnas (born 1917) was a pivotal figure, standing halfway between the older trends and the new directions taken by the "earth" group of writers, centering around the magazine *Literatūros lankai,* which Bradūnas helped to organize in Buenos Aires in 1952. This group did not begin with a common ideology, except for the desire to pass beyond the realistic-patriotic mode into a new kind of art, responsive to aesthetic developments in the west, which would reach toward the depths of universal human experience. Bradūnas, a prolific writer, still draws his inspiration from a poetic conception of "the soil," the native Lithuanian earth, but he defines the meaning of existence in religious-mythological terms, as an ancient ritual in which man offers his works to God in return for the sacrifice of Christ.

The most prominent of the earth poets has been Alfonsas Nyka-Niliūnas (born 1919). His poetry combines the landscapes of home, transfigured in an exile's longing memory, with universal symbolic and mythological allusions expressive of man's total existential solitude. Both Nyka-Niliūnas and the novelist and playwright Antanas Škėma (1911–1961) were very responsive to French existentialism. Škėma's main theme was the destruction of man's creative consciousness, together with his very existence, by the inexorable action of the life-denying laws that govern the universe. His novel *Balta drobulė* (1958, The White Shroud) depicted a Lithuanian exile who retreats into insanity among the broken pieces of his life, past and present. In Škėma's plays the theme of man's defeat by the universe was presented in terms of Lithuanian resistance to Soviet occupation.

The playwright and novelist Algirdas Landsbergis (born 1924) has been closely related to the earth group, but his own work at times has passed beyond philosophical existentialism into a comic-grotesque playfulness that seems like a revenge against the terrible absurdity of the human condition. Landsbergis's novel *Kelionė* (1954, The Journey) dealt with the chaotic experiences of a slave laborer in Germany, and his play *Penki stulpai turgaus aikštėje* (1966, Five Posts in the Market Place) portrayed Lithuanian anti-Soviet guerillas, torn between their human needs and the iron necessities of their chosen, hopeless struggle.

The absurdity of death itself has been the main concern of the playwright Kostas Ostrauskas (born 1926). His avant-garde drama was influenced by Ionesco and Beckett. But Ostrauskas, in such plays as *Pypkė* (1954, The Pipe) and *Duobkasiai* (1967, The Gravediggers), called for a defiant reassertion (tempered somewhat by self-mockery) of the values of human life against death's meaningless oblivion.

Similarly preoccupied with death was the poet Algimantas Mackus (1932–1964), who pursued the theme of exile in brooding, complex

poems in which he reversed the traditional connotations of poetic metaphors to create a kind of anti-language, where all the images of life
signified death. Mackus felt that such a radical alienation from all hope and
faith constituted the perfection of exile, the true purification of man's
homeless soul from all the comforting illusions built up in the history of
civilization.

The poet Henrikas Radauskas (1910–1970) remained apart from all
Lithuanian literary movements and traditions. Although the techniques of
his art showed traces of such modern Polish poets as Julian Tuwim and of
Russian writers like Pasternak and Mandelstam, Radauskas can only be
approached as himself alone, a brilliant poet totally committed to the
values and realities of art itself. Radauskas's poetry consisted of a variety
of highly complex, carefully balanced formal structures, with many interesting planes of thought and emotion, fused into an artistic whole by the
heat of intellectual passion. He found in art a third absolute reality, as he
passed through the two other absolutes of life and death, transforming the
one and the other into poetic images embodying the beautiful and the
grotesque, the chill of frozen eternity and a wild, Dionysian joy in the
dynamic processes of destruction and creation.

SOVIET LITHUANIAN LITERATURE

The literature of contemporary Soviet Lithuania can be divided into three
different categories.

First, there is the heritage of leftist writers who, in the years of independence, formed a cohesive group called the Third Front. Prominent among
these was the novelist and short-story writer Petras Cvirka (1909–1947),
whose works were full of bitter social satire against the Lithuanian bourgeoisie and great admiration for the Soviet people and their political
system. Also in the Third Front was the poet Salomėja Neris (1904–
1945), who committed her graceful, limpid verses to the service of the new
Soviet order.

The second group consists of established writers who had not previously
shown leftist or communist convictions but who submitted after World War
II to party dictates in art. Antanas Vienuolis (1882–1957), well known
before the war for his realistic novels and short stories, continued in the
same vein. But his pictures of Lithuanian country life became Marxist,
giving prominence to class struggles.

Vincas Mykolaitis-Putinas (1893–1967) had been a poet with sym-
bolist tendencies and a novelist who in his *Altorių šešėly* (1933, In the
Shadow of the Altars) produced the first Lithuanian psychological novel.
During his later career as a Soviet writer he devoted much effort to the

creation of another novel, *Sukilėliai* (1957, The Rebels), which described, in the spirit of respect for the liberal Russian traditions, the events on the eve of the Lithuanian-Polish uprising against the Russians in 1863.

One of the best writers of this second group is Jonas Avyžius (born 1922). His short stories, as well as the novel *Kaimas kryžkelėj* (1964, Village at the Crossroads), have often dealt with crucial changes in Lithuanian peasant life, set in motion by modern economic and ideological forces, in particular the collectivization of agriculture.

The third group includes writers of various ages who first came to prominence during the postwar period, especially after 1956, with the loosening of some party restrictions upon literature. Lithuanian history, old mythology, a new awareness of the native soil, conflicts in the present—these themes began to be treated with primary attention to their artistic value. Among the first to set the new standards was Eduardas Mieželaitis (born 1919). His poetry has been especially concerned with human dignity and with Lithuanian national identity as it has emerged from the tumultous changes in the country's history. His collection of poems *Žmogus* (1961, Man) received the Lenin prize.

Justinas Marcinkevičius (born 1930), in his narrative poem *Kraujas ir pelenai* (1960, Blood and Ashes), assessed the strengths and weaknesses of the Lithuanian national character against the background of Nazi atrocities in World War II. Marcinkevičius has also produced significant works in fiction and in drama.

Juozas Grušas (born 1901), an important playwright of this younger group of Soviet Lithuanian writers, has dealt with both ancient and modern subjects. The play *Herkus Mantas* (1957, Herkus Mantas) dealt with a crucial period in medieval Lithuanian history; the orientation was clearly Lithuanian. On the other hand, Grušas presented the modern theme of alienation among the young from the Soviet point of view, and asserted the continuing validity of socialist ideas, in the avant-garde comedy *Meilė, džiazas ir velnias* (1967, Love, Jazz, and the Devil). Grušas has also written a number of short stories that use irony and fantasy as tools for the exploration of men's dreams and their consciences.

Janina Degutytė (born 1928), a warm, humane poet, has written with deep feeling and conviction about the survival of human values through wars and persecutions in her own country and throughout the world. Sigitas Geda (born 1943) utilizes the verbal resources of the peasant idiom in the creation of a modern, intensely metaphorical poetic language, in which the simplicity and ordinariness of the life of country folk is transformed into a mythology of the national ethos.

Judita Vaičiūnaitė (born 1937), perhaps the most interesting of the younger poets, has written intellectually complex, yet essentially light-hearted verse. Vaičiūnaitė is interested in conveying her happy perception of life in its totality by means of varied, structurally coordinate verbal textures. For example, hot summer pavements and ancient streets become metaphors for the passions of love, rising like a fountain in the city square. This same love, directed toward her country, acquires depth in the mythological overtones of native landscapes. In Soviet Lithuanian literature, Vaičiūnaitė was one of the first to use urban imagery successfully.

Future Lithuanian literature would be much enhanced if it were possible for it to regain a single identity by uniting in some way the exile branch with the main stem at home. This would require radical changes in the present system and policies of the Soviet Union, changes that would put personal freedom and creativity before political ideology. As it is, the sources of the exile literature must eventually dry up, as the ethnic Lithuanian communities become fully integrated into adopted cultures, principally in the United States. Possibly, at some later date, there may be "Lithuanian writers" in English, in the sense that one speaks of "Jewish writers" today. At home, the Lithuanian language and ethnic values, thus also the literature, are likely to endure and prosper only insofar as the Soviet system permits a return to traditional humanistic concerns in the arts.

LITHUANIAN WORKS IN ENGLISH TRANSLATION

ANTHOLOGIES

Landsbergis, Algirdas and Clark Mills, eds. *The Green Oak.* New York, 1962
Zobarskas, Stepas, ed. *Lithuanian Quartet.* New York, 1962
————. *Selected Lithuanian Short Stories.* New York, 1959

INDIVIDUAL WORKS MENTIONED IN ARTICLE

Donelaitis, Kristijonas. *Metai* as *The Seasons.* Los Angeles, 1967
Landsbergis, Algirdas. *Penki stulpai turgaus aikštėje* as *Five Posts in the Market Place.* New York, 1968
Ostrauskas, Kostas. *Duobkasiai* as *The Gravediggers.* Chicago (in the journal *Lituanus*), 1967
————. *Pypkė* as *The Pipe.* New York (in the journal *Arena*), 1963

SECONDARY WORKS

Bradūnas, Kazys, ed. *Lietuvių literatūra svetur 1945–1967*. Chicago, 1968

Dobrynin, M. K., K. P. Korsakas, et al. *Ocherk istori litovskoi sovietskoi literatury*. Moscow, 1955

Korsakas, Kostas, ed. *Lietuvių literatūrinai ryšiai ir sąveikos*. Vilnius, 1969

Kubilius, Vytautas, ed. *Šiuolaikines lietuvių literatūros bruožai*. Vilnius, 1969

Lietuvių literatūros istorija, 4 vols. Vilnius, 1957–68

Naujokaitis, Pranas. *Lietuvių literatūra*. Tübingen, 1948

Rubulis, Aleksis. *Baltic Literature*. Notre Dame. Ind., 1970

Senn, Alfred. *Storia della letteratura lituana*. In Giacomo Devoto, ed., *Storia delle letterature baltiche*. Milan, 1957

Šilbajoris, Rimvydas. *Perfection of Exile: Fourteen Contemporary Lithuanian Writers*. Norman, Okla., 1970

AD DEN BESTEN

Netherlandic Literature

NETHERLANDIC LITERATURE is often regarded as two separate entities—
Dutch and Flemish—much as Austrian literature is distinguished from the
literature of Germany. In the case of Netherlandic literature, however, the
separation has frequently arisen from the mistaken premise that Flemish
and Dutch are separate languages. While the centuries-long divergence
between predominantly Protestant Holland and the Catholic Spanish
Netherlands (an independent kingdom of Belgium only since 1839) certainly affected the language, Netherlandic specialists have always regarded
Holland and Flanders (the Netherlandic region of bilingual Belgium) as a
single linguistic and literary unit. It is of little significance that, according
to the criteria of the written language established in Holland, Flemish
writers have tended to use the spoken language more than their Dutch
colleagues. The great Flemish writers have always belonged to Netherlandic literature. Furthermore, since the turn of the twentieth century
almost all the important Flemish writers have been published by Dutch
publishers. Since around 1960 dialectic differences have been disappearing,
and today, more than ever, Dutch and Flemish writers see themselves as
part of a single Netherlandic literature.

Liberal ideas had a harder time in Flanders than in Holland, where
Calvinism never aspired to the cultural authority that Catholicism exerted
in Belgium. Moreover, even the effects of international politics have been
different in Holland and in Flanders. During World War II both Holland

and Belgium were occupied by the Germans; but Belgium was simply placed under military government, while in Holland an oppressive political administration harassed the Dutch people endlessly. As a consequence, in Flanders politically uncontroversial books could be published without going through a censor. In Holland, however, the administration attempted to enforce an extreme—and clumsy—reorganization of cultural life. Thus, by 1943 Dutch literature was forced underground, and an extensive, though not particularly significant, resistance literature developed.

The disorientation of Dutch literature during the war was as much the result of individual deaths as of repression. Three leading writers died in the German invasion of May, 1940: Menno ter Braak (1902–1940), Charles Edgar du Perron (1899–1940), and Hendrik Marsman (1899–1940). The poet Jan R. T. Campert (1902–1942) and the novelist Johan Brouwer (1898–1943) were executed for their participation in the resistance. Flemish literature suffered no such catastrophic losses. For Flemish writers, therefore, the year 1945 represented a new beginning to a far less degree than it did for their Dutch colleagues. And literary conventions, particularly in poetry, could hold their grip more tenaciously in Flanders than in Holland.

While the expressionist movement, generally known in Holland as "vitalism," survived in both Holland and Flanders into the 1930s, a strong rationalist trend developed after 1930, modeled to some extent on contemporary French literature; the major representatives of this rationalism were Menno ter Braak, Charles Edgar du Perron, Ferdinand Bordewijk (1884–1965), Simon Vestdijk (1898–1971), and Gerard Walschap (born 1898). A reaction against this trend began shortly before World War II. In 1940, Cola Debrot (born 1902), H. G. Hoekstra (born 1906), and Eduard Hoornik (1910–1970) founded the journal *Criterium* (1940–43), which was dedicated to "romantic rationalism." Since their most important works did not appear until after 1945, they may be regarded as postwar writers. In addition, many writers of the older generation—such as Simon Vestdijk, Theun de Vries (born 1907), Marnix Gijsen (born 1899), Gerrit Achterberg (1905–1962), and Gaston Burssens (1896–1965)—wrote some of their finest work after the war and had a direct influence on younger writers.

FICTION

TRADITION: THE MAIN CONCERNS OF OLDER NOVELISTS

The break with the past was less noticeable in fiction than in poetry, largely because the leading prewar novelists continued to write well into the postwar period. The prolific Simon Vestdijk was the unchallenged master of the novel of psychological realism, rooted in depth psychology. His works often drew upon recollections of his own youth. The autobiographical element was particularly pronounced in the Anton Wachter cycle, composed of eight novels, four of which appeared before 1940. *De koperen tuin* (1950, The Garden Where the Brass Band Played), a pitiless account of an unsuccessful love affair and a miscarried attempt to escape from the narrow-mindedness of a small town, also contained autobiographical details. In the trilogy *Symfonie van Victor Slingeland* (1958–60, Symphony of Victor Slingeland) the first-person narrator, a musician, analyzes his own creative genius.

Among Vestdijk's psychoanalytically oriented novels, which sometimes seem too contrived, the eschatological *De kellner en de levenden* (1949, The Waiter and the Living) was particularly noteworthy. A shared vision of Doomsday leads the tenants of a high-rise apartment building into a ghastly journey through the abyss of their own fears, during which they confront a series of infernal horrors. A young waiter who serves these "displaced persons" represents their only hope.

Vestdijk also demonstrated his psychological interests in his panoramic historical novels. The central question of his novel about Voltaire, *De filosoof en de sluipmoordenaar* (1961, The Philosopher and the Assassin), is whether the poetic man does not always tend to present his own imaginative view of things as the definitive one, thus obscuring reality for other people as well as for himself. The demythologizing *De held van Temesa* (1962, The Hero of Temesa) showed how the traces of vengeful gods were effaced as Greek culture declined in Asia Minor. In his theological novels Vestdijk tried to unmask religious cults while showing considerable understanding for religious feelings.

The historical novels of Theun de Vries, who also began to publish before World War II, have presented the past from a distinctly socialist viewpoint, though not without sympathy and understanding for the nonsocialist characters. Vries's native province of Friesland in northern Holland has been the usual setting of his novels. The lives, thoughts, and actions of twentieth-century people in Friesland have been the subjects of his broadly conceived—and still unfinished—cycle *Fuga van de tijd* (1952ff., Fugue of Time). Vries's fascination with the lives of medieval artists inspired *Het motet van de kardinaal* (1960, The Motet of the Cardinal), which was based on the life of Josquin Desprez, and *Moergrobben* (1964, Marsh Specters), about Hieronymus Bosch.

Vries's novels have been fairly conventional in structure, as were the successful early works of Hella S. Haasse (born 1918), in which time is handled in a traditional, chronological manner. *Het woud der verwachting* (1950, The Forest of Expectation), a colorful, gripping description of the times of Charles d'Orléans, was a good example of her early approach. In her later work, however, brisk storytelling for its own sake yielded to declared commitment. *De ingewijden* (1957, The Initiates) dealt with the woman artist's problems as wife and mother.

All Haasse's novels have shown a keen insight into history. This can be seen most clearly in *Een nieuwer testament* (1966, A Newer Testament), a novel about the decline of the Roman empire, whose structure has a triptychlike prismatic quality. *A Newer Testament* showed how the establishing of Christianity as the official religion forces non-Christians, like the writer Claudianus, who represents the freedom of the creative personality, into difficult positions.

Helma Wolf-Catz (born 1900) has also liked to draw upon history for her novels, as in her seven-volume "Sidonia cycle." *Diepzee* (1960, Deep Sea) begins in the present; and Wolf-Catz returns to the present by way of a wide network of past associations, so that the final volume, *Luchtkristal* (1964, Air Crystal), has the same central character as the first volume of the cycle. This old-fashioned *roman fleuve* was an unusual high point in postwar Netherlandic literature. Wolf-Catz had earlier written one of the best novels about life under the Hitler terror—*De dreiging* (1946, The Threat). Her basic stance is humanistic, like that of Hella Haasse, but Wolf-Catz has focused more on man's moral abysses.

Wolf-Catz's contemporary Marnix Gijsen resembles her in his humanism. Most of his books constitute a progressive stripping away of all a priori dogmas and conventions, so as to find life's true values. The protagonists of his work are always ready to abandon themselves totally to situations, however dangerous they may be. In *Het boek van Joachim van Babylon* (1947, The Book of Joachim of Babylon) the husband of the chaste Susannah recounts his tragedy and his struggle toward a skeptical affirmation of life. In *Er gebeurt nooit iets* (1956, Nothing Ever Happens) one of the characters turns into a murderer behind the façade of daily life. *Klaaglied om Agnes* (1951, Lament for Agnes) dealt with memories of a youthful love affair, whose tenderness is heightened by the World War I background. Admittedly, many of Gijsen's novels have served as mere pretexts for his theses; an example is *De vleespotten van Egypte* (1952, The Fleshpots of Egypt), in which he offered an analysis of America.

Johan Daisne's (born 1912) powerful imagination has given his realism a magical quality, but, of his postwar work, only *De man die zijn haar kort liet knippen* (1947, The Man Who Had His Hair Cut Short) has reached the level of his first novel, *De trap van steen en wolken* (1942, The Staircase of Stone and Clouds). In *The Man Who Had His Hair Cut Short,* the narrator, a man suspected of murder, tries to analyze the crime he is accused of. This structurally interesting novel consists of three sharply defined parts: the idyllic description of a never-admitted youthful love, the

bluntly realistic account of an inquest, and the hallucinations of the narrator, who believes he has killed the woman he once loved.

Anna Blaman's (1905–1960) *Eenzaam avontuur* (1948, Lonely Adventure), another work in which the central character becomes inextricably
involved in someone else's life, was similar to *The Man Who Had His Hair
Cut Short. Lonely Adventure* was the first work in postwar Dutch fiction to
use the novel-within-a-novel technique successfully. After dealing primarily
with homosexual problems in her early novels, Blaman extended her
sympathies to man in general and his unbearable loneliness. Her most
important work, *Op leven en dood* (1954, Of Life and Death), in which
psychological analysis transcended the danger of clinical intellectuality,
ends with the realization that the only thing man has left is the illusion of
happiness.

In *De nacht der Girondijnen* (1957, The Night of the Girondists), a
novella about the persecution of the Jews, Jacob Presser (1899–1970)
combined psychological analysis with great sympathy for his characters.
The problem of being a Jew was also a dominant theme in *Het wilde feest*
(1952, The Wild Feast) by Adriaan van der Veen (born 1916), which
described how an apolitical refugee moves toward commitment. Sartre's
statement that to seek to avoid decisions is to opt for self-deception could
serve as the epigraph for this novel and other similar works of Veen, such
as *Een idealist* (1966, An Idealist), in which evasion of a decision leads
directly to hypocrisy and inhumanity.

Cola Debrot's *Bewolkt bestaan* (1948, Overcast Existence) also depicted man as seeking a way out of the despair of being polarized between
body and soul, earth and heaven. Debrot strove to solve existentially a
basic Christian problem. The novels of the Catholic literary critic Jos
Panhuysen (born 1900) have usually taken the daily life of the common
man as a point of departure for positing Christian problems. In *Iedereen
weet het beter* (1955, Everybody Knows Better) a simple man falls into the
trap that awaits everyone; he casts himself into the wheel of fate and
becomes a criminal. Maria Rosseels (born 1916), in *Ik was een christen*
(1957, I Was a Christian), approached the crises of a Christian existence
in a different way.

Through the historical subject of the novel *Een vinger op de lippen*
(1952, A Finger on the Lips) Pierre H. Dubois (born 1917) traced his
own development from Catholicism to agnosticism. An imprisoned monk
awaiting death renders an account to himself and to his former god, articu-
lating the philosophical doubt of modern man. Dubois, an ethical agnostic
who prizes human dignity above all else, has upheld humanism and has
longed for a meaningful spiritual reality, a world of perfection and pure
humanity. Dubois's work embodies the tragic sense of life of "romantic

rationalism" and an awareness of the unbridgeable abyss between the acquirable knowledge here and an unattainable life beyond the spiritual boundaries of our time.

Hubert Lampo (born 1920) has been less strongly influenced by existentialism, but cares more about the use of language. *Terugkeer tot Atlantis* (1953, Return to Atlantis) convincingly presented his search for another, more meaningful reality. His novel about a messiah, *De komst van Joachim Stiller* (1960, The Coming of Joachim Stiller), also had a transcendental dimension. On the other hand, his first novel, *Hélène Defraye* (1945, Hélène Defraye), a profound analysis of the mind of a young girl, had linked him to psychological realism.

FANTASY AND EXOTICISM

Netherlandic fiction has traditionally taken reality as its point of departure, and even the most fabular works usually retain a trace of it. This is true of Alfred Kossmann (born 1922), whose partly autobiographical novel *De nederlaag* (1950, The Defeat) dealt with his experiences in German camps for foreign workers. Kossmann's tendency toward fantasy first expressed itself in very original poetry, then in a series of short novels in which realism is blended with fantasy in fascinating combinations, sometimes with Kafka-like effects.

Writers of playfulness and fantasy have generally preferred shorter prose forms. The stories of Belcampo (born 1902, pseudonym of Herman Schönfeld Wichers) reflect a logical, philosophical mind, which gives an overt seriousness to his absurd fantasies. Godfried Bomans (1913–1971) built on the deliberate discrepancy between the comic nature of what he says and the rather solemn, serious tone in which he says it; his humor stems from rather tenacious willfulness. While Bomans creates types, Simon Carmiggelt (born 1909) confronts his readers with individual characters whose fates concern them. Carmiggelt sees comedy in tragedy and vice versa. The most characteristic feature of his numerous short stories is their gentle resignation rather than their predominantly linguistic humor. Carmiggelt and another writer of short prose, Anton Koolhaas (born 1912), have been among the most individualistic personalities in postwar Netherlandic literature. Koolhaas has put his stamp on the genre of animal stories. Like Aesop, he projects human themes and problems into the animal world; his primary aim has been to show the role of instinct in man's behavior and help us to recognize it the better through this process of projection.

Adriaan Morriën (born 1912) won recognition for *Een slordig mens* (1951, An Untidy Man) and *Een bijzonder mooi been* (1955, An Unusually Beautiful Leg)—light prose pieces that are more profound than they appear at first sight. The works of Willem G. van Maanen (born 1920) have an element of fantasy reminiscent of Kafka's *Die Verwandlung*. Maanen's ironic novel *De onrustzaaier* (1954, Disturbers of the Peace) was a welcome break from the ponderousness of so many Netherlandic novels. A passionate feud over a school transforms an outwardly charming Dutch town into a morass of malice and smear campaigns. The dispassionate narrator uses this behavior to expose all the forces that obstruct spiritual renewal.

Fantasy has sought neither to transform reality nor to evade it, although the possibility of such escapism certainly exists in modern literature. Without falling into unworldly idyllicism, Clare Lennart (born 1899), a late neoromantic, has shown her characters discovering the fundamental goodness of the earth and of human life, as in *Stad met rose huizen* (1954, Town with Pink Houses) and *De ogen van Roosje* (1957, Roosje's Eyes).

Maria Dermoût (1888–1962) was more mysterious and exotic. She did not begin to publish until 1951, when several prose works in a distinctly East Indian vein appeared; these were well received abroad as well as in the Netherlands. Dermoût had a special talent for suggesting the presence of invisible forces that affect the lives of men. Reminiscing about the Netherlands East Indies was also a major concern in *De eilanden* (1952, The Islands), a collection of short stories by Albert Alberts (born 1911) written in a brittle style. His short novel *De bomen* (1953, The Trees) tells the story of a boy growing up in the depths of the country; he enters into a pact with the trees, and the pact seems to protect him from all the dangers that beset him.

Memories of Holland's lost colonial possessions have produced varied reactions, not necessarily reflecting particular political viewpoints. *Vergeelde portretten* (1954, Faded Portraits) by E. Breton de Nijs (born 1908), some of Hella S. Haasse's works, and *Het laatste uur* (1953, The Final Hour), a more critical novel by Albert van der Hoogte (1909–1970), transfigured the past by recreating the relatively unthreatened colonial world when these writers were children.

Quite unlike this mainstream of "colonial" literature has been the work of a younger writer, Jef Geeraerts (born 1930). He has described the disastrous effect of European civilization on the people of Africa in two linked novellas, *Ik ben maar een neger* (1962, I Am Only a Negro) and *Het verhaal van Matsombo* (1966, The Story of Matsombo). Geeraerts's language is often as brutal as his subject matter.

NEONATURALISM

For those born after 1920, World War II was a formative experience. After the radical unmasking of man by war and terror, the traditional ethical values of literature were not entirely adequate to such gross realities as force, deception, corruption, and sadism. Thus, many younger writers tended to interpret man primarily in the light of his brutish side. This led to a neonaturalism, whereby the writer considered it his duty to shock those who had not as yet recognized that the bourgeois, Christian, humanist system of values was a monstrous fraud and to unmask those who upheld it. Even when the war, the occupation, and the Nazi terror were not the direct subjects of these black novels, violent strife was taken as the mode of human behavior.

The works of Piet van Aken (born 1920), however, have shown that this view was by no means one-dimensional. While Aken has had an eye for the bestial, demonic forces in man, he is far from tarring all humanity with the same brush, even in his harshest work, the peasant novel *Het begeren* (1953, Desire), set in the nineteenth century. He conceives these passions as sublimated in the service of the great humanist idea of socialism.

Another champion of socialism—though one with far fewer illusions—has been Louis Paul Boon (born 1920). In his major works, the novels *De Kapellekensbaan* (1953, Kapellekens Road) and *Zomer te Termuren* (1956, Summer in Termuren), he dealt, from a committed viewpoint, with the misery of the proletariat in the recent past, adapting his style and narrative technique as closely as possible to the teeming life of the common people.

Willem Frederik Hermans (born 1921) can match Boon's realism—and sometimes his blasphemy and obscenity too—but this "mannerist of nausea" has shown no signs of social commitment and not much love for his fellow men. His characters, who almost without exception are peculiarly aggressive, are motivated by an insistent hatred for untruthful or absurd life. In *De tranen der acacia's* (1949, The Tears of the Acacias) Hermans painted a horrifying picture of the Nazi-occupation years in Amsterdam and the week of the liberation by the Allies in Brussels. *De donkere kamer van Damocles* (1958, The Dark Room of Damocles) was an oppressive account of a young member of the resistance who is suspected of collaborating with the Nazis. Its underlying theme is that people do not really know one another but merely perceive each other's façades. Hermans's novellas, collected under a characteristic title, *Paranoia* (1953, Paranoia), have also depicted a sadistic universe. His recent novel, *Nooit meer slapen* (1965, Never Sleep Again), dealt with a mysterious expedition, which suddenly seems to its participants to symbolize life itself and man's inadequate equipment for it. This novel introduced a new element into Hermans's work: man's shock when he is confronted with the annihilating power of nature.

Gerard Kornelis van het Reve's (born 1923) first novel, *De avonden*

(1947, The Evenings), has been unsurpassed as a self-portrait of a member of the war and postwar generation. It paints a moving yet ruthless picture, with flashes of humor, of the inner experiences, the fears and revulsions, of a young man who cannot understand how adults can keep on living unaffected in their bourgeois comfort. The atmosphere of world weariness, introversion, and defensive behavior was even more strikingly rendered in Reve's later novels, the epistolary *Op weg naar het einde* (1964, On the Way to the End) and *Nader tot U* (1966, Nearer to You). In these novels religious feelings alternate with sadistic impulses, and the sublime and the vulgar constantly enter into peculiar but fascinating combinations. Reve has expressed morbid gloom in a remarkably cool style.

In his distaste for life and in his malicious humor, Harry Mulisch (born 1927) is not far behind Hermans and Reve. *De versierde mens* (1957, The Decorated Man) was a collection of excellent novellas on the theme of man's isolation. Through the story of a former American bomber pilot, the novel *Het stenen bruidsbed* (1959, The Stone Bridal Bed) posed the question of human responsibility. Most of Mulisch's works have combined an inexhaustible inventiveness and a brilliant, sometimes visionary style with a touch of charlatanism. In recent years he has been vociferously proclaiming the death of the novel.

Many younger writers' pursuit of naturalism has gone hand in hand with a liking for autobiographical material. Jan Wolkers's (born 1926) Calvinist past has retained an oppressive relevance for him, and sex represents a no less powerful elemental force in relationships between men and women. These obsessions formed the basis of his strikingly suggestive and successful novellas, such as *Serpentina's petticoat* (1961, Serpentina's Petticoat). His short novel *Een roos van vlees* (1963, A Rose of Flesh) was a gripping description of a man plunged into terrible isolation. In his openly autobiographical *Terug naar Oegstgeest* (1965, Back to Oegstgeest) Wolkers seemed to be taking leave of the experiences of his own youth. Unfortunately, this was not a final farewell, and his subsequent works have been little more than facile repetitions.

In the works of Hugo Claus (born 1929) the obsession with sex and animalism has also been dominant, but his range of subjects is greater than Wolkers's. Claus's first, almost expressionistic, novel, *De Metsiers* (1951, The Metsiers), depicted an asocial peasant family addicted to all kinds of evil. Claus's strong talent for observation and his eruptive, cinematic narrative style, with sudden flashes of brilliance, have continued to characterize his work. Although the negative side of human nature seems to dominate his work, a yearning for innocence began to show through the gloom. A modulation of naturalism by more humane touches has marked Claus's more recent novels, such as *De verwondering* (1962, The Astonishment) and *Omtrent Deedee* (1963, Concerning Deedee), both of which dealt with the problematic nature of loyalty.

The Flemish Claus has had a number of followers in his own country. Astère Michel Dhont's (born 1937) *God in Vlaanderen* (1965, God in Flanders) was an attempt to supplant the traditional Flemish novel, as represented by Felix Timmermans's (1886–1947) *Het kindeke Jezus in Vlaanderen* (1917, The Christ Child in Flanders).

Ward Ruyslinck's (born 1929) *De ontaarde slapers* (1957, The Degenerate Sleepers), the story of a man deranged by war who tries to escape from the brutality and senselessness of the modern world in sleep, and his novel *Het dal van Hinnom* (1961, The Valley of Hinnom) were further examples of the contemporary black novel. Jan Walravens (1920–1965), Flemish literature's untiring champion of modernism, received only posthumous recognition for his bleak, despairing novels *Roerloos aan zee* (1951, Motionless by the Sea) and *Negatief* (1958, Negative).

NEW DIRECTIONS

Many of the younger novelists have written largely autobiographical works, in which they identify completely with today's drifting urban generation. Because their fiction is in many ways experimental, it can no longer be described as purely neonaturalistic.

Out of the alienation of youth, Andreas Burnier (born 1931) created in *Een tevreden lach* (1965, A Contented Smile) a picaresque *Bildungsroman* whose hero attains his own authenticity after suffering the "twelve blows of fate." *Het jongensuur* (1969, The Hour of Youth) was a retrospective account of the psychological troubles of a rather masculine Jewish girl during the war. The problems of homosexuality dealt with in *The Hour of Youth* could also be found in *De getatoeeerde Loreley* (1968, The Tattooed Loreley) by Jaap Harten (born 1930).

A number of younger writers have created lyrical novels by allying techniques of poetry with those of fiction. Andreas Burnier is one. The subjective novels of Judicus Verstegen (born 1933), such as *De koekoek in de klok* (1969, The Cuckoo in the Clock), are further examples.

The aim of Willem Brakman (born 1922) has been to examine some previously unexplored questions. *Een winterreis* (1961, A Winter Journey) dealt with the Pyrrhic victory that modern technological society has achieved in prolonging life. *De opstandeling* (1963, The Rebel) criticized the frequently close connection between sex and violence and also prepared the way for Brakman's later attacks on Christianity. At the heart of his work lies a religion of nature, in which life and death, desire and loyalty, weave endlessly changing patterns.

A faith in nature rooted in sex has found its clearest expression in a long polemical novel by Jacques Hamelink (born 1939), *Ranonkel, de geschiedenis van een verzelving* (1969, Ranonkel, the Story of Becoming Oneself), in which Hamelink saw the stamping out of civilization through the overgrowth of nature as the only hope for human salvation. In the novella collection *Het plantaardig bewind* (1964, The Plant Regime) he had already addressed himself to the theme of man's close ties to nature— although here he concentrated on the threatening aspect of nature. The short stories in *Horror vacui* (1966, the title is in Latin: Horror of Emptiness) also combined an irrational faith in the dark forces of plant life with excursions into pathology.

Skepticism about the traditional novel's photographic rendering of reality, together with misgivings about the traditional novel as an art form capable of revealing a deeper dimension of life, led a number of writers to make a radical turn toward experimental fiction. Bert Schierbeek (born 1918) was one of the first, with two difficult books inspired by James Joyce, whose very titles—*Het boek Ik* (1951, The Book i) and *De derde person* (1953, The Third Person)—indicate their predominantly linguistic nature. Schierbeek has also used "automatic writing," passively giving himself over to streams of consciousness, which express the state of mind of contemporary man, shifting from fear to ecstasy, from rebellion to tranquillity. In *Het dier heeft een mens getekend* (1960, The Animal Drew a Man) all Schierbeek's "voices" blended: narrative, myth, and lyrical impulses.

Ivo Michiels's (born 1923) works have been akin to Schierbeek's. In *Het afschied* (1957, The Leave Taking) a ship's crew members, who have already taken leave of their families but wait for days for the order to sail, represent the psychic tensions and insecurities of mankind. In *Het boek Alfa* (1963, The Book Alpha) the stream of consciousness of a soldier on guard duty reflects the uncertainty of modern man. Michiels does not probe the inner psychology of his characters but rather projects them onto outward reality.

The poet Sybren Polet's (born 1924) novels have been both playful and profound. The elderly title character of the novel *Breekwater* (1962, Breekwater) is born in the true sense only when he becomes aware of his self, and this leads to some amusing confusions.

Paul de Wispelaere (born 1928) has been a leading theoretician and practitioner of the experimental Netherlandic novel. In the hope of finally mastering the past, the first-person narrator of *Een eiland worden* (1963, To Become an Island) brings his consciousness to bear on it in various ways. In *Paul Tegenpaul* (1970, Paul Antipaul) Wispelaere blurred all distinctions between reader, writer, and characters. Cees Nooteboom's (born 1933) presentation of poetic uncertainty in *De ridder is gestorven* (1963, The Knight Is Dead) was somewhat mannerist. It is a book about a dead novelist engaged in writing a book about a dead novelist.

Many of these experimental novels might be called novels of situation in the existential sense: the human being exists only by virtue of ever-new situation-determined decisions that lead to ever-new experiences of the self, so that the personality represents the sum of all these time-and-place-determined concrete situations. Hugo Raes's (born 1929) *Een faun met kille horentjes* (1967, A Faun with Cold Little Horns) was a good example of the novel of situation; an anonymous narrator reflects upon the unending battle of the sexes, and the faun, like an accomplished puppeteer of fate, manipulates the strings that control events.

The hero in *Grillige Kathleen* (1966, Capricious Kathleen) by René Gysen (1927–1969) is a man involved in a *Lolita*-like situation; he realizes with dismay that his youth is over and tries to overcome the situation by using three different linguistic modes. Jacq Firmin Vogelaar (born 1944) presented a young woman in a state of utter psychological confusion in the noncausally related, associative series of mosaiclike fragments that make up *Anatomie van een glasachtig lichaam* (1966, Anatomy of a Glasslike Corpse). But the most successful Netherlandic experimental novel so far may well be Jeroen Brouwers's (born 1940) *Joris Ockeloen en het wachten* (1966, Joris Ockeloen and Waiting), which portrayed a man whose own sexuality has become repulsive to him because it has been so commercialized that it no longer bears any relation to his unconscious archetype of sacred love.

POETRY

POETS OF THE 1940s: A PERIOD OF TRANSITION

While Flanders has always been a land of storytellers, Holland has traditionally been a land of poets. In Flanders, where the threats to the language from French have been serious, poetic conventions have survived much longer than in Holland, where a combination of experimentation and tradition has proved very fertile, especially since World War II. In Flanders during the 1940s, one of the staunchest advocates of the poetry of the younger generation was Gaston Burssens, a champion of the fruitful mixture of tradition and renewal generally so rare in Flemish poetry. Burssens's collection *Het neusje van de inktvis* (1956, The Little Nose of the Cuttlefish) documented the steady growth of his fine talent; Burssens has rhythm and sound play an integral part in his poetic statement.

This interweaving of traditional and experimental elements, which could almost be called a prerequisite of modern poetry, is lacking in the works of the other Flemish poets who came to the fore after the war, including Christien d'Haen (born 1923), Herwig Hensen (born 1917), Hubert van Herreweghen (born 1920), and Karel Jonckheere (born 1906). Without departing from tradition, Jos de Haes (born 1920) nonetheless tried to renew his poetry through greater intensity and clarity. His volume *Azuren holte* (1964, Azure Grottoes) built a bridge to experimental poetry through its dense language and unusual, condensed metaphors.

The key position of linking the old and the new in Holland was held by Gerrit Achterberg. His major postwar collections were *Doornroosje* (1947, Sleeping Beauty), *Sneeuwwitje* (1949, Snow White), *Spel van de wilde jacht* (1957, Game of the Wild Hunt), and *Vergeetboek* (1961, Forget Book). For Achterberg, the central goal of the poem was to transcend the boundary between life and death, which has claimed his beloved, to call her back from beyond this boundary, and to resurrect her in its very words. Out of this Orphic inspiration Achterberg wrote hundreds of poems, some of which are like magical incantations. His attempts to heighten the magical function of language by making it very dense led him to experiments with language and form and to an increasingly rigorous prosody. The conquest of death seems to stand for the ultimate realization of what is normally impossible, yet within the province of poetry.

All postwar Dutch poetry with any claim to modernity has had to come to terms with Achterberg's achievements in language. Indeed, the other poets of his generation were no match for him linguistically, with the possible exception of Margarethe Vasalis (born 1909), who—in such works as *Vergezichten en gezichten* (1954, Views and Faces)—sought to discern eternal, death-defying qualities. Ida Gerhardt (born 1905), who has written in a classically austere style, has shown a kinship to Vasalis in such volumes as *Het levende monogram* (1954, The Living Monogram) and *De ravenveer* (1970, The Raven Feather).

This generation of poets that came to the fore in the 1940s included several who had undergone horrifying wartime experiences. Maurits Mok (born 1907) has confined himself almost exclusively to the subject of a Jewish survivor of Nazi terrorism, as in *Gedenk de mens* (1957, Think of Man). For Eduard Hoornik the Dachau concentration camp became an inescapable symbol of reality. Yet he could not easily cope with the idea of the death of God and accepted it only reluctantly—and never completely. Gabriël Smit (born 1910) has confronted similar religious problems in *Dichterbij* (1964, Coming Closer) and *Op mijn woord* (1968, Upon My Word). In Smit's work, however, as well as in the novelist Adriaan Morriën's *Vriendschap voor een boom* (1954, Friendship for a Tree), a new closeness to nature began to make itself felt. The best erotic poems in

Morriën's *Het gebruik van een wandspiegel* (1968, The Use of a Wall Mirror) also conveyed wonder at the closeness of things.

Een voetreis naar Rome (1946, To Rome on Foot), a long poem by Bertus Aafjes (born 1912), extolled uncomplicated earthly love and beauty; but in the graceful sonnets of *Het koningsgraf* (1948, The Royal Grave), in which Thanatos joined Eros, Aafjes struck a deeper note. The striking poetry in Pierre Kemp's (1886–1967) collection *Bloemlezing uit zijn kleine liederen* (1953, Harvest from His Small Songs), with its bold metaphors, presented a seemingly problem-free attitude to man and the world, albeit with a hint of regret (which has grown more marked as Kemp gets older) for the transitoriness of all beauty. His *Engelse verfdoos* (1956, English Paint Box) ranks among the best postwar Dutch poetry.

The poetry of Christiaan Johannes van Geel (born 1917) derives its originality from language which sometimes verges on the bizarre and which seeks to render extraordinary experiences of nature. His collections have included *Spinroc, en andere gedichten* (1958, Spinroc, and Other Poems) and *Uit de hoge boom geschreven* (1967, Written from the High Tree). His work is related to that of Leo Vroman (born 1915), whose scientific viewpoint has left its unmistakable stamp on his poetry. An extremely precise critical perception combined with a boundless imagination has made Vroman a modern-day magician: he is able to dissect the phenomena of life analytically, and then to reassemble and poetically reanimate the components, so that we seem to find ourselves in a new, curiously recognizable world very close to our own but never identical with it. Vroman's tendency toward the bizarre has increased recently and made his second collection, *114 gedichten* (1969, 114 Poems), less valuable than the earlier *126 gedichten* (1965, 126 Poems).

Other poets of the 1940s also developed specific styles. Nes Tergast (born 1896) has created sequences of associative images in the tradition of the French surrealists. The deliberately antipoetic texts of Louis Theodoor Lehmann (born 1919) have a certain brashness and tired skepticism. C. Buddingh' (born 1918) began as a writer of light verse and a supporter of dadaism and surrealism, as in *Gorgelrijmen* (1945–53, Jugular Rhymes). But he later turned entirely to the poetry of daily life, although without losing his eye for the poetic in the midst of the mundane. Buddingh''s most successful book, *Wil het bezoek afscheid nemen?* (1968, Do the Guests Wish to Say Goodbye?), contained poems written in a parlando style, which may well have future possibilities for Netherlandic poetry. A. Marja (1917–1964) also had doubts about the honesty of literary language and a suspicious attitude toward "beautiful words." What was irony for Marja became in J. B. Charles's (born 1910) poetry biting sarcasm; this sarcasm has also been evident in his polemical attacks on fascism, such as *Volg het spoor terug* (1953, Retrace the Tracks).

EXPERIMENTALISTS OF THE 1950S: ANTIRATIONALISTS AND
MYTHOLOGICAL POETS

The period of experimental antirationalism, which began about 1948
and ended soon after 1960, was unquestionably the most important period
in postwar Netherlandic poetry, especially in Holland. It was paralleled by
another trend, usually known as the "mythological school." Experimental
poetry began on the margins of experimental painting and received significant support from the journal *Het woord*.

The experimentalists were not interested in playing games unrelated to
their world and times; they wanted to open up new possibilities for poetic
expression and unknown dimensions of human existence long buried under
layers of rationalistic thinking. They were greatly helped by the publication, in 1950, of a crucial little volume of poetry *Het innerlijk behang* (The
Inner Wallpaper) by Hans Lodeizen (1924–1950). Here world-weariness
heightened by an awareness of sexual abnormality and a premonition of
death were expressed in novel metaphors without any wrenched striving for
effect.

Yet Lodeizen had an insidious influence on the young poets of the late
1950s and early 1960s. The early work of Simon Vinkenoog (born 1928),
such as *Wondkoorts* (1950, Wound Fever), full of hatred and sadness,
was an example. Nevertheless, *Wound Fever* was better than Vinkenoog's
later "public" poetry, which has often been too vociferous.

Remco Campert's (born 1929) early work also owed something to
Lodeizen. Campert was the first to attempt a deliberately prosaic style, and
even disguised himself as a nonpoet; and, indeed, he was unfortunately
caught up by the strong antipoetic trend of the 1960s. His early poetry,
Bij hoog en bij laag (1959, High and Holy), whose moods ranged from
tenderness to irony, was quite different from his later work. An older poet
who shared Campert's liking for understatement was Jan Hanlo (1912–
1969), who, with a chameleonlike talent, tackled sophisticated experiments with language as readily as traditional forms.

Hans Andreus (born 1926), like Hanlo, avoided a radical break with
tradition. His early, playful poetry, *Muziek voor kijkdieren* (1951, Music
for Peeping Animals), posed the same haunting metaphysical questions he
confronted more completely in *Sonnetten van de kleine waanzin* (1957,
Sonnets of Small Madness), which brought new prestige to the out-of-
fashion sonnet form. In his more recent poems nature and love seem
rooted in a deeper dimension that can only be called mystical.

A number of Flemish poets, including Ben Cami (born 1920), Erik van
Ruysbeek (born 1915), Marcel Wauters (born 1921), and Albert Bont-
ridder (born 1921), the ecstatic of his generation, have also been haunted
by serious existential notions. The fondness of the Flemish experimentalists

for ponderous sentence structure and logical syntax generally keeps them closer to the rationalist tradition than their colleagues in Holland.

The Flemish Hugo Claus is no less significant as a poet than as a novelist and dramatist. Despite its aggressive tone, *Een huis, dat tussen nacht en morgen staat* (1951, A House That Stands between Night and Morning) openly expressed his fear of life and attacked what he saw as the threats of society, civilization, old age; he came to the bitter realization that paradise was irrevocably destroyed and lost. In *De Oostakkerse gedichten* (1955, The Oostakker Poems) Claus's attacks became even more violent.

A romantic urge for the elemental and a desire to return to the beginnings were probably the major stimuli for the experimentalists. Any philosophical, moral, or literary conventions that stood in their way had to be abolished; closed forms were discarded, rigid syntax and punctuation eliminated, and previously formulated metaphors rejected in favor of autonomous imagery.

The work of Lucebert (born 1924), certainly the most radical poet of the 1950s, has been the clearest illustration of this experimentalism. His profound agonizing mistrust of the pleasures of this world has led him to protest against the times and even, in *Apokrief* (1952, Apocrypha), to proclaim a strange revolution. Lucebert wants to help his contemporaries break through into another reality, which he calls the "realm of complete life"—a more essential reality in which man must recognize himself as totally insignificant. Many of Lucebert's poems describe this awareness of his own unimportance as an ecstatic joy. Instead of self-aggrandizement and human arrogance he has urged loss of self and absorption in the immensity of nature.

Lucebert's revolution demands prostration rather than revolt. Only by casting off the self can man become so light that he can conquer the abyss by soaring above it, Lucebert announced in *Van de afgrond en de luchtmens* (1953, Of the Abyss and Ethereal Man). Lucebert's increasing closeness to Taoism and Zen Buddhism has not, however, prevented him from writing political verse and poems of social criticism.

The socialist convictions of Lucebert's former "comrade-in-arms" Jan G. Elburg (born 1919) made him immune to Lucebert's mythic and mystical ideas. The revolution Elburg proclaimed in *Laag Tibet* (1952, Lower Tibet), for instance, was purely political. The poems of Sonja Prins (born 1912) have reflected a similar political commitment.

Gerrit Kouwenaar (born 1923), insofar as he can be called a political poet, has been chiefly concerned with creating a sense of human solidarity. This was most clearly expressed in the urban poetry of *De stem op de 3e etage* (1960, The Voice on the Third Floor). Kouwenaar has always been preoccupied with problems of verbal communication. For him, words contain the interpretations of reality of bygone generations; thus, to speak meaningfully, one would have to free oneself from all "names." In *Zonder namen* (1962, Without Names) Kouwenaar sought a solution in the form of a "language of the flesh." Later, he proposed an intellectually filtered language, which, by rejecting all the dead "names" that kill communication, could question the substance of contemporary life.

Sybren Polet has also been in search of an adequate language to deal with present-day reality. In such works as *Geboorte-Stad* (1958, Home Town) he set up a sort of science-fiction future to which he exposes the speaker or subjects of his poems. This interaction produces his "new homoid," whose abilities include many of the potentialities of the robot. Polet appropriately called one section of the collection *Konkrete poëzie* (1962, Concrete Poetry) "mutation poetry."

Gust Gils's (born 1924) *Drie partituren* (1962, Three Scores) contained poems in the vein of black humor. But Gils is interested in reconciling man with civilization and helping him to adjust to the logic of our time. Ellen Warmond's (born 1930) terse, "unpoetic" poems, collected in 1969 in *Mens: Een inventaris* (Man: An Inventory) have avoided any attempt to escape into a world where life can be lived more fully than in the city. She has used preponderantly urban imagery with a coolly calculated effect.

Paul Rodenko (born 1920) has become one of the leading theoreticians of experimental poetry. His own poems have been intellectual in tone and have reflected his interest in surrealism and expressionism.

After some appealing landscape poetry and love lyrics, Hans Warren (born 1921) published *Leeuw lente* (1954, Lion Spring), which revealed his striking shift to experimentation. In *Tussen hybris en vergaan* (1969, Between Hubris and Disappearance) nothing troubles the philanthropic seeker of beauty more than the idea of ugly death. Nico Verhoeven (born 1925), another poet with a message, has been firmly committed to the myth of nature; so have H. J. van Tienhoven (born 1923), whose *Flessengroen* (1958, Bottle Green) evoked a Pan-like attitude to landscape, and Leo Herberghs (born 1924), whose *Lessen in landschap* (1968, Lessons in Landscape), with great verbal economy, turned landscape into a multi-dimensional myth.

Man and nature have always been the dominant themes of W. J. van der Molen (born 1923), the poet of homelessness straining his ears in the silent universe to catch the dying footfall of a once-perceived god. Out of the emptiness expressed in *Sous-terrain* (1950, Basement) Molen broke through to the paradoxical hopefulness of *De onderkant van het licht* (1956, The Underside of the Light).

Coert Poort's (born 1922) poetry—*Mannenwerk* (1961, Man's Work), for example—stands in striking contrast to expansive European civilization. For Poort, poetry's sole function is to reveal secrets, but he has been wary of extracting them from external reality. He is fascinated by the primeval, not in the sense of distant origins but as an ever-present possibility.

The most important of these myth-oriented poets has been Guillaume van der Graft (born 1920). His *Mythologisch* (1950–54, Mythological) took the nature myth as its point of departure, while still denying its truth. Behind this attitude lay Graft's early acquaintance with Nazism's mythical interpretation of life. In *Vogels en vissen* (1953, Birds and Fish) he dealt with man's freedom in renouncing the myth of the "life that resides within itself." He expressed the wish to be a poetic presence for others in *Woorden van brood* (1956, Words of Bread); this represented an attempt to break out of the vicious circle of individualism.

Like Graft, Jan Wit (born 1914) came to poetry from theology. But many of Wit's poems are satirical, and he has a sharp sense of humor. *In den metalen stier* (1954–55, In the Metal Bull) offered a comprehensive display of his talents.

While Wit and Graft have used both free verse and fixed forms, Jan Willem Schulte Nordholt (born 1920), who is closely akin to them intellectually, has stuck to strict meter. Volumes such as *Een lichaam van aarde en licht* (1961, A Body of Earth and Light) have included nature and landscape poems as well as religious ones well adapted to our nonreligious age. Similar themes have been taken up in the free-form sonnets of the Catholic poet Michel van der Plas (born 1927).

THE 1960s: FURTHER EXPERIMENTS AND A NEW RELIGIOUSNESS

In the 1950s Netherlandic poetry made an unprecedented advance. This was followed in the 1960s by an unfortunate regression, both in the form of a depressing imitativeness and in the form of a second, but much less fruitful wave of experimentalism.

The second generation of experimentalists includes Paul Snoek (born 1934) and Hugues C. Pernath (born 1932); Pernath's *Instrumentarium voor een winter* (1963, Instruments Needed for a Winter) communicated an immense loneliness. But for these younger writers, the poem no longer corresponded to any kind of objective reality, so that it became its own subject; aestheticism has taken over, while pretending to do just the opposite. *Geachte Muizenpoot, en andere gedichten* (1965, Esteemed Mouse Paw, and Other Poems) by F. ten Harmsen van der Beek (born 1927), with its weird, logic-defying view of the world, was less sterile.

The coldness of so-called objective and informative poetry during the 1960s can be explained by the decision of a group of younger poets to eliminate personal statement of any kind, even personally chosen words. This resulted in a revival of the "chance object" technique, which dates back to shortly after World War I. The poem becomes a montage of preexisting texts; in fact the word "text" replaces the word "poem." It is no longer important to pursue the creative process to the end; the reader can do this for himself. The artist's function is limited to the selection and arrangement of the textual components.

The only one of these "textual" poets worth mentioning—for his inconsistency—is Hans Verhagen (born 1939). In *Rozen & motoren* (1963, Roses & Motors) he attempted impersonal, "unmanned" poetry. Unintentionally, however, his matter-of-fact tone did not prevent a romantic longing for the "damned time of roses" from breaking through.

The objective poetry of the group around the journal *Barbarber* has shown greater intelligence and, more importantly, more humor and sense of proportion. Its most successful representative is J. Bernlef (born 1937), who often skillfully exploits the potentialities of the "chance object" without absolutely accepting the technique. Since ultimately nothing can exist except concrete reality, the objective poet is obliged to give up any idea of a mysterious reality behind, above, or within the physical world. Despite such premises, Bernlef has often succeeded, especially in *Dit verheugd verval* (1963, This Joyful Decay) and *Bermtoerisme* (1968, Sidewalk Tourism), in discovering or creating unexpected relationships between "facts" by constantly changing his angle of vision.

This "concrete reaction" can be explained as a rebellion against the mythic, often highly subjective linguistic creations of the experimental poetry of the 1950s; but it also shows a deep inner uncertainty .The poetry of the 1950s was closely connected with existentialism. With the ascendancy of a more realistic, neopositivist way of thinking, poetry faced the choice of trying to hold its own, unaided, in the prevailing climate, or of relinquishing its intrinsically poetic character and accommodating itself to new developments.

The journal *Raster* was the center of a group of poets who accepted the new science of linguistics, with its emphasis on modern logic, and conceived the poem purely as a word structure. H. C. ten Berge (born 1939) is typical of this group, with his rigorously constructed poems and poem sequences, full of modifying clauses, which seek to fuse heretogeneous elements into a convincing rendering of multilevel reality. The novelist Jacques Hamelink enjoys a high reputation within this group, although his mythomania is out of line with its cool way of thinking.

A refreshing dislike for big words has linked Judith Herzberg (born 1934), whose austere poems show an aristocratic distaste for the uglification of life, with Rutger Kopland (born 1934), who has drawn his melancholy recollections from the almost inexhaustible well of his own youth. Youthful memories have also been a major subject of Jaap Harten's (born 1930) poetry.

Peter Berger (born 1936) has made a reputation not only as a poet but also as a polemical essayist. His poems have evoked a highly visible and audible world—the concrete reality of a town by the sea—with a delicate sensitivity to the invisible and the inaudible. Mystery and revelation, both in the city and in nature, were the themes of Berger's *Op tegenspraak* (1968, Until We Speak Again). He is interested in the evolution of language from the anthropological point of view and in the origins of life. The hypothesis of *Perm* (1965, Permian System) was that world, life, and humanity are closely connected with one another, an hypothesis that links him to some extent with the mythological poets of the 1950s.

A similar feeling of unity has marked the works of the priest-poet Huub Oosterhuis (born 1933), whose prayer book for a contemporary liturgy, *Bid om vrede* (1966, Send Us Peace), attracted international notice. Themes of exodus and birth have dominated his poetry. A "you" is nearly always involved, whether in the form of his fellow men, his beloved, or God. Only when the hero of Oosterhuis's epic *Parcival* (1970, Perceval) is cast out of the heaven of metaphysics does he find his way to mankind.

Maria de Groot (born 1937) has attracted much attention with very personal religious poems in an unmistakably mystical vein, such as those in *Amsterdams getijdenboekje* (1966, Little Amsterdam Breviary). Her more recent work has shown a turn toward contemporary social and political problems. Another writer of the humanely committed poetry of the 1960s, Mischa de Vreede (born 1936), has shown a coolness that is clearly only the underside of an immense sensibility. In *Binnen en buiten* (1968, Inside and Outside) the inner world of a woman preoccupied with her household and child interacts with the outer world of inhumanity and strife.

DRAMA

Netherlandic dramatic literature has never been overly rich. The theatrophobic attitude of Calvinism, which dominated Holland for many centuries, still shows its traces today. It is strange, however, that Catholic Flanders, which has always been traditionally more receptive to the theater, has hardly an edge on Holland; indeed the important plays of the postwar period, with one noteworthy exception, have all been Dutch, not Flemish.

Only a few Netherlandic works have become part of world theater. Several plays by Jan de Hartog (born 1914), a Dutchman who moved to the United States, were successful in America during the early postwar period. Outstanding among them was *Schipper naast God* (1945, Skipper next to God), which was considered at the time to be a prime example of the Dutch intellectual inheritance, shaped by the eternal struggle with the sea. More commercially successful was *Het hemelbed* (1952, The Four-poster), which was a triumph on Broadway.

World War II has been the subject of several Netherlandic authors, among them August Defresne (1893–1961), whose *De naamlozen van 1942* (1945, The Nameless of 1942) is still worthy of interest. The Flemish Tone Brulin (born 1926) dramatized the retaliatory destruction of the Czech village of Lidice by the Nazis in *Nu het dorp niet meer bestaat* (1958, Now That the Village Does Not Exist Any More). The threat that the atomic bomb poses to mankind was the focus of Maurits Dekker's (1896–1962) *De wereld heeft geen wachtkamer* (1950, The World Has No Waiting Room).

Max Croiset (born 1912), a gifted actor, used a classical setting to discuss specific problems of the war and the postwar period in *De medeplichtigen* (1957, The Helper's Helpers). He reinterpreted the Iphigenia legend in terms of questions of treason and collaboration. The Iphigenia Goethe had idealized appears in *The Helper's Helpers* as a person driven by her hatred for her country, who gladly sheds Greek blood in the service of the barbarian Taurians. Catharsis is completely lacking. Earlier, Croiset had written plays in which the Oedipus and Amphitryon myths received psychological interpretations. *Oidipous en zijn moeder* (1951, Oedipus and His Mother) showed man as prisoner of his own free will.

Jeanne van Schaik-Willing's (born 1895) verse play *Odysseus weent* (1953, Odysseus Cries), a play about marital fidelity, deviated from the classical version of the myth insofar as Odysseus admits that he shares the guilt of Penelope's unfaithfulness and Penelope chases Antinoüs away. The use of a chorus gave *Odysseus Cries* the flavor of a classical play.

Other contemporary reworkings of classical subjects have included the novelist Hella S. Haasse's *Een draad in het donker* (1964, A Thread in the Dark), based on the Ariadne myth, and *Geen bacchanalen* (1971, No Bacchanalia). Although twice removed from its classical source, *No Bacchanalia* transposed the frenzy of the ancient Bacchic rites to the modern city high school. The prolific poet and novelist Hugo Claus also wrote a myth play—*Thyestes* (1966, Thyestes). And the novelist Harry Mulisch has announced a play on the Oedipus theme for the near future.

Various contemporary playwrights have been inspired by biblical subjects. Abel Herzberg's (born 1893) *Herodes* (1954, Herod) and *Sauls dood* (1959, Saul's Death) are more effective when read than when performed because they are so philosophically complex.

Martinus Nijhoff (1895–1953), one of the outstanding poets of the interwar years, wrote three verse plays during the war and immediately thereafter for the principal Christian holidays. The plays gave a new impulse to Netherlandic religious drama. These plays by Nijhoff were published together under the title *Het heilige hout* (1950, The Holy Wood). The plays of T. S. Eliot clearly influenced Nijhoff, as they did the poet Guillaume van der Graft, who published highly original, somewhat pretentious experiments in verse drama under the title *Schijngestalten* (1962, Shining Figures). His "one-act play for three angels," *Het eerste kwartier* (1957, The First Quarter), and the full-length play *Een ladder tegen de maan* (1954, A Ladder against the Moon), inspired by Jacob's dream, can be considered as a further elaboration of Graft's mythological poetry. Graft and Nijhoff wanted to return the drama to its function within the liturgy, where it originated, but they were hardly successful.

Eduard Hoornik showed himself to be a follower of the English verse dramatist Christopher Fry in his first dramatic works; but Hoornik gave stronger emphasis to social relationships than did Fry. In *De bezoeker* (1952, The Visitor) he was able to create an eerie tension. Two married couples wait for an announced visitor, who never appears but whose presence makes itself felt so strongly that one of the characters confesses that he is a murderer. In a way, *The Visitor* anticipated Beckett's *En attendant Godot* (1953). In *Kains geslacht* (1955, Cain's Progeny), Hoornik continued to use verse, but afterward he turned to prose because he realized not only that there was less of an audience for verse drama but also that verse no longer served his goals as playwright. Yet, Hoornik's last works—*Het water* (1957, The Water), *De overlevende* (1968, The Survivor)—were not at all excursions into an antipoetic realism; these plays still showed traces of the mythopoetic.

Also in the vein of the mythopoetic play is the dramatic work of the novelist Bert Schierbeek, who offered a very provocative linguistic innovation in *Een groot dood dier* (1963, A Big Dead Animal). *A Big Dead Animal* was a drama of rebirth, celebrating an erotic ecstasy that has withstood all civilization and has become the last chance to regenerate our doomed existence.

To the category of mystical play also belongs Lodewijk de Boer's (born 1937) extensive dramatic oeuvre. Many of his plays have been performed by student theaters. Boer's early plays—such as *Het gat* (1964, The Hole) and *De verhuizing* (1965, The Move)—showed the influence of Pinter, but his more recent work has been more akin to Artaud's theater of cruelty. *Darts* (1967, Darts), a short "score for actors, voice, and pictures," centers on a pretended Indian legend of a king who has such a lecherous love for his own sister that he has her put to death and then presides unmoved over the fall of his throne and empire.

The audience's feeling of attending a black mass was even more intense in Boer's *Lijkensynode* (1968, Synod of Corpses), which used myths of the early medieval church. Pope Stephanus VI has the corpses of his predecessors disinterred so he can stage a trial and accuse them of a crime of which he feels himself guilty. He is tormented by the thought that at his election as pope the proceedings had something strange about them. In *Borak valt* (1968, Borak Falls) Boer was considerably less under Artaud's influence. His predilection for creating shocking scenes gave way to a desire to tell a continuous story.

Otto Dijk (born 1925) has focused much more on the present in his extremely cleverly constructed absurdist one-act plays. These plays were originally written for television but were soon performed on stage, even abroad. In 1966 seven of Dijk's short plays were published under the title *De laatste der kolonialen* (The Last of the Colonialists).

The fascination of Dijk's plays lies in the tension between the real and the unreal; the plays of the novelist and poet Sybren Polet—such as *Het huis* (1959, The House) and *De koning komt voorbij* (1964, The King Passes By)—however, are so divorced from reality that one can hardly understand them. In these plays the absurd has overstepped its boundaries and has reached a realm in which everything is possible and therefore does not engage our interest any longer.

Much more tenable have been the semiabsurdist plays of Tone Brulin, most notably *Ogen van krijt* (1963, Eyes of Chalk), which dealt with early-American religious hysteria. In a similar absurdist vein was *De Babel* (1963, The Babels) by the novelist Jan Wolkers. In this play space travel becomes an absurd search for God, but the absurdism does not mask the author's seriousness about such a search. More grotesque and more closely related to Wolkers's fiction was his black comedy *Wegens sterfgeval gesloten* (1966, Closed Because of Death).

Harry Mulisch's *De knop* (1959, The Button), which he called a "farce," satirized the insanity of the arms race extremely effectively through a dialogue between two generals. But Mulisch firmly established his reputation as a playwright with his "chronicle of a heretic," *Tanchelyn* (1960, Tanchelyn), which posed the question of the death of God in a historical setting. *Tanchelyn* is a drama about a twelfth-century anti-Christ, who had a tremendous influence through his power over women. An excommunicated priest, Everwachter, a Hitler-like Puritan, uses Tanchelyn as a tool for his own designs. In the end, he eliminates Tanchelyn to save his own life. The dramatic techniques of *Tanchelyn* showed the influence of Brecht (one of the very few plays in the contemporary Netherlandic theater to reflect Brecht's innovations).

The writer of fiction Anton Koolhaas's choice of historical subjects superficially suggests Brecht's influence. But his most powerful play, *Niet doen, Sneeuwwitje* (1966, Don't Do It, Snow White), probably owed more to Jean Anouilh's *L'alouette*. This dramatization of the experiences of a young girl exposed to a jungle of emotions and pursued by maternal jealousy was rich in its psychological perceptions.

The traditions of realistic-naturalistic theater, which was given a distinctly Dutch stamp by Herman Heijermans (1864–1924) during the first quarter of the century, were continued by Jan Staal (born 1925). His first play, *De laatste verlofganger* (1958, The Last One to Be Retired) nostalgically told the story of a plantation owner who has been driven out of Indonesia. She and her daughters are unable to adapt to the alien environment of Holland. Nostalgia and loneliness also characterize the Polish émigré protagonist of Staal's *Terug naar Warschau* (1963, Back to Warsaw), who struggles to make a living in a working people's district of Rotterdam.

Even superior to Staal's technically excellent plays have been the realistic dramas of Hugo Claus. His first play, *Een bruid in de morgen* (1955, A Bride in the Morning), was a great success. It is the tragic story of a forbidden love between an asocial young man, a poetic dreamer, and his sister, who wants to protect him from the evil world of strangers and relatives. *Suiker* (1958, Sugar), a less poetic play, also portrayed a genuine but impossible love. It is the story of a young man from the north of France working as a laborer during the sugar harvest, who falls in love with a provocatively flirtatious girl. The girl is threatened by her former lover.

In *Vrijdag* (1969, Friday), a work deeply rooted in Flemish folklore, Claus again came to grips with the problem of incest. Despite its realism, this play had another dimension, which one can only call religious. It was concerned with the guilt and atonement of two people who have sinned against each other; by passing through purgatory, they find a new way of living together. Also religious, although in a negative sense, was Claus's "imitation" of Seneca's tragedy *Thyestes*. On the surface, this seems to be a play intended to shock, even going as far as advocating cannibalism, as Artaud did; but Claus mainly aimed at depicting the existential problem of man being "thrown" into an absurd world. Claus has been trying to transcend the reality of modern life, which he considers to be meaningless and truthless. He has advocated with great intensity the irrational as the primal cause of human existence; we must relate anew to the irrational if we want to survive.

The recent work of Hugo Claus, like that of Lodewijk de Boer and Harry Mulisch, points to a return to spiritual concerns, which seemed to be buried and forgotten during the 1960s. It is a moot question whether one should rejoice over the rediscovery of the primeval and mythical qualities to which various works, mainly in lyric poetry, seem to point. Should literature see its main mission as a "return to nature," which after all is bound to result in a deification of nature? One should remember an earlier regression of this kind, one that surrendered much of the world to Hitler's terror for many years. That such revaluations of the "natural life" are tied to Marxist thought does not make them more palatable to me. Without doubt this ancient, yet ever-new realm of myth is where decisions about human existence are made. But what is crucial is *how* we decide.

NETHERLANDIC LITERATURE IN ENGLISH TRANSLATION

ANTHOLOGIES

Barnouw, Adriaan Jacob, ed. *Coming After: An Anthology of Poetry from the Low Countries.* New Brunswick, N.J., 1948

Greshoff, Jan, ed. *Harvest of the Lowlands: An Anthology in English Translation of Creative Writing in the Dutch Language, with a Historical Survey of the Literary Development.* New York, 1945

Literary Holland (a periodical). Amsterdam, 1956–59

Wolf, Manfred, ed. *Change of Scene: Contemporary Dutch and Flemish Poems in English Translation.* San Francisco, 1969

Writing in Holland and Flanders (a periodical). Amsterdam, 1959ff.

INDIVIDUAL WORKS MENTIONED IN ARTICLE

Hartog, Jan de. *Het hemelbed* as *The Fourposter.* New York, 1954

―――. *Schipper naast God* as *Skipper next to God.* In John Chapman, ed., *The Best Plays of 1947–48.* New York, 1948

Mulisch, Harry. *Het stenen bruidsbed* as *The Stone Bridal Bed.* New York, 1963

Ruyslinck, Ward. *De ontaarde slapers* as *The Deadbeats.* London, 1968

Timmermans, Felix. *Het kindeke Jezus in Vlaanderen* as *The Christ Child in Flanders.* Chicago, 1960

Veen, Adriaan van der. *Het wilde feest* as *The Intruder.* New York, 1958

Vestdijk, Simon. *De koperin tuin* as *The Garden Where the Brass Band Played.* New York, 1965

Wolkers, Jan. *Een roos van vlees* as *A Rose of Flesh.* New York, 1967

SECONDARY WORKS

BIBLIOGRAPHIES AND GUIDES

Bibliographie van de Nederlandse taal- en literatuurwetenschap. Antwerp, Brussels, and The Hague, 1970ff.

Knuvelder, G. P. M. *Handboek tot de moderne letterkunde,* 2nd ed. 's-Hertogenbosch, 1954–62

Laarschot, K. van der. *Malmbergs bibliographie der Nederlandse kritiek in Noord- en Zuid-Nederland I: Betref-* *fende kritieken in boekvorm verschenen.* 's-Hertogenbosch, 1968

GENERAL WORKS

Brachin, Pierre. *La littérature néerlandaise.* Paris, 1961

Calis, Piet. *Daling van temperatuur: Twaalf Nederlandse dichters 1880–1960.* The Hague, 1964

Hermanowski, Georg. *Die Stimme des schwarzen Löwen: Geschichte des flämischen Romans.* Starnberg, 1961

Lissens, R. F. *De Vlaamse letterkunde van 1780 tot heden,* 4th ed. Brussels and Amsterdam, 1967

Vooys, C. G. N. de and G. Stuiveling. *Schets der Nederlandse letterkunde,* 30th ed. Groningen, 1967

Weevers, T. *Poetry of the Netherlands in Its European Context.* London, 1960

Weisberger, Jean. *Formes et domaines du roman flamand.* Brussels, 1963

WORKS ON CONTEMPORARY LITERATURE

Bernlef, J. *Wie a zegt.* Amsterdam, 1970

Besten, Ad den. *Ik uw dichter: Een hoofd-stuk uit de immanente poetica van de dichters van vijftig.* Haarlem, 1968

———. *Stroomgebied: Een inleiding tot de poëzie van de naoorlogse dichter-generatie.* Amsterdam, 1954

Brandt Corstius, J. C. and Karel Jonckheere. *De literatuur van de Nederlanden in de moderne tijd.* Amsterdam, 1961

Dinaux, C. J. E. *Auteurs van nu.* Amsterdam, 1969

———. *Gegist bestek,* 2 vols. The Hague, 1958–61

Fens, Kees. *De eigenzinnigheid van de literatuur.* Amsterdam, 1964

———. *De gevestigde chaos.* Amsterdam, 1966

Fens, Kees et al. *Literair lustrum: Een overzicht van vijf jaar Nederlandse literatuur.* Amsterdam, 1967

Hermanowski, Georg. *Die moderne flämische Literatur.* Bern, 1963

———. *Säulen der modernen flämischen Prosa.* Bonn, 1969

Jessurun d'Oliveira, H. U. *Vondsten en bevindingen.* Amsterdam, 1967

Jonckheere, Karel. *De Vlaamse letteren vandaag.* Antwerp, 1958

Jonckheere, Karel and Erik van Ruysbeek. *Poëzie en experiment: Dialoog in briefvorm over oud en nieuw in de dichtkunst.* Antwerp, 1956

Rodenko, Paul. *De sprong van Münchhausen.* The Hague, 1958

———. *Tussen de regels: Wandelen en spoorzoeken in de moderne poëzie.* The Hague, 1958

Vestdijk, Simon. *Voor en na de explosie.* The Hague, 1960

Walravens, Jan. *Phenomenologie van de moderne poëzie.* Brussels, 1951

Wispelaere, Paul de. *Facettenoog.* Brussels and The Hague, 1968

———. *Met kritisch oog.* The Hague, 1966

WILHELM FRIESE

Norwegian Literature

WHEN NORWEGIAN LITERATURE entered the "modern" phase (toward the end of the nineteenth century), it still remained intimately tied to the political and social development of the country. In the numerous dramas of Bjørnstjerne Bjørnson (1832–1910) and Henrik Ibsen (1828–1906) and in some of the novels of Jonas Lie (1833–1908) and Alexander Kielland (1849–1906), the authors were concerned less with aesthetic than with social, ethical, and moral problems.

Norwegian authors of the twentieth century have not denied this heritage, and they have made no secret of their wish to communicate a message to their fellow citizens. Knut Hamsun (1859–1952) proclaimed the gospel of the "blessings of the earth." Sigrid Undset (1882–1949) contrasted the world of faith and the chaos of the times. Helge Krog's (1889–1962) dramas subjected Ibsen's rigorous individualism to critical examination. And Nordahl Grieg's (1902–1943) plays put communist doctrines onto the stages of his country. Like drama and fiction, poetry also followed traditional patterns. The prevailing poetic mode remained the epic, characterized by normal syntax, regular stanzaic structure, and rhyme. Until the mid-1950s authors, critics, and readers generally disapproved of all literary experiments.

There are several reasons for this unbroken tradition of realism despite crises and changes. For an author who wants to address a message to a large audience, aesthetic experiments must take a secondary role. A writer

489

cannot enter into an esoteric linguistic world; he must communicate in an understandable language.

But there is another, decisive reason for the tenacity of realism in Norway, and this has to do with an unusual linguistic phenomenon: there are two official forms of the Norwegian language—*nynorsk,* "new Norwegian" (formerly called *landsmål,* "rural language") and *bokmål,* "book language" (formerly called *riksmål,* "state language"). Until the middle of this century changes in both *nynorsk* and *bokmål* seemed to indicate the development of a uniform Norwegian literary language. But many contemporary authors have been reluctant to abandon the particular expressiveness of the linguistically conservative *nynorsk* or of dialect. Thus, a linguistic division still remains, and this split precludes the same kind of experimenting with language one finds in countries in which the literary language had been unequivocally fixed.

Another special feature of Norway is its relative isolation. Living at the geographical and political fringe of Europe, Norwegian writers did not discover the risk and menace to human existence and, consequently, the questionableness of a realistic manner of writing until several decades after the writers of most of the rest of Europe.

The occupation of Norway by German troops during World War II, the end of the war, and the succeeding years of reconstruction did not bring about any major changes in the literary climate. But there was a change of faces. Older writers—Ronald Fangen (1895–1946), Sigurd Christiansen (1891–1947), Knut Hamsun, and Sigrid Undset—fell silent. A middle generation—consisting of authors who had begun publishing in the 1930s—now wrote its most important books, and in these works these writers showed themselves surprisingly more susceptible to the currents of modern world literature than did even younger authors who first began writing in the 1940s. Ironically, the younger authors—as opposed to the middle generation—still used prewar norms to describe our radically changed world.

FICTION

Many writers of fiction had to write their experiences of the war out of their systems, for the dark years of the occupation by Nazi Germany refused to disappear quickly from memory. Sigurd Hoel (1890–1960) published the first critical, indeed relentless, assessment of the "heroic period" of his country (the resistance) in the novel *Møte ved milepelen* (1947, Meeting at the Milestone). In *Stevnemøte med glemte år* (1954, Rendezvous with Forgotten Years) he took up again the problem of the struggle of the Norwegian resistance during Nazi occupation. Like all his novels, these two were in the mode of psychological realism.

Aksel Sandemose's (1899–1965) novels were less traditional. Of the midcentury novelists, he was the one who moved farthest from the epic style of narration. In *Det svundne er en drøm* (Swedish 1944, Norwegian 1946; Whatever Has Disappeared Is a Dream) he took up again the central themes of his earlier novels: he described, harshly and remorselessly, the inner division of man and his evil nature, however repressed it may appear. Variations on this theme kept recurring in Sandemose's subsequent works, including *Varulven* (1958, The Werewolf) and its sequel, *Felicias bryllup* (1961, Felicia's Wedding), in both of which the main figures were victims and murderers at the same time. The mythological creature in *The Werewolf* symbolizes man's destructive spirit, his capacity for hatred, and his will to power.

Many novels of Tarjei Vesaas (1897–1970), the most significant *nynorsk* author of our time, also dealt with the secret driving forces behind human actions. Yet, because of Vesaas's compressed and concise language, his style differed fundamentally from the expansive, convoluted prose of Sandemose. The tension in Vesaas's early novels between realism and symbolism shifted gradually toward symbolism, but the idea of sacrifice and self-sacrifice for one's fellow man remained central, even in Vesaas's late work.

Vesaas's *Kimen* (1940, The Seed) told of man's dark, primitive forces but also of the good within him, a power capable of saving his dignity in the midst of hysteria and mass delusion. The parable *Bleikeplassen* (1946, The Pale Girl), recorded an individual's delusion and his subsequent deliverance. *Huset i mørkret* (1945, The House in the Dark) depicted allegorically the condition of an oppressed country and made clear how difficult it is to assert oneself against evil and terror without becoming like the oppressor oneself.

The simple composition, the condensed and lyrical language, the stylized milieu, and the mood-laden symbols of *The House in the Dark* characterized Vesaas's following novels, although in *Tårnet* (1948, The Tower) and *Signalet* (1950, The Signal) the overly abstract images were not very successful. *Vårnatt* (1954, Spring Night), *Fuglane* (1957, The Birds), and *Is-slottet* (1963, Palace of Ice) described the defenselessness of the individual and the lack of understanding between men. But they showed the overcoming of the individual's isolation and the responsibility of one man for another—ideas also expressed by the title of the novel *Bruene* (1966, The Bridges).

In his many stories published during the 1940s and 1950s, Johan Borgen (born 1902) portrayed the loneliness of man and the power of love to make him find his own identity. Borgen first succeeded as a novelist in the trilogy consisting of *Lillelord* (1955, Little Lord), *De mørke kilder* (1956, The Dark Sources), and *Vi har ham nå* (1957, We Have Him Now). In this trilogy, a broad study of the decline of the Norwegian middle class in the first half of the twentieth century, Borgen illustrated, through his male protagonist, the modern phenomenon of the loss of identity. In the search for true individuality, the first-person narrator in *"Jeg"* (1959, "I"), who is divided into an acting "I" and an observing "I," moves in a world that is partly real and partly fabular and symbolic. Borgen's subsequent novels have likewise made the problem of identity the center of attention. In *Blåtind* (1964, Blue Spire) the self-sacrifice of the main figure achieves positive results; in *Den røde tåken* (1967, The Red Fog), on the other hand, the moment of insight costs the protagonist his life.

The novels of Sigurd Evensmo (born 1912) have been less complicated and far more on the surface than the sociological and psychological explorations of evil and fascism in the works of Hoel, Sandemose, Vesaas, and Borgen. Evensmo's *Englandsfarere* (1945, Travelers to England) was a suspensefully narrated portrayal of an ill-fated attempt to escape to England. Here, as in his next novel concerning the resistance effort, *Oppbrudd etter midnatt* (1946, Escape after Midnight), the theme of the surrender of the individual to the fellowship of a group played an important role. But in *Escape after Midnight* Evensmo lapsed into clichés and simple black-and-white contrasts.

In the trilogy consisting of *Grenseland* (1947, Borderland), *Flaggermusene* (1949, The Bats) and *Hjemover* (1951, Going Home), Evensmo described the failure of a man in the personal and political realm: coming from the borderland, both literally and figuratively, the protagonist does not feel at home anywhere. Evensmo presented a variation on this theme in the melodramatic political thriller *Femten døgn med Gordona* (1963, Fifteen Days with Gordona); yet the tragic ending of the novel showed that there is no individual happiness, since each man is too deeply entangled with the social structures. If the turbulent action of *Fifteen Days with Gordona* was somewhat reminiscent of Graham Greene's novels, George Orwell's horrible vision in *1984* seems to have been the pattern for the futuristic novel *Miraklet på Blindern* (1966, The Miracle of Blindern), even though Evensmo was far less pessimistic than Orwell.

Finn Havrevold (born 1905) presented the dangers of total individualism and the resultant brutality and contempt for other people through the title character of his novel *Walter den fredsommelige* (1947, Walter, the Peaceable Man). In *Skredet* (1949, The Collapse) he explored the uncompromising egocentricity of male-dominated, success-oriented society. In the allegory *Den ytterste dag* (1963, The Last Day), he envisioned the destruction of human society. In the novel *Den blå rytter* (1968, The Blue Rider), suspended between dream and reality, the perversity and aggressiveness of the main character threw a piercing light on the age that produces such people.

The works of Torborg Nedreaas (born 1906) have treated the loneliness of man and his constant yearning for happiness. She explored these themes again and again—from *Bak skapet står øksen* (1945, Behind the Cupboard Stands the Ax) to *Den sista polka* (1965, The Last Polka). The tragedy of a young woman who refuses to forsake her love even when she is abused was the subject of *Av måneskinn gror det ingenting* (1947, Nothing Grows from Moonlight). This same animal need for the warmth of a fellow human being also motivates the artist-heroine Herdis in *Trylleglasset* (1950, The Magic Glass) and *Musikk fra en blå brønn* (1960, Music from a Blue Fountain). Nedreaas has indulged in occasional sentimentality, but her soberness and realism have kept the sentimentality under control.

Nedreaas's contemporary Nils Johan Rud (born 1906) has made love and nature the central themes of his books, from *Jakten og kvinnen* (1939, The Hunt and the Woman) on. One of Rud's titles—*Eros leker* (1969, Eros Plays)—could be applied to almost all of his stories and novels. The psychologically realistic novels of Solveig Christov (born 1918) have likewise been concerned with the existential necessity of love. For Finn Bjørnseth (born 1924) as well—from his volume of stories *Unge netter* (1951, Young Nights) on—love and sex have played an important role. In *Franceska* (1968, Franceska), a work written in lyrical prose, Bjørnseth went so far as to describe love as the only way to human salvation.

In his very first volume of short stories, *Taustigen* (1948, The Rope Ladder) Agnar Mykle (born 1915) described the difficulties of communication, the loneliness of the individual, and the bitter awakening from a beautiful dream world caused by confronting the reality of life. In one variation or another, these themes have recurred again and again in his work. We find them in the longer of the two stories in *Largo* (1967, Largo), which made clear, through the use of a taboo subject, the profound isolation of a young man. These themes were also present in the novels *Lasso rundt fru Luna* (1954, Lasso around Mrs. Luna) and *Sangen om den røde rubin* (1956, The Song of the Red Ruby). Ask Burlefot, the protagonist of *A Lasso around Mrs. Luna* and *The Song of the Red Ruby,* yearns for a lasting love. The detailed naturalistic descriptions of his gymnastics in bed do not obscure his more profound yearnings. But he finds only passion, sexual satisfaction, and ultimately emptiness. In the end, however, his desire for a great and pure love is fulfilled. In *Rubicon* (1965, Rubicon) Mykle once again produced a variation on the theme of the Burlefot novels.

The central motif in Kåre Holt's (born 1917) fiction was articulated in the title and action of his first important novel, *Det store veiskillet* (1949, The Great Crossroad). Holt likes to place his characters before a decisive choice that determines the future course of their lives. Other Holt characters who have to make momentous choices are the two old comrades-in-arms of the workers' movement in the spy story *Mennesker ved en grense* (1954, People at the Border) who have gone different ways and who now stand opposed to each other. Between 1956 and 1960 Holt published a trilogy about the development of the workers' and trade-union movement in Norway from its beginnings in the middle of the nineteenth century through the 1920s.

A more important later trilogy by Holt, whose overall title was *Kongen* (The King), was about King Sverrir, one of the most controversial figures of the Norwegian Middle Ages. The first part, *Mannen fra utskjæret* (1965, The Man from the Cliffs Outside), described Sverrir's youth in the Faeroe Islands, his journey to Norway, and his decision to become the leader of the rebel Birkebeiners. *Fredløse menn* (1967, Warlike Men), the second part of the trilogy, narrated Sverrir's battles, portraying the victories, defeats, and the final triumph of the king. In *Hersker og trell* (1969, Lord and Servant) Holt followed the life of Sverrir up to his death. Holt has the trilogy narrated by an invented character, who is a companion of Sverrir. But Holt by and large remained faithful to his twelfth-century model, the *Sverris saga* (Sverrissaga).

Events from the more recent history of Norway provided the material for Alfred Hauge's (born 1915) most comprehensive work, the Cleng Peerson Trilogy. Each volume of the trilogy depicted a different stage in the emigration of Norwegians to America during the first half of the nineteenth century: *Hundevakt* (1961, Dog Watch), the situation before emigration; *Landkjenning* (1964, Landmarks), the departure and the journey; and *Ankerfeste* (1965, Lying at Anchor), the encounter with the new world. The suspense of the plot resulted more from the inner contradictions of the protagonist than from the representation of the people leaving their homeland. Since the Cleng Peerson trilogy, religious and ethical questions, which always played an important role in Hauge's novels, have occupied him more and more. The religious answers in *Mysterium* (1967, Mystery), in which the spiritual crisis of a fifty-year-old man was described, became specifically Christian solutions in *Legenden om Svein og Maria* (1968, The Legend of Svein and Maria).

Like the most recent work of Hauge, Finn Carling's (born 1925) works published in the early 1950s took the form of fairy tales, legends, or parables. These "novels of another reality" dealt with life and death, dreams and reality, and the passivity of man. Carling pursued these themes, in a stylized lyrical prose, in *Fangen i det blå tårn* (1955, Captured in the Blue Tower) and *Desertøren* (1956, The Deserter). Subsequently Carling turned away from the lyrical and allegorical mode, but all of his works have centered around similar problems. Human beings find no

proper relationship to their fellow man. They live constantly with unfulfilled hopes and yearnings and are not capable of breaking through the
walls of isolation surrounding them, which they have erected themselves.

Images from the fantasy world of dreams collided with the world of real
existence in Gunnar Bull Gundersen's (born 1929) novels *Martin* (1959,
Martin) and *Judith* (1963, Judith). He described the experiences of an
artist in *Fabelnetter* (1961, Nights of Fables), *Kjære Emanuel* (1965,
Dear Emanuel), and *Han som ville male havet* (1968, He Who Wanted to
Paint the Ocean). These works portrayed the egocentric behavior of the
artist, which is destructive to human relationships; to an even greater
degree, they demonstrated the problematic character of his creativity.

The flight from the reality of everyday life and from the shadows of the
past was Terje Stigen's (born 1922) central subject in his first novels.
Stigen showed more individuality in *Vindstille underveis* (1956, Calm
while Underway), a volume of novellas held together by a frame story.
These novellas, although presented in the form of legends and sagas and
concerned with the destinies of the characters, were also explorations of
the minds of the narrators. Stigen, who enjoys storytelling, has also experimented with historical novels and portraits of simple people in the far
north, whose everyday life is interrupted only by the joys and sorrows of
love. *Til ytterste skjær* (1964, To the Farthest Shore), the tragicomic story
of an old fisherman, was followed by *Timer i grenseland* (1966, Hours in
the Borderland), an exciting narrative of the flight of a young couple to the
Norwegian border during the years of the German occupation.

Stigen's most artistically successful novel to date has probably been
Det flyktige hjerte (1967, The Flighty Heart), in which the protagonist is
confronted with the most disparate forms of love. But love brings neither
happiness nor sorrow into his life. For him, Eros is nothing but a tool of
his artistic creation. This story about love and art, about the flight from
love and life, which is set toward the end of the eighteenth century, was
presented in a fragmented narrative form. Stigen, however, returned to his
epic style in *De tente lys* (1968, The Lighted Lamps), set in the Middle
Ages, and in the melancholy, romantic *Det siste paradis* (1969, The Last
Paradise). In *The Last Paradise* modern civilization intrudes on the "last
paradise."

Stigen writes in the narrative tradition of Knut Hamsun; Jens Bjørneboe
(born 1920), on the other hand, has reflected the heritage of the naturalism of the end of the nineteenth century. In his first works his attacks
were directed against specific deficiencies of modern society: *Før hanen
galer* (1952, Before the Rooster Crows) dealt with the social irresponsibil-
ity of scientists, and *Den onde hyrde* (1960, The Bad Shepherd) polemi-
cized against Norway's penal system and its orphanages. Bjørneboe revealed a passionate temperament as well as a social consciousness in the

realistic-symbolic novel *Frihetens øyeblikk* (1966, Moment of Freedom). For the first-person narrator in *Moment of Freedom,* the modern world is a combination of the latrine and the torture chamber. Yet, as Bjørneboe showed in *Kruttårnet* (1969, The Tower of Power), the sequel to *Moment of Freedom,* the degradation of human life was also true of past centuries.

Axel Jensen's (born 1932) discontent with the world was directed toward the purely personal and private realm in *Ikaros* (1957, Icarus) and *Line* (1959, Line). In the tale *Epp* (1965, Epp), which is set in the future, however, Jensen sketched the horrifying picture of a perfected world. In the story of Epp, who is a pensioner because of automation and who appears to be completely satisfied with his status in that social paradise, there is also veiled criticism of the present—of the welfare society.

Finn Alnæs (born 1932) also viewed our age pessimistically in his overly ambitious first work, *Koloss* (1963, Colossus). His male protagonist, living in a world in which decency and love are dead, ultimately goes mad. Although in *Colossus* Alnæs still used the techniques of psychological realism, in *Gemini* (1968, Gemini) he questioned the language and forms of contemporary literature.

POETRY

The social involvement of poets in the years between the two world wars and the literature on war and resistance during the period of Nazi occupation almost precluded the adoption by Norwegian poets of the stylistic elements of modern world poetry. Nevertheless, during this time some evidence of the beginnings, even if very timid, of a modern language was discernible. Rolf Jacobsen (born 1907) spoke of the "metaphysics of the city," and Claes Gill (born 1910) broke with customary meter and metaphorical language under the influence of English poetry.

The development of modern poetry in Norway can be traced most clearly in the work of Gunnar Reiss-Andersen (1896–1964). In the 1920s he wrote in elegant, sonorous verse about the loneliness, yearnings, and love among the young. In the 1930s his poetry expressed his sharp reaction to contemporary political events. His *Kampdikte fra Norge* (1943, War Poems of Norway) and *Norsk røst* (1944, Voice of Norway) were published in Sweden, where, like many of his literary colleagues, he had to flee from the German occupation forces. In 1945 the two collections appeared in Norway under the title *Dikt fra krigstiden* (Poems from Wartime). Later, in the title poem in *Prinsen av Isola* (1949, The Prince of Isola), Reiss-Andersen showed a receptivity to modern imagery. But in *Usynlige seil* (1956, Invisible Sails) and *År på en strand* (1962, Years on a Beach), he returned to a more traditional lyrical language.

Traditionalism also characterized the resistance poetry of Inger Hagerup (born 1905), as well as her collections devoted to more general human themes—from *Den syvende natt* (1947, The Seventh Night) to *Fra hjertets krater* (1964, From the Crater of the Heart). Traditionalism has also marked the poems of Gunvor Hofmo (born 1921) from her first publication, *Jeg vil hjem til menneskene* (1946, I Want to Go Home to People). In this collection Hofmo spoke of the perversion of a man because of war and of the senselessness of its horrors. Later, in *Fra en annen virkelighet* (1948, Of Another Reality), Hofmo's speaker encountered the redeeming happiness of mystical union and the liberating nearness of Christ. A continuing influence on Hofmo has been Sigbjørn Obstfelder (1866–1900). Like Obstfelder's poetry, Hofmo's work through *Testamente til en evighet* (1955, Testament to an Eternity) was marked by powerful intensity and visionary and dreamlike imagery.

The verse of Tor Jonsson (1861–1951) was unadorned and spare. His major themes were loneliness and the yearning for the unknown beyond all boundaries. In the work of Jan-Magnus Bruheim (born 1914)—from *Spegelen* (1950, The Mirror) to *Menneskehagen* (1965, The Garden of Men)—feelings of perplexity and fear yielded more and more to a sense of responsibility for what happens in our world.

Jarl André Bjerke (born 1918) emerged as a modern troubadour in his first collection of verse. The titles of two of Bjerke's poems written twenty years apart—*Regnbuen* (1946, The Rainbow) and *Det finnes ennu seil* (1968, There Still Are Sails)—suggest his favorite themes: summer and sun, adventure and unquenchable yearning. In addition to these poems, Bjerke has published successful children's books, several novels, and collections of essays. He has also translated into Norwegian masterpieces of world literature, such as Shakespeare's plays and the first part of Goethe's *Faust*.

The shattered verse structure and the fragmented language of modern poetry appeared for the first time in Norway in the collection *Skyggefektning* (1949, Shadow Boxing), which Paal Brekke (born 1923) published after intensive preoccupation with the contemporary poetry of Sweden (he had also translated T. S. Eliot's *The Waste Land*). After several novels written in the early 1950s—little-noticed harbingers of nonrealistic fiction —Brekke created in *Løft min krone, vind fra intent* (1957, Lift My Crown, Wind of Nothing) images of the emptiness, coldness, and barrenness of the time. In the cycle *Roerne fra Itaka* (1960, The Rowers of Ithaca) Brekke contrasted motifs from the Odyssey with the reality of today's world; yet the irony and satire in this work finally yielded to an avowal of simplicity, beauty, and love. Brekke's always critical attitude toward modern society was intensely expressed in *Det skjeve smil i rosa* (1965, The Crooked Smile in Pink) and in his verses and prose texts that were composed like collages. In *Granatmannen kommer* (1968, The

Granite Man Is Coming) he used the language of contemporary news-papers and advertising to unmask the emptiness of existence.

Astrid Hjertenæs Andersen (born 1915) also used modern verse forms in *Strandens kvinner* (1955, Women of the Beach), in which—as in her other works—she showed a deep concern for nature. The poems in later collections, however, especially those in *Frokost i det grønne* (1964, Break-fast Outdoors), were simpler in form.

Harald Sverdrup (born 1923) also returned to stanza and rhyme in his works of the 1960s—*Isbjørnfantasi* (1961, Polar Bear Fantasy) and *Sang til Solen* (1964, Song to the Sun)—although earlier he had liked free verse. Even so eloquent an advocate of modern poetry as Erling Christie (born 1928) strove for a less abstract symbolic language in *Tegnene slukner* (1960, The Signs Disappear).

The poetry of a younger writer, Peter R. Holm (born 1931), has undergone a development similar to that of Paal Brekke. His poems pub-lished in the 1950s showed the influence of modern Swedish and English verse. In *Det plutselige landskapet* (1963, The Sudden Landscape) and his following works, however, Holm returned to a more concrete imagery and to fixed verse forms. The title of *Øyeblikkets forvandlinger* (1965, Trans-formations of the Moment) established immediately one of the central themes of Holm's poetry—the few moments between rest and action that can lead to liberation. In *Befrielse* (1966, Liberation) the poetic speaker sees the face of the hidden God in a mystical vision.

Stein Mehren (born 1935), whose first collection of poems, *Gjennom stillheten en natt* (Through the Silence of a Night), appeared in 1960, has also wanted to illuminate the "transformations of the moment." He has tried to capture and preserve the sudden and rapidly fleeting moments in which worlds encounter each other (either two people or inner and exter-nal reality) and to impart to them a new reality through strange combina-tions and paradoxical leaps. Always an issue for Mehren has been the difficult position of the poet: powerless as the poet is, he still resorts to words; for, with all its inadequacies, verse still does provide communica-tion. The word can, to be sure, also paralyze the individual; it creates distance and alienation. This alienation is experienced with particular intensity by a person in love.

Mehren adapted the Tristan and Isolde legend in quite a few of the poems in *Alene med en himmel* (1962, Alone with a Heaven) and *Mot en verden av lys* (1963, Toward a World of Light). In *Gobelin Europa* (1965, Gobelin Europe) the speaker has become more conscious of his position in society and history. Along with Mehren's earlier themes, the poems in *Gobelin Europe* bitterly criticized the superficiality of a society oriented exclusively toward productive efficiency. *Tids alder* (1966, Age of Time) and *Vind runer* (1967, Wind Runes) did not contain new themes, but the verse became simpler and more comprehensible: Mehren is aware of the artist's responsibility to his reader. For Mehren, the artist is on a "journey into language"—as he described it in *Aurora, det niende mørke* (1969, Aurora, the Ninth Darkness)—and is the "eternally restless man," a voice of hope and freedom in the everyday life of activity and politics.

For Georg Johannesen (born 1931) there has been no difference between political and artistic effect. From his first volume, *Dikt* (1959, Poems), to *Nye dikt* (1966, New Poems) his passionate social commitment was directed toward the oppressed in bourgeois-capitalistic society. A title like *Ars Moriendi, eller de syv dødsmåter* (1965, Ars Moriendi, or The Seven Ways of Dying) was clearly reminiscent of Bertolt Brecht, whom Johannesen introduced to Norway through several translations. Furthermore, Johannesen's matter-of-fact, sober style could not have existed without the model of the German playwright: Johannesen has described the decline of bourgeois morality ironically and satirically. But his most penetrating work to date has been the poems in *New Poems*. In a world full of brutality—as a warning Johannesen calls attention admonishingly to the destruction of the Jews in World War II—aesthetic feelings only turn one's glance away from blood-spattered reality.

Jan Erik Vold (born 1939) has questioned the ability of language to communicate because of the obvious discrepancy between language and reality. The short prose work *Fra rom til rom: Sad & Crazy* (1967, From Room to Room: Sad & Crazy) demonstrated this discrepancy even more than did the linguistic experiments in *Blikket* (1966, The Glance). For Vold, reality consists only of fragments, yet even these have become questionable and cannot be simply classified. Vold offered straightforward, even naïve poems in *kykelipi* (1969, kykelipi), in which he did not use the usual patterns of language. He tested the capacity of images, words, sentences, and verses, but without losing his infectious sense of humor.

Kollisjon (1966, Collision), the first volume of poetry of Tor Obrestad (born 1938), who writes in *nynorsk,* also contained simple and laconic verses. In *Vårt daglige brød* (1968, Our Daily Bread) he observed the modern world critically and pondered anxiously the future of the individual. For Obrestad, man has already become often nothing more than a marionette—*Marionettar* (1969, Marionettes) is the title of one of Obrestad's novels—who cannot escape the entanglements of his surroundings.

DRAMA

Many of the novelists and poets I have discussed have also written plays. In the travesty *Vikingar* (1949, Vikings) Johan Borgen unmasked the still-extant romanticism with which the Vikings are regarded. In addition to the dramatizing of his novel *The Pale Girl* in 1953, Tarjei Vesaas wrote several more plays, all of which, however, were not effective theater. The same lack of theatricality marked the plays of Tore Ørjasæter (1886–1968), which were too abstract and unreal. Typical of Ørjasæter's drama was the passion play *Den lange bryllaupsreisa* (1949, The Long Wedding Trip), which was modeled on the medieval mystery play.

More effectively constructed, but too closely tied to events of the day to transcend topicality, were the plays of Axel Kielland (1907–1963). Shortly after the end of the war Odd Eidem (born 1913) strove for new dramatic forms. His later plays were more traditional. Eidem was more effective as a critic, particularly in his witty, irreverent observations on the characteristics and prejudices of his countrymen.

More recently, in the plays of younger authors, there has been no lack of attempts to escape from the realistic-naturalistic theater. However, no significant play has resulted, and none of these experimental plays has achieved much popular success. Tormod Skagestad's (born 1920) play *Under treet ligg øksa* (1955, Under the Tree Lies the Ax), based on the *Oresteia*, brought a striking rhythmic prose dialogue to the modern Norwegian drama. Skagestad also achieved an unusual effect by using a chorus in *Byen ved havet* (1962, The City by the Sea), a play about the fear of the atom bomb in a fishing village in southern Norway.

Using the techniques of Brechtian theater, Jens Bjørneboe reworked his novel *The Bad Shepherd* into a play with songs, *Til lykke med dagen* (1965, Much Happiness for the Day). In *Fugleelskerne* (1966, The Bird Lovers) he also used Brechtian dramaturgy to attack the neo-Nazi tendencies of the 1960s and the latent aggressiveness in people. The play *Semmelweis* (1968, Semmelweis) was based on documentary material (the life of the great nineteenth-century obstetrician), but had contemporary relevance.

Finn Carling's play *Gitrene* (1966, The Fences) went beyond the limitations of time and space. As in his fiction, Carling was concerned in this play with the isolation of man and his inability to use roads of communication available to him, especially love: man is not capable of opening the gate in the fence.

The experimental plays of the poets Georg Johannesen and Stein Mehren have treated the situation of man in the past and present. With bitter irony Johannesen, in his revue-like play *Kassandra* (1967 Cassandra), commented on our world, which conjures up its own destruction. Mehren set the action of his play *Narren og hans hertug* (1968, The Fool and His Duke), a lyric-symbolic drama of ideas, in the second half of the fifteenth century. In *The Fool and His Duke* the individual is conceived of as a prism in which the light of history is gathered and refracted.

It took longer than in neighboring Sweden and Denmark for Norwegian literature to become receptive to contemporary international trends. Even when Norwegian authors finally began to adopt the styles and themes of postwar world literature, the epic-realistic narrative style—especially in the popular genre of the historical novel—still continued to predominate in fiction. In poetry a period of receptivity to modern forms seems to have been followed by a return to traditional verse. In the drama the few attempts to establish a modern theater have not met with critical or popular success.

On the whole, Norwegian literature of the present shows a pronounced awareness of tradition. And, as has been true in Norway since the late nineteenth century, psychological and social questions continue to occupy writers far more than do aesthetic problems.

NORWEGIAN WORKS IN ENGLISH TRANSLATION

ANTHOLOGY

Allwood, Inga, ed. *Modern Norwegian Poems.* New York, 1949

INDIVIDUAL WORKS MENTIONED IN ARTICLE

Evensmo, Sigurd. *Englandsfarere* as *A Boat for England.* London, 1947
Hoel, Sigurd. *Møte ved milepelen* as *Meeting at the Milestone.* New York, 1952
Jensen, Axel. *Ikaros* as *Icarus: A Young Man in the Sahara.* London, 1959
Mykle, Agnar. *Lasso rundt fru Luna* as *Lasso Round the Moon.* New York, 1961

————. *Sangen om den røde rubin* as *The Song of the Red Ruby.* New York, 1961
Sandemose, Aksel. *Varulven* as *The Werewolf.* Madison, Wisc., 1966
Sverris saga as *Sverrissaga.* London, 1899
Vesaas, Tarjei. *Bruene* as *The Bridges.* New York, 1970
————. *Fuglane* as *The Birds.* New York, 1969
————. *Is-slottet* as *Palace of Ice.* New York, 1968
————. *Kimen* as *The Seed* (together with *Spring Night*). New York, 1964
————. *Vårnatt* as *Spring Night* (together with *The Seed*). New York, 1964

SECONDARY WORKS

Beyer, Edvard. *Utsyn over norsk litteratur,* 2nd rev. ed. Oslo, 1971
Beyer, Harald. *A History of Norwegian Literature.* New York, 1956
Beyer, Harald and Edvard. *Norsk litteraturhistorie,* 3rd rev. ed. Oslo, 1970

Brinchmann, Alex and Sigurd Evensmo. *Norske forfattere i krig og fred.* Oslo, 1968
Bull, Francis et al. *Norsk litteraturhistorie,* 6 vols., rev. ed. Oslo, 1957–63

Christiansen, Hjalmar. *Norwegische Literaturgeschichte*. Berlin, 1953

Dahl, Willy. *Fra 40-tall til 60-tall: Norsk prosa gjennom 25 år.* Oslo, 1969

———. *Fra Vinje til Vold.* In *Ordene og verden: Ti analyser av moderne norske dikt.* Oslo, 1967

———. *Stil og struktur: Utviklingslinier i norsk prosa gjennom 150 år,* rev. ed. Oslo, 1969

Dale, J. A. *Nynorsk dramatikk i hundre år.* Oslo, 1964

Dalgard, Olav. *Norsk etterkrigsdrama i støypeskeia.* In *Norsk litterær årbok 1968.* Oslo, 1968

Friese, Wilhelm. *Nordische Literaturen im 20. Jahrhundert.* Stuttgart, 1971

Huom, Philip. *Norsk litteratur efter 1900.* Stockholm, 1951

Lescoffier, Jean. *Histoire de la littérature norvégienne.* Paris, 1952

Longum, Leif. *Et speil for oss selv.* Oslo, 1968

Øksnevad, Reidar. *Norsk litteraturhistorisk bibliografi 1900–45, 1946–55.* Oslo, 1951–58

Schneider, Hermann. *Geschichte der norwegischen und isländischen Literatur.* Bonn, 1948

GEORGE GÖMÖRI

Polish Literature

TWO DOMINANT TRENDS in nineteenth-century Polish literature have proved significant for the character of modern Polish literature: the romantic tradition created by the poets Adam Mickiewicz (1798–1855), Juliusz Słowacki (1809–1849), Zygmut Krasiński (1812–1859), all living in exile; and the rationalist and positivist tradition represented by such writers as Bolesław Prus (1845–1912) and Eliza Orzeszkowa (1841–1910). Of these two trends, romanticism, which played a disproportionately large part in the revitalization of Polish national consciousness, continued to influence the novels of the immensely popular Henryk Sienkiewicz (1846–1916) and even those of Stefan Żeromski (1864–1925), whose sharp social criticism reflected the intelligentsia's growing concern with society and politics.

More recently, Polish writers—especially poets—began to regard Cyprian Norwid (1821–1883) as their most characteristic precursor. Norwid, a postromantic, was hardly known in his lifetime; his assessments of social and aesthetic questions and his experiments in increasing the symbolic force of language produced a poetry that transcended both romanticism and positivism. Norwid's greatness has been recognized only in our century, among others by the critic Stanisław Brzozowski (1878–1911), another outstanding, and isolated, figure in Polish literature. Both Norwid and Brzozowski, while believing in the desirability of Polish independence, tried to ground their work in supranational values.

503

With some simplification, it can be said that if any major (other than purely stylistic) division exists in twentieth-century Polish literature, it is the difference between "Polonocentrics" and "universalists." This is not a simple continuation of the romantic/antiromantic dichotomy. For instance, while the program of the poets around the journal *Skamander,* the most influential group between the wars, was antiromantic, they proved to be no less Polonocentric in their themes and outlook than had previous genera-tions. Their main opponents in the Cracow avant-garde postulated but could never reach their ideal of universalism: the best-known poet of this group, Julian Przyboś (1901–1970), wrote his most accomplished verse on patriotic themes during World War II. In retrospect, one can see that universalism, with its quest for untraditional ideas and new ways of expres-sion, was given shape between the wars by only a very few writers: the philosopher-playwright Stanisław Ignacy Witkiewicz (1885–1939), the esoteric "linguistic" poet Bolesław Leśmian (1879–1937), and the bril-liant novelist Witold Gombrowicz (1904–1969), who rebelled against convention in the name of "immaturity." On the whole, Polish literature before 1939 was more traditional than modern, more inward-looking than European, more dignified than innovative.

The war, feared and expected for a long time, finally broke out in 1939 and buried under its debris the literary experiments and controversies of twenty years. During the German occupation literature was suppressed in Poland and either went underground or reappeared in emigration. Most poets of the *Skamander* group escaped to the west. Gombrowicz, who had left Poland on a trip to South America before the war, remained in Argen-tina. Some writers escaped to Hungary and enjoyed comparative safety there until the last months of the war. Others, who in 1939–40 found themselves in Soviet-occupied territory, had different experiences. Some of them, like Władysław Broniewski (1897–1962) and Aleksander Wat (1900–1967), although communists, were imprisoned and treated badly by the Russians. The luckier ones managed to stay at large until 1943, when the Soviets needed their services in the army.

During the war Polish literature, both inside and outside Poland, by and large reverted to its old national patterns. The tribulations of the nation and of individual Poles recalled the martyrology of the great romantics, and a new martyrology asserted itself both inside and outside Poland. The former members of the *Skamander* group now wrote patriotic poetry. A similar romanticism throbbed in the verse of Władysław Broniewski, who left Russia and managed to reach the middle east with the Polish-nation-alist Anders Army; romanticism likewise informed the somber poems of the youthful activists of the resistance who wrote for mimeographed under-ground newspapers. At such trying times the return to the sources of national consciousness was not at all surprising. As in France, where the former surrealists Aragon and Éluard now wrote traditional poems exhorting anti-German resistance, poetry gained a new popularity in Poland, although now the author's name was less important than the message of the poem. Underground verse anthologies—such as *Pieśń niepodległa* (1942, Independent Song), edited by Czesław Miłosz (born 1913), and *Słowo prawdziwe* (1942, A True Word), edited by Jerzy Zagórski (born 1907)—were filled with tragic accounts of life and of sudden, unexpected death in an occupied country, reflecting the authors' determination to fight Nazi barbarism with pen and bullet.

The toll of the war among writers was considerable. The Lublin poet Józef Czechowicz (1903–1939) died in an air raid at the beginning of the war. The Kafka-like Jewish novelist Bruno Schulz (1892–1942) and the excellent critic and translator Tadeusz Boy-Żeleński (1874–1941) were shot by the Germans. Another critic, Karol Irzykowski (1873–1944), also a novelist, died during the Warsaw uprising, in which many young writers died. Among poets who fell on the barricades were Tadeusz Gajcy (1922–1944) and Krzysztof K. Baczyński (1921–1944), the most promising talent of his generation. Baczyński's poetry, intensely romantic in the vein of Juliusz Słowacki and at the same time bitterly resigned and pessimistic (a painful poetic catalogue of the deprivations of his generation), became popular shortly after the war, but it was well over a decade until his collected works were published: *Utwory zebrane* (1961, Collected Works) resulted in a resurgence of interest in him.

The period in Poland since the end of World War II cannot be discussed as a coherent whole. Within the literature of this period four different phases can be distinguished, each largely the result of changes in the political climate. In the first postwar years (1945–49) Polish literature within Poland was engaged in a self-therapeutic exercise: wartime experiences were told and slowly digested, and a cautious groping began toward recognition of the altered world.

This period of relatively democratic "personal adjustment" came to an end in 1949, when with the Szczecin Congress of the Polish Writers' Association the communists, who had taken power in 1947, embarked upon a program of the total subordination of literature to political aims. This meant the forcible introduction and aggressive propagation of the Soviet model of socialist realism, which, party spokesmen claimed, was the only creative method true to reality. A nonacceptance of this point of view spelled decreasing opportunities for publication, or no publication at all. Surprisingly, most well-known Polish writers and poets seemed to take the demand of the regime seriously and underwent a phase of ideological commitment.

This state of affairs changed during the mid-1950s, when after Stalin's death Polish literature reemerged from its short period of ideological puritanism and facile optimism. The political reform movement, which culminated in 1956 with the "Polish October" and Władysław Gomułka's return to power, was paralleled by an improvement in the cultural atmosphere. These years of "thaw" lasted in the arts (although the political impetus was lost more quickly) from 1955 to 1959. During this time some of the leading older writers freed themselves from rigid dogma, younger writers made their debuts, different trends flourished, the Polish film and theater gained international renown.

The rest of the Gomułka era (1959–70) came to be known as the period of "small stabilization," although this stability was more imaginary than real. It was seriously upset by the political events of 1968 (Poland's participation in the invasion of Czechoslovakia; the campaigns against "Zionism" and "revisionism" at home) and ended with what has become a stagnation in literary life.

POETRY

The poetry of the war years and to some extent that of the initial postwar period was characterized, at least among writers of the older generation, by a return to the traditional genres and modes of expression. Julian Tuwim (1894–1953), a master of satirical verse and of metaphysical love lyrics before the war, wrote a long epic poem in emigration—*Polskie kwiaty* (Polish Flowers)—published in 1949, about the Poland of his youth. Tuwim's nostalgic reminiscences turned into hopeful expectation in the parts in which he imagined the new, "democratic" Poland of the future. When he returned to his devastated homeland, under communist rule, he published only a handful of affirmative poems praising the work of reconstruction.

Antoni Słonimski (born 1895), another leading member of the *Skamander* group, who before the war wrote witty satirical plays and light, sentimental poems, also borrowed the mantle of the Polish romantics during the war. Besides his patriotic verse, he wrote a long elegiac poem of great charm about Warsaw, *Popiół i wiatr* (1941, Ashes and Wind). Słonimski was less active in the 1950s, but his poems published after 1956 (between 1956 and 1959 he was president of the Polish Writers' Association) showed him to be a staunch defender of his old rationalist and liberal ideals.

Jarosław Iwaszkiewicz (born 1894), a prolific poet of the same generation, has reflected in his poems a life-long love of nature and a preoccupation with aesthetics; his work is enriched by erudite cultural allusions.

Maria Pawlikowska-Jasnorzewska (1894–1945), who wrote short, impressionistic poems, died in England soon after the end of the war, while two other poets of the *Skamander* group, Kazimierz Wierzyński (1894–1969) and Jan Lechoń (1899–1956, pseudonym of Leszek Serafimowicz) remained in the United States after 1945, although Wierzyński moved to London, the largest center of Polish émigré intellectuals, shortly before his death. Of the two, Wierzyński's development was the more interesting: during the war a passionate nationalist romantic, he switched to free verse in later years, and alongside poems voicing a defiant but frustrated patriotism he wrote short nature lyrics and meditative poems of great beauty. Lechoń's rigid and recherché classicism confined him to a narrow range of subjects, and his postwar poetry is considered, on the whole, inferior to his early work.

The most famous of the poets who stayed in Poland during the war was Leopold Staff (1878–1957). His long poetic career was marked by creative eclecticism; he learned not only from the art-for-art's-sake poets of Młoda Polska (Young Poland) and from the *Skamander* group but also from his youngest colleagues. His best collection of verse was probably *Wiklina* (1954, Osiers), the short, subtle, and tender poems of which are similar to oriental drawings and watercolors.

Staff's vision was too ahistorical to reflect the tragic experiences of the Nazi occupation; this was left to such poets as Mieczysław Jastrun (born 1903), Czesław Miłosz, and Tadeusz Różewicz (born 1921). Jastrun's *Godzina strzeżona* (1944, A Guarded Hour)—together with Miłosz's *Ocalenie* (1945, Rescue)—described the martyrdom of Poles and Jews, underground fighters and ordinary citizens, in a simple language of tragic feeling. In later years Jastrun departed from his high artistic standards and contributed to the communist propaganda poetry of the 1950s, but in 1956 in *Gorący popiół* (Hot Ashes) he responded to the thaw with a cycle of searching and embittered poems questioning the whole mythology of Stalinist totalitarianism. He later returned to the aesthetic and moral preoccupations that informed his poetry before and soon after the war, and evolved a new symbolism, the hero of which was man shaped by the forces of history and culture.

Czesław Miłosz, a native of the Polish-inhabited part of Lithuania, also lived in Warsaw during the occupation. A poet with a critical mind, a strong sense of proportion, and a fascination with the dialectics of history, Miłosz could have become a respected figure in an "open Marxist" society, but not in the dogmatic communist dictatorship of the 1950s. After a stretch of diplomatic service abroad, in 1951 Miłosz resigned, remained in France, and wrote *Zniewolony umysł* (1953, The Captive Mind), in his words an "analysis of mental acrobatics" of eastern European intellectuals seeking accommodation with Stalinism. Despite his political commitment, Miłosz has remained first and foremost an artist. His is a tormented classicism, forged in a constant struggle between his European self, "objective" and historically aware; and his Lithuanian self, "subjective," Dionysian, and irrational. While *Światło dzienne* (1953, Daylight) is probably his best single collection, Miłosz's later books of poetry—reflecting his experiences in California and showing a self-analytical introversion—confirmed the opinion that he is the leading poet of his generation.

The most interesting poetic newcomer of the first postwar years was Tadeusz Różewicz, whose first two collections, *Niepokój* (1947, Anxiety) and *Czerwona rękawiczka* (1948, The Red Glove), were the very opposite of the verbose romanticism of some of the older poets. Różewicz used his terse and simple free verse to rediscover the world shorn of its old values, full of memories of the dead. His faith in a more humane society of the future through socialism, together with his hatred of war, spurred him to write "antiimperialist" verse in the 1950s. But his development since 1955 has shown that the essence of his commitment was not political but moral and philosophical. His influence on younger poets has been considerable.

It was not Różewicz, however, but Władysław Broniewski and Adam Ważyk (born 1905) who were the most favored poets of the socialist-realist period. In Broniewski's prewar work two traditions blended: romanticism and revolutionary internationalism. A prewar communist, Broniewski, when he returned from the middle east to liberated Poland, was in conflict for some time between private frustrations and a strong sense of civic duty. Duty won out, and soon Broniewski wrote rousing poems about Warsaw's reconstruction and also a eulogy to Stalin. His best postwar work, including poems on the beauty of his native region of Mazovia, was collected in *Mazowsze, i inne wiersze* (1952, Mazovia, and Other Poems). Broniewski's poetry was traditional both in form and content, and he found few followers in the 1960s. Adam Ważyk had been a surrealist before the war, but became a spokesman of socialist realism during the early years of communist rule in Poland. His most remembered work, however, is the politically explosive poem *Poemat dla dorosłych* (A Poem for Adults), which showed—in 1955—the darker side of Polish society.

Another poet of the older generation whose name became connected with the thaw in literature was Aleksander Wat, who finally emigrated in 1962 and died in Paris. A futurist and communist activist during the interwar period, Wat had his share of harrowing experiences in Soviet jails during the war. His sufferings and a recurring illness he contracted in the Soviet Union left a deep imprint on his poetry, collected in the volumes *Wiersze* (1957, Poems) and *Ciemne świecidło* (1968, A Dark Knick-Knack). Wat's poetry, with its echoes of the Old Testament and its existentialist gloom, is basically pessimistic, although there are occasional moments of serenity or exuberance.

Apart from Różewicz, Staff, and to some extent Broniewski, the only poet who managed to create something of value even in the worst years of compulsory propaganda doggerel was K. I. Gałczyński (1905–1953), a true bohemian intellectual and jester. Well known for the volatility of his political views, he created a half-grotesque, half-sentimental style of his own, which suited the tastes of apolitical readers rather well. His best book after the war, *Zaczarowana dorożka* (1948, The Enchanted Cab), was followed by a spate of bad political verse. But the long poem *Wit Stwosz* (1952, Wit Stwosz) and the cycle of lyrical poems written shortly before his death demonstrated Gałczyński's creative synthesis of different styles and cultural values. His popularity, which was great during the years of the thaw, has decreased in recent years.

The year 1955 was an *annus mirabilis* for Polish poetry: in that year a whole new generation of poets made its, on the whole belated, debut. The most unconventional and striking of them was Miron Białoszewski (born 1922), whose *Obroty rzeczy* (1956, Turns of Things) revealed the hidden poetry of objects and of everyday life. In his following books Białoszewski pursued his interest in the structure of the Polish language, which he dissected and reassembled in grotesque and often enigmatic patterns.

Another "linguistic" poet, Tymoteusz Karpowicz (born 1921), in addition to his experiments with language, has shown a precision reminiscent of the Italian hermetics. The Cracow poet Wisława Szymborska (born 1923) is also more impressive in the exactness of her observations and in the great economy of her language—especially in the volume *Sól* (1962, Salt)—than in flights of imagination.

Perhaps the best (certainly the most translated) poet of this generation, Zbigniew Herbert (born 1924) fought in the resistance during the war; studied law, philosophy, and history of art afterward; and traveled extensively in western Europe. His poetry has shown an awareness of cultural continuity and a contemplative but ironic approach to history. His "anthropological" symbolism, reminiscent of the Greek poet Kavafis, and his sensitive use of the language place Herbert into the mainstream of modern Polish poetry. His best single volume is probably *Studium przedmiotu* (1961, The Study of the Object).

Other poets who found their definitive styles in the mid-1950s were Witold Wirpsza (born 1918), whose attitude toward the language is also questioning and analytical; and Artur Międzyrzecki (born 1922) and Wiktor Woroszylski (born 1927), both of whom have experimented with a less detached, more autobiographical kind of modernism.

Almost simultaneously with the generation of Herbert and Białoszewski there appeared a still younger group of poets, whose diverse interests almost defy classification. Among this younger group are poets exploring the enchantments of unspoiled nature and of all things bizarre, such as Jerzy Harasymowicz (born 1933); poets mingling grotesque baroque imagery with crude naturalism, such as Stanisław Grochowiak (born 1934); poets trying to forge a new style out of pseudoarchaic ironic statements, such as Ernest Bryll (born 1935). A new version of classicism has been set forth by Jarosław Marek Rymkiewicz (born 1935) in *Metafizyka* (1963, Metaphysics). Premature death prevented Andrzej Bursa (1932–1957) from becoming more than the vigorous promise of a good poet. Tadeusz Nowak (born 1930) is a poet of peasant origin, whose personal mythology cherishes remnants of a reconstructed and partly imaginary past; his metaphors have a near-surrealistic quality. Urszula Kozioł (born 1935), on the other hand, has preferred a clear-cut and concise verse. Kozioł, who has an affinity with such poets as Szymborska and Karpowicz, has been determined to fight her way to the core of the language and of human thought.

The 1960s saw a general stagnation of poetry among younger writers; the "small stabilization" of the regime encouraged eclecticism rather than bold experimentation. The most interesting recent debut of this period was that of Ewa Lipska (born 1945).

Polish poetry has, of course, had a second life in emigration. Apart from Miłosz, Wierzyński, and Wat, one could single out Marian Czuchnowski (born 1909), Wacław Iwaniuk (born 1916), and Marian Pankowski (born 1919); traumatic war experiences left their imprint on the work of all three. As a rule, émigré poets cannot be published in Poland. An exception is Jan Brzękowski (born 1903), whose connections with the Cracow and French avant-garde made him a forerunner of certain postwar trends in Poland. Among the young émigrés, only one poet of real promise has emerged—Bogdan Czaykowski (born 1932). Czaykowski, for a time editor of the London-based cultural review *Kontynenty,* at present teaches Polish literature in Canada.

FICTION

The traumatic events of World War II became the central subject of Polish fiction for well over a decade. During the war "everything happened" that could possibly happen to human beings; initially, however, only a handful of writers dared to confront the worst aspects of this vast inferno. One of the first to do so was Tadeusz Borowski (1922–1951), who began his career as an underground poet, less romantic and more scornfully sober than most of his contemporaries. Borowski's terrifying and grim stories about Auschwitz, where he was sent in 1943, are among the best of their kind. After two books of stories—*Pożegnanie z Marią* (1948, Farewell to Maria) and *Kamienny świat* (1948, Stone World)—Borowski turned to political journalism. But he was unable to find his place within an increasingly regimented Poland, and he committed suicide in 1951.

Zofia Nałkowska (1884–1954), who before the war wrote the socially critical novel *Granica* (1935, Boundary), published in 1946 a factual account of Nazi atrocities—*Medaliony* (Medallions). The genocide of Polish Jews found its chronicler in Adolf Rudnicki (born 1912), a novelist of prewar fame, who lived in Warsaw on false documents during the occupation and fought in the 1944 Warsaw uprising. After the war his main literary ambition became to erect a literary monument to the sufferings and martyrdom of his fellow Jews. Rudnicki's long stories, rich and flamboyant in style and full of psychological insights, were collected in several volumes, of which *Żywe i martwe morze* (1952, The Living and the Dead Sea) is the best known.

Other writers bearing witness to the tragedy of the Warsaw ghetto and to the mass extermination of Poland's Jewish population were Stanisław Wygodzki (born 1907) and Jerzy Andrzejewski (born 1909). Among the works of younger writers who took up the same subject, the two autobiographical novels of Henryk Grynberg (born 1936), who emigrated to the United States in 1968, have been the most successful.

Many books about the war were devoted to the exploits of the Polish soldier in different parts of the world; of these Melchior Wańkowicz's (born 1892) "literary reportage" *Monte Cassino* (1957, Monte Cassino) and his novel *Westerplatte* (1959, Westerplatte) enjoyed great popularity. A very versatile writer on similar themes was Ksawery Pruszyński (1907–1950), the author of *Karabela z Meschedu* (1948, The Sabre from Meshed). Whether based on an anecdote or on a medieval legend, Pruszyński's stories usually included an element of the supernatural, which blended surprisingly well with his realistic and frequently amusing descriptions of the soldier's life.

One of the major omissions of Polish fiction during the first ten years after the war was any full literary account of the Warsaw uprising. This important event was tackled in a politically slanted manner by Kazimierz Brandys (born 1916) in *Miasto niepokonane* (1946, The Indomitable City). But generally, both the uprising and the armed resistance of the Armia Krajowa (the nationalist underground army, which recognized the Polish government in London) were regarded as themes too dangerous for objective discussion. This danger was mainly the result of political circumstances in a postwar Poland divided between a Soviet-sponsored communist regime with relatively few supporters and a hostile, nationalist majority. Indeed, some units of the Armia Krajowa had taken to the woods and continued fighting against the new authorities long after the peace treaties had been concluded.

It was under such political circumstances that Jerzy Andrzejewski, known as a Catholic writer before the war, wrote *Popiół i diament* (1948, Ashes and Diamonds). Its popular success could be partly attributed to the fact that it told at least some truth about the young people who fought in the Polish underground army. Maciej, the youthful hero of *Ashes and Diamonds,* is ordered to kill the new district party secretary, a former concentration camp inmate and a man of great integrity. While planning the assassination, Maciej meets a girl and falls in love with her. Eventually he kills the party secretary, but he himself is also killed, by mistake. While Andrzejewski wanted to demonstrate the futility of armed struggle against the new order, his young hero (especially in the film version of the book made in 1957, which was reputedly closer to the author's original manuscript) turns out to be the most attractive character of the story. Indeed, both the young nationalist and the elderly communist receive the author's sympathies: their tragedy springs from the historical situation opposing "national independence" to "social justice." Though not a flawlessly constructed book, *Ashes and Diamonds* remains an important novel of those years.

A number of writers did not feel the necessity of being committed for or against the new regime. Stanisław Dygat's (born 1914) popular *Jezioro Bodeńskie* (Lake Constance), written during the war but not published until 1946, used the war theme as a framework for the investigation of national myths. His hero is a Pole who holds a French passport and is interned by the Germans near Lake Constance, where a flirtatious liaison with a Frenchwoman makes him more and more assume the somewhat inflated role of the "romantic Pole," which he had previously detested. The protagonists of Dygat's later novels—*Pożegnania* (1948, Farewells), *Podróż* (1958, The Journey)—are equally nonheroic in their pursuit of a more meaningful and fulfilled life, which always seems to be attained by others. Dygat's mildly self-mocking tone and his ordinary characters, who live fully only in daydreams, make him one of the most entertaining and least pretentious Polish writers.

The first postwar years witnessed a minor renascence of a genre popular in Poland ever since Henryk Sienkiewicz—the historical novel. For some reason, the leading practitioners of this genre have tended to be Catholics and traditionalists. Typical is Antoni Gołubiew (born 1907), who began his grand cycle on the medieval King Bolesław I in 1947 with the novel *Puszcza* (Deep Forest). Here Gołubiew focused on the process of psychological adaptation the pagan Slavs had to undergo in order to fit into the organized framework of Christianity. In later volumes of the cycle, Gołubiew's realism suffered from a too-apologetical interpretation of the role of the early church. Other Catholic novelists, such as Zofia Kossak (1890–1970) and Hanna Malewska (born 1911), also looked for themes either to Poland's pagan past or to later Polish and European history; Jan Dobraczyński (born 1910) gained recognition with numerous novels on biblical themes and personalities.

The most intriguing historical novelist in contemporary Polish literature has been Teodor Parnicki (born 1908), who spent many years in emigration before his return to Poland after the loosening of repressions in the mid-1950s. Parnicki does not want to re-create history in small, often naturalistic details like Gołubiew: he is more interested in change and structure. His characters live in ages of transition, whether it be medieval Europe or the Hellenistic east of the second century B.C., and they all seem to have far-reaching political and cultural interests. Parnicki's plots are intricate, and not everyone can follow him in his sophisticated and somewhat tortuous psychological expeditions into the depths of history; indeed, his technique of deliberate obfuscation sometimes resembles such western contemporaries as Lawrence Durrell. Among Parnicki's numerous novels, *Koniec "Zgody Narodów"* (1955, The End of the "Covenant of the Nations") and *Tylko Beatrycze* (1962, Only Beatrycze) have had the greatest critical acclaim. *Only Beatrycze,* the tale of a mysterious hero's unending search for his elusive identity, was called by the critic Andrzej Kijowski a "many-storeyed labyrinth of thought."

The atmosphere of the early 1950s did not favor the development of a contemporary fiction comparable in spirit or style to the fiction of western Europe. Apart from the tedious and propagandistic "production novels," with their schematic plots and cardboard heroes, the only kind of fiction that flourished was novels and stories critical of prewar Poland. One of the more ambitious attempts to describe this much-maligned epoch was that of Kazimierz Brandys, whose tetralogy *Między wojnami* (1948–51, Between the Wars) mainly dealt with the failings and indifference of the prewar intelligentsia. Neither these tendentious novels nor the artistically poor *Obywatele* (1954, Citizens) managed to impress Polish readers, many of whom became interested in Brandys only after the publication of the short novel *Obrona Grenady* (1956, The Defense of Granada). *The Defense of Granada* and *Matka Królów* (1957, The Mother of the Króls) were typical of the anti-Stalinist wave of writing that flooded Poland in the mid-1950s. Brandys's psychologically well-motivated stories were collected in the volume *Romantyczność* (1960, Romanticism).

Another long novel devoted to the life of the Polish intelligentsia in the twentieth century was the poet Jarosław Iwaszkiewicz's *Sława i chwała* (1956–62, Fame and Glory), a trilogy firmly rooted in the realistic tradition. Iwaszkiewicz's most congenial prose genre, however, is perhaps the short story: his psychological insights and the masterful use of language make some of his stories unusually impressive. Igor Newerly's (born 1903) best novel, *Pamiątka z Celulozy* (1952, Souvenir from the Cellulose

Factory) evoked the political struggle of the Polish communists against the semiauthoritarian Piłsudski regime during the 1930s. While the narrative was conventional enough, Newerly's style and the humanity of his characters lifted the novel out of the literary wreckage of the socialist-realist years.

During the thaw Maria Dąbrowska (1889–1965), who had achieved an international reputation for *Noce i dnie* (1932–34, Nights and Days), a *roman fleuve,* published a collection of new stories. This volume, *Gwiazda zaranna* (1955, Morning Star), included a long story depicting life in the country in the spirit of critical realism, showing both the farmers' improved living conditions and their fears and anxieties. Dąbrowska believed that human solidarity and well-done work were values independent from and more important than political considerations.

Childhood reminiscences became once again fashionable in the 1950s, and Dąbrowska's volume of stories on her childhood, *Uśmiech dzieciństwa* (1923, A Smile of Childhood) was reprinted many times after the war. A classic among postwar childhood reminiscences was a book written by an émigré, Czesław Miłosz—*Dolina Issy* (1955, The Valley of the Issa). Other writers, such as Wilhelm Mach (1917–1965) with *Życie duże i małe* (1959, Life, Big and Small), wrote their best work in this genre.

Expressions of political disillusionment were heard during the mid-1950s, and the most forceful of these came not from such established writers as Brandys or Andrzejewski, but from the young, who created a grim and savage "black literature." Marek Hłasko (1934–1969) was the most impressive of this group. His stories were a mixture of crude naturalism, macabre humor, and hooliganish romanticism. His first collection, *Pierwszy krok w chmurach* (1956, The First Step in the Clouds) was an immediate success. His short novel *Cmentarze* (1958, The Graveyard), a mordant caricature of the Stalinist police state, proved to be too explosive for publication even in the relatively free atmosphere of 1957, and it was published in Paris after Hłasko's decision to defect to the west. His later work included thrillers about Israel, where he lived for some time, and an extremely funny if muddled autobiography, *Piękni, dwudziestoletni* (1966, Beautiful Twenty-Year-Olds). Although Hłasko had undeniable talent, his writing was impaired by his impatience and his nostalgic desire to live up to the imaginary role of the "noble bandit."

Unlike Hłasko's work, Marek Nowakowski's (born 1935) short stories have eschewed politics as well as heroics; they focus on the everyday life of social outcasts, petty criminals, and "marginal" people.

In Polish fiction during the last fifteen years three main trends can be distinguished: the traditional (realistic or lyrically impressionistic) novel, with straightforward plot and characters; an innovative attempt to widen the structure of the novel (desynchronization, the introduction of nonfictional elements); and historical or social parables, which, although they adopt some innovative techniques, have kept the traditional plot.

Not surprisingly, most of the Polish novelists belong to the first group—traditionalists. These writers have included the classical philologist Jan Parandowski (born 1895); Maria Kuncewicz (born 1899), who lived for many years in England and in the United States; and Kornel Filipowicz (born 1913). Another traditionalist is Julian Stryjkowski (born 1905); his *Czarna róża* (1962, Black Rose) was about the revolutionary movement in prewar Lvov, and his *Austeria* (1966, The Inn) dealt with the fate of a Jewish community during the turmoil of World War I. Jan Józef Szczepański's (born 1919) novel on the collapse of independent Poland in 1939, *Polska jesień* (1955, Polish Autumn), is thought to be the best treatment of this subject, but he is probably a better story writer, his best collection being *Buty, i inne opowiadania* (1956, Shoes, and Other Stories).

After 1956 the ban imposed on certain controversial themes was temporarily lifted, and the new freedom gave the chance to Roman Bratny (born 1921) to describe the 1944 Warsaw uprising from the point of view of its fighting participants in *Kolumbowie rocznik 20* (1957, The Columbus Boys Born in 1920). Although this novel has some artistic flaws, it is vividly written and was a great popular success. The less heroic and more grotesque aspects of the uprising were ably depicted by Jerzy Stefan Stawiński (born 1921) in the story *Węgrzy* (1956, Hungarians).

Among the traditionalists, Wojciech Żukrowski (born 1916) has had a reputation as the talented author of stories on the occupation. But his most ambitious work to date, *Kamienne tablice* (1966, Stone Tablets), a romantic love story set in India that develops into a conflict of political loyalties, is entertaining but unconvincing in its resolutions.

Jerzy Putrament's (born 1910) ideological commitment is stronger than his respect for artistic truth. His political novels—such as *Rozstaje* (1954, Crossroads) and *Małowierni* (1967, Those of Too Little Faith)—although much debated in Poland, suffer from psychological primitivism and from the journalistic impurities of the author's language.

Anna Kowalska (1903–1969), Bohdan Czeszko (born 1923), and Andrzej Braun (born 1923) have all been adherents of a broadly conceived realism, although Kowalska's was more psychological, and Czeszko's and Braun's has been more social and political. Individual moral decisions have played a central role in Janusz Krasiński's (born 1928) fiction; his *Haracz szarego dnia* (1959, The Extortion of Everyday) was greeted by critics as a very promising debut.

Two poets, Tadeusz Nowak and Urszula Kozioł, are also writers of fiction; both have drawn largely on autobiographical material. Kozioł's *Postoje pamięci* (1965, Stations of Memory) was called by Czesław Miłosz "one of the most authentic testimonies" of village life.

Among the younger novelists, those who have shown narrative skill or an original use of language in one or more books are Eugeniusz Kabatc (born 1930), Bogdan Wojdowski (born 1930), Stanisław Stanuch (born 1931) and Władysław Terlecki (born 1933).

Realistic fiction—and, of course, romantic fiction as well—has also been flourishing in emigration. Some of it has been published in the excellent France-based journal *Kultura,* edited by Jerzy Giedroyć. Most of the émigré fiction is politically outspoken and thus unpublishable in Poland, such as Józef Mackiewicz's (born 1902) novels, of which the best is *Droga do nikąd* (1955, Road to Nowhere), an account of Lithuania's lurid annexation by the Soviet Union, with all the human suffering that accompanied it.

The all-pervading terror of Stalin's Russia, with its "underworld" of concentration camps, was the subject of Gustaw Herling-Grudziński's (born 1919) *Inny świat* (1953, A World Apart), an autobiographical account of great persuasive force. Leo Lipski (born 1919), writing on the same subject, introduced a surrealistic, macabre element, which has made his stories peculiarly haunting. A less grave, more playful tone characterized Czesław Straszewicz's (1911–1963) *Turyści z bocianich gniazd* (1953, Tourists from A Crow's Nest), with its resourceful Polish sailors and pompous party functionaries. Also less somber has been the work of Tadeusz Nowakowski (born 1918); he has written sarcastic and witty stories, as well as a best-selling émigré novel, *Obóz Wszystkich Świętych* (1957, The Camp of All Souls).

The most influential Polish émigré writer and the chief representative of the second—experimental—trend in contemporary Polish fiction was Witold Gombrowicz. His first novel, *Ferdydurke* (1938, Ferdydurke) was a literary event of the first magnitude. A year after the publication of this controversial novel Gombrowicz left Poland forever; all the same, it was he who set the tone for innovation in Polish fiction. Through careful cultivation of certain myths and obsessions, Gombrowicz developed a highly subjective style of his own. But it was more his vision than his style that appealed to postwar generations.

Ferdydurke remained Gombrowicz's best novel, with *Pornografia* (1960, Pornography) a worthy second. But Gombrowicz's oeuvre also included several plays, such as *Ślub* (1953, The Marriage), containing a central statement of Gombrowicz's existential philosophy, and the grandhistorical parody *Operetka* (1966, Operetta). The three volumes of his diaries, *Dziennik* (1957–66, Diary), all published by Instytut Literacki in Paris, brim with intellectual excitement and pungent irony; they also provide an invaluable commentary to Gombrowicz's life and work. Although his books have not been published in Poland (save for a period of "grace" between 1956 and 1968), his work is well known in intellectual circles.

There is an element of the absurd in Gombrowicz's art; and like Gombrowicz in *Operetta,* many of his compatriots found a veritable treasure mine of the absurd in Polish history. One of these was Stanisław Jerzy Lec (1909–1966), a master of philosophical aphorisms, which he collected under the title *Myśli nieuczesane* (1957, Unkempt Thoughts). Others are Stanisław Zieliński (born 1917) and Sławomir Mrożek (born 1930). Mrożek's collection of satirical sketches, *Słoń* (1957, The Elephant), took a pot shot at the bureaucratic incompetence and power worship during the first decade of postwar Poland; his symbol of irrationalism was an "official" rubber elephant kept in the zoo. Mrożek's more recent collections of stories, such as *Deszcz* (1962, Rain) and *Dwa listy, i inne opowiadania* (1970, Two Letters, and Other Stories), showed his interest in mental structures and in "eternal" human situations.

On the whole, contemporary Polish fiction has had few genuine experimentalists; Włodzimierz Odojewski (born 1930) is one of them. His free-flowing, sensuous, Faulkner-like prose has been well suited to his presentation of the wartime disintegration of a Polish family in the western Ukraine. Another author whose prose verges on lyrical verse in its chaotic subjectivism and fragmentariness is Leopold Buczkowski (born 1905). A recurrent setting in Buczkowski's work is a small Jewish community during the German occupation, in which the characters are involved in elaborate and irrational play acting, preparing for murder or for death. Buczkowski's best known novel is *Czarny potok* (1954, Black River), but his most experimental novel has been *Młody poeta w zamku* (1959, Young Poet in the Castle).

Tadeusz Konwicki's (born 1926) first important book, *Rojsty* (Marshes), written in 1948, but not published until 1956, while a revelation in its undiluted account of the anti-Soviet partisan movement in the Vilnius region, did not go beyond the conventions of realism. His *Sennik współczesny* (1963, A Dreambook for Our Time), however, signaled a change: its narrative slides back and forth in time; the dividing line between reality and dream is constantly blurred. By these devices Konwicki was able to suggest that the war is still very much present in the Polish soul and that his generation is suffering from "memoritis," a compulsion to remember and relate the past to the present. The same obsession was present in *Wniebowstąpienie* (1967, Ascension), a strange book about the world of Warsaw's "night people," in which the hero is struck by temporary amnesia.

The writers representative of the third trend in contemporary Polish fiction—historical and social parables—seem less interested in individual destinies than in the workings of an institution, of an idea, or of power in general. Tadeusz Breza (1905–1970) gained recognition with *Spiżowa brama* (1960, The Bronze Gate) and *Urząd* (1961, The Post), describing the present-day power structure of the Vatican. Breza neither attacks nor defends the church: he simply describes it on the basis of firsthand experiences in a style remarkably cool and collected.

The prolific Jerzy Andrzejewski turned to historical parables in the mid-1950s. In *Ciemności kryją ziemię* (1957, Darkness Covers the Earth) and *Bramy raju* (1959, The Gates of Paradise), he explored the connections between faith and sacrifice; *The Gates of Paradise* revealed the hidden sexual basis of fanatical commitment to a cause. *Idzie skacząc po górach* (1963, He Cometh Leaping upon the Mountains) was a satire about certain French artistic circles and also an attack on the myth surrounding the outstanding artist. *Apelacja* (1968, The Appeal), published in Paris, was a fascinating contribution to the diagnosis of the Polish national psychosis, manifested, among other ways, by the government-sponsored witch hunt following the student protests of March, 1968.

Among the younger writers of parables Jacek Bocheński (born 1926) is outstanding because of his intelligent and incisive prose. His novels, which have included *Boski Juliusz* (1961, The Divine Julius) and *Nazo poeta* (1969, Naso the Poet) are fictionalized essays about the mechanism of power, dissected by the writer with cool detachment, and studies in the situation of the artist in "benevolent" dictatorships. The philosopher Leszek Kołakowski (born 1927), at present living in Oxford, has written some remarkable biblical tales and dialectical parables about the dilemmas and antinomies inherent in human existence, in addition to his essays promoting a "noninstitutional Marxism." A selection of these essays was published in English as *Toward a Marxist Humanism* (1968).

DRAMA

Polish playwrights reacted to the war much more slowly than did poets or novelists. The first postwar years were dominated by the leading prewar dramatists, such as Jerzy Szaniawski (1886–1970), whose *Dwa teatry* (1946, Two Theaters), a rather conventional play that skillfully used the dream technique of the symbolists, became very popular.

Two Catholic playwrights, Jerzy Zawieyski (1902–1969) and Roman Brandstaetter (born 1906), used traditional techniques to pose relevant and daring questions. Zawieyski's main theme was man's struggle for integrity and for independence from institutional control. He was also drawn to exotic themes and even to science fiction, as in *Ziemia nie jest jedyna* (1960, The Earth Is Not Unique). Brandstaetter was a prolific writer; his twenty-odd plays in verse and prose included biographical dramas on Rembrandt, Copernicus, and Mickiewicz as well as plays on more modern themes, such as *Dzień gniewu* (1962, Day of Wrath), about the crises of conscience arising from extreme situations during World War II.

The poet Jarosław Iwaszkiewicz and Wacław Kubacki (born 1907) also wrote biographical plays, selecting their subject matter mainly from the romantic period. Their plays, full of dramatic events and peopled by great artists, had strong appeal to the popular imagination.

The prewar political theater was revived and developed by Leon Kruczkowski (1900–1962), whose *Niemcy* (1949, Germans) was a successful dramatization of the problem of individual moral responsibility for war crimes. In two later plays—*Pierwszy dzień wolności* (1959, The First Day of Freedom) and *Śmierć gubernatora* (1961, The Death of the Governor)—Kruczkowski managed to move beyond immediate political issues and to create a kind of "morality play." Other plays by Kruczkowski could not avoid the pitfalls of schematic simplification inherent in their propagandistic aims.

In the mid-1950s the Polish theater underwent a striking change. Right after the war the center of theatrical life was Łódź, where Leon Schiller's (1887–1954) productions of classics were in the best traditions of the Polish theater; later the "Schiller approach" was denounced as "too western" and the so-called Stanislavski method of acting was enforced in a rigid imitation of the Soviet theater.

During the thaw, experimentation regained its claims to legitimacy, and Adam Mickiewicz's national masterpiece, *Dziady* (1832, Forefathers), could at last be staged, for the first time since the war. It was presented at the People's Theater in Nowa Huta, a new workers' town near Cracow, produced by Krystyna Skuszanka and Jerzy Krasowski. Kazimierz Dejmek, director of Teatr Narodowy in Warsaw from 1961 to 1968, began to put on exciting productions of old Polish mystery plays and contemporary dramas.

The most important figure of the renascence of the Polish theater was Jerzy Grotowski (born 1933), whose "poor theater" started out in a small town in western Poland, Opole, and moved to Wrocław some years later. Grotowski's austere, remarkably disciplined, and almost hypnotic productions of Polish classics (which he regarded as mere scenarios rather than set texts) brought him international fame.

During the thaw the excellent theatrical review *Dialog* was launched (in 1956). Under the editorship of Adam Tarn (born 1902), it provided a forum for new and unconventional dramatic texts and criticism. After 1968 Tarn had to resign; he now lives in Canada.

Two new plays were among the more significant theatrical events of the thaw. One was *Święto Winkelrida* (Winkelried's Feast), written in 1944 but not performed until 1956, by Jerzy Andrzejewski and Jerzy Zagórski; a satire on the fascist establishment when written, it had in the meantime become applicable to the communist establishment. Jerzy Broszkiewicz's (born 1922) *Imiona władzy* (1956, The Names of Power) was devoted to the investigation of political power throughout history. Innovation and experimentation in the theater were effectively supported by the biting, witty theatrical reviews of Jan Kott (born 1914), whose essays in *Szekspir współczesny* (1965, Shakespeare Our Contemporary) won him an international reputation.

The most important development in contemporary Polish drama has been the emergence of a native theater of the absurd. Its best representatives are undoubtedly Sławomir Mrożek and Tadeusz Różewicz, both of whom had earlier established themselves in other genres, Mrożek in fiction and Różewicz in poetry.

Mrożek's *Policja* (1958, The Police) was a satire on a police state that achieves its aim of eliminating all opposition and therefore makes itself superfluous; consequently, a policeman has to "impersonate" a political dissenter. After *The Police*, Mrożek wrote some excellent one-act plays and *Tango* (1964, Tango), a full-length play on the eternal clash of generations. Mrożek has been an astute critic of slogans, routine, and mechanistic patterns of behavior. In his hands, the "theater of the absurd" has become an instrument of meaningful social criticism. Since 1968 Mrożek has been living in Paris. Because of his public protest against Poland's participation in the invasion of Czechoslovakia, his plays have been taken off the Polish stage.

While Mrożek's characters are more often than not conformists who act out "logical" schemes inherent in absurd situations, Różewicz's theater, especially in the nameless and fragmented existence of his anti-heroes, reminds us more of the plays of Samuel Beckett. Różewicz's most successful plays—*Kartoteka* (1960, The Card Index) and *Świadkowie, czyli nasza mała stabilizacja* (1962, The Witnesses, or Our Small Stabilization)—showed a deep pessimism about human life, which sprang partly from the grim experiences of Różewicz's generation, partly from the unrepenting frivolity of the world. These plays are documents of the mechanization of postwar society, in which individual existence has lost its authenticity. *Stara kobieta wysiaduje* (1968, The Old Woman Broods), which takes place in part on a huge rubbish heap after a devastating war, showed Różewicz's vision pushed to its extreme.

Besides Różewicz, there are other poets writing for the theater (and for the mass media). Tymoteusz Karpowicz has been interested in the often absurd and unreal situations of everyday life, while Zbigniew Herbert has examined the tragic inadequacy in human relationships, as in *Drugi pokój* (1958, The Other Room). Probably under the influence of Gombrowicz, poets like Jarosław Marek Rymkiewicz and Stanisław Grochowiak (in his *Król IV* [1963, King IV]) created a mythical history within which grotesque situations can be evolved, not without a moral as to the nature of convention or power.

The poet Ernest Bryll's attempt to revive Polish romantic drama in a modern context has so far produced only questionable results. Bohdan Drozdowski (born 1931) is another poet-playwright; his best play to date, *Kondukt* (1960, The Funeral Convoy), showed conflicts between different social groups with considerable realism. Jarosław Abramow (born 1933) and Jerzy Krzysztoń (born 1940) have also been followers, by and large, of realism. Both Krzysztof Choiński (born 1940), the author of *Krucjata* (1961, Expedition), and Maciej Zenon Bordowicz (born 1941) have wedded their psychological insights to mysterious situations, showing a new interest in the stage thriller, paralleling recent developments in western theater.

The achievement of Polish literature during the last thirty years has been split between Poland proper and the Poles in emigration. Between 1939 and 1945 the émigré branch dominated. Although after the war many writers returned to Poland, others preferred to stay abroad permanently, or at least until 1956. And the Polish cultural diaspora continues to exist, absorbing many distinguished newcomers (Miłosz, Hłasko, Wat, Mrożek, Kołakowski).

Poetry reacted rather quickly to the changes in Poland during and after the war, but the promising start of 1945–46 was interrupted by the imposition of socialist realism around 1949. Only after 1955–56 did Polish poetry reach and even surpass its prewar standards. While the most popular poets of the first postwar decade were Broniewski and Gałczyński, in retrospect the work of Miłosz, Jastrun, and Różewicz seems to have been of greater importance. Their poetry, as well as that of Herbert and Szymborska, was informed by a new awareness of history; and "objectivity" replaced the subjective, albeit richly varied, tone of the poets of the prewar *Skamander* group. A later trend, which developed during the 1960s, concentrated on the exploration of hidden semantic and syntactic aspects of the language (Białoszewski).

In fiction there was a crop of good, mostly realistic or naturalistic, short stories soon after the war, but the best novels were written later, after 1956, when experimentation with art forms once again became possible. Perhaps it is significant that one of the most modern Polish novelists (Parnicki) lived abroad until 1967, that another one (Gombrowicz) never returned from his self-chosen exile, and that several young writers (among them Hłasko) stayed in the west, where they were not hampered in their urge to describe the seamier sides of Polish life. In the 1960s there was relatively little fiction written on life in contemporary Poland: parables, allegories, and satirical tales filled the gap between the reader and his experience of reality that was officially negated.

After a period during which the theater was dominated by plays within the realist-impressionist convention (Kruczkowski, Szaniawski), the Polish theater suddenly caught up with the rest of Europe. Thanks to the appearance of some outstanding playwrights (particularly Różewicz and Mrożek) and a group of ambitious and gifted directors, Polish theatrical life became extremely lively and interesting between 1955 and 1968. The last years of the Gomułka era (following Kazimierz Dejmek's politically explosive production of Mickiewicz's *Forefathers* in 1968) saw the stagnation of the theater and the suppression of plays—old or new—that contained too much social criticism. As of 1972 there is hope that the return of a more relaxed political atmosphere, which has already permitted the publication of some poetry and fiction previously suppressed, will lead to more propitious conditions for the theater as well.

POLISH WORKS IN ENGLISH TRANSLATION

ANTHOLOGIES

Gillon, Adam and Ludwik Kryżanowski, eds. *Introduction to Modern Polish Literature: An Anthology of Fiction and Poetry.* New York, 1964

Gömöri, George and Charles Newman, eds. *New Writing of East Europe.* Chicago, 1968

Kijowski, Andrzej, ed. *Contemporary Polish Short Stories.* Warsaw, 1960

Kuncewicz, Maria, ed. *The Modern Polish Mind: An Anthology of Stories and Essays.* Boston, 1962

Mayewski, Paweł, ed. *The Broken Mirror: A Collection of Writings from Contemporary Poland.* New York, 1958

Miłosz, Czesław, ed. *Post-war Polish Poetry.* Garden City., N.Y., 1965

Peterkiewicz, Jerzy and Burns Singer, eds. *Five Centuries of Polish Poetry, 1450–1970.* New York, 1970

Stillman, Edmund, ed. *Bitter Harvest: The Intellectual Revolt behind the Iron Curtain.* New York, 1959

Tyrmand, Leopold, ed. *Explorations in Freedom: Prose, Narrative, and Poetry from Kultura.* New York, 1970

Wieniewska, Celina, ed. *Polish Writing Today.* Baltimore, 1967

INDIVIDUAL WORKS MENTIONED IN ARTICLE

Andrzejewski, Jerzy. *Bramy raju* as *The Gates of Paradise.* London, 1962

———. *Ciemności kryją ziemię* as *The Inquisitors.* New York, 1960

———. *Idzie skacząc po górach* as *A Sitter for a Satyr.* New York, 1965

———. *Popiół i diament* as *Ashes and Diamonds.* London, 1962

Brandstaetter, Roman. *Dzień gniewu* as *Day of Wrath.* Warsaw, 1962

Brandys, Kazimierz. *Matka Królów* as *Sons and Comrades.* New York, 1961

———. *Obrona Grenady* as *The Defense of Granada.* In Paweł Mayewski, ed., *The Broken Mirror.* New York, 1958

Broszkiewicz, Jerzy. *Imiona władzy* as *The Names of Power.* In *Dialog,* no. 7, 1957

Choiński, Krzysztof. *Krucjata* as *Expedition.* In *Dialog,* no. 9, 1961

Gombrowicz, Witold. *Ferdydurke* as *Ferdydurke.* New York, 1961

———. *Operetka* as *Operetta.* London, 1971

———. *Pornografia* as *Pornografia.* New York, 1967

————. *Ślub* as *The Marriage*. New York, 1969

Herbert, Zbigniew. *Drugi pokój* as *The Other Room*. In *Dialog*, no. 4, 1958

Herling-Grudziński, Gustaw. *Inny świat* as *A World Apart*. New York, 1952

Hłasko, Marek. *Cmentarze* as *The Graveyard*. New York, 1959

Kołakowski, Leszek. *Toward a Marxist Humanism*. New York, 1968

Konwicki, Tadeusz. *Sennik współczesny* as *A Dreambook for Our Time*. Cambridge, Mass., 1969

Kott, Jan. *Szekspir współczesny* as *Shakespeare Our Contemporary*. Garden City, N.Y., 1964

Kruczkowski, Leon. *Pierwszy dzień wolności* as *The First Day of Freedom*. In *Dialog*, no. 11, 1959

Lec, Stanisław Jerzy. *Myśli nieuczesane* as *Unkempt Thoughts*. New York, 1962

Mackiewicz, Józef. *Droga do nikąd* as *Road to Nowhere*. Chicago, 1964

Mickiewicz, Adam. *Dziady* as *Forefathers*. London, 1968

Miłosz, Czesław. *Zniewolony umysł* as *The Captive Mind*. New York, 1953

Mrożek, Sławomir. *Policja* as *The Police*. In *Six Plays*. New York, 1967

————. *Słoń* as *The Elephant*. New York, 1963

————. *Tango* as *Tango*. New York, 1968

Newerly, Igor. *Pamiątka z Celulozy* as *A Night of Remembrance*. Warsaw, 1957

Różewicz, Tadeusz. *Kartoteka* as *The Card Index*. In *The Card Index, and Other Plays*. New York, 1970

————. *Niepokój* as *Faces of Anxiety*. Chicago, 1969

————. *Stara kobieta wysiaduje* as *The Old Woman Broods*. In *The Witnesses, and Other Plays*. London, 1970

————. *Świadkowie, czyli nasza mała stabilizacja* as *The Witnesses*. In *The Witnesses, and Other Plays*. London, 1970

Rudnicki, Adolf. *Żywe i martwe morze* as *The Dead and the Living Sea, and Other Stories*. Warsaw, 1957

Szczepański, Jan Józef. *Buty* as *Shoes*. In *Poland* (Warsaw), Aug., 1959

Ważyk, Adam. *Poemat dla dorosłych* as *A Poem for Adults*. In Edmund Stillman, ed., *Bitter Harvest*. New York, 1959

SECONDARY WORKS

BIBLIOGRAPHIES AND GUIDES

Coleman, Marion Moore. *Polish Literature in English Translations: A Bibliography*. Cheshire, Conn., 1963

Korzeniewska, Ewa et al. *Słownik współczesnych pisarzy polskich*, 4 vols. Warsaw, 1963–66

Maciuszko, Jerzy. *The Polish Short Story in English: A Guide and a Critical Bibliography*. New York, 1968

Pelcowa, J. and M. Lenartowicz, eds. *Bibliographie sur la Pologne*. Warsaw, 1964

Taborski, Bolesław. *Polish Plays in English Translations: A Bibliography*. New York, 1968

GENERAL WORKS

Bersano Begey, Marina. *Storia della letteratura polacca*. Milan, 1953

Herman, M. *Histoire de la littérature polonaise*. Paris, 1963

Istoriya pol'skoi literatury, 2 vols. Moscow, 1968–69

Krejči, Karel. *Dějiny polské literatury*. Prague, 1953

Kridl, Manfred. *A Survey of Polish Literature and Culture*, 2nd ed. The Hague, 1965

Krzyżanowski, Julian. *Dzieje literatury polskiej od początków do czasów najnowszych*. Warsaw, 1970

Miłosz, Czesław. *The History of Polish Literature*. New York, 1969

Pilat, R. *Historia literatury polskiej*. Warsaw, 1962

Štefan, R. *Poljska književnost*. Ljubljana, 1960

Żółkiewski, S. Z. et al. *Z problemów literatury polskiej XX wieku: Księga zbiorowa*. Warsaw, 1965

WORKS ON CONTEMPORARY LITERATURE

Gillon, Adam and Ludwik Krzyżanowski. *Introduction of Modern Polish Literature*. New York, 1964

Gömöri, George. *Polish and Hungarian Poetry 1945 to 1956*. Oxford, 1966

Goriély, B. *Littérature de la république populaire de Pologne*. Paris, 1956

Hartmann, Karl. *Des polnische Theater nach dem zweiten Weltkrieg*. Marburg, 1964

Jakubowski, J. Z. *La littérature polonaise contemporaine*. Warsaw, 1955

Kunstmann, Heinrich. *Moderne polnische Dramatik*. Cologne, 1965

Mąciag, Włodzimierz. *16 pytań*. Cracow, 1961

Matuszewski, R. *Portraits d'écrivains polonais contemporains*. Warsaw, 1959

Rusinek, M. and Z. Grabowski, eds. *Polish Literature and Art Today*. Special issue of *Arena* (London), March, 1967

Scherer-Virski, O. *The Modern Polish Short Story*. The Hague, 1955

WOLF-DIETER LANGE

Portuguese Literature

IN THE NINETEENTH CENTURY, during the age of romanticism, Portugal made important literary strides that brought it once again into the mainstream of European literature. By 1871 younger writers were organizing an articulate protest movement against the extremes of romanticism and becoming increasingly receptive to the new forms—realism, naturalism, and symbolism—that were developing in France.

Around 1910 the poet Teixeira de· Pascoais (1877–1952) began to resist this foreign influence through *saudosismo* (the word *saudade* means "yearning"). *Saudosismo*'s evocation of the traditionally popular themes of suffering, sorrow, and yearning had a special appeal to the Portuguese people. Foreign observers could see *saudosismo* as a typically Portuguese reaction: situated between European tradition and the new world across the ocean, and beset by its own political and social problems, Portugal had tended to withdraw within itself at times of threatening intellectual conflict.

The age of *modernismo*—which was particularly espoused by Mário de Sá-Carneiro (1890–1916) and Fernando Pessoa (1888–1935)—was firmly established by the group of writers associated with the journal *Presença* (1927–40). It brought renewed contact with French literary trends. Internationalism was furthered by neorealism in Portuguese fiction, which began about the time of World War II and whose models (apart from Russian and French writers) were the Brazilian writers Jorge Amado, José Lins do Rêgo, and Graciliano Ramos.

525

POETRY

A group of young poets created its own style of neorealistic, socially committed poetry in the periodical *Novo cancioneiro* (1941–44), but this group could not succeed in prevailing over the modernists. But Portuguese poetry did depart from the psychological approach of the *Presença* group after World War II, to revive an intellectual adventure dating back more than twenty years—surrealism.

The revival of surrealism was first noticeable in the work of Mário Cesariny de Vasconcelos (born 1924), a poet with a strong feeling for language and structure. His volume *Corpo visível* (1950, Visible Body) dealt with subjects suggested by Breton and other French surrealists. The title poem was a typical example of the way Cesariny de Vasconcelos has combined specific themes (love) and imagery (eyes and seeing) from traditional Portuguese poetry with a more somber note of horror and soberly stated suffering.

In Cesariny de Vasconcelos's poems, although space and physical objects are drastically stripped of reality, thought generally remains ascertainable, within the limits of association. This poet of surreal love has also been in search of an all-encompassing explanation of the world, which, as he said himself, he is more apt to find in the French poet Lautréamont or in Picasso than in Rilke. Cesariny de Vasconcelos has mixed humor and a vulnerable yet ironic sensibility with such typical elements of surrealism as experimental language and deliberate nonsense. He is an authentic successor of the undogmatic French surrealists, whose poetry has been characterized equally by concrete reality and surreality.

Alexandre O'Neill (born 1924), who is also a compiler of anthologies, has been another member of Portugal's surrealist movement. Although his oeuvre has not been extensive, he has broadened the scope of surrealism through his gift for minute observation. The poem *Um adeus português* (A Portuguese Farewell) in *No reino da Dinamarca* (1958, In the Kingdom of Denmark) was an outstanding example of O'Neill's technique. Predictably, O'Neill likes to use the surrealist device of sequences of associated words. A follower of the French surrealists Jacques Vaché and André Breton, he wrote a poem on a revolver; but its bitter, derisive tone of resignation took it far beyond the playful mood of its models. In other surrealist poems, O'Neill displayed a delightful sense of humor.

O'Neill, who later turned away from surrealism, has shown the same tendency to make his personal life an increasingly specific part of his work as has António Maria Lisboa (1928–1953), the most influential of the Portuguese surrealists. Lisboa's models were Rimbaud and Jarry, and his deliberate adoption of Breton's theories brought him close to the realm of dreams and visionary reflection. Again and again, Lisboa's prose and verse poems circled around the theme of his search for secure ground in a constantly shifting world, which only friendship or love can render tolerable. These ideas achieved particular intensity when he brought into play his powerful verbal talents.

Other theories besides surrealism have influenced Portuguese poetry since 1945. It has also been dominated by two other groups: one associated with the journal *Távola redonda,* the other with the journal *Árvore.*

The twenty issues of *Távola redonda* (from 1950 to 1954) were full of references to the renewal of poetry achieved by Fernando Pessoa; numerous articles in *Távola redonda* sought to link Pessoa and his work with Portugal's traditions. *Távola redonda* was edited by Manuel Couto Viana (born 1923) and David Mourão-Ferreira (born 1927), who since 1956 have expressed their gradually diverging views in other journals: Couto Viana in *Graal,* edited by himself; and Mourão-Ferreira in *Tempo presente,* edited by Fernando Guedes (born 1928).

Manuel Couto Viana made his debut in 1948 with the collection *O avestruz lírico* (The Lyrical Ostrich). His voice has been simple and modest from the beginning. His strophic, often rhymed poems have been little vivid renderings of impressions, perceptions, and momentary bewilderments. Couto Viana has followed his own poetic bent, turning the morality of everyday life into rhyme, and often using autobiographical material as a point of departure for a lyrical statement.

David Mourão-Ferreira, in addition to writing poetry, has also written short stories (*Gaivotas em terra* [1959, Seagulls on Land]) and plays (*O irmão* [1965, The Brother]). More clearly than Couto Viana, he has fitted his broadly conceived poetry into the larger framework of nationalism (in the best sense of the word). Mourão-Ferreira has clearly been a supporter of literary traditions, both popular and scholarly, and has handled them— in such works as *Os quatro cantos do tempo* (1958, The Four Songs of Time)—with dynamic freshness and earnest emphasis.

In contrast to the writers of the *Távola redonda* group, with their relatively narrow appeal to a strictly Portuguese public, the poets who published the four voluminous issues of *Árvore* (1951–53) advocated a program of integration into the mainstream of European literature. Their chief interest was the place of poetry in the age. The one and only issue of *Cassiopeia* (1955), a journal closely linked with *Árvore,* was not able to revive the goals of the *Árvore* program.

One of the editors of *Árvore,* Raul Maria de Carvalho (born 1920), typifies the poets who belonged to this group. Carvalho saw a fundamental piety in the daily acts of resignation he observed in individual lives, while the alienation of the city of Lisbon suggested to him images vaguely reminiscent of the Spanish poet Dámaso Alonso's *Hijos de la ira.* For Carvalho, poetry is a bulwark against the horror and fear of life and against its hopelessness, because it helps one to see details as symbols of a discoverable unity. Proud of the vocation that links him with Fernando Pessoa, Carvalho in metric prose has brought Portuguese poetry back to a pure, lyrical tone, keyed to timeless traditions.

Poetry, which has contributed so much to the special character of Portuguese literary life, also initiated the avant-garde attempt to combine image and word in a new unity. This aim was first formulated for Portuguese-language literature by the Brazilian Noigandres group, founded in 1952. The poems of the Noigandres writers were inspired by Anton Webern's *Klangfarbenmelodie* (sound-color melody) and Ezra Pound's ideogram techniques. In 1962 the first anthology of Brazilian concrete poetry, *Poesia concreta* (Concrete Poetry), appeared in Lisbon, and in 1963 Ernesto Manuel Geraldes de Melo e Castro (born 1932)—who had written *Sismo* (1952, Earthquake), *Salmos* (1953, Psalms), and *Queda livre* (1961, Free Fall)—published a concrete poem, *Monumento* (Monument), in which he constructed a monument to freedom around the *e*'s in the English words "men" and "free." The visual base of the poem reverses into its opposite the relationship between "free" and "men"—all men shall be free—implied by the vertical axis.

Salette Tavares de Aranda (born 1922), author of *Espelho cego* (1957, Tarnished Mirror) and *Concerto em mi maior para clarinete e bateria* (1961, Concert in E Major for Clarinet and Percussion), is another concrete poet of international stature. Her concrete poem *arrranhisso* (a play on the word *"aranhiço,"* meaning an ugly or feeble-minded person), published in 1966 and modeled on Apollinaire's *Calligrammes,* was printed in the form of a spider (*aranha*). The visual image dynamically reinforced and enriched the associations suggested by linguistic variations on the root of the word.

In Portugal such literary experiments—the quest to find a form appropriate to this multimedia age—have been chiefly confined to poetry, and then only cautiously. Some experimental poets have found an outlet in the journal *Poesia experimental* (1964). Fiction and drama have engaged only sporadically in such experimentation.

FICTION

Nearly all the writers who gained an international reputation for twentieth-century Portuguese fiction were closely associated with the journal *Presença,* which flourished between the two world wars. Among others, these writers included José Régio (1901–1969), Adolfo Casais Monteiro (born

1909), Miguel Torga (born 1907), Branquinho da Fonseca (born 1905), João Gaspar Simões (born 1903), and Vitorino Nemésio (born 1901).

Since World War II, however, the modernistic *Presença* school has been less influential than that of the neorealist generation that gradually began to compete with it. The neorealist writers have been more interested than the *Presença* writers in social questions; their pursuit of realism has linked them with the much-translated work of José Maria Ferreira de Castro (born 1898), who had encouraged in Portuguese readers of the 1930s a new appreciation for literature dealing with the tangible realities of history and society, nature and the individual.

Soeiro Pereira Gomes (1909–1949)—whose major works were *Esteiros* (1941, Estuaries), *Refúgio perdido* (1950, Lost Refuge), and *Engrenagem* (1951, Clockwork)—was a precursor of neorealism who continued to use naturalistic descriptive techniques. By the end of World War II neorealism was fully accepted. Furthermore, instead of remaining isolated from postwar European developments, it tried, for example, to make use of the ideological principles of existentialism and, more recently, of the formal theories of the *nouveau roman.*

What might be called the opening chord of neorealistic fiction was the novel *Gaibéus* (1940, Weed Picker) by António Alves Redol (born 1911), an extremely prolific writer whose early works were strongly indebted to the Brazilian Jorge Amado. *Weed Picker* dealt with life on the land—its human problems and hard physical labor—depicted through a typical group of three farmhands. Its enthusiastic reception by Portuguese readers led Alves Redol to publish one book after another, not always with regard for stylistic elegance. But *O barranco de cegos* (1961, The Ravine of the Blind), which the critics have unanimously considered Alves Redol's finest work, offered irrefutable proof of his literary talent. It described the gradual transformation of the behavior of people on an estate in Ribatejo.

Carlos de Oliveira (born 1921), Manuel da Fonseca (born 1911), and Fernando Gonçalves Namora (born 1919), earlier associated with the *Novo cancioneiro* school of poetry, later turned more and more to fiction. The widely read, highly praised novels and short stories of these three writers have dealt with such subjects as the decline and fall of a family, the drabness of provincial life and the conflicts and drastic social change it breeds, and the contrast between city and country. They have treated these subjects in a regionalist style, often enriched with elements of folklore.

Of the three, Fernando Gonçalves Namora, some of whose books have been widely translated, seems to be the most distinctive literary personality. After a first book that was close to the intellectual line of *Presença* and some poems published in *Novo cancioneiro,* he made an early contribution to neorealism with *Fogo na noite escura* (1943, Fire in the Dark Night), a novel about the student generation of the time. Namora is a self-conscious, self-critical stylist, as can be seen from the revisions he has made on some of his works. He is familiar with the world of day laborers, and he has described his own experiences as a country doctor and a city doctor in the two volumes of *Retalhos da vida de um médico* (1949–63, Fragments from a Doctor's Life).

Openly concerned with the social world of human relationships, Namora has also evoked—in *Minas de São Francisco* (1946, Mines of São Francisco) and *O trigo e o joio* (1954, The Wheat and the Chaff)—a serenely poetic world that is not out of harmony with the committed tone of his work. He has also dealt successfully with existentialist ideas in *Cidade solitária* (1959, Lonely City). His prize-winning novel *Domingo à tarde* (1961, Sunday Afternoon), which focused on the conflicts of a doctor constantly confronted with morbidity and hopelessness, showed how far he developed from the simple neorealism of his early work.

In a certain sense, Namora's refinement of neorealism served as a model for Virgílio Ferreira (born 1916), who has made a particular effort to adapt contemporary intellectual trends from other countries. Ferreira's work has drawn upon existentialist and phenomenological ideas. He has also experimented with form as well as content, out of a desire to transcend the limitations of neorealism so that it could accommodate a metaphysical treatment of the theme of death. His major works have included *O caminho fica longe* (1943, The Way Is Long) and *Alegria breve* (1965, Brief Pleasure).

The scope of neorealism was broadened in a different way by certain writers seeking an effective vehicle for a subjective point of view, which challenged the objective historical laws generally accepted by the neorealists. The leading representative of this movement, which the critics named "ethical realism," has been José Rodrigues Miguéis (born 1901). He has made use of a variety of literary techniques, and his semiautobiographical works have an admirable density. Rodrigues Miguéis can be said to be in the line of the relatively traditional fiction associated with Aquilino Ribeiro (1885–1963), a key figure in the development of regional literature in Portugal.

Irene Lisboa (1892–1958) was also a representative of ethical realism. She published expository works under the name of Manuel Soares, and poetry and fiction under the name of João Falco. These masculine pseudonyms suggest the difficult social position of the woman writer. One of the main subjects of her novels was the life of simple people in Lisbon and in the mountain regions.

Irene Lisboa was by no means the only important woman writer in Portugal. Indeed, there has been a significant increase in women writers since 1950. Among the most gifted, internationally recognized writers have been Sophia de Melo Breyner Andresen (born 1919); Maria Agustina Bessa Luís (born 1922), whose short stories have recalled the worlds of Kafka and the surrealists; Maria Fernanda Botelho de Faria e Castro (born 1926), the sober chronicler of a meaningless bourgeois way of life; and Maria Judite de Carvalho (born 1928), who has described, in moving and perceptive prose, man's forlornness and hopeless vulnerability.

Two other contemporary writers, who started from fundamentally different premises, have given the heterogeneous group of writers associated with ethical realism a clearer profile. One is João de Araújo Correia (born 1899), author of *Contos bárbaros* (1939, Wild Tales), *Contos durienses* (1941, Tales of the Douro), and *Montes pintados* (1964, Painted Mountains). A vigorous, original regionalism has characterized Araújo Correia's descriptions of the social atmosphere in which the inhabitants of the Douro valley live.

Joaquim Paço d'Arcos (born 1908, pseudonym of Joaquim Belford Correia da Silva), unlike Araújo Correia, has shown—at least in his short stories—the openmindedness of the much-traveled man, an important asset for a novelist who has dealt with all sides of Lisbon society. Paço d'Arcos's works have included *Herói derradeiro* (1932, Last Hero), *Memórias de uma nota de banco* (1962, Memoirs of a Banknote), and *Cela 27* (1965, Cell 27).

Among the most widely read short-story writers in Portugal today are Mário Braga (born 1921); José Cardoso Pires (born 1925), and Augusto Abelaira (born 1926). Braga began to write in the 1940s. His books have included *Nevoeiro* (1944, Mist), *Serranos* (1948, Mountain People), *Quatro reis* (1957, Four Kings), and *Viagem incompleta* (1963, Unfinished Journey). He has described the stifling narrowness of life in the provinces of northern Portugal from a committed viewpoint, but he has hidden his personal dismay behind a factuality that has given his indictment tremendous impact.

While Braga stands squarely in the tradition of Portuguese realistic fiction, José Cardoso Pires—in *Os caminheiros, e outros contos* (1949, The Wanderer, and Other Stories), *O anjo ancorado* (1958, The Anchored Angel), and *O livro de Job* (1963, The Book of Job)—has relied heavily on American short-story techniques in his detached treatment of intellectual confrontation. Although he has never lost touch with the traditional subject matter of Portuguese fiction, his approach has brought him close to the types of the *nouveau roman* that do not exclude plot.

Augusto Abelaira's *As boas intenções* (1962, The Good Intentions) was evidence of his fondness for experimentation. Abelaira's work has brought into focus the intellectual controversies that have challenged his generation.

Despite the many signs of independence, Portuguese fiction is still strongly influenced by French writers. The productive and versatile Urbano

Tavares Rodrigues (born 1923)—whose major works have been *Exílio perturbado* (1962, Restless Exile) and *Dias lamacentos* (1965, Dirty Days)—has been a follower of existentialism (now superseded in France by structuralism). Alfredo Margarido (born 1928) clearly modeled *As portas ausentes* (1963, The Absent Doors) on the *nouveau roman*. Margarido coedited an historically important anthology of the modern French novel, published in 1962. But insofar as there has been a new orientation of Portuguese fiction, the most promising figure is the young Almeida Faria (born 1943), whose first book, *Rumor branco* (1962, White Clamor), tried to elucidate various levels of human experience on different but intersecting time planes through the application of phenomenological and existentialist ideas.

DRAMA

The drama has had more limited opportunities than poetry and fiction in contemporary Portugal. While social and political factors are partly to blame, the main reason for the lack of vitality is the structure of the Portuguese theater. Financial support from either private or public sources is very hard to find. What little interest in serious playwriting there is has come mainly from amateur theaters, which also produce foreign plays. Thus, most Portuguese dramatists must assume from the outset that their work will be only read, not produced.

Modern Portuguese drama is seeking a style of its own and trying its best to involve the audience. Its use of both traditional and contemporary forms and subjects gives it a strongly syncretic character. Man in his isolation; social man at the mercy of fate; an unstable reality that rises toward the unreal and even the absurd—these are the themes of the postwar Portuguese drama. Brecht, Miller, O'Neill, Priestley, and Artaud, along with Pirandello and García Lorca, were the foreign dramatists who contributed to its intellectual shape.

Contemporary Portuguese drama may be said to have begun with Luís Francisco Rebelo (born 1924), who has been concerned with the isolation of modern man. Rebelo's *O mundo começou às 5 e 47* (The World Began at 5:47), first performed at the Teatro do Salitre in 1947, contrasted the exuberant hopefulness of the postwar years with the despair of the years preceding World War II. In this play, a new world founded on an absolute humanism is about to arise. Rebelo returned to this theme in *O dia seguinte* (1946, The Following Day). His other plays, expressionistic in language and almost allegorical in structure, have also dealt with man's isolation. Although man is forced into a manicheistic dualism, a new day may still dawn for him at any time, regardless of good or evil.

The outstanding playwright in contemporary Portugal is Bernardo Santareno (born 1924, pseudonym of António Martinho do Rosário). He has a striking talent for combining in his plays essentially disparate phenomena. A careful observer with an eye for folkloristic detail, yet one who has avoided regionalism, Santareno has exposed the underlying causes of his country's inner problems and has ripped off the veils shrouding the age-old conflicts of the flesh in dialogue with psychological overtones that have recalled Tennessee Williams. Santareno's major plays—*O judeu* (1966, The Jew) and *O inferno* (1968, Hell)—were most distinguished by their characterization of the heroes, who are as lifelike as those of the "Portuguese Balzac," Camilo Castelo Branco (1825–1890).

Romeu Correia (born 1917), who earned his reputation with neorealistic short stories and novels, may justifiably be ranked with Rebelo and Santareno. He has used to his own purposes the formal techniques of experimental drama and has drawn his subjects largely from traditional, popular art forms, such as the *romanceiro* and the Portuguese puppet play. Nonetheless, his tendency toward abstraction has made some of his plays difficult to grasp. As his most recent, unfavorably reviewed play *Bocage* (1965, Bocage) showed, he also has a scholarly interest in Portugal's literary tradition.

Luís de Sttau Monteiro's (born 1926) *Auto da barca do motor fora da borda* (1966, One-Act Play about a Boat with an Outboard Motor) alluded ironically to the eschatological trilogy of one-act plays (*autos*)— *Barca do Inferno* (1517, The Ship of Hell), *Barca do Purgatorio* (1518, The Ship of Purgatory), and *Barca da Gloria* (1519, The Ship of Glory)—by the great Renaissance Portuguese dramatist Gil Vicente (c. 1470–1536). Monteiro has recently come to the fore as a dramatist of great promise. In 1962 he won the coveted drama prize of the Sociedade Portuguesa de Escritores for his *Felizmente ha luar!* (1961, Fortunately There's a Moon!), which treated nineteenth-century Portuguese liberalism along Brechtian lines.

Fiama Hasse Pais Brandão (born 1938) also received the prize of the Sociedade Portuguesa de Escritores—for the play *Os chapéus de chuva* (1961, The Umbrellas). She has also written *O museu* (1962, The Museum) and *O golpe de estado* (1964, The Coup d'Etat). Hasse Pais Brandão has borrowed from Brecht and Ionesco to create a Portuguese theater relevant to the times.

Although traditionalism and stylistic conservatism still are dominant in Portuguese literature, there is sufficient evidence to suggest that the Portuguese intelligentsia is trying to bring foreign aesthetic and philosophical trends to the literature of their country. It is to be hoped that further liberalization in Portuguese political life will provide a climate in which the country's readiness for new literary departures can bear a rich harvest.

PORTUGUESE   WORKS   IN
ENGLISH   TRANSLATION

ANTHOLOGY

Longland, Jean R., ed. *Selections from Contemporary Portuguese Poetry: A Bilingual Collection.* New York, 1966

INDIVIDUAL WORKS MENTIONED
IN ARTICLE

Namora, Fernando Gonçalves. *O trigo*

e o joio as *Fields of Fate.* New York, 1970
Paço d'Arcos, Joaquim. *Memórias de uma nota de banco* as *Memoirs of a Banknote.* Chicago, 1968
Vicente, Gil. *Barca do Inferno, Barca do Purgatorio,* and *Barca da Gloria* as *The Ship of Hell.* In Robert O'Brien, ed., *Early Spanish Plays.* New York, 1964

SECONDARY   WORKS

BIBLIOGRAPHIES AND GUIDES

Coelho, Jacinto do Prado. *Dicionário de literatura,* 2 vols. Oporto, 1969–72
Moisés, Massaud. *Bibliografia da literatura portuguesa.* São Paulo, 1968

GENERAL WORKS

Franzbach, Martin. *Abriß der spanischen und portugiesischen Literaturgeschichte in Tabellen.* Frankfurt, 1968
Le Gentil, G. *La littérature portugaise.* Paris, 1951
Rossi, Giuseppe Carlo. *Storia della letteratura portoghese.* Florence, 1953
Saraiva, António José and Óscar Lopes. *História da literatura portuguesa,* 5th ed. Oporto, 1967
Simões, João Gaspar. *História da poesia portuguesa do século XX.* Lisbon, 1959
Stegagno Picchio, Luciana. *Storia del teatro portoghese.* Rome, 1964

WORKS ON CONTEMPORARY LITERATURE

Ameal, J. *Panorama de la littérature portugaise contemporaine.* Paris, 1949
Azevedo Filho, Leodegário A. de. *Situação atual do romance português.* In *I Congresso brasileiro de língua e literatura.* Rio de Janeiro, 1970
Mendonça, Fernando. *Situação atual do teatro português.* In *I Congresso brasileiro de língua e literatura.* Rio de Janeiro, 1970
Neves, João Alves das. *Situação atual do conto português.* In *I Congresso brasileiro de língua e literatura.* Rio de Janeiro, 1970
Oliveira, J. Osório de. *Visão incompleta de meio século de literatura portuguesa.* Lisbon, 1951
Rebelo, Luís Francisco. *Imagens do teatro contemporâneo.* Lisbon, 1964
Rodrigues, António Basílio. *Situação atual da crítica portuguesa.* In *I Congresso brasileiro de língua e literatura.* Rio de Janeiro, 1970
Tânger, Manuel. *Situação atual da poesia portuguesa.* In *I Congresso brasileiro de língua e literatura.* Rio de Janeiro, 1970

PAUL MIRON

Rumanian Literature

RUMANIAN CULTURAL LIFE between the two world wars seemed full of promise. Such observers as the philosopher Count Keyserling and the novelist Paul Morand, among others, were surprised by the variety of intellectual activity that emanated from this little-known culture. Rumania offered classicism when one expected barbarism. It also offered an archaically harmonious view of the world.

This world view was reflected in creative literature. Primary value was placed on harmony with the universe: revolt flares up only when the cosmic order is disturbed, and conflicts result from the betrayal of the "law," which in this context meant not rigidly imposed rules of behavior but regulators that make man into a human being. Rumanian writers of the period accepted the fashionable and the modern as long as they did not interfere with the relationship to the universal. Provincialism, whether of time or of space, was therefore rejected in favor of inherent values. The boundaries between concrete things and abstractions, between this world and the world beyond, were effaced to such a degree that surrealism was at home in Rumania before it became a specific genre in the west. And one can find examples of dadaism in Rumania before it was ever "proclaimed" in France. In many ways, the Rumanian language uses words not so much as communication but as communion of a society of initiates.

The prophecies about the "hour of Rumanian culture" have, to be sure,

535

not been fulfilled. History, which, according to the poet and philosopher Lucian Blaga (1895–1961), is being boycotted by the Rumanians, proved it to be unpropitious. When the Soviet invasion in 1944 led to a communist takeover of Rumania, writers were put into a painful situation: the hastily installed official critics had no firm standards with which to measure the value of a literary work. Writers were unsure about how to comply with official demands, and mistakes later became fateful. Even imitating Soviet-approved Russian writers was no guarantee against the caprices of censorship, for in the Soviet Union under Stalin there were shifts and reversals. Now we are discovering in greater detail how literature was treated in the period immediately following World War II, as, for example, in a report in 1971 in the journal *Tribuna* by Mihai Beniuc (born 1907), the long-term president of the Rumanian Writers' Association.

At first writers restricted themselves to two genres that offered less risk: in poetry it was the ode, which used the entire arsenal of Rumanian adjectives; in prose the favored genre was a bloodthirsty literature of "unmasking," in which wholesale denunciation for its own sake became each author's objective. Reportage, understood as a mixture of these two categories, likewise became a popular form and has flourished continuously to the present day. It is unnecessary to note any names from this period immediately following World War II. Only the distressing phenomenon itself, because of its uniqueness in European postwar literature, is worthy of mention.

Many writers—both established names and younger people who were just beginning to write—whose work could have made an impact on the new situation, either were abroad and remained there or hurried to emigrate. Aron Cotruș (1891–1961), a poet of social revolt, of workers' marches, and of justice, died in the United States. Paul Celan (born 1920) became a German author; Eugen Ionescu (born 1912), the French writer Eugène Ionesco. In France Constantin Virgil Gheorghiu (born 1916) won acclaim for *La vingt-cinquième heure* (1949, The Twenty-fifth Hour); and Vintilă Horia (born 1915), for *Dieu est né en exil* (1960, God Was Born in Exile). Mircea Eliade (born 1907), who could have best interpreted the intrusion of Russia into Rumanian history, moved to the United States. Horia Stamatu (born 1912), the grandiose lyricist and bridger of epochs, chose western Europe (France, Spain, Germany).

The authors who remained in Rumania either kept silent at first or accepted the new political line. The most striking example of conformity was Mihail Sadoveanu (1880–1961), who won the Lenin prize for an artistically worthless novel—*Mitrea Cocor* (1949, Mitrea Cocor). Gradually, almost all writers "joined the ranks," albeit with occasional lapses in some of their work.

POETRY

Contemporary Rumanian poetry has been dominated by four authors, who represent four different directions.

Ion N. Theodorescu (1880–1967), a former monk, characteristically chose the pseudonym Tudor Arghezi, which means roughly "he who has lost charisma." In 1927 he achieved deserved recognition with the volume of poetry *Cuvinte potrivite* (Matched Words). There followed *Flori de mucigai* (1931, Flowers of Mold), *Cărticică de seară* (1935, The Little Evening Book), and eleven other volumes, the last of which was *Ritmuri* (1966, Rhythms). Arghezi was an eclectic, trying out many different approaches to the world. Since he was not an original thinker, what he has mainly bequeathed is the magic of his language, the power of his expression, and the vitality of his verses. These qualities were always evident, whether he burrowed in the filth of the prisons, played the role of a singer of psalms, or announced his dissatisfaction with some form of society.

Arghezi believed himself to be a Balkan Baudelaire, yet his genius flashed precisely in what he tried to repudiate—in his organic attachment to the God of eastern Christianity, whom he daily betrayed and worshiped, cursed and then invited as his guest. Precisely in this vacillation lay the depth of his inner drama. Nowhere in world literature has the tragic destiny of Judas been reiterated in one man's complete work with such intensity. Quarreling with God, documenting evil, giving vent to blasphemy, establishing a different moral code, attempting to drive God himself out of paradise, along with glorifying creation, summoning God in humility, and lamenting lost grace—Arghezi presented all of this with gripping metaphysical restlessness.

Arghezi's poems also contained despair and fear, which were intended to reconcile us with death. The more Arghezi emphasized the physical nature of man, the more tormenting became the hidden questions. No matter how much poison he spread, how much misery and decay he described, he still did not succeed in preaching hatred, because he could not shed the inherent kindliness of the peasant, which he always retained. To criticize society, he turned to burlesque, in which historical revolt was drowned in verbosity. He remained a virtuoso in language, but did not bring anything new to it.

Dan Barbilian (1895–1961) published poetry under the pseudonym Ion Barbu, the name of his grandfather, a world-famous mathematician. He began as a Parnassian, as he described himself, but without the formalism of the French Parnassians. He was later intrigued by Nietzsche's vision of the "platonic heaven"; he was not interested in the things in themselves, but in the original idea of things, the world of pure spirit. Hence the title of his most mature volume of poetry, *Joc secund* (1931, Mirrored Play). Reality is not the result of chance but of a reflection onto a sublimated plane. Barbu explained what he meant in a poem at the beginning of the collection. Although poetry is a reflection of life, it is not a copy of it, but a pure and beneficent "counterpart." The new level causes the old one to disappear; poetry has become the reality.

Barbu's very first poems were compared to those of José-Maria de Hérédia, Richard Dehmel, and particularly Paul Valéry. But he then experienced a "Balkan conversion." In the cycle *Isarlîc* (1924, Isarlîc) he found inspiration in Anton Pann (1794–1854), a latter-day Rumanian Villon. From Pann, Barbu adopted subject matter, symbolism, and a pleasure in telling stories. From the west, however, he took the formality of his style, the virtually mathematical rigidity of language, and the art of abstraction. The east did not conquer the west, as some critics claimed. Instead, east and west met in a powerful but harmonious tension, which has characterized Rumanian literature since the time of Mihai Eminescu (1850–1889), the "father" of Rumanian literature.

The writings of Lucian Blaga, an important philosopher and dramatist as well as a poet, were banned in Rumania in 1947, and Blaga was not "rehabilitated" until after his death. His first poems—*Poemele luminii* (1919, Poems of Light) and *Pașii profetului* (1921, Steps of the Prophet) —established his importance as a Rumanian poet. Although his verses, which were written to illustrate a philosophical system, sprang more out of intellect than emotion, they have poetic value because of their originality of images and bold use of metaphors. Blaga, a mystical poet, was a contemplative wise man, a bucolic poet, whose words transformed his village in Transylvania into an infinite cosmic landscape. Archangels plow the gardens of man, God arises from the scattered seed, the animals are tamed, as are the ancient gods, especially wild Pan. The grapevines become more productive, and the vegetation of the pastures and fields grows greener. The joyful, purified world banishes restlessness and fear. Death is not a separation, but a return. Apocalyptic scenes make the reader shudder only because of their beauty.

Nothing was gloomy in Blaga's mystical world, because he always walked under the light of the "cosmic crown of miracles." His path was illuminated by love, which, for him, was the sign of recognition among the initiated and the bond between existence and transcendence. On his journey everything was a sign from the beyond and at the same time a signpost of the absolute, whose proximity we can sense by premonition, since it is deeply imprinted in our memory. An early brittleness, which was perhaps caused by Blaga's leanings toward German expressionism, gradually disappeared from his language.

George Bacovia (1881–1957), who greatly influenced contemporary

Rumanian literature, was an important exponent of symbolism. A poet of decay, twilight, and despair, he described hell in the manner of the *"poètes maudits"*: it is located in a desolate, provincial city, which is wasting away because of triviality and illness. The themes and images of Bacovia's poetry were taken from the storehouse of banalities. But through a polished technique, involving repetition, his poems took on the intensity of an hallucination. The intense colors of his simplified spectrum caused pain. Sudden snatches of melody in an otherwise atonal language had the effect of signs of hope or at least of fragments of memory. Because of this, hell became more painful but not final. Bacovia did not write much, and to date no complete edition of his poetry has been published, only several collections including *Poezii* (1956, Poems).

All recent Rumanian poetry, however original it may be, has been a coming to terms with these four poets—with their world of ideas and their language.

A year after the émigré journal *Prodromos* devoted an issue to Dan Botta (1907–1957), a four-volume edition of his works—*Scrieri* (1968, Writings)—appeared in Bucharest. The very small edition, which sold out the first day, revealed to the younger generation in Rumania a self-assured poet who gave names to their yearnings, who interpreted their dreams through his own inner tumult. Botta was both an innovator and a classicist, who strove for the magical purity of words and also freed poetry from the chains of the provincial and the ephemeral. Classical form gave his poetry beauty—the crystalline sonority of Thrace and of Hellas rediscovered. For Botta, primeval thought and primeval form were more real than everyday reality. He probably fulfilled the requirements of Barbu's poetic standards more than any other Rumanian poet.

Constant Tonegaru (1919–1952), whose life brought him nothing but misery, hunger, imprisonment, and an early death, was influenced by Bacovia and Apollinaire. He was a spokesman for absolute freedom, which he celebrated in his poetry with insouciance. Beneath his aloof irony and gallows humor there was a marked sensitivity. The fearful premonitions expressed in his work were understandable because of the constant threats of death. His volume of poetry *Plantații* (1945, Plantings) was not followed until 1969, when the collection *Steaua Venerii* (The Star of Venus) was published long after his death.

Among the many poets who established their reputations before 1947, those particularly deserving mention include Alexandru Philippide (born 1900), a meditative intellectual; Miron Radu Paraschivescu (1911–1971), whose gypsy songs in *Cântice țigănești* (1941, Gypsy Songs) were written in the manner of García Lorca; and Mihai Beniuc, who sacrificed his literary gifts, which shone so brilliantly in *Cântece de pierzanie* (1938, Songs of Doom), to become a political functionary.

Emil Botta (born 1912), one of the most important actors in the country and a follower of Mihai Eminescu, has preserved the world view and specific themes of Eminescu in a modern idiom falling somewhere between Blaga and Barbu. Virgil Gheorghiu (born 1905), a metaphysician, recently began publishing poetry again after a long pause during which he devoted himself to music. Geo Dumitrescu (born 1920) published in 1946 *Libertatea de a trage cu pușca* (The Freedom to Shoot a Gun). Anatol E. Baconsky (born 1925 celebrated ceremonial and pleasurable contemplation in *Fluxul memoriei* (1957, The Tide of Memory).

Among poets who cannot be published in Rumania are Sandu Tudor (1889–1960?), who became a monk after the war and died in prison; Nichifor Crainic (born 1889), cofounder of the journal *Gândirea*, which had great influence on Rumanian culture between the wars; and Radu Gyr (born 1905). All three were important authors of predominantly Christian poetry, which, although unpublished, has been disseminated orally.

A number of émigré poets, whose residence abroad has opened them up to the influence of foreign literatures, have continued nonetheless the traditions of Rumanian poetry. Dumitru Bacu (born 1924), a late romantic, found his inspiration for *Aiud* (1961, Aiud) in the past. Nicu Caranica (born 1911), in *Povestea foamei* (1965, The Tale of Hunger) populated the paradise of Botticelli with earthy Balkan characters. Ioan Cușa (born 1925), in *Plângeri* (1967, Laments), recreated the Old Testament patriarch. Virgil Ierunca's (born 1922) restrained poems have muffled the torment of existential questions through intellectual solutions. Numerous journals have also revealed a lively cultural activity among the émigrés: *Caete de dor, Limite, Ființa românească, Destin, Revista scriitorilor români,* and *Prodromos.*

Within Rumania the emergence of a new generation and, indeed, the rebirth of poetry after the war began with Nicolae Labiș (1935–1956), of whose work only the little volume *Primele iubiri* (1956, Early Loves) was published during his lifetime. Labiș meditated on the purity of childhood, which he described with the melancholy of the people of Moldavia. The masterful poem *Moartea căprioarei* (The Death of the Deer) became a symbol to his generation after his early death.

Nichita Stănescu (born 1937) has presented surprises in every new volume of poetry because of the persistence and depth of his questioning. His works have included *Sensul iubirii* (1960, The Meaning of Love), *11 elegii* (1966, 11 Elegies), and *Necuvintele* (1969, Nonwords). Stănescu wants to lead his contemporaries back to the original source, to the unborn state. With the power of a founder of a religion, he incites, convinces, enchants, converts. Indeed, everything he addresses himself to becomes winged, begins to float, prepares for salvation through poetry. But poetry is not the final goal: we enter the infinity of the inexpressible.

Ion Alexandru (born 1942) is another disquieting seeker. His collections of poetry—*Cum să vă spun?* (1964, How Shall I Tell You?), *Viaţa deocamdată* (1965, Life Thus Far), and *Vămile pustiei* (1969, The Bounds of the Desert)—have been proof of a highly gifted literary talent. The starting point in Alexandru's poetry is the exigencies of his Transylvanian homeland—the basic problem of survival. From here begin his flight into the heights and his concern for the survival of the spirit. After he goes through skepticism and irony, his view clears and his intention is fortified. He strives toward the eternally valid, a goal that can be reached only through a difficult crisis of beliefs comparable to that of the Israelites in the desert: hence the title of one of his collection of poems—*The Bounds of the Desert*. In the Bible the desert was the place in which union with the godhead occurred, the beginning of the exodus from bondage; but it was and has remained a place of great temptations. The conquering of the desert is achieved by gifts of love.

Alexandru's striving for inexpressible shores has led him to conclude that the tangible and demonstrable part of man is not his essence. The poet seeks salvation not as an individual but as a member of the mystical community of all who have gone before and of those who will come later. Like Stănescu, Alexandru wants to destroy poetry to make perceptible the inexpressible. Other poets seeking a new approach to reality are Ana Blandiana (born 1942) and Gheorghe Pituţ (born 1940), who with the precision of a watchmaker has taken objects, feelings, and landscapes apart, in order to reconstruct them again in a new arrangement of beauty and grace.

Marin Sorescu (born 1936)—who has published several much-discussed books, including *Moartea ceasului* (1966, The Death of the Clock), *Tinereţea lui Don Quijote* (1968, The Youth of Don Quixote), and *Tuşiţi* (1970, Cough)—has hidden under a fool's cap to avoid giving solutions. Instead, he has torn down the walls of human inadequacies with the sharpness of his irony and has mercilessly exposed weaknesses and uncovered all forms of bondage.

Ion Gheorghe (born 1935) has been a dynamic creator of myths. His language has the density of swamp forests. Leonid Dimov (born 1926) has assumed the role of an oriental wise man, a magician of colorful Balkan reveries; his cheerful verse contains clever recommendations for overcoming time and space. Other interesting contemporary Rumanian poets are Romulus Vulpescu (born 1933), Ştefan Augustin Doinaş (born 1922), Ion Caraion (born 1923), Alexandru Andriţoiu (born 1929), Nina Cassian (born 1924), Teodor Mihădaş (born 1923), Adrian Păunescu (born 1923), and—among the youngest poets—George Alboiu (born 1941) and Alexandru Grigore (born 1949).

DRAMA

The drama has not attained the same level as poetry in Rumania. In 1967 Horia Lovinescu (born 1917), who until recently was considered the most important dramatist of the postwar period, published a collection of plays. But the plays that received praise—*Citadela sfărîmată* (1955, The Crumbling Fortress), *Surorile Boga* (1959, The Boga Sisters), and *Febre* (1962, Fever)—had unbelievable characters and unsuspenseful conflicts. These plays were boring because of the transparency of their didacticism. That Lovinescu was capable of better work was demonstrated by his historical plays; an example was *Petru Rareş* (1967, Petru Rareş), which went beyond clichés and slogans and provoked genuine thinking.

Teodor Mazilu (born 1930), who has also written several satirical novels, published a number of his best-known comedies in a volume entitled *Teatru* (1971, Theater). In these plays barbed irony alternated with a striving for clever remarks at any price. Mazilu has displayed antipathy toward saviors of the world, pedagogues, and preachers, who, according to his plays, rob man of his freedom through their proselytizing fanaticism. Mazilu believes in man, not in systems of morality.

Some younger playwrights have shown promise. The poet Marin Sorescu's *Iona* (1967, Jonas), a modern mystery play, had more value than as a mere topical allusion to the present. Other interesting recent plays have included *Fotografii mişcate* (1969, Moving Pictures) by Ilie Păunescu (born 1920); *Autostop* (1970, Hitchhiking), a suspenseful, contemporary parable by Iosif Naghiu (born 1934); and the plays of Gheorghe Astaloş (born 1941), such as *Vin soldaţii* (1970, The Soldiers Are Coming), a very contemporary play full of symbolism and poetry.

FICTION

Fiction has not regained the same quality it achieved during the period between the two world wars. Among older writers, Camil Petrescu (1894–1957) tried to write an historical novel in terms of the new socialist ideology: *Un om între oameni* (1953, A Man amongst Men) was the story of Nicolae Bălcescu, a Rumanian revolutionary leader of 1848. George Călinescu (1900–1965), an important literary critic and essayist, succeeded in *Bietul Ioanide* (1953, Wretched Ioanide) in telling the tragic story of an intellectual who tried to preserve his freedom.

Five older writers have remained yardsticks for measuring every new arrival. They formed the bridge between tradition and such young writers as Petru Popescu (born 1944), and Radu Petrescu (born 1949), both of whom offer hope for the future of Rumanian fiction.

Zaharia Stancu (born 1902), president of the Rumanian Writers' Association, a poet and an outstanding translator of Yesenin, has written several novels and stories. Works such as *Descuļ* (1948, 1961; Barefoot) and *Rădăcinile sînt amare* (1958–59, The Roots Are Bitter)—which contained autobiographical features and a clearly lyrical background—were intended as frescoes of Stancu's rural homeland.

Radu Tudoran (born 1910) has written entertaining social novels with passionate heroes, suffering women, and exotic landscapes. His major works have been *Un port la răsărit* (1939, A Harbor in the East), *Anotimpuri* (no date, Seasons), and *Intoarcerea fiului risipitor* (no date, The Return of the Prodigal Son).

Geo Bogza (born 1907) began as a dadaist and then devoted himself increasingly to journalism. His committed socialism, which has made him soar to pompous metaphors, has become gentle and humanitarian when he turns his attention to the powerless and the humiliated. Bogza's most important work remains *Cartea Oltului* (1945, The Book of the River Olt).

Mircea Eliade, a philosopher and religious scholar, is the only writer living in exile who has had some of his works reprinted in Rumania. His books written before the war were best sellers. The world of his fiction moves under the constant sun of humanity's myths; the fantastic and the erotic are accepted as harmonious components of its reality. There is always the possibility of escape from the closed circle of existence through mysticism; this has been the secret of the attraction of Eliade's works. His major works have included *Huliganii* (1935, Hooligans), *Nopțile de Sân-ziene* (1954, The Eves of Saint John), and *Pe strada Mântuleasa* (1968, On Mântuleasa Street).

Vasile Voiculescu (1884–1963), who died shortly after being released from prison, left behind a manuscript with some of the most beautiful love poems ever written in the Rumanian language—*Ultimele sonete închipuite ale lui Shakespeare în traducere imaginară de V. Voiculescu* (1964, The Last Conceived Sonnets of Shakespeare in the Imaginary Translation of V. Voiculescu). His *Povestiri* (1966, Stories), also published posthumously, rivaled the poems in poetic content. Voiculescu's tone was reminiscent of Hemingway, yet his world was always consecrated; in it the holy spirit participates a thousandfold in the action, determines its course, or is influenced by it.

The way to the top was not easy for the new generation of talented novelists, except for perhaps Eugen Barbu (born 1924), Marin Preda (born 1922), and Petru Dumitriu (born 1924). Dumitriu was the star author of the communist regime until he fled to the west in 1960, at which time he ceased to write in Rumanian. His best book, *Incognito* (1962, Incognito), was published in French.

In 1957 Eugen Barbu published *Groapa* (The Pit), a naturalistic novel set in the suburbs of Bucharest, in which misery, intrigues, and individual destinies were described with a compassion comparable to John Steinbeck. After several additional novels and stories, many of them in several versions, Barbu published the mature novel *Principele* (1969, The Prince), which depicted the atmosphere of Bucharest during the eighteenth century with unequivocal allusions to the present. *The Prince* was a Balkan-Levantine counterpart of Robert Penn Warren's *All the King's Men*. The author himself defined his book as "a synthesis, a fairy tale, and a lyrical work." The modernity of Barbu's technique is bedazzling. He created out of countless books, tracts, letters, and documents a collage in which inventiveness and narrative talent conceal a weak intellectual content. Barbu, who has also written plays, is a clever, self-satisfied journalist who provides a relief from the general monotony of the cultural magazines.

Marin Preda, in his novel *Morome\c{t}ii* (1954, The Morometes), continued the tradition of the Rumanian village epic. Ilie Moromete, the chief protagonist, could have come out of a book by Sholokhov, and the entire atmosphere of the book points in other ways to Russian models. The most impressive thing about *The Morometes* was not the facts and their consequences but the manner in which Preda portrayed them. The characters of his fiction do not feel that existence is absurd (in the existential sense), but they are defeated somehow in their confrontation with life's problems. Their happiness withers away, and it is never possible to discover where the blame lies—in the estrangement caused by the forces of history or in the inadequacy of man.

Not until the middle of the 1960s did fiction begin to flower again in Rumania. Ştefan Bănulescu's (born 1926) six stories in the volume *Iărna bărba\c{t}ilor* (1965, The Winter of Men) earned him acclaim as the master of narrative art in postwar literature. Bănulescu is a great stylist. His extraordinary control of language has permitted him to create, by means of the rhythm, position, and function of words, an inseparable unity between expression and content without a mannerist effect. Nothing is capricious in the flow of his story or in the dynamics of his statement, and, thus, nothing can be changed or transposed. The word receives a new energy from the content; conversely, the topicality of the language determines the vitality of the action. Thus, we find, for example, that a picturesque description can conceal dramatic suspense, that the boundaries between such traditional categories as time and space, natural and supernatural, or animal, mineral, and vegetable melt to form a kaleidoscope which is modern but which at the same time reflects the original qualities of Rumanian culture.

The most important work of Fănuş Neagu (born 1935) has been the novel *Ingerul a strigat* (1968, The Angel Cried Out). The colorful, exotic, seething world of this tale is so fascinating that one almost overlooks the tragic core of the pulsating action. It is the epic of a society chained to an unrelenting destiny from which there is no escape. The "callings of the angel" are the opposite of a happy message; in every instance they signal the descent into the depths of unhappiness.

Dumitru Radu Popescu (born 1935), a dramatist and journalist, has also written stories and novels, among others *F* (1969, F), always with sensitive empathy with the souls of his characters, each one a "case." The problem of freedom and of making decisions, as well as the problematic situation of the split personality, was analyzed by Leonid Plămădeală (born 1926) in *Trei ceasuri în iad* (1970, Three Hours in Hell). Nicolae Breban (born 1928) presented a panopticon of madmen in the manner of Dostoevski in *Animalele bolnave* (1968, The Sick Animals). In this work evil is not explained by external circumstances; it slumbers in the deepest reaches of the human soul, which the author does not describe but uncovers and explains.

A number of philosophical novels have recently appeared in Rumania, including *Cunoașterea de noapte* (1969, Cognition by Night) by Alexandru Ivasiuc (born 1923) and *Viața si opiniile lui Zacharias Lichter* (1969, The Life and Opinions of Zacharias Lichter) by Matei Călinescu (born 1934). Ion Lăncrăjan (born 1928) has been fond of mass scenes and conglomerations of characters and situations, as in *Cordovanii* (1963, Cordovans). Mircea Ciobanu (born 1943) in *Epistole* (1969, Letters) and *Martorii* (1968, Witnesses), Dumitru Țepeneag (born 1933) in *Exerciții* (1966, Exercises), and Aurel Dragoș Munteanu (born 1944) in *Scarabeul sacru* (1969, The Holy Scarab) turned to the convoluted labyrinths of their own psyches in writing parables, accounts of dreams, and symbol-laden "confessions."

If one had to summarize briefly the main characteristics of contemporary Rumanian literature, the following should be cited: a delicate feeling for sacred things that is not limited by religious dogma; a harmony between the modern and the rational on one hand and the archaic and the fabular on the other; and a meeting of genesis and apocalypse in the creative act.

RUMANIAN WORKS IN ENGLISH TRANSLATION

ANTHOLOGIES

MacGregor-Hastie, Roy, ed. *Anthology of Contemporary Romanian Poetry.* Chester Spring, Pa., 1969

Popa, Eli, ed. *Romania Is a Song: A Sampler of Verse in Translation.* Cleveland, 1966

Short Stories, 2 vols. Bucharest, 1955–56

Steinberg, Jacob, ed. *Introduction to Rumanian Literature*. New York, 1966

INDIVIDUAL WORKS MENTIONED IN ARTICLE

Dumitriu, Petru. *Incognito* as *Incognito*. New York, 1964
Gheorghiu, Virgil. *La vingt-cinquième heure* as *The Twenty-fifth Hour*. New York, 1950

Lovinescu, Horia. *Citadela sfărîmată* as *The Crumbling Fortress*. In *Rumanian Review*, 10, 2, 1956
Petrescu, Camil. *Un om între oameni* as *A Man amongst Men*, 2 vols. Bucharest, 1958
Preda, Marin. *Moromeţii* as *The Morometes*. Bucharest, 1957
Stancu, Zaharia. *Descuļ* as *Barefoot*. London, 1951

SECONDARY WORKS

Balotă, Nicolae. *Euphorion*. Bucharest, 1969
Bibliografia literaturii romîne (1948–1960). Bucharest, 1965
Bote, Lidia. *Simbolismul românesc*. Bucharest, 1966
Călinescu, Matei. *Eseuri critice*. Bucharest, 1967
Damian, S. *Intrarea la castel*. Bucharest, 1970
George, Alexandru. *Marele Alpha*. Bucharest, 1970
Ierunca, Virgil, *Românește*. Paris, 1964
Lupi, Gino. *Storia della letteratura romena*. Florence, 1955
Manolescu, Nicolae. *Metamorfozele poeziei*. Bucharest, 1968
Micu, Dumitriu and Nicolae Manolescu.

Rumänische Literatur der Gegenwart 1944–1966. Munich, 1968
Negoiţescu, Ion. *Scriitori moderni*. Bucharest, 1967
Paleologu. *Spiritul şi litera*. Bucharest, 1970
Piru, Alexandru. *Panorama deceniului literar 1940–1950*. Bucharest, 1968
Regman, Cornel. *Cică niște cronicari*. Bucharest, 1970
Schroeder, Klaus-Henning. *Einführung in das Studium des Rumänischen: Sprachwissenschaft und Literaturgeschichte*. Berlin, 1967
Vianu, Tudor. *Studii de literatură română*. Bucharest, 1965
Zaciu, Mircea. *Glose*. Cluj, 1970

GLEB STRUVE

Russian Literature

FUTURE HISTORIANS of twentieth-century Russian literature will have to reckon with two cardinal factors that determined and shaped its fortunes. One of its characteristics is that ever since the early 1920s it has led a double life. This double life was a result of the impact the Bolshevik revolution of October, 1917, had on Russian life. The repercussions of that revolution were felt (and are still felt today) throughout the world. But nowhere was its impact on literature so powerful, so profound, and so total as in Russia. It split Russian literature into two separate, parallel-flowing streams.

Ever since the early 1920s, when the civil war in Russia ended and the victory of bolshevism led to a mass exodus of Russians who were opposed to the new order, Russian literature has been divided in two. The division was both geographical and spiritual. Alongside literature inside Russia—Soviet Russian literature—there sprung up and developed, scattered all over the world but at various periods gravitating toward this or that main center—Berlin, Paris, and New York in turn, in that order—literature in exile, or émigré literature. Except for a brief spell at the very outset, between 1921 and 1924, there was no osmosis, no real intercourse and

---

The transliteration and capitalization in this article reflect the publisher's style and are consistent with other articles in this reference work. They do differ in some details, however, from Dr. Struve's preferences and practice in other publications.

interaction between these two branches of Russian literature. At least, there was no two-way communication, let alone influence: while émigré writers, both old and young, knew, read, often admired, and were sometimes influenced by what was going on in Soviet literature, émigré literature remained, to those living in Soviet Russia, a closed book and a forbidden fruit. The policy of exclusion of émigré literature from the Soviet Union began to change—very gradually and in the face of great obstacles—only in the late 1950s, when a new dimension was added to both branches of literature in the shape of "émigré books" by nonémigré writers. The best-known examples of these "exiled" books are Boris Pasternak's (1890–1960) *Doktor Zhivago* (1957, Doctor Zhivago), Abram Terts's (born 1925, pseudonym of Andrei Sinyavski) *Sud idyot* (1960, The Trial Begins), and the works of Aleksandr Solzhenitsyn (born 1919). In the late 1960s there were also several cases of more-or-less established Soviet writers, born between 1920 and 1930, "defecting" to the west.

The second distinctive feature of postrevolutionary Russian literature has been the almost complete dependence of nearly the whole literary output inside the country on the "political climate" of the day, if not—as was often the case during the past fifty years—on the specific policies of the ruling members of the Communist Party in the most narrow sense. Certain developments in Soviet literature cannot therefore be understood fully without reference to the political background.

SOVIET RUSSIAN LITERATURE

It was natural that during World War II the war theme itself dominated Soviet literature almost to the exclusion of everything else. It was not surprising, for instance, that the publication, in 1943, of Mikhail Zoshchenko's (1895–1958) autobiographical fragments, *Pered voskhodom solntsa* (Before the Sunrise), attracted immediate critical attention and came to be sharply attacked: the work had nothing to do with the war and showed a strange and "untimely" concern with the theories of Pavlov and Freud. Most Soviet writers, however, placed themselves wholeheartedly in the service of the national war effort and produced a vast number of war reportages, front-line sketches, poems, and topical political articles. There were also several war plays and some war novels, of semifictional and semidocumentary nature.

Much of the wartime literature reflected the concessions the Soviet government had begun to make not long before the war, in the face of the German threat, to Russian patriotism and national feelings. During the war the government made full use of those sentiments in bolstering the war effort of the Russian people. In literature nationalism found expression in some historical novels dealing with World War I (those of Sergei Sergeev-Tsenski [1876–1958] for instance, the last of which—*Pushki zagovorili* [The Guns Have Spoken]—was published in 1945, just before the war was over). The equation of Soviet patriotism with Russian patriotism also became a key theme in the journalistic writings of two other prerevolutionary writers: Aleksei N. Tolstoi (1882–1945) and Ilya Ehrenburg (1891–1967).

Two important works were produced in the last year of the war. *Molodaya gvardiya* (1945, The Young Guard) by Aleksandr Fadeev (1901–1956), one of the best known postrevolutionary writers, was a novel about the activities of a group of young communists who worked for the Soviet underground behind the German lines during the war. It was based on actual events disclosed after the advancing communist forces had reoccupied the territory. The novel, well written, was at first enthusiastically received by Soviet critics. But in the postwar period it came to be severely criticized from above for the author's failure to give full credit to the role of the party leadership in the underground activities he described. Fadeev was forced to revise the novel and bring out a new edition in 1951.

The other important work was *V okopakh Stalingrada* (1946, In the Trenches of Stalingrad), by Viktor Nekrasov (born 1911), then a newcomer to literature, later a very well-known writer. Barely disguised as a fiction, *In the Trenches of Stalingrad* was one of the best accounts of the Battle of Stalingrad to come from the pen of one of the participants; it showed both Nekrasov's literary ability and his psychological insight.

A new period in Soviet literature was inaugurated on August 14, 1946, when the Central Committee of the Communist Party of the Soviet Union passed a resolution that would set loose violent "political" passions and was to become the starting point of what has come to be generally regarded as the bleakest, most sterile period in the history of Soviet literature. This period lasted over six years, until after Stalin's death in 1953. It came to be associated with the name of Andrei Zhdanov (1896–1948), even though Zhdanov himself died only two years after the resolution. Nevertheless, from 1946 to 1948 he played the role of cultural dictator in the Soviet Union, and the policies initiated by him were continued after his death.

The original resolution of the Central Committee was concerned, on the face of it, with two specific cases, and it was published under the seemingly innocuous title, "About the Magazines *Zvezda* and *Leningrad.*" The two Leningrad magazines, the first of which was to be thoroughly shaken up and the second suppressed, were accused of having wrought "ideological havoc" among the Leningrad writers and given a bad example to all other Soviet periodicals by publishing "ideologically harmful" works, full of "anti-Soviet innuendoes." Two writers were chosen as targets for a particularly venomous attack: Mikhail Zoshchenko and Anna Akhmatova (1889–1966).

Zoshchenko, one of the most popular Soviet satirists of the 1920s and 1930s, was attacked for his *Priklyucheniya obez'yany* (1946, The Adventures of a Monkey), a fable that was interpreted as a satirical portrait of the Soviet regime. His *Before the Sunrise* was recalled. These autobiographical fragments had been previously denounced as "vulgar," "antinational," "amoral," "profoundly alien to the spirit and character of Soviet literature." It was said that there was no place for a writer like Zoshchenko in Soviet literature.

Akhmatova was described as a "typical representative of vacuous poetry, devoid of any ideas and alien to our people." The attack on both writers was developed and sharpened by Zhdanov himself in his speeches to the Leningrad branch of the Union of Soviet Writers—on whose leaders much of the blame for the state of things in the two magazines was laid—and to the Leningrad City Committee of the Communist Party. Speaking of Akhmatova's poetry, he described her as a "cross between a nun and a harlot."

In those two notorious speeches Zhdanov laid down the new party line in matters of arts and letters. The immediate result of all this was the expulsion of both Zoshchenko and Akhmatova from the Union of Soviet Writers and from Soviet literature itself. Zoshchenko never really succeeded in reintegrating himself into it, although he was officially "rehabilitated" after 1956. Toward the end of his life some new stories of his were published, and some of his earlier work was reissued, although much of his inimitable satire was pruned by censorship.

Akhmatova found her way back into print in 1950, with a cycle of poems glorifying Stalin and the Soviet peace effort in connection with the Stockholm Peace Congress. It was, however, well known that with those poems she was trying to buy freedom for her son, Lev Gumilyov, who had been sent to a concentration camp in 1945. Her paeans to Stalin, in which it is difficult to recognize her poetic voice, were one of the saddest illustrations of the poet's plight under Stalin. (They were not included in the 1961 and 1965 editions of Akhmatova's collected works.)

The real comeback of Akhmatova to literature did not take place until later, during the de-Stalinization of 1956. Akhmatova's importance as a poet was heightened in the 1960s, with the publication of many short poems, as well as the major work *Poema bez geroya* (Poem without a Hero), which was written from 1940 to 1942 and thus far published more or less in its entirety only outside Russia (in 1967). Much of Akhmatova's work, including parts of *Poem without a Hero* and the cycle *Rekviem* (Requiem)—written between 1935 and 1940, destroyed after the war, and restored from memory—remains unpublished to this day in the Soviet

Union. Thus, many works by Akhmatova belong to the category of "émigré books" by nonémigré writers. The latest Soviet edition of her collected poems, *Beg vremeni* (1965, The Course of Time), published not long before her death, is far from complete.

The resolution of August 14, 1946, and its aftermath meant much more than the expulsion of Zoshchenko and Akhmatova from literature. The resolution was fully endorsed by the board of the Union of Soviet Writers. In its own resolution the board abjectly admitted its own responsibility in encouraging the infiltration of alien tendencies and moralities into Soviet literature and stressed the "un-Soviet spirit of servility before the bourgeois culture of the west" that had characterized the activities of some of the Leningrad writers. Rabid antiwesternism was to become the keynote of the Zhdanov cultural policies during the next five years.

The party resolution on *Zvezda* and *Leningrad* was followed by two others: "On the Repertory of Dramatic Theaters, and Measures for Its Improvement" and "On the Motion Picture *Bol'shaya zhizn'* (Big Life)." The resolution on the dramatic repertory attributed the main weakness of Soviet theatrical life to the almost complete absence of Soviet plays on topical contemporary themes and to the undue prominence of plays by foreign writers, such as Somerset Maugham, Arthur W. Pinero, George S. Kaufman, and Moss Hart. The second resolution dealt specifically with the shortcomings of Pavel Nilin's film *Big Life,* but it also criticized a number of other films on ideological grounds, including some by Eisenstein, Pudovkin, Kozintsev, and Trauberg. The result was the withdrawal of *Big Life,* followed by Nilin's recantation. Eisenstein confessed to having distorted historical truth in the second part of his *Ivan Grozny* (Ivan the Terrible), and the showing of it was prohibited.

After these resolutions, the response to Zhdanov's directives rapidly mounted in pitch and violence, with Soviet writers, critics, and literary scholars vying with party spokesmen in castigating any departure from the new party line. The few voices raised in doubt or opposition were immediately silenced. Although the number of those from literature and literary scholarship who were "purged" in those years, that is, those who were put to death or who perished in labor camps, was not as great as during the great purge of 1937–38, it was still a fairly large number. Much larger, however, was the number of those who were reduced to silence unless they joined in what became a veritable orgy of antiwesternism in literature and the other arts.

This antiwestern campaign took three principal directions. First, those guilty of "servility before the west" were ferreted out. They were soon to be branded as *bezrodnye kosmopolity* (rootless cosmopolitans). Second, the "decadent west" was directly attacked and denounced. These attacks had a strong political flavor and were directed mainly against the United

States, although the list of "decadent" writers was very extensive and included not only Proust, Joyce, and Kafka but also Sartre, Camus, Mauriac, Malraux, Henry de Montherlant, Valéry Larbaud, Jules Romains, Edwin Muir, and Stephen Spender. Third, everything Russian was glorified, and the superiority of Russia in every field, including its priority in many a scientific invention, was unquestioningly asserted. By 1948–49 this antiwestern campaign acquired Gargantuan proportions. After that it began to peter out, but it was only after Stalin's death that an end was put to it.

Under these conditions, it was not surprising that there was little literary value in the great majority of works written between 1946 and 1953—be they novels, poems, or plays (in the plays the antiwestern bias was particularly prominent; all the above-mentioned three trends were somehow embodied in them). The majority of these works are now deservedly forgotten.

Some mention should be given to a few works by older writers that appeared during the period 1946–53. These older writers did not write "to order." Nevertheless, they did try to avoid tackling ticklish themes. Konstantin Fedin (born 1892), who was the author of one of the first full-scale Soviet novels (and at that, rather experimental in construction and style), became during the 1950s one of the pillars of the literary establishment. He undertook, at the end of the war, a vast chronicle of Russian life, which, without being autobiographical, coincided with the span of his own adult life and contained a great deal of material based on personal experiences and reminiscences—a device Fedin had readily resorted to in his earlier works. The first part of what was to become a trilogy was called *Pervye radosti* (1945, First Joys); the second, *Neobyknovennoe leto* (1948, No Ordinary Summer). Both novels were in the tradition of the realistic, social-psychological novel.

In *First Joys* the action takes place in Saratov (Fedin's native town) on the eve of World War I. The hero, Kiril Izvekov, appears here as a schoolboy. Alongside Izvekov, Fedin presented a great number of secondary characters, of whom the most important are Ragozin, a revolutionary workman, somewhat reminiscent of Maksim Gor'ki's (1868–1936) "positive" characters; and two representatives of the intelligentsia: the writer Pastukhov and the actor Tsvetukhin. (Izvekov falls in love with a girl who later becomes an actress, and the theatrical milieu plays an important part in the novel.) Fedin painted a broad panorama of Russian provincial life, with a stress on the milieu in which the revolution was being preached and nurtured. Under the influence of Ragozin, Izvekov is drawn into this underground revolutionary movement. At the end of the book he is arrested.

In *No Ordinary Summer* the story is advanced by several years and set in the midst of the civil war, in the summer of 1919, when the fate of that conflict was decided. Writing his novel when he did, Fedin could not refrain from distorting the historical truth and portraying Stalin as the military hero of the day, at the expense of Trotski (in the post-1956 editions of the novel all such passages were revised or cut out). Izvekov is shown in this second novel as a good Bolshevik. The writer Pastukhov plays an important role. Just as in his two earliest novels, Fedin was concerned with the problems of the intelligentsia, of its place and role in the revolution. He did not simplify or overschematize this problem. But, unlike Andrei Startsov, the hero of Fedin's first novel, *Goroda i gody* (1924, Cities and Years), who was in many ways the author's alter ego, Pastukhov is not shown as an out-and-out "superfluous man" in the revolution. He sheds his individualism and adheres to the revolution, deciding that one must take a stand in the shaping of a nation's history.

Fedin posed the problem of the relationship between revolution and art, and he solved it in an orthodox way. Unlike Nikita Karev, the hero of Fedin's second novel *Brat'ya* (1928, Brothers), both Pastukhov and Tsvetukhin overcome their inner contradictions and find their own artistic revitalization in the revolution.

By comparison with Fedin's first two novels—especially with the very first, *Cities and Years,* in which he experimented with narrative technique and took great liberties with chronology—Fedin's postwar novels sounded old-fashioned. This was particularly true of *No Ordinary Summer,* in which the action is set in the same year as in *Cities and Years.*

Only much later did Fedin go back to the trilogy and publish the first part of the third volume—*Kostyor* (1962, Bonfire). The action here is set on the eve of World War II and during its first stages. There are some new characters, but most of the action is centered around the same principal figures. The novel's structure, however, differed from the first two parts: in *Bonfire* Fedin pursued several separate lines of narrative, and there are no encounters between some of the principal characters.

Another novel by a well-known prewar Soviet writer that was attacked and had to be issued in a revised edition was *Za vlast' Sovietov* (1949, 1951; For the Power of the Soviets), by Valentin Kataev (born 1897). It was also the first part of a trilogy, with the action set during World War II, in German-occupied Odessa. The principal character was the son of the hero of Kataev's very popular earlier novel *Beleet parus odinoki* (1936, Lonely White Sail). In *For the Power of the Soviets* both the son and the father's friend Gavrik are members of the Soviet resistance against the Germans. The charge brought against Kataev was similar to the one against Fadeev's *The Young Guard:* he was accused of having committed a political mistake by minimizing the role of the party in the anti-German underground activities.

Another bulky work written during the Zhdanov period was the autobiographical trilogy by Fyodor Gladkov (1883–1958): *Povest' o detstve* (1949, Story of a Childhood), *Vol'nitsa* (1950, Freebooters), and *Likhaya godina* (1954, Hard Times). The influence of Gor'ki and of Gor'ki's autobiography is clearly felt in this work, but it will probably survive as Gladkov's best work.

One of the few newcomers to literature to attract attention during this period was Vera Panova (born 1905). Her short war novel, *Sputniki* (1946, Traveling Companions), for which she was awarded the Stalin Prize, described a group of people working on an ambulance train that evacuated the wounded from the front. The novel had an objectivity and detachment reminiscent of Chekhov. Panova's second novel, *Kruzhilikha* (1948, the title is the name of a factory), was written in response to the demand for works on contemporary themes. But *Kruzhilikha* showed the same concern with human beings, their personal problems and their mutual relationships, and the same predilection for Chekhovian understatement. Rather characteristically for this period, some critics blamed Panova for her "dispassionateness," for her failure to "decipher" for the readers her own characters.

One of the most prolific Soviet writers, and the most western-oriented among them, Ilya Ehrenburg wrote two novels during this period: *Burya* (1948, The Storm) and *Devyaty val* (1953, The Ninth Wave). Both of them can be described as "international" journalistic novels. The contrast between the two worlds, the capitalist and the Soviet, is central, particularly in *The Ninth Wave,* where the action is set in Moscow, Paris, the United States, Prague, and Bonn. The events are shown partly through the eyes of a French journalist, who changes his attitude toward the Soviet Union from skeptically negative to positive. Both novels, especially *The Ninth Wave,* reflected Ehrenburg's response to the antiwestern "social command"; they were fictional counterparts of the role he played in those days as the official Soviet peace propagandist. The portrayal in *The Ninth Wave* of a United States senator and his daughter was an obviously overdone caricature. But the novel was not devoid of documentary interest, and through some of his negative or uncommitted characters Ehrenburg manages at times to subject the Soviet regime to convincingly ruthless criticism.

The survival of Ehrenburg, a Jew and a man with a strong and genuine attachment to the west (he lived there for many years before the revolution and often returned in the 1930s), through all the vicissitudes of Stalin's reign, was one of the minor miracles of that time. He shed some light on those years in his multivolumed memoirs, *Lyudi, gody, zhizn'* (1960–64, People, Years, Life), a typical Ehrenburgian mixture of truths, half-truths, and untruths. There is no doubt that all through those years he showed himself to be extraordinarily adaptable and keen-sighted. More than once his works of fiction served as a barometer of the literary weather. But luck was on his side, too.

It was no wonder that one of Ehrenburg's works, with its "meterologi-cal" title, gave the name to the whole period in Soviet literature that followed Stalin's death. Called *Ottepel'* (1954, The Thaw), this short novel was not actually the first symptom of a spring after the long Zhdanov winter. It was preceded by several poems by Olga Bergholz (born 1910) and other writers in which a new personal note could be detected; by Ehrenburg's own article about some modern western writers, which was a complete breaking away from the Zhdanovite antiwesternism; by a similar article on western music by Aram Khachaturian; by an article by Vladimir Pomerantsev (born 1907) about "sincerity in literature," advocating a sincere and truthful portrayal of Soviet life, a depiction "without varnish"; and by an article by Fyodor Abramov (born 1920) attacking several recent prize-winning novels about collective farms, on the grounds that they showed reality through rose-colored spectacles.

It later became a commonplace to say that there were at least three thaws in Soviet literature in the period between Stalin's death and the downfall of Khrushchev in 1964 (in 1953–54, in 1956, and in 1961–62) and that they alternated with new freezes. The first part of Ehrenburg's *The Thaw* was the high point of the first thaw. Its main significance lay in its defense of free, unregimented art, personified in the contrast between two young artists. But some other aspects of Soviet society, such as over-bureaucratization, arbitrary reprisals, and injustice, were also subjected to criticism. The work was at once attacked by the Soviet "conservatives," and the attacks induced Ehrenburg to tack on a second part when *The Thaw* appeared in book form in 1955 (a great number of Soviet novels are first published in magazines). Here some of the criticisms were toned down, but the main issue of "free art" stood out even more clearly.

The year 1953 saw the publication of *Russki les* (The Russian Forest) by Leonid Leonov (born 1899), one of the leading Soviet novelists of the 1920s and 1930s. Serialized for the most part after Stalin's death, it was written earlier, ostensibly in response to Stalin's ecological appeal for the preservation of Russia's forests (a similar response came from Dmitri Shostakovich in the form of a cantata).

The Russian Forest was Leonov's first novel since his *Doroga na okean* (1935, Road to the Ocean). In the interim he had written several plays, some war stories, and many journalistic articles. But the ecological theme was a purely external framework: as usual, Leonov was primarily con-cerned with multiple human destinies, problems, and conflicts, while at the same time he used the forest as an overall symbol. The main narrative of the novel covers the period before and during the Soviet-German war, but there are long and important flashbacks, involving the two principal antagonists in the novel and taking the reader well into the prerevolutionary period (Leonov had done the same in *Road to the Ocean*).

Leonov's overriding concern was with a moral problem. As in his earlier works, one could sense, if not the influence, at least the lurking shadow of Dostoevski. In addition, one of the most perspicacious students of Leonov in the west, R. D. B. Thomson, saw in all of Leonov's works a new approach to the Pushkinian theme of Mozart versus Salieri, of creative "flights" versus sheer diligence. Thomson came to the conclusion that in *The Russian Forest* Leonov's treatment of this theme "comes full circle," that his would-be positive hero, Professor Vikhrov, turns out to be a Salieri, whereas his rival, the "villain" Gratsianski, even though no Prometheus and only "half alive," achieves the illusion of an "almost creative" life.

In the view of Thomson, it was in the same spirit that Leonov proceeded, in the 1950s, to rewrite several of his most important earlier works: the plays *Metel'* (1940, Snowstorm), which had been violently denounced while it was being rehearsed, and *Zolotaya kareta* (1946, The Golden Coach); and his best-known and most ambitious pre-1930 novel, *Vor* (1927, The Thief). The revised, highly controversial version of *The Thief* (1959) was Leonov's most important contribution to the literature of the post-Stalin period. Whether it signified, as asserted by some western students of Soviet literature, Leonov's "surrender" to the new order or, as some Soviet critics have said, his ideological "maturing," it was, as nearly everything Leonov has ever written, very interesting and thought-provoking.

The only works Leonov has published since are the play *Begstvo g-na Mak-Kinli* (1961, Mr. McKinley's Escape), which has been described as both "unworthy and unrepresentative" of Leonov, and a short, well-written narrative, *Evgenia Ivanovna* (1963; the title is in Latin characters in the original), a rather curious, intriguing story of a young Russian woman. Evgenia Ivanovna is evacuated with her husband, soon after their marriage at the end of the civil war, from the Crimea to Constantinople. She is "abandoned" by him almost immediately (he "disappears"), leads a life of poverty in Paris, but ends by marrying a much older British archeologist with whom, on one of his expeditions to Mesopotamia, she revisits the Soviet Union and during a short stay in the Caucasus meets her former husband, who acts as their guide and interpreter.

Leonov may have meant *Evgenia Ivanovna* to be an illustration of the theme of homesickness (Soviet critics even saw in it "a passionate reflection on the importance of one's home country"). But its "message," if any, remains vague and mysterious, and the ending is inconclusive: we only know that Evgenia Ivanovna (as she is called throughout) wants to go back to England and make her home there—after discovering, during a solitary walk with her former husband, that she is pregnant. The dates Leonov placed under the last line of *Evgenia Ivanovna* (1938–1963) may mean that the story was originally written in 1938 and then revised or perhaps just polished. One of the principal figures in Soviet literature before and during the war, Leonov seems to have almost withdrawn from it after 1960.

The 1956 thaw was heralded by Khrushchev's speech denouncing Stalin and the iniquities of his rule at the Twentieth Congress of the Communist Party. Although delivered in a closed session, the speech soon became widely known. Whether expected or not, its repercussions were far-reaching. One of its immediate effects on literature was the accelerated process of "rehabilitation" of those numerous writers who had become "unpersons" during the purges of the late 1930s and the Zhdanov period. It was now admitted that these writers perished either by being executed outright (although this was seldom actually spelled out) or by dying in remote labor camps. The official standard formula in their biographies in *Kratkaya literaturnaya entsiklopediya* (1962–68, The Concise Literary Encyclopedia, volumes 1–5 published thus far) and in introductions to their reissued works now ran, with slight variations, as follows: "Repressed during the period of the cult of personality [that is, the dominance of Stalin]; posthumously rehabilitated."

Some of the "unpersons" who remained alive were also rehabilitated and readmitted into literature, but in their cases the repression was seldom mentioned in print. At least a partial rehabilitation was also accorded to a few deceased émigré writers, such as Ivan Bunin (1870–1953) and Marina Tsvetaeva (1892–1941). The rehabilitations had in fact begun earlier: some of them (including Bunin's) were announced at the Second Congress of Soviet Writers at the end of 1954. But in 1956, as a direct result of Khruschchev's speech, their scope was expanded, their pace accelerated, and the whole procedure regularized, with special commissions set up, under the chairmanship of prominent writers, to deal with the literary legacy of the former "unpersons."

In some cases, however, the rehabilitation process proved to be slow and tortuous, as in the case of Tsvetaeva, who had returned to Russia in 1939 and committed suicide soon after the outbreak of the war in 1941. In 1956 Ehrenburg published a very warm tribute to her in *Literaturnaya Moskva* (Literary Moscow), accompanied by some of her early poems, and announced the forthcoming publication of a volume of her collected poetry. This volume did not, however, appear until five years later. (True, in 1965 it was followed by another, and much fuller, collection, although still with some poems and passages censored.)

The rehabilitation of another outstanding poet, Osip Mandelstam (1891–1938), whose work spanned the years 1909–37 and who died a miserable death in a transit camp in the far east, stopped short at the publication of his works, although such publication was announced on more than one occasion, with the name of the prospective editor (a different name with each announcement).

The high point of the 1956 thaw in literature was the publication of the novel *Ne khlebom yedinym* (1956, Not by Bread Alone), by Vladimir Dudintsev (born 1918), until then a little-known writer. *Not by Bread Alone* became something of a literary sensation and was translated into many languages. Its literary value was rather overrated in the outside world, while its significance as a work of dissent was exaggerated at home. Its publication was followed by strong attacks on Dudintsev, by new enjoinders to writers to adhere to the methods of socialist realism, and by fresh denunciations of the "decadent" literature of the west.

There was, however, no question of a return to the antiwesternism of the Zhdanov period. Ever since the death of Stalin, and still more so after the 1956 de-Stalinization, the "acceptance" of modern western literature became one of the features of Soviet literary life. It found its expression in the ever-growing number of translations from contemporary foreign writers —European, American, and others. When it came to pass that even Kafka was translated into Russian, Soviet critics began to discuss his work in a more or less objective way. Plays by such avant-garde writers as Ionesco were staged in Moscow, and a film of Fellini's was shown there. This did not prevent these artists from being labeled "decadent," as before; and Soviet writers were discouraged from imitating them. And the line seems to be still drawn at such writers as Joyce, though back in the late 1920s he did have some admirers among Soviet writers, including such a stalwart communist as Vsevolod Vishnevski (1900–1951).

The freeze that followed the publication of Dudintsev's novel was still further intensified as a result of the appearance in 1957 of Boris Pasternak's great novel *Doctor Zhivago,* first in translation into Italian and other languages and then in the original Russian edition published outside Russia. The freeze was aggravated a year later: Pasternak was awarded the Nobel Prize for literature, which he had to turn down and which led to his "excommunication" and vilification at home. This ostracization lasted until after his death.

The next thaw began four years later. One of its first signs was the partial rehabilitation of Pasternak. A volume of his poetic works, with an introduction by Andrei Sinyavski (known abroad by his pseudonym, Abram Terts), was published in 1961. It was almost complete and even included most of the poems from *Doctor Zhivago*. (Soviet critics and scholars to this day insist that there is no necessary connection between those poems and the novel; yet, ironically, the ban is still retained on some of the poems.)

The high point of this thaw came late in 1962 when Aleksandr Tvardovski (1910–1971) published in the November issue of his *Novy mir*—and
it was generally known that the publication had been authorized by
Khrushchev himself—*Odin den' Ivana Denisovicha* (One Day of Ivan
Denisovich). This publication marked the entrance into Soviet literature of
Aleksandr Solzhenitsyn, a hitherto unknown writer and someone quite
unlike any of his fellow writers. He soon became the best-known living
Russian author throughout the world and received the Nobel Prize for
literature in 1970.

In the words of one western critic, Solzhenitsyn "has laid bare a whole
new world." The existence of that world had, of course, been known for a
long time, but the western world preferred to shut its eyes to it, and to
Soviet writers it remained taboo, even though among its countless victims
had been many of their friends and colleagues. This world was the vast
system of concentration camps created under Stalin. Directly or indirectly,
these camps were, for over twenty years, part of the daily life of all Soviet
citizens. And yet their workings, if not their existence, were virtually
ignored by Soviet literature: the doctrines of socialist realism implicitly
demanded their concealment. After 1953 a few shamefaced references to
the camps began to crop up in Soviet literature (some can be found in
Ehrenburg's *The Thaw*). After 1956 we see some former inmates of concentration camps passing briefly through the pages of Soviet novels.

Solzhenitsyn's *One Day of Ivan Denisovich,* however, was the first work
that described camp life as it was. Its subject is one typical day in the life
of an average inmate of a Soviet concentration camp. It is not written in
the first person, but we see the camp, its daily routine, its other inmates, as
they are seen by the protagonist—Ivan Denisovich Shukhov, a simple,
uneducated, almost illiterate Russian peasant. His name will probably
become as familiar to readers throughout the world as those of some of the
characters in Tolstoi and Dostoevski.

Solzhenitsyn, who had himself spent many years in camps and prisons,
wrote from inside knowledge. He did not dwell on any horrors or nightmares. If anything, he was given to understatement. In introducing the
work to its readers, Tvardovski spoke of its "unusual honesty" and "harrowing truth," and said that its effect was "to unburden our minds of things
thus far unspoken but which had to be said." *One Day of Ivan Denisovich*
was at once hailed as not only a startling revelation of a long-concealed
truth but also a great and original work of literature, remarkable in its
psychological insight and interesting and original in its language and narrative technique.

The three stories that followed *One Day of Ivan Denisovich*—*Sluchai na
stantsii Krechetovka* (Incident at Krechetovka Station), *Matryonin dvor*
(Matryona's House), and *Dlya pol'zy dela* (For the Good of the Cause)—

all published in the same *Novy Mir* in 1963, showed that Solzhenitsyn was by no means a writer of one theme. At least one of those stories—*Matryona's House*—was a masterpiece, recalling some of the best short works of Russian nineteenth-century literature. Although it had nothing to do with concentration camps and Soviet terror, the light it threw on ordinary Soviet life was even more cruel. Its heroine, Matryona, a simple peasant woman, is unforgettable, both as a human being and as a symbol.

The 1962 literary thaw, although it seemed to have carried over briefly into 1963, was of quite short duration: Soviet writers spoke of it bitterly as a "coffee break." Its end was prefigured by Khrushchev's violent outburst at the abstract art exhibit in Moscow soon after the publication of Solzhenitsyn's first story. By the spring of 1963 the winter had returned, and since then the Soviet cultural barometer has been pointing to changeable weather. Various manifestations of dissent have been growing in scope and number, but the counterreaction has usually been swift and emphatic.

The literature of the thaw, be it of 1953–54 or of 1956–57, did not bring with it any radical change in the nature of Soviet literature, any tendency to innovation, any desire to experiment with form, with narrative techniques. Essentially, Soviet writers stuck to realism. What changes there were concerned the subject matter and themes. There was a widening of the scope, a loosening of inhibitions, a gradual lifting of certain taboos. There was more interest in the characters—whoever they might be—and more emphasis on their personal affairs and problems, on their idiosyncrasies. Still, the characters were shown mainly as members of certain social groups, against the background of wider, impersonal destinies. Nonetheless, more attention was given to internal conflicts, either within a family or within this or that social group.

Several writers who published novels in the 1950s seemed to be responding to Pomerantsev's appeal for "sincerity in literature." Typical in this respect were such novels as Vera Panova's *Vremena goda* (1953, The Seasons), centered around the family of a high-ranking communist; and *Bitva v puti* (1957, Battle on the Way), by Galina Nikolaeva (1911–1963), which portrayed a dedicated communist whose husband is falsely accused and arrested, whereupon she begins to lose her faith in the party.

World War II was approached in a new, more outspoken, spirit by some writers, such as Vasili Grossman (1905–1964) in his novel *Za pravoe delo* (1953–54, For the Just Cause), which remained unfinished, apparently through no fault of the author. Konstantin Simonov (born 1915), earlier the author of a rather conventional novel about Stalingrad, in *Zhivye i myortvye* (The Living and the Dead), published in 1960 but written much earlier, treated the war theme more complexly. In *V rodnom gorode* (1955, In the Home Town), a story of Red Army soldiers returning to war-ruined Kiev, Viktor Nekrasov introduced the delicate theme of those who remained behind when the Russian army had retreated. His bold manner, his stark presentation of reality, recalled the neorealism of Italian postwar films. Indeed, it was not coincidental that Italian was the first language into which *In the Home Town* was translated. Ever since, Nekrasov has been a favorite with the Italian critics. Some of his works have been compared with Hemingway's.

Some younger writers also tried to approach World War II in a new, less conventional way: Grigori Baklanov (born 1923), in *Pyad' zemli* (1959, An Inch of Ground) and *Myortvye srama ne imut* (1961, The Dead Have No Shame); and Yuri Bondarev (born 1924), in *Batal'ony prosyat ognya* (1957, The Battalions Are Asking for Fire) and *Poslednie zalpy* (1959, The Last Salvos). Bondarev later wrote an interesting novel, called *Tishina* (1962, Silence), in which he introduced the theme of arbitrary reprisals in the last years of Stalin's rule. It preceded by several months Solzhenitsyn's *One Day of Ivan Denisovich*. Unfortunately, in the second part of that novel, published after a rather long interval, the effect of the first part was neutralized by the rather conventional happy ending.

Konstantin Paustovski (1892–1968) also played an important part in the thaw literature. He had always tried to avoid writing to order and did his best to adhere to the nineteenth-century canons of artistic objectivity while not introducing any anti-Soviet themes into his writings. His main contribution to the literature of the 1950s and 1960s was his colorful, vivid autobiography, *Povest' o zhizni* (1945–63, Story of a Life), a six-volume opus. His love for the Russian countryside, about which he wrote many fine stories, his sensitive use of the language, and his artistic integrity made him one of the most popular writers of the post-Stalin period. He stated his views on the art and craft of writing in *Zolotaya roza* (1955, The Golden Rose).

In the 1960s Paustovski was regarded as a likely candidate for the Nobel Prize, and there was much disappointment when in 1964 the prize was awarded not to him but to Mikhail Sholokhov (born 1905), whose work after the war was confined to a partially published war novel, *Oni srazhalis' za rodinu* (1946, 1966; They Fought for Their Country), and a short war story, *Sud'ba cheloveka* (1956, The Fate of a Man). Sholokhov holds the sorry distinction of having attacked both Pasternak and Solzhenitsyn, his predecessor and his successor as Soviet Nobel laureates.

Veniamin Kaverin (born 1902), one of the most promising newcomers to literature during the 1920s, a member of the Serapion Brotherhood, published after World War II a long three-part novel, *Otkrytaya kniga* (1949–56, Open Book). *Open Book* was the life story of a young Soviet woman doctor. Into the framework of a social-psychological novel, more or less traditionally constructed, Kaverin worked in his favorite elements from adventure and detective stories. The last part of the novel, *Poiski i nadezhdy* (Quests and Hopes), was first published in the 1956 collection *Literary Moscow,* which became an important landmark in the de-Stalinization of literature. In it, Kaverin made one of his characters, the husband of the heroine, a victim of a false denunciation: he is arrested and sent to a labor camp. Although there was no detailed description of camp conditions in *Quests and Hopes,* it was, at the time, one of the most outspoken references to a common phenomenon of Soviet life under Stalin, one then regarded as a more-or-less forbidden subject; and Kaverin was taken to task for it.

During the 1962 thaw, Kaverin wrote a short novel, *Sem' par nechistykh* (Seven Pairs of the Unclean), in which the principal characters were inmates of concentration camps. The main theme was the patriotic behavior of these underprivileged citizens after the outbreak of war against Hitler's Germany. The positive effects of de-Stalinization were also shown in Kaverin's short novel *Kosoy dozhd'* (1962, Slanting Rain).

Kaverin chose a very unusual subject for his novel *Pered zerkalom* (In Front of a Mirror), published in 1970 in the magazine *Zvezda.* Much of it was written in the form of an epistolary novel: letters are exchanged between a young girl, Liza, who is a talented artist, and her boy friend (who later becomes her lover), a student of mathematics from the same provincial town in northeastern Russia. *In Front of a Mirror* begins in Russia, during the years preceding the 1917 revolution; but later Liza, who had gone to the Crimea, emigrates—first to Istanbul and then to Paris. Through her eyes Kaverin introduced the subject of the everyday life of Russian émigrés in France—the first treatment of this subject by a Soviet writer. Kaverin was not unsympathetic, even though he showed his heroine as homesick most of the time.

One of the peripheral characters in *In Front of a Mirror* is Marina Tsvetaeva, the remarkable Russian woman poet, who, as I mentioned, returned to Russia for personal reasons in 1939 and hanged herself in 1941. (Kaverin's novel, however, stops in 1934—with the death of Liza in Corsica.) Although Tsvetaeva has a fictitious name in the novel, she is unmistakably recognizable. Liza and the man she lives with in Paris and Corsica were modeled after a couple of artists who were Tsvetaeva's neighbors in a Parisian suburb and who figure in her still-unpublished correspondence.

In Front of a Mirror may not be a great work, but it is an unusual, pleasant, and well-written story. Possibly Kaverin based it on actual correspondence. Whether Liza's Russian mathematician friend had a prototype in real life we do not know. In the second part of the novel he comes to Paris on a scientific assignment and renews his relationship with Liza.

An important part in the thaw literature was a whole series of works about collective farms, done in a spirit of stark, unvarnished realism. The catalyst for these novels was the previously mentioned article by Fyodor Abramov attacking untruthful idealizations of collective farms. Abramov's article was soon followed by a number of works, mostly in the form of nonfictional or semifictional *ocherki* (sketches) by Valentin Ovechkin (1904–1968), Vladimir Tendryakov (born 1923), Yefim Dorosh (born 1908), and others. Later, Abramov himself contributed an interesting story about the post-Stalin conditions in rural Russia—*Vokrug da okolo* (1963, Round and About). One of the most effective stories of the 1956 thaw was *Rychagi* (Levers) by Aleksandr Yashin (1913–1969, pseudonym of Aleksandr Popov), which described a typical meeting of a village soviet. Tendryakov did not confine himself to the subject of collective farming and wrote several other interesting works that also belonged to the thaw literature.

Another group of works, characteristic of the post-1956 period, dealt with the younger generation and its problems. Most of them came from younger writers: *Prodolzhenie legendy* (1957, Sequel to a Legend), by Anatoli Kuznetsov (born 1929), who later wrote *Babi Yar* (1966, Babi Yar), and in 1969 defected to the west; *Kollegi* (1960, Colleagues), *Zvyozdny bilet* (1962, A Ticket to the Stars), and several short stories by Vasili Aksyonov (born 1932); *Bud' zdorov, shkolyar!* (1961, Hail, Schoolboy!), by Bulat Okudzhava (born 1924), who is better known as a poet. Aksyonov, in whose work the romance of travel and a certain restlessness play an important part, has been said to have been influenced by Heinrich Böll as well as by Hemingway. Okudzhava's novel, written in the form of a diary of a young soldier, was criticized for the alleged "infantility" of its protagonist.

A number of younger writers of fiction of the 1950s and 1960s shunned the political or even the predominantly social orientation of their elders. Their work was often lyrical, showing an interest in nature, in country life, in personal emotions. Their masters seemed to be Bunin (and to some extent Prishvin) among the prerevolutionary writers and Paustovski among the Soviet ones. Among these younger writers, one may single out Yuri Nagibin (born 1920), Yuri Kazakov (born 1927), and Georgi Vladimov (born 1931).

There has been some kinship to these lyrical writers in the work of Vladimir Soloukhin (born 1924), who began by writing verse and purely lyrical prose—for example, the volume of short stories *Kaplya rosy* (1960, A Drop of Dew). Characteristic of Soloukhin's later work, as well as of a whole new trend in Soviet literature (and also in historical scholarship), was a renewed and intensified interest in Russia's past, especially in the early period of its history—among other things, in its art, including ikon painting and church architecture. This interest was reflected, for instance, in Soloukhin's *Pis'ma iz Russkogo Museya* (Letters from the Russian Museum), serialized in 1966 and reissued, in a somewhat censored version, in book form in 1967. In Soloukhin's case, interest in the past seemed not only aesthetic and historical but also genuinely religious.

The new interest in the country's past met, on the whole, with encouragement from above: from the point of view of the government, its aspects of Russian nationalism were to be welcomed. This interest took on a practical manifestation in campaigns to preserve various kinds of historical monuments. There was also a counterpart in poetry, as in the work of Viktor Sosnora (born 1935?). Sosnora's *Vsadniki* (1969, Riders)—to which Professor D. Likhachev, a well-known authority on early Russian literature, wrote an introduction called *Poet and History*—was devoted entirely to historical themes, with allusions to such early works of literature as *The Lay of Igor's Campaign* and the Chronicles.

As I said before, there was little formal innovation in post-Stalinist fiction. One exception was Valentin Kataev's *Svyatoi kolodets* (1966, The Holy Well). In it Kataev transposed temporal and spatial planes. The narrative is in the form not so much of stream-of-consciousness as of a sequence of dream images. This form, it is true, is realistically based in the narrator's state of pre- and postoperational anaesthesia. Yet it enabled the author to flout the norms of realistic narrative, to dispense with the usual conventions of plot and characterization, and to mix an account of a sojourn in paradise, a trip across the United States, and an evocation of a youthful love affair in Odessa, the partner of which the narrator revisits as an old widow in Los Angeles.

All these techniques of Kataev's were something quite new, coming as they did from the pen of an established Soviet writer. Thrown in here and there were also some grotesque satirical quips at the Soviet literary scene (for example, the narrator's repulsive phantom double, the pitifully ludicrous "talking cat"). Kataev himself described his new literary manner, with tongue-in-cheek irony, as *mauvisme* (from the French word *"mauvais"*), the essence of which he saw in the blending of two worlds—the real world and the world of imagination: "Only the blending of the two elements can produce truly beautiful art." Kataev mentioned the name of Fellini in passing, suggesting the possible influence of his films. Tame as all this may sound to the western ear, a more drastic breakaway from socialist realism, to which Soviet critics and theorists continue to pay lip service and which is still regarded as the official artistic credo, would be difficult to imagine.

There were also references to *mauvisme* in Kataev's *Trava zabven'ya* (The Grass of Oblivion), written in 1964–67 and published in book form together with *The Holy Well* in 1968. *The Grass of Oblivion* was, however, less experimental in form: much of it consisted of autobiographical reminiscences, in which the central figures are Ivan Bunin, whom Kataev knew in Odessa in 1918–19 and regarded then as his literary master, and Vladimir Mayakovski (1893–1930), who became, in later days, Kataev's literary idol. Superimposed on the evocation of these literary encounters is a quaint story of an old love affair. Toward the end Kataev returns to Bunin and describes a visit to Bunin's widow in Paris and a pilgrimage to Bunin's grave in Ste. Geneviève-des-Bois. Unfortunately, some of these passages are in rather poor taste, and one cannot help suspecting that the narrator-author's vulgar double from *The Holy Well* (his inner censor?) was peeking over his shoulder when he wrote them.

Kataev mentioned a young Soviet writer, Anatoli Gladilin (born 1935), as another exponent of *mauvisme*. But the only things Kataev and Gladilin seem to have in common is plotlessness and a multiplicity of means of expression. In Gladilin's *Dym v glaza: Povest' o chestolyubii* (1959, Smoke in the Eyes: A Tale about Ambitiousness), the narrative incorporates reminiscences, bits of the hero's diary, tape recordings, newspaper reports, letters from, to, and about the hero, and the authorial text. But the effect was quite unlike Kataev's blend of the real and the fantastic. It is not clear whether Kataev was joking in his mentioning of Gladilin or whether he saw such multivoiced, fragmented narrative as a distinctive feature of *mauvisme*.

There are perhaps more reasons for putting Bulat Okudzhava in Kataev's company. Okudzhava made his second foray into fiction with a would-be historical novel, *Bedny Abrosimov* (1969, The Poor Abrosimov). Its background is the Decembrist uprising of 1825, and the story is centered around its aftermath and the investigation of the case of one of its leaders, Pavel Pestel'. The whole book is an exercise in *ostranenie* ("making it strange"), beginning with the point of view, which is that of a minor scribe in the Investigating Commission, a slightly ludicrous, somewhat Gogolian figure who becomes involved in all sorts of hardly believable adventures—half-comic, half-tragic. There is a general Gogolian air about the whole work; at the same time the reader feels the seriousness of Okudzhava's intentions. Some Soviet readers may feel inclined to read between the lines and to see a second—hidden—political plane in *The Poor Abrosimov*.

In poetry, the effects of the post-Stalin literary thaw were felt more clearly than in any other genre. The liberation took the form of emancipation from the constraints and inhibitions of socialist realism and its concomitant, party-mindedness; of a widening of thematic scope; of a greater freedom in experimenting in form. The thaw made possible the reemergence of Akhmatova after a period of enforced silence. It was a case of a veritable poetic rebirth. The only major prerevolutionary poet to live into the post-Stalin period, she wrote some of her best work during the last years of her life.

Another poet who began writing and publishing before the revolution, Nikolai Aseev (1889–1963), the last Mohican of Russian futurism, made no significant contribution to poetry after 1945, but he played a not unimportant part as an influence and a heartening example to younger poets. Of the older postrevolutionary poets, Semyon Kirsanov (born 1906), like Aseev a poet in the Mayakovski tradition, full of verbal exuberance and satirical wit, contributed to the early thaw literature with his satirical fantasy *Sem' dnei nedeli* (1956, Seven Days of the Week). Two volumes of his poetry were published in the 1960s.

Pavel Antokol'ski (born 1896), an heir to the acmeist tradition, with strong ties to western culture, was able, in the post-Stalin period, to follow his natural bent more freely. Nikolai Tikhonov (born 1896), a poet of the same style but of greater natural gifts, who since the 1930s turned more and more toward prose although he continued to write verse, seemed to be a spent force and never regained the level of his early books of poetry. This may have been the price he had to pay for capitulating before the regimented art.

An interesting case was that of Nikolai Zabolotski (1903–1958), one of the most original avant-garde poets of the late 1920s and early 1930s. In contrast to Tikhonov, he had to redeem his avant-gardism; he disappeared from literature for several years, and when he came back after the war, he seemed a quite different poet. This change was often attributed to purely external pressures, but it may, in fact, have reflected a natural evolution toward more classical diction. Even before the war there was a certain kinship between Zabolotski and Fyodor Tyutchev (1803–1873); in Zabolotski's postwar poetry he remained a poet of bold and original imagery. In 1965 two editions of his collected poetry appeared almost simultaneously, one in Russia (where some of his early poetry is still under a ban), the other in the United States. The American edition, which included all his early poetry known to exist, gave a better picture of his evolution.

Of the poets of the middle generation, Olga Bergholz, Margarita Aliger (born 1915), and Leonid Martynov (born 1905) all showed the positive effects of the thaw in their post-1953 poetry, mainly in a much freer choice of themes: poetry as a personal expression was back in favor.

A place apart among the poets of this generation belonged to Aleksandr Tvardovski, who before the war made a name for himself through a long narrative poem about collectivization—*Strana Murav'ya* (The Muravya Land), a blend of Nekrasovian realism and whimsical fancy, of spicy satire and gentle humor. During the war Tvardovski wrote another long poem, in a somewhat similar vein, about a typical Red Army soldier—Vasili

Tyorkin. A cycle of Tvardovski's poems, *Za dal'yu dal'* (Vista beyond Vista) began to be published in 1954. More poems were added to this cycle later: it became a kind of Tvardovski lyrical diary, mixing personal motifs with reflections about the topics of the day.

Vista beyond Vista was symptomatic of the first thaw, when Tvardovski was editor of *Novy mir* (at the end of 1954 he lost that position to Konstantin Simonov, but soon won it back). Another important landmark of the post-Stalin period was Tvardovski's bitingly satirical poem, *Tyorkin na tom svete* (1963, Tyorkin in the Other World). Tvardovski played a very important role as the liberal editor of *Novy mir* in 1953–54 and again after 1957. It was he who was responsible for the publication of the works of Dudintsev, Bondarev, Solzhenitsyn, and other thaw writers. Tvardovski's dismissal as editor in 1970 was seen as a great blow to the liberalizing movement in Soviet literature.

But it was the younger poets—or at any rate those who came into literature after 1954—who helped most to create a new climate in Soviet poetry. The first to attract wide attention was Yevgeni Yevtushenko (born 1933)—with his poem *Stantsiya Zima* (1956, Zima Junction), in which private and public themes were blended in a kind of lyrical monologue. This blending, or alteration, of private, autobiographical and "public," social motifs became a salient characteristic of Yevtushenko's poetry. Some poems appealed to the readers, especially the young, by their subject matter, by the poet's readiness to tackle delicate, if not forbidden, themes. These included such poems as *Nasledniki Stalina* (1961, Stalin's Heirs) and *Babi Yar* (1962, Babi Yar), for which Dmitri Shostakovich wrote music.

Much of Yevtushenko's success and popularity, both at home and abroad (he was the first young Soviet poet to travel extensively in the west and visited the United States more than once) depended on his outgoing, exuberant personality and on his effectively flamboyant manner of reciting poetry. To many people, both Russians and foreigners, Yevtushenko became a living symbol of dissent of the younger generation. But with years, as the dissent movement began to take deeper roots, people noticed all the concessions he made, and his image gradually paled. While he often found himself in deep waters, he always managed somehow to surface and to live down his "transgressions," by conforming again and again.

Yevtushenko's technical innovations in verse have been greatly over-rated: they were largely confined to taking certain liberties, not always felicitous, with rhymes. His rhythmical effects, his verbal tricks, his neologisms, and his use of slang were no advance on Mayakovski and some other poets of the 1920s. In some respects he has been much more traditional than Tsvetaeva, and he lacks Mandelstam's or Akhmatova's combination of verbal and rhythmic inventiveness with deep-seated culture.

Another young poet who became a symbol of nonconformity, of a revolt against the literary establishment, was Andrei Voznesenski (born 1933). Even in his first volumes—*Mozaika* (Mosaics) and *Parabola* (Parabola), both published in 1960—there was more genuine formal daring than in Yevtushenko. This was still truer of his later books: *Treugol'naya grusha* (1962, Triangular Pear), *Antimiry* (1964, Antiworlds), and *Akhillesovo serdtse* (1966, The Heart of Achilles). Like Yevtushenko, Voznesenski traveled to western Europe and to America and gave recitals of his poetry. His poetry is both more hermetic and more sophisticated than Yevtushenko's. If Yevtushenko's poetic ancestry can be traced back to Mayakovski, Voznesenski has greater affinity with Pasternak. Although not completely unconcerned with specific Soviet issues, he is cosmopolitan and may be seen as a Soviet counterpart of some western modernists.

Among the gifted younger poets there are also four women: Rimma Kazakova (born 1932), Novella Matveeva (born 1934), Yunna Morits (born 1937), and Bella Akhmadulina (born 1937). Akhmadulina, although uneven, is perhaps the most important of the four. Some critics have spoken of her as a worthy successor to Akhmatova and Tsvetaeva; indeed, Akhmatova may have had some influence on her. Only one small volume of Akhmadulina's verse, *Struna* (1962, A Chord), has appeared in Russia, but a large volume of her selected poetry, previously scattered in various periodicals, was published abroad under the title *Oznob* (1968, Fever). This volume also includes some unpublished poems that the author has read at poetry recitals.

Boris Slutski (born 1919), who began to publish rather late in life, has excelled particularly in topical satire. Some of his satirical poems—about World War II and about the Jews in the Soviet Union—have yet to be published in Russia. One of his latest volumes, written in colloquial, often deliberately unpoetic language and full of wry humor, is characteristically entitled *Sovremennye istorii* (1969, Contemporary Stories).

Arseni Tarkovski (born 1907) is something of a foreign body in Soviet poetry. Although he started writing and publishing much earlier (some of his original poems and many translations appeared in the 1930s), he did not bring out his first book, *Pered snegom* (1962, Before the Snow), until he was well advanced in age. It was followed by two others: *Zemle—zemnoe* (1966, To the Earth, Things Earthly) and *Vestnik* (1969, The Messenger). He has continued some of the prerevolutionary traditions, including acmeism (it is known that his poetry was greatly appreciated by Akhmatova). His philosophical poems show some kinship with Tyutchev. Compared to Voznesenski and some other young poets, Tarkovski may appear to be "old-fashioned" and classical. Yet his poetry has very contemporary accents. Among his themes are the mission of the poet and the relationship between word and thought and word and deed.

Tarkovski's emergence in the post-Stalin period was in itself significant. As Boris Runin (born 1912), a Soviet critic, observed, it was no accident that Tarkovski's entry into Soviet poetry coincided with the reintegration in it of such poets as Tsvetaeva, Akhmatova, Pasternak, Zabolotski, and Mandelstam. Tarkovski has portrayed Tsvetaeva and her tragic fate, without naming her, in several of his poems. In one poem, *Poet* (1963, The Poet), with a motto from Pushkin about "the poor knight," he gave tribute, without naming him, to Osip Mandelstam.

Some of the other older poets, such as Pavel Antokol'ski, Olga Bergholz, and Margarita Aliger, also felt free now to follow their natural bent and avoid hackneyed themes. Some of the younger ones—Konstantin Vanshenkin (born 1925), for example—introduced philosophical motifs into their poetry.

Another unconventional poet is Bulat Okudzhava, who is also an important novelist. Okudzhava erupted into Soviet poetry at the height of the de-Stalinization and soon became one of the idols of the younger generation. His first volume, *Lyrika* (1956, Lyrics), was followed by several more: *Ostrova* (1959, Islands), *Vesyoly barabanshchik* (1964, The Gay Drummer), *Po doroge k Tinatin* (1964, On the Way to Tinatin), and *Mart velikodushny* (1967, March the Generous). Okudzhava's great popularity partly arises from his skill as an entertainer: many of his poems are songs that he half sings, half recites, accompanying himself on a guitar. His poetry may be seen as a Soviet equivalent of pop poetry, but a deep earnestness underlies it. It is fresh and musical. Its naïve romanticism alternates with wry humor.

Aleksandr Galich (born 19??) has also written popular songs for guitar accompaniment. These songs belong to the "dissent" literature and circulate clandestinely in tape-recordings and manuscripts. Two collections of them have been published abroad: *Pesni* (1971, Songs) and *Pokolenie obrechennykh* (1972, The Doomed Generation). He has been expelled from the Union of Soviet writers.

Given the scientific and technological developments in the Soviet Union, it is not surprising that it has produced in recent years a substantial body of science fiction. Little of it is of lasting literary value. Some of it may have served as a kind of escape, a safety valve for those writers who were reluctant to deal with the realities of Soviet life or could find little inspiration in it. It has offered, at the same time, a welcome variety of reading matter to those who wanted to escape the drabness of their own lives.

The majority of science-fiction writers have concentrated either on the purely scientific or on the adventure aspect of the story. But there are also those who have combined the themes of scientific progress and discovery, of achievements in space exploration, with social themes, sometimes giving them a satirical treatment. Both Soviet and western critics have noted that the two non-Russian science-fiction writers who have had the strongest appeal to and greatest influence on their Soviet counterparts are the Polish writer Stanisław Lem and the American Ray Bradbury.

The most successful exponents of socially-oriented science fiction in Soviet literature have been the brothers Arkadi Strugatski (born 1925) and Boris Strugatski (born 1933). In some of their works they introduced not only the element of social utopia but also that of social satire. Indeed, one of their works, *Skazka o troyke* (The Tale of the Three) could not be published inside the country. It was smuggled out and serialized in *Grani* a Russian-language periodical published in Germany, in 1970.

Some of the works of Ivan Yefremov (born 1907) have presented a positive social utopia, depicting the future achievements of communism and laying stress on human values rather than on technology. Yefremov, a well-known paleontologist, enjoyed great success with the novel *Tumannost' Andromedy* (1959, The Nebula of Andromeda).

ÉMIGRÉ LITERATURE

By 1945, many émigré writers of the older generation had either died or were lapsing into silence. Ivan Bunin, who was the first Russian writer to receive the Nobel Prize, published the last volume of his short stories, *Tyomnye allei* (Dark Avenues) in 1943. It contained some of his best love stories. After *Dark Avenues* he wrote only two works: *Vospominaniya* (1950, Memoirs), very subjective and in parts rather spiteful; and a volume of fragmentary reminiscences and reflections about Chekhov, *O Chekhove* (1955, About Chekhov), which remained unfinished and was published posthumously, with an introduction by Mark Aldanov (1886–1957, pseudonym of Mark Landau).

A little over a year after Bunin's death, at the Second Congress of Soviet Writers in December, 1954, he was officially reintegrated into Russian literature. Soon after that, a volume of his selected works, in which his *Zhizn' Arsen'eva* (The Life of Arsen'ev) was heavily censored, was brought out—the first publication in the Soviet Union of any of his works since the late 1920s. This volume was followed by an edition of his collected works (1965–67) in nine volumes, and by several studies about him. In 1970 the centenary of his birth was commemorated by a special volume of *Literaturnoe nasledstvo* (Literary Heritage) devoted to his life and work. Bunin was the first prominent émigré writer to be thus rehabilitated, and this in itself was a symptom of a new climate in Soviet literature. Although attempts made after the war to lure Bunin back to Russia had failed and the Zhdanov regime made his lifetime rehabilitation impossible, today he is regarded as one of the glories of Russian literature.

Bunin's younger contemporary Aleksei Remizov (1877–1957) did not receive the same rehabilitation. One of the most original, versatile, and influential of modern Russian writers, Remizov's impact on many Soviet writers of the 1920s—Yevgeni Zamyatin (1884–1937), Boris Pil'nyak (1894–1938?), some of the Serapion Brothers, and others—was much greater than that of Bunin. In addition, Remizov's political commitment to anti-Bolshevism was much less pronounced than Bunin's. The explanation of the difference in treatment is to be found in an examination of the two writers' styles. While Bunin was very much in the nineteenth-century classical tradition and therefore fitted rather well into the framework of post-Stalin literature, Remizov, despite his close links to such writers as Gogol', Dostoevski, Nikolai Leskov (1831–1895), and a few minor realists, was also very much in the mainstream of modern literature: his "realism" was sometimes questionable; he was easily carried away by the "fantastic"; he was interested in word play.

Much of Remizov's later work would hardly fit into the "realistic" tradition. Some of it was autobiographical: *Podstrizhennymi glazami* (1951, With Narrowed Vision) and *Myshkina dudochka* (1953, A Mouse's Pipe). *A Mouse's Pipe* was the story of Remizov's life in wartime Paris. Remizov himself called it "an interlude, a funny act amid the storms of tragedy," and used in it a kind of film technique, what he called *"kurmetrazh"* (*court métrage,* that is, short subject), to great effect.

Some other works by Remizov defy classification, such as *Plyashushchi demon: Tanets i slovo* (1949, The Dancing Demon: Dance and Word) and *Ogon' veshchei* (1954, The Fire of Things). Remizov's long-standing interest in dreams found its reflection in the book *Martyn Zadeka: Sonnik* (1954, Martyn Zadeka: A Dream Book). But there was hardly a single book by Remizov in which dreams did not play some part.

During the last years of his life Remizov was also given to retelling, in his own inimitable way, various stories and legends from world literature. These retellings included biblical apocrypha, stories from Panchatantra (via Old Russian literature), medieval romances (including Tristram and Isolde), and *Savva Grudtsyn* (Savva Grudtsyn), the Russian seventeenth-century version of the Faust legend.

Some of these books were illustrated with Remizov's own whimsical dream drawings. Several of Remizov's illustrated "albums," written in his beautiful calligraphic script, remain unpublished to this day. None of his work has been published in Russia since the early 1920s. Much of it is almost untranslatable, which accounts for his not having the reputation he deserves in the west. Still, he was very much appreciated in certain French literary circles.

Ivan Shmelyov (1873–1950) has to date received only partial rehabilitation. His principal prerevolutionary work, the novel *Chelovek iz restorana*

(1910, The Waiter) and a few stories of the émigré period have been published in Russia. But the bulk of his émigré work did not find a way back: some of it, such as his powerful *Solntse myortvykh* (1926, The Sun of the Dead), because of the unrelieved picture of the cruelty of the revolution; some, because of its religious inspiration. Those religiously inspired works included Shmelyov's autobiographical, nonfictional tales of childhood: *Bogomol'e* (1935, Pilgrimage) and *Leto Gospodne* (1933, Anno Domini). These two works were superior to Shmelyov's fiction, and he will be remembered mainly for them. His only work published after 1945 was the second volume of his long and ambitious novel *Puti nebesnye* (1948, Celestial Ways), which was, for the most part, an artistic failure.

The oldest émigré writer to live well into the contemporary period, Boris Zaytsev (1881–1971), completed his long and frankly autobiographical family chronicle after World War II. He published three parts of it since the war: *Puteshestvie Gleba* (1947, Gleb's Journey), *Tishina* (1948, Stillness), and *Drevo zhizni* (1953, The Tree of Life). Zaytsev also wrote two fictionalized biographies—of Chekhov and of Vasili Zhukovski (1783–1853). Even more than Zaytsev's prewar *Zhizn' Turgeneva* (1932, The Life of Turgenev), these works differed from the *biographie romancée* pattern set by André Maurois. There was less of the "romancing" element in them and a little more stylization. In both works (especially the one on Zhukovski) Zaytsev communicated a deeply felt affinity with his subjects.

In his old age Zaytsev was given more and more to reminiscing. His volume of literary reminiscences, *Dalyokoe* (1965, Far-Off Things); his recollections of travels in Italy; his portrait of the two Veras, his own wife and the wife of his friend Bunin—these all have their legitimate place in artistic memoir literature. In the volume of stories *Reka vremyon* (1968, River of Time) there were only three stories written after World War II. One of them, the title story—about two old monks in a monastery near Paris—was among the best ever written by Zaytsev; it would have done credit to Chekhov.

Of the writers of the middle generation, Mark Aldanov, a prolific author of historical novels, continued along the same path after emigrating from France to the United States during World War II. His two most interesting novels of the post-1945 period were *Istoki* (1950, The Sources) and *Samoubiystvo* (1958, Suicide). In *The Sources* the central event is the assassination of Alexander II in 1881, and the title refers to the sources of the Russian revolutionary movement. Its characters, apart from the fictional ones, include Alexander II and the Russian terrorists implicated in the plot, the anarchist Mikhail Bakunin and Dostoevski, Marx and Engels, Bismarck and Gladstone.

The action of *Suicide* is set between 1903 and 1924, but with big chronological gaps. Aldanov made no attempt to give an extended picture of the 1917 revolution (he had already done this earlier). Much of the action is concerned with fictional characters, all of whom did not appear in any earlier novel of Aldanov (in this sense this novel differed from Aldanov's series of novels covering the Russian revolution). Among the historical figures there are Lenin, Stalin, Wilhelm II, and the Russian statesman Count Sergei Witte.

Suicide begins with Lenin's arrival in Brussels to take part in the Second Congress of Social Democrats and ends with Lenin's death. Thus, Lenin, in a way, is the dominating figure in the novel, although he plays but little part in its plot. The dominant theme of the novel is the theme of death, and the account of Lenin's death is preceded by the story of the double suicide, in revolutionary Moscow, of two of the most attractive of Aldanov's fictional characters, a husband and a wife.

The theme of death dominates another late novel of Aldanov's—*Povest' o smerti* (1952–53, A Story about Death). This novel was meant to be part of an earlier historical series (the historical event around which it is centered is the collapse of the French monarchy in 1848). Two other novels—*Zhivi kak khochesh'* (1952, Live as You Wish) and *Bred* (serialized 1954–55 and 1957; Nightmare)—have contemporary settings. They were among Aldanov's least successful works, with overly-involved plots. In *Live as You Wish* an important part is played by the United Nations, for which the main Russian character, an émigré, works. Into this drawn-out novel Aldanov introduced two complete plays written by his hero, but their relevance to the novel is unconvincing, and this "innovative" device is just boring. In more than one way the novel was unworthy of Aldanov.

At the same time that Aldanov was working on these novels, he wrote a philosophical book—*Ul'mskaya noch* (1953, The Night of Ulm). It was subtitled "The Philosophy of Chance," and in it Aldanov set forth his ideas about history, which made *The Night of Ulm* important for understanding the concepts behind his historical fiction.

Of the younger émigré writers, those who did not make a name for themselves until after the revolution, the most talented one, Vladimir Nabokov (born 1899), was virtually lost to Russian literature after emigrating to the United States in 1940 and becoming an English-language writer. One slim volume of verse, containing, with a few exceptions, poems written while he was still in Europe, and a partial autobiography, *Drugie berega* (1954, Other Shores)—which was a rewriting in Russian of the original English version published as *Conclusive Evidence* and later revised and renamed *Speak, Memory*—were Nabokov's only postwar contributions to the literature of his native tongue, if one discounts his own translation of *Lolita* into Russian (1967).

The translation of *Lolita* was a great disappointment to those of his Russian readers who had admired him as a stylist. Nabokov himself called the history of that translation "a history of disappointment" and sought consolation for the "clumsiness" of his Russian version in the assumption that the fault lay not only in the translator, who had got "disused" to his native instrument, but also in the spirit of the language into which the translation was being made. One was reminded of Turgenev's statement that he could never understand how a writer could write works of art in two languages, that such a work was bound to be a "tour de force." Be that as it may, it looks as if the birth of Nabokov the American writer, hailed by the critics as a genius, meant the end of Nabokov the Russian writer.

Of the younger émigré writers of fiction, Nabokov was undoubtedly the most talented, even though it took Russian critics some time to recognize this. (We must not forget, however, that Nabokov's English writings and a few of his translated novels found relatively little critical acclaim before the staggering success of *Lolita*.) Of the others, very few have gone on writing after the War. Yet some works of merit were produced by former Parisian writers, most of whom had, during or after the war, moved to the United States, where the focus of Russian émigré life had shifted. Nina Berberova's (born 1901) *Mys bur'* (1950–51, The Cape of Storms) was a novel about three young women, one of them an adolescent, daughters of the same man but from different wives, who come to live in Paris with their father and his last wife (the initial scenes of the novel are set in Russia at the time of the civil war, but the rest takes place in Paris).

Berberova has not sought any structural or stylistic innovative effects, and the only departure from the straightforward third-person narrative is the interpolation of portions of the diary of one of the three half-sisters, through which she is almost exclusively shown, which makes the reader identify her, more than the others, with the author.

While some of Berberova's earlier work showed evidence of a strong dependence on Dostoevski, *The Cape of Storms* and some of her later shorter works owed some of their features to French writers of the 1920s and 1930s. At the same time Berberova is very much in the main tradition of Russian psychological realism and owes nothing to Nabokov, even though she has voiced unbounded admiration for his work, especially for *Lolita*.

The same traditionalism was true, on the whole, of Gayto Gazdanov (1903–1972), although his first novel showed the influence of Proust, and some of his later novels had a rather western flavor, partly because many characters in them were non-Russian and partly because of his undisguised interest in the plot. His principal novels included *Prizrak Aleksandra Vol'fa* (1948, The Specter of Alexander Wolf), *Vozvrashchenie Buddy* (1950, Buddha's Return), *Piligrimy* (1954, The Pilgrims), and *Probuzhdenie* (1968, The Awakening).

Much less conventional and much more Russian is Vasili Yanovski (born 1906), who has combined the writing of fiction with the practice of medicine. In *Portativnoe bessmertie* (Portable Immortality), written before the war but published in 1953, the setting is the Parisian slums, and the characters are cosmopolitan. Yanovski's manner can be described as symbolic realism, although it also contains elements of surrealism and, of course, naturalism.

Amerikanski eksperiment (1948, An American Experiment) was the story of a white American, Bob Caster, whose skin turns suddenly black. In the end he turns white again and founds a strange sect bent on saving the world, as did one of the characters, Jean Doute, in *Portable Immortality*. Both Caster and Doute reappeared in Yanovski's even more intensely symbolic work, *Zalozhnik* (1961–62, The Hostage), in which there are utopian motifs.

Even stranger is Yanovski's short novel *Chelyust emigranta* (1957, Homo Emigrans's Jaw—the author's own English rendering of the title), which was built around a complex of nightmarish "dental" images. The distinguished Russian critic Fyodor Stepun felt that the sinister pictures of émigré life in *Homo Emigrans's Jaw* were written "with undoubted talent, but also with such malice and at times with such cynicism and such needless emphasis on shameless sexual greed that they become heavy reading." Stepun also called Yanovski the "most solitary" of all Russian émigré writers. Yanovski's work has sometimes been marred by a tendency to didacticism, but he is always interesting and worth reading.

In the late 1920s there appeared abroad some stories signed "B. Temiryazev," and in 1934 the same signature was placed on a long novel—*Povest' o pustyakakh* (A Story About Trifles), set partly in Soviet Russia and partly among the émigrés. Their tone, texture, and contents made several critics suspect that they had been written in Russia. Later, the identity of the author was revealed: he turned out to be the well-known portrait painter and stage designer Yuri Annenkov (born 1889), a friend of Zamyatin and a follower of his "neorealism." After the war Annenkov published, under the same pseudonym, the novel *Rvanaya epopeya* (1960, A Tattered Epic), which had the same characteristics and showed a close similarity between Temiryazev the storyteller and Annenkov the draftsman.

Among the younger writers, Leonid Zurov (1902–1971) occupied a place apart. Although he lived in France in the late 1920s (earlier he had lived in Estonia, in close proximity to the Russian border), he remained, unlike Berberova and Gazdanov, completely untouched by contemporary western literature, even by his French environment; he continued to write only about Russian life. Because of his personal proximity to Bunin, he was sometimes seen as Bunin's disciple, but he certainly should not be regarded as a mere imitator. After 1945 Zurov did not write much, publishing only one volume of short stories—*Mar'yanka* (1958, Maryanka).

Although the ranks of Russian émigrés were, numerically speaking, greatly swollen after World War II by the "displaced persons" who chose not to return to their country and were lucky enough to escape forcible repatriation, and although many of them came to play an important part in the cultural activities of their adopted countries, there were only three men among them who, when they left, were known outside Russia as men of letters. One of them was the well-known prerevolutionary literary critic Razumnik Ivanov-Razumnik (1878–1945). He died, however, in 1945, while the war was still on. The two others were relatively little-known writers: Rodion Akul'shin (born 1896), who changed his name subsequently to Beryozov and became an extremely prolific writer of little intrinsic value; and Gleb Glinka (born 1903), a member of the Pereval literary group, who has published, since emigrating, two volumes of verse, as well as his reminiscences of Soviet literary life and of his fellow Pereval writers.

Several wartime émigrés established reputations only after they left Russia. One of the first to attract attention among writers of fiction was Sergei Maksimov (1917–1967). His novel *Denis Bushuev* (1953, Denis Bushuev), recalling his native Volga region, reminded some critics of Gor'ki. The novelty of its treatment of a Soviet theme led to its being somewhat overpraised by the critics.

To some extent this overpraising was also true of another novel— *Mnimye velichiny* (1952, Imaginary Values), by N. Narokov (1887–1969, pseudonym of Nikolai Marchenko). In this case there was more justification for the praise: *Imaginary Values* was the first novel in Russian émigré literature to deal with the subject of Stalin's secret police and its impact on Russian life during the notorious purges of the 1930s. The book created quite a stir and was immediately translated into several languages. Although *Imaginary Values* was marred by didacticism, it was important as a pioneering effort in fiction to portray Stalinist terror. Later it was, of course, eclipsed by some works from the Soviet Union itself, written not by outsiders but by victims of that terror.

Leonid Rzhevski (born 1905) made his debut with the novel *Mezhdu dvukh zvyozd* (1953, Between the Two Stars), in which he painted a vivid picture of the last stages of World War II and of the life of Russian displaced persons in German camps. His . . . *pokazavshemu nam svet* (1960, To Thee Who Showed Us Light) was a shorter and more mature work, with less of a plot. Subtitled "An Optimistic Story," this later work presented the same background as *Between the Two Stars,* but with more restraint and less emphasis on the externals.

Rzhevski also published two volumes of stories—*Dvoe na kamne* (1960, The Two on the Rock) and *Cherez proliv* (1966, Across the Straits)—in which Soviet themes alternated with those of émigré life. The best of them combined a fine sense of language, skill in storytelling, and keen psychological insights. Rzhevski's writings on Pasternak, Solzhenitsyn, Mikhail Bulgakov (1891–1940), and other modern Russian writers showed his understanding of subtle problems of language and style.

Another wartime émigré to attract almost immediate attention by his fiction was Nikolai Ul'yanov (born 1904). His historical novel *Atossa* (1952, Atossa) dealt with the invasion, in the sixth century B.C., of Scythia by the Persian king Darius Hystaspis. Some critics thought that Ul'yanov, a professional historian, while he used Herodotus as a source, at the same time was tempted by certain parallels to our own times. Another quasihistorical novel, *Sirius* (Sirius), about Russia on the eve of the revolution, introducing the last tsar as one of the characters, has so far been known only through fragments published between 1958 and 1972 in the New York *Novy zhurnal.*

Ul'yanov's versatility was demonstrated in the volume of stories *Pod kamennym nebom* (1970, Under the Stony Sky), in which limpid prose was combined with a certain dreamlike atmosphere. The longest story in the collection—*Solntse* (Sun)—transposes temporal planes; a modern inventor, kidnapped by secret police, is questioned by Emperor Nero.

Another postwar newcomer to Russian literature outside Russia was Alla Ktorova (a pseudonym). As far as is known, she did not publish anything before coming to live in the United States. Her principal work has been *Litso Zhar-Ptitsy* (1969, serialized earlier; The Face of the Firebird), which she herself described as an "anti-novel," although its affinity with the work of Alain Robbe-Grillet and Nathalie Sarraute is not easy to perceive. At any rate, it is as far removed from the tradition of the Russian novel as it is from a typical contemporary Soviet novel, although its themes and all its characters are Soviet.

The Face of the Firebird is the story of a group of young Soviet people, mostly teenagers ("Firebird" is the nickname of the heroine, who in the end marries a foreigner and goes to live abroad). The story is told against the background of Soviet everyday life, painted in the spirit of lighthearted, yet sharp satire (one may well suspect the autobiographical background of the story). Ktorova, who has also written some short stories, more or less in the same vein, has a clearly individualized manner and style. She has not as yet tackled any non-Soviet subject.

Even before World War II poetry occupied a more important place in Russian émigré literature than did fiction. This was caused, no doubt, by the ever-growing difficulties of publishing and marketing long novels or volumes of short stories. After the war, these difficulties became even more pronounced. They affected the publication of verse, too, for the number of periodicals that were outlets for poetry was drastically reduced. In the 1950s and 1960s there was only one such periodical in the United States (*Novy zhurnal,* a quarterly), one in France (*Vozrozhdenie,* a monthly), and one in Germany (*Grani,* a quarterly). *Grani,* however, was becoming, by the 1960s, mainly an outlet for Soviet literary works smuggled out of the country.

Few prerevolutionary poets were still living after World War II. The oldest representative of Russian symbolism in poetry to survive the war, Vyacheslav Ivanov (1866–1949), continued writing until his death in Rome (he had emigrated to Rome in 1924 and soon after became a convert to Roman Catholicism). Ivanov's last work, the ambitious *Povest' o Svetomire Tsareviche* (The Tale of Svetomir the Prince), remained incomplete at his death, but he bequeathed its completion to Olga Deschartes, his close friend and companion during the last forty-five years of his life. It was published posthumously, as completed by Olga Deschartes, in Russian in the first volume of his collected works (Brussels, 1971).

The Tale of Svetomir the Prince is a long epic, partly in verse but mostly in prose, written in skillfully archaicized language and deeply rooted in Russian folklore and in hagiographic and other traditional literature. The story, put into the mouth of a monk, is deceptively simple but fraught with deep symbolic meaning. Its chronology and historicity are rather arbitrary, and there are no truly historical characters in it. One of the main episodes involves the stay of Prince Svetomir, the hero of the epic, in the mythical kingdom of White India, under the rule of John the Presbyter.

In *The Tale of Svetomir the Prince* Ivanov displayed fully his impressive historical, linguistic, and philosophical erudition. At the same time the work was inspired with genuine poetic sense. It may one day come to be regarded as Ivanov's magnum opus and as an important extension and new development in the history of Russian literary symbolism. Olga Deschartes's introduction to the Brussels volume threw an interesting light on Ivanov's work and on this swan song. She also wrote a commentary to an earlier published posthumous volume, *Svet vecherni* (1962, The Evening Light), which contained all his previously uncollected poetry, including the beautiful poems of his 1944 *Rimski dnevnik* (Roman Diary).

Georgi Ivanov (1894–1958), one of the younger acmeists, had a poetic "second birth" in the 1950s and was (and still is) regarded by many Russian critics and readers in the west as one of the finest modern Russian poets. Ivanov's poignant poetry of nihilistic despair was clothed in exquisitely musical lines. Through all of it ran the motif of the utter, hopeless meaninglessness of life. His later poetry was collected in two volumes: *Portret bez skhodstva* (1950, A Portrait without Resemblance) and *1943–1958: Stikhi* (1958, 1943–1958: Poems).

An older and lesser poet, Sergei Makovski (1877–1962), the founder and editor of the famous magazine *Apollon* (1909–17), for a long time better known as an art critic, proved to be extraordinarily fertile in his old age. Of the seven volumes of poetry Makovski published after the war, five consisted entirely of previously unpublished, and presumably new, poems. In contrast to Ivanov, Makovski's verse was cold, chiselled, Parnassian.

Another survivor of what has often been referred to as a Silver Age, but was more like a second Golden Age of Russian poetry (1900–14), was Georgi Adamovich (1894–1972). Unlike Makovski, he wrote, as time went by, fewer and fewer verses. But many young Russian poets in France, where Adamovich lived, looked upon him as their master, and he became the presiding spirit of what was termed the "Parisian note" in poetry. The Parisian note, which can be described as a poetic existentialism of sorts, was a highly subjective poetry concerned primarily with ultimate problems of being (Georgi Ivanov's poetry was an extreme development of this trend). Adamovich's later poetry was collected in a small volume *Yedinstvo* (1967, Unity). Adamovich's reputation as an émigré writer rests mainly on his activities as a critic and on the influence he exerted on many younger writers, especially poets.

Two poets of the younger émigré generation have been rather prominent in recent years: Igor Chinnov (born 1909) and Yuri Ivask (born 1910). Chinnov began as a follower of the Parisian note but gradually developed further and further away from it. His recent poetry, written since the publication of his third volume, *Metafory* (1968, Metaphors), has shown signs of disintegrating into an arbitrary, undisciplined play, not so much of words as of alogical associations. There is no doubt that he has been under the influence of certain trends in western, particularly German, poetry.

Ivask, much of whose poetry is derivative, drawing inspiration from literature or from the visual arts, is more eclectic. He is a self-avowed admirer of George Herbert and John Donne, of Osip Mandelstam and W. H. Auden. His latest volume, *Zolushka* (1970, Cinderella), is a modernist's tribute to the baroque. He revels in word play that combines the futurism of Velimir Khlebnikov (1885–1922) with baroque conceits. The whole has at times an air of coy artificiality and smacks of parody.

Both Chinnov and Ivask often indulge in rather questionable experiments with rhymes, resembling those of Yevtushenko—hardly necessary in a language that has such a natural wealth of rhyming possibilities. Their poetry is poles apart from the simplicity Pasternak aimed for toward the end of his life.

The posthumous publication of the poetry of Vladimir Korvin-Piotrovski (1901–1966), entitled *Pozdni gost'* (1968–69, The Late Visitor), revealed him as an interesting poet of distinct individuality, capable of achieving great poetic effects with seemingly old-fashioned means. Korvin-Piotrovski not only adhered to traditional meters and strict rhymes but wrote the overwhelming majority of his poems in iambs, thus showing what a rich, flexible, and varied instrument they could be. He was one of the few émigré poets who also wrote longer narrative and dramatic poems. One of his dramatic poems, *Beatriche* (1929, Beatrice) earned high praise from Vladimir Nabokov.

Two leading émigré women poets of today, Irina Odoevtseva (born 1900) and Lidiya Alekseeva (born 1907, pseudonym of Lidiya Ivannikova) are very different. Odoevtseva began publishing in Russia in 1919. A pupil of Nikolai Gumilyov (1886–1921), she romantically combined the poetic discipline of acmeism with refracted Soviet themes. After emigrating in 1922, she wrote little poetry and published several novels. She has, however, published three volumes of verse since World War II: *Kontrapunkt* (1951, Counterpoint); *Desyat' let* (1961, Ten Years), with its cycle of *Stikhi, napisannye vo vremya bolezni* (Poems Written during Illness); and *Odinochestvo* (1965, Solitude). The poetry in these volumes was very fine. It had a certain affinity with that of Georgi Ivanov, to whom she was married, but was distinctly feminine. Instead of Ivanov's nihilistic rejection of life, there was a slightly unreal, mirrorlike reflection of it.

Lidiya Alekseeva, who was practically unknown until she moved from Yugoslavia to the United States after World War II, has published four slim volumes: *Lesnoe solntse* (1954, Forest Sun), *V puti* (1959, On the Road), *Prozrachny sled* (1964, The Transparent Vestige), and *Vremya razluk* (1971, The Time of Partings). Her poetry, which recalls Akhmatova, has continued some of the best traditions of Russian poetry. She is by no means old-fashioned but does not seek innovation for innovation's sake.

Of the poets who first came to the free world during World War II and have become part of émigré literature, Dmitri Klenovski (born 1892, pseudonym of Dmitri Krachkovski) was not exactly a newcomer. His first book of poems and some translations from Henri de Régnier were published before the revolution. After destroying his second book, which was ready for the press, he stopped writing and resumed doing so only when he began to breathe free air. Between 1950 and 1971 he published eight volumes, and another is on the way. In 1967, a volume of his selected poems, covering the period from 1945 to 1966, was published in Munich.

Brought up in the acmeist school, rooted in western cultural tradition, both Germanic and Romance (he had traveled in Europe before the revolution), Klenovski has flowered in his old age into a poet transcending all schools and movements. For him, poetry is not a game. He may seem old-fashioned, but he has not shunned innovations and should be described as classical in the best sense of the word. He has a great many admirers both among the émigrés and in the Soviet Union, where his poetry has been penetrating in recent years.

Two other wartime émigré poets differ both from Klenovski and from each other. Ivan Yelagin (born 1918), the first to attract attention among the newcomers, is perhaps the only one who can claim a Soviet pedigree. His poetry owes much to Mayakovski, both in theme and in style, although he has less concern with words. His poetry is often loud, rhetorical. He does not shun political themes. His principal books of verse have been *Po doroge ottuda* (1947, On the Road from There), *Politicheskie fel'etony v stikhakh* (1959, Political Feuilletons in Verse), and *Otsvety nochnye* (1963, Night Reflections).

N. Morshen (born 1917, pseudonym of Nikolai Marchenko, Jr.), the son of writer Nikolai Marchenko (N. Narokov), has been publishing rather sparingly, and his two volumes of verse were separated by eight years: *Tyulen'* (1959, Seal), and *Dvoetochie* (1967, Colon). In *Seal* reminiscences of his Soviet childhood and adolescence predominated, but the treatment of this theme was purely personal, lyrical, nonpolitical. One of the characteristics of Morshen's poetry is the keenness of his vision of the world. At the same time, he is fascinated by words and likes to play with them, but his word play has a semantic, rather than phonetic, orientation. Wit is one of its indispensable ingredients. Sometimes his witty effects are a little overdone, especially in his more recent poetry, which also reflected his personal scientific interests—in physics, mathematics, and cybernetics.

Morshen's poetic experiments do not resemble the avant-garde "trans-sense" poetry of Khlebnikov and other Russian futurists of the 1910s and early 1920s; they are along entirely different lines. But one wonders sometimes whether they may not also lead to a poetic dead end. At its best, fortunately, Morshen's poetry is free from these excesses.

In the 1960s what looked to many people like a new name began to appear under poems published in émigré periodicals. The name was Valeri Pereleshin (born 1913, pseudonym of Valeri Salatko-Petryshche). Actually, its bearer had published before World War II, in Manchuria and China where he then lived, four books of original poetry and a translation of Coleridge's *The Rime of the Ancient Mariner*. In his two recent books of poetry—*Yuzhny dom* (1968, The Southern Home) and *Kachel'* (1971, The Swing)—and in various poems published since then in periodicals, Pereleshin has shown himself to be a poet with an individual voice and original themes, and a fastidious master of technique. Unlike most of his contemporaries, he has tried to revive certain traditional verse forms, especially the sonnet. An erudite Sinologist, Pereleshin has also published a volume of translations of classical Chinese poetry—*Stikhi na veere* (1970, Poems on a Fan).

"ÉMIGRÉ BOOKS" FROM THE SOVIET UNION

On the whole, the literary production of the Russian emigration has been showing signs of a decline in the last thirty years or so. The communist revolution in Russia has passed its fiftieth anniversary, and émigré literature, despite the influx of new blood after World War II, is drawing close to its natural age limit. Its prospects of having a natural succession are rather dim. But there is no doubt that its best achievements will be one day incorporated in the general treasure of Russian literature.

What is more important is that in the last decade there has been developing a kind of dialogue between the two branches of Russian literature. The two are beginning to interpenetrate. What is written on this side of the iron curtain is for the first time becoming accessible to the Russians on the other side (of course, to a small elite minority only), while unpublishable books written there reach the free world in ever-growing numbers.

Before World War II the number of works written in the Soviet Union but first published abroad was minimal (one of them was Yevgeni Zamyatin's [1884–1937] anti-utopian novel *My* [1922, We]). Since 1956 such works, "émigré books" by nonémigré writers (Zamyatin did in the end emigrate, but long after the publication of *We* abroad), can be counted by the dozen. They include such major works of literature as Pasternak's *Doctor Zhivago* (1957) and Solzhenitsyn's *Rakovy korpus* (1968, Cancer Ward) and *V kruge pervom* (1968, In the First Circle). Pasternak's novel was rejected by the most liberal Soviet magazine, *Novy mir,* and ten years after his death it still remains taboo and almost unmentionable, although Pasternak himself was posthumously rehabilitated, and a volume of his poetry (including some poems from the banned novel, as I mentioned earlier) was published in 1961.

Things had changed since 1959, and when Solzhenitsyn was awarded the Nobel Prize in 1970, the brunt of the Soviet attack had to be borne by the Swedish Academy: of Solzhenitsyn, who had been earlier expelled from the writers' organization, it was only said that he was a "mediocre" writer, "unworthy" of the honor. Earlier, he had been allowed to protest to the Union of Soviet Writers against the ban on his writings and to state his case at a special meeting, and he found a few defenders among his fellow writers and many supporters in that constantly growing section of Soviet society that has been championing the rights of man in the last four or five years. And the famous cellist Mstislav Rostropovich wrote a spirited and courageous letter, in defense of Solzhenitsyn and his writings, to the principal Soviet newspapers, but they refused to publish it. Significantly, in 1959 no one came out openly in Pasternak's defense!

Having, unlike Pasternak, accepted the Nobel Prize, Solzhenitsyn, although unable to attend the ceremony, wrote an acceptance speech. It was published by the Swedish Academy, in August, 1972, in the original Russian and in translations. The speech (or "lecture," as it has been described) was a passionate vindication of human freedoms and a scourging attack not only on the Soviet totalitarian regime but also on the prevailing spirit of the modern world. One of its targets was the United Nations: the organization was accused of never having even tried to make acceptance of the declaration of human rights obligatory for membership. The speech was also a lament for a whole generation of Russian writers "cast into oblivion not only without a grave but even without underclothes—naked, with a number tagged onto its toe." "Woe to that nation whose literature is disturbed by the intervention of power," said Solzhenitsyn.

Doctor Zhivago, Cancer Ward, and *In the First Circle* were the three most significant works of this new *free* Soviet literature. There already exists a vast literature about them. One can argue whether they are or are not "old-fashioned," whether they represent a throwback to nineteenth-century realism or are expressive of a new symbolic realism. To me, both *Doctor Zhivago* and *In the First Circle* seem fresh rather than traditional. Whatever they are, these books are almost unanimously recognized in the outside world as great books, not only opening new worlds before the reader but also using, by and large, new means of expression. The greatness of Solzhenitsyn is known to be recognized by many of his Soviet readers, including some well-known writers.

In *Doctor Zhivago* the main action is set before the revolution and during the first decade of the Soviet republic (the hero, a practicing young physician and poet, dies in 1929). The worst years of the Stalin rule and the war with Germany are touched on only briefly in the epilogue. Pasternak covers a vast geographical ground. The pre-1917 chapters are situated in Moscow and at the Russo-German front during World War I. In the post-1917 period the action is transferred first back to Moscow and then to a large city in the Urals and an estate nearby where Zhivago and his family find temporary refuge from the turmoil and hardships of the revolution. Then comes an interlude during which Zhivago is shown as a kidnaped prisoner of the guerrillas who are fighting the Whites in the Siberian forests. After an escape, he makes his way on foot to the same city in the Urals and the estate nearby, only to find that his family has left in the meantime. For a time he lives there with a woman he had fallen in love with before his kidnaping. Later, when she is taken away—for her own good!—by her former lover, Zhivago makes a long trek on foot to Moscow in the company of a young man whom he and his family had met earlier on the way out east and whom he now meets again by pure chance.

These rapidly changing settings enable Pasternak to introduce a great variety of characters (something he had never done before in his fiction), as well as some wonderful descriptions of nature. *Doctor Zhivago* is a great love story. It is also a portrait of a Russian intellectual, not unlike Pasternak himself, at odds with the revolution.

An essential part of the novel is the poems written by Yuri Zhivago. They are not incorporated into the novel but are appended to it. Yet they form an integral part of it. This technique alone makes the novel anything but traditional. Quite apart from this, Pasternak's "realism," which some western critics described as old-fashioned, is also untraditional. It is a symbolic realism of its own kind. Also symbolic is the character of Zhivago's half-brother Yevgraf. That the book became a best seller in the west does credit to the reading public.

Solzhenitsyn's *Cancer Ward* and *In the First Circle* were undoubtedly based on personal experiences: *Cancer Ward,* of a hospital in central Asia; *In the First Circle,* of a very special labor camp outside Moscow for the scientific elite among the so-called enemies of the people, where, although deprived of their freedom and forced to do the research demanded by the government, they enjoyed all sorts of privileges and fringe benefits that the ordinary inmates of Stalin's labor camps never dreamed of.

The protagonists of both of these novels—Kostoglotov in *Cancer Ward* and Nerzhin in *In the First Circle*—can be, with a few alterations, identified with Solzhenitsyn himself. But neither of the two works was an autobiographical memoir. They are novels; they are works of art—and great works of art at that—showing Solzhenitsyn as a writer of the first caliber. In both there are some marvelous character creations. In *In the First Circle* the range of characters is wider and richer, and all things considered, it is probably the more powerful of the two novels. But not all critics have agreed on this.

Whereas all of Solzhenitsyn's earlier works—both those which had been published in Russia and those later ones which appeared only abroad— dealt with contemporary Soviet realities and were drawn, by and large, from the author's personal experience, his most recent work published is totally different. *Avgust chetyrnadtsatogo* (1971, August Fourteen) is intended to be the first volume (Solzhenitsyn called it "the first knot") of an ambitiously planned long novel that is to cover an important period in recent Russian history.

The chronological framework of this new novel was not made quite clear, but judging by the names of places, as listed in the author's "post-face," in which the future action is to be set, it will apparently cover the events of 1917 and the civil war in the south of Russia. The events described in the first volume are condensed within a few days of August, 1914, and center around the Russian defeat in east Prussia, the encirclement and near annihilation of General Samsonov's army, and the tragic suicide of the general himself.

Alongside other historical characters—Grand Duke Nicholas, several Russian generals, the commander of the first corps of the German Eighth Army, General von François, who played a very important part in the German victory and upon whose book about the Battle of Tannenberg Solzhenitsyn undoubtedly drew—Solzhenitsyn introduces a great number and variety of invented characters—Russian officers, soldiers, and civilians—some of whom we assume will reappear in subsequent volumes. Although the military happenings during this fateful month of August dominate in this volume, its initial and final chapters also provide a very interesting picture of what was going on in the rear, and introduce a number of fascinating characters, undoubtedly called upon to play an important part in the following "knots." The reader can already sense the ties that are going to bind together the destinies of some of these characters.

Despite various minor factual inaccuracies noted by Russian émigré critics, Solzhenitsyn showed, in *August Fourteen,* a remarkable mastery of the material seemingly quite new to him as a writer. Some of the military chapters, including the suicide of General Samsonov, are very powerfully written.

Both in its structure and in its language *August Fourteen* is characterized by certain innovative features that met with a mixed reception on the part of Russian émigré critics; but in any case these features disproved the widespread notion of Solzhenitsyn as an old-fashioned writer. It is still too early for a final critical judgment of *August Fourteen.* But there can be no doubt about its being one of Solzhenitsyn's most interesting and significant works. It was also his first book to be published abroad with his full knowledge, in a duly authorized and copyrighted edition.

Vsyo techyot (1970, Everything Flows), by Vasili Grossman, is a relatively short work. Possibly the author had no chance to complete it, or at least to put the finishing touches on it: the manuscript was confiscated by the KGB and began circulating, much later, in a *samizdat* (self-publishing) edition.

Before World War II Grossman was known as a perfectly orthodox writer. After the war he wrote *For the Just Cause,* which I mentioned earlier as an example of the new approach to the war. Severely criticized at first, it came to be viewed, after Khrushchev's de-Stalinization program, as one of the best Soviet war novels. In its center stood the battle for Stalingrad. Apparently, Grossman intended to write a sequel to *For the Just Cause,* but it is unknown whether he gave up the idea, whether he was prevented from carrying it out, or whether whatever he had written of it was also confiscated.

Everything Flows is the story of a political prisoner, an old man, Ivan Grigor'evich (the reader never learns his last name), who regains his freedom after thirty years of prisons and labor camps. Grossman does not retell Ivan Grigor'evich's experiences in the prisons and the camps, but only hints at them: the author is primarily concerned with Ivan Grigor'evich's resumption of his normal, free life. We see him on the train to Moscow, and Grossman sketches satirical portraits of his traveling companions. We see him visiting his cousin in Moscow, a successful scholar who has managed to save his life and his position by knowingly going from one inglorious compromise to another. (Grossman gives a short but devastating account of the so-called Zhdanov era, in the last six or seven years of Stalin's rule.)

The two men cannot find a common language, and Ivan Grigor'evich declines the invitation extended by his cousin and the cousin's wife to stay with them. Instead, he goes to Leningrad, finds a modest job, and begins a new life. The only real action in the novel concerns his meeting with a cook who works in the canteen of the place at which he is employed. Even this episode is projected mainly in the past: on their first night together she tells him of her experiences in the collectivization of 1929–30.

Nothing much happens after this. The woman dies. Left alone, Ivan Grigor'evich decides to visit the place on the Black Sea where he grew up. On the way there he muses about the destiny of Russia and the meaning of the revolution.

There are two highlights of the novel. The first is the cook's story of Stalin's forcible collectivization in the south of Russia, in which she, then a young girl and an enthusiastic communist, took part as an "activist." The story takes up some twenty pages and is the most powerful and the most harrowing account of this event in all of Soviet literature, next to which Sholokhov's *Podnyataya tselina* (1932, 1955–59; Virgin Soil Upturned) seems a very tame affair.

The second highlight is Ivan Grigor'evich's denunciation of Lenin as the real great villain of the Russian revolution, with Stalin and all his iniquities as only a logical outcome of Lenin's concept of the revolution. This idea—alongside some more general reflections on Russian history, on the absence of the "theme of freedom" in it (some of these reflections are highly controversial even from an anti-Soviet point of view)—is presented to the reader as what is going on in the mind of Ivan Grigor'evich as he travels south; but through him it is Grossman who is speaking. Despite some rather obvious structural weaknesses, *Everything Flows* is one of the most interesting *samizdat* works.

There are many other "émigré books." Here is a partial list of them: Akhmatova's *Requiem* and *Poem without a Hero* (only parts of *Poem without a Hero* have been published in Russia), as well as a number of her shorter poems; *The Trial Begins* and *Fantasticheskie povesti* (1961, Fantastic Stories), by Abram Terts (his works were collected in a volume entitled *Fantasticheski mir Abrama Tertsa* [1967, The Fantastic World of Abram Terts], which also included the Russian text of his famous essay on socialist realism, published anonymously in French and Polish in 1959, in which he exposed and ridiculed the falsehood and vacuity of the official Soviet literary doctrine); *Govorit Moskva* (1962, Moscow Speaking) and *Ruki* (1963, Hands), by Nikolai Arzhak (born 1925, pseudonym of

Yuli Daniel); Yevtushenko's *Primechaniya k avtobiografii* (1963, Footnotes to an Autobiography); *Skazanie o siney mukhe* (1963, The Tale of the Bluebottle) and *Palata No. 7* (1966, Ward No. 7), by Valeri Tarsis (born 1902); *Opustely dom* (1965, The Deserted House), by Lidiya Chukovskaya (born 1902?); *Stikhotvoreniya i poemy* (1965, Poems), by Iosif Brodski (born 1940), followed later by another volume—*Ostanovka v pustyne* (1970, A Halt in the Desert); Varlaam Shalamov's (born 1907) *Kolymskie rasskazy* (Stories of Kolyma), serialized in *Novy zhurnal* from 1966 to 1972; and two very different volumes of memoirs—Yevgeniya Ginzburg's (born 19??) *Krutoy marshrut* (1968, Arduous Journey) and Nadezhda Mandelstam's (born 1899) *Vospominaniya* (1970, Memoirs).

All these works found their way abroad. Most of them had been previously circulating clandestinely, in *samizdat* editions. (This does not apply to *Doctor Zhivago* and to the works by Terts, Arzhak, and Tarsis.) To one extent or another, they all bespeak the liberation of Soviet Russian writers from the yoke of socialist realism and various extraliterary shackles imposed on literature by the totalitarian communist regime. They opened up for readers new areas and new dimensions of Soviet reality, and they returned Russian literature to the fountainhead of true humanism. At the same time, the works of Terts, and to a lesser extent of Arzhak, with their predilection for fantasy and the grotesque, recall some of the best Soviet works of the 1920s and are not unrelated to some modern western trends.

These authors of "émigré books" come from different strata of Soviet society; their backgrounds vary, although many of them are (or were) known to each other. Their fates have also differed. Pasternak was vilified and ostracized because of his novel, and he died in disgrace. The identity of Terts and Arzhak remained for a long time a mystery (even in the west they were suspected to be living not in the Soviet Union but in Israel or somewhere else). When they were at last identified—Terts, as Andrei Sinyavski, a well-known literary critic who was as late as 1961 entrusted with writing the introduction to the posthumous collection of Pasternak's poetry; Arzhak, as Yuli Daniel, a little-known Jewish translator of verse—the two were arrested, put on trial, and sentenced respectively to seven and five years of hard labor.

Lidiya Chukovskaya was apparently left alone and was able to take a very active part in the dissent movement, protesting against the persecution of Solzhenitsyn, against trials of young dissenters, against the invasion of Czechoslovakia, and so on. Valeri Tarsis was allowed to emigrate to the west soon after the publication of *Ward No. 7,* a fictionalized account of his detention in a psychiatric hospital, and was then deprived of his Soviet citizenship.

Iosif Brodski, who had been tried as a "parasite" prior to the publication of his poems abroad, was exiled to the far north but was eventually released. He then lived at large but was not allowed to publish his work, even though much of it had no political implications but was simply out of tune with the prevalent trends. Some of it has been religious in inspiration (biblical themes and images play an important part in his poetry), and some of it metaphysical in the spirit of Donne, who is one of Brodski's favorite poets. In 1972 Brodski was expelled from the Soviet Union and invited by the University of Michigan to be its poet in residence.

The fate of Varlaam Shalamov, who spent some twenty years in Soviet camps and whose stories have a great documentary value, apart from being well written, is not known, but his work continues to reach the free world.

Yevgeniya Ginzburg's *Arduous Journey* was a powerfully written and harrowing account of her experiences in Stalin's prisons and labor camps. It stood apart from many similar accounts in *samizdat* literature because it came from the pen of the wife of a high-ranking Soviet official, who was himself liquidated. Ginzburg, a dedicated communist and the mother of a well-known Soviet writer (Vasili Aksyonov), did not have to pay a price for the publication of her book abroad (it was apparently smuggled out without her knowledge and first published in an Italian translation). But there was no question of its publication inside the Soviet Union.

Nadezhda Mandelstam is the widow of the poet Osip Mandelstam, now generally recognized by critics in the west as one of the most remarkable modern Russian poets, although his work has been taboo in Russia since the early 1930s and the only quasi-complete edition of his work has been published in the United States. Nadezhda Mandelstam is living in retirement in Moscow on her pension (she used to teach English in various schools and colleges). Her memoirs, written in 1964–65, circulated in *samizdat* for a few years despite their bulkiness (some 500 typewritten pages) before reaching the west. This work is perhaps the most remarkable account of the terrible years of Stalin's rule and its deadening and dehumanizing impact on Soviet literary intelligentsia to come from the pen of one who was part and parcel of it but who, unlike the overwhelming majority, did not succumb and capitulate.

An even more slashing indictment of all of Soviet society was Nadezhda Mandelstam's sequel to her memoirs, called *Vtoraya kniga* (1972, Second Book). Chronologically overlapping the earlier volume, but much longer and of a more general nature, *Second Book* took the Soviet Union to task in the name of Christian humanism (a Jew by birth, Mrs. Mandelstam converted to Christianity). Of particular interest in *Second Book* was the picture of the literary community, which she accused of near-total capitulation, even during the first decade of the Soviet period, which is usually exempted from such charges. The few individual exceptions, including Osip Mandelstam (although, toward the end, even he was on the point of capitulating), made the overall situation look even more dismal. Circulated clandestinely in manuscript before its publication abroad, *Second Book* seemed to provoke controversy even among Soviet dissenters.

Somewhat apart from the rest of the *samizdat* fiction stood Vladimir Maksimov's (born 1932) book *Sem' dnei tvoreniya* (1971, Seven Days of Creation). Until its publication Maksimov, who had been brought up in children's colonies and had gone through a factory school, was not regarded as a nonconformist writer. He began writing in 1952, and his first volume of poetry appeared in 1956. Later, he switched to writing fiction and plays. His short novel *My obzhivaem zemlyu* (1961, We Are Assimilating the Land) and his play *Pozyvnye tryokh parallelei* (1964, The Call Signs of the Three Parallels) attracted favorable attention but did not stand out from the rest of Soviet fiction and drama of that period.

For a time Maksimov was a member of the editorial board of *Oktyabr'*, the most "conservative"—that is, ultraorthodox—of all Soviet literary periodicals. His name, however, disappeared from its masthead in 1967, and in the same year one of the six stories that were to form *Seven Days of Creation* was published anonymously in the émigré magazine *Grani* under the title *Dvornik Lashkov* (The Janitor Lashkov).

Seven Days of Creation is not a novel in the strict sense of the word: it consists of six separate stories plus a one-sentence epilogue. These seven pieces are named after the days of the week; in addition, each of the six stories has a subtitle of its own. There is no unifying plot. All the stories, however, deal with different members of the Lashkov family in its three generations, but within the same chronological framework: except for a few flashbacks, the action is set in the postrevolutionary period.

Besides the Lashkovs, some other characters appear in several stories. Maksimov paints a vast panorama of Soviet life as he follows the fortunes of Pyotr Lashkov; of his two brothers, each of whom stands in the center of one of the stories; of his grandson Vadim, who, in the story entitled *Thursday,* is shown as a patient in a psychiatric hospital, many of whose inmates are, like Vadim, quite sane (this episode is said to be based on one in Maksimov's own life); and of Pyotr's daughter Antonina, a deeply religious woman, who, together with her husband, takes part in the construction of a giant prison in the steppes of central Asia and in the last story returns, after the arrest of her husband, to the home of her father.

Maksimov did not bring up directly any political issues, but among his characters there are several who are critical of existing conditions. And the overall effect of Maksimov's description of life in the Soviet Union is most depressing. The principal value of the book is in the variety of its characters and the richness of Maksimov's characterization. Despite the overall gloominess of Maksimov's picture, his one-sentence epilogue sounds an optimistic note: "And the seventh day came—the day of hope and resurrection. . . ." In addition to several religious characters besides Antonina in *Seven Days of Creation,* the whole work is imbued with a religious spirit.

To the list of current books that are copied and recopied and occasionally smuggled out of Russia must be added a large body of what may be called "submerged" literature—those works which were written earlier but which were suppressed and are now floating to the surface. A few of them were eventually published in Russia. An example was the very remarkable novel by Mikhail Bulgakov, *Master i Margarita* (1967, The Master and Margarita), although it was published there with cuts. Later another work by Bulgakov, still considered unpublishable, *Sobach'e serdtse* (written in 1928, Heart of a Dog), cropped up and was published abroad in 1969. Two of Bulgakov's satirical plays, which were produced but then banned—*Zoykina kvartira* (1926, Zoyka's Apartment) and *Bagrovy ostrov* (1928, Crimson Island)—were published in Paris in 1971. *Crimson Island* was successfully staged in Prague in 1967.

A special case was that of Anatoli Kuznetsov. When he "defected" in 1969 he brought with him a microfilm of the uncensored versions of some of his works. *Babi Yar* was published in its entirety, in both Russian and English, in 1970. This edition included the text that was originally published in *Yunost'* in 1966, the passages that were censored at the time, and new material added by the author between 1967 and 1969. Typographical means were used to distinguish among the different texts.

The process of interpenetration between the two Russian literatures goes both ways. Readers in the Soviet Union have been receiving, in the last eight or so years, such forbidden works as the complete, or quasi-complete, editions of the works of Pasternak, Akhmatova, Gumilyov, Mandelstam, Nikolai Klyuev (1887–1957), Khlebnikov, as well as Zamyatin's *We* and the works of Terts and Arzhak. Of course, this movement in reverse is unofficial, but it does go on all the time, and it is known that those foreign editions of Russian writers find an enthusiastic response on the other side of the curtain. This must be a unique case in the history of Russian—or, for that matter, any other—literature: in the worst days of the old regime, under Nicholas I, only a few individual poems—usually blasphemous or licentious—had to be printed abroad.

RUSSIAN WORKS IN ENGLISH TRANSLATION

INDIVIDUAL WORKS MENTIONED IN ARTICLE

Akhmadulina, Bella. *Oznob* as *Fever, and Other New Poems.* New York, 1969

Aksyonov, Vasili. *Kollegi* as *Colleagues.* Moscow, 1962

———. *Zvyozdny bilet* as *A Ticket to the Stars.* New York, 1963

Aldanov, Mark. *Istoki* as *Before the Deluge.* New York, 1947

————. *Zhivi kak khochesh'* as *To Live as We Wish.* New York, 1952

Arzhak, Nikolai. *Govorit Moskva* as *This Is Moscow Speaking, and Other Stories.* New York, 1969

Baklanov, Grigori. *Pyad' zemli* as *The Foothold.* Philadelphia, 1964

Bondarev, Yuri. *Tishina* as *Silence.* Boston, 1966

Bulgakov, Mikhail. *Bagrovy ostrov* as *Crimson Island.* In *The Early Plays of Mikhail Bulgakov.* Bloomington, Ind., 1972

————. *Master i Margarita* as *The Master and Margarita.* New York, 1967

————. *Sobach'e serdtse* as *Heart of a Dog.* New York, 1968

————. *Zoykina kvartira* as *Zoyka's Apartment.* In *The Early Plays of Mikhail Bulgakov.* Bloomington, Ind., 1972

Bunin, Ivan. *Tyomnye allei* as *Dark Avenues, and Other Stories.* London, 1949

————. *Vospominaniya* as *Memories and Portraits.* New York, 1968

————. *Zhizn' Arsen'eva* as *The Well of Days.* New York, 1934

Dudintsev, Vladimir. *Ne khlebom yedinym* as *Not by Bread Alone.* New York, 1957

Ehrenburg, Ilya. *Burya* as *The Storm.* New York, 1949

————. *Devyaty val* as *The Ninth Wave.* London, 1955

————. *Lyudi, gody, zhizn'* as *People and Life 1891–1921.* New York, 1962; *Memoirs 1921–1941.* Cleveland, 1964; *The War 1941–1945.* Cleveland, 1964; *Postwar Years 1945–1954.* Cleveland, 1967

————. *Ottepel'* as *A Change of Season.* New York, 1962

Fadeev, Aleksandr. *Molodaya gvardiya* as *The Young Guard.* Moscow, 1958

Fedin, Konstantin. *Goroda i gody* as *Cities and Years.* New York, 1962

————. *Kostyor* as *The Conflagration.* Moscow, 1968

————. *Neobyknovennoe leto* as *No Ordinary Summer.* Moscow, 1967

————. *Pervye radosti* as *Early Joys.* New York, 1960

Gazdanov, Gayto. *Prizrak Aleksandra Vol'fa* as *The Specter of Alexander Wolf.* New York, 1950

————. *Vozvrashchenie Buddy* as *Buddha's Return.* New York, 1951

Ginzburg, Yevgeniya. *Krutoy marshrut* as *Journey into the Whirlwind.* New York, 1967

Gladkov, Fyodor. *Povest' o detstve* as *Restless Youth.* Moscow, n.d.

Grossman, Vasili. *Vsyo techyot* as *Forever Flowing.* New York, 1972

Kataev, Valentin. *Beleet parus odinoki* as *Lonely White Sail, or Peace Is Where the Tempest Blows.* New York, 1937

————. *Svyatoi kolodets* as *The Holy Well.* New York, 1967

————. *Trava zabven'ya* as *The Grass of Oblivion.* New York, 1970

Kaverin, Veniamin. *Otkrytaya kniga* as *Open Book.* London, 1955

Kuznetsov, Anatoli. *Babi Yar* as *Babi Yar.* New York, 1970

————. *Prodolzhenie legendy* as *Sequel to a Legend.* Moscow, 1959

Leonov, Leonid. *Doroga na Okean* as *Road to the Ocean.* New York, 1944

————. *Russki les* as *The Russian Forest.* Moscow, 1966

————. *Vor* as *The Thief.* New York, 1960

Maksimov, Sergei. *Denis Bushuev* as *The Restless Heart.* New York, 1951

————. *Dvornik Lashkov* as *House in the Clouds.* In Michael Scammell, ed., *Russia's Other Writers.* London, 1970

Mandelstam, Nadezhda. *Vospominaniya* as *Hope Against Hope: A Memoir.* New York, 1970

Nabokov, Vladimir. *Drugie berega* as *Speak Memory.* New York, 1966

Narokov, N. *Mnimye velichiny* as *The Chains of Fear.* Chicago, 1958

Panova, Vera. *Kruzhilikha* as *The Factory.* London, 1949

————. *Vremena goda* as *Span of the Year.* London, 1956

Pasternak, Boris. *Doktor Zhivago* as *Doctor Zhivago.* New York, 1958

Paustovski, Konstantin. *Povest' o zhizni* as *The Story of Life: Years of Hope.* New York, 1969

————. *Zolotaya roza* as *The Golden Rose.* Moscow, 1957

Sholokhov, Mikhail. *Podnyataya tselina* as *Virgin Soil Upturned.* New York, 1959

————. Sud'ba cheloveka as The Fate of Man. Moscow, 1967

Simonov, Konstantin. Zhivye i myortvye as The Living and the Dead. New York, 1968

Solzhenitsyn, Aleksandr. Avgust chetyrnadtsatogo as August 1914. New York, 1972

————. Dlya pol'zy dela as For the Good of the Cause. New York, 1970

————. Matryonin dvor as Matryona's House. In "We Never Make Mistakes." Columbia, S.C., 1963

————. Odin den' Ivana Denisovicha as One Day in the Life of Ivan Denisovich. New York, 1971

————. Rakovy korpus as Cancer Ward. New York, 1969

————. Sluchai na stantsii Krechetovka as Incident at Krechetovka Station. In "We Never Make Mistakes." Columbia, S.C., 1963

————. V kruge pervom as The First Circle. New York, 1968

Tarsis, Valeri. Palata No. 7 as Ward 7. New York, 1965

————. Skazanie o siney mukhe as The Bluebottle. New York, 1963

Terts, Abram. Fantasticheskie povesti as Fantastic Stories. New York, 1967

————. Sud idyot as The Trial Begins. New York, 1960

Voznesenski, Andrei. Antimiry as Antiworlds and The Fifth Ace. New York, 1967

Yefremov, Ivan. Tumannost' Andromedy as Andromeda: A Space-Age Tale. Moscow, 1963

Yevtushenko, Yevgeni. Primechaniya k avtobiografii as A Precocious Autobiography. New York, 1963

Zamyatin, Yevgeni. My as We. New York, 1972

SECONDARY WORKS

BIBLIOGRAPHIES AND GUIDES

The American Bibliography of Slavic and East European Studies. Bloomington, Ind., 1960–68

Dox, George. Die russische Sowjetliteratur. Berlin, 1961

Harkins, William E. Dictionary of Russian Literature. New York, 1957

Lewanski, Richard C., ed. The Literatures of the World in Translation: A Bibliography, Vol. II: The Slavic Literatures. New York, 1965

Surkov, A., ed. Kratkaya literaturnaya entsiklopediya, 5 vols. Moscow, 1962–68

Tarasenkov, A. Russkie poety XX veka, 1900–1955: Bibliografiya. Moscow, 1956

GENERAL WORKS

Alexandrova, Vera. A History of Soviet Literature. New York, 1963

Blair, Katherine Hunter. A Review of Soviet Literature. London, 1967

Brown, Edward J. Russian Literature since the Revolution, 2nd ed. New York, 1968

Drawicz, A. Literatura radziecka: 1917–1967. Warsaw, 1968

Gasiorowska, Xenia. Women in Soviet Fiction 1917–1964. Madison, Wis., 1968

Gorchakov, Nikolai A. The Theatre in Soviet Russia. New York, 1957

Hayward, Max and Leopold Labedz, eds. Literature and Revolution in Soviet Russia: 1917–1962. New York, 1963

Herling, G. Da Gorki a Pasternak: Considerazioni sulla letteratura sovietica. Rome, 1958

Holthusen, Johannes. Twentieth-Century Russian Literature. New York, 1972

Lettenbauer, Wilhelm. Russische Literaturgeschichte, 2nd ed. Wiesbaden, 1958

Lo Gatto, Ettore. Storia della letteratura russa, 5th ed. Florence, 1964

Mathewson, Rufus W. The Positive Hero in Russian Literature. New York, 1960

Messina, Giuseppe L. *La letteratura sovietica.* Florence, 1950

Mihailovich, Vasa D., ed. *Modern Slavic Literatures,* Vol. I. New York, 1972

Mirsky, Dmitrii S. *A History of Russian Literature,* 4th ed. London, 1960

Muchnic, Helen. *From Gorky to Pasternak.* New York, 1961

————. *Russian Writers: Notes and Essays.* New York, 1971

Reavey, George. *Soviet Literature Today.* New Haven, 1947

Rühle, Jürgen. *Das gefesselte Theater.* Cologne, 1957

————. *Literature and Revolution: A Critical Study of the Writer and Communism in the Twentieth Century.* New York, 1969

Setschkareff, Vsevolod. *Geschichte der russischen Literatur,* 2nd ed. Stuttgart, 1962

Simmons, Ernest Joseph, ed. *Through the Glass of Soviet Literature.* New York, 1961

Slonim, Marc. *Modern Russian Literature.* New York, 1953

————. *An Outline of Russian Literature.* Oxford, 1958

————. *Soviet Russian Literature: Writers and Problems, 1917–1967,* 3rd ed. London, 1969

Stender-Petersen, Adolf. *Geschichte der russischen Literatur,* 2 vols. Munich, 1957

Strada, V. *Tradizione e rivoluzione nella letteratura russa.* Turin, 1969

Struve, Gleb. *Geschichte der Sowjetliteratur.* Munich, 1957

————. *Russian Literature under Lenin and Stalin: 1917–1953.* Norman, Okla., 1971

————. *Russian Writers in Exile: Problems of an Émigré Literature.* In Werner P. Friedrich, ed. *Comparative Literature: Proceedings of the Second Congress of the International Comparative Literature Association at the University of North Carolina,* Vol. II. Chapel Hill, N.C., 1959

————. *Russkaya literatura v izgnanii: Opyt istoricheskogo obzora.* New York, 1956

————. *Soviet Russian Literature 1917–1950.* Norman, Okla., 1951

Tatu, Michel. *Power in the Kremlin.* New York, 1969

Yarmolinsky, A. *Literature under Communism.* Bloomigton, Ind., 1960

WORKS ON CONTEMPORARY LITERATURE

Boffa, Giuseppe. *Inside the Khrushchev Era.* New York, 1959

Bosley, Keith and Dmitry Pospielovsky, eds. *Russia's Underground Poets.* New York, 1970

Brumberg, Abraham. *In Quest of Justice.* New York, 1970

Conquest, Robert. *The Great Terror.* New York, 1968

————. *The Pasternak Affair: Courage of Genius.* Philadelphia, 1962

Dement'ev, A., ed. *Istoriya russkoi sovietskoi literatury,* Vol. III (1941–53), 2nd ed. Moscow, 1968; Vol. IV (1954–65), 2nd ed. Moscow, 1971

Gibian, George. *Interval of Freedom: Soviet Literature during the Thaw, 1954–1957.* Minneapolis, 1960

Hayward, Max, ed. *On Trial: The Soviet State versus "Abram Tertz" and "Nikolai Arzhak."* New York, 1967

Hayward, Max and Edward L. Crowley, eds. *Soviet Literature in the Sixties.* New York, 1964

Johnson, Priscilla. *Khrushchev and the Arts: The Politics of Soviet Culture, 1962–1964.* Cambridge, Mass., 1965

Kuckhoff, Armin. *Sowjetische Dramatik 1946–1952.* Berlin, 1953

Marchenko, Anatoly. *My Testimony.* New York, 1969

Medvedev, Roy. *Let History Judge.* New York, 1972

Nivat, Georges and Michel Aucouturier, eds. *L'Herne: Soljénitsyne.* Paris, 1971

Reddaway, Peter, ed. *Uncensored Russia: Protest and Dissent in the Soviet Union.* New York, 1972

Rothberg, Abraham. *The Heirs of Stalin: Dissidence and the Soviet Regime, 1953–1970.* Ithaca, N.Y., 1972

Scammell, Michael, ed. *Russia's Other Writers: Selections from "Samizdat" Literature.* New York, 1971

Shub, Anatole. *The New Russian Tragedy.* New York, 1969

Ssachno, Helen von. *Der Aufstand der Person: Sowjetliteratur seit Stalins Tod.* Berlin, 1965

Steininger, Alexander. *Literatur und Poli-*

tik in der Sowjetunion nach Stalins Tod. Wiesbaden, 1965

Swayze, Ernest Harold. *Political Control of Literature in the USSR, 1946–1959.* Cambridge, Mass., 1962

Vickery, Walter N. *The Cult of Opti-mism: Political and Ideological Problems of Recent Soviet Literature.* Bloomington, Ind., 1963

Werth, Alexander. *Russia: Hopes and Fears.* New York, 1969

MANUEL DURÁN-GILI

Spanish and Catalan Literature

SPANISH LITERATURE

A DISASTER, swift and devastating as a tidal wave, may strike a group of people, a civilization, at any time. Individuals are hopelessly lost: they die or are fated to go on living without hope. Yet, if the civilization is strong enough, it will survive, though perhaps not in the same form. Lizards and polyps endure terrible mutilations and are able to go on living; they regenerate the lost limbs. Spain suffered such a mutilation in war: from 1936 to 1939, the civil war was almost an act of national suicide, certainly a gruesome self-mutilation.

Spanish culture has been slowly recovering ever since the end of the civil war. Many of the wounds inflicted by the war are still not completely healed. Much of what was lost then (in talent, in hopes, in courage) cannot be brought back to life. What we see now is a new animal: its torn limbs are growing back, although in a different shape.

Before the war Spanish cultural life had reached a level that we might designate as a second golden age. It was a time during which such writers as José Ortega y Gasset (1883–1955), Miguel de Unamuno (1864–1936), and Federico García Lorca (1898–1936) were setting the pace for a growing number of new literary talents. Poetry had reached a pinnacle; Antonio Machado (1875–1939), Jorge Guillén (born 1893), Rafael

Alberti (born 1902), Pedro Salinas (1892–1951), and Federico García Lorca were only the very summit of a vast edifice of lyrical accomplishments. A generation of great poets, Lorca's generation, added its insights to a generation of philosophical writers, the generation of Unamuno. But suddenly the orchard became a desert. The Spanish civil war, the most tragic and devastating war Spain had ever endured, not only interrupted with its violence the normal development of Spanish literature but also placed on opposite sides almost all the writers, old and young. Political polarization was a preface to chaos and destruction.

Many left Spain after Franco's victory. Others stayed. With the exception of a few noteworthy émigrés, such as the first-rank writers Machado and Juan Ramón Jiménez (1881–1958), the writers of the Generation of 1898 (roughly, those writers born between 1864 and 1880) either gave up their liberal philosophy and lent their support to the new political regime or gave it their approval in a passive way. On the other hand, the great majority of young writers rallied to the side of the republic and left the country at the end of the civil war.

Spanish literature was thus considerably weakened. Its most eminent writers, those of the Generation of 1898, either died shortly before the war (as did Ramón del Valle-Inclán [1869–1936]) or during the war (Miguel de Unamuno) or immediately after the war (Antonio Machado, who died in exile). José Ortega y Gasset also went into exile and did not return to Spain until 1954. The novelists Pío Baroja y Nessi (1872–1956) and Azorín (1874–1967, pseudonym of José Martínez Ruiz) went briefly into exile but eventually made peace with the regime. However, they tried little new in their late works. Federico García Lorca was murdered in 1936. Pedro Salinas, Jorge Guillén, and Rafael Alberti fled from Spain.

Literary life thus became divided; the émigrés produced important works, especially in the fields of poetry and fiction, yet for a long time their works remained unknown to the reading public in Spain. Meanwhile, at home, after several years of almost totally mediocre output, a new awakening took place. First the novel, then lyric poetry, and finally the essay and the drama regained vitality, wholly or in part.

The years immediately following the civil war were especially gloomy for Spaniards. At home, a cruel dictatorship crushed all dissent. Hunger and social disintegration added to create the climate of anguish and frustration. Outside Spain, World War II, which started shortly after the end of the Spanish civil war (but in which Spain was not directly involved), seemed to add intensity to the apocalyptic mood of despair that had seized many Spaniards. Recovery was slow and painful.

Contemporary Spanish literature can be divided into three periods: the 1940s, during which an existentialist mood of sullen frustration prevailed; the 1950s, a period that saw the first signs of hope and even a partial rebirth of prosperity (due in part to American loans and an increase in tourism); and the 1960s, a decade of growing wealth and partial liberalization in governmental regulations and censorship, a trend that so far has been largely carried into the 1970s.

Each period made a specific contribution to Spanish literature. During the 1940s, following the chaos of the war period, new trends were slow in developing. It can be said that Spanish literature after the civil war did not begin properly inside Spain until 1944 or 1945, thus at around the same time when other countries were witnessing the end of the ravages of World War II. What had been lost during the civil war and after it was an intellectual climate of openness, gaiety, self-confidence, and optimism. Before the civil war Spain, without renouncing her unique personality, was becoming "modern," catching up with the rest of Europe. The setback created by the war and its aftermath explains in part the gloomy character of most Spanish literature of the 1940s.

An overview of the period brings to mind labels for each decade: for the 1940s, "existential realism"; for the 1950s, "social or critical realism"; and for the 1960s, a time of "experimentation and synthesis." These labels are particularly useful for the evolution of fiction. In poetry the period of existential and personal poetry was succeeded by a period of socially committed poetry, and finally by a period in which personal, subjective values seem to have regained the ascendency. Similar classifications could be applied to the Spanish drama. The evolution of the essay is harder to define, but it, too, has reflected the changing moods of the times.

FICTION

Camilo José Cela (born 1916), a writer of great talent and individuality, dominated Spanish fiction of the 1940s. His first novel, *La familia de Pascual Duarte* (1942, The Family of Pascual Duarte), has often been compared to Albert Camus's *L'étranger*. The resemblance is the result more of the general intellectual climate of the war years than of a direct influence. Cela's anti-hero, Pascual Duarte, whose wretched life has been scarred by the indifference or the cruelty of society, reminisces about his past in crude, colloquial language, while awaiting execution for the murder of his own mother. Cela used some of the traditional techniques of Spanish picaresque novels—such as the first-person narrative and the abundance of cruelty and the grotesque—but he blended them with modern psychological insights.

Cela's next major novel, *La colmena* (1951, The Hive), was an ambitious attempt to depict a whole city, post-civil-war Madrid, through a collective portrait: 116 characters moving around in ever-widening circles at the center of a great city, living out their gray lives within a framework of hunger, sex, and noncommunication. The mosaic structure and the jumping from one character to the next create a panoramic view of society in Spain after the civil war.

Cela has written other interesting novels. *Pabellón de reposo* (1944, Rest Home) was a slow-paced love story taking place in a tuberculosis rest home. *Mrs. Caldwell habla con su hijo* (1953, Mrs. Caldwell Speaks to Her Son), in a surrealistic, stream-of-consciousness narrative, depicted a delirious mother who manages to convince herself that her dead son is still alive. In *La catira* (1955, The Fair One) Cela dealt with the backlands of Venezuela, telling a tragic tale in local dialect.

After *The Fair One* Cela abandoned the novel for many years, writing instead short stories and books about travel. But in 1969 he published another major novel, *San Camilo, 1936* (Saint Camilo's Day, 1936), by far his best work thus far, a masterpiece that holds its own against the best novels of the last twenty years in all of western literature. As ambitious and vast as *The Hive, Saint Camilo's Day, 1936* makes use of a more complex collage technique in which newspaper and radio commercials intrude upon the narrative, creating ironic contrasts and producing comic effects that soften the brutal impact of the events on the eve of the civil war. The metaphysical and existential introspection of the hero provides continuity in an otherwise fragmented narrative. Humor and pathos are intermingled. Violence and the grotesque are always present. Human madness is fully depicted; stupidity and heroism stand side by side. But the final pages transcend folly and horror in a modern version of Greek catharsis.

Cela is a prolific author, and he keeps publishing minor works at the rate of one or two a year. Among these, some have genuine lasting interest, especially his books about travel, the best of which is still *Viaje a la Alcarria* (1948, Journey to Alcarria). In this book Cela appears as a hobo, a vagabond wandering through some of the least-frequented corners of the Spanish countryside and narrating his reactions to the landscape and the country people in a style both ironic and tender, which fully reflects his sympathy for the poor and downtrodden, for the humble and backward peasants who nevertheless manage to hold on to their self-respect and their dignity.

Cela's work has been characterized by alienation, cruelty, irony, and satire—but not at the expense of tenderness and lyricism. His early critical analysis of Spanish society made possible the development of a new Spanish realism. His interest in experimental methods has kept him abreast with recent trends. He is today an undisputed master—at the same time a social critic, a great artist, and a buffoon. He has given much to Spanish literature, and more is expected from him.

Following Cela's initial success, another writer made a major contribution to the contemporary Spanish novel. Carmen Laforet (born 1921) wrote a best seller, *Nada* (1945, Nothing), at the age of twenty-three. Her main theme, and one she has expressed in several other novels—*La isla y los demonios* (1952, The Island and the Devils), *La mujer nueva* (1955, The New Woman), *La insolación* (1963, Sunstroke)—has been the conflict between the hopes of an adolescent and the dreary world around him or her. The outcome is disenchantment. Laforet is a sensitive psychologist. What is lacking in her novels has been a fresh approach to our modern world in her ideas and her literary techniques. Yet her intuition and her poetic gift for description go a long way to compensate for these shortcomings. Her novels remain appealing, and *Nothing* is historically important as the first valid Spanish existentialist novel. *Sunstroke* is a better novel, a more complex approach to the problem of misunderstanding and disillusion; it deserves more attention than it has received so far.

Miguel Delibes (born 1920) also brought to the contemporary Spanish novel a new realism. His production is not only large in quantity; he has maintained from the very beginning a consistently high quality. Delibes's first novels were realistic, analytical, and, although highly readable and excellent in parts, somewhat conventional by twentieth-century standards; they belong to the realistic school of the turn of the century. In *La sombra del ciprés es alargada* (1948, The Cypress Tree Casts a Long Shadow) the hero, Pedro, afraid of death and disappointment, refuses to love anyone. He becomes a sailor, persistently rejects the love of a woman, but finally agrees to marry her. A few days after the wedding, she dies in an accident, thus confirming his premonitions and fears. *Aún es de día* (1949, It Is Still Light) was a bitter tale of an ugly salesman who loves a beautiful society girl from a distance. *Mi idolatrado hijo Sisí* (1950, My Beloved Son Sisí) was a rather prosaic story of a selfish businessman who dotes on his only son and commits suicide when the son dies in the civil war.

El camino (1950, The Path) marked the beginning of a second period in Delibes's art, characterized by a more subjective approach and a keener insight into social problems. *The Path* was much more than a tale about an eleven-year-old boy growing up in a Castilian village. Alongside descriptions of the pastoral setting are satirical vignettes of the villagers. Innocence and wisdom are fused in the thoughts and deeds of the young boy Daniel and his friends. *Las ratas* (1962, The Rats) was also a description of rural life in Castile. Its two heroes are an old man, who lives in a cave, and a young boy, intelligent and warm-hearted. Yet the real protagonist is the whole village. Poverty has not degraded its inhabitants; instead, it has created a curiously Spanish mixture of dignity and picaresque attitudes. *La hoja roja* (1959, The Red Slip) was a melancholy tale about a retired municipal employee who fears the approach of death. He finds consolation in giving advice to a young servant girl, whom he finally marries. The sad mood of this fine novel is relieved by amusing critical and satirical sections.

Delibes's masterpiece thus far has perhaps been *Cinco horas con Mario* (1966, Five Hours with Mario). It is a satire, often amusing, at times bordering on pathos, of a segment of Spanish society symbolized here by a stupid woman, Carmen, whose bigotry and narrowminded attitude toward life are slowly revealed in a long monologue. Her husband, Mario, has just died. Carmen sits in wake beside his body and for five hours relives her past life, argues incessantly in her mind with her dead husband, reproaching him for his failures and defending her own conduct. The more she talks, the more she exposes her shallowness and cruelty. Colloquial language and the expressions typical of the uneducated middle class have never been put to better use. Through the stupidity of the main character the reader acquires insight into Spanish history and society.

Parábola del náufrago (1969, The Drowning Sailor's Parable) was in many ways just as good as *Five Hours with Mario*. More symbolic and less concerned with the minutiae of everyday life than *Five Hours with Mario,* its subject was the alienation of modern man exploited by an autocratic regime. A worker who questions the meaning of his factory job is turned by a mysterious, remote supervisor into a speaking goat. Through experimental techniques, elliptical language, and inventive words Delibes created in this Kafkaesque novel a cumulative and total effect of irony and chaos.

Delibes, through his novels, has become a profound analyst of Spanish society and of the modern world in general. Each of his latest novels has added to his stature as a stylist and experimental writer, a writer with a wealth of ideas, keen observations, and an expert capacity to handle irony, satire, and symbolism. Moreover, neither the experimental nature of his latest work nor the use of parables and symbols has prevented him from creating memorable characters.

Camilo José Cela, Carmen Laforet, and Miguel Delibes were without a doubt the most important novelists to appear in Spain in the years that followed closely the end of the civil war. But two more traditional novelists also contributed to the Spanish novel of the 1940s and 1950s: Ignacio Agustí (born 1913) and Juan Antonio Zunzunegui (born 1901). Moreover, the prolific group of exiled novelists, to whom we owe several major novels, also published during the 1940s and 1950s.

Ignacio Agustí's four-part novel, *La ceniza fue árbol* (1944–65, These Ashes Were Once a Tree), the story of the rise of a Catalan family of industrialists, was a "period novel," reminiscent of John Galsworthy's *Forsyte Saga.* Agustí's novel was a deliberate and honest attempt to continue the traditions of nineteenth-century realism. Highly readable in spite of its limitations, the first volume, *Mariona Rebull* (1945, Mariona Rebull) was by far the best of the tetralogy.

The first novels of the prolific Juan Antonio Zunzunegui, including *La úlcera* (1949, The Ulcer), were humorous. Later Zunzunegui wrote numerous novels describing the Spanish bourgeoisie after the civil war. The best of these was probably *Esta oscura desbandada* (1952, This Dark Rout). In the manner of Zola and Vicente Blasco Ibáñez (1867–1928), Zunzunegui's novels have been accumulations of details, descriptions, anecdotes, all with varying effectiveness. Indeed, these accumulations have often not resulted in a distinctive style or a clear focus.

The exiled novelists have offered rich and varied perspectives. For them, the subject of the Spanish civil war has been of paramount importance. Pío Baroja, already mentioned as a member of the older Generation of 1898, was in exile only briefly, returning to Spain in 1940. The only noteworthy work he wrote from his return until his death in 1956 was his memoirs, *Desde la última vuelta del camino* (1944, From the Road's Last Bend), which is of interest mainly to the literary historians. Baroja's friend Azorín returned to Spain in 1939. Before his death in 1967, Azorín published several books of memoirs and essays and one notable novel, *María Fontán* (1943, María Fontán). Ramón Gómez de la Serna (1891–1963), who lived for a while in Buenos Aires, came back to Spain in 1949. With the exception of *Automoribundia* (1948, The Art of Dying), a semiautobiographical novel that displayed his great talent as a humorist and as an avant-garde stylist, his late works were marred by self-plagiarism.

The "true exiles" are those writers who did not make their peace with the Franco regime and therefore did not come back to Spain. The first work to appear from this group of writers was Arturo Barea's (1897–1957) *La forja de un rebelde* (The Forging of a Rebel), a semiautobiographical trilogy written in Spanish but published first in English between 1941 and 1944. (It was finally published in Spanish in 1951, in Buenos Aires.) Barea evoked successfully the Madrid of his childhood, his years as a soldier in north Africa, the gathering storm of the civil war, the years of struggle and chaos. His style was graceless but expressive.

Max Aub (born 1903) made an outstanding contribution to the war novel in *El laberinto mágico* (The Magic Labyrinth), a long panoramic work with epic and lyrical overtones, divided into five books: *Campo cerrado* (1943, Closed Field), *Campo de sangre* (1945, Bloody Field), *Campo abierto* (1951, Open Field), *Campo del Moro* (1963, Field of the Moor), and *Campo de los almendros* (1968, Field of Almond Trees). Aub used modern techniques: psychological introspection, slow descriptions, prose poems, dream analyses, and colloquial conversations. Yet the rhythm is often fast, because of the mosaic fragments and kaleidoscopic visions. Through Aub's descriptions we relive the poignant moments of the street fighting in Barcelona, the birth of human cruelty and human solidarity, the theoretical discussions about discipline and friendship, the bitter fighting around Teruel and Madrid, rear-guard intrigue, espionage and chaos, and finally the despair and defeat of the republican fighters. This monumental work was the closest Spanish literature has come to *War and Peace*.

Aub has written other noteworthy novels. *Las buenas intenciones* (1954, Good Intentions) was both a love story and a panoramic novel about life in Madrid and several other Spanish cities from 1924 to 1939. *Jusep Torres Campalans* (1958, Jusep Torres Campalans) was the "biography" of a Catalan painter, a friend of Picasso. Everything in the book has the appearance of reality: notes, bibliography, news items of the period. Yet the painter whose story is told was invented by Aub; hence, the novel is a joke on the reader. *La calle de Valverde* (1961, Valverde Street) was a multilayered panorama of Madrid around 1927, with its intellectuals and its café crowds talking incessantly at all hours. Aub has also written numerous short stories, including those collected in *Cuentos ciertos* (1955, True Tales) and *Cuentos mexicanos* (1959, Mexican Tales).

Francisco Ayala (born 1906) is another great émigré novelist. Already a writer before the civil war, Ayala's style underwent a change, and his art reached maturity after 1939. *El hechizado* (1944, The Bewitched), a tale of mystery set in the Spanish royal court of the seventeenth century, can be compared in its metaphysical dimensions and literary beauty with the best short stories of Jorge Luis Borges. *La cabeza del cordero* (1949, The Sheep's Head) was a sensitive and poignant book of short stories dealing with war and hatred, often indirectly or symbolically. Ayala's style here was spare and sober, yet subtle and almost poetic. *Historia de macacos* (1955, Monkey Tale) contained some of the most amusing and original stories written in Spanish.

Ayala's humor has often verged on the grotesque, on cruelty. *Muertes de perro* (1959, A Dog's Deaths) was a caricature of a "banana republic" in the Caribbean, complete with a cruel tyrant and a court of abject flatterers. *El fondo del vaso* (1962, The Bottom of the Glass) tied together the loose ends of *A Dog's Deaths* and extracted the philosophical and ethical consequences of the chaos and cruelty that *A Dog's Deaths* had revealed. In *El jardín de las delicias* (1971, The Garden of Delights), a collection of short stories, Ayala's versatility, his gifts as a psychologist and as a stylist, and his cruel humor were once more brought into play.

Another important novelist in exile, Ramón Sender (born 1902), published before the civil war realistic novels of social criticism, such as *Imán* (1929, Magnet). *Contraataque* (Counterattack), one of the first Spanish novels to deal with the civil war, appeared in 1938. Since 1939 Sender's talent has matured, and his subject matter has become more philosophical and universal. *Crónica del alba* (1942, Chronicle of Dawn), perhaps Sender's most successful novel, was classical in its simplicity, serene and pastoral in its setting, tender and poignant in its description of childhood in a magic Spanish village. Almost a prose poem, it justified the label "magic realism," which has sometimes been applied to Sender.

In *El Rey y la Reina* (1947, The King and the Queen) Sender wove a symbolic tale around wartime Madrid and the relationship of two human beings—a duchess alone in her palace and her gardener Romulo, whom she had hardly looked upon as a man, because of the social barriers, but who proves to be a hero and a respectful admirer of the duchess. Amidst the struggle that is tearing Spain apart, the two protagonists build an island of peace and confidence.

Sender's *La esfera* (1947, The Sphere) was an ambitious philosophical novel, in which a Spanish refugee pursues the elusive relationship between dreams and reality during a sea voyage. Eroticism and metaphysics are mingled in its pages. The ship, symbolizing perhaps life, civilization, human reason, is wrecked, and the would-be philosopher drowns. In *Requiem por un campesino español* (1960, Requiem for a Spanish Peasant), Sender used a flashback technique and a chorus of washerwomen, who comment on the past and the present, to evoke the life of a man who fights for justice and is finally betrayed and executed.

Among lesser works by Sender were *Mexicayotl* (1940, Mexicayotl), a volume of myths and tales with a Mexican setting, and *Los cinco libros de Ariadna* (1957, Ariadna's Five Books), a complicated and sometimes confusing novel about intrigue and espionage in republican Spain during the civil war. Sender's fiction is uneven, and some of it may not pass the test of time; but three or four of his novels rank with the best contemporary Spanish fiction.

While the exiled novelists were developing their art outside Spain, mainly during the 1950s, their contemporaries in Spain were creating a new literary movement. The novel of social protest, or the committed novel, was their goal. Their technique was far from uniform; it included behaviorism, poetic realism, perspectivism—often a combination of several of these approaches. Their aim, however, was common: to write novels in which social injustice was denounced, and individual and political freedom defended. At its best, this trend produced real works of art, not propaganda novels. It engaged the talents of some of the best writers in post-civil-war Spain. They included not only mature writers, such as Cela and Delibes, but also younger writers: Ana María Matute (born 1926), Rafael Sánchez Ferlosio (born 1927), Luis Martín-Santos (1924–1964), Juan Goytisolo (born 1931).

Luis Romero (born 1916) is the oldest author to belong wholly to this group of committed novelists. He acquired sudden fame after winning the Nadal Prize for his novel *La noria* (1951, The Water Wheel). In this ambitious work Romero tried to present faithfully a vast number of characters in contemporary Barcelona. He used a technique reminiscent of Cela's *The Hive,* but with a faster pace, since all the events take place in one single day. *The Water Wheel* remains probably Romero's best novel. Later came *Carta de ayer* (1953, Yesterday's Letter), a love story, and *Los otros* (1956, The Others), a complex novel dealing with a robbery and the death of its perpetrator, in which Romero thoroughly explored life in the Barcelona slums. Romero has talent but is often denigrated as an epigone of Cela.

Ana María Matute has great skill as a short-story writer and as a novelist, endowed with imagination, sensitivity, and a gift for poetic language. Her recurring subjects have been the difficulty of communication, violence, injustice, death, time, loneliness, and the world of children. *Los Abel* (1948, The Abel Brothers) was a saga of seven brothers confined in an obscure village, each one of whom struggles, often in vain, to find his identity and his vocation. *Fiesta al Noroeste* (1953, A Fiesta at the Northwest) was a poetic tale centered around the opposition between two brothers, one of them deformed and obsessed by avarice, the other an heroic outcast. It is a parable about envy and greed, with overtones of mystery and magic.

Matute's most important work to date has been the trilogy *Los mercaderes* (The Merchants). The first book, *Primera memoria* (1960, First Memory) was a delicate semiautobiographical narrative, in which a woman remembers a few months of her adolescence in Mallorca during the civil war. The description of Mediterranean landscapes softens somewhat the cruelty and violence of a country divided by hatred. *Los soldados lloran de noche* (1964, Soldiers Cry at Night) projected many of the same characters against the confused panorama of the end of the war. *La trampa* (1969, The Trap) was perhaps the best novel of the trilogy. The war has ended; in spite of their adaptation to the new authoritarian society that has now been created, and perhaps because of their adaptation, all the characters feel prostituted and frustrated. Mario, an idealistic intellectual out of work, wishes to take revenge upon the man who tricked him into revealing the hiding place of Mario's father (who was then executed by the Franquists). Mario desists from his purpose, but to no avail: one of his disciples carries out the murder.

Matute has also published several books of short stories: *Los niños tontos* (1957, The Stupid Children), *El tiempo* (1957, Time), *Tres y un sueño* (1961, Three Characters and a Dream), *Historias de la Artámila* (1961, Tales from Artámila), and *Algunos muchachos* (1969, Some Boys). In these stories, almost all about children, Matute has no peer in modern Spanish literature.

Another representative of the new trend toward critical realism is Rafael Sánchez Ferlosio, who, though far from prolific, has managed to have a great impact upon Spanish literary life. His first book, *Industrias y andanzas de Alfanhuí* (1951, Alfanhuí's Tricks and Travels), was a neopicaresque narrative about the adventures of an imaginative young man who, after roaming Spain and serving different masters, decides to play with creation to produce new and unexpected combinations in the forms of nature. He is at once Lazarillo de Tormes and Paracelsus, Gil Blas and Merlin. The novel is witty and even dazzling at times.

Sánchez Ferlosio's best work to date has been *El Jarama* (1956, The Jarama River), a behavioristic novel in which the Sunday picnic of a group of young people belonging to Madrid's lower middle class is explored in depth. Sánchez Ferlosio in this novel was both a camera and a tape recorder: every word sounds authentic; every gesture is faithfully reported, without comment. The general impression is one of subdued sadness, of mediocrity and impotence. Hence the impact of the novel as a document of social criticism, as an indictment of a society and a government in which people are compelled to be mediocre and meek.

Jesús Fernández Santos (born 1926) is another practitioner of the social or committed novel. His *Los bravos* (1954, The Valiant People) was an objective travelogue dealing with a few days in the life of a Spanish village. *The Valiant People* was a literary translation of *cinéma vérité,* in which human weakness and the exploitation of man by man were exposed without rhetoric. *Cabeza rapada* (1959, Shaven Head) proved Fernández Santos's mastery of the short-story form. *El hombre de los santos* (1969, The Man of the Saints), a complex tale about a frustrated painter who tries in vain to make his life meaningful and rekindle his love for an old sweetheart, explored the debasing grip that a mediocre society holds upon its members.

Luis Martín-Santos became famous, and justly so, after writing only one novel, *Tiempo de silencio* (1962, Time of Silence). A scathing criticism of the Spanish bourgeoisie, it was much more. The plot is simple. A young biologist becomes accidentally embroiled in a sordid case of abortion and is briefly jailed; his fiancée is murdered by a hoodlum bent on revenge; his career is destroyed. The style and composition are far from simple. Martín-Santos employed the full range of the Spanish language, from slang to scientific jargon. Symbolic elements and situations abound. Words and syntax undergo deep transformations. This tale of a young man exploring a city in search of his destiny can be compared to Joyce's *Ulysses*. Martín Santos masterfully fused caricature, parody, puns, invented words, irony, and satire.

The realism of Ignacio Aldecoa (1925–1969) was more down-to-earth. In *El fulgor y la sangre* (1954, The Glow and the Blood) he described the lonely life of a squad of rural policemen and their dependents in an isolated outpost up in the mountains. *Gran sol* (1957, The Big Sun), a slowly paced reconstruction of the life of Spanish fishermen, reminds one occasionally of *Moby Dick*.

Juan Marsé's (born 1933) first novel, *Encerrados con un solo juguete* (1960, Locked Up with Only One Toy), dealt with the sexual obsessions of Spanish youth, incapable of finding any other outlet for their energies. In the best seller *Últimas tardes con Teresa* (1966, Last Afternoons with Teresa) a gullible pseudointellectual woman is duped by a scoundrel posing as an anti-Franco resistance hero. Marsé's satirical approach is as amusing as it is biting.

The distasteful side of Spanish life has also occupied Ángel María de Lera (born 1912). His *Los olvidados* (1957, The Forgotten People) depicted, in the manner of Gor'ki, life in the poorest suburbs of Madrid. *Los clarines del miedo* (1958, The Horns of Fear), an existential study of corruption in the sport of bullfighting, dealt with death and sensuality without glamour or rhetoric. *Bochorno* (1960, Shame) and *Trampa* (1962, Cheating) projected into a city landscape the troubled atmosphere of *The Horns of Fear*. *Las últimas banderas* (1967, The Last Flags) treated with honesty the last weeks of republican Spain in 1939, Franco's victory, and its repercussions upon the novel's hero. Honesty is rewarded, even in today's Spain: this novel has become a best seller.

Another author with wide readership is José Gironella (born 1917), whose three novels to date—*Los cipreses creen en Dios* (1953, The Cypresses Believe in God), *Un millón de muertos* (1961, One Million Dead), and *Ha estallado la paz* (1966, Peace Has Broken Out)—purported to be objective, panoramic descriptions of Spain at war with itself. Although they were commercially successful, a journalistic superficiality and a hidden bias largely undermined the artistic value of these novels.

Much more rewarding is the work of Juan Benet (born 1927), whose *Volverás a Región* (1967, Thou Shalt Go Back to Región) was an attempt to combine realism with myth, fable, and mystery. In his experimental techniques Benet has emulated the best recent fiction of the western hemisphere. There are echoes of Faulkner and García Márquez in *Thou Shalt Go Back to Región*. This novel was far from flawless, yet implicit in it was great promise.

Juan García Hortelano (born 1928) has achieved considerable international success through the translations of two of his novels: *Nuevas amistades* (1959, New Friendships) and *Tormenta de verano* (1962, Summer Storm). A book of tales, *Gente de Madrid* (1967, People of Madrid), showed García Hortelano's continuing interest in the upper middle class of urban Spain.

Among Spanish novelists who have established substantial reputations, one of the youngest, and one of the most active and significant, practitioners of the art of fiction is Juan Goytisolo. His first novel, *Juegos de manos* (1954, Violent Games), established him as a writer committed to social criticism, yet interested in the complex interaction between dreams and reality, illusion and disenchantment. Goytisolo is always looking for his identity—and that of his country—behind the social masks. *Violent Games* deals with a gang of young "bourgeois anarchists" who plan a political murder. The would-be assassin does not have the courage to go through with the murder and as a punishment is in turn executed by one of his friends.

Goytisolo's *Duelo en el paraíso* (1955, Grief in Paradise), a dramatic account of a child's crime in a school during the civil war, is reminiscent of William Golding's *Lord of the Flies,* as well as of the French film *Jeux interdits* (indeed, the influence of cinematographic techniques has been very strong in Goytisolo's generation). *El circo* (1957, The Circus), *Fiestas* (1958, Fiestas), and *La resaca* (1958, The Undertow) formed a trilogy dealing with poverty, squalor, and abandoned children who play at being adult and imitate the most corrupt and depraved aspects of adult society. In spite of his somber subjects, Goytisolo managed to create poetic moods. His gifts for characterization and the dramatic tension that pervades his novels has made them highly readable.

Fin de fiesta (1962, The Party's Over), a volume of four novellas about four couples whose marriages are disintegrating, showed Goytisolo's talent as a psychologist and a social critic. *La isla* (1961, The Island) was an exposé of the Spanish bourgeoisie, without ideals or ethical principles, living a meaningless *dolce vita* on the Costa del Sol.

Like Camilo José Cela, Goytisolo is a great traveler and often looks for remote sections of Spain untouched by tourism. His travel books are almost as lively and as dramatic as his novels. Among them are *Campos de Níjar* (1960, The Fields of Níjar), *La Chanca* (1962, The Chanca Region), and *Pueblo en marcha* (1963, A People in Motion [about Cuba]).

In 1966 Goytisolo published *Señas de identidad* (Marks of Identity), one of his most important and difficult novels. It is conceived on a grand scale, making use of shifting viewpoints, counterpoint technique, flashbacks to the turn of the century, geographical zigzagging: Barcelona—Andalusia—Cuba—Paris—Barcelona. A man, the author's double, is looking at himself in the mirror of the society that gave birth to him. The prize of his effort—and the reader's—is an insight into the nature of the hero and into the society whose product he is.

Reivindicación del Conde Don Julián (1969, An Apology for Count Julián), as well as *Marks of Identity,* had to be published outside of Spain because of its controversial and critical viewpoint. Though stylistically complex, the theme of *An Apology for Count Julián* is simple. A young man, self-exiled, looks at the far-away Spanish coast from the African city of Tangiers and dreams about the Spain he knew. In a subtle love-hate relationship, he examines his present surroundings, experiments with hashish, goes through delirious visions and nightmares, in which the essence of the Spanish past is analyzed and satirized. Imaginative, grotesque, amusing—these adjectives come to mind, and yet they are incapable of describing the overwhelming power of this novel.

Goytisolo and Cela are the two contemporary Spanish novelists with the greatest international reputations. Goytisolo has now reached the peak of his creative powers, and he seems to have the capacity to continue to produce innovative and important works.

POETRY

Spanish poetry today can compare favorably with Spanish fiction. Many critics rate it higher, although its impact upon the reading public is considerably lower.

The aftermath of the civil war was equally devastating on poetry and fiction. Most of the first-rank poets were either annihilated or exiled. García Lorca was murdered in 1936, and Antonio Machado died in exile in 1939. Many of the best poets belonging to Lorca's generation left Spain at the end of the war.

Among poets who stayed behind, one of the best, Miguel Hernández (1910–1942), soon died in jail. A victim of the civil war, like so many other Spaniards, his swan song, *Cancionero y romancero de ausencias* (Songs and Ballads about Absent Ones) was written between 1938 and 1941: the best and most poignant poems were composed from jail while he was awaiting death. Hernández was a great erotic poet, but here he became a philosophical voice, questioning destiny and justice, saying "yes" and "no" to fate.

In the meantime, a new climate in poetry was slowly spreading throughout Spain. It is not easy to label the movement, but there were some common characteristics. Most of the poets of this group were religious. Most of them wanted to effect a rebirth of classicism. Many turned for inspiration to the great Spanish poet of the Renaissance, Garcilaso de la Vega (1501–1536).

Perhaps the best practitioner of this return to classicism was Luis Rosales (born 1909). Certainly he was, for a few years, the most influential lyrical voice. His first book, *Abril* (1935, April), had already established a joyful mood of religiosity before the explosion of the civil war. His *Retablo sacro del Nacimiento del Señor* (1940, Holy Altar Depicting Our Lord's Birth) was a clear, simple call to piety in the aftermath of the war. His best book of poetry by far has been *La casa encendida* (1949, Lighted

Home), a long autobiographical poem in which nostalgia and love are like huge crenellated walls protecting man against the powers of darkness.

Luis Felipe Vivanco (born 1907) is another simple and direct poet, whose subjects—nature, love, tenderness, the pleasures of being a father—are eternal sources of wonder for him. In *Los ojos de Toledo* (1953, Toledo's Eyes) and *Lecciones para el hijo* (1961, Lessons for My Son) he developed his favorite subjects: the joys of adolescence and the dialogue with the poet's child, the one person who will continue the quest for truth and beauty.

Germán Bleiberg (born 1915) began his career as a poet, with *Sonetos amorosos* (1963, Love Sonnets), in an intimate, tender, and subtle style in the tradition of Garcilaso. *Más allá de las ruinas* (1947, Beyond the Ruins) contained several powerful love poems, but here happiness was replaced by loneliness and anguish since the poet was writing from jail. *Himno de transfiguración* (1945, Transfiguration Hymn) had a biblical quality. In it, hope and serenity tried to reassert themselves.

Leopoldo Panero (1909–1962), another poet very active after the civil war, created in *Escrito a cada instante* (1949, Written from Moment to Moment) a poetry rooted in the home, family life, religious experiences, and country landscapes. At its best, Panero's poetry expressed serenity and perfect balance. Antonio Machado was the main influence upon Panero. In *Canto personal* (1953, A Personal Song) the smooth surfaces of Panero's thoughts were ruffled by politics and polemics as the poet tried to defend contemporary Spain against the attacks of the Chilean poet Pablo Neruda.

Dionisio Ridruejo (born 1912) is another member of the classical or "Garcilaso" group. His *Sonetos a la piedra* (1943, Sonnets to Stone) and *En once años* (1950, Eleven Years' Work) showed him to be a virtuoso of classical forms, especially the sonnet. Ridruejo is a poet distinguished by cold elegance, stylized aesthetic descriptions, and well-tuned musical effects.

Ridruejo's early poetry was typical of the period immediately following the civil war. In 1944 the calm was shattered by the publication of *Hijos de la ira* (Children of Wrath) by the great critic and poet Dámaso Alonso (born 1898). This whole book was a long cry of anguish, an existential outburst. Life is but a "horrible trip," a "nightmare without exit." Only religious feelings could briefly calm Alonso's tormented heart. The influence of this work, a genuine masterpiece, was profound. In *Hombre y Dios* (1955, Man and God), a book less original and less powerful than *Children of Wrath*, Alonso expressed his quest for religious answers to chaos and death.

This second mood, the "existential quest" in contemporary Spanish poetry, displayed less orthodoxy in religion than that of the group of Rosales, Vivanco, Bleiberg, Panero, and Ridruejo. To the second group belonged José Luis Hidalgo (1917–1947), who died young, the same year in which his book *Los muertos* (The Dead Ones) appeared. Melancholy, resignation in the face of death, and the mystery and adventure of dying were Hidalgo's subjects. At his best he was both poignant and serene.

Vicente Gaos (born 1919) is also a metaphysical poet in the existential and religious sense. His *Arcángel de mi noche* (1944, Archangel of My Night) and *Profecía del recuerdo* (1956, Prophecy of Memory) were treasure troves of polished, elegant sonnets, in which emotion was not stifled but rather enhanced by the formal style.

Carlos Bousoño (born 1923) is a less intense poet than Gaos. He has carried on a long dialogue with God and nature in his books of poetry: *Subida al amor* (1945, Ascent toward Love), *Primavera de la muerte* (1946, Spring of Death), *Hacia otra luz* (1950, Toward Another Light), and *Noche del sentido* (1957, Night of Sense). But this long dialogue has failed to solve the poet's doubts and questions. On the contrary, Bousoño's skepticism seems to have grown with the passing of time.

José María Valverde (born 1926) has also written religious poetry: *Hombre de Dios* (1945, Man of God) and *Voces y acompañamientos para San Mateo* (1956, Voices and Music for Saint Matthew). In *Versos del domingo* (1954, Sunday Verses) he turned his attention to everyday life and household objects. Valverde's combination of sensitivity and a Franciscan-like feeling of brotherhood made for an ideal approach to these homely interests. *Enseñanzas de la edad: Poesía 1945–1970* (What the Years Can Teach: Poems 1945–1970), an anthology of Valverde poems published in 1971, contained his best earlier poetry and also included some excellent previously unpublished material, such as *El profesor de español* (The Professor of Spanish), in which Valverde showed himself to be a social and cultural critic.

Two major poets, both active before the war, were both important influences in what I have called the existential wave: Gerardo Diego (born 1896) and Vicente Aleixandre (born 1898). Diego is a Janus-like poet, both surrealistic and classical. In *Alondra de verdad* (1941, True Lark) his poetic emotion was expressed in technically flawless sonnets. *Amazona* (1955, Amazon) was a colder book. In many of his poems, Diego has been too far removed from everyday life. *Amor solo* (1958, Only Love) was an exception: the poet has fallen in love with a young girl and sings this love without restraint. Of the two tendencies inside the poet's soul—the surrealistic and the classical—the classical seems to have won out in Diego's recent poetry. Yet he has retained a playful, whimsical attitude, piercing through rhetoric, which has exerted a healthy influence upon younger poets.

Vicente Aleixandre is more central to contemporary Spanish poetry—and more influential. For years he was the very incarnation of poetry to the younger generation of poets. A member of Lorca's generation, he bridged the gap left by the war and the exile of so many other poets and almost singlehandedly established a continuity in Spanish poetry. Aleixandre shared with Jorge Guillén and Federico García Lorca an exposure to pure poetry, surrealism, and intellectual poetry. Before the civil war Aleixandre had a highly individualistic and irrational view of the cosmos; his poetry was basically erotic and, if I may say so, selfish: the poet made of love, of his love, the beginning and end of all things. He wanted to fuse himself with the universe, and love was his means. Love and death were but two sides of the same coin.

A change took place in Aleixandre's poetry after the war. In *Sombra del paraíso* (1944, Shadow of Paradise) he tried to escape from a cold, cruel civilization by returning to a primitive world, the world as it was before man appeared. In *Shadow of Paradise* innocence is the essence of this world, and the world's tragedy is that innocence does not last forever. In his postwar books of poems Aleixandre has tried to correct the imbalance of his early poems: matter was too important; minerals, the sea, air, were placed at the center of his world. Now man has become important. In his universal love, Aleixandre concentrates on man's existential and social problems: this was the message of *Historia del corazón* (1954, Heart's Story). Man is an historical being, time corrodes his existence, and only love and pity can heal the wounds time has opened. In *En un vasto dominio* (1962, In a Vast Realm) Aleixandre found a reconciliation between man and creation. Death must be accepted stoically. Through fusion with the universe, composed of one single material in spite of appearances, man can also become eternal.

Aleixandre is both a great erotic poet and a nature poet. He is also one of the greatest philosophical poets in Spanish literature, a modern Lucretius. His poems, if read from beginning to end, evaluate man's place in the cosmos, define all creation, and sing of the communion of men, as temporal beings, with the universe and with other men; only in such communion can man endure and become eternal. Through his difficult symbolic and visionary imagery, derived mainly from dreams and surrealism, Aleixandre has managed to unify realities that seemed irreconcilable. Not unlike William Blake, in Aleixandre the "marriage of Heaven and Hell" appears as a possibility; chaos is but one aspect of order; love and communion accept—and transcend—death.

Aleixandre's poetry therefore provides a good transition to the next movement in contemporary Spanish poetry—socially committed poetry. Perhaps the most typical poet of this group is Blas de Otero (born 1916). His first book, however, belongs to the earlier, "metaphysical" period. *Ángel fieramente humano* (1950, A Fiercely Human Angel) presented a metaphysical void that is but a prelude to a dialogue with God. In this work there were occasional echoes of Miguel de Unamuno's anguished attempts to communicate with God—or even to argue with him. Nihilism seems to have taken over more often than not in his next book, *Redoble de conciencia* (1951, My Conscience Is a Drum). In *Pido la paz y la palabra* (1955, I Want Peace, I Want the Floor) a new Otero emerged, socially committed and politically oriented, a man for whom poetry became a weapon with which to fight hunger and injustice.

Otero's art has become increasingly direct and artless. Yet his power to communicate has grown with each new book. In *En castellano* (1960, Written in Spanish) and *Esto no es un libro* (1963, This Is Not a Book) he made further strides along the path of committed poetry. *Que trata de España* (1964, Dealing with Spain) was an attempt, on the whole successful, to find poetry and meaning out of Spanish geography: the names of towns, rivers, mountains. The prose work *Expresión y reunión* (1969, Expression and Friendship) described Otero's travels and was a partial autobiography.

Blas de Otero's evolution has taken him from the general and abstract to the immediate and concrete, from metaphysics to brotherhood, from God to Marxism. He is a master craftsman of the Spanish language. His vocabulary is uncommonly vast. He knows how to make the best use of alliteration, puns, repetition, punctuation. His images are often unusual and startling. He has stated that his poems are meant to be recited to a nonliterary public rather than read: they are meant for the masses. We might define Otero's art as a cross between Unamuno's anguished metaphysical questioning and Mayakovski's political appeals to human solidarity. Otero's poetry is concise, spartan, sharp, even harsh. Whatever musical elements in it are purposefully dissonant. His alliterations sound like the rolling of drums, the clashing of cymbals, the loud blare of trumpets, martial music to a vast parade, the gathering of crowds in a huge bacchanalia of brotherhood.

Gabriel Celaya (born 1911, pseudonym of Rafael Múgica) is, like Blas de Otero, a northerner, a Basque, and a poet committed to the masses, to freedom, to leftist causes. His first book of poetry, *Marea del silencio* (1935, Tide of Silence) appeared just before the civil war. After many years of silence he has become, since 1946, one of the most prolific—one might almost say most "professional"—of contemporary Spanish poets. *Tentativas* (Attempts) appeared in 1946. Eroticism, symbolism, and a flowing poetic discourse were the ingredients of this mature work, which was really a prose poem. *Movimientos elementales* (1947, Elementary Motions) gave further proof of his imagination, his verve, his enthusiasm. In 1948 he published both *La soledad cerrada* (Close Loneliness), probably written around 1936, and *Objetos poéticos* (Poetic Objects).

Celaya, an engineer by profession, has been interested in matter, space, mathematical relationships. This can be seen in *Las cosas como son* (1949, Things as They Really Are), *Deriva* (1951, Drift), and *Las cartas boca arriba* (1951, Cards on the Table). From 1953 to 1968 Celaya published thirteen volumes. The best were *Paz y concierto* (1953, Peace and Harmony), *Cantos iberos* (1955, Iberian Songs), *Las resistencias del diamante* (1958, A Diamond's Hardness), and *Los espejos transparentes* (1968, Transparent Mirrors).

Lírica de cámara (Chamber Music), published in 1969, was perhaps Celaya's most original recent book. In it he commented, sometimes wittily and at times poignantly, on aspects of modern physics—ions, particles, atoms—and on parallel phenomena in man's mind. Celaya's poetic gifts are many: a vivid imagination; a zest for life that allows him to see truth and beauty in the most prosaic objects and commonplace situations; a language that, although often direct, is seldom artless. His art is radically different from that of Blas de Otero—much closer perhaps to the art of Pablo Neruda—since Otero's poetry is sparse, concentrated, while Celaya's is diffuse, abundant, full of detail.

Besides these two leaders, Otero and Celaya, there are several other important socially oriented poets. One of them is Victoriano Cremer (born 1910), who in *La espada y la pared* (1949, The Sword and the Wall) and *Furia y paloma* (1956, Fury and a Dove) made vibrant aggressive statements about man's injustice and cruelty. Another socially committed poet, Eugenio de Nora (born 1923), in *España, pasión de vida* (1954, Spain, a Lifelong Passion) mingled indignation with hope, love with wrath. Also a committed poet is Ángel González (born 1925), whose *Aspero mundo* (1955, Harsh World) and *Sin esperanza, con convencimiento* (1962, Without Hope, with Conviction) were startling in their wit, their passion, their mastery of language.

Gloria Fuertes (born 1918), in like manner, in *Todo asusta* (1958, Everything Frightens Us) and in her anthology, . . . *Que estás en la tierra* (1962, . . . Who Art on Earth), used colloquial language, humor, and a description of the alienated life of the poor to make a case against social injustice. Equally committed to social change is Ángela Figuera (born 1902), who, in *Belleza cruel* (1958, Cruel Beauty) and *Toco la tierra* (1962, I Touch the Earth), opposed motherhood to a world that menaces the young through war and frustration. Another important woman poet, Concha Zardoya (born 1914) has published critical essays and translations as well as such excellent books of poetry as *El desterrado ensueño* (1955, Exiled Dream) and *Corral de vivos y muertos* (1967, A Back Yard for the Living and the Dead). Grief, nostalgia, elegy, description of plastic beauty—these have been major elements in her mature art. Concha Lagos (born 1913), in *Los anales* (1966, The Annals), *Diario de un*

hombre (1970, Diary of a Man) and *El cerco* (1971, The Siege), combined her delicate Andalusian sensitivity with her interest in philosophical
and existential questions.

José Hierro (born 1922) is hard to classify. No one doubts his rank: he
is among the best contemporary Spanish poets. Is he socially or politically
committed? This is far from clear, especially in his recent collections.
Hierro is perhaps committed to one goal: to find meaning to man's existence, to define something in man—whether it be hope, art, or song—that
will make it possible to endure pain and the ceaseless flow of time. Clear,
with a minimum of rhetorical tricks, his simple and direct poetry has often
been profound and touching. His major works include *Tierra sin nosotros*
(1947, Land without Us), *Alegría* (1947, Joy), *Quinta del 42* (1953, The
Draftees of 1942), and *Cuanto sé de mí* (1957, All I Know about Myself). In 1962, a collected edition of Hierro's poetry was published—
Poesías completas 1944–1962 (Complete Poems 1944–1962). Hierro has
classified his poems in two groups: "reporting poems," that is, poems
describing something he has witnessed; and "hallucinations," or purely
subjective and imaginary poems.

One cannot write an account of Spanish poetry after the civil war without mentioning the great poets who left Spain after the war: León Felipe
(1884–1968, pseudonym of León Felipe Camino), Juan Ramón Jiménez,
Jorge Guillén, Pedro Salinas, and Rafael Alberti.

León Felipe, a torrential, passionate poet, described his bitter experiences of the war and exile in *El hacha* (1939, The Hatchet), *Español del
éxodo y del llanto* (1939, Spaniard of Exile and Tears), *El gran respon-
sable* (1940, The Guilty One), and—most importantly—*Ganarás la luz*
(1943, Thou Shalt Earn Thy Light), perhaps his best book. His *Antología
rota* (Broken Anthology) was published in 1947, *Llamadme publicano*
(Call Me a Publican) in 1950, *El ciervo* (The Stag) in 1958, *Oh, este
viejo y roto violín* (Oh, This Old Broken-Down Violin) in 1968. The two
great influences on Felipe were the Bible and Walt Whitman. The main
traits of his poems were verbal violence, a cosmic imagination, and a
somewhat proselike expression.

Jorge Guillén, a member of Lorca's generation, added to his international stature by publishing some of his best books in exile, including the
third and fourth enlarged editions of *Cántico* (Canticle) in 1945 and
1950; *Huerto de Melibea* (Melibea's Garden) in 1954; *Clamor* (Clamor),
in three parts, published in 1957, 1960, and 1963; finally a magnum
opus, *Aire nuestro: Cántico, Clamor, Homenaje* (Our Air: Canticle,
Clamor, Homage), published in 1968—1698 pages long. A short volume,
Guirnalda civil (A Civic Garland) appeared in 1970.

Although some of Guillén's poetic roots go back to Valéry, Mallarmé,
and the symbolist tradition, he also owes a poetic debt to two great Castil-

ian poets: Garcilaso and San Juan de la Cruz (1542–1591). Guillén's first poems (in *Canticle,* which appeared in its first form in 1928), were joyful, luminous celebrations of reality. In his most recent works (*Clamor, A Civic Garland*) the modern world, war, and oppression have made the poet's voice less serene.

Guillén has been called an absolute poet, one seeking to express fundamental laws. In his verse we can always find a dialogue between the poet and the world around him. If Guillén had written only *Canticle,* we could claim that he is the poet of being—just as we could claim that Aleixandre is the poet of becoming, of evolution. Guillén has remained faithful to his fascination with being, the absolute, joy, beauty. Yet he has also recognized man's imperfections, his limitations, his gropings for power. Hence *Clamor,* which does not oppose *Canticle,* as we might believe at first sight, but enlarges the poet's vision of man and history. *Clamor* often reveals a "wounded world," a dramatic, chaotic universe. Therefore, it deals with the effort and the pain of "becoming" in the modern era. The unifying trait is an attitude of wonder: the joyful Guillén is astonished by being, the critical Guillén is astonished by becoming in the middle of chaos and anguish. As a bridge between these two moods, the *Homage* section of *Our Air* reemphasizes the poet's clarity of thought, his sympathy, and his compassion.

Juan Ramón Jiménez, the great Andalusian poet who won the Nobel Prize in 1956, left Spain during the civil war and lived in various countries of the western hemisphere. Among his last books, the most outstanding were *La estación total* (1946, The Total Season), in which he perfected his "simple" style, and *Animal de fondo* (1949, Animal at the Bottom of the Sea), an extraordinary attempt to express metaphysical experiences. In *Animal at the Bottom of the Sea* an attitude of lyrical pantheism brought Jiménez to celebrate the union of the "eternal whole," as he puts it, with the "internal whole."

Pedro Salinas also died in exile. During his years away from Spain he published two important poetic works: *El contemplado* (1945, The Contemplated Sea) and *Todo más claro* (1949, Everything Is Clearer). *The Contemplated Sea* was an intense, quasimystical description of his experiences by the sea in Puerto Rico. *Everything Is Clearer* dealt with modern life, often critically and ironically. Salinas also wrote several valuable books of literary and social criticism and several plays, as well as novellas and short stories. He is the only member of his generation who contributed to all genres.

Rafael Alberti, another great poet of the Lorca group, has also fulfilled in exile his early promise. His most important volumes published in exile have been *Entre el clavel y la espada* (1941, Between a Carnation and a Sword), *A la pintura* (1948, Ode to Painting), *Retornos de lo vivo lejano*

(1952, Memories of the Living Past), and *Roma, peligro para caminantes* (1968, Rome, Dangerous for Pedestrians). Alberti's poetry is often simple, direct, and remarkably effective in its rendition of musical and pictorial imagery. Alberti has also written several interesting plays: *La gallarda* (1940, The Handsome Woman), *El adefesio* (1944, The Monster), *El trébol florido* (1946, Flowering Clover), and *Noche de guerra en el Museo del Prado* (1956, Night of War in the Prado Museum), in all of which a surrealist style often became a vehicle for social criticism.

Luis Cernuda (1904–1963) published in exile in 1958 an enlarged edition of his early book, *La realidad y el deseo* (Reality and Desire). *Ocnos el alfarero* (Ocnos the Potter) had appeared in 1942. *La desolación de la quimera* (The Desolate Chimera) was published in 1962, one year before Cernuda's death. Exile made his last poems either nostalgic or bitterly critical. Another exiled poet was Emilio Prados (1899–1962). Andalusian by birth, Prados's subjects were nostalgia, dreams, the landscape of southern Spain. Outstanding among his books written in exile (all published in Mexico) were *Jardín cerrado* (1946, Enclosed Garden) and *Signos del ser* (1962, Signs of Being). Manuel Altolaguirre (1905–1959) contributed *Fin de un amor* (1946, The End of a Love Affair) and *Poemas en América* (1955, American Poems).

The younger poets living in Spain are hard to classify and difficult to single out: each year many new names appear, and of these only a few will survive the test of time. José Ángel Valente (born 1929) has written *A modo de esperanza* (1955, A Kind of Hope), *Poemas a Lázaro* (1960, Poems to Lazarus), *La memoria y los signos* (1966, Memory and Signs) and *Siete representaciones* (1967, Seven Representations). His dry, ironic style is sometimes reminiscent of José Hierro. Valente has combined social criticism with a subtle subjective vision of existential man.

Claudio Rodríguez (born 1934), in *Don de la ebriedad* (1953, The Gift of Drunkenness), *Conjuros* (1958, Spells), and *Alianza y condena* (1965, Alliance and Condemnation), showed himself to be a gifted poet in the Castilian tradition—sober and precise. He has also conveyed a deep pity for modern man. Carlos Barral (born 1928) has published, among other works, *Las aguas reiteradas* (1952, Incessant Waters) and *Metropolitano* (1957, Metropolitan). His satire and his social comments can be amusing and biting.

An anthology by the well-known critic José María Castellet, *Nueve novísimos* (1970, Nine Brand-new Poets), emphasized the importance of several young poets who form a coherent literary movement, as yet unnamed, which many observers find promising but which others reject as irritating. These poets make use of automatic writing, elliptical techniques, syncopation, collages, "pop" culture, "camp" subjects, names and places found in newspaper headlines. They have read Marshall McLuhan and the

Italian critic Umberto Eco. Their poems are often amusing, frequently outrageous. The most promising members of this group are Manuel Vázquez Montalbán (born 1939), who has written *Una educación sentimental* (1967, A Sentimental Education), *Movimientos sin éxito* (1970, Movements without Success), and *Manifiesto subnormal* (1970, Subnormal Manifesto); and Pedro Gimferrer (born 1945), who has written *Arde el mar* (1966, The Sea on Fire) and *La muerte en Beverly Hills* (1968, Death in Beverly Hills).

DRAMA

Spanish drama since the civil war has been less interesting than poetry or fiction. This has partly been the result of censorship, which has been especially harsh toward the drama: it is rumored that several important plays languish in the desk drawers of their authors, having been suppressed by the censors. Another reason is the social nature of the theater. Spanish society has undergone a difficult period after the war, one in which hypocrisy and the pressures of politics and economics have produced a demand for escapist or innocuous plays. Be that as it may, one can, nevertheless, compile a substantial list of gifted playwrights and noteworthy plays.

It is tempting to classify today's Spanish theater into two broad categories: escapist comedies and serious drama. Yet the oldest of the post-civil-war playwrights defies such a classification. Alejandro Casona (1903–1965), exiled after the war, continued his brilliant career as a playwright in South America. His plays were always well constructed, and his tricks never failed to please the public. He has been accused of being too sentimental and even melodramatic. Yet his blend of fantasy, poetry, and serious dramatic situations created some memorable plays: *La dama del alba* (1944, The Lady of Dawn), a poetic vision of the mystery of death; *La barca sin pescador* (1945, The Boat without a Fisherman), a drama about greed, evil, and the devil; and *Los árboles mueren de pie* (1949, Trees Die Standing Up), a play about the fortitude and courage of an old woman. A year before his death, Casona returned to Spain, and his last play, *El caballero de las espuelas de oro* (The Knight with Golden Spurs), was a great success when it was produced in 1966. The play dramatized the life of Francisco de Quevedo (1580–1645), the great Golden Age writer.

Antonio Buero Vallejo (born 1916) began writing plays only after the civil war. *Historia de una escalera* (The Story of a Staircase), acclaimed in 1949, was the first major play of the contemporary Spanish theater. A realistic drama about mediocrity, frustrations, and the lack of social mobility, it was well constructed and convincing. *En la ardiente oscuridad*

(1950, In Burning Darkness) was an even better play, both realistic and allegorical, about love and hatred in a school for the blind. *Un soñador para un pueblo* (1958, A Dreamer for the People) was a strong historical drama set in eighteenth-century Spain, about political reform and its drawbacks. *La doble historia del doctor Valmy* (1964, The Double History of Doctor Valmy) was too didactic to be entirely successful. Buero Vallejo is at his best when, as in *In Burning Darkness,* his thesis is stated ambiguously.

Alfonso Sastre (born 1926), the author of such successful dramas as *Escuadra hacia la muerte* (1953, Squad toward Death), *La cornada* (1960, The Goring), and *Guillermo Tell tiene los ojos tristes* (1963, Sad Are the Eyes of William Tell), is, like Buero Vallejo, a playwright with a social message—the need to fight injustice and oppression. In *Sad Are the Eyes of William Tell,* Tell's arrow pierces his son's forehead, not the apple. The spectators then, indignant, topple the cruel ruler who had been responsible for this act. This allegorical play was dramatically effective.

If Buero Vallejo and Sastre represent the group of serious, committed playwrights at its best, the rival school—the uncommitted playwrights of comedies—can boast writers as popular as Miguel Mihura (born 1905) and Alfonso Paso (born 1926). Mihura has written some of the most amusing comedies of the modern Spanish stage, plays that are fast-paced, relevant to our times, full of surprises: *Tres sombreros de copa* (1952, Three Top Hats), *Maribel y la extraña familia* (1959, Maribel and the Strange Family), *La bella Dorotea* (1963, Beautiful Dorothy). Mihura was also one of the founders and directors of the popular humor magazine *La codorniz.*

Alfonso Paso, who came from a theatrical family, has certainly been the most prolific, and probably the most applauded, Spanish playwright of our era. He knows all the tricks of the trade. More a great craftsman than an artist, Paso has always managed to find the right formula to please his public. Among his almost innumerable plays are *Los pobrecitos* (1947, The Poor Ones), *El cielo dentro de casa* (1950, Heaven at Home), and *Por lo menos tres* (1968, At Least Three).

The *enfant terrible* of the Spanish stage is indisputably Fernando Arrabal (born 1932). Deeply traumatized as a child by the civil war, in which his father, a career officer, disappeared mysteriously, Arrabal turned as a young man to black humor and the theater of the absurd. His first plays—such as *Fando y Lis* (1953, Fando and Lis) and *La tricicleta* (1954, The Tricycle)—were so poorly received by Spanish audiences—judged offensive and in bad taste—that in 1955 he left Spain to live in Paris. He has remained there, writing in French ever since. Today Arrabal is famous (or perhaps notorious, as some of his detractors would have it) in international theater circles. Arrabal has great talent, and although his plays are compared with those of Ionesco, with whom he has much in common, Arrabal's Spanish roots—reflected in his obsessions with death, religion, and sensuality—are clear.

Experimental playwrights are not too numerous in the Spanish stage, if we except Arrabal. One of the best young experimental authors is José María Bellido (born 1922), whose *Tren a F . . .* (1964, Train to F . . .) was a political and social allegory reminiscent of both Kafka and some of Alfonso Sastre's plays. The play depicts an imaginary country, a vast barren plain being crossed by a train whose passengers are traveling toward F (Felicidad [Happiness]?—perhaps everyone's private dreams). The train, alas, frequently and inexplicably breaks down. The people on the train are both travelers and shareholders in the railroad company. What keeps the company in business is the belief of all the passengers that only the trains belonging to the company have access to a tunnel, which happens to be the only access to F. Both religion and the authoritarian state are the targets of this witty play.

José Ruibal's (born 1925) *El asno electrónico* (1968, The Electronic Jackass), which the author called "a pocket opera," was in the genre of the political cabaret skit, dealing with the American exploitation of Spain. Ruibal was probably inspired by Brecht's *The Threepenny Opera*. Nonetheless, Ruibal's play was original, amusing, and biting. Another of Ruibal's plays, *El hombre y la mosca* (1969, The Man and the Fly), takes place in a mythical country ruled for seventy "peaceful" years by El Hombre, a dictator who is creating and training a double inside a huge glass dome, in which both the dictator and his double remain insulated from the outside world. The double is supposed to carry on his work after El Hombre's death and thus create the myth of his immortality. A fly penetrates the dome and the project collapses, because the double turns out to be a coward, afraid of the fly.

Antonio Martínez Ballesteros's (born 1929) *El héroe* (1965, The Hero), was a cynical play about human motivations. With sardonic irony, the author showed the official hero to be exactly the opposite in his private life. Martínez Ballesteros's plays have been largely based on a contrast between opposites, and they consequently have lacked the psychological subtlety in characterization that is the strength of José Ruibal's plays.

THE ESSAY

The Spanish essay has suffered in these last decades from the same drawbacks that have affected the Spanish drama: both censorship and the relative isolation from international intellectual currents of the 1940s. Recovery has been slow and is yet incomplete. Some of the great essayists already famous before the war, however, have helped bridge the gap. Among the well established, the most prominent were Ramón Menéndez Pidal (1869–1968), Eugenio D'Ors (1882–1954), José Ortega y Gasset, and Américo Castro (born 1885).

Menéndez Pidal continued, after the civil war, his research on Spain's language, history, and culture. Among his numerous works were *La epopeya castellana a través de la literatura española* (1945, Castilian Epic Poems in Spanish Literature) and *El torno al Poema del Cid* (1963, Concerning the Poem of the Cid). Menéndez Pidal's works were characterized by a scrupulous attention to historical details and a positivistic attitude, which was not, however, devoid of artistic sensitivity.

Eugenio D'Ors continued after the civil war to develop his famous yardstick—"Whatever has not been inspired by tradition is plagiarism"—in brilliant, although arbitrary, essays on aesthetics, among which the most noteworthy was *La ciencia de la cultura* (The Science of Culture), published posthumously in 1964. Eugenio D'Ors's influence is now on the wane.

The influence of José Ortega y Gasset on Spanish readers also has diminished since 1940, in spite of the fact that he returned from exile in 1954. A brilliant writer, never lacking for ideas, Ortega wrote some very rewarding books after the civil war. Among them were *Papeles sobre Velázquez y Goya* (1950, Writings on Velázquez and Goya), a psychological and historical interpretation of the art of these two painters and of the times that produced them. Less successful was his ambitious attempt at a sociological theory, *El hombre y la gente* (Man and People), published posthumously in 1957. *Idea del teatro* (The Essence of the Stage) also appeared after Ortega's death, in 1958. Two essential qualities combined to give the prose of Ortega its great distinction: clarity and elegance. Both qualities were enhanced by a frequent use of well-chosen metaphors, which were employed not only as a literary ornament but also as a means of facilitating the understanding of any given idea. Through metaphor, Ortega's style acquired an almost baroque brilliance. Moreover, his metaphors made his most difficult philosophical concepts accessible to the nonspecialist.

The philologist and literary historian Américo Castro's massive book *España en su historia: Cristianos, moros y judíos* (1948, Spain in Its History: Christians, Moors, Jews) was a vast synthesis of Spanish medieval culture. Castro's thesis was that during the centuries in which Spaniards were slowly shaping their national identity and their culture a pluralistic society formed by three different religious groups was bound to give birth to a peculiar system of values, as different from the oriental one as from the system of values of other western cultures. Castro's theories were founded on solid erudition and were developed with imagination and even passion. Although controversial from time to time, his ideas were often convincing, offering a new, dramatic view of Spanish history. *La realidad histórica de España* (1953, Spain's Historic Reality) continued this line of thought and offered further proof of Castro's masterly scholarship.

Gregorio Marañón (1887–1960) was both a scientist—a doctor of medicine and a biologist—and a humanist. In addition to medical publications, he wrote many works that combined his biological knowledge with his interest in social and historical problems. Since the civil war, he published *El Greco y Toledo* (1957, El Greco and Toledo) a sensitive yet scholarly reconstruction of Spanish life in the sixteenth century, and *Antonio Pérez* (1947, Antonio Pérez), a brilliant study of Philip II and his court. The value of Marañón's scientific works should not overshadow his importance as a man of letters. His essays were easy to read, thought-provoking, and persuasive.

Pedro Laín Entralgo (born 1908) is also both a scientist and a humanist. He has published important philosophical essays, such as *La espera y la esperanza* (1956, Waiting and Hoping) and *Teoría y realidad del otro* (1961, Theory and Reality of Otherness). He has combined philosophy, existentialism, and metaphysics with shrewd sociological and scientific observations. Perhaps the most important contribution by Laín Entralgo to literature is his fine study *La generación del 98* (1945, The Generation of 1898).

Julián Marías (born 1914) is Ortega y Gasset's foremost disciple and in some ways has inherited Ortega's position and prestige. A prolific author, he writes clearly and often elegantly. His major works have been *Historia de la filosofía* (1941, History of Philosophy), *Miguel de Unamuno* (1943, Miguel de Unamuno), *El método histórico de las generaciones* (1949, Generations: A Historical Method), *La estructura social* (1955, The Social Structure), *Ortega: Circunstancia y vocación* (1960, Ortega: Circumstance and Vocation).

José Luis Aranguren (born 1909), a professor of ethics, has published numerous essays and studies marked by a desire to expound from a Catholic viewpoint the problems of present-day society, especially within the aesthetic, moral, and religious spheres. These works have included *Catolicismo y protestantismo como formas de existencia* (1952, Catholicism and Protestantism as Forms of Existence), *Catolicismo día tras día* (1955, Catholicism Day by Day), and *La juventud europea, y otros ensayos* (1961, European Youth, and Other Essays).

Also prominent among the philosophical essayists is José Ferrater Mora (born 1912), author of a voluminous *Diccionario de la filosofía* (1941, Dictionary of Philosophy), *Cuatro visiones de la historia universal* (1945, Four Views of Universal History), and *El hombre en la encrucijada*

(1952, Man at the Crossroads)—all of which revealed a keen interest in the current problems of mankind.

In literary criticism two writers have made outstanding contributions: Dámaso Alonso and Guillermo de Torre (1900–1969). Dámaso Alonso, already discussed as a poet, is a first-rank literary critic, both scholarly and intuitive. His major critical works have been *La poesía de San Juan de la Cruz* (1942, The Poetry of San Juan de la Cruz), *Ensayos sobre poesía española* (1944, Essays on Spanish Poetry), *Poesía española: Ensayo de métodos estilísticos* (1950, Spanish Poetry: Essays on Stylistic Methods), and *Góngora y el "Polifemo"* (1960, Gongora and "Polifemo"). Guillermo de Torre's main subject was the study of modern literary trends. Outstanding among his numerous works have been *La metamórfosis de Proteo* (1956, The Metamorphosis of Proteus), *Claves de la literatura hispanoamericana* (1959, Keys to Spanish American Literature), and the definitive *Historia de las literaturas de vanguardia* (1965, A History of Avant-Garde Literature).

If we take into account the almost insurmountable obstacles that existed in Spain at the beginning of the contemporary period, the renascence of Spanish literature is remarkable. A devastating war, the exile of some of the country's best minds, an almost total isolation of nearly a decade from international cultural trends, a harsh repressive regime that made censorship into a permanent weapon of control—these conditions all had to be surmounted. Little by little, progress was made.

On the material side, the improvement of the economy has allowed Spanish publishers to regain their old preeminence in the Spanish-speaking world. Books are being produced in ever-increasing quantities: new titles can reach the impressive figure of 20,000 annually (which is comparable to that of France), and an important percentage of these new titles are works of literature. Literary prizes, almost unknown before the war, are now awarded on a regular basis and have become an important stimulus to creation, especially in the field of fiction.

Spain has now more writers and more readers than before the civil war. But the development has been uneven. Certain genres, such as fiction and poetry, are flourishing. The drama and the essay, on the other hand, are lagging behind. The two major achievements of the last thirty years were the development of a fiction that is at the same time realistic and imaginative, and the sustained high level of poetry. The last five years have witnessed the birth of new experimental trends—in fiction (perhaps because of the influence of the new Latin American novelists) and in poetry. The drama and the essay are also evolving rapidly toward a freer, less traditional approach.

CATALAN LITERATURE

The image of the phoenix rising from its ashes well suits the progress of Catalan literature during the past thirty years. In 1939, at the end of the civil war in Spain, Catalan culture was in ruins. The Franco regime had decreed that it should be destroyed, since most of its leaders had been allied to the Spanish republic. Catalan culture thus became a forbidden culture in a conquered part of Spain, a culture that had flowered in the Middle Ages, hibernated for three centuries, and slowly rose again during the nineteenth century, nurtured by the bourgeois wealth of Barcelona, yet with its roots firmly planted in the Catalan countryside.

The political and military defeat in 1939 seemed to spell total ruin. The Catalan language could no longer be taught in schools. Catalan books could not be published. Yet the Franco regime could not destroy essences so easily. Catalan identity has flowered again, against great odds. Slowly but steadily, victories have been won, permissions have been obtained, books and even magazines have managed to appear.

The tempo quickened during the 1960s. Local prosperity and increasing tolerance from Madrid brought forth a flow of publications. According to the Spanish Book Institute, more than 5,000 books in Catalan appeared between 1939 and 1969, and almost half of the titles were of books in the fields of literature and belles lettres. Talent and stubbornness won the day: Catalan literature has become once again significant, not only for Catalonia but for the whole Iberian peninsula. For Catalan literature is now, as it was in the past, the bedrock of identity for the most active and forward-looking minority in Spain, and a bridge between Iberian culture and the rest of western Europe.

POETRY

In the quest for identity and influence Catalan poetry has played the major role. In the nineteenth century such poets as Jacint Verdaguer (1845–1902) and Joan Maragall (1860–1911) were the leading voices in Catalan literature. Since World War II, two great poets reached their peaks—but in exile: Josep Carner (1884–1969) and Carles Riba (1893–1959).

Carner was perhaps the quintessential Catalan poet: sensuous, sensitive, learned, ironic, generous, true to his origins—both provincial and universal. *Nabí* (1947, The Seer) and *Obres completes* (1957–67, Complete Works) have increased Carner's influence.

Carles Riba was perhaps more learned, more subtle than Carner. His *Elegies de Bierville* (1943, The Bierville Elegies) re-created classical sensitivity in modern terms. Riba's poems remind us of Paul Valéry in French poetry, Jorge Guillén in Spanish poetry, and Giuseppe Ungaretti in Italian poetry. Like them, he brought the symbolist style to its utmost refinement. In Riba's poetry, intelligence and elegance devolved around a core of sensitivity, of human experience, and this experience could be tragic and heroic.

Unlike the exiled Carner and Riba, Josep Maria de Sagarra (1894–1961) remained in Catalonia. Also a major influence, Sagarra turned toward tradition. There was nothing contrived or deliberately modern in his poetry, only a consistent quality in style and a boundless love for the Catalan landscape, traditions, and attitudes.

Mariá Manent (born 1898), a friend and follower of Josep Carner, has also translated poetry and has written literary criticism. He has written very few poems, but they are outstanding. Tomás Garcés (born 1901) developed his sensuous visions along lines reminiscent of the Spanish poet Luis Cernuda. Under the serene surface of images of the sea, of "pure" poetry, of Platonic beauty lies a deep dissatisfaction.

Josep Vicens Foix (born 1894), although of the Carner-Riba generation, has used a much more modern, more experimental style. Influenced perhaps by Éluard and the surrealists, he has turned each poem into a quest, an adventure in the land of mystery, dreams, and death. His descriptions remind us of Dali's landscapes. *Les irreals omegues* (1949, Unreal Omegas) has been his best book to date. Foix's other important works have included *On he deixat les claus* (1953, Where Did I Leave the Keys?) and *Obres poètiques* (1964, Poetic Works). Foix, who has been translated into several languages, has perhaps been the most original Catalan poet of the twentieth century.

Pere Quart (born 1899) is second only to Foix in his importance as an innovator. *Terra de naufragis* (1956, Land of Shipwrecks), *Vacances pagades* (1960, Paid Vacations), and *Obres de Pere Quart* (1963, Works by Pere Quart) were permeated by Quart's sardonic wit and black humor.

Agustí Bartra (born 1908), who has written novels and plays as well as poems, recently returned to Catalonia. He published many books of poetry in exile: *L'arbre de foc* (1946, Tree of Fire), *Marsias i Adila* (1948, Marsias and Adila), *L'evangeli del vent* (1956, The Wind's Gospel), *Odisseu* (1953, Ulysses [prose poems]), *Poemes* (1954, Poems), and *Doso* (1970, Doso). Bartra has both imagination and power. Although his dream images were indebted to surrealism, his intense interest in classical culture has brought him in contact with the Greek myths. Bartra has managed to express the essence of the Mediterranean past in a modern poetic language.

Salvador Espriu (born 1913) started his literary career as a writer of short stories. He has become perhaps the most significant and influential poet of the postwar period. Elegy, satire, and social criticism have been Espriu's major devices to convey his dark humor, his existential anguish, his sense of modern chaos. He can elevate a Catalan village, Arenys de Mar, into an archetypal setting, "Sinera," and listen to its critical, prophetic voices. Espriu's style is lean, intense, subtle. He writes for the "happy few"; yet his message has been transferred to and enlarged by the stage. A sequence of his poems has become a play, *Cementiri de Sinera* (1946, Sinera's Churchyard), which can be compared favorably to such works as Dylan Thomas's *Under Milk Wood*. A popular singer of protest folk songs, Raimon, has helped make Espriu's poetry known to the masses. Espriu's major works have been *Les cançons d'Ariadna* (1949, Ariadna's Songs), *La pell de brau* (1960, The Bull's Hide), and *Obres completes* (1968, Complete Works).

Joan Vinyoli (born 1914), an avid reader, may have been influenced by Rilke and Carles Riba. Outstanding among his works have been *De vida i somni* (1948, On Life and Dreams), *Les hores retrobades* (1951, The Found Hours), *El Callat* (1956, The Silent One), and *Realitats* (1963, Realities). Vinyoli has become progressively less symbolic and obscure, increasingly more enamored of commonplace objects, of everyday life.

Gabriel Ferrater (born 1922) has written poignant autobiographical poems. His *Les dones i els dies* (Women and Days) appeared in 1968. Blai Bonet (born 1926) is perhaps the best representative of religious poetry. In *Entre el coral i l'espiga* (1953, Between Coral and Wheat) and *L'evangeli segons un de tants* (1968, The Gospel According to a Copy) he used sensuous imagery to reach spiritual elevation.

PROSE

The two masters of contemporary Catalan fiction have been Josep Pla (born 1897) and Pere Calders (born 1912). Pla, a prolific writer, has written novels, essays, and travel books. One of his best novels was *El carrer estret* (1951, The Narrow Street), a slow, rambling description of the inhabitants of a street in a Catalan village. It reminds us of the Spanish novelist Pío Baroja at his best. In *Girona: Un llibre de records* (1952, Girona: A Book of Reminiscences) Pla combined autobiography with history to re-create the past. Some sections are reminiscent of Proust.

Pla's books are hard to classify; many of them are hybrids, part travelogue and part novel or autobiography. Pla is both a skeptic and a sensualist. His conception of the novel is an "objective" one: it should be a mirror of society. His power to re-create an environment or paint a landscape has been unequaled. This is due partly to his vast knowledge of the Catalan language. His vocabulary is one of the richest in modern Catalan literature.

Brevity and wit are the outstanding qualities of Pere Calders. He has published some of the funniest short stories in Catalan literature, such as *L'arbre domèstic* (1964, Domestic Tree). His sentences are short and devoid of anything that is not strictly relevant. His humor reminds us of Kafka and of surrealism. The absurd and the unexpected play a large role in Calders's fiction. His most important book, *Tots els contes* (Collected Short Stories), appeared in 1968.

Another major writer of fiction, Llorenç Villalonga (born 1897), a native of Mallorca, has written what is perhaps the best Catalan novel of the modern period, *Bearn* (1963, Bearn). Much like the Italian novel *Il gattopardo* by Giuseppe Tomasi di Lampedusa, *Bearn* described with irony, but not without tenderness, the downfall of an old family.

Another important Catalan novelist was Joan Puig i Ferreter (1882–1956), whose picaresque novel *Camins de França* (1934, French Roads) appeared before the civil war. After the war, Puig i Ferreter published an uneven yet powerful *roman fleuve, El pelegrí apassionat* (1955–62, The Passionate Pilgrim), in twelve volumes.

Manuel de Pedrolo (born 1918) is a prolific novelist who has also written short stories and plays. In his novels, such as *Es vessa una sang fàcil* (1953, Blood Easily Spilled), he has often used a realistic style to treat existential situations. Pedrolo also enjoys experimenting with reversals of time.

Jordi Sarsanedas (born 1924) is a subtle short-story writer of great imagination. His *Mites* (1954, Myths) and *El balcó* (1969, The Balcony) were in some ways reminiscent of the work of Henri Michaux and Kafka.

The poet Agustí Bartra is also an important prose writer. His novel *Crist de 200,000 braços* (1968, Christ with 200,000 Arms) described life in a French concentration camp for Spanish republican soldiers after the war. The prose poems in *Doso* re-created Homeric myths.

The *enfant terrible* of Catalan literature is Terenci Moix (born 1943), whose short stories and novels have been influenced by "pop" art, the comics, and the movies. His *La torre dels vicis capitals* (1967, The Tower of Capital Sins) and *Onades sobre una roca deserta* (1969, Waves on a Bare Rock) were often witty, always relevant.

Among writers who are primarily essayists, I would like to single out four: the critic and historian Joan Fuster (born 1922), who wrote *Nosaltres els valencians* (1962, We People from Valencia); the philosopher Josep Ferrater Mora (born 1912); and the historians Jaume Vicens Vives (1910–1960) and Ferran Soldevila (born 1892).

Thus, despite official persecution, Catalan literature has entered a period of expansion and is becoming, day by day, richer, more complex, more creative, and more influential—both inside and outside Catalonia.

SPANISH AND CATALAN WORKS IN ENGLISH TRANSLATION

INDIVIDUAL WORKS MENTIONED
IN ARTICLE

Alberti, Rafael. *Noche de guerra en el Museo del Prado* as *Night and War in the Prado Museum.* In Michael Benedikt and George Wellwarth, eds., *Modern Spanish Theatre.* New York, 1969

Alonso, Dámaso. *Hijos de la ira* as *Children of Wrath.* Baltimore, 1971

Arrabal, Fernando. *Fando y Lis* as *Fando and Lis.* In *Four Plays.* London, 1966

———. *La tricicleta* as *The Tricycle.* In *Guernica, and Other Plays.* New York, 1969

Aub, Max. *Jusep Torres Campalans* as *Jusep Torres Campalans.* Garden City, N.Y., 1962

Ayala, Franciso. *Muertes de perro* as *Death as a Way of Life.* New York, 1964

Ballesteros, Antonio Martínez. *El héroe* as *The Hero.* In George Wellwarth, ed., *The New Wave Spanish Drama.* New York, 1970

Barea, Arturo. *La forja de un rebelde* as *The Forging of a Rebel.* New York, 1946

Bellido, José María. *Tren a F . . .* as *Train to H . . .* In George Wellwarth, ed., *The New Wave Spanish Drama.* New York, 1970

Casona, Alejandro. *La barca sin pescador* as *The Boat without a Fisherman.* In Marion P. Holt, ed., *The Modern Spanish Stage: Four Plays.* New York, 1970

Castro, Américo. *España en su historia: Cristianos, moros y judíos* as *The Structure of Spanish History.* Princeton, N.J., 1954

Cela, Camilo José. *La colmena* as *The Hive.* New York, 1965

———. *La familia de Pascual Duarte* as *The Family of Pascual Duarte.* Boston, 1964

———. *Mrs. Caldwell habla con su hijo* as *Mrs. Caldwell Speaks to Her Son.* Ithaca, N.Y., 1968

———. *Pabellón de reposo* as *Rest Home.* New York, 1961

Delibes, Miguel. *El camino* as *The Path.* New York, 1961

———. *Las ratas* as *Smoke on the Ground.* Garden City, N.Y., 1972

Ferrater Mora, José. *El hombre en la encrucijada* as *Man at the Crossroads.* Boston, 1957

García Hortelano, Juan. *Tormenta de verano* as *Summer Storm.* New York, 1962

Gironella, José. *Los cipreses creen en Dios* as *The Cypresses Believe in God.* New York, 1955

———. *Ha estallado la paz* as *Peace after War.* New York, 1969

———. *Un millón de muertos* as *One Million Dead.* Garden City, N.Y., 1963

Goytisolo, Juan. *Duelo en el paraíso* as *Children of Chaos.* London, 1959

———. *Fiestas* as *Fiestas.* New York, 1960

———. *Fin de fiesta* as *The Party's Over.* New York, 1967

———. *La isla* as *Island of Women.* New York, 1962

———. *Juegos de manos* as *The Young Assassins.* New York, 1959

———. *Señas de identidad* as *Marks of Identity.* New York, 1969

Laforet, Carmen. *Nada* as *Andrea.* New York, 1964

Lera, Ángel María de. *Los clarines del miedo* as *The Horns of Fear.* New York, 1961

Marías, Julián. *Historia de la filosofía* as *History of Philosophy.* New York, 1967

———. *El método histórico de las generaciones* as *Generations: A Historical Method.* University, Ala., 1970

———. *Miguel de Unamuno* as *Miguel de Unamuno.* Cambridge, Mass., 1966

———. *Ortega: Circunstancia y vocación* as *Jose Ortega y Gasset: Circumstance and Vocation.* Norman, Okla., 1970

Martín-Santos, Luis. *Tiempo de silencio* as *Time of Silence.* New York, 1964

Matute, Ana María. *Primera memoria* as *Ana Maria: School of the Sun.* New York, 1963

Mihura, Miguel. *Tres sombreros de copa* as *Three Top Hats.* In Michael Benedikt and George Wellwarth, eds., *Modern Spanish Theatre.* New York, 1969

Ortega y Gasset, José. *El hombre y la gente* as *Man and People.* New York, 1957

Paso, Alfonso. *El cielo dentro de casa* as *Blue Heaven.* New York, 1962

Ruibal, José. *El asno electrónico* as *The Jackass.* In George Wellwarth, ed., *The New Wave Spanish Drama.* New York, 1970

———. *El hombre y la mosca* as *The Man and the Fly.* In George Wellwarth, ed., *The New Wave Spanish Drama.* New York, 1970

Salinas, Pedro. *El contemplado* as *Sea of San Juan: A Contemplation.* Boston, 1950

Sánchez Ferlosio, Rafael. *El Jarama* as *The One Day of the Week.* New York, 1962

Sastre, Alfonso. *La cornada* as *Death Thrust.* In Robert Corrigan, ed., *Masterpieces of the Modern Spanish Theatre.* New York, 1967

———. *Guillermo Tell tiene los ojos tristes* as *Sad Are the Eyes of William Tell.* In George Wellwarth, ed., *The New Wave Spanish Drama.* New York, 1970

———. *Escuadra hacia la muerte* as *The Condemned Squad.* In Marion P. Holt, ed., *The Modern Spanish Stage: Four Plays.* New York, 1970

Sender, Ramón. *Crónica del alba* as *Chronicle of Dawn.* In *Before Noon: A Novel in Three Parts.* Albuquerque, N.M., 1957

———. *La esfera* as *The Sphere.* New York, 1949

———. *Requiem por un campesino español* as *Requiem for a Spanish Peasant.* New York, 1960

———. *El Rey y la Reina* as *The King and the Queen.* New York, 1948

SECONDARY WORKS

BIBLIOGRAPHIES AND GUIDES

Bleiberg, Germán and Julián Marías, eds. *Diccionario de literatura española,* 4th ed. Madrid, 1971

Foster, David W. and Virginia. *Manual of Hispanic Bibliography.* Washington, D.C., 1970

Foulché-Delbosc, Raymond and Louis

Barrau-Dihigo. *Manuel de l'hispanisant,* 2 vols., new ed. New York, 1959

Newmark, Maxim. *A Dictionary of Spanish Literature.* New York, 1956

Sainz de Robles, Federico Carlos. *Ensayo de un diccionario de la literatura.* Vol. II: *Autores españoles e hispanoamericanos,* 2nd ed. Madrid, 1953

Serís Homero, Manuel de. *Bibliografía*

de la literatura española, 2 vols. New York, 1948–54

Simón, Díaz, José. *Bibliografía de la literatura hispanica,* 6 vols., 2nd ed. Madrid, 1960ff.

———. *Manual de bibliografía de la literatura española.* Barcelona, 1963 (supplement 1962–64. Barcelona, 1968)

GENERAL WORKS

Antón Andrés, Ángel. *Geschichte der spanischen Literatur vom 18. Jahrhundert bis zur Gegenwart.* Munich, 1961

Brenan, Gerald. *The Literature of the Spanish People,* 2nd ed. Cambridge, 1953

Cano, José Luis. *De Machado a Bousoño.* Madrid, 1955

———. *Poesía española del siglo XX.* Madrid, 1960

Castelltort, Ramón. *La poesía lírica española del siglo XX.* Barcelona, 1957

Chabás Marti, Juan. *Historia de la literatura española.* Havana, 1953

———. *Literatura española contemporánea: 1898–1950.* Havana, 1952

Chandler, Richard E. and Kessel Schwartz. *A New History of Spanish Literature.* Baton Rouge, La., 1961

Del Río, Ángel. *Historia de la literatura española,* 2 vols., 2nd ed. New York, 1963ff.

Descola, Jean. *Histoire littéraire de l'Espagne.* Paris, 1966

Díaz Plaja, Guillermo, ed. *Historia general de las literaturas hispanicas,* 7 vols. Barcelona, 1944ff.

Díez Echarri, E. and José M. Roca Franquesa. *Historia de la literatura española e hispanoamericana.* Madrid, 1960

Fitzmaurice-Kelly, James. *A New History of Spanish Literature,* 4th ed. New York, 1968

Franzbach, Martin. *Abriß der spanischen und portugiesischen Literaturgeschichte in Tabellen.* Bonn, 1968

Gallo, Ugo. *Storia della letteratura spagnola,* 2 vols. Milan, 1952

García López, José. *Historia de la literatura española,* 9th ed. Barcelona, 1965

Giese, Wilhelm. *Geschichte der spanischen und portugiesischen Literatur.* Bonn, 1949

Guillén, Jorge. *Language and Poetry: Some Poets of Spain.* Cambridge, Mass., 1961

Larrieu, Robert and R. Thomas. *Histoire illustrée de la littérature espagnole.* Paris, 1952

Mancini, Guido. *Storia della letteratura spagnola.* Milan, 1961

Marín, Diego and Ángel Del Río. *Breve historia de la literatura española.* New York, 1966

Montoliu y de Togores, Manuel de. *Manual de historia de la literatura castellana.* Barcelona, 1957

Niedermayer, Franz. *Spanische Literatur des 20. Jahrhunderts.* Bern, 1964

Northup, George Tyler. *An Introduction to Spanish Literature,* 3rd ed. Chicago, 1960

Romera-Navarro, Miguel. *Historia de la literatura española,* 2nd ed. Boston, 1949

Sainz de Robles, Federico Carlos. *La novela española en el siglo XX.* Madrid, 1957

Salinas, Pedro. *Literatura española: Siglo XX,* 2nd ed. Mexico City, 1949

Stamm, James R. *A Short History of Spanish Literature.* New York, 1967

Valbuena Prat, Angel. *Historia de la literatura española,* 3 vols., 8th ed. Barcelona, 1969

Valverde, José María. *Storia della letteratura spagnola.* Turin, 1955

WORKS ON CONTEMPORARY LITERATURE

Alborg, Juan Luis. *Hora actual de la novela española,* 2 vols. Madrid, 1958–61

Alonso, Dámaso. *Poetas españoles contemporáneos.* Madrid, 1952

Aub, Max. *Discurso de la novela española contemporánea: Jornadas 50.* Mexico City, 1945

Borel, Jean-Paul. *Théâtre de l'impossible.* Neuchâtel, 1961

Buckley, Ramón. *Problemas formales en la novela española contemporánea.* Barcelona, 1968

Cano, José Luis. *Poesía española contemporánea: De Unamuno a Blas de Otero.* Madrid, 1960

Castellet, Josep Maria. *La hora del lector.* Barcelona, 1957

———. *Notas sobre literatura española contemporánea.* Barcelona, 1955

Cernuda, Luis. *Estudios sobre poesía española contemporánea.* Madrid, 1957

Eoff, Sherman H. *The Modern Spanish Novel.* New York, 1961

Goytisolo, Juan. *Problemas de la novela.* Barcelona, 1959

Iglesias Laguna, A. *Treinta años de novela española (1938–1968).* Madrid, 1969

Marra-López, J. R. *Narrativa española fuera de España (1939–1961).* Madrid, 1963

Nora, Eugenio G. de. *La novela española contemporánea,* 3 vols. Madrid, 1958–62

Pastor-López, Mateo. *Modern spansk litteratur.* Stockholm, 1960

Siebenmann, Gustav. *Die moderne Lyrik in Spanien.* Stuttgart, 1965

Torrente Ballester, Gonzalo. *Panorama de la literatura española contemporánea,* 4th ed. Madrid, 1969

———. *Teatro español contemporáneo,* 2nd ed. Madrid, 1967

Vivanco, Luis Felipe. *Introducción a la poesía española contemporánea.* Madrid, 1957

Zardoya, Concha. *Poesía española contemporánea.* Madrid, 1961

WORKS ON CATALAN LITERATURE

Andújar, M. *La literatura catalana en el destierro.* Madrid, 1949

Cardó, C. and J. Romeu Figueras. *Tres estudios sobre literatura catalana.* Barcelona, 1955

Castellet, Josep Maria and Joaquim Molas. *Poesia catalana del segle XX.* Barcelona, 1964

Díaz-Plaja, Guillermo. *De literatura catalana.* Barcelona, 1956

Goytisolo, José Agustín. *Poetas catalanes contemporáneos.* Barcelona, 1968

Martín de Riquer, M. *Història de la literatura catalana.* Barcelona, 1964ff.

Montoliu, M. de. *Cuatro etapas en la evolución de la literatura catalana moderna.* Barcelona, 1956

———. *Les grans personalitats de la literatura catalana,* 8 vols. Barcelona, 1957–62

Ruiz i Calonja, J. *Història de la literatura catalana.* Barcelona, 1954

Vila, Albert. *Compendi de literatura catalana.* Barcelona, 1968

GEORGE SCHOOLFIELD

Swedish Literature

SWEDISH LITERATURE
IN SWEDEN

IN THE FIRST DECADES of the twentieth century Swedish literature attracted considerable attention abroad, primarily in Germany but also in England, the United States, France, Italy, and Spain. This popularity was a part of the general enthusiasm for literature from northern countries, which had begun with the discovery of Ibsen by non-Scandinavian audiences and critics.

While a number of major Swedish writers found readers abroad, the overwhelming figure was August Strindberg (1849–1912), whose work had, and has, a range and force without parallel in Swedish literature. As a playwright (and he was much else: novelist, essayist, poet, polemicist, autobiographer, and amateur scientist), he was more quickly and fully appreciated abroad than at home. Perhaps he was too large and too violent a figure for the relatively serene Sweden of his day. Sweden's social problems, although increasingly evident, had not yet become acute, thanks not least to the safety valve of migration to America. Moreover, Sweden had not been at war since its brief alliance with England and Prussia against Napoleon in 1813–14; the union with Norway was dissolved without bloodshed (1905), and Sweden did not become involved in World War I.

After Strindberg's death there appeared other disturbers of the literary peace: Ludvig Nordström (1882–1942), who saw the seamy side of "pioneer" society in Norrland (the northern provinces); Hjalmar Bergman (1883–1931), the jaundiced chronicler of a central Swedish town; Birger Sjöberg (1885–1929), the subtle satirist of the Swedish idyll; and Pär Lagerkvist (born 1891), whose efforts at "expressionism" (a personalized orthography, a lapidary style, a stern avoidance of detail) bewildered his first readers. Yet it turned out that Nordström and Bergman loved the worlds they castigated. And Lagerkvist revealed himself as an admirer of Sweden's great classical poet, Esaias Tegnér (1782–1846), and he developed a direct and forceful language that won him a very large audience.

Moreover, literary criticism—very influential in a small and highly literate nation—lay in the hands of men with conservative tastes. Their goal was a "healthy literature"—a literature that was essentially uncritical of established society, that met accepted standards of good taste, and that avoided technical experiment or innovation. Most authors seemed of the same mind. However, a new spirit—of constructive revolution, one might say—was entering Swedish letters and Swedish life; and it is this spirit that has made Swedish writers of the past four decades an increasingly important part of European literature.

No new Strindberg has emerged, and Swedish literature simultaneously suffers from, and is inspired by, an awareness of Strindberg's greatness. Yet the absence of a contemporary giant may be to the good. Instead of equating literary Sweden with a single name, the outside world has learned that the country now possesses a "major literature," many-faceted and constantly changing. This transformation and expansion of Swedish literature has been the result of various forces: the slow but thorough democratization of Swedish society; the pressures of political, social, and sometimes military developments abroad, which compelled Sweden to abandon its stance of noninvolvement, if not its traditional neutrality; and a desire to be in contact with—and to rival—European and American literature.

During the late 1920s and 1930s a major new phenomenon entered Swedish literature, that is, authors who were autodidacts and who frequently used their bitter experiences of childhood and youth as the material of their books. Among these writers were Harry Martinson (born 1904), Artur Lundkvist (born 1906), Vilhelm Moberg (born 1898), Jan Fridegård (born 1897), Rudolf Värnlund (born 1900), Ivar Lo-Johansson (born 1901) and Eyvind Johnson (born 1900).

Like his contemporaries, Eyvind Johnson used autobiographical material: his northern Swedish proletarian background was central to his tetralogy *Romanen om Olof* (1934–37, The Novel about Olof). Johnson, however, was also aware of the political crisis that culminated in World War II, and he demonstrated this awareness in a gargantuan set of novels about a Stockholm anti-Nazi group—*Krilon* (1941–43, Krilon). Johnson became interested in experiments with narrative technique very early in his career. Two works fully displayed his technical virtuosity as well as the fact that he had become an extremely learned man: *Strändernas svall* (1948, The Seashores' Surge), about Odysseus; and *Hans Nådes tid* (1960, The Days of His Grace), about both the Carolingian age and twentieth-century totalitarianism.

Two other members of the generation of the 1930s also wrote masterpieces after World War II. Vilhelm Moberg's "emigrant" tetralogy (1949–59) dealt with one of the most important and most ignored events in Swedish history—the mass migration to the United States. Harry Martinson's long poem *Aniara* (1956, Aniara) described a space ship's flight to nowhere. Martinson had prepared for *Aniara,* a work on the empty triumph of technology, both in his early seaman's reminiscences—*Resor utan mål* (1932, Journeys without Destination) and *Kap Farväl* (1933, Cape Farewell)—and in the long title poem of his best collection of verse, *Passad* (1945, Trade Winds).

An altogether different kind of novelty—at a great remove from the autodidacts' farms, factories, and tramp steamers—was presented to a shocked public during the 1930s by Agnes von Krusenstjerna (1894–1940). Her two works of fiction about the decadent nobility—*Fröknarna von Pahlen* (1930–35, The von Pahlen Ladies) and *Fattigadel* (1935–38, Impoverished Nobility)—destroyed a good many taboos by their depictions of sexual abnormalities. Through the emotional subtleties of these works, Krusenstjerna prepared for the introspective novels of the 1940s and 1950s.

The fascination with new currents from the continent, England, and America—characteristic of the zest for culture of the autodidacts Martinson, Lundkvist, and Johnson—also marked the work of the principal new poet of the 1930s, Gunnar Ekelöf (1907–1968). He came, however, from an affluent home and enjoyed an excellent formal education, acquiring a close knowledge of Persian and Byzantine history. Ekelöf's first master was Rimbaud, as can be seen in the "exploded poetry" of *Sent på jorden* (1932, Late on the Earth). But Ekelöf never stayed with one style very long, and both the variety and depth of his oeuvre have made him the most influential Swedish poet of the mid-twentieth century.

After a romantic interlude, Ekelöf found an analytical-lyrical style, not unlike T. S. Eliot's, in *Färjesång* (1941, Ferry Song) and *Non serviam* (1945, the title is in Latin: I Will Not Serve). He later displayed a jocular mysticism in *Strountes* (1955, a punning title—*"strunt"* means "nonsense"—borrowed from the Swedish romantic C. J. L. Almqvist [1793–1866]). Ekelöf's *Opus incertum* (1959, another Latin title: An Uncertain Work) and *En natt i Otočac* (A Night in Otočac, 1961), with their intentional "un-beauty," were examples of "anti-poetry," a development of the greatest importance for Swedish poetry, because the very mellifluousness of the language has often been a snare.

In his later collections—*Dīwān över Fursten av Emgión* (1965, Divan Concerning the Prince of Emgión) and *Sagan om Fatumeh* (1966, The Tale of Fatumeh)—Ekelöf used the near-eastern studies of his youth to construct, with philological exactness, a Byzantine-Turkish world of unbelievable cruelty—an aspect of human nature that had haunted Ekelöf throughout his life. The popularity of even so difficult a work of Ekelöf's as his long-prepared *En Mölna-elegi* (1960, A Mölna Elegy), was a noteworthy phenomenon. Not so long ago, the Swedish public was seldom given hard intellectual or artistic nuts to crack. But through the tutelage offered by Ekelöf, Eyvind Johnson, and others, the public has shown a surprising ability to accept, and even to demand, complicated literature.

Indeed, taste has lately become so fastidious that even the elegant Hjalmar Gullberg (1898–1961), who treated many of the same themes and locales as Ekelöf in a less complex fashion, has gone out of fashion. The popularity once held by Gullberg's earlier work—religious-mystical poetry, erotic verse, mild satire, and political criticism—began to fade in the 1940s. Gullberg was aware of his loss of popularity, but he continued undauntedly to publish well into the postwar period: *Dödsmask och lustgård* (1952, Death Mask and Pleasure Garden), *Terziner i okonstens tid* (1958, Terzinas in the Time of Un-Art), and *Ögon, läppar* (1959, Eyes, Lips).

Gullberg's undeserved fall from critical and popular grace was partly because of his virtuosity with rhyme, a skill that seemed out of date. Ironically, the work of his contemporary Nils Ferlin (1898–1961)—not a product of Lund's university, as Gullberg was, but a jack-of-all-trades and cabaret artist—has recently enjoyed a renascence, although Ferlin employed rhyme brilliantly in his satirical songs and ballads of the 1930s. Perhaps a similarity in form and tone to Brecht has been detected in his work; he was not, however, politically committed. And the central theme of his latter collections—such as *Med många kulörta lyktor* (1944, With Many Chinese Lanterns) and *Kejsarens papegoja* (1951, The Emperor's Parrot)—was an overwhelming fear of death.

Still another poet who has remained relatively faithful to the old gods of rhyme, regular rhythm, and lucidity is Johannes Edfelt (born 1904), who, with erotic poems more passionate than Gullberg's, won a name for himself in the 1930s. Unlike Gullberg and Ferlin, Edfelt has been determined to make his poems as compressed as possible, something that gives added force to the pessimism of much of his work.

If the 1930s showed a broadening of social and literary horizons, the 1940s began with an enforced isolation: Sweden underwent its *beredskaps-*

tid (time of preparedness) for an invasion that never came. Through good luck, and a governmental policy not wholly unhelpful to Germany, Sweden was able—to her great material gain—to maintain her neutrality. The ill-defined feelings of anxiety and guilt arising from this special situation left an imprint on literature, infusing the "Swedish idyll" with a nervousness and a pessimism it had never known so completely before.

POETRY

The most important poet to emerge in Sweden during the 1940s was unquestionably Erik Lindegren (1910–1968), who had made a false start with *Posthum ungdom* (1935, Posthumous Youth), a collection he later disowned. After a period of self-discipline, he published *mannen utan väg* (1942, the man without a way), a cycle of forty "exploded sonnets," each composed of seven pairs of unrhymed couplets, in which he described mankind pursued by the twin terrors of dictatorship and war, mankind in grave danger of losing whatever dignity, and whatever humanity, it had left. Because of the pounding monotony of the cycle's structure and the abruptness with which image came hurtling after image, the collection was judged unacceptable by commercial publishers; Lindegren brought it out himself in 200 copies. The poems, once so forbidding, are familiar now, often anthologized and often quoted.

In 1947 a romantic Lindegren emerged with *Sviter* (Suites), whose portrait and role poems, eulogies, and love poems became models for the poets of the next decade. Then, in 1954, Lindegren published *Vinteroffer* (Winter Sacrifices), the third part of his small but important oeuvre. Here the mood was elegiac, sometimes chilly, sometimes tired.

Like Lindegren, Karl Vennberg (born 1910) made a practically un-noticed debut in the 1930s. With *Halmfackla* (1944, Straw Torch) and *Tideräkning* (1945, Chronology) he joined Lindegren in singing the despair of the 1940s. The poet is placed before the choice between "the indifferent and the impossible." He is distrustful of large phrases but not unwilling to use obscurity, calm but intense, yet with a mocking bite that is peculiarly his own. In 1949 Vennberg published the collection of poems *Fiskefärd* (1949, Fishing Trip), which, like Lindegren's *Suites,* heralded the nostalgia and learnedness of the 1950s. Vennberg's poem on the Latin author Ausonius showed unmistakable signs of this relaxation (or perhaps, in Vennberg's case, renunciation) and prefigured the gentle passion of the 1950s for figures, preferably poets, of another time and place.

Werner Aspenström (born 1918) began as the bitter squire of Venn-berg, and of the whole frightened decade, as one of the editors of the journal *40-tal* (1944–47) and the poet of *Skriket och tystnaden* (1946,

The Cry and the Silence). But Aspenström lacked Vennberg's ironic salt. In its stead, he had a refined sense of the image and a wide emotional range, talents that have sustained his career over the years and have given him the rare ability to combine beauty of language and subtlety of emotion with social comment, as was so well demonstrated by poems in *Om dagen om natten* (1961, At Day, at Night).

At first glance, the career of Sven Alfons (born 1918) would seem to be in quiet opposition to that of his contemporaries: in an age of *"ångest,"* he forewent technical novelties and wrote love poetry: *Ensamhets himmelshuva* (1942, Skyhood of Loneliness) and *Sommaren och döden* (1943, Summer and Death). Yet the despairing spirit of the 1940s was and has remained part of his work. A professional art historian, Alfons imparted to *Backspegel mot gryningen* (1949, Rear-View Mirror toward the Dawn; the title bespeaks his affection for the past) his sense of the fragility of the idyll that allows the treasures of the past to continue their existence.

Ragnar Thoursie (born 1919), on the other hand, gave his *Emaljögat* (1945, The Enamel Eye) the enigmatic language and the sense of catastrophe common during the war years and their immediate aftermath. The book was distinguished by common sense, and a sense of humor, both of which have grown steadily more apparent in Thoursie's work, as a lyrical commentator on Sweden's realities.

Around these writers who formed the core of Swedish poetry during the 1940s there were others, in the time but not necessarily of it. Critics have called them the "outsiders." The oldest of these outsiders was Sten Hagliden (born 1905), who had a premature debut in the 1930s. Thereupon, like Lindegren and Vennberg, he fell silent, until he could return with the extremely concentrated language that has become his trademark. The poet and critic Göran Printz-Påhlson (born 1931) has noted a resemblance in "methodic style" between Hagliden and Stig Sjödin (born 1917). Sjödin's compactness, as seen in *Sotfragment* (1949, Soot Fragment), offered fewer problems of penetration for the reader, since he describes Swedish workers in the portrait style of Edgar Lee Masters.

Quite unlike Hagliden and Sjödin, who have been pretty well convinced of life's hardness, there are some for whom existence has been a wonder never ceasing. Harald Forss's (born 1911) many poems have all expressed an undying and cosmic affection for existence. Bernt Erikson (1921) has been equally and volubly enamored of himself and his gigantic word constructions (his knowledge of Joyce is apparent). The miniaturist Lars Englund (1917–1959), as reticent and careful as Forss and Erikson have been uncontrolled, wrote four volumes of *kortdikt* (short poems) from *Säg du* (1941, Say Thou) to *Svala* (1950, Swallow). His special charm lay in his openness to his surroundings and his ability to capture them in a quick grasp. One can find in Englund's poems parallels to Japanese poetry (which he translated) and to the "matchbox poetry" of the Finland-Swede Rabbe Enckell (born 1903).

The "romantic" tone, evident in the works of the late 1940s by Linde-gren, Vennberg, Aspenström, and Alfons, flourished as the new decade dawned. The "time of preparedness" had paused, and the necessary adjust-ments to Sweden's new affluence had been made. The idyll was wholly reinstated, but it was a well-planned and prosperous idyll now. Of course, Sweden was keenly aware of the atom bomb, the cold war, of Korea. And the "third standpoint"—a position between east and west in the cold war—began slowly to grow, championed by, among others, Karl Vennberg and the novelist Sivar Arnér (born 1909). But the dangers seemed somehow more remote than before, and Swedish literature had a great deal of cul-tural catching-up to do. The result was a literature—particularly a poetry —more varied than that of the 1940s, but surely less intense.

Lars Forssell (born 1928)—who summed up the 1950s as "safety and insecurity, idyll and express telegrams from above"—became the special poetic voice of the 1950s. In *Ryttaren* (1949, The Rider) and *Narren* (1952, The Fool) he demonstrated that he was a learned poet, full of allusions, but never obscure, at least not in the way of the poets of the 1940s. However, he was a role player rather than single piercing voice. He wanted and found a large audience, not least by means of his poses, such as the fool, through which he expressed a constantly shifting view of things. Moreover—again a characteristic of the 1950s—he tried a number of styles instead of forging his own. In *The Fool* he showed, among other things, what a masterly student he was of the Lindegren of *Suites*. After translating Ezra Pound, Forssell wrote *F. C. Tietjens* (1954, F. C. Tietjens), with its many echoes of the *Cantos*. In an effort to lift the cabaret song to a serious literary level, he wrote the collections *Snurra min jord* (1958, Turn, My Earth) and *Jack Uppskäraren* (1966, Jack the Ripper), in both of which the influence of Brecht was plain.

Ever aware of what the time wanted and eager to try out new trends, Forssell embraced sexual frankness in *En kärleksdikt* (1960, A Love Poem). An inveterate globetrotter, like so many other Swedish writers of the 1950s, some of his collections were veritable albums of his travels. But it was in the "dramatis personae" of his more recent poetry (portrait and role poems again) that Forssell continued to demonstrate one of his two main strengths—his ability to play roles. His other strength has been his drive to clarity and immediacy of expression, which has had an effect on the "new simplicity" of the 1960s.

Curiously, two other major poets of the 1950s, Sandro Key-Åberg (born 1922) and Tomas Tranströmer (born 1931), have been much less aware of their public than has Forssell—or rather, they have treated the reader with respect, instead of trying to woo him. Indeed, the reader of Key-

Åberg's earlier collections will find himself battered by the poet's insistence upon the small and large brutalities of life, and unnerved by Key-Åberg's constant awareness of death. His first four volumes, culminating with *Bittergök* (1954, Bitter Cuckoo), seem almost a remnant of the time of *ångest* just past. Recently he has attempted to create "personae"—in the prose poems of *Bildade människor* (1964, Cultured People)—similar to Forssell's. He has also tried his hand at the drama.

Tranströmer, like Key-Åberg, has been his own man, filled from the start with confidence in his own poetic vision. The volume *17 dikter* (1954, 17 Poems) indicated that he was at ease in the world he perceived (not the same, of course, as being at peace with it), that he was able to express his ease in original but by no means enigmatic images, and that he knew precisely how to choose between his images and to control them. His oeuvre has been small: his fourth volume, *Klanger och spår* (Sounds and Traces), appeared only in 1968. But, as in Ekelöf and Lindegren, every poem has value. On this account, he has been attacked by some antielitist poetic spirits of the 1960s who object to poetry that cannot be thrown away after using it.

Like Tranströmer, Folke Isaksson (born 1927) seemed from the outset to know exactly what he was about. But, on closer examination, his verse (*Vinterresa* [1951, Winter Journey]) and poetic prose (*Irrfärder* [1953, Wanderings]) showed him to be very much in thrall to Rilke, just then at the peak of his Scandinavian popularity. In the landscape poems of *Det gröna året* (1954, The Green Year) Isaksson almost found himself, by emulating those Swedish prose writers who had recently rediscovered special poetic qualities in the individual Swedish provinces. But more recently Isaksson's muse has depended on derivation (which resulted, to be sure, from his valuable work as a translator of Wallace Stevens) and incessant travel.

The same problems have beset other poets: Lasse Söderberg (born 1931), who, imitating the Latin American "accessions" of Artur Lundkvist, has made Spain and Spanish poetry his bailiwick; Urban Torhamn (born 1931), who sent his poetic creation, the peripatetic dandy David Heron, on a trip through the world viewed ironically through Heron's, then Torhamn's, and, one fears, ultimately T. S. Eliot's eyes; and Petter Bergman (born 1934), who learned about cool elegance from Alexander Pope. Söderberg, Torhamn, and Bergman were all members of Metamorfos, a literary club that flourished in Stockholm in the early 1950s; its great hope was Paul Andersson (born 1930), who won fame on the strength of a single poem—*Elegi till en förlorad sommar* (1953, Elegy to a Lost Summer). He then, like so many others of the time, traveled the world, seeking new material.

The enormous cultivation of these poets cannot be denied, nor can the care with which they have wrought their works. Yet they lack the ultimate talent that has distinguished Forssell, Key-Åberg, Tranströmer. Other laborers in the vineyard, aware of their lack of poetic fury, have turned the fault into a virtue, writing satiric and parodic verse of a high order. These include Bengt Jahnsson (born 1928), who viewed a Swedish town in *Dikter till Wäxiö* (1955, Poems to Wäxiö); Björn Julén (born 1927), who cartooned Sweden's skalds in *Dagtingan* (1955, Bargaining); and Kjell Espmark (born 1930), who turned his vision to current events in *Världen genom kameraögat* (1958, The World through the Camera's Eye). Espmark would have been a precursor of the committed poets of the 1960s if he did not find the world so amusing. His talent, small but genuine, has lately been used to advantage in the Stockholm poems of *Det offentliga samtalet* (1968, The Public Conversation).

"Parody" of another sort—"devoted re-creation" might be a better term—has been the hallmark of Gustaf Adolf Lysholm (born 1909), who has been able to enter so completely into the literary spirit of other times that he has composed books of poetry that seem to come from the turn of the century, or from the age of romanticism, or even from the rococo period. He has also written prose guidebooks to a vanished Stockholm.

The religious strain that could be detected in some of the most serious Swedish fiction of the 1940s revealed itself unashamedly in the poetry of the 1950s, partly as an accompanying phenomenon to the new "romanticism," partly in imitation of the Catholic revival in French and British literature, partly, of course, out of personal conviction.

The Catholic-convert poet, Osten Sjöstrand (born 1925), had the great advantage of not being altogether convinced. He could argue his doubts in poem after poem. Staffan Larsson (born 1927) was nonsectarian, more like what German literature once called a *Gottsucher*. He was also very much a poet of his time with his elegant phraseology and his admiration for idols, particularly musical idols, of the cultural past.

Bo Setterlind (born 1923) has used religion more unabashedly than Sjöstrand or Larsson. Recently, he has written miracle plays. Setterlind, however, has tried almost every genre, attracting attention, not always friendly, from every side. He has written novellas, half a dozen novels, including *Pandoras ask* (1957, Pandora's Box), father of the Swedish anti-American novels of the 1960s; polemics (in defense of the monarchy and against social welfare); and book after book of poetry, whose high points have been the nature lyrics and the imitation folksongs.

Much of Setterlind's verse is given over to portraits of other artists, and tributes to them, as well as to travel poetry—again the frantic pursuit of food for an overproductive pen. Because of his febrile activity, his desire to embrace unpopular attitudes, and his religious bent, he might be called a Strindberg resurrected, if he possessed Strindberg's genius. Because of his will to variety, and the lucidity of his best poetic work, he can be compared to Lars Forssell.

In the middle 1950s, a poetic school developed in Lund, the university town of the south. It had an organ in *Vox* and a program opposed to "the pathos of middle Sweden." It built directly on the Lund traditions of breadth of humanistic interests, of humor (seen in the tradition of the student comedies, or *spex*), and of the well-made work of art.

The leader of this "school" was Göran Printz-Påhlson, whose *Dikter för ett barn i vår tid* (1956, Poems for a Child in Our Time), like Tranströmer's *17 Poems,* was one of the essential poetry collections of the 1950s. The first line of the first poem can serve as a summary of the best and the worst in the poetry of the time: "The wisdom of satire lies in its elegance."

Printz-Påhlson was not just a poet: his essays on modern Swedish poetry, *Solen i spegeln* (1958, The Sun in the Mirror), explored the subject with intelligence and only occasional obscurity. His single collection of poems from the 1960s, *Gradiva* (1966, the title is in Latin: The Goddess Who Walks into Battle), was learned (with notes) and finely wrought. He has written sociopolitical commentary and has even essayed verses in English. This desire to write in English, which Printz-Påhlson shares with a number of contemporary Swedish poets, marks a return to the multiplicity of tongues of the baroque poets, who believed they could write the same "international style" in several languages.

Printz-Påhlson has lived away from Sweden for many years, as a teacher in America and England. It is to be hoped that the publications in 1971 of three of his volumes, one of poetry (*16 dikter* [16 Poems]) and two of essays (*Slutna världar öppen rymd* [Closed Worlds Open Space] and *Förtroendekrisen* [Crisis of Confidence]), will mark his return to a central position in Swedish literary life, which has need of his keen and open-minded intelligence.

Printz-Påhlson's "costar" during the halcyon days at Lund, Majken Johansson (born 1930), withdrew from direct participation in literary battles in a different way—by enlisting in the Salvation Army. After beginning with macabre *spex* wit in *Buskteater* (1952, Rustic Theater), Johansson then made despair her subject in *I grund och botten* (1956, Basically). *Liksom överlämnad* (1965, As it Were, Surrendered) was a collection of well-constructed, even overpolished, poems, which commented on the times. Johansson's religious standpoint has provided a leavening that Printz-Påhlson neither has nor needs.

The poetry of the 1960s can be said, speaking in very general terms, to have followed two lines of development: "concrete poetry," in which language exists for its own sake, and is frequently treated as clay, or as paint on canvas, or as sheer sound; and a "new simplicity," a directness and clarity of diction, often unadorned by images, and aimed at communication.

Concrete poetry attracted some amused attention in the early 1960s with the "word-list" poems of Carl Fredrik Reuterswärd (born 1934) in *På samma gång* (1961, At the Same Time). He had already won a reputation for the playful naïveté of his *Abra Makabra* (1955, Abra Makabra). Later, Reuterswärd succeeded in making an "ultimate" collection of concretism with *Prix Nobel* (1966, Prix Nobel), composed entirely of punctuation marks.

Reuterswärd is a professor of painting; Öyvind Fahlström (born 1928) is a well-known artist living in New York; Åke Hodell (born 1919), the Nestor of the group and its boldest member, has worked in the graphic arts, as has Jarl Hammarberg-Åkesson (born 1940). Bengt-Emil Johnson (born 1936) and Mats G. Bengtsson (born 1944) have been active as composers of avant-garde music. Since all art forms are reduced to their sensuous components, it does not matter much which form one employs. Thus, Bengtsson has held an "art exhibit" of his poems as graphic objects; Hammarberg-Åkesson has published his doodles as poems; Hodell has pasted together collage-poems, and has issued a "book"—*igevär* (1963)—composed of a single nonsense word, whose vowels are stretched out over several pages.

The popularity of concrete poetry is an interesting literary-sociological phenomenon in Swedish culture, a culture in which fads—and keeping up with the never-ceasing "artistic debate"—play an unusually large role. The unfriendly critic is tempted to think of the emperor's new clothes. In fairness, attention must be called (as it often is) to the "liberation of language" and, in the less concrete examples of concretism, to the creation of new words. However, did not the unpretentious genius of the cabaret lyric of the 1930s, Nils Ferlin, do something of the same?

The concretist, of course, wanted to rebel against the limitations even of modernist poetry. The poet of the "new simplicity" was similarly inspired, but he had the further intention of reaching as large an audience as possible with a message readily graspable.

Kai Henmark (born 1932) was a member of the Träffpunkt group from suburban Stockholm. He issued a manifesto in *Dagens Nyheter* (August, 1960) against "the tyranny of form," which was seen as a barrier to those poets who, above all else, had something to tell their audience. In practice, Henmark has been sometimes gnomic, sometimes platitudinous, as in the collection *Spott i ditt öga* (1963, Spit in Your Eye; the title may be a pun, since *"spott"* also means mockery).

Sonja Åkesson (born 1926) was writing poems in the "neo-simple" style before the phrase was coined: *Situationer* (1957, Situations) and

Glasveranda (1959, Glass Veranda). Because of her wry view of life, especially of woman's life, she has won a wide following. *Jag bor i Sverige* (1966, I Live in Sweden) was a typical example of her poetic work.

Another member of the Träffpunkt group, Reidar Ekner (born 1929), may affect simplicity. But his poems have been closer to the traditional mode of lyrical poetry: they attempt to capture a moment, or a mood, and avoid the prose catalogues that have swelled so many poems of the movement.

The poetry of Lars Gustafsson (born 1936) has been a welcome broadening of the new simplicity. He is able, as in his novels, to write simply of the things of the world around him, as in *Ballongfararna* (1962, The Balloon Travelers) and *En förmiddag i Sverige* (1963, A Forenoon in Sweden). But his tendency toward the abstract and the intellectual, reminiscent of the 1950s, has led him more and more, like a figure in one of his novels, down his private path. *Bröderna Wright uppsöker Kitty Hawk,* (1968, The Wright Brothers Visit Kitty Hawk) was an example of these tendencies.

In contrast to Gustafsson and Ekner, Bengt Nerman (born 1922) has stayed true to the unadorned and unphilosophical style. Of the older and less politically committed representatives of the group, he has probably been the most straightforward. He most clearly represents the pedagogical strain at the heart of much of this neo-simple verse.

A classical example of the neo-simple style can be also found in the early works of Björn Håkanson (born 1937), whose early verse showed points of contact with the experimental novelist Per Olof Sundman (born 1922), down to the title for a poem such as *Undersökning* (Investigation) in *Rymd för ingenting* (1962, Space for Nothing). Later, he was drawn more and more to polemical verse, as in *Kärlek i vita huset* (1967, Love in the White House).

The "angry young men" of the neo-simple movement have chosen, above all else, the United States as their target. Göran Sonnevi (born 1939) made his reputation on the strength of a poem about the Vietnam war. How interested he is in communication, and persuasion, can be seen from his "collected poems" from 1959 to 1968, *Det gäller oss* (1969, It Concerns Us), equipped with notes explaining his by no means obscure allusions.

Göran Tunström (born 1937) has given evidence of a more active poetic intellect than Sonnevi. In his early collections he presented naïvely charming poetry, using a simple line. In *De andra, de till hälften synliga* (1966, The Others, the Half-Visible Ones) he committed himself directly to contemporary affairs. Although more inclined to self-dramatization than Tunström, Thomas Tidholm (born 1943) has followed a similar path,

producing poems of what seems a genuine childlike innocence and simultaneously revolting against a society he considers overmechanized and
overorganized.

Göran Palm (born 1931), who distinguished himself as a critic of great
common sense during the 1950s, albeit less learned than Printz-Påhlson,
turned his attention to poetry in the 1960s—*Hundens besök* (1961, The
Dog's Visit) and *Världen ser dig* (1964, The World Sees You)—in an
effort to capture his surroundings in an "imageless and conversational
language." At the same time, Palm established himself as an important
political voice with his attacks, in the essays of *En orättvis betraktelse*
(1966, An Unjust Observation), on the "western orientation" of the
Swedish press and other media, an argument that has not gone unheard by
his poetic colleagues, or by some sectors of the Swedish public.

An unusual contemporary poet is Lars Norén (born 1944), who, having
once spent some six months of regimented and senseless "treatment" in a
Swedish mental hospital, has good reason to consider himself a victim of
the antihuman society presented by Tidholm. Norén's poetry, however, has
gone more in the direction of prophecy than criticism, and his chaotic
recitation of tormented images—as, for example, in *De verbala resterna av
en bildprakt som går* (1964, The Verbal Remnants of an Imagery that
Passes)—has won him, if not a large audience, then the reputation of
being a "poetic genius." Perhaps the Swedish public, after all, wants its
poets to be bards instead of propagandists.

FICTION

The prose author whose works repeatedly bespoke the *ångest* of the 1940s
was Stig Dagerman (1923–1954). Gnawing and ambiguous fear was
incorporated into the serpent of his first book's title, *Ormen* (1945, The
Serpent), and surrounded the barracks and training vessels described in its
pages. In *De dömdas ö* (1946, The Isle of the Damned) Dagerman left
Sweden for an abstract milieu, bearing some relation to Kafka's world and
paralleling that used by William Golding in *The Lord of the Flies:* seven
castaways on a hideous island slowly destroy themselves.

Dagerman's own childhood—like so many of the autodidact writers of
the 1930s, he came from poverty—surfaced in *Bränt barn* (1948, A Burnt
Child) and *Bröllopsbesvär* (1949, Wedding Difficulties), and, supported
by his keen observations of the seamier sides of Stockholm life, ran
through his collection of short stories *Nattens lekar* (1947, The Games of
Night). Dagerman also tried his hand at the drama, producing "late expressionistic" plays close in spirit and in form to those of his German

contemporary Wolfgang Borchert. He also wrote the reportage *Tysk höst* (1947, German Autumn), which will remain an essential account of that wretched time.

This creative outburst left Dagerman empty, a condition exacerbated by the Swedish public's (and Swedish criticism's) demand for overproduction, a demand that has damaged more promising talents than one. Before his suicide, Dagerman was at work on a novel about the Swedish romantic C. J. L. Almqvist, who was fast becoming a cultural hero of the 1940s, by reason of the mixture of fantasy and desperation in his work. Dagerman's book had the working title *Tusen år hos Gud* (1955, A Thousand Years with God), and it was published as fragments after his death.

Another of the "early dead" was Gösta Oswald (1926–1950). His *En privatmans vedermödor* (1949, A Private Person's Difficulties) was built on the pattern of "confessions of a sensitive young man," a form dear to turn-of-the-century writers, which was given new subtleties by Gide in *André Walter* and Rilke in *Malte*. The narrative complications and literary allusions adorning both *A Private Person's Difficulties* and *Rondo* (1951, Rondo) have contributed to Oswald's steadily increasing popularity. A 1963 collected edition of his works included *Christinalegender* (Legends of Christina), centered around the thirteenth-century German mystic, Christina of Stommeln, and having as its theme an "escape" from the limitations of flesh and intellect—an escape also sought by Dagerman in his less pretentious and more humanly sympathetic work.

A central concern for Sivar Arnér has been human responsibility. He has debated this question throughout his extensive oeuvre, beginning with his double debut in 1943: with the collection of historical novellas *Skon som krigaren bar* (The Shoe the Warrior Wore); and with the simple and laconic prose of *Plånbok borttappad* (Lost Wallet), in which Arnér showed himself to be a master of restrained brevity, in the style of Tage Aurell (born 1895), the supreme artist of understatement from the previous decade, and of Pär Lagerkvist himself. Arnér also addressed himself in these works to the question, a particularly thorny one at the time, of whether or not tyranny should be resisted.

Later Arnér expanded his range to include other variations on the theme of domination, and response to it—especially in marriage—from *Du själv* (1946, You Yourself), to *Tvärbalk* (1963, Crossbeam). He has also shown an ability to use almost every form of fiction, from the psychological dissection of a sadomasochistic teacher in *Egil* (1948, Egil) to the allegory of *Fyra som var bröder* (1955, Four Who Were Brothers). In *Four Who Were Brothers* Arnér appeared as a spokesman of the "third standpoint," thus anticipating standard Swedish literary-political attitudes of the 1960s. Everywhere, he has worked with his special combination of intensity and what may be called dryness, seen to special advantage in his short stories and in his many radio plays.

Lars Ahlin (born 1915) made his debut with the novel *Tåbb med Manifestet* (1943, Tåbb with the Manifesto), in which a young depression victim of the 1930s examines not only Marxism but also Christianity. Thus, because of its theorizing and its interest in the transcendental, *Tåbb with the Manifesto* was a workers' novel quite unlike those of the previous decade. Like so many of his contemporaries, Ahlin cultivated the short story; *Inga ögon väntar mig* (1944, No Eyes Await Me) showed another side of his rich personality, his concern with small, stunted, or even grotesque existences. His next novel, *Min död är min* (1945, My Death Is Mine) fully demonstrated the characteristic style of Ahlin (in complete contrast to Arnér's terseness): full of digressions and jokes, learned and yet popular, turgid but never dull.

In *Om* (1946, If), in which (as not infrequently in Ahlin) a boy attempts to lead his father onto more orderly ways, the narrative is repeatedly interrupted in an effort to show how "all the heavens have collapsed," an effort typical of Swedish writers during the 1940s. During the next decade, with *Fromma mord* (1952, Pious Murders) and *Natt i marknadstältet* (1957, Night in the Market Tent), Ahlin's pedagogy took a more hopeful bent. Always a champion of humanity, he tried to indicate the dangers inherent in a failure, however small, to answer humanity's demands.

In addition to these difficult but important novels and short stories, Ahlin has written a number of more accessible works, dealing with problems of love and marriage and, in particular, growing up: *Kanelbiten* (1953, The Cinnamon Bit) and *Stora glömskan* (1954, The Big Forgetting). In his most recently published novel, *Bark och löv* (1961, Bark and Leaf), Ahlin argued for the work of art as communication, against the work of art for its own sake. Paradoxically, this novel by an artist who is by no means lucid has inspired authors of the 1960s who write an astringent "nonartistic" style quite unlike Ahlin's and who must find the ebullient delight in storytelling of much of his work embarrassing.

The interest of Dagerman, Arnér, and Ahlin in shorter fiction is quite understandable: Hemingway and other American masters of the short story had recently been introduced into Sweden through the essays and the tales of Thorsten Jonsson (1910–1950), who also wrote the war novel *Konvoj* (1947, Convoy), a sensitive, Swedish revision of the hard-boiled school. Another Hemingway graduate was Olof Jonason (born 1919), whose collection *Parabellum* (1943, Revolver) became a classic of the "time of preparedness," considerably more realistic, though less suggestive, than Dagerman's work.

The third important author in this tough line was Peder Sjögren (born 1905), who used his experiences in Finland's Winter War (1939–40) for *Kärlekens bröd* (1945, Bread of Love), a book whose symbolism and involved narrative technique made it quite different from Peter Nisser's (born 1919) more elementary *Blod och snö* (1941, Blood and Snow). Toughness of a different kind, and more shocking to its contemporary audience, could be found in the novel *Kain* (1948, Cain) of Bengt Anderberg (born 1920), a book surprisingly close to the spirit of the 1960s in its determined pacificism and its frankness in erotic matters.

Alongside these many innovations, a traditional fiction was being written: about Norrland by Stina Aronson (1892–1956) and Björn-Erik Höijer (born 1907), about Norrland and the west-central province Värmland by Sven Rosendahl (born 1913), about the southern province Blekinge by Sven Edvin Salje (born 1914), and about Stockholm by Owe Husáhr (1921–1958) and Per Anders Fogelström (born 1917).

The novel of psychological realism also had its practitioners during the 1940s. The human psyche, put under the pressures of a difficult age, was the subject of Bengt V. Wall's (born 1916) *Vännen Patrik* (1948, Friend Patrik) and Per Erik Rundquist's (born 1912) *Kalla mig Ismael* (1950, Call Me Ishmael). And the social realm favored in the 1930s, the world of the worker, was entered anew, by Walter Dickson (born 1916), whose best books have dealt with the lot of Swedish immigrants in New Haven's building trade during World War I, and Folke Fridell (born 1904), who, eschewing the historical view, addressed himself to the Swedish working man after 1945, confronted rather suddenly by the welfare state—its blessings and its problems.

In one of its two main currents, the fiction of the 1950s had features in common with the poetry of the Lund school, but these resemblances may well have been purely accidental. It distrusted the simple chronicling of reality; it was highly intellectualized, usually polished, sometimes cruelly ironic and sometimes playful; and it appears not to have been concerned with the fate of its fictional characters. However, beneath the chilly indifference—a quality cultivated earlier by Eyvind Johnson—there may well have been a genuine compassion.

Lars Gyllensten (born 1921) entered Swedish literature by making fun of it, in a parody of the poetry of the 1940s called *Camera obscura* (1946, Camera Obscura). An exponent of the preference of the 1950s for relativity, for playing roles, Gyllensten, gifted with a keen eye and ear and an imposing intelligence, has slipped from one garb to another, all in illustration of his refusal to believe in any final solution. His program of intellectual and spiritual "infidelity" has provoked protracted debate.

Gyllensten's *Barnabok* (1952, Children's Book), reminiscent of Stig Dagerman's work, depicted emotional impotence and barbarism in the midst of Swedish order. *Carnivora* (1953, the title is in Latin: Carni-vores), a collection of prose poems, took another step along the same dark path. It would have seemed that Gyllensten was a permanent pessimist. However, the pessimist went through a series of metamorphoses: the aging main figure of *Senilia* (1956, Senilia); the title character of *Senatorn* (1958, Senatorn), about a would-be idealist functionary in some east European dictatorship; the philosopher in *Sokrates död* (1960, Socrates' Death).

In these three books Gyllensten argued that life is indeed wretched, but that one must find a role, or roles, to meet it, all the same. We may become intellectual desperados (a short-story collection from 1962 bears the name), or "Cainites," heretics refusing to believe anything with utter firm-ness (*Kains memoarer* [1963, Cain's Memoirs]). Or we may split our-selves into separate personalities, as the hero of *Juvenilia* (1965, Juvenilia) does. All this amounts to what Gyllensten called a *Nihilistiskt credo* (1964, Nihilistic Credo), the title of a collection of essays that should be read in conjunction with *Carnivores* if one wishes to catch the drift of Gyllensten's work.

Sven Fagerberg (born 1918) has, like Gyllensten, written books that are more intellectual and more intricately constructed than are the works of authors whose first calling is belles lettres. Fagerberg entered literature with an essay on Joyce, whose great appeal for him was not Joyce's vitality and humor but his use of myth. Yet, for Fagerberg, myth would be only one of the several tools (oriental spiritual exercises are another) by which the advanced mind can find a meaning to life.

Fagerberg's *Höknatt* (1957, Hawk Night) was a very sophisticated kind of *Bildungsroman,* in which a flier, moving through various parts of the world, learns about the development of the intellect and the soul (thanks to Zen Buddhism) before he meets a sacrificial death. In other works, Fager-berg has delivered oblique lectures to a materialist Sweden. His thought returned to the east in *Svärdfäktarna* (1963, The Swordsmen).

In certain respects, the way for Fagerberg's involved structures was prepared by Willy Kyrklund (born 1921), a Finland-Swede whose entire literary career has taken place in Sweden. Kyrklund's little books are enter-tainments in the best sense. Among them was *Solange* (1951, Solange), the story of resigned love. The heroine learns Persian in a desire to be different (a thrust, perhaps, at an obvious feature of literature during the 1950s). In the quasi-document *Mästaren Ma* (1952, Mah the Master), the analects of a Chinese scholar are commented upon by his wife, by his friends, and by later scholars. The pastiche *Polyfem förvandlad* (1964, Polyphemus Transformed) showed the drying up of Kyrklund's talent.

Fagerberg and Kyrklund have used known myths. Arne Sand (1927–1963), who had begun by writing moderately successful realistic-psychological novels, wanted to create his own mythical world. However, he refused to leave the realistic home base of Sweden altogether. His gallant gesture in this direction was *Ljugarstriden* (1956, The Battle of the Liars), whose central figure is a Swedish country woman of the middle nineteenth century, a teller of tall tales. Sand's effort at mythologizing was of great interest to critics, less to the public: he weighed down his tale with numerous and often obscure political references.

Another author who tried to mix myth, reality, and allusion was Knut Nordström (born 1930). His ponderous *En fördömds memoarer* (1963, A Condemned Man's Memoirs) was the feigned autobiography of a man who tries to set himself beyond the limits of good and evil. Sand and Nordström, it would seem, lack what Gyllensten and Fagerberg possess in large measure—an intellect in iron control of narrative complications. All four are tired of linear narration, but Sand and Nordström—perhaps because they need its support—have been unwilling to abandon it altogether.

Other writers were content simply to continue as unabashed tellers of tales, combining this "old-fashioned" narrative impulse not infrequently with a commitment to one or several causes. Per Wästberg (born 1933) was only fifteen when he published his first book, and, quite naturally, depicted adolescence therein. The next phase in his semiautobiographical work concerned young love in Stockholm (*Halva kungariket* [1955, Half the Kingdom]) and then a youthful Swede in a renascent Germany (*Arvtagaren* [1958, The Heir]). In *The Heir* the hero realizes that he owns a share in European culture.

Ultimately, Wästberg found a special field in Africa, and, with factual books and anthologies, has become the leading Swedish voice on this topic, while at the same time he continues to produce novels drawing on his intimate knowledge of Stockholm. His latest Stockholm narratives—the much-discussed *Vattenslottet* (1968, The Water Castle) and *Luftburen* (1969, The Air Cage)—argued against such municipal evils as pollution and thoughtless urban renewal on the one hand, and for a complete freedom in sexual matters on the other. The novels' hero is an air-traffic controller at Arlanda Field: competent, cool-headed, and useful to the world's travelers as they stream into Stockholm. He toys, however, with the notion of helping Africa's new nations.

Sara Lidman (born 1923) made a village in her native province of Västerbotten her literary home ground, as Stockholm has been Wästberg's. *Tjärdalen* (1952, The Tar Pit), written in dialect, was a notable accomplishment, both because of the accuracy of its character portrayals and the sense of inevitability that the author gave to her tragicomedy about worthy ambitions foiled, worthy moral aims betrayed. Lidman's portrayal of the same milieu, but written in more standard Swedish, continued in *Hjortron-*

landet (1965, The Cloudberry Patch), in which she tried to portray a whole village instead of individual inhabitants. Two later books—*Regnspiran* (1958, The Rain Bird) and *Bära mistel* (1960, To Carry Mistletoe)—portrayed a sensitive young woman who has the misfortune (in the second book) of falling in love with a homosexual.

Sara Lidman then turned her sympathies to the benighted lands beyond the seas. In a far more emotional manner than Wästberg she made Africa the subject of her next books: *Jag och min son* (1961, I and My Son), about South Africa; and *Med fem diamanter* (1964, With Five Diamonds), about Kenya. The expectations of the Swedish public were met by her painting the whites as villains, blacks as the stuff of which martyrs are made. The Vietnam war then led her to visit the orient, from which she issued *Samtal i Hanoi* (1966, Conversations in Hanoi). Lidman has an enormous following, thanks to the artistic quality of her first works and her ability to champion popular causes. Most recently, she has focused (in the play *Marta, Marta* [1970, Marta, Marta]) on social problems in which Sweden has a share.

Another woman writer, whose career has resembled Lidman's up to a point, is Brigitta Trotzig (born 1929). Her sympathies with the oppressed are of a similar intensity, and she has likewise staked out a special Swedish literary province for herself—south Sweden, especially in the days when it passed back and forth between Danes and Swedes. *De utsatta* (1957, The Exposed Ones) and *En berättelse från kusten* (1961, A Tale from the Coast), written in Trotzig's biblically influenced prose, were filled to the brim with human suffering, which the author viewed sometimes with utter hopelessness, sometimes with a dark-hued Christianity.

Wästberg, Lidman, and Trotzig all have in common a certain romanticism, as well as a vein of lyricism in their prose. Kurt Salomonson (born 1929), on the other hand, has been closer in his technique to the novels about workers of the 1930s and 1940s and more concerned than Wästberg, Lidman, or Trotzig with Sweden's immediate problems. Salomonson discussed the plight of Swedish miners in *Hungerdansen* (1955, The Hunger Dance) and *Grottorna* (1956, The Grottoes). He refused to romanticize physical labor, and, indeed—going against a chief tenet of the genre in its earlier form—he was aware of a selfishness among the proletariat, with every man for himself, quite as vicious as that of the bosses. Parallels can be seen in the British novel of the "I'm all right, Jack" school. Salomonson is less interested in his protagonists than in the forces that beset and dehumanize them.

Åke Wassing (born 1919) has been closer to the practice of Eyvind Johnson's Olof novels through his concentration on a single figure, such as the title figure in *Dödgrävarens pojke* (1958, The Gravedigger's Son), who is exposed to the numberless humiliations of life's underside, but is not broken by them. Wassing's novels about the boy from the poorhouse—continued in *Slottet i dalen* (1960, The Castle in the Vale) and *Grimman* (1963, The Halter)—looked back in time to the "poor Sweden" of the 1920s and 1930s. Salomonson, on the other hand, has probed determinedly into the untreated social sores of his own day.

Three gifted novelists of the 1950s have been lost to literature: one through death (Pär Rådström [1925–1963]); two through defection to another art form (Bo Widerberg [born 1930] and Vilgot Sjöman [born 1924]).

Pär Rådström published a long series of short novels, in which he worked with an international cast of characters and a foreign milieu: *Paris, en kärleksroman* (1955, Paris, A Love Novel); *Ballong till månen* (1958, Balloon to the Moon), set in a grotesque America; and *Översten* (1961, The Colonel), in which the last of the Vasa dynasty, the wretched Gustaf IV Adolf, appears in modern times. Rådström was something of a riddle to critics. His books were written with apparent haste and carelessness. And it was remarked that he seemed most at home in the sketch: the collection *Ro utan åror* (1961, Row without Oars) contains a section with the motto, "This story must be told in a hurry." However, Rådström's use of black humor, before the term was invented, has given him an ever-increasing reputation in the 1960s, as has his detestation of literary poses.

Bo Widerberg began with the virtues of the Lund school's verse—humor, understatement, fine craftsmanship—as in *Kejsaren av Capri* (1955, The Emperor of Capri), about Swedish tourists on a bus tour in Italy. In 1957 he published the distinguished novel on adultery's torments, *Erotikon* (Eroticon), which at the same time, in its depiction of the southern towns of Malmö and Falsterbo, was one of the best examples of regionalism during the 1950s. After writing a critical study on the film, Widerberg went over to the form altogether, winning an international reputation with *Kvarteret Korpen* (1963), *Elvira Madigan* (1967), and *Ådalen 31* (1968).

Vilgot Sjöman's fiction was more expansive than Widerberg's. His long novel *Lektorn* (1948, The Lector) dealt with a dizzying variety of themes, against a school background. A technical innovation (for the Swedish novel) in *The Lector* was that each chapter was written from the standpoint of one of the book's many characters. Sjöman then pursued the fate of Rolf Thörner, his hero and alter ego, in other books. As his interest in fiction slowly palled, Sjöman turned to films, first publishing a report on Hollywood in 1961, then a diary of his participation with Ingmar Bergman on *Nattvardsgästerna*. Subsequently, Sjöman achieved international fame with his two *I Am Curious* films—as a director, author, and actor.

There are reasons for this transfer of affection to the cinema: the example of Ingmar Bergman himself, whose scenarios made increasingly greater literary claims; dissatisfaction with the novel (and the written word in general); and the desire to reach a very large public both at home and abroad.

Without himself turning to the film—although he is the author of a television play, *Resa* (1965, Journey)—Per Olof Sundman has succeeded in speaking to the very widest circles, while at the same time winning critical esteem (even in France) as an experimental novelist. Sundman started as a regionalist, having taken the north-central province of Jämtland as his special setting. In the novella cycle *Jägarna* (1957, The Hunters), the Jämtland wilderness provides the scene for the chase—of a man, an animal, an ideal. In *Undersökningen* (1958, The Investigation) a minor official is dispatched to look into the report that an engineer at an isolated power plant is an alcoholic, a report never verified or denied in the book's course.

Sundman continued the themes of investigation and pursuit in *Skytten* (1960, The Marksman), about an apparently accidental shooting (of one hunter by another) and the points of view on it. Nor did the twin themes lose their fascination in the short stories of *Sökarna* (1963, The Searchers), or in *Två dagar, två nätter* (1965, Two Days, Two Nights), a novel about the hunt for a criminal.

With the short novel *Expeditionen* (1962, The Expedition) Sundman left Jämtland, following a safari modeled on Stanley's into the black heart of Africa, but not out again. In *Ingeniör Andrées luftfärd* (1968, Engineer Andrée's Flight), about S. A. Andrée's ill-fated balloon flight toward the North Pole, Sundman investigated—what book of his has not engaged in investigation at manifold levels?—the meaning of exploration and of technical knowledge. In his objectivity, his apparent simplicity, and his sometimes tiresome attention to the smallest mechanical details, Sundman has been compared to French novelists Michel Butor and Alain Robbe-Grillet; he claims to have been the student of the saga style and no more.

Erik Beckman's (born 1935) and Torsten Ekbom's (born 1938) fiction has likewise been called experimental, and has richly earned the name. It can be read, as Sundman's tales often are, as one would a boy's adventure book. To be sure, Beckman's *Någon något* (1964, Someone Something) was a wilderness story, about elk poaching. But Beckman provided a wealth of blind paths, of narrative twists, turns, and contradictions, all intended to make the reader "write his own book." In *Hertigens kartonger* (1965, The Duke's Squares), the squares are the orderly formations of sailors, to be admired and mocked, in the cortege accompanying Winston Churchill's casket. Here, as in *Someone Something,* the love for the burlesque, and for tormenting the reader, distinguished Beckman's work from Sundman's. (One of Beckman's penates, he has said, is Rabelais.)

Beckman is convinced that, however hard the author may try, his words cannot capture or reproduce any "reality." Thus, the reader of *Inlandsbanan* (1968, The Inland Railroad) is invited to participate in a "eulogy of perfidy": neither the author, his language, nor his audience can have a fixed standpoint. Lars Gyllensten's credo of faithlessness has begot children.

In Torsten Ekbom's *Negationer* (1963, Negations) and *Spelöppning* (1964, Opening Move) the influence of the French *nouveau roman* was patent. While *Negations* bore a resemblance to Sundman's investigations (a man comes to town on a mission whose nature we never learn), in *Opening Move* Ekbom turned to a collage technique, by which (according to his own statement) he wrote a "normal novel," cut it up, and then put together the fragments that had "made an impression" on him. In *Signalspelet* (1965, The Signal Game) a data machine has been fed with material from a juvenile tale of derring-do, and has produced its own novel. Does a machine have a standpoint, a controlling intellect? Only the language is left.

Per Olov Enquist (born 1934) has followed an experimental path somewhere between Sundman's misleading and utter simplicity and the fractured worlds of Beckman and Ekbom. He claims to have learned to admire lucidity and directness of style from Thorsten Jonsson. In addition, he says that he has acquired from Robbe-Grillet the conviction that "it is not what happened but how it happened" that is important. The result has been an apparent crystal clearness in the separate sections of Enquist's books, and a frightening complexity in their total structure.

Enquist's *Färdvägen* (1963, Thoroughfare), a *Bildungsroman,* was couched in a sequence of styles, including conscious parodies, in order to see how "reality" can best be reproduced. The picaresque novel *Magnetisörens femte vinter* (1964, The Mesmeriser's Fifth Winter) was closer to traditional storytelling in that the search for "reality," or the "truth," was put into the events themselves and the manner of narration was relatively straightforward. But in *Hess* (1966, Hess)—a novel in disconnected sections, something in the fashion of Beckman's *The Duke's Squares*—the fragments deal not only with Hitler's sometime satrap and the prisoner of Spandau, but with Robinson Crusoe, with the Franco-Prussian war, with Stockholm in the 1920s, all in an effort to make the reader participate in Enquist's debate on the nature of "freedom," a concept now grown as difficult to define as "reality."

In 1968 Enquist won a large readership with his documentary novel *Legionärerna* (The Legionaries), about the delivery of Baltic refugee soldiers into Russian hands by the Swedish authorities in 1945. His attempt to make a "wholly objective and exact picture" left the impression of being an apologia for the Swedish action, if not an exculpation. From the Balts, Enquist turned to sports, a field about which he knew a good deal more, and the result was still another documentary novel, *Sekonden* (1971, The Second).

The affection for the grotesque and the absurd, one of the possibilities pursued by Beckman and Ekbom, has flourished in the 1960s under some gifted hands. These authors have pursued the absurd (and, as in Rådström's case, entertain the reader rather than putting him through gymnastics) in an effort to make their quite serious points about contemporary life.

Per Christian Jersild (born 1935) filled his first book, *Räknelära* (1960, Arithmetic) with funny and painful vignettes of life in welfare Sweden, a milieu he continued to explore in the story of a housewife who yearns for a sunnier life—*Till varmare länder* (1961, To Warmer Lands). Sweden was also taken to task in *Ledig lördag* (1963, Free Saturday), whose pair of characters gets acquainted while trapped in a subway car; *Prins Valiant och Konsum* (1966, Prince Valiant and the Cooperative Store), about a girl's dreams of a comic-strip hero and the sterile monotony of the omnipresent Swedish grocery store; and *Grisjakten* (1968, The Pig Hunt), an "honorary butcher's" journal of the rational, ridiculous, very Swedish preparations for a pig hunt. (Can this book be a parody on Sundman?)

Jersild ventured abroad in his cycle of exuberant fables concerning an immortal and much transformed picaro, in *Calvinols resa genom världen* (1965, Calvinol's Journey through the World). Calvinol, whose conception and birth reminds one of Gargantua and of Günter Grass's Oskar, participates in the Thirty Years War, as filmed by Cecil B. De Mille; takes part in the first months of World War I, depicted as an archaeological expedition; becomes "Doc," an American gasoline station owner, and a Swedish school boy during World War II. *El Alamein* (El Alamein), a story in *Calvinol's Journey through the World* about the battle for the school lavatory, was a dirty jewel of the Swedish short story.

Sven Delblanc's (born 1931) *Eremitkräftan* (1962, The Hermit Crab) was yet another variation on the *Bildungsroman:* a young man leaves one ideological shell, and, unprotected, must find another. There are prefigurations of Enquist's thoughts on freedom; the hero returns to the tyranny he had left, after a flight to a city of absolute license. The allegory admits an interpretation not necessarily out of keeping with the disaffection toward the west, grown fashionable now in Sweden.

Next, Delblanc tried another of the popular narrative forms, the picaresque. *Prästkappan* (1963, Clergyman's Gown), like Enquist's *The Mesmeriser's Fifth Winter,* is set in the Germany of duodecimo princes, and the runaway pastor Hermann, accompanied by his gigantic attendant, Lång

Hans, sees the world from almost every perspective, like Jersild's Calvinol. Hermann ends on the heights, as heir to Waldstein, and no longer a human being. *Homunculus* (1964, Homunculus) was reminiscent of the movie *Dr. Strangelove.* Sebastian creates a homunculus, which both the Pentagon and the Kremlin want to get for their own destructive ends. The maker destroys his "son," so that he will not be misused.

Delblanc's *Nattresa* (1967, Night Journey) was an antinihilist novel, set mostly in a radical California. "Its intention," according to Delblanc's afterword, "was to seek to give a positive alternative to . . . *Clergyman's Gown.*" Delblanc continued his search for a positive alternative in *Åsnebrygga* (1969, Asses' Bridge), called a "diary novel." It offered a plea for a "conservatism of values," using the author's Berkeley experiences.

In *Åminne* (1970, River Memory) Delblanc returned to the countryside of his youth (in Södermanland, near Stockholm) and to the peasants' annual ceremony of "cleaning the river." Because of its boisterous good humor, and its nostalgia for a lost world, *River Memory* immediately became a popular success. Delblanc knows how to keep the public's interest alive. His *Zahak: Persiska brev* (1971, Zahak: Persian Letters) once again gave his readers the chance, as with *Asses' Bridge,* to feel pious shock at a society less perfect than theirs, and at the same time added the spice of the exotic—a not unfamiliar combination in contemporary Swedish literature.

Beside such rambunctious writers as Jersild and Delblanc, Lars Gustafsson, whose poetry I discussed earlier, may seem at first glance to be both overintellectual and overromantic, a remnant from the gentler days of the 1950s. *Poeten Brumbergs sista dagar och död* (1959, The Poet Brumberg's Last Days and Death), subtitled "a romantic tale," purported to be the posthumously published novel by a contemplator of life, together with observations by his friends on the work left behind. Brumberg, a collector of eighteenth-century cookbooks, would seem to be out of place in the cruel and combative world of the new Swedish literature, but, quite like Enquist's and Delblanc's characters, the dead Brumberg had meant to find a way, or several ways, to live. The quiet man continued his existence in *Bröderna* (1960, The Brothers), in which he tries to make a close contact with the *things* around him (however unfashionable Rilke has grown, some of his thoughts live on). In *Den egentliga berättelsen om herr Arenander* (1966, The True Story about Mr. Arenander), the sketchbook of a man trying to go his own way, Gustafsson employed the fragmented technique also used by Enquist in *Hess.*

There are, of course, novelists who have used the new technical accomplishments to write what may be called entertainment literature. But Swedish readers require opinions on contemporary problems even from lighter writers, such as Bosse Gustafson (born 1924) and Stig Claesson (born 1928). Other writers, more sincere in their commitment to penetrate the worst sides of the welfare state, abandoned technical brilliance to make their arguments more directly. The journalist and polemicist Jan Myrdal (born 1927) made a move in this direction with his *"folkhemsromaner"* ("novels of the welfare state") of the middle 1950s, recently given more attention.

A popular hero in the same tradition was Lars Görling (1931–1966), whose novel *491* (1963, 491) became a *succès de scandale* because of its unmercifully detailed description of the life led by teen-age boys at an internment home in Stockholm. Filmed by Vilgot Sjöman, it spread Görling's name in Europe and America. Compared with Görling's brutal visions, the eroticism of Annakarin Svedberg (born 1934) and Loka Enmark (born 1931), like the tales of wild adolescence by Birgitta Stenberg (born 1932), seemed a little tame, if not banal. Likewise, the jaundiced regional humor of Sven Christer Swahn (born 1933) and of Max Lundgren (born 1937), both of whom have looked askance at Lund, has a reformatory point to make, but lacks Görling's intensity.

Of novelists with a social-critical bent, Svante Foerster (born 1931) offered great promise of a wider range with *Klasskämpen* (1964, The Struggler for His Class), a panorama of Stockholm on the eve of the entrance of the Vietnam war into the Swedish consciousness. The work may turn out, however, to be regarded as merely a historical document.

Like Bosse Gustafson and Stig Claesson, Björn Runeborg (born 1937) has taken up a series of dilemmas, book by book, instead of putting all his observations into a single compendium, as did Foerster. After *Utflykten* (1962, The Excursion), which discussed freedom and responsibility, and *Koltrasten* (1963, The Blackbird), which presented various points of view on violent death in a small community, Runeborg became more completely himself in *De bländade* (1964, The Blinded Ones), about the unintentional cruelty of a frozen society, and *Matthyddan* (1967, The Carpet Hut), about a young mother's retreat into fantasy from a gray world she cannot find interesting, or even intelligible. The spark of humor, albeit bitter, one detected in *The Carpet Hut* flourished more in *Statsbesöket* (1965, The State Visit), about a Bulgarian deputation's official visit to the Swedish provincial town of Falköping.

It may be significant that Max Lundgren's *Gangsterboken* (1965, The Gangster Book), about the coming of a Swedish-American racketeer to the fictional town of Slättköping in southern Skåne, appeared in the same year. However sophisticated Swedish fiction and its authors may become, the temptation to make sympathetic fun of Swedish provincialism will never perish. Indeed, this spirit adds some necessary color to the all-too-earnest world of social comment and criticism.

DRAMA

Although Sweden is a nation with a highly developed theater and the model of Strindberg (as well as of the successful plays of Hjalmar Bergman), the contemporary drama has not attracted the best literary talents. Or, according to an argument presented recently (1969) by four prominent novelists—Lars Ardelius (born 1926), Sven Delblanc, Per Christian Jersild, and Björn Runeborg—it is the fault of Sweden's directors that men of letters seem to shun the theater: the attitude of these professional theater people is that "Swedish drama is provincial, pointless, boring, and clumsy."

To demonstrate what sins of omission the theaters of Sweden were committing, the four authors then printed an anthology of four plays—under the title *Refuserat* (1969, Refused)—one by each of them, that had been rejected, "in some cases as many as ten times." Examining the anthology, one concludes that each of the plays would indeed provide an interesting evening of theater—but perhaps because one knows other works by these authors.

Ardelius's *Guiden* (The Guide), about a young Catherine the Great and her wretched husband Peter, reminds one of Ardelius's concern with marital problems in his novels. Delblanc's *Fångvaktare* (Prison Guards) dealt with the relativity of freedom, a central theme in his fiction. Jersild's *Fänrik Duva: En fars* (Ensign Duva: A Farce) could easily be turned into an episode in *Calvinol's Journey through the World*. And Runeborg's *Macken* (The Gas Station) takes place in the milieu Runeborg knows best and detests most, the Sweden of highways, trucks, and their dehumanized servants.

In short, the plays are useful ancillary material for students who someday will write dissertations about the principal oeuvre of the authors in question, a fate that may also fall to the theatrical efforts of other worthwhile or even distinguished authors.

The verse plays of the poet Elsa Grave (born 1918), as well as the plays of the novelists Björn-Erik Höijer and Bengt V. Wall, have not become a living part of the repertory, and the stage and radio work of Stig Dagerman was subsidiary to his fictional production. The plays of Vilhelm Moberg (who tried the theater in the 1930s and again in the 1960s), of Sara Lidman (the previously mentioned *Marta, Marta*), of Lars Gustafsson (*Två maktspel* [1970, Two Plays about Power]) fall into the same category: they are, in a way, by-blows.

Who then are the "professional dramatists"? Erland Josephson (born 1923), drawing upon his extensive practical knowledge of the theater, has written competent but not memorable plays. In the 1950s and later, Tore

Zetterholm (born 1915) made a small mark with his topical plays: on motorcycle gangs (*Tiger-Harry* [1952, Tiger Harry]), on Africa (*Det brinnande spjutet* [1960, The Burning Spear]), and on Mao's China (*Kvinnorna från Shanghai* [1967, The Women from Shanghai]).

Sandro Key-Åberg and Lars Forssell have ventured away from their lyric calling for the theater. Of the two, Key-Åberg has been the more experimental, using the techniques of late medieval drama in *Härliga tid som randas: Ett skådespel i tolv stunder* (1968, Great Day Coming: A Play in Twelve Moments), about the hydrogen bomb. Lars Forssell has been more traditional, and also more persistent. He has ranged from the cabaret sketch to the full-scale historical drama: *Galenpannan* (1964, The Madcap), another contemporary work on Gustav IV Adolf, and *Christina Alexandra* (1968, Christina Alexandra), about Sweden's seventeenth-century queen. His short play *Charlie McDeath* (1961, Charlie McDeath), a dialogue in which the dummy swallows the ventriloquist's soul, and a much more complex work about family conflicts, *Söndagspromenaden* (1963, The Sunday Promenade), have attracted attention outside Sweden. Forssell is a master of tragicomedy, beginning by making the audience laugh and ending by demonstrating, as in *The Sunday Promenade,* the vanity of man's dreams.

The laudable attempt to continue the Strindbergian traditions of compression and suggestion and of attention to the anti-hero has been quite obvious in Forssell's dramatic work. Also like Strindberg, Forssell has been fascinated by the use of music on the stage, and has perhaps gone further than Strindberg would have wanted to go in this direction, writing, among other things, the Grand Guignol "musical comedy," *Flickan i Montréal* (1967, The Girl in Montreal).

Because of his vitality, his many-sidedness, and (at his best) his humanity, Forssell is easily the dominant creative figure in the Swedish theater. He has inspired at least one gifted imitator, and perhaps rival, in Arne Törnqvist (born 1932). Like Forssell, Törnqvist has a penchant for the historical fantasy on a scarcely heroic main figure. His first play, *Carl XVI Joseph* (1969, Carl XVI Joseph), depicted the mental decay of the Swedish painter-poet Ernst Josephson (1851–1906). His second, *Leo Tolstojs testamente* (1970, Lev Tolstoi's Will) let the ancient and bewildered Tolstoi fumble his way between tsarist despotism, which he detests and endures, and the revolutionary spirit, to which he has given inspiration and which he fears.

Both Forssell and Törnqvist have seldom let political attitudes override their sense of poetry in the theater. This is not true of the work of the playwrighting team of Ronny Ambjörnsson (born 1936) and Agneta Pleijel (born 1940). Their *Ordning härskar i Berlin* (1970, Order Prevails in Berlin), about the events leading to the deaths of German socialists

Rosa Luxemburg and Karl Liebknecht, was simply a vehicle for the presentation of not very subtle political propaganda, as the authors readily admitted. They called it "cabaret rather than drama," in which the music of Kai Chydenius was almost as important as the text.

What Ambjörnsson, Pleijel, and Chydenius have created is, of course, the work of a team. An even more "democratic" mode of dramatic creation has been fashionable in Sweden for some time. In 1962, at the Norrköping City Theater, Tore Zetterholm asked the actors to "write the play" along with himself, a practice supported by references to the supposed mode of composition of Shakespeare and Molière. The notion of group theater has subsequently taken hold at Göteborg's municipal theater.

Bengt Bratt (born 1937), one of the Göteborg playwrights, has, like a number of Swedish dramatists, written for television. His *Exercis* (1967, Maneuver) was about Sweden's compulsory military service. Critical in the extreme of the military system, even in its mild Swedish form, aware (like Kurt Salomonson) that shared misery does not create comradeship, Bratt is very much a child of his time. The television plays of older writers, such as the psychological novelist Per Erik Rundquist and Erland Josephson, have been more interested in atmosphere and in emotional nuances than in argumentation and conversion.

The lure of television is strong, of course, and Sivar Arnér, for one, has successfully tried it in his handsome, semihistorical play *En satans person* (1970, A Devil of a Fellow), about an imaginary encounter of the aging and Mephistophelean C. J. L. Almqvist with the young idealist Viktor Rydberg (1828–1895) and the revivalist preacher P. L. Sellergren (1769–1843). In this play, Almqvist (whose lure for Swedish writers will surely never die) is in flight to America, after having tried to poison his chief creditor. Arnér has pointed out that *A Devil of a Fellow* was not intended for the television screen alone. Evidently, he hopes—like so many of his colleagues—to win a place on the live stage.

SWEDISH LITERATURE IN FINLAND

There have been Swedish speakers in Finland since prehistory—well before the twelfth century, when the Finnish wilderness was incorporated into the kingdom of Sweden. Even when Finland fell into Russian hands in the early nineteenth century, the language of culture and administration of the country remained Swedish. Only during the emergence of a strong national spirit toward the end of the nineteenth century was Finnish accepted as a pedagogical, legal, and literary language.

Although many Finland-Swedes were early supporters of Finnish nationalism, the demand of some extremists for "one language, one spirit" led to a long and bitter feud between Finns and Finland-Swedes. When Finland became independent during the Russian civil war, the new constitution guaranteed the linguistic rights of the minority, probably the best outcome the Finland-Swedes could have hoped for in an unequal contest.

The percentage of the Swedish-speaking population of Finland has been on the decline for many years. The main reasons have been a higher Finnish birth rate, mixed marriages, social pressures, and migration to Sweden. The change has been especially marked in Helsinki ("Helsingfors" in Swedish) and its environs. Helsinki's population was 50 percent Swedish-speaking in 1890 (and, doubtless, near 90 percent in 1830). By 1970 only 10 percent of Helsinki's residents spoke Swedish, and only 6.4 percent of the entire country's.

For many years, Finland-Swedish authors had a keen sense of isolation as a result of the language quarrels and the population decline, a sense coupled, in some cases, with an equally keen awareness of mission—the preservation of an old and worthy culture. Currently, a certain indifference to the once all-important language question has become apparent.

Finland-Swedish literature's greatest age came during the 1920s, following the establishment of Finland's independence. During the hey-day of modernism, as the literary movement of the 1920s came to be called, the political and social background of the Finland-Swedes combined to foster a literature of high quality and great originality.

The modernists tried to maintain a conciliatory attitude toward the Finnish extremists, while at the same time they attempted by example to show the value of Finland-Swedish literature. They did at least succeed in showing the value of their work to *Swedish* writers. Such Swedish poets as Gunnar Ekelöf made pilgrimages to the grave of the modernist "high priestess," Edith Södergran (1892–1923). Elmer Diktonius (1896–1961) and Rabbe Enckell, respectively the most vigorous and the subtlest members of the modernist group, became the admired friends and colleagues of Ekelöf, Eyvind Johnson, Artur Lundkvist, and others; Diktonius in particular had almost the stature of a cultural hero in Swedish eyes.

The Swedish-language literature of Finland grew somewhat paler during the 1930s. The careers of two of the modernists, Södergran and Henry Parland (1908–1930), had been cut short by death; Diktonius had already produced his best poetry, although he was still to publish several works of fiction and some fine music criticism. Rabbe Enckell, however, entered a new phase in his poetry, and Gunnar Björling's (1887–1960) production of syntactically fragmentary verse continued unabated, although more serene than it had been earlier.

The most interesting new writers of the 1930s were the religious novelist

Tito Colliander (born 1904), who, a Finland-Swedish refugee from Soviet Russia, drew heavily on the Dostoevskian tradition, and Solveig von Schoultz (born 1907), who wrote sensitive novellas and poetry. Both these authors have written some of their best work during the last ten years or so. Colliander published a series of invaluable memoirs, and von Schoultz's collections of tales will probably become classics: *Den blomstertid* (1959, That Time of Flowers), *Även dina kameler* (1965, Your Camels Too), and *Rymdbruden* (1971, The Space Girl).

The most interesting single development of the 1930s was a "Karelian romanticism"—a burning interest in Finland's easternmost province. The passion for Karelia was fostered by the novels and travel books of Rabbe Enckell's older brother Olof (born 1900). But a culmination of the Karelian enthusiasm was reached in Hagar Olsson's (born 1893) *Träsnidaren och döden* (1940, The Woodcarver and Death). By such efforts, the Finland-Swedes, who had suffered unusually bitter attack during the wretched final phases of the language strife in the 1930s, could prove that they were as good patriots as their Finnish-speaking colleagues.

The events of the Winter War (1939–40) and the "Continuation War" (1941–44) helped to bring the language factions closer to one another. All the same, the immediate postwar period was anything but hopeful for Finland's Swedish culture. The essayist Hans Ruin (born 1891) left for a post at Lund. Younger men, Willy Kyrklund and the critic Bengt Holmqvist (born 1924), established their literary careers in Sweden, an example followed shortly by the historical novelist and essayist Lorenz von Numers (born 1913), the poetess Ulla Olin (born 1920), and Ralf Parland (born 1914). Parland wrote apocalyptic and futuristic poetry, and, like Numers (in *Basturesan* [1953, The Sauna Trip]), he was a teller of tales with deep roots in Finland (*Hem till sitt hav* [1957, Home to His Sea]).

The new works of importance came from already established writers, such as Rabbe Enckell and Kerstin Söderholm (1897–1943), whose diaries were published in 1947–48.

Modernism's hand lay heavy on those who attempted to enter poetry. And fiction followed the line of psychological analysis against an abstract background, practiced with some power by Mirjam Tuominen (1913–1967), and with great skill, if less force, by Disa Lindholm (born 1916), Marianne Alopaeus (born 1918), Viveca Hollmerus (born 1920), Ole Torvalds (born 1916), and Carl-Fredrik Sandelin (born 1925).

Probably the most memorable fiction came from writers with a political orientation to the left: the Helsinki vignettes of Eva Wichman (born 1908) in *Där vi går* (1949, Where We Go); and the little novel *Klyftan* (1946, The Chasm) by Anna Bondestam (born 1907), in which she portrayed the "other side," the Reds, in Finland's civil war (1918)—a deed of fairness and humanity performed some time before Väinö Linna made a similar attempt on a broader epic scale in Finnish.

Other writers who first published during the 1940s came to dominate the next decade. The poetry of Bo Carpelan (born 1926)—from *Som en dunkel värme* (1946, Like a Warm Darkness) to *Gården* (1969, The Courtyard)—established him as Rabbe Enckell's crown prince, or, indeed, a monarch in his own right, a creator of images readily to be ranked with Sweden's Tomas Tranströmer. The urge toward excessive subtlety in his earlier books has given way to simplicity and force. The macabre humor has abated, letting us perceive the mature poet, a major elegist, but never lachrymose, never sentimental.

And in Carpelan, it turns out, we may find a major novelist as well. In 1971 he published the novel *Rösterna i den sena timmen* (The Voices in the Late Hour), about a group of people on the eve of an accidental nuclear catastrophe. This work not only avoided the peril of sensationalism but had a solid intellectual texture relatively rare in the Finland-Swedish novel.

Other poets followed in Carpelan's footsteps: the fragile Peter Sandelin (born 1930); the quietly pessimistic Åke Gulin (born 1906); Inga-Britt Wik (born 1930), who has brought restrained emotions and, in her latest collection, *Långa längtan* (1969, Long Longing), a style that is at last completely her own; Kurt Sanmark (born 1927), with his aphoristic brevity; and the dryly elegant Lars von Haartman (born 1919). All have written verse of quality, but none has been able to employ, and to over-come, the modernist burden as Carpelan had.

Two poets who established clear contours by drastic means were Sebastian Lybeck (born 1929), who moved to Norway's Lofoten Islands and used the fishermen there as models in his poetry; and Carolus Rein (born 1935), whose conversion to Roman Catholicism gave him a wealth of images, which even today are swept along in the shapeless flood of his poetry.

Walentin Chorell (born 1912) composed some insignificant poetry before turning to fiction and drama. His long string of novels—from *Jörgen Hemmelinks stora augusti* (1947, Jörgen Hemmelink's Great August) and *Calibans dag* (1948, Caliban's Day) to *Agneta och lumpsamlaren* (1968, Agneta and the Ragman) and *Sista leken* (1970, The Last Game)—with their rundown cafés, exconvicts, and traveling peddlers, have dealt (as Diktonius had) with a Finland of sordidness and deprivation. But his novels are never social tracts. Nor do they provide, except to the careful eye, a key to the particular milieu on which they draw—the life of those numerous Finland-Swedes who, contrary to Finnish myth, are neither wealthy nor powerful.

Chorell is concerned with individuals: the unhappy adolescent, the blind and the lame, the mentally ill, the emotionally maimed. Similar themes can be found in his radio plays and in his works for the stage, such as *Systrarna* (1955, The Sisters) and *Gräset* (1958, The Grass). Chorell expanded his cast, but not his range of concern, with *Kattorna* (1961, The Cats), about women workers in a factory opposed to their female chief. Together with Lars Forssell, Chorell is one of the few Swedish-language dramatists of recent times to have achieved some notice in the outside world.

Two other prose writers rivaled Chorell in popularity in the 1950s, both of them—in contrast to Chorell—coming from the Finland-Swedish upper class, and reflecting that background in quite distinct ways. Oscar Parland (born 1912) has written memoir-novels of a high order—*Den förtrollade vägen* (1953, The Enchanted Way) and *Tjurens år* (1962, Year of the Bull)—about a well-to-do and eccentric family's life at Viborg, the quadri-lingual capital of old Karelia. Parland views his caste with gentle affection.

Jörn Donner (born 1933), much of whose creative work has been written in exaggerated reaction against his patrician background and "Fin-land-Swedishness" in general, produced a series of autobiographical novels in the 1950s, and then went on to first-rate journalism and to films, interspersed with still further "factual" books. Thanks to his films, Don-ner's name is known in England and America. Tove Jansson (born 1914) has achieved a comparable fame, with her children's books about the Mumin-trolls, which may be read, it has been discovered, as serious parables for adults.

Regionalism, never a particularly strong factor in so small a language group, suddenly flourished in the 1950s in Ostrobothnia (the area along the northwestern coast of Finland) with the establishment of Österbottens Svenska Författarförening (Ostrobothnia's Swedish Authors' Union), through the efforts of Evert Huldén (1895–1968), a poet in whom good humor and a sense of the country life had made a very happy union. Under the auspices of the Union, the literary journal *Horisont* has appeared since 1954.

The "Ostrobothnian renascence" could look back to a similar if less organized movement in the Finland-Swedish Åland Islands some fifteen to twenty years earlier, with the appearance of the enormously popular books of Sally Salminen (born 1906) and the technically sophisticated historical novels of Valdemar Nyman (born 1904). In 1955, Aili Nordgren (born 1908) continued in the same tradition with the "documentary novel" *Väl-jer du stormen* (If You Choose the Storm), about events in Åbo (Turku) and the Åland Islands during the Finnish civil war.

The Ostrobothnian group likewise had sympathies with the economically unfortunate, as were shown by the novels, mostly historical, of Leo Ågren (born 1928) and the poetry (which presaged the neo-simple poetry in Sweden) of his brother Gösta (born 1936). Still another member of the circle was the first editor of *Horisont,* Sven Olof Högnäs (1910–1961), whose *Vägen till verkligheten* (1954, The Road to Reality), was about Ostrobothnian discontent, both at home and in Finland's capital.

In the 1960s the sober tradition of narratives about life on the Ostrobothnian coastal plain and in the islands was continued by authors who, whatever their technical shortcomings, knew whereof they spoke. In *Brytningstid* (1967, Time of Transition) Levi Sjöstrand (born 1920) used a collection of tales, rather than the customary novel, to talk about Ostrobothnia's hard past and scarcely more hopeful present, including the chronic drain of migration—formerly to America, now to nearby Sweden. Anni Blomqvist (born 1909) has begun a series of novels describing the life of isolated fishermen and island farmers. The fourth volume is called, appropriately, *I kamp med havet* (1971, In Battle with the Sea).

Some of the regionalists have also tried to go beyond the limits of their home region: after a long silence, Leo Ågren published a short novel, *Krigshistoria* (1971, War Story), about the "Continuation War," seen from the standpoint of a Russian soldier. In a story in his latest collection, *Ohördas rop* (1970, Cry of the Unheard), the Ostrobothnian Hans Fors (born 1933) has gone as far afield as Spain. In tales from milieus closer to him Fors has shown a skill in the short narrative rivaling that of Solveig von Schoultz.

According to many literary historians, the Finland-Swedish novel has been pale and bloodless, as if Finland-Swedes were loath to confront the outside reality in which they lived, and preferred instead to look inside themselves. It is one of the literature's curiosities that the two wars against Russia have been rarely depicted in Finland-Swedish fiction (in contrast to the spate of Finnish writing on the subject), and then only in such books as the surrealistic *Djungel* (1950, Jungle) of Lars Hjalmarsson Dahl (born 1920), or, very recently, in Rolf Sandqvist's (born 1919) *Mitt kära krig* (1967, My Dear War). Sandqvist was earlier a practitioner of rather abstract fiction—as in the novel about a future war, *Taskspelaren* (1957, The Sleight-of-Hand Artist).

In the early 1960s an unaccustomed vigor entered the Finland-Swedish novel, emanating, in large part, from Anders Cleve (born 1937) and Christer Kihlman (born 1930). In his rowdy novellas about Finn and Finland-Swede alike in Helsinki in *Gatstenar* (1959, Paving Stones) and in his expansive novels about Helsinki—*Vit eld* (1962, White Fire), *Påskägget* (1966, The Easter Egg), and *Labyrint* (1971, Labyrinth)—Cleve made the "White Queen of the Baltic," albeit somewhat disheveled and besmudged, come alive. His faulty sense of structure (it should be noted that his latest book contains a tribute to Thomas Wolfe) is outweighed by the altogether unfashionable frankness with which he discusses contemporary Finnish methods of making the Swedish minority disappear.

Christer Kihlman has not shared Cleve's devotion to Swedish Finland. His *Se upp Salige!* (1960, O Blest, Look Up!), about the nastier sides of the Finland-Swedish establishment in a small cultural center (the town of Borgå, "Finland's Weimar"), got him fame in Sweden and some enmity among his own group: the book's representatives of the Finland-Swedish spirit were human, all too human. (It should be added that Kihlman's books are best sellers in Finnish, while Cleve's novels have not been translated.)

Kihlman's next book, *Den blå modern* (1963, The Blue Mother), with its analysis of perverted tendencies and practices and its continuation of the sordid fable of *O Blest, Look Up!,* caused greater consternation still. Many overlooked its clearly humane core. *Madeleine* (1965, Madeleine) dealt with an author's personal problems of adultery and alcoholism. In *Människan som skalv* (1971, The Man Who Trembled) Kihlman removed the fictional mask entirely, publishing a confessional book, pure and simple; intentionally or not, he has followed in the footsteps of Strindberg's autobiographical novels. The horror and the repugnance of what Kihlman talks about is heightened by his mastery of Swedish prose.

Younger novelists who would like to emulate Kihlman have not so far proved that they are of his caliber. Ralf Nordgren's (born 1937) autobiographical series about the life of a Finland-Swedish communist—thus far, *Med* (1968, Along), and *Fjärilsörat* (1971, The Butterfly's Ear)—is interesting in its special standpoint. But this standpoint is not exclusively Nordgren's. Jarl Sjöblom's (born 1932) *Vägen till Hangö* (1968, The Way to Hangö) brought another communist, an amputee-veteran of the two wars, up against his pacifist son.

Johan Bargum (born 1943) has chosen to investigate violence in everyday life. Thus far, he has looked at a draftee's humiliations (*Svartvitt* [1965, Black-White]), at a somewhat nasty television cameraman (*Tre två ett* [1968, Three Two One]), and at a vacation in the skerries (*Finsk rulett* [1971, Finnish Roulette]).

The sensationalist Gunnar Mattsson (born 1937) has not even pretended to be a thinker, gladly turning from the sentimental *Prinsessan* (1965, The Princess) to the mildly pornographic "social study" of suburban housewives, *Eden* (1967, Eden). Mattsson, to be sure, has solved a problem that has kept Kihlman, Cleve, and many other Finland-Swedish authors from working full time at their art: How can the serious writer survive economically?

If the quality of Finland-Swedish literature is to be measured by the attention it attracts in Sweden, then the 1960s was its best decade since the flowering of modernism. Cleve and, particularly, Kihlman have won a limited Swedish following, while, more recently, Claes Andersson (born 1937) has found his way into the annals of the new simplicity.

In 1965, a new magazine *FBT* (the meaning of the initials was kept a secret throughout *FBT*'s brief life) gave a forum to those writers who wanted to throw off the now ancient cloak of "modernism" and to shake Finland-Swedish society to its foundations. Ironically, they bore a strong resemblance to the more radical modernists of forty years earlier, in their awareness of social injustice and in their determination not to be Finland-Swedes any longer but rather citizens of Finland writing in Swedish. Thus, together with their Finnish colleagues, they have published the bilingual anthology *Lyrik i Finland nu/ Suomen lyriikkaa tänään* (1969, Poetry in Finland Now), in which each poem has been translated into the other language.

Among the poets themselves, two lines can be discerned: one of playfulness, in which puns, jokes, and parodies are used to criticize Finnish society or the world at large; and a second, in which both the social message and the means of expression are more direct.

Lars Huldén (born 1926) can be considered the chieftain of the playful group. He has brought his special skills to bear in his small but important books of comic poetry. Mauritz Nylund (born 1925), a quick-tongued man, has similar but less finely honed gifts. And the subtle Tom Sandell (born 1936) has written both verse (the brevity and lucidity of which is misleading) and reflective prose, such as *Ur clownens garderob* (1965, From the Clown's Wardrobe) and *N. N.* (1967, N. N.). A woman's intelligent voice has been raised by Wava Stürmer (born 1929), an Ostrobothnian like Huldén and with a sense of humor more inclined to indignation than his.

Among the activists, the principal writers are Robert Alftan (born 1940), who has often been lured into intellectualism; Gösta Ågren, whose most recent volume of verse was simply called *Ågren* (1968, Ågren); and Claes Andersson. Andersson's six collections of poetry—among them *Staden heter Helsingfors* (1965, The City Is Called Helsingfors) and *Samhället vi dör i* (1967, The Society We Die In)—have paraded an interest in social welfare and an awareness of the uneasiness of modern culture.

Andersson's poetry is sometimes perceptive, sometimes a bid for attention. But he himself has said that much of his poetry is written for a special purpose, meant to arouse interest in a problem and then to be thrown away. In a society as tied to tradition as the Finland-Swedish has been, and maybe as needful of tradition for survival, Claes Andersson's work (to use the title of one of Mauritz Nylund's collections) is indeed *"ofinlandssvensk verksamhet"* ("un-Finland-Swedish activity").

SWEDISH WORKS IN
ENGLISH TRANSLATION

ANTHOLOGY

Bäckström, Lars and Göran Palm, eds. *Sweden Writes: Contemporary Swedish Poetry and Prose, Views on Art, Literature and Society.* Stockholm, 1965

INDIVIDUAL WORKS MENTIONED
IN ARTICLE

Dagerman, Stig. *Bränt barn* as *A Burnt Child.* New York, 1950
———. *Nattens lekar* as *The Games of Night: Ten Stories and an Autobiographical Piece.* Philadelphia, 1961
Delblanc, Sven. *Homunculus* as *Homunculus: A Magic Tale.* Englewood Cliffs, N.J., 1969
Forssell, Lars. *Söndagspromenaden* as *The Sunday Promenade.* In Robert Corrigan, ed., *The New Theatre of Europe 3.* New York, 1968
Görling, Lars. *491* as *491.* New York, 1966

Gyllensten, Lars. *Kains memoarer* as *The Testament of Cain.* London, 1967
Johnson, Eyvind. *Hans Nådes tid* as *The Days of His Grace.* London, 1968
———. *Nu var det 1914* (Part 1 of *Romanen om Olof*) as *1914.* London, 1970
———. *Strändernas svall* as *Return to Ithaca.* New York, 1952
Lidman, Sara. *Regnspiran* as *The Rain Bird.* New York, 1962
Martinson, Harry. *Aniara* as *Aniara.* London, 1963
———. *Kap Farväl* as *Cape Farewell.* London, 1934
Olsson, Hagar. *Träsnidaren och döden* as *The Woodcarver and Death.* Madison, Wisc., 1965
Sjögren, Peder. *Kärlekens bröd* as *Bread of Love.* Madison, Wisc., 1965
Sundman, Per Olof. *Expeditionen* as *The Expedition.* London, 1967
Wästberg, Per. *Luftburen* as *The Air Cage.* New York, 1972

SECONDARY WORKS

BIBLIOGRAPHIES AND GUIDES

Åhlén, Bengt. *Svenskt författarlexikon,* 7 vols. Stockholm 1942ff.
Runnquist, Åke. *Litterära tidskrifter 1920–1960.* Stockholm, 1964
———. *Moderna svenska författare,* 2nd ed. Stockholm, 1967
Svenskt litteraturlexikon, 2nd ed. Lund, 1970
Vem skrev vad? Stockholm, 1948

GENERAL WORKS

Alving, H. and Gudmar Hasselberg. *Svensk litteraturhistoria,* 4th ed. Stockholm, 1957

Brandell, Gunnar. *Svensk litteratur 1900–1950,* 2nd ed. Stockholm, 1967
Gustafsson, Alrik. *A History of Swedish Literature.* Minneapolis, Minn., 1961
Henriques, Alf. *Svensk litteratur efter 1900,* 2nd ed. Stockholm, 1947
Holm, Ingvar and Magnus von Platen. *La littérature suédoise.* Stockholm, 1957
Linder, Erik H. *Fem decennier av nittonhundratalet,* I–II, 4th rev. ed. Stockholm, 1965 (Published as vol. 5, 1–2, of E. N. Tigerstedt, ed. *Ny illustrerad svensk litteraturhistoria,* 5 vols., 2nd rev. ed. Stockholm, 1967
Tigerstedt, E. N. *Svensk litteraturhistoria,* 3rd ed. Stockholm, 1960

WORKS ON CONTEMPORARY LITERATURE

Anderson, Carl L. *The Swedish Acceptance of American Literature.* Stockholm, 1957

Bäckström, Lars. *Klippbok: Litterärt in i sextitalet.* Stockholm, 1965

———. *Under välfärdens yta: Litterärt under femtitalet.* Stockholm, 1959

Franzén, L. O. *40-talsförfattare.* Stockholm, 1965

Gustafsson, L. *The Public Dialogue in Sweden.* Stockholm, 1964

Lagerlöf, Karl Erik. *Samtal med 60-talister.* Stockholm, 1965

Lagerlöf, Karl Erik, ed. *Femtitalet i backspegeln.* Stockholm, 1968

Schoolfield, George C. *Canals on Mars:*

The Recent Scandinavian Lyric. In *Books Abroad,* Winter–Spring, 1962

Wizelius, I. *Swedish Literature: 1956–1960.* Stockholm, 1960

WORKS ON FINLAND-SWEDISH LITERATURE

Holmqvist, Bengt. *Modern finlandssvensk litteratur.* Stockholm, 1951

Laitenen, Kai. *Finlands moderna litteratur.* Helsinki, 1968

Lindström, Hans. *Finlandssvensk nittonhundratalslitteratur.* Stockholm, 1965

Schoolfield, George C. *The Postwar Novel of Swedish Finland.* In *Scandinavian Studies,* May, 1962

Warburton, Thomas. *Finlandssvensk litteratur 1898–1948.* Helsinki, 1951

GEORGE S. N. LUCKYJ

Ukrainian Literature

DURING WORLD WAR II all Ukrainian territories were incorporated into the
Soviet Union. This has had a profound influence on the literature of the
country. On the one hand, the union of western Ukraine (which had been
largely under Polish rule since 1920) and eastern Ukraine (always under
Russian control, except for a brief period of independence after the Russian revolution) had some positive effects; on the other hand, the contacts
with western Europe that had existed before 1939 came to an end. When
Czechoslovakia and Poland became communist states in the late 1940s, it
was clear that these two countries would no longer offer a haven to Ukrainian émigré writers, who earlier had been quite active in Prague and
Warsaw. New Ukrainian émigrés had to settle further west—in western
Europe and later in America.

Those Ukrainian writers who remained within the Soviet Union had to
face ideological readjustments. During the war political controls over
literature were somewhat relaxed, and Ukrainian ethnic identity was
encouraged as part of the resistance to German invasion. Immediately after
the end of the war, however, strict political controls were reimposed (after
Zhdanov's speech in 1946) and some writers were accused of nationalism,
which had been a common charge against Ukrainian writers in the 1930s.
Until Stalin's death in 1953 strict conformity to the principles of socialist
realism prevailed, but after 1953 new trends emerged.

The desire for greater freedom of expression was intensified by the partial rediscovery—through republication—of writers who had perished in the late 1930s and 1940s. These writers included Mykola Zerov (1890–1941), Oleksa Slisarenko (1891–1937), Mykola Kulish (1892–1937), Yevhen Pluzhnyk (1898–1936), and Hryhori Kosynka (1899–1934). The Khrushchev era was relatively liberal, permitting great advances to be made, especially by the young poets in the early 1960s. After 1964 the political control of literature was intensified, and many Ukrainian writers had to resort to underground publication. At present no literary thaw is in sight. The official doctrine of literature as "socialist in content and national in form" meant in practice that Ukrainian literature was dependent on Russian models.

Against the background of these political developments, Ukrainian literature of the period 1945–70 can best be studied in its various themes, as they reflect or run contrary to the official ideology. From the point of view of form there has been very little new or different from the period 1930–45, except in poetry. For a long time after the war, victory was depicted in heroic terms both by poets (Mykola Bazhan [born 1904], Andri Malyshko [1912–1969], Platon Voron'ko [born 1913]) and by novelists (Oles' Honchar [born 1918] and Mykhaylo Stel'makh [born 1912]). Faithful to socialist realism, these writers represented war as an ennobling experience; their positive heroes were frequently communists or those who followed the party line.

Oles' Honchar, in his novel *Praporonostsi* (1948, The Standard-Bearers), produced a good example of what may be called "socialist romanticism." Other war novels, such as Leonid Pervomays'ky's (born 1908) *Dyky med* (1963, Wild Honey), expressed a spirit of genuine humanism.

An older poet, Maksym Ryl's'ky (1895–1964), who wrote two memorable poems during the war—*Slovo pro ridnu matir* (1941, A Song about Mother) and *Zhaha* (1943, Thirst)—proclaimed the popular theme of the friendship of Soviet peoples in his collection of verse *Chasha druzhby* (1946, Chalice of Friendship). In the Ukraine writers handling this theme tended to glorify Russia to the point of complete obsequiousness. Perhaps the most notable work in this category was Natan Rybak's (born 1910) novel *Pereyaslavs'ka rada* (1949–53, The Council of Pereyaslav).

Other historical novels—such as Petro Panch's (born 1891) *Homonila Ukrayina* (1954, The Echo of the Ukraine) and Anton Khyzhnyak's (born 1907) *Danylo Halyts'ky* (1951, Danylo of Halych)—also extolled Ukrainian-Russian contacts in the past. On the other hand, some novels dealt with the history of the Ukrainian revolution in 1917–18 and were directed against the regime of the nationalist Ukrainian People's Republic. These included Yuri Smolych's (born 1900) *Myr khatam, viyna palatsam*

(1958, Peace to Houses, War to Palaces) and *Reve ta stohne Dnipr shyroky* (1960, The Wide Dnieper Roars and Groans).

Occasionally, historical fiction possessed humor and lyricism; an example was Oleksandr Il'chenko's (born 1909) novel about the legendary figure Cossack Mamay, *Kozats'komu rodu nema perevodu* (1958, There Is No End to the Cossack Breed). Other outstanding examples of historical fiction were Semen Sklyarenko's (1901–1962) two novels about the Kiev Rus—*Svyatoslav* (1959, Svyatoslav) and *Volodymyr* (1962, Volodymyr). The profusion of historical novels attested in some measure to the interest taken by Ukrainians in their national identity. One such novel, Honchar's *Sobor* (1968, The Cathedral), was severely criticized for overindulgence in historical sentiments. In both content and form, these works continued the populist tradition of the nineteenth century.

A great deal of contemporary Ukrainian literature is crudely propagandist, concentrating on such themes as the glorification of Lenin and, up to 1953, of Stalin; the behavior of the ideal communist; or the campaign against western European and American influences. An example was Andri Malyshko's *Sa synim morem* (1950, Beyond the Blue Sea). Most works dealing with life in factories and on collective farms also belonged to this category. Among them is the cycle by Mykhaylo Stel'makh: *Velyka ridnya* (1949–51, Great Family), *Krov lyuds'ka ne vodytsya* (1957, Human Blood Is Not Water), *Khlib i sil'* (1959, Bread and Salt), and *Pravda i kryvda* (1961, Truth and Falsehood). He received the Lenin prize for this cycle.

Sometimes, despite tendentiousness, novels of peasant life preserved a degree of realism; an example is *Vyr* (1959–61, Whirlpool), by Hryhori Tyutyunnyk (1920–1961). Yuri Yanovs'ky (1902–1954) tried to portray a village's postwar reconstruction in his novel *Zhyva voda* (1947, Living Water), which was severely attacked by official critics and subsequently rewritten as *Myr* (1950, Peace).

Rewriting works to suit the demands of socialist realism is a common phenomenon. One such example was Volodymyr Gzhyts'ky's (born 1895) *Chorne ozero* (1929, 1959, The Black Lake). Gzhyts'ky was one of the few writers who, in the 1940s, were released from concentration camps or exile. Many more perished there before or during the war. Three others who were released were Ostap Vyshnya (1889–1956), a writer of humorous stories; Zinayida Tulub (1890–1964), an historical novelist; and Borys Antonenko-Davydovych (born 1899), author of the novel *Za shyrmoyu* (1963, Behind the Screen).

Another older writer who continued to create was the world-famous film producer, Oleksandr Dovzhenko (1894–1956). His autobiographical novel *Zacharovana Desna* (1954, The Enchanted Desna), a lyrical masterpiece, was especially interesting. His film scenario *Poema pro more* (1957, Poem about the Sea) received the Lenin prize.

Dovzhenko also wrote some interesting memoirs (*Zapysni knyzhky* [1958, Notebooks] and *Shchodennyk* [1962, Diary]). Other important reminiscences, especially of the 1920s, were Antonenko-Davydovych's *Zdaleka i zblyz'ka* (1969, From Far and Near) and Yuri Smolych's *Rozpovid' pro nespoki* (1968, A Tale about Restlessness) and *Rozpovid' pro nespoki tryvaye* (1969, A Tale about Restlessness Continues). It is a pity that, because of political restraints, these memoirs were not as informative as they could be.

Until the thaw, developments in Soviet Ukrainian literature reflected the changes in Russian literature of the time. The post-Stalin thaw in the Ukraine did not produce as many original, nonconformist works as it did in Russia. On the whole, Ukrainian writers seemed more timid than their Russian colleagues. Some of the works of protest in the Ukraine against Stalinist practices came from the pens of faithful party followers who simply went along with the new Khrushchev policy (for example, Oleksandr Korniychuk's [born 1905] play *Kryla* [1954, Wings]).

In spite of the great number of new writers, the quality of literature remained low. The significant exception is poetry written in the 1960s. Some members of the older generation of poets, who had reached their zenith in the 1920s, were still creative, although their works tended to be rather uneven. The greatest of them, Pavlo Tychyna (1891–1967), was reduced to composing panegyrics on communism in his collection *Komunizmu dali vydni* (1961, Communism's Ranges Are Visible). On the other hand, Ryl's'ky managed to produce some moving lyrics in his *Holosiyivs'ka osin'* (1959, Autumn at Holosiyiv). He also gave active support to the younger poets. Volodymyr Sosyura (1898–1965) was criticized for his poem *Lyubit' Ukrayinu* (1944, Of Love for Ukraine). Mykola Bazhan occasionally rose to the level of his best prewar poetry, as in *Opovidannya pro nadiyu: variyatsiyi na temu R. M. Rilke* (1966, A Tale about Hope: Variations on a Theme by R. M. Rilke).

Yet the real innovations in poetry came from a group of poets who without any formal affiliation were often referred to as "Shestydesyatnyky" ("the 1960-ers"). What they had in common was a desire to turn away from political ideology and toward universal themes. In both language and style, their poems were much more sophisticated than those of their immediate predecessors. At their best, they equaled the leading young Russian poets, whose influence was visible not so much in specific instances but in the general revival of poetry as an art in the Soviet Union.

The most gifted in this group has been Lina Kostenko (born 1930), whose collections include *Prominnya zemli* (1957, Earthly Rays), *Vitryla*

(1958, Sails), and *Mandrivky sertsya* (1961, The Wandering Heart). Sometimes she found it difficult to get her poems accepted for publication. Unlike Kostenko, who is basically a lyricist, Ivan Drach (born 1936) is an intellectual poet of great power. This power was revealed in *Sonyashnyk* (1961, Sunflower) and *Protuberantsi sertsya* (1965, Protuberances of the Heart). He has also written film scenarios. Less profound but quite versatile is Vitali Korotych (born 1936), whose art was shown by *Zoloti ruky* (1961, Golden Hands) and *Vulytsya voloshok* (1963, The Street of Cornflowers).

Quite different from these poets, because of his talent for satire, was Vasyl' Symonenko (1935–1963), author of *Zemne tyazhinnya* (1964, Earth's Gravity). Some of his best poems were published abroad and did not appear in the Soviet Union. Mykola Vinhranovs'ky (born 1936), whose first collection was *Atomni prelyudy* (1962, Atomic Preludes), is another strong, original talent.

Among still younger poets, the following have shown great promise: Borys Mamaysur (born 1938), Ihor Kalynets' (born 1939), Irena Zhylenko (born 1941), and Vasyl' Holoborod'ko (born 1942). A particularly fine poetic achievement was Kalynets''s collection *Pidsumovuyuchy movchannya* (Summing Up Silence), clandestinely circulated and later published in Munich in 1971. It is a great pity that this resurgence of Ukrainian poetry has not been matched in prose. In fiction, only three young short-story writers stand out: Yevhen Hutsalo (born 1937), Volodymyr Drozd (born 1929), and Valeri Shevchuk (born 1939).

In the mid-1960s several Ukrainian writers and intellectuals were arrested for alleged anti-Soviet activities. Among them was Vyacheslav Chornovil (born 1938), whose collection of protest literature, *Lykho z rozumu* (1967, Woe from Wit), was smuggled out and published in America. It included some literary works by the intellectual dissenters. The well-known literary critic Ivan Dzyuba (born 1931) wrote another underground work, *Internatsyonalizm chy rusyfikatsiya* (1968, Internationalism or Russification). Another critic, Yevhen Sverstyuk, circulated clandestinely an essay on Honchar's *The Cathedral,* in which he discussed many problems connected with literary freedom.

Ukrainian underground literature, although smaller in volume than in Russia, shows strong originality in the genre of the essay. A good example is the work of Valentyn Moroz (born 1936), who recently received a fourteen-year jail sentence. The tone of Moroz's essays is extremely defiant and nationalistic. Many voices from the underground plead for more creative freedom and abolition of russification.

No survey of contemporary Ukrainian literature can ignore the émigré writers. Many of them were in western Europe by the end of World War II.

Some belonged to the artists' movement MUR (Mystets'ky ukrayins'ky rukh), which published several anthologies in Germany in the late 1940s. Among the contributors were the poets Yuri Klen (1891–1947), Todos' Os'machka (born 1895), Yevhen Malanyuk (born 1899), Mykhaylo Orest (born 1901), Vasyl' Barka (born 1908), and Vadym Lesych (born 1909); the novelists and short-story writers Viktor Domontovych (1894–1969), Dokiya Humenna (born 1904), Ulas Samchuk (born 1905), Yuri Kosach (born 1909), and Ivan Bahryany (born 1907); and the critics Volodymyr Derzhavyn (1899–19??) and Yuri Sherekh (born 1908). Some of them are now living and writing in America.

The younger generation of Ukrainian writers in America has been best represented by the so-called New York Group of poets: Bohdan Boychuk (born 1927), Emma Andiyevs'ka (born 1931), Yuri Tarnavs'ky (born 1934), Bohdan Rubchak (born 1935), and Patrytsiya Kylyna (born 1936). These and other writers have been frequent contributors to the magazine *Suchasnist'*, published in Munich. Among the younger émigré writers there is a strong tendency toward experimentation, a quality sadly lacking in Soviet Ukraine.

UKRAINIAN WORKS IN ENGLISH TRANSLATION

ANTHOLOGIES

Browne, M., ed. *Ferment in the Ukraine.* London, 1971
Luckyj, George, ed. *Modern Ukrainian Short Stories.* Littleton, Colo., 1972
Slavutych, Yar, ed. *The Muse in Prison: Eleven Sketches of Ukrainian Poets Killed by Communists and Twenty-two Translations of Their Poems.* Jersey City, N.J., 1956
Stories of the Soviet Ukraine. Moscow, 1970

The Ukrainian Poets 1189–1962. Toronto, 1963

INDIVIDUAL WORKS MENTIONED IN ARTICLE

Sosyura, Volodymyr. *Lyubit' Ukrayinu* as *Of Love for Ukraine.* In Yar Slavutych, ed. *The Muse in Prison.* Jersey City, N.J., 1956
Stel'makh, Mykhaylo. *Krov lyuds'ka ne vodytsya* as *Let the Blood of Man Not Flow.* Moscow, 1968

SECONDARY WORKS

Deržavyn, V. *Post War Ukrainian Literature in Exile.* In *Ukrainian Review,* 4–5, 1957–58
Istoriya ukrayins'koyi radyans'koyi literatury. Kiev, 1964
Koshelivets', Ivan. *Suchasna literatura v URSR.* New York, 1964

Literature. In V. Kubijovyč, ed. *Ukraine: A Concise Encyclopaedia.* Toronto, 1963
Ukrayins'ki pys'mennyky. Vols. IV–V. Kiev, 1965

CHARLES MADISON

Yiddish Literature

THE MIGRATION OF JEWS over Europe and other parts of the western world, forced upon them largely by persecution, has given Yiddish literature a character radically different from that of any other literature. Yiddish literature was also unusual in its pattern of growth: after growing slowly from the early Middle Ages through the middle of the nineteenth century, it suddenly and vigorously flowered after 1860. With the restrictions of orthodox Judaism loosened by the surge of modern enlightenment, the energies of the east European Jews, which had been directed almost exclusively to religious study, were released to other pursuits, enabling those with creative talent to express themselves with great vitality.

The progenitors of modern Yiddish literature—Mendele Moikher Sforim (1835–1917), I. L. Perets (1851–1915), and Sholem Aleichem (1859–1916)—wrote original works of high quality. Scores of other writers followed, each seeking to express in Yiddish the life he knew intimately. Coming from the yeshiva and the synagogue, but also familiar with the work of major European authors, Yiddish writers readily adopted the prose and verse forms of modern literature. Persecution and economic hardship before World War II sent many Jews to the Americas, some even as far as Australia; everywhere they established centers of Yiddish literature.

After 1945, with a third of the world's Jews dead in gas chambers, Jewish writers—both those writing in Yiddish and those writing in other languages—reacted with soul-searing anguish to the catastrophe. Overpowered by the guilt of their own survival, they relived the horrors of the martyrs. This traumatic experience was aggravated when Stalin, once the war was over, sought to expunge Jewish cultural life in the Soviet Union by completely strangulating artistic and intellectual activity in the Yiddish language. Prominent writers and scholars were arrested and subsequently executed. In recent years, therefore, the horror of genocide, both German and Russian, has dominated Yiddish writing. Even when writers turned to other events in the past, they tended to choose those having a similarly tragic content.

Halpern Leivick (1888–1962) wrote outstanding poetry after the war expressing his empathy with the victims. Viewing events from his adopted city of New York, Leivick never ceased agonizing over the slaughter of Jews in Europe. In the collection *In Treblinke bin ikh nit geven* (1945, In Treblinka I Never Was) he expressed in poem after poem his guilt at not having been consumed by the "fire in Treblinka." Leivick's elegy on the Warsaw ghetto reminded readers that the desperate Jews there exclaimed heroically in their fatal uprising, *"Gevalt,* Jews, don't despair!" In *Maaram fun Rotenberg* (1945, Rabbi Mair of Rothenburg) he treated the same theme of resistance and martyrdom during an earlier time of woe in Jewish history. *Di khasune in Fernvald* (1949, The Wedding in Fernwald) again dealt with the holocaust, depicting, symbolically and mystically, the celebration of a wedding among the hapless survivors in a displaced-persons camp in Bavaria.

Grief over the holocaust continued to permeate Leivick's subsequent writing. In *In di teg fun Eyov* (1953, In the Days of Job) he considered mystically and philosophically the question of how God could permit the sacrifice of Isaac and the tortures of Job. In his last two volumes of verse—*A blat oifn appleboim* (1955, A Leaf on the Apple Tree) and *Lieder fun eybigkeit* (1959, Songs of Eternity)—the concentration camp still dominated, but its presence was softened by nature lyrics of great beauty.

A close friend of Leivick's, Joseph Opatoshu (1886–1954), a leading writer of fiction, was also shattered by the dreadful events in Europe, especially by the news from his native Poland. In story after story, Opatoshu expressed his agony over the torture and killing of defenseless Jews, but he also portrayed the courage and heroism of individual Jews in the face of Nazi brutalities. His distinguished novel *Der letster oifshtand* (1948–52, The Last Uprising) portrayed the patriotic boldness of an earlier group of martyrs, inspired by Rabbi Akiba and Bar Kokhba, who resisted Hadrian's legions in 132 A.D.

In 1945 Sholem Asch (1880–1957) was the Yiddish writer best known to non-Yiddish-speaking readers. His *Der man fun Notseres* (1943, The Man from Nazareth [but first published in English as *The Nazarene*] and

Paulus (1943, Paul, the Apostle) were esteemed the world over. Asch was privately affected by the holocaust, but he was somehow unable to write much about it. Eager to effect a reconciliation, he discussed in *One Destiny: An Epistle to the Christians* (1945) Judeo-Christian relations over the centuries and stressed dependence of the two religions on one another: "Only the Judeo-Christian idea contains in itself the possibility for salvation for our tortured world." In *Der brenender dorn* (1946, The Burning Bush) Asch wrote about Nazi atrocities with poignancy but without Leivick's emotional intensity. *East River* (1946, East River) which described Jewish life in New York, focused on the problems of intermarriage. *Maria* (1949, Mary) was the simplest and least controversial of his trilogy about the origins of Christianity. After 1950 Asch devoted himself to Old Testament themes. In *Moshe* (1951, Moses) and *Der novi* (1955, The Prophet) he enlivened biblical material with legendary, mythological, and anthropological embellishments.

Jacob Glatstein (1896–1971) was perhaps the greatest Yiddish writer of the contemporary period. Living in New York since 1914, fully Americanized but with a strong Jewish identity, he long gave voice to his Jewishness in a pure, musical Yiddish. Glatstein wrote both poetry and prose with eloquence and passion. In *A gute nakht, welt* (Good Night, World), published in the late 1930s, he foresaw the oncoming genocide and exclaimed, with a combination of despair and disdain: "Good night, broad world, big stinking world, not you but I shut fast the gate." Poems like *Millionen toit* (Millions Dead), written in the early 1950s, were outcries of pain against the killing of his fellow Jews. In *Di freyd fun yiddish vort* (1961, The Joy of the Yiddish Word) and in his other late poems he both continued to lament the tragedy and celebrated the state of Israel.

Isaac Bashevis Singer (born 1904), the Yiddish writer currently most popular among non-Yiddish readers, depicted in his first book, *Soten in Gorey* (1935, Satan in Goray), the psychotic aspects of the behavior of Hasidic Jewry at a time of persecution during the seventeenth century. After Singer settled in New York in 1935, he became a journalist for the next fifteen years. *Di familie Moskat* (1950, The Moskat Family) established him as a major writer of fiction. Since then he has published a number of novels and collections of short stories as well as children's books, all of them translated into numerous languages. His fiction, steeped in Hasidic life and embellished with exotic folklore, has a charm that gives his subject matter greater significance than it intrinsically has.

Relatively early, modern Yiddish literature had to confront the problem of survival. Unlike other literatures, which find sustenance and inspiration from a native land and a more or less homogeneous population, works in

Yiddish have been written by men and women in various parts of the world who originally came from eastern Europe and who adhered less to their adopted countries than to the culture and history of the Jewish people. But by now, most Jews speak the language of the land in which they live, and cultural assimilation is almost unavoidable. Moreover, genocide, plus the anti-Jewish policies of Iron Curtain countries, almost completely destroyed the eastern European sources of the Yiddish language.

In recent years few new Yiddish writers have replaced those who were gassed or were shot or died of natural causes. Most of the current Yiddish writers were born before 1910. One of the younger writers of this group is Khaim Grade (born 1910), who published his first volume of poetry in 1936. He found refuge in Soviet Russia during the war years and came to New York in 1948. His poems in *A mames tsavoeh* (1949, A Mother's Will) and his stories in *Der mames shabosim* (1955, The Mother's Sabbaths) jolted readers with tortured reflections on human life in a world of chaos and evil. His most recent novel, the two-volume *Reb Tsemakh Atlas* (1969, Reb Tsemakh Atlas), was a monumental narrative of Jewish life in eastern Europe before 1939.

Kadia Molodowsky (born 1894) is perhaps the most distinguished of Yiddish women poets. Moved by the poverty of Jews in her native Poland, she reacted to this on a metaphysical plane. The grief caused by the slaughter of many close to her led her to write numerous laments. Coming to New York after the war, she wrote distinguished poetry and fiction, including *Lieder fun khurban* (1962, Songs of the Holocaust) and the novel *Beim toyer* (1967, At the Gate).

Many Yiddish writers, including some I have already discussed, now live in the United States. Eliezer Greenberg (born 1896) is an important poet and critic. His three postwar volumes of verse—*Di lange nakht* (1946, The Long Night), *Beinakhnitiges dialog* (1953, Night Dialogue), and *Eybigker dorsht* (1968, Eternal Thirst)—were quietly lyrical and showed a mastery of prosody. His critical studies of Yiddish writers have been perceptive.

Itsik Manger (1901–1969) was quite a different writer—a word magician with a humorous turn of phrase and a serious undertone. After coming to New York (in 1951), he published *Lied un balade* (1951, Song and Ballad) and *Nohente geshtalten, un andere shriften* (1961, Intimate Portraits, and Other Writings). These and later poems combined pathos with subtle satire; they had the flow and spontaneity of the folk song and the purity of tone and musicality of sophisticated verse.

An eager experimenter in literary forms, Aaron Glantz-Leyeles (1889–1966) was equally at home in romantic verse and journalistic prose. In *A Yid oifn yam* (1946, A Jew at Sea) and *Amerike un ikh* (1961, America and I) he did not achieve the poetic authenticity for which he strove.

Aaron Tzeitlin (born 1898) wrote prose and poetry in both Yiddish and Hebrew, and produced a major study of Byron. Since reaching New York after the war, he has published three volumes of polished verse.

In Russia, where Yiddish literature first came into flower, the Bolshevik revolution at first led to official encouragement of Yiddish culture. In the 1930s, however, during the years of the political purges, Stalin's censors began to restrict Yiddish writing and publishing. This repression was intensified after the Russo-German pact of 1939. Yiddish writers were not permitted to mention the Nazi atrocities. Once this restriction was relaxed, after the German armies invaded Russian soil, Yiddish writing became a cry of anguish and anger over the slaughter of innocent Jews.

After the war, Aron Kushnirov (1891–1949) and Perets Markish (1895–1952) brought out volumes of poems, each titled *Milkhome* (War) —Kushnirov's in 1946, Markish's in 1948—in which they expressed the grief of the Jews in Soviet Russia. Itsik Kipnis (born 1896), a humorist in the tradition of Sholem Aleichem, described the wholesale murder of Jews in Babi Yar with great power. Itsik Fefer (1900–1952), a prominent poet and devoted communist, wrote *Di sotens fun wharshever ghetto* (1945, Shadows of the Warsaw Ghetto), a long chronicle of beastly brutality and heroic resistance. Numerous other Yiddish writers in Russia added to the literary lament for the millions barbarously destroyed.

Two Yiddish writers in Russia require special mention: Der Nister (1884–1950, pseudonym of Pinkhas Kahanovich) and Dovid Bergelson (1884–1952). Der Nister, mystical and apolitical, consistently refused to join the communist bandwagon and suffered accordingly. His chief work, *Di familie Mashbir* (1939–48, The Mashbir Family), treated Hasidic life in the nineteenth century with masterly insight and artistic depth. His stories about the war remained unpublished until a volume was brought out in New York in 1957. Another collection, *Di milkhome fun yiddishe partizaner* (1956, The War of the Jewish Partisans), was issued in Buenos Aires. Bergelson, long the most distinguished Yiddish novelist in Russia, could not get his stories of the holocaust published in the Soviet Union, but they were issued in Buenos Aires as *Neie dertseylungen* (1949, New Stories).

In 1948 Der Nister, Dovid Bergelson, and many other writers and intellectuals were arrested, and most of them were exiled to Siberia, where they were shot in 1952. From 1948 to 1959 nothing in Yiddish was printed in the Soviet Union. Then, in 1959, four Yiddish books, three reprints of classics and an account of Birobizhan (the Jewish autonomous region in eastern Siberia), were issued in Moscow. A few additional volumes have been published since, and several of the executed writers were officially rehabilitated. In 1961 *Sovietish heymland* began to appear, first as a bimonthly and later as a monthly. Edited by Aron Vergelis (born 1918), a poet who is a devoted communist, it remains the only Yiddish periodical now being published in Soviet Russia.

Some of the Yiddish writers who survived the war found their way to Israel and to countries in western Europe, the Americas, and Australia, where they joined fellow writers who had previously migrated from eastern Europe. Yiddish books were published in all these Jewish centers. In Paris, for instance, Mendel Man (born 1916) and Mordekhai Litwin (born 1903) are among the active writers. In Canada today Melekh Ravitch (born 1893) is one of a number of interesting Yiddish writers. Mexico City, Buenos Aires, and other Latin American cities, as well as the big cities in Australia, also have groups devoted to furthering Yiddish literature and culture. These oases notwithstanding, assimilation—forced in eastern Europe and voluntary elsewhere—is drying up the sources of the Yiddish language and thus of Yiddish literature in the diaspora.

In Israel, however, Yiddish writing is increasing, although this hospitality to Yiddish is recent. The early Jewish settlers in Palestine, determined to make Hebrew the national language, were actively hostile to the use of Yiddish. It was only after World War II, when Hebrew was already fully established, that the Israelis became more tolerant toward the mother tongue of the tens of thousands of refugees from concentration camps who migrated to Palestine. Yiddish began to be regarded as "the martyr's tongue"—in contrast to Hebrew as "the holy tongue"—and welcomed accordingly.

In 1949 a quarterly, *Di goldene keyt* was established in Israel and quickly became the most prestigious periodical in Yiddish, printing contributions from writers in every part of the world. Another enterprise, the Perets Ferlag, was active from the outset and now publishes more Yiddish books than all Yiddish book firms outside Israel. In 1951 a chair in Yiddish was established at the Hebrew University—after it had been rejected twenty years earlier; more such chairs are now being established at other educational institutions. A Yiddish newspaper has a wide circulation. Several literary "houses," named after leading Yiddish writers, also contribute to furthering Yiddish culture. All this activity points to an increase, not a decline, of Yiddish literature in Israel.

In the early years of this century Yiddish writers who settled in Palestine learned to write in Hebrew because of the hostility toward Yiddish. Outstanding among them is Uri Tsvi Greenberg (born 1894), one of the most talented poets in Israel. In 1956 he resumed writing in Yiddish. Many of his Yiddish poems were dirges bewailing the millions dead in a Jeremian lament. Yosef Papiernikov (born 1897), always a staunch Yiddishist, continued to write poems in praise of Israel in his mother tongue—knowing well he would have difficulty getting them published. Another early settler in Palestine who did not abandon Yiddish was the poet Malke Locker (born 1897). Among her postwar publications are *Di velt is on a hieter* (1947, The World Is without a Keeper) and biographies of Jean Arthur Rimbaud (1950) and Charles Baudelaire (1970).

Undoubtedly the most prominent of the present Yiddish writers in Israel is Abraham Sutzkever (born 1913). His early poems established him as a notable young eastern European poet. During the war he was flown to Moscow at the request of Soviet Jewish writers who had read his latest poems. He entered Palestine illegally in 1947. Two years later he was largely instrumental in founding *Di goldene keyt,* of which he has remained chief editor. *Geheymshtot* (1952, Secret City), one of his best works, depicted graphically the ordeal of Jews hiding in sewers during the Nazi terror. He celebrated the emergence of Israel as a nation in *Di geistige erd* (1961, Spiritual Soil). *Lieder fun yam hamoves* (1968, Songs of the Holocaust) were further accounts of the tragic years of war and bestiality. In his dual capacity of writer and editor, Sutzkever has been one of the main forces in promoting the growth of Yiddish literature in Israel, and thus offsetting its decline in other parts of the world.

YIDDISH LITERATURE IN ENGLISH TRANSLATION

ANTHOLOGIES

Betsky, Sarah, ed. *Onions and Cucumbers and Plums: Forty-six Yiddish Poems in English.* Freeport, N.Y., 1969

Cooperman, Jehiel B. and Sarah H., eds. *America in Yiddish Poetry.* New York, 1967

Howe, Irving and Eliezer Greenberg, eds. *A Treasury of Yiddish Poetry.* New York, 1969

———. *A Treasury of Yiddish Stories.* New York, 1965

———. *Voices from the Yiddish.* Ann Arbor, Mich., 1972

Landis, Joseph C., ed. *The Dybbuk, and Other Great Yiddish Plays.* New York, 1966

Rosenfeld, Max, ed. *Pushcarts and Dreamers.* Cranbury, N.J., 1969

Schmuller, Aaron, ed. *Treblinka Grass: Poetical Translations from the Yiddish and with an Introductory Essay and Notes on Nazi and Soviet Anti-Semitism.* New York, 1957

Whitman, Ruth, ed. *An Anthology of Modern Yiddish Poetry.* New York, 1966

INDIVIDUAL WORKS MENTIONED IN ARTICLE

Asch, Sholem. *Der brenender dorn* as *The Burning Bush.* New York, 1946

———. *East River* as *East River.* New York, 1946

———. *Der man fun Notseres* as *The Nazarene.* New York, 1939

———. *Maria* as *Mary.* New York, 1949

———. *Moshe* as *Moses.* New York, 1951

———. *Der novi* as *The Prophet*. New
York, 1955
———. *Paulus* as *The Apostle*. New
York, 1943
Glatstein, Jacob. *A gute nakht, welt* as
Good Night, World. In *Poems*. Tel
Aviv, 1970
———. *Millionen toit as Millions Dead*.
In *Poems*. Tel Aviv, 1970

Opatoshu, Joseph. *Der letster oifshtand*
as *The Story of Rabbi Akiba*. Philadelphia, 1952
Singer, Isaac Bashevis. *Di familie Moskat*
as *The Family Moskat*. New York,
1950
———. *Soten in Gorey* as *Satan in
Goray*. New York, 1955

SECONDARY WORKS

*Almanakh fun di yiddishe shreiber in
Yisroel*. Tel Aviv, 1962
Landmann, Salcia. *Jiddisch: Das Aben-
teuer einer Sprache*. Olten, 1962
*Leksikon fun der neier yiddisher litera-
tur,* 8 vols. New York, 1956–60
Liptzin, Sol. *The Flowering of Yiddish
Literature*. New York, 1963
Madison, Charles. *Yiddish Literature: Its
Scope and Major Writers*. New York,
1968
Pat Jacob. *Shmusen mit shreiber in Yis-
roel*. New York, 1960
Pomerantz, Alexander. *Di sovietishe
Harugay-Malkhus*. Buenos Aires, 1962

Rivkin, B. *Grund-tendentzen in der
amerikaner yiddisher literatur*. New
York, 1948
———. *Unsere prosayiker*. New York,
1951
Roback, A. A. *Haintige yiddishe litera-
tur*. London, 1957
Tabatchnick, A. *Dikhtung un dikhter*.
New York, 1965
Tzinberg, Isroel. *Di geshikhte fun der
yiddisher literatur*, 10 vols. New York,
1968
Yasanowitch, I. *Mit yiddishe shreiber in
Russland*. Buenos Aires, 1959

V A S A   D .   M I H A I L O V I C H

Yugoslav Literature

THERE IS NO SINGLE ENTITY called Yugoslav literature. Four separate literatures—Serbian, Croatian, Slovenian, and Macedonian—plus the literatures of several minorities (Albanian, Hungarian, Italian, and others) comprise what is sometimes called Yugoslav literature when literature is classified by political boundaries rather than languages. Moreover, the Bosnians, Herzegovinians, and Montenegrins, although they write in Serbian or Croatian, often speak of their literatures as separate units. While all these literatures have developed since 1918 under similar external circumstances, they have also been governed by their specific natures, which can be traced back even to the time when, centuries ago, these south Slavic tribes spoke one language. Today only Serbs and Croats can read each other's literatures without difficulty (Serbian and Croatian are virtually the same language, but written in different alphabets). The literatures of Slovenes and Macedonians, not to speak of various minorities, are frequently as foreign to the Serbs and Croats as are those of other Slavic nationalities. Nevertheless, because of considerable kinship and common political ties, Yugoslav literature is often discussed as a whole.

Yugoslav literature has a history of a thousand years. It was founded in the ninth century, when Cyril and Methodius brought the alphabet they had devised to the Macedonians and Serbs to the north. Approximately at the same time the Croats began to develop their own literature. In the early period, the biographies of Serbian monarchs and church leaders were the highest achievements. During the Turkish occupation of Serbia, which lasted four and a half centuries, the only possible literature was oral. The Serbian folk epics attained high artistry and unusual beauty. While the Serbs were kept enslaved, an interesting literature blossomed in the republic of Dubrovnik. After the liberation of Serbia at the beginning of the nineteenth century Serbian literature was reborn, while the Croats were still fighting for their independence within the Austro-Hungarian empire. At this time, too, Slovenian literature began to take a firmer shape after centuries of dormancy. Macedonian literature officially joined the ranks only after World War II.

In the early modern period, Yugoslav literature showed a close kinship to other Slavic literatures. Like the others, it had its roots in the oral tradition, and it was closely associated with national aspirations. This kinship was enhanced in the second half of the nineteenth century through a similar concern for political and social problems. But despite these ties, Yugoslav literature remained self-contained and self-centered until recently. It became somewhat cosmopolitan only after World War I, and more so after World War II. Ties with neighboring countries, which had always existed, widened into connections with both the west, especially France, and the east, mainly Russia. Originality was hard to achieve and sustain. Since the growth of Yugoslav literature has always been dictated by external events, by the cultural level of the Yugoslav people, and by its size, it looked for models to the major European literatures. The greatest originality is to be found in folk poetry and in the works of Vuk Karadžić (1787–1864), Petar Petrović Njegoš (1813–1851), and Ivo Andrić (born 1892).

At the beginning of the twentieth century Yugoslav writers were under the heavy influence of western literatures, especially French and German. This process continued after World War I, when many writers, especially avant-garde writers, reacted adversely to the war. A small group imitated the French surrealists, while others followed other trends in European literatures. English and American literature had some influence, while Soviet Russian literature had an impact only on the leftist writers. Additional currents in the interwar period were provided by a traditional realistic school, by socially concerned writers, by a strong folklorist orientation among some writers, and by several lone individualists. Many of these authors remained active after 1945; indeed, some of them set the mood for postwar writing, by providing contemporary Yugoslav literature with its first significant works and by influencing new writers.

Since the year 1945 represents a historical watershed, it is a convenient starting point for a survey of contemporary Yugoslav literature. During the first few years after the war there were attempts to install socialist realism as the official literary theory, to coincide with the newly emerged political situation. These attempts proved unsuccessful. After a few years of bitter struggle between the proponents of socialist realism, called the "realists," and their opponents, the "modernists," the modernists were victorious. From the mid-1950s on, there have been no further attempts to impose prescribed formulas on Yugoslav writers. At the same time, however, there is a certain uniformity, in that no new literary movements have come into being.

Today, although literature is to a certain degree dependent on social and political forces, writers have a considerable amount of freedom. They are not considered mere tools of the state or society, as in other communist countries. They are allowed to express themselves, within the limits set by the system governing the country, to acquaint themselves with the literatures of the world, and to experiment. But they are expected to accept the system and help preserve it. Direct opposition, that is, questioning the right of the Communist Party to rule or criticizing Tito, is still not tolerated. Still, very few writers—and none of the leading ones—have suffered greatly because of their political views, at least insofar as an outside observer can be privy to the internal relationships between artists and authorities. In short, the lot of Yugoslav writers today is a much better one than in other socialist countries in which a one-party system prevails. Writers, especially poets, enjoy public respect, although they have to struggle financially. They are in a constant search for readers, who seem to prefer light, insubstantial reading. For the most part, they depend on the publicly owned publishing houses, although there are some private publishers as well.

SERBIAN LITERATURE

POETRY

Of the poets who wrote both before and after World War II, some added relatively little to their prewar oeuvre, while others reached their full potential only after the war. Miloš Crnjanski (born 1893), one of the leading prewar modernists, published only one significant poetic work after the war, a long poem called *Lament nad Beogradom* (1962, Lament over Belgrade). In this poem Crnjanski continued from where he had left off almost four decades before. Although he showed little change in his basic approach to poetry, he added serenity, a wider scope, and a richer experience to his elegiac, reflective poetry, a poetry full of vivid metaphors and genuine emotions. With *Lament over Belgrade* Crnjanski secured a prominent position in contemporary Serbian poetry.

Stanislav Vinaver (1891–1955), another prewar modernist, also published only one collection of poetry after the war—*Evropska noć* (1952, The European Night)—in which he added little new but did maintain his earlier ingenuity. Desanka Maksimović (born 1898), on the other hand, wrote her best poetry after the war. She combined patriotic feelings with sensitivity, subtle lyricism, and reverence for nature. Her most recent book of poems, *Tražim pomilovanje* (1965, I Seek Mercy), evoked the reign of the medieval Serbian emperor Stevan Dušan and commented on his famous Book of Laws.

A very talented, dynamic, and prolific poet, Oskar Davičo (born 1909), an exponent of surrealism before the war, reached his full potential only after the war. In his numerous collections of poems he gave expression to his revolutionary spirit. Unable or unwilling to restrain his muse, he always went to the heart of the matter, attacking, changing positions, and often preaching. He was a decisive figure in the victory of the modernists over the realists in the 1950s. His uncanny mastery over words—manifested in unexpected metaphors, paradoxical twists, and boldness in diction—have made Davičo one of the most significant contemporary poets.

Another former surrealist, Dušan Matić (born 1898), attained full stature only after the war. Matić, an erudite intellectual and aesthetician, has written contemplative, and at times playful, poetry, which has influenced younger poets. He is interested primarily in the reality behind appearance. He has been highly cosmopolitan both in dealing directly with foreign literatures, especially French, and in implementing this foreign influence in his own works. Milan Dedinac (1902–1966), after writing turbulent poetry during the surrealist era, found peace of mind in his mature years. He combined an avant-garde spirit with a deep interest in man and nature.

Of the generation of poets who first began writing after the war, Vasko Popa (born 1922) and Miodrag Pavlović (born 1928) were enormously important, not only because they wrote excellent poetry but also because they were crucial figures in the struggle between the modernists and the realists.

Vasko Popa is considered the best living Serbian poet. His poems—collected in *Kora* (1953, The Crust), *Nepočin polje* (1956, The Fields of No Rest), and *Sporedno nebo* (1968, The Secondary Sky)—have shown many unusual features: a predilection for concrete objects; a curt, crisp verse style; and, above all, the creation of new myths. Despite his seeming traditionalism, everything about Popa is unconventional, almost revolutionary. Even his patriotic poetry is unlike anyone else's. His concern for the universal—even the metaphysical—and his attempt to pierce the "crust" of things have given Popa's poetry lasting value. He has already received international recognition.

Miodrag Pavlović, a poet, essayist, playwright, and short-story writer, found the sources of his contemplative poetry in English and American literature and in classical myths. Intellectual and neoclassical, he has endeavored to overcome the romantic, bohemian tradition of overemotionalism. Pavlović's fine sense for form and for the musical quality of the word, as well as his concern for universal questions, have been evident in his various collections of poetry: *87 pesama* (1952, 87 Poems), *Stub sećanja* (1953, The Pillar of Memory), *Oktave* (1957, Octaves), and *Mleko iskoni* (1962, Primeval Milk). In *Velika skitija* (1969, Great Wandering) he reached back to the Serbian Middle Ages in an effort to find answers to present problems. His most recent books have been *Hododarje* (1971, Pilgrimage) and *Svetli i tamni praznici* (1971, Bright and Dark Holidays).

A third important poet of the first postwar generation, Stevan Raičković (born 1928) has been a representative of the neoromantic wing in contemporary Serbian poetry. His collections of poetry, marked by simplicity and sincerity, have included *Pesma tišine* (1952, The Song of Silence), *Kasno leto* (1958, The Late Summer), *Kamena uspavanka* (1963, A Stony Lullaby), and *Prolazi rekom ladja* (1967, The Boat Sails on the River). Several motifs keep recurring in his poems: nature as perfection, a passion for loneliness, and a yearning for soothing silence. Raičković's anxiety over man's losing ties with nature have led him sometimes to pessimism and to a retreat from city life.

Like Miodrag Pavlović, the younger poet Jovan Hristić (born 1933) has followed the English and American as well as neoclassical tradition. Contemplative, rationalistic, and erudite, he has focused on philosophical themes and such contemporary problems as alienation and loneliness. His best collection has been *Aleksandrijska škola* (1963, The Alexandrian School). Ivan V. Lalić (born 1931), a poet of subdued pathos and great technical skill, has also inclined toward classical motifs and intellectualism. His verse has been complex and refined, and his poems have been vehicles of thoughts rather than emotions. In *Argonauti, i druge pesme* (1961, Argonauts, and Other Poems), *Vreme, vatre, vrtovi* (1962, Time, Fires, Gardens), and *Čin* (1963, The Act) Lalić not only invoked old myths but created new ones—an inclination prevalent in many contemporary Serbian poets. Božidar Timotijević (born 1932) is a pure lyricist, somewhat romantic but always personal and direct. Avoiding extravagance and exhibitionism, he has been content to write about his inner world in a traditional, unobtrusive manner.

One of the best postwar Serbian poets, Branko Miljković (1934–1961), committed suicide and thus became a somewhat legendary figure. Influenced by the French and Russian symbolists, as well as by the surrealists, Miljković attained near perfection in form and a considerable depth in theme. He was concerned with the role of a poet and poetry, which led him to pessimism and rebelliousness. He has influenced many young poets.

Among younger poets, Borislav Radović (born 1935) has combined emotionalism with calm thoughtfulness, showing an inclination to rationalistic treatment of poetic material. He also has striven for a high artistic standard and linguistic virtuosity, especially in his best collection, *Maina* (1964, Maina). Ljubomir Simović (born 1935) has dealt with old national myths (*Slovenske elegije* [1958, Slavic Elegies]), as well as with militant pacifism (*Šlemovi* [1967, Helmets]). His poetic work has been marked by nuances of subtle emotions and thoughtful lyricism. He is very interested in maintaining Serbian traditions. Branislav Petrović (born 1937), with studied irreverence, brought to Serbian poetry freshness, ingenuity, and the passionate tempo of city life, expressed in a mixture of commonplace and surrealistic language. Matija Bećković (born 1939) has recently entered the front ranks of contemporary Serbian poetry because of the boldness of his themes and his linguistic virtuosity.

FICTION

The giant of contemporary Serbian fiction has been Ivo Andrić, who began publishing short stories long before the war. In his stories as well as in his great novels—*Na Drini ćuprija* (1945, The Bridge on the Drina) and *Travnička hronika* (1945, The Chronicle of Travnik)—he has depicted the tragic and lonely existence of his fellow Bosnians. His Bosnia, with its many races, nationalities, and religions, is replete with harshness, violence, fear, alienation, and futility. The external predicaments are often accompanied by his characters' inability to find themselves in the maze of obstacles. Yet there is implied optimism in all the bleakness, best expressed by Andrić's beautiful metaphor of a bridge that spans opposites, symbolizing hope. Andrić has used his settings and references to the past to expound his own philosophical views and ethical values. An accomplished prose stylist as well as a writer of intellectual depth, he received the Nobel Prize in 1961.

Veljko Petrović (1884–1967) also attained both maturity and acclaim decades ago. In addition to poetry and essays, he wrote short stories about his native Vojvodina, depicting the life of this fertile region during war and peace.

Miloš Crnjanski has written novels as well as poetry. His main postwar contribution has been the novel *Druga knjiga Seoba* (1962, The Second

Book of Migrations), the first volume of which appeared in 1929. This novel described the efforts of the Serbs living in Austria-Hungary during the middle of the eighteenth century to preserve their identity while at the same time dreaming about migration to Russia. Crnjanski used this semi-historical panorama to express his belief that the whole of mankind is constantly migrating somewhere in search of its true identity. At his venerable age, Crnjanski still continues to publish novels that draw on his rich experiences.

The poet Oskar Davičo's best work of fiction is the novel *Pesma* (1952, The Poem), in which he treated, through the character of a high-school youth, the theme of revolution and the awakening of a young man as a revolutionary. The novel's importance was its articulation of a topic that has usually collapsed under the weight of socialist realism. Davičo's ambitious tetralogy *Robije* (1963–66, Penitentiaries) was similar in theme— the plight of Communist Party members in prewar prisons. Like his poetry, Davičo's novels have bedazzled the reader with their artistry, although in the novels this often has become overdone and self-defeating. The novels of another former surrealist, Aleksandar Vučo (born 1897), have dealt with the attempts of an intellectual to understand war and revolution.

The most popular contemporary Serbian writer, Branko Ćopić (born 1915), has written numerous poems, stories, and novels about the common man from Bosnia and his exploits during the war and the ensuing peacetime. Ćopić's early novel *Prolom* (1952, Breakthrough) was an epic tale about the partisan war and the gradual winning of the peasant masses to the cause of the partisans. His later novels—*Cluvi barut* (1957, Noiseless Gunpowder) and *Osma ofanziva* (1964, The Eighth Offensive)—have dealt with difficulties the victorious peasants encountered in city life after the war. The popular and somewhat superficial nature of Ćopić's writings has been offset by a warm sympathy for his characters and genuine humor. Ćopić has also been a prolific writer of children's books.

The Montenegrin Mihailo Lalić (born 1914) has written almost exclusively about World War II. *Svadba* (1950, The Wedding), *Zlo proljeće* (1953, The Evil Spring), *Raskid* (1955, The Break), *Lelejska gora* (1957, The Wailing Mountain), and *Hajka* (1960, The Chase) were all variations on the same theme—the fratricidal war in Montenegro during World War II. In his best novel, *The Wailing Mountain,* Lalić presented the tribulations of a partisan leader who, hunted behind enemy lines like a wild animal, is stripped of the last veneer of civilization and reaches that primordial stage at which the only concern is one's own naked self. After Andrić, Lalić is considered the best living Serbian novelist.

Dobrica Ćosić (born 1921) achieved sudden fame with his first novel, *Daleko je sunce* (1952, Far Away Is the Sun), in which he treated the partisan war with objectivity for the first time in Yugoslav literature, thus contributing greatly to the victory over the abortive socialist realism. Among his other novels, *Koreni* (1954, Roots) traced the history of a Serbian family at the end of the nineteenth century, and *Deobe* (1961–63, Divisions) treated those who opposed the communists in the partisan war not as criminals but as victims of their own weaknesses and mistakes. His most recent novel, *Bajka* (1966, A Fairy Tale), presented a utopian vision of a future society.

Erih Koš (born 1913) is one of the few satirists in contemporary Serbian literature. His *Veliki Mak* (1956, The Great Mak), an allegorical story about a stranded whale, has enjoyed international success. The Bosnian writer Mehmed Selimović (born 1910) has published three collections of short stories as well as three novels: *Tišine* (1961, Silences), *Derviš i smrt* (1966, The Dervish and Death), and *Tvrdjava* (1970, A Fortress). *The Dervish and Death* was an allegorical tale about the basic dilemmas of existence: life and death, the contemplative versus the active life, and the effects of power on both the ruler and the ruled.

Of the younger writers of fiction, Radomir Konstantinović (born 1928) has written philosophical novels, in which he grapples with such existential problems as the relationship between an individual and society, immortality, personal responsibility, alienation, and the dangers man has brought upon himself. Antonije Isaković (born 1923) has written short stories exclusively about the partisans in World War II, using this specific subject to deal with man in general.

By far the most outstanding of the younger writers of fiction has been Miodrag Bulatović (born 1930). His books of short stories—*Djavoli dolaze* (1955, The Devils Are Coming) and *Vuk i zvono* (1958, The Wolf and the Bell)—foreshadowed the eerie world in which his characters are held captive through their own shortcomings and idiosyncrasies. He has explored this eerie world in three novels: *Crveni petao leti prema nebu* (1959, The Red Cock Flies to Heaven), *Heroj na magarcu* (1964, A Hero on a Donkey), and *Rat je bio bolji* (1969, The War Was Better). Bulatović has exposed the animal side of man, overemphasizing sex and linking it with violence and war. Despite certain imperfections, he has an international reputation: he is the second most translated Yugoslav author (after Andrić).

Among the writers of fiction to emerge recently, perhaps the most promising has been Borislav Pekić (born 1929). With only a few works, he has established himself as a mature writer of fiction. In *Vreme čuda* (1965, The Times of Miracles) he presented old religious themes in a modern fashion, and in *Hodočašće Arsenija Njegovana* (1970, The Pilgrimage of Arsenije Njegovan) he dealt with modern themes in a traditional, realistic fashion with fine psychological twists. Radomir Smiljanić (born 1934) has created myths to analyze contemporary problems. Danilo Kiš (born 1935) has wrestled with reminiscences of his traumatic childhood experiences. And Branimir Šćepanović (born 1937) has mused philosophically about the fate of his alienated characters. Mirko Kovač (born 1938) and Filip David (born 1940) are other leading young Serbian writers.

DRAMA

Drama has always been weaker than other genres in Serbian literature, although it flowered at various times during the nineteenth century. During the last decade there has been a renascence, thanks largely to two outstanding playwrights.

Velimir Lukić (born 1936) has written several farces that used classical myths to allude to the problems of the present. In addition to his ideas, the form of his plays—disconnected scenes, lack of rapport among characters in the dialogue, a depersonalized non-hero—has expressed his modernity. His best plays have been *Dugi život kralja Osvalda* (1963, The Long Life of King Osvald) and *Bertove kočije ili Sibila* (1964, Bert's Coach or Sybil).

Aleksandar Popović (born 1929) has written prolifically—farces, comedies, and satires. His plays have been largely plotless, the characters not individualized, and the message veiled. He likes to use street jargon and to present the little man with all his vain hopes and at times grotesque behavior. *Razvojni put Bore Šnajdera* (1967, The Development of Bora the Tailor) and *Druga vrata levo* (1969, The Second Door to the Left) have been his best plays to date.

There are many one- or two-play dramatists; they have not as yet written enough to make a permanent mark on Serbian literature. An interesting new phenomenon in the drama has been the emergence of the radio and television drama.

CROATIAN LITERATURE

POETRY

During the first few years after World War II Croatian poetry was dominated by established writers. Foremost among them was Vladimir Nazor (1876–1949), who in his old age joined the partisans and wrote poems extolling their struggle. In postwar poetry, small in quantity, Nazor continued to create myths and to glorify nature, but he was also inspired to write about everyday politics. Still, his best works were written in the first decades of this century. Augustin-Tin Ujević (1891–1953), important both as a translator and as an original poet, wrote his best poetry before the war as did Nazor, but he contributed to postwar poetry as well. He was a poet of unusual talent: linguistic virtuosity, great imagination, and innovative spirit. He has had great influence on younger Croatian poets.

Gustav Krklec (born 1899) established himself before the war, but he has remained active to this day. His collections of rather conventional poetry have shown him to be a poet of personal experiences, attempting to impart to a basically tragic existence lighter, more philosophical overtones. Dobriša Cesarić (born 1902) has written simple and conventional but unquestionably beautiful poetry, devoid of rhetoric and full of intimate allusions to a rich inner life. He has also written poetry of social protest. Although Dragutin Tadijanović's (born 1905) prewar free-verse poetry lamented the loss of childhood innocence and dwelled on the loneliness of his native countryside, his postwar poetry has been more contemplative, grappling with the perennial problems of transience and death. In a very different mode has been the poetry of Drago Ivanišević (born 1907). A versatile writer, Ivanišević is a cosmopolitan intellectual and an avant-gardist. A writer apart from all currents and schools, he has been concerned with metaphysical questions and man's inability to escape his fate.

Prominent among writers who began their careers after World War II have been Jure Kaštelan (born 1919) and Vesna Parun (born 1922). Jure Kaštelan is considered the leading postwar poet of all Yugoslavia. With his collections *Pijetao na krovu* (1950, Rooster on the Roof), *Biti ili ne* (1955, To Be or Not), and *Malo kamena i puno snova* (1957, A Few Stones and Plenty of Dreams) he brought a new and unquestionably individual tone into Croatian poetry, especially in his compact poems about the partisans, their suffering and sacrifices. In his most recent poetry he has been searching for a modern poetic diction, and his themes have shifted from the horrors of war to the anxiety of modern man.

Vesna Parun has created from emotionalism and sensuousness the rich texture of her spiritual world. Her numerous collections have attested to an insatiable desire for self-expression and to an inexhaustible capacity for love and compassion. She is without doubt the leading woman poet in contemporary Croatia.

Four eminent younger poets soon achieved levels of artistic achievement comparable to the standards set by Kaštelan and Parun. Slavko Mihalić (born 1928), a neoromantic with intellectual inclinations, has attempted to overcome the absurdity of life through his ardent belief in the humanistic role of a poet. Two of his most important collections—*Ljubav za stvarnu zemlju* (1964, Love for the Real Earth) and *Prognana balada* (1965, A Banished Ballad)—showed him to be a poet who described with subtlety his rich inner experiences. Milivoj Slaviček (born 1929), is an antithesis of Mihalić, in that he is a rationalist and a nonconformist. Yet his proselike poems have not been devoid of warmth and concern for man. Slaviček seems to be carrying on a running dialogue with his contemporaries and with himself about the basic problems of existence expressed in everyday terms. Ivan Slamnig (born 1930) similarly has used a proselike language, mainly to play with serious problems of life, to point out the supremacy of reason, and to experiment with form. Primarily an intellectual, he has adapted the English and American tradition to Croatian poetry. Antun Šoljan (born 1932) is related to Slamnig in many ways, although he is less cerebral and more experimental. Of late, he has turned more to fiction and drama.

Zvonimir Golob (born 1927) and Vladimir Gotovac (born 1930) are antithetical in several ways. Golob has used his own brand of surrealism to explore both existential and social problems. His love poems, perhaps the best he has written, are emotionally charged and suffused with passion. Gotovac, on the other hand, has dealt with ideas, often abstract ones, and has probed man's relationship to them. Such an attitude has sometimes forced him into hermetic situations, in which he ponders the fate of man and the problems of love and death.

Among younger poets, Daniel Dragojević (born 1934), in his several collections, has combined an interest in philosophical and religious specu-lation with fine sensitivity and a sense of rhythm.

FICTION

By far the most important contemporary Croatian writer of fiction has been Miroslav Krleža (born 1893). Active for many decades and strongly influential on other Croatian writers, he has contributed to contemporary literature in many genres, most importantly fiction and drama. Most of his novels and short stories were written between the wars. Since World War II, in addition to fiction, Krleža has also written diaries, reminiscences, and essays. *Djetinjstvo u Agramu* (1952, Childhood in Zagreb) and *Davni dani* (1956, Days Long Past) were fascinating collages, encyclopedic in scope and erudition, of his reminiscences and views on various subjects. In 1952, he added a third volume to his prewar *Banket u Blitvi* (The Banquet in Blitvia). The best work of his entire career, the multivolume novel *Zastave* (1963–65, Flags), amply illustrated Krleža's main preoccupation— the downfall of the Austro-Hungarian empire and its bourgeoisie. His concern for social problems and revolutionary causes has been augmented by an accomplished, individual style.

Vjekoslav Majer (born 1900) also published most of his fiction before the war. He has been interested mainly in the banal everyday life of man in a capitalistic society. The title of his most recent book, *Osamljeni čovjek u Tingletanglu* (1965, A Lonely Man in the Honky-Tonk), concisely described his major concerns. Slavko Kolar (1891–1963), a humorist and satirist, exclusively wrote realistic short stories. He showed compassion for the little man, while at the same time lambasting the forces of officialdom that oppress him.

Ivan Dončević (born 1909) wrote some of the best short stories about World War II in the collection *Bezimeni* (1945, The Nameless). His novel *Mirotvorci* (1956, Peacemakers) was a satire on the Croatian middle class before World War II. Novak Simić (born 1906), whose prewar stories were set in his native Bosnia, has set his more recent works in Zagreb. His best novel, *Braća i kumiri* (1955, Brothers and Idols), dealt with the dehumanization brought about by the capitalistic system. This potentially tendentious theme was enlivened by Simić's lyricism and compassion.

Vjekoslav Kaleb (born 1905) published his first stories just before the war but came into his own only after the war. His best works—the novel *Divota prašine* (1954, Glorious Dust) and the stories collected in *Ogledalo* (1962, Mirror)—were characterized by introspection, psychological realism, and a heavy style. Ranko Marinković (born 1913) also wrote his major works after World War II. The short stories in the successful volume *Ruke* (1953, Hands) approached reality by way of symbols and psychological illumination. Marinković's best work, the novel *Kiklop* (1965, Cyclops), depicted the monstrosity of a big city and the evils it brings: anxiety, alienation, and aimlessness. Marinković's inventiveness, his black humor, and his stylistic excellence have made him one of the leading contemporary Croatian writers.

Petar Šegedin (born 1909) has written about his native island off the Dalmatian coast. His early novels—*Djeca Božja* (1946, God's Children) and *Osamljenici* (1947, Lonely People)—were psychological studies of people plagued by weaknesses and ridden with complexes. His later collections of short stories—*Na istom putu* (1963, On the Same Road) and *Orfej u maloj bašti* (1964, Orpheus in a Small Garden)—were also psychological studies, but in miniature. Šegedin has written travel books, too, notable for their sharp observations and polished style.

Vladan Desnica (1905–1967) won acclaim for his first works: the novel *Zimsko ljetovanje* (1950, Summer Vacation in Winter) and the short stories collected in *Olupine na suncu* (1952, Wrecks in the Sun). Further stories, especially the collection *Fratar sa zelenom bradom* (1959, A Monk with a Green Beard), established him as an accomplished short-story writer. The novel *Proljeća Ivana Galeba* (1957, The Springs of Ivan Galeb) combined various novelistic techniques with the story of a musician's search for the meaning of life and art.

Slobodan Novak (born 1924) has focused in his stories on moral deformities and the evils of war. His most recent novel, *Mirisi, zlato i tamjan* (1968, Scents, Gold, and Incense), analyzed a crippled war hero as he muses about the meaning of his sacrifice and implicitly criticized the conditions under which he is forced to live.

DRAMA

Contemporary Croatian drama, as well as the fiction, has been dominated by Miroslav Krleža. In addition to his numerous prewar plays, he has written one new play, *Aretej* (1960, Aretheus) and has rewritten some of his earlier plays. *Aretheus* brought back to life the third-century humanist, placing him in a totalitarian state of the late 1930s. Like his fiction and essays, Krleža's drama has been primarily concerned with moral and social problems.

The prolific playwright Marijan Matković (born 1915) has continued Krleža's tradition. He, too, is preoccupied with social problems, notably with the decay of the Croatian middle class preceding and during World War II. In addition to the cycle of plays *Igra oko smrti* (1955, Dance around Death), he wrote a trilogy, *I bogovi pate* (1962, Gods Also Suffer), which reinterpreted the legends of Prometheus, Hercules, and Achilles.

Mirko Božić (born 1919), on the other hand, has used war themes to discuss moral issues. Although his plays have been conventionally realistic, they have contained many philosophical—notably existentialist—treatments of the basic problems of life.

SLOVENIAN LITERATURE

POETRY

The greatest Slovenian poet of the twentieth century, Oton Župančič (1878–1949), died without making a contribution to the postwar world. Another venerable poet, Alojz Gradnik (1882–1967), also remained silent after the war. Edvard Kocbek (born 1904) has written sparingly, but his postwar poems have revealed his faith in man to find the way out of the impasse brought on by war and alienation. Matej Bor's (born 1913, pseudonym of Vladimir Pavšič) war poetry proved him to be one of the most committed of contemporary Slovenian poets. He showed a similar attitude in his recent poems about the horrors and dangers of the atomic age, against which he protested in the name of threatened mankind.

Of the younger poets, Ivan Minatti (born 1924) also began by writing partisan poetry, but later turned to his own disillusionment and mild despair, unable to get away from war experiences. His subjective reaction to these experiences has given his poems an individual and very lyrical voice. Similar to Minatti is Lojze Krakar (born 1926), except that Krakar has been more optimistic and concrete in both subject matter and theme. Cene Vipotnik (born 1914) began writing late in life and has written relatively few poems. In his collection *Drevo na samem* (1956, A Tree Alone) the war penetrated the poet's secluded world. His later poems have turned for the most part to love and the changes love elicits in the poet's sensitive soul.

Ciril Zlobec (born 1925), Dane Zajc (born 1929), and Gregor Strniša (born 1930), signaled a decisive change in Slovenian poetry. Ciril Zlobec at first lamented the loss of childhood and tried to find solace in love; later he turned to the wider problems of the world in all its insensitivity and ugliness, protesting man's incapability to escape them. Dane Zajc has similarly shown a strongly individualistic attitude, not letting the war trauma dominate and burden his outlook. He has arrived at the conclusion that man's loneliness leads him to negation, even self-destruction. The existentialist views of Zajc have been shared by Gregor Strniša, an unusual and highly articulate poet. He has expressed reaction to fear and alienation through beautiful metaphors and dream sequences.

Of several promising younger poets, Tomaž Šalamun (born 1941) can be cited as the best representative of the avant-garde in Slovenian poetry. He has grappled with the most fundamental existential problems of our chaotic world, protesting, often in irreverent terms, against its inhumanity while at the same time attempting to find meanings and solutions.

FICTION

The prolific author France Bevk (1890–1970), a strict realist, wrote historical fiction as well as stories and novels about village and city life. He is one of the most popular of Slovenian writers. Miško Kranjec (born 1908), also very prolific, made his reputation before the war for socially tinged and regionally oriented fiction. He has continued to write in the same vein, following the tradition of Ivan Cankar (1876–1918), the greatest twentieth-century Slovenian writer, by extolling the dignity of his people living in desperate poverty and humiliation.

Ciril Kosmač (born 1910) has also been concerned with social problems. But his lyricism, his touches of humor, and his excellent characterization have made his stories special achievements in contemporary Slovenian fiction. His collection of autobiographical stories, *Sreča in kruh* (1946, Happiness and Bread), and his novel *Pomladni dan* (1953, A Day in Spring) depicted the life in his native western Slovenia, showing the great strength of the people and their patriotic feelings for Slovenia.

Among the younger writers, Lojze Kovačič (born 1928) has depicted the lives of simple people in the big city in the stories *Ljubljanske razglednice* (1954, Picture Cards of Ljubljana). His latest work, the novel *Deček in smrt* (1969, A Boy and Death), was an ambitious psychological study of a boy's first encounters with tragedy. Andrej Hieng (born 1925), who has probed the psychological states of his characters and grappled with moral problems, has borrowed technical innovations from western European literatures. His novel *Gozd in pečina* (1966, A Forest and a Cave) was a psychological portrait of a musician's downfall. Pavle Zidar (born 1932), a temperamental defender of moral values in his short fiction, has not been reluctant to employ new forms and a bold, dramatic language. His best works are the short novels *Sveti Pavel* (1965, Saint Paul) and *Oče naš* (1967, Our Father).

DRAMA

The major Slovenian playwrights of today are Bratko Kreft (born 1905) and the poet Matej Bor. Both have written many successful plays, which are frequently performed in Slovenian theaters. Dominik Smole (born 1929) has written perhaps the best recent Slovenian play, *Antigona* (1961, Antigone), in which he used the classical subject and form to express his views on contemporary social and political questions. The novelist Andrej Hieng recently turned to radio and television drama and wrote a trilogy of plays about three Spanish figures: *Cortesova vrnitev* (1967, Cortes's Return), *Burleska o Grku* (1968, Burlesque About the Greek [about El Greco]), and *Gluhi mož na meji* (1968, The Deaf Man at the Border [about Goya]).

MACEDONIAN LITERATURE

One of the most interesting developments in contemporary Yugoslav literature is the emergence of Macedonian literature after centuries of underground existence. For political reasons, mainly the efforts of the Serbs and Bulgarians to appropriate these people, Macedonian writers were not allowed to publish in their own language. They nevertheless wrote in various Macedonian dialects, and either published abroad or waited for more propitious times. After World War II they were finally allowed to work out their dialectal differences and to publish in literary Macedonian. An entirely new written language had to be created for this purpose.

In a relatively short time, Macedonian literature has almost reached the level of other, much older written Yugoslav literatures. Although their achievements understandably stand somewhat below those in other literatures, the Macedonians have already developed all genres and have created models upon which younger and future writers can build. One can already speak of a Macedonian tradition.

POETRY

The three poets most instrumental in the founding and early development of Macedonian poetry are Aco Šopov (born 1923), Slavko Janevski (born 1920), and Blaže Koneski (born 1921). Aco Šopov published the first book of poetry in the newly created literature—*Pesni* (1944, Poems). His effort to move the fledgling poetry away from a socially and politically committed literature and toward personal expression in his *Stihovi za makata i radosta* (1952, Verses of Sorrow and Joy) touched off a heated controversy but also started Macedonian poetry on a more sophisticated road. His subsequent poetry has been pronouncedly subjective and intimate, testing the possibilities of the new literary language.

Slavko Janevski's early poetry was also pioneering. He was somewhat less subjective than Šopov, but bolder in his choice of subjects and themes. Of late, he has turned more to fiction. Blaže Koneski has pioneered not only in poetry but also in scholarly, especially linguistic, endeavors. His poems have shown a somewhat limited range—the Macedonian landscape and man's reaction to it—but he is much more direct and genuine in his poetic approach to reality than the other two founders of Macedonian poetry.

Mateja Matevski's (born 1929) two important collections—*Doždovi* (1956, Rains) and *Ramnodenica* (1963, Equinox)—combined quiet reflection and sensitivity with economical structure. Matevski is considered the best of the second generation of Macedonian poets.

Of the many younger Macedonian poets, Radovan Pavlovski (born 1934) and Bogomil Djuzel (born 1939) are noteworthy. Pavlovski has employed powerful images and an anthropomorphic approach to the natural world, while Djuzel has been a more contemplative poet, but equally deep-rooted in nature.

FICTION

The poet Slavko Janevski wrote the first Macedonian novel, *Selo zad sedumte jaseni* (1952, The Village beyond the Seven Ash Trees). In this novel he treated the life in a village commune with remarkable objectivity. His second novel, *Dve Marije* (1956, Two Marijas), showed Janevski's transition from his early realism to a more modern method.

Another early Macedonian writer of fiction was Vlado Maleski (born 1919). His early stories were about the war and the aspirations of his people. Both these stories and his later works have been marked by a talent for creating female characters. Dimitar Solev (born 1930) and Živko Čingo (born 1936) are two promising writers who have brought to Macedonian fiction modern tendencies and fresh approaches.

DRAMA

Undoubtedly the best Macedonian playwright has been Kole Čašule (born 1921). He started out as a writer of fiction but later turned to drama. He is a realist who has depicted the Macedonian working man in Macedonia, in Bulgaria, and in America. Even though his plays have focused on social and political themes, they have not lacked psychological insight. Many other writers have written plays, both for the stage and for radio and television; but Macedonian drama is still in the process of establishing itself as a full-fledged genre.

In this survey of contemporary Yugoslav literature, I could have mentioned many other deserving names and titles of works. But my intention was to keep the four literatures in perspective by stressing major writers and works.

All four Yugoslav literatures have made giant strides in the postwar era. Yugoslav writers have shown a remarkable variety, not only because of the various regions and cultures but, more importantly, because of the versatility in approaching them. Despite some degree of regionalism, the four literatures have demonstrated that they are related in character and purpose. Yugoslav writers have succeeded in keeping political pressures pretty much out of their domain. They have read and learned from foreign writers eagerly. Finally, they have brought the literature of Yugoslavia, more than in any previous period, to the level of a world literature. With new writers constantly emerging, the chances are very good that Yugoslav literature will progress even further in all areas of growth.

YUGOSLAV WORKS IN
ENGLISH TRANSLATION

ANTHOLOGIES

Johnson, Bernard, ed. *New Writing in Yugoslavia.* Baltimore, 1970
Koljević, Svetozar, ed. *Yugoslav Short Stories.* New York, 1966
Lavrin, Janko, ed. *An Anthology of Modern Yugoslav Poetry.* London, 1962
Lenski, Branko, ed. *Death of a Simple Giant, and Other Modern Yugoslav Short Stories.* New York, 1965
Menart, Janez, ed. *Slovene Poets Today.* Ljubljana, 1965
Mihailovich, Vasa et al., eds. *Introduction to Yugoslav Literature.* New York, 1972
Simic, Charles, ed. *Four Yugoslav Poets.* Northwood Narrows, N.H., 1970

INDIVIDUAL WORKS MENTIONED
IN ARTICLE

Andrić, Ivo. *Na Drini ćuprija* as *The Bridge on the Drina.* New York, 1959

————. *Travnička hronika* as *Bosnian Chronicle.* New York, 1963
Bulatović, Miodrag. *Crveni petao leti prema nebu* as *The Red Cock Flies to Heaven.* New York, 1962
————. *Heroj na magarcu* as *A Hero on a Donkey.* New York, 1970
————. *Rat je bio bolji* as *The War Was Better.* New York, 1972
Ćosić, Dobrica. *Daleko je sunce* as *Far Away Is the Sun.* Belgrade, 1963
Davičo, Oskar. *Pesma* as *The Poem.* London, 1959
Kaleb, Vjekoslav. *Divota prašine* as *Glorious Dust.* London, 1970
Koš, Erih. *Veliki Mak* as *The Strange Story of the Great Whale, also Known as Big Mac.* New York, 1962
Kosmač, Ciril. *Pomladni dan* as *A Day in Spring.* London, 1959
Lalić, Ivan V. *Vreme, vatre, vrtovi* as *Fire Gardens.* New York, 1970
Lalić, Mihailo. *Lelejska gora* as *The Wailing Mountain.* New York, 1965

SECONDARY WORKS

GENERAL WORKS

Barac, Antun. *A History of Yugoslav Literature.* Belgrade, 1955
Cronia, Arturo. *Storia della letteratura serbo-croata.* Milan, 1956
Janež, Stanko. *Istorija slovenačke književnosti.* Sarajevo, 1959
Kadić, Ante. *From Croatian Renaissance to Yugoslav Socialism.* The Hague, 1969
Koneski, Blaže. *Makedonska književnost.* Belgrade, 1961
Marjanović, M. *Hrvatska moderna,* 2 vols. Zagreb, 1951

Savković, M. *Jugoslavenska književnost,* 3 vols., 2nd ed. Belgrade, 1954
Skerlić, J. *Istorija nove srpske književnosti,* 4th ed. Belgrade, 1953
Slodnjak, Anton. *Geschichte der slowenischen Literatur.* Berlin, 1958
Trogrančić, F. *Povijest književnosti naroda Jugoslavije.* Pula, 1952

WORKS ON CONTEMPORARY LITERATURE

Bandić, Miloš I. *Srpska književnost u književnoj kritici: Savremena proza.* Belgrade, 1965

Kadić, Ante. *Contemporary Croatian Literature*. The Hague, 1960
———. *Contemporary Serbian Literature*. The Hague, 1964
Lukić, Sveta. *Contemporary Yugoslav Literature: A Sociopolitical Approach*. Urbana, Ill., 1972
———. *Srpska književnost u književnoj kritici: Savremena poezija*. Belgrade, 1966
Palavestra, Predag. *Posleratna srpska književnost*. Belgrade, 1972
Paternu, Glušič, and Kmecl. *Slovenska književnost, 1945–1965*, 2 vols. Ljubljana, 1967

Pavletić, Vlatko, ed. *Panorama hrvatske književnosti XX stoljeća*. Zagreb, 1965
Peleš, Gajo. *Poetika suvremenog jugoslavenskog romana, 1945–1961*. Zagreb, 1966
Schmaus, Alois. *Die literarischen Strömungen in Jugoslawien*. In *Osteuropa-Handbuch: Band Jugoslawien*. Cologne, 1954.
Šicel, Miroslav. *Pregled novije hrvatske književnosti*. Zagreb, 1966
Trifković, Risto. *Savremena književnost u Bosni i Hercegovini*. Sarajevo, 1968

Index of Authors

Noncapitalized prepositions in French, Spanish, Portuguese, Italian, German, Icelandic, and Dutch names (*de, di, von, van,* and so forth) are neither alphabetized nor cross-referenced. Thus, for example, Heinz von Cramer is listed only under "Cramer, Heinz von." Spanish compound surnames are alphabetized under the first element only: "García Márquez, Gabriel." Portuguese compound surnames, because of mixed usage, are listed under both elements and are cross-referenced.

701